Business Foundations
WCOB 1023

Carl McDaniel
University of Texas, Arlington

Lawrence J. Gitman
San Diego State University

Robert W. Ingram
University of Alabama

Thomas L. Albright
University of Alabama

Bruce A. Baldwin
Arizona State University West

Ralph Stair

George Reynolds

Jeff Madura

SOUTH-WESTERN
™
THOMSON LEARNING

Printed in the United States of America

South-Western College Publishing
5191 Natorp Boulevard
Mason, OH 45040
USA

For information about our products, contact us:
Thomson Learning Academic Resource Center
1-800-423-0563
http://www.swcollege.com

International Headquarters
Thomson Learning
International Division
290 Harbor Drive, 2nd Floor
Stamford, CT 06902-7477
USA

UK/Europe/Middle East/South Africa
Thomson Learning
Berkshire House
168-173 High Holborn
London WCIV 7AA

Asia
Thomson Learning
60 Albert Street, #15-01
Albert Complex
Singapore 189969

Canada
Nelson Thomson Learning
1120 Birchmount Road
Toronto, Ontario MIK 5G4
Canada
United Kingdom

ISBN 0-324-21581-9

The Adaptable Courseware Program consists of products and additions to existing South-Western College Publishing products that are produced from camera-ready copy. Peer review, class testing, and accuracy are primarily the responsibility of the author(s).

Custom Contents

1

ACCOUNTING AND ORGANIZATIONS

What do we need to know to start a business?

In December of 2003, Maria and Stan were very excited about starting a company to sell cookies made using their mother's recipes. To honor their mother, they decided to call the business Mom's Cookie Company. Realizing they did not have much money and had little business experience, the brother and sister made plans to start with a small company. They hope the business will grow as more customers become aware of their products. Maria and Stan know that accountants provide advice to help managers of companies better understand their businesses. Because they had never started a company before, they made an appointment with Ellen Coleman, an accountant who had provided helpful business advice to several of their friends.

FOOD FOR THOUGHT

Suppose you were in Maria and Stan's position. What would you want to know in order to start a business? What goals would you have for the business, and how would you plan to reach those goals? What resources would you need in your business, and how would you finance those resources? How would you organize your company? Who would your customers be? How would you know whether you are reaching your goals or not? These are issues Ellen poses to Maria and Stan.

Ellen: *Creating a successful business is not an easy task. You need a good product, and you need a plan to produce and sell that product.*

Maria: *Stan and I think we have an excellent product. We don't have a lot of money for equipment and other resources, but we have identified a bakery that could produce our products using our recipes and according to our specifications.*

Stan: *Also, we have spoken with several local grocery chains that have been impressed with samples and have agreed to sell our products.*

Ellen: *Good. A primary goal of every successful business is to create value for customers. If you focus on delivering a product that customers want at a price they are willing to pay, you are also likely to create value for yourselves as owners of the company. You have to make sure you know what it will cost to run your company and decide how you will obtain the money you need to get started.*

Stan: *We have some money in savings, and we plan to obtain a loan from a local bank. Those financial resources should permit us to rent a small office and purchase equipment we need to manage the company. Also, we will need to acquire a truck for picking up the cookies from the bakery and delivering them to the grocery stores.*

Ellen: *You will need a system for measuring your costs and the amounts you sell. That system is critical for helping you determine whether you are accomplishing your goals.*

Maria: *Stan and I don't know much about accounting. Can you help us get started?*

Ellen: *I'll be happy to help you. First, let's explore in more detail some of the issues you need to consider.*

OBJECTIVES

Once you have completed this chapter, you should be able to:

1. Identify how accounting information helps decision makers.
2. Compare major types of organizations and explain their purpose.
3. Describe how businesses create value.
4. Explain how accounting helps investors and other decision makers understand businesses.
5. Identify business ownership structures and their advantages and disadvantages.
6. Identify uses of accounting information for making decisions about corporations.
7. Explain the purpose and importance of accounting regulations.
8. Explain why ethics are important for business and accounting.

INFORMATION FOR DECISIONS

OBJECTIVE 1

Identify how accounting information helps decision makers.

All of us use information to help us make decisions. ***Information*** **includes facts, ideas, and concepts that help us understand the world.** To use information, we must be able to interpret it and understand its limitations. Poor information or the improper use of information often leads to poor decisions.

As an example, assume you wish to drive from Sevierville to Waynesville. The drive will take several hours and require several turns on unfamiliar secondary roads. Therefore, you use a map, as illustrated in Exhibit 1, to provide information to help guide you along the way.

Exhibit 1
Map from Sevierville to Waynesville

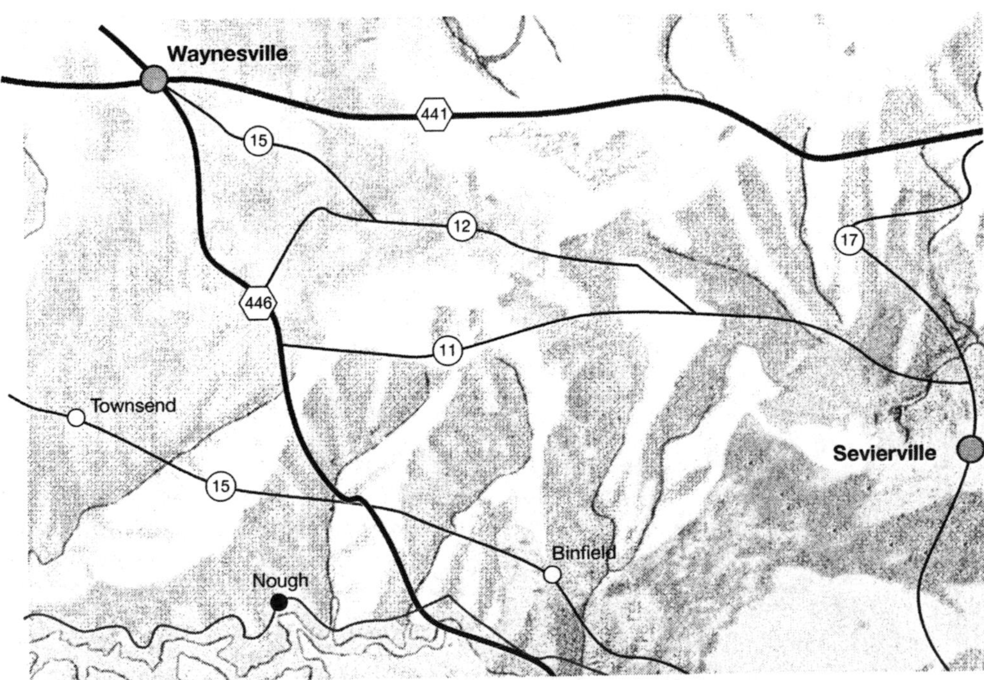

Why is the map useful? The map can help you plan your trip. You have selected a primary goal: arrive at Waynesville. You may have other goals as well, such as getting there as quickly as possible. Or perhaps you wish to stop at various points along the way. The map provides information about alternative routes so that you can select the one that is shortest, fastest, or most scenic. Using the map along the way helps you make decisions about where to turn or stop. It helps you determine how far you have traveled and how much farther you have left to go. It helps you decide whether you are on the right road or where you made a wrong turn. It helps you decide where you are, how you got there, and where you are going.

INTERNATIONAL

Accounting provides information to help in making decisions about organizations. This information is like a map of an organization. **Accounting information helps decision makers determine where they are, where they have been, and where they are going.** Rather than measuring distances in miles or kilometers, accounting measures an organization's activities by the dollar amounts associated with these activities. The primary measurement unit for accounting information is dollars in the United States or the local currency for other countries.

Maria and Stan have decided to start a business selling cookies. Their company will pay a bakery to produce the cookies and will sell the cookies to local grocery stores. An early decision they have to make is to identify the resources they will need to start and run their business. They will need merchandise (cookies) to sell and will purchase those products from a supplier (the bakery). They will need a place to operate the business and someone to pick up the products and deliver them to sellers (grocery stores). They will need money to pay for the merchandise, rent for their office, wages, equipment, and miscellaneous costs such as supplies and utilities.

As an initial step in deciding whether to start the business, Maria and Stan might consider how much they expect to sell. Suppose that after discussing this issue with grocery store owners, they determine that the company will sell about $12,000 of merchandise each month.

Next, they consider how much money they will need to operate their business. A discussion with the bakery indicates the cost of the merchandise will be $8,000 each month. After consideration of their other needs, they calculate their monthly costs will be:

Merchandise	$ 8,000
Wages	1,000
Rent	600
Supplies	300
Utilities	200
Total	$10,100

From this information, they decide they should expect to earn a profit of $1,900 ($12,000 – $10,100) each month as shown in Exhibit 2. Profit is the amount left over after the cost of doing business is subtracted from sales.

Exhibit 2
Expected Monthly Earnings for Mom's Cookie Company

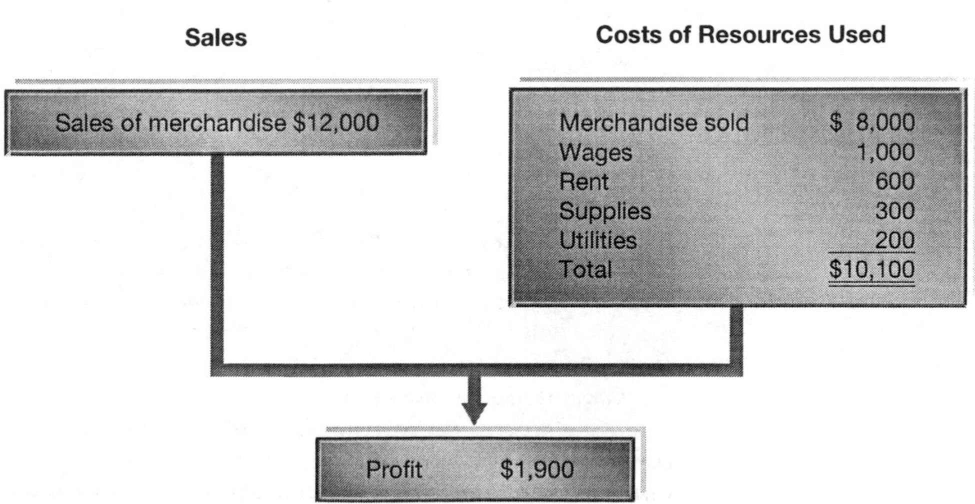

Does this appear to be a good business for Maria and Stan? Suppose they each have $5,000 to invest in the business. They will use this money to purchase merchandise and to pay for rent, wages, and the miscellaneous costs for the first month. Would investing their money in the business be a good idea?

If they don't invest in the business, they could earn interest of about $50 a month on their $10,000 of combined savings. The expected profit of $1,900 is considerably larger. However, they also should consider the wages they could earn if they worked for someone else instead of working in their own company. Additionally, they should consider how certain they are about the amount they can earn from their business and how much risk they are willing to take. Investing in a business is always risky. ***Risk* is uncertainty about an outcome,** such as the amount of profit a business will earn. If the company sells less than Maria and Stan expect, its earnings also will be less than expected. If the company does not do well, they could lose their investments. Are they willing to take that risk? **Accounting can help with these decisions by providing information about the results that owners and other decision makers should expect will occur.** Decision makers then have to evaluate that information and make their decisions.

Accounting is a way of looking at a business. It measures the activities of a business by the dollars it receives and spends. It helps decision makers determine where they started and where they should end up. It helps determine whether expectations are being met. In the case of Mom's Cookie Company, accounting identifies the company's starting point by the $10,000 Maria and Stan invest in their business. It identifies an expected ending point as the amount of profit of $1,900 they expect to earn each month. It provides a means of determining whether expectations are being met by measuring business activities each month to determine whether the company is actually earning $1,900 each month. Like a map, accounting can help decision makers determine that they are not where they want to be. It can help them determine what went wrong and what they might do to get back on the proper route.

Accounting provides a model of a business by measuring the business activities in dollar amounts. Underlying this model is an information system. This system provides a process for obtaining facts that can be converted into useful information. Understanding the system and its processes will help you understand the information provided by accounting.

The purpose of accounting is to help people make decisions about economic activities. Economic activities involve the allocation of scarce resources. People allocate scarce resources any time they exchange money, goods, or services. These activities are so common that almost every person in our society uses the accounting process to assist in decision making.

Accounting provides information for managers, owners, members, and other stakeholders who make decisions about organizations. ***Stakeholders* include those who have an economic interest in an organization and those who are affected by its activities. An *organization* is a group of people who work together to develop, produce, and/or distribute goods or services.** The next section of this chapter discusses the purpose of organizations and the role of accounting in organizations.

THE PURPOSE OF ORGANIZATIONS

OBJECTIVE 2

Compare major types of organizations and explain their purpose.

Many types of organizations exist to serve society. Why do these organizations exist? Most exist because people need to work together to accomplish their goals. The goals are too large, too complex, or too expensive to be achieved without cooperation. All organizations provide goods and/or services. By working together, people can produce more and better goods and services.

Organizations differ as to the types of goods or services they offer (Exhibit 3). ***Merchandising* (or *retail*) *companies* sell to consumers goods that are produced by other companies.** Grocery, department, and hardware stores are examples. Mom's Cookie Company is a merchandising company. It purchases merchandise from a bakery and sells the merchandise to grocery stores. ***Manufacturing companies* produce goods that they sell to consumers, to merchandising companies, or to other manufacturing companies.** Examples include automobile manufacturers, petroleum refineries, furniture manufacturers, computer companies, and paper companies. The bakery from which Mom's Cookie Company purchases its cookies is a manufacturing company. ***Service companies* sell services rather than goods.** These companies include banks, insurance companies, hospitals, universities, law firms, and accounting firms. Some companies may be a combination of types. For example, many automobile dealers are both retail and service companies. Restaurants are both manufacturing and service companies.

Exhibit 3
Types of Organizations

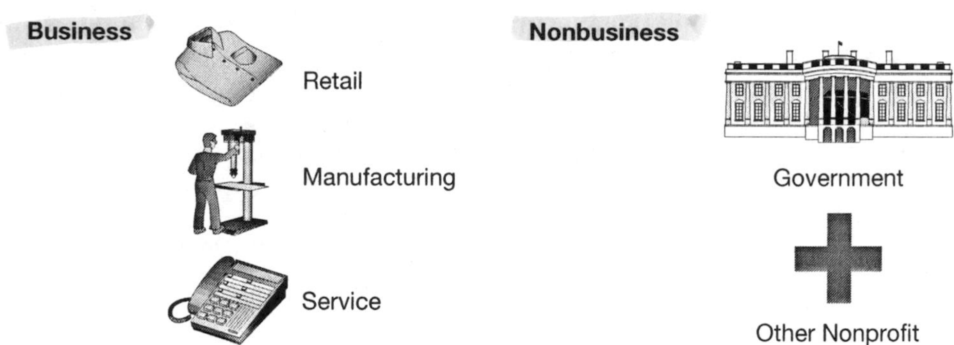

Organizations may be classified by whether or not they attempt to earn a profit. Profits result from selling goods and services to customers at prices greater than the cost of the items sold. **Organizations that sell their goods and services to make a profit are *business organizations. Governmental and nonprofit organizations,* sometimes referred to as nonbusiness organizations, provide goods or, more typically, services without the intent of making a profit.** Nonbusiness organizations include civic, social, and religious organizations. Some types of services, such as education and healthcare services, are provided by both business and nonbusiness organizations. Although the products are similar, the goals of the organizations providing these services are different. Nevertheless, all organizations need accounting information for decision making. This book focuses primarily on accounting for business organizations.

Transformation of Resources

A common purpose of organizations is to transform resources from one form to a different, more valuable, form to meet the needs of people. Resources include natural resources (such as minerals and timber), physical resources (such as buildings and equipment), management skills, labor, financial resources, legal rights (such as patents and trademarks), information, and the systems that provide information. The transformation process combines these resources to create goods and services. Transformation may involve making goods or services easier or less expensive for customers to obtain, as in most merchandising and service companies. Or it may involve physically converting resources by processing or combining them, as in manufacturing companies. An easy way to understand the transformation of resources is by thinking about how a bakery takes resources like flour and sugar and transforms them through the mixing and baking process to become cookies. Exhibit 4 illustrates this transformation process.

Organizations are created because many transformations are too difficult or too expensive for individuals to accomplish without working together. By combining their managerial skills, labor, and money, individuals create organizations to provide value that otherwise would be unavailable. Value is added to society when an organization transforms resources from a less desirable form or location to a more desirable form

Exhibit 4
Transformation of Resources into Goods and Services

or location. **The transformation, if it meets a need of society, creates value because people are better off after the transformation than before.** For example, a company that manufactures shirts creates value because the shirts are more useful to those who purchase them than the material from which the shirts are made or the cotton or synthetic fibers used to make the material.

To improve its welfare, a society must encourage organizations to increase the value they create. Because resources are in scarce supply, a society should attempt to use its resources wisely. A major purpose of accounting information is to help decide how to get the most value from scarce resources.

Creating Value

OBJECTIVE 3
Describe how businesses create value.

How can society determine how to use its resources? Decisions about using scarce resources wisely are not easy. Because society is made up of many individuals, disagreement often exists as to how resources should be used. In our society and many others, markets are the means used to promote the wise use of many resources.

Markets exist to allocate scarce resources used and produced by organizations. **A *market* is any location or process that permits resources to be bought and sold.** Competition in a market determines the amount and value of resources available for exchange. The more valuable a resource is in meeting your needs, the more you are willing to pay for it as a buyer, or the more you want for it as a seller.

The price paid for a resource in a competitive market is an indication of the value assigned to it at the particular time the buyer and seller negotiate an exchange. For example, when you buy a box of cookies, you exchange money for it. The amount of money is a measure of the value you place on the product. Thus, the price of goods and services in a market is a basis for measuring value. **Accounting measures the increase in value created by a transformation as the difference between the total price of goods and services sold and the total cost of resources consumed in developing, producing, and selling the goods and services.**

What value results when you purchase cookies? The amount you pay for the cookies is an indication of the value you expect to receive. However, resources were consumed in producing the cookies and making them available to you as illustrated in Exhibit 5.

LEARNING NOTE

Distinguish between prices charged by a business to its customers and prices paid by a business for resources it consumes. A price charged by a business is a **sales price**. A price paid by a business to purchase resources that will be consumed in providing goods and services is a **cost** to the business.

Exhibit 5
Value Created by Transforming Resources

Sales Price of Box of Cookies		Total Cost of Resources Consumed to Produce and Make Box of Cookies Available		Value Added
\$3.50	–	\$3.00	=	\$0.50

If you pay $3.50 for a box of cookies and the total cost of producing the cookies and making them available to you is $3.00, the value added by the transformation is $0.50. The difference between the price you pay and the total cost of the cookies is profit for those who produce and sell the cookies. ***Profit* is the difference between the price a seller receives for goods or services and the total cost to the seller of all resources consumed in developing, producing, and selling these goods or services during a particular period.** Thus, profits are the net resources generated from selling goods and services (resources received from the sales minus resources used in making the sales).

Several types of markets are important in our economy. Markets exist for resources used by organizations. Organizations compete in **financial markets** for financial resources. Investors choose where to put their money to work by selecting among competing organizations. Organizations compete in **supplier markets** for other resources needed to produce goods and services. Competition in these markets determines the costs of materials, labor, equipment, and other resources available to organizations. Organizations compete in **product markets** (markets for goods and services). These markets determine the prices of goods and services available to customers. From the perspective of organizations, financial and supplier markets are input markets; product markets are output markets. All of these markets allocate scarce resources.

Exhibit 6 reports the actual profit earned by Mom's Cookie Company in January, its first month of operations. (Keep in mind, the information presented earlier was the estimated amount of sales, costs, and profit.) The profit of $1,700 represents the difference between the amount of resources created by selling goods to customers and the total cost of resources consumed in providing those goods. Of course, a business venture may not produce a profit. It produces a loss if it consumes more resources than it creates.

Exhibit 6
Profit Earned by Mom's Cookie Company in January

Mom's Cookie Company
Profit Earned
For January

Resources created from selling cookies		$11,400
Resources consumed:		
Cost of merchandise sold	$7,600	
Wages	1,000	
Rent	600	
Supplies	300	
Utilities	200	
Total cost of resources consumed		9,700
Profit earned		$ 1,700

This exhibit reports results of activities that occurred during January. These results can be compared with expected results. Mom's Cookie Company had sales of $11,400 compared with expected sales of $12,000. The cost of merchandise sold during January was $7,600 rather than the expected amount of $8,000, and profit earned by the company was $1,700 rather than the expected amount of $1,900. By examining the differences between expected and actual results, Maria and Stan can determine whether they need to make changes in their business. Perhaps they need to find more stores to sell their products, or perhaps they need to advertise their products.

THE ROLE OF ACCOUNTING IN BUSINESS ORGANIZATIONS

Businesses earn profits by providing goods and services demanded by society. Owners invest in a business to receive a return on their investments from profits earned by their business. By investing in a business, owners are forgoing the use of their money for

OBJECTIVE 4

Explain how accounting helps investors and other decision makers understand businesses.

other purposes. In exchange, they expect to share in a business's profits. ***Return on investment (ROI)*** **is the amount of profit earned by a business that could be paid to owners.** Return on investment often is expressed as a ratio that compares the amount of profit to the amount invested in a business by its owners:

$$\text{Return on Investment} = \frac{\text{Profit}}{\text{Amount Invested}}$$

Profits represent net resources that have been earned through sales transactions. A business may distribute profits to its owners. Alternatively, owners (or managers acting on their behalf) may decide to reinvest profits in a business to acquire additional resources. The business can use the additional resources to earn more profits by expanding its size or by expanding into new locations or product lines. Either way, the owners are usually better off. They receive cash from their investments if profits are withdrawn, or they add value to the business if profits are reinvested.

As shown in Exhibit 6, Mom's Cookie Company earned $1,700 during January. As the owners, Maria and Stan may choose to withdraw some or all of this amount for personal use. It is their return on investment. Alternatively, they might choose to reinvest all or a portion of this profit to enlarge their company by buying a larger amount of merchandise for sale in February.

Return on investment for Mom's Cookie Company for January was $1,700, or 17% ($1,700 ÷ $10,000), relative to the owners' initial investment. If Maria and Stan withdraw more than $1,700 from their business, the additional amount withdrawn is a **return *of* investment,** not a return on investment. That additional amount is a return of a portion of the amount they originally invested. **For a company to maintain its capital (the amount invested by its owners), it must pay a return to owners from profits the company has earned. Otherwise, the company is reducing its capital by returning a portion of owners' investments to them.**

The amount of return owners receive from a company depends on the company's success in earning a profit. If you are the primary owner of a business, you are actively involved in managing the business, and its success depends largely on your ability and effort. If you are one of many who invest in a company, you probably are not actively involved in the business, and its success depends largely on the abilities and efforts of those who are managing the business. When you invest in a business, you have no guarantee that it will be successful. You are taking a risk that you may not receive a return on your investment, that the return may be smaller than you expected, or even that you might lose your investment.

Why invest in a business if the investment is risky? If a business is successful, its owners can expect to earn a higher rate of return on their investments than they could earn on a safer alternative, such as a savings account. By investing $10,000 in Mom's Cookie Company, Maria and Stan expect to earn $1,900 each month from their investment. If they invested their money in a savings account, they would expect to earn $50 each month. In general, it is necessary to take greater risks in order to earn higher returns. Accounting information helps owners evaluate the risks and returns associated with their investments so they can make good decisions.

To earn profits and pay returns to owners, businesses must operate effectively and efficiently. **An *effective business* is one that is successful in providing goods and services demanded by customers.** Effective management involves identifying the right products and putting them in the right locations at the right times. **An *efficient business* is one that keeps the costs of resources consumed in providing goods and services low relative to the selling prices of these goods and services.** Managers must control costs by using the proper mix, qualities, and quantities of resources to avoid waste and to reduce costs. The risk of owning a business is lower if the business is effective and efficient than if it is ineffective or inefficient. Efficient and effective businesses are competitive in financial, supplier, and product markets.

Mom's Cookie Company will be effective if it sells products desired by customers and if the products are made available in locations convenient for customers to purchase them. The company will be efficient if it can keep the costs of resources it consumes low relative to the price of the goods it sells. During January, the company was less effective than Maria and Stan had planned because it sold fewer goods than expected. The company was efficient in controlling the cost of resources consumed because its costs were less than the prices of goods sold, thus permitting the company to earn a profit.

Business owners expect to receive a return on their investments. Investors choose among alternative investments by evaluating the amount, timing, and uncertainty of the returns they expect to receive. Businesses that earn high profits and are capable of paying high returns have less difficulty in obtaining investors than other businesses. A business that cannot earn sufficient profits will be forced to become more effective and efficient or to go out of business.

The accounting information system is a major source of the information investors use in making decisions about their investments. Accounting information helps investors assess the effectiveness and efficiency of businesses. It helps them estimate the returns that can be expected from investing in a business and the amount of risk associated with their investments. Financial, supplier, and product markets create incentives for businesses to provide products that society demands. These markets help ensure that scarce resources are used to improve society's welfare. Markets help allocate scarce resources to those organizations that can best transform them to create value.

Accounting **is an information system for the measurement and reporting of the transformation of resources into goods and services and the sale or transfer of these goods and services to customers.** Accounting uses the prices and costs of resources to measure value created by the transformation process and to trace the flow of resources through the transformation process. By tracing the flow of resources, managers and other decision makers can determine how efficiently and effectively resources are being used.

1 SELF-STUDY PROBLEM

WebTUTOR™ Advantage

John Bach owns a music store in which he sells and repairs musical instruments and sells sheet music. The following transactions occurred for Bach's Music Store during December 2004:

1. Sold $8,000 of musical instruments that cost the company $4,300.
2. Sold $1,400 of sheet music that cost the company $870.
3. The price of repair services provided during the month was $2,200.
4. Rent on the store for the month was $650.
5. The cost of supplies used during the month was $250.
6. The cost of advertising for the month was $300.
7. The cost of utilities for the month was $200.
8. Other miscellaneous costs for December were $180.

Required

A. Determine the profit earned by Bach's Music Store for December.
B. Explain how profit measures the value created by Bach's Music Store.

The solution to Self-Study Problem 1 appears at the end of the chapter.

THE STRUCTURE OF BUSINESS ORGANIZATIONS

OBJECTIVE 5

Identify business ownership structures and their advantages and disadvantages.

Many types of decisions are made in organizations. Accounting provides important information to make these decisions. For example, organizations require financial resources to buy other resources used to produce goods and services. Primary sources of financing for businesses are owners and creditors.

Business Ownership

Businesses may be classified into two categories: those that are distinct legal entities apart from their owners and those that are not distinct legal entities. A ***corporation*** is

a legal entity with the right to enter into contracts; the right to own, buy, and sell property; and the right to sell stock. Resources are owned by the corporation rather than by individual owners.

Corporations may be very large or fairly small organizations. Small corporations often are managed by their owners. The owners of most large corporations do not manage their companies. Instead, they hire professional managers. These owners have the right to vote on certain major decisions, but they do not control the operations of their corporations on a day-to-day basis. One reason most large businesses are organized as corporations is that corporations typically have greater access to financial markets than other types of organizations.

A corporation may be owned by a large number of investors who purchase shares of stock issued by the corporation. **Each share of *stock* is a certificate of ownership that represents an equal share in the ownership of a corporation.** An investor who owns 10% of the shares of a corporation owns 10% of the company and has a right to 10% of the return available to stockholders. ***Stockholders*, or *shareholders*, are the owners of a corporation.**

INTERNATIONAL

Shares of stock often are traded in stock markets, such as the New York, London, and Tokyo stock exchanges, which are established specifically for this purpose. These markets facilitate the exchange of stock between buyers and sellers. Therefore, unlike other businesses, ownership in many corporations changes frequently as stockholders buy or sell shares of stock. Major corporations, such as **General Motors, Exxon,** or **IBM,** have received billions of dollars from stockholders.

***Proprietorships* and *partnerships* are business organizations that do not have legal identities distinct from their owners. Proprietorships have only one owner; partnerships have more than one owner.** For most proprietorships and partnerships, owners also manage the business. Owners have a major stake in the business because often much of their personal wealth is invested in it. The amount of a proprietor's personal wealth and his or her ability to borrow limit the size of a proprietorship. If a proprietorship is profitable, profits earned by the proprietor can be reinvested, and the business can become fairly large.

Partnerships can include several partners; therefore, the money available to finance a partnership depends on the money available from all the partners. New partners can be added, making new money available to the business. While most partnerships are small, large businesses (with as many as a thousand or more owners) sometimes are organized as partnerships. The profit of most proprietorships and partnerships is not taxed. Instead, the profit is income for the owners, who pay income taxes on the profit as part of their personal income taxes.

Percentage of Companies and Volume of Sales by Type of Organization

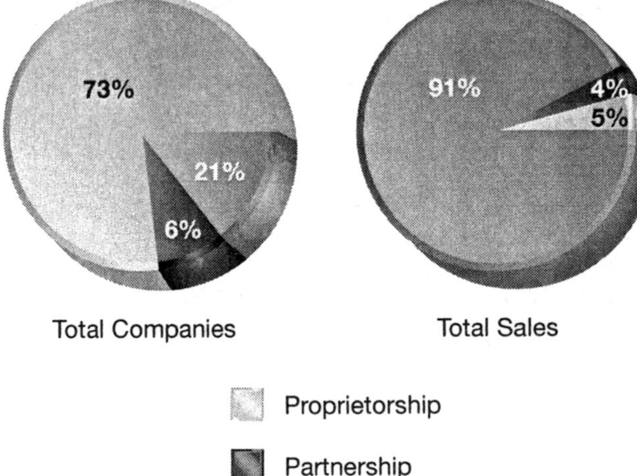

(Data source: U.S. Census Bureau Web site (http://www.census.gov)

Management of Corporations

Exhibit 7 describes the organizational structure of a typical corporation. A **board of directors** oversees the decisions of management and is responsible for protecting the interests of stockholders. Normally, the board is appointed by management with the approval of stockholders. Top managers often serve on the board along with outside directors who are not part of the corporation's management. The **chairman of the board** often holds the position of **chief executive officer** (**CEO**) with the ultimate responsibility for the success of the business. The **president**, as **chief operating officer** (**COO**), is responsible for the day-to-day management of a corporation. In some cases, the president also may be the CEO. The company may appoint any number of **vice presidents**, who are responsible for various functions in the organization. The titles and roles of these managers will vary from corporation to corporation. Along with the CEO and the president, the vice presidents constitute the top management of a corporation. Together, they make planning decisions and develop company goals and policies.

Exhibit 7
Corporate Management Functions

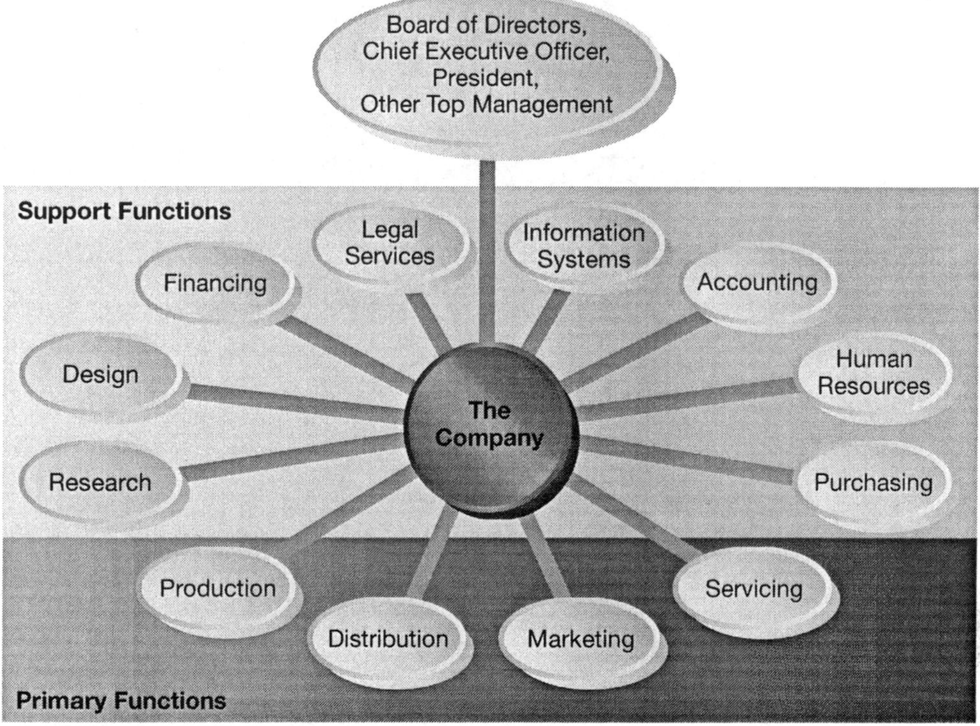

Functions performed within a corporation may be separated into support functions and primary functions. Support functions assist the primary functions by providing information and other resources necessary to produce and sell goods and services. Primary functions are those actually involved in producing and selling goods and services. These functions include distribution of goods and services to customers and servicing the goods and services to meet customer needs.

Among the support functions are research and development, product and production design, finance, legal services, accounting, purchasing, and human resources. The **chief financial officer (CFO)**, who also may be the **treasurer**, is responsible for obtaining financial resources and managing a corporation's cash. The **controller**, as the chief accounting officer, is responsible for accounting and financial reporting, developing and maintaining the accounting information system, and reporting to tax and regulatory authorities.

Primary functions involve production, distribution, sales, and service. **Plant managers** oversee production for specific product lines or geographical locations. These managers often have their own staffs at the divisional or plant level. For example, divisional or plant level controllers exist in many corporations. Research, design, and development staffs also exist at the divisional or plant level in some organizations.

Corporations may be organized by functions such as those described in Exhibit 7. Other corporations are organized primarily by region or product line. For example, multinational companies may be organized into North American, European, and Pacific divisions. Functional areas, such as development and production, report to regional or product managers. Many corporations are finding advantages in changing from a traditional organization structure to teams of managers working together on specific projects. Thus, the idea for a new product may be the responsibility of a team of employees from a company's functional areas, such as engineering, accounting, and marketing. Together, the team decides on a design for the product and on a production process to create efficiency and product quality.

Advantages of Corporations

A corporate form of organization has several advantages over proprietorships or partnerships. Corporations have **continuous lives** apart from those of their owners. If a proprietor or partner sells her or his share of a business or dies, the business ceases to exist as a legal entity. The new owner of the business must reestablish the business as a new legal entity. Most corporations, however, continue unchanged if current owners sell their stock, donate it to charity, give it to relatives, or otherwise dispose of their shares.

Shareholders normally are not liable personally for the debts of a corporation. This is a characteristic known as **limited liability.** If a corporation defaults on debt or enters bankruptcy, its owners may lose a portion or all of their investments in the company, but they are not obligated to use their personal wealth to repay creditors for losses the creditors incurred. In many cases, proprietors and partners are personally liable for the debts of their companies and can be required to use their personal wealth to repay their creditors.

Shareholders of most corporations do not manage the company. They elect members of the board of directors, who then hire **professional managers** to run the corporation. Investors can own part of a corporation or parts of many corporations without having to participate in the day-to-day decisions of running those companies. Many Americans own stock in corporations through personal investments and retirement plans, but they are not required to commit large amounts of their personal time to corporate concerns.

Shareholders cannot enter into contracts or agreements that are binding on a corporation unless they are managers or directors. Therefore, investors in a corporation do not have to be concerned about the abilities of other stockholders to make good business decisions. In contrast, bad decisions by one partner can result in the personal bankruptcy of all partners in a partnership. This problem arises because partners normally are in a mutual agency relationship. ***Mutual agency* permits a partner to enter into contracts and agreements that are binding on all members of a partnership.**

By selling shares to many investors, a corporation can obtain a large amount of financial resources. The **ability to raise large amounts of capital** permits corporations to become very large organizations. Thus, corporations can invest in plant facilities and undertake production activities that would be difficult for proprietorships or partnerships.

LEARNING NOTE

A partnership can be organized as a **limited liability partnership (LLP).** The LLP restricts the personal liability of each partner for obligations created by the company. Many professional service companies, particularly accounting and legal firms, are organized as LLPs. A business also can be organized as a **limited liability company (LLC).** An LLC combines certain advantages of a partnership and a corporation in that it combines the tax treatment of a partnership with the limited liability of corporations. While a corporation can have as few as one shareholder, an LLC usually must have at least two owners. Both LLPs and LLCs are separate legal entities from their owners.

Disadvantages of Corporations

There are several disadvantages to the corporate form of ownership. Most corporations must pay **taxes** on their incomes. Corporate taxes are separate from the taxes paid by shareholders on dividends received from the company. (Some corporations, however, especially smaller ones, are not taxed separately.) Another disadvantage is that corporations are **regulated** by various state and federal government agencies. These regulations require corporations to comply with many state and federal rules concerning business practices and reporting of financial information. Corporations must file many reports with government agencies and make public disclosure of their business activities. Compliance with these regulations is costly. Also, some of the **required disclosures** may be helpful to competitors. Partnerships and proprietorships are regulated also, but the degree of regulation normally is much less than for corporations.

Owners of corporations usually do not have access to information about the day-to-day activities of their companies. They depend on managers to make decisions that will increase the value of their investments. However, managers' personal interests sometimes conflict with the interests of stockholders. This problem produces a condition known as moral hazard. Moral hazard arises when one group, known as **agents** (such as managers), is responsible for serving the needs of another group, known as **principals** (such as investors). ***Moral hazard* is the condition that exists when agents have superior information to principals and are able to make decisions that favor their own interests over those of the principals.**

Without disclosure of reliable information, corporations would have difficulty in selling stock, and investors would be unable to determine whether managers were making decisions that increased stockholder value or were making decisions that took advantage of the stockholders. Accounting reports are major sources of information to help stockholders assess the performance of managers. For example, profit information helps owners evaluate how well managers have used owners' investments to earn returns for the owners. Moral hazard imposes costs on corporations because managers must report to stockholders and, generally, these reports are audited. **An audit verifies the reliability of reported information.**

The size of many corporations makes them **difficult to manage**. An individual manager cannot be involved directly with all the decisions made in operating a large organization. Top-level managers depend on low-level managers to make decisions and to keep them informed about a corporation's operations. This process is costly because coordination among managers may be difficult to achieve. Moral hazard also exists among managers and employees, not just between managers and investors. Corporate goals and policies provide guidance for manager decisions, but communicating goals and policies and providing incentives for managers to implement them often is difficult and expensive. Employees and low-level managers may not report reliable information about their activities to high-level managers if the information is not in their best interests. Multinational corporations, in particular, are complex and difficult to manage. Distant locations for facilities and differences in language and local custom can cause special problems.

The profits of corporations, except for those of small privately-owned ones, referred to as Subchapter S corporations, are taxed separately from taxes paid by the owners of the corporation. The federal government and most state governments impose a corporate income tax on the profits of corporations. This tax is paid by the corporation. In addition, amounts distributed to shareholders are taxed as part of their personal income. Thus, the profits of corporations often are subject to **double taxation**: taxation of the corporation and taxation of the shareholders.

Creditors

In addition to money provided by owners, businesses (and other organizations) may borrow money. Money may be obtained from banks and other financial institutions, or it may be borrowed from individual lenders. **A *creditor* is someone who loans financial resources to an organization.**

Most organizations depend on banks and similar institutions to lend them money. Corporations often borrow money from individuals or other companies. Exhibit 8 shows the amount of money several large corporations have received from owners and creditors. The amounts and proportions of financing from owners and creditors vary greatly across companies.

Creditors loan money to organizations to earn a return on their investments. They usually loan money for a specific period and are promised a specific rate of return on their investments. Usually, this is a fixed rate (say 10%). In contrast, owners invest for a nonspecific period (until they decide to sell their investments) and receive a return that depends on the profits earned by the business.

The success of a business determines whether creditors will receive the amount promised by the borrower. When a business fails to generate sufficient cash from selling

Exhibit 8
Sources of Financing for Selected Corporations

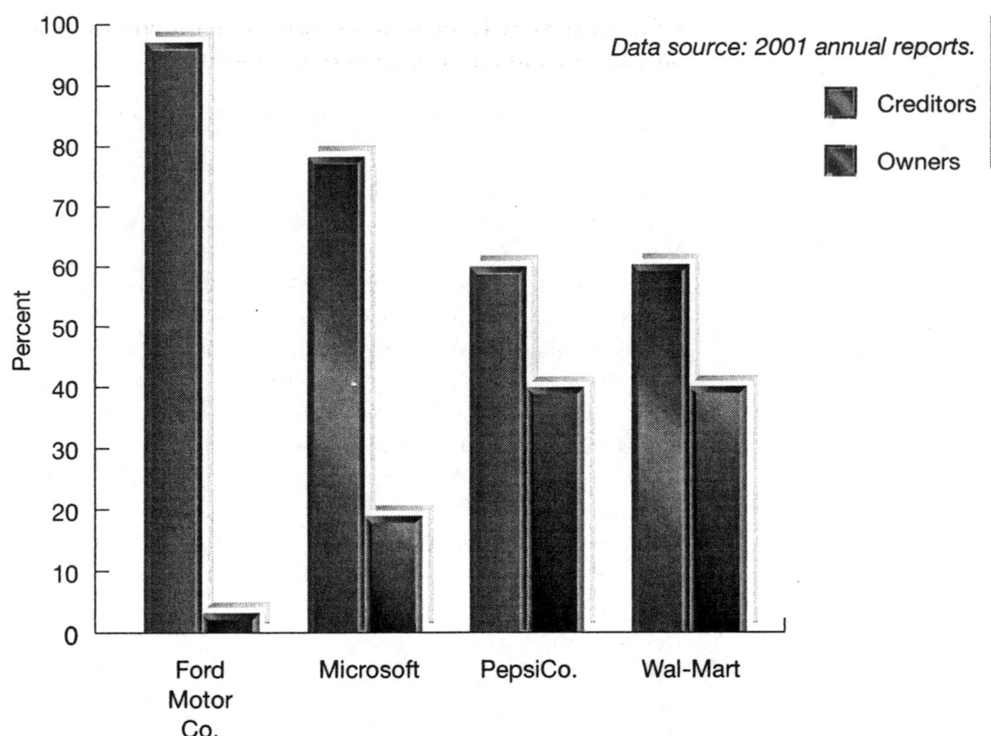

goods and services to pay for resources it consumes and to pay its creditors, the creditors may not receive the amount promised. Therefore, creditors estimate the probability that an organization will be able to repay debt and interest. Risk is a concern of both creditors and owners, and accounting information is key in evaluating the risk. Exhibit 9 illustrates the role of owners and creditors in providing financial resources for businesses.

Exhibit 9
Obtaining Financial Resources

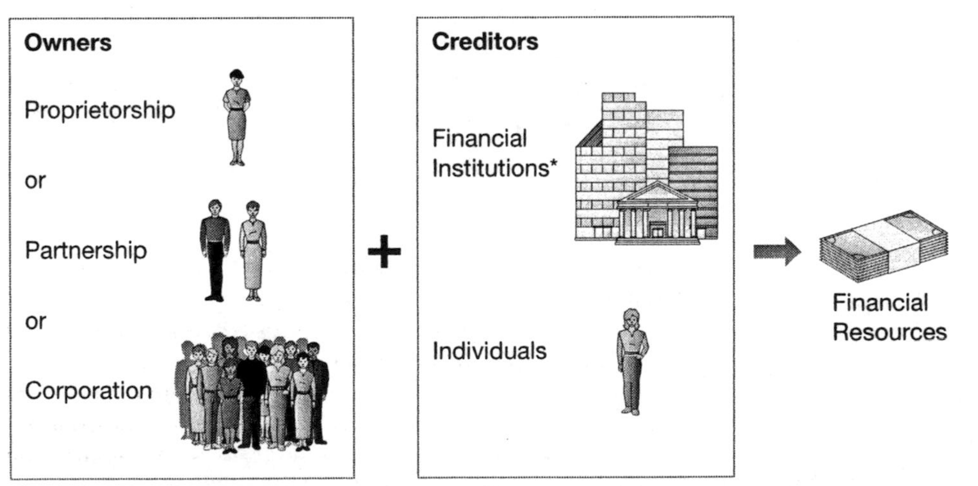

*The term "financial institutions" refers to banks, savings and loans, and similar companies.

2 SELF-STUDY PROBLEM

Hammer Hardware Company and **Home Depot** are both retail stores that sell tools, hardware, and household items. Hammer Hardware is owned by Harvey Hammer and is organized as a proprietorship. Home Depot is organized as a corporation and is owned by thousands of investors.

Required Why is the form of ownership different for these companies? What are the advantages and disadvantages of each form?

The solution to Self-Study Problem 2 appears at the end of the chapter.

ACCOUNTING AND BUSINESS DECISIONS

OBJECTIVE 6

Identify uses of accounting information for making decisions about corporations.

The value of accounting information is determined by how well it meets the needs of those who use it. Accounting information describes economic consequences of the transformation process. Information needs of decision makers arise from the many relationships that occur within the transformation process among an organization's stakeholders: managers, investors, suppliers, employees, customers, and government authorities. These stakeholders compete in markets for resources, or they regulate these markets. They exchange resources or services with an organization as part of its transformation process.

Contracts **are legal agreements for the exchange of resources and services.** They provide legal protection for the parties to an agreement if the terms of the agreement are not honored. Contract terms establish the rights and responsibilities of the contracting parties. Contracts are "give and get" relationships. Each party to the contract expects to receive something in exchange for something given. For example, a contract by an employee to provide labor to a company involves the giving of labor services by the employee in exchange for wages and benefits. Contracts with proprietorships and partnerships are between the owners/managers and other contracting parties. In contrast, because corporations are legal entities, contracts can be formed with the corporation as one of the contracting parties. Managers make contracts on behalf of corporations and their owners.

Contracts are enforceable only to the extent that contracting parties can determine whether the terms of the contract are being met. Assume that you sign a contract with a company that calls for you to invest $1,000 in the company and for the company to pay you 10% of the amount the company earns each year. Unless you have reliable information about the company's earnings, you cannot determine whether it is paying you the agreed amount. Therefore, you probably would not agree to the contract. Contracts require information that the contracting parties accept as reliable and sufficient for determining if the terms of the contract have been met. **Accounting information is important for forming and evaluating contracts.**

Exhibit 10 identifies examples of exchanges among stakeholders for which contracts and information about organizations are important. The following sections discuss these exchanges.

LEARNING NOTE

Products can be either goods or services or both. While often we talk about companies that sell goods, you should keep in mind how accounting is important to service companies also.

Risk and Return

Contracts are formed to identify rights and responsibilities. These rights and responsibilities establish how risk and return will be shared among contracting parties. Information about risk and return is needed to determine contract terms. Return is the amount a party to a contract expects as compensation for the exchange outlined in the contract. As noted earlier in this chapter, risk is uncertainty about an outcome; it results from uncertainty about the amount and timing of return. Exhibit 11 describes the returns of two investments (A and B) over several time periods. Which investment is riskier? Returns for investment A are relatively stable and predictable; they are growing at a steady rate. Returns for investment B are less predictable. Investment B is riskier than A, although it may produce higher returns over time than A.

Those who invest in a company expect to earn returns on their investments. At the same time, they must evaluate the risk inherent in investing in the company. What

Exhibit 10
Examples of Exchanges Requiring Information

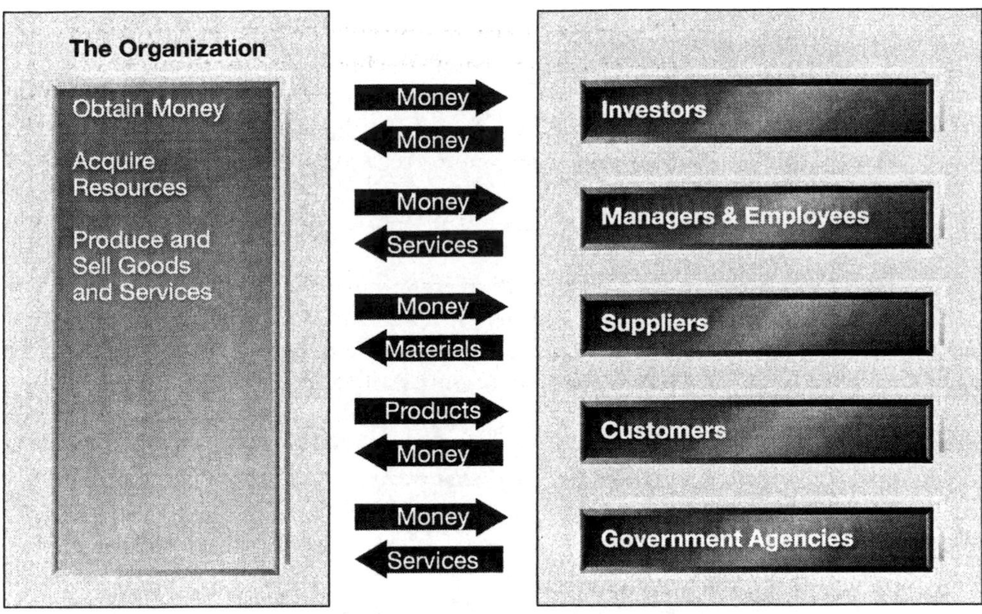

Exhibit 11
An Illustration of Risk and Return

	Returns	
Time Period	**Investment A**	**Investment B**
1	$6	$10
2	6	12
3	7	7
4	7	3
5	8	8
6	8	11

should they earn if the company does well? What might happen if the company does poorly? Risk and return are related in most situations; investors expect to earn higher returns on riskier investments. The higher returns compensate them for accepting higher risk. However, actual returns may differ from expected returns, and so riskier investments may actually result in higher or lower returns than less risky investments. On average, however, higher return should be associated with greater risk; otherwise, investors will not participate in risky investments. Accounting information helps investors predict risk and return associated with investments. The following sections consider the risk and return evaluations made by those who contract with an organization.

Investors and Creditors. Investors and creditors contract with companies to provide financial resources in exchange for future returns. They need information to decide whether to invest in a company and how much to invest. **Accounting information helps investors evaluate the risk and return they can expect from their investments. Also, it helps them determine whether managers of companies they invest in are meeting the terms of their contracts.**

If a company does not earn sufficient profits, it may be unable to repay its creditors, and creditors can force a company to liquidate (sell all its noncash resources) to repay its debts. On the other hand, if a company is profitable, stockholders (investors) normally earn higher returns than creditors because stockholders have a right to share in a company's profits. Creditors receive only the amount of interest agreed to when debt is issued. Consequently, investors and creditors choose between risk and return.

Managers. Owners generally do not manage large corporations. Instead, they hire managers who operate the businesses for them. Managers contract with owners to provide management services in exchange for salaries and other compensation. Owners, or directors who represent them, need information to determine how well managers are performing and to reward managers when they do well. To provide incentives for managers to perform well, owners may offer managers bonuses when a company is profitable. **Accounting information provides a means for owners and managers to determine the amount of compensation managers will receive.**

Compensation arrangements also encourage managers to present their companies' performances in the best light. Often, compensation is linked to profits and other accounting information, giving managers incentives to report numbers that will maximize their compensation. The combination of management control over information and manager incentives to make their companies look good provides an ethical dilemma for managers. Sometimes, they must choose between the company's best interests and their own best interests.

http://ingram.swlearning.com

Learn more about Enron.

Moral Hazard—Mismanagement by Managers

In 2001, **Enron Corporation**, the seventh largest U.S. corporation at the time, declared bankruptcy after revealing that its profits had been overstated for several years and that it had failed to report large amounts of debt. The debt was used by the corporation to expand its business operations into new markets and products. Some of these new ventures resulted in losses that were not properly reported by the corporation's management. When revealed, these losses made it difficult for the corporation to obtain additional financing, and it was unable to meet its debt obligations. As a result of these events, the market value of the corporation decreased dramatically, creating losses for many investors. Many employees lost their jobs and retirement savings, and many creditors were unable to collect amounts owed them.

Enron's investors and creditors sued the company's managers, claiming that they had been misled by information reported by the managers. The managers had earned high salaries and other compensation associated with the high profitability and growth they reported for the company. Investors and creditors, and many members of Congress who investigated the collapse of Enron, argued that managers had profited by operating the business for personal gain rather than for the benefit of the company's owners.

Decisions by managers have a direct effect on the risk and return of those who contract with a company. Managers decide which resources to acquire, when to acquire them, and how much to pay for them.

Each investment in a resource involves decisions about the risk and return associated with the investment. An organization is a portfolio (collection) of individual resources. In combination, the risks and returns on the investments in these resources help determine the risk and return of the organization as a whole. One task of management is to select a portfolio of resources that will yield a desired amount of return at a level of risk that managers and owners find acceptable. Investments in proven technology and established products generally are less risky than investments in new technology or products. Investments in resources in some countries are riskier than those in other countries because of those countries' political and economic environments. **Accounting information is useful for identifying the types and locations of an organization's resources.**

A major purpose of accounting is to measure costs associated with the flow of resources through the transformation process. Accounting also measures resources obtained from selling goods and services. The profits earned by a corporation are a major determinant of risk and return. **Information about the results of the operations of a business is used to estimate, compare, and manage companies' risks and returns.**

Employees. Employees have a major effect on a company's risk and return. Wages and quality of work directly affect product quality, sales, costs, and profits. Companies evaluate the cost and productivity of their employees. They compare employee performance with management expectations, examine changes over time, and compare different divisions with each other. **Accounting information helps managers assess employee performance.**

Employees negotiate for wages, benefits, and job security. Compensation is affected by a company's performance and financial condition. Labor unions and other employee groups use accounting information to evaluate a company's ability to compensate its employees. Like other contracting parties, employees evaluate risk and return in an employment relationship. If a company does well, employees expect to be rewarded. If it does poorly, they may face layoffs, wage and benefit cuts, and loss of jobs. **Accounting information helps employees assess the risk and return of their employment contracts.**

Suppliers. An organization purchases materials, merchandise, and other resources from suppliers. These resources are a major cost for most companies. Careful negotiation of prices, credit, and delivery schedules between management and suppliers is required. If a company cannot obtain quality materials when they are needed, it may incur major losses as a result of idle production, waste, lost sales, and dissatisfied customers. If a supplier goes out of business or cannot fulfill its commitments, a company may have difficulty obtaining needed resources. **Accounting information helps companies evaluate the abilities of their suppliers to meet their resource needs.**

Suppliers often sell resources to companies on credit. These suppliers are creditors who are financing the sale of resources to a company in anticipation of future payments. Usually, these loans are for short periods (30 to 60 days), although longer financing sometimes is arranged. When a company is not profitable, its suppliers may have difficulty collecting the amounts owed them. Therefore, suppliers evaluate the risk they are taking in selling on credit to other companies. **Suppliers often use accounting information about their customers to evaluate the risk of a buyer not being able to pay for goods and services acquired.**

Customers. A company is a supplier to its customers. Thus, it evaluates customers in the same way it is evaluated by suppliers. Managers decide the terms of sales by evaluating the risk and return associated with the sales. Riskier customers normally receive less favorable terms. For example, a customer with good credit can purchase a house, car, appliances, and other goods on more favorable terms than can a customer with bad credit.

Customers' decisions to buy products often are affected by their perception of quality and dependability, as well as price. These decisions also may depend on the financial reputation of the seller. Will the company be in business in the future when maintenance, repair, or replacement is needed? Will it be able to honor warranties? Are its profits sufficient to invest in new technology and maintain quality products? **Accounting information is used to assess the risks of buying from specific companies and selling to specific customers.**

Government Agencies. Organizations are required to provide information to government agencies. Governments require businesses to purchase licenses for selling goods and services and to pay fees and taxes for various government services. Often these amounts are determined by the amount of sales or the profitability of an organization. Governments collect information about organizations as a basis for economic forecasts and planning at the local, state, and national levels. Businesses are required to report information to state and federal authorities that regulate business activities to ensure fair trade, fair treatment of employees, and fair disclosure to investors.

Businesses report information to taxing authorities at various levels of government. Reports are required in filing sales, property, payroll, excise, and income taxes. The amount of these taxes is determined by a company's sales, the costs it incurs, and amounts paid to employees. **Government agencies use accounting information to make taxation and regulatory decisions.**

THE REGULATORY ENVIRONMENT OF ACCOUNTING

OBJECTIVE 7

Explain the purpose and importance of accounting regulations.

Accounting information prepared for use by external decision makers is financial accounting information. ***Financial accounting*** **is the process of preparing, reporting, and interpreting accounting information that is provided to external decision makers.** It is a primary source of information for investors and creditors. Thus, it is very important to the organization when it wants to obtain resources from those external decision makers. It also may affect the decisions of suppliers, customers, and employees. Because of concerns about information reliability and moral hazard, managers of major corporations prepare financial accounting information according to specific rules called *generally accepted accounting principles* (GAAP). ***GAAP*** **are standards developed by professional accounting organizations to identify appropriate accounting and reporting procedures.** GAAP establish minimum disclosure requirements and increase the comparability of information from one period to the next and among different companies.

LEARNING NOTE

GAAP apply only to information prepared for use by external decision makers. Because managers control information available inside an organization, accounting standards such as GAAP are not necessary for this information.

This textbook emphasizes financial accounting for corporations. Moral hazard resulting from the separation of owners and managers has led to the creation of a strong regulatory environment for corporations. This environment oversees the development of accounting and reporting requirements for corporations. We will examine this environment and the resulting requirements.

Financial accounting usually is distinguished from managerial accounting. ***Managerial*** **(or** ***management*****)** ***accounting*** **is the process of preparing, reporting, and interpreting accounting information that is provided to internal decision makers.** Because managers have control over the information they use internally, this information does not have to be prepared according to GAAP. Accounting information reported by managers to owners and other external decision makers is the subject of financial accounting. It is important to keep in mind, however, that this information also is used by managers. Although managers have access to information that extends beyond that reported to external decision makers, internal and external decisions are related. Therefore, this book will consider internal and external decisions that rely on financial accounting information.

LEARNING NOTE

Managers, as internal decision makers, use financial accounting information to evaluate the performance of their companies. Also, they are concerned about the effect of financial accounting information on the decisions of the other stakeholders because these decisions can affect their companies.

Accounting information reported by corporations to investors must be audited. **An** ***audit*** **is a detailed examination of an organization's financial reports.** It includes an examination of the information system used to prepare the reports and involves an examination of control procedures organizations use to help ensure the accuracy of accounting information. The purpose of an audit is to evaluate whether information reported to external decision makers is a **fair presentation** of an organization's economic activities. Standards (GAAP) for the preparation and reporting of information help ensure the reliability of accounting information. The auditors, who are independent **certified public accountants (CPAs)**, examine this information to confirm that it is prepared according to GAAP. To be a CPA, a person must pass a qualifying exam and meet education and experience requirements. CPAs are independent of the companies they audit because they are not

http://ingram.swlearning.com

Learn more about the CPA exam.

company employees. Rather, they work for an accounting firm that is hired by the company's owners to perform the audit. In the case of a corporation, it is the board of directors, with the approval of stockholders, that hires the auditor. Also, CPAs should have no vested interests in the companies that might bias their audits.

LEARNING NOTE

GAAP apply to all business organizations. As long as accounting information produced by the business is used for internal purposes only, the company's managers can elect whether or not that information complies with GAAP. Conformity with GAAP is required for information produced for external users, such as creditors. Many privately-owned businesses are audited because they are required to provide accounting information to banks and other financial institutions that lend money to the businesses.

Many corporations must report audited financial accounting information to governmental agencies. Corporations whose stock is traded publicly in the United States report to the **Securities and Exchange Commission (SEC)**. This agency examines corporate financial reports to verify their conformance with GAAP and SEC requirements. If the SEC believes a company's reports have not been prepared in conformance with GAAP, it can refer the company to the Justice Department for criminal and civil charges. In addition, the corporation's auditors can be prosecuted if they fail to meet their responsibilities for ensuring that a corporation's reports are a fair representation of its economic activities.

Case In Point

http://ingram.swlearning.com

Learn more about auditor responsibilities.

Auditor Responsibility

Enron Corporation's audit firm, **Andersen**, was investigated for its role in the misstatement of Enron's financial information. The audit firm admitted that it made mistakes in the audit but argued that Enron's managers had failed to report fully to the auditors about its questionable business activities. Andersen also was charged by the Federal government with destroying information that would have assisted the government in its investigation of Enron's activities. In addition, this industry leader can no longer perform SEC audits. Consequently, Andersen lost a major portion of its business as former clients awarded their audits to other audit firms and as many Andersen employees left the firm.

Critics also questioned Andersen's independence in the audit because the firm earned large consulting fees from Enron. The critics argued that Andersen did not press Enron for proper disclosure of its business activities for fear that it would lose Enron as a client, thereby losing the consulting fees in addition to its audit fees. It is important that audit firms be *perceived* as being independent of their clients, in addition to actually *being* independent. Auditors must continuously assess their independence.

Financial accounting is critical for the operations of a market economy. **Full and fair disclosure** of business activities is necessary for stakeholders to evaluate the returns and risks they anticipate from investing in and contracting with business organizations. **Capital markets,** markets in which corporations obtain financing from investors, in particular, require information that permits investors to assess the risks and returns of their investments. If that information is not available or is unreliable, investors are unable to make good decisions. **Without reliable information about companies' business activities, investors cannot determine which companies are most efficient and effective and are making the best use of resources.** Consequently, resources may be allocated to less efficient and effective companies, resulting in a loss of value for society.

Without good information, contracts cannot be evaluated, and markets cannot function properly. Consequently, accounting plays a critical role in our society. For our society to continue to prosper, it is essential that those who make decisions about resource allocations understand accounting information and how to use that information to evaluate business activities. They need to understand how accounting information is created and the limitations inherent in this information. Failure to understand accounting properly is likely to lead to poor decisions and unsatisfactory economic outcomes.

This book will help you understand why accounting information is important, how this information is produced, and how you can use this information to make good business decisions. It will help you learn to evaluate business activities and to determine which companies are operating most efficiently and effectively. It will help you contribute to improving our society by becoming an informed participant in our market economy.

THE IMPORTANCE OF ETHICS

OBJECTIVE 8

Explain why ethics are important for business and accounting.

Ethics are important in business organizations. Ethics involve living by the norms and rules of society. In business, those norms and rules identify appropriate behavior for managers, employees, investors, and other stakeholders. Keeping their investors and other stakeholders fully informed about their business activities is an important ethical norm for managers. Managers who conceal their activities or who misrepresent those activities make it difficult for stakeholders to assess how well a business is performing. Overstating profits, for example, may result in investors allocating more resources to a company than actual results would justify. This misallocation results in a loss of value to society and often leads to financial harm for those who use this information.

Ethical behavior is particularly important for accounting because the reliability of accounting information depends on the honesty of those who prepare, report, and audit this information. Managers may make decisions that benefit themselves at a cost to investors or other stakeholders. If they then attempt to conceal these decisions by reporting incorrect information, that information is not an accurate description of the economic activities of a business. If employees steal money or other resources from a business and the thefts are not detected, the company's accounting information also will not properly reflect the company's economic situation. If those who audit a company do not ensure that reported information is a fair representation of the company's business activities, those who rely on the information are likely to be disadvantaged.

Those who contract with businesses must consider the ethics of those who manage them. Managers who are willing to bend rules or operate outside of accepted norms are likely to be untrustworthy. An important role of accounting is to evaluate whether appropriate rules are being followed in accounting for reporting business activities. Failure to follow these rules can result in significant economic consequences, as evidenced by the collapse of Enron Corporation. Generally accepted accounting principles and other accounting and auditing rules have been created to help ensure that companies fairly report their business activities. In addition, corporations and other organizations are required to maintain elaborate systems of controls to make it difficult for managers and employees to engage in unethical behavior or misrepresent business activities. We examine ethical issues and controls throughout this book as we consider proper accounting rules and procedures.

3 SELF-STUDY PROBLEM

R. Floorshine is a manufacturer of shoes. The company operates as a corporation and has issued shares of stock to its owners and debt to creditors. It has purchased and leased buildings and equipment. It purchases materials on short-term credit and converts the materials into shoes. The shoes are sold to retail stores, also on a short-term credit arrangement.

Required Identify the primary exchanges and contracts between the company and its stakeholders. Describe the primary information needs associated with these exchanges and contracts.

The solution to Self-Study Problem 3 appears at the end of the chapter.

Appendix A SHORT INTRODUCTION TO EXCEL

SPREADSHEET

This introduction summarizes some of the primary operations and functions of a spreadsheet. It is intended to get you started if you have not had previous experience with Excel. There are many operations and functions in addition to those mentioned here.

Identifying and Selecting Cells

A spreadsheet consists of rows and columns. Rows are identified by numbers, and columns are identified by letters. An intersection of a row and column is a cell. A cell is identified by the column letter and row number that intersect at that cell.

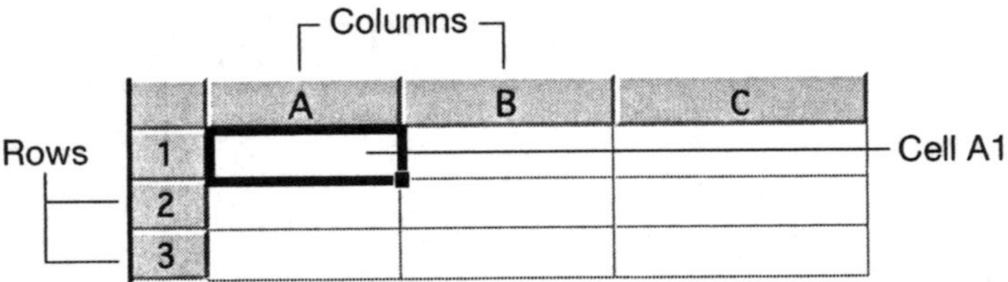

To select a cell, click on the cell using the left mouse button. A cell must be selected before you can enter data or format the cell. Enter data by typing numbers, words, or characters. Enter numbers without commas. Commas can be added using formatting procedures described later. An entire row or column can be selected by clicking on the row or column header. The row header is the leftmost cell in a row that contains the row number. A column header is the topmost cell in a column that contains the cell letter. A group of neighboring cells can be selected by clicking with the left mouse button on the cell in the upper, left corner of the group, then dragging the cursor over all the cells to be selected.

Referencing and Mathematical Operations

The contents of one or more cells can be referenced in another cell. To reference a cell, enter the equal sign followed by the cell being referenced. For example, entering =A1 in cell B1 will copy the contents of cell A1 in cell B1. If the contents of cell A1 are changed, these changes also will appear in cell B1. A common use of cell referencing is to calculate totals from data in a series of cells. For example, the following spreadsheet contains sales data for the first three months of a year. The total appears in cell B5. To calculate the total, you would enter a formula in cell B5. The formula would be =B2+B3+B4.

	A	B
1		Sales
2	January	3,457.38
3	February	3,892.90
4	March	3,204.07
5	Total	10,554.35

Normal mathematical operations can be entered in a cell:

=B2+B3 adds the contents of cells B2 and B3.
=B2−B3 subtracts the contents of cell B3 from cell B2.
=B2*B3 multiplies the contents of cell B2 by the contents of cell B3.
=B2/B3 divides the contents of cell B2 by the contents of cell B3.
=B2^B3 raises the number in cell B2 to the power of the number in cell B3.

Copying Cell Contents

The contents (including a formula) can be copied from one cell or group of cells to another cell or group of cells. To copy the contents, select the cells containing the data to be copied and click on Edit/Copy. Then select the cell you want to copy to (or the upper, left cell of a group of cells) and click Edit/Paste.

The contents of a cell also can be copied to a neighboring cell using a shortcut procedure. In the following example, we want to copy the contents of cell B4 to cell C4. Cell B4 contains the formula =B2+B3. To copy the contents, we select cell B4 and drag the cursor over the box in the lower, right corner of cell B4. The cursor changes shape and appears as crosshairs (+). If we click on the left mouse button while the cursor is in this shape, we can drag the contents of cell B4 to cell C4. The formula =B2+B3 is copied to cell C4, except that the references are automatically adjusted for the new column, and the formula appears as =C2+C3.

	A	B	C
1		Cash	Merchandise
2	Store 1	1,543.02	16,794.23
3	Store 2	4,587.45	24,586.50
4	Total	6,130.47	

Box

When you enter a formula in a cell, such as =B2+B3, the cell addresses are relative addresses. When the formula is copied to another cell, the relative addresses change. Copying the contents of cell B4 above to cell C4 results in an adjustment in the formula so that =B2+B3 is changed to =C2+C3. You can also enter absolute addresses. An absolute address results from entering a dollar sign ($) before a cell address. For example, if you enter =$B2+$B3 in cell B4 and then copy cell B4 to cell C4, the formula in C4 remains =$B2+$B3. You can use absolute addresses for the column (=$B2), the row (=B$2) or both (=B2).

Changing Column Widths

You can make a column wider or narrower using the Format/Column/Width menu. A simpler approach is to move the cursor to the right-hand side of the column header of the column you wish to adjust. The cursor changes to appear as ↔. Click and drag the cursor to the right or left to adjust the column width. The same procedure can be used for row height adjustments.

Menus

The top of an Excel spreadsheet contains menus. A brief description of the menu items you are likely to use on a regular basis follows.

File. Use the File menu to open a **New** spreadsheet, to **Open** an existing spreadsheet, to **Save** a spreadsheet, to **Print** a spreadsheet, and to **Close** the Excel program.

Edit. Use the Edit menu to **Delete** a row, column, or cell. Select the row, column, or cell and click Edit/Delete. You can delete the contents of a particular cell by selecting the cell and pressing the Backspace or Delete key.

View. Use the View menu to select which Toolbars appear on the spreadsheet. The Header and Footer command permits you to add titles and comments to spreadsheets that will appear on printed output. The Zoom command allows spreadsheets to be resized as they appear on the monitor to make them easier to see. This command does not affect printed output.

Insert. Use the Insert menu to insert **Rows, Columns,** and **Cells**. To enter a new row, select the row *below* the row you wish to add and click on Insert/Row. To enter a new column, select the column to the *left* of the column you want to add and click on Insert/Column. To enter a new cell, click on the cell where you want to add a new cell and click on Insert/Cell. A dialog box will ask whether you want the existing cell moved to the right or down. When you enter a new cell, all existing cells to the right or below the entered cell will be moved to make room for the new cell.

Format. Use the Format menu to format **Cells.** Select the cells and click on Format/Cells. A dialog box provides options. The **Number** tab provides various formatting options. The **Alignment** tab provides options for how numbers or text will be aligned. The Wrap text box can be checked (click on the box) to allow for more than one line of text to appear in a particular cell.

Tools. Use the Tools menu to check your **Spelling.**

Data. Use the Data menu to **Sort** data. To sort, select all the columns in the spreadsheet and click Data/Sort. A dialog box lets you select the column or columns you want to use to sort the data.

Help. Use the Help menu to get additional directions about using Excel. Click on Help/Contents and Index. Select a topic from the **Contents** tab or click on the **Index** tab. Type the keyword for an item to get additional information and click on the Display button.

Buttons

Several of the buttons under the menu are particularly useful. The identity of each button and its use are described below.

Save. Click to save your spreadsheet. **Save your work often.**

Copy. Copies the contents of a selected cell or group of cells.

Paste. Pastes the contents of a copied cell or group of cells into a selected cell or group.

Format Painter. Copies the format of a selected cell into another cell or group of cells. Select the cell with the format to be copied and click the button. Then click on the cell or click and drag over the cells where the format will be copied.

Σ **AutoSum.** Select a cell to contain the sum of a neighboring set of cells (above or to the left of the selected cell). For example, we want to sum the contents of cells E10 and E11 into cell E12. Select cell E12 and click on the AutoSum button. The =Sum formula appears in cell E12 as shown below. You can change the cells to be included in the sum by clicking on the top cell to be included and dragging the cursor over the cells to be added as part of the sum.

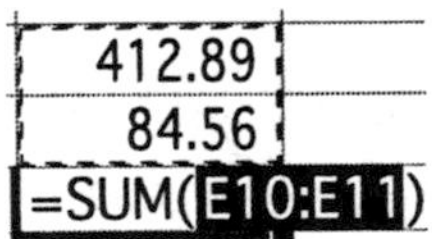

Once the sum formula is correct, click on the checkmark in the selection box at the top of the spreadsheet:

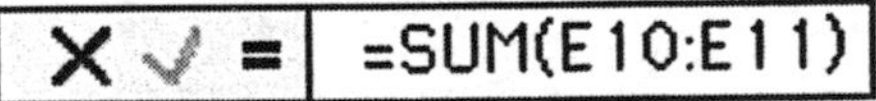

Click on the green checkmark to accept the cell contents. Click on the red X to remove the cell contents.

B I U **Format.** Select a cell or group of cells and click on B for bold, I for italics, and U for underline.

Align. Select a cell or group of cells and click on a button to align the cell contents to the left, center, or right of the cell.

Merge and Center. Select two or more neighboring cells in a row and click on the button to merge the cells into a single cell and center the cell contents. For example, the caption (The Book Wermz) in the following example was created by selecting cells B1 and C1 and clicking on the Merge and Center button.

	A	B	C
1		The Book Wermz	
2	Store 1	1,543.0	Merchandise
3	January	4,528.23	145,360.98

$ % , **Number Formatting.** Select a cell or group of cells and click on a button to include a dollar sign in the cell(s), to convert from decimals to percentages, or to add comma separators between thousands' digits in numbers.

Decimal Places. Select a cell or group of cells and click on a button to increase or decrease the number of decimal places showing in the cell(s).

Indent. Select a cell or group of cells and click on a button to indent the cell contents or to remove the indentation.

Borders. Select a cell or group of cells and click on the down arrow. Select the type of border you want for the cell(s) from the options provided. If the option you want is already showing on the button, click on the button to select that option.

REVIEW

SUMMARY of IMPORTANT CONCEPTS

1. The accounting process provides information about business activities to help decision makers allocate scarce resources.
   a. Accounting measures profits created by a business as the dollar amount of resources created from selling goods and services minus the dollar amount of resources consumed in producing and making the goods and services available to customers.
   b. Accounting helps decision makers determine the risk and return they should anticipate from a business investment or activity.

2. Organizations serve the needs of society by providing a means for people to work together to accomplish their goals.
   a. Businesses operate as merchandising, manufacturing, and service companies. Other organizations, like governments and nonprofit organizations, are nonbusiness organizations.
   b. All organizations benefit society by transforming resources from one form to another form that is more valuable in meeting the needs of people.

3. Businesses sell their products and acquire resources in competitive markets.
   a. Markets provide a way for people to express their perceptions of the value of goods and services by the products they purchase and the prices they pay. Markets allocate resources to those companies and activities that market participants believe best meet their needs.
   b. Value created by a business is measured by the difference between the dollar amount of resources created from selling goods and services and the dollar amount of resources consumed in producing and making the goods and services available to customers.

4. Owners invest in a business to receive a return on their investments from business profits. Businesses that operate effectively and efficiently normally will earn higher profits.
   a. Businesses that are not profitable will have difficulty attracting investors and will be forced to change their behavior or to go out of business.

b. Markets make financial and other scarce resources available to organizations that can best transform them to maximize their value for society.

5. Businesses operate as corporations, proprietorships, and partnerships.
   a. Corporations can obtain large amounts of capital by selling stock to many investors.
   b. Owners of corporations usually hire professional managers to run their businesses. They depend on these managers to run the business for the benefit of owners and to report reliable information about their business activities.

6. Accounting information is used in corporations and other organizations to create and evaluate contracts and other agreements between a company and its stakeholders.
   a. Accounting information helps investors and creditors assess the return and risk associated with their investments and loans.
   b. Accounting information is useful for determining management compensation, determining an organization's resources, and evaluating results of its operating activities.
   c. Accounting information helps managers evaluate employee performance and helps employees evaluate the risk and return of their employment contracts.
   d. Accounting information helps companies evaluate their suppliers and helps customers evaluate the companies from which they make purchases.
   e. Accounting information helps government agencies make taxation and regulatory decisions.

7. Because investors and other external stakeholders have limited access to business information, information reported to external parties is regulated.
   a. Companies must prepare financial accounting information in conformity with generally accepted accounting standards.
   b. This information is audited by an independent accountant to ensure that it fairly represents a company's business activities.
   c. Reliable accounting information is essential for the proper operation of markets that depend on the information to determine how to allocate resources.

8. Ethical behavior is important to ensure that businesses are managed properly and that accounting information is reliable. Accounting rules and controls have been created to help monitor and enforce ethical behavior.

DEFINE

TERMS and CONCEPTS DEFINED in this CHAPTER

accounting (F10)
audit (F20)
business organization (F6)
contracts (F16)
corporation (F10)
creditor (F14)
effective business (F9)
efficient business (F9)
financial accounting (F20)
generally accepted accounting principles (GAAP) (F20)
governmental and nonprofit organizations (F6)
information (F3)
management accounting (F20)
managerial accounting (F20)
manufacturing companies (F6)
market (F7)
merchandising companies (F5)
moral hazard (F14)
mutual agency (F13)
organization (F5)
partnerships (F11)
profit (F8)
proprietorships (F11)
retail companies (F5)
return on investment (ROI) (F9)
risk (F5)
service companies (F6)
shareholders (F11)
stakeholders (F5)
stock (F11)
stockholders (F11)

SELF-STUDY PROBLEM SOLUTIONS

SSP1-1 A.

Bach's Music Store
Profit Earned
For December 2004

Resources created from selling goods and services:		
Musical instruments	$8,000	
Sheet music	1,400	
Repair of instruments	2,200	
Total resources created		$11,600
Resources consumed:		
Cost of instruments sold	4,300	
Cost of sheet music sold	870	
Rent	650	
Supplies used	250	
Advertising	300	
Utilities	200	
Miscellaneous	180	
Total resources consumed		6,750
Profit		$ 4,850

B. The value created by a transformation of resources is the difference between the total price of the goods and services sold and the total cost of the resources consumed in producing these goods and services. This difference is profit for the seller.

SSP1-2 Hammer Hardware is owned and managed by Harvey Hammer. As a small company, Hammer Hardware does not need access to large amounts of capital. Harvey is probably more interested in maintaining control of his company rather than having others invest in it. As a proprietorship, Harvey has total control of the business. All company profits belong to him. A primary disadvantage of the proprietorship is that Harvey is personally liable for all of the company's obligations. He is responsible for paying the company's debts, even if they require use of his personal resources.

Home Depot is a large corporation. To obtain the financial resources the company needs, it sells stock to a large number of investors. These investors expect a return from their investments but have no interest in managing the company. Instead, they hire professional managers to run the company for them. Corporations permit access to large amounts of capital. Also, individual owners are not responsible for the corporation's debt, thus reducing the risk of ownership. A primary disadvantage of corporations is that owners have little access to information about the company. They depend on managers to run the business for the benefit of owners and to provide reliable information about their business activities.

SSP1-3 A. **Exchanges and contracts between managers, owners, and creditors:** Owners and creditors exchange money with Floorshine for the right to receive cash in the future from the company. Contracts exist among managers, owners, and creditors. Managers contract with owners and creditors for money to acquire resources that will generate profits for the company and to employ the resources effectively and efficiently. Managers expect to be rewarded for their effectiveness and efficiency, and owners and creditors expect a fair return on their investments. These contracting parties need information to assess how well managers have performed and to determine how much cash from the company's operations should be distributed to each party. Managers, owners, and creditors decide whether the terms of contracts are being met. Owners hire independent auditors (CPAs) to examine the financial information provided by managers to owners and creditors to ensure its reliability.

B. **Exchanges and contracts between suppliers and managers:** Suppliers exchange goods and services with the company for the right to receive cash. Contracts between suppliers and managers require information to determine that the company receives the correct types and quantities of goods and services at the appropriate times. Also, information is needed to demonstrate that the company has made timely payments for these goods and services.

C. **Exchanges and contracts between employees and managers:** Employees exchange labor services with the company for wages and benefits. Contracts between employees and managers describe the payments, benefits, and rights employees have negotiated with managers. Information is needed to demonstrate that labor services have been provided and employees have been treated fairly. The demands of employees for future wages and benefits depend, in part, on the profitability of the company. Employees and managers need information about the performance of the company to negotiate future contracts.

D. **Exchanges and contracts between customers and managers:** Customers exchange cash for goods and services provided by the company. Customers, such as retail stores, may receive the goods and pay for them later, say within 30 or 60 days. Managers expect to receive the payments when they are due. Contracts between customers and managers call for the delivery of goods to customers and payment to the company. Customers decide whether to continue to purchase the company's goods. The quality and costs of the goods and future prospects for obtaining the goods when needed are relevant pieces of information. Information about the payment history of customers helps managers decide whether to continue to extend credit to customers.

E. **Exchanges and contracts between government agencies and managers:** Government agencies monitor companies to determine if they are engaged in fair trade and labor practices. Managers provide information to demonstrate that the company is conforming to government regulations. Governments provide services to companies in the form of police and fire protection, utilities, sanitation, and streets and roads. Companies pay taxes and fees for these services. Information is required to verify that appropriate amounts of taxes and fees are being paid.

Thinking Beyond the Question

What do we need to know to start a business?

The chapter introduction asked you to consider what you would need to know in order to start a company. This chapter identified several important considerations. How would your answer to this question differ if you were starting a service business or a nonprofit service organization as opposed to a retail business?

QUESTIONS

Q1-1 *Obj. 1* What is the purpose of accounting? How does accounting accomplish that purpose?

Q1-2 *Obj. 1* How can accounting information help investors understand risk?

Q1-3 *Obj. 2* How does the purpose of merchandising, manufacturing, and service companies differ? How do they each create value?

Q1-4 *Obj. 2* List an example of each of the following types of organization. Describe how each type of organization differs from each of the others.

a. Merchandising
b. Manufacturing
c. Service
d. Governmental
e. Nonprofit

Q1-5 *Obj. 3* Sandy Dune overheard some friends from your accounting class discussing the "transformation of resources." She is curious about what this term means and how it applies to organizations and accounting. Explain to Sandy your understanding of the transformation of resources and why it is an important concept in accounting.

Q1-6 *Obj. 3* Accounting is an information system that measures and reports the value created when a company transforms resources. Does an accounting system create value? If so, how? If not, why do companies have them?

Q1-7 *Obj. 4* Phillip invested $3,000 in a business at the beginning of the year. By the end of the year, the value of this investment had risen to $4,100. Near year-end, the business sent Phillip a check for $2,000. Describe the difference between a return *on* investment and a return *of* investment. What portion of the $2,000 is return on investment and what portion is return of investment?

Q1-8 *Obj. 4* How are effectiveness, efficiency, return on investment, and accounting interrelated? Be specific.

Q1-9 *Obj. 6* What is a contract, and why are contracts important for business organizations?

Q1-10 *Obj. 6* What is meant by risk, and why is it an important concept for decision makers to understand? What is the relationship between risk and accounting?

Q1-11 *Obj. 6* Your friend is puzzled that the topic of contracts has come up in your accounting class. Says he, "Contracts are the business of lawyers, not accountants. Why are we studying contracts in an accounting class?" Educate your friend.

Q1-12 *Obj. 6* Your uncle tells you that risk is to be avoided when considering potential investments. In fact, he believes the government should ban risky investments to protect the public. Do you agree with your uncle? Why or why not?

Q1-13 *Obj. 6* It is often said that there exists a risk-return tradeoff. That is, to obtain a higher return, one must be willing to accept higher risk. If one wishes to incur little risk, one must be willing to accept a smaller return. What evidence of this do you observe in the world around you, either in investments or other aspects of life?

Q1-14 *Obj. 6* Why do owners invest in businesses even though such an investment is more risky than investing in U.S. Savings Bonds? If you had $3,000 to invest, how would you decide whether to invest it in businesses or whether to invest it in U.S. Savings Bonds?

Q1-15 *Objs. 6, 7* What is the interrelationship among the concepts of risk, moral hazard (when setting executive compensation), and generally accepted accounting principles?

Q1-16 *Obj. 7* How does an audit increase the credibility of financial statements?

Q1-17 *Obj. 7* An accounting classmate notes that adherence to GAAP is not required for managerial accounting reports. She observes, "If it's so important for financial accounting, it seems reasonable that it would also be useful for managerial reporting." Explain to her why it's more important that financial accounting reports adhere to GAAP than it is for managerial accounting reports to do so. In what ways is managerial accounting different from financial accounting?

EXERCISES

If your instructor is using Personal Trainer in this course, you may complete online the assignments identified by PT.

E1-1 Write a short definition for each of the terms listed in the *Terms and Concepts Defined in This Chapter* section.

E1-2 *Obj. 1* Assume you have a friend, Edwina Polinder, who has no knowledge of accounting. Draft a short memo to Edwina that will help her understand the purpose of accounting.

DATE: (today's date)
TO: Edwina Polinder
FROM: (your name)
SUBJECT: Inquiry about accounting
(your response)

E1-3 *Objs. 1, 6* Wilma Borrelli is a stockholder of Essex International, a major supplier of building materials. Wilma received information that Essex sustained a large loss during the most recent quarter and is expecting bigger losses during the coming quarter. How might this information affect those who contract with Essex?

E1-4 *Obj. 2* PT Match the type of organization with the characteristics and examples provided below:

Type of organization:

1. Merchandising (or retail) companies
2. Manufacturing companies
3. Service companies
4. Governmental and nonprofit organizations

Characteristics and examples:

a. Provide goods or services without the intent of making a profit. Examples include the **IRS** and the **United Way**.
b. Produce goods that are sold to consumers or to merchandising companies. Examples include **Ford Motor Company** and **PepsiCo.**
c. Sell to consumers goods that are produced by other companies. Examples include **Wal-Mart** and **Sears.**
d. Sell services rather than goods. Examples include **H&R Block** and **Delta Air Lines.**

E1-5 *Obj. 3* PT Leonardo has started a small business making sundials. The following transactions occurred for the business during a recent period. How much profit did the company earn for this period?

Sales to customers	$970
Rent for the period	450
Supplies used during the period	225
Wages for the period	180

E1-6 *Obj. 3* PT Soft Light Company produces specialty lamps and sells them to retail stores. During the latest year, the company sold 40,000 lamps at an average price of $70 per lamp. The production and distribution costs per lamp were $25, on average. Other costs for the year were $1,200,000 for management salaries and facilities. Total investment in the company is $3,000,000. How much profit did Soft Light earn for the year? Describe the steps you went through to get your answer.

E1-7 *Obj. 3* PT Fashion Threads Company uses the following four steps to make a particular pair of cotton slacks:

a. Cotton is planted, grown, harvested, and shipped to a textile manufacturer. The cost to produce the cotton associated with the slacks is $5. This amount of cotton is sold to the manufacturer for $5.50.
b. Raw cotton is processed into cotton fabric. The cost of producing the fabric for the slacks, including the cost of the raw cotton, is $13.25. This fabric is sold to a garment manufacturer for $17.
c. Cotton fabric is cut and sewn to produce a pair of slacks. The cost of making the slacks, including the cost of the fabric, is $25. The slacks are sold to a retailer for $30.
d. The cost to the retailer of making the slacks available for sale, including the cost of the slacks, is $34. The retailer sells the slacks for $56.

(Continued)

Use Exhibits 5 and 6 to help you answer the following questions. How much profit is earned at each step in the production and selling process? How much total profit is earned by those involved in making and selling the slacks? Why are customers willing to pay the amounts involved in this process?

E1-8 *Obj. 3* Alexander makes professional baseball gloves by hand. He buys leather for $80 a yard. Padding costs $6 a pound; thread and other materials cost $16 for a month's supply. He pays $500 a month rent for a small shop, and utilities average $150 a month. Shipping costs are about $4.50 per glove. In an average month, Alexander produces and sells 8 gloves. Each glove requires a half yard of leather and a half pound of padding. What is the average cost of a glove made by Alexander? How much profit does Alexander earn on each glove if he sells them for $475 each? How much profit does Alexander earn each month, on average? Exhibits 5 and 6 will help you answer these questions.

E1-9 *Obj. 3* Mario's Restaurant specializes in Italian food. During February, Mario's recorded the following sales to customers and costs of doing business:

Sales to customers	$19,500
Cost of food products used	5,750
Cost of rented building and equipment	4,376
Cost of employee labor services used	3,750
Maintenance and utilities used	2,000

Prepare a schedule that shows the amount of profit (or loss) earned by Mario's Restaurant during February. (Hint: See Exhibit 6.)

E1-10 *Obj. 3* The Quick Stop is a fast-food restaurant. During March, Quick Stop recorded the following sales to customers and costs of doing business:

Sales to customers	$4,400
Cost of food products used	2,100
Cost of rented building and equipment	1,250
Cost of employee labor services used	1,000
Maintenance and utilities used	600

Prepare a schedule that shows the amount of profit (or loss) earned by Quick Stop during March. (Hint: See Exhibit 6.)

E1-11 *Obj. 3* Pam Lucas is a high school student who delivers papers to earn spending money. During May, she received $450 from customers in payment for their subscriptions for the month. She paid $300 for the papers she delivered. In addition, she paid $45 to her parents for use of their car to deliver the papers, and she paid $30 for gas. Prepare a statement to compute the amount of profit Pam earned from her paper route in May. (Hint: See Exhibit 6.)

E1-12 *Obj. 4* On January 1, 2004, Alicia invested $4,000 in a savings account. At the end of January, the account balance had increased to $4,020. The balance at the end of February was $4,040.10. The balance at the end of March was $4,060.30. The increases occurred because of interest earned on the account. What was Alicia's return on investment, in dollars and cents, for each of the three months? What was the total return for the three months taken together?

E1-13 *Obj. 4* Davy Crockett invested $15,000 in Mike Fink Rafting Company. At the end of the year, Crockett's investment was worth $17,250 because of earnings during the year. Fink paid Crockett $3,000 at the end of the year. What was Crockett's return *on* investment (in dollars) for the year? What was his return *of* investment (in dollars) for the year? Did Mike Fink Rafting maintain its capital as a result of these events? Explain.

E1-14 *Obj. 4* Flick and Flack are two companies that sell identical products. They are located in different parts of the same city. During September, Flick sold $24,000 of goods, while Flack sold $18,000. Flick's profit was $8,000, and Flack's profit was $2,000. Compare the efficiency and effectiveness of the two companies.

E1-15 *Obj. 4* Rogers and Hornsby are two companies that compete in the same market with the same product, a brand of steak sauce. The companies are the same size and sell to the same grocery retailers. Both products are sold by the retailers at the same price. During 2004, Rogers sold 500,000 bottles of its sauce at a profit of 10 cents per bottle. Hornsby sold 425,000 bottles at a profit of 15 cents a bottle. Which company was more effective? Which was more efficient? Which company was more profitable?

E1-16 *Obj. 4* You have a choice of investing in either of two companies, Lewis or Clark. Both companies make the same products and compete in the same markets. Over the last five years, the operating results for the two companies have been:

	Lewis	Clark
Sales to customers	$4,500,000	$5,625,000
Profit	$412,500	$675,000
Return on investment per dollar invested	4.5%	7.5%

Which company is more efficient? Which is more effective? In which company would you invest? State the reasons for your answers.

E1-17 *Obj. 5* Identify each of the following as describing corporations, proprietorships, and/or partnerships. Some items have more than one answer.

a. Distinct legal entity separate from its owners.
b. More than one owner.
c. Ownership by stockholders.
d. Controlled by a board of directors.
e. Legal identity changes when a company is sold.
f. Limited liability.
g. Mutual agency.
h. Access to large amounts of capital.
i. Direct taxation of profits.
j. Moral hazard usually not a major problem.

E1-18 *Obj. 6* Yashiko Takawsa is a loan officer at a major bank. Hendrick Swindler recently applied for a small business loan for his dry cleaning company, Take 'Em to the Cleaners. As part of the application, Swindler was asked to provide financial information about his company. The financial reports revealed that the company had been fabulously profitable. What concerns might Yashiko have about the information provided by Swindler? What actions might she take to relieve these concerns?

E1-19 *Obj. 6* Wendy Hu is considering two new products for her office products manufacturing business. One is a laser printer. Wendy has had numerous calls for the product, which will compete with existing well-known brands. The other product is a new computer projection system that permits a presenter to display color computer images without the need of a regular computer or projection system. The product would have little competition. Wendy believes the market will be receptive to this product. What are some of the risks that Wendy must consider in deciding whether to produce the two products?

E1-20 *Obj. 7* To encourage its managers to earn a profit for its stockholders, Primrose Mining Company pays a bonus to top managers if the company earns at least a 15% return on investment each year. Management prepares financial reports from which the return on investment is calculated. Should the board and the stockholders be concerned about the reliability of the financial reports? Discuss. What can they do to make sure the reports faithfully represent the company's economic activities?

E1-21 *Obj. 8* Andy attends college on a full-time basis and works part-time for Meredith's Garden Center. The owner, Jim Meredith, asked Andy to work late into the night to move merchandise from one warehouse to an empty warehouse located across town. Andy thought his assignment was unusual but was happy to get the extra hours of work.

The next day, Andy overheard the company's auditors discussing their visit to the warehouse where he had moved the merchandise. Apparently, Mr. Meredith was attempting to fool the auditors. They had counted the merchandise on the previous day. On the following day, they had counted the same merchandise a second time but at a different warehouse. Meredith was attempting to acquire a bank loan and wanted to impress the loan officer with a strong financial report. Andy knew Meredith would mislead the auditors and banker but did not know what to do.

What may happen to Andy if he informs the auditors of his activities from the night before? Who may be harmed by Meredith's actions?

PROBLEMS

If your instructor is using Personal Trainer in this course, you may complete online the assignments identified by PT.

P1-1 Obtaining Funding
Obj. 1

Betsy wants to start a business making flags. She has calculated that she will need $62,500 to start the business. The money will be used to rent a building, purchase equipment, hire workers, and begin production and sales. Betsy has $12,500 in savings she can invest in the business.

Required

A. What alternatives might Betsy have for obtaining the additional $50,000 she needs for her business?
B. What information about her business will lenders or investors want to have?

P1-2 Types of Organizations
Obj. 2
PT

Provided below are four types of organizations and a list of organizations with which you are probably familiar. Associate each organization with a type of organization.

Types of organizations
Merchandising companies
Manufacturing companies
Service companies
Governmental or nonprofit organizations

Organizations

United Parcel Service (UPS)	Internal Revenue Service (IRS)
Amazon.com	March of Dimes
Dow Chemical Company	JCPenney
United States Postal Service (USPS)	DaimlerChrysler
PepsiCo	Sears
Federal Express (FedEx)	Verizon Communications

P1-3 Determining Profit and Return on Investment
Obj. 3
PT

Harry Honda owns a small car dealership. He rents the property he uses, buys cars from a manufacturer, and resells them to customers. During July, Harry sold 14 cars that cost him a total of $189,000. The total amount he received from the sale of these cars was $224,000. Other costs incurred by Harry for the month included rent, $2,550; utilities, $800; insurance, $825; maintenance of property and cars, $500; advertising, $1,000; and property taxes and business license, $200.

Required

A. Prepare a profit report that calculates the amount of profit earned during July.
B. What can Harry do with the profit he earned?
C. Assuming he invested $1,200,000 in the dealership, what was the return on his investment for July expressed as a percentage of his investment?

P1-4 Developing Profit and Return on Investment
Objs. 3, 4
PT

Through hard work and careful saving, Hans and his family have $152,000 to start a small specialty foods business. The family estimates sales to customers will be about $4,500 per month during the first year. On the average, expected costs per month are budgeted as follows:

Wages for occasional labor	$ 700	Utilities	$100
Rent on land and buildings	1,200	Advertising	300
Supplies	75	Delivery costs	225

Required

A. What is the projected monthly profit?
B. What is the expected annual return on investment?

P1-5 The Relationship between Profit and Value Created

Obj. 3

PT

Marty and Judi own and operate Tender Sender Company, a store providing private mail boxes, contract shipping services on commission, and a wide variety of gift and novelty items. The following transactions occurred during the month of February.

1. Sold $6,000 of gift items for which the company had paid $3,100.
2. Advertising, both newspaper and radio, was $1,500.
3. Rent for the month received from mail box customers totaled $1,640.
4. The cost of monthly rent for the store location was $2,200.
5. The cost of utilities for the month was $475.
6. Commissions earned from shipping services for the month totaled $1,588.
7. Sold $3,200 of novelty items that had cost the company $1,450.
8. The cost of supplies used during the month was $384.
9. Other miscellaneous costs for the month of February totaled $250.

Required

A. Prepare a schedule that shows the amount of profit earned by the company during the month of February.
B. Has the company created value? Explain your answer.

P1-6 How Businesses Create Value

Objs. 1, 3

PT

You are considering opening a shop in a nearby mall that will sell specialty T-shirts. T-shirts, containing designs and words selected by customers, will be produced for customers on order. You will need to borrow $25,000 to begin operations. A local bank has agreed to consider a loan and has asked for a summary plan to demonstrate the performance you expect from your company and your ability to repay the loan. You will pay $5.50 for T-shirts and will sell them for $8. The cost of paint and supplies will be $0.50 per shirt. An examination of similar stores at other malls indicates that you should be able to sell an average of 1,000 shirts per month. Rent for your store will be $300 per month. Utilities will be $150 per month, on average. Wages will be $800 per month.

Required

A. Calculate the expected profit of your company for the first year of operation.
B. Explain how a bank loan officer may use your profit projections to help make the lending decision.

P1-7 Measuring Value Created

Obj. 3

PT

T. Edison owns her own business and had the following activity during September. She earned $2,600 from royalties on inventions. She consumed resources as follows: $525 for rent, $300 for clerical salaries, $124 for legal services, $100 for office supplies, $90 for utilities, $70 for fuel, and $200 for insurance.

Required

A. Prepare a report in good form, following the example of Exhibit 6, to describe Edison's financial activities for September.
B. How might this information be useful for Edison?
C. Identify some decisions Edison might make using this information.

P1-8 The Results of the Transformation Process

Obj. 3

PT

Betsy started Betsy's Flag Co. on September 1. During September, Betsy consumed the following resources:

Rent	$ 625	Utilities	250
Supplies	3,000	Repairs	1,500
Fabric	8,750	Wages	2,500
Business license	500		

Betsy created resources by selling flags for $22,000 during the month of September.

Required Determine the profit earned by Betsy during September.

P1-9 *Objs. 1, 4*

Using Accounting Information for Decisions

The chief financial officer (CFO) of Flash Bulb and Seed Company has prepared the following projections for the month of August.

Expected sales		$480,000
Projected monthly resources consumed:		
Rent	$ 85,000	
Utilities	2,900	
Wages	274,000	
Advertising	115,000	
Repairs	12,000	
Supplies	2,500	
Total cost of resources consumed		491,400
Projected loss		$ (11,400)

Although Flash Bulb and Seed Company predicts a loss for August, the CFO is confident that sales will increase in the future.

Required

A. Why is it important that the CFO prepare a document like this?
B. If the company came to your bank requesting a loan, how would you respond? From the data given, does the firm appear that it is likely to be able to repay a loan? Why?

P1-10 *Obj. 4* P/T

Return on Investment and Return of Investment

John invested $250,000 into a business that earned a profit of $2,250 during the past month as shown below. John believes the business will earn an annual profit equal to twelve times the monthly profit. Assume John wants to take $20,000 from the business each year for his personal use.

Resources created from sales		$17,000
Resources consumed:		
Materials	$7,500	
Insurance	1,500	
Rent	2,000	
Utilities	950	
Wages	2,800	
Total cost of resources consumed		14,750
Profit earned		$ 2,250

Required

A. Determine the company's return on investment.
B. Determine John's return of investment.

P1-11 *Obj. 5*

Choosing a Form of Business Organization

Below are three independent situations.

A. Larry, Ulysses, and Irene are three college student friends planning to set up a summer business at a nearby resort to sell T-shirts, souvenirs, and novelties to tourists. While they have no assets (to speak of) of their own, Larry's uncle has agreed to finance them with upfront capital to acquire merchandise and so on. They plan to operate for only one summer, as all expect to graduate soon and take permanent jobs in a nearby state.
B. Molly and Vicky are twin sisters who have decided to start a computer software consulting firm. Molly is the "techie," and a bit unreliable. Vicky is a highly successful manager gifted with organizational and business skills. Between the two, they believe they can attract and serve a profitable clientele. In fact, they envision rapid expansion of their practice and diversification into a variety of related business activities. Between them, they have only enough liquid capital to start a small operation.

C. Reginald and Ruth Ann are ne'er-do-well offspring of a deceased industrialist who left them each $400 million—most of which they still have. Ever the optimists, they think there is money to be made in the steel business. A friend they met at the country club has persuaded them to provide $10 million to set up a business that would manufacture and distribute a line of lightweight steel kites. Operations would be located in a nearby state.

Required For each of the three independent situations, recommend the form of business organization that you believe would be most appropriate. Explain your reasoning in each case, both in favor of your selection and any reasons against your choice.

P1-12 Business Ownership Structures

Obj. 5

Mary Jackson is graduating with a degree in business administration. She has scheduled interviews with a variety of companies. Mary found the following diagram in the packet of information provided by one of the companies:

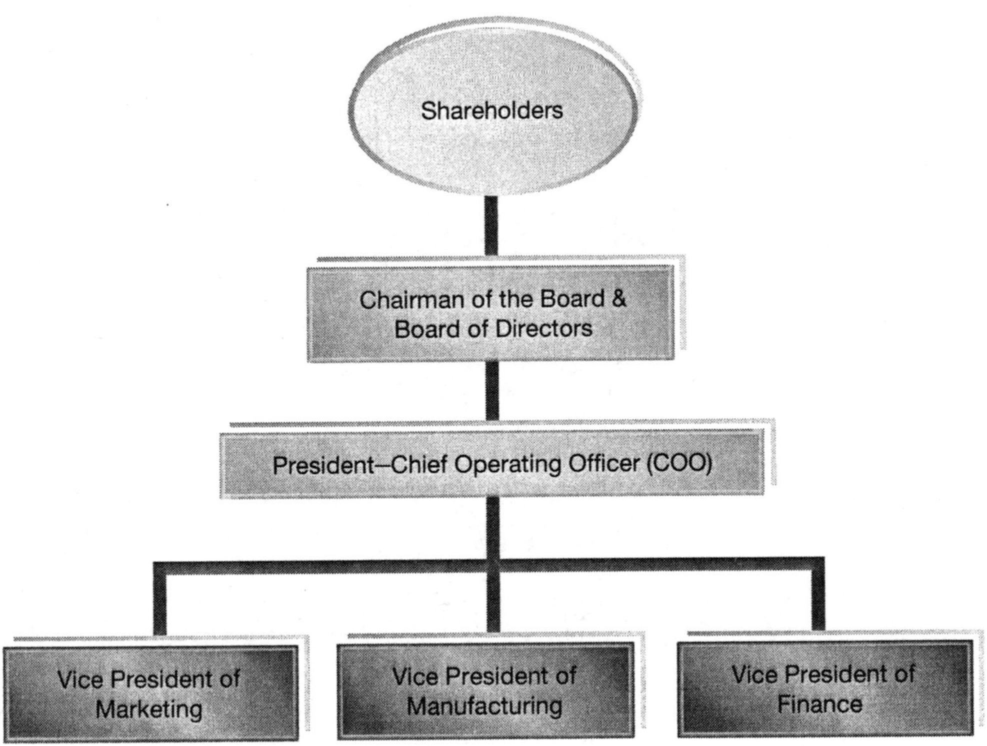

Required

A. Is Mary interviewing with a proprietorship, partnership, or corporation?
B. What are the advantages of this form of organization?
C. In this form of organization, management ultimately is responsible to whom?

P1-13 Contracts, Risk, and Uses of Accounting Information

Obj. 6

Sonny Beam established Solar Supply Corporation earlier in the current year. To obtain resources, he contributed $5,000 of his savings to the company, had the company borrow $8,000 from his mother, sold shares of company stock to friends totaling $10,000, and obtained a $25,000 bank loan. The company is obligated to buy out all investors and repay the two loans within 12 months of the business becoming profitable. Sonny located space in a nearby business park and leased it for monthly rent of $1,000 plus 1% of his company's sales. Several competing manufacturers tried to attract him as a distributor of their products. He signed an exclusive agreement with one that offered its products at 52% off their normal sales prices

(Continued)

with 30-day free credit. Sonny hired a sales manager at a salary of $3,000 per month and promised her a profit-sharing plan payable each December 31. Sonny's credit policy is that commercial customers receive 60-day free credit and that retail customers must pay by cash or credit card. All goods carry the manufacturer's warranty and Sonny's secondary warranty of "satisfaction guaranteed or your money back." Because the company is a corporation, it will pay corporate income tax to the city, state, and federal governments. In addition, the state will levy a merchandise tax each July 1.

Required

A. Identify the primary exchanges and contracts between the company and those that interact with it.
B. Which of the parties have taken on risk? For each such party, describe that risk.
C. Which contracts will require the parties to rely on accounting information to verify performance according to the contract? Be specific.

P1-14 Using Information About Risk to Make Decisions

Objs. 4, 6

Nancy and Mauro are reviewing the information given below for different reasons. Nancy is a bank loan officer who has received a 2-year, $50,000 loan application from both firms. Mauro is an independently wealthy investor who is considering investing $50,000 in a company. The information below is just one part of a complete data set about the companies that both persons are reviewing. The data reveal the profit history of the two firms over the last seven years. The companies are very similar except for the way in which their profits vary over the years. (All dollar amounts are in thousands.)

	Profits							
	2004	**2003**	**2002**	**2001**	**2000**	**1999**	**1998**	**Total**
Hill Country Enterprises	337	315	303	268	207	225	201	1,856
Low Land Associates	730	(55)	(10)	598	(131)	619	498	2,249

Required

A. Explain the concept of risk and its usual relationship to return on investment.
B. If you were Nancy, would you be more likely to make the loan to Hill Country or to Low Land? Why?
C. If you were Mauro, would you be more likely to invest in Hill Country or Low Land? Why?
D. Suppose the financial information of Low Land Associates (but not that of Hill Country Enterprises) has been audited and verified as being in conformance with generally accepted accounting principles. Would that change your responses to parts (b) and (c) above?

P1-15 Using Financial Information to Assess Risk

Obj. 6

Assume you are the credit manager for a manufacturing company that sells its products to retail businesses. One of your company's sales representatives has been working hard to establish business relationships with two different retailers. Both businesses are interested in marketing your products. Summary earnings information is presented below for each business.

	Profits (losses)			
	2001	**2002**	**2003**	**2004**
Company A	80,000	20,000	(10,000)	70,000
Company B	30,000	32,000	40,000	43,000

Required

A. Based on the summary financial information, which company is a better credit risk?
B. When a new relationship is established between two businesses, would the customer be interested in information about the supplier's financial condition? Why or why not?

P1-16 Accounting Information and Management Compensation

Objs. 6, 8

Taylor Grey is the sales manager of an electronics manufacturing company. His annual bonus is based on profits earned by the company. On December 30, Taylor is inquiring about the status of a very large order that he would like to include in the year-end profit figures. Unfortunately, a production machine has broken down. Taylor has been advised the order will not be completed and shipped by the end of the year. The profit figures including and excluding the order appear below.

Profit Including the Order	Profit Excluding the Order
$2,300,000	$1,500,000

Taylor's bonus is 3% of profits.

Required

A. Using the financial information provided, calculate Taylor's bonus under both scenarios.
B. Why do companies use accounting information to evaluate managerial performance?
C. Is there an economic incentive for Taylor to misrepresent the annual sales?

P1-17 The Value of an Audit

Obj. 7

Assume you have inherited a sum of money from a distant relative and are looking for good investment opportunities. You are considering investing in one of two companies, Wonderworks or Hoffstetter's. Both companies are retailing organizations that have earned profits during the month of January as follows:

	Wonderworks		Hoffstetter's	
Resources created		$50,000		$60,000
Resources consumed:				
Cost of merchandise sold	$30,000		$35,000	
Wages	5,000		4,000	
Rent	2,000		2,500	
Supplies	1,500		1,700	
Utilities	700		500	
Total cost of resources consumed		39,200		43,700
Profit earned		$10,800		$16,300

You learn that a CPA examined the financial information provided by Wonderworks and confirmed the information was prepared according to GAAP.

"I don't see any reason to pay a CPA to examine my company's books," Patty Hoffstetter tells you. They add to the cost of conducting business. Hoffstetter's brother-in-law prepared the company's financial information. He has no formal training in accounting but followed the instructions provided in the accounting software package that he purchased from an office supply company.

Required

A. Do you agree that the audit adds no value? Why or why not?
B. GAAP help ensure that users can compare the financial information of two different companies. The two sets of financial information appear identical in format. Are they comparable?

P1-18 The Importance of Accounting Regulations

Obj. 7

http://ingram.swlearning.com

Learn more about the SEC.

In its 2001 annual report, **Qwest Communications International Inc.** ("Qwest") stated that because of an SEC investigation, it couldn't guarantee that it would not have to restate its earnings (*to make them consistent with GAAP*). A restatement could wipe out more than $500 million of earnings, bringing Qwest close to violating agreements with its creditors. The biggest problem with a restatement is that Qwest faces lawsuits alleging that company executives made misleading statements to prop up the stock price.

Source: www.msnbc.com

(Continued)

Required

A. What is the SEC? What is its mission?
B. If a company's management believes they have reported earnings in a meaningful way, why can the SEC force them to restate earnings?
C. If management issued misleading financial information, do the shareholders have a reason to be upset with the company? Explain.

P1-19 *Obj. 8*

Ethics and Moral Hazard

You are the manager of a retail electronics store. Recently, you purchased 200 What-A-Sound portable CD players from a wholesaler in a going-out-of-business sale. These units cost you $80 each, about half of the normal cost of other brands that you sell for $260. You expected to sell these units at the regular price and earn an above-normal profit. After your purchase, you discovered that the units were poorly constructed and would probably last about a third as long as other major brands.

Customers often ask you for a recommendation when considering the purchase of a portable CD player. If you tell them the truth about the What-A-Sound model, you may have difficulty selling these units, even if you offer a steep discount.

Required

A. What will you tell a customer who asks about these units?
B. What are the short-run and long-run implications for your company's profits if (a) you conceal the quality of the units and sell them at their regular price or (b) reveal the quality problem? If you were to choose alternative b, what options might you consider in an effort to minimize the effect of these units on your profits?

P1-20 *Obj. 8*

Ethics and Moral Hazard

You manage an auto service store. One of your major services is brake replacement. You purchase replacement parts at an average cost of $30 per set. Each set contains parts for four wheels and will repair one car. You charge an average of $100 per car for replacing worn brakes, including an average labor cost of $40. Your current volume for brake replacements is about 700 jobs per month. A new vendor has contacted you with an offer to sell you replacement parts at an average cost of $22.50 per set. After checking on the quality of these parts, you find that their average life is about two-thirds that of the parts you are currently using.

Required

A. What are the short-run profit implications of using the $22.50 brakes instead of the $30 brakes?
B. What are the long-run profit implications?
C. What ethical issues should be considered in choosing which brakes to use?

P1-21 *P/T*

Excel in Action

SPREADSHEET

Millie and Milo Wermz are the owners and managers of a small bookstore, The Book Wermz, near a college campus. The store specializes in rare and out-of-print books. During September 2004, the company sold $40,000 of books. The books cost the company $28,000. The cost of other resources used during September included:

Wages	$4,200
Supplies	2,000
Rent	1,500
Utilities	300

Required Use a spreadsheet to prepare a report describing profit earned by The Book Wermz for September. The spreadsheet should contain the following heading:

The Book Wermz
Profit Earned
For September 2004

The merge and center button [merge icon] can be used to center the heading in the first three rows of the spreadsheet. Select the cells that will contain the heading, and then click the merge button to combine these cells.

The report should list each resource created or consumed during September and should include a formula to automatically calculate the profit earned as the difference between resources created and resources consumed. Use the appropriate format buttons to format the numbers to include commas. Show resources consumed as negative amounts. The first and last numbers in the column should include dollar signs.

The completed worksheet should look like the following example:

	A	B
1	The Book Wermz	
2	Profit Earned	
3	For September 2004	
4		
5	Sales	$ 40,000
6	Cost of goods sold	(28,000)
7	Wages	(4,200)
8	Supplies	(2,000)
9	Rent	(1,500)
10	Utilities	(300)
11	Profit	$ 4,000

Use formula to calculate total

It is important to **save your work on a regular basis.** Save your work before you make any major changes so that mistakes will not require you to redo a lot of work.

P1-22 Multiple-Choice Overview of the Chapter

P/T

1. The basic purpose of accounting is to:
   a. minimize the amount of taxes a company has to pay.
   b. permit an organization to keep track of its economic activities.
   c. report the largest amount of earnings to stockholders.
   d. reduce the amount of risk experienced by investors.

2. A primary purpose of all organizations in our society is to:
   a. make a profit.
   b. minimize the payment of taxes.
   c. provide employment for the largest number of workers possible.
   d. create value by transforming resources from one form to another.

3. Value is created when organizations:
   a. raise capital by borrowing funds from banks, individuals, or other businesses.
   b. pay cash to suppliers, employees, owners, and government.
   c. sell products or services at prices that exceed the value of resources consumed.
   d. invest in machinery.

4. Which of the following are features of the corporate form of business organization?

	Mutual Agency	Limited Liability
a.	Yes	Yes
b.	Yes	No
c.	No	Yes
d.	No	No

5. Tammy Faye invested $2,000 in a partnership. One year later, the partnership was sold, and cash from the sale was distributed to the partners. On that date, Tammy received a check for her share of the company in the amount of $2,250. What was Tammy's return on investment?

(Continued)

a. $0
b. $250
c. $2,000
d. $2,250

6. Sternberg Enterprises developed a new type of roller skate that is very popular because of its high quality and reasonable price. Sternberg is losing money on the product, however, because several key production personnel recently resigned and replacements are not as skilled. Which of the following terms properly describe the firm?

	Effective	**Efficient**
a.	Yes	Yes
b.	Yes	No
c.	No	Yes
d.	No	No

7. The *transformation of resources* refers to:
   a. the assessment of employee performance.
   b. converting resources from one form to a more valuable form.
   c. procedures designed to reduce a company's risk.
   d. training methods by which unskilled workers become efficient and effective.

8. An investor is evaluating the potential investments described below. Past financial results of these two companies are judged to be indicative of future returns and risk.

Year	Abercrombie Profits	Fitch Profits
A	$16	$ 6
B	18	48
C	20	3

From the information provided, which investment appears to have the higher return and which the higher risk?

	Highest Return	**Highest Risk**
a.	Abercrombie	Abercrombie
b.	Abercrombie	Fitch
c.	Fitch	Abercrombie
d.	Fitch	Fitch

9. SEC stands for:
   a. Securities Excellence Commission
   b. Securities and Exchange Commission
   c. Standard Executive Compensation
   d. Salaried Executive's Council

10. Ethical behavior is particularly important for accounting because:
   a. companies cannot detect unethical behavior.
   b. if the reports are wrong, accountants may have to go to jail.
   c. the SEC cannot carefully audit each company's financial statements.
   d. the reliability of accounting information depends on the honesty of those who prepare, report, and audit this information.

CASE

C1-1 Understanding the Transformation Process

Obj. 2

Environmental Housing Company designs and builds log homes. It purchases logs and other building materials from other companies. The logs are cut to the dimensions called for in a design and shipped to the customer's building site with other materials for assembly. Environmental Housing employs construction and assembly workers, maintenance personnel, and marketing and service personnel, in addition to its management and office staff. The company is in charge of the construction process until the home is completed and ready for occupancy.

Required Identify the resources, transformation activities, and goods of Environmental Housing's transformation process. Construct a diagram similar to Exhibit 4 that shows the flow of resources through the transformation process.

2

BUSINESS ACTIVITIES—THE SOURCE OF ACCOUNTING INFORMATION

How do we know how well our business is doing?

After developing an understanding of the purpose of a business and the considerations involved in starting a business, Maria and Stan officially began Mom's Cookie Company in January of 2004. Their first task was to obtain financial resources for the business. Then, they acquired equipment and other resources for the business, and they began to produce and sell their products. In addition, they needed an accounting system to record their business activities and to report how the business was performing.

FOOD FOR THOUGHT

If you were starting a business, what kinds of information would you want to know about your business? How would you keep track of where the company obtained financial resources, how those resources were used, and the amounts of other resources the company has available for use? How would you know how much of your product you were selling and how much it was costing you to acquire and sell the product? For answers to these questions Maria and Stan are meeting with their accountant, Ellen.

Ellen: *Once you start your business, you will need an accounting system for recording business activities and for providing reports to help you understand how your business is performing.*

Maria: *Is this something we can do ourselves?*

Ellen: *Yes, for now, since your business will not be very complicated. You can set up a basic accounting system and keep track of your activities. The system will help you understand your business and events that affect how well you are doing.*

Stan: *How do we get started?*

Ellen: *We will start with a simple set of accounts and look at how these accounts are related. As your company acquires and uses resources, we will record each event. At the end of the month, we will summarize these activities and prepare financial statements.*

Maria: *What will the statements tell us?*

Ellen: *The statements will report the resources available to your company, how you financed those resources, and how the resources were used.*

Stan: *Will we know whether our company is making money?*

Ellen: *Yes, we can prepare a statement that will tell you how much profit the company earns each month. By the time we are finished, you'll have a pretty good idea of whether the company is performing as well as you hope it will.*

OBJECTIVES

Once you have completed this chapter, you should be able to:

1. Identify financing activities and explain why they are important to a business.
2. Demonstrate how accounting measures and records business activities.
3. Identify investing activities and explain why they are important to a business.
4. Identify operating activities and explain how they create profits for a company.
5. Describe how financial reports summarize business activities and provide information for business decisions.

FINANCING ACTIVITIES

OBJECTIVE 1

Identify financing activities and explain why they are important to a business.

A business is an organization that exists for the purpose of making a profit for its owners. A business creates a profit if it can sell goods and services to customers at prices that are greater than the total costs incurred to provide those goods and services. To be successful, a business must be effective in meeting the needs of customers by providing goods and services demanded by customers at prices they are willing to pay. Also, a business must be efficient in controlling costs so that the prices charged to customers exceed the costs to the company of acquiring and selling its products. If a company is successful, it creates value for its owners as well as for other stakeholders. Profit is a measure of the value created by a business for its owners.

Maria and Stan started Mom's Cookie Company in January of 2004. The goods they sell are prepared from their mother's recipes. It is important to keep in mind that a business is a separate entity from its owners. The resources and activities of the business should be kept separate from those of the owners or managers of a business. Throughout this book we will discuss accounting issues related to Mom's Cookie Company. We will be accounting for the company, not for the owners or other stakeholders.

To start their business, Maria and Stan invested $10,000 from their savings. This money enabled the company to acquire resources it would need to operate. **A contribution by owners to a business, along with any profits that are kept in the business, is known as *owners' equity*.** The contribution provides resources to the company and represents a claim by the owners. Owners have a claim to profits earned by a business and to the resources owned by the business.

Because they needed more money to get started, Maria and Stan borrowed $8,000 from a local bank to help finance the business. Borrowing is another source of money for a company and represents a claim by the lender of the money. As noted in Chapter F1, those who lend money to a business are referred to as creditors of the business. Creditors have a claim for repayment of amounts the company borrows and for interest on amounts borrowed. **The amount a company borrows is the *principal* of a loan. *Interest* is the cost of borrowing and is paid to creditors in addition to the repayment of principal.**

LEARNING NOTE

Keep in mind that the business is an accounting entity separate from its owners. From an accounting perspective, the bank lends the $8,000 to the business, Mom's Cookie Company, not to Maria and Stan.

Contributions by owners and loans from creditors are examples of business activities, as illustrated in Exhibit 1. ***Business activities* are events that occur when a business acquires, uses, or sells resources or claims to those resources.** Exhibit 1 illustrates business activities as the exchange of resources and claims between creditors and owners and the company.

Contributions by owners and loans from creditors are examples of financing activities. ***Financing activities* occur when owners or creditors provide resources to a company or when a company transfers resources to owners or creditors,** as in the repayment of a loan principal. Financing activities provide financial resources for businesses. How

Exhibit 1
Business Activities: Financing from Owners and Creditors

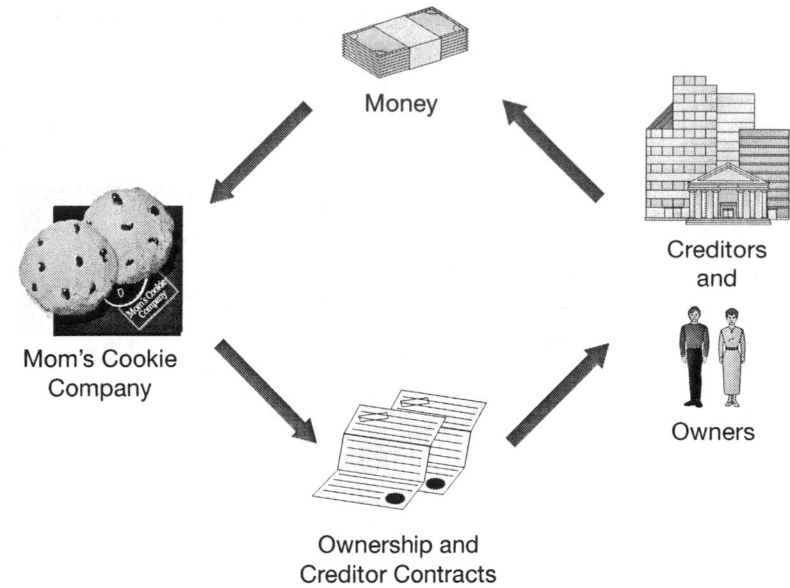

businesses use those resources is a topic discussed later in this chapter when we examine investing and operating activities. First, we look at how we account for financing and other business activities.

Accounting for Business Activities

OBJECTIVE 2

Demonstrate how accounting measures and records business activities.

Accounting provides a basis for describing business activities. Accounting measures, records, reports, and analyzes business activities using accounts. **An *account* is a record of increases and decreases in the dollar amount associated with a specific resource or activity.** Accounting ***transactions*** **are descriptions of business activities (or events) that are measured in dollar values and recorded in accounts.** In general, the amount recorded for an event is the cash value of resources transferred or used in a business activity.

Financial accounting records transactions by using the accounting equation. The accounting equation shows the fundamental relationship between resources and claims to those resources:

ASSETS = LIABILITIES + OWNERS' EQUITY

Assets **are the resources controlled by a business.** ***Liabilities*** **are the claims of creditors to a company's resources.** Liabilities are the resources a company would have to transfer to creditors to satisfy those claims. As noted earlier, owners' equity is the claim of owners to a company's resources. Accounts are specific types of assets, liabilities, or owners' equity.

Exhibit 2 illustrates financing activities of Mom's Cookie Company. The company received $10,000 from Maria and Stan. Then, it borrowed $8,000 from a bank. Consequently, the company has assets (cash) valued at $18,000. Creditors have a claim of $8,000, and owners have a claim of $10,000 on the company's assets.

LEARNING NOTE

"Account" is the root of "accounting." The root of "account" is "count." Thus, we can observe that accounting is a process of quantifying ("counting") business activities and recording them in specific information categories as a means of understanding these activities.

Exhibit 2
The Effect of Financing Activities on the Accounting Equation

Assets $18,000 = Liabilities $8,000 + Owners' Equity $10,000

Exhibit 3 provides an accounting representation of financing activities. On January 2, 2004, Mom's Cookie Company received $10,000 from the company's owners. On January 3, 2004, the company received $8,000 from the bank. These events are recorded as increases (or decreases, if needed) in specific accounts.

Exhibit 3
Accounting Representation of Financing Activities

Date	Accounts	ASSETS	=	LIABILITIES	+	OWNERS' EQUITY
	Beginning Amounts	0	=	0	+	0
Jan. 2	Cash	10,000				
	Contributed Capital					10,000
Jan. 3	Cash	8,000				
	Notes Payable			8,000		
	Ending Amounts	18,000	=	8,000	+	10,000

Accounts associated with these transactions include Cash, Contributed Capital, and Notes Payable. ***Cash* refers to financial resources in the form of coins and currency, bank deposits, and short-term investments that can be converted easily into currency and that can be used to pay for resources and obligations of a company. *Contributed Capital* is an owners' equity account and identifies amounts contributed to a company by its owners. *Notes Payable* is a liability account used to identify amounts a company owes to creditors with whom a formal agreement, or note, has been signed.**

As Exhibit 3 illustrates, accounting measures business activities in terms of dollar values, and records these activities in accounts. Thus, accounting provides a systematic way for a business to keep track of its activities. A review of a company's transactions reveals the events that occurred, when they occurred, the amounts involved, and the resources and claims that were exchanged. Good business decisions depend on accurate and timely information about business activities. Decision makers need to know what the business did and how the business was affected by those activities. Accounting is a primary source of this information. It is important that accounting provide a complete record of a company's business activities. Only then do decision makers have a full and fair description of those activities.

Case In Point

http://ingram.swlearning.com

Visit the Enron site for the latest news.

Consequences of Unreported Liabilities

One of the primary criticisms of **Enron Corporation**'s accounting was that it failed to report large amounts of debt (liabilities) that the company was responsible for repaying. The company's owners and other stakeholders were not easily able to identify or measure the amount of debt owed by the corporation. Consequently, their investments in Enron were riskier than they thought. When some of Enron's business operations proved to be less profitable than anticipated, the corporation had difficulty meeting its obligations. If owners and other stakeholders had known the true amount of the company's debt, they may have been less willing to purchase the company's stock or lend money to the company, and some owners and creditors may have avoided losses they incurred when the company's actual financial condition became known.

INVESTING ACTIVITIES

Before a company can sell goods and services to customers, it must acquire resources needed to operate the business. The particular resources a business needs depends on what the business is. Maria and Stan do not have sufficient resources to produce their cookies. Instead, they have contracted with a local bakery to make the cookies from

OBJECTIVE 3

Identify investing activities and explain why they are important to a business.

their mother's recipes. The bakery will order containers and package the cookies with the Mom's Cookie Company label. Maria and Stan have arranged to sell the cookies to local grocery stores.

The primary resources Mom's Cookie Company needs are office equipment and delivery equipment. Maria and Stan will use the office equipment to maintain information about the business and to make contacts with the bakery and grocery stores. Delivery equipment will be used to pick up cookies from the bakery and to deliver them to stores. Resources such as office equipment and delivery equipment are long-term resources because they can be used for more than one year. These resources enable a company to acquire and sell its products but are not products themselves. **Activities involving the acquisition or disposal of long-term resources used by a business are *investing activities.*** Exhibit 4 illustrates investing activities for Mom's Cookie Company. Long-term resources (such as office and delivery equipment) are acquired from suppliers. Money, or a promise of future payment, is transferred to suppliers of these resources.

Exhibit 4
Business Activities: Investing in Long-Term Resources

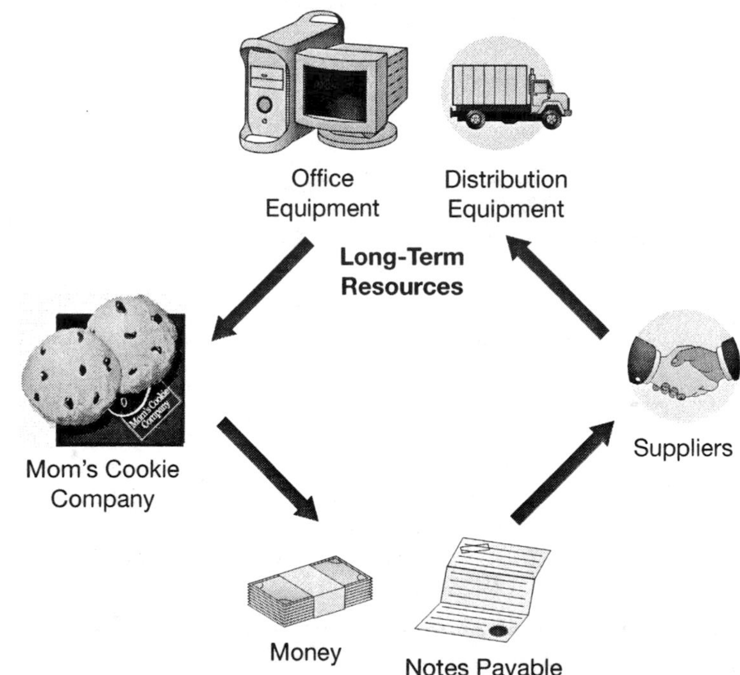

Exhibit 5 provides an accounting representation of investing activities. On January 5, Mom's Cookie Company paid $6,000 for office equipment. On January 6, the company bought a delivery van for $25,000. It paid $3,000 in cash and financed the remaining $22,000 of the purchase price with a note payable.

Exhibit 5
Accounting Representation of Investing Activities

Date	Accounts	ASSETS	=	LIABILITIES	+	OWNERS' EQUITY
	Beginning Amounts	18,000	=	8,000	+	10,000
Jan. 5	Equipment	6,000				
	Cash	−6,000				
Jan. 6	Equipment	25,000				
	Cash	−3,000				
	Notes Payable			22,000		
	Ending Amounts	40,000	=	30,000	+	10,000

The January 6 entry above shows the equipment purchase as a single transaction involving both the borrowing of $22,000 from the bank and the payment of an additional $3,000. An alternative way to record the purchase of the delivery van shows the transaction as a two-step process. First the $22,000 is borrowed from the bank and then the full $25,000 is paid to purchase the van. Recording the transaction in two steps is presented below.

Date	Accounts	ASSETS	=	LIABILITIES	+	OWNERS' EQUITY
	Beginning Amounts	18,000	=	8,000	+	10,000
Jan. 5	Equipment	6,000				
	Cash	−6,000				
Jan. 6	**Cash**	**22,000**				
	Notes Payable			**22,000**		
Jan. 6	**Equipment**	**25,000**				
	Cash	**−25,000**				
	Ending Amounts	40,000	=	30,000	+	10,000

LEARNING NOTE

Account titles vary in practice depending on the needs of a company. Accounts can be divided into as many subcategories as a business needs. For example, Mom's Cookie Company could use separate accounts for Office Equipment and Delivery Equipment if it chose to do so. Although you should not get too concerned about specific account titles, certain titles, such as Notes Payable, are used by most businesses. You should learn the titles that are listed as terms in this book. Remember, what is most important is that the account titles correctly represent the transactions.

Accounts used to record these transactions include Equipment, Cash, and Notes Payable. Observe that the second transaction involves both an investing activity (purchase of equipment) and a financing activity (borrowing to purchase van).

In each transaction, the accounting equation must balance. The January 5th transaction balances because the $6,000 increase in Equipment offsets the amount of the decrease in Cash. The January 6th transaction involves three accounts. Together the net increase in assets of $22,000 ($25,000 − $3,000) equals the increase in liabilities of $22,000.

The ending amounts in Exhibit 5 indicate that the accounting equation is in balance. Each transaction and all transactions taken together must preserve the relationship:

ASSETS = LIABILITIES + OWNERS' EQUITY

Maintaining the accounting equation is an important accounting control. If individual transactions or all transactions as a whole do not preserve the equality, an error has occurred in recording one or more of the business activities.

1 SELF-STUDY PROBLEM

WebTUTOR® Advantage

Delphi Co. was started in 2004 when its owners contributed $100,000 to the business and borrowed $120,000 from creditors. These resources were used to purchase equipment at a cost of $160,000. In addition, the company purchased a building at a cost of $400,000, paying $40,000 in cash and signing a note for $360,000 with a local bank.

Required Using the format of Exhibit 5, record these financing and investing activities. Demonstrate that the accounting equation is in balance after the transactions have been recorded.

The solution to Self-Study Problem 1 appears at the end of the chapter.

Operating Activities

OBJECTIVE 4

Identify operating activities and explain how they create profits for a company.

Financing and investing activities are necessary for a company to obtain the resources it needs to operate, but these activities do not involve operating the business. A business operates by obtaining or creating products or services and selling those products or services to customers. Mom's Cookie Company acquires cookies from a bakery and sells the cookies to grocery stores. ***Operating activities*** **are those activities necessary to acquire and sell goods and services.** When goods or services are sold to customers, revenue is created. ***Revenue*** **is the amount a company expects to receive when it sells goods or services.** Revenue can be thought of as the reward earned by serving customers. In addition to goods and services for sale, operating activities use a variety of resources, including employee labor, supplies, and utilities. The consumption of these resources creates expenses. ***Expense*** **is the amount of resources consumed in the process of acquiring and selling goods and services.** Not all operating activities create revenues or expenses, but most do.

Exhibit 6 illustrates the purchase of goods to sell, which is one aspect of operating activities that does not create a revenue or expense. Cookies are purchased from the bakery in exchange for cash.

Exhibit 6
Operating Activities: Purchase of Goods for Sale

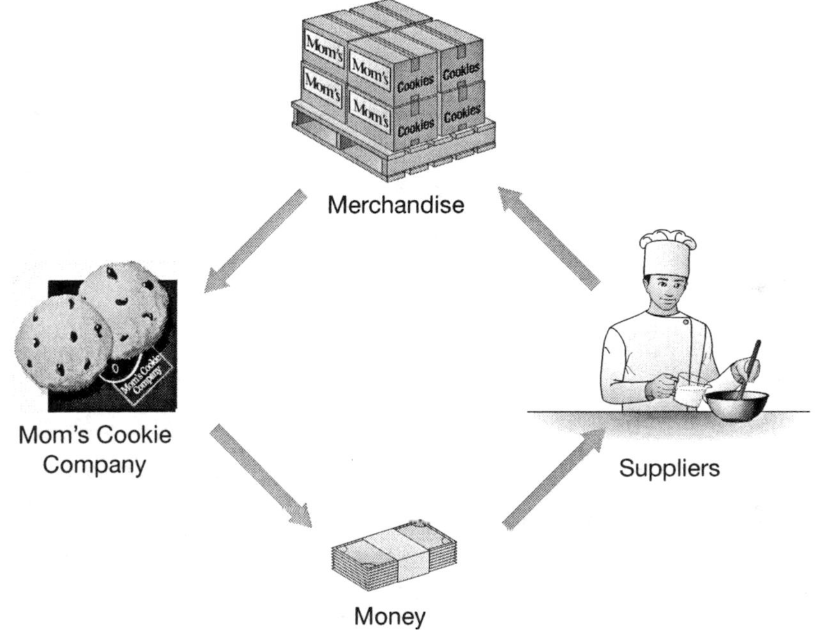

Exhibit 7 describes how this type of transaction might be recorded. Mom's Cookie Company purchased cookies from the bakery at a cost of $9,000 on January 7. ***Merchandise Inventory*** **is an asset account and identifies the cost of goods a company has purchased that are available for sale to customers.** Observe that in this transaction the company's total assets have not changed. The particular assets controlled by the com-

Exhibit 7
Accounting Representation of Purchase of Merchandise

Date	Accounts	ASSETS	=	LIABILITIES	+	OWNERS' EQUITY
	Beginning Amounts	40,000	=	30,000	+	10,000
Jan. 7	Merchandise Inventory Cash	9,000 −9,000				
	Ending Amounts	40,000	=	30,000	+	10,000

pany have changed. The company now has $9,000 of goods for sale but $9,000 less cash than before. In fact, the company's cash balance is now zero ($18,000 cash raised from financing activities minus $6,000 spent on office equipment, $3,000 for the down payment on a delivery van, and $9,000 spent on merchandise).

Exhibit 8 illustrates a company's sale of goods to a customer. When goods or services are sold to a customer, revenue is earned. The amount of revenue earned is equal to the amount of resources received from the customer in exchange for the goods. In this example, Cash is received from the customer and merchandise is delivered to the customer.

Exhibit 8
Operating Activities: Selling Goods to Customers

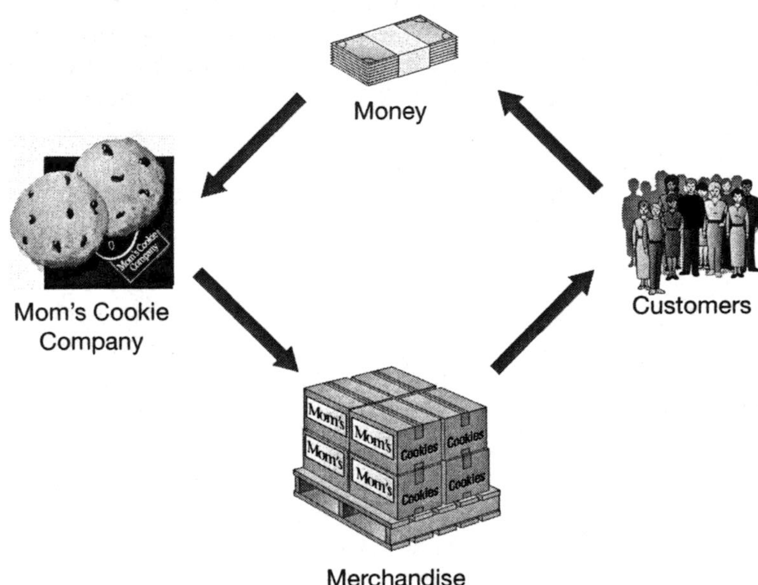

Exhibit 9 describes how this type of transaction can be recorded. Assume Mom's Cookie Company sells 380 boxes of cookies to grocery stores during January in exchange for cash. Each box, which contains several bags of cookies, costs Mom's Cookie Company $20, the amount the company pays the bakery for producing and packaging the cookies. Mom's Cookie Company sells each box to the store for $30. Therefore, 380 boxes cost the company $7,600 (380 boxes × $20) and are sold for $11,400 (380 boxes × $30).

Exhibit 9 Accounting Representation of Operating Activities

		ASSETS		=	LIABILITIES	+	OWNERS' EQUITY	
Date	**Accounts**	**Cash**	**Other Assets**				**Contributed Capital**	**Retained Earnings**
	Beginning Amounts	0	+40,000	=	30,000	+	10,000	+0
Jan. 31	Cash	11,400						
	Sales Revenue							11,400
Jan. 31	Cost of Goods Sold							−7,600
	Merchandise Inventory		−7,600					
	Ending Amounts	11,400	+32,400	=	30,000	+	10,000	+3,800

Because revenues and expenses occurred in this transaction, we expand the accounting equation to include them. ***Retained Earnings,* a subcategory of Owners' Equity, are the accumulated profits of a business that have been reinvested in the business.** Revenues increase Retained Earnings and expenses decrease Retained

Earnings. Amounts paid to owners from a company's profits also decrease Retained Earnings. We distinguish Retained Earnings from Contributed Capital because this subcategory identifies the profits earned by a company rather than amounts contributed directly by owners.

Also, notice in Exhibit 9 that Assets have been divided into two categories: Cash (beginning amount is $0) and Other Assets (beginning amount is $40,000). They still total to $40,000, the ending amount in Exhibit 7. Because many transactions involve Cash, separating it from Other Assets makes it easier to keep track of the cash received and paid by a company.

In Exhibit 9, the sale of goods is recorded in two transactions. One records the revenue earned from the sale. The other records the cost of the goods sold. These transactions are central to business operations and should be examined closely.

LEARNING NOTE

The sales transaction in Exhibit 9 is a summary transaction for all sales during January. In reality, sales occur throughout the month, and each sale should be recorded as it occurs. Each transaction would follow the same pattern shown in Exhibit 9. Therefore, to avoid repeating the same transaction several times, we record one summary transaction.

***Sales Revenue* identifies the amount a company earns from selling its products.** Revenue ordinarily is measured by the amount of cash received or expected from a customer in exchange for the goods or services transferred. Revenue normally is recorded at the time goods are transferred to customers. A company earns revenue for its owners. Remember that owners have a claim to profits earned by a company. Accordingly, revenue is part of owners' equity. It is an increase in the value of a company for its owners.

***Cost of Goods Sold* identifies the cost to the company of the goods transferred to customers.** It is an example of an expense. Expense normally is measured by the cost of resources consumed and is recorded at the time the resources are consumed. Thus, when merchandise is sold to customers, it is consumed from the seller's viewpoint. The seller no longer has control of the resource. Consequently, merchandise has been "used up." An expense reduces owners' equity because it identifies the use of resources for which owners have a claim. It is a decrease in the value of a company for its owners. Thus, **revenues increase owners' equity and expenses decrease owners' equity**.

Revenue minus expense equals profit. Profit results from operating activities and is the difference between revenues earned from selling goods and services and expenses incurred in acquiring and selling those goods and services. Note that in Exhibit 9 the sale resulted in profit of $3,800 ($11,400 − $7,600). The company's assets and owners' equity each increased by $3,800 as a result of the sale.

Remember, Owners' Equity represents the claims of owners to a business. Those claims include contributions made by the owners (Contributed Capital) plus profits earned by the business minus amounts paid by the business to its owners (Retained Earnings).

Other common expenses for a company like Mom's Cookie Company include wages paid to employees, plus the cost of supplies, rent, and utilities. To illustrate, assume the following activities for Mom's Cookie Company during January:

January	6	Paid $300 for supplies used during January
	8	Paid $600 for rent for January
	31	Paid $1,000 for wages for January
	31	Paid $200 for utilities for January

Exhibit 10 illustrates how these activities are recorded. An expense is recorded for the amount of resources used in each transaction. Because these resources were paid for at the time they were consumed, Cash decreases in each transaction.

Exhibit 10 Accounting Representation of Expenses

		ASSETS		=	LIABILITIES	+	OWNERS' EQUITY	
Date	**Accounts**	**Cash**	**Other Assets**				**Contributed Capital**	**Retained Earnings**
	Beginning Amounts	11,400	+32,400	=	30,000	+	10,000	+3,800
Jan. 6	Supplies Expense							−300
	Cash	−300						
Jan. 8	Rent Expense							−600
	Cash	−600						
Jan. 31	Wages Expense							−1,000
	Cash	−1,000						
Jan. 31	Utilities Expense							−200
	Cash	−200						
	Ending Amounts	9,300	+32,400	=	30,000	+	10,000	+1,700

2 SELF-STUDY PROBLEM

The following events occurred for Mega Co. during January, its first month of business:

WebTUTOR Advantage

Jan.	3	Owners contributed $40,000 to the business.
	5	The company received $25,000 from a bank in exchange for a note payable.
	8	The company paid $35,000 for equipment.
	10	The company paid $20,000 for merchandise.
	11	The company paid $2,000 for supplies used in January.
	15	The company received $12,000 from customers for the sale of merchandise. The merchandise cost Mega Co. $8,000.
	22	The company received $9,000 from customers for the sale of merchandise. The merchandise cost Mega Co. $6,000.
	31	The company paid $3,000 to employees for wages earned in January.
	31	The company paid $800 for utilities used in January.

Required Use the format of Exhibit 10 to record the transactions of Mega Co. for January. The beginning account balances will all be zero.

The solution to Self-Study Problem 2 appears at the end of the chapter.

FINANCIAL REPORTING AND ANALYSIS

OBJECTIVE 5

Describe how financial reports summarize business activities and provide information for business decisions.

The purpose of measuring and recording business activities is to provide useful information to those who need to make decisions. Accounting reports information to decision makers in the form of financial statements. ***Financial statements* are reports that summarize the results of a company's accounting transactions for a fiscal period.** Exhibit 11 lists all of Mom's Cookie Company's transactions for January using the expanded format.

To prepare financial statements, a company needs to identify the balances in its accounts at the end of the fiscal period being reported. Exhibit 12 provides a summary of account balances for Mom's Cookie Company at January 31. Balances for expenses, which reduce owners' equity, are shown in parentheses. All of the summary balances shown in this exhibit are the results of the transactions recorded for the company in Exhibit 11.

Exhibit 11 Transactions for Mom's Cookie Company for January

		ASSETS		=	LIABILITIES	+	OWNERS' EQUITY	
Date	**Accounts**	**Cash**	**Other Assets**				**Contributed Capital**	**Retained Earnings**
	Beginning Amounts	0	+0	=	0	+	0	+0
Jan. 2	Cash	10,000						
	Contributed Capital						10,000	
Jan. 3	Cash	8,000						
	Notes Payable				8,000			
Jan. 5	Equipment		6,000					
	Cash	−6,000						
Jan. 6	Equipment		25,000					
	Cash	−3,000						
	Notes Payable				22,000			
Jan. 6	Supplies Expense							−300
	Cash	−300						
Jan. 7	Merchandise Inventory		9,000					
	Cash	−9,000						
Jan. 8	Rent Expense							−600
	Cash	−600						
Jan. 31	Cash	11,400						
	Sales Revenue							11,400
Jan. 31	Cost of Goods Sold							−7,600
	Merchandise Inventory		−7,600					
Jan. 31	Wages Expense							−1,000
	Cash	−1,000						
Jan. 31	Utilities Expense							−200
	Cash	−200						
	Ending Amounts	9,300	+32,400	=	30,000	+	10,000	+1,700

Exhibit 12
Summary of Account Balances for Mom's Cookie Company at January 31

Account	January 31 Balance	Explanation
Assets:		
Cash	9,300	column total
Merchandise Inventory	1,400	\$9,000 − \$7,600
Equipment	31,000	\$6,000 + \$25,000
Liabilities:		
Notes Payable	30,000	\$8,000 + \$22,000
Owners' Equity:		
Contributed Capital	10,000	
Sales Revenue	11,400	
Cost of Goods Sold	(7,600)	
Wages Expense	(1,000)	
Rent Expense	(600)	
Supplies Expense	(300)	
Utilities Expense	(200)	

The Income Statement

The *income statement* reports revenues and expenses for a fiscal period as a means of determining how well a company has performed in creating profit for its owners. An income statement reports revenues, expenses, and profit for a fiscal period.

A *fiscal period* **is any time period for which a company wants to report its financial activities.** Typical periods are months, quarters (three months), and years. Fiscal months usually correspond with calendar months (January, February, etc.). Fiscal years do not have to correspond with calendar years, however. For example, a company may prepare an income statement for the year ended June 30 that would report operating activities for July 1 through June 30 of the following year. Some companies choose months that end on particular days of the week, such as Sunday. Thus, a company might prepare an income statement for the month ended January 29 if the 29th were the last Sunday in the month. For example, **General Mills'** fiscal year always ends on the last Sunday of May. Therefore, fiscal year 2002 ended on May 26, 2002 and included all operating activities since the previous year ended on May 27, 2001. General Mills' 2002 income statement is shown on page 24 of Appendix B at the end of this book.

Exhibit 13 provides an example of an income statement for Mom's Cookie Company for the month ended January 31, 2004. The statement includes all the revenues and expenses recorded for January. *Net income* **is the amount of profit earned by a business during a fiscal period.** It is a measure of the value created for the owners of a business by the operating activities of the business during a fiscal period. Net income (revenue minus expense) increases owners' equity as we observed in the transactions in Exhibit 9. Information in financial statements is summarized from the transactions recorded for a fiscal period. All the sales revenue transactions are added together, for example, to calculate the total sales revenue for January.

Exhibit 13
Income Statement

Mom's Cookie Company
Income Statement
For the Month Ended January 31, 2004

Sales revenue	$11,400
Cost of goods sold	(7,600)
Wages expense	(1,000)
Rent expense	(600)
Supplies expense	(300)
Utilities expense	(200)
Net income	$ 1,700

An income statement provides information about the results of a company's operating activities for a fiscal period. Owners and other decision makers can use the statement to evaluate how well a company has performed.

The Balance Sheet

A *balance sheet* **identifies a company's assets and claims to those assets by creditors and owners at a specific date.** It is a summary of the accounting equation and, like the equation, the total of assets reported on the balance sheet must equal the combined total of liabilities and owners' equity. Exhibit 14 provides a balance sheet for Mom's Cookie Company at January 31, 2004. It reports dollar amounts associated with a company's assets and the sources of financing for those assets. It reports resources and claims at a particular point in time rather than results of activities over a period of time.

A balance sheet usually is prepared at the end of each fiscal period. It reports amounts of assets, liabilities, and owners' equity at that time. We examine the procedure for determining these amounts in more detail in Chapter F3.

Profit is earned by a business for its owners. It may be paid to the owners as a return on their investments, or it may be retained in the business as a means of acquiring additional assets. Thus, retained earnings is the total amount of net income earned

Exhibit 14
Balance Sheet

Mom's Cookie Company Balance Sheet At January 31, 2004	
Assets	
Cash	$ 9,300
Merchandise inventory	1,400
Equipment	31,000
Total assets	$41,700
Liabilities and Owners' Equity	
Notes payable	$30,000
Contributed capital	10,000
Retained earnings	1,700
Total liabilities and owners' equity	$41,700

over the life of a company minus the portion of net income paid out to owners. January is the first month of operations of Mom's Cookie Company, so the company has earned net income for only one month. The income statement reported net income for January of $1,700. None of the net income was paid out to owners. Consequently, retained earnings at the end of January is $1,700.

Retained earnings, January 1	$ 0
Net income for January	1,700
Less: Payment to owners in January	0
Retained earnings, January 31	$1,700

Retained earnings is separated from contributed capital in Exhibit 14 to distinguish between the amount paid into the company by Maria and Stan from the amount of profit earned and retained by the company. Amounts paid to owners normally should come from the company's profits. If a company pays its owners more than the company has earned, it is returning a portion of their investment to them. Owners need to know whether amounts paid to them are a return *on* their investments, from profits, or a return *of* their investments, from amounts invested directly by the owners. Thus, Mom's Cookie Company could pay Maria and Stan up to $1,700 from profits earned in January as a return on their investment. Any amount paid in excess of $1,700 would be a return of their investment.

The Statement of Cash Flows

A third financial statement prepared by businesses is the statement of cash flows. **The *statement of cash flows* reports events that affected a company's cash account during a fiscal period.** The statement contains three sections corresponding to operating, investing, and financing activities. The operating activities section reports cash from selling goods and services and cash paid for expense-related activities. The investing activities section reports cash paid for equipment and other long-term assets and cash received from selling these assets. The financing activities section reports cash received from creditors and owners, cash paid to creditors as a repayment of amounts borrowed by the company, and cash paid to owners.

Exhibit 15 provides a statement of cash flows for Mom's Cookie Company for January 2004. The source of data for the statement is the cash column for the transactions recorded in Exhibit 11. The results of these transactions are organized into the sections contained in the statement of cash flows.

Exhibit 15
Statement of Cash Flows

Mom's Cookie Company
Statement of Cash Flows
For the Month Ended January 31, 2004

Operating Activities		
Received from customers	$11,400	
Paid for merchandise	(9,000)	
Paid for wages	(1,000)	
Paid for rent	(600)	
Paid for supplies	(300)	
Paid for utilities	(200)	
Net cash flow from operating activities		$ 300
Investing Activities		
Paid for equipment*		(31,000)
Financing Activities		
Received from creditors**	30,000	
Received from owners	10,000	
Net cash flow from financing activities		40,000
Net cash flow for January		9,300
Cash balance, January 1		0
Cash balance, January 31		$ 9,300

*Office Equipment of $6,000 + Delivery Van of $25,000
**Notes Payable of $8,000 + Notes Payable of $22,000

The statement of cash flows describes the events that affected a company's cash account during a fiscal period. The amount reported as net cash flow for the period is the change in the cash balance. The final line of the statement reports the cash balance at the end of the month and corresponds with the amount reported on the company's balance sheet (see Exhibit 14). Thus, the statement of cash flows is useful for identifying how much cash a company has, where that cash came from, and how the company used its cash during a fiscal period.

LEARNING NOTE

As noted in the discussion of Exhibit 5, the purchase of the delivery van involved both investing and financing activities. On the statement of cash flows these are treated as two events. The financing transaction is treated as though the company received cash from borrowing money, and the investing transaction is treated as though the company paid cash for the delivery van.

The Transformation Process

Businesses transform resources into goods and services for sale to customers. Accounting measures and reports the results of that transformation process. Financing activities describe how a company obtains financial resources from owners and creditors. Investing activities describe how a company uses financial resources to acquire long-term assets to be used by the company. Operating activities describe how a company uses its financial resources and long-term assets to acquire and sell its products.

LEARNING NOTE

The statement of cash flows often is prepared using a format different than that described in Exhibit 15. We examine the alternate format in a later chapter.

Exhibit 16 illustrates the relationship among these activities as they are described in the income statement and balance sheet. The balance sheet describes a company's assets. Financial resources to acquire these assets are obtained from (1) financing activities (liabilities and owners' equity) and from (2) revenues earned by the company. When assets are consumed (3), expenses are created that reduce a company's profits. The profits earned during a period (4) increase owners' equity, as reported in retained earnings. The total amount of assets is equal to the total amount of liabilities and owners' equity (5).

Exhibit 16
Reporting the Transformation Process

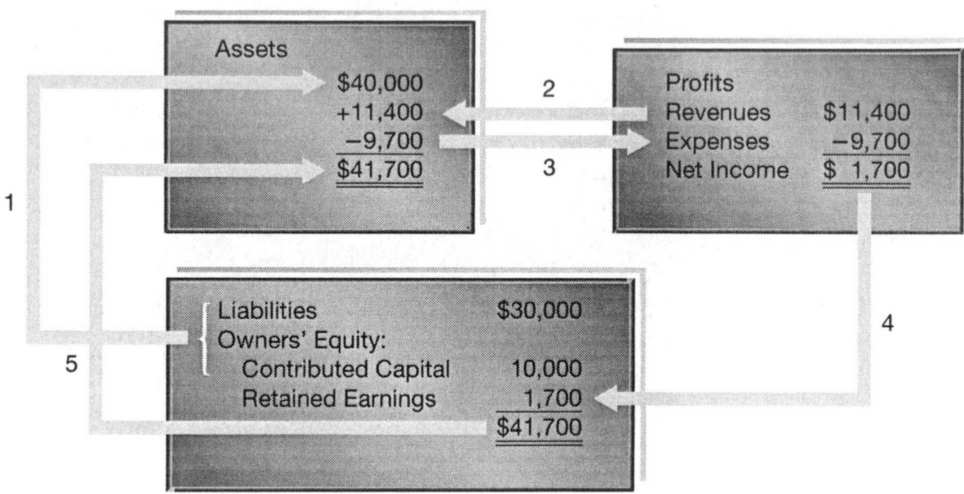

Financial Analysis

Many business decisions rely on accounting information. Decision makers use accounting information to evaluate a company's performance. A variety of analysis tools are available for this purpose. We examine these in later chapters. Financial statement numbers themselves provide useful information. For example, managers need to know how much cash or merchandise inventory a company has available so they can determine whether purchases can or should be made. Creditors need to know about a company's liabilities and profits to determine whether to make additional loans. Analysis often involves a comparison of accounting numbers, such as net income, with other numbers. Sometimes comparisons are made among fiscal periods or among companies. Comparisons are also made among different divisions of a company. For example, a decision maker may be interested in how the East division of a company compares with the West division, or how the U.S. division compares with the European division.

A common analytical tool involves the calculation of ratios. Most ratios compare one financial statement number with another. One example is return on assets. ***Return on assets (ROA)*** **is the ratio of net income to total assets.** Because total assets are equal to the total investment in a company from creditors and owners, return on assets measures return on total investment in a company. We can calculate return on assets for Mom's Cookie Company at January 31, 2004, as:

$$\text{Return on Assets} = \frac{\text{Net Income}}{\text{Total Assets}} = \frac{\$1{,}700}{\$41{,}700} = 4.1\%$$

We can interpret the ratio as the amount a company earned for each dollar of total investment. Thus, Mom's Cookie Company earned 4.1 cents for each dollar of investment in January. It is common to report many ratios, especially those expected to be less than one, as percentages, as shown above. Whether 4.1% is a good return or not can be assessed by comparing the amount with expectations of owners, with returns for similar companies, and with returns for other periods. A good return for one company is not necessarily good for another, particularly if the companies operate in different industries, countries, or geographic regions.

Owners, creditors, and other decision makers can examine return on assets for Mom's Cookie Company to decide whether the company is earning a reasonable profit. If the return is not satisfactory, Maria and Stan can make changes in the business. We examine various means of analyzing a company's performance in this book.

Business analysis relies on accounting and other information to understand how a business is performing and to determine future business activities. Exhibit 17 describes the role of accounting in business organizations. Accounting measures and records business activities. It converts data about business activities into useful information that is reported to decision makers. The information is analyzed to evaluate the performance of a company. Then, decisions are made that affect the company's future business activities. **A primary purpose of accounting is to help people make decisions about business activities. Accounting is the link between business activities and business decisions.**

Exhibit 17
A Model of the Accounting Process

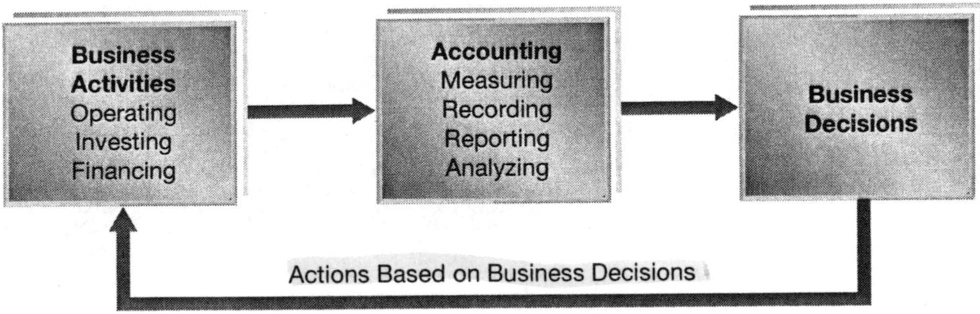

3 SELF-STUDY PROBLEM

WebTUTOR Advantage

Philistine Co. reported the following information for its first month of operations ended August 31, 2004:

Cash	$ 25,000
Merchandise inventory	200,000
Equipment	425,000
Notes payable	350,000
Investment by owners	250,000
Sales revenue	520,000
Cost of goods sold	300,000
Other expenses	140,000
Payments to owners	30,000

Required

A. Prepare an income statement using the format of Exhibit 13.
B. Determine how much retained earnings the company should report at the end of August.
C. Prepare a balance sheet using the format of Exhibit 14.
D. Calculate return on assets for the company for August.

The solution to Self-Study Problem 3 appears at the end of the chapter.

Appendix DEBITS AND CREDITS: ANOTHER WAY TO RECORD TRANSACTIONS

For most of its history, accounting has recorded transactions using debits and credits. They were particularly useful to facilitate the calculation of account balances prior to the advent of computers. Though the accounting process is largely computerized today, debits and credits remain part of the language of accounting. To understand this method, begin with the accounting equation, including revenues and expenses as subcategories of owners' equity, as described in Exhibit 18.

Debits **are increases in elements on the left (assets) side of the accounting equation and decreases in elements on the right (liabilities and owners' equity) side.** ***Credits*** **are decreases in elements on the left (assets) side of the accounting equation and**

Exhibit 18
Defining Debits and Credits

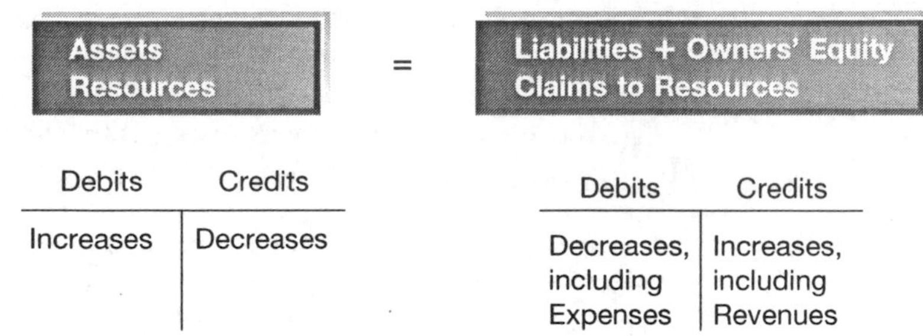

increases in elements on the right (liabilities and owners' equity) side. Because expenses decrease owners' equity, they are recorded as debits (unless expense amounts are being eliminated or offset). Because revenues increase owners' equity, they are recorded as credits (unless revenue amounts are being eliminated or offset).

Each account can be divided into a debit side (on the left) and a credit side (on the right). Transactions are recorded as debits and credits to the appropriate accounts. For example, (a) an owner's contribution of $10,000 to a company could be recorded as in Exhibit 19.

Exhibit 19
Recording a Transaction with Debits and Credits

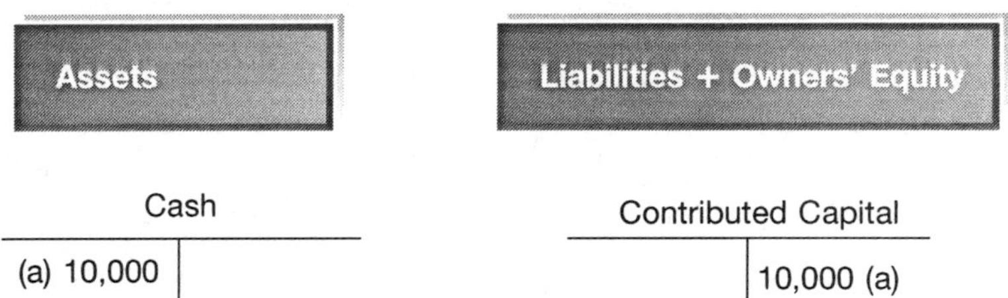

Cash is increased, and because it is an asset account, the increase is represented by a debit to the cash account. Contributed Capital is increased, and because it is an owners' equity account, the increase is represented by a credit to the contributed capital account.

For the accounting equation to balance, every transaction must have an equal amount of debits and credits. Therefore, total debits must always equal total credits for a company's transactions or accounts taken as a whole. Consequently, debits and credits provide a useful control to help ensure integrity of the accounting process. If debits do not equal credits, an error has been made.

The T-account format illustrated in Exhibit 19 often is used to describe transactions. This format makes it easy to observe the debit and credit effects of a transaction. If several transactions involve the same account, this format also makes it easy to observe the cumulative effect of the transactions. For example, (b) assume that the company borrowed $8,000 from a bank. Exhibit 20 includes the effect of this transaction, in addition to the transaction shown in Exhibit 19.

Exhibit 20
Recording Additional Transactions with Debits and Credits

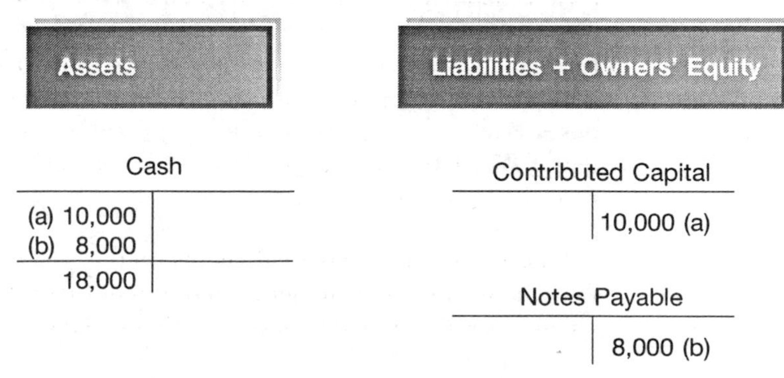

The addition of $8,000 to the cash account is represented by an additional debit entry. The combined effect of the two transactions is apparent after adding the two debit entries.

A third transaction (c), payment of $12,000 for equipment, is illustrated in Exhibit 21. The payment decreases Cash and is recorded as a credit to the cash account. The balance of the account decreases to a debit balance of $6,000. Equipment increases by $12,000, as represented by the debit to that account. Asset accounts normally have debit balances. Liability and owners' equity accounts normally have credit balances. Keep in mind that expenses are decreases in owners' equity and normally have debit balances.

Exhibit 21
Recording a Decrease in an Asset Account

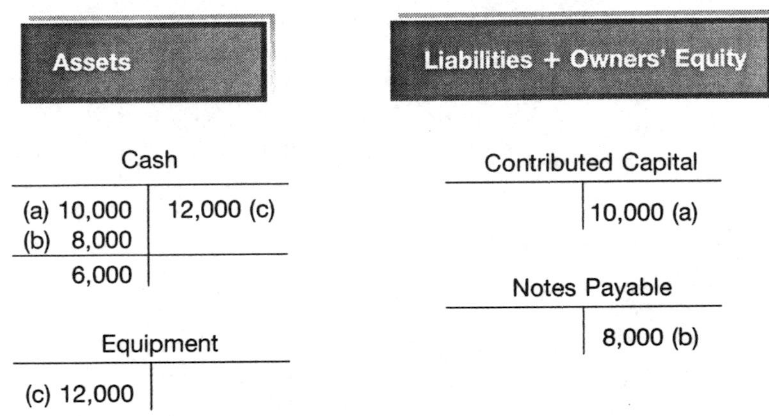

Exhibit 21 illustrates the advantages of a debit and credit system of recording transactions when transactions are recorded manually. Because increases in accounts are separated from decreases, it is simpler to calculate balances than if increases and decreases are recorded in one column. Remember that for most of our history, computers, calculators, and other electronic devices were not available. Account balances had to be determined using basic rules of math. Debits and credits facilitated that process.

Observe from Exhibit 21 that each transaction involves recording debits and credits of equal magnitude. Also note that the accounting equation remains in balance after each transaction. In Exhibit 21, total assets of $18,000 ($6,000 + $12,000) equals total liabilities and owners' equity ($10,000 + $8,000).

An alternative to the T-account approach is the traditional journal format. **The journal is a book (or computer file) in which transactions are recorded individually.** The journal provides for each transaction to be recorded using debits and credits without having to set up T-accounts. T-accounts are useful for simple transactions but become unwieldy when many transactions are being recorded.

Transactions considered in this chapter can be recorded using the traditional journal format as shown in Exhibit 22. The first transaction records cash received by Mom's Cookie Company from the owners. Observe that the total amount of debits equals the total amount of credits. Debits are listed first, and credits are indented to the right. Cash is debited because assets have increased. Contributed Capital is credited because owners' equity has increased. The cells to the right side of the transaction (labeled Effect on Accounting Equation) are not part of the journal entry. We include them as a reminder of the effect the transaction has on the equation. We abbreviate the elements of the accounting equation as follows: A = Assets, L = Liabilities, OE = Owners' Equity, CC = Contributed Capital, and RE = Retained Earnings. Refer to Exhibit 5 for comparison.

The purchase of a delivery van on January 6 by Mom's Cookie Company is shown in Exhibit 23. The purchase increased Equipment, decreased Cash, and increased Notes Payable. Observe that negative signs are not used with debits and credits because the credit to an asset or expense or the debit to a liability, owners' equity, or revenue identifies the amount as a decrease in the account balance.

Exhibit 22 Journal Representation of Financing Transaction

Journal

Date	Accounts	Debits	Credits
Jan. 2	Cash	10,000	
	Contributed Capital		10,000

Effect on Accounting Equation

A	=	L +	OE	
			CC +	RE
+10,000				
			+10,000	

Exhibit 23 Journal Representation of Investing Transaction

Journal

Date	Accounts	Debits	Credits
Jan. 6	Equipment	25,000	
	Cash		3,000
	Notes Payable		22,000

Effect on Accounting Equation

A	=	L +	OE	
			CC +	RE
+25,000				
−3,000				
		+22,000		

As a final example, Exhibit 24 provides the journal entries for the sale of goods from Exhibit 9. Cash and Sales Revenue increase, thus increasing both assets and owners' equity. Cost of Goods Sold and Merchandise Inventory decrease when goods are sold. Since Cost of Goods Sold is an expense, owners' equity decreases. The decrease in inventory reduces assets.

Exhibit 24 Journal Representation of Sales Transaction

Journal

Date	Accounts	Debits	Credits
Jan. 31	Cash	11,400	
	Sales Revenue		11,400
Jan. 31	Cost of Goods Sold	7,600	
	Merchandise Inventory		7,600

Effect on Accounting Equation

A	=	L +	OE	
			CC +	RE
+11,400				
				+11,400
				−7,600
−7,600				

REVIEW

SUMMARY of IMPORTANT CONCEPTS

1. Accounting provides information about business activities
   a. Accounting is an information system for measuring, recording, reporting, and analyzing business activities.
   b. Financing activities provide financial resources for a company from creditors and owners. Claims to resources by creditors and owners are recorded in liability and owners' equity accounts.
   c. The accounting equation, Assets = Liabilities + Owners' Equity, provides a basis for recording transactions.
   d. Accounting measures business activities by the cash value of resources transferred or consumed in a transaction.

   e. Investing activities involve acquiring and disposing of long-term assets.
   f. Operating activities involve acquiring and selling goods and services. Revenues identify the amount of goods and services sold to customers. Expenses identify the amount of resources consumed in acquiring and selling goods and services. Profit or net income for a fiscal period is the revenue earned during the period minus expenses incurred during the period.

2. Accounting reports business activities in the form of financial statements.
   a. An income statement reports revenues, expenses, and net income for a fiscal period as a measure of operating results.
   b. A balance sheet reports the assets controlled by a company and the claims to those assets by creditors and owners at a particular time, usually the end of a fiscal period.
   c. A statement of cash flows reports the events that resulted in cash being received or paid by a company during a fiscal period.
   d. Accounting measures and reports the results of the company's transformation of resources into goods and services for sale to customers.

3. Financial analysis involves the interpretation and use of accounting information to make business decisions.
   a. Analysis involves the comparison of accounting numbers with other numbers and comparison among companies or time periods.
   b. Financial ratios compare one financial statement number with another. Return on assets is one ratio used to evaluate a company's performance.

DEFINE

TERMS and CONCEPTS DEFINED in this CHAPTER

account (F46)
assets (F46)
balance sheet (F55)
business activities (F45)
cash (F47)
contributed capital (F47)
cost of goods sold (F52)
credits (F59)
debits (F59)
expense (F50)
financial statements (F53)
financing activities (F45)
fiscal period (F55)
income statement (F54)
interest (F45)
investing activities (F48)
liabilities (F46)
merchandise inventory (F50)
net income (F55)
notes payable (F47)
operating activities (F50)
owners' equity (F45)
principal (F45)
retained earnings (F51)
return on assets (ROA) (F58)
revenue (F50)
sales revenue (F52)
statement of cash flows (F56)
transactions (F46)

SELF-STUDY PROBLEM SOLUTIONS

SSP2-1

Accounts	ASSETS	=	LIABILITIES	+	OWNERS' EQUITY
Beginning Amounts	0	=	0	+	0
Cash	220,000				
Notes Payable			120,000		
Contributed Capital					100,000
Equipment	160,000				
Cash	−160,000				
Building	400,000				
Cash	−40,000				
Notes Payable			360,000		
Ending Amounts	580,000	=	480,000	+	100,000

SSP2-2

		ASSETS		=	LIABILITIES	+	OWNERS' EQUITY	
Date	Accounts	Cash	Other Assets				Contributed Capital	Retained Earnings
	Beginning Amounts	0	+0	=	0		+0	+0
Jan. 3	Cash	40,000						
	Contributed Capital						40,000	
Jan. 5	Cash	25,000						
	Notes Payable				25,000			
Jan. 8	Equipment		35,000					
	Cash	−35,000						
Jan. 10	Merchandise Inventory		20,000					
	Cash	−20,000						
Jan. 11	Supplies Expense							−2,000
	Cash	−2,000						
Jan. 15	Cash	12,000						
	Sales Revenue							12,000
Jan. 15	Cost of Goods Sold							−8,000
	Merchandise Inventory		−8,000					
Jan. 22	Cash	9,000						
	Sales Revenue							9,000
Jan. 22	Cost of Goods Sold							−6,000
	Merchandise Inventory		−6,000					
Jan. 31	Wages Expense							−3,000
	Cash	−3,000						
Jan. 31	Utilities Expense							−800
	Cash	−800						
	Ending Amounts	25,200	+41,000	=	25,000	+	40,000	+1,200

SSP2-3 A.

Philistine Co.
Income Statement
For the Month Ended August 31, 2004

Sales revenue	$ 520,000
Cost of goods sold	(300,000)
Other expenses	(140,000)
Net income	$ 80,000

B.

Retained earnings, August 1	$ 0
Net income	80,000
Less: Payment to owners	30,000
Retained earnings, August 31	$50,000

C.

Philistine Co.
Balance Sheet
At August 31, 2004

Assets	
Cash	$ 25,000
Merchandise inventory	200,000
Equipment	425,000
Total assets	$650,000
Liabilities and Owners' Equity	
Notes payable	$350,000
Investment by owners	250,000
Retained earnings	50,000
Total liabilities and owners' equity	$650,000

D. Return on Assets = $80,000 ÷ $650,000 = 12.3%

Thinking Beyond the Question

How do we know how well our business is doing?

At the beginning of the chapter we asked how a business can determine how well it is performing. This chapter has described the key elements of a basic accounting system. Accounts are used to record business activities. Account balances are summarized at the end of a fiscal period, and those balances are used to prepare financial statements. Those statements help owners, creditors, and other stakeholders understand the resources available to a company, how the resources were financed, how they were used in the business, how much profit the business earned, and the events that affected the company's cash during the period.

The procedures described in this chapter may appear mechanical. Some of them are. However, sometimes judgments have to be made about when certain

events should be recorded. Assuming you are making the accounting decisions for a company, what information do you think would tell you when revenues have been earned and expenses have been incurred? What events would be important for determining when to recognize revenues and expenses?

QUESTIONS

Q2-1 *Obj. 1* Joan Hoyt is considering opening a small retail store to sell knives and other kitchen utensils. She has a small amount of money to invest and wants to maintain as much control over the business as she can. She has asked you to help her decide how to finance her business. Describe the primary issues you would suggest Joan to consider.

Q2-2 *Obj. 1* Hardly Moving and Storage Corporation needs an additional $1,000,000 in financing to build new facilities. How might Hardly get the money? What issues should company management consider in deciding on the type of financing to use?

Q2-3 *Obj. 1* Jerrilyn has invested $5,000 in shares of the stock of Ambitious Enterprises, Inc. From the corporation's perspective, was this a financing activity, an investing activity, or an operating activity? Why?

Q2-4 *Obj. 2* Discuss the effect on the accounting equation if a company accurately reports its assets, yet understates its liabilities.

Q2-5 *Obj. 2* How are liabilities and owners' equity similar?

Q2-6 *Obj. 3* Explain why the accounting equation must balance after each transaction.

Q2-7 *Objs. 3, 4* Is purchasing merchandise inventory considered an investing or operating activity? Explain.

Q2-8 *Obj. 4* If owners contribute resources to a company, Owners' Equity increases. If a company records Sales Revenue, Owner's Equity also increases. How are Contributed Capital and Sales Revenue dissimilar?

Q2-9 *Obj. 4* While reviewing a company's balance sheet, John observed the Retained Earnings account with a balance of $850,000. "Wow," he thought. "That's a lot of cash!" Has John correctly interpreted the company's financial information? Explain.

Q2-10 *Obj. 5* Think of a company that operates in the same city as the college you are attending. With that company in mind, identify two examples each of assets, liabilities, owners' equity, revenues, and expenses that the company is likely to report on its financial statements.

Q2-11 *Obj. 5* Assume you are reviewing a balance sheet that has assets listed on the left side and liabilities and owners' equity on the right side. What question or questions can you answer by looking at the information on the left side of the balance sheet? What question or questions can you answer by looking at the information on the right side of the balance sheet?

Q2-12 *Obj. 5* What types of information are reported, respectively, on the balance sheet, income statement, and the statement of cash flows? Be specific.

Q2-13 *Obj. 3* A balance sheet identifies assets and claims to assets. Typically, who has claims on a company's assets?

Q2-14 *Obj. 5* Both the income statement and the statement of cash flows provide information about operating activities during a fiscal period. Why are both statements included in a company's financial report? How can decision makers use information in each statement?

Q2-15 *Obj. 5* Why are account balances summarized into financial statements? Why don't companies simply distribute a list of year-end account balances?

EXERCISES

If your instructor is using Personal Trainer in this course, you may complete online the assignments identified by PT.

E2-1 Write a short definition for each of the terms listed in the *Terms and Concepts Defined in this Chapter* section.

E2-2 *Objs. 1, 3, 4* PT Leonetta Garcetti owns and manages a large construction company. This morning she is faced with the following issues.

1. The office manager just submitted his resignation and the search for a replacement must be organized.
2. A loan officer from the company's bank just phoned saying that the company's application for a $400,000 loan has been approved.
3. Bids from several vendors have been received regarding installation of a new computerized information system. One proposal must be selected.
4. Because the new bank loan has been approved, two short-term loans can be paid off.
5. Old office furniture is awaiting disposal.
6. A long-time customer is unhappy with the firm's latest architectural drawings for a new shopping center complex.
7. A new construction crane is being purchased.
8. An investor has approached Leonetta offering to purchase 20% of her company in exchange for cash.
9. The firm is considering the purchase of exclusive regional rights to a patented construction process.
10. One of the company's customers is behind on scheduled payments. The amounts are large and Leonetta must decide whether to suspend construction on the project involved.

Identify each of the issues above as involving a financing activity, an investing activity, or an operating activity.

E2-3 *Objs. 1, 3, 4* PT For each of the following items, identify which part of the transformation process is involved. Use *F* to indicate a financing activity, *I* to indicate an investing activity, or *O* to indicate an operating activity.

a. ____ New manufacturing equipment was purchased for installation in the factory.
b. ____ Three new salespersons were hired.
c. ____ A loan was obtained from a local bank.
d. ____ A $500 down payment was received from a customer on goods sold.
e. ____ The Human Resources department hired three new employees.
f. ____ The company's worn-out delivery truck was sold to the junk yard for $400.
g. ____ The owner contributed more cash to the business.
h. ____ Refunds totaling $450 were given to several customers.
i. ____ Goods were shipped to a customer in a neighboring state.
j. ____ The remaining balance of a loan was repaid in full.

E2-4 *Obj. 2* PT Popovich Company had the following transactions during June.

June	1	$20,000 of merchandise inventory was purchased with cash.
	15	Sold merchandise for $60,000 cash. The merchandise had cost Popovich $28,000.
	23	Borrowed $200,000 from a bank.
	25	Paid $2,000 for supplies used in June.
	28	June wages of $6,000 were paid.
	30	$100,000 of equipment was purchased using cash.
	30	Paid $4,000 for utilities consumed in June.

Indicate the amount of cash, other assets, liabilities, and/or owners' equity that would result from each transaction by completing the table provided on the next page.

(Continued)

		ASSETS		=	LIABILITIES	+	OWNERS' EQUITY	
Date	Accounts	Cash	Other Assets				Contributed Capital	Retained Earnings
June 1	Beginning Amounts	$40,000	+60,000	=	30,000	+	50,000	+20,000
	Ending Amounts							

E2-5 *Obj. 1, 3, 4* P/T Identify each transaction in E2-4 as financing, investing, or operating.

E2-6 *Obj. 2* P/T Perez Company had the following selected transactions during the month of May. Show how the financial effects of each transaction would be recorded using the following format. The first transaction has been completed as an example.

Juanita Perez invested $10,000 in the company on May 1.

		ASSETS		=	LIABILITIES	+	OWNERS' EQUITY	
Date	Accounts	Cash	Other Assets				Contributed Capital	Retained Earnings
	Beginning Amounts	70,000	+90,000	=	60,000	+	60,000	+40,000
May 1	Cash	10,000						
	Contributed Capital						10,000	

May 5 Sold goods for $30,000 cash. The goods had cost $14,000.
10 Purchased merchandise inventory for $45,000 cash.
15 Paid back part of a bank loan, $1,500 (decrease Notes Payable).
22 Purchased equipment for $4,000 using cash.
31 Paid the utility company for services consumed, $600.
31 Paid $7,500 wages for labor services consumed.

E2-7 *Objs. 1, 3, 4* P/T Identify each transaction in E2-6 as financing, investing, or operating.

E2-8 *Obj. 2* Rosy Cheeks Company distributes perfumes and cosmetics. The following account changes were made in the company's accounting records during March. For each item, describe the transaction that caused the changes. The first item has been completed as an example.

a. Cash increased $18,000; Contributed Capital increased $18,000.
The owners invested $18,000 in the company.
b. Equipment increased $10,500; Cash decreased $10,500.
c. Cash increased $8,500; Notes Payable increased $8,500.
d. Supplies inventory increased $13,500; Cash decreased $13,500.
e. Merchandise Inventory decreased $9,500; Cost of Goods Sold increased $9,500.
f. Cash increased $23,500; Sales Revenue increased $23,500.
g. Supplies Expense increased $2,250; Supplies inventory decreased $2,250.

E2-9 *Obj. 2* P/T Amelio has operated a one-person law firm for many years. During the first week of February, the following events occurred in his business.

Feb. 2 Collected $1,800 from a client for legal work performed.
3 February's office rent of $1,200 was paid to the landlord.
4 A $300 payment was made on a loan previously obtained from a local bank.
4 The monthly subscription to *Lawyer's Monthly* magazine (a Miscellaneous Expense) was paid: $35.
5 Collected $4,250 for legal services performed.
5 Purchased a computer for $3,200 using cash.
6 Wages were paid to the office staff totaling $525.
6 Office supplies of $128 were purchased for cash and were consumed.

Show how the events above would be recorded using the format demonstrated in the chapter. Beginning account balances were as follows: Cash $5,000, Liabilities $1,500, Contributed Capital $3,000, and Retained Earnings $500. Prepare an income statement for the first week of February.

E2-10 *Objs. 1, 3, 4* P/T Identify each transaction in E2-9 as financing, investing, or operating.

E2-11 *Obj. 2* P/T Balance sheet accounts for Dale's Delightful Florist Shoppe at the end of a recent fiscal year are listed below. Prepare a schedule demonstrating that assets = liabilities + owner's equity for the company.

Supplies Inventory	$ 4,150
Buildings	79,500
Cash	1,200
Equipment	12,750
Flowers and Plants	24,780
Notes Payable	58,000
Proprietor's Capital	64,380

E2-12 *Obj. 2* P/T Harmony Cabot opened a music store in a local mall, selling CDs and tapes. She invested $80,000 in the business and borrowed $140,000 from a local bank. The following additional events occurred during April, the first month of operations:

a. Paid cash for equipment costing $45,150.
b. Purchased an inventory of CDs and tapes for $129,600 in cash.
c. Sold one-third of the CDs and tapes for a cash sales price of $85,000.
d. Paid expenses as follows:

Employee wages	$12,300
Rent	15,500
Utilities	4,800
Postage	650
Insurance	1,290

Record the transactions using the format shown in the chapter.

E2-13 *Obj. 4* P/T Chang Pottery Works began November with a Retained Earnings balance of $95,000. During November the company earned $15,000 and returned $4,000 to the owners. Prepare a schedule that reports the beginning balance, changes, and ending balance of retained earnings.

E2-14 *Obj. 5* P/T The following events occurred during December for Christmas Cookie Company:

a. Purchased and consumed $60,000 of flour, sugar, and other ingredients for cookies sold.
b. Paid $97,500 for December wages.
c. Paid $24,000 for utilities consumed in December.
d. Sold $234,000 of cookies and received cash.

Prepare an income statement for Christmas Cookie Company.

E2-15 *Obj. 5* PT Wheatgerm Healthfoods reported the following information:

Proceeds from issuance of notes payable	$13,057
Additions to plant and equipment	5,379
Proceeds from owners	30,957
Proceeds from sales of plant and equipment	1,986
Payments of debt	80,323

Calculate the net cash flow from (a) financing and (b) investing activities for Wheatgerm.

E2-16 *Obj. 5* PT Darden Bottling Company has the following information available for the first six months of 2004:

Cash collected from customers	$268,000
Cash paid merchandise inventory	83,500
Cash paid for utilities	20,000
Cash paid for insurance	23,000
Cash paid for equipment	76,500
Cash paid to employees	57,500
Cash paid for postage	7,500
Cash paid to owners	5,000
Cash received from sale of old equipment	18,500

Determine the cash flow from operating activities for the six-month period.

E2-17 *Obj. 5* PT Listed below are typical accounts or titles that appear on financial statements. For each item, identify the financial statement(s) on which it appears.

Wages expense
Cost of goods sold
Sales revenue
Merchandise inventory
Net income
Retained earnings
Contributed capital
Rent expense
Cash
Notes payable

E2-18 *Obj. 5* PT After six months of operation, Brother's Lawn Service had the following revenue and expense account balances:

Supplies expense	$ 4,000
Wages expense	6,000
Service revenue	12,300
Utilities expense	500
Rent expense	1,000

Prepare an income statement for Brother's Lawn Service for the first six months of operation that ended June 30, 2004.

E2-19 *Obj. 5* PT On June 30, 2004, Brothers' Lawn Service had the following account balances:

Cash	$3,000
Notes payable	1,000
Contributed capital	6,700
Retained earnings	800
Supplies inventory	500
Equipment	5,000

Prepare a balance sheet for Brother's Lawn Service.

E2-20 *Obj. 2, appendix* PT Record each transaction described in E2-4, using the debit and credit format illustrated in the appendix.

E2-21 *Obj. 2, appendix* PT Record each transaction described in E2-6, using the debit and credit format illustrated in the appendix.

PROBLEMS

If your instructor is using Personal Trainer in this course, you may complete online the assignments identified by PT.

P2-1 Recording Transactions
Obj. 2 PT

Surf-The-Net.com had the following events occur during October:

1. Paid $5,800 for utilities.
2. Made cash sales to customers that totaled $89,460. The merchandise had cost Surf-The-Net.com $60,000
3. Paid $28,600 for new equipment.
4. Repaid a $4,900 bank loan.
5. Borrowed $65,000 from local bank.
6. Paid $59,430 to employees for salaries.
7. Paid $11,900 for maintenance and repair.
8. Received $48,600 from investors.
9. Paid $3,750 for supplies that were used.

Required

A. Record transactions 1–9 using the format illustrated in the chapter.
B. What issues must a manager consider before making a financing decision or investing decision?

P2-2 Classifying Activities as Operating, Investing, or Financing
Objs. 1, 3, 4 PT

Refer to the information provided in P2-1.

Required Identify each transaction in P2-1 as a financing, investing, or operating activity.

P2-3 The Accounting Equation
Obj. 2 PT

Apollo Corporation reported the following accounts and balances in its financial statements:

Cash	$10,000
Merchandise Inventory	30,000
Equipment	45,000
Notes Payable	20,000
Contributed Capital	35,000
Retained Earnings	30,000

Required Arrange the accounts and balances into the accounting equation as shown below:

Assets = Liabilities + Equity

P2-4 Recording Transactions
Obj. 2 PT

Davidson Enterprises had the following transactions during its first month of business, June 2004.

June 1	Lynne Davidson set up a bank account in the business name and deposited $8,000 of her personal funds to it.
2	June's rent of $525 per month for a store-front location was paid in cash.
7	Goods for resale costing $3,600 were purchased using cash.
12	Paid advertising costs of $1,000 for the firm's Gala Grand Opening.
26	Goods costing $3,000 were sold during June for $7,200 in cash.
30	Workers were paid $850 and the utility company was paid $228 for June services.

(Continued)

Required

A. Use the format illustrated below to show how these transactions would be recorded.
B. Prepare an income statement that reports the firm's profit during June.
C. Prepare a balance sheet that reports the firm's assets, liabilities, and equity at June 30.

		ASSETS		=	LIABILITIES	+	OWNERS' EQUITY	
Date	Accounts	Cash	Other Assets				Contributed Capital	Retained Earnings
	Beginning Amounts	0	+0	=	0	+	0	+0

P2-5 Classifying Transactions as Financing, Investing, or Operating

Objs. 1, 3, 4

Refer to the information provided in P2-4.

Required Identify each transaction in P2-4 as financing, investing, or operating.

P2-6 Recording Transactions

Obj. 2

Carmen Bay Company sells a variety of souvenirs to tourists on the beach. Teenagers are paid 20 percent of the sales price to hawk the wares up and down the beach and are paid daily. The company was formed only recently and given approval by the local city council to operate. The following events are the first in the company's short history:

1. The company was formed when Carmen Bay contributed $2,150 to the firm.
2. A local bank loaned the firm $4,000 in exchange for the firm's one-year note payable.
3. Merchandise costing $4,100 was purchased with cash.
4. Goods costing $825 were sold to tourists for a total of $2,250 in cash, and the teenagers were paid their commissions.
5. A payment of $1,500 was made to the local bank on the note payable.
6. Carmen Bay withdrew $500 cash for personal use (Hint: reduce retained earnings).

Assume the company uses the following set of accounts:

Cash	Notes Payable
Cost of Sales	Merchandise Inventory
Sales	Contributed Capital
Retained Earnings	Commissions Expense

Required Determine how each event affects the company, and record the events using the format shown below.

		ASSETS		=	LIABILITIES	+	OWNERS' EQUITY	
Date	Accounts	Cash	Other Assets				Contributed Capital	Retained Earnings
	Beginning Amounts	0	+0	=	0	+	0	+0

P2-7 Recording Transactions

Obj. 2

Randi had a hard time finding a summer job when she went home from college, so she decided to go into business for herself mowing lawns. She had the following business activities during the month of June.

June 1 Used $200 of her own money and borrowed $450 from her father to start the business.

2 Rented a used pickup truck from an uncle for $85 per month. Paid for the first month's use.

3 Rented a lawnmower ($75 per month), an edger ($50 per month), and a wheelbarrow ($10 per month) at an equipment rental store. Paid the first month's rental fees in full.

16 During the first two weeks, performed $528 of lawn-mowing services. Customers paid in cash. Paid out $52 for gas, oil, and other supplies.

18 Paid $35 for a newspaper advertisement that had appeared earlier in the month.

30 During the last half of the month, performed $507 of lawn-mowing services and collected the cash.

30 Paid out $107 for gas, oil, and other supplies.

30 Paid back one-half of the amount she had borrowed from her father plus $5 for interest.

Randi knew from taking an accounting class at college that the following accounts would be needed to keep track of her business activities.

Cash	Equipment Rental Expense
Note Payable—Dad	Contributed Capital
Service Revenue	Retained Earnings
Gas and Oil Expense	Advertising Expense

Required

A. Show how each event would be entered into the accounting system.
B. Prepare an income statement for Randi's Lawn-mowing Service for the month of June.
C. Prepare a balance sheet as of June 30.
D. Did Randi make a smart decision when she started her own business? What factors might be considered in making that evaluation?

P2-8 *Obj. 2*

Reconstructing Events from Information in the Accounting Database

Jill Jones has just established a security alarm maintenance service. She charges $20 per hour per person and is paid by check upon completion of the job. Her expenses are rather low—usually only supplies and transportation. Following are the entries to the accounting system that were made for the first seven transactions of the company.

		ASSETS		=	LIABILITIES	+	OWNERS' EQUITY	
Date	**Accounts**	**Cash**	**Other Assets**				**Contributed Capital**	**Retained Earnings**
1	Cash	5,000						
	Contributed Capital						5,000	
2	Supplies Inventory		300					
	Cash	−300						
3	Cash	4,200						
	Service Revenues							4,200
4	Utilities Expense							−450
	Cash	−450						
5	Transportation Expense							−500
	Cash	−500						
6	Insurance Expense							−700
	Cash	−700						
7	Retained Earnings							−1,300
	Cash	−1,300						
	Ending Amounts	5,950	+300	=			5,000	+1,250

(Continued)

Required

A. For each transaction, describe the event that caused the entry to be made.
B. How much income (or loss) did the company earn?

P2-9 Understanding Information in the Accounting Information System

Obj. 2

Jacqueline owns and operates a specialty cosmetics manufacturing firm. Distribution is primarily through boutique shops in regional shopping centers, although some items are sold directly through a network of beauty consultants. Raw materials consist of various lotions, potions, fragrances, oils, and powders. The transactions that occurred during the month of March were entered into the accounting system as follows.

		ASSETS		=	LIABILITIES	+	OWNERS' EQUITY	
Date	**Accounts**	**Cash**	**Other Assets**				**Contributed Capital**	**Retained Earnings**
Mar. 1	Cash	10,000						
	Contributed Capital						10,000	
Mar. 3	Cash	7,000						
	Notes Payable				7,000			
Mar. 5	Merchandise Inventory		8,100					
	Cash	−8,100						
Mar. 18	Cash	15,250						
	Sales Revenue							15,250
	Cost of Goods Sold							−7,500
	Merchandise Inventory		−7,500					
Mar. 18	Wages Expense							−650
	Cash	−650						
Mar. 23	Notes Payable				−2,500			
	Cash	−2,500						
Mar. 31	Retained Earnings							−2,000
	Cash	−2,000						
	Ending Amounts	19,000	+600	=	4,500	+	10,000	+5,100

Required

A. Describe each of the firm's transactions. Specify as much detail about each transaction as you can.
B. Assume an income statement and balance sheet are prepared immediately after the last transaction.
   1. What amount of net income would be reported?
   2. What total amount of owners' equity would be reported on the balance sheet?

P2-10 Reconstructing Events from the Financial Statements

Obj. 2

Costantino Company just started in business. The first seven transactions have been entered into and processed by the company's computerized accounting information system. To be sure the accounting system is operating properly, Jim Costantino, the owner, has printed out the financial statements as produced by the accounting system after seven transactions.

Assets:		Liabilities and Equity:	
Cash	$22,850	Payable to bank	$ 6,285
Equipment	11,000	Payable for equipment	11,000
		Owner investment	15,000
		Retained earnings	1,565
Total assets	$33,850	Total liabilities and equity	$33,850
Revenues	$ 2,250		
Expenses:			
Rent	(400)		
Wages	(250)		
Internet service	(35)		
Net income	$ 1,565		

Required Identify the seven transactions and as much detail about each transaction as you can.

P2-11 Recording Transactions and Preparing Financial Statements

Objs. 2, 5

P/T

Assume that you began a small business in May 2004 by (1) investing $10,000 and (2) borrowing $30,000 from a bank. You (3) purchased equipment for $25,000 cash and (4) purchased merchandise for $12,000 using cash. During the first month of operations, your company (5) sold merchandise for $27,000 in cash. (6) The cost of merchandise sold during the month was $10,000. You (7) repaid $300 of the amount borrowed from the bank. You (8) withdrew $800 from the business for personal use. The name of your business is Sand Dune Trading Company.

Required

A. Record transactions 1–8 using the format illustrated in the chapter.
B. Prepare an income statement for May 2004, the first month of operations.
C. Prepare a balance sheet at the end of the first month.

P2-12 Identifying Financial Statements

Obj. 5

P/T

Refer to the information about financial statements below.

1. The statement provides information about resources consumed during an accounting period.
2. The statement is dated as of a specific point in time.
3. The amounts that are owed to other organizations or individuals are reported.
4. The total amount of capital that has been contributed to the organization is reported.
5. The cash used for investing activities is reported.
6. Information is reported regarding the rewards that have been earned from serving customers during the accounting period just ended.
7. The cash received from financing activities is reported.
8. The statement is not as of a specific date, but covers a period of time.
9. The statement contains information about the financial obligations that were made to acquire resources.
10. The statement reports cash inflows and outflows.

Required For each item above, indicate the financial statement for which the information is true. Use *I* to indicate income statement, *B* to indicate balance sheet, *C* to indicate cash flow statement. If an item is not true for any of the three financial statements, indicate with an *N*.

P2-13 Summarizing the Results of Financial Activities

Obj. 5

P/T

The accounting staff at Moonbeam Enterprises prepares monthly financial statements. At the end of April 2004 the company had the following account balances:

(Continued)

Land	$45,000
Notes payable	33,000
Merchandise inventory	12,480
Buildings	50,000
Cash	10,360
Contributed capital	38,770
Retained earnings, April 30	46,070
Cost of goods sold	15,050
Sales revenue	26,000
Supplies expense	1,300
Income tax expense	1,060
Wage expense	1,500
Insurance expense	550
Interest expense	900

Required Prepare an income statement and balance sheet in good form. For each statement, use a three-line heading on the statement that includes (a) the name of the company, (b) the name of the statement, and (c) the appropriate time period or date.

P2-14 Recording Transactions

Objs. 2, 5

Larrisa Enterprises, Inc., owns and operates a chain of mini-mart stores in a popular summer resort area. Business is highly seasonal with about 80% of annual sales occurring during June, July, and August. Shown below are transactions that occurred during the first week of June.

June 3 Merchandise costing $120,000 was purchased from a supplier using cash.
4 Dividends of $25,000 were distributed to owners for their own personal use. (Hint: Dividends reduce Retained Earnings.)
5 Goods costing $112,000 were sold to customers for $140,000 cash.
5 Advertising was run in local newspapers during the first week. The bill, for $9,000, was paid on June 5.
6 Electricity, water, natural gas, and Internet charges totaling $450 were paid in cash.
6 Display equipment was purchased for $15,000 cash.
7 Employees were paid a total of $12,900 for all work performed through the end of the first week of June.

Required Show how the events above would be entered into the accounting system using the format demonstrated in the chapter. Beginning balances are provided below:

		ASSETS		=	LIABILITIES	+	OWNERS' EQUITY	
Date	Accounts	Cash	Other Assets				Contributed Capital	Retained Earnings
	Beginning Amounts	90,000	150,000		80,000		60,000	100,000

P2-15 Classifying Transactions as Financing, Investing, or Operating Activities

Objs. 1, 3, 4

Refer to the information provided in P2-14.

Required Identify each transaction in P2-14 as a financing, investing, or operating activity.

P2-16 Preparing a Statement of Cash Flows

Obj. 5

Crimson Florist had the following cash flows for the month of July 2004.

Cash paid for wages	$ 5,000
Cash paid for supplies	2,500
Cash received from sales to customers	15,000
Cash paid for equipment	5,000
Cash received from owners	13,000
Cash paid for utilities	3,500
Cash received from creditors	8,500

The cash balance on July 1 was $3,200.

Required

A. Prepare a statement of cash flows for Crimson Florist.
B. What is the purpose of the statement of cash flows?

P2-17 Preparing a Statement of Cash Flows

Obj. 5

During January, The College Shop had the following cash flows:

Cash paid for merchandise	$ 4,000
Cash paid for rent	5,300
Cash received from sales to customers	13,000
Cash paid for utilities	200
Cash received from owners	9,000
Cash paid for equipment	7,000
Cash paid for insurance	2,500
Cash received from a bank loan	10,500
Cash paid for wages	1,200

The beginning cash balance was $4,000.

Required Prepare a statement of cash flows for The College Shop.

P2-18 Financial Analysis

Obj. 5

Holiday Travel Store is a retailer that sells merchandise at a family campground. The company's most recent income statement and balance sheet are presented below:

Holiday Travel Store
Income Statement
For the Year Ended December 31, 2004

Sales revenue	$75,000
Cost of goods sold	(43,000)
Wages expense	(15,000)
Supplies expense	(3,500)
Utilities expense	(2,000)
Rent expense	(8,000)
Net income	$ 3,500

Holiday Travel Store
Balance Sheet
December 31, 2004

Assets	
Cash	$ 900
Merchandise inventory	7,000
Equipment	20,000
Total assets	$27,900
Liabilities and Owners' Equity	
Notes payable	$15,500
Contributed capital	10,000
Retained earnings	2,400
Total liabilities and owners' equity	$27,900

Required

A. Calculate Holiday Travel Store's return on assets.
B. Explain what the ratio means.
C. What kinds of changes might the owners make if the return on assets is not acceptable?

P2-19 Obj. 2, Appendix

Recording Transactions Using the Debit and Credit Format

Refer to the information provided in P2-6.

Required For each transaction described in P2-6, record the transaction using the debit and credit format illustrated in the appendix.

P2-20 Obj. 2, Appendix

Recording Transactions Using the Debit and Credit Format

Refer to the information provided in P2-7.

Required For each transaction described in P2-7, record the transaction using the debit and credit format illustrated in the appendix.

P2-21

Excel in Action

SPREADSHEET

Millie and Milo Wermz are the owners of The Book Wermz. The business is operated as a corporation. The Wermz invested $100,000 in the company when they started it in 1996. This investment represents the company's stockholders' equity. The company's account balances on September 30, 2004—the end of the fiscal year—were: Cash $4,238.72, Inventory of Books $235,892.35, Supplies $2,343.28, Equipment $43,297.00, Notes Payable $123,452.88, Investment by Owners $100,000, and Retained Earnings $62,318.47.

Summary transactions for The Book Wermz for October 2004 included:

Cash sales	$38,246.50
Cost of goods sold	27,318.93

Required Use a spreadsheet to keep track of account balances for The Book Wermz. Enter the titles of accounts in row 1. Use column A for dates. Enter account balances for September 30, 2004 in row 2. A partial spreadsheet is illustrated below as an example:

	A	B	C
1	Date	Cash	Inventory
2	9/30/04	4,238.72	235,892.35

Use the Format menu to adjust cell formats as needed to wrap text for long titles. Use the comma button to format dollar amounts. See instructions from Chapter 1 if you need help with formatting. Include columns for Sales and Cost of Goods Sold. The beginning balances for these two accounts will be $0.

In Row 3, enter the sales transaction for October, and in Row 4 enter the Cost of Goods Sold transaction. Use 10/31/04 as dates for these transactions. Using the illustration of closing the accounts in this chapter, close the revenue and expense accounts for October in Row 5. In Row 6, calculate the account balance for each account at October 31, 2004. Use the Sum function [=Sum(B2:B5)] or button Σ for this purpose. Note that =Sum(B2:B5) performs the same operation as =B2+B3+B4+B5. The ending balances for revenue and expense accounts should be $0 after these accounts have been closed.

Beginning in Row 9, prepare a balance sheet and income statement for The Book Wermz for October 2004. Use the format illustrated in Exhibits 13 and 14 in this chapter. You may need to make some of the columns in the spreadsheet wider to accommodate captions. Format cells with the currency format so that they display $, as shown in Exhibits 13 and 14. You can use the Currency $ and Comma , buttons for this purpose. Cells containing totals should be formatted to contain double underlines. Use the Borders button for this purpose.

Use cell references in the financial statements to identify amounts for each account. For example: | Cash | =B6 |

Also, use the Sum function or button to calculate totals in the balance sheet and income statement. You should be able to change any of the numbers in the transactions at the top of the spreadsheet and have the financial statements change automatically in response to the new amounts.

P2-22 Multiple Choice Overview of the Chapter

1. Which of the following is a financing activity?
   a. A manufacturing company purchases supplies.
   b. A retail company borrows $40,000 from a bank.
   c. A manufacturing company acquires a new building.
   d. A service organization pays the monthly utility bill.

2. If a company borrows cash from a bank, the effect on the accounting equation is as follows:
   a. Assets increase, Liabilities increase
   b. Assets decrease, Liabilities increase
   c. Assets increase, Liabilities decrease
   d. Assets decrease, Liabilities decrease

3. The balance sheet describes a company's assets. Financial resources to acquire these assets are obtained from
   a. investing activities.
   b. financing activities and revenues earned.
   c. investing activities and expenses paid during a fiscal period.
   d. none of the above.

4. Which of the following is an investing activity?
   a. A manufacturer borrows from creditors.
   b. A service firm pays a return to its stockholders.
   c. A retailer sells goods to a not-for-profit agency at cost.
   d. A government agency purchases a new mainframe computer system.

5. Which of the following is *not* an operating activity?
   a. Merchandise is sold to customers.
   b. Utility bills are paid.
   c. Merchandise is shipped to customers.
   d. Equipment is purchased for use in manufacturing.

6. Return on assets represents
   a. cash that is returned to investors.
   b. merchandise that is returned by customers.
   c. the ratio of income to total assets.
   d. the ratio of merchandise returned by customers to sales.

7. Accounting information is

	Needed by managers for internal decision making	Needed by managers for persons outside the firm
a.	Yes	Yes
b.	Yes	No
c.	No	Yes
d.	No	No

8. Liability and owners' equity accounts usually arise from which type of activities?
   a. Investing activities
   b. Financing activities
   c. Operating activities
   d. Manufacturing activities

9. Expresso Delivery Service purchased a new delivery truck for $21,000 by making a $4,000 cash payment and giving a $17,000 note payable to the seller. How were each of the following affected when this event was recorded in the firm's accounting information system?

	Assets	Liabilities
a.	Increased	Increased
b.	No change	Increased
c.	Increased	Decreased
d.	Decreased	Increased

10. The statement of cash flows for the Halyard Exploration Company reported the following:

Cash paid for equipment	$ 300,000
Cash paid to employees	400,000
Cash paid to owners	150,000
Cash paid to suppliers	560,000
Cash received from customers	1,200,000

What were Halyard's net cash flows from operating, investing, and financing activities?

	Operating	Investing	Financing
a.	$240,000	($300,000)	$(150,000)
b.	$500,000	($860,000)	$200,000
c.	$640,000	($860,000)	$200,000
d.	$240,000	($860,000)	$200,000

11. When an investor contributes cash to a business, the transaction is recorded as follows:

	Debit	Credit
a.	Cash	Retained Earnings
b.	Cash	Contributed Capital
c.	Contributed Capital	Cash
d.	Retained Earnings	Cash

CASE

C2-1 Designing an Accounting Information System

Obj. 6

For about a year, Frank Poppa has been operating a hot dog stand in the parking lot of a major discount retailer in a suburban area. The stand appears to be a pushcart but is actually a small trailer that is towed from home each day. Frank cleverly designed the stand to include storage compartments, napkins, and the like. What started out as a "weekend gig" to pick up a few extra bucks has turned into a full-time occupation. Frank soon found that on a hot summer day, he could easily take in more than $1,000 from sales of a full line of fancy hot dogs and cold sodas.

About four months ago, Frank decided to expand to more locations. He found that large discount retailers were quite happy to provide him adequate space near the front door because customers enjoyed the convenience and the stand helped build traffic for the retailer. Frank formed Poppa's Dogs Company and negotiated contracts with several retailers to provide pushcart operations outside their stores. The contracts generally call for Poppa's Dogs to pay a location fee to the retailer plus 3% of the pushcart's sales.

Frank plans to be very careful when hiring the people necessary to operate the five new pushcart locations. He is confident that he can assess good moral character and avoid hiring anyone who would take advantage of him. Frank will have to spend about $3,000 for each new pushcart and related equipment. In addition, he will have to finance an inventory of hot dogs, condiments, and sodas for each location. A local bank has agreed to provide financing.

Until now, Frank has maintained an informal accounting system consisting of an envelope full of receipts and his personal checking account. The system has served him well enough so far, but he is finding that more and more he is getting his personal financial activities confused with those of his business. Frank is positive that the business is profitable because he seems to have more money left at the end of the month than he did when he was working full time as an auto mechanic. He has decided he needs a better accounting system and has decided to consult with a CPA he knows to see what she might recommend.

Required What information does Frank's current accounting system provide him? What additional information should Frank want from an improved accounting system? Make recommendations to Frank regarding how he can improve his accounting system and identify a chart (list) of accounts that you would expect to find in Frank's new accounting system. For each account, identify whether it is an asset, liability, owner's equity, revenue, or expense.

C2-2 Financing, Investing, and Operating Activities as Part of the Transformation Process

Objs. 1, 3, 4

Environmental Housing Company designs and builds log homes. Financing is provided by owners and creditors, primarily banks. The company owns buildings and equipment it uses in the management, design, transportation, and construction process. It purchases logs and other building materials from other companies. These materials are shipped by the sellers. Homes are designed for customers. Logs are cut to the dimensions called for in a design and shipped to the customer's building site with other materials for assembly. Environmental Housing employs design engineers, construction and assembly workers, maintenance personnel, and marketing and service personnel, in addition to its management and office staff. The company is in charge of the construction process until the home is completed and ready for occupancy. The company gives warranties for one year after completion that state the completed home is free of defects from materials or construction.

Required List decisions involving the acquisition, use, or disposal of resources that Environmental Housing's managers would make at each stage (financing, investing, and operating) of the transformation process.

3

Measuring Revenues and Expenses

How do we know how much profit our business has earned?

With their accountant's help, Maria and Stan set up an accounting system for recording the business activities of Mom's Cookie Company. They prepared financial statements for January from information recorded in their accounting system. However, certain types of transactions were not considered in preparing those statements. A business requires an accounting system that ensures that all revenues and expenses are recorded in the appropriate fiscal period.

FOOD FOR THOUGHT

If you were running a business, how would you know when to record revenues and expenses? It's easy to keep track of cash when your business receives it at the time goods are sold or services are provided. What would you do if your goods are transferred or services are provided to customers in one fiscal period and cash is received in a different period? You might consume resources in one fiscal period but pay for those resources in a different period. When should you recognize the expense? Now that they understand some basic accounting procedures, Maria and Stan discuss the appropriate recognition of revenues and expenses with their accountant, Ellen.

Stan: *We recorded transactions and prepared financial statements for January, but it seems like we haven't included all the business activities that occurred during January. We owe interest on our loan to the bank, and we used equipment we purchased in January without recording any expense.*

Ellen: *You're correct. We created a basic accounting system for recording transactions in January. Now we need to expand that system to include all transactions that should be recorded each month.*

Maria: *Does it really matter that much if we don't include everything in the appropriate month?*

Ellen: *Businesses are required to record revenues and expenses in the fiscal period in which revenues are earned and expenses incurred. Careful identification of the proper amount of revenues and expenses is important to provide accurate and reliable information about your company's performance. If you fail to do so, you may report misleading information. That could cause you to make bad decisions and it may affect decisions by creditors and other stakeholders.*

Stan: *How can we know if we have recorded all the transactions we need to record each month?*

Ellen: *You need to follow the proper accounting rules and procedures. Once you identify the kinds of events that need to be recorded each month, following these rules and procedures will help make sure your financial statements are accurate and reliable. Let's look at these rules and procedures and learn how to apply them to your company.*

OBJECTIVES

Once you have completed this chapter, you should be able to:

1. Explain the concept of accrual accounting and why it is used.
2. Record revenue transactions using accrual accounting.
3. Record expense transactions using accrual accounting.
4. Identify and record adjusting entries at the end of a fiscal period.
5. Prepare closing entries and financial statements at the end of a fiscal period.
6. Identify steps in the accounting cycle.

ACCRUAL ACCOUNTING

OBJECTIVE 1

Explain the concept of accrual accounting and why it is used.

Almost all of the transactions we examined in Chapter F2 involved receipt or payment of cash. Cash often is received from customers at the time goods are sold. Cash often is paid when equipment, merchandise inventory, and supplies are purchased. These transactions involve increasing or decreasing the cash account and recording an offsetting amount to the revenue or expense account that explains the cause of the increase or decrease in cash.

In many cases a company earns revenue or incurs expenses in a fiscal period other than the one in which cash is received or paid. Consider the following examples for Mom's Cookie Company for the first three months of operation:

- Money was borrowed in January, but repayment of principal was not made until later.
- Interest was incurred on debt in January and February, but the interest was not paid until March.
- Goods were sold to customers on credit in February, but cash was not received until March.
- Employees worked in February and earned wages, but the wages were paid in March.
- Customers ordered goods in February and paid cash at the time of the order, but the goods were not delivered to the customers until March.
- Rent was paid on a building in February for use of the building in February, March, and April.

These types of transactions are common for most companies. To accommodate these types of events, businesses use a form of accounting known as accrual accounting. ***Accrual accounting*** **is a form of accounting in which revenues are recognized when they are earned and expenses are recognized when they are incurred.** To recognize revenues and expenses means to record them as accounting transactions. Normally, revenues are earned when goods are transferred or when services are provided. Expenses are incurred when resources are consumed in the processes of acquiring and selling goods and services. Accrual accounting focuses on business activities to determine when to record revenues and expenses.

A company does not have to receive or pay cash at the time revenues or expenses are recorded. However, the accounting process is more complicated when revenues or expenses are recorded in one period and cash is received or paid in another. Let's consider some examples for Mom's Cookie Company.

REVENUE TRANSACTIONS

OBJECTIVE 2

Record revenue transactions using accrual accounting.

On February 12, 2004, Mom's Cookie Company sold boxes of cookies to a customer for $600 on credit. The boxes cost Mom's Cookie Company $400. The customer paid for the goods on March 10, 2004. Because the revenue was earned in February, Mom's Cookie Company must recognize the revenue in February. The transaction to record the sale would be as follows:

		ASSETS		=	LIABILITIES	+	OWNERS' EQUITY	
Date	Accounts	Cash	Other Assets				Contributed Capital	Retained Earnings
Feb. 12	Accounts Receivable		600					
	Sales Revenue							600
Feb. 12	Cost of Goods Sold							−400
	Merchandise Inventory		−400					

Neither of these transactions involves cash. Cash was not received from the customer at the time of the sale. Cash was not paid by Mom's Cookie Company for the merchandise at the time of sale, either. The company was selling merchandise that it had already purchased.

***Accounts Receivable* is an asset account that increases when goods are sold on credit.** It represents an amount a customer owes to a company. Revenue is recognized because the goods have been transferred to the customer. Mom's Cookie Company has done the work necessary to earn revenue, and accrual accounting requires revenue to be recognized when it is earned.

The sale transaction is linked to a second transaction that occurs on March 10. When the customer pays for the goods, Mom's Cookie Company records the following:

		ASSETS		=	LIABILITIES	+	OWNERS' EQUITY	
Date	Accounts	Cash	Other Assets				Contributed Capital	Retained Earnings
Mar. 10	Cash	600						
	Accounts Receivable		−600					

Cash increases because it has been received from the customer. Accounts Receivable decreases because the customer has fulfilled the obligation to pay for the goods sold in February. **Revenue is not recognized at the time cash is received because it has already been recognized when goods were sold.** Because the sale occurs at one time and cash is received at a different time, two transactions are needed to record the sale and cash receipt. Accounts Receivable provides a means of linking the two transactions. It records the amount the customer owes the company until the customer pays for the goods. Exhibit 1 describes the effect of the transactions on the Cash, Accounts Receivable, and Sales Revenue accounts.

Accounts Receivable increases at the time of sale in February. The amount the customer owes is decreased when the customer pays cash in March, reducing the Accounts Receivable balance for this sale to zero. The net result of the two transactions is the same as if the customer had paid cash for the goods. However, two transactions are necessary to achieve this result. The first transaction is important because Maria and Stan and other decision makers are interested in when a company sells goods. All of the sales that oc-

Exhibit 1
Linking Revenue and Cash through Accounts Receivable

Date	Cash	Accounts Receivable	Sales Revenue
Feb. 12		600	600
Mar. 10	600	−600	
Net result	600	0	600

cur in February should appear on Mom's Cookie Company's income statement for February. The income statement provides information about business activities that occurred during a particular fiscal period. If a company waited until cash was received from customers to record revenues, it would appear that the business sold the goods in the period when cash was received. Instead, accrual accounting ensures that decision makers have information about sales activities for the period in which the sales occurred. In addition, recording accounts receivable provides information about the amount owed by customers that a company expects to collect in a future fiscal period.

Sometimes a company receives cash from a customer before a sale is made. For example, Mom's Cookie Company received an order from a customer on February 24, 2004, for more goods than the company had in its inventory. Maria and Stan agreed to fill the order for the customer but required the customer to pay for the goods at the time of the order. The customer paid $3,000 on February 24, and Mom's Cookie Company ordered the goods from its supplier. The goods were delivered to the customer on March 3.

The payment transaction would be recorded as follows:

		ASSETS		=	LIABILITIES	+	OWNERS' EQUITY	
Date	**Accounts**	**Cash**	**Other Assets**				**Contributed Capital**	**Retained Earnings**
Feb. 24	Cash	3,000						
	Unearned Revenue				3,000			

Cash increases by the amount received from the customer. Revenue has not been earned, however, because goods have not been transferred to the customer. Instead, Mom's Cookie Company has incurred a liability as represented by the Unearned Revenue account. ***Unearned Revenue* is a liability account that results when a company receives cash from a customer for goods or services to be provided in the future.** The liability results from the obligation Mom's Cookie Company has to order the goods and provide them to the customer. If the company fails to complete the obligation, it will be required to refund the $3,000 to the customer.

The sales transaction is recorded on March 3 when goods are transferred to the customer.

		ASSETS		=	LIABILITIES	+	OWNERS' EQUITY	
Date	**Accounts**	**Cash**	**Other Assets**				**Contributed Capital**	**Retained Earnings**
Mar. 3	Unearned Revenue				−3,000			
	Sales Revenue							3,000
Mar. 3	Cost of Goods Sold							−2,000
	Merchandise Inventory		−2,000					

Once the goods are transferred to the customer on March 3, the obligation has been fulfilled and the liability is eliminated. **In most sales transactions, Sales Revenue is recognized when the goods are transferred to the customer.** The cost of the merchandise to Mom's Cookie Company of $2,000 is also recognized when the goods are transferred to the customer. Again, this process results in revenue being recognized in the period in which it is earned rather than when cash is received. Expenses are recognized when resources are consumed. Exhibit 2 illustrates the effects of these activities on the company's accounts.

Exhibit 2
Linking Cash and Revenue through Unearned Revenue

Date	Cash	Unearned Revenue	Sales Revenue
Feb. 24	3,000	3,000	
Mar. 3		−3,000	3,000
Net result	3,000	0	3,000

Unearned Revenue is an account used to link the receipt of cash in February with the revenue earned in March. This time, cash was received before revenue was recognized. Like Accounts Receivable, amounts are added or subtracted from Unearned Revenue as needed to ensure the proper timing of revenue recognition. The net result of these transactions is the same as if goods were sold for cash.

Transactions in which cash is received before revenue is earned are common for some types of companies. Examples include airlines, magazine publishers, and communications companies. Passengers often purchase airline tickets prior to their flights. At the time of the purchase, the airline records unearned revenue. When the passenger uses the ticket, the airline eliminates the unearned revenue and records passenger revenue. Similarly, subscribers often pay for magazine subscriptions before receiving the issues. At the time of purchase, the magazine records unearned revenue. As issues are published and mailed to subscribers, the amount of unearned revenue is reduced and subscription revenue is recognized. As an example, **AOL Time Warner**, owner of *Time*, *Life*, and other magazines, reported unearned revenues of $1.456 billion for the fiscal year ended December 31, 2001.

To summarize, companies recognize revenues in the period in which they are earned. Typically, the earnings process is considered complete at the time goods are transferred to customers or services are provided to customers. Exhibit 3 illustrates the relationship between revenue recognition and cash inflow.

LEARNING NOTE

Account titles vary in practice. For example, Unearned Revenue might appear as Customer Deposits, Air Traffic Liability, Prepaid Subscriptions, or Deferred Revenues.

Exhibit 3
Revenue Recognition and Cash Flows

Timing Effect	First Period	Second Period	Linking Account
No Accrual or Deferral Needed	Revenue Earned Cash Received		None
Accrued Revenue	Revenue Earned	Cash Received	Accounts Receivable
Deferred Revenue	Cash Received	Revenue Earned	Unearned Revenue

Three possibilities exist concerning the relationship. In all three possibilities, revenue is recognized when it is earned. Cash may be received at the time revenue is earned. In this situation, Revenue and Cash are the only accounts necessary for the transaction. If revenue is earned before cash is received, the revenue is accrued. ***Accrued revenue* is revenue recognized prior to the receipt of cash.** In this situation, Accounts Receivable is used to connect Revenue and Cash. If cash is received before revenue is earned, the revenue is deferred. ***Deferred revenue* is revenue recognized after cash has been received.** Unearned Revenue is used to connect Cash and Revenue.

EXPENSE TRANSACTIONS

OBJECTIVE 3

Record expense transactions using accrual accounting.

In addition to recognizing expenses at the time cash is paid, expenses may also be accrued or deferred. ***Accrued expenses* result when expenses are recognized prior to the payment of cash. *Deferred expenses* result when expenses are recognized after the payment of cash.**

For example, assume Mom's Cookie Company purchases $400 of supplies on February 16, 2004. The supplies are not consumed at the time they are purchased. Instead of paying cash for the supplies, the company purchases them on credit, agreeing to pay the supplier by March 16. On March 15, 2004, Mom's Cookie Company sends a check to the supplier. Mom's Cookie Company should record this purchase of supplies as follows:

		ASSETS		=	LIABILITIES	+	OWNERS' EQUITY	
Date	**Accounts**	**Cash**	**Other Assets**				**Contributed Capital**	**Retained Earnings**
Feb. 16	Supplies		400					
	Accounts Payable				400			

This transaction records the supplies as an asset and the amount owed the supplier as a liability. ***Accounts Payable* is a liability account that identifies an obligation to pay suppliers in the near future.**

When Mom's Cookie Company uses the supplies, it records an expense. Suppose that the supplies have been consumed by the end of February. The company would record this amount as:

		ASSETS		=	LIABILITIES	+	OWNERS' EQUITY	
Date	**Accounts**	**Cash**	**Other Assets**				**Contributed Capital**	**Retained Earnings**
Feb. 28	Supplies Expense							−400
	Supplies		−400					

This transaction records the expense in the fiscal period in which resources were consumed.

Another transaction is necessary to record payment for the supplies. If Mom's Cookie Company sends a check to the supplier on March 15, it would record this:

		ASSETS		=	LIABILITIES	+	OWNERS' EQUITY	
Date	**Accounts**	**Cash**	**Other Assets**				**Contributed Capital**	**Retained Earnings**
Mar. 15	Accounts Payable				−400			
	Cash	−400						

LEARNING NOTE

In Chapter F2, we recorded the purchase of supplies as an expense at the time the supplies were acquired because the supplies were used in January. In theory, it is preferable to record the purchase as an asset and then expense the supplies when they are used. Practically, however, it does not matter whether the supplies are recorded as an asset initially if all of the supplies are consumed in the same fiscal period as they were acquired. Either way, the amount will be an expense by the end of the fiscal period.

An expense is not recorded at the time the payment is made because the supplies were consumed in February. Exhibit 4 illustrates the use of the Accounts Payable account to link expenses recognized in one period with cash paid in a subsequent period. The net result of these transactions is the same as if cash had been paid for supplies at the time they were consumed. The transaction was recorded initially to the supplies account. Since the supplies were consumed in February, the transaction could have been recorded initially to supplies expense.

Exhibit 4
Linking Expense and Cash through Accounts Payable

Date	Cash	Supplies	Accounts Payable	Supplies Expense
Feb. 16		400	400	
Feb. 28		−400		−400
Mar. 15	−400		−400	
Net result	−400	0	0	−400

Expenses also may be recognized after cash is paid. For example, assume Mom's Cookie Company pays $600 for rent for use of a building on February 26. However, the rent is for March. The payment would be recorded as follows:

		ASSETS		=	LIABILITIES	+	OWNERS' EQUITY	
Date	**Accounts**	**Cash**	**Other Assets**				**Contributed Capital**	**Retained Earnings**
Feb. 26	Prepaid Rent		600					
	Cash	−600						

LEARNING NOTE

Accounts Payable is an example of a general category of liabilities known as accrued liabilities. *Accrued liabilities* record the obligation to make payments for expenses that have been incurred or for assets that have been acquired but for which payment has not been made. Other examples of accrued liabilities include Wages Payable, Interest Payable, and Income Taxes Payable.

The February transaction records the payment for rent. Prepaid Rent is an example of a prepaid expense account. **A *Prepaid Expense* is an asset account that identifies a resource that has been paid for but not used.** The purchase is an asset because a resource has been acquired that will be used in the future. The March transaction records use of the resource. The expense should be recognized in March, when the resource is consumed, rather than in February when cash is paid. The expense has been deferred from the time of the payment to March, when the building is used. By the end of March the rental service has been consumed and the expense would be recorded as follows:

		ASSETS		=	LIABILITIES	+	OWNERS' EQUITY	
Date	**Accounts**	**Cash**	**Other Assets**				**Contributed Capital**	**Retained Earnings**
Mar. 31	Rent Expense							−600
	Prepaid Rent		−600					

Exhibit 5 illustrates the use of the prepaid rent account to link cash paid in one period with expense recognized in a subsequent period. Prepaid Rent increases when cash is paid for next month's rent and decreases when the rent is consumed.

Exhibit 5
Linking Expense and Cash through Prepaid Rent

Date	Cash	Prepaid Rent	Rent Expense
Feb. 26	−600	600	
Mar. 31		−600	−600
Net result	−600	0	−600

In summary, accrual accounting records expenses when resources are consumed, not necessarily when cash is paid for those resources. Exhibit 6 illustrates the relationship between expense recognition and cash outflow.

Exhibit 6
Expense Recognition and Cash Flows

Timing Effect	First Period	Second Period	Linking Account
No Accrual or Deferral Needed	Expense Incurred Cash Paid		None
Accrued Expense	Expense Incurred	Cash Paid	Accounts Payable
Deferred Expense	Cash Paid	Expense Incurred	Prepaid Expense

Three possibilities exist concerning the relationship. In all three possibilities, expense is recognized when it is incurred. Cash may be paid at the time expense is incurred. In this situation, Expense and Cash are the only accounts necessary for the transaction. If expense is incurred before cash is paid, the expense is accrued. That is, it is recognized prior to the payment of cash. In this situation, Accounts Payable is used to connect Expense and Cash. If cash is paid before expense is incurred, the expense is deferred. That is, it is recognized after the cash is paid. Prepaid Expense is used to connect Cash and Expense.

By recording revenues when earned and expenses when incurred, a company matches resources consumed by business activities with revenues created by those activities. Consequently, net income (revenues minus expenses) measures business activity for a fiscal period. It is not a measure of how much cash a company received or paid. **An important concept in accounting is the *matching principle*, which requires companies to recognize the expenses used to generate revenue in the same accounting period in which the revenues are recognized.**

An important responsibility of accountants is to make decisions about when revenues and expenses should be recognized. They examine a company's business activities and use appropriate accounting rules to ensure the proper recording of revenue and expense transactions in the fiscal period in which those transactions occur.

1 SELF-STUDY PROBLEM

WebTUTOR® Advantage

The following events occurred for Kirkland Co. in January and February:

1. Goods priced at $5,000 were sold on credit on January 15.
2. The cost of the goods sold in transaction 1 was $3,000.

3. Cash of $400 was received on January 23 for goods that will be transferred to customers in February.
4. Cash of $750 was paid on January 25 for supplies that will be used in February.
5. By January 31, employees had earned wages of $2,500 that will be paid in February.
6. On February 3, cash of $2,500 was paid to employees for wages earned in January.
7. On February 6, cash was collected from customers for the sales on January 15.
8. On February 8, goods were transferred to customers that had been paid for on January 23.
9. By February 28, the supplies purchased on January 25 had been consumed.

Required Record all transactions associated with these events in the order in which they occurred.

The solution to Self-Study Problem 1 appears at the end of the chapter.

Adjusting Account Balances

OBJECTIVE 4

Identify and record adjusting entries at the end of a fiscal period.

Some revenues and many expenses are associated with the passage of time. Rent, insurance, and equipment are resources that are purchased in one period and used during future periods. Wages relate to specific periods in which employees work, whether or not they are paid during those periods. Interest on debt accumulates over time. Revenues associated with some services, such as repair and maintenance contracts, also may be earned over time.

These activities often result in an expense or revenue that must be recognized for a fiscal period even though no specific event occurs to create the expense or revenue other than the passage of time. In these situations, a company must adjust its accounts at the end of a fiscal period to record the expenses and revenues that should be recognized for that period.

Let's consider some examples of adjustments for Mom's Cookie Company. Suppose in mid-February, Mom's Cookie Company decided to move to a new building on March 1. The rent for the new offices is $600 a month. On February 24 rent is paid for March and April. The transaction for February would be:

		ASSETS		=	LIABILITIES	+	OWNERS' EQUITY	
Date	Accounts	Cash	Other Assets				Contributed Capital	Retained Earnings
Feb. 24	Prepaid Rent		1,200					
	Cash	−1,200						

The transaction involves payment of rent for two months. The Prepaid Rent account is an asset that identifies the resource available for future use. At the end of March and April, Mom's Cookie Company must record Rent Expense for each month:

		ASSETS		=	LIABILITIES	+	OWNERS' EQUITY	
Date	Accounts	Cash	Other Assets				Contributed Capital	Retained Earnings
Mar. 31	Rent Expense							−600
	Prepaid Rent		−600					
Apr. 30	Rent Expense							−600
	Prepaid Rent		−600					

The accounting entries for March and April are adjusting entries. **An *adjusting entry* is a transaction recorded in the accounting system to ensure the correct account balances are reported for a particular fiscal period.** Usually, adjusting entries are made at the end of the fiscal period.

Another example of adjusting entries for Mom's Cookie Company involves interest. As indicated in Chapter F2, the company borrowed $30,000 ($8,000 + $22,000) in January. The bank charges $200 of interest each month but permits the interest to be paid the day after the end of each quarter. Accordingly, Mom's Cookie Company's first interest payment is not due until April 1, 2004. Nevertheless, interest expense accrues each month and should be recognized in the fiscal period in which it is incurred. Mom's Cookie Company would record the following adjusting entries at the end of January, February, and March:

		ASSETS		=	LIABILITIES	+	OWNERS' EQUITY	
Date	Accounts	Cash	Other Assets				Contributed Capital	Retained Earnings
Jan. 31	Interest Expense							−200
	Interest Payable				200			
Feb. 28	Interest Expense							−200
	Interest Payable				200			
Mar. 31	Interest Expense							−200
	Interest Payable				200			

An expense is recorded each month for the interest incurred on the loan. A liability is recorded as well because the interest is not being paid until the end of March. Consequently, an obligation exists for the unpaid interest. **Every adjusting entry, like the three above, includes at least one balance sheet and at least one income statement account.** Adjusting entries always involve recognition of a revenue or expense during a fiscal period.

Another transaction at the beginning of April records payment of the liability that accumulated over the three months. This entry is not an adjusting entry; it is a payment of an obligation when it becomes due. The payment is recorded as follows:

		ASSETS		=	LIABILITIES	+	OWNERS' EQUITY	
Date	Accounts	Cash	Other Assets				Contributed Capital	Retained Earnings
Apr. 1	Interest Payable				−600			
	Cash	−600						

Another example of adjustments involves the use of equipment. Mom's Cookie Company purchased equipment in January for $31,000 ($6,000 + $25,000). The equipment was recorded as an asset at that time. However, equipment and other physical assets usually wear out over time and eventually need to be replaced. Because resources are consumed over a number of fiscal periods, the usage should be recognized as an expense of each of the periods that benefits from that use. ***Depreciation* is the allocation of the cost of assets to the fiscal periods that benefit from the assets' use.** Mom's Cookie Company expenses its equipment at the rate of $520 per month. Consequently, it would record the following adjustments at the end of January and February:

		ASSETS		=	LIABILITIES	+	OWNERS' EQUITY	
Date	Accounts	Cash	Other Assets				Contributed Capital	Retained Earnings
Jan. 31	Depreciation Expense Accumulated Depreciation		-520					-520
Feb. 28	Depreciation Expense Accumulated Depreciation		-520					-520

Depreciation Expense identifies the estimated amount of the asset consumed. ***Accumulated Depreciation* is a contra-asset account used to identify the total amount of depreciation recorded for a company's assets.** It is subtracted from the related asset accounts on the company's balance sheet, and therefore is known as a contra account. **A *contra account* is an account that offsets another account.**

To understand Accumulated Depreciation, consider the effect the adjusting entries would have on the Accumulated Depreciation account. At the end of January, the account will have a balance of −$520, depreciation for January. At the end of February, the account will have a balance of −$1,040, depreciation for January and February.

Mom's Cookie Company's balance sheet for January and February will report the following:

	January	February
Equipment, at cost	$31,000	$31,000
Less: accumulated depreciation	520	1,040
Equipment, net of depreciation	$30,480	$29,960

The cost of the equipment continues to be reported at its cost of $31,000. The amount of accumulated depreciation increases each month, and the net amount of equipment reported each month decreases at the rate of $520 per month. We examine how depreciation amounts are determined in a later chapter.

The process of recording and reporting depreciation is necessary to make sure a company reports the appropriate expense each fiscal period. The use of Accumulated Depreciation provides useful information to decision makers. Examination of the balance sheet data for Mom's Cookie Company provides Maria and Stan with information about the cost of equipment and about how long the equipment has been used. Creditors and other external users of the company's financial statements might be especially interested in this information. They may want to know if a company's assets are replaced on a regular basis and if plans are being made for replacement as assets age.

Companies record transactions throughout each fiscal period. Accountants determine necessary adjustments for a company and develop and maintain information systems that allow them to determine interest, depreciation, and other expenses and revenues accurately. They adjust accounts at the end of each fiscal period prior to preparing financial statements. The next section considers the final steps in preparing these statements.

2 SELF-STUDY PROBLEM

The following events occurred for Davis Co. during 2004:

WebTUTOR® Advantage

1. On September 27, the company paid rent for the following three months of $1,500 per month.
2. The company incurs interest expense of $800 per month. Interest was paid on October 31 for a three-month period, ending with October.
3. The company purchased equipment for $200,000 on January 2, 2004. The equipment is depreciated at the rate of $4,000 per month.

4. The company paid $12,000 for property insurance on January 4, 2004. The insurance is for the 12 months ended December 31, 2004.

Required Record the adjusting entries associated with these events for October.

The solution to Self-Study Problem 2 appears at the end of the chapter.

LEDGER ACCOUNTS

Transactions, like those in this and the preceding chapter, are initially recorded by a company in a journal. **A *journal* is a chronological record of a company's transactions.** The format we have used in this chapter to record transactions is an example of a particular journal format. Each transaction is recorded according to the date the transaction occurred. The accounts affected by the transaction are listed along with the amounts associated with each account. Most companies use a computerized accounting system. Journal entries are recorded on a computer using a format that provides a place for each account to be identified and the amount to be entered. Regardless of the format, journal entries provide for a means of entering transactions in an accounting system.

Once transactions have been entered into a journal, the effects of transactions on particular accounts need to be transferred to those accounts. **A *ledger* is a file in which each of a company's accounts and the balances of those accounts are maintained.** A record is maintained for each account. Each time a transaction is recorded, the effects of that transaction are transferred to the ledger. ***Posting* is the process of transferring transactions to specific accounts in a company's ledger.** Exhibit 7 illustrates this process.

Exhibit 7 Posting Transactions to the Ledger

Journal

		ASSETS		=	LIABILITIES	+	OWNERS' EQUITY	
Date	**Accounts**	**Cash**	**Other Assets**				**Contributed Capital**	**Retained Earnings**
Jan. 31	Depreciation Expense							−520
	Accumulated Depreciation		−520					
Feb. 28	Depreciation Expense							−520
	Accumulated Depreciation		−520					

Ledger

Accumulated Depreciation

Date	Amount	Balance
Jan. 31	−520	−520
Feb. 28	−520	−1,040

Initially a transaction is recorded using the journal format. The transaction is then posted to the ledger accounts affected by the transaction. The balance of the account is updated to show the effect of the transaction. Thus, after transactions have been posted, the ledger provides a current record of the balance of each of a company's accounts. These balances are the primary source of data for preparing a company's financial statements.

The primary ledger a company uses to record its account balances is referred to as the *general ledger*. Companies often use other special ledgers to maintain information about specific types of account balances. For example, each customer who has purchased goods from a company on credit would be listed in the company's accounts receivable ledger. The accounts in the special ledger are referred to as subsidiary accounts. Subsidiary accounts are accounts of a specific type that are associated with a control account in the general ledger. The total of the balances of all of the subsidiary accounts of a specific type is equal to the balance of the general ledger control account. To illustrate, assume Mom's Cookie Company sells goods on credit to three stores: Hopkins' Grocery, Lori's Market, and Samson's Foods. Mom's Cookie Company maintains a subsidiary accounts receivable account for each store. The amounts owed by each of these stores at the end of February is the subsidiary account balance. The total of these amounts is the balance of accounts receivable for Mom's Cookie Company.

Subsidiary Accounts Receivable:	
Hopkins' Grocery	$1,300
Lori's Market	600
Samson's Foods	900
Accounts Receivable Control	$2,800

The subsidiary accounts are used to keep track of amounts owed by each customer. The control account balance is the amount reported in the company's financial statements.

Closing Entries and Financial Statements

OBJECTIVE 5

Prepare closing entries and financial statements at the end of a fiscal period.

At the end of each month, Maria and Stan, with the help of their accountant, prepare financial statements for Mom's Cookie Company. The financial statements report a company's business activities to help managers, creditors, and other stakeholders make decisions.

Summary of Account Balances

To illustrate this process, we begin with a review of all the transactions for Mom's Cookie Company for January. These are presented in Exhibit 8 and include the adjusting entries for interest expense and depreciation expense described in this chapter.

Next we examine a summary of general ledger account balances for Mom's Cookie Company at the end of January. Exhibit 9, on page F96, provides balances for each of the company's general ledger accounts at January 31. The amounts shown are those from Exhibit 12 in Chapter F2, adjusted for interest and depreciation, as described in this chapter.

A purpose of the summary is to make sure that the accounting equation is in balance prior to preparing the financial statements. We can determine that the equation is in balance by reference to Exhibit 9 because:

Assets = Liabilities + Owners' Equity
$41,180 = $30,200 + $10,980

Income Statement

Balances of revenue and expense accounts appear in Mom's Cookie Company's Income Statement for January. Exhibit 10, on page F96, provides this statement. As discussed in Chapter F2, the income statement reports results of operating activities for a particular fiscal period. The statement shows that Mom's Cookie Company earned $980 of profit in January. This amount is less than that reported in Chapter F2 because of the adjusting entries that were considered in this chapter.

Exhibit 8 Transactions for Mom's Cookie Company for January

		ASSETS		=	LIABILITIES	+	OWNERS' EQUITY	
Date	**Accounts**	**Cash**	**Other Assets**				**Contributed Capital**	**Retained Earnings**
	Beginning Amounts	0	+0	=	0	+	0	+0
Jan. 2	Cash Contributed Capital	10,000					10,000	
Jan. 3	Cash Notes Payable	8,000			8,000			
Jan. 5	Equipment Cash	−6,000	6,000					
Jan. 6	Equipment Cash Notes Payable	−3,000	25,000		22,000			
Jan. 6	Supplies Expense Cash	−300						−300
Jan. 7	Merchandise Inventory Cash	−9,000	9,000					
Jan. 8	Rent Expense Cash	−600						−600
Jan. 31	Cash Sales Revenue	11,400						11,400
Jan. 31	Cost of Goods Sold Merchandise Inventory		−7,600					−7,600
Jan. 31	Wages Expense Cash	−1,000						−1,000
Jan. 31	Utilities Expense Cash	−200						−200
Jan. 31	Interest Expense Interest Payable				200			−200
Jan. 31	Depreciation Expense Accumulated Depreciation		−520					−520
	Ending Amounts	9,300	+31,880	=	30,200	+	10,000	+980

Closing Entries

An intermediate step in preparing financial statements is closing the revenue and expense account balances. Before preparing a balance sheet, the company's accountant closes Mom's Cookie Company's revenue and expense account balances at the end of February. Closing these accounts transfers the balances in these accounts to Retained Earnings. Exhibit 11, on page F97, provides the closing entries for January.

The closing process includes two transactions. In the first, revenue accounts are transferred to Retained Earnings. The closing transaction leaves the revenue account with a zero balance by subtracting the amount of revenue earned during the month from the Sales Revenue account and transferring the balance to Retained Earnings.

In the second transaction in Exhibit 11, expense account balances are transferred to Retained Earnings. The balances of these accounts also are zero after they are transferred to Retained Earnings.

If revenues are greater than expenses for the period, Retained Earnings increases. If revenues are less than expenses, Retained Earnings decreases. Remember that Retained Earnings is an accumulation of a company's profits. If profits are earned during

Exhibit 9
Summary of Account Balances for Mom's Cookie Company at January 31

Mom's Cookie Company
Account Balances
January 31, 2004

Account	Balance
Assets:	
Cash	9,300
Merchandise Inventory	1,400
Equipment	31,000
Accumulated Depreciation	(520)
Total Assets	**41,180**
Liabilities:	
Interest Payable	200
Notes Payable	30,000
Total Liabilities	**30,200**
Owners' Equity:	
Contributed Capital	10,000
Sales Revenue	11,400
Cost of Goods Sold	(7,600)
Wages Expense	(1,000)
Rent Expense	(600)
Depreciation Expense	(520)
Supplies Expense	(300)
Utilities Expense	(200)
Interest Expense	(200)
Total Owners' Equity	**10,980**

Exhibit 10
Income Statement for Mom's Cookie Company

Mom's Cookie Company
Income Statement
For the Month Ended
January 31, 2004

Sales revenue	$11,400
Cost of goods sold	(7,600)
Wages expense	(1,000)
Rent expense	(600)
Depreciation expense	(520)
Supplies expense	(300)
Utilities expense	(200)
Interest expense	(200)
Net income	$ 980

a fiscal period, Retained Earnings increases. If losses are incurred during a fiscal period because revenues are less than expenses, Retained Earnings decreases.

Exhibit 12 illustrates the effect of closing entries on ledger account balances. Each account contains the balance of that account prior to the closing entry. ***Closing entries* reset the balances of each revenue and expense account to zero and transfer these balances to Retained Earnings.**

The closing entries zero out the revenue and expense account balances at the end of a fiscal period. Consequently, the next fiscal period begins with zero balances and accumulates revenues and expenses for the new fiscal period. The closing process also transfers the amount of net income for a fiscal period to Retained Earnings. Keep in mind that revenues and expenses are subcategories of owners' equity. The closing process transfers amounts from the income statement accounts to owners' equity on

Exhibit 11 Closing Entries for January for Mom's Cookie Company

		ASSETS		=	LIABILITIES	+	OWNERS' EQUITY	
Date	Accounts	Cash	Other Assets				Contributed Capital	Retained Earnings
Jan. 31	Retained Earnings							11,400
	Sales Revenue							−11,400
Jan. 31	Retained Earnings							−10,420
	Cost of Goods Sold							7,600
	Wages Expense							1,000
	Rent Expense							600
	Depreciation Expense							520
	Supplies Expense							300
	Utilities Expense							200
	Interest Expense							200

Exhibit 12
Effect of Closing Entries on Revenue and Expense Account Balances

Ledger

Retained Earnings

Date	Amount	Balance
		0
Jan. 31	11,400	11,400
Jan. 31	−10,420	980

Sales Revenue

Date	Amount	Balance
		11,400
Jan. 31	−11,400	0

Cost of Goods Sold

Date	Amount	Balance
		−7,600
Jan. 31	7,600	0

Wages Expense

Date	Amount	Balance
		−1,000
Jan. 31	1,000	0

Rent Expense

Date	Amount	Balance
		−600
Jan. 31	600	0

Depreciation Expense

Date	Amount	Balance
		−520
Jan. 31	520	0

Supplies Expense

Date	Amount	Balance
		−300
Jan. 31	300	0

Utilities Expense

Date	Amount	Balance
		−200
Jan. 31	200	0

Interest Expense

Date	Amount	Balance
		−200
Jan. 31	200	0

the balance sheet so that the accounting equation (Assets = Liabilities + Owners' Equity) balances at the end of a fiscal period.

Because revenue and expense accounts are zeroed-out at the end of a fiscal period, they are referred to as temporary accounts. They are used during a fiscal period to collect the results of operating activities. These results are transferred to Retained Earnings at the end of the period. Retained Earnings and other balance sheet accounts are referred to as permanent accounts because their balances continue to accumulate from period to period.

Payments to Owners

Another transaction that affects the balance of Retained Earnings is a payment by a company to its owners. For example, if Maria and Stan decide to withdraw $500 from Mom's Cookie Company at the end of January, the transaction would be recorded like this:

		ASSETS		=	LIABILITIES	+	OWNERS' EQUITY	
Date	Accounts	Cash	Other Assets				Contributed Capital	Retained Earnings
Jan. 31	Retained Earnings							−500
	Cash	−500						

The retained earnings account accumulates profits earned by a company for its owners. The owners may choose to leave the profits in the company or withdraw some of them for personal use. Amounts withdrawn reduce Retained Earnings. The balance of Retained Earnings and Cash for Mom's Cookie Company after the withdrawal would be as follows:

Ledger

Retained Earnings

Date	Amount	Balance
		980
Jan. 31	−500	480

Cash

Date	Amount	Balance
		9,300
Jan. 31	−500	8,800

Post-Closing Account Balances

Let's look at the effects of the closing and withdrawal entries by preparing a summary of account balances after these entries have been posted to ledger accounts. Exhibit 13 provides a post-closing summary for Mom's Cookie Company at the end of February. At this point, the revenue and expense accounts have zero balances.

Balance Sheet

The balance sheet can now be prepared from the post-closing account balances. Exhibit 14 provides the balance sheet for Mom's Cookie Company at January 31, 2004. Observe that the amounts in the balance sheet for January 31 are those in the post-closing summary from Exhibit 13.

Along with the income statement, the balance sheet helps users determine how well the company performed during January. From the income statement, users can

Exhibit 13
Post-Closing Summary of Account Balances for Mom's Cookie Company

Mom's Cookie Company
Post-Closing Summary of Account Balances
February 28, 2004

Account	Balance
Assets:	
Cash	8,800
Merchandise Inventory	1,400
Equipment	31,000
Accumulated Depreciation	(520)
Total Assets	**40,680**
Liabilities:	
Interest Payable	200
Notes Payable	30,000
Total Liabilities	**30,200**
Owners' Equity:	
Contributed Capital	10,000
Retained Earnings	480
Sales Revenue	0
Cost of Goods Sold	0
Wages Expense	0
Supplies Expense	0
Rent Expense	0
Depreciation Expense	0
Interest Expense	0
Total Owners' Equity	**10,480**

Exhibit 14
January 31 Balance Sheet for Mom's Cookie Company

Mom's Cookie Company
Balance Sheet
At January 31, 2004

Assets	
Cash	$ 8,800
Merchandise inventory	1,400
Equipment	31,000
Accumulated depreciation	(520)
Total assets	$40,680
Liabilities and Owners' Equity	
Interest payable	$ 200
Notes payable	30,000
Total liabilities	30,200
Contribution by owners	10,000
Retained earnings	480
Total liabilities and owners' equity	$40,680

determine the major sources of revenue and expense. From the balance sheet, they can determine the assets controlled by the company and claims to those resources by creditors and owners. When statements for additional months become available, decision makers can compare the statements to determine whether the company is performing better or worse over time. Users can determine how much change there is in assets, liabilities, and owners' equity from one month to the next.

Statement of Cash Flows

A third financial statement, the statement of cash flows, also should be prepared. The adjusting transactions described in this chapter are associated with revenue and expense recognition, not with cash flows. Therefore, the statement of cash flows at the end of January is almost identical to the one in Chapter F2. Exhibit 15 includes the effect of the payment of $500 cash to owners. This payment is a financing activity.

Exhibit 15
A Statement of Cash Flows

Mom's Cookie Company
Statement of Cash Flows
For the Month Ended January 31, 2004

Operating Activities		
Received from customers	$11,400	
Paid for merchandise	(9,000)	
Paid for wages	(1,000)	
Paid for rent	(600)	
Paid for supplies	(300)	
Paid for utilities	(200)	
Net cash flow from operating activities		$ 300
Investing Activities		
Paid for equipment		(31,000)
Financing Activities		
Received from creditors	30,000	
Received from owners	10,000	
Paid to owners	(500)	
Net cash flow from financing activities		39,500
Net cash flow for January		8,800
Cash balance, January 1		0
Cash balance, January 31		$ 8,800

SUMMARY OF ACCOUNTING CYCLE

OBJECTIVE 6

Identify steps in the accounting cycle.

The procedures we have examined in this chapter are often referred to as the accounting cycle. **The *accounting cycle* is the process of recording, summarizing, and reporting accounting information.** As we have discussed in this chapter, the cycle consists of eight steps, as illustrated in Exhibit 16.

Once the accounting cycle is completed for one fiscal period, the accounting records are ready to begin recording transactions for the next fiscal period. As noted in Chapter F2, a fiscal period can be any time period for which managers want accounting information. Most companies prepare financial statements monthly and combine these to prepare statements for quarterly and annual periods.

ACCOUNTING AND ETHICS

The accounting system described in this chapter provides a way for Maria and Stan to monitor their business activities and to make decisions about their company's performance. Also, it provides a means for them to communicate with creditors about the performance of their company. An accounting system with adequate controls to ensure reliable information is expected by stakeholders of most companies and is a legal requirement for companies that sell shares of stock to the public and for many other companies that are regulated by state and local authorities.

These requirements are intended to protect owners, creditors, and other stakeholders from receiving inaccurate or improperly prepared financial information. A good accounting system helps ensure that all transactions are recorded properly and that stakeholders

Exhibit 16 Steps in the Accounting Cycle

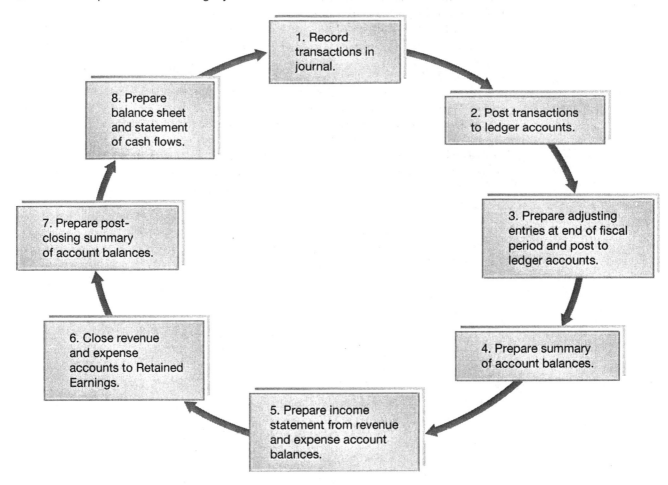

receive information that describes a business's activities on a timely basis. Most businesses are expected to comply with generally accepted accounting principles (GAAP) in preparing financial accounting information. GAAP require the use of the accrual rules and procedures described in this chapter. Making sure that a company's accounting procedures conform with GAAP and creating an accounting system that records and reports all transactions in the appropriate fiscal periods is a major responsibility of a company's management. Failure to understand and implement appropriate accounting procedures is, itself, unethical. Management is responsible for proper use of a company's resources and for proper reporting of its business activities. Managers who fail to take these responsibilities seriously leave a company vulnerable to improper behavior, such as fraud and theft, that reduces the value of the company for its owners and other stakeholders.

Case in Point

http://ingram.swlearning.com

Learn more about Enron.

Economic Effects of Poor Accounting Practices

The failure of **Enron Corporation's** management to properly account for and report its business activities resulted in an understatement of the company's liabilities and an overstatement of profits. When the company's bad accounting practices became apparent in October 2001, creditors were unwilling to lend additional money to the company and investors tried to dump their stock. The value of Enron's stock dropped rapidly, resulting in losses of millions of dollars for owners. Many of Enron's owners were employees of the company who had invested in the company's stock as part of their retirement plans. Many employees lost their jobs and their retirement savings as a result of these events.

Unethical behavior may occur in businesses because appropriate accounting controls are not in place or are not enforced. For example, an employee sells goods to a customer but does not record the sale and pockets the cash. This behavior leads to incorrect accounting information. Sales Revenue, Cost of Goods Sold, Merchandise Inventory, and Cash are all misstated in this example. In general, unethical behavior by employees and managers leads to misstated accounting information. Protecting a company's accounting records and assets is an important management task. Procedures should be in place to make it difficult for employees at all levels of the organization to engage in unethical behavior. For example, cash registers and scanning devices help ensure that sales made by employees are recorded. Supervisors should compare sales records with cash receipts to make sure cash has not been stolen. **Good accounting is the first line of defense against unethical behavior in business.**

3 SELF-STUDY PROBLEM

Howard Co. provided the following summary of account balances at the end of December 2004.

WebTUTOR™ Advantage

Howard Co.
Summary of Account Balances
December 31, 2004

Account	Balance
Cash	37,450
Accounts Receivable	2,300
Merchandise Inventory	140,000
Supplies	30,000
Equipment	75,000
Accounts Payable	2,000
Notes Payable	200,000
Investment by Owners	65,000
Retained Earnings	15,000
Sales Revenue	20,000
Cost of Goods Sold	(13,000)
Wages Expense	(2,000)
Depreciation Expense	(750)
Interest Expense	(1,500)

Required Prepare closing entries and a post-closing summary of account balances for Howard Co.

The solution to Self-Study Problem 3 appears at the end of the chapter.

REVIEW

SUMMARY of IMPORTANT CONCEPTS

1. Accrual accounting requires companies to recognize revenues in the fiscal period in which they are earned and to recognize expenses in the period incurred.
2. Accrual accounting requires the use of accounts such as Accounts Receivable and Unearned Revenue to link Cash received in one period with revenues earned in another period.
3. Accrual accounting requires the use of accounts such as Accounts Payable and Prepaid Expenses to link Cash paid in one period with expenses incurred in another period.

4. Adjusting entries record revenues and expenses that occur because of the passage of time to ensure that these revenues and expenses are recognized in the appropriate fiscal period.

5. At the end of a fiscal period, a company closes its revenues and expense accounts to transfer these account balances to retained earnings. The balance sheet reports retained earnings after the accounts have been closed.

6. The accounting cycle is the process of recording transactions, preparing summaries of account balances, closing accounts, and preparing financial statements.

DEFINE

TERMS and CONCEPTS DEFINED in this CHAPTER

accounting cycle (F100)
accounts payable (F87)
accounts receivable (F84)
accrual accounting (F83)
accrued expense (F87)
accrued liabilities (F88)
accrued revenue (F87)
accumulated depreciation (F92)
adjusting entry (F91)
closing entries (F96)
contra account (F92)
deferred expense (F87)
deferred revenue (F87)
depreciation (F91)
general ledger (F94)
journal (F93)
ledger (F93)
matching principle (F89)
posting (F93)
prepaid expense (F88)
unearned revenue (F85)

SELF-STUDY PROBLEM SOLUTIONS

SSP3-1

		ASSETS		=	LIABILITIES	+	OWNERS' EQUITY	
Date	**Accounts**	**Cash**	**Other Assets**				**Contributed Capital**	**Retained Earnings**
Jan. 15	Accounts Receivable		5,000					
	Sales Revenue							5,000
Jan. 15	Cost of Goods Sold							−3,000
	Merchandise Inventory		−3,000					
Jan. 23	Cash	400						
	Unearned Revenue				400			
Jan. 25	Supplies		750					
	Cash	−750						
Jan. 31	Wages Expense							−2,500
	Wages Payable				2,500			
Feb. 3	Wages Payable				−2,500			
	Cash	−2,500						
Feb. 6	Cash	5,000						
	Accounts Receivable		−5,000					
Feb. 8	Unearned Revenue				−400			
	Sales Revenue							400
Feb. 28	Supplies Expense							−750
	Supplies		−750					

SSP3-2

		ASSETS		=	LIABILITIES	+	OWNERS' EQUITY	
Date	**Accounts**	**Cash**	**Other Assets**				**Contributed Capital**	**Retained Earnings**
Oct. 31	Rent Expense							−1,500
	Prepaid Rent		−1,500					
Oct. 31	Interest Expense							−800
	Interest Payable				800			
Oct. 31	Depreciation Expense							−4,000
	Accumulated Depreciation		−4,000					
Oct. 31	Insurance Expense							−1,000
	Prepaid Insurance		−1,000					

Note: A transaction to record the payment of interest in October for the period August, September, and October also would be recorded. This transaction is not an adjusting entry, however.

SSP3-3

		ASSETS		=	LIABILITIES	+	OWNERS' EQUITY	
Date	**Accounts**	**Cash**	**Other Assets**				**Contributed Capital**	**Retained Earnings**
Dec. 31	Retained Earnings							20,000
	Sales Revenue							−20,000
Dec. 31	Retained Earnings							−17,250
	Cost of Goods Sold							13,000
	Wages Expense							2,000
	Depreciation Expense							750
	Interest Expense							1,500

Howard Co.
Post-Closing Summary of Account Balances
December 31, 2004

Account	**Balance**
Assets:	
Cash	37,450
Accounts Receivable	2,300
Merchandise Inventory	140,000
Supplies	30,000
Equipment	75,000
Total Assets	**284,750**
Liabilities:	
Accounts Payable	2,000
Notes Payable	200,000
Total Liabilities	**202,000**
Owners' Equity:	
Investment by Owners	65,000
Retained Earnings	17,750
Sales Revenue	0
Cost of Goods Sold	0
Wages Expense	0
Depreciation Expense	0
Interest Expense	0
Total Owners' Equity	**82,750**

Thinking Beyond the Question

How do we know how much profit our business has earned?

At the beginning of the chapter we asked how you can know how much profit a company has earned. This chapter described the rules and procedures of accrual accounting. The rules specify when revenues and expenses should be recognized. The procedures help ensure that all revenues and expenses of a fiscal period have been recorded and reported. Understanding accrued and deferred revenues and expenses and adjusting and closing entries help ensure that the proper amount of profit is reported each fiscal period and that other accounting information is correct.

These rules may seem relatively simple. For example, it may be easy to identify when goods are transferred to customers. However, that may not always be the case. Suppose you agree to provide services to a customer over several fiscal periods. You negotiate a price with the customer that covers all of the services to be provided. How much revenue would you recognize each fiscal period while you are providing the services?

QUESTIONS

Q3-1 *Obj. 1* Why isn't cash basis accounting the preferred method of reporting on the economic consequences of an organization's activities?

Q3-2 *Obj. 1* A friend observes that "in the long run, accrual and cash flow measurements equal out to the same amount. It's only in the short run that they differ." Do you agree or disagree? Explain.

Q3-3 *Obj. 1* How is it possible that a company could be very profitable yet be forced to go out of business because it cannot pay its bills?

Q3-4 *Obj. 2* How does Accounts Receivable "link" Revenue and Cash?

Q3-5 *Obj. 2* Where does the account Unearned Revenue appear in the financial statements? How does Unearned Revenue link Cash with Sales Revenue?

Q3-6 *Obj. 2* Accrued revenue and deferred revenue are both accrual concepts. Explain the order in which cash is received and revenue is recognized for each concept.

Q3-7 *Obj. 3* On May 31, a company paid $900 rent for June to its landlord. Would you recommend that this expenditure be presented in the end-of-May financial statements as an asset (Prepaid Rent) or as an expense (Rent Expense)? Why?

Q3-8 *Obj. 3* Quick Computer Company just spent $35,000 of its cash to purchase merchandise for later resale to customers. Would you agree that since $35,000 of cash has been used up, a $35,000 expense has been incurred in this transaction? Why or why not?

Q3-9 *Obj. 4* What is the difference between a subsidiary account and a control account?

Q3-10 *Obj. 4* Why are control account balances reported in external financial statements while subsidiary account balances are not? Are subsidiary account balances useful to anyone? Who?

Q3-11 *Obj. 4* The textbook lists depreciation as an example of a period cost that often must be updated in the accounting records at the end of a fiscal period. What other examples of period costs that must be updated at period-end can you identify? Why is it necessary to update these items?

Q3-12 *Obj. 5* A friend observes that "one of the most useful pieces of information found on a balance sheet is the current market value of assets such as buildings and land." Do you agree or disagree? Why?

Q3-13 *Obj. 5* Explain why accountants prepare a summary of general ledger account balances prior to preparing the financial statements.

Q3-14 *Obj. 5* Why do accountants close revenue and expense accounts prior to preparing the financial statements?

Q3-15 *Obj. 5* Is a payment to owners considered an expense? Explain.

Q3-16 *Obj. 6* Why are good accounting practices the first line of defense against unethical behavior in business?

Q3-17 *Obj. 6* Why is an accounting system with adequate controls a legal requirement for companies that sell shares of stock to the public?

Q3-18 *Obj. 6* Accountants prepare a post-closing summary of account balances as one step of the accounting cycle. Which types of accounts have non-zero balances? Which types of accounts have zero balances?

EXERCISES

If your instructor is using Personal Trainer in this course, you may complete online the assignments identified by P/T.

E3-1 Write a short definition for each of the terms listed in the *Terms and Concepts Defined in this Chapter* section.

E3-2 *Obj. 1* P/T Jon Harland is a wheat farmer. He owns farm equipment and buildings that cost $600,000 when purchased several years ago. He owes a local bank $425,000 for loans used to purchase these assets. In 2004, Jon sold $650,000 of wheat he raised during the year. He incurred operating costs of $585,000 to produce the wheat. This amount included $33,750 of interest on the bank loans and $52,500 of depreciation on the plant assets. In addition, Jon repaid $40,000 of the outstanding loan balance. The sales and all operating costs, except depreciation, were for cash. How much net income did Jon earn in 2004? What was his net cash flow for the year? Explain the difference.

E3-3 *Obj. 1* P/T Jeni Arrington drives for a large moving company. The company contacts Jeni when it has a job for her and furnishes a truck for her use. Jeni picks up the truck, drives to the customer's home, and loads, transports, and delivers the customer's belongings. She returns the truck to the company and receives her pay. Jeni is paid $4.50 per mile for the job. She is responsible for paying for her own gas, food, and lodging. Also, she must hire any helpers she needs to load and unload the truck. Jeni traveled 2,400 miles on a recent job that was completed on June 30. She paid $500 for gas, $116 for food, $204 for lodging, and $100 for helpers. Jeni expects to receive payment on July 5. How much did Jeni earn for the job? How much cash did Jeni spend while providing the service? Why is there a difference in cash flow and net income?

E3-4 *Obj. 2* P/T The Hardware Shoppe sold $222,500 of goods during September. It collected $75,000 from these sales plus $165,000 from sales of prior months. Complete the following table:

	Cash Flow for September	Cash Flow in Future	Sales Revenue for September
Cash from prior sales			
Cash from September sales			?
Total cash received in September	?		

E3-5 *Objs. 2, 3*

Holes 'R' Us, a blasting services company, has the following information available on December 31, the last day of the company's fiscal year. Each item involves an adjusting entry that must be made before financial statements can be prepared and the books closed for the year. Show how these adjusting entries would be entered into the accounting system.

1. A $35,000 note payable, incurring 9% interest, has been outstanding for the entire year. The note payable was properly recorded when it arose, but no entries regarding this event have been made since.
2. A $12,000 check was received on November 2 from a tenant that subleases part of the company's headquarters building. The amount was in payment of rent for November, December, and January. When the check was received, Cash was increased and Rent Revenue was increased. (Hint: Use a liability account titled Unearned Rent.)
3. On April 1 of the current year, the company purchased a two-year fire insurance policy for $7,200. When the policy was purchased, Cash was decreased and Prepaid Insurance was increased for the entire amount.
4. Wear and tear on the buildings and machinery for the year is estimated to be $42,000.

E3-6 *Objs. 2, 3*

Record each transaction of Rose's Flower Shop.

a. Purchased merchandise for sale on October 1 for $3,600, to be paid by October 30.
b. Sold merchandise for $900 cash on October 3. The merchandise cost Rose's $270.
c. Sold merchandise for $1,800 on credit on October 6. The merchandise cost Rose's $590.
d. Ordered $2,150 of merchandise on October 7 from a supplier.
e. $400 of the merchandise purchased on October 1 spoiled on October 9 and had to be trashed, resulting in spoilage expense.
f. Paid $1,800 on October 10 to suppliers for merchandise purchased on October 1.
g. Received $1,200 on October 16 from customers for sales on October 6.

E3-7 *Obj. 4*

Complete the following table. Each column represents a different company. All receivables are collected in the year following sale.

	Company A	Company B	Company C
Cash received from customers during 2004	$300,000	$625,000	
Sales revenue for 2004	$352,500	$580,000	$260,000
Accounts receivable at beginning of 2004	$31,000		$35,000
Accounts receivable at end of 2004		$85,000	$53,000

E3-8 *Objs. 2, 3*

The following information is available at December 31, the end of the fiscal year. It requires that adjusting entries be identified and entered into the accounting system. Unless specifically noted, none of this information has been previously entered into the accounting system. If the information below were ignored, net income for the year would be $72,400.

1. Employees are owed $9,500 for wages they have earned but will not receive until the next regular payroll distribution in five days.
2. A physical count reveals that there is $5,000 of office supplies remaining on hand at the end of the period. The company started the year with $3,500 of office supplies recorded in the Office Supplies Inventory account. During the year, $14,000 of office supplies was purchased, paid for, and charged to Office Supplies Expense.
3. The basement of the building is rented out to another firm and used for storage. At year end, the $2,000 rent for the month of December had not yet been collected.
4. At the end of the year, the company has long-term assets on which $13,600 of depreciation must be recorded.
5. Earlier in the year, a bank loan was obtained and recorded in the accounting system. Since then, interest of $5,200 has been incurred on that loan but it has not yet been recorded or paid.

(Continued)

(a) Using the spreadsheet format, show how this information would be entered into the accounting system. (b) After considering the effects of all five adjusting entries, what is the proper amount of net income that should be reported for the year?

E3-9 *Objs. 2, 3* Silberman Company transactions are listed below. Indicate the amount of revenue, expense, and cash flow that results from each. Use the format provided, and place the appropriate amount in each section of the table. Use a separate table for each transaction.

a. $5,000 of supplies were purchased in August for cash. $1,500 of the supplies were consumed in August, and $2,500 were consumed in September.
b. $15,000 of merchandise was sold in September. $6,000 of the sales were on credit.
c. Merchandise that cost Silberman $7,500 was sold in September. Silberman had paid $5,000 for the merchandise in August. The rest was paid for in September.
d. $50,000 was borrowed in August. $2,500 will be repaid each month for 20 months beginning in September. (Ignore interest.)
e. $25,000 of equipment was purchased and paid for in August. $500 of the equipment's revenue-generating ability was consumed in September; the remainder will be consumed in the future.

	Past	September	Future	Total
Revenues				
Expenses				
Cash received				
Cash paid				

E3-10 *Obj. 3* The Get Well Medical Clinic paid $50,000 in wages during June. Of this, $5,800 was for wages earned in May. An additional $4,200 of wages was owed to employees for services provided in June. These wages will be paid in July. Complete the following table:

	Cash Flow for June	Cash Flow in July	Wages Expense for June
Cash paid for prior wages	5800		
Cash paid for June wages	44,200	4200	48,400
Total cash paid in June for wages	50,000		

E3-11 *Obj. 3* George Carver borrowed $150,000 on January 1 to open a peanut processing plant. Interest on the loan is $3,750 each quarter. The first interest payment will be made on March 31. Complete the following table:

	January	February	March	Total for Quarter
Cash paid for interest	?	?	?	?
Interest expense	?	?	?	?

E3-12 *Obj. 3* Rapid Recovery Chemical Company manufactures prescription drugs. On January 1, 2003, the company purchased new equipment for $450,000 in cash. The company will depreciate the equipment over a 3-year period at $150,000 each year. Complete the following table:

	2003	2004	2005	Total for 3 Years
Cash paid for equipment	?	?	?	?
Depreciation expense	?	?	?	?

Explain the difference between cash flows each year and the amount of depreciation expense recorded.

E3-13 *Obj. 3* Tasaka Company manufactures oriental rugs. It pays utility bills at the end of the month in which services are received. The company received the following bills for April, May, and June, respectively: $850, $1,025, $1,150. Complete the following table:

	April	May	June	Total for 3 Months
Cash paid for utilities	?	?	?	?
Utilities expense	?	?	?	?

When are cash and accrual basis measures different? When are they the same?

E3-14 *Obj. 4* Each of the following independent situations relates to information available on the last day of the year. Each involves an adjustment that must be made to the accounting system before financial statements can be prepared. Show the effects of each adjusting entry on the accounting system.

a. A $15,000 note payable, incurring 8% interest, has been outstanding the entire year. The note payable was properly recorded when it arose.
b. A $3,000 check was received 2 months ago from a tenant that subleases part of a building. The amount was for 6 months' rent beginning the day the check was received. When received, the entire amount of the check was recorded in a liability account titled Unearned Rent.
c. Exactly halfway through the year just ended, the company purchased a 2-year fire insurance policy for $8,000. When the policy was purchased, the entire amount was recorded in the Prepaid Insurance account.
d. Wear and tear on the buildings and machinery for the year is estimated to be $35,000.

E3-15 *Obj. 4* On August 30, 2004, Goya Co. purchased $20,000 of canvas material from a supplier, Ramirez, Inc., on credit. The material is cut into smaller pieces for sale to customers. Prior to the purchase, Goya's merchandise inventory account had a balance of $135,000 and its accounts payable account had a balance of $17,000. Answer each of the following questions: (a) What subsidiary accounts are affected by the purchase and how are they affected? (b) What control accounts are affected and how are they affected? (c) If Goya Co. prepared a balance sheet immediately after recording the purchase, how would the balance sheet report the information associated with the purchase event?

E3-16 *Obj. 4* On December 31, 2004, the Washington Music Store reported net income of $1,500 and the following account balances.

(Continued)

Cash	$1,375
Accounts receivable	2,100
Prepaid insurance	900
Equipment & furnishings	3,225
Less: Accumulated depreciation	(500)
Accounts payable	1,100
Wages payable	1,080
Owners' equity	4,920

After this information was prepared, the bookkeeper discovered that he had forgotten to make two necessary adjusting entries for the year and, therefore, they were not reflected in the balances shown. Information concerning the two missing adjusting entries follows:

a. The prepaid insurance involves a 3-year fire insurance policy that was purchased (and went into effect) on January 1, 2004. By the end of the year, a portion of the insurance policy had been used up.
b. The wages payable does not include the wages that were owed at year-end to two workers who had been temporarily assigned to work off the premises. This amount totaled $450.

Using the following schedule, determine the correct year-end amount of (1) total assets, (2) total liabilities, (3) owners' equity, and (4) net income.

	Assets	Liabilities	Equity	Net Income
Year-end amounts before correction				
Adjusting entry (a):				
Adjusting entry (b):				
Year-end corrected amounts	$	$	$	$

E3-17 *Obj. 5* On December 31, 2004, Bert's Farm Store had the following account balances in its accounting system. All year-end adjustments had been entered, but the books had not yet been closed.

Bert's Farm Store
Account Balances Before Closing
December 31, 2004

Account	Balance	Account	Balance
Cash	$ 700	Sales Revenue	$2,200
Merchandise	2,800	Cost of Goods Sold	900
Supplies	925	Wages Expense	400
Prepaid Insurance	450	Utilities Expense	150
Equipment	3,550	Depreciation Expense	50
Accumulated Depreciation	1,750	Insurance Expense	100
Interest Payable	150	Supplies Expense	150
Notes Payable	2,000	Interest Expense	100
Owners' Equity	4,175		

a. What is the purpose of closing the books?
b. Prepare all necessary closing entries.
c. After closing, what is the amount of owners' equity that will be reported on the balance sheet?

E3-18 Constantino Company presented the following general ledger account balances for the month ended December 31, 2005.
Obj. 5

Assets:	
Cash	20,600
Accounts Receivable	2,250
Equipment	11,000
Total Assets	**33,850**
Liabilities:	
Wages Payable	250
Payable to Internet Service	35
Notes Payable	17,000
Total Liabilities	**17,285**
Owners' Equity:	
Contributed Capital	13,000
Retained Earnings	1,000
Service Revenue	3,315
Rent Expense	(400)
Wages Expense	(315)
Internet Service Expense	(35)
Total Owners' Equity	**16,565**

a. Close the books for Constantino Company.
b. Prepare a post-closing summary of account balances similar to Exhibit 13.

E3-19 Hydrangea Nurseries had the following general ledger balances at December 31, 2004:
Obj. 5

Assets:	
Cash	10,000
Accounts Receivable	25,000
Inventory	50,000
Prepaid Insurance	5,000
Equipment	300,000
Accumulated Depreciation	(80,000)
Total Assets	**310,000**
Liabilities:	
Accounts Payable	35,000
Notes Payable	130,000
Total Liabilities	**165,000**
Owners' Equity:	
Contributed Capital	90,000
Retained Earnings	45,000
Sales Revenue	300,000
Cost of Goods Sold	(140,000)
Insurance Expense	(5,000)
Wages Expense	(75,000)
Utilities Expense	(40,000)
Interest Expense	(10,000)
Depreciation Expense	(20,000)
Total Owners' Equity	**145,000**

a. Prepare the entry to close the revenue and expense accounts at the end of the year.
b. Prepare a post-closing summary similar to Exhibit 13.

E3-20 *Obj. 5* The accounting staff at Taiwan Manufacturing have prepared the following summary of account balances at year end. The balances include all transactions for the fiscal year except for closing entries.

Account	Balance	Account	Balance
Cash	$ 1,850	Sales Revenue	$7,600
Merchandise	8,435	Cost of Goods Sold	2,840
Supplies	2,955	Wages Expense	1,015
Prepaid Insurance	1,375	Utilities Expense	550
Equipment	9,650	Depreciation Expense	660
Accumulated Depreciation	4,100	Insurance Expense	495
Interest Payable	425	Supplies Expense	525
Notes Payable	7,000	Interest Expense	300
Owners' Equity	11,525		

a. What is the purpose of closing the books?
b. Prepare all necessary closing entries.
c. After all closing entries are entered into the accounting system, what will be the amount of owners' equity reported on the balance sheet?

PROBLEMS

If your instructor is using Personal Trainer in this course, you may complete online the assignments identified by PT.

P3-1 Explaining the Difference between Cash and Accrual Accounting

Obj. 1

The accounting department at Klinger Realty sent the financial reports, as shown below, to Robin Garrison, general manager. Attached was a note indicating that both sets of data are based on the same set of events, which occurred during the quarter just completed. Robin was only recently promoted to this position and is not very knowledgeable about accounting information.

After reviewing this report, Robin was somewhat disturbed because she always had thought accounting was an exact process. How, she wondered, can there be two different results from the same set of facts? Furthermore, how could they be so different? Which one is the "true" or "correct" report?

Klinger Realty
Results of Operating Activities
Third Quarter, 2004

	Cash Basis		Accrual Basis	
Cash receipts/revenues:				
Sales commissions	$300,000		$400,000	
Property management	210,000		165,000	
Total		$510,000		$565,000
Cash payments/expenses:				
Office employee wages	(53,000)		(48,000)	
Advertising	(10,000)		(90,000)	
Office supplies	0		(3,400)	
Depreciation—office equipment	0		(1,800)	
Rent	(6,000)		(6,000)	
Sales staff commissions	(150,000)		(200,000)	
Property managers' salaries	(116,000)		(90,000)	
Total		(335,000)		(439,200)
Net cash flow		$175,000		
Net income				$125,800

Required Assume that you are called in to advise Ms. Garrison. Write a memo to her explaining why there can be two measures of operating results and why they differ.

P3-2 Ethics and Accounting Measurement

Obj. 1

Hardy Rock is proprietor of a jewelry store. In January, he applied for a bank loan and was asked to submit an income statement for the past year, ending in December. Near the end of the prior year, Hardy had purchased merchandise for resale that cost him $60,000. He still owed $45,000 for this merchandise at year end. Half of the merchandise was sold during the Christmas holidays for $75,000. Customers owed Hardy $50,000 for these purchases at year end. Hardy included these transactions as part of his financial statements as follows:

Added to revenues	$75,000
Added to expenses	7,500
Added to net income	$67,500

Hardy reasoned that because he had sold half the merchandise in December, he should report it as revenue, though he had not received all of the cash from customers. Also, he reasoned that because he had paid $15,000 for the merchandise by year end and had sold half of the merchandise, he should report $7,500 of this amount as cost of goods sold.

Required What problems do you see with Hardy's reasoning? Is there an ethical problem with Hardy's treatment of these transactions? What should the effect of these transactions have been on net income?

P3-3 Revenue Recognition and Accrual Accounting

Obj. 2

Daisy Political Consultants has been in existence for many years. During the month of November, the following events occurred:

1. The owners contributed an additional $6,500 to the business to finance an expansion of operations.
2. Consulting services totaling $11,000 were performed on credit during November and billed to customers.
3. A loan in the amount of $25,000 was obtained from a wealthy campaign contributor.
4. Expenses in the amount of $6,000 were incurred during the month. One-third had been paid for by month end.
5. Cash of $18,500 was collected from customers for whom services had been performed during September and October.
6. Services totaling $4,500 were performed for customers who had paid in the previous month for the services.

Required Daisy uses accrual basis accounting. For which of the events above should revenue be recorded in November? In each case, how much revenue should be recorded? If an event does not involve revenue, specify why not.

P3-4 How Unearned Revenue Links Cash and Sales Revenue

Obj. 2

On March 15, the Spinnaker Company received $4,000 in cash from a customer who ordered a custom sail for her racing yacht. The company completed the sail and delivered it on April 30. The Spinnaker Company incurred costs of $2,500 in making the sail. Assume the company recorded the manufacturing costs in the Merchandise Inventory account.

Required

A. Record the transaction on March 15.
B. Record the transaction on April 30.
C. Prepare a table similar to Exhibit 2 that illustrates how Unearned Revenue links Cash with Sales Revenue.

P3-5 How Prepaid Insurance Links Cash and Insurance Expense

Obj. 3

On January 1, Taylor Manufacturing Company purchased a 12-month insurance policy for $1,200 and recorded it as Prepaid Insurance. On December 31 the bookkeeper observed the prepaid insurance account had a $1,200 balance representing the insurance purchased on January 1.

Required

A. Record the insurance purchase on January 1.
B. Prepare the entry required to record insurance expense for the year appropriately.
C. Prepare a table similar to Exhibit 5 that illustrates how Prepaid Insurance links Insurance Expense and Cash.

P3-6 Expense Recognition and Accrual Accounting

Obj. 3

The local chapter of Helping Hands, a social service organization, had the following economic events occur during the month of May:

1. A luncheon honoring volunteers was held at a cost of $950. By month end the bill hadn't been received or paid.
2. New letterhead and envelopes were printed at a cost of $625 and paid for. The new items will not be used, however, until the old supply is exhausted sometime in June.
3. The executive director was paid her usual salary of $3,800 during May.
4. Prizes, ribbons, and awards for events upcoming in July were delivered by the supplier, who charged $10,175. The amount was paid in cash.
5. The electric bill for April totaled $163 and was paid in full.
6. Radio, TV, and newspaper advertising related to a special fund-raising campaign ran during May. The $7,550 cost had been paid in April.

Required Helping Hands uses accrual basis accounting. For which of the events above should an expense be recorded in May? In each case, how much expense should be recorded? If an event does not involve an expense, specify why not.

P3-7 Converting Net Income to Cash Flow

Objs. 1, 2, 3

Middle East Importers reports the following accrual basis information for a recent month.

Total revenue from sales to customers	$90,000
Total expenses	69,000
Net income	$21,000

In addition, the following account information is known:

	Accounts Receivable	Accounts Payable
Beginning of month balance	$ 9,000	$15,000
End of month balance	21,000	9,000

Required Determine (a) the amount of cash collected from customers during the month, (b) the amount of cash paid out for expenses during the month, and (c) the net cash flow for the month.

P3-8 Converting Net Cash Flow to Net Income

Objs. 1, 2, 3

Khim Lee Company reported the following cash flow information at the end of its first year in business:

Cash received from customers	$235,000
Cash paid out to suppliers of inventory	(55,000)
Cash paid out to employees	(77,500)
Cash paid out for advertising	(12,500)
Cash paid out for taxes	(30,000)
Net cash flow for the year	$ 60,000

Also known at year end was the following:

Amounts not yet collected from customers	$85,000
Amounts owed to suppliers	15,000
Wages owed to employees	22,500
Additional taxes still owed	10,000
Amount remaining in inventory	0

Required Prepare an accrual basis income statement for the company's first year in business.

P3-9 Ethics and Accounting Measurement

Objs. 1, 2, 3

Tinker, Evers, and Chance are partners in a sports equipment megastore. Tinker keeps the accounting records for the partnership because he is skilled in accounting and the other partners are not. The partners have agreed that they will share equally in the company's profits (or losses) at the end of each year. For fiscal 2004, the first year of operations, the company sold $7,600,000 of merchandise. Of this amount, $1,400,000 was still owed to the company by customers at year end. The company purchased and paid for merchandise costing $4,300,000 during 2004; $1,000,000 of this merchandise remained in inventory at year end. The company purchased and paid for $1,400,000 of equipment during the year. The equipment should have a useful life of 7 years. Thus depreciation expenses would be $200,000 each year. Other expenses amounted to $650,000, all paid for in cash. Tinker has prepared the following income statement and distribution of profits for 2004:

Tinker, Evers, and Chance
Income Statement
For Year 2004

Revenues		$6,200,000
Expenses:		
Merchandise	$4,300,000	
Equipment	1,400,000	
Other	650,000	
Total expenses		6,350,000
Net loss		$ 150,000
Distribution of net loss:		
Reduction in owners' capital:		
Tinker		$ 50,000
Evers		50,000
Chance		50,000
Total distribution of net loss		$ 150,000

Evers and Chance are mystified by these results because they thought the company had been performing above their expectations. Tinker assured his partners that his numbers were correct. Tinker has offered to buy out his partners, explaining that "he got 'em into this and should do the right thing." Of course, the other partners will lose half of their original investment if they sell.

Required

A. What problems do you see with Tinker's financial report?
B. Advise the other partners as to whether they should sell out. To support your advice, prepare a revised income statement incorporating any changes you think appropriate to support a prudent decision.

P3-10 Accrual versus Cash Flow

Objs. 2, 3, 4

The Water Fun Store is a retailer of water sports products for backyard swimming pools. During August, the firm had the following operating activities:

Date	Event
Aug. 1	Bought $5,000 of goods for resale from Pinetree Wholesalers on credit.
5	Paid $450 to the local newspaper for advertising that ran during July.
6	Paid $975 rent for the month of August.
9	Sold goods to customers for $7,350 on credit. These goods had cost the firm $3,600.
10	Paid $3,000 to Pinetree Wholesalers in partial payment for goods purchased August 1.
11	Collected $5,350 from goods sold on August 9.
13	Bought $9,200 of goods for resale from Stanley Company. Paid cash.
16	Paid employees for their work so far in August, $1,050.
19	Sold goods to customers on credit for $6,350. These goods had cost the firm $2,400.
25	Collected $3,700 from the sales made on August 19.
29	Paid $975 rent for the month of September.
31	Employees had earned an additional $1,200 of wages but would not be paid until September 1.

Required

A. Prepare a report of net cash flow from operating activities.
B. Prepare an accrual basis income statement.
C. Which statement documents a more realistic or complete picture of August's activity? Why?

P3-11 Determining Transactions from Changes in Financial Statements

Objs. 2, 3, 4

The Loc-Tite Correctional Facility is a private enterprise prison that contracts services to a midwestern state. At October 1, the beginning of its fiscal year, the organization had the following balance sheet.

Loc-Tite Correctional Facility
Balance Sheet
at October 1

Assets:		Liabilities and Owners' Equity:	
Cash	$ 43,725	Accounts payable	$ 28,350
Supplies	65,700	Bonds payable	450,000
Equipment	350,000	Owners' investment	1,050,000
Building	1,400,000	Retained earnings	883,575
Accumulated depreciation	(100,000)		
Land	652,500		
Total	$2,411,925	Total	$2,411,925

During the month of October, a number of economic events occurred and were entered into the accounting system. At the end of October, the company prepared the following financial statements.

Loc-Tite Correctional Facility
Financial Statements

Balance Sheet (at Oct. 31)				Income Statement (for Oct.)	
Assets:		Liabilities and Owners' Equity:		Revenues	$810,000
Cash	$ 58,725	Accounts payable	$ 28,350	Expenses:	
Supplies	28,200	Bonds payable	0	Supplies	37,500
Equipment	350,000	Owners' Investment	1,050,000	Depreciation	8,625
Building	1,400,000	Retained earnings	1,302,450	Wages	345,000
Accumulated depreciation	(108,625)				
Land	652,500				
Total	$2,380,800	Total	$2,380,800	Net income	$418,875

Required

A. Identify the transactions that occurred during October.
B. Prepare a schedule that explains the changes in cash balance during October.

P3-12 Understanding Going Concern and Accounting Measurement

Objs. 2, 3, 4

On March 1, Carl Caldwell started Caldwell Furniture Repair Company. He invested $2,000 of his own money, borrowed $16,000 from his father-in-law at 9% annual interest, and obtained an additional $3,000, 12% loan from Maxibank. He purchased $15,000 of tools and equipment (some new, some used) and bought $5,200 of supplies such as paints, resins, and glue, all for cash. He rented a shop at a local business park by paying $3,600 in advance for the months of March, April, and May. During March he performed repairs totaling $7,600 and used up $2,400 of supplies. Of the repair services performed, 75% were paid for in cash by the end of the month and the balance was expected to be collected in April. Carl estimated that wear and tear on the equipment and tools during March was $250. On March 31, he owed $332 to the electric company and $78 to the water company for services consumed. Also on that date, he paid interest totaling $150 on the two loans.

Required

A. Prepare an income statement for Caldwell Furniture Repair for the month of March.
B. Prepare a separate schedule that explains the changes in cash balance during March.
C. Is the transformation cycle complete or incomplete at the end of March? Explain your answer.

P3-13 Accrual versus Cash Flow

Objs. 2, 3, 4

Consider each of the five independent situations below.

1. Asia Tea Company purchased a 3-month property insurance policy on March 1 at a cost of $3,600. The insurance became effective immediately although payment was due and paid 45 days later.
2. On February 1, Big Bang Chemical Company signed a contract with a customer. Big Bang agreed to deliver each month, for 3 months, goods priced at $7,500. The first delivery was made on April 1. The customer paid $22,500 for these goods on May 15.
3. Turning Tire Company borrowed $15,000 from a bank on February 1. Terms of repayment are that $1,000 of the principal amount must be repaid on the first day of each following month. In addition, interest at 2% per month on the unpaid balance must accompany each payment.
4. Bureaucrats, Inc. consumes large amounts of office supplies. On February 1, a $10,000 order of supplies was received and paid for. 60% of these supplies were used in March and the rest were used in April. On April 20, a $12,000 order of office supplies was received. The invoice for these goods was paid in May. 30% of these goods were consumed in May and the rest were consumed in June.

(Continued)

5. Sales at the High-Price Furniture Store totaled $45,000 for the month of February. Of this amount, 20% was cash sales, 40% was collected during March, 30% during April, and 10% during May.

Required

A. Determine the proper amount of revenue, expense, and cash flow that should be entered into the accounting system during each month shown. Use the format shown below. The first event is completed as an example.
B. What does this information suggest to you about the pattern in which accrual-based measures are recognized versus cash-based measures?
C. What does this suggest to you about a manager's need for both accrual information and cash flow information?

Event	Revenue, Expense, or Cash Flow?	Month of February	Month of March	Month of April	Month of May	Month of June
1.	Expense Cash Flow	-0- -0-	$1,200 -0-	$1,200 3,600	$1,200 -0-	-0- -0-
2.						
3.						
4.						
5.						

P3-14 *Objs. 2, 3, 4* PT

Preparing Financial Statements and Making Decisions

The Desert Harbor Inn has been in business for more than 100 years but was recently renovated. On January 1, 2004, the balance sheet of the company was as shown on the next page.

During 2004, the inn earned $165,000 from room rentals and another $35,000 from parking, the gift shop, and other guest services. Of this amount, $187,000 was received in cash by year end; $13,000 was still collectible from credit card companies and one very reliable corporate account. Expenses incurred during the year included staff wages, $49,000; utilities, $10,400; supplies used, $4,300; depreciation on furniture and fixtures, $1,500; depreciation on the building, $3,500; interest on note payable, $4,700; cost of goods sold by gift shop, $11,000; and other miscellaneous expenses of $3,300.

Except for depreciation, supplies consumed, and $890 of wages still owed to employees, all expenses were paid for in cash. Other cash payments included $800 for purchase of supplies and $35,000 paid on the principal of the note payable. Owners withdrew $45,000 from the business for living expenses during the year.

Desert Harbor Inn
Balance Sheet
January 1, 2004

Assets		Liabilities and Owners' Equity	
Cash	$ 4,900	Notes payable	$ 56,500
Supplies on hand	8,800	Investment by owners	60,000
Furniture and equipment	25,000	Retained earnings	19,200
Buildings	95,000		
Accumulated depreciation	(10,000)		
Land	12,000		
Total	$135,700	Total	$135,700

Required

A. Prepare year-end financial statements for the company for 2004. Include an income statement, statement of cash flows, and a balance sheet.
B. From a financial perspective, does this company appear to be one that you would like to own? Why or why not?

P3-15 Identifying Problems in Financial Reporting

Objs. 2, 3, 4

Alma Zorditch started an Internet company and has computed the first year's profit as shown below. She is distressed. She thought the business had been going fairly well but does not know how she can live on the meager profit the company has earned. She is considering going out of business. Alma doesn't have any formal training in accounting but once took a 4-hour seminar on the subject. That seminar impressed on her the importance of keeping detailed and accurate records. All the numbers reported below are accurate, but there may be other problems that you can identify.

Zorditch.com
Profits I Made the First Year

Revenue:		
Cash collected from customers	$173,400	
Accounts receivable at year end	18,200	
Total revenue		$191,600
Expenses:		
Money I contributed to start the firm	15,000	
Purchase of office furnishings & equipment	28,500	
Purchase of office supplies	1,560	
Rent on the office space	13,000	
Loan from the bank	50,000	
Wages paid to employees	36,200	
Advertising and promotion	24,280	
Miscellaneous	11,300	
Total expenses		179,840
Profit		$ 11,760

After talking with Alma, you discover the following additional information.

1. When purchased, the office furnishings and equipment have an expected useful life of 5 years. That estimate still appears reasonable.
2. All office supplies have been used up.
3. The rent amount includes $1,000 rent paid in advance for the first month of Year 2.
4. Half of the advertising and promotion amont is for a campaign that will begin 3 months from now.

(Continued)

Required

A. Study the information given and prepare a new income statement making all changes you believe are appropriate.
B. Wherever your report differs from Alma's, justify the change you have made.
C. Based on your revised income statement, what advice would you have for Alma? List two or three specific suggestions.

P3-16 Adjusting Entries and Closing Entries: Effects on Financial Statements

Objs. 4, 5

P/T

The Flash Pan Company manufactures cooking products. On August 1, 2004, the company borrowed $125,000 from creditors. Semiannual interest payments of $7,500 are to be made to creditors beginning January 31, 2005. On July 1, 2004, the company purchased a 1-year insurance policy for $10,000 and recorded it as prepaid insurance. On January 1, 2004, the company purchased equipment for $50,000. The equipment has an expected life of 4 years. On October 1, 2004, the company rented some of its unused warehouse space to another company. The other company agreed to pay $15,000 for the space every 6 months beginning April 1, 2005. Balance sheet and income statement information reported by Flash for the fiscal year ended December 31, 2004 included:

Assets	$625,000
Liabilities	250,000
Owners' equity	337,500
Revenues	150,000
Expenses	112,500
Net income	37,500

The balance sheet did not balance but it was distributed anyway. Later, it was discovered that the company's accounting staff had failed to record any adjusting entries at the end of 2001 for interest, insurance, depreciation, or rent. In addition, no closing entries had been made.

Required

A. Record the adjusting entries that should have been made at year end 2004.
B. Explain why the balance sheet did not balance and whether this was caused by the failure to record adjusting entries or the failure to record closing entries.
C. Identify the corrected amounts for the balance sheet and income statement. Show your work.

P3-17 End-of-Period Adjustments and Closing

Objs. 4, 5

At December 31, 2004, the accountant at Puget Sounds, a recording studio, has entered all the firm's transactions into the accounting system and is beginning the end-of-period process. He asks your help in identifying the necessary adjusting entries. In the first column on page F121, the accountant has listed the company's account balances before considering adjustments. In addition, he has provided other information that may cause you to recommend that certain adjusting entries be made.

1. $4,350 of wages earned by employees during December have not been recorded or paid.
2. The prepaid insurance is for a 3-year policy purchased on the first day of the year just ending.
3. Unearned revenues are for contracts for the use of studio facilities. $12,000 of this amount has been earned by December 31.
4. A count at year-end shows that $10,050 of supplies remain on hand.
5. The note payable was issued on October 1, 2004. Interest accumulates in the amount of $3,000 per month. Interest has not yet been recorded for December.
6. Depreciation on equipment is $1,500 per month. Depreciation on buildings is $600 per month. No depreciation has yet been recorded for the quarter (3 months) just ended.

	Account Balance Before Adjustment	Adjustments	Account Balance After Adjustment
Cash	$ 52,500		
Accounts receivable	35,250		
Supplies	19,200		
Prepaid insurance	4,050		
Equipment	468,000		
Accumulated depreciation—equipment	(129,000)		
Buildings	649,500		
Accumulated depreciation—buildings	(85,500)		
Land	58,500		
Total assets	**$1,072,500**		
Unearned revenues	$ 36,000		
Accounts payable	27,900		
Interest payable	6,000		
Wages payable	0	(1) +4,350	4,350
Notes payable	420,000		
Common stock	300,000		
Retained earnings *(a)*	224,100		
Total liabilities & stockholders' equity	**$1,014,000**		
Rent revenues	$ 100,500		
Wages expense	(36,000)	(1) −4,350	(40,350)
Supplies expense	0		
Insurance expense	0		
Interest expense	(6,000)		
Depreciation expense	0		
Net income	**$ 58,500**		
(a) Net income has not been added for the current year.			

Required

A. Identify any adjustments you believe necessary and enter their effects in the adjustments column of the table above. Code each adjustment with the number to which it relates. The first item is completed for you as an example.

B. Record the proper ending amount for each account in the final column.

C. On the table you have completed, why doesn't the total of all asset accounts equal the total of all liability and equity accounts?

D. What additional step(s) needs to be performed before financial statements can be prepared? Explain how this will solve the imbalance identified in part (C) above.

E. By what amount (and percentage) would net income have been misstated if no adjusting entries had been recorded by this company?

P3-18 Types and Treatment of Accounts

Obj. 5

Encanto Properties, Inc., uses the accounts listed below.

A. Prepaid Insurance
B. Retained Earnings
C. Accumulated Depreciation
D. Wages Expense
E. Commissions Revenue
F. Interest Payable
G. Supplies
H. Insurance Expense
I. Unearned Rent
J. Prepaid Advertising
K. Notes Payable
L. Cost of Goods Sold
M. Machinery
N. Owners' Capital
O. Accounts Receivable
P. Bonds Payable
Q. Supplies Expense
R. Depreciation Expense

Required (a) For each account above, indicate whether it is an asset, liability, owners' equity, revenue, or expense account. (b) Indicate whether the account is closed at the end of the fiscal year.

P3-19 Ethical Issues in an Accounting System

Obj. 6

Ethel Spikes works for Hard Rock Candy Company. She enters customer orders in the company's accounting system. The orders are written on prepared forms by the company's sales representatives (reps). The company employs ten sales reps, who work different territories. The reps are paid on a commission basis for sales made during the preceding month. Sales reports prepared by the accounting department supervisor are used to determine the commissions. Sales reps drop off the forms with the accounting supervisor each week. The supervisor then delivers the forms to Ethel. She enters the orders in a computer and prints out a sales report and sales invoices for each customer. These are picked up by the supervisor, who delivers them to payroll and to shipping. The result of entering the orders in the accounting system is to increase accounts receivable and to increase sales revenue.

Ethel has discovered an interesting regularity in some of the orders. One of the sales reps always reports abnormally high orders from a particular customer. A few days after the end of each month, the rep submits a cancelation form for the customer to eliminate a large portion of the customer's order. The supervisor directs Ethel to record the cancelation by reducing accounts receivable for the customer and recording an increase in an operating expense account. Ethel doesn't know much about accounting. When she asked her supervisor about this procedure, she was told that it was standard for this customer and not to worry about it.

Ethel smells a rat, however, and has considered discussing the matter with the vice president for finance. But she is concerned she may simply be making waves that will alienate her supervisor.

Required Ethel has sought your advice, as a friend, about this matter. What would you recommend to Ethel? What problems do you see in Hard Rock's accounting system? How might these problems be solved?

P3-20 Describing Processes in an Accounting System

Obj. 6

Flora Wiser is the daughter of the owner of Wiser Florist Company. She recently completed college with a major in biology and has taken the job of assistant manager. Her primary duties involve purchasing inventory from suppliers. Flora has little understanding of accounting, and you have been asked to help her become familiar with the company's accounting system and how the system processes information.

Required Write a memo to Flora describing the purpose of an accounting system. Describe each of the basic processes that occur within financial accounting systems and how these processes accomplish the purpose of the system.

P3-21 Excel in Action

The problem in Chapter F2 provided account balances for The Book Wermz on September 30, 2004, the end of the company's fiscal year: Cash $4,238.72, Inventory of Books $235,892.35, Supplies $2,343.28, Equipment $43,297.00, Notes Payable $123,452.88, Investment by Owners

SPREADSHEET

$100,000, and Retained Earnings $62,318.47. Chapter F2 also listed summary transactions for October 2004:

Cash sales	$38,246.50
Cost of goods sold	27,318.93

The Equipment account balance of $43,297.00 is net of accumulated depreciation of $12,353.00. Therefore, the Equipment balance before considering the effect of depreciation is $55,650.00.

Other transactions for the month ended October 31, 2004, include:

Cash paid for books purchased	$18,243.27
Cash paid for supplies	1,750.92
Cost of supplies used in October	2,129.48
Employee wages earned and paid in October	3,620.83
Employee wages earned in October but unpaid	527.12
Cash paid for portion of Notes Payable	1,122.77
Cash paid for interest incurred on Notes Payable	823.02
Cash paid for October rent	1,534.86
Depreciation on equipment for October	721.62

In addition, The Book Wermz held classes on book binding for local civic organizations in October. The organizations agreed to a $500 fee for these services but did not make the payment in October.

Required Add the transactions described above to those created in Chapter F2. Additional rows should be added to the spreadsheet for the transactions. Additional columns also will be needed for accounts not included in Chapter F2. The following accounts should be included in the spreadsheet in the order indicated: Cash, Accounts Receivable, Supplies, Inventory, Equipment, Accumulated Depreciation, Wages Payable, Notes Payable, Investment by Owners, Retained Earnings, Sales, Service Revenues, Cost of Goods Sold, Supplies Expense, Wages Expense, Rent Expense, Depreciation Expense, and Interest Expense. The beginning balance of all new accounts except Accumulated Depreciation is $0. The beginning balance of the Accumulated Depreciation account is $12,353 (note this is a negative amount because it is a contra account), and the beginning balance of the Equipment account should be changed to $55,650 (to permit Accumulated Depreciation to be included as a separate account). Column sums should be recalculated to determine totals at October 31. Make sure to close the revenue and expense accounts to Retained Earnings. Use October 31 as the date for all transactions.

Update the balance sheet and income statement by including the effects of the transactions recorded for October. Use cell references in the financial statements to identify amounts for each account. Add captions to identify each statement. The statements should include the name of the company on the top line. The next line should identify the financial statement as a balance sheet or income statement. The third line should identify the date (October 31, 2004 for the balance sheet) or period (for October 2004 for the income statement). List total revenues and total expenses as subtotals on the income statement. Use underlines to separate the subtotals from other numbers. The Borders button can be used for this purpose.

P3-22 Multiple-Choice Overview of the Chapter

P/T

1. The primary difference between control accounts and subsidiary accounts is that
   a. control accounts appear on the balance sheet but subsidiary accounts appear on the income statement.
   b. subsidiary accounts provide detailed information; control accounts provide summary information.
   c. control account balances are reported on the financial statements but subsidiary accounts appear only in the general ledger.
   d. subsidiary accounts are necessary in a manual accounting system but not in a computerized system.

2. At the beginning of the year, Lagos Importers had $750 of office supplies on hand. During the year, an additional $3,250 of supplies were purchased and recorded in

(Continued)

Office Supplies Inventory. At year end, $900 of supplies remained on hand. Just prior to preparing the year-end adjusting entry, the balance in the Office Supplies Inventory account was $1,200. Which of the following is a true statement about the necessary adjusting entry?
a. An asset account must be decreased by $300.
b. An asset account must be decreased by $3,250.
c. An expense account must be increased by $1,200.
d. An expense account must be increased by $900.

3. The balance of the merchandise inventory account increased by $3,000 during February. Which of the following statements can be made as a result of this information?
   a. Credit sales for the month were $3,000 greater than cash received from customers.
   b. Purchases of inventory for the month were $3,000 less than the cost of merchandise sold for the month.
   c. Purchases of inventory for the month were $3,000 greater than the cost of merchandise sold for the month.
   d. Merchandise purchased for the month totaled $3,000.

4. Which of the following accounts should always have a zero balance after all closing entries are completed?
   a. Interest Expense
   b. Interest Payable
   c. Prepaid Interest
   d. Accounts Payable

5. Tempel Manufacturing uses accrual accounting. Each of the following events occurred during the month of February. Which one of them should be recorded as a revenue or expense for the month of February?
   a. Sales of $30,000 were made on credit. They will be collected during March.
   b. Collections of $10,000 were made from sales that occurred during January.
   c. Materials costing $18,000 were purchased and paid for. It is expected that they will be used during March.
   d. A bill in the amount of $8,600 was received from a supplier for goods purchased during January. It was paid immediately.

6. Zinsli Company uses the accrual basis of accounting. Each of the following events occurred during July. Which one of them should be reported as an expense for July?
   a. Office supplies costing $800 were used up. They had been purchased and paid for during April.
   b. A new delivery truck was purchased on the last day of July. It was not put into use until August.
   c. On the third day of the month, $8,000 was paid to employees for hours worked during the month of June.
   d. Near the end of the month, August's rent of $1,500 was paid in advance.

7. The following information is available for two companies for the year 2004:

	Handle-Bar Mustache Co. Cash Operating Statement For the Year 2001	Pencil-Thin Mustache Co. Accrual Income Statement For the Year 2004
Receipts/Revenues	$50,000	$55,000
Payments/Expenses	38,000	31,000
Net Cash/Net Income	$12,000	$24,000

Which of the following statements can be determined from the information provided?

a. Pencil-Thin collected more cash from customers during 2004 than did Handle-Bar.
b. Pencil-Thin was profitable during 2004, whereas Handle-Bar may have been profitable.
c. Pencil-Thin was twice as profitable as Handle-Bar.
d. Handle-Bar consumed more total resources during 2004 than did Pencil-Thin.

8. Are the following accounts a liability?

	Depreciation expense	Accounts receivable
a.	Yes	Yes
b.	Yes	No
c.	No	Yes
d.	No	No

9. Using accrual-basis measurement, expenses should be recognized when
   a. a business owner recognizes that the firm is generating too much profit.
   b. resources are used rather than when they are paid for.
   c. cash is paid for resources.
   d. sufficient revenue is earned to offset the expenses.

10. Match the account name to the financial statement on which it is reported.

	Accumulated Depreciation	Depreciation Expense
a.	Statement of stockholder's equity	Balance sheet
b.	Balance sheet	Balance sheet
c.	Income statement	Balance sheet
d.	Balance sheet	Income statement

CASES

C3-1 Ethical Issues Involving Revenue Recognition

Obj. 4

Flash Newton is national sales director at Bright & Shiny Toothpaste Company. The firm manufactures and distributes a full line of premium-priced personal care products sold through a carefully selected set of distributors nationwide. The popularity and profit margins of the Bright & Shiny product line make distributorships very profitable and there is intense competition when one becomes available.

Flash, and the regional sales directors working for him, are compensated by a base salary and a significant bonus tied to percentage increases in yearly sales. Because of an impending recession, sales have been mostly flat during the first three quarters of the year. On October 3, Flash convened a national sales meeting with representatives of all distributors. At that meeting, he presented the distributors with Bright & Shiny's newest sales plan. All distributors would be required to buy, during the 4th quarter, up to 2 years' worth of inventory of the firm's products. Further, the prices charged on these special purchases would be 10% greater than usual. Any distributors not agreeing to the proposal would automatically lose their distributorship. Because most distributors are not expected to have cash readily available to pay for these additional purchases under the usual 30-day credit terms, Bright & Shiny will allow up to 12 months to pay.

The new policy has been a huge success and by year end, total orders and shipments to distributors are up by 12% over the previous year. Bright & Shiny recorded all shipments as revenue even though some distributors were told by lower-level managers that they could return unsold products. Because many distributors could not handle the large shipments in their usual storage facilities, many orders have been shipped to third-party warehouses for storage at Bright & Shiny's expense. At Flash's suggestion, and to obtain maximum benefit of this new sales program, the company held the books open for a few days after December 31 to obtain and ship additional orders.

Required Identify and explain any problems you see with the sales plan. If you were Bright & Shiny's CEO, which aspects of the sales plan would you have approved and which would you have denied? Why?

C3-2 Evaluating the Results of an Organization's Transformation Process

Objs. 1, 5

SoftwareSolutions.com has been in business for several years and is publicly traded on a major U.S. stock exchange. It is an Internet wholesaler of a variety of commercial software applications. On January 1, 2004, the company's balance sheet appeared as follows (all amounts are in thousands of dollars):

SoftwareSolutions.com
Balance Sheet
January 1, 2004

Assets		**Liabilities & Stockholders' Equity**	
Cash	$ 4,240	Wages payable	$ 640
Accounts receivable	6,800	Capital stock (owner's investment)	33,000
Inventory	15,200	Retained earnings	13,600
Buildings & equipment	16,780		
Accumulated depreciation	(4,780)		
Land (for plant expansion)	9,000		
Total assets	$47,240	Total liabilities and stockholders' equity	$47,240

During the first quarter of the current year (January, February, March), the following events occurred.

A. New office furniture costing $500 was purchased on the last day of March. This was to be used in a new sales office that was scheduled to open April 1. The office furniture was paid for in cash.
B. Wages and salaries totaling $3,200 were paid. Of this amount, 20% was to liquidate wages payable that arose in the fourth quarter of the previous year. The company has a policy of not making wage or salary advances to employees.
C. All accounts receivable outstanding at January 1 were collected.
D. The company's advertising agency billed the firm $1,000 for a campaign that had run during the current quarter. The company is planning to pay the bill during April.
E. Sales totaling $18,000 were made to customers. Of these sales, 60% was collected during the first quarter, and the balance is expected to be collected during the next quarter. The goods that were sold had cost the company $13,000 when they were purchased.
F. Dividends were declared and paid to stockholders in the amount of $1,500.
G. Inventory (software programs) costing $10,500 was purchased, of which 10% was paid for by the end of the quarter.
H. A 3-year, $4,000, 12% loan was obtained from a local bank on the last day of the quarter.
I. New shares of stock were sold by the company for $2,000 in cash.
J. A new 3-year lease agreement was signed and executed. The lease required that a $900 monthly rental be paid in advance for the first 2 quarters of the current year. (Total paid is $5,400 = $900 × 6 months.)
K. The accountants calculated that depreciation totaling $350 should be recorded for the quarter for the firm's buildings and equipment.
L. The land that had been held for plant expansion was sold for $9,000.

Required Prepare any summary documents you believe might help management (or interested external parties) better understand the effectiveness or efficiency of the firm's first quarter transformation process. Did the company have a satisfactory first quarter?

COMPREHENSIVE REVIEW

CR3-1 Financial Statement Preparation and Closing Process

Summary account balances for Mom's Cookie Company at the end of February are presented below. The summary includes all transactions for February, not just those described in this chapter. In particular, additional sales transactions have been included.

Mom's Cookie Company
Account Balances
February 28, 2004

Account	Balance
Assets:	
Cash	7,740
Accounts Receivable	1,580
Merchandise Inventories	7,520
Supplies	60
Prepaid Rent	1,200
Equipment	31,000
Accumulated Depreciation	(1,040)
Total Assets	**48,060**
Liabilities:	
Accounts Payable	1,400
Unearned Revenue	3,000
Interest Payable	400
Notes Payable	30,000
Total Liabilities	**34,800**
Owners' Equity:	
Contribution by Owners	10,000
Retained Earnings	480
Sales Revenue	17,160
Cost of Goods Sold	(11,440)
Wages Expense	(1,000)
Rent Expense	(600)
Depreciation Expense	(520)
Supplies Expense	(400)
Utilities Expense	(220)
Interest Expense	(200)
Total Owners' Equity	**13,260**

Required Use the account balances to (a) prepare an income statement for February, (b) close the revenue and expense accounts (show journal transactions and ledger accounts), (c) prepare a post-closing summary of account balances, and (d) prepare a balance sheet.

4
Reporting Earnings and Financial Position

How do we report earnings and financial position to stockholders?

Previous chapters described business activities of Mom's Cookie Company and the system the company used to account for those activities. As the business grew during 2004, Maria and Stan needed additional financial resources to take advantage of opportunities to sell more of their product. In October, they decided to issue shares of stock in their company to other individuals. Cash received from issuing the stock was used to acquire additional equipment, particularly delivery vans, and to increase the amount of inventory the company could purchase. Because the company has external investors (stockholders who are not managers of the company), it must report its business activities in conformance with generally accepted accounting principles to ensure these stockholders are properly informed of the company's earnings and financial position.

FOOD FOR THOUGHT

Assume you own shares of stock in Mom's Cookie Company. What information about the company is important to you? As the company prepares to report accounting information to you and its other owners at the end of its 2004 fiscal year, what information must it include in its income statement and balance sheet? What information do corporations report, especially about their earnings and stockholders' equity, that other companies do not? Is there any information about the company that does not have to be disclosed?

Maria and Stan have arranged to meet with their accountant, Ellen, to discuss these issues.

Maria: ***We have prepared monthly financial statements for our use in managing the company. I suspect that those statements are not adequate for reporting to our other stockholders.***

Ellen: ***That's correct. The statements you have been preparing are fine for internal use and contain correct information. However, formal financial statements for external users need to follow a somewhat different format than those you have been using.***

Stan: ***Does this mean we have to redo our accounting system and learn a new way of accounting for our company?***

Ellen: ***No. Your accounting system is fine. You just need to modify the format of your statements to organize the information a bit differently, and you need to include more information about earnings and stockholders' equity than you have been reporting.***

Maria: ***Will these changes be hard for us to make?***

Ellen: ***No. You will need to understand how information is classified in formal financial statements and how corporations report such matters as earnings per share and changes in stockholders' equity. Now that you understand the basic content of financial statements and how business activities are reported in these statements, you shouldn't have much trouble preparing statements for your stockholders.***

OBJECTIVES

Once you have completed this chapter, you should be able to:

1. Identify the primary financial statements issued by businesses.
2. Explain information presented on a company's income statement.
3. Explain information presented on a company's balance sheet.
4. Explain information presented on a company's statement of stockholders' equity.
5. Identify some of the primary limitations of financial statements.

THE PURPOSE OF FINANCIAL STATEMENTS

OBJECTIVE 1

Identify the primary financial statements issued by businesses.

Accounting information may serve general and specific purposes. Financial statements are the primary means organizations use to report general-purpose accounting information to external decision makers. Most business organizations prepare three financial statements:

1. An income statement
2. A balance sheet
3. A statement of cash flows

Many corporations also prepare a statement of stockholders' equity because of the variety and complexity of their ownership transactions. This chapter examines the purpose and content of the income statement, the balance sheet, and the statement of stockholders' equity. Chapter F5 examines the statement of cash flows. Information contained in financial statements and in the notes accompanying the statements is the primary focus of financial accounting. Specific-purpose accounting reports and other information used by internal decision makers are subjects of managerial accounting.

The form and content of financial statements evolved throughout the twentieth century and continue to change to meet user needs. Financial statements are used by internal and external decision makers. The format and content of the statements used by managers to make financing, investing, and operating decisions often follow those of statements prepared for external users. Statements for internal use, however, may be prepared in any form and with any content desired by management.

For many years the balance sheet was the primary financial statement reported to external users. It was designed to meet the needs of creditors, who wanted information about resources and claims to these resources. The income statement developed to meet the needs of corporate investors, who wanted information about earnings. Earnings information is useful for evaluating management decisions that affect payments to stockholders and stock values. The statement of stockholders' equity describes transactions affecting stock and the amount and use of retained earnings. The statement of cash flows, which is a more recent addition to external reports, provides information that enables creditors, investors, and other users to assess a company's ability to meet its cash requirements.

Financial statements for general-purpose external reporting normally are prepared according to generally accepted accounting principles (GAAP). As noted previously, GAAP are accounting and reporting standards established by authoritative agencies and monitored and enforced by the federal government. GAAP specify the format and content of the statements, though they permit managers to choose among alternative methods of reporting some transactions. The establishment and enforcement of accounting standards are discussed in Chapter F6.

An income statement (sometimes called an earnings statement, a statement of operations, or a profit and loss (P&L) statement) reports a company's revenues and expenses for a fiscal period. The income statement presents operating results on an accrual basis. It measures the amount of goods and services provided to customers during a fiscal period and resources consumed in providing those goods and services. Revenues and expenses result from the sale and consumption of resources for a fiscal period. Therefore, the income statement reports the results of operating activities for a particular period, such as a month, quarter, or fiscal year.

A balance sheet reports the balances of the asset, liability, and owners' equity accounts at a particular date. Other names for the balance sheet are statement of financial position and statement of financial condition. These names are good descriptions of the statement because it reports the amount of resources available to an organization at a particular date and the sources of financing used to acquire those resources. In combination, the resources and financing are the financial position, or condition, of the organization at the report date.

A *statement of stockholders' equity* reports changes in a corporation's owners' equity for a fiscal period. Owners of corporations are known as stockholders or shareholders because they acquire ownership by purchasing shares of stock issued by the corporation. Each share of stock represents an equal share of ownership in a corporation. The primary changes in stockholders' equity result from profits earned during a period, from dividends paid to owners, and from the sale or repurchase of stock by a corporation. ***Dividends* are distributions of cash or stock by a corporation to its stockholders.** The statement of stockholders' equity links the income statement to the balance sheet because it describes how much net income was reinvested as part of retained earnings.

THE INCOME STATEMENT

OBJECTIVE 2

Explain information presented on a company's income statement.

The income statement reports the revenues, expenses, and net income for a fiscal period. Exhibit 1 provides the income statement of Mom's Cookie Company for the year ended December 31, 2004. The income statement reports revenues and expenses that are measured on an accrual basis. Revenues indicate the sales price of goods and services sold during a fiscal period. They do not indicate how much cash was received from the sales during that period. Expenses identify the cost of resources consumed in producing and selling goods and services sold during a fiscal period. They do not identify how much cash was paid for resources during that period. **Net income is not cash.** As a first step in understanding Exhibit 1, observe the general format of the statement. Unlike the statements we described in Chapters 2 and 3 that simply listed revenues and

Exhibit 1

A Corporate Income Statement

Mom's Cookie Company
Income Statement
For the Year Ended December 31, 2004

Sales revenue	$ 686,400
Cost of goods sold	(457,600)
Gross profit	228,800
Selling, general and administrative expenses	(148,300)
Operating income	80,500
Interest expense	(4,800)
Pretax income	75,700
Income taxes	(22,710)
Net income	$ 52,990
Earnings per share	$ 13.25*
Average number of common shares	4,000

*rounded

expenses, the income statements prepared by most companies are divided into several sections. The following paragraphs describe the sections commonly found on income statements.

Gross Profit

The income statement reports *gross profit,* **the difference between the selling price of goods or services sold to customers during a period and the cost of the goods or services sold.** For a merchandising company, the cost of goods sold is the cost of the merchandise inventory sold during a period. For a manufacturing company, cost of goods sold includes the dollar amounts of materials, labor, and other resources that are consumed directly in producing the goods sold during a period. These costs are **product costs.** Product costs are recorded as an asset (Inventory) until goods are sold. Then the costs are matched against the revenues generated from the sale by recording an expense (Cost of Goods Sold) during the same fiscal period as the sale.

Cost of services sold, rather than cost of goods sold, is important for service companies. **The *cost of services sold* is the cost of material, labor, and other resources consumed directly in producing services sold during a period.** For example, in a hospital, the cost of nursing is a cost of services. This cost cannot be held as inventory and, therefore, is expensed in the period in which the services are provided.

Gross profit is a measure of how much a company earned directly from the sale of its products during a fiscal period. Every company would like to earn a large gross profit by selling its products at a much higher price than their cost. Competition prevents most companies from being able to do so. Companies must price their products at amounts their customers are willing to pay, which is determined in part by prices of other similar products that customers could buy from other companies. Mom's Cookie Company cannot sell its cookies at a price that is much higher than that of other companies that sell similar cookies. Therefore, Mom's Cookie Company has to purchase the goods it sells at a cost that allows it to earn a reasonable gross profit. The amount of gross profit a company can earn depends on the kinds of products it sells and the markets in which it operates. Some markets are more competitive than others. For example, many competing companies sell computers, but not many sell the operating systems for computers.

Operating Income

The second section of an income statement lists operating expenses other than cost of goods sold or cost of services sold. ***Operating expenses* are costs of resources consumed as part of operating activities during a fiscal period and that are not directly associated with specific goods or services.** Most operating expenses are **period costs** because they are recognized in the fiscal period in which they occur. Operating expenses include selling, general, and administrative expenses incurred during a period.

Corporations usually do not identify specific operating expenses in detail. Salaries for managers and their support staffs who are not involved directly in producing goods and the cost of resources used by managers are operating expenses. These expenses include depreciation, taxes, and insurance on office buildings and equipment, and the costs of supplies and utilities consumed in operating these facilities. Operating expenses also include marketing and product development costs. GAAP require most marketing and selling costs and research and development costs incurred during a fiscal period to be reported as operating expenses of the period in which they occur. Because identifying how much of these costs is associated with benefits of future periods is difficult, GAAP require that these amounts be expensed to avoid an overstatement of profits during the current fiscal period.

The excess of gross profit over operating expenses is *operating income.* If operating expenses are greater than gross profit, a loss from operations results. Operating income is a measure of how much a company earned from its basic business activities.

A company is in the business of acquiring and selling products. Cost of goods sold and other operating expenses include the cost of acquiring and making its products available to customers. Sales revenues, sometimes referred to as operating revenues, are the total prices of the goods sold during a fiscal period. Therefore, operating income is a measure of how much a company made from selling its products, after considering normal and reoccurring expenses of doing business.

Other Revenues and Expenses

Revenues and expenses may occur that are not directly related to a company's primary operating activities. These are considered **non-operating** items and are reported separately on the income statement following operating income. The item listed in this category most often is interest expense. Borrowing money is frequently necessary for an organization's operations; however, except for financial institutions, it is not part of most businesses' primary operating activities. Accordingly, other expenses and revenues are reported on the income statement after operating income. This separate listing distinguishes them from revenues and expenses that result from a business's primary operating activities.

Income Taxes

Most corporations pay income taxes on their earnings. The amount of income tax expense is determined by applying tax rates required by current tax laws and regulations to the income earned by a company during a fiscal period. Exhibit 1 reports that Mom's Cookie Company incurred income taxes of 30% on its pretax income ($22,710 = $75,700 × 0.30).

As noted in Chapter F1, direct taxation of income is one of the disadvantages of corporations. Proprietorships and partnerships do not pay income taxes on their profits directly. Instead, those profits are treated as personal income of the owners. Owners pay income tax on a proprietorship's profits or on their share of the profits of a partnership as part of personal taxes.

LEARNING NOTE

Not all U.S. corporations pay income taxes on profits. Certain small corporations, known as Subchapter S corporations in the tax laws, are treated like partnerships for tax purposes. Each stockholder is taxed on his or her share of the corporation's profits.

Net Income

Net income, or net earnings, is the amount of profit earned by a company during a fiscal period. It represents an increase in owners' or stockholders' equity, and it can be either distributed to owners or reinvested in the company. Distributions to owners, such as dividends, are not an expense. They are a deduction from retained earnings when a transfer is made to owners of a portion of a company's earnings. Undistributed earnings are included in retained earnings on a company's balance sheet.

LEARNING NOTE

It is important to note that cash dividends and cash withdrawals are paid out of cash. Therefore, a company must have sufficient cash available before it can pay dividends or before owners can withdraw money. Remember that net income does not guarantee that a company will have favorable cash flows during a period.

Earnings Per Share

GAAP require that corporate income statements prepared for distribution to stockholders and other external users present earnings per share as part of the statement. ***Earnings per share* is a measure of the earnings performance of each share of common stock during a fiscal period. *Common stock* is the stock that conveys primary ownership rights in a corporation.** We examine other types of stock in a later chapter. In general, earnings per share is computed by dividing net income by the average number of shares of common stock outstanding during a fiscal period. By multiplying earnings per share times the number of shares they own, stockholders can identify the amount of profit or loss associated with their individual investments.

The average number of common shares is based on the number of shares a company has outstanding, weighted by the portion of the fiscal period the stock is outstanding. To illustrate, assume Mom's Cookie Company was formed on January 1, 2004, as a corporation by issuing 1,000 shares of stock to Maria and Stan (500 shares each). Then, on September 1, 2004, the company issued an additional 9,000 shares of stock to other stockholders. Consequently, the company had 1,000 shares outstanding for 8 months (January through August) and 10,000 shares outstanding for 4 months (September through December).

The **average number of shares outstanding** was:

$$4{,}000 \text{ shares} = (1{,}000 \text{ shares} \times 8/12) + (10{,}000 \text{ shares} \times 4/12)$$

Earnings per share for Mom's Cookie Company was computed as follows:

$$\$13.25^{*} \text{ earnings per share} = \frac{\$52{,}990 \text{ net income}}{4{,}000 \text{ average common shares}}$$

*rounded

Other Reporting Issues

Income statements of actual companies vary in format and terminology from that presented in Exhibit 1. Though it is not possible to present all the possibilities that you may encounter in practice, certain issues are common for most corporate reports. These are apparent from a review of an actual corporate income statement. Exhibit 2 provides the income statement for **Krispy Kreme Doughnuts, Inc.**, from its 2002 annual report.

Exhibit 2 Income Statement for Krispy Kreme

Krispy Kreme Doughnuts, Inc.
Consolidated Statements of Operations

(In thousands, except per share amounts)

Year ended	Jan. 30, 2000	Jan. 28, 2001	Feb. 3, 2002
Total revenues	$220,243	$300,715	$394,354
Operating expenses	190,003	250,690	316,946
General and administrative expenses	14,856	20,061	27,562
Depreciation and amortization expenses	4,546	6,457	7,959
Income from operations	10,838	23,507	41,887
Interest income	293	2,325	2,980
Interest expense	(1,525)	(607)	(337)
Equity loss in joint ventures	—	(706)	(602)
Minority interest	—	(716)	(1,147)
Loss on sale of property and equipment	—	(20)	(235)
Income before income taxes	9,606	23,783	42,546
Provision for income taxes	3,650	9,058	16,168
Net income	$ 5,956	$ 14,725	$ 26,378
Basic earnings per share	$ 0.16	$ 0.30	$ 0.49
Diluted earnings per share	$ 0.15	$ 0.27	$ 0.45

First note that the title of Krispy Kreme's statement is labeled "consolidated statements of operations." Most large corporations include a number of companies owned by the corporation. **The controlling corporation is referred to as the *parent* and the companies owned or controlled by the parent are its *subsidiaries. Consolidated financial statements* include the activities of the parent and its subsidiaries as though they were one company.** Thus, Krispy Kreme's income statement reports profits for the entire corporation, including all subsidiaries it owns.

Most corporations, like Krispy Kreme, report income statements for three fiscal years. Krispy Kreme's fiscal year ends with the Sunday closest to the end of January. Three years of data permit readers to evaluate how company performance has changed in recent years. Also observe that amounts, except per share amounts, are in thousands of dollars. Thus, revenues for 2002 were greater than $394 million. ***Total revenue* is the amount earned from selling goods and services.**

The items presented in a company's income statement vary depending on the type of company. Any items that are uncommon and that are important relative to the total income of the company should be reported as a separate income statement item. For example, Krispy Kreme reports store operating expenses and depreciation and amortization as separate operating expenses. ***Amortization expense,*** like depreciation expense, **is the allocation of the cost of long-term intangible assets to the fiscal periods that benefit from their use.** We consider intangible assets later in this chapter and amortization expense in Chapter F11. Krispy Kreme also lists "equity loss in joint ventures" as a separate item. This loss resulted from a cooperative effort between Krispy Kreme and other companies and represents Krispy Kreme's share of the loss from these ventures.

Krispy Kreme also reports "minority interest" as a separate item. Minority interest on the income statement is that portion of the income of Krispy Kreme's subsidiaries that cannot be claimed by Krispy Kreme. For example, if Krispy Kreme owns 90% of a subsidiary and the subsidiary's net income is $1 million, Krispy Kreme's share of the net income would be $900,000. The remaining $100,000 would be the minority interest in the income. Because the reported revenues and expenses on the consolidated statement include the subsidiary amounts in them, Krispy Kreme subtracts the minority interest on the income statement. This indicates Krispy Kreme does not have a claim to that share of subsidiary income.

Items appearing after income from operations represent revenues and expenses that are not part of a company's primary operating activities. Interest, joint venture income or loss, minority interest, and gain or loss on sale of property and equipment are nonoperating revenues and expenses because they are not part of a company's primary operating activities. Many companies report "net interest" by combining interest revenue and interest expense into one item.

For some corporations, earnings per share is complicated because the company has issued financial instruments, such as long-term liabilities, that can be exchanged for shares of common stock or that might result in the issuance of additional shares if certain conditions are met. If issued, the additional shares of common stock would reduce earnings per share. These companies, like Krispy Kreme, report two sets of earnings per share numbers, **basic and diluted earnings per share**. Basic earnings per share (as described above) is calculated without considering the effect of the additional shares that could be issued. Diluted earnings per share is adjusted for the effects of additional shares that could be issued. Diluted earnings per share is never greater than basic earnings per share. It is a more conservative measure of earnings per share during a period than is basic earnings per share.

LEARNING NOTE

You should become familiar with the variety of terms that are used by companies in their financial statements. "Net earnings" is often substituted for "net income" for example. Real companies do not follow textbook formats in presenting their statements. As you increase your understanding of the basic content of these statements, you will be able to determine the meaning of terms used by most companies.

1 SELF-STUDY PROBLEM

WebTUTOR Advantage

An income statement for **IBM Corporation** for a recent fiscal year is provided below.

IBM Corporation
Income Statement

(Dollars in millions except per share amounts)	
FOR THE YEAR ENDED DECEMBER 31:	*2001*
REVENUE:	
Global Services	$34,956
Hardware	33,392
Software	12,939
Global Financing	3,426
Enterprise Investments/Other	1,153
TOTAL REVENUE	85,866
COST OF SALES AND SERVICES:	
Global Services	25,355
Hardware	24,137
Software	2,265
Global Financing	1,693
Enterprise Investments/Other	634
TOTAL COST OF SALES AND SERVICES	54,084
GROSS PROFIT	31,782
OTHER EXPENSE AND INCOME:	
Selling, general and administrative	17,197
Research, development and engineering	5,290
Intellectual property and custom development income	(1,535)
Other (income) and expense	(361)
Interest expense	238
TOTAL OTHER EXPENSE AND INCOME	20,829
INCOME BEFORE INCOME TAXES	10,953
Provision for income taxes	3,230
NET INCOME	$ 7,723
EARNINGS PER SHARE OF COMMON STOCK:	
ASSUMING DILUTION	$4.35
BASIC	$4.45

Required Use this statement to answer the following questions:

1. How much revenue did IBM earn from selling computers?
2. How much revenue did IBM earn from other operating activities?
3. How much gross profit did IBM earn?
4. How much expense did IBM incur for non-operating activities?
5. Approximately how many shares of stock did IBM have outstanding?
6. What were IBM's total product costs?
7. How much net income did IBM earn?
8. How much cash did IBM receive from its operating activities during the year?

The solution to Self-Study Problem 1 appears at the end of the chapter.

THE BALANCE SHEET

OBJECTIVE 3

Explain information presented on a company's balance sheet.

A balance sheet reports the asset, liability, and owners' equity account balances for a company at the end of a fiscal period. Exhibit 3 provides a balance sheet for Mom's Cookie Company for the year ended December 31, 2004.

Recall that the total amount of assets reported on the balance sheet at the end of a fiscal period must be equal to the total amount of liabilities and owners' equity. This relationship, assets = liabilities + owners' equity, is the fundamental balance sheet equation.

Exhibit 3 provides a **classified** balance sheet in which assets and liabilities are separated by type. The primary sections of the balance sheet are described in the following paragraphs.

LEARNING NOTE

An organization's **operating cycle** is the period from the time cash is used to acquire or produce goods until these goods are sold and cash is received. The operating cycles of most organizations are less than 12 months. A fiscal year is the primary reporting period for these companies. Occasionally, a company's operating cycle is longer than 12 months. In such cases, which are rare, current assets are defined as those that a company expects to convert to cash or consume during the next operating cycle.

Current Assets

GAAP require companies to report their current assets separately from their long-term assets. ***Current assets*** **are cash or other resources that management expects to convert to cash or consume during the next fiscal year.** Some current assets are liquid assets. ***Liquid assets*** **are resources that can be converted to cash in a relatively short period.** Cash equivalents include securities that are easily converted to cash and that have a short maturity, usually less than three

Exhibit 3

A Corporate Balance Sheet

Mom's Cookie Company
Balance Sheet
At December 31, 2004

Assets	
Current assets:	
Cash	$ 10,680
Accounts receivable	8,570
Merchandise inventory	23,600
Supplies	690
Prepaid rent	2,000
Total current assets	45,540
Property and equipment, at cost	215,660
Accumulated depreciation	(25,500)
Total assets	$235,700
Liabilities and Stockholders' Equity	
Current liabilities:	
Accounts payable	$ 9,610
Unearned revenue	4,250
Interest payable	650
Notes payable, current portion	5,000
Total current liabilities	19,510
Notes payable, long-term	73,200
Total liabilities	92,710
Stockholders' equity:	
Common stock, 10,000 shares issued	100,000
Retained earnings	42,990
Total stockholders' equity	142,990
Total liabilities and stockholders' equity	$235,700

months. In addition to cash and equivalents, current assets include (1) accounts receivable for which a company expects to receive cash during the next fiscal year, (2) inventory a company expects to sell during the next fiscal year, and (3) resources a company expects to consume during the next fiscal year, such as supplies and prepaid insurance, generally referred to as prepaid expenses.

Property and Equipment

Property and equipment, **often called** *fixed assets* **or** *plant assets,* **are long-term, tangible assets that are used in a company's operations.** (*Long-term intangible assets* **are those that provide benefits to the company for more than one fiscal period.**) Unlike inventory, these assets are not intended for resale. U.S. GAAP require fixed assets, other than land, to be depreciated over their estimated useful lives. Depreciation allocates the cost of these assets to the fiscal periods that benefit from their use as a means of matching expenses with revenues. The net value of fixed assets is the cost of the assets minus accumulated depreciation.

Land is not depreciated because it is not used up. Natural resources, such as petroleum, minerals, or timber, are accounted for separately from land and other property assets. The costs of these assets are allocated to expense over the periods that are expected to benefit from the use of the assets. **The process of allocating the cost of natural resources to expenses is known as** *depletion.* We examine depletion in Chapter F11.

Liabilities

GAAP require companies to report their current liabilities separately from their long-term liabilities. *Current liabilities* **are those obligations that management expects to fulfill during the next fiscal year.** *Long-term liabilities* **are those obligations not classified as current liabilities.**

Current liabilities include amounts owed by a company that will be paid during the coming fiscal year. Accounts, wages, interest, and income taxes payable all fit in this category. Unearned revenues that will be earned during the coming fiscal year also are classified as current assets.

The portion of long-term debt that will become due and be paid during the next year is a current liability. Exhibit 3 identifies this amount as "Notes payable, current portion." For example, assume Mom's Cookie Co. issued $80,000 in long-term notes payable during 2004. The notes are to be repaid in annual installments of $5,000. Therefore, $5,000 of the notes would be reported as a current liability on a balance sheet prepared at December 31, 2004. The unpaid balance would be reported as a long-term liability. From Exhibit 3 you can determine that $1,800 ($80,000 borrowed less $5,000 current portion and $73,200 long-term portion) of the notes was repaid in 2004, the year of issue.

The difference between current assets and current liabilities is known as *working capital.* Because current assets include those assets that are likely to produce cash inflows for a company and current liabilities include those liabilities that are likely to produce cash outflows, working capital is a measure of a company's liquidity. A company with a large amount of working capital should have little difficulty meeting its short-term obligations. Mom's Cookie Company reports $26,030 ($45,540 of current assets − $19,510 of current liabilities) of working capital in 2004.

Working capital often is reported as a ratio. **The ratio of current assets to current liabilities is the** *working capital ratio* **or** *current ratio.* Mom's Cookie Company's current ratio for 2004 is 2.33 ($45,540 ÷ $19,510).

Stockholders' Equity

Stockholders' equity includes (1) amounts paid by owners to a corporation for the purchase of shares of stock and (2) retained earnings, profits reinvested in the corporation.

Common stock, as noted earlier, conveys basic ownership rights in a corporation. We examine other types of stock in Chapter F9.

Other Balance Sheet Content

Like the income statement, the balance sheet may appear in a variety of formats. Companies may use reporting rules that differ from those previously described. Some types of companies—many utilities, for example—report fixed assets prior to current assets and report stockholders' equity prior to liabilities. Companies in the United States often use formats that differ from those used in other countries. The items included on a balance sheet depend on the activities of a company.

Exhibit 4 provides the balance sheet from Krispy Kreme's 2002 annual report. Krispy Kreme's balance sheet is **comparative** because it contains information for more than one year. Also, it is consolidated because it includes all the companies owned by the parent corporation.

Other Current Assets

In addition to current assets we considered earlier, Krispy Kreme reports short-term investments and deferred income taxes. **Short-term investments** are stocks or debt of other companies owned by Krispy Kreme that it expects to sell in the near future. **Deferred income taxes** listed as current assets are prepaid taxes. These are taxes that the company has paid but that are associated with income tax expense of the coming fiscal period. The deferred taxes will be written off to income tax expense in a future period.

Krispy Kreme reports its accounts receivable net of allowances. The allowances are **estimated uncollectible accounts.** (These are sometimes referred to as **allowance for doubtful accounts** or **allowance for bad debts.**) When companies sell goods on credit, thus creating accounts receivable, it is likely that some customers will be unable to pay for their purchases. Companies are required by GAAP to estimate the amount of uncollectible receivables each fiscal period and to subtract that amount from their gross accounts receivable. The amount reported on the balance sheet for accounts receivable is the gross amount (total accounts receivable) minus the expected uncollectible amount (allowance). The net amount is the amount the company expects to collect from customers. We examine receivables in more detail in Chapter F13.

Other Long-Term Assets

In addition to property and equipment, long-term assets may include non-current receivables; fixed assets held for sale; prepaid expenses not expected to be consumed in the next fiscal year; long-term legal rights such as patents, trademarks, and copyrights; and long-term investments. These types of assets may be listed on the balance sheet under separate headings if they constitute a significant portion of a company's assets. Otherwise, they often are listed simply as Other Assets.

Accounts and notes receivable that a company does not expect to collect during the next fiscal year are not included among current assets. These items are reported as long-term assets. Fixed assets that a company is not using currently but is holding for future use, disposal, or sale also are included in this category. For example, land held for a future factory site would be listed here.

Long-term legal rights resulting from the ownership of patents, copyrights, trademarks, and similar items are known as *intangible assets*, in contrast to tangible assets such as property and equipment. Goodwill is a special type of intangible asset that can occur when one company acquires another company. ***Goodwill* is the excess of the price paid for a company over the fair market value of the net assets (assets less liabilities) of the acquired company.**

***Long-term investments* occur when a company lends money to or purchases stock issued by other organizations and does not intend to sell those investments in the**

Exhibit 4 Balance Sheet for Krispy Kreme

Krispy Kreme Doughnuts, Inc.
Consolidated Balance Sheets

(In thousands)	**Jan. 28, 2001**	**Feb. 3, 2002**
ASSETS		
Current Assets:		
Cash and cash equivalents	$ 7,026	$ 21,904
Short-term investments	18,103	15,292
Accounts receivable, less allowance for doubtful accounts of $1,302 (2001) and $1,182 (2002)	19,855	26,894
Inventories	12,031	16,159
Prepaid expenses and other current assets	6,787	16,913
Deferred income taxes	3,809	4,607
Total current assets	67,611	101,769
Property and equipment, net	78,340	112,577
Long-term investments	17,877	12,700
Investment in joint ventures	2,827	3,400
Intangible assets	—	16,621
Other assets	4,838	8,309
Total assets	$171,493	$255,376
LIABILITIES AND SHAREHOLDERS' EQUITY		
Current Liabilities:		
Accounts payable	$ 8,211	$ 12,095
Book overdraft	5,147	9,107
Accrued expenses	21,243	26,729
Revolving line of credit	3,526	3,871
Current maturities of long-term debt	—	731
Income taxes payable	41	—
Total current liabilities	38,168	52,533
Deferred income taxes	579	3,930
Long-term debt, net of current portion	—	3,912
Other long-term obligations	5,950	4,843
Total long-term liabilities	6,529	12,685
Minority interest	1,117	2,491
SHAREHOLDERS' EQUITY:		
Common stock, no par value, 100,000 shares authorized; issued and outstanding — 51,832 (2001) and 54,271 (2002)	85,060	121,052
Accumulated other comprehensive income and other items	(1,928)	(2,310)
Retained earnings	42,547	68,925
Total shareholders' equity	125,679	187,667
Total liabilities and shareholders' equity	$171,493	$255,376

coming fiscal year. Companies often invest in other companies to share in their earnings or to obtain access to resources, management skills, technology, and markets available to other companies. If management expects to hold these investments beyond the next fiscal year, they are classified as long-term investments. We examine accounting for each of these assets in later chapters.

Joint ventures reported on the balance sheet is the amount Krispy Kreme has invested in these ventures. **Joint ventures** involve cooperative efforts among two or more companies, with each company providing some of the financing for the venture, and each company sharing in the profits or losses from these ventures.

Other Current Liabilities

The current liabilities listed on Krispy Kreme's balance sheet are similar to those we have discussed for Mom's Cookie Company. The titles used for these liabilities are different, however. Accrued expenses is simply another name for liabilities such as wages payable and rent payable. One of the challenges of reading financial statements is becoming familiar with the wide variety of labels companies use.

The current liability, book overdraft, is a bit unusual. It suggests the company has overdrawn its checking accounts. In actuality it reflects the fact that Krispy Kreme has many bank accounts it uses to pay for business activities in various locations. It moves money from its primary bank accounts to these other accounts daily, as needed to meet operating expenses. At times, checks are written on these local accounts before cash is transferred to the accounts. These amounts are reported in the book overdraft category and indicate timing differences between when checks were written and cash was transferred. The category does not indicate a financial problem for the company. **A careful review of notes to the financial statements sometimes is important to understand the items reported by a company in those statements.**

Other Long-Term Liabilities

In addition to long-term debt, Krispy Kreme reports deferred taxes and minority interest. When **deferred taxes** are reported as a long-term liability, they represent income tax expenses that have not been paid and will not be paid during the coming year. Deferred taxes occur because of timing differences between when corporations recognize revenues and expenses for tax purposes and when those revenues and expenses are recognized for financial reporting purposes. If pretax income on a company's income statement exceeds its taxable income for tax purposes, a portion of the income tax expense a company recognizes will not be paid until some future fiscal period.

Minority interest, also known as **noncontrolling interest** (or **NCI**), represents the portion of a corporation's subsidiaries not owned by the parent corporation. Krispy Kreme reports $2,491,000 of minority interest on its 2002 balance sheet. This is the value of that portion of the subsidiaries not owned by Krispy Kreme. Note that the balance sheet amount refers to the book value of the subsidiary (assets less liabilities) owned rather than to the portion of income associated with noncontrolling owners that is reported on the income statement. Valuation of noncontrolling interest is a topic covered in advanced financial accounting texts.

Stockholders' Equity and Comprehensive Income

Like Mom's Cookie Company, Krispy Kreme reports common stock and retained earnings. The number of shares of common stock authorized is the maximum number of shares the company could issue under its current charter. The number of shares issued (54,271,000 for 2002) is the total number of shares that the company has sold to stockholders.

In addition to net income reported on the income statement, companies must report other comprehensive income. ***Comprehensive income* is the change in a company's owners' equity during a period that is the result of all non-owner transactions and activities.** Comprehensive income includes profits resulting from normal operating activities. It includes any event that changes owners' equity except those arising from dealings with the company's own stockholders. Accordingly, it excludes events such as selling stock or paying dividends. Comprehensive income also includes some activities that are not reported on the income statement.

Three items that are not included in net income are included as part of **other comprehensive income**. These are (a) gains or losses from holding certain marketable securities, (b) certain gains or losses from foreign currency effects on foreign subsidiaries, and (c) certain changes in the minimum liability for employee pensions. These items are reported as part of other comprehensive income that is included in stockholders' equity. Gains and losses from holding marketable securities are discussed in Chapter F11.

INTERNATIONAL

Foreign currency transactions occur when a corporation operates in other countries or owns subsidiaries outside of the U.S. These international activities involve currencies other than U.S. dollars. To prepare financial statements that are stated in U.S. dollars, those activities have to be translated from foreign currency amounts using exchange rates that are appropriate for the transaction. In some cases, U.S. currency must be exchanged for foreign currency or vice versa. Gains or losses can occur from changes in exchange rates. Gains or losses associated with foreign currency translations and exchanges are reported as part of other comprehensive income.

Changes in employee pension liabilities occur when estimates change about the amount a company can earn on assets it has invested to cover these liabilities or when other estimates change that affect the amount employees will receive in pension payments. These changes result in gains or losses that are reported as part of other comprehensive income.

Keep in mind that financial statements of actual companies can be complex because of the many types of business activities in which companies are involved. Understanding basic concepts of assets, liabilities, and owners' equity will help you interpret this information.

2 SELF-STUDY PROBLEM

Listed below are account balances, cash receipts and payments, and other data for Lewy Pasture, Inc., a company that distributes pharmaceutical supplies, for the fiscal year ended October 31, 2004.

WebTUTOR™ Advantage

Accounts payable	$ 22,000
Accounts receivable	11,000
Accumulated depreciation	164,000
Buildings	412,000
Cash	16,000
Common stock	300,000
Cost of goods sold	146,000
Dividends (declared and paid)	17,000
Equipment	245,000
General and administrative expenses	96,000
Goodwill	13,000
Income tax expense	14,000
Income tax payable	6,000
Interest expense	25,000
Interest payable	14,000
Land	35,000
Long-term investments	35,000
Merchandise inventory	62,000
Notes payable, current portion	10,000
Notes payable, long-term	278,000
Prepaid insurance	7,000
Retained earnings, October 31, 2003	25,000
Sales revenue	357,000
Selling expenses	47,000
Supplies	13,000
Wages payable	18,000

The average number of shares of common stock outstanding during the year was 10,000.

Required From the data presented on the previous page, determine the amount of each of the following items for Lewy Pasture's financial statements:

1. Gross profit
2. Income from operations
3. Net income
4. Earnings per share
5. Current assets
6. Land, buildings, and equipment
7. Other assets
8. Total assets
9. Current liabilities
10. Total liabilities
11. Retained earnings, October 31, 2004
12. Total stockholders' equity
13. Total liabilities and stockholders' equity

The solution to Self-Study Problem 2 appears at the end of the chapter.

THE STATEMENT OF STOCKHOLDERS' EQUITY

OBJECTIVE 4

Explain information presented on a company's statement of stockholders' equity.

The statement of stockholders' equity provides information about changes in owners' equity for a corporation during a fiscal period. Exhibit 5 provides an example of this statement for Krispy Kreme. Though Krispy Kreme, like other corporations, presents three years of data for this statement in its annual report, only one year is included in Exhibit 5.

Exhibit 5 reports the number of shares of stock issued by Krispy Kreme at the beginning and end of the 2002 fiscal year, and describes changes in the amount associated with stock options, sale of stock, and other activities. The dollar amount of stock issued increased during 2002, as well. The amount of common stock issued at the end of the 2002 fiscal year ($121,052,000) is equal to the amount reported for common stock on the balance sheet in Exhibit 4.

A primary reason for the increase in common stock was related to **stock options**. Corporations often use stock option plans to provide an opportunity for employees to receive shares of stock for achieving corporate goals. To provide stock to employees and for other purposes, corporations repurchase shares from stockholders.

Retained earnings increased by the amount of net income earned in 2002. Retained earnings would decrease by the amount of dividends paid or promised (declared) during the fiscal year. However, Krispy Kreme did not pay any dividends during its 2002 fiscal year. Dividends are not reported on the income statement because they are not expenses. They are a distribution of net income to owners. **Dividends are a reduction in retained earnings and are reported on the statement of stockholders' equity.**

Accumulated other comprehensive income increases (or decreases) by the amount of other comprehensive income reported during a fiscal period. Krispy Kreme reported a holding loss of $111,000 and foreign currency translation losses of $42,000 during 2002. Remember that these losses are not reported on the income statement in the calculation of net income. The holding loss reported by Krispy Kreme is unrealized because the securities that created the holding loss have not been sold. Their market value decreased during the period, and the amount of the decrease is reported as a holding loss. When Krispy Kreme actually sells the securities, any gain or loss from the sale will be reported on the income statement. Krispy Kreme's other comprehensive income decreased during 2002 and the balance of its accumulated other comprehensive income is negative (a loss). The balance considers the effects of previous years' gains and losses. These gains and losses are added together from year to year to obtain the total reported on the statement of stockholders' equity. The ending balance also is reported on the balance sheet as part of stockholders' equity, see Exhibit 4.

Exhibit 5 Changes in Corporate Equity

Krispy Kreme Doughnuts, Inc.
Consolidated Statement Of Shareholders' Equity

(In thousands)	Common Shares	Common Stock	Retained Earnings	Accumulated Other Comprehensive Income & Other	Total
Balance at January 28, 2001	51,832	$ 85,060	$42,547	$(1,928)	$125,679
Net income			26,378		26,378
Unrealized holding loss, net				(111)	(111)
Translation adjustment				(42)	(42)
Total comprehensive income					26,225
Proceeds from sale of stock	1,086	17,202			17,202
Exercise of stock options	1,183	13,678			13,678
Other	170	5,112		(229)	4,883
Balance at February 3, 2002	54,271	$121,052	$68,925	$(2,310)	$187,667

The ending balances on the statement of stockholders' equity are the amounts reported on the corporation's balance sheet for the same date. Compare the ending balances in each column of Exhibit 5 with the amounts in Exhibit 4. The statement of stockholders' equity describes the events that changed Krispy Kreme's stockholders' equity during its 2002 fiscal year.

USE OF FINANCIAL STATEMENTS

Financial statements are a primary source of accounting information for external decision makers. External users analyze statements to evaluate the ability of an organization to use its resources effectively and efficiently. By comparing changes in assets, liabilities, earnings, and cash flows over time, users form expectations about return and risk. Comparisons across companies help determine which companies are being managed effectively and provide the best investment opportunities.

Later chapters of this book describe methods of analyzing and interpreting financial statements. The remainder of this chapter considers attributes of financial statements that decision makers should understand when interpreting them.

Interrelationships among Financial Statements

Taken as a whole, financial statements describe business activities that changed the financial condition of a company from the beginning to the end of a fiscal period. Information on the income statement and statement of cash flows explains changes in balance sheet accounts during a period.

The summary information presented in financial statements does not always provide sufficient detail to explain the change in every balance sheet account. Access to individual account balances would be necessary to provide a complete explanation. Nevertheless, the relationships among the financial statements are important. Balance sheets for the beginning and ending of a fiscal period reveal changes in a company's resources and finances. The company's income statement and statement of cash flows reveal major events that caused these changes. **The relationship among financial statements in which the numbers on one statement explain numbers on other statements is called *articulation*.** You should remember that a company's financial statements are not independent of each other. They work together to explain the events that changed the company's financial condition.

Limitations of Financial Statements

OBJECTIVE 5

Identify some of the primary limitations of financial statements.

In spite of the abundant information financial statements provide, their usefulness is limited by certain constraints of the reporting process. Some of these limitations include:

1. Use of estimates and allocations
2. Use of historical costs
3. Omission of transactions
4. Omission of resources and costs
5. Delay in providing information

These constraints result primarily from costs associated with reporting financial information. Information is a resource, and it is costly to provide. Its value is determined by the benefits derived by those who use the information. For information to be valuable, its cost must be less than the benefits it provides to users. Therefore, the amount and type of reported information are constrained by costs and benefits.

The following paragraphs consider these limitations. Users should keep these limitations in mind when interpreting financial statement information.

Use of Estimates and Allocations. **Many of the numbers reported in financial statements result from estimates and allocations.** For example, depreciation is the allocation of asset costs to expenses over the estimated lives of the assets. These estimates often are not exact because the amount of the asset consumed in a particular fiscal period is difficult to determine. Decisions about when to recognize revenues and expenses frequently require management judgment. These subjective decisions and estimates mean that accounting numbers are not as precise as they might appear.

Use of Historical Costs. **Financial statements report primarily the historical cost of assets and liabilities. *Historical cost* is the purchase or exchange price of an asset or liability at the time it is acquired or incurred.** The recorded values are not adjusted for changes in the purchasing power of money or for changes in the current value of the assets or liabilities. The purchasing power of money changes over time because of inflation; for example, a dollar in 2003 buys less than a dollar bought in 1983. The current value of an asset is the amount at which that asset, in its current condition, could be bought or sold at the present time.

INTERNATIONAL

Certain assets and liabilities, particularly financial securities such as investments in stocks, are reported at market value in the United States. We will examine these reporting rules in a later chapter. Some countries, such as the United Kingdom and the Netherlands, permit plant assets and other items to be reported using current values. In these countries, assets and liabilities are restated to approximate their market values at the end of a fiscal period.

Omission of Transactions. Financial statements include the primary transactions that occur as part of a company's business activities. Nevertheless, **there is no guarantee that all important transactions are fully reported in a company's financial statements.** Some transactions do not result from specific exchanges. They result when revenues or expenses are allocated to fiscal periods. Accountants and managers sometimes disagree about when certain activities should be recognized. Also, they may disagree about the amount that should be reported in the financial statements for these activities. The accounting profession has debated extensively issues such as how to recognize the costs of employee retirement benefits. Today, companies report certain liabilities, assets, and expenses associated with these items that were not reported 10 years ago. Undoubtedly, other issues will arise that will alter information reported in the financial statements.

The importance of information changes over time. Companies develop new financing and compensation arrangements. Reporting rules for these arrangements may not be covered by existing GAAP. If the arrangements become common and new reporting rules would increase the benefits of information for users, GAAP may be created for transactions involving these new arrangements. GAAP are dynamic. They change as the needs of users and economic activities of organizations change.

Omission of Resources and Costs. **Certain types of resources and costs are not reported in financial statements.** The value of employees is not an asset listed on most balance sheets. Nevertheless, a well-trained and stable workforce and skilled managers may be the resource that adds the most to the value of many companies. Without skilled labor and management, the remaining resources of a company often would have little value. Financial statements do not report these human resources. They are not owned by a company, and their values are difficult and costly to determine. A major portion of the value of many companies derives from their research and development activities, which create new and improved products. The costs of these efforts are expensed when they are incurred each fiscal period even though they may have a major effect on the future earnings of a company. Such costs are expensed because of difficulty in identifying the timing and amount of future benefits a company will receive from these efforts. Nevertheless, the economic value of a company differs from the amount reported on its financial statements because of these measurement limitations.

Delay in Providing Information. **Financial statement information is not always timely.** Annual financial statements may lag actual events by a year or more; even monthly statements may lag events by several weeks. While such delays may not be a problem for certain types of decisions, they may be critical for others. Users often need more timely sources. Managers, in particular, may need information on an ongoing basis to make effective decisions. Traditional financial statements are only one type of accounting information. Because financial statements are costly to produce and distribute, external reporting is limited to distinct fiscal periods. In addition to annual financial reports, major corporations provide quarterly reports to stockholders. As information technology reduces the cost of reporting, more frequent reporting to external users may become feasible.

Though a variety of problems impair their usefulness, financial statements continue to be a primary source of information for managers and external users about a company's activities. But these problems mean that considerable care is needed to understand accounting information and to use it correctly in making decisions.

3 SELF-STUDY PROBLEM

A series of financial statement items is listed below.

Accounts payable
Accounts receivable
Buildings
Common stock
Cost of goods sold
Depreciation expense
Dividends
Interest expense
Interest payable
Merchandise
Notes payable
Patents
Prepaid insurance
Retained earnings
Sales revenue
Stock issued
Stock repurchased
Supplies
Wages expense
Wages payable

Required For each account, indicate the financial statement (income statement, balance sheet, or statement of stockholders' equity) on which the account would appear.

The solution to Self-Study Problem 3 appears at the end of the chapter.

REVIEW

SUMMARY of IMPORTANT CONCEPTS

1. Financial statements report business activities.
   a. Financial statements include the balance sheet, the income statement, the statement of cash flows, and the statement of stockholders' equity.
   b. The income statement reports on the accrual basis the results of a company's operations for a fiscal period. It reports information about the creation and consumption of resources in producing and selling goods and services.
   c. A balance sheet identifies asset, liability, and owners' equity account balances at the end of a fiscal period. Balance sheets classify accounts into current and long-term asset and liability categories. Comparative balance sheets report account balances for more than one fiscal period.
   d. The statement of stockholders' equity describes the results of transactions that have changed the amount of stockholders' equity of a corporation during a fiscal period.

2. The interrelated financial statements, as a set, describe the financial effects of business activities of a company from the beginning to the end of a fiscal period.

3. Consolidated financial statements report the economic activities of a parent and its subsidiaries as though they were one business entity.

4. Financial statements have limitations that affect the usefulness of the information the statements report. These limitations include the need for estimates of financial results, the use of historical costs for representing asset values, and incomplete measures for some resources or transactions that might affect a company's value.

DEFINE

TERMS and CONCEPTS DEFINED in this CHAPTER

SELF-STUDY PROBLEM SOLUTIONS

SSP-1 (Answers in millions except numbers of shares)

1. Revenue from sale of computers	$33,392
2. Other operating revenue:	
Services	$34,956
Software	12,939
Financing	3,426
Enterprise investments and other	1,153
Total	$52,474
3. Gross profit	$31,782
4. Interest expense*	$238
5. Number of shares outstanding ($7,723 net income ÷ $4.45 basic earnings per share) = 1,736 million shares	
6. Total product costs	$54,084
7. Net income	$7,723
8. Net cash from operations cannot be determined from the income statement.	

*Other (income) and expense of $(361) may or may not be from non-operating activities. The notes to the income statement would provide more information.

SSP-2

1. Gross profit:	
Sales revenue	$357,000
Cost of goods sold	146,000
Gross profit	$211,000
2. Income from operations:	
Gross profit	$211,000
General and administrative expenses	96,000
Selling expenses	47,000
Income from operations	$ 68,000
3. Net income:	
Income from operations	$ 68,000
Interest expense	25,000
Income tax expense	14,000
Net income	$ 29,000
4. Earnings per share: Net income ÷ shares of common stock ($29,000 ÷ 10,000) = $2.90	
5. Current assets:	
Cash	$ 16,000
Accounts receivable	11,000
Merchandise inventory	62,000
Supplies	13,000
Prepaid insurance	7,000
Current assets	$109,000
6. Land, buildings, and equipment:	
Land	$ 35,000
Buildings	412,000
Equipment	245,000
Accumulated depreciation	(164,000)
Land, buildings, and equipment	$528,000
7. Other assets:	
Long-term investments	$ 35,000
Goodwill	13,000
Other assets	$ 48,000

8. Total assets:

Current assets	$109,000
Land, buildings, and equipment	528,000
Other assets	48,000
Total assets	$685,000

9. Current liabilities:

Accounts payable	$ 22,000
Wages payable	18,000
Interest payable	14,000
Income tax payable	6,000
Notes payable, current portion	10,000
Current liabilities	$ 70,000

10. Total liabilities:

Current liabilities	$ 70,000
Notes payable, long-term	278,000
Total liabilities	$348,000

11. Retained earnings, October 31, 2004:

Retained earnings, October 31, 2003	$ 25,000
Net income	29,000
Dividends	(17,000)
Retained earnings, October 31, 2004	$ 37,000

12. Total stockholders' equity:

Common stock	$300,000
Retained earnings	37,000
Stockholders' equity	$337,000

13. Total liabilities and stockholders' equity:

Total liabilities	$348,000
Stockholders' equity	337,000
Total liabilities and stockholders' equity	$685,000

SSP-3

Item	Financial Statement
Accounts payable	Balance sheet
Accounts receivable	Balance sheet
Buildings	Balance sheet
Common stock	Balance sheet and statement of stockholders' equity
Cost of goods sold	Income statement
Depreciation expense	Income statement
Dividends	Statement of stockholders' equity
Interest expense	Income statement
Interest payable	Balance sheet
Merchandise	Balance sheet
Notes payable	Balance sheet
Patents	Balance sheet
Prepaid insurance	Balance sheet
Retained earnings	Balance sheet and statement of stockholders' equity
Sales revenue	Income statement
Stock issued	Statement of stockholders' equity
Stock repurchased	Statement of stockholders' equity
Supplies	Balance sheet
Wages expense	Income statement
Wages payable	Balance sheet

Thinking Beyond the Question

How do we report earnings and financial position to stockholders?

This chapter describes important rules for corporations and other businesses when they report financial information to external users. We considered the need for separating ordinary revenues and expenses from those, such as interest revenue or expense, that are secondary to a business's primary purpose. Corporations report corporate taxes and earnings per share as part of their income statements. Balance sheets should distinguish between current and long-term assets and liabilities and should report details about common stock issued by a corporation. Changes in stockholders' equity should be described in the statement of stockholders' equity.

Why is it important for businesses to follow specific rules and use common formats in reporting their business activities? What would be the consequences for businesses and the economy if individual companies were permitted to select their own reporting rules?

QUESTIONS

Q4-1 *Obj. 1* Are dividends an expense? Sometimes? Always? Never? Explain.

Q4-2 *Obj. 1* Identify three questions that can be answered by reviewing a firm's income statement but that cannot be answered by reviewing the firm's balance sheet or statement of stockholders' equity. Be specific.

Q4-3 *Obj. 1* Identify three questions that can be answered by reviewing a firm's balance sheet but that cannot be answered by reviewing the firm's income statement or statement of stockholders' equity. Be specific.

Q4-4 *Obj. 2* Why are there so many different sections of information on an income statement?

Q4-5 *Obj. 2* Why does a parent company prepare consolidated financial statements?

Q4-6 *Obj. 2* A friend says, "The income statement doesn't reveal anything about the amount of cash that was received from sales during a fiscal period." Do you agree with this statement? Why or why not?

Q4-7 *Obj. 3* Explain the difference between a classified balance sheet and a comparative balance sheet.

Q4-8 *Obj. 3* In what way are the depreciation of plant, property, and equipment and the amortization of intangible assets alike? In what way are they different?

Q4-9 *Obj. 3* Assume you are reviewing a balance sheet that has assets listed on the left side and liabilities and owners' equity on the right side. What question or questions are answered by looking at the information on the left side of the balance sheet? What question or questions are answered by looking at the information on the right side of the balance sheet?

Q4-10 *Obj. 4* If all of the stockholders' equity accounts are reported on the balance sheet, why is the statement of stockholders' equity necessary?

Q4-11 *Obj. 4* The statement of stockholders' equity can be thought of as a bridge between the income statement and the balance sheet? Why?

Q4-12 *Obj. 4* What does the term *articulation* mean as applied to accounting and financial reporting?

Q4-13 *Objs. 3, 4* How do the purpose of the income statement, the purpose of the balance sheet, and the purpose of the statement of stockholders' equity differ?

Q4-14 *Obj. 5* Why is the use of historical cost information a limitation of financial statements?

Q4-15 *Obj. 5* It is often said that measuring performance for a fiscal period requires periodic measurement and the use of estimates and approximations. Do you agree that this is true? Why or why not?

EXERCISES

If your instructor is using Personal Trainer in this course, you may complete online the assignments identified by PT.

E4-1 Write a short definition for each of the terms listed in the *Terms and Concepts Defined in this Chapter* section.

E4-2 *Obj. 1* PT A list of information contained in financial statements is provided below. For each item, indicate which financial statement provides the information.

a. Changes in a corporation's stockholders' equity for a fiscal period
b. The dollar amount of resources available at a particular date
c. The amount of credit sales not yet collected
d. Accrual-based operating results for a fiscal period
e. The cost of resources consumed in producing revenues for a period
f. The sources of finances used to acquire resources
g. The effect of issuing stock on the amount of contributed capital during a period
h. The amount of profit earned during a period
i. Revenues generated during a fiscal period

E4-3 *Obj. 1* PT For each of the items listed below, indicate the financial statement (or statements) for which the information is true. Use *I* to indicate income statement, *B* to indicate balance sheet, and *SE* to indicate statement of stockholders' equity. If the item below is not true for any of the three financial statements, indicate with an *N*.

1. The statement provides information about resources consumed during an accounting period.
2. The portion of profits that were distributed to owners of the firm is disclosed.
3. The current market value of the firm's resources is reported.
4. The statement is dated as of a specific point in time.
5. The amounts that are owed to other organizations or individuals are reported.
6. The total amount of capital that has been contributed to the organization is reported.
7. The amount of capital that has been contributed to the organization during the accounting period just ended is reported.
8. Information is reported regarding the rewards that have been earned from serving customers during the accounting period just ended.
9. The statement is not as of a specific date, but covers a period of time.
10. Reports information that has been developed on the accrual basis.
11. The statement contains information about the financial sacrifices that were made to acquire resources.
12. The statement contains information concerning contributed capital.
13. The statement contains information concerning the results of operating activities.
14. The amount of stock sold during the accounting period just ended is disclosed.
15. The information provided links two other statements.

E4-4 *Obj. 2* Alex didn't study very hard when he took accounting because he thought he wouldn't ever use it on the job at Valentine Company. Yesterday, after preparing all end-of-the-month adjusting entries, both of the company's accounting staff became ill. The company owner, knowing that Alex had taken accounting as part of his college major, asked him to finish the job by preparing the financial statements. The owner needs the statements tomorrow to present to her banker. Alex isn't sure that his income statement is prepared properly.

Valentine Company Income Statement at September 30, 2004	
Sales revenue	$48,500
Wages expense	11,369
Operating income	**37,131**
Operating expenses:	
Advertising	3,133
Cost of goods sold	30,070
Insurance	670
Interest expense	240
Utilities	1,250
Gross profit	**1,768**
Depreciation expense	282
Pretax income	**1,486**
Income tax expense	519
Net income	$ 967

Alex is confident that each revenue account and expense account balance is correct because those were determined by the accounting staff. He is unsure, however, that he has organized them properly on the income statement. Therefore, he is unsure about the summary amounts listed in bold-faced print on the statement.

Rearrange the accounts into proper income statement format. Be sure to date the statement correctly.

E4-5 *Obj. 2* P/T Slotnick Company sells, rents, and services ski equipment. Information about the company's financial performance for a recent fiscal period is provided below.

Average shares outstanding	20,000
Cost of goods sold	$34,000
Debt outstanding	65,000
General and administrative expenses	12,000
Income tax expense	20,000
Interest expense	8,000
Payments to owners	30,000
Rental revenue	45,000
Sales revenue	79,000
Selling expense	27,000
Service revenue	23,000

From the information provided, compute the following amounts for the period:

a. Gross profit
b. Operating expenses
c. Income from operations
d. Pretax income
e. Net income
f. Earnings per share

E4-6 *Obj. 2* Flowers by Freddie presented the income statement below for its most recent fiscal year. The items have been numbered for convenience in analysis.

(1) Sales revenue	$371,923
(2) Cost of goods sold	201,668
(3) Gross profit	170,255
(4) Operating expenses	72,853
(5) Operating income	97,402
(6) Other revenues	538
(7) Other expenses	(13,227)
(8) Pretax income	84,713
(9) Income taxes	29,650
(10) Net income	$ 55,063

(Continued)

Answer the following questions. Be specific. Give examples to clarify.

a. What is the difference between the revenue listed in item 1 and that listed in item 6?
b. What does item 3 represent, and why is it important?
c. What do items 2, 4, and 7 have in common?
d. How are items 2, 4, and 7 different from one another?
e. How is item 9 similar to items 2, 4, and 7?
f. Why do you think items 2, 4, 7, and 9 are listed separately on an income statement rather than being lumped together as one item?

E4-7 *Obj. 2* An income statement for **Delta Air Lines, Inc.**, for a recent fiscal year is provided below:

Delta Air Lines, Inc.
Consolidated Statements of Operations
For the Year Ended December 31, 2001

(In millions, except per share data)	
OPERATING REVENUES:	
Passenger	$12,964
Cargo	506
Other, net	409
Total operating revenues	13,879
OPERATING EXPENSES:	
Salaries and related costs	6,124
Aircraft fuel	1,817
Depreciation and amortization	1,283
Passenger commissions	540
Contracted services	1,016
Landing fees and other rents	780
Aircraft rent	737
Aircraft maintenance materials and outside repairs	801
Passenger service	466
Other	1,917
Total operating expenses	15,481
OPERATING INCOME (LOSS)	(1,602)
OTHER INCOME (EXPENSE):	
Interest expense, net	(410)
Other income	148
LOSS BEFORE INCOME TAXES	(1,864)
INCOME TAX BENEFIT	648
NET LOSS	$ (1,216)
BASIC EARNINGS (LOSS) PER SHARE	$(9.99)
DILUTED EARNINGS (LOSS) PER SHARE	$(9.99)

Note: Modifications have been made to the statement to simplify the presentation.

Use this income statement to answer the following questions:

a. What was Delta's primary source of revenue?
b. What percentage of Delta's revenue came from this source?
c. What were its largest expenses?
d. How much revenue did Delta earn from transporting passengers?
e. How much revenue did it earn from operating activities other than transporting passengers?
f. How much revenue did it earn from nonoperating activities?
g. How much operating income did Delta earn (or lose)?
h. How much expense did it incur for nonoperating activities?
i. Approximately how many shares of stock did Delta have outstanding during the year?
j. How much profit or loss did Delta report during the fiscal year?

E4-8 *Obj. 2* A recent income statement for **Applebees International** (a restaurant chain) is provided below. It operates both company-owned and franchised restaurants.

Applebees International, Inc.
Income Statement
For the Year Ended December 30, 2001

(Dollars in thousands except per share amounts.)	
Revenues:	
Company restaurant sales	$651,119
Franchise income	93,225
Total operating revenues	744,344
Cost of company restaurant sales:	
Food and beverage	175,977
Labor	208,996
Direct and occupancy	164,965
Pre-opening expense	1,701
Total cost of company restaurant sales	551,639
Operating expenses:	
General and administrative expenses	72,935
Amortization of intangible assets	5,851
Loss on disposition of restaurants and equipment	1,492
Operating earnings	112,427
Other income (expense):	
Investment income	1,650
Interest expense	(7,456)
Other expense	(3,993)
Total other expense	(9,799)
Earnings before income taxes	102,628
Income taxes	38,227
Net earnings	$ 64,401
Basic net earnings per common share	$1.74
Diluted net earnings per common share	$1.70

Use this financial statement to answer the following questions:

a. How much revenue did Applebees earn from food and drinks?
b. How much revenue did it earn from other operating activities?
c. How much revenue did it earn from nonoperating activities?
d. What amount of gross profit did Applebees earn? Express your answer both in dollars and as a percentage of total revenues.
e. How much expense did it incur for nonoperating activities?
f. Approximately how many shares of stock did Applebees have outstanding during the year?
g. How much operating income and net income did Applebees earn during the fiscal year? Express your answers both in dollars and as a percentage of total revenues.
h. Can the amount of cash Applebees received from its operating activities during the year be determined from the income statement? If so, what is that amount? If not, why not?

E4-9 *Obj. 2* SuperQuick Computer Corporation reported the following income statement for a recent quarter.

Consolidated Statement of Income
For the Quarter Ended December 31, 2004

Sales	$719,150
Cost of sales	549,313
	169,837
Research and development costs	16,900
Selling general and administrative expense	83,771
Other income and expense, net	7,685
	108,356
Income before income taxes	61,481
Provision for income taxes	15,451
Net income	$ 46,030
Earnings per share	$0.93

Assume that Other Income and Expense are nonoperating.

a. What was the company's gross profit for the quarter?
b. What was the amount of the company's product costs expensed during the quarter?
c. What was the amount of its operating expenses?
d. What was the amount of its operating income?
e. What was the amount of its nonoperating income or expense?

E4-10 *Obj. 2* BioTek's 2005 annual report included the following income statement information.

(In millions, except earnings per share)

Year Ended June 30	**2003**	**2004**	**2005**
Revenue	$8,671	$11,358	**$14,484**
Operating expenses:			
Cost of revenue	1,188	1,085	**1,197**
Research and development	1,432	1,925	**2,502**
Acquired in-process technology	0	0	**296**
Sales and marketing	2,657	2,856	**3,412**
General and administrative	316	362	**433**
Other expenses	19	259	**230**
Total operating expenses	5,612	6,487	**8,070**
Operating income	3,059	4,871	**6,414**
Interest income	320	443	**703**
Income before income taxes	3,379	5,314	**7,117**
Provision for income taxes	1,184	1,860	**2,627**
Net income	$2,195	$ 3,454	**$ 4,490**
Earnings per share	$0.86	$1.32	**$1.67**

Ratios often are used to assess changes in financial statement information over time. Use Bio-Tek's income statements to answer the following questions. Express your answers as percentages.

a. What was the ratio of net income to net revenues each year?
b. What was the ratio of cost of revenues (cost of goods sold) to net revenues each year?
c. What was the ratio of operating expenses to net revenues each year?
d. What was the percentage change in net income between 2003 and 2004 and between 2004 and 2005? (Hint: Divide the increase in net income from one year to the next by the net income for the earlier year.)
e. Did Bio-Tek's operating results improve between 2003 and 2005? Explain your answer.

E4-11 Listed below are selected account balances for Hemmingway Company for June 30, 2004.
Obj. 3

Accounts payable	$95,300	Land	$250,000
Accounts receivable	78,100	Merchandise inventory	390,000
Accumulated depreciation	318,000	Notes payable, current portion	50,000
Buildings	750,000	Notes payable, long-term	571,300
Cash	34,500	Prepaid insurance	38,000
Contributed capital	700,000	Retained earnings	279,000
Cost of goods sold	840,000	Supplies on hand	52,000
Equipment	450,000	Trademarks	45,000
Interest payable	38,000	Wages expense	375,000
		Wages payable	36,000

Determine each of the following amounts. (Hint: Not all items will be used.)

a. Current assets
b. Current liabilities
c. Property, plant, and equipment
d. Total assets
e. Long-term liabilities
f. Total liabilities
g. Stockholders' equity
h. Total liabilities and stockholders' equity
i. Working capital

E4-12 Styles Unlimited reported the following information at January 31.
Obj. 3

Accounts payable	$ 250
Accounts receivable	1,057
Accrued expenses (current)	348
Cash and equivalents	321
Contributed capital	319
Deferred income taxes (liabilities)	275
Income taxes payable (current)	93
Inventories	734
Long-term debt	650
Other current assets	109
Other current liabilities	16
Other long-term assets	248
Other long-term liabilities	61
Property and equipment, net of depreciation	1,667
Retained earnings, net of adjustments	2,124

Accrued expenses are current liabilities. Deferred income taxes are long-term liabilities.

Use the information provided to prepare a balance sheet for Styles Unlimited in good form.

E4-13 The accounting staff at Marvelous Enterprises prepares monthly financial statements. At the end of April, the company's ledger accounts have the following balances. All adjusting entries have been made and the next step is to prepare the financial statements. The company has 18,200 shares of stock outstanding.
Obj. 3

(Continued)

Accounts payable	$17,000	Land	$45,000
Accounts receivable	14,700	Long-term notes payable	33,000
Accumulated depreciation	13,100	Merchandise inventory	12,480
Buildings	50,000	Notes payable, current portion	14,200
Cash	10,360	Patents	3,300
Contributed capital	38,770	Prepaid insurance	1,100
Copyrights and trademarks	5,000	Retained earnings, March 31	8,400
Cost of goods sold	15,050	Sales revenue	26,000
Depreciation expense	1,100	Supplies	3,570
Dividends declared	1,200	Supplies expense	1,300
Income tax expense	1,060	Wage expense	1,500
Insurance expense	550	Wages payable	17,700
Interest expense	900		

Prepare a classified balance sheet in proper format. (Show land separately.) Use a three-line heading on the statement that includes (1) the name of the company, (2) the name of the statement, and (3) the appropriate date. Explain how you determined the April 30 balance in Retained Earnings.

E4-14 *Obj. 3* P/T Jenny didn't study very hard when she took accounting because she thought she would never use it on the job at Tech-Noid Company. Yesterday, after preparing all end-of-the-month adjusting entries, the company's accountant became ill. The company asked Jenny to finish the job by preparing the financial statements. The owner needs the statements tomorrow to present to his banker. Jenny is having trouble getting the balance sheet to balance.

Tech-Noid Company
Balance Sheet
January 31, 2004

Assets		**Liabilities and Stockholders' Equity**	
Current assets:		**Current liabilities:**	
Inventory	$1,121	Accounts payable	$ 231
Interest payable	100	Accounts receivable	691
Land	2,200	Wages payable	636
Noncurrent assets:		**Long-term liabilities:**	
Buildings and equipment	4,990	7%, 10-year note payable	2,000
Retained earnings	1,398	Accumulated depreciation	531
		Stockholders' equity:	
		Contributed capital	4,230
		Cash	124
Total assets	$9,809	Total liabilities and equity	$8,443

(a) Help Jenny by making a list of the five account categories that are printed in bold-face type on the balance sheet. Leave three lines between each category listed. For each category, write the names of Tech-Noid's accounts that should be reported under it on the balance sheet.
(b) Determine the correct balance sheet amounts for:

1. total current assets
2. total noncurrent assets
3. total assets
4. total current liabilities
5. total long-term liabilities
6. total stockholders' equity
7. total liabilities and equity

E4-15 *Objs. 2, 3*

Listed below are account balances and other data for Hands & Eyes, Inc., a company that sells crafts and decorative supplies, for the fiscal year ended December 31, 2004.

Accounts payable	$ 41,000	Land	$ 65,000
Accounts receivable	29,000	Long-term investments	46,000
Accumulated depreciation	180,000	Merchandise inventory	79,000
Buildings	430,000	Notes payable, current portion	25,000
Cash	35,000	Notes payable, long-term	307,000
Contributed capital	315,000	Prepaid insurance	22,000
Cost of goods sold	130,000	Retained earnings, Dec. 31, 2003	19,000
Dividends (declared and paid)	22,000	Sales revenue	373,000
Equipment	262,000	Selling expenses	34,000
General and administrative expenses	98,000	Supplies	25,000
Income tax expense	8,000	Trademarks	31,000
Income tax payable	22,000	Wages payable	36,000
Interest expense	33,000	Interest payable	31,000
Shares of common stock outstanding:	20,000		

From the data presented above, determine the amount of each of the items that follow. (Hint: Pretax income for the year 2004 = $78,000.)

1. Gross profit
2. Operatintg income
3. Net income
4. Earnings per share
5. Current assets
6. Property, plant, and equipment
7. Other assets
8. Total assets
9. Current liabilities
10. Working capital and working capital ratio
11. Total liabilities
12. Retained earnings, December 31, 2004
13. Total stockholders' equity
14. Total liabilities and stockholders' equity

E4-16 *Objs. 2, 3, 4*

Listed below are typical accounts or titles that appear on financial statements. For each item, identify the financial statement(s) on which it appears.

a. Loss on sale of equipment Income statement
b. Taxes payable balance sheet
c. Trademark balance sheet (other assets)
d. Accumulated other comprehensive income St. of Stockholders' Equity
e. Current assets balance sheet
f. Investments balance sheet
g. Rental revenue income st.
h. Gross profit income st.
i. Earnings per share income st.
j. Accumulated depreciation balance sheet
k. Net income income st.
l. Minority interest income / balance
m. Contributed capital balance / stock. equity
n. Operating income income
o. Common stock issued during year stock. equity

E4-17 *Objs. 2, 3, 4*

A list of financial statement items is given below.

1. Accounts receivable
2. Rent payable

(Continued)

3. Retained earnings
4. Cost of sales
5. Prepaid rent
6. Supplies expense
7. Equipment
8. Dividends
9. Depreciation expense
10. Copyrights
11. Accrued liabilities
12. Wages payable
13. Land
14. Notes payable
15. Service revenue
16. Inventory
17. Advertising expense
18. Common stock

Use the format shown below. (a) For each account, indicate the financial statement on which the account would appear. (b) Identify the information provided by the account. The first item is completed as an example:

Item	*Financial Statement*	*Information Provided*
1. Accounts receivable	Balance sheet	Cash to be received in the future from prior sales

E4-18 *Obj. 4* Listed below are financial statements for the Sunflower Company.

Income Statement
For the Year Ended December 31, 2004

Sales revenue	$ 20,000
Cost of sales	(12,000)
Gross profit	8,000
Operating expenses	(4,000)
Selling and administrative expenses	(3,000)
Net income	$ 1,000

Statement of Stockholders' Equity
For the Year Ended December 31, 2004

	Contributed Capital	Retained Earnings	Total
Balance at December 31, 2003	$5,000	$13,000	$18,000
Common stock issued	2,000		2,000
Net income		1,000	1,000
Dividends		(4,000)	(4,000)
Balance at December 31, 2004	$7,000	$10,000	$17,000

Balance Sheet
as of December 31, 2004

Assets:		Liabilities and Stockholders' Equity	
Cash	$ 9,000	Accounts payable	$ 5,000
Accounts receivable	3,000	Notes payable	8,000
Inventory	2,000	Common stock	7,000
Land	16,000	Retained earnings	10,000
Total	$30,000	Total	$30,000

(a) Describe what is meant by the term *articulation.* (b) What evidence of articulation is there in this set of financial statements?

E4-19 *Obj. 4* PT Crane Pool Corporation reported the following selected information for its 2004 fiscal year.

Contributed capital at June 30, 2003	$ 657
Retained earnings at June 30, 2003	1,536
Dividends	222
Net income	953
Common stock issued	243

Use this information to prepare a statement of stockholders' equity for Crane Pool for the year ended June 30, 2004.

E4-20 *Objs. 2, 4* PT Use the information provided in Exercise 4-13.

a. Prepare an income statement following the format shown in Exhibit 1. (List expenses separately.)
b. Prepare a statement of stockholders' equity in good form.

(Hint: There was no change in contributed capital during the month.) For each statement, use a three-line heading on the statement that includes (1) the name of the company, (2) the name of the statement, and (3) the appropriate time period or date.

PROBLEMS

If your instructor is using Personal Trainer in this course, you may complete online the assignments identified by PT.

P4-1 Identifying the Purpose of Financial Statements

Obj. 1

Assume you are a financial manager with a U.S. corporation. A. Suliman is a recently employed manager in the Middle Eastern division of your corporation and a visitor to the United States. He has little familiarity with financial reporting practices in the United States. Your boss has given you the responsibility of explaining financial reports to Mr. Suliman.

Required Write a short report describing each of the four basic corporate financial statements for Suliman. Make sure you are clear about the purpose of each statement, its contents, and its relationships to the other financial statements.

P4-2 Ethical Issues in Financial Reporting

Obj. 1

Flower Childs is a regional sales manager for Green-Grow, Inc., a producer of garden supplies. The company's fiscal year ends on April 30. In mid-April, Flower is contacted by the president of Green-Grow. He indicates that the company is facing a financial problem. Two years ago, the company borrowed heavily from several banks to buy a competing company and to increase production of its primary products: insecticides and fertilizers. As a part of the loan agreement, Green-Grow must maintain a working capital ratio of 1.5 to 1 and earn a net income of at least $2 per share. If the company fails to meet these requirements, as reflected in its annual financial statements, the banks can restrict future credit for the company or require early payment of its loans, potentially forcing the company into bankruptcy.

The president explains that this fiscal year has been a difficult one for Green-Grow. Sales have slipped because of increased competition, and the rising prices of chemicals have increased the company's production costs. The company is in danger of not meeting the loan requirements. The company could be forced to make drastic cuts or to liquidate its assets. The president informs Flower that her job could be in danger. The president asks her to help with the problem by dating all sales invoices that clear her office during the first half of May as though the sales had been made in April. May is a month of heavy sales volume for the company as retail stores stock up for the coming season. The president believes that the added sales would be sufficient to get the company past the loan problem. He explains that this procedure will be used only this one time. By next year, the company will be in better shape because of new products it is developing. Also, he reminds Flower that her bonus for the year will be higher because of the additional sales that will be recorded for April. He points out that the company is fundamentally in sound financial shape, and that he would hate to see its future jeopardized by a minor bookkeeping problem. He is asking for the cooperation of all of the regional sales managers. He argues that the stockholders, employees, and managers will all be better off if the sales are predated. He wants Flower's assurance that she will cooperate.

Required

A. What effect will predating the sales have on Green-Grow's balance sheet, income statement, and statement of cash flows? Be specific about which accounts will be affected and why.
B. How will this practice solve the company's problem with the banks?
C. What would be the appropriate behavior for the company president under the circumstances the company is facing?
D. What would be the appropriate behavior for Flower?

P4-3 Identifying and Correcting Errors in an Income Statement

Obj. 2
P/T

Just after preparing the adjusting entries for the year, the long-time controller at Parrot Company took a leave of absence. Her inexperienced assistant did his best to prepare financial statements from the information the controller had left behind. He had particular difficulty with the income statement.

The item labeled sales expense is the sum of the amounts charged customers during the year for goods and services provided.

Income Statement
December 31, 2004

Sales expense		$260,722
Cost of goods sold		102,690
Net profit		$158,032
Operating expenses:		
Wages	$59,780	
Utilities	9,002	
Interest	14,420	
Depreciation	13,510	
Total operating expense		97,712
Operating income		$ 60,320
Advertising expense		9,968
Pretax income		$ 50,352
Income tax expense		13,150
Net income		$ 63,502
Earnings per share of common stock ($64,502 ÷ 15,000 shares)		$4.30

Required

A. Identify and list the errors in the income statement above.
B. Prepare a corrected income statement.

P4-4 Interpreting an Income Statement

Obj. 2
P/T

Microsoft Corporation's 2002 annual report included the following income statement information.

Microsoft Corporation
Income Statements

(In millions, except earnings per share)			
Year Ended June 30	**2000**	**2001**	**2002**
Revenue	$22,956	$25,296	$28,365
Operating expenses:			
Cost of revenue	3,002	3,455	5,191
Research and development	3,772	4,379	4,307
Sales and marketing	4,126	4,885	5,407
General and administrative	1,050	857	1,550
Total operating expenses	11,950	13,576	16,455
Operating income	11,006	11,720	11,910
Losses on equity investees and other	(57)	(159)	(92)
Investment income (loss)	3,326	(36)	(305)
Income before income taxes	14,275	11,525	11,513
Provision for income taxes	4,854	3,804	3,684
Income before accounting change	9,421	7,721	7,829
Cumulative effect of accounting change (net of income taxes of $185)		(375)	
Net income	$ 9,421	$ 7,346	$ 7,829
Basic earnings per share:			
Before accounting change	$ 1.81	$ 1.45	$ 1.45
Cumulative effect of accounting change		(0.07)	
	$ 1.81	$ 1.38	$ 1.45
Diluted earnings per share:			
Before accounting change	$ 1.70	$ 1.38	$ 1.41
Cumulative effect of accounting change		(0.06)	
	$ 1.70	$ 1.32	$ 1.41
Weighted average shares outstanding:			
Basic	5,189	5,341	5,406
Diluted	5,536	5,574	5,553

Required Ratios often are used to assess changes in financial statement information over time. Use Microsoft's income statements to answer the following questions. Express your answers as percentages.

A. What was the ratio of net income to net revenues each year?
B. What was the ratio of cost of revenues (cost of goods sold) to net revenues each year?
C. What was the ratio of operating expenses to net revenues each year?
D. What was the percentage change in net income between 2000 and 2001, and between 2001 and 2002? (Hint: Divide the increase in net income from 2000 and 2001 by the net income for 2000.)
E. Did Microsoft's operating results improve between 2000 and 2001? Between 2001 and 2002? Explain your answers.

P4-5 Comprehensive Income

Objs. 2, 3, 4

The Lo Company imports and sells Chinese furniture in the United States. Its new accountant has been assigned the task of preparing the income statement. She knows that the FASB is now requiring that certain unrealized gains and losses be reported as part of comprehensive income. She has the following information available for the year just ended.

1. Loss on cumulative effect of change of depreciation method, net of tax	$ 840
2. Gain from disposal of discontinued operations, net of tax	3,500
3. Cost of goods sold	180,000
4. Revenue received in advance	2,500
5. Work in process inventory	135,000
6. Interest expense	4,000

(Continued)

7. Provision for income tax	11,700
8. Sale of treasury stock at a price greater than cost	5,050
9. Sales revenue	250,000
10. Unrealized gain on increase of market value of investment	1,240
11. Sale of stock to investors	60,300
12. General and administrative expense	27,000
13. Extraordinary gain on retirement of debt, net of tax	4,200
14. Unrealized loss on foreign currency translation (regarding foreign subsidiary)	3,600
15. Cash received from customers	75,000
16. Dividends paid to shareholders	8,000

Required

A. From the information given above, decide which items should appear in the income statement, which would appear on a separate statement of comprehensive income, and which would not appear on either. If an item does not appear on either statement, indicate where it would be found. Also indicate which are transactions with owners.

B. Using the information above, prepare an income statement and a separate statement of comprehensive income.

P4-6 Reading and Interpreting a Balance Sheet

Obj. 3

PT

A recent balance sheet for **Walt Disney Company** is provided below.

Walt Disney Company
Consolidated Balance Sheets

(In millions, except per share data)

September 30	2001	2000
ASSETS		
Current Assets		
Cash and cash equivalents	$ 618	$ 842
Receivables	3,343	3,599
Inventories	671	702
Television costs (current)	1,175	1,162
Other assets	1,222	1,258
Total current assets	7,029	7,563
Film and television costs	5,235	5,339
Investments	2,061	2,270
Parks, resorts and other property, at cost		
Attractions, buildings and equipment	20,635	19,202
Accumulated depreciation	(7,728)	(6,892)
	12,907	12,310
Intangible assets, net	14,540	16,117
Other assets	1,927	1,428
Total assets	$43,699	$45,027

(Continued)

September 30	2001	2000
LIABILITIES AND STOCKHOLDERS' EQUITY		
Current Liabilities		
Accounts payable and other accrued liabilities	$ 4,603	$ 5,161
Current portion of borrowings	829	2,502
Unearned royalties and other advances	787	739
Total current liabilities	6,219	8,402
Borrowings	8,940	6,959
Other noncurrent liabilities	5,486	5,210
Minority interests	382	356
Stockholders' Equity		
Common stock	12,096	12,101
Retained earnings	12,171	12,767
Adjustments	(1,595)	(768)
Total stockholders' equity	22,672	24,100
Total liabilities and stockholders' equity	$43,699	$45,027

Note: Slight modifications have been made to the format of the statement to simplify the presentation.

Required Respond to the following questions.

A. Do you agree that Disney's balance sheet is both classified and comparative? Explain why or why not.
B. At year-end 2001, what percentage of total assets was composed of current assets? Had this percentage increased or decreased since year-end 2000?
C. What was Disney's amount of working capital at year-end 2001? Did it change significantly from year-end 2000?
D. Compute the working capital ratio at year-end 2001 and year-end 2000. Did it improve or deteriorate between 2000 and 2001?
E. Film and television costs is the amount paid to produce movies or television shows. Explain why it appears in two places on the balance sheet.
F. What were the amounts of total assets, total liabilities, and stockholders' equity at year-end 2001 and year-end 2000?
G. Did Disney's overall financial position improve between 2000 and 2001? Explain.

P4-7 Identifying and Correcting Errors in a Balance Sheet

Obj. 3

Ceramics, Inc. reported the following balance sheet for the year 2004.

Balance Sheet
For the year ending December 31, 2004

Assets:	
Cash	$ 2,000
Accounts payable	500
Inventory	900
Equipment	1,000
Land	1,500
Total assets	$ 6,000
Liabilities:	
Accounts receivable	$ 3,000
Accrued liabilities	1,000
Total liabilities	4,000
Stockholders' equity:	
Common stock	1,800
Retained earnings	5,100
Total stockholders' equity	6,900
Total liabilities and stockholders' equity	$10,900

(Continued)

Required

A. Identify and list the errors in the balance sheet above.
B. Prepare a corrected balance sheet.

P4-8 Interpreting an Income Statement

Obj. 2

A recent Consolidated Statement of Income for the **Coca-Cola Company** and Subsidiaries is presented below.

Consolidated Statements of Income
The Coca-Cola Company and Subsidiaries

Year Ended December 31	2001	2000	1999
(In millions except per share data)			
NET OPERATING REVENUES	$20,092	$19,889	$19,284
Cost of goods sold	6,044	6,204	6,009
GROSS PROFIT	14,048	13,685	13,275
Selling, administrative and general expenses	8,696	8,551	8,480
Other operating charges	0	1,443	813
OPERATING INCOME	5,352	3,691	3,982
Interest income	325	345	260
Interest expense	(289)	(447)	(337)
Other income (loss)	282	(190)	(86)
INCOME BEFORE INCOME TAXES AND CUMULATIVE EFFECT OF ACCOUNTING CHANGE	5,670	3,399	3,819
Income taxes	1,691	1,222	1,388
INCOME BEFORE CUMULATIVE EFFECT OF ACCOUNTING CHANGE	3,979	2,177	2,431
Cumulative effect of accounting change, net of income taxes	(10)	0	0
NET INCOME	$ 3,969	$ 2,177	$ 2,431
BASIC NET INCOME PER SHARE			
Before accounting change	$1.60	$0.88	$0.98
Cumulative effect of accounting change	0.00	0.00	0.00
	$1.60	$0.88	$0.98
DILUTED NET INCOME PER SHARE			
Before accounting change	$1.60	$0.88	$0.98
Cumulative effect of accounting change	0.00	0.00	0.00
	$1.60	$0.88	$0.98
AVERAGE SHARES OUTSTANDING	2,487	2,477	2,469
Dilutive effect of stock options	0	10	18
AVERAGE SHARES OUTSTANDING ASSUMING DILUTION	2,487	2,487	2,487

Note: Slight modifications have been made to the statement to simplify the presentation.

Required

A. What is the amount of cost of goods sold for 1999, 2000, and 2001? What kinds of costs are included in cost of goods sold?
B. What does gross profit represent? Calculate gross profit as a percentage of net operating revenues for each year. What do you observe?
C. How does gross profit differ from operating income?
D. Is Coca-Cola more profitable in 2001 than in 1999? Explain.

P4-9 Understanding Working Capital and Long-Term Debt

Obj. 3

A recent Consolidated Balance Sheet for the Coca-Cola Company and Subsidiaries is presented on the following page.

Required

A. Is Coca-Cola a larger or smaller company in 2001 than in 2000? Explain.
B. What is the total amount of long-term debt? Explain why Coca-Cola classifies long-term debt into two categories.
C. What is working capital?
D. How much working capital does Coca-Cola report in 2001 and 2000? What conclusions can you make as a result of your calculations? (Note: This problem takes an interesting twist. Think about the implication of your calculations.)

Consolidated Balance Sheets
The Coca-Cola Company and Subsidiaries

December 31	2001	2000
ASSETS		
CURRENT		
Cash and cash equivalents	$ 1,866	$ 1,819
Marketable securities	68	73
	1,934	1,892
Trade accounts receivable, less allowances of $59 in 2001 and $62 in 2000	1,882	1,757
Inventories	1,055	1,066
Prepaid expenses and other assets	2,300	1,905
TOTAL CURRENT ASSETS	7,171	6,620
INVESTMENTS AND OTHER ASSETS		
Investments	5,422	5,765
Other assets	2,792	2,364
	8,214	8,129
PROPERTY, PLANT AND EQUIPMENT		
Land	217	225
Buildings and improvements	1,812	1,642
Machinery and equipment	4,881	4,547
Containers	195	200
	7,105	6,614
Less allowances for depreciation	2,652	2,446
	4,453	4,168
TRADEMARKS AND OTHER INTANGIBLE ASSETS	2,579	1,917
	$22,417	$20,834

(Continued)

December 31	2001	2000
LIABILITIES AND SHARE-OWNERS' EQUITY		
CURRENT		
Accounts payable and accrued expenses	$ 3,679	$ 3,905
Loans and notes payable	3,743	4,795
Current maturities of long-term debt	156	21
Accrued income taxes	851	600
TOTAL CURRENT LIABILITIES	8,429	9,321
LONG-TERM DEBT	1,219	835
OTHER LIABILITIES	961	1,004
DEFERRED INCOME TAXES	442	358
SHARE-OWNERS' EQUITY		
Common stock, $.25 par value; Authorized: 5,600,000,000 shares; Issued: 3,491,465,016 shares in 2001; 3,481,882,834 shares in 2000	873	870
Capital surplus	3,520	3,196
Reinvested earnings	23,443	21,265
Accumulated other comprehensive income and unearned compensation on restricted stock	(2,788)	(2,722)
	25,048	22,609
Less treasury stock, at cost (1,005,237,693 shares in 2001; 997,121,427 shares in 2000)	13,682	13,293
	11,366	9,316
	$22,417	$20,834

Note: Slight modifications have been made to the statement for purposes of simplifying the presentation.

P4-10 Using the Balance Sheet to Determine Asset Composition

Obj. 3

Recent Balance Sheets for **Microsoft Corporation** are presented below.

Microsoft Corporation
Balance Sheets
(In millions)

June 30	2001	2002
Assets		
Current assets:		
Cash and equivalents	$ 3,922	$ 3,016
Short-term investments	27,678	35,636
Total cash and short-term investments	31,600	38,652
Accounts receivable, net	3,671	5,129
Inventories	83	673
Deferred income taxes	1,522	2,112
Other	2,334	2,010
Total current assets	39,210	48,576
Property and equipment, net	2,309	2,268
Equity and other investments	14,361	14,191
Goodwill	1,511	1,426
Intangible assets, net	401	243
Other long-term assets	1,038	942
Total assets	$58,830	$67,646

(Continued)

June 30	2001	2002
Liabilities and stockholders' equity		
Current liabilities:		
Accounts payable	$ 1,188	$ 1,208
Accrued compensation	742	1,145
Income taxes	1,468	2,022
Short-term unearned revenue	4,395	5,920
Other	1,461	2,449
Total current liabilities	9,254	12,744
Long-term unearned revenue	1,219	1,823
Deferred income taxes	409	398
Other long-term liabilities	659	501
Commitments and contingencies		
Stockholders' equity:		
Common stock and paid-in capital-shares authorized 12,000; shares issued and outstanding 5,383 and 5,359	28,390	31,647
Retained earnings, including accumulated other comprehensive income of $587 and $583	18,899	20,533
Total stockholders' equity	47,289	52,180
Total liabilities and stockholders' equity	$58,830	$67,646

Required

A. Microsoft reports property and equipment, net on the balance sheet. Calculate property and equipment as a percentage of total assets for 2001 and 2002.
B. Microsoft reports cash and short-term investments as a current asset. Calculate cash and short-term investments as a percentage of total assets.
C. Comment on your analysis from Requirements A and B.
D. Calculate the working capital ratio for 2001 and 2002. Discuss your results.

P4-11 Preparing Financial Statements

Objs. 2, 3
P/T

Argyle Company has the following account balances at December 31, 2004. During the year, Argyle had 10,000 shares of stock outstanding.

Argyle Company
Account Balances
at December 31, 2004

Account	Balance
Cash	$ 4,650
Accounts receivable	16,350
Inventory	30,500
Supplies	7,700
Prepaid insurance	3,550
Equipment	42,500
Accumulated depreciation—equipment	17,500
Buildings	170,000
Accumulated depreciation—buildings	105,000
Land	10,000
Patents	3,000
Accounts payable	18,250
Wages payable	3,450
Interest payable	1,700
Income taxes payable	4,050
Notes payable, current portion	2,500

(Continued)

Account	Balance
Notes payable, long-term	37,500
Owners' investment	25,000
Retained earnings, December 31, 2003	60,150
Dividends	15,000
Sales revenue	130,000
Cost of goods sold	62,500
Wages expense	16,000
Utilities expense	2,000
Depreciation expense	1,050
Insurance expense	1,500
Supplies expense	2,300
Interest expense	3,650
Advertising expense	1,450
Patent expense	400
Income tax expense	11,000

Required

A. Prepare an income statement in good form based on Argyle Company's account balances.
B. Prepare a classified balance sheet as of December 31, 2004. Include appropriate headings and subheadings.

P4-12 Preparing Financial Statements

Objs. 2, 3

The following account balances are provided for Rustic Company at December 31, 2004. Revenues and expense accounts cover the fiscal year ending on that date. All numbers are dollars except shares outstanding.

Account	Amount
Accounts payable	$ 14,000
Accounts receivable	18,000
Accumulated depreciation	30,000
Cash	6,000
Common stock, par value	20,000
Cost of goods sold	35,000
Current portion of long-term debt	2,000
Income taxes	6,000
Interest expense	4,000
Interest payable	500
Inventory	34,000
Long-term debt	40,000
Net income	12,000
Paid-in capital in excess of par	30,000
Patents and trademarks	4,000
Prepaid insurance	2,500
Property, plant and equipment, cost	150,000
Retained earnings	78,000
Sales revenues	110,000
Selling, general, and administrative expenses	65,000
Service revenues	12,000
Supplies	3,000
Wages payable	3,000
Shares outstanding	20,000

Required

A. Prepare an income statement in good form for Rustic Company.
B. Prepare a classified balance sheet.

P4-13 *Obj. 4*

Information in the Statement of Stockholders' Equity

A recent annual report for **Wal-Mart Stores, Inc.** and its subsidiaries is provided below.

Required From the information provided, answer the following questions:

A. What is the total amount of contributed capital as of January 31, 1999?
B. Did total contributed capital increase or decrease between January 31, 1999 and January 31, 2001? By what amount?
C. How much profit has been distributed to owners in cash during the three years covered by this statement?
D. Has stockholders' equity increased or decreased over the three years and what is the main reason?
E. Compute the ratio of cash dividends to net income for each year. Did the portion of profits paid out in dividends each year increase, decrease, or stay about the same?
F. Compute the percentage change in net income between 2000 and 2001, and between 2001 and 2002. (Hint: Divide the increase in net income from 2000 to 2001 by the net income for 2000.) Do you believe this is an encouraging sign or a discouraging sign?
G. Compute the percentage change in dividends between 2000 and 2001, and between 2001 and 2002. Is the rate of dividend increase greater or smaller than the rate of profit increase?

Wal-Mart Stores, Inc.
Consolidated Statements of Shareholders' Equity

(Amounts in millions)	Number of shares	Common stock	Capital in excess of par value	Retained earnings	Other accumulated comprehensive income	Total
Balance January 31, 1999	4,448	$445	$ 435	$20,741	($509)	$21,112
Comprehensive Income						
Net income				5,377		5,377
Other accumulated comprehensive income					54	54
Total Comprehensive Income						**5,431**
Cash dividends ($.20 per share)				(890)		(890)
Purchase of Company stock	(2)		(2)	(99)		(101)
Stock options exercised and other	11	1	281			282
Balance January 31, 2000	4,457	446	714	25,129	(455)	25,834
Comprehensive Income						
Net income				6,295		6,295
Other accumulated comprehensive income					(229)	(229)
Total Comprehensive Income						**6,066**
Cash dividends ($.24 per share)				(1,070)		(1,070)
Purchase of Company stock	(4)		(8)	(185)		(193)
Issuance of Company stock	11	1	580			581
Stock options exercised and other	6		125			125
Balance January 31, 2001	4,470	447	1,411	30,169	(684)	31,343
Comprehensive Income						
Net income				6,671		6,671
Other accumulated comprehensive income					(584)	(584)
Total Comprehensive Income						**6,087**
Cash dividends ($.28 per share)				(1,249)		(1,249)
Purchase of Company stock	(24)	(2)	(62)	(1,150)		(1,214)
Stock options exercised and other	7		135			135
Balance January 31, 2002	**4,453**	**$445**	**$1,484**	**$34,441**	**($1,268)**	**$35,102**

Note: Slight modifications have been made to the statement for purposes of simplifying the presentation.

P4-14 Understanding Stockholders' Equity

Obj. 4

Recent stockholders' equity statements for Microsoft are presented below.

Required

A. What was the amount of common stock and paid-in capital at June 30, 2000, 2001, and 2002?
B. Does Microsoft pay dividends on common stock?
C. How can you explain the increase in Common stock and paid-in capital over the three-year period?
D. Without consulting Microsoft's Statement of Income, can we determine net income reported in 2000, 2001, and 2002? Why or why not?
E. Microsoft's Stockholders' Equity Statements report Common stock repurchased. Why do you think a company would repurchase its own shares? If the shares are later reissued at a higher price, do you think Microsoft should report a gain on shares reissued?

Microsoft Corporation
Stockholders' Equity Statements

(In millions)

Year Ended June 30	2000	2001	2002
Convertible preferred stock			
Balance, beginning of year	$ 980	$ 0	$ 0
Conversion of preferred to common stock	(980)		
Balance, end of year	0	0	0
Common stock and paid-in capital			
Balance, beginning of year	13,844	23,195	28,390
Common stock issued	3,554	5,154	1,801
Common stock repurchased	(210)	(394)	(676)
Other, net	6,007	435	2,132
Balance, end of year	23,195	28,390	31,647
Retained earnings			
Balance, beginning of year	13,614	18,173	18,899
Net income	9,421	7,346	7,829
Other comprehensive income:			
Cumulative effect of accounting change		(75)	
Other, net	(283)	(826)	(86)
Translation adjustments and other	23	(39)	82
Comprehensive income	9,161	6,406	7,825
Preferred stock dividends	(13)		
Common stock repurchased	(4,589)	(5,680)	(6,191)
Balance, end of year	18,173	18,899	20,533
Total stockholders' equity	$41,368	$47,289	$52,180

Note: Slight modifications have been made to the statement to simplify the presentation.

P4-15 Using Interrelationships among Financial Statements

Objs. 2, 3, 4

Corey Issacson is an investor in Stone Cold Enterprises. Last week he received the company's most recent financial statements but some of the numbers were smudged and unreadable. Each of the unreadable numbers is represented with a letter on the following page.

Stone Cold Enterprises
Comparative Balance Sheet
December 31, 2004 and 2005

(In thousands)	December 31, 2005	December 31, 2004
Assets		
Cash	$ 2,940	$ 1,020
Accounts receivable	1,850	1,225
Merchandise	2,855	1,000
Prepaid insurance	*(a)*	3,000
Property, plant and equipment	25,000	*(b)*
Accumulated depreciation	*(c)*	(6,250)
Other assets	8,400	3,000
Total assets	$35,545	$ *(d)*
Liabilities and equity:		
Accounts payable	$ 1,580	$ 950
Wages payable	125	700
Rent payable	500	500
Long-term notes payable (8%)	12,000	12,000
Common stock	*(e)*	*(f)*
Retained earnings	*(g)*	10,845
Total liabilities and equity	$ *(h)*	$ *(i)*

Stone Cold Enterprises
Statement of Stockholders' Equity
Year Ended December 31, 2005

	Common Stock	Retained Earnings	Total
Balance, December 31, 2004	$3,000	$ *(j)*	$ *(k)*
Issued common stock	*(l)*		*(m)*
Net income		14,495	14,495
Dividends paid		(9,000)	(9,000)
Balance, December 31, 2005	$5,000	$ *(n)*	$21,340

Stone Cold Enterprises
Income Statement
Year Ended December 31, 2005

Sales revenue		$103,000
Cost of goods sold		66,000
Gross profit		37,000
Operating expenses:		
Wages	$5,490	
Interest	*(o)*	
Rent	*(p)*	
Insurance	1,000	
Depreciation	1,250	
Total operating expenses		*(q)*
Pretax income		*(r)*
Income taxes (35%)		*(s)*
Net income		$ *(t)*

(Continued)

Additional information:

1. No items of plant, property and equipment were purchased or sold during the year.
2. The prepaid insurance account represents the remaining portion of a four-year policy purchased on January 1, 2004.
3. The rent payable account at year end (both years) represents December's rent that had not yet been paid.

Required Use your knowledge regarding the interrelationships among financial statements to determine each of the missing amounts.

P4-16 Preparing Financial Statements

Objs. 2, 3, 4
PT

ABC, Inc. has the following account balances at December 31, 2004.

Accounts payable	$17,080	Income tax expense	$ 1,300
Accounts receivable	9,400	Land	50,000
Accumulated depreciation	26,100	Notes payable	30,000
Buildings	60,000	Retained earnings,	
Cash	20,880	December 31, 2003	17,000
Contributed capital	31,000	Sales revenue	26,000
Cost of goods sold	15,600	Supplies	7,500
Depreciation expense	2,200	Wages expense	3,000
Dividends paid	1,200	Wages payable	23,900

During the year 2004, the company issued $6,000 of new common stock.

Required From this information, prepare (A) an income statement, (B) a statement of stockholders' equity, and (C) a classified balance sheet. (D) Show how the three financial statements articulate. (Note: In parts (A), (B), and (C), include appropriate headings and subheadings in the financial statements that you prepare.)

P4-17 Understanding the Information in Financial Statements

Objs. 2, 3, 4

Today is April 1 and Dale has just received the annual report of Clam Chowder Company, in which he owns stock. Displayed below are the comparative balance sheet and income statement that have drawn his attention.

Balance Sheet	Dec. 31, 2005	Dec. 31, 2004
Cash	$ 1,244	$ 1,512
Accounts receivable	6,914	5,886
Inventory	11,211	9,099
Buildings and equipment	49,900	46,500
Accumulated depreciation	(5,319)	(2,497)
Land	22,000	22,000
Total assets	$85,950	$82,500
Accounts payable	$ 2,313	$ 1,988
Interest payable	-0-	2,563
Wages payable	7,364	6,327
7%, 10-year note payable	20,000	20,000
Contributed capital	42,300	42,300
Retained capital	13,973	9,322
Total liabilities and equity	$85,950	$82,500

Income Statement	For Year 2005
Sales revenue	$485,000
Cost of goods sold	300,700
Gross profit	184,300
Operating expenses:	
Advertising	31,330
Depreciation	2,822
Utilities	19,200
Wages	113,698
Operating income	17,250
Interest expense	2,400
Pretax income	14,850
Income tax expense	5,200
Net income	$ 9,650
Earnings per share	$ 3.86

After reviewing this information, Dale makes the following comments.

1. I'm surprised that the value of the company's land has not increased. Prices have been increasing rapidly in the area the company is located.

2. I'm sure that I received a dividend from this company, but they don't report that they paid any.
3. I don't see how the company's cash balance could have declined when it took in $485,000 in cash from sales to customers.
4. I see that the value of the buildings and equipment declined by $2,822. That seems about right.
5. I don't understand why the company's highly trained workforce is not listed as an asset. It is one of the most important resources that the company has.
6. One thing I really like about this company is the up-to-the-minute financial reports it provides.
7. It's good to see that the value of the inventory has increased since last year.

Required

A. Help Dale better understand these financial statements by responding to each of his comments. Explain whether you agree or disagree with each comment and why.
B. Did the company declare and pay cash dividends during the year just ended? If so, what total amount was distributed?
C. Approximately how many shares of stock does the company have outstanding?

P4-18 The Transformation Process as Reported in Financial Statements

Objs. 2, 3, 4

Far East Specialties is an import company, financed primarily by stockholders and bank loans. It imports handmade goods from Central and East Asia to the United States, where they are sold to retail stores. The company's buyers contract with small companies for goods, which the buyers ship to a central location in the United States. The goods are inventoried and then redistributed as orders are received from retailers. The company receives a bill from the manufacturers along with the goods it receives. Payment is made each month. Bills are sent to retailers along with orders. Most retailers pay their bills each month, as well. It can be several months from the time goods are shipped to the United States until cash is received from retailers.

Required

A. Explain how the various aspects of Far East Specialties' transformation process are reported in its financial statements. That is, consider the events just described and identify where information about each event is reported in the financial statements. In particular, consider the relationship the company has with its investors, suppliers, and customers.
B. Why is it important that time, and the timing of events, be considered in reporting accounting information?

P4-19 Limitations on Financial Statements

Obj. 5

Markus O'Realius is considering the purchase of Caesar Company. The potential seller has provided Markus with a copy of the business's financial statements for the last three years. The financial statements reveal total assets of $350,000 and total liabilities of $150,000. The seller is asking $300,000 for the business. Markus believes that the business is worth only about $200,000, the amount of owners' equity reported on the balance sheet. He has asked your assistance in determining a price to offer for the business.

Required Write a memo to Markus explaining why he should not interpret the balance sheet as an accurate measure of the value of the business. Describe limitations of financial statements that might mean that the market value of the business was higher (or lower) than the financial statement amounts.

P4-20 Limitations of Financial Statements

Obj. 5

Limits, Ltd. had the following financial statements for the fiscal year ending December 31, 2004 (the statement of stockholders' equity and the statement of cash flows are not shown).

(Continued)

Limits, Ltd.
Income Statement
For the Year Ending December 31, 2004

Sales revenue		$20,000
Operating expenses:		
Cost of sales	$1,000	
Wages expense	800	
Advertising expense	100	
Depreciation expense	300	
Research and development expense	300	
Total operating expense		2,500
Operating income		17,500
Other expenses:		
Interest expense		500
Income before taxes		17,000
Income tax		5,100
Net income		$11,900

Limits, Ltd.
Balance Sheet
as of December 31, 2004

Assets		*Liabilities and stockholders' equity*	
Current assets:		Current liabilities:	
Cash	$ 2,300	Accounts payable	$ 3,000
Accounts receivable	8,000	Wages payable	7,600
Inventory	15,000	Interest payable	900
Total current assets	25,300	Total current liabilities	11,500
Property, plant and equipment:		Notes payable, long-term	9,000
Equipment	21,000	Total liabilities	20,500
Accumulated depreciation	(8,000)	Stockholders' equity:	
Buildings	90,000	Owners' investment	9,700
Accumulated depreciation	(85,000)	Retained earnings	13,100
PP&E	18,000	Total stockholders' equity	22,800
Total assets	$43,300	Total liabilities and stockholders' equity	$43,300

Required The text lists several limitations of financial statements. Using the financial statements given here, identify as many examples of limitations or items that relate to limitations of financial statements as you can.

P4-21 Excel in Action

P/T

SPREADSHEET

Listed below are account balances and other data for The Book Wermz at the close of November 30, 2004. Revenue and expense account balances are for the month of November. All amounts are dollars except shares of common stock. The Book Wermz operates as a corporation.

Accounts payable	$ 6,131.77
Accounts receivable	375.00
Accumulated depreciation	13,891.82
Cash	12,307.99
Contributed capital	100,000.00
Cost of goods sold	30,937.32
Depreciation expense	817.20
Dividends paid	1,500.00

Equipment	57,650.00
Income tax expense	897.45
Interest expense	932.03
Inventory	235,255.06
Notes payable, current portion	1,122.77
Notes payable, long-term	120,084.57
Rent expense	1,738.15
Sales	43,312.25
Service revenues	1,566.23
Shares of common stock	1,000
Supplies	2,130.12
Supplies expense	2,411.53
Wages expense	4,697.35
Wages payable	1,150.68

Required Use the account balances to produce an income statement, a statement of stockholders' equity, and a balance sheet for The Book Wermz in a spreadsheet. The financial statements should follow the examples illustrated in Chapter F4. The balance sheet should contain columns for November and October. October 31 balances should be obtained from data provided in the Chapter F3 spreadsheet problem.

Enter account titles in column A. Use columns B, C, and D as necessary for amounts. Use the Borders button to produce single and double lines by selecting the cell to be formatted, using the button down arrow to select the proper line type, and clicking on the button. Use the Indent button to indent titles and captions as needed by selecting the cell and clicking on the button. Use the Comma and Currency buttons to format amounts by selecting the cell and clicking on the appropriate buttons. The Comma button also formats numbers so that negative amounts appear in parentheses. The first and last amounts in a column of numbers should include dollar signs as illustrated in the chapter. Set column widths by placing the cursor at the right edge of a column header so the Change Width cursor appears. Then click and drag the column to the right or left as needed. Use functions to sum subtotals and totals, =SUM(B5:B8) for example, so the spreadsheet will automatically recalculate any changes in account numbers. To merge adjacent cells for titles, select the cells to be merged and click on the Merge Cells button. Put titles in bold type by selecting the cell containing the title and clicking on the Bold Type button **B**.

Suppose sales for November had been $45,000 and the cash balance at November 30 had been $13,995.74. How much net income would the company report for November? How much total assets and stockholders' equity would it report at November 30?

P4-22 Multiple-Choice Overview of the Chapter

1. Which of the following is *not* a statement you would expect to find in a corporate annual report?
   a. Statement of financial position
   b. Statement of earnings
   c. Statement of stockholders' equity
   d. Statement of accounts receivable

2. The following information was reported on the income statement of Wagon Wheel Company.

Sales revenues	$450,000
Cost of goods sold	200,000
Selling, general, and administrative expenses	150,000
Interest expense	30,000

Wagon Wheel's gross profit and operating income would be

	Gross profit	Operating income
a.	$300,000	$70,000
b.	$250,000	$70,000
c.	$250,000	$100,000
d.	$100,000	$70,000

(Continued)

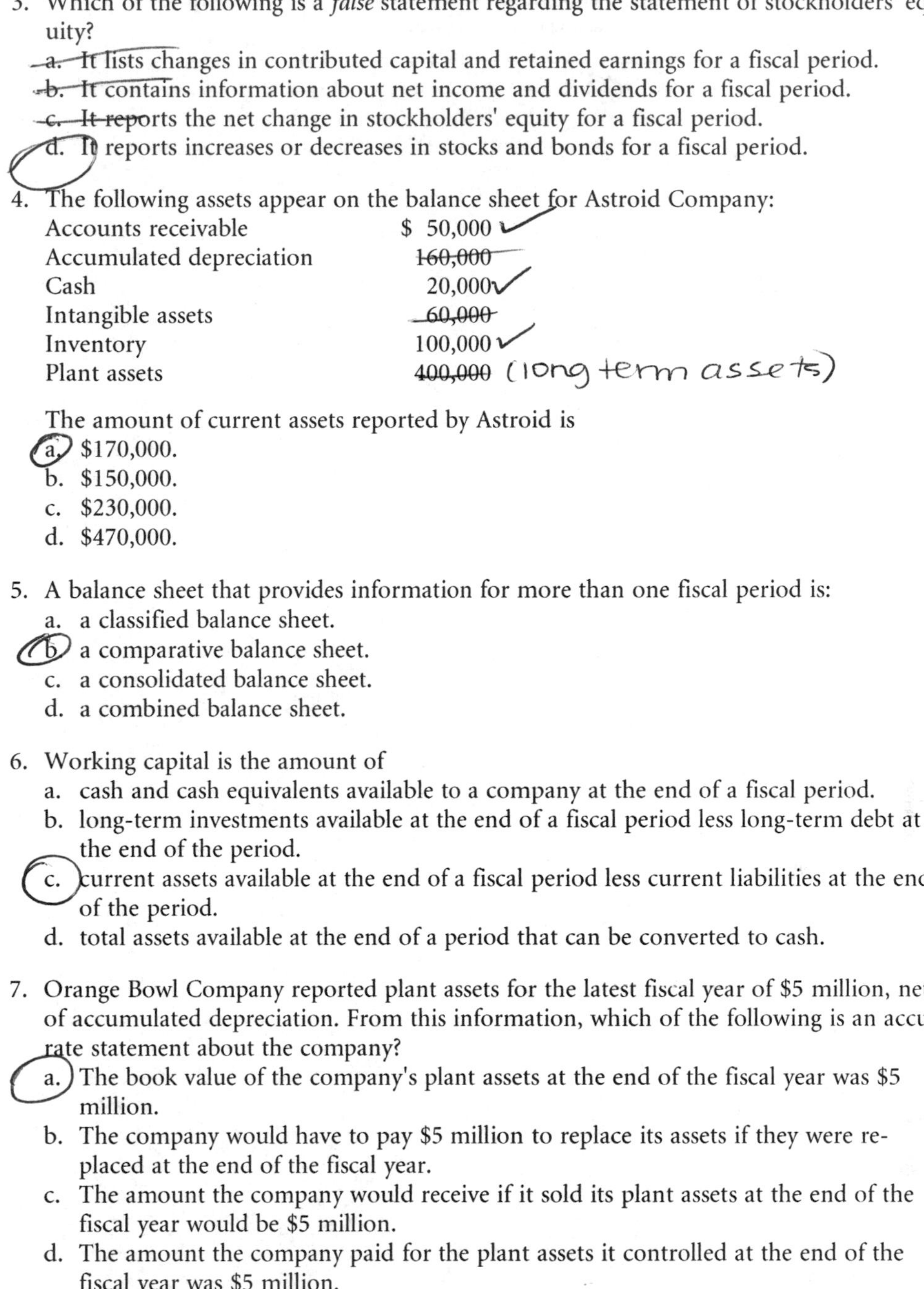

3. Which of the following is a *false* statement regarding the statement of stockholders' equity?
   a. It lists changes in contributed capital and retained earnings for a fiscal period.
   b. It contains information about net income and dividends for a fiscal period.
   c. It reports the net change in stockholders' equity for a fiscal period.
   d. It reports increases or decreases in stocks and bonds for a fiscal period.

4. The following assets appear on the balance sheet for Astroid Company:

Accounts receivable	$ 50,000
Accumulated depreciation	160,000
Cash	20,000
Intangible assets	60,000
Inventory	100,000
Plant assets	400,000

   The amount of current assets reported by Astroid is
   a. $170,000.
   b. $150,000.
   c. $230,000.
   d. $470,000.

5. A balance sheet that provides information for more than one fiscal period is:
   a. a classified balance sheet.
   b. a comparative balance sheet.
   c. a consolidated balance sheet.
   d. a combined balance sheet.

6. Working capital is the amount of
   a. cash and cash equivalents available to a company at the end of a fiscal period.
   b. long-term investments available at the end of a fiscal period less long-term debt at the end of the period.
   c. current assets available at the end of a fiscal period less current liabilities at the end of the period.
   d. total assets available at the end of a period that can be converted to cash.

7. Orange Bowl Company reported plant assets for the latest fiscal year of $5 million, net of accumulated depreciation. From this information, which of the following is an accurate statement about the company?
   a. The book value of the company's plant assets at the end of the fiscal year was $5 million.
   b. The company would have to pay $5 million to replace its assets if they were replaced at the end of the fiscal year.
   c. The amount the company would receive if it sold its plant assets at the end of the fiscal year would be $5 million.
   d. The amount the company paid for the plant assets it controlled at the end of the fiscal year was $5 million.

8. A consolidated financial statement is one in which
   a. more than one year's financial data is included.
   b. the personal financial activities of the owner are combined with those of the company.
   c. the income statement and the balance sheet are combined into a single statement.
   d. the financial information of multiple corporations is reported as if they were a single firm.

9. Which of the following is *false*?
   a. Financial statement information is not always presented in a timely manner.
   b. The purpose of a balance sheet is to report the market value of assets and liabilities.
   c. Certain types of resources and costs are not reported in financial statements.
   d. Many of the numbers reported in financial statements result from estimates and allocations.

10. Where on an income statement would you expect to find administrative salaries expense?
    a. just after cost of goods sold
    b. grouped with other operating expenses
    c. as part of cost of goods sold
    d. following income taxes

CASES

C4-1 Evaluating the Transformation Process

Objs. 1, 5

Italiano Pizza Company has just completed its first month in business. The owners, Charla and Maria, had previously worked for a major pizza chain but were convinced that they could offer a better product in a better atmosphere. They knew the importance of accurate financial records and hired a bookkeeper. Yesterday, the bookkeeper hand-delivered financial statements to the owners and announced her resignation. You have been retained by Charla and Maria to interpret the following financial information and explain its significance.

Italiano Pizza Company
Financial Statements
After One Month in Business

Balance sheet accounts				**Income statement accounts**	
Assets:		Liabilities + Owners' Equity:		Revenues	$ 4,000
Cash	$ 2,240	Wages payable	$ 180	Expenses:	
Food products	980	Advertising payable	400	Store rent	800
Supplies	1,000	Loan from bank	6,800	Food products	1,475
Prepaid rent	2,400	Owners' investment	4,340	Wages	990
Equipment	5,150			Advertising	1,430
Accumulated				Interest	40
depreciation	(50)			Supplies	375
Total	$11,720	Total	$11,720	Depreciation	50
				Net income	$(1,160)

Required

A. Discuss whether the information provided could be helpful to the owners and, if so, describe how. If not, describe why not.
B. Identify at least 10 events that occurred as part of the transformation process during the firm's first month in business. For each event, identify the amount of cash involved.
C. Did Charla and Maria make a good judgment when they decided to get into this business? Would you recommend that they continue with the pizza business or discontinue it? What additional information would be helpful to you in making such a recommendation?

C4-2 The Financial Statements of General Mills, Inc.

Objs. 2, 3, 4

The **General Mills** 2002 Annual Report is reproduced in Appendix B at the end of the text.

Required

A. Answer the following questions about the General Mills Consolidated Statements of Earnings:
   1. General Mills recorded sales of almost $8 billion. Is this the amount of cash collected? Explain.
   2. Sales increased each year from 2000 to 2002. Compute the percentage increase for each year.

(Continued)

3. What is the largest expense for General Mills? Compute this expense as a percentage of sales for each of the three years. Is there a trend?
4. Compare the net income figures for three years. What do you observe?
5. Explain why a company's stock price generally is influenced by the amount of net income.
6. General Mills paid dividends in 2002, 2001, and in 2000, yet the corresponding total dividend payments do not appear as expenses on the income statement. Why not?

B. Answer the following questions about the General Mills Consolidated Balance Sheets:
   1. Why does a company have assets?
   2. What is the total amount of assets at the end of 2002?
   3. For 2002, compare the assets at the beginning of the year to the assets at the end of the year.
      a. Compute the percentage increase in assets during the year.
      b. Which type of assets account for most of the increase?
   4. What two groups have contributed assets to General Mills and have claims on the company's assets?

C. Answer the following questions about the General Mills Consolidated Statement of Stockholders' Equity:
   1. General Mill's total stockholders' equity has increased significantly from May 27, 2001 to May 26, 2002. What is the major cause of the increase in stockholders' equity?
   2. The consolidated statement of stockholders' equity identifies comprehensive income. Briefly explain the concept of comprehensive income. What kinds of activities are included in comprehensive income?

5

REPORTING CASH FLOWS

How is cash flow information determined and reported to external users?

Chapter F4 examined the reporting of operating results and financial position to stockholders and other external users. Corporations and other companies also report information about their cash flows for a fiscal period to external users. The statement of cash flows identifies the cash created by and used for operating, investing, and financing activities. Stan and Maria realize it is important for their company to provide information about how much cash is generated from business activities and how this cash was used. In addition to helping them, as managing owners of the firm, this information helps external stockholders and other decision makers determine whether a company is likely to grow and to meet its financial obligations.

FOOD FOR THOUGHT

As a stockholder of Mom's Cookie Company, what information about cash flows do you need to make decisions about your investment? How do companies determine how much cash they received and paid during a fiscal period? Knowing they need to provide key cash flow information to stockholders and others, Maria and Stan have arranged to meet with their accountant, Ellen, to discuss these issues.

Stan: *We prepared an income statement, balance sheet, and statement of stockholders' equity for our stockholders. I understand we also need to report cash flow information.*

Ellen: *Yes, the statement of cash flows is an important part of your total financial report. This statement requires you to look carefully at your business activities to identify activities that created cash and those that used it.*

Maria: *We know how much cash the company had at the end of the year. Many of our transactions during the year involved cash. Do we have to look at all of these transactions to prepare the statement of cash flows?*

Ellen: *No. You can summarize your cash flows without looking at individual transactions. Most of the information for the statement can be obtained from the income statement and balance sheets you have already prepared.*

Stan: *Those statements don't include much cash information. How can they tell us anything about cash flows?*

Ellen: *The income statement contains information about the results of operating activities measured using the accrual basis. Timing differences between when revenues and expenses were recognized and when cash was received and paid are reported on the balance sheets for this fiscal year end and the prior one. Preparing the statement of cash flows is largely a matter of adjusting income statement numbers for these timing differences and looking at other activities that increased or decreased balance sheet amounts during the year.*

Maria: *That sounds complicated.*

Ellen: *It requires a good understanding of accrual accounting and working systematically with the income statement and balance sheet numbers. Once you learn how the statement is prepared, you'll have a good understanding of how accrual and cash flow information is related. Also, you will see how valuable cash flow information can be for understanding your company.*

OBJECTIVES

Once you have completed this chapter, you should be able to:

1 Explain information reported on a statement of cash flows using the direct format.

2 Explain information reported on a statement of cash flows using the indirect format.

3 Interpret cash flow information as a basis for analyzing financial performance.

THE STATEMENT OF CASH FLOWS

The purpose of the statement of cash flows is to identify the primary activities of a fiscal period that resulted in cash inflows and outflows for a company. The statement describes the cash flow results of financing, investing, and operating activities for a company for a fiscal period, and it explains the change in a company's cash balance during the period. GAAP permit the statement of cash flows to be presented in either of two formats: direct or indirect. The two formats differ only with respect to the presentation of operating activities.

THE DIRECT FORMAT

OBJECTIVE 1

Explain information reported on a statement of cash flows using the direct format.

Some companies, especially smaller companies, use the direct format to present the statement of cash flows. Most large corporations use the indirect format. Exhibit 1 provides an example of the cash flow statement for Mom's Cookie Company using the direct format.

The direct format of the statement of cash flows presents each major source and use of cash. The statement of cash flows is divided into three sections corresponding to the three primary types of business activities: operating, investing, and financing.

The source of data for the direct format of the statement of cash flows is the transactions that affect the cash account. The operating cash flow section of the statement includes those transactions that affected cash and were associated with operating activities: sales to customers, purchases of merchandise, wages, and other operating activities. GAAP require that interest payments be included in the operating activities section of the statement of cash flows because interest expense is reported on the income statement. Thus, **operating cash flows are the cash equivalent of the accrual results reported on the income statement**. That is, they represent a cash-basis income statement for the fiscal period.

The investing activities section includes cash transactions associated with the purchase or sale of long-term assets. The financing activities section includes cash transactions associated with debt (short- or long-term) and owners' equity, including payments to owners.

The direct format of the statement of cash flows lists the direct effects of transactions that affect the cash account during a period. It answers the question, "Where did cash come from and where did cash go?" Therefore, it is an explanation of business activities that resulted in an increase or decrease in cash. In total, these activities explain the change in a company's cash account balance for a fiscal period. Because 2004 was Mom's Cookie Company's first year of operations, the beginning cash balance was $0.

The company's ending cash balance was equal to the net increase in cash for 2004, $10,680. The net increase (or decrease) in cash for a fiscal period is the sum of net cash flow from operating, investing, and financing activities.

Exhibit 1
Statement of Cash Flows, Direct Format

Mom's Cookie Company
Statement of Cash Flows
For the Year Ended December 31, 2004

Operating Activities	
Receipts: Collections from customers	$ 682,080
Payments:	
For inventory	(471,590)
To employees	(70,800)
For rent	(24,000)
For utilities	(4,500)
For supplies	(15,990)
For insurance	(3,700)
For advertising	(6,500)
For interest	(4,150)
For income tax	(22,710)
Net cash flow from operating activities	58,140
Investing Activities	
Payments for purchase of equipment	(216,000)
Receipts from sale of equipment	340
Net cash flow for investing activities	(215,660)
Financing Activities	
Receipts from sale of common stock	100,000
Payment of dividends	(10,000)
Receipts from borrowing	80,000
Repayments of debt	(1,800)
Net cash flow from financing activities	168,200
Net increase in cash	10,680
Cash balance, December 31, 2003	0
Cash balance, December 31, 2004	$ 10,680

Operating Activities

Operating activities are transactions involving the acquisition or production of goods and services and the sale and distribution of these goods and services to customers. Cash flow from operating activities identifies cash received from the sale of goods and services. Also, it identifies cash paid for resources used to provide goods and services. An important relationship exists between the income statement and the operating activities section of the statement of cash flows—both are based on the same set of activities. On the income statement, operating activities are measured on an accrual basis. On the cash flow statement, these activities are measured on a cash basis. These amounts can be compared to determine timing differences between accrual basis recognition of revenues and expenses and cash flows for the period.

To understand how the cash flow numbers in Exhibit 1 were computed, we need to refer to the income statement and balance sheet from Chapter F3. These are reproduced in Exhibit 2.

Selling, general and administrative expenses are as follows:

Wages	$ 70,800
Utilities	4,500
Insurance	3,700
Advertising	6,500
Depreciation	25,500
Rent	22,000
Supplies	15,300
Total	$148,300

Exhibit 2
Income Statement and Balance Sheet for Mom's Cookie Company

Mom's Cookie Company
Income Statement
For the Year Ended December 31, 2004

Sales revenue	$ 686,400
Cost of goods sold	(457,600)
Gross profit	228,800
Selling, general and administrative expenses	(148,300)
Operating income	80,500
Interest expense	(4,800)
Pretax income	75,700
Income taxes	(22,710)
Net income	$ 52,990

Mom's Cookie Company
Balance Sheet
At December 31, 2004

Assets	
Current assets:	
Cash	$ 10,680
Accounts receivable	8,570
Merchandise inventory	23,600
Supplies	690
Prepaid rent	2,000
Total current assets	45,540
Property and equipment, at cost	215,660
Accumulated depreciation	(25,500)
Total assets	$235,700
Liabilities and Stockholders' Equity	
Current liabilities:	
Accounts payable	$ 9,610
Unearned revenue	4,250
Interest payable	650
Notes payable, current portion	5,000
Total current liabilities	19,510
Notes payable, long-term	73,200
Total liabilities	92,710
Stockholders' equity:	
Common stock, 10,000 shares issued	100,000
Retained earnings	42,990
Total stockholders' equity	142,990
Total liabilities and stockholders' equity	$235,700

Of these items, wages, utilities, insurance, and advertising were paid in cash. Observe that there are no noncash assets or liabilities (prepaid insurance or wages payable, for example) on the balance sheet associated with these items. **Depreciation expense does not require the payment of cash.** Rent and supplies expenses were not completely paid in cash because prepaid rent and supplies are reported on the balance sheet. Income tax also was paid in cash. Again, observe that there are no noncash assets or liabilities associated with income taxes, such as income taxes payable. There are noncash assets and liabilities associated with sales revenue, cost of goods sold, and interest expense. These assets and liabilities result from timing differences between when revenues and expenses are recognized and when cash is received or paid. Therefore, they must be adjusted to determine cash flows. Exhibit 3 explains the calculation of operating cash flows from the data in Exhibit 2.

Exhibit 3 Calculation of Operating Cash Flows for Direct Method

Accounts	Accrual	Adjustment	Cash Flow	Explanation
a. Sales Revenue	$ 686,400			Accrual
Less: Accounts Receivable		$ (8,570)		Sales for which cash not received
Add: Unearned Revenue		4,250		Cash received but not yet earned
Cash Collected from Customers			$ 682,080	Cash flow
b. Cost of Goods Sold	(457,600)			Accrual
Add: Merchandise Inventory		(23,600)		Cash paid but goods not sold
Less: Accounts Payable		9,610		Goods purchased but cash not paid
Cash Paid for Merchandise			(471,590)	Cash flow
c. Wages	(70,800)			Cash paid equals accrual amount
Utilities	(4,500)			Cash paid equals accrual amount
Insurance	(3,700)			Cash paid equals accrual amount
Advertising	(6,500)			Cash paid equals accrual amount
Income Taxes	(22,710)			Cash paid equals accrual amount
Cash Paid for Other Operating Items			(108,210)	Cash paid equals accrual amount
d. Rent Expense	(22,000)			Accrual
Prepaid Rent		(2,000)		Cash paid but not expensed
Cash Paid for Rent			(24,000)	Cash flow
e. Supplies Expense	(15,300)			Accrual
Supplies		(690)		Cash paid but not expensed
Cash Paid for Supplies			(15,990)	Cash flow
f. Interest Expense	(4,800)			Accrual
Interest Payable		650		Cash not paid in 2004
Cash Paid for Interest			(4,150)	Cash flow
g. Depreciation Expense	(25,500)		0	Accrual
		25,500		Cash not paid
			0	Cash flow
Net Income	$ 52,990			
Net Cash Flow from Operating			$ 58,140	

To determine cash collected from customers (a), revenue is adjusted for cash not received (because it is still owed) and for cash received that has not been earned. To determine cash paid for merchandise (b), cost of goods sold is adjusted for cash paid for merchandise that has not been sold and for amounts owed suppliers. It is important in these computations that expenses and cash outflows are shown as negative amounts.

Other operating cash flows are either accrued expenses that were paid in cash, as those in (c), or expenses that require adjustment, as with rent, supplies, and interest.

To determine cash paid for rent (d), rent expense is adjusted for cash paid for rent of future periods. To determine cash paid for supplies (e), supplies expense is adjusted for supplies that have been purchased but that have not been used. To determine cash paid for interest (f), interest expense is adjusted for interest that has not been paid.

Depreciation and amortization expenses (g) are tied to operating activities but are not cash flow items. When the direct format is used, these expenses are not listed in the statement of cash flows.

Investing Activities

Investing activities involve acquisition or sale of long-term assets and financial investments during a fiscal period. As noted above, depreciation and amortization expenses are not part of investing activities. Cash flow for investing activities occurs when fixed assets are purchased or sold, not when these assets are depreciated.

Calculation of investing cash flow in Exhibit 1 is straightforward. Mom's Cookie Company purchased $216,000 of equipment for cash in 2004. It sold equipment for $340 in cash. Investing cash flow is simply the amount paid for long-term assets minus the amount received from selling these assets.

Some transactions affect investing and financing activities without affecting cash directly. For example, suppose a company borrows $300,000 from a bank to purchase a building. The transaction increases Buildings and Notes Payable but does not have a direct effect on Cash. GAAP require that such transactions be reported. Most of these events are reported as though they were cash transactions: cash received from borrowing and then paid for property and equipment.

Financing Activities

Financing activities are transactions between a company and its owners or creditors. The financing activities section reports only the cash flow effects of transactions associated with borrowing or repaying debt and investments by owners. Cash flows result when debt is issued or repaid and when stock is issued or repurchased. Payment of dividends or other cash distributions to owners also are financing activities.

The calculation of financing cash flow for Mom's Cookie Company is straightforward. The company received $100,000 from issuing common stock and paid $10,000 of dividends to stockholders. It received $80,000 of cash from borrowing and paid back $1,800 of the amount borrowed. (It is important to remember the repayment of debt is the repayment of the amount actually borrowed, not the payment of interest on the borrowed money. As noted above, the payment of interest is an operating activity.)

GAAP require a schedule to reconcile cash flows from operating activities with net income when the direct format is used. This schedule is similar to the presentation of the statement of cash flows using the indirect format described in the next section of this chapter.

1 SELF-STUDY PROBLEM

WebTUTOR Advantage

Listed below are cash activities for Jerome, Inc. for a recent fiscal period. Jerome's cash balance at the beginning of the period was $16,350.

Paid for dividends	$ 2,500
Paid to employees	4,000

Paid for utilities	2,200
Paid for equipment	13,500
Received from sale of stock	100,000
Paid for supplies	1,800
Paid for inventory	8,400
Received from customers	14,750
Paid for debt repayment	35,000
Received from sale of land	20,000
Paid for building	75,000

Required Use these activities to prepare a statement of cash flows for Jerome, Inc., using the direct format. What were Jerome's primary sources and uses of cash for the period?

The solution to Self-Study Problem 1 appears at the end of the chapter.

THE INDIRECT FORMAT

OBJECTIVE 2

Explain information reported on a statement of cash flows using the indirect format.

The direct format of the statement of cash flows identifies the sources of cash received and the purposes for which cash is paid during a period. Thus, operating activities identify cash received from customers and paid to suppliers, employees, and so on. In practice, however, this format is rarely used by major corporations.

Instead, nearly all major corporations use the indirect format for reporting the statement of cash flows. **The differences between the direct and indirect formats are in the operating activities section only.** The indirect format reconciles net income on an accrual basis with cash flow from operating activities on a cash basis. It answers the question, "Why was cash flow from operations different from net income?" Consequently, operating cash flows are presented as the indirect result of changes in current assets, current liabilities, and other accounts.

Exhibit 4 provides the statement of cash flows for Mom's Cookie Company using the indirect method. In this method, the operating activities section begins with net income. This is the amount reported on the company's income statement (see Exhibit 2). The indirect format begins with the results of operating activities reported on an accrual basis (net income) and adjusts this amount to arrive at the amount that explains the results of operating activities on a cash basis (net cash flow from operating activities). Adjustments are made for activities that had a different effect on net income than they had on cash flow. Observe that **the net cash flows in each section (operating, investing, and financing) are the same as those reported using the direct method** in Exhibit 1. In fact, the investing and financing sections are identical in the two methods.

The operating activities section looks quite different, however. To understand this method, refer to Exhibit 2. The adjustments column of the exhibit identifies the differences between the accrual amounts from the income statement and the cash flow amounts. Starting with net income, we can simply list these adjustments to compute cash flow from operating activities. The indirect method does just that. It starts with the accrual amount (net income) and lists the adjustments necessary to determine cash flow from operating activities.

Though the determination of the adjustments may seem somewhat complicated, they are actually fairly simple. They consist of subtracting any revenues that did not result in cash inflow or adding any expenses that did not require cash outflow. Most adjustments are associated with current assets and current liabilities, with the exclusion of financial resources such as cash and investments.

When current assets increase during a fiscal period, one of two things has occurred:

- Revenue was earned but cash was not received—increase in accounts receivable, or
- Cash was paid for resources that have not been expensed—increase in inventory or prepaid expenses.

Exhibit 4
Indirect Format of Statement of Cash Flows

Mom's Cookie Company Statement of Cash Flows For the Year Ended December 31, 2004	
Operating Activities	
Net income	$ 52,990
Depreciation expense	25,500
Increase in accounts receivable	(8,570)
Increase in merchandise inventory	(23,600)
Increase in supplies	(690)
Increase in prepaid rent	(2,000)
Increase in accounts payable	9,610
Increase in unearned revenue	4,250
Increase in interest payable	650
Net cash flow from operating activities	58,140
Investing Activities	
Payments for purchase of equipment	(216,000)
Receipts from sale of equipment	340
Net cash flow for investing activities	(215,660)
Financing Activities	
Receipts from sale of common stock	80,000
Payment of dividends	(1,800)
Receipts from borrowing	100,000
Repayment of debt	(10,000)
Net cash flow from financing activities	168,200
Net increase in cash	10,680
Cash balance, December 31, 2003	0
Cash balance, December 31, 2004	$ 10,680

In either case, cash flow is less than net income. Therefore, **increases in current assets are subtracted from net income to calculate operating cash flow.**

When current assets decrease, the opposite has occurred, either:

- Cash has been received from customers that was not earned this period—decrease in accounts receivable, or
- Resources have been used that were not paid for this period—decrease in inventory or prepaid expenses.

In either case, cash flow is greater than net income. Therefore, **decreases in current assets are added to net income to calculate operating cash flow.**

When current liabilities increase, either:

- Cash has been received from customers but has not been earned—increase in unearned revenue, or
- Resources have been used but payment has not been made—increase in accounts and other payables.

In either case, cash flow is greater than net income. Therefore, **increases in current liabilities are added to net income to calculate operating cash flow.**

When current liabilities decrease, either:

- Revenue has been earned but cash was received in a previous period—decrease in unearned revenue, or
- Payment has been made for resources that were used in a previous period—decrease in accounts and other payables.

In either case, cash flow is less than net income. Therefore, **decreases in current liabilities are subtracted from net income to calculate operating cash flow.**

Exhibit 5 summarizes these rules. The rules apply to changes in current asset and current liability accounts during a fiscal period. Because 2004 was the first year of operations for Mom's Cookie Company, the beginning balances of all current asset and current liability accounts was zero. Consequently, the changes in these accounts were equal to the ending balances. When working with a company that has beginning and ending balances, it is necessary to compute the change in current asset and current liability balances and use these in the calculations in Exhibit 2. Also keep in mind that some current asset and current liability accounts, such as short-term investments and short-term debt (including the current portion of notes payable), are not associated with operating activities. These accounts are associated with financial resources and involve investing activities (for assets) or financing activities (for liabilities). Finally, some revenue and expense items, depreciation and amortization expenses in particular, do not require cash payments. Therefore, they are always added to net income to calculate operating cash flow.

Exhibit 5
Rules for Adjusting Net Income to Calculate Operating Cash Flow

Event	Rule
Increase in Current Assets	Subtract from Net Income
Decrease in Current Assets	Add to Net Income
Increase in Current Liabilities	Add to Net Income
Decrease in Current Liabilities	Subtract from Net Income

Exhibit 6 provides the statement of cash flows for Krispy Kreme Doughnuts, Inc., from the company's 2002 annual report. Though the statement contains more items than that for Mom's Cookie Company, the interpretation is similar. For each operating cash flow adjustment, a note identifies why the amount was added (or subtracted). All of these items identify either revenues for which cash was not received, cash received that was not earned, expenses for which cash was not paid, or cash paid for which expenses were not incurred. In short, all are timing differences between when revenue or expense was recognized and when cash was received or paid.

We can determine from Exhibit 6 that, usually, all of Krispy Kreme's current assets and current liabilities increased. Observe that receivables, inventories, and prepaid expenses were all subtracted, and accounts payable and other current liabilities were added.

It is not uncommon for a company to report a noncash revenue (or gain) or a noncash expense (or loss). Gains are always subtracted because they increase net income but do not provide cash inflow, and losses are always added because they decrease net income but do not require cash outflow. Gains and losses from sales of long-term assets (plant assets or investments) are subtracted (for gains) or added (for losses) because these gains and losses do not provide or use cash as part of operating activities. Cash received or paid from these transactions is correctly reported in the investing activities section.

The investing activities section of Krispy Kreme's cash flow statement is similar to that for Mom's Cookie Company. Purchases of property and equipment and other long-term assets decrease cash flow. Sale of these items increases cash flow. The financing activities section also is similar. Borrowing and issuing stock increase cash flow, and repayment of debt and payments to owners decrease cash flow.

The net increase in cash of $14,878,000 in 2002 explains the change in Krispy Kreme's cash account reported on its balance sheet. (See Exhibit 4 in Chapter F4.)

Exhibit 6 Indirect Format of Statement of Cash Flows

Krispy Kreme Doughnuts, Inc.
Consolidated Statements of Cash Flows

In thousands

Year ended	**Jan. 30, 2000**	**Jan. 28, 2001**	**Feb. 3, 2002**
CASH FLOW FROM OPERATING ACTIVITIES:			
Net income	$ 5,956	$ 14,725	$ 26,378
Items not requiring (providing) cash:			
Depreciation and amortization	4,546	6,457	7,959
Deferred income taxes	258	1,668	2,553
Loss on disposal of property and equipment, net	—	20	235
Other	1,012	2,357	11,573
Change in assets and liabilities:			
Receivables	(4,760)	(3,434)	(13,317)
Inventories	(93)	(2,052)	(3,977)
Prepaid expenses	(1,619)	1,239	(682)
Income taxes, net	(2,016)	902	(2,575)
Accounts payable	540	2,279	3,884
Accrued expenses	4,329	7,966	4,096
Deferred compensation	345	(15)	83
Net cash provided by operating activities	8,498	32,112	36,210
CASH FLOW FROM INVESTING ACTIVITIES:			
Purchase of property and equipment	(11,335)	(25,655)	(37,310)
Proceeds from disposal of property and equipment	—	1,419	3,196
Acquisitions	—	—	(20,571)
Investments in joint ventures	—	(4,465)	(1,218)
(Increase) decrease in other assets	1,309	(3,216)	(4,237)
(Purchase) sale of investments, net	—	(35,371)	7,877
Net cash used for investing activities:	(10,026)	(67,288)	(52,263)
CASH FLOW FROM FINANCING ACTIVITIES:			
Repayment of long-term debt	(2,400)	(3,600)	—
Net short-term (repayments) borrowings	—	(15,775)	345
Borrowings of long-term debt	4,282	—	4,643
Proceeds from stock offering	—	65,637	17,202
Proceeds from exercise of stock options	—	104	3,906
Cash dividends paid	(1,518)	(7,005)	—
Other	934	(144)	5,483
Net cash provided by financing activities:	398	39,019	30,931
Net increase (decrease) in cash and cash equivalents	(1,130)	3,843	14,878
Cash and cash equivalents at beginning of year	4,313	3,183	7,026
Cash and cash equivalents at end of year	$ 3,183	$ 7,026	$ 21,904

Note: Modifications have been made to the original format to simplify the presentation.

2 SELF-STUDY PROBLEM

The following information appears on the income statement and balance sheet of Bryson Co. for a recent fiscal period.

WebTUTOR Advantage

Net income	$16,540
Depreciation and amortization expense	3,560
Increase in accounts receivable	2,500
Decrease in merchandise	3,200
Increase in supplies	430
Increase in accounts payable	660
Decrease in wages payable	375
Increase in interest payable	280
Decrease in income tax payable	700

Required Use the information provided to prepare the operating activities section of the statement of cash flows for Bryson Co. using the indirect format.

The solution to Self-Study Problem 2 appears at the end of the chapter.

INTERPRETING CASH FLOWS

OBJECTIVE 3

Interpret cash flow information as a basis for analyzing financial performance.

Understanding a company's cash flows and the reasons for the cash flows is critical to investors, managers, and other decision makers. To survive and prosper, a company must create sufficient cash flows to pay its bills, repay its debt, and provide a reasonable return to its owners. The statement of cash flows provides important information for evaluating past decisions and future prospects.

A company's net income and operating cash flow are seldom equal. A major difference between the two amounts is Depreciation and Amortization Expense. This expense reduces net income but does not require the use of cash. As shown in Exhibit 6, much of the difference between Krispy Kreme's net income and its operating cash flows is due to its depreciation and amortization expense. Other differences are explained by changes in current asset and current liability accounts. Changes in these accounts can provide useful information about a company's operations. Increases in current assets (Accounts Receivable and Inventory) and increases in Accounts Payable are common for companies that exhibit increases in net income. Higher sales lead to more receivables and require larger amounts of inventories. Payables also increase because of the increased demand for inventories. Increases in operating cash flows over time and large operating cash flows relative to net income (as seen in Exhibit 6) usually indicate good financial performance.

The amount of cash flow from operating activities normally is approximately equal to the amount of cash flow from (for) investing activities plus the amount of cash flow from (for) financing activities. A company depends on its operating activities to meet most of its cash flow needs. In the long run, operating cash flows must be sufficient to meet the cash needs of a company. If net operating cash flows are negative, a company is normally facing serious financial problems. In the short run, the company may be able to borrow cash or sell long-term assets to generate cash. But in the long run, it will be unable to stay in business using these methods. Creditors will refuse to lend money to a company that cannot create operating cash flows to ensure repayment of the debt. Also, the company will run out of assets that it can sell and still stay in business. Accordingly, negative operating cash flows combined with cash inflows from investing activities (from selling assets) and cash inflows from financing activities (from borrowing) is clearly a negative sign.

A company that is performing well normally creates net cash flow from operating activities. This excess cash can be used for expansion (to buy additional assets) or for financing purposes (to repay debt, repurchase stock, or pay dividends to stockholders). Accordingly, a combination of positive net cash flows from operating activities and negative cash flows for investing activities normally is a sign of good performance **and growth**. A growing company usually is increasing in value. As the company expands by purchasing more assets, it has the ability to produce and sell more products, which may result in additional profitability and increased operating cash flows. Observe that Krispy Kreme is using most of its operating cash flows for investing purposes. The company is acquiring additional assets each year.

If a company creates more cash from operating activities than it can use for investing purposes, it normally will use the cash to repay debt or to make payments to stockholders. If these payments are large, they may be an indication that the company is performing well but does not have a lot of good investing opportunities. Krispy Kreme was not able to generate sufficient cash flows from operating activities to meet its investing needs. Additional cash was obtained from financing activities.

A company with a lot of good investing opportunities may borrow money or sell stock to provide additional cash to take advantage of these opportunities. Thus, cash inflow from financing activities is a positive sign if a company is using this cash to purchase additional assets (for investing activities). Cash inflow from financing activities is a bad sign if the cash is used for operating activities. This may indicate that the company cannot create enough cash from its operations to meet ongoing needs.

The cash flow information presented in Exhibit 6 suggests that Krispy Kreme was performing well during the three years reported. Operating cash flows were large and generally increasing, and cash was being invested in additional assets. The company was not experiencing any difficulty in repaying debt or in meeting any of its cash flow needs.

Exhibit 7 summarizes the types of information provided by a cash flow statement. Other cash flow combinations are possible, but these are the most common and the most likely to provide a clear indication of how well a company is performing.

Exhibit 7
Cash Flow Patterns and the Financial Health of a Company

Operating Cash Flows	Investing Cash Flows	Financing Cash Flows	Normal Interpretation
+	−	+	The company is prosperous and growing. Financing cash flow is used to take advantage of growth opportunities.
−	+	+	The company is facing serious financial problems. It is selling assets and using financing activities to meet current cash needs.
+	+ or −	−	The company is prosperous but may not have a lot of good growth opportunities. It is using operating cash to pay off debt and pay stockholders.
+ or −	+	−	The company may be facing a current cash flow problem. It is selling assets to supplement current cash flows to cover its financing needs. This is especially a problem if the company is short of cash to repay debt.

The amount of change in a company's cash balance usually is not of major importance. This change usually is small, and a small increase or decrease does not signal financial problems or strengths. In particular, you should not assume that a net decrease in cash is an indication of a major financial problem for a company. You should **focus instead on changes in operating, investing, and financing cash flows.**

Case in Point

http://ingram.swlearning.com

Find out more about United Airlines.

Cash Flow Problems

The airlines industry faced financial problems in 2001 because of the declining economy. As economic activity decreases, fewer people travel and airline revenues decrease. The tragic events of September 11 were catastrophic for the industry. Many flights were cancelled, and passenger mileage dropped dramatically. The result of these events was a sharp decrease in profits and operating cash flows, leaving many airlines struggling for survival.

The following information was reported by United Airlines in its 2001 annual report:

(In millions) Year Ended December 31	2001	2000	1999
Net earnings (loss)	$(2,145)	$ 50	$ 1,235
Cash flows from (for) operating activities	(160)	2,472	2,421
Cash flows from investing activities	(1,969)	(2,521)	(1,624)
Cash flows from (for) financing activities	2,138	1,418	(877)

Profits decreased steadily from 1999 to 2001. Operating cash flow became negative in 2001. To meet its investing cash flow needs, the company increased its borrowing in 2001. The company's assets did not increase much from 2000 to 2001. Most of its investing activities were to replace existing assets. Most of United's assets were airplanes that it could not sell, since there was a surplus among all airlines. Some of the airplanes were mothballed pending an increase in demand.

Borrowing to meet operating and investing needs is a short-term solution. A company cannot stay in business long if it does not generate sufficient cash from operating activities to cover ordinary operating costs, replace assets, and repay creditors.

3 SELF-STUDY PROBLEM

WebTUTOR Advantage

A statement of cash flows is provided below for Sound Bytes Company.

Sound Bytes Company
Statement of Cash Flows
For the Year Ended December 31, 2004

Operating Activities	
Net income	$ 40,698
Adjusted for:	
Increase in accounts receivable	(23,034)
Increase in merchandise	(36,780)
Increase in accounts payable	22,479
Increase in prepaid expenses	(12,340)
Decrease in other payables	(3,982)
Depreciation and amortization	35,612
Net cash flow from operating activities	22,653
Investing Activities	
Sale of plant assets	86,511
Financing Activities	
Repayment of debt	(115,240)
Net decrease in cash	(6,076)
Cash balance, December 31, 2003	15,495
Cash balance, December 31, 2004	$ 9,419

Required Use the statement to answer the following questions.

A. How much cash flow did the company create from its operating activities?
B. What are the primary explanations for the difference between the company's net income and operating cash flow?
C. How did the company use its cash flows?
D. How well does the company appear to be performing based on its cash flow information?

The solution to Self-Study Problem 3 appears at the end of the chapter.

REVIEW

SUMMARY of IMPORTANT CONCEPTS

1. The statement of cash flows reports the cash inflows and outflows associated with the operating, investing, and financing activities of a company for a fiscal period. The statement may be presented in a direct or indirect format.
   a. The direct format lists cash activities associated with operating activities for a fiscal period.
   b. The indirect format reports cash flow from operating activities by adjusting net income for operating activities that did not generate or use cash during a fiscal period. These adjustments consist of revenues or expenses (such as depreciation) that did not have a cash effect and changes in current asset and current liability accounts.

2. Cash flow information is important to decision makers.
   a. Information about the sources and uses of cash indicates a company's ability to meet its payment obligations now and in the future.
   b. Cash flow information, along with information on the income statement and balance sheet, provides insight into a company's operating, investing, and financing activities.

SELF-STUDY PROBLEM SOLUTIONS

SSP5-1

Jerome, Inc.
Statement of Cash Flows

Operating Activities	
Received from customers	$ 14,750
Paid for merchandise	(8,400)
Paid to employees	(4,000)
Paid for utilities	(2,200)
Paid for supplies	(1,800)
Net cash flow for operating activities	(1,650)
Investing Activities	
Received from sale of land	$ 20,000
Paid for building	(75,000)
Paid for equipment	(13,500)
Net cash flow for investing activities	(68,500)
Financing Activities	
Received from sale of stock	$100,000
Paid for debt repayment	(35,000)
Paid for dividends	(2,500)
Net cash flow from financing activities	62,500
Net decrease in cash	(7,650)
Cash balance at beginning of period	16,350
Cash balance at end of period	$ 8,700

The company's primary sources of cash were from selling stock, selling land, and from sales of goods to customers. Its primary uses of cash were the purchase of a building and equipment and the repayment of debt.

SSP5-2

Bryson Co. Statement of Cash Flows	
Operating Activities	
Net income	$16,540
Adjustments to reconcile net income to cash flows:	
Depreciation and amortization expense	3,560
Increase in accounts receivable	(2,500)
Decrease in merchandise	3,200
Increase in supplies	(430)
Increase in accounts payable	660
Decrease in wages payable	(375)
Increase in interest payable	280
Decrease in income tax payable	(700)
Net increase in operating cash flows	$20,235

SSP5-3

A. Net cash flow from operating activities was $22,653.
B. Primary explanations of the differences are increases in current assets (merchandise and receivables), an increase in accounts payable, and depreciation and amortization expense.
C. Cash flows from operating and investing activities were used to repay debt.
D. The company does not appear to be performing very well. Its operating cash flows were much less than its net income. The increase in merchandise and receivables and the increase in payables suggest that the company was not selling the inventory it was acquiring, was having difficulty collecting from its customers, and was having difficulty paying its suppliers. Selling plant assets to meet current cash needs is also a sign of poor financial performance. The company apparently needed more cash than it could create from its operating activities to meet its obligations. It was forced to sell assets to raise cash. In the long run, a company cannot survive by selling assets to repay debt.

Thinking Beyond the Question

How is cash flow information determined and reported to external users?

This chapter examined the opening question by describing two methods of preparing the statement of cash flows. Both methods use income statement and balance sheet amounts to determine cash flows. It is important to understand the relationships among the statements to obtain a complete picture of a business.

Is it possible for a profitable business to fail? What do you think are the primary causes of business failure? How are a company's financial statements useful for identifying financial problems that may lead to failure? What role does the statement of cash flows play in decision making by investors and creditors?

QUESTIONS

Q5-1 *Obj. 1* What question is the direct format of the statement of cash flows designed to answer?

Q5-2 *Objs. 1, 2* If a company acquires machinery in exchange for a long-term note payable, both a financing activity and an investing activity have taken place. Explain how this is true.

Q5-3 *Objs. 1, 2* If long-term assets are acquired in exchange for shares of stock, no cash is involved. Will this transaction be reported on the statement of cash flows? If not, why not? If so, how?

Q5-4 *Objs. 1, 2* The direct format and indirect format relate only to the operating activities section of the statement of cash flows. Regarding the investing and financing activities sections, are they presented in a direct-type format or an indirect-type format?

Q5-5 *Objs. 1, 2* Why does the cash effect of interest appear as an operating activity, rather than a financing or investing activity?

Q5-6 *Obj. 2* Explain why depreciation expense and amortization expense are added back to net income in the determination of cash flows from operations when the indirect format is used.

Q5-7 *Obj. 2* In indirect format, why is an increase in accounts receivable subtracted from net income in computing cash flow from operations?

Q5-8 *Obj. 2* What question is the indirect format of the statement of cash flows designed to answer? Explain.

Q5-9 *Obj. 1* Why would one usually expect a growing company to have negative cash flow from investing activities?

Q5-10 *Obj. 3* Why is it a bad sign if cash flow from operations is consistently negative?

Q5-11 *Obj. 3* Why is it a bad sign if cash flow from investing activities is consistently positive?

Q5-12 *Obj. 3* Assume a company consistently produces net cash inflow from operations. To what uses might this cash inflow be applied?

Q5-13 *Obj. 3* Assume a company consistently reports a net cash outflow from financing activities. What does this suggest about the company?

Q5-14 *Obj. 3* Upon studying its statement of cash flows, you note that over the last three years a firm has consistently reported negative cash flow from operating activities, positive cash flow from investing activities, and negative cash flow from financing activities. What does this combination of cash flows suggest to you about the firm?

Q5-15 *Obj. 3* Explain how a company can have a net loss for a fiscal period but have a net increase in cash from operating activities.

Q5-16 *Obj. 1* A company operating in a mature industry with few opportunities for growth or expansion will generally report negative cash flow from financing activities. Why? Where might this cash be going?

EXERCISES

If your instructor is using Personal Trainer in this course, you may complete online the assignments identified by PT.

E5-1 *Obj. 1* The following information reflects cash flow and other activities of Better Vision Eyeglass Company for three months ended March 31, 2004.

Paid for equipment	$42,000	Paid to owners	$12,000
Paid for income taxes	3,000	Paid to suppliers	39,000
Paid for insurance	200	Depreciation expense	13,000
Paid for interest	450	Received from customers	87,500
Paid for utilities	790	Received from issuing long-term debt	23,000
Paid for advertising	300	Received from sale of land	19,500
		Paid to employees	18,000

Use this information to answer the following questions:

a. What was net cash flow from operating activities for the period?
b. What was net cash flow from financing activities for the period?
c. What was the net cash flow from investing activities for the period?
d. What was the net change in cash for the period?

E5-2 *Obj. 1* For each of the items listed below, identify whether the item would appear on the statement of cash flows (direct format) as part of the computation of cash flow from operating activities, investing activities, financing activities, or would not appear at all. Also, indicate whether the item is added or subtracted in computing cash flow using the direct method of preparing the statement of cash flows.

a. Purchase of plant assets
b. Cash paid to suppliers
c. Cash collected from customers
d. Payment of long-term debt
e. Net income
f. Depreciation expense
g. Payment of dividends
h. Issuing stock
i. Cash paid to employees
j. Cash paid for income taxes
k. Disposal of plant assets

E5-3 *Obj. 1* Northport Bottling Company has the following information available for the first six months of 2004.

Cash collected from customers	$268,000
Cash paid to suppliers	82,500
Cash paid for utilities	20,000
Cash paid for insurance	23,000
Cash paid for equipment	75,000
Cash paid to employees	57,500
Cash paid for interest	9,000
Cash paid for dividends	5,000
Cash received from disposal of equipment	18,500

Determine the cash flow from operating activities for the six-month period.

E5-4 *Obj. 1* Bay View Company reported the following information at the end of its most recent fiscal year.

Cash paid for fire insurance	$ 5,000
Cash paid for dividends	22,600
Cash paid to suppliers of inventory	119,850
Cash paid for interest	3,750
Cash collected from customers	187,200
Cash received from disposal of equipment	38,000
Cash paid for utilities	9,400
Cash paid to employees	31,500
Cash paid for equipment	65,100

(Continued)

Determine each of the following amounts. Show your work neatly and clearly.

a. Net cash flow from operating activities (direct format)
b. Net cash flow from financing activities
c. Net cash flow from investing activities

E5-5 *Obj. 1* Eden Healthfoods reported the following information.

Proceeds from issuance of long-term debt	$13,057
Additions to plant and equipment	5,500
Proceeds from sales of businesses	30,957
Proceeds from sales of plant and equipment	1,986
Payments of debt	83,000

Calculate the net cash flow from (a) financing and (b) investing activities for Eden.

E5-6 *Objs. 1, 2* All of the following statements apply to the statement of cash flows covering a given period. If a statement applies only to the direct format, write *D* in the space allowed. If a statement applies only to the indirect format, write *I* in the space allowed. If a statement applies to both formats, write *B* in the space allowed.

____________ a. The amount of cash received from customers is listed.
____________ b. A purpose of the statement is to reconcile the amount of cash generated by operating activities to the amount of net income generated by operating activities.
____________ c. The amount by which cash receipts from customers differed from sales is reported.
____________ d. Certain revenues and expenses that did not generate or consume cash are listed.
____________ e. The amount of net income is listed on the face of the statement.
____________ f. The amount of cash paid to suppliers of inventory is included.
____________ g. The amount of cash paid for taxes is reported.
____________ h. The amount of cash raised from selling bonds to investors is listed on the face of the statement.
____________ i. The purpose of the statement is to reveal the amount of cash received from or paid out for specific operating activities.
____________ j. The amount of cash paid to acquire land and buildings is included.

E5-7 *Objs. 1, 2* Each of the items found below might appear on a statement of cash flows.

	Statement Section	Statement Format	Added or Subtracted?
1. Decrease in taxes payable			
2. Cash paid to suppliers of inventory			
3. Dividends declared and paid			
4. Depreciation expense			
5. Sale of stock			
6. Increase in accounts receivable			
7. Cash collected from customers			
8. Purchase of plant assets			
9. Payments on long-term debt			
10. Cash paid for taxes			
11. Increase in wages payable			
12. Purchase of treasury stock			

For each item, indicate answers as shown.

a. Would it appear on the statement of cash flows under the operating activities (*O*), investing activities (*I*), or financing activities (*F*) section?
b. Would it appear in the direct format (*D*), indirect format (*I*), or in both formats (*B*)?
c. Would it be added (*1*) or subtracted (*2*) in computing cash flow?

E5-8 *Obj. 2* For each item in the following list, identify whether it would appear on the statement of cash flows (indirect format) as part of the computation of cash flow from operating activities, cash flow from investing activities, or cash flow from financing activities. Also, indicate whether the item is added or subtracted in computing cash flow using the indirect method of preparing the statement of cash flows.

a. Purchase of plant assets
b. Increase in accounts payable
c. Decrease in accounts receivable
d. Payment of long-term debt
e. Net income
f. Depreciation expense
g. Payment of dividends
h. Issuing stock
i. Increase in inventory
j. Decrease in taxes payable
k. Disposal of plant assets

E5-9 *Obj. 2* The following information is available for Guardian Company for the first month of 2004.

Revenues	$15,000
Expenses	8,000
Increase in accounts receivable	700
Decrease in inventory	1,200
Decrease in supplies	400
Increase in accounts payable	1,100
Decrease in wages payable	900
Depreciation expense	800
Patent expense	300

Determine the cash flow from operating activities for the month.

E5-10 *Obj. 2* Use the information provided in each of the following independent situations to answer the questions. For each situation, briefly explain the reasoning behind each of your calculations.

a. Cash paid to suppliers for merchandise during a period was $37,500. Accounts payable decreased during the period by $3,000. Inventory increased during the period by $3,500. What was the cost of goods sold for the period?
b. Interest paid during a period was $4,000. Interest payable decreased during the period by $1,200. What was the interest expense for the period?
c. Cash flow from operations for a period was $28,000. Current assets decreased during the period by $6,000. Current liabilities decreased during the period by $2,000. What was net income for the period?
d. Cash collected from customers for a fiscal period was $27,000. Accounts receivable increased during the period by $3,000. What was sales revenue for the period?

E5-11 *Obj. 2* Use the information provided in each of the following independent situations to answer the questions. For each situation, briefly explain the reasoning behind each of your calculations.

a. Net cash flow from operations for a period was $30,000. Noncash revenues for the period were $11,000. Noncash expenses for the period were $13,200. What was net income for the period?
b. Wages expense for a period was $69,000. Wages payable increased during the period by $10,500. How much cash was paid to employees during the period?
c. Cash collected from customers for a fiscal period was $224,500. Sales revenue for the period was $241,000. Accounts receivable at the beginning of the period was $36,000. What was the balance in accounts receivable at the end of the period?
d. Net income for a period was $45,000. Current assets increased during the period by $7,500. Current liabilities increased during the period by $10,000. How much was cash flow from operations for the period?

E5-12 *Obj. 2* Changes in account balances are shown in the following chart. For each item, where appropriate, indicate the adjustment that would be made to net income in the operating cash flow

(Continued)

section of a cash flow statement using the indirect method and the reason for the adjustment. Item *a* is provided as an example.

Account Balance	Adjustment and Reason
a. Accounts receivable increased $10,000	Subtract $10,000 from net income because cash collected from customers was $10,000 less than sales for the period.
b. Accounts payable increased $7,500	
c. Inventory decreased $50,000	
d. Notes payable increased $100,000	
e. Equipment decreased $80,000	
f. Prepaid insurance decreased $22,000	
g. Wages payable decreased $8,000	
h. Unearned revenue increased $13,000	

E5-13 *Obj. 2* P/T The following information was reported by **The Boeing Company** in its 2000 annual report (in millions of dollars).

Decrease in inventories	$1,097
Decrease in short-term investments	100
Depreciation and amortization	1,479
Decrease in accounts payable	311
Increase in accounts receivable	768
Increase in income taxes payable	421
Net earnings	2,128
Other additions to net income	1,796

What was Boeing's cash flow from operating activities for the fiscal year?

E5-14 *Obj. 2* Martha Rosenbloom holds stock in several major corporations. Each year she receives a copy of the companies' annual reports. She looks at the pictures, reads the discussion by management, and examines some of the primary financial statement numbers. She has a pretty good understanding of some of the financial statement information. She tells her friends that she doesn't know how to make heads or tails of the statement of cash flows, however. She doesn't understand how depreciation and changes in current assets and liabilities have anything to do with cash. A mutual friend, Arthur Doyle, has found out that you are taking accounting and asks you to help Martha. Write Martha a letter explaining the cash flow from operating activities section of the statement of cash flows found in most annual reports. Martha's address is 945 Oak Lane, Anytown, USA.

E5-15 *Obj. 2* Great Adventure Travel Company had the following adjustments to net income when computing its cash flow from operations for the year just ended.

Net income		$326,000
Add: Adjustments		
(1) Depreciation	$13,000	
(2) Decrease in accounts receivable	2,000	
(3) Increase in inventory	(4,500)	
(4) Decrease in accounts payable	(3,000)	7,500
Cash flow from operations		$333,500

a. Explain why it is generally necessary to make additions to and subtractions from net income when computing cash flow from operations in the indirect format.
b. For each adjustment (labeled 1 through 4), explain why that specific adjustment was necessary to determine cash flow from operations.

E5-16 *Obj. 3* Bingle, Bangle, and Bungle all manufacture toys. At year end 2004, they reported the following information.

	Bingle	Bangle	Bungle
Cash flow from operating activities	$ 6,862	$ 14,656	$ 3,052
Cash flow from (for) investing activities	(4,409)	457	938
Cash flow from (for) financing activities	(834)	(12,476)	(2,307)

Respond to each of the following questions.

a. Which company had the largest amount of cash flow from operating activities? Which had the smallest?
b. Would you generally expect cash flow associated with investing activities to be negative? Why or why not?
c. In what ways does Bingle appear to be different from the other two companies? What do these differences suggest about the companies?

E5-17 *Obj. 3* Consider the pattern in following selected year-end data for Landsdowne Company.

Year	1	2	3	4	5	6
Cash flow from operating activities	$20,000	$25,000	$18,000	$12,000	$ 6,000	$ 2,000
Receivables	35,000	37,000	42,000	45,000	50,000	53,000
Inventory	70,000	76,000	80,000	84,000	86,000	90,000
Payables	24,000	28,000	32,000	46,000	57,000	66,000
Net income	50,000	53,000	55,000	59,000	63,000	55,000

Provide an explanation for the changes over the six-year period. Year 6 is the most recent year. What difficulties do you believe the company is facing?

E5-18 *Obj. 3* Sommer Company has experienced the following results over the past three years.

Year (In thousands)	1	2	3
Net income (loss)	$ 2,000	$(10,000)	$ (8,000)
Depreciation and amortization	(9,000)	(11,000)	(14,000)
Net cash flow from operating activities	13,000	15,000	18,000
Net expenditures for plant assets	9,000	6,000	5,000

The price of Sommer's common stock has declined steadily over the three-year period. At the end of year 3, it is trading at $10 per share. Early in year 4, Bottom Fischer, who specializes in taking over poorly performing businesses, has offered shareholders of Sommer $18 per share for their stock. Why would Fischer be willing to pay such an amount? What does he see in the company that suggests value?

E5-19 *Obj. 3* Rockman Associates has reported the following selected account balances on its most recent balance sheet.

Account and balance	Anticipated future event and cash flow
a. Accounts receivable, $12,000	$12,000 of cash should be received from customers during the next fiscal year. This will appear in the operating activities section.
b. Prepaid insurance, $22,000	no cash flow; reduce over time
c. Merchandise, $50,000	CASH FLOW
d. Treasury stock, $33,000 (companies buy their own stock back)	
e. Accounts payable, $6,500	CASH outflow; Oper. Activity
f. Machinery, $92,000	cash flow
g. Notes payable, long-term, $88,000	NO cash flow this year; Fin.
h. Unearned revenue, $10,000	NO cash flow; will disappear
i. Taxes payable, $7,800	oper.; cash flow
j. Retained earnings, $56,000	

For each item, describe the anticipated future event and cash flow (if any) that is expected to occur and in which section of a future statement of cash flows it will appear. The first item is completed as an example.

PROBLEMS

If your instructor is using Personal Trainer in this course, you may complete online the assignments identified by PT.

P5-1 Preparing a Statement of Cash Flows (Direct Format)

Obj. 1

PT

San Garza Properties has been in business for many years. On December 31, 2003, the firm's cash balance was $9,121. During January of 2004, the 14 events below were recorded in the company's accounting system.

		ASSETS		=	LIABILITIES	+	OWNERS' EQUITY	
Date	**Accounts**	**Cash**	**Other Assets**				**Contributed Capital**	**Retained Earnings**
1	Cash	18,000						
	Bank Loan Payable				18,000			
2	Rent Expense							−3,000
	Cash	−3,000						
3	Office Furniture		5,500					
	Cash	−5,500						
4	Merchandise		9,000					
	Accounts Payable				9,000			
5	Cash	10,000						
	Common Stock						10,000	
6	Advertising Expense							−2,200
	Cash	−2,200						
7	Accounts Receivable		18,000					
	Sales Revenue							18,000
8	Merchandise		−7,500					
	Cost of Goods Sold							−7,500
9	Cash	8,100						
	Accounts Receivable		−8,100					
10	Accounts Payable				−7,000			
	Cash	−7,000						
11	Computer Equipment		4,800					
	Cash	−4,800						
12	Wages Expense							−1,400
	Wages Payable				1,400			
13	Dividends							−2,000
	Cash	−2,000						
14	Bank Loan Payable				−5,000			
	Interest Expense							−135
	Cash	−5,135						

Required Prepare a statement of cash flows for the month of January 2004. Use good form and the direct format.

P5-2 Preparing the Statement of Cash Flows (Direct Format)

Obj. 1

PT

Planet Accessories Company reported the following balance sheet and income statement at year-end 2004. In addition, dividends totaling $1,000 were paid.

Required

A. Assume the company uses the direct format to prepare its statement of cash flows. What amounts would be reported on the 2004 statement of cash flows for each of the following?

1. Cash collections from customers (Hint: Inspect Sales Revenue and the change in Accounts Receivable.)
2. Cash paid to suppliers of inventory (Hint: Assume all purchases were made for cash.)
3. Cash paid for insurance (Hint: Inspect the insurance expense account and the change in the prepaid insurance account.)
4. Cash paid for rent (Hint: Inspect Rent Expense and the change in Rent Payable.)
5. Cash paid for depreciation
6. Cash paid for wages

B. What items and amounts would be reported under cash flow from investing activities? (Hint: Inspect the changes in long-term asset accounts.)

C. What items and amounts would be reported under cash flow from financing activities? (Hint: Inspect the changes in long-term liability and stockholders' equity accounts.)

D. Prepare a statement of cash flows using the direct format.

Balance Sheets at December 31	**2004**	**2003**
Cash	$ 826	$ 553
Accounts receivable	8,950	8,000
Inventories	11,600	10,100
Prepaid insurance	400	300
Property, plant and equipment	8,750	3,735
Less: Accumulated depreciation	(2,900)	(1,900)
Land	5,850	4,850
Total assets	$33,476	$25,638
Rent payable	$ 3,750	$ 4,000
Wages payable	1,750	1,400
Loan payable, long-term	9,200	5,200
Common stock, $1 par value	5,400	4,400
Retained earnings	17,950	12,212
Treasury stock	(4,574)	(1,574)
Total liabilities and shareholders' equity	$33,476	$25,638

Income Statement for 2004	
Sales revenue	$135,800
Cost of goods sold	54,300
Gross profit	81,500
Operating expenses:	
Advertising	17,029
Depreciation	1,000
Insurance	4,800
Rent	14,255
Wages	33,400
Operating income	11,016
Interest expense	650
Income before taxes	10,366
Taxes	3,628
Net income	$ 6,738

P5-3 Reconciling Net Income and Cash Flow from Operations

Obj. 2

P/T

For the fiscal year just completed, Dollar Sine Enterprises had the following summary information available concerning operating activities. The company had no investing or financing activities this year.

Sales of merchandise to customers on credit	$307,400
Sales of merchandise to customers for cash	88,250
Cost of merchandise sold on credit	200,000
Cost of merchandise sold for cash	57,400
Purchases of merchandise from suppliers on credit	233,700
Purchases of merchandise from suppliers for cash	48,100
Collections from customers on accounts receivable	321,000
Cash payments to suppliers on accounts payable	293,600
Operating expenses (all paid in cash)	93,500

Required

A. Determine the amount of:
1. net income for the year.
2. cash flow from operations for the year (direct format).

B. Indicate the direction and amounts by which each of these accounts changed during the year.
1. Accounts receivable
2. Merchandise inventory
3. Accounts payable

C. Using your results above, prepare the operating activities section of the statement of cash flows (indirect format).

P5-4 *Obj. 2* PT

Preparing a Statement of Cash Flow (Indirect Format)

Reuben Corporation has completed its comparative balance sheet and income statement at year-end 2004.

Comparative Balance Sheet	December 31, 2004	December 31, 2003
Cash	$ 4,400	$ 3,550
Accounts receivable	4,100	5,300
Inventory	5,700	4,100
Prepaid advertising	900	1,200
Buildings and furnishings	20,000	20,000
Accumulated depreciation	(6,000)	(5,000)
Land	14,000	10,000
Total assets	$43,100	$39,150
Rent payable	$ 2,800	$ 2,600
Taxes payable	1,600	2,000
Wages payable	2,000	900
Loan payable, long-term	14,000	22,250
Common stock	16,000	10,000
Retained earnings	6,700	1,400
Total liabilities and equity	$43,100	$39,150

Income Statement for 2004	
Sales revenue	$355,000
Cost of goods sold	241,400
Gross profit	$113,600
Operating expenses:	
Advertising	8,300
Depreciation	1,000
Insurance	3,500
Rent	31,200
Wages	57,380
Operating income	12,220
Interest expense	1,450
Income before tax	10,770
Taxes	3,770
Net income	$ 7,000

Additional information:

1. A payment of $8,250 was made on the loan principal during the year.
2. Just before year-end, a dividend was distributed to stockholders.
3. A parcel of land was acquired early in the year.
4. New shares of common stock were sold during the year.

Required Prepare a statement of cash flows in good form using the indirect format.

P5-5 *Obj. 2* PT

Preparing the Statement of Cash Flows (Indirect Format)

Refer to the financial statement information in Problem P5-2 and use it to complete the requirements below.

Required

A. Assume the company uses the indirect format to prepare its statement of cash flows. What amounts would be reported on the 2004 statement of cash flows for each of the following?
   1. Net income
   2. Adjustment for depreciation expense
   3. Adjustment for accounts receivable
   4. Adjustment for inventories
   5. Adjustment for prepaid insurance
   6. Adjustment for rent payable
   7. Adjustment for wages payable
B. What items and amounts would be reported under cash flow from investing activities? (Hint: Inspect the changes in long-term asset accounts.)
C. What items and amounts would be reported under cash flow from financing activities? (Hint: Inspect the changes in long-term liability and stockholders' equity accounts.)
D. Prepare a statement of cash flows using the indirect format.

P5-6 **Interpreting Cash Flows**

Obj. 3

The statement of cash flows for **Rowe Furniture Corporation** is shown below. Based in Salem, Virginia, the firm manufactures upholstered household furniture including sofas, sofa beds, and chairs.

Required Use the statement of cash flows to answer the following questions.

A. What were Rowe's primary sources of cash in 2001? Were these different than in the prior two years?
B. What were Rowe's primary uses of cash in 2001? Were these different than in the prior two years?
C. What were the primary reasons for the decrease in cash flow from operating activities between 2000 and 2001?
D. Evaluate Rowe's cash flows over the period shown. Has the company been able to finance its growth, dividends, and acquisition of treasury stock out of cash flow from operations? Explain.
E. Over the past three years, what were the primary reasons that cash flows from operations differed so much from net income?
F. The portion of the statement titled "Reconciliation of net earnings to net cash provided by operating activities" is a required disclosure. Of what does this section and presentation remind you? Might this disclosure requirement help explain why so few companies use the direct method? Explain.

The Rowe Companies Annual Report 2001
Consolidated Statements of Cash Flows

	Year Ended		
	12/2/01 (52 weeks)	**12/3/00 (53 weeks) (in thousands)**	**11/28/99 (52 weeks)**
Increase (Decrease) In Cash			
Cash flows from Operating Activities			
Cash received from customers	$ 329,683	$ 379,400	$ 295,563
Cash paid to suppliers and employees	(328,948)	(354,570)	(274,870)
Income taxes paid, net of refunds	585	(6,183)	(7,726)
Interest paid	(4,642)	(5,693)	(2,686)
Interest received	480	288	159
Other receipts—net	1,109	1,156	1,684
Net cash and cash equivalents provided by (used in) operating activities	(1,733)	14,398	12,124
Cash flows from Investing Activities			
Proceeds from sale of property and equipment	1,056	21	19
Capital expenditures	(3,317)	(9,155)	(8,830)
Payments to acquire businesses	—	(5,160)	(8,892)
Net cash used in investing activities	(2,261)	(14,294)	(17,703)
Cash flows from Financing Activities			
Net borrowings (payments) under line of credit	5,368	(164)	2,071
Proceeds from issuance of long-term debt	6,865	13,020	25,132
Payments to reduce long-term debt	(3,821)	(11,922)	(14,522)
Proceeds from loans against life insurance policies	3,014	—	—
Proceeds from issuance of common stock	27	51	460
Dividends paid	(1,379)	(1,849)	(1,714)
Purchase of treasury stock	(16)	(951)	(3,224)
Net cash provided by (used in) financing activities	10,058	(1,815)	8,203
Net increase (decrease) in cash and cash equivalents	6,064	(1,711)	2,624
Cash at beginning of year	3,393	5,104	2,480
Cash at end of year	$ 9,457	$ 3,393	$ 5,104

(Continued)

The Rowe Companies Annual Report 2001
Reconciliation of Net Earnings (Loss) to Net Cash
Provided by (Used In) Operating Activities:

	Year Ended		
	12/2/01 (52 weeks)	**12/3/00 (53 weeks) (in thousands)**	**11/28/99 (52 weeks)**
Net earnings (loss)	$ (6,189)	$ 3,544	$13,901
Adjustments to reconcile net earnings (loss) to net cash provided by (used in) operating activities, net of acquisition and disposition of businesses			
Loss on disposition of Wexford	—	5,455	—
Depreciation and amortization	8,569	8,581	6,165
Provision for deferred compensation	173	816	1,083
Payments made for deferred compensation	(813)	(160)	(319)
Deferred income taxes	1,001	(2,099)	(472)
Provision for losses on accounts receivable	4,421	1,485	413
Loss (gain) on disposition of assets	15	29	4
Change in operating assets and liabilities net of effects of acquisition and disposition of businesses			
Decrease (increase) in accounts receivable	4,649	5,564	(9,379)
Decrease (increase) in inventories	227	(832)	(5,692)
Decrease (increase) in prepaid expenses and other	1,679	(887)	(795)
Decrease (increase) in other assets	(352)	472	(1,210)
Increase (decrease) in accounts payable	(10,277)	(4,750)	3,830
Increase (decrease) in accrued expenses	(4,433)	(1,715)	2,170
Increase (decrease) in customer deposits	(403)	(1,105)	2,425
Total adjustments	4,456	10,854	(1,777)
Net cash provided by (used in) operating activities	$ (1,733)	$14,398	$12,124

Note: Slight modifications have been made to the format of the statement to simplify the presentation.

P5-7 Errors in Reporting Cash Flow from Operating Activities

Obj. 3

Starkovich Architects, Inc. uses the direct format to prepare the statement of cash flows. At year-end 2004, the following comparative balance sheet and abbreviated income statement were available as shown.

	December 31	
Comparative Balance Sheet	**2004**	**2003**
Cash	$ 3,400	$ 2,750
Accounts receivable	5,800	4,300
Inventory	4,700	5,100
Land	10,000	10,000
Total assets	$23,900	$22,150
Rent payable	$ 2,500	$ 2,900
Taxes payable	1,600	1,600
Wages payable	3,200	1,050
Common stock	15,000	15,000
Retained earnings	1,600	1,600
Total liabilities and equity	$23,900	$22,150

Income Statement for 2004	
Service revenue	$ 73,000
Commission revenue	42,100
Advertising expense	(13,400)
Rent expense	(24,000)
Wages expense	(42,600)
Taxes expense	(12,000)
Net income	$ 23,100

From this information, the accounting staff prepared the operating activities section of the statement of cash flows shown on the following page using the direct format.

Starkovich Architects, Inc. Operating Activities (Direct Format) Year Ending December 31, 2004	
Operating Activities	
Cash received from customers	$115,100
Cash paid for advertising	(13,400)
Cash paid for rent	(23,600)
Cash paid for wages	(40,450)
Cash paid for taxes	(11,000)
Cash provided by operating activities	$ 26,650

Required

A. What evidence can you identify to suggest that certain items are misstated in the computation of cash flow from operating activities? For each item that you believe is misstated, specify why you know this. (You may assume that the income statement and balance sheets are correct as presented.)
B. Prepare a revised computation of cash flow from operating activities incorporating the necessary changes.

P5-8 Depreciation and Cash Flow

Obj. 3

A colleague is about to make a presentation to the management group regarding a $2 million capital investment proposal. She is quite sure that the management group will press her to identify a new source of financing to support the proposed investment. She shows you the operating activities section of the company's most recent statement of cash flows. (Amounts are in thousands of dollars.)

Your colleague is aware that there are a variety of methods acceptable under GAAP by which depreciation expense can be computed. Further, she knows that the company currently uses a very conservative method that results in low depreciation expense, especially in the early years of an asset's life. Your colleague is going to suggest that the firm use a more aggressive depreciation policy that will result in higher depreciation expense for the next several years. Says she, "The higher depreciation expense will generate more cash from operating activities. According to the cash flow statement here, adding back greater depreciation expense will result in more cash provided by operating activities. See?" Assume it's quite reasonable that the firm use a more aggressive depreciation method.

Required

A. What format is this company using to prepare the statement of cash flows?
B. Do you agree with your colleague's thinking? Why or why not?
C. Construct a numerical example to prove your argument.

P5-9 Interrelationships among Financial Statements

Objs. 2, 3

P
T

Avnet, Inc. is a manufacturer of electronic instruments and controls with corporate headquarters in Phoenix, Arizona. Following are comparative income statements and comparative statements of cash flow from a recent annual report.

(Continued)

Avnet, Inc. and Subsidiaries
Consolidated Statements of Operations

(In thousands, except per share amounts)	June 28, 2002	Years Ended June 29, 2001	June 30, 2000
Sales	$8,920,248	$12,814,010	$9,915,042
Cost of sales	7,697,434	10,948,484	8,470,257
Gross profit	1,222,814	1,865,526	1,444,785
Selling, general and administrative expenses	1,225,799	1,611,874	1,076,793
Operating income (loss)	(2,985)	253,652	367,992
Other income, net	6,755	25,495	10,452
Interest expense	(124,583)	(191,895)	(94,798)
Income (loss) from continuing operations before income taxes	(120,813)	87,252	283,646
Income tax (provision) benefit	36,377	(87,155)	(121,082)
Income (loss) from continuing operations	(84,436)	97	162,564
Income from discontinued operations, net of income taxes of $0, $1,611 and $100, respectively	—	2,416	828
Gain on disposal of discontinued operations, net of income taxes of $0, $8,611 and $0, respectively	—	12,889	—
Income (loss) before cumulative effect of change in accounting principle	(84,436)	15,402	163,392
Cumulative effect of change in accounting principle	(580,495)	—	—
Net income (loss)	$ (664,931)	$ 15,402	$ 163,392
Earnings (loss) per share from continuing operations:			
Basic	$ (0.71)	$ —	$ 1.52
Diluted	$ (0.71)	$ —	$ 1.50
Earnings (loss) per share before cumulative effect of change in accounting principle:			
Basic	$ (0.71)	$ 0.13	$ 1.53
Diluted	$ (0.71)	$ 0.13	$ 1.51
Net earnings (loss) per share:			
Basic	$ (5.61)	$ 0.13	$ 1.53
Diluted	$ (5.61)	$ 0.13	$ 1.51
Shares used to compute earnings (loss) per share:			
Basic	118,561	117,263	106,627
Diluted	118,561	118,815	108,257

Note: Slight modifications have been made to the format of the statement to simplify the presentation.

Avnet, Inc. and Subsidiaries
Consolidated Statements of Cash Flows

(In thousands)	June 28, 2002	Years Ended June 29, 2001	June 30, 2000
Cash flows from operating activities:			
Net income (loss)	$ (664,931)	$ 15,402	$ 163,392
Income from discontinued operations, net of income taxes	—	(2,416)	(828)
Gain on disposal of discontinued operations, net of income taxes	—	(12,889)	—
Cumulative effect of change in accounting principle	580,495	—	—
Net income (loss) from continuing operations	(84,436)	97	162,564
Non-cash and other reconciling items:			
Depreciation and amortization	103,879	119,398	83,516
Deferred taxes	10,828	(79,659)	(40,159)
Other, net	121,240	296,450	43,339
	151,511	336,286	249,260
Changes in (net of effects from businesses acquisitions and dispositions):			
Receivables	433,863	315,669	(453,330)
Inventories	552,621	248,978	(535,844)
Payables, accruals and other, net	(161,690)	(714,733)	245,532
Net cash flows provided from (used for) operating activities	976,305	186,200	(494,382)
Cash flows from financing activities:			
Sales (repayments) of accounts receivable	(150,000)	350,000	—
Issuance of notes in public offerings, net	394,328	572,389	358,326
(Repayment) issuance of debt, net	(1,051,375)	(453,210)	695,966
Cash dividends	(26,546)	(27,387)	(18,180)
Other, net	24,225	10,834	29,157
Net cash flows (used for) provided from financing activities	(809,368)	452,626	1,065,269

(Continued)

(In thousands)	Years Ended June 28, 2002	June 29, 2001	June 30, 2000
Cash flows from investing activities:			
Purchases of property, plant and equipment	(83,750)	(125,421)	(92,488)
Acquisitions of operations, net	(31,547)	(858,851)	(675,030)
Investments in non-consolidated entities, net	(2,544)	(2,955)	(42,972)
Proceeds from sale of discontinued operations	—	226,390	—
Net cash flows used for investing activities	(117,841)	(760,837)	(810,490)
Effect of exchange rate changes on cash and cash equivalents	12,859	(7,468)	(995)
Net decrease in cash from discontinued operations	—	(25,073)	(11,082)
Cash and cash equivalents:			
-(decrease) increase	61,955	(154,552)	(251,680)
-at beginning of year	97,279	251,831	519,924
-at end of year	$ 159,234	$ 97,279	$ 268,244

Note: Slight modifications have been made to the format of the statement to simplify the presentation.

Required Answer the following questions.

A. Which reporting format does Avnet use for the statement of cash flows?
B. Compare the three-year trends of sales and net income. Do they exhibit an encouraging pattern? Why or why not? Discuss.
C. How does the pattern of cash flow from operations match up with the trends of net income and sales for the most recent three years?
D. During the most recent year shown, determine whether the following balance sheet accounts increased or decreased.
   1. Cash
   2. Receivables
   3. Inventory
   4. Payables
E. Study the overall pattern and components of financing cash flows. What have been the major sources and uses of cash during the three years shown? What do you conclude from this information?
F. Study the overall pattern and components of investing cash flows. What have been the major sources and uses of cash during the three years shown? What do you conclude from this information?

P5-10 Evaluating Information from a Statement of Cash Flows

Obj. 3

Circuit City is the nation's largest retailer of brand-name consumer electronics and major appliances. Its headquarters are in Richmond, Virginia. The company's comparative statements of cash flows from a recent annual report are shown on the next page.

Required Answer the following questions.

A. For the three years shown, compare the trend in net income to the trend in cash provided by operations.
B. What were the three most significant reasons that cash provided by operations was positive for fiscal 2002?
C. Inspect the information shown under investing activities. Also note the amount of depreciation and amortization reported under operating activities. Does this company's long-term asset base appear to be expanding, shrinking, or staying about the same size? Explain your answer.

Circuit City Stores, Inc.
Consolidated Statements of Cash Flows

(In thousands)	Years Ended February 28 or 29 2002	2001	2000
OPERATING ACTIVITIES:			
Net earnings	$ 218,795	$ 160,802	$ 197,590
Adjustments to reconcile net earnings to net cash provided by operating activities of continuing operations:			
Loss from discontinued operations	—	—	16,215
Loss on disposal of discontinued operations	—	—	114,025
Depreciation and amortization	150,711	153,090	148,164
Unearned compensation amortization of restricted stock	15,678	11,365	12,096
Loss on disposition of property and equipment	13,735	4,674	17
Provision for deferred income taxes	31,166	19,765	43,053
Changes in operating assets and liabilities, net of effects from business acquisitions:			
(Increase) decrease in net accounts receivable and retained interests in securitized receivables	(140,766)	7,541	(18,922)
Decrease (increase) in inventory	124,337	(67,655)	(184,507)
Decrease (increase) in prepaid expenses and other current assets	16,312	(41,426)	81,316
(Increase) decrease in other assets	(720)	1,012	240
Increase (decrease) in accounts payable, accrued expenses and other current liabilities and accrued income taxes	336,774	(64,193)	244,559
Increase (decrease) in deferred revenue and other liabilities	71,186	(17,855)	(15,565)
NET CASH PROVIDED BY OPERATING ACTIVITIES OF CONTINUING OPERATIONS	837,208	167,120	638,281
INVESTING ACTIVITIES:			
Cash used in business acquisitions	—	(1,325)	(34,849)
Purchases of property and equipment	(213,997)	(285,556)	(222,268)
Proceeds from sales of property and equipment, net	187,426	115,695	100,151
NET CASH USED IN INVESTING ACTIVITIES OF CONTINUING OPERATIONS	(26,571)	(171,186)	(156,966)
FINANCING ACTIVITIES:			
Proceeds from (payments on) short-term debt, net	9,037	(1,805)	(5,011)
Principal payments on long-term debt	(132,388)	(178,060)	(2,707)
Issuances of Circuit City Group Common Stock, net	17,920	26,912	6,942
Issuances of CarMax Group Common Stock, net	(1,958)	(263)	1,914
Proceeds from CarMax Group Common Stock offering, net	139,546	—	—
Dividends paid on Circuit City Group Common Stock	(14,556)	(14,346)	(14,207)
NET CASH PROVIDED BY (USED IN) FINANCING ACTIVITIES OF CONTINUING OPERATIONS	17,601	(167,562)	(13,069)
CASH USED IN DISCONTINUED OPERATIONS [NOTE 15]	(22,837)	(26,174)	(90,193)
Increase (decrease) in cash and cash equivalents	805,401	(197,802)	378,053
Cash and cash equivalents at beginning of year	446,131	643,933	265,880
Cash and cash equivalents at end of year	$1,251,532	$ 446,131	$ 643,933

Note: Slight modifications have been made to the format of the statement to simplify the presentation.

P5-11 Evaluating Income and Cash Flows

Objs. 2, 3

Selected financial statement information is reported below for Office Decor Company. All amounts are in thousands.

For the Year Ended December 31, 2004	
Sales revenue	$11,200
Cost of goods sold	6,400
Operating expenses	2,800
Net income	2,000
Dividends paid	1,000

(Continued)

December 31	2004	2003
Cash	$ 1,340	$1,940
Accounts receivable	4,600	2,200
Inventories	9,400	5,000
Accounts payable	3,800	2,600
Notes payable	10,000	6,000

Required Prepare a statement of cash flows (indirect format) for Office Decor, assuming that all important cash flow activities are reflected in the information provided above. Examine the financial information presented for Office Decor Company. What financial problems do you see? What are some potential causes of these problems?

P5-12 Interpreting a Cash Flow Statement

Obj. 3

Sara Lee Corporation, a food products company headquartered in Chicago, Illinois, recently reported the following cash flow statement.

Consolidated Statements of Cash Flows

Dollars in millions	Years Ended	June 29 2002	June 30, 2001	July 1, 2000
Operating Activities				
Income from continuing operations		$ 1,010	$ 1,603	$ 1,158
Adjustments for non-cash charges included in income from continuing operations				
Depreciation		471	392	402
Amortization of intangibles		111	207	200
Unusual items				
Gain on disposal of Coach business		—	(967)	—
Charges for exit activities and business dispositions		101	500	—
Increase in deferred taxes		21	88	48
Other non-cash credits, net		7	(62)	(38)
Changes in current assets and liabilities, net of businesses acquired and sold				
Decrease (increase) in trade accounts receivable		93	42	(116)
Decrease (increase) in inventories		304	25	(152)
Decrease (increase) in other current assets		7	(11)	(47)
(Decrease) in accounts payable		(417)	(133)	(56)
Increase (decrease) in accrued liabilities		27	(164)	57
Net cash from operating activities—continuing operations		1,735	1,520	1,456
Operating cash flows (used by) from discontinued operations		—	(24)	84
Net cash from operating activities		1,735	1,496	1,540
Investment Activities				
Purchases of property and equipment		(669)	(532)	(647)
Acquisitions of businesses and investments		(1,930)	(300)	(743)
Dispositions of businesses and investments		23	1,819	21
Sales of assets		113	65	64
Other		(12)	13	9
Net cash (used in) from investment activities		(2,475)	1,065	(1,296)
Financing Activities				
Issuances of common stock		109	104	84
Purchases of common stock		(138)	(643)	(1,032)
Borrowings of long-term debt		1,362	1,023	725
Repayments of long-term debt		(503)	(390)	(502)
Short-term borrowings (repayments), net		124	(1,914)	1,022
Payments of dividends		(484)	(486)	(485)
Net cash from (used in) financing activities		470	(2,306)	(188)
Effect of changes in foreign exchange rates on cash		20	(21)	(21)
(Decrease) increase in cash and equivalents		(250)	234	35
Cash and equivalents at beginning of year		548	314	279
Cash and equivalents at end of year		$ 298	$ 548	$ 314

Required Use the information from the statement of cash flows for Sara Lee Corporation to answer the following questions.

A. What was the amount of change in Sara Lee's cash account for 2002?
B. What were the primary sources of cash for the company?
C. What were the primary uses of cash?
D. Why were depreciation and amortization added to net income in computing cash flow from operating activities?
E. Why were the decreases in inventories and trade accounts receivable added to net income in computing cash flow from operating activities?
F. Why were the purchase of property and equipment, sales of assets and acquisitions of businesses listed as investing activities?
G. Did short-term debt increase or decrease during the year?
H. How much new long-term debt was issued during the year? How much old long-term debt was paid off?
I. Does the company appear to be facing a cash flow problem? Explain your answer.

P5-13 Interpreting Cash Flows

Obj. 3

The operating activities section of Bernstein Company's cash flow statement is reported below.

(In millions)	**2004**	**2003**	**2002**
Net income	$ 391	$ 455	$467
Depreciation and amortization	258	247	223
Special and nonrecurring items	(3)	0	0
Changes in current assets and liabilities:			
Accounts receivable	(220)	(102)	(66)
Inventories	(112)	(73)	(45)
Accounts payable	15	(22)	19
Income taxes	6	(7)	30
Other accrued expenses	(17)	26	11
Cash flow provided by operations	$ 318	$ 524	$639

Required What does this information reveal about why cash flow from operations has decreased by 50% over the three-year period? Be specific and explain the basis for your conclusions.

P5-14 Interpreting the Cash Flow Statement

Obj. 3

Best Buy Company, Inc., a retailer of consumer electronics headquartered in Minnesota, recently reported the following partial cash flow statement and income statement.

	(Dollars in millions) Year Ended March 2, 2002
Cash flows from operating activities	
Net income	$ 570
Adjustments to reconcile net income to net cash:	
Depreciation and amortization	309
Increase in accounts receivable	(18)
Decrease in inventories	(330)
Increase in other assets	(39)
Increase in accounts payable	529
Increase in accrued expenses and other	557
Net cash provided by operating activities	$1,578

	(Dollars in millions) Year Ended March 2, 2002
Revenues	$19,597
Cost of goods sold	15,167
Gross profit	4,430
Selling, general, and administrative expenses	3,493
Interest expense, net	1
Income before provision for income taxes	936
Provision for income taxes	366
Net income	$ 570

Required Use the information from the financial statements to answer each of the following questions.

A. How much cash did Best Buy collect from customers in the fiscal year ended March 2, 2002?
B. How much cash did Best Buy pay out for inventory in the fiscal year ended March 2, 2002? The increase in Accounts Payable arose from purchases of inventory that had not yet been paid for.
C. How much cash did Best Buy pay out for selling, general, and administrative expenses in the fiscal year ended March 2, 2002? The changes in other assets and in accrued expenses and other are related to selling, general, and administrative expenses.

P5-15 Comparing Cash Flows

Obj. 3

Summarized cash flow statements for 2001 are shown below for two computer industry firms: **Intel Corporation**, based in Santa Clara, California, and **Apple Computer**, headquartered in Cupertino, California.

(In millions)	Intel Corporation	Apple Computer
Net income	$ 1,291	$ (25)
Adjustments:		
Depreciation and amortization	6,469	102
(Increase) decrease in accounts receivable	1,561	487
(Increase) decrease in inventories	24	22
(Increase) decrease in other assets	898	118
Increase (decrease) in payables	(2,484)	(416)
Changes in taxes	(84)	(36)
Other adjustments	979	(67)
Net cash provided by operating activities	8,654	185
Net cash provided by (used in) investing activities	(195)	892
Net cash provided by (used in) financing activities	(3,465)	42
Net change in cash	4,994	1,119

Required Write a short report comparing the financial performance of the two companies. In what important ways were the results for both companies similar? In what important ways were the results different?

P5-16 Interpreting Cash Flows

Obj. 3

P/T **Required** Identify whether each of the following statements is true or false. Explain your answers. Write in complete sentences. Computations may be used as part of your explanation.

A. When a company prepares a cash flow statement using the indirect method, it adds depreciation expense to net income because depreciation is a source of cash during a fiscal period.
B. Alpha Company reported an increase in Accounts Receivable of $2 million during 2004. As a result, Alpha's cash flow from operating activities was $2 million less than its operating revenues.
C. Beta Company purchased $40 million of merchandise inventory during 2004. Beta's accounts payable increased from $5 million to $8 million during the year. Beta's cash flow statement (indirect method) would report an adjustment to net income of −$3 million.
D. Delta Company reported cost of goods sold of $27 million for 2004. Its merchandise inventory increased by $8 million during the year. If all inventory purchased was paid for in cash, then Delta's cash payments to suppliers of inventory during the year were $35 million.
E. Gamma Company reported the following:

Net cash flow for operating activities	$80
Net cash flow from investing activities	35
Net cash flow from financing activities	50
Net change in cash	$ 5

From this information, it appears that Gamma is facing financial problems.

P5-17 The Differential Effect of Transactions on Net Income and Cash Flow
Obj. 3

PT During March, each of the following events occurred at Frolic Park, Inc.

Event	Type of Activity	Effect on March's Net Income	Effect on March's Cash Flow
1. Sold $18,000 of goods on credit to customers. Received a 25% down payment with the balance on account.			
2. Paid $500 cash for office supplies that will be used during April.			
3. Received $3,000 from a customer in full payment of her account balance.			
4. Borrowed $80,000 from a local bank to be repaid in monthly installments plus interest starting in April.			
5. Paid rent on the office space ($1,200 per month) for the months of February, March, and April.			
6. Distributed monthly paychecks to employees totaling $13,300. 30% was for work performed in February and the balance for work performed in March.			
7. Purchased new Internet server equipment at a cost of $50,000.			
8. Purchased a 3-year fire insurance policy at a total cost of $10,800. Its coverage began on March 1.			
9. Purchased merchandise from suppliers on credit at a cost of $70,000.			
10. Collected $22,000 from customers in payment of their accounts. 80% of this amount was from sales recorded in February and the balance was from March sales.			
11. Collected four months' rent in advance (at $700 per month) from a tenant who will move in on April 1.			
12. Paid $45,000 to suppliers in partial payment for goods purchased in #9 above.			
13. Sold $33,000 of merchandise to customers on credit.			
14. Sold an investment in stocks and bonds for $28,000; the same amount that had been paid for it. A 3-year, 9% note receivable was accepted in full payment.			
Totals for March			

(Continued)

Required

A. Identify whether each transaction is an operating, investing, or financing activity.
B. For each event, identify the effect it had on March's net income and on March's cash flow from operations.
C. What does this problem suggest to you about the hazards of trying to manage an organization with accrual-basis accounting information only? Discuss.

P5-18 Comparing Cash Flow Statements Among Firms

Obj. 3

Sheik, Speer, and Love are three companies in similar industries. Five years of summarized cash flow data are available for each firm. Year 5 is the most recent.

	Year 5	Year 4	Year 3	Year 2	Year 1
Sheik Company:					
Operating activities	$ 30	$ 31	$ 28	$ 26	$ 28
Investing activities	3	1	6	5	4
Financing activities	(31)	(28)	(33)	(30)	(32)
Speer Company:					
Operating activities	(15)	(3)	7	14	26
Investing activities	8	4	(9)	(17)	(35)
Financing activities	6	0	3	4	11
Love Company:					
Operating activities	9	6	3	2	(1)
Investing activities	(13)	(12)	(11)	(10)	(10)
Financing activities	8	7	8	10	9

Study the information carefully. What clues can you find in the information concerning what is (or has been) going on with each firm? Do their business histories appear similar or dissimilar? Does the situation of one or more firms appear more favorable than one or more of the others?

Required For each firm, describe and discuss what you have learned from reviewing its summarized cash flow information.

P5-19 Interpreting the Cash Flow Statement

Obj. 3

PT

Embarcadero Company's most recent statement of cash flows is shown on the next page.

Required Use Embarcadero's statement of cash flows to answer the following questions.

A. What was the primary source of cash inflow for the company?
B. Why was the company able to report a net cash inflow from operations when it incurred a net loss for the period?
C. What were the primary uses of cash during the period?
D. Did Receivables, Inventories, and Accounts Payable increase or decrease during the year?
E. If revenues (as reported on the income statement) were $3,960 for the year, how much cash was collected from customers during the year?

Embarcadero Company Consolidated Statement of Cash Flows For the Year Ended December 31, 2004	
Operating activities	
Net loss	$ (682)
Adjustments to reconcile NI to cash flows:	
Depreciation and amortization	592
Noncash gains and losses, net	(136)
Changes in:	
Accounts receivable	172
Inventories	110
Other current assets	(24)
Accounts payable	98
Other current liabilities	148
Cash provided by operations	278
Investing activities	
Investments and acquisitions	(424)
Capital expenditures	(42)
Sales of investments	206
Cash used by investing activities	(260)
Financing activities	
Increase in long-term debt	1,014
Repurchase of common stock	(740)
Dividends paid	(402)
Cash provided by financing activities	(128)
Decrease in cash	$ (110)

P5-20 **Interrelationships among the Income Statement, Balance Sheet, and Statement of Cash Flow**
Objs. 2, 3
P/T

Frontera Corporation reported the following income statement and comparative balance sheet for the year ended December 31, 2004.

Income Statement (for the Year Ended December 31, 2004) (In thousands)	
Sales revenue	$6,930
Cost of goods sold	3,660
Gross profit on sales	3,270
Operating expenses:	
Wages	855
Depreciation	102
Rent	546
Advertising	1,224
Operating income	543
Other revenues and expenses:	
Interest revenue	84
Interest expense	(24)
Income before taxes	603
Income tax expense	210
Net income	$ 393

(Continued)

Balance Sheet (at December 31)	2004	2003
Assets:		
Cash	$ 482	$ 318
Accounts receivable	246	189
Inventory	471	483
Prepaid advertising	54	21
Total current assets	1,253	1,011
Buildings and equipment	2,811	1,974
Accumulated depreciation	(922)	(820)
Land	350	300
Investments, long-term	250	400
Total assets	$3,742	$2,865
Liabilities and stockholders' equity:		
Rent payable	$ 450	$ 478
Wages payable	32	24
Total current liabilities	482	502
Notes payable, long-term	1,150	750
Common stock	1,400	1,100
Retained earnings	710	513
Total liabilities and equity	$3,742	$2,865

Frontera Corporation used the indirect format to prepare the statement of cash flows, but it has been misplaced and is not available.

Required Use your knowledge of financial statements to answer each of the questions that follow. For each item you list as part of your answer, describe fully why the item appears on the statement of cash flows.

A. Which line items from the income statement will also be found in the operating activities section of the statement of cash flows?
B. Which line items from the balance sheet contain information that will be reflected in the operating activities section?
C. Which line items from the income statement will also be found in the investing activities section?
D. Which line items from the balance sheet contain information that will be reflected in the investing activities section?
E. Which line items from the income statement will also be found in the financing activities section?
F. Which line items from the balance sheet contain information that will be reflected in the financing activities section?

P5-21 Evaluating Income and Cash Flows

Obj. 3

Selected financial statement information is reported on the next page for Beltway Distributors, Inc.

Required

A. Prepare a statement of cash flows (indirect format) for Beltway Distributors, assuming that all important cash flow activities are reflected in the information provided.
B. Assume this has been the pattern of cash flows for several years. What does this imply about the firm's business situation?

For the Fiscal Year Ended January 30, 2004 (In thousands)		
Sales revenue	$35,400	
Cost of goods sold	22,700	
Operating expenses (except depreciation)	4,500	
Depreciation expense	2,900	
Net income	5,300	
Dividends declared and paid	5,000	
For January 30	**2004**	**2003**
Cash	$ 2,050	$ 1,950
Accounts receivable	8,600	13,400
Inventories	23,500	27,100
Accounts payable	8,600	8,800
Bank loan payable	18,700	30,000

P5-22 **Excel in Action**

P/T

SPREADSHEET

The following information is available for The Book Wermz for November, 2004. All numbers are dollar amounts.

Cash balance, November 30	$12,307.99
Cash balance, October 31	15,389.55
Cash paid for debt repayment	1,122.77
Cash paid for dividends	1,500.00
Cash paid for equipment	2,000.00
Cash paid for interest	932.03
Cash paid for merchandise	33,243.92
Cash paid for rent	1,738.15
Cash paid for supplies	2,576.93
Cash paid for taxes	897.45
Cash paid for wages	4,073.79
Cash received from customers	45,003.48
Decrease in accounts receivable	125.00
Depreciation expense	817.20
Increase in accounts payable	6,131.77
Increase in inventory	8,438.37
Increase in supplies	165.40
Increase in wages payable	623.56
Net income	2,447.45

Required Use the data provided to prepare a statement of cash flows for The Book Wermz for November using a spreadsheet. Prepare the statement using both the direct and indirect formats. Show cash outflows as negative amounts. Use the appropriate formatting buttons to include commas and dollar signs as needed. Use the Merge Cells and Bold buttons to position and format titles. The captions for the direct format statement should appear in column A and the amounts should appear in column B. The captions for the indirect format should appear in column D and the amounts should appear in column E. Use functions to sum subtotals and totals, such as =SUM(B5:B8), so that changes to any of the amounts being totaled will be automatically recalculated.

Suppose net income had been $2,600 and the amount of cash received from customers had been $45,156.03. What would operating cash flow have been?

P5-23 Multiple-Choice Overview of the Chapter

PT

1. The primary difference between a statement of cash flows prepared in direct format and one prepared in indirect format is
   a. in how net cash flow from operations is computed.
   b. that the indirect approach always results in higher net cash flow.
   c. in how net cash flow from investing activities is reported.
   d. that the beginning-of-the-year cash balance is included in direct format but not in indirect.

2. The statement of cash flows for the Halyard Exploration Company reported the following:

Cash paid for equipment	$ 300,000
Cash paid to employees	400,000
Cash paid to owners	150,000
Cash paid to suppliers	560,000
Cash received from creditors	200,000
Cash received from customers	1,200,000

What were Halyard's net cash flows from operating, investing, and financing activities?

	Operating	Investing	Financing
a.	$240,000	($300,000)	$ 50,000
b.	$500,000	($860,000)	$200,000
c.	$640,000	($860,000)	$200,000
d.	$240,000	($860,000)	$200,000

3. Haddad Company is a well-established, growing company. Which categories of activities would you generally expect to generate positive cash flows?
   a. Operating activities only
   b. Financing activities only
   c. Investing activities only
   d. Both operating activities and financing activities
   e. Both financing activities and investing activities

4. A statement of cash flows has been prepared in the indirect format. Depreciation expense has been added back to net income because depreciation is
   a. not really an expense and to list it as such understates profitability.
   b. an investing activity and should be reported in that section.
   c. a source of cash for the company.
   d. a noncash expense.

5. Zeff Company reports positive operating cash flows, near zero investing cash flows, and negative financing cash flows. This may indicate that the company
   a. is raising new capital to purchase long-term assets for expansion.
   b. does not have many good growth opportunities.
   c. has severe cash flow problems caused by too-rapid growth.
   d. is unable to provide goods and services that customers want.

6. A statement of cash flows prepared using the indirect format would report an increase in Accounts Receivable as
   a. an addition to cash flow from financing activities.
   b. a subtraction from cash flow from financing activities.
   c. an addition to net income in computing cash flow from operating activities.
   d. a subtraction from net income in computing cash flow from operating activities.

7. Flag Ship Company reported depreciation and amortization expense of $300,000 for the latest fiscal year. The depreciation and amortization expense
   a. increased cash flow for the year $300,000.
   b. decreased cash flow for the year $300,000.
   c. had no effect on cash flow for the year.
   d. had an effect on cash flow if assets were purchased during the year.

8. Rust Iron Company purchased a three-month insurance policy on March 1, 2004. The company paid $3,000 for the policy. The amount of insurance expense and cash outflow the company should report for March would be

	Insurance Expense	Cash Outflow
a.	$3,000	$3,000
b.	3,000	1,000
c.	1,000	3,000
d.	1,000	1,000

9. Micro Fish Company recognized $10,000 of interest expense in 2002. The balance of the company's interest payable account decreased $2,000. The amount of cash paid by the company for interest in 2002 was
   a. $10,000.
   b. $12,000.
   c. $2,000.
   d. $8,000.

10. Operating activities are reflected on a company's balance sheet primarily in
   a. plant assets.
   b. current assets and liabilities.
   c. income from operations.
   d. cash flow from operating activities.

CASES

C5-1 General Mills, Inc., Statement of Cash Flows
Objs. 2, 3

The General Mills 2002 Annual Report is reproduced in Appendix B at the end of the text.

Required Answer the following questions about the General Mills Consolidated Statement of Cash Flows.

A. What are the three categories of cash flows shown on the company's cash flow statement?
B. Compare the net income figure to the amount of net cash provided by operating activities for each of the three years. What do you observe?
C. Has the net cash provided by operating activities been large enough to meet the net investing cash outflow? Explain where the difference came from (or went).
D. Compare the dividend payments to the income amounts for the current year. (Note: You may find it helpful to calculate the dividend payout ratio, which is the total dividends for the period ÷ net income for the period. This ratio is explained further in Ch. F10.)

C5-2 Analysis of Corporate Financial Statements
Obj. 3

The 2002 financial statements for **General Mills, Inc.** are provided in Appendix B near the end of this text. Examine these statements and answer the following questions.

Required

A. What were General Mills' major operating activities during 2002? What were the major differences between the accrual and cash flow effects of these activities?
B. What were the company's returns on total assets (net income ÷ total assets) for 2002 and 2001? Did the return improve or deteriorate from 2001?
C. If you owned 10,000 of the company's common stock, what would be your claim on the company's earnings for 2002? Was this a larger or smaller claim than you would have had for 2001?
D. What were the company's major sources of cash for 2002? In general, what did the company do with the cash it received?
E. What were the major financing activities during 2002? In general, how would you describe the company's financing activities overall during the last three years?
F. What major investing activities occurred in 2002?
G. As of the end of 2002, what were the company's most important reported assets? What other resources may be important to the company that are not reported on its balance sheet?

C5-3 Interpreting Cash Flows

Obj. 3

Review the financial report of General Mills, Inc., in Appendix B.

Required Prepare a short report analyzing each of the following issues.

A. What were the accrual and cash basis results of operating activities for 2002? Explain any major differences between the two results.
B. Inspect the balance sheet to identify which current assets and liabilities increased and decreased during 2002. What was the amount of cash collected from customers during 2002?
C. What have been the relative amounts and trends in net income and cash flow from operating activities over the 2000–2002 period? What accounts for the differences you observe?
D. How would you assess the company's financial performance for 2002?

C5-4 Comparing Direct Format and Indirect Format Statements of Cash Flow

Objs. 1, 2, 3

ABM Industries, headquartered in San Francisco, sells a wide variety of industrial and commercial services. Its 2001 statement of cash flows (**direct format**) is shown below exactly as it appeared in the firm's annual report. If ABM Industries had chosen to use the **indirect format**, it would have appeared as shown on page F221. All amounts are in thousands of dollars.

ABM Industries Incorporated and Subsidiaries
Consolidated Statements of Cash Flows

YEARS ENDED OCTOBER 31 (in thousands)	2001	2000	1999
CASH FLOWS FROM OPERATING ACTIVITIES:			
Cash received from customers	$ 1,918,558	$ 1,739,297	$ 1,589,775
Other operating cash receipts	5,523	2,347	1,491
Interest received	859	580	870
Cash paid to suppliers and employees	(1,822,629)	(1,686,988)	(1,522,495)
Interest paid	(2,991)	(3,209)	(2,025)
Income taxes paid	(33,524)	(33,102)	(32,311)
Net cash provided by operating activities	65,796	18,925	35,305
CASH FLOWS FROM INVESTING ACTIVITIES:			
Additions to property, plant and equipment	(16,922)	(18,717)	(19,451)
Proceeds from sale of assets	1,253	1,164	922
Decrease (increase) in investments and long-term receivables	49	370	(1,885)
Purchase of businesses	(23,401)	(14,191)	(10,980)
Proceeds from sale of business	12,000	—	—
Net cash used in investing activities	(27,021)	(31,374)	(31,394)
CASH FLOWS FROM FINANCING ACTIVITIES:			
Common stock issued, including tax benefit	26,688	16,381	17,178
Common stock purchases	—	(8,390)	(5,448)
Preferred stock redemption	(6,400)	—	—
Dividends paid	(16,202)	(14,539)	(13,055)
(Decrease) increase in bank overdraft	(15,952)	10,985	2,492
Long-term borrowings	108,000	126,000	57,064
Repayments of long-term borrowings	(133,857)	(118,127)	(61,847)
Net cash (used in) provided by financing activities	(37,723)	12,310	(3,616)
Net increase (decrease) in cash and cash equivalents	1,052	(139)	295
Cash and cash equivalents beginning of year	2,000	2,139	1,844
CASH AND CASH EQUIVALENTS END OF YEAR	$ 3,052	$ 2,000	$ 2,139

Reconciliation of Net Income to Net Cash Provided by Operating Activities:			
Net income	$ 32,826	$ 44,343	$ 39,667
ADJUSTMENTS:			
Depreciation	13,710	12,265	10,815
Amortization	12,618	11,259	9,883
Provision for bad debts	6,134	2,971	2,257
Gain on sale of assets	(41)	(265)	(160)
Gain on sale of business	(718)	—	—
Increase in deferred income taxes	(12,138)	(5,517)	(6,537)
Increase in trade accounts receivable	(24,340)	(65,555)	(39,304)
Increase in inventories	(3,223)	(2,217)	(331)
Increase in prepaid expenses and other current assets	(3,045)	(1,200)	(1,950)
(Increase) decrease in other assets	40	2,475	(3,295)
(Decrease) increase in income taxes payable	(1,267)	765	1,791
(Decrease) increase in retirement plans accrual	(903)	3,092	3,320
Increase in insurance claims liability	18,872	7,155	4,500
Increase in trade accounts payable and other accrued liabilities	27,271	9,354	14,649
Total adjustments to net income	32,970	(25,418)	(4,362)
NET CASH PROVIDED BY OPERATING ACTIVITIES	$ 65,796	$ 18,925	$ 35,305
SUPPLEMENTAL DATA:			
Non-cash investing activities:			
Common stock issued for net assets of business acquired	$ 1,666	$ 1,581	$ 1,710

Required Study the two statements of cash flow and answer the following questions.

A. Describe how the statements are similar. Be specific.
B. Describe how the statements are dissimilar. Be specific.
C. Note the reconciliation of net income to net cash provided by operating activities that appears at the bottom of the direct format statement. Of what does this disclosure remind you? What information does it provide?
D. What questions can be answered by reading one of the statements that cannot be answered by reading the other?
E. Which statement format do you believe presents more understandable information? Describe and discuss your beliefs.
F. If you had the power to dictate that one format should be used in financial reporting instead of the other, which would you recommend? Why?

If the indirect format had been used:

Years Ended October 31 (In thousands)	**2001**	**2000**	**1999**
Cash flows from operating activities:			
Net income	$ 32,826	$ 44,343	$ 39,667
Adjustments to reconcile net income to cash flow from operating activities:			
Depreciation and amortization	26,328	23,524	20,698
Provision for bad debts	6,134	2,971	2,257
Gain on sale of assets	(41)	(265)	(160)
Gain on sale of business	(718)	—	—
Increase (decrease) in deferred income taxes	(12,138)	(5,517)	(6,537)
Increase in accounts receivable	(24,340)	(65,555)	(39,304)
Increase in inventories	(3,223)	(2,217)	(331)
Increase in prepaid expenses and other current assets	(3,045)	(1,200)	(1,950)
Decrease (increase) in other assets	40	2,475	(3,295)
Increase (decrease) in income taxes payable	(1,267)	765	1,791
(Decrease) increase in retirement plans accrual	(903)	3,092	3,320
Increase (decrease) in insurance claims liability	18,872	7,155	4,500
Increase in accounts payable and other accrued liabilities	27,271	9,354	14,649
Net cash provided by operating activities	65,796	18,925	35,305

(Continued)

Years Ended October 31 (In thousands)	2001	2000	1999
Cash flows from investing activities:			
Additions to property, plant and equipment	(16,922)	(18,717)	(19,451)
Proceeds from sale of assets	1,253	1,164	922
Increase (decrease) in investments and long-term receivables	49	370	(1,885)
Purchase of businesses	(23,401)	(14,191)	(10,980)
Proceeds from sale of business	12,000	—	—
Net cash used in investing activities	(27,021)	(31,374)	(31,394)
Cash flows from financing activities:			
Common stock issued	26,688	16,381	17,178
Common stock purchases	—	(8,390)	(5,448)
Preferred stock redemption	(6,400)	—	—
Dividends paid	(16,202)	(14,539)	(13,055)
Increase (decrease) in bank overdraft	(15,952)	10,985	2,492
Long-term borrowings	108,000	126,000	57,064
Repayments of long-term borrowings	(133,857)	(118,127)	(61,847)
Net cash (used in) provided by financing activities	(37,723)	12,310	(3,616)
Net (decrease) increase in cash and cash equivalents	$ 1,052	$ (139)	$ 295
Cash and cash equivalents beginning of year	2,000	2,139	1,844
Cash and cash equivalents end of year	$ 3,052	$ 2,000	$ 2,139

COMPREHENSIVE REVIEW

CR5-1 Preparing Financial Statements

Alice Springs Merchandise is a retail company that sells general household products. Account balances for the company's fiscal years ended January 31, 2004, and 2005 are provided on the next page. Changes in balance sheet account balances also are provided. Additional information for the 2005 fiscal year includes the following:

- The company paid $38,802 for additional property and equipment and received cash from the sale of equipment of $1,967.
- Amounts borrowed or repaid are equal to changes in Notes Payable, Current and changes in Notes Payable, Long-Term.
- The change in Common Stock is the amount of stock issued or repurchased during the year.
- The balance of Retained Earnings includes the effects of net income and dividends.

Required From the information provided, prepare the following in good form.

A. An income statement containing separate columns for 2005 and 2004.
B. A balance sheet containing separate columns for 2005 and 2004.
C. A schedule like Exhibit 3 in this chapter (page F183) that includes the adjustments necessary to calculate operating cash flow. The adjustments should be the changes in the appropriate account balances.
D. A statement of cash flows for 2005 using the direct method.
E. A statement of cash flows for 2005 using the indirect method.

	2005	2004	Change
Sales Revenue	$ 589,351	$ 530,666	
Cost of Goods Sold	(359,504)	(328,343)	
Wages Expense	(123,764)	(117,136)	
Rent Expense	(30,116)	(28,052)	
Depreciation Expense	(24,871)	(22,628)	
Supplies Expense	(13,555)	(10,751)	
Cash	63,172	57,845	5,327
Accounts Receivable	48,386	43,106	5,280
Merchandise Inventory	130,247	117,202	13,045
Prepaid Rent	2,530	2,314	216
Supplies	1,129	952	177
Property and Equipment	365,398	328,563	36,835
Accumulated Depreciation	(43,848)	(18,977)	(24,871)
Accounts Payable	25,953	23,674	2,279
Wages Payable	10,272	9,500	772
Unearned Revenue	12,966	11,675	1,291
Notes Payable, Current	47,249	44,249	3,000
Notes Payable, Long-Term	214,838	222,467	(7,629)
Common Stock	102,629	95,581	7,048
Retained Earnings	153,105	123,860	29,245
Dividends Paid	8,297	5,250	

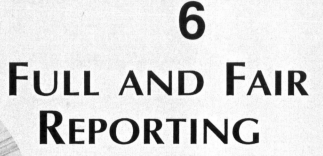

6
FULL AND FAIR REPORTING

How do we ensure that reports to external users fairly present business activities?

Previous chapters examined how businesses collect and record information about their activities and report this information in the form of financial statements. Maintaining a reliable accounting system and reporting information that fairly presents a company's business activities is an important task. Because stockholders and other external users rely on a corporation's managers to provide this information, the financial reporting process is regulated. Corporations and other businesses must conform with regulations and standards that describe accounting procedures, the content and format of financial statements, and other information that must accompany those statements.

Maria and Stan, like other managers, must ensure that their corporation conforms with these requirements. Maintaining an accounting system and producing financial statements is not sufficient. Maria and Stan must be aware of the requirements that ensure that businesses fairly present their activities and make sure they conform with those requirements.

FOOD FOR THOUGHT

As a stockholder, what information, in addition to financial statements, do you and other external users need to understand the business activities of Mom's Cookie Company? How can you be sure information provided by the business is accurate and reliable? Maria and Stan are discussing these issues with Ellen, their accountant.

Maria: ***I've noticed that many corporations produce elaborate annual reports for their stockholders. Is this something we need to do for Mom's Cookie Company?***

Ellen: ***Providing financial statements is not all you have to do to report to your stockholders. An annual report that contains those statements is necessary. It does not have to be elaborate, but it does have to contain certain information.***

Stan: ***Our financial statements describe our business activities. Why aren't these adequate?***

Ellen: ***You need to help your stockholders understand the information in your statements. You must discuss and analyze the financial statement information to identify activities that are key to understanding the performance of your company. And, you must provide disclosures about assumptions you made and methods you used in preparing the statements. In some cases, the statements may not fully inform users about your activities. You may need to provide details about some of your business activities.***

Maria: ***Once we prepare all this information, do we simply have it printed and mail it to our stockholders?***

Ellen: ***Before you send any financial information to external users for your fiscal year, you must have that information audited.***

Stan: ***Who do we get to do the audit?***

Ellen: ***The audit must be performed by an independent Certified Public Accountant. The CPA must be someone who is not employed by your company and who has no financial ties to your company. I'll help you identify someone for the job. First, let's examine the broader picture of corporate financial reporting and the regulations that govern that activity.***

OBJECTIVES

Once you have completed this chapter, you should be able to:

1 Explain the purpose of accounting regulation.

2 Describe how accounting standards are established in the United States.

3 Explain the purpose of the Financial Accounting Standards Board's conceptual framework.

4 Identify supplementary information to the financial statements in a corporate annual report.

5 Describe the purpose of internal controls and types of controls that should be evident in business organizations.

THE PURPOSE OF ACCOUNTING REGULATION

OBJECTIVE 1

Explain the purpose of accounting regulation.

Decision makers who are not managers of a business have limited access to information about the business. These external users rely on financial reports for much of the information they need to make decisions. Stockholders and creditors use accounting information to decide whether to purchase or sell stock and whether to make loans to a company. Suppliers also make decisions about whether to sell goods and provide services to a business on credit. Government authorities use accounting information to determine taxes owed by businesses and whether companies have met legal requirements and regulations. Even customers and employees may use accounting information to determine the financial viability of a company from which they purchase goods and services or for which they work.

Accounting regulations protect the interests of external decision makers by ensuring that information for evaluating the performance and financial condition of a business is available and that the information is prepared according to specific guidelines. These guidelines provide assurance that the information is reliable and comparable over time and across companies.

Though many accounting regulations apply to any business that provides financial reports to external users, they are particularly applicable to publicly traded corporations. These are businesses whose stock can be bought and sold in stock markets. Because owners of these businesses are not involved in their day-to-day operations, they have special information needs. Shareholders of most corporations do not manage the companies in which they invest. They elect members of a corporation's board of directors, who then hire professional managers to run the corporation. Investors can own part of a corporation or parts of many corporations without having to participate in the day-to-day decisions of running those companies. Many Americans own stock in corporations through personal investments and retirement plans, but they are not required to commit large amounts of their individual time to these businesses.

Corporations have continuous lives apart from those of their owners. If a proprietor or partner dies or sells her or his share of a business, the business ceases to exist as a legal entity. The new owner of the business must reestablish the business as a new legal entity. Most corporations, however, continue unchanged if current owners sell their stock. Thus, while proprietorships and partnerships are separate accounting entities from their owners, most are not separate legal entities. They have no legal identity apart from their owners. Most corporations *are* separate accounting and legal entities.

The purchaser of a corporation's stock needs assurance that the shares are reasonably priced and represent a legitimate business. To ensure access to capital markets, corporations prepare accounting information in conformity with generally accepted accounting principles (GAAP). Accounting regulations assure investors of the financial integrity of a corporation. Compliance with these regulations is costly. Large corporations maintain large staffs to handle financial reporting requirements and pay large fees to independent auditors who report on the reliability of financial information reported to external users.

Sources of Accounting Regulation

http://ingram.swlearning.com

Learn more about the NYSE.

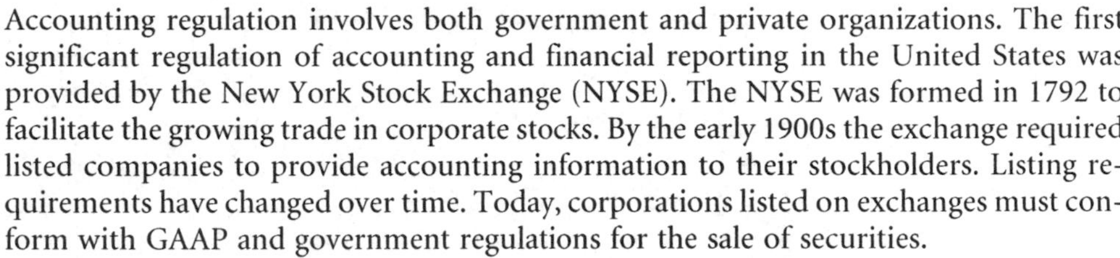

Accounting regulation involves both government and private organizations. The first significant regulation of accounting and financial reporting in the United States was provided by the New York Stock Exchange (NYSE). The NYSE was formed in 1792 to facilitate the growing trade in corporate stocks. By the early 1900s the exchange required listed companies to provide accounting information to their stockholders. Listing requirements have changed over time. Today, corporations listed on exchanges must conform with GAAP and government regulations for the sale of securities.

Adoption of the 16th Amendment to the U.S. Constitution in 1913 permitted federal taxation of individual and corporate income. Taxation of income is not possible without rules and reporting requirements that determine how income will be computed. Consequently, the U.S. government and state governments have an interest in ensuring that businesses comply with accounting standards.

The early 1900s was a period of intense corporate activity. Many corporations were created, and many individuals invested in stock. During the 1920s the average price of corporate shares increased dramatically for many companies. That growth ended abruptly in late 1929, when stock prices plummeted to levels below those of the early 1920s. Many stockholders lost their life savings, and many companies were forced out of business. The collapse of the stock market in 1929 resulted in a demand for increased regulation of corporate financial reporting. Many people believed a cause of the collapse was a lack of sufficient information about corporate activities and a lack of government oversight of the stock markets.

http://ingram.swlearning.com

Learn more about the SEC.

In response to these concerns, the U.S. Congress passed the *Securities Act of 1933*. This legislation **required most corporations to file registration statements before selling stock to investors.** As a part of these statements, corporations were required to provide financial reports containing balance sheets and income statements. Additional legislation, the *Securities Exchange Act of 1934*, **required corporations to provide annual financial reports to stockholders.** The legislation also required that these reports be audited by independent accountants. The 1934 act also created the *Securities and Exchange Commission (SEC)*, a federal agency that reports to Congress. The SEC **was given responsibility for overseeing external financial reporting by publicly traded corporations.**

Currently, the SEC requires publicly traded corporations to publish annual and quarterly financial reports. In addition, annual and quarterly registration statements must be filed by corporations with the SEC. Annual registration statements filed by corporations with the SEC are known as Form 10-K reports. They are required by Section 10-K of the 1934 act. Quarterly statements are known as 10-Q reports.

During the twentieth century, financial accounting has become a highly regulated and formalized process. Publicly traded corporations must provide audited financial reports to stockholders. The managers and auditors of companies who fail to provide this information, or who do so fraudulently, are subject to civil and criminal prosecution. The SEC reviews corporate reports to ensure they conform with GAAP. The SEC can require corporations that do not conform with GAAP to restate their financial statements. Under extreme circumstances, the SEC can halt the trading of a company's stock. If it believes a corporation's managers have attempted to mislead stockholders by their reports, the SEC can refer the matter to the Justice Department for criminal and civil proceedings. An announcement that the SEC is opening an investigation of a company's accounting practices often has a major impact on the company's stock price. Evidence of improper accounting practices is a major cause of lawsuits by investors against corporate managers and their auditors.

Case in Point

http://ingram.swlearning.com

Learn more about Enron.

The Effect of an SEC Investigation

In October 2001, Enron Corporation announced that it was being investigated by the SEC for its accounting and reporting practices. On the day of the announcement, its stock price dropped 20%.

USA Today reported that, on October 22, Enron's stock closed at $20.65 per share, a drop of $5.40 or 21%. That effectively decreased the company's market capitalization by $4.1 billion, which was the NYSE's largest percentage loser that day. The stock price actually fell below $20 per share at one point during the day. Enron's stock had not traded that low for almost four years.

Enron's stock had experienced very heavy losses throughout the prior week. The closing price on October 22 reflected a 75% drop for the year to date. This was very different from the same time during 2000 when the stock price rose by 87%.*

The Rise and Fall of Enron's Stock Price

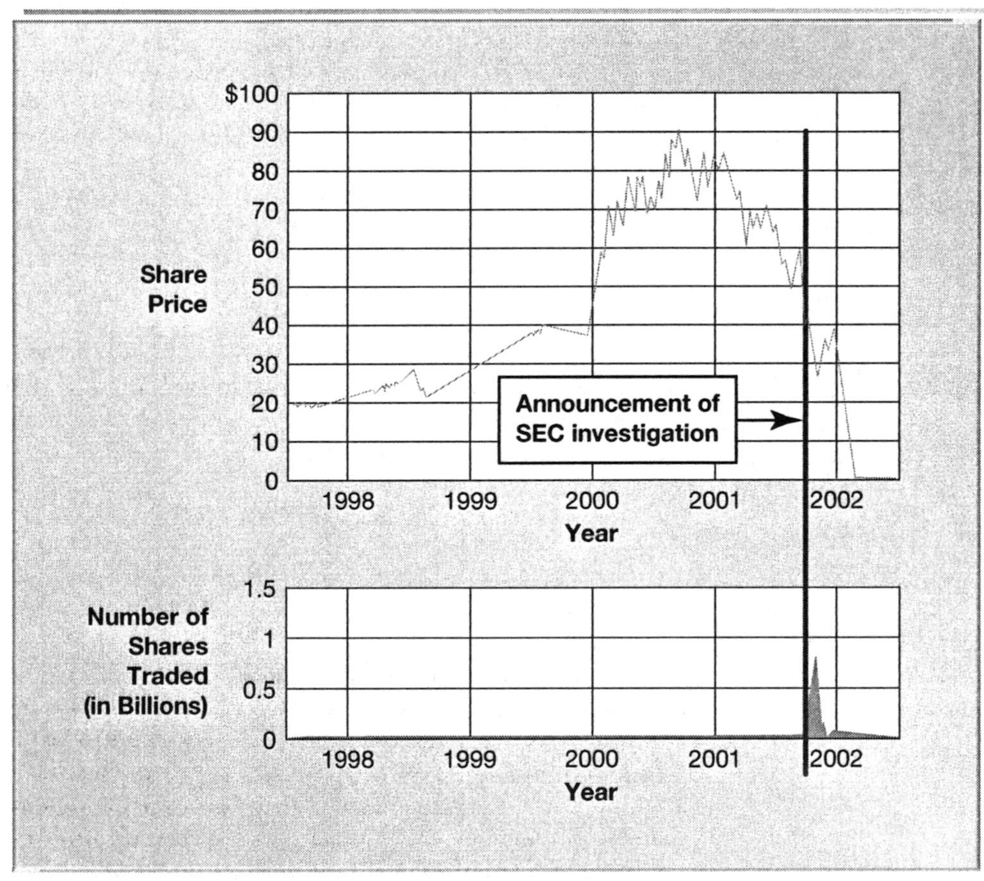

The decline in stock price was one of the major causes of Enron's bankruptcy and the primary cause of lawsuits against the company by its stockholders. The restatement resulted in a reduction in Enron's stockholders' equity of approximately $1.2 billion resulting from a write-down of earnings from 1997 through 2000. In addition, the company's reported debt increased by over $600 million.†

*Source: *USA Today*, 10/22/01, www.usatoday.com/money/energy/2001-10-22-enron.htm.

†Source: www.enron.com/corp/pressroom/releases/2001/ene/78-SECReleaseLtr.html.

The failure of corporations to report fairly their activities to stockholders is a major concern in a capitalistic economy. The stock markets are a primary mechanism for the allocation of financial resources. Society benefits when resources are allocated to the most efficient and effective companies. Misleading information can result in markets allocating resources to companies that are not efficient or effective. When investors become aware that information is misleading, they may suffer losses as many investors attempt to sell their shares.

These problems can lead to a crisis of confidence in the markets if investors are unsure of whom they can trust and whether they are being treated fairly. Improper and inadequate reporting affect everyone. The economy suffers because resources are not being properly allocated. The decrease in economic activity has a ripple effect that leads to decreased sales and profits for other companies, loss of jobs for employees, and loss of taxes for government organizations.

Accounting regulations are important because they provide standards for determining whether corporations are reporting their activities fairly to stockholders. The next section examines the processes and organizations associated with establishing accounting standards.

1 SELF-STUDY PROBLEM

Abe Milton is the owner and sole proprietor of Honest Abe's Used Cars. Abe needs a loan to help finance an expansion of his business. You are the loan manager of a local bank where Abe has applied for a loan. The loan application requires financial statements, which Abe has supplied. You asked Abe whether the statements were prepared according to GAAP and whether they have been independently verified. Abe says he doesn't know anything about GAAP and that he does not permit anyone else to examine his financial information because he is afraid competitors will find out how well he is doing. He notes, however, that he is "Honest" Abe and that the financial statements are accurate.

Required Briefly explain to Abe why GAAP is important and why moral hazard is an issue of concern in making a loan decision.

Creating Accounting Standards

OBJECTIVE 2

Describe how accounting standards are established in the United States.

This section considers organizations responsible for setting accounting standards in the United States and the organization that coordinates accounting standards among many of the world's most developed countries.

The Securities and Exchange Commission is authorized by law to establish and enforce accounting standards in the United States. From time to time, the SEC uses that authority to issue standards on matters it considers to be important and in need of authoritative guidance. For the most part, however, the SEC has delegated the setting of accounting standards to private (non-government) organizations. The United States differs from most other countries in this respect. In most countries, accounting standards are set by the country's central government.

INTERNATIONAL

Standard-Setting Organizations

Several organizations are responsible for establishing accounting standards in the United States. Different organizations set standards for businesses and other non-governmental organizations than the ones that establish standards for governments. In addition, an international organization exists for coordinating standards across countries and for establishing standards that are used in some countries.

LEARNING NOTE

Accounting standards are established by the government in most countries. These standards are part of the nation's laws and are the responsibility of government agencies.

http://ingram.swlearning.com

Learn more about the FASB.

The *Financial Accounting Standards Board (FASB)* **has been the primary organization for setting accounting standards for businesses in the United States since 1973.** The FASB has seven full-time members and is privately funded. It is not a government organization. The FASB also sets accounting and financial reporting standards for nonprofit organizations other than governmental units. It is headquartered in Norwalk, Connecticut. The FASB employs a research staff to study accounting problems. It periodically issues *Statements of Financial Accounting Standards*, which are authoritative guidelines for accounting and financial reporting in the United States.

http://ingram.swlearning.com

Learn more about the GASB and the GAO.

The *Governmental Accounting Standards Board (GASB)* **sets accounting standards for state and local governmental units.** Like the FASB, the GASB is a private rather than a governmental organization. The GASB also is headquartered in Norwalk, Connecticut, and shares staff and facilities with the FASB. The federal government is not subject to FASB or GASB standards but establishes its own accounting rules. The *General Accounting Office (GAO)* **is the primary federal government agency that oversees accounting in the federal government.**

http://ingram.swlearning.com

Learn more about the IASB.

The regulation of financial accounting and reporting is an international activity. Considerable diversity exists in accounting standards among nations. The International Accounting Standards Committee (IASC) was created in 1973 as an international effort to study accounting issues and to reduce the diversity of standards. The IASC was reconstituted as the *International Accounting Standards Board (IASB)* in 2001. The IASB **recommends accounting standards that it believes are appropriate for a broad range of global activities involving companies in many nations.** The IASB describes itself on its website (http://www.iasb.org.uk) as follows:

> . . . [A]n independent, privately-funded accounting standard setter based in London, UK. Board Members come from nine countries and have a variety of functional backgrounds. The Board is committed to developing, in the public interest, a single set of high quality, understandable and enforceable global accounting standards that require transparent and comparable information in general purpose financial statements. In addition, the Board cooperates with national accounting standard setters to achieve convergence in accounting standards around the world.

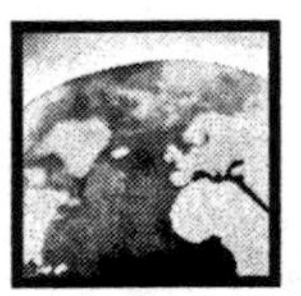

INTERNATIONAL

Accounting standards are important to protect the interests of investors, managers, and the general public. Therefore, the standards must be perceived as being reasonable and responsive to the needs of different constituents. Arbitrary and unnecessary standards do not serve the needs of society. For these reasons, accounting standards are established through a political process. This process gives interested parties an opportunity to express their opinions and to provide information that may have a bearing on prospective standards. The fact that accounting standards are referred to as generally accepted accounting principles is not accidental. To serve the needs of society, accounting standards must be accepted by those who are affected by them.

LEARNING NOTE

The IASB has issued accounting standards that identify preferred accounting methods. Many countries have adopted these standards for accounting and financial reporting.

The Standard-Setting Process

The process used by the FASB to create accounting standards is typical of that used by other organizations, such as the GASB and the IASB. The process consists of the following steps:

1. Accounting issues are identified and evaluated for consideration.
2. A discussion memorandum is issued and responses are solicited.
3. Public hearings are held.
4. An exposure draft is issued and responses are solicited.
5. Additional public hearings are held as needed.

6. A standard is issued.
7. Existing standards are reviewed and modified as needed.

Accounting issues may be identified by accounting professionals, managers, investors, or the FASB staff. The staff evaluates the issues, and the board determines those issues that appear to be important enough to address.

A *discussion memorandum* is a document that identifies accounting issues and alternative approaches to resolving the issues. All interested parties are encouraged to respond to a discussion memorandum. The board develops a proposed standard after reviewing responses to a discussion memorandum and issues its proposal in the form of an exposure draft. **An *exposure draft* is a document that describes a proposed accounting standard.** It identifies requirements that may be contained in an actual standard. Responses again are solicited, and public hearings sometimes are held.

Once the board reviews responses to an exposure draft, it may modify and reissue the exposure draft or issue a standard. **An accounting standard is an official pronouncement establishing acceptable accounting procedures or financial report content. FASB standards are known as *Statements of Financial Accounting Standards.*** To issue a standard, at least five of the seven members of the board must agree to it. Once a standard has been issued, it becomes part of GAAP. Standards can be reviewed at any time to determine if they are serving their intended purposes and can be modified or replaced if they are found to be ineffective.

The FASB's Conceptual Framework

OBJECTIVE 3

Explain the purpose of the Financial Accounting Standards Board's conceptual framework.

The conceptual framework was developed by the FASB in the late 1970s and early 1980s to provide guidance in the development of accounting standards. **The *FASB conceptual framework* is a set of objectives, principles, and definitions to guide the development of new accounting standards.**

The FASB conceptual framework includes four major components:

1. Objectives of financial reporting
2. Qualitative characteristics of accounting information
3. Elements of financial statements
4. Recognition and measurement in financial statements

Objectives of financial reporting provide an overall purpose for financial reports. The purpose of financial reports is to provide information useful to current and potential investors, creditors, and other users. Financial reports should help these decision makers assess the amounts, timing, and uncertainty of prospective cash flows. Financial reports should also provide information about resources, claims to resources, and changes in resources for business organizations.

Qualitative characteristics are attributes that make accounting information useful. **Understandability** and **usefulness** for decision making are the most important characteristics. **Relevance** and **reliability** are considered to be the two primary qualities that result in accounting information being useful. **To be relevant, information should be timely and have predictive or feedback value. To be reliable, information should faithfully represent economic events and should be verifiable and neutral.** Information about an organization is more valuable when it can be compared with information from other organizations and when it is prepared using consistent methods over time.

Elements of financial statements provide definitions of the primary classes of items contained in financial statements. Elements include assets, liabilities, equity, investments by owners, distributions to owners, revenues, expenses, gains, and losses.

Recognition and measurement criteria identify information that should be contained in financial statements. The primary financial statements are described in the conceptual framework, along with the items that should be contained in each statement.

LEARNING NOTE

The accounting systems of most organizations report periodically the estimated results of financing, investing, and operating activities. Such **periodic measurement** is needed to ensure the timely reporting of financial information that is needed for effective decision making.

DISCLOSURE AND FAIR REPRESENTATION

OBJECTIVE 4

Identify supplementary information to the financial statements in a corporate annual report.

In addition to establishing acceptable accounting procedures and methods and guidelines for the format and content of financial statements, GAAP require companies to include information in addition to their financial statements in annual reports to stockholders. This information includes management's discussion and analysis of the company's business activities and disclosures about methods used in determining accounting information and details about those activities that are not evident in the financial statements.

Corporate annual reports usually include the following:

- a letter from the president or chief executive officer of the company
- a description of the company's products and business activities
- a summary of selected business data
- a discussion by management of the company's performance
- financial statements
- notes to the financial statements
- a statement of management responsibility for the financial statements
- an audit report

The president's letter and the description of a company's products and business are not part of the financial section of a company's annual report. Management has a fair amount of discretion in what to include in these sections. The president's letter often summarizes the company's financial performance for the year. As long as information contained in the letter is consistent with that reported in the financial section, it is not subject to accounting regulation.

The following paragraphs describe the financial section items contained in an annual report, with the exception of financial statements that were examined in Chapters 4 and 5. Appendix B of this book contains the financial section of General Mills' 2002 annual report. You may wish to refer to the appendix for a better idea of the contents of each item in the financial section.

Summary Business Data

Financial and non-financial data often are included for various periods beyond those covered by the primary financial statements. For example, Exhibit 1 provides a five-year summary reported in Krispy Kreme's annual report.

Krispy Kreme, like Mom's Cookie Company, sells products through stores. The amount the company sells depends on the number of stores selling its products. Some of these stores are stand-alone businesses that specialize in Krispy Kreme's products. Others are small shops that are part of another business. These shops are located in service stations, grocery stores, and similar locations.

The summary data reported in Exhibit 1 is useful for determining trends in Krispy Kreme's business activities. The data indicate a steady growth in sales, income, assets, and stores over the five years. The company has grown substantially over this period in most categories.

Management's Discussion and Analysis

Corporate annual reports should include discussion and analysis of the company's financial performance. This section, known as ***management's discussion and analysis (MD&A)*****, explains important events and changes in performance during the years presented in the financial statements.**

Typical issues considered in the MD&A include the following:

- a comparison of operating results among the data provided in the company's income statement

Exhibit 1 Summary Business Data from a Corporate Report

	In Thousands, Except Per Share Data and Store Numbers				
YEAR ENDED	Feb. 1 1998	Jan. 31 1999	Jan. 30 2000	Jan. 28 2001	Feb. 3 2002
Statement of Operations Data:					
Total revenues	$158,743	$180,880	$220,243	$300,715	$394,354
Operating expenses	140,207	159,941	190,003	250,690	316,946
General and administrative expenses	9,530	10,897	14,856	20,061	27,562
Depreciation and amortization expenses	3,586	4,278	4,546	6,457	7,959
Provision for restructuring	—	9,466	—	—	—
Income (loss) from operations	5,420	(3,702)	10,838	23,507	41,887
Interest expense (income), net, and other	895	1,577	1,232	(1,698)	(2,408)
Equity loss in joint ventures	—	—	—	706	602
Minority interest	—	—	—	716	1,147
Income (loss) before income taxes	4,525	(5,279)	9,606	23,783	42,546
Provision (benefit) for income taxes	1,811	(2,112)	3,650	9,058	16,168
Net income (loss)	$ 2,714	$ (3,167)	$ 5,956	$ 14,725	$ 26,378
Net income (loss) per share:					
Basic	$ .09	$ (.09)	$ .16	$ .30	.49
Diluted	.09	(.09)	.15	.27	.45
Shares used in calculation of net income (loss) per share:					
Basic	29,136	32,996	37,360	49,184	53,703
Diluted	29,136	32,996	39,280	53,656	58,443
Cash dividends declared per common share	$ .04	$ .04	$ —	$ —	$ —
Operating Data (Unaudited):					
Systemwide sales	$203,439	$240,316	$318,854	$448,129	$621,665
Number of stores at end of period:					
Company	58	61	58	63	75
Franchised	62	70	86	111	143
Systemwide	120	131	144	174	218
Average weekly sales per store:					
Company	$ 42	$ 47	$ 54	$ 69	$ 72
Franchised	23	28	38	43	53
Balance Sheet Data (at end of period):					
Working capital	$ 9,151	$ 8,387	$ 11,452	$ 29,443	$ 49,236
Total assets	81,463	93,312	104,958	171,493	255,376
Long-term debt, including current maturities	20,870	21,020	22,902	—	4,643
Total shareholders' equity	38,265	42,247	47,755	125,679	187,667

Source: Krispy Kreme 2002 annual report.

- liquidity and cash flows as indicated by cash and short-term investments and the statement of cash flows
- major business risks
- financial risks such as foreign currency exchange rates, equity security prices, and interest rate changes on debt securities
- changes in accounting methods used by the company
- subsequent events

Exhibit 2 provides excerpts from the MD&A section of Krispy Kreme's 2002 annual report. The items in this section of the annual report describe the company's performance for the last year compared with previous years. Business risk issues, such as Krispy Kreme's exposure to changes in interest rates, are identified. The section also identifies new accounting standards the company has adopted and the effects of these standards.

Exhibit 2
Management's Discussion and Analysis from a Corporate Report

MANAGEMENT'S DISCUSSION AND ANALYSIS OF FINANCIAL CONDITION AND RESULTS OF OPERATIONS

OVERVIEW

As noted above, we operate on a 52 or 53-week fiscal year. Our operations for fiscal 2002 contained 53 weeks while fiscal 2001 contained 52 weeks.

Systemwide sales for the fiscal year increased 38.7% to $621.7 million compared to $448.1 million in the prior year. The increase was comprised of an increase of 24.6% in Company Store sales, to $266.2 million, and an increase of 51.6% in Franchise Store sales, to $355.5 million. The increase was the result of sales from new stores opened during the fiscal year and an increase in systemwide comparable sales. . . . The total number of stores at the end of the fiscal year was 218. Of those, 52 are Associate franchise stores, 91 are Area Developer franchise stores and 75 are Company stores. Systemwide comparable store sales increased 12.8% in the fiscal year. We believe continued increased brand awareness and growth in off-premises sales contributed significantly to this increase in our systemwide comparable store sales. Adjusting for the number of weeks in fiscal 2002, the increase in systemwide sales was 35.8%.

LIQUIDITY AND CAPITAL RESOURCES

We funded our capital requirements for fiscal 2000, 2001 and 2002 primarily through cash flow generated from operations, as well as proceeds from the initial public offering completed in April 2000 and follow on public offering completed in early February 2001. Over the past three years, we have greatly improved the amount of cash we generate from operations. We believe our cash flow generation ability is becoming a financial strength and will aid in the expansion of our business.

CASH FLOW FROM OPERATIONS

Net cash flow from operations was $8.5 million in fiscal 2000, $32.1 million in fiscal 2001 and $36.2 million in fiscal 2002. Operating cash flow in each year has benefited from an improvement in our net income and was offset by additional investments in working capital, primarily accounts receivable and inventories.

QUANTITATIVE AND QUALITATIVE DISCLOSURE ABOUT MARKET RISKS

We are exposed to market risk from changes in interest rates on our outstanding bank debt. Our revolving line of credit bears interest at either our lender's prime rate minus 110 basis points or a rate equal to LIBOR [London InterBank Offered Rate] plus 100 basis points. We can elect the rate on a monthly basis.

RECENT ACCOUNTING PRONOUNCEMENTS

In July 2001, the Financial Accounting Standards Board (the "FASB") issued SFAS No. 141, "Business Combinations". SFAS No. 141 addresses financial accounting and reporting for business combinations and supersedes APB Opinion No. 16, "Business Combinations", and SFAS No. 38 "Accounting for Preacquisition Contingencies of Purchased Enterprises". All business combinations in the scope of this Statement are to be accounted for using one method, the purchase method. The Company adopted the provisions of this pronouncement for all business combinations subsequent to June 30, 2001. Its adoption did not have a significant impact on the consolidated financial statements.

Notes to the Financial Statements

Notes to the financial statements are important for helping readers interpret the statements. They describe how some of the numbers were computed and provide additional information about items reported in the statements. Exhibit 3 contains example notes

Exhibit 3
Notes to the Financial Statements from a Corporate Report

NATURE OF BUSINESS AND SIGNIFICANT ACCOUNTING POLICIES

NATURE OF BUSINESS. Krispy Kreme Doughnuts Inc. and its subsidiaries (the "Company") are engaged principally in the sale of doughnuts and related items through Company-owned stores. The Company also derives revenue from franchise and development fees and the collection of royalties from franchisees. Additionally, the Company sells doughnutmaking equipment and mix and other ingredients and supplies used in operating a doughnut store to Company-owned and franchised stores.

BASIS OF CONSOLIDATION. The consolidated financial statements include the accounts of the Company and its wholly-owned subsidiaries. All significant intercompany accounts and transactions are eliminated in consolidation.

FISCAL YEAR. The Company's fiscal year is based on a fifty-two/fifty-three week year. The fiscal year ends on the Sunday closest to the last day in January. The years ended January 30, 2000 and January 28, 2001 contained 52 weeks. The year ended February 3, 2002 contained 53 weeks.

PROPERTY AND EQUIPMENT. Property and equipment are stated at cost less accumulated depreciation. Major renewals and betterments are charged to the property accounts while replacements, maintenance, and repairs which do not improve or extend the lives of the respective assets are expensed currently. Interest is capitalized on major capital expenditures during the period of construction.

USE OF ESTIMATES IN PREPARATION OF FINANCIAL STATEMENTS. The preparation of financial statements in conformity with generally accepted accounting principles requires management to make estimates and assumptions that affect the reported amounts of assets and liabilities and disclosure of contingent assets and liabilities at the date of the financial statements and the reported amounts of revenues and expenses during the reporting period. Actual results could differ from those estimates.

ADVERTISING COSTS. All costs associated with advertising and promoting products are expensed in the period incurred.

REVENUE RECOGNITION. A summary of the revenue recognition policies for each segment of the Company is as follows:

- Company Store Operations revenue is derived from the sale of doughnuts and related items to on-premises and off-premises customers. Revenue is recognized at the time of sale for on-premises sales and at the time of delivery for off-premises sales.
- Franchise Operations revenue is derived from: (1) development and franchise fees from the opening of new stores; and (2) royalties charged to franchisees based on sales. Development and franchise fees are charged for certain new stores and are deferred until the store is opened. The royalties recognized in each period are based on the sales in that period.

from the 2002 annual report of Krispy Kreme. These notes identify when certain revenues and expenses were recognized and the amounts of certain expenses that were not reported individually in the financial statements. We will examine other notes in future chapters as we examine specific accounting and reporting issues.

Notes to the financial statements provide information about how amounts reported in the financial statements were determined and provide more detailed information about some income statement items. Exhibit 3 contains only a few of these notes. They describe such matters as when revenue is recognized, how the company's fiscal year is defined, and how advertising expenses are determined and reported. Other notes provide similar information about other financial statement items. These notes are intended to assist readers in understanding and interpreting the information reported in the financial statements. They are an important part of the financial statement presentation and should be included when audited financial statements are presented.

The Auditors' Report

The auditors' report is an important item accompanying a company's financial statements. Auditors issue an audit report upon completion of their audit work. **An *audit* involves a detailed, systematic investigation of a company's accounting records and procedures for the purpose of determining the reliability of financial reports.** The auditor attempts to verify that the numbers and disclosures made by management in its financial reports are consistent with the company's actual financial position, operating results, and cash flows. Records, operating procedures, contracts, resources, and management policies and decisions are examined to provide evidence of the fairness of financial report information. Auditors determine if control procedures to ensure the integrity of accounting information exist and are being used. They compare the information in financial reports with information from prior years and other sources to confirm the fairness of the reports.

***Attestation* occurs when an auditor affirms the fairness of financial statements and other information.** The audit report, or audit opinion, provides public notice of the auditors' belief about the fairness of the accompanying financial information. Exhibit 4 provides the auditors' report from Krispy Kreme's annual report.

Exhibit 4
Independent Auditors' Report

KRISPY KREME DOUGHNUTS, INC.
REPORT OF INDEPENDENT ACCOUNTANTS

To the Board of Directors and Shareholders of Krispy Kreme Doughnuts, Inc.

In our opinion, the accompanying consolidated balance sheets and the related consolidated statements of operations, of shareholders' equity and of cash flows present fairly, in all material respects, the financial position of Krispy Kreme Doughnuts, Inc. and its subsidiaries (the Company) at January 28, 2001 and February 3, 2002, and the results of their operations and their cash flows for each of the three years in the period ended February 3, 2002, in conformity with accounting principles generally accepted in the United States of America. These financial statements are the responsibility of the Company's management; our responsibility is to express an opinion on these financial statements based on our audits. We conducted our audits of these statements in accordance with auditing standards generally accepted in the United States of America, which require that we plan and perform the audit to obtain reasonable assurance about whether the financial statements are free of material misstatement. An audit includes examining, on a test basis, evidence supporting the amounts and disclosures in the financial statements, assessing the accounting principles used and significant estimates made by management, and evaluating the overall financial statement presentation. We believe that our audits provide a reasonable basis for the opinion expressed above.

PricewaterhouseCoopers LLP

Greensboro, North Carolina
March 8, 2002, except Note 21 for
which the date is March 27, 2002

The auditors' report is addressed to the board of directors and shareholders of the company. Normally, an audit is performed on behalf of the shareholders and other external parties. Audits may be requested for special purposes also—for example, to secure a bank loan or as part of merger negotiations. In such a case, the auditors' report would be addressed to the intended users.

The audit report states the auditor's opinion. Most audit reports provide an **unqualified opinion**. Such an opinion states that the auditor believes that the financial statements fairly present the company's actual economic events for the period covered by the audited statements. Fair presentation means that the financial statements are prepared in conformity with GAAP and are free from material omissions and misstatements. An unqualified opinion means that the auditor has not stated any qualifying (limiting) conditions or exceptions in the opinion. If the financial statements do not fully conform to GAAP or if serious concerns exist as to the ability of a company to continue as a going concern, the auditor lists qualifications to the opinion that the reader should consider in interpreting the financial information.

The auditors' report identifies the statements and fiscal periods covered by the audit. A typical audit will cover all the primary financial statements: income statement, balance sheet, and statement of cash flows. The audit normally covers the most recent three years of operations. For most large corporations, the audited financial statements are the consolidated statements of the parent and its subsidiaries.

The auditors' report describes the responsibilities of auditors and management. Management is responsible for preparing the statements. Auditors are responsible for competently using the technology available to them to confirm (or disconfirm) the assertions of management made in its financial statements and related disclosures.

The report summarizes the audit process. ***Generally accepted auditing standards (GAAS)* include procedures used in conducting an audit to help auditors form an opinion about the fairness of the audited statements.** GAAS are developed in the United States by the Auditing Standards Board (ASB). The ASB is a division of the American Institute of Certified Public Accountants (AICPA). Auditing standards are published and updated periodically by the AICPA. Failure to conform to GAAS in an independent audit is a major violation of a CPA's responsibilities.

From evidence collected from applying GAAS, auditors assert that the financial statements are free of material misstatement. Materiality is a criterion for establishing the importance of a potential misstatement in audited financial statements. Financial statements contain estimates and allocations that depend on management judgment. In addition to finding errors in accounting records, auditors may disagree with managers about their estimates and allocations. Unless these errors and disagreements are material (important) to the overall amounts reported on the financial statements, however, auditors are not required to take action on these issues.

Auditors examine accounting records on a "test basis." Auditors do not examine 100% of a company's transactions. Instead, they use sampling techniques to select representative transactions. By verifying these transactions, auditors form an opinion about the financial statements as a whole. Sampling is necessary because the cost of auditing all of a company's records would be prohibitive.

The content of the auditors' report is standard for most corporations. Some audit firms issue an audit report that contains several paragraphs. The paragraphs contain the same type of information as that included in the paragraph in Exhibit 4.

Auditors' reports must be signed by the public accounting firm that performed the audit, thus indicating its responsibility. The date of the auditors' report is the date on which all audit work was completed for the periods covered by the report. The auditor is responsible for disclosing any material information that might affect a decision maker's interpretation of the financial statements through the date of the audit report.

LEARNING NOTE

Unless information is found that raises doubts about a company's ability to continue operating in the future, it is assumed to be a ***going concern***. This means the company is **an organization with an indefinite life that is sufficiently long that, over time, all currently incomplete transactions will be completed.**

LEARNING NOTE

Auditors' reports for foreign corporations differ from those for U.S. corporations. Different countries establish their own auditing and accounting standards. The format of the auditors' report depends on the auditing standards of the country in which a company has its principal operations.

INTERNATIONAL

The auditor certifies that financial statements present fairly a company's business activities. The audit is not a guarantee that a company will be successful. If a company is not performing well, the financial statements should reveal the company's problems. It is up to stockholders to interpret the statements and assess the company's performance. Good information should lead to informed decisions about whether to invest in a company or not. Good information does not mean a company is doing well or that investors are likely to earn high returns. The audit certifies the quality of financial information, not the quality of management or the ability of management to make good business decisions.

Report of Management Responsibilities

In addition to the auditors' report, the annual report usually contains a statement of management responsibilities. Exhibit 5 contains a typical statement of management responsibilities.

Management is responsible for preparing financial statements and related information that fairly reports the business activities of a corporation. This information should be prepared in conformity with GAAP. Management is also responsible for developing and implementing a system of internal controls. ***Internal controls* are procedures a company uses to protect its assets and ensure the accuracy of its accounting information.** The next section of this chapter describes internal controls in more detail.

Exhibit 5
Report of Management Responsibilities

The management of Mom's Cookie Company is responsible for the preparation and integrity of the financial statements included in this Annual Report to Shareholders. The financial statements have been prepared in conformity with accounting principles generally accepted in the United States of America and include amounts based on management's best judgment where necessary. Financial information included elsewhere in this Annual Report is consistent with these financial statements.

Management maintains a system of internal controls and procedures designed to provide reasonable assurance that transactions are executed in accordance with proper authorization, that transactions are properly recorded in the Company's records, that assets are safeguarded and that accountability for assets is maintained. The concept of reasonable assurance is based on the recognition that the cost of maintaining our system of internal accounting controls should not exceed benefits expected to be derived from the system. Internal controls and procedures are periodically reviewed and revised, when appropriate, due to changing circumstances and requirements.

Independent auditors are appointed by the Company's Board of Directors and ratified by the Company's shareholders to audit the financial statements in accordance with auditing standards generally accepted in the United States of America and to independently assess the fair presentation of the Company's financial position, results of operations and cash flows. Their report appears in this Annual Report.

The Audit Committee, all of whose members are outside directors, is responsible for monitoring the Company's accounting and reporting practices. The Audit Committee meets periodically with management and the independent auditors to ensure that each is properly discharging its responsibilities. The independent auditors have full and free access to the Committee without the presence of management to discuss the results of their audits, the adequacy of internal accounting controls and the quality of financial reporting.

A corporation's board of directors should establish an audit committee. The committee should be made up of members of the board who are not part of the corporation's management. The audit committee is responsible for receiving information from the independent auditors and from those in the corporation who implement and evaluate internal controls. Accounting and auditing problems should be reported to the audit committee. The committee can discuss problems with management and can take steps to correct the problems if necessary.

2 SELF-STUDY PROBLEM Listed below are statements about auditing:

A. An independent audit guarantees the accuracy of financial information.
B. An auditor does not have to examine all of an audited company's transactions to certify the reliability of the company's financial statements.
C. An auditor must follow generally accepted auditing standards in performing an audit.
D. An auditor is responsible only for the period covered by the financial statements audited when preparing an audit report.

Required Identify each statement as true or false and explain your reasoning.

INTERNAL CONTROLS

OBJECTIVE 5

Describe the purpose of internal controls and types of controls that should be evident in business organizations.

An essential requirement of any accounting system is that it provide accurate data. Incorrect data are not useful and can lead to poor decisions. Consequently, controls are important in a company to help ensure that data are accurate. Incorrect data can result from errors in recording data or from events that affect a company's assets. For example, if Mom's Cookie Company purchased inventory at a cost of $1,200, it would be incorrect to record the amount owed the supplier as $1,150. It is correct to record an increase in Accounts Payable and Merchandise Inventory of $1,200. However, if the merchandise is stolen from the company, the accounting data are in error because they are not consistent with the amount of the asset actually available to the company. Accordingly, a company uses a system of internal controls both to protect assets and to ensure accuracy of accounting information.

Management Philosophy

A strong system of internal controls begins with a management philosophy that encourages appropriate security and behavior in a company. If top management takes a lax attitude about these matters, it is unlikely that it will develop and enforce an effective system. Accordingly, top management should develop policies and ensure that these are communicated throughout the company. It should also ensure that procedures are developed to monitor and enforce control policies. If Maria and Stan want their company's employees to act with integrity, they must establish a tone of ethical conduct by acting with integrity themselves and by creating and enforcing policies and procedures that require ethical behavior in conducting business activities.

Part of management philosophy should involve developing rewards and incentives that encourage employees to take appropriate actions. For example, a bonus system that places too much emphasis on sales quotas could encourage employees to create false sales, to predate sales orders, and to make credit sales to risky customers. A good system of rewards will encourage employees to focus on the value and ongoing success of a company.

Business Ethics

Management should create a code of ethics and other documents that establish company policy and inform employees of acceptable and expected behavior. These policies should consider the relationship between a company and its customers, employees, suppliers, stockholders, and community. As an example, Exhibit 6 identifies the contents of **United Technologies Corporation's** Code of Ethics.

http://ingram.swlearning.com

Learn more about the Foreign Corrupt Practices Act.

A major purpose of internal controls is to ensure compliance with laws and regulations. If a company fails to comply with laws, it can be subject to civil and criminal penalties resulting in significant losses. Antitrust laws prohibit collaboration among competitor companies that leads to unfair pricing or trade practices. Companies that sell similar products in the same markets cannot collude to set prices or limit competition. The Foreign Corrupt Practices Act prohibits companies from offering or accepting bribes or other payments to obtain business or influence the behavior of customers or government authorities.

Ethical behavior involves treating individuals and companies fairly and providing full disclosure of information that might affect their decisions. Moral hazard is a potential problem in dealing with customers, suppliers, employees, and others who interact with a company. The company often has access to information that is not available to external stakeholders. Full disclosure is often a remedy for moral hazard. In the long run, fair treatment and disclosure will create a reputation for a company that will lead to financial benefits.

Exhibit 6
Ethical Issues Associated with Corporate Conduct

Relationships between the Company and:	**Important Issues:**
Customers	• Quality and safety of products • Honesty in dealings • Avoid conflicts of interest • Protection of confidential information • Comply with Foreign Corrupt Practices Act
Employees	• Equal opportunity in hiring, compensation, and treatment • Privacy of information about employees • Treatment with dignity and respect • Provide a safe and healthy work environment • Provide opportunity for development
Suppliers	• Fair competition
Stockholders	• Provide superior returns • Protect and improve investment value • Protect assets • Accurate accounting information and disclosure of business activities
Competitors	• Fairness • Comply with antitrust laws
Communities	• Responsible corporate citizenship • Abide by laws • Participate in civic affairs • Support through corporate philanthropy • Comply with laws concerning political donations • Comply with export laws • Protect environment

Source: www.utc.com/profile/ethics.

Computer System Controls

Many internal controls should be built into computer information systems. These **controls protect a company's information resources from unauthorized access, improper use, and destruction.** System controls determine who can gain access to various parts of a company's database. Users should have **appropriate identification and passwords** to log onto networks or to use network resources. Users typically are assigned to groups based on the type of work they perform. For example, data entry personnel in the sales division are permitted access to those files in the database that need to be updated when customers submit orders. They should not have access to other data in the system that they do not need in the course of their work.

System controls also manage databases to prevent several users from trying to update particular records at the same time. While one user is accessing a record or file, other users are locked out so that conflicting or incomplete changes cannot be made.

Other controls **check data for errors** to make sure that data entered in a system are reasonable and appropriate. For example, a system may refuse to prepare a check for an amount larger than $1,000. This control prevents a clerk from accidentally writing large checks by mistyping data or omitting a decimal. **Automatic numbering** should be used to identify transactions and source documents such as sales orders, invoices, and purchase orders. Each transaction or document is assigned a number that follows a preset sequence. Consequently, each item can be tracked and missing items can be identified. Using automatic numbering makes it more difficult for employees to create fictitious transactions or falsify data by recording transactions and then deleting them from the system. Missing numbers are easily identified, and those responsible for deleting the numbered items can be held responsible.

Many other controls can be built into computer systems. Examples include the use of software and hardware to make it difficult for unauthorized users to break into computer networks and databases. The software and hardware also can monitor systems to detect attempts to gain unauthorized access.

Duplicate copies of databases often are maintained so that if one database system fails, the other is available for use. **Backup systems and data** are necessary to prevent data from being lost if a database system fails and to permit a company to continue to operate even if it has computer problems. Databases are backed up on a regular basis. Data are copied to tape or other permanent storage devices so they can be retrieved in case of a major problem with the active database. These backup data are stored in locations away from where the working database is maintained.

Complete computer systems must be protected. Many companies maintain centralized computer information system facilities. These facilities must be protected from destruction by natural disasters (fire, flood, earthquake) and from those who might attempt to destroy a company's systems (terrorists, disgruntled employees, competitors). An important control is a **disaster recovery plan** that a company can rely on to get its computer systems back into working order in case of a major disaster. Such a plan usually requires access to facilities, hardware, and software at locations other than those normally used.

Human Resources Controls

Many internal controls focus on a company's human resources. Important controls involve **hiring qualified employees** who have the appropriate skills for a particular job. **Background checks** can identify employees who have a history of improper behavior. A **good training program** can ensure that employees develop and maintain the skills needed for their jobs.

An important control involves **segregation of duties** so that an employee does not have access to resources and information that would make it easy for the employee to misuse those resources. For example, an employee should not have access both to a resource and to the accounting for that resource. If an employee has control over merchandise, supplies, or cash, that employee should not have control over records showing the amount of the resources received or transferred. Computer programmers and systems developers should not have access to actual operations of computer systems. Developers create the systems and can use them to create improper transactions that can transfer cash or other resources to improper persons. Developers can also destroy systems by creating programs to erase data or corrupt program logic. Disgruntled employees can be a major risk to an organization, especially if they understand and have access to a company's computer system.

Employees should understand their responsibilities and authority. They should know what they are permitted to do in their jobs and what they are not permitted to do. They should clearly understand lines of authority in a company. **Employees should be supervised** and inappropriate behavior should be reported and addressed.

Physical Controls

Safeguarding assets often involves controlling physical access. Merchandise and materials can be secured in warehouses or display cases. Merchandise can be tagged electronically to make shoplifting or theft difficult. Surveillance equipment can monitor important resources. Cash registers, vaults, and safety deposit boxes secure financial resources.

Conclusion

A strong system of internal controls is essential for protecting any information system. Though not all controls relate directly to how information is processed, the integrity of accounting information depends on controls that protect data and the systems used to process those data. An internal control system is an important part of an accounting information system. Without internal controls, users could not rely on accounting information as an accurate description of a company's economic activities.

The Responsibilities of Accountants

Throughout this chapter we have considered various regulatory functions associated with accounting. Accountants and the accounting profession have primary responsibility for these functions. Accountants work to prepare **financial information** contained in companies' annual reports. They **manage the information systems** used to record and report this information. They help other managers **interpret information** reported by the accounting system and make sure the information is reliable and conforms with GAAP and legal requirements.

Accountants serve on organizations like the FASB and SEC that **establish and monitor accounting standards.** They research accounting issues, prepare standards, and research company financial reporting practices. Independent CPAs **audit business financial reports** to ensure that they fairly present the companies' business activities. The audit is an important tool in maintaining strong capital markets. If managers fail in their responsibilities to report fairly to external users, independent audits are a major line of defense to prevent misleading information from reaching investors. Consequently, auditors are held to a high standard of professional responsibility and integrity. Audit failure is a major source of concern for the SEC and society in general. CPAs and the audit firms in which they work are required to maintain current professional knowledge and are reviewed on a regular basis to make sure their practices are consistent with current standards.

Case in Point

http://ingram.swlearning.com

Learn more about the largest public accounting firms.

The Consequences of Audit Failure

Concerns about Enron Corporation's accounting practices led to close scrutiny of the company's audit firm, Arthur Andersen. Congressional hearings raised concerns that the auditor failed to protect the public interest and was involved in business activities with Enron that reduced the audit firm's independence. The Justice Department indicted Andersen for obstruction of justice because its employees destroyed documents that the Justice Department believed were important for its investigation of Enron's and Andersen's activities. In addition, Andersen was sued for billions of dollars by Enron stockholders and creditors. Because of these events, many of Andersen's other audit clients replaced the firm as their independent auditors. Andersen was forced to lay off many of its employees, and many others resigned to take positions with other audit firms or companies.

Prior to these events, Andersen was one of the "Big Five" accounting firms, along with Deloitte & Touche, Ernst & Young, KPMG, and PricewaterhouseCoopers. The events associated with Enron removed Andersen from the ranks of the "Big Five" and seriously jeopardized its ability to continue as an audit firm.

In addition to working as external auditors, accountants also work as **internal auditors**. Internal auditors work for businesses and are responsible for developing and monitoring internal control systems and for auditing a company's divisions for compliance with accounting rules, company policies, and legal requirements. They also may evaluate the performance of a division or company to improve efficiency and effectiveness.

3 SELF-STUDY PROBLEM

Deborah Stinger works in the systems development department of a major company. She helped develop the company's computerized accounting system. Occasionally, she fills in for one of the operators in the accounts payable department. This operator is responsible for processing checks to suppliers for purchases made by the company. While filling in, Deborah created an account of a fictitious company, just to see if the system could be tricked into writing checks for nonexistent purchases. She added data to the company's file and entered some phony purchases. The computer wrote the checks, and they were mailed to a post office box Deborah opened. Over the last few years, Deborah has written over $80,000 in checks to her fictitious company.

Required Identify some internal control deficiencies in the accounting system that have allowed Deborah to embezzle money from her company.

REVIEW

SUMMARY of IMPORTANT CONCEPTS

1. Accounting regulations are important to protect the interests of external users of accounting information who have limited access to business information. GAAP help ensure that reliable information is available to control moral hazard on the part of corporate managers.

2. Several events and organizations are important for the development of accounting regulations in the United States.
   a. The first regulations were established by the New York Stock Exchange.
   b. The Securities Act of 1933 and the Securities and Exchange Act of 1934 are major laws that affect accounting and financial reporting in the United States.

3. Several organizations play a role in setting and enforcing accounting standards.
   a. The SEC has the authority to establish and enforce accounting standards in the United States.
   b. The FASB is a private-sector organization that is largely responsible for setting accounting standards in the United States.
   c. The GASB is a private-sector organization that establishes accounting standards for state and local governments in the United States.
   d. The IASB is a private-sector organization that helps develop global accounting standards.

4. Accounting standards are set through a process of public discussion that permits those affected by standards to have input into the standard-setting process.

5. The FASB's conceptual framework provides guidance for the development of financial accounting standards for business organizations.

6. Annual reports contain information supplemental to financial statements that is important for understanding and interpreting those statements.
   a. Supplemental financial disclosures provide information about business activities and for periods other than those covered by the primary financial statements.
   b. Notes to the financial statements provide additional information about business activities and explain methods used in preparing financial statements.
   c. The auditors' report describes the audit and expresses an opinion as to whether the financial statements are a fair presentation of a company's business activities in conformity with GAAP.
   d. The report of management's responsibilities identifies responsibilities of managers for financial statements and internal controls and describes a company's audit committee.

7. Internal controls are designed to protect a company's assets and ensure the reliability of its accounting information.
   a. Management is responsible for establishing an environment of integrity in which internal controls are important.
   b. Management should establish a code of ethics and inform employees of expected and appropriate behavior.
   c. Computer controls are important for protecting a company's data and computer systems.
   d. Human resource controls are designed to control the behavior of employees and managers and to provide expectations about appropriate behavior.
   e. Physical controls are designed to protect assets and to limit access to important resources.

8. Accountants and the accounting profession are responsible for development and enforcement of accounting regulations.

DEFINE

TERMS and CONCEPTS DEFINED in this CHAPTER

attestation (F235)
audit (F235)
discussion memorandum (F230)
exposure draft (F230)
FASB conceptual framework (F230)
Financial Accounting Standards Board (FASB) (F229)
General Accounting Office (GAO) (F229)
generally accepted auditing standards (GAAS) (F236)
going concern (F236)
Governmental Accounting Standards Board (GASB) (F229)
internal controls (F237)
International Accounting Standards Board (IASB) (F229)
management's discussion and analysis (MD&A) (F231)
Securities Act of 1933 (F226)
Securities and Exchange Commission (SEC) (F226)
Securities Exchange Act of 1934 (F226)
Statements of Financial Accounting Standards (F230)

SELF-STUDY PROBLEM SOLUTIONS

SSP6-1 GAAP are guidelines for the preparation of financial statements and other accounting information. They are important because they provide standards for the content and format of financial reports. How earnings and other accounting information are measured is important for determining the reliability and usefulness of the information. If each company chose its own accounting rules, it could select those rules that made the company appear successful.

Moral hazard results when a person, like Abe, has incentives to behave in ways that can be harmful to others, such as creditors, who have a financial stake in the person's activities. To get a loan, Abe has an incentive to make his company appear financially strong. If he fails to repay the loan, the bank will lose money. Reliable financial information is a means of controlling moral hazard so that the bank can make a decision based on an accurate view of the company's business activities. GAAP help ensure that financial information is reliable.

SSP6-2

A. False. An independent audit provides reasonable assurance about the reliability of audited financial information. Auditors rely on information provided by management and on evidence collected from a sample of a company's transactions.
B. True. The cost of examining all of a company's transactions is usually too high. Auditors examine a representative sample of transactions.
C. True. GAAS are procedures that auditors must follow in performing an audit to help ensure the audit has been performed properly.
D. False. The auditor is responsible for making sure a company notifies readers of its financial reports of any events occurring between the end of the period covered by the financial statements and the date of the audit report that would have a material affect on interpretation of the financial statements.

SSP6-3 Internal control deficiencies include access to the accounting system by an employee who should not have access. Limitations on physical access, passwords, and employee identification numbers should have prevented Deborah from gaining access to the system. Deborah should not have authority to use the system. Another deficiency was the failure to separate systems development from computer operations personnel. Deborah was able to embezzle funds because she understood the computer programs that created accounting files. Computer operators normally do not have sufficient knowledge of the system to manipulate it in this manner. An additional deficiency was the failure of the system to verify transactions or compare amounts from one part of the system to another. For example, use of sequentially numbered purchase orders should make it difficult for an employee to create fictitious data without the system identifying a problem.

Thinking Beyond the Question

How do we ensure that reports to external users fairly present business activities?

Full and fair reporting involves reliable financial statements that accurately report a company's business activities. Information to describe, interpret, and extend that information also is important. Audits and internal controls also help ensure full and fair reporting. To what extent should full and fair reporting protect external users from poor management decisions? Does full and fair reporting guarantee that stakeholders will not suffer losses from their contractual relations with a business? Why or why not?

QUESTIONS

Q6-1 *Obj. 1* Other than business managers, who relies on financial reports to make decisions?

Q6-2 *Obj. 1* Compliance with regulations is costly. Why are public companies required to comply with GAAP?

Q6-3 *Obj. 2* Why does the FASB issue a discussion memorandum prior to releasing an exposure draft of a new pronouncement?

Q6-4 *Obj. 2* The SEC is authorized by law to establish and enforce accounting standards in the United States. Why are most accounting standards used by businesses issued by the FASB?

Q6-5 *Obj. 3* What are the elements of financial statements, according to the FASB's conceptual framework? Where would an investor find these elements?

Q6-6 *Obj. 3* One of the major components of the FASB conceptual framework is the objectives of financial reporting. What are the objectives of financial reporting?

Q6-7 *Obj. 4* A friend has been reviewing the annual report of a firm in which he has invested. He says, "I'm worried because the auditors gave an unqualified opinion on the financial statements. You'd think a big company like this would have auditors that were qualified." Clear up your friend's misunderstanding.

Q6-8 *Obj. 4* What is the purpose of notes to financial statements? If a firm does a good job presenting its financial statements, why are notes necessary?

Q6-9 *Obj. 4* What is an audit and why is it important?

Q6-10 *Obj. 5* Why is it necessary for managers and other decision makers to understand how accounting information is developed and reported? Shouldn't it just be management's job to manage and the accountant's job to account? Explain.

Q6-11 *Obj. 5* What are the two primary purposes of internal controls?

Q6-12 *Obj. 5* Explain why internal controls are important to a computerized management information system and identify several such controls that are commonly used.

Q6-13 *Obj. 5* Why is management philosophy an important internal control issue?

Q6-14 *Obj. 5* Identify some human resource controls that can be used in a company and explain why they are important.

Q6-15 *Obj. 5* Identify some physical controls that can be used in a company and explain why they are important.

EXERCISES

If your instructor is using Personal Trainer in this course, you may complete online the assignments identified by PT.

E6-1 *Objs. 1–5* Write a short definition for each of the terms listed in the *Terms and Concepts Defined in this Chapter* section.

E6-2 *Obj. 1* Three major developments in the history of accounting involved the development of the New York Stock Exchange, the 16th Amendment to the U.S. Constitution, and the events subsequent to the stock market crash of 1929. Explain briefly the significance of each of these events for contemporary accounting.

E6-3 Identify the major reporting requirements associated with each of the following:
Obj. 1

a. Securities Act of 1933
b. Securities and Exchange Act of 1934
c. 10-K report
d. 10-Q report

E6-4 Identify each of the following:
Obj. 2
P/T

a. The private sector organization currently responsible for setting financial accounting standards in the United States.
b. The private sector organization currently responsible for setting state and local governmental accounting standards in the United States.
c. The organization that exists to influence the development of international accounting standards.
d. The federal agency that oversees accounting at the federal government.
e. The organization responsible for the enforcement of financial accounting standards in the United States.

E6-5 How would you react to the following statement? "Accounting standards impose costs on corporations and their managers to protect the interests of investors."
Obj. 2

E6-6 What is meant by the term "generally accepted accounting principles?" What is the significance of the phrase "generally accepted?"
Obj. 2

E6-7 What is the purpose of the qualitative characteristics of financial reports? What are the primary qualitative characteristics as defined by the FASB?
Obj. 3

E6-8 What is the FASB's conceptual framework?
Obj. 3

E6-9 Identify each of the sections of an auditors' report and explain its purpose.
Obj. 4

E6-10 Corporate annual reports include a discussion and analysis of the company's financial performance. What is the purpose of this discussion?
Obj. 4

E6-11 General Mills Corporation had sales of almost $8 billion in fiscal year 2002 from Betty Crocker, Pillsbury, Wheaties, Cheerios, Pop Secret popcorn, and other products. The company reported total assets of more than $16.5 billion. Inspect the General Mills' balance sheet found in Appendix B at the back of this book. (a) Does it seem strange to you that such a big company is able to report all of its assets using only nine different accounts? How is this possible? (b) Why is this done? (c) Would this level of detail meet the needs of the general manager of the Pillsbury division, or the managers in other divisions of the company? Discuss.
Obj. 4

E6-12 Quick Transport Company owns a large fleet of trucks that move freight throughout the country. Some of these trucks cost hundreds of thousands of dollars and are operated for 15 years or more before being replaced. The company issues long-term debt to pay for most of its equipment. The company's fiscal year ends on June 30. For each fiscal year, the company prepares financial reports that include estimates of its results of operations for the year. How do the operations of Quick illustrate the periodic measurement and going concern principles of accounting?
Obj. 4

E6-13 Bill's grandparents have been buying shares of stock for his college education fund since the day he was born. Yesterday, Bill received the annual report of Thompson Consolidated Shoulderpads, Inc., and is telling you about it. Bill says:
Obj. 4

> "I feel really good about the company because its financial statements were prepared and audited by a well-known national accounting firm. Not only that, but the firm received an unqualified audit report. This means that the auditor checked out all the company's transactions and that the company is healthy. Since the auditors think the company is doing well, I think I'll invest some of my summer job savings in it."

How would you respond to your friend? Do you believe he has a good understanding of what information is conveyed by an auditors' report? Discuss.

E6-14 *Obj. 5* What is the role of an accountant who works for a business organization?

E6-15 *Obj. 5* PT Selma Fromm is a recent graduate in accounting. She has taken a position with Hand Writer Company. The company has three divisions that manufacture three products: pencils, pens, and colored markers. Financial information for the most recent fiscal period for each division includes the following:

	Pencils	Pens	Markers
Division revenues	$200,000	$ 300,000	$100,000
Division expenses	140,000	160,000	60,000
Division assets	600,000	1,000,000	200,000

One of Selma's regular duties is to prepare an analysis of the performance of each division. Prepare an analysis of division performance from the information provided. Which of the divisions appears to be most profitable? Is this responsibility typical of the tasks often performed by accountants who work for business organizations? Explain.

E6-16 *Obj. 5* What is the purpose of internal auditing? Why is it important to an organization?

E6-17 *Obj. 5* List and briefly describe the primary internal control procedures discussed in the chapter.

E6-18 *Obj. 5* What is the role of an independent CPA?

E6-19 *Obj. 5* Mag's Pie Shop is a rapidly growing baker and distributor of specialty pies for festive occasions. Mag's CPA adviser keeps recommending that Mag install better internal controls over the business. Specifically, the CPA recommends that Mag separate the company's record-keeping function from the physical control of cash and other assets. The CPA also recommends that Mag use only preprinted and prenumbered forms for all business transactions.

a. What is the purpose of internal controls? Be specific.
b. For each internal control suggested by the CPA, give one example of an unsatisfactory situation or event that the control would prevent.

E6-20 *Obj. 5* Ima Crook is a sales clerk for Free Cash Company. Ima runs a cash register. Each day she obtains $200 from a supervisor and places the money in the cash register to make change. Customers bring goods to the sales counter, where Ima takes their money and writes out a sales slip using a form provided for this purpose. If requested by the customer, she writes out a separate slip for the customer. Ima works from 9 A.M. to 5 P.M. except for breaks and lunch when she is replaced by a coworker who runs the cash register for her. At 5 P.M. Ima takes all the cash from her cash register and puts it in an envelope along with the sales receipts and hands the envelope to a supervisor. Ima just bought a new $50,000 car and paid cash. What internal control problems exist in this situation? What can be done to solve the problems?

PROBLEMS

If your instructor is using Personal Trainer in the course you may complete online the assignments identified by PT.

P6-1 The Importance of Financial Accounting Standards

Obj. 1

Accounting and financial reporting is highly regulated in the United States. Standards specify the types of information to be reported and how accounting numbers are to be calculated. Listed below are groups who benefit from these standards.

A. managers
B. stockholders
C. creditors
D. governmental authorities
E. employees

Required Explain why financial accounting standards are important to each of these groups.

P6-2 The Role of Accounting Regulation
Obj. 1

On Wednesday, July 10, 2002, the *Wall Street Journal* reported the following headlines:

> *Securities Threat*[1]
> *Bush Crackdown on Business Fraud Signals New Era*
> *Stream of Corporate Scandals Causes Bipartisan Outrage; Return of Big Government?*
> *Fiery Rhetoric on Wall Street*

President Bush's tongue-lashing of big business marks a swing of the American political pendulum away from a quarter-century of bipartisan deference to capitalists. "We will use the full weight of the law to expose and root out corruption."

"Book-cooking" has eroded "the trust and the confidence that is absolutely vital to the function of our capital markets," Rep. Patrick Toomey, a Republican from Pennsylvania, said.

Required Discuss the role of accounting regulation. Why is trust vital to the function of our capital markets?

P6-3 Setting Accounting Standards
Obj. 2

Accounting standards are set in the United States in the private sector. Public hearings and written documents provide feedback during development of the standards. Opportunity is provided to those affected by standards to contribute information to standard-setting organizations such as the FASB.

Required List the major steps in the standard-setting process. Explain the purpose of each of the primary documents that results from the process.

http://ingram.swlearning.com

Access the FASB and IASB sites through the text's Website.

P6-4 Obtaining the Most Recent Information about FASB Activities
Obj. 2

Visit the FASB's website at http://www.fasb.org and prepare a report that summarizes the various types of information available on the site.

P6-5 Obtaining the Most Recent Information about IASB Activities
Obj. 2

Visit the International Accounting Standards Board's website at http://www.iasb.org.uk and prepare a report that summarizes the various types of information available on the site. Are there similarities between the processes of developing standards used by the IASB and the FASB? Explain.

P6-6 The Purpose of the Conceptual Framework
Obj. 3

The Financial Accounting Standards Board developed a conceptual framework to provide guidance in the development of financial accounting standards.

Required Identify the primary components of the conceptual framework for business organizations and explain the purpose of each component.

P6-7 The Conceptual Framework—Qualitative Characteristics
Obj. 3

Draw a diagram that describes the relationships among the qualitative characteristics as defined in the FASB conceptual framework. Explain your diagram.

P6-8 Ethical Issues in Auditing
Objs. 3, 4

Larry Clint is the president of Hometown Bank. The bank has several thousand depositors and makes loans to many local businesses and homeowners. Blanche Granite is a partner with a CPA firm hired to audit Hometown Bank. The financial statements the bank proposes to issue for the 2004 fiscal year include the following information.

[1] *The Wall Street Journal*, Wednesday, July 10, 2002, Eastern Edition, p. A1.

Loans receivable	$4,000,000
Total assets	5,000,000
Net income	1,000,000

During the audit, Blanche discovers that many of the loans were made for real estate development. Because of economic problems in the region, much of this real estate remains unsold or vacant. The current market value of the property is considerably less than its cost. Several of the developers are experiencing financial problems, and it appears unlikely that the bank will recover its loans if they default. Blanche described this problem to Larry and proposed a write-down of the receivables to $2,800,000. The $1,200,000 write-down would be written off against earnings for 2004.

Larry is extremely upset by the proposal. He notes the write-off would result in a reported loss for the bank for 2004. Also, the bank would be in jeopardy of falling below the equity requirements imposed by the bank regulatory board to which the bank is accountable. He fears the board would impose major constraints on the bank's operations. Also, he fears depositors would lose confidence in the bank and withdraw their money, further compounding the bank's financial problems. He cites several economic forecasts indicating an impending improvement in the region's economy. Further, he notes the bank's demise would be a major economic blow to the local economy and could precipitate the bankruptcy of some of the bank's major customers.

Blanche acknowledges that Larry is correct in his perceptions of the possible outcomes of the write-off. Larry proposes an alternative to Blanche. The bank will write down the receivables by $300,000 for 2004. The remaining losses will be recognized over the next three years, assuming property values have not improved. Larry also tells Blanche that if she is unwilling to accept his proposal, he will fire her firm and hire new auditors. The bank has been a long-time client of Blanche's firm and is one of its major revenue producers. Blanche also recognizes Larry's proposal is not consistent with accounting principles.

Required What are the ethical problems Blanche faces? What action would you recommend she take?

P6-9 Evaluating the Quality of Financial Reports

Obj. 4

The following statements describe the annual report issued by Short Sheet Company for the fiscal year ended December 31, 2004.

A. The report was issued on October 1, 2005.
B. The balance sheet included management's estimates of the increased value of certain fixed assets during 2004.
C. Procedures used to calculate revenues and expenses were different for 2004 than for 2003 and earlier years.
D. Short's financial statements were audited by an accounting firm owned by the president's brother.
E. Some of the company's major liabilities were not included in the annual report.

Required For each statement, identify the qualitative characteristic that has been compromised.

P6-10 Understanding the Auditors' Report

Obj. 4

A standard auditors' report contains reference to each of the following:

A. Responsibility
B. Generally accepted auditing standards
C. Material misstatement and material respects
D. A test basis
E. Present fairly . . . in conformity with generally accepted accounting principles

Required Explain why each of these terms is important for understanding the auditors' report and the audit process.

P6-11 Distinguishing Among Types of Accounts

Obj. 4

Bonner Systems uses the following accounts when preparing its financial reports.

	Type of Account					Financial Statement	
	Asset	Liability	Equity	Revenue	Expense	Income Statement	Balance Sheet
1. Wages Payable							
2. Accounts Receivable							
3. Retained Earnings							
4. Buildings							
5. Supplies Used							
6. Inventory							
7. Sales (for cash)							
8. Accumulated Depreciation							
9. Loan from Bank							
10. Land							
11. Owners' Investment							
12. Supplies							
13. Sales (on credit)							
14. Bonds Payable							
15. Unearned Revenue							
16. Wages Earned by Employees							
17. Utilities Consumed							

Required

A. Place a mark in the appropriate column to indicate the type of account.
B. Place a mark in the appropriate column to indicate on which financial statement that account is reported.

P6-12 Interpreting Information Reported on Financial Statements

Obj. 4

The two most recent monthly balance sheets of Strauss Instrument Company are shown below. Also shown is the most recent monthly income statement.

Balance Sheet	**May 31**	**June 30**		**May 31**	**June 30**
Assets:			Liabilities and Owners' Equity:		
Cash	$ 3,200	$ 1,375	Accounts payable	$ 2,300	$ 2,300
Accounts receivable	5,700	5,900	Wages payable	1,900	1,400
Equipment	26,300	26,300	Notes payable	48,600	40,100
Building	115,000	115,000	Owners' investment	43,000	47,000
Accumulated depreciation	(28,000)	(28,500)	Retained earnings	26,400	29,275
Total	$122,200	$120,075		$122,200	$120,075

Income Statement for June	
Service revenues	$ 7,300
Rent expense	(1,300)
Wages expense	(1,900)
Supplies expense	(400)
Depreciation expense	(500)
Interest expense	(325)
Net income	$2,875

Required From the financial statements presented, identify and record the transactions that occurred during June. Use the spreadsheet format shown on the next page to record the transactions. One transaction is shown as an example.

	Accounts	Cash	Other Assets	=	LIABILITIES	+	Contributed Capital	Retained Earnings
		ASSETS					OWNERS' EQUITY	
	Beginning Amounts	3,200	+119,000	=	52,800	+	43,000	+26,400
1	Cash	+7,100						
	Accounts Receivable		+200					
	Service Revenues							+7,300

P6-13 Management Discussion and Analysis

Obj. 4

The letter to the shareholders from Douglas N. Daft, Chairman, Board of Directors, and Chief Executive Officer of Coca-Cola is provided on the text's Web site and on the student CD that accompanies this text. This letter appeared in the company's 2001 annual report.

Required Read Chairman Daft's letter and comment on the following:

A. To whom is the letter addressed?
B. What is the overall tone of the letter?
C. What time periods are addressed in the letter? (past, present, future)
D. What are the accomplishments mentioned in the letter?

P6-14 Management Discussion and Analysis

Obj. 4

The letter to the shareholders from Douglas N. Daft, Chairman, Board of Directors, and Chief Executive Officer of Coca-Cola is provided on the text's Web site and on the student CD that accompanies this text. This letter appeared in the company's 2001 annual report.

Required Read Chairman Daft's letter and comment on the following:

A. Which segments of the market represent the largest growth for Coca-Cola?
B. Comment on the level of detail contained in the letter. For example, are the bulleted points shown on the last page of the letter detailed, or general in nature?
C. The second paragraph of the chairman's letter makes reference to the nature of the competitive environment. What is the tone of the second paragraph? What is Chairman Daft telling the reader?

P6-15 Earnings Restatement and Stock Prices

Objs. 4, 5

In April, 2001, the management of U.S. Aggregates, Inc., a producer of aggregates made of a combination of crushed stone, sand, and gravel, announced that the company would be restating its earnings for the first three quarters of 2000. After the announcement, the company's stock price per share dropped more than 75% from its high for the period affected by the company's restatement of earnings.

Financial irregularities of other companies have been announced in recent years. In late May, 2001, trading of the stock of U.S. Wireless Corporation was halted on the Nasdaq Stock Exchange when its share price dropped significantly. This sudden drop occurred when the company announced irregularities had been uncovered and it had replaced its chairman and chief executive. The price went from a high of $24.50 in March, 2000 to a low of $2.91.

Required

A. Did these companies practice full and fair disclosure? Why did the stock price of U.S. Aggregates and U.S. Wireless Corporation fall when investors learned that the company had produced financial information that was incorrect?
B. Do you believe "financial shenanigans" by management is an ethical issue? Explain.

P6-16 Evaluating Internal Control Procedures

Obj. 5

Consider each of the following situations.

A. Sales clerks in a retail store are assigned to a specific cash register. They are given a cash drawer containing $100 in change at the beginning of their shifts. They are required to record the amount of each purchase in the cash register. The cash register records an identification and price for each item purchased. Cash payments are collected from customers and placed in the cash drawer. A copy of the cash register sales slip is given to the customer. At the end of each shift, the employee takes the cash drawer and cash register tape to a supervisor who counts the cash, verifies the sales, and signs an approval form. The sales clerk also signs the form that identifies the amount of cash and amount of sales for the day.
B. A ticket seller at a movie theater is issued a cash drawer with $100 in change and a roll of prenumbered tickets when the theater opens each day. The seller collects cash from customers and issues the tickets. Each customer hands a ticket to a ticket taker who tears the ticket in half and gives half back to the customer. At the end of the day, the ticket seller returns the cash drawer and tickets to a supervisor.

Required For each situation, discuss why the procedures are used and how they provide effective internal control.

P6-17 Evaluating Internal Control

Obj. 5

The Spring Valley Church is a small congregation with about 50 members. The church is financed by member donations. Most of these donations are collected during the Sunday morning service. Many of the donations are in cash. Other donations are by checks made payable to the church. Harvey Plump has served as treasurer for the church since becoming a member a few years ago. The church accepted Harvey's offer to serve as treasurer as an indication of his interest in being active in the church. Harvey listed several previous experiences with financial matters on his resume as qualifying him for the position.

Once donations are collected each week, Harvey takes the money to the church office where he counts it. He makes out a deposit slip and deposits the money in the church's account at a local bank. He records the deposit in the church's check register. He writes checks to pay the church's expenses. In some cases, he writes small checks to himself as reimbursement for incidental expenses he pays for the church. He opens bank statements received by the church each month and reconciles them with the church's check register. Harvey prepares a monthly statement of cash received and disbursed that is distributed to members of the congregation.

The church always seems to be lacking sufficient financial resources. A recent meeting was held to discuss expansion of the church's building, but current finances seem to make expansion impossible. Some members don't understand why the church's financial condition appears to be so bleak, since they believe they are making large donations.

The church has asked you to help them evaluate their financial situation.

Required Evaluate the internal control problems of the Spring Valley Church. What explanation can be provided for the church's financial problems?

P6-18 Internal Controls for Cash Sales

Obj. 5

You and a friend have finished your Christmas shopping at the mall and have decided to relax and have lunch in a small restaurant in the food court. After selecting your entrees, you notice a sign on the cash register that reads "If you do not receive a receipt, your meal is free." Your friend is puzzled by the sign and asks you the purpose of giving away a free meal if a cashier forgets to give you a receipt.

Required Is the policy of providing a free meal if a receipt is not given a form of internal control? Why or why not?

P6-19 Multiple-Choice Overview of the Chapter

PT

1. To protect its assets and accounting information, a company should
   a. give one person sole responsibility for the accounting system.
   b. control access to its networks and databases.
   c. permit access to accounting records only by top managers.
   d. hire only employees with college degrees.

2. The purpose of an auditors' report is to show that
   a. a CPA has prepared the company's financial statements.
   b. all of the company's transactions have been inspected for accuracy.
   c. an independent party believes that the financial statements do not contain any significant errors.
   d. the company is healthy, profitable, and likely to remain that way into the foreseeable future.

3. An organization's plan and the procedures used to safeguard assets ensure accurate information, promote efficiency, and encourage adherence to policies is its
   a. internal control system.
   b. cost accounting system.
   c. financial accounting system.
   d. management information system.

4. An auditors' report made by an independent accounting firm
   a. is addressed to a company's managers.
   b. must contain only three paragraphs.
   c. is dated at the balance sheet date of the audited financial statements.
   d. identifies the responsibilities of the auditor.

5. The Securities and Exchange Act of 1934 established the
   a. FTC.
   b. SEC.
   c. FASB.
   d. GAO.

6. A 10-K report is
   a. a quarterly financial report for the SEC.
   b. a registration for a new stock issue with the SEC.
   c. an annual financial report for the SEC.
   d. a report of change in auditors for the SEC.

7. Financial accounting standards for businesses currently are established in the United States primarily by the
   a. Federal Accounting Standards Board.
   b. Financial Accounting Standards Board.
   c. Securities and Exchange Commission.
   d. Accounting Principles Board.

8. All of the following are qualitative characteristics of financial reporting except
   a. relevance.
   b. reliability.
   c. representational faithfulness.
   d. conservatism.

9. The Governmental Accounting Standards Board (GASB) sets standards for
   a. not-for-profit organizations.
   b. state and local governments.
   c. state and federal governments.
   d. the federal government.

10. The FASB releases the following document(s) as part of creating new standards.
    a. discussion memorandum
    b. exposure draft
    c. b only
    d. a and b

CASES

C6-1 Obj. 4

Examining an Audit Report

Examine the auditors' report provided as part of the 2002 annual report of **Nike, Inc.**, and answer the following questions.

REPORT OF INDEPENDENT ACCOUNTANTS

To the Board of Directors and Shareholders of Nike, Inc.

In our opinion, the consolidated financial statements listed in the index appearing under Item 14(A)(1) on page 55 present fairly, in all material respects, the financial position of Nike, Inc. and its subsidiaries at May 31, 2002 and 2001, and the results of their operations and their cash flows for each of the three years in the period ended May 31, 2002 in conformity with accounting principles generally accepted in the United States of America. In addition, in our opinion, the financial statement schedule listed in the index appearing under Item 14(A)(2) on page 55 presents fairly, in all material respects, the information set forth therein when read in conjunction with the related consolidated financial statements. These financial statements and financial statement schedule are the responsibility of the Company's management; our responsibility is to express an opinion on these financial statements and financial statement schedule based on our audits. We conducted our audits of these statements in accordance with auditing standards generally accepted in the United States of America, which require that we plan and perform the audit to obtain reasonable assurance about whether the financial statements are free of material misstatement. An audit includes examining, on a test basis, evidence supporting the amounts and disclosures in the financial statements, assessing the accounting principles used and significant estimates made by management, and evaluating the overall financial statement presentation. We believe that our audits provide a reasonable basis for our opinion.

As discussed in Note 1 to the consolidated financial statements, effective June 1, 2001, the Company changed its method of accounting for derivative instruments in accordance with Statement of Financial Accounting Standards No. 133 Accounting for Derivative Instruments and Hedging Activities and Statement of Financial Accounting Standards No. 138, Accounting for Certain Derivative Instruments and Certain Hedging Activities.

PRICEWATERHOUSECOOPERS LLP
Portland, Oregon
June 27, 2002

Required

A. Who was Nike's external auditor? What date did the auditor complete its audit work?
B. What was the auditor's responsibility with respect to the company's financial statements? What was the responsibility of management?
C. What kind of opinion did Nike's auditors issue? Why is this opinion important to the company?
D. How does PricewaterhouseCoopers' audit opinion differ from the Krispy Kreme's opinion shown in this chapter?

C6-2 Objs. 4, 5

General Mills, Inc., Management Responsibilities and Audit Opinion

The General Mills 2002 Annual Report is reproduced in Appendix B at the end of the text.

Required Answer the following questions about the General Mills Report of Management Responsibilities and the Report of the Independent Public Accountants.

A. Who is responsible for the accounting numbers in the annual report?
B. What safeguards are in place to ensure the accuracy of the reported numbers?
C. Does the independent accountant state that the reported amounts are correct? What does the CPA assure?
D. Why does General Mills hire a CPA to audit the financial statements?

7

COMPUTERIZED ACCOUNTING SYSTEMS

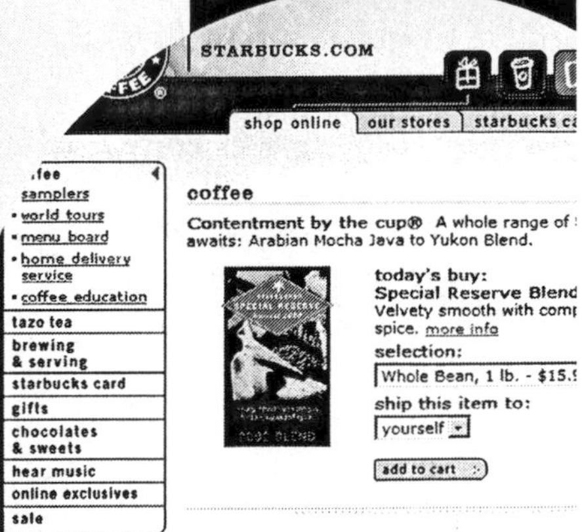

How do we implement a computerized accounting system?

As Mom's Cookie Company has grown and become more complex, a simple accounting system kept with pencil and paper has become increasingly inadequate. Large numbers of transactions, more customers and products, and more complex business activities mean that the company is likely to benefit from a computerized accounting system. Maria and Stan are now realizing that their manual system needs to be replaced by a computerized one.

FOOD FOR THOUGHT

How does a computerized accounting system differ from a manual system? What issues must a company consider with regard to a computerized system? Maria and Stan discuss these questions with Ellen, their accountant.

Maria: *Recording transactions and preparing financial reports with our current accounting system is labor intensive and a bit slow. It takes us several hours a week to record transactions and prepare reports. Sometimes we are several days or even weeks behind in updating our accounts. Should we be looking at a computerized accounting system?*

Ellen: *Yes, there are a number of good systems on the market that are not expensive and that will meet your needs.*

Stan: *How different are these systems from what we have been using? Will a computerized system be difficult for us to learn?*

Ellen: *No, computerized systems use similar concepts to the manual approach you have been using. The computer will provide a means for you to record data. The main advantage of a computer system is that the system can do much of the work for you. Once data are recorded, the system automatically updates account balances and prepares financial statements.*

Maria: *That sounds easy. Are there problems with computer systems that we will need to avoid?*

Ellen: *You need to make sure the system is secure and that you have good backup procedures to protect your data in case the system fails. Let's look at some key issues that are important for understanding these systems.*

OBJECTIVES

Once you have completed this chapter, you should be able to:

1 Identify the primary components of a computerized accounting system.

2 Describe the components of a computerized accounting system used to process data and produce useful information.

3 Describe how data are processed in various modules of an accounting system.

4 Explain the use of relational databases to perform accounting functions.

5 Describe how a database system can be used to create a simple accounting system.

COMPONENTS OF A COMPUTERIZED ACCOUNTING SYSTEM

OBJECTIVE 1

Identify the primary components of a computerized accounting system.

Many of the mechanical functions of an accounting system—posting to ledger accounts, updating account balances, and preparing schedules and reports from account balances—can be automated. Computers are capable of processing data through a series of steps to produce standard outputs such as reports. Consequently, certain accounting functions are automated in most companies.

Computerized accounting systems, even those for small companies like Mom's Cookie Company, are composed of modules. Each module provides a mechanism for recording and reporting specific types of business activities. Common modules are those associated with the most common business activities: sales and customer relations, purchasing and inventory management, production (for manufacturing companies), human resources, asset management, and financial management. A separate module is usually responsible for the general ledger and external financial reporting (GAAP-based financial statements) functions. Exhibit 1 illustrates an accounting system as a set of component modules.

All of the components in the system are linked so they share data with each other. Some businesses use one software application that integrates all of these functions. **Systems that integrate most of the business information functions as a basis for management decisions are referred to as *enterprise resource planning (ERP) systems.*** Many large companies have implemented these systems from ERP developers such as SAP®, Peoplesoft®, and Oracle® Financials. Other companies may rely on software from different vendors for different components of their systems. Many smaller companies rely on software that handles most of the company's accounting functions. These systems lack the capabilities of larger systems but provide for most of the common accounting and financial reporting functions small businesses need. Thus, computerized accounting systems can be small basic systems such as QuickBooks®, MAS, Peachtree®, or Simply Accounting®; middle market systems such as Microsoft® Great Plains or ACCPAC®; or large-scale systems such as SAP and Oracle Financials. Regardless of size, each of these systems is made up of component modules.

http://ingram.swlearning.com

Learn more about these ERP developers and other computerized accounting systems.

Each component in the information system has a particular role. This role depends on the stakeholders who interact with the component.

- The **sales module** receives sales order data from customers and maintains accounts receivable information.
- The **purchases and inventory management module** provides purchase order data to vendors. Vendors are those who supply specific products to a company. This module maintains accounts payable and inventory information.
- The **human resources module** maintains data about employees, including hours worked and wage rates. It is used for preparing payroll and payroll tax information.

Exhibit 1 Components of an Accounting Information System

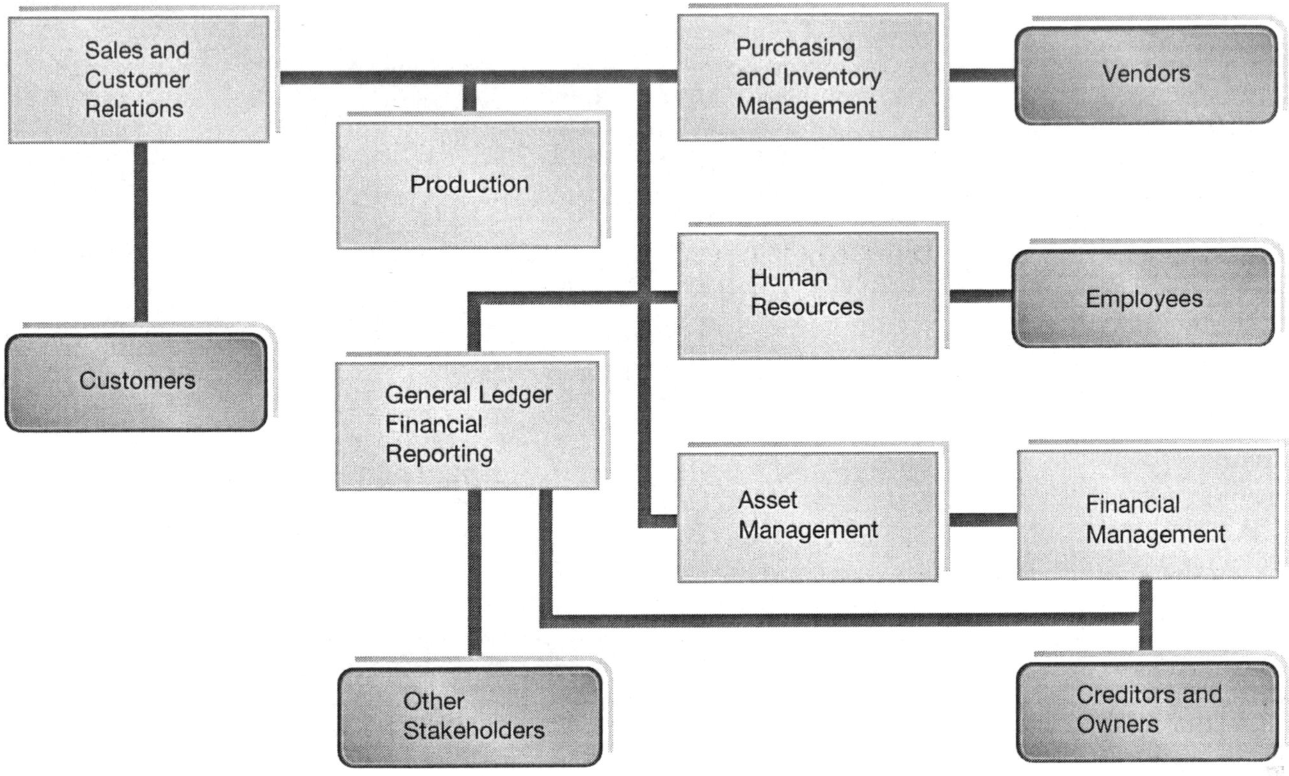

- The **production module** tracks the flow of costs through the manufacturing process.
- The **asset management module** identifies long-term asset costs, their expected useful lives, and where these assets are located in a company.
- The **financial management module** keeps track of debt, repayment schedules, interest rates, and shareholder information.
- The **general ledger/financial reporting module** provides information for use by external stakeholders, including shareholders and government regulators.

The accounting process in a computerized system involves all modules. Each module maintains data for specific entities and activities. **The computerized system records financial data about individual items of importance to a company in *subsidiary accounts.*** These accounts include transactions for individual customers, suppliers, or products. Thus, when Mom's Cookie Company sells goods to a customer on credit, it uses the system to record customer and product identification data so that it can determine what was sold and to whom it was sold. A separate subsidiary account is maintained for each customer to keep track of that customer's sales and payments. **Records for all subsidiary accounts of a particular type are maintained in a subsidiary ledger.** A subsidiary accounts receivable ledger, for example, would consist of all the individual customer accounts, with data about purchases and payments for each customer. In a computerized accounting system, a subsidiary ledger is a file that provides records for a particular type of entity or activity. Thus, a customer file would contain data for the amount owed by that customer and when payment was due.

***Control accounts* are summary accounts that maintain totals for all subsidiary accounts of a particular type.** For example, the balance of the accounts receivable control account is the sum of the balances of all accounts receivable subsidiary accounts for the company's customers. The same is true for inventory accounts for products a company sells and for accounts payable accounts for amounts owed to vendors.

A company maintains subsidiary accounts for management purposes. For example, Mom's Cookie Company must be able to respond when a specific customer inquires about his current account balance or wishes to dispute a billing statement. A company reports control account balances in financial statements to external users and in reports for higher level management decisions. Accordingly, account balances for both subsidiary and control accounts are updated on a regular basis. Control account balances are maintained in a company's general ledger. **Records for each control account are maintained in a company's *general ledger*.** The general ledger/financial reporting module keeps track of each control account and the balances in each account. The general ledger module uses these data to prepare general purpose financial statements for a company.

We examine modules in greater detail later in the chapter. First, we consider the processing of data in computerized systems.

DATA PROCESSING IN A COMPUTERIZED SYSTEM

OBJECTIVE 2

Describe the components of a computerized accounting system used to process data and produce useful information.

http://ingram.swlearning.com

Visit the online shopping sites of Amazon.com, Southwest Airlines, and Banana Republic.

Each component of an information system receives data, stores the data, processes the data to create useful information, and reports that information, as indicated in Exhibit 2.

Input originates in business activities and can come from a variety of sources. It may originate as paper documents, such as **sales orders** prepared by or for customers or **sales receipts** indicating the sale of goods to customers. Data must be entered into the computer system. Data entry may take place when clerical personnel transfer data by typing, or keying, information from paper documents to computer files. Increasingly, data are entered directly into computer systems. For example, many retail stores use scanners to read bar code data from products. The bar codes are linked to the company's inventory data so that sales prices, costs, and inventory amounts are recorded without data having to be keyed.

Many companies provide web-based input systems that permit customers to place orders directly using the Internet. Companies like **Amazon.com**, **Southwest Airlines**, and **Banana Republic** provide for online shopping, reservations, and sales. Data entered by customers updates company order and inventory files. Customers also can retrieve information about their orders from these systems.

Exhibit 2 Data Processing in a Computerized Information System

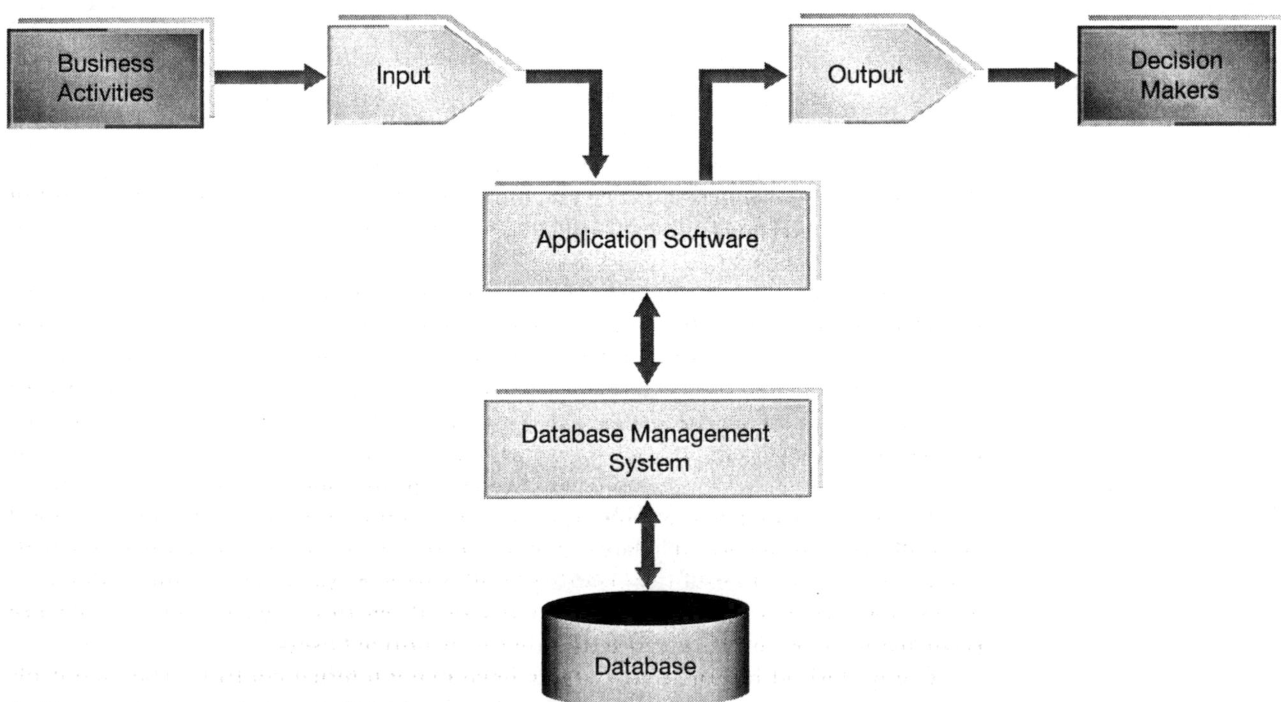

Exhibit 3 provides a web page from **Starbucks'** web site. It provides options for online shopping such as selection of products and shipping information. Other web pages provide for payment using a credit card. These pages are connected to Starbucks' accounting system so that sales, inventory, and customer information can be updated automatically.

Exhibit 3
Example of Web-Based Input

Using computer networks, such as the Internet, to make customer sales is referred to as *E-business.* Some E-business systems, like Starbucks', provide a means for a company to receive sales orders from customers. These systems are referred to as business-to-customer, or b2c, systems. Other systems permit companies to order goods from vendors and to track order information. These systems are referred to as business-to-business, or b2b, systems. In either system, customers do most of their own data entry. These data become the basis for recording sales, accounts receivable, cost of goods sold, and related transactions. Thus, many routine transactions are recorded and processed automatically without the seller having to take special steps.

***Application software* includes the computer programs that permit data to be recorded and processed.** If a customer enters an order using a web browser, application software is needed to collect that data, to record it in the company's files, and to process the data to ensure that the appropriate actions occur. For example, a customer order must be recorded, the shipping department must be notified of the order so the goods can be shipped, a bill may need to be prepared and sent to the customer, and sales and accounts receivable accounts need to be updated. Application software automates these functions.

Databases store data used by various components of a system. Data are transferred by application software to databases. **A *database* is a set of computerized files in which company data are stored in a form that facilitates retrieval and updating of the data. A *database management system* controls database functions to ensure data are recorded properly and are accessed only by authorized users.**

Computerized information systems have many internal controls. These controls are important for protecting data and for helping to prevent errors. Controls, such as passwords, ensure that data are not accessed or modified by unauthorized personnel. Controls built into database management systems prevent more than one user from updating a particular record at the same time and make sure that all appropriate parts of a database are updated when a transaction is recorded.

Other controls require management action. For example, databases must be backed up on a regular basis so data will not be lost if a computer system fails or is destroyed. A company also must have a plan in case its computer system is destroyed because of natural disaster, sabotage, or terrorism. Failure to provide backup systems can result in a company being unable to do business if its primary system is unusable.

Output from information systems often is in the form of reports. These reports may contain prescribed information and may be prepared automatically by a system. They may be print reports or electronic documents that are sent to users. Many output reports can be modified and retrieved as needed by users. For example, managers at Mom's Cookie Company need to know which customer accounts are overdue by more than 30 days. They need a report that gives them an up-to-date listing of grocery stores that are late in paying their accounts. Other managers need to know how much of each type of cookie the company sold in the last month. Database systems are useful because they allow users to query the database to obtain current information.

Regardless of which of the modules in a company's accounting system is involved, data flow through the system from inputs to outputs. How the data are processed depends on the module. Data flows are initiated by business activities, but they also stimulate these activities. For example, a customer order creates data that are processed by the system. Also, data about the order result in goods being shipped to the customer. Thus, business activities create data that are processed to create additional business activities.

Computerized systems rely on networks for processing data. **A** ***computer network*** **is a set of hardware devices that are linked so they can exchange data among themselves using software.** Exhibit 4 illustrates a computer network. Input devices, such as scanners, and client workstations allow data input as well as data access. A **client** is a computer or other network device that uses software to request services from other software.

Exhibit 4

A Computer Network

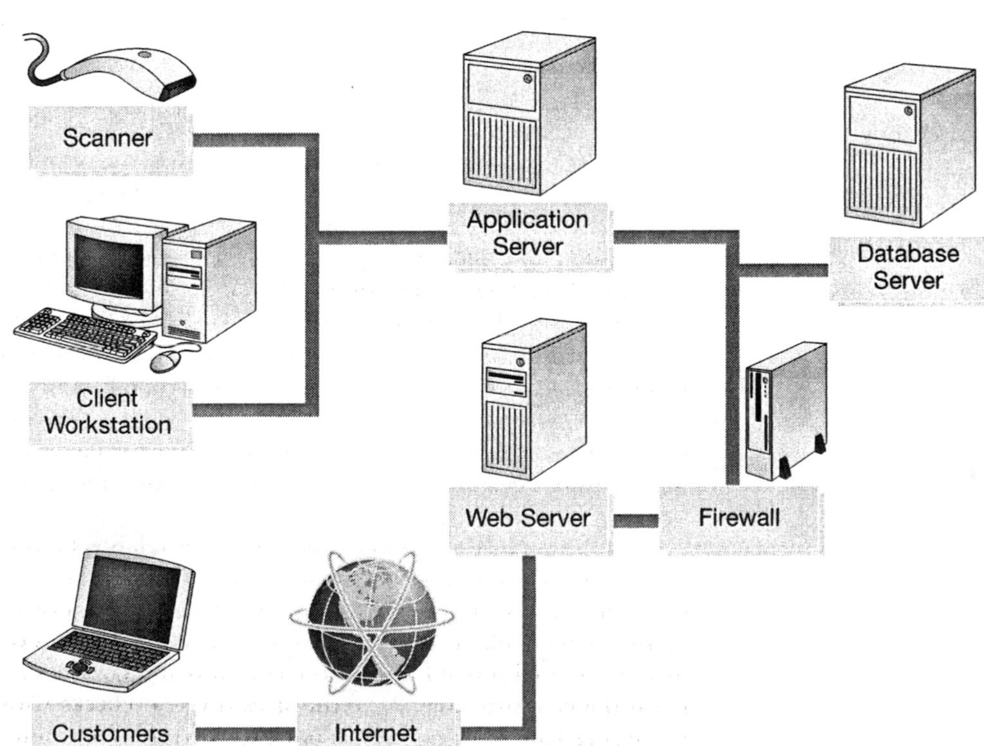

The services are provided by server software that resides on another computer, referred to as a **server**. Networks involve the cables that connect the clients and servers and the hardware and software needed to make the networks function properly. Most networks are client-server networks because they provide for the exchange of data between clients and servers.

Application software usually resides on one or more **application servers** on the network. Application servers are connected to **database servers**, which store and manage data. Companies engaged in E-business or that permit their employees to connect to their network from locations outside of the business, often use web servers to provide the software needed to interact across the Internet. The Internet provides a network so that almost any computer can connect to a company to do business.

Networks pose security problems, especially when they are connected to the Internet. A **firewall** usually is special software running on a computer that makes it difficult for unauthorized users to gain access to a company's internal network. Data must pass through the firewall, where they are examined and filtered to determine whether they should be passed to the internal network. Firewalls can be placed at many locations in a network. Typically they are placed between devices that provide services to external users and the internal network to prevent unauthorized access to data and devices inside the firewall.

The next section examines various modules in a company's accounting system.

1 SELF-STUDY PROBLEM

Lavender's is a plant nursery that supplies specialty plants to other nurseries around the country. It also sells plants to customers from a retail store.

Required Describe the components of a computer network that Lavender's might use to run its business. Explain the purpose of each component.

ACCOUNTING SYSTEM MODULES

OBJECTIVE 3

Describe how data are processed in various modules of an accounting system.

The following section examines each of several primary modules in an accounting system. Each module obtains, processes, and reports information for a particular type of business activity.

The Sales Module

Accounting systems are designed to meet information needs associated with business activities. These needs vary from company to company. For example, a retail company that sells goods directly to customers for cash relies primarily on point-of-sales systems that provide for collecting data about the goods that are sold and the amount received from customers. A company like **McDonalds** does not need to maintain data about its customers, for example. However, a company that sells goods using an order system, like Amazon.com, General Mills, or Southwest Airlines, must maintain customer data that identifies customers, addresses, billing information, and, perhaps, shipping information.

Exhibit 5 illustrates a sales and customer relations module for a company that receives orders from customers and sells goods on credit. To illustrate, Mom's Cookie Company permits its commercial customers, such as grocery stores, to submit orders by phone or by mail. When Fair-Price Foods submits a sales order, that order is received by the sales division at Mom's Cookie Company. The sales division checks to make sure the product is available. Also, the sales division checks with the credit department to make sure Fair-Price Foods has not exceeded its credit limit and that its payments are not overdue. If the sale is approved, the sales division notifies the shipping division at

Exhibit 5
A Sales Processing Module

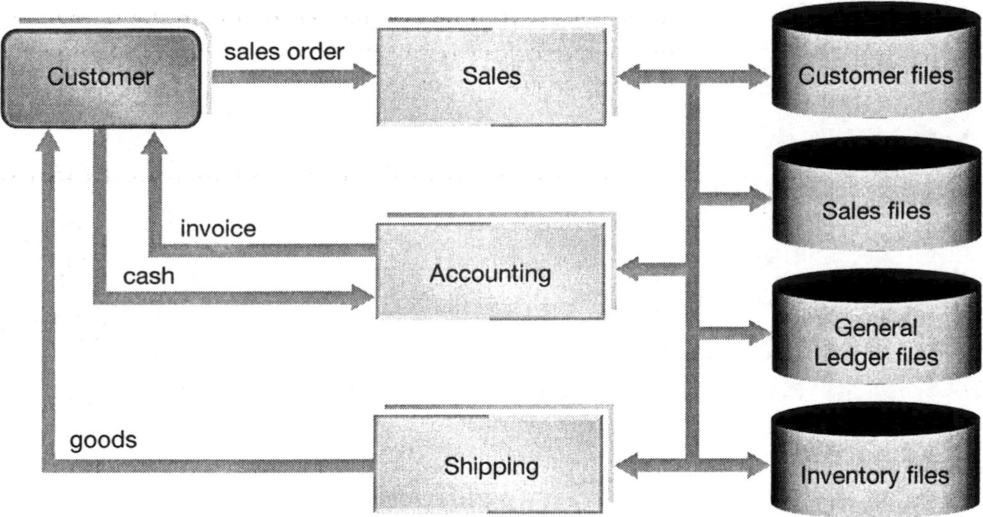

Mom's Cookie Company, which ships the cookies to the customer. The sales division also notifies the accounting department of the order. Accounting updates the customer file for the amount the customer owes. The transaction is recorded to sales revenue and accounts receivable. The general ledger accounts are posted either at the time the transaction is recorded or on a periodic basis. Inventory files are updated for the goods shipped to the customer. Accounting sends an **invoice** to the customer for the amount of the sale. The invoice notifies Fair-Price Foods of the amount owed and requests payment. When Fair-Price Foods pays for the order, the accounting department updates the customer's account and accounts receivable in the general ledger. The cash is transferred to a bank.

Good internal control requires that the personnel who account for the cash should not also have physical access to the cash. Therefore, these functions should be separated within the accounting department.

How much human intervention is needed in the processing of these data depends on the company and the sophistication of its computer systems. In many companies, the computer system handles most of these activities.

Sales, accounting, and shipping functions all are sources of data in the sales module. In addition, these functions also receive information from the system. An important part of this system is its ability to provide information to decision makers. The database files provide up-to-date data about sales activities. The sales department retrieve data about particular customers, such as what they purchased and how much they have purchased. These data guide decisions about advertising and promotion campaigns and about sales bonuses and commissions. Purchasing and production use this information to determine which products to purchase or produce and the amounts needed. The profitability of products and profits earned from sales to certain customers may help a company determine its strategy for which products or types of customers to emphasize. Customers who do not pay their accounts on a timely basis may be flagged to prevent future sales. A company can also use these data to evaluate performance. For example, a company may monitor how long it takes to process orders and ship goods. Unnecessary delays may help explain decreased sales or dissatisfied customers.

Accounting for transactions is an important part of each systems module. The sales department notifies accounting of a customer order. Shipping notifies accounting of goods shipped to customers. Accounting compares data from sales and shipping and bills the customer. **Accounts receivable and sales revenue transactions are recorded at the time goods are shipped to customers. Cash and accounts receivable transactions are recorded when cash is received.** These transactions update the general ledger account balances in the General Ledger files. However, they are a relatively small part of the overall data processing that occurs in the sales module. A considerable amount of data are collected and processed to keep track of customers, sales, shipments, inventory, receivables, and cash flow.

The Purchasing and Inventory Management Module

The purchasing and inventory management functions are responsible for the acquisition of merchandise and supplies. In a manufacturing company, these functions indicate when to acquire materials that are used in the products the company manufactures. Inventory management involves keeping track of the amounts and locations of inventories and making sure these inventories are available when needed.

Exhibit 6 illustrates the purchasing and inventory management module. Purchasing is responsible for placing orders with vendors when additional merchandise or materials are needed. Vendor files identify approved vendors for each type of merchandise or material. Mom's Cookie Company purchases cookies from several bakeries. As additional cookies are needed to sell to grocery stores, orders are placed with the bakeries. Vendor files identify the names, locations, and contacts for each vendor. Also, they keep track of amounts owed to each vendor and when payments are due. Inventory files identify each type of cookie and the number of cases Mom's Cookie Company has available for sale. When inventory levels fall below a predetermined minimum, the purchasing department contacts a vendor and orders additional cookies. The receiving department receives cookies from the bakeries. The vendor sends a bill to the accounting department. Accounting compares the bill with information from the receiving department to verify that the goods were received. Once the billing information is verified, the vendor records are updated. Accounting also uses information from the receiving department to update inventory records to show the number of cases of each type of cookie available for sale.

Exhibit 6
A Purchases and Inventory Management Module

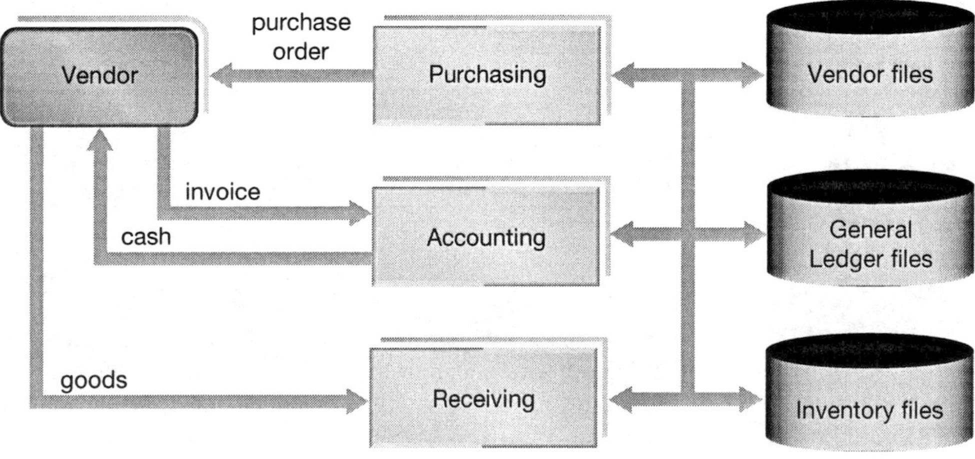

When accounts payable become due to vendors, cash is transferred to the vendors in the form of checks or electronic transfers to the vendor bank accounts. Accounts payable and cash accounts are updated for these transfers.

The system permits appropriate personnel to determine the amount of each inventory item available, the cost of these items, and amounts owed to each vendor. In addition, the efficiency of vendors in responding to orders can be determined. Thus, the purchasing department may be interested in which vendors respond promptly and provide the best service in response to a company's orders.

Many vendors now permit their customers to place orders online. The purchaser can identify the items to be purchased and the cost of these items and submit an order directly to the vendor's computer system. The customer may also be able to connect to the vendor's system to determine product availability and when goods are expected to be shipped.

The interaction of a company and its suppliers is known as *supply-chain management*. Companies reduce purchasing and inventory costs by developing relationships with vendors to supply needed products promptly and efficiently. Many companies rely on close relationships with suppliers to make sure materials and merchandise are available when they are needed. If suppliers are reliable, the purchasing company can place orders and receive goods as they are needed rather than having to maintain large amounts of inventory. In addition, companies depend on their suppliers to provide inventory of the type and quality they need. Companies also work with suppliers to make sure they are getting the best deal possible on the goods they need.

If Mom's Cookie Company cannot get the cookies it needs from bakeries, if the quality of the cookies is not satisfactory, or if the costs are too high, it will not meet the needs of its customers.

The Human Resources Module

The human resources function in a business is responsible for hiring and training employees. The data needed to account for employee activities involve employees' hours and their wages or salaries. How these data are obtained and processed depends on the type of company and the type of work employees perform.

Exhibit 7 illustrates the processing of employee wages for a manufacturing company, such as Parma's Bakery, one of Mom's Cookie Company's suppliers. Employees' hours are collected from time sheets or are entered automatically as employees log into computer systems to obtain data and perform tasks. The wage rate data are maintained by the personnel department. Accounting receives time data from the production division and wage rate information from personnel to determine how much each employee has earned each pay period.

Exhibit 7
A Human Resources Module

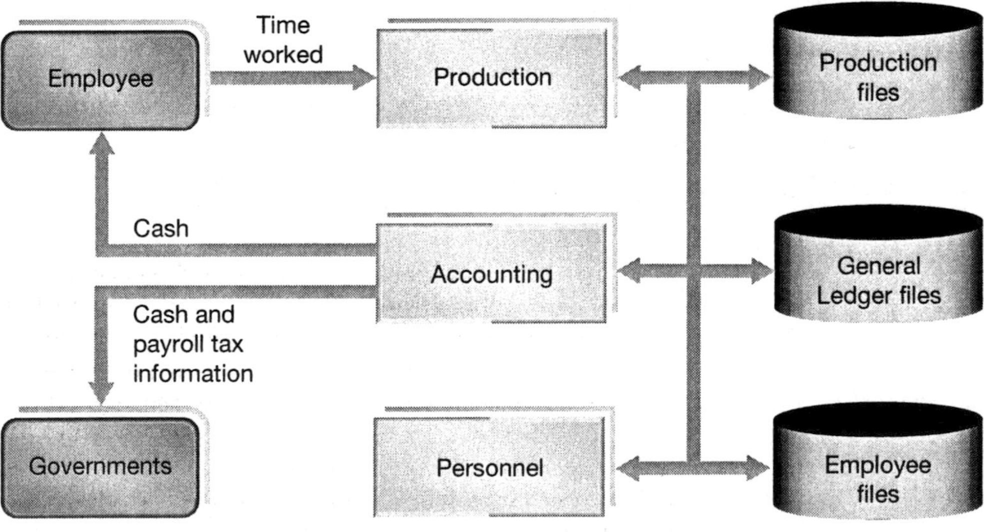

Wage data are important for several activities. Amounts earned by and owed to each employee are in employee files. These data are used to process payroll information and to prepare paychecks or to transfer cash to employee bank accounts. Payroll taxes, such as income taxes, and benefits, such as retirement and health insurance, also usually are tied to amounts earned by employees. A company must keep track of taxes and other amounts associated with wages and provide information about these amounts to governments and other organizations. Payments also must be made to these organizations for payroll taxes and benefits.

Wage information also is important for determining production costs. Labor costs become part of the cost of manufacturing, as examined in the discussion of the production module in the next section. Amounts paid to employees and governments affect wages and taxes payable accounts and cash in a company's general ledger accounts.

The Production Module

Manufacturing companies carry out many complex activities and transactions. These companies may produce many different products, and each product may require numerous types of materials and processing activities. Many costs have to be recorded and many events have to be tracked by a manufacturing company's information system.

Exhibit 8 illustrates basic components of a production module. The manufacturing process usually responds to the actual or expected demand for a company's products. Sales orders or forecasts are inputs for the production planning and scheduling process. Planning and scheduling functions determine which products, how much of each, and when various products will be produced.

Exhibit 8
A Production Module

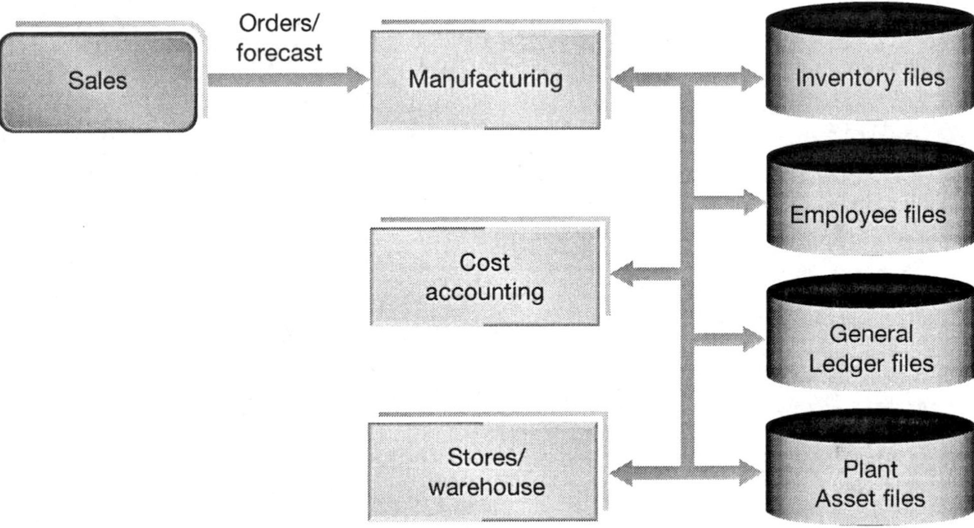

A special accounting function, known as **cost accounting**, keeps track of the costs of resources used in the manufacturing process. Materials, labor, and the costs of other resources used in producing goods must be identified and tracked throughout the manufacturing process. Materials and supplies are obtained from stores (or the manufacturers' storage facilities) and placed into production. The costs of these materials must be identified in association with particular jobs or goods that are being produced. The wages earned by employees who work on these jobs or goods also must be identified. Other costs are associated with plant assets used in the production process, including utilities, insurance, and other resources used during a production period. Once goods are completed, they are shipped to customers or transferred to warehouses for storage until they are shipped.

Cost accounting identifies and records these costs. They are used to determine the costs of goods produced during a period or the cost of completing a particular order. These data become cost of goods sold once goods are completed and sold to customers. For example, Parma's Bakery keeps track of all the ingredients used in preparing an order for Mom's Cookie Company. Also, it keeps track of the labor costs associated with producing the cookies. These costs, along with other production costs, are used to identify Parma's cost for the goods prepared for Mom's Cookie Company. These costs are important for Parma to make sure it has earned a profit from the order.

Each module in an accounting system is responsible for data associated with certain business activities. As noted earlier, each module collects, records, and processes data and provides information to decision makers. The next section considers how a database system functions to provide these information services.

2 SELF-STUDY PROBLEM Suppose you were in charge of production at Parma's Bakery.

Required What actions would you perform that would require you to interact with the company's computer system?

THE STRUCTURE OF ACCOUNTING SYSTEMS

OBJECTIVE 4

Explain the use of relational databases to perform accounting functions.

Most computerized accounting systems are constructed as relational databases. **A *relational database* is a set of related files that are linked so that files can be updated and information can be retrieved from the files efficiently.**

A relational database stores data in tables. **A *table* is a file that contains data represented as rows and columns.** Each column identifies a particular attribute of the entity or process described in the table. Each attribute in the table is referred to as a **field**. A customer table would include customer name and address attributes, for example. Each row in the table contains a record of data for a particular entity. Rows in a customer table would contain data for each customer, for example. Separate tables are used for specific types of entities (customers and products) and processes (sales orders and shipping). Each table contains one or more **primary keys** that uniquely identifies the entities or processes recorded in the rows of the table. These primary keys are used to connect the tables into relationships. The primary key in one table connects to the primary key or a **foreign key** in another table. A foreign key is a field that is a primary key in a different table.

Exhibit 9 illustrates the tables and relationships in a database. The boxes represent tables, identified by their captions at the top. Fields stored in each table are listed in the boxes. Fields in bold are primary keys. Lines connect the primary and foreign keys that form the relationships in the database.

Exhibit 9 Tables in a Relational Database

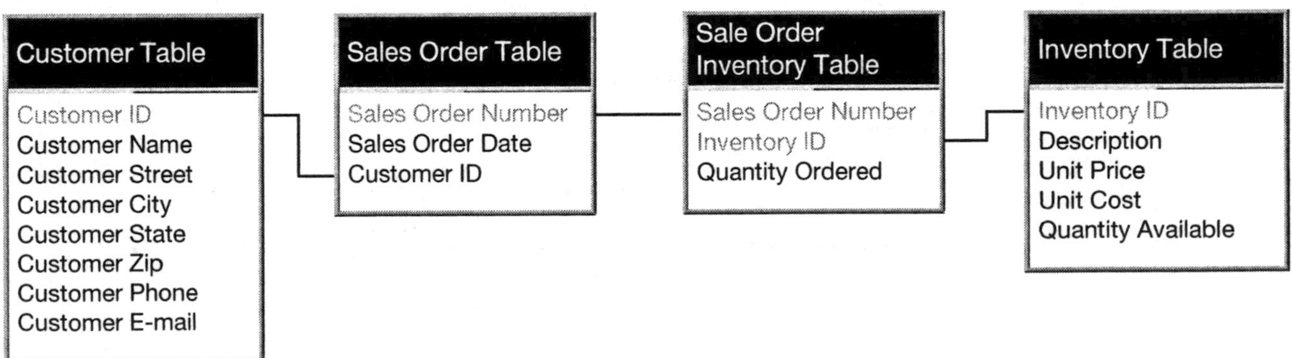

The relationships permit a change to a field to affect each table containing that field. For example, when a sales order number is entered into the system, the Sales Order Number field is updated in the Sales Order and Sales Order Inventory tables. The relationships also permit a user to obtain data from more than one table. For instance, by using a particular sales order number, a user can obtain data from the Sales Order and Sales Order Inventory tables because these tables are linked by the sales order number. The sales order number can then be used to identify the customer and the items the customer has ordered.

Thus, a relational database is a network of information objects that permits efficient storage and retrieval of data. Knowing the relationships in the database, a user can retrieve any combination of fields to serve a particular decision need.

Individual tables in the database store data about a particular entity or activity. Exhibit 10 provides an example of a simple table. The top row identifies the attributes stored in the table. The remaining rows are records. The first column of each record identifies the sales order number that identifies that record. Records are listed sequentially by sales order number, which is the primary key for the table. Other fields identify other attributes associated with each sales order, such as the date and an identifier for the customer who placed the order.

Exhibit 10
A Table in a Database

	Sales Order Number	Sales Order Date	Customer ID
▶	SO12473	04/12/04	CU3452
	SO12474	04/12/04	CU2490
	SO12745	04/13/04	CU2873

Data are entered into a database using **forms**. Forms are computer screens that provide templates for entering data. Exhibit 11 provides an illustration of a simple form. The form provides input areas where data are keyed into the system. Form fields are linked to attributes in tables in the database. Thus, when a new sales order number is entered in the form in Exhibit 11, data are added to the sales order table in the company's database.

Exhibit 11
A Form for Data Entry

Sales Order Number SN001

Sales Order Date 9/2/04

Customer ID CID001 ▼

Name Moore Clothing Co.

	Product ID	Type	Style	Quantity On Hand	Quantity Ordered
▶	PID01010 ▼	Blanket	Blue	44	10
*	▼				

Record: |◀ ◀ ▶ ▶| ▶* of 1

As noted earlier, most data needed by a computerized system may be entered automatically through scanning devices. Customers enter data in forms when they place orders using web-based systems. However, most data needed in database systems are entered by company employees who are responsible for various data entry functions.

Each module of a computerized accounting system consists of tables and forms that collect and store data for the activities associated with that module. Individual tables often are part of more than one module. For example, an inventory table may be accessed by the sales module to determine product availability and price. It may be accessed by the purchasing module to update it for goods received from vendors.

The following section illustrates a database accounting system that is typical of real accounting systems, though it uses simple examples with limited transactions and examines only a small part of a total accounting system. The illustration is designed to help you see how accounting data are processed in a real system from data entry to storage and financial reporting.

AN ILLUSTRATION OF AN ACCOUNTING SYSTEM

OBJECTIVE 5

Describe how a database system can be used to create a simple accounting system.

This section illustrates various components of a computerized accounting system. The illustration examines the sales module of Mom's Cookie Company's accounting system. Example transactions are provided for September 2004 to illustrate sales activities: receiving sales orders, shipping goods to customers, updating inventory files, invoicing customers, receiving cash, updating accounting records, and producing summary reports.

The electronic file used in this module is a Microsoft® Access database, which can be found in the CD that accompanies this text or which can be downloaded from http://ingram.swlearning.com. Directions for use of the software are provided as part of the description that follows. To use the database, you must have a computer with a Microsoft® Windows®) operating system and Access 2000 or a more recent version.

Access is application software built around a database system. It is inadequate for large-scale accounting applications but is useful for illustrating database systems. Unlike most business systems, all of the software runs on a workstation. Though it can be configured to run on a network with separate client and server components, it is easier to use and easier to understand when it is operated from a single computer.

Copying and Opening the Database

It is highly recommended that the database be copied to a hard disk before it is used. To copy the database, open Windows® Explorer and select the drive where the database is located. Click on MomsCookies.mdb and drag it to a folder. Release the mouse button, and the database will be copied. It is a good idea to make several copies of the database under different names (MomsCookies1.mdb, MomsCookies2.mdb, and so on). If the database is modified or accidentally corrupted, you still have an unmodified version for use.

Use one of the following options to open the database.

Option 1. Open Access by clicking Start, Programs, Microsoft Access. Once Access has opened, click File, Open Database. Double-click MomsCookies.mdb in the folder to which it was copied.

Option 2. Open Windows Explorer. Select the folder in which the database was copied. Double-click on MomsCookies.mdb.

Database files can become large when they are modified through use. It is a good idea to compact the database periodically. To compact the database, open it in Access, click Tools, Database Utilities, Compact Database. The database will be compacted automatically. Compacting removes unused space in the database. Running a database from a floppy disk requires frequent compacting.

Database Contents

A database consists of objects. Once you open MomsCookies.mdb database, these objects appear in various categories: tables, queries, forms, reports, macros, and modules. Examine these categories. **Tables** contain the data stored in the system. **Queries** are short programs that permit a user to obtain data from one or more tables. **Forms** provide a means for entering or reading data stored in the database. **Reports** provide summary information intended primarily to be printed. **Macros** are sequences of steps a user performs to complete a particular task. A macro runs a task without the user having to enter each keystroke separately. **Pages** provide a means of creating web documents for accessing a database. **Modules** are computer programs (written in Visual Basic) to provide higher level functions in the database. The Mom's Cookie Company database contains no macros or modules. Also, pages are not included in this illustration.

Tables

Tables are the key to understanding a database. Tables contain the data in the database. Other objects manipulate these data by adding new data, modifying existing data, deleting data, or retrieving data.

Begin by examining the tblProduct table. Click on the Tables tab in the Database window. Double-click on tblProduct or click on tblProduct and then click the Open button. Columns in the table identify categories (also known as fields or attributes) of data. The Product ID is a code that uniquely identifies each product. Name and Size describe the products. Unit Price and Unit Cost indicate the selling price and cost per unit. Quantity on Hand indicates the number of units available for sale. Units for Mom's Cookie Company are cases. Each case contains 20 bags of cookies that the grocery store sells individually. The stores must purchase the cookies in cases rather than as individual bags of cookies, however. Additional products could be added to the table by entering data in the bottom row. Existing data can be modified by entering the data in the appropriate cell. For example, if the unit price for PID0201 increased to $35.00, the new price could be entered in the Unit Price column for this product. Close the table by clicking the **X** box in the upper right corner of the table window. Do not click the **X** box in the Access window (top right of screen) or you will close the Access program. If you close Access by mistake, reopen it and the MomsCookies.mdb database.

Next examine the tblCustomer table. This table identifies Mom's Cookie Company's existing customers. Each customer is identified by a Customer ID. The table includes name and address data to identify where to ship goods and mail invoices. Close the table.

The tblProduct and tblCustomer tables are examples of master files. Master files contain data that are relatively stable and that may be updated periodically.

You can examine the relationships among all the tables in the database by clicking on the relationships button in the top row (toolbar) of buttons in the Database window. (This looks similar to Exhibit 9.) The relationship diagram that appears contains the tables and identifies the fields in each table. Lines in the diagram link the primary and foreign keys. Close the relationship window by clicking on the bottom X in the upper right corner of the screen.

Entering Transactions

You will have a chance to examine other database objects as you work through the process of entering transactions and producing information.

Sales Orders

Begin with a sales order. Open the tblSalesOrder table. Each order is identified by a Sales Order Number. The Order Date and Customer ID also are listed for each order. (This is similar to Exhibit 10.) The Customer ID connects each sales order to a specific customer. Close this table and open the tblSOProduct table. This table identifies the Sales Order Number, Product ID, and Quantity Ordered. This table connects to both the tblSalesOrder and tblProduct tables. Scroll down the table to the final row. Note the data for the last sales order. Once a new sales order is entered, new rows will appear in the tblSalesOrder and tblSOProduct tables. Close the table.

Personnel in the sales department would normally enter sales orders. To enter a transaction, click on the Forms tab of the Database window. Then open the frmSalesOrder form. Notice that the form identifies the Sales Order Number, Date, and Customer ID. (This is similar to Exhibit 11.) It also identifies customer name and address information and information about the products ordered. You can click on the Record selector arrow ▶ at the bottom of the form window to view existing orders. To enter a new order, click on the New Record selector arrow ▶* at the bottom of the form window. Two sets of arrows appear near the bottom of the form. Use the bottom set of arrows to move among the sales orders. Enter a new Sales Order Number, *SN010*, at the top of the form. You may wish to press the Caps Lock key when entering transaction data. Press the Tab key to go to the Sales Order Date box. Type *09/30/04* in the box. Click on the Customer ID selector arrow ▼ to see a list of customers. Click on CID003. The name of the customer appears on the form as confirmation of the customer's identity. Click on the Product ID selector arrow, and click on PID0201. The product Type, Style, and Quantity on Hand appear on the form. Tab to the Quantity Ordered box and enter *12*. Click on the second Product ID selector arrow, click on PID0202, tab to the Quantity Ordered box, and enter *9*. To save the order, you can click the new record selector arrow ▶* at the bottom of the form or close the form window.

To view the data entered for the order, open the tblSalesOrder and tblSOProduct tables, scroll to the last row, and observe the new data. Close each table after you view it.

You can view a summary of sales orders, including the one just entered, by selecting the Reports tab on the Database window and double-clicking on rptSalesOrders. A report appears listing the orders for September. To see the entire report you may need to enlarge the window and set the zoom control on the menu bar to 75% [75% ▼]. Sales orders are listed in the report by date. The order you just entered is listed at the bottom of the report. If you wish, print a copy of the report. Only transactions occurring in September 2004 are included in reports in this tutorial. Close the report when you have finished examining it.

Reports in the Mom's Cookie Company database are derived from queries. Queries obtain data from tables, manipulate these data in some cases to produce new data items, and store them temporarily. Click on the Queries tab to view the queries. Double-click on qrySalesOrders and view the data that appear in the rptSalesOrders report. Queries can be used to present data in table form when a formal report is not needed. Each of the reports described in this tutorial is associated with a query. Close the query.

Shipping Information

Once an order is received, personnel in the shipping department can review the order information. Review can take place on screen or from a printed copy of the sales order report. The shipping department then selects the goods and prepares them for shipment. Also, they update shipping records and prepare a shipping report.

To view shipping data, click on the Tables tab in the Database window and double-click on the tblShipping table. The table contains the Sales Order Number, Product ID, Date Shipped, and Quantity Shipped for each order shipped. The table also contains an Inventory Updated field. When a shipment is entered in this table, the Updated field is set to No, indicating that inventory records have not been updated. Observe that all the fields contain Yes in the tblShipping table, indicating that inventory records have been updated for all shipments. Close the table.

To enter a shipment, click on the Forms tab in the database window and double-click on the frmShipping form. This form indicates the Sales Order Number, customer information, and product information for each shipment. You can review previous entries by clicking on the selection arrow at the very bottom of the Form window ▶. To enter data for the sales order you just completed, click on the Last Record arrow at the bottom of the form window ▶|. The form will display the Sales Order Number of the order you just entered, SN010. The customer information also is displayed for this order. Click on the Product ID selection arrow and click on the product being shipped,

PID0201. Press the Tab key and enter 09/30/04 for the shipping date. Press the Tab key again and enter 12 for quantity shipped. Click on the second Product ID selection arrow and repeat the process for the second item ordered (PID0202, 09/30/04, 9). Close the form to save the data.

You can view a report of shipments by clicking on the Reports tab of the Database window and double-clicking on rptShipping. You may need to expand the Report window and set the zoom to 75% to see the entire report. Use the Record selection arrows at the bottom of the Report window to view each page of the report. To see the most recent shipment, click on the Last Record selection arrow ▶|. A copy of the shipping report can be printed and enclosed with the goods shipped to the customer. A copy also may be sent to the billing department, or the shipping data may be viewed electronically by that department. Close the report.

Open the tblShipping table and scroll to the bottom of the table to view the data. Observe that the Inventory Updated field contains No for the items just shipped. It is important for the shipping personnel to update the inventory records so that the quantity of each product available is correct. Quantity available data are contained in the tblProducts table. Close the tblShipping table and open the tblProducts table. Note the Quantity on Hand for the products associated with the sales order you entered, PID0201 (29 units) and PID0202 (47 units). Close the table.

To update the inventory records, click on the Queries tab of the Database window and double-click on the qryUpdateShipments query. If you are asked if you want to run an update query, click the YES button. A dialog box appears asking for the sales order number associated with the records to be updated. Enter the number for the shipment, SN010, and click the OK and Yes buttons. The inventory records have now been updated. Verify the update by opening the tblProducts table and viewing the Quantity on Hand for PID0201 (29 − 12 = 17 units) and PID0202 (47 − 9 = 38 units). Also, if you examine the tblShipping table, you will find that the Inventory Updated field has been changed to Yes for the last shipment. The change to this field is an important control. Once inventory quantity has been updated for a particular Sales Order Number, it cannot be updated again. Close any tables you have open.

Receiving Goods

As goods are shipped, the quantity of goods available for sale decreases. The supply of goods must be increased periodically. In the case of Mom's Cookie Company, the increase occurs when goods are received at the warehouse from the supplier's manufacturing division. When goods are received, the receiving department places the goods in the appropriate location to be retrieved by shipping personnel. In addition, they update inventory records by completing the frmProductReceipt form. Click on the Forms tab of the Database window and double-click on frmProductReceipt to open this form. Review the form contents, then click on the New Record arrow ▶* at the bottom of the form window. Enter the following data in the form: Product Receipt Number, 10906; Product ID, PID0201; Receipt Date, 9/30/04; and Quantity Received, 25. Close the form.

The data entered in the form update the tblProductReceipt table. Open this table to see the items received. The Inventory Updated field is set to No for the most recent acquisition to indicate that the inventory records have not been updated for this receipt. Close the table.

To update the inventory records, click on the Queries tab of the Database window and double-click on the qryUpdateReceipts query. If you are asked if you want to run an update query, click the YES button. Enter the Product Receipt Number for the inventory item you entered in frmProductReceipt, 10906. Click the OK and Yes buttons and the inventory records are updated. To verify the update, open the tblProduct table and examine the Quantity On Hand value for PID0201 (17 + 25 = 42 units). Close the table. Open the tblProductReceipt table and confirm that the Inventory Updated field has changed to Yes. Close the table.

A report of available inventory is provided by rptInventory. Click on the Reports tab and double-click rptInventory. Each product is listed with quantity and cost data. The balance of the inventory account is the total cost for all products. Close the report.

Billing Customers

Once a shipment is made, the accounting department prepares a sales invoice to mail to the customer. The accounting department also creates the accounting transactions associated with the sale of goods to the customer. These transactions involve recording Sales and Accounts Receivable for the sales price of the goods shipped. In addition, Cost of Goods Sold and Inventory are adjusted for the cost of the goods shipped.

To view sales invoice data, click on the Tables tab of the Database window and double-click on the tblSalesInvoice table. This table contains Sales Invoice Number, Date, Sales Order Number, and Amount Billed associated with each invoice. Close the table.

Before preparing an invoice, the accounting department needs to determine the amount a customer owes. This information is found on the sales order and shipping reports. The Mom's Cookie Company database allows users to calculate the amount associated with each sales order. Click on the Queries tab and double-click on qrySales-Amount. Each sales order is listed with the amount owed. Close the query.

To prepare a sales invoice, click on the Forms tab of the Database window and double-click on frmSalesInvoice. You can review previously entered invoice data by clicking on the selection arrow at the bottom of the form. To enter a new sales invoice, click on the New Record arrow ▶* at the bottom of the form. Enter 10910 for the sales invoice number, 9/30/04 for the sales invoice date, and SN010 for the sales order number. Click the Tab key. Customer information appears on the form. Enter Amount Billed, 765. Do not enter the dollar sign. Close the form to save the data. You can verify that the data have been saved by clicking on the Tables tab of the Database window and double-clicking on the tblSalesInvoice table. Scroll down to view the last record in the table. Close the table.

View or print sales invoices from the rptSalesInvoice report on the Reports tab. Double-click on the report and scroll through the records to view each sales invoice. The last entry is the sales invoice you just prepared. Close the report.

Reporting Sales and Income

Once goods are shipped to customers, the accounting system updates Sales and Cost of Goods Sold. Obtain a list of sales from the rptSalesbyCustomer report. Double-click on the report. All sales for September are listed for each customer, including the most recent sale to customer CID003. Close the report.

A simple income statement is provided by rptIncomeStatement. The only income statement accounts included in this tutorial are Sales and Cost of Goods Sold. The simplified income statement lists these accounts, which have been updated for all transactions in September. Close the report.

Cash Receipts and Accounts Receivable

The last step in the revenue cycle is recording cash received from customers. The rptAccountsReceivable report lists the amounts sold to each customer, the cash received from these sales, and the amount the customer owes. Double-click on the report to view this information. Note the amount owed by customer CID001, $3,180. Close the report.

To record a cash receipt, open the frmCashReceipts form in the Forms tab. Use the Record selection arrow at the bottom of the form to scroll through the cash receipts. Go to record number 4. Observe that the sales order number and customer information appear on the form. Sales invoice number and cash receipts data do not appear because the cash has not been received. When a customer pays an invoice, a check is mailed to Mom's Cookie Company along with a copy of the sales invoice (the copy is known as a remittance advice). The accounting department receives the remittance advice and records the sales invoice number and amount of cash received. The check is deposited in a bank account.

To record a cash receipt for SN004, enter the sales invoice number associated with this sales order, 10904. Enter the cash receipt date, 9/30/04, and enter the cash receipt amount, 2280. Do not enter a dollar sign or comma. Close the form to update the records.

The tblCashReceipts table contains data on the amounts paid for each invoice. The rptAccountsReceivable report has been updated for the amount paid by customer CID001. Review the table and report to confirm that the cash receipt has been recorded. Close the table and report. Close the Access program.

Summary

Most companies use computerized accounting systems. These systems contain modules to handle the business activities that are accounted for in the system. Network components and database systems in accounting modules capture, store, and process data.

3 SELF-STUDY PROBLEM

The accounting system described in the last section of this chapter did not provide separate accounts for sales revenue and accounts receivable. Suppose you wanted to determine the accounts receivable for Mom's Cookie Company at the end of September.

Required Describe the steps you would go through to obtain the data necessary to determine accounts receivable for the company as reported in an accounts receivable report.

REVIEW

SUMMARY of IMPORTANT CONCEPTS

1. Accounting systems contain modules. Each module handles data collection, processing, and reporting for a particular type of business activity, such as sales or purchasing.

2. Computer systems receives input from data entry sources, use application software to process the data, and store the data in databases. Database management systems control database operations as well as access to the database. Application software obtains data from the database and provides information as output to decision makers.

3. Accounting systems are implemented on computer networks. Client workstations and input devices, such as scanners, provide input to the system. Application servers, web servers, and database servers respond to client requests by processing and storing data, and by making information available to users.

4. The sales module receives customer orders, processes shipments, bills customers, and maintains data about customer purchases and receivables.

5. The purchasing and inventory management module is responsible for the acquisition of merchandise, materials, and supplies. It tracks available inventories, processes orders, and identifies goods received and on hand. It also determines amounts owed to vendors.

6. The human resources module maintains employee information, processes payroll, and monitors amounts owed to employees and to government agencies for payroll taxes.

7. The production module tracks the flow of costs from materials, labor, and other sources into the production process. It tracks these costs until goods are completed and shipped to customers. It may also assist managers with scheduling production jobs and monitoring the availability of materials for use in the production process.

8. Accounting systems usually are implemented as relational database systems. These systems contain tables that are linked through primary and foreign keys to facilitate the processing of data. Data are input in electronic forms. Queries allow users to access data and produce reports for decision makers.

DEFINE

TERMS and CONCEPTS DEFINED in this CHAPTER

application software (F259)
computer network (F260)
control accounts (F257)
database (F259)
database management system (F259)
E-business (F259)
enterprise resource planning (ERP) systems (F256)
general ledger (F258)
relational database (F266)
subsidiary accounts (F257)
supply-chain management (F264)
table (F266)

SELF-STUDY PROBLEM SOLUTIONS

SSP7-1 A client workstation and scanning device might be used to input data from local customers. A web server would be needed to provide access for web orders. An application server would provide the software needed to collect and process the data and convert data into reports. A database server would store data for customer orders, plant inventories, and shipments. A network would connect the servers and the client workstation and scanning device. An Internet connection would be needed to connect the web server to the Internet.

SSP7-2 To produce a product, such as cookies, you would need data about the materials needed to produce the product, availability of these materials, and production processes. You would need to schedule the production to make sure materials, labor, and equipment, such as mixers and ovens, are available. You would need information about sales orders so you know how much of each product to produce. Also, you would need to transfer goods from process to process as they are manufactured, and eventually you would need to transfer completed goods to shipping or to retail outlets. As you engage in these activities, you would need to update the company's information system so that the cost of goods produced could be determined.

SSP7-3 To determine accounts receivable, you would need to compare the amount shipped to each customer with the amount paid by the customer at a particular date. This comparison would require a query that retrieved data from several tables. The fields involved in this query are underlined in the following diagram.

The Customer ID would be needed to identify each customer. All sales orders for each customer would need to be examined, using the Sales Order Number. Each sales order would be used to identify the product ordered, based on the Product ID, the cost per unit of each product (Unit Cost), and the Quantity Shipped. The total of unit cost times quantity shipped would determine the amount of each order for each customer. The Date Shipped field or the Sales Invoice Date would be used to establish the date of each receivable. The Cash Receipt Date and Cash Receipt Amount would determine when the customer made a payment. Comparing the total of the sales to each customer minus the total of cash received at a particular date would determine how much the customer owes at that date. A total of amounts owed for all customers would determine total accounts receivable.

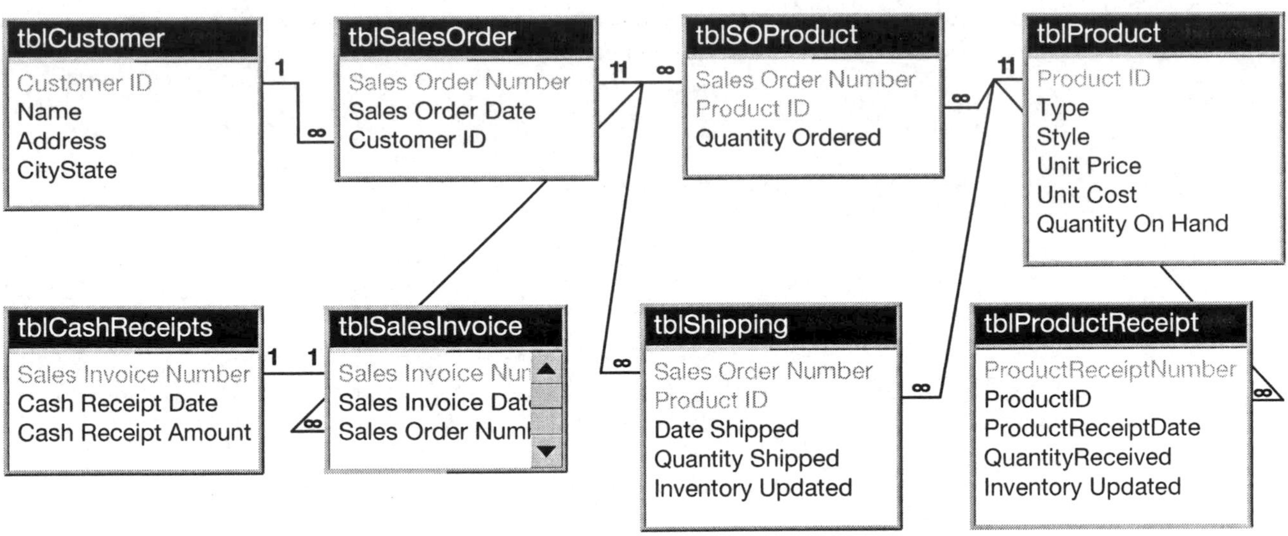

Thinking Beyond the Question

How do we implement a computerized accounting system?

Computerized accounting systems reduce the labor needed to record accounting information and prepare accounting reports. How can computerized systems also help managers, investors, and other stakeholders with their analysis and decision making tasks?

QUESTIONS

Q7-1 *Obj. 1* Why are integrated business systems more efficient than using individual systems for different functions in a business?

Q7-2 *Obj. 3* Suppose a company sells to customers on-line. Customers are required to pay for their orders with credit cards at the time of the order. What primary activities would be required of the sales module to process and account for these orders?

Q7-3 *Obj. 3* The human resources module described in Exhibit 7 is for a manufacturing company. How would the module differ for a retail or service company?

Q7-4 *Obj. 2* What is a computer network? Why are they used by businesses to maintain accounting systems?

Q7-5 *Obj. 2* What is the purpose of a database management system?

Q7-6 *Obj. 3* Irmo Company's asset management module lists each piece of equipment the company has purchased, when it was purchased, its cost, its expected life, and its location in the company. Why would the company want this information?

Q7-7 *Obj. 3* Kreel Company's financial management module lists each loan the company has outstanding, when the money was borrowed, the amount borrowed, the interest rate, the dates payments were made, and the amounts of these payments. Why is this information important to the company?

Q7-8 *Obj. 3* What purposes does a retail company's purchasing module serve? What accounts and types of transactions are associated with this module?

Q7-9 *Obj. 3* What purposes does a service company's human resources module serve? What accounts and types of transactions are associated with this module?

Q7-10 *Obj. 3* Street Inc.'s financial management module lists each stockholder's name, address, the number of shares owned, and when the stock was purchased. How might the company use this information?

Q7-11 *Obj. 3* Why would the sales module of **Burger King** differ from the sales module of the mail order clothing company, **Lands' End**? What transactions would Lands' End record as part of its sales process that would differ from those of Burger King?

Q7-12 *Obj. 3* Why is it important for the accounting department of a company to receive data from sales and shipping? What internal control function is served by this process?

Q7-13 *Obj. 3* Why is it important for the accounting department of a company to receive data from purchasing and receiving? What internal control function is served by this process?

EXERCISES

If your instructor is using Personal Trainer in this course, you may complete online the assignments identified by PT.

E7-1 Write a short definition for each of the terms listed in the *Terms and Concepts Defined in this Chapter* section.

E7-2 *Objs. 1, 2, 3, 4, 5* PT Complete each sentence with the appropriate term.

1. Systems that integrate most of the business information functions are referred to as ____________.
2. Financial data about individual items of importance to a company are recorded in ____________.
3. Summary accounts that maintain totals for all subsidiary accounts of a particular type are called ____________.
4. A ____________ is an accounting record of each (control) account and the balance of each such account.
5. The use of computer networks, such as the Internet, to provide for customer sales is referred to as ____________.
6. A computer program that permits data to be recorded and processed is one kind of ____________.
7. A ____________ is a set of computerized files in which company data are stored in a form that facilitates retrieval and updating of the data.
8. A ____________ controls database functions to ensure data are recorded properly and can be accessed only by those authorized to record, update, or retrieve the data.
9. The interaction of a company and its suppliers is known as____________.
10. A ____________ is a set of related files that are linked so the files can be updated and information can be retrieved from the files efficiently.

E7-3 *Objs. 1, 2, 3, 4, 5* PT Match each term with the appropriate definition.

a. application software
b. control accounts
c. database management system
d. database
e. E-business
f. enterprise resource planning (ERP) systems
g. general ledger
h. relational database
i. subsidiary accounts
j. supply-chain management

___ 1. A set of computerized files in which company data are stored in a form that facilitates retrieval and updating of the data
___ 2. A set of related files that are linked so the files can be updated and information can be retrieved from the files efficiently
___ 3. An accounting record of each (control) account and the balance of each such account

___ 4. Controls database functions to ensure data are recorded properly and can be accessed only by those authorized to record, update, or retrieve the data
___ 5. Includes the computer programs that permit data to be recorded and processed
___ 6. Type of account in which financial data about individual items of importance to a company are recorded
___ 7. Summary accounts that maintain totals for all subsidiary accounts of a particular type
___ 8. Systems that integrate most of the business information functions
___ 9. The interaction of a company and its suppliers
___ 10. Term that refers to the use of computer networks, such as the Internet, to provide for customer sales

E7-4 *Obj. 1* A friend is confused about entries to computerized accounting systems. She says, "I understand that there are both subsidiary accounts and control accounts, but why are the effects of individual transactions entered only into the subsidiary accounts? Doesn't this cause the subsidiary accounts and the control to report different information?" Explain the difference between a general ledger and a subsidiary ledger and the difference in how the information contained in each is used.

E7-5 *Obj. 2* **Lands' End, Inc.**, is a large, well-known mail-order retailer. Assume you logged onto its web site, ordered three pairs of shorts, and paid for them by credit card. Describe the business activities that would occur at Lands' End, including linkages to the accounting system, in handling your order.

E7-6 *Objs. 2, 3* Great Plains Manufacturing recently ordered 100 tons of raw materials including steel, aluminum, glass, and various plastics. Today, the goods were received via rail at the company's warehouse. Identify the documents that will be handled today (either by hand or electronically) and identify the specific and/or control accounts affected by this event.

E7-7 *Obj. 4* Modern accounting information systems often are maintained as relational databases. What is a relational database and what are the advantages of these database systems? Identify parts of a relational database and explain the purpose of each part.

E7-8 *Obj. 2* Computerized accounting systems create special control problems for an organization. Common control procedures used by organizations include the following:

a. Use of passwords to access terminals and programs
b. Limits placed on amounts that the computer will accept for various transactions
c. Backing up of data and programs regularly
d. Separation of design from operation of systems

Explain the purpose of each control procedure.

E7-9 *Obj. 4* P/T Howard Company sells woolen goods and maintains its accounting system using a relational database. To prepare information about sales transactions, the company uses the following tables in its database. The fields that appear in each table are in brackets following the table.

- customers [customer ID, name, shipping address, phone number]
- sales orders [sales order number, customer ID, order date, product ID, order quantity]
- inventory [product ID, product name, quantity on hand, unit price]
- customer shipments [sales order number, shipping date]
- sales invoice [sales invoice number, sales order number, invoice date]
- cash receipts [sales invoice number, cash receipt amount, receipt date]

For each of the following events, identify the tables that would be needed to record the event.

1. Received an order from Jones & Sons for 12 blankets on November 3.
2. Shipped the blankets to Jones & Sons and billed the customer on November 6.
3. Received cash from Jones & Sons for the purchase on December 5.

E7-10 *Obj. 4* Refer to information provided in E7-9 as you answer the following questions.

1. If a manager for Howard Company wanted to query the company's database to obtain information about customer sales during November, which tables should she use to obtain the information? Explain why.
2. If the same manager wanted to query the database to obtain information about amounts owed by customers at the end of November, which tables should she use to obtain the information? Explain why.

E7-11 *Obj. 2* Computer networks in many organizations include client software, business management programs and databases on servers, and connections among the computers running these programs. For each of the following activities, identify the portions of the computer system that would be affected. Explain how the portions are affected.

1. Access to company data is requested
2. Records are updated
3. Data are transferred between a client and a server
4. New data for processing are entered
5. Data being used by another user are required
6. Data to print a report are obtained

E7-12 *Obj. 2* One Star Co. recently lost all of its customer and accounts receivable records. An irate customer walked into the company's sales office and took a sledge hammer to the company's computer. The company now has no basis for determining which customers owe it money or how much they owe. Identify control problems that permitted the loss to occur and controls that should have been in place to prevent the loss. Why is this an accounting problem?

PROBLEMS

If your instructor is using Personal Trainer in this course, you may complete online the assignments identified by $^{P}_{T}$.

P7-1 Purpose of Relational Databases

Obj. 4

Barbury Company sells machine parts to manufacturing companies. Parts usually are purchased to replace worn or broken parts. Most of Barbury's customers order goods by phone or through Internet connections from regional sales offices throughout North America. Sales are made on credit and are shipped immediately to avoid manufacturing delays at customer plants. Barbury uses a relational database for its accounting system.

Required Explain the purpose of a relational database and why it is useful to a company. Describe the parts of a relational database and identify specific examples of how these parts would be used by Barbury to obtain and fill customer orders.

P7-2 Tables and Forms in Relational Databases

Obj. 4

Exhibit 9 in this chapter provides examples of tables that might appear in a company's relational database. Exhibit 11 provides an example of a sales order form.

Required Using these exhibits as examples, explain the purpose of tables and forms in a relational database. Be specific about what the rows and columns in a table represent and how individual entities are identified in tables. Explain how forms are related to tables.

P7-3 Computer Networks

Obj. 2

You have just been hired as an account representative for a large financial institution. Your supervisor shows you to your desk that contains a workstation. She explains that the workstation is part of a wide-area network connecting all of the bank's offices through a client-server system. All of the bank's data are maintained in databases on servers and are accessed through a database management system. To obtain account information, you must log on to the network and use the bank's account service program on your workstation to retrieve data from the database.

Required What is the supervisor talking about? Explain the function of each part of the bank's computer network. Why do most companies use computer networks for their accounting systems?

P7-4 Controlling Networks

Obj. 2

Dora Company uses a client-server network for its accounting system. The company's database servers are kept at a central computer center. Users of the system access the company's database through workstations on their desks. Data are updated continuously throughout the day based on sales, production, billing, and other transactions recorded by users. Dora is a large company and its network connects offices in several states.

Required Identify four threats to the accounting system and accounting data that exist in Dora's network system that should be managed through internal controls. Identify an internal control that would be useful for dealing with each threat.

P7-5 Web Interfaces to Relational Databases

Obj. 4

Connect to http://www.amazon.com on a web browser.

Required Identify the data items that are collected and processed by Amazon's web interface as part of selecting and placing an order for a book. How might these items be stored in a relational database? Identify potential tables and fields in the tables associated with these items.

P7-6 Tables in Relational Databases

Obj. 3

You have been assigned the responsibility of developing a purchasing module for a retail company.

Required Identify the tables that you think would be necessary as part of a relational database that will store data for the module. Identify the fields that will be important in each table and the primary and foreign keys that will link the tables together.

P7-7 Application Software

Obj. 2

An Excel spreadsheet provides an example of an application program that can be used as a simple database.

Required Describe the applications that a spreadsheet can provide and how a spreadsheet could be used as a database. How do the application functions in the software differ from the database functions?

P7-8 Database Management Systems

Obj. 2

Open an Access database like the Mom's Cookie Company database described in this chapter. Examine the Tools menu in the database window.

Required What database management functions are provided by the Tools menu options? Based on your examination, what are some of the primary purposes of a database management system?

P7-9 Network Components

Obj. 2

Trainor Company has decided to market its pet supplies on the Internet. It has developed a web site so that customers can identify products and order them online.

Required Describe a network configuration that Trainor might use to support its E-business activities.

P7-10 Fields in a Relational Database

Obj. 4

Linden Company sells more than 100 different types of nuts, bolts, and screws. Each product has an identification number and is described by its type, size, and material composition. Each product is purchased from one vendor.

Required Linden Company is developing a database system for its inventory. What fields would be important to include in the database for the inventory items? Why would these fields be important?

P7-11 *Obj. 4*

Relational Database Design

Niven Company manufactures and sells ornamental flamingoes. The flamingoes come in one color, pink, but come in three sizes, small, medium, and large. Customers order the products through the web by specifying the quantity of each product, and by providing a shipping address and credit card number. The credit card is verified and the customer's account is charged when the order is placed. Orders are rejected if the card cannot be charged.

Required Design a relational database system that Niven might use for its products and orders. Identify the tables, fields, and primary and foreign keys that would be part of the database.

P7-12 *Obj. 4*

Diagramming a Relational Database

Plaxa Company developed a design for its order system that consisted of three tables. Tables and associated fields are listed below. The primary keys for each table are underlined.

Product Table [<u>Product ID</u>, Size, Price, Quantity Available]
Customer Table [<u>Customer ID</u>, Name, Address, City, State, Zip, email]
Order Table [<u>Customer ID</u>, <u>Product ID</u>, Order Date, Quantity Ordered]

Required Provide a relational diagram for the order system like that illustrated in Exhibit 9.

P7-13 *Obj. 4*

Determining Revenue in a Relational Database System

Refer to P7-12. Plaxa ships its products on the same day orders are received.

Required Describe the process that Plaxa would use to determine the amount of sales it made during a particular period.

P7-14 *PT*

Multiple-Choice Overview of the Chapter

1. Which of the following statements does NOT describe an advantage of a computerized accounting system?
   a. Many accounting cycle steps are performed by the computer.
   b. It is easier to control than a manual system.
   c. It is faster than a manual system.
   d. Fewer opportunities for error exist than in a manual system.

2. Which of the following is NOT part of a computer network?
   a. transmitters
   b. clients
   c. servers
   d. databases

3. Data needed by a computerized accounting system may be entered
   a. automatically through scanning devices.
   b. by customers who enter data in forms when they place orders using web-based systems.
   c. by a company's employees.
   d. by all of the above.

4. An information system that integrates most of the business information functions of a company is known as an
   a. enterprise resource planning system.
   b. enterprise manufacturing relations system.
   c. enterprise resource module system.
   d. enterprise business planning system.

5. The part of a computer system that controls access to data and ensures reliability of processing in the system is the
   a. relational database.
   b. application software.
   c. database management system.
   d. control module.

6. The part of a client-server system that requests services from the system is the
   a. database server.
   b. application server.
   c. web server.
   d. client.

7. The Internet is an example of a
   a. client.
   b. network.
   c. server.
   d. database.

8. The module in an accounting system that is most concerned with vendors is the
   a. sales module.
   b. purchases module.
   c. human resources module.
   d. financial management module.

9. The field in a table that uniquely identifies records in the table is the
   a. primary key.
   b. foreign key.
   c. relation key.
   d. access key.

10. The part of a relational database system that permits users to define the information provided as output from the system is a
    a. form.
    b. table.
    c. query.
    d. report.

CASE

C7-1 Working with a Relational Database System

Obj. 5

Mom's Cookie Company received an order from Fair-Price Foods on September 30, 2004 for seven boxes of Terrific Cookies, 24 oz. size.

Required Use the Mom's Cookie Company database to record the sale. Begin with the Sales Order form. Use 09/30/04 for all dates. Follow the example in the chapter for processing the order. Once the order has been recorded, complete the Shipping form, and then the Sales Invoice form. Print the Sales Invoice for this sale.

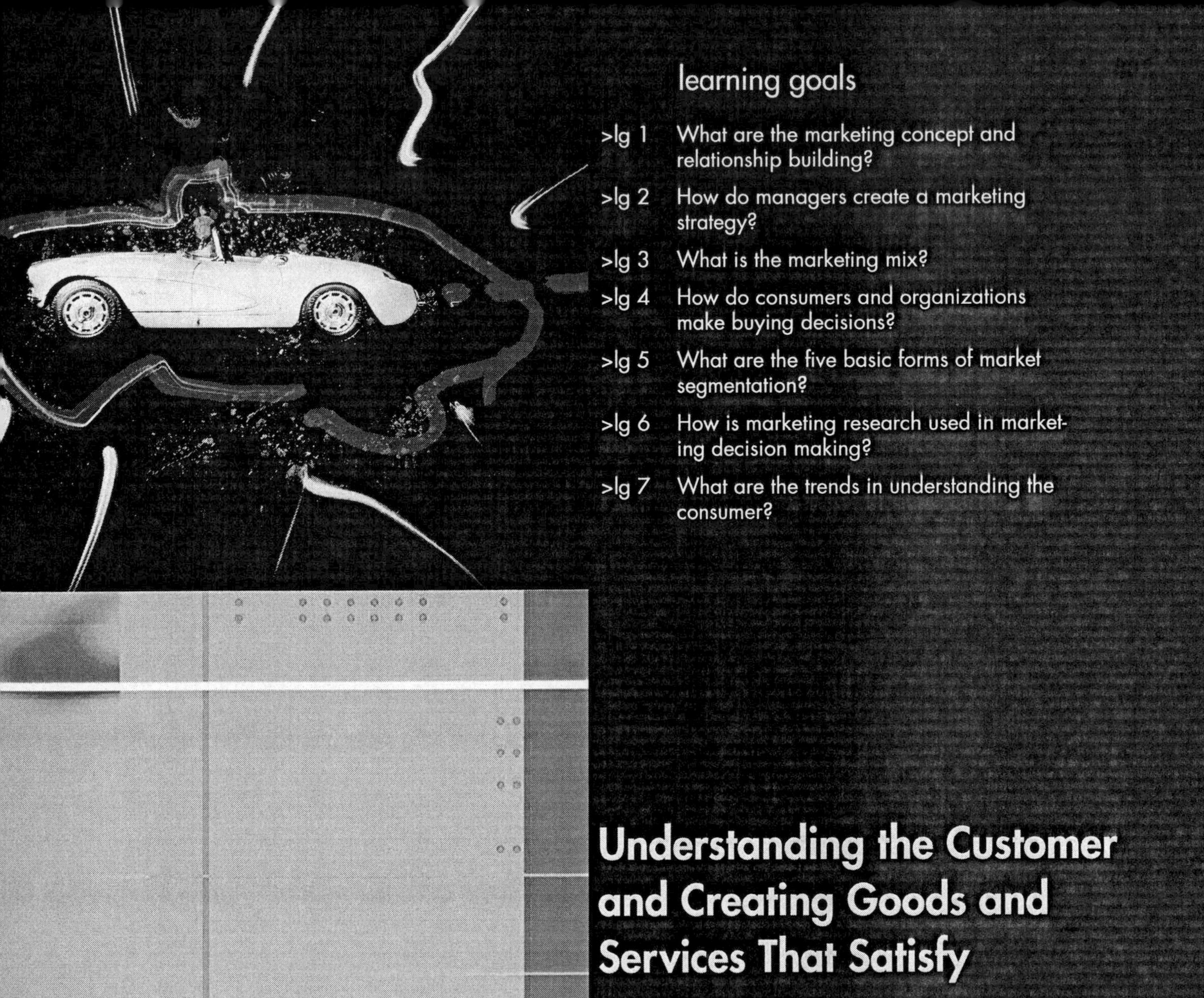

learning goals

>lg 1 What are the marketing concept and relationship building?

>lg 2 How do managers create a marketing strategy?

>lg 3 What is the marketing mix?

>lg 4 How do consumers and organizations make buying decisions?

>lg 5 What are the five basic forms of market segmentation?

>lg 6 How is marketing research used in marketing decision making?

>lg 7 What are the trends in understanding the consumer?

Understanding the Customer and Creating Goods and Services That Satisfy

8

Targeting Baby Boomers at DaimlerChrysler

In 1955, Chrysler needed an icon. It had no Corvette, no Thunderbird for crew cut young men in blue jeans to drool over. That year the company found its muscle car: the C-300. Touted as "America's most powerful car," the C-300 tore up the tracks at NASCAR and Daytona, positioning Chrysler as a leader in high-performance, upscale American automobiles. The company launched a new model in its "letter-car" series every year until 1965's 300L and then discontinued the line.

Now, 45 years later, Chrysler had merged with Germany's Daimler-Benz, and the new company, DaimlerChrysler (**http://www.daimlerchrysler.de/**) needed an icon to catch the attention of 40-something baby boomers. "Bringing a car to market is a $1 billion to $4 billion investment," says Steven Bruyn, large-car marketing executive at the Chrysler division of Daimler-Chrysler. "As a result, you like to be right." The company didn't have to go far for its concept: it resurrected the 300 letter series from the 1950s and 1960s, and simply picked up where it left off in the alphabet. After three years of development, engineering tinkering, and intense market research, the car maker launched the 300M in 1998. Sales have been booming since, and it was named the *Motor Trend* 1999 Car of the Year.

Steering the 300M from drafting table to dealer has been no easy task. At the start of the project, Bruyn and his team studied the potential of the near-luxury car market by looking at population trends and forecasts for its target customers. America's baby boomers were aging and well educated, and their personal income was growing, courtesy of a strong national economy. They wanted room for their expanding waistlines—and were willing to pay for it.

Factors like these indicated a robust future for near-luxury car sales, but how did the 300M fit into the picture? Through marketing research, DaimlerChrysler honed its profile of the car's typical driver. "To 300M drivers, the car is more than just something to get them from point A to point B," says Bruyn.

Target customers are real car enthusiasts. They read *Motor Trend* and other car magazines. And, says Paul Leinberger, senior vice president at Roper Starch Worldwide, they're looking for a product that represents who they are. "It's not about status, but their sense of identity," he says.

America's mood swing toward nostalgia also influenced the design of the 300M, both inside and out. The egg-crate grille harks back to earlier styles in the letter series, and simple analog dials dot the dashboard. Chrysler restored the series's vintage silver-winged badge, which now appears on the hood of all of the brand's cars and trucks. Of course, not everything about the 300M recalls the 1950s—standard features include leather seats, climate control, and a stereo system with nine speakers. "We marketed the 300M with an 'American heritage' wrapper," Bruyn says. "It differentiated us from the others in the market."[1]

Critical Thinking Questions

As you read this chapter, consider the following questions as they relate to DaimlerChrysler:

- Why do companies identify target customers for their products?
- Why is it important to differentiate a product?
- How does a company like DaimlerChrysler find out what customers and potential customers want in a car?

BUSINESS IN THE 21ST CENTURY

marketing
The process of discovering the needs and wants of potential buyers and customers and then providing goods and services that meet or exceed their expectations.

exchange
The process in which two parties give something of value to each other to satisfy their respective needs.

In marketing its 300M model, DaimlerChrysler conducted research to find out what potential buyers wanted and needed and then designed the car to satisfy those wants and needs.

Marketing played an important role in DaimlerChrysler's successful launch of its 300M. Marketing is the process of getting the right goods or services to the right people at the right place, time, and price, using the right promotion techniques. This concept is referred to as the *"right" principle.* We can say that **marketing** is finding out the needs and wants of potential buyers and customers and then providing goods and services that meet or exceed their expectations. Marketing is about creating exchanges. An **exchange** takes place when two parties give something of value to each other to satisfy their respective needs. In a typical exchange, a consumer trades money for a good or service.

To encourage exchanges, marketers follow the "right" principle. If your local DaimlerChrysler dealer doesn't have the right car for you when you want it, at the right price, you will not exchange money or credit for a new car. Think about the last exchange (purchase) you made: What if the price had been 30 percent higher? What if the store or other source had been less accessible? Would you have bought anything? The "right" principle tells us that marketers control many factors that determine marketing success. In this chapter, you will learn about the marketing concept and how organizations create a marketing strategy. You will learn how the marketing mix is used to create sales opportunities. Next, we examine how and why consumers and organizations make purchase decisions. Then, we discuss the important concept of market segmentation, which helps marketing managers focus on the most likely purchasers of their wares. We conclude the chapter by examining how marketing research and decision support systems help guide marketing decision making.

THE MARKETING CONCEPT

marketing concept
Identifying consumer needs and then producing the goods or services that will satisfy them while making a profit for the organization.

If you study today's best organizations, you'll see that they have adopted the **marketing concept,** which involves identifying consumer needs and then producing the goods or services that will satisfy them while making a profit. The marketing concept is oriented toward pleasing consumers by offering value. Specifically, the marketing concept involves:

- Focusing on customer wants so the organization can distinguish its product(s) from competitors' offerings.
- Integrating all of the organization's activities, including production, to satisfy these wants.

- Achieving long-term goals for the organization by satisfying customer wants and needs legally and responsibly.

Today, companies of every size in all industries are applying the marketing concept. McDonald's, for example, found that burger eaters like to determine what's on their burger rather than buying a hamburger that is already dressed in a heated bin. Now, its restaurants deliver fresh sandwiches made to order. After McDonald's changed its procedures to satisfy this customer need, its sales rose 9 percent and profits increased 25 percent.[2]

production orientation

An approach in which a firm works to lower production costs without a strong desire to satisfy the needs of customers.

Firms have not always followed the marketing concept. Around the time of the Industrial Revolution in America (1860–1910), firms had a **production orientation,** which meant that they worked to lower production costs without a strong desire to satisfy the needs of their customers. To do this, organizations concentrated on mass production, focusing internally on maximizing the efficiency of operations, increasing output, and ensuring uniform quality. They also asked such questions as What can we do best? What can our engineers design? What is economical and easy to produce with our equipment?

There is nothing wrong with assessing a firm's capabilities. In fact, such assessments are necessary in planning. But the production orientation does not consider whether what the firm produces most efficiently also meets the needs of the marketplace. By implementing the marketing concept, an organization looks externally to the consumers in the marketplace and commits to customer value, customer satisfaction, and relationship marketing as explained in this section.

Customer Value

customer value

The ratio of benefits to the sacrifice necessary to obtain those benefits, as determined by the customer; reflects the willingness of customers to actually buy a product.

Customer value is the ratio of benefits to the sacrifice necessary to obtain those benefits. The customer determines the value of both the benefits and the sacrifices. Creating customer value is a core business strategy of many successful firms. Customer value is rooted in the belief that price is not the only thing that matters. A business that focuses on the cost of production and price to the customer will be managed as though it were providing a commodity differentiated only by price. In contrast, businesses that provide customer value believe that many customers will pay a premium for superior customer service. Sir Colin Marshall, chairman of the board of British Airways (BA), is explicit about his commitment to superior customer service, insisting that BA can succeed only by meeting all of its customers' value-driven needs, not just price. In a highly competitive industry, BA has used this customer-value-based strategy to become the world's most profitable airline.[3]

The automobile industry also illustrates the importance of creating customer value. To penetrate the fiercely competitive luxury automobile market, Lexus adopted a customer-driven approach, with particular emphasis on service. Lexus stresses product quality with a standard of zero defects in manufacturing. The service quality goal is to treat each customer as one would treat a guest in one's home, to pursue the perfect person-to-person relationship, and to strive to improve continually. This strategy has enabled Lexus to establish a clear quality image and capture a significant share of the luxury car market.

Customer Satisfaction

customer satisfaction

The customer's feeling that a product has met or exceeded expectations.

Customer satisfaction is the customer's feeling that a product has met or exceeded expectations. New York State Electric and Gas Corp. says that its top priority is customer satisfaction. "We're committed to providing superior customer service and earning our customers' business every day," said Ralph Tedesco, president of NYSEG. "We're very proud that our customers acknowledge our restoration efforts following devastating storms and give us high marks for customer service."[4]

Read Embassy Suites's Guest Guarantee at

http://www.embassysuites.com

At DoubleTree Hotels, guests are asked to fill out a CARE card several times during their stay to let staff know how they are doing. Managers check the cards daily to solve guests' problems before they check out. Guests can also use a CARE phone line to call in their complaints at the hotel. A CARE committee continually seeks ways to improve guest services. The goal is to offer a solution to a CARE call in 15 minutes. Embassy Suites goes one step further by offering a full refund to guests who are not satisfied with their stay.

Customer satisfaction may indicate how consumers feel about a product, but it may not indicate their willingness to actually purchase that product. General Motors' Cadillac Division, for example, was quite pleased that more than 90 percent of its customers reported that they were either "satisfied" or "highly satisfied" with their recent purchase of a new Cadillac, figures comparable with those reported by purchasers of Japanese automobiles. But Cadillac was quite dismayed to learn that only 30 to 40 percent of these new Cadillac owners would buy another Cadillac, compared with more than 80 percent of Japanese auto purchasers.[5] GM had been asking only about customer satisfaction, not customer value, the willingness of customers to actually buy a new Cadillac.

Building Relationships

relationship marketing
A strategy that focuses on forging long-term partnerships with customers by offering value and providing customer satisfaction.

Relationship marketing is a strategy that focuses on forging long-term partnerships with customers. Companies build relationships with customers by offering value and providing customer satisfaction. Companies benefit from repeat sales and referrals that lead to increases in sales, market share, and profits. Costs fall because it is less expensive to serve existing customers than to attract new ones. Keeping a customer costs about one-fourth of what it costs to attract a new customer, and the probability of retaining a customer is over 60 percent, whereas the probability of landing a new customer is less than 30 percent.[6]

Customers also benefit from stable relationships with suppliers. Business buyers have found that partnerships with their suppliers are essential to producing high-quality products while cutting costs. Customers remain loyal to firms that provide them greater value and satisfaction than they expect from competing firms.

Frequent buyer clubs are an excellent way to build long-term relationships. All major airlines including American and United have frequent flyer programs. After you fly a certain number of miles, you become eligible for a free ticket. Now, cruise lines, hotels, car rental agencies, credit card companies, and even mortgage companies give away "airline miles" with purchases. Consumers patronize the airline and its partners because they want the free tickets. Thus, the program helps to create a long-term relationship with the customer.[7]

concept check

- What is marketing?
- Explain the marketing concept.
- Explain the difference between customer value and customer satisfaction.
- What is meant by relationship marketing?

If an organization is to build relationships with customers, its employees' attitudes and actions must be customer oriented. Any person, department, or division that is not customer oriented weakens the positive image of the entire organization. An employee may be the only contact a potential customer has with the firm. In that person's eyes, the employee is the firm. If greeted discourteously, the potential customer may well assume that the employee's attitude represents the whole firm.

Building long-term relationships with customers is an excellent way for small businesses to compete against the big chains. Some-

FOCUSING ON SMALL BUSINESS

IF YOU WANT TO BUY A CROCK-POT, TRY SOMEPLACE ELSE

With Wal-Marts and Home Depots overrunning the landscape, it looked as though Josh and Michael Bracken's small nursery in Dallas, Texas, would quickly wilt. So how is it that profit at the Brackens' Nicholson-Hardie Nursery & Garden Center rose 11 percent last year and the brothers are talking of expansion? Well, they make house calls, for one thing. One afternoon, 29-year-old Josh responds to a plea from retiree Jon Bauman, who is fretting over a bed of withering azaleas. "These are way dry," the nurseryman says, prodding the brittle plants and snapping off a twig. He advises Bauman to either water his shrubs more often or find a plant that is better suited to the dense clay soil. "At the Gap, anyone with a smile can sell a shirt," Josh boasts. "But it takes a couple of years to learn about plants."

In industry after industry, chain competitors have driven independents into the ground. The same thing almost happened in the nursery business, where big retailers now control two-thirds of the $71 billion lawn-and-garden market. But today, many of the nation's 10,000 independent nurseries are stubbornly holding their own by stocking plants suited for local conditions, pampering customers, and luring them with inventive promotions. Homestead Gardens in Davidsonville, Maryland, holds an herb festival, with local chefs demonstrating how to make herbal marinades and garnishes.

Because the Brackens can't buy in bulk as the chains do, they don't even attempt to match the chains' prices. Instead, they offer superior customer service by stocking more than 1,000 plant varieties, far more than the chains carry. Rare perennial flowers such as Tapien verbena and Mount Fuji phlox, which sell for between $3 and $6, can be found only at Nicholson-Hardie.

To distinguish themselves, the brothers aim for the sort of customer who "would buy a Land Rover versus a Chevrolet," says Josh. Thus, the stores stock top-of-the-line tools one might find in Martha Stewart's garden, including $35 British sheep shears for trimming grass and $45 Swiss pruners. There are dozens of brass and animal-shaped fountains, some selling for thousands of dollars. Nicholson-Hardie even carries a $20.95 imported British rosemary-scented herbal hand cream. It can't be found anywhere else in Dallas except at Neiman Marcus. Michael Bracken, who handles the company's finances, says he loves the association with the fancy retailer. "It adds to the aura."

Critical Thinking Questions

1. What else could the Brackens do to build long-term relationships with customers?
2. Would a frequent purchaser program work?
3. What about giving away airline miles with purchases?

times small firms, with few employees, are in a better position to "go the extra mile," as explained in the Focusing on Small Business box.

CREATING A MARKETING STRATEGY

>lg 2

There is no secret formula for creating goods and services that provide customer value and customer satisfaction. An organization that is committed to providing superior customer satisfaction puts customers at the very center of its marketing strategy. Creating a customer-focused marketing strategy involves four main steps: understanding the external environment, defining the target market, creating a competitive advantage, and developing a marketing mix. This section will examine the first three steps, and the next section will discuss how a company develops a marketing mix. The marketing mix is explained in detail in Chapter 12.

Understanding the External Environment

Unless marketing managers understand the external environment, a firm cannot intelligently plan for the future. Thus, many organizations assemble a team of specialists to continually collect and evaluate environmental information, a process called **environmental scanning.** The goal in gathering the environmental data is to identify future market opportunities and threats.

environmental scanning
The process in which a firm continually collects and evaluates information about its external environment.

For example, as technology continues to blur the lines between personal computers, television, and compact disc players, a company like Sony may find itself competing against a company like Compaq. Research shows that children would like more games bundled with computer software, while adults desire various types of word-processing and business-related software. Is this information an opportunity or a threat to Compaq marketing managers?

In general, six categories of environmental data shape marketing decisions:

- *Social forces* such as the values of potential customers and the changing roles of families and women working outside the home.
- *Demographic forces* such as the ages, birth and death rates, and locations of various groups of people.
- *Economic forces* such as changing incomes, inflation, and recession.
- *Technological forces* such as advances in communications and data retrieval capabilities.
- *Political and legal forces* such as changes in laws and regulatory agency activities.
- *Competitive forces* from domestic and foreign-based firms.

target market
The specific group of consumers toward which a firm directs its marketing efforts.

Defining the Target Market

Managers and employees focus on providing value for a well-defined target market. The **target market** is the specific group of consumers toward which a firm directs its marketing efforts. It is selected from the larger overall market. For instance, Carnival Cruise Lines says its main target market is "blue-collar entrepreneurs," people with an income of $25,000 to $50,000 a year who own auto supply shops, dry cleaners, and the like. Unlike other cruise lines, it does not seek affluent retirees. Quaker Oats targets its grits to blue-collar consumers in the South. Kodak targets Ektar color print film, designed for use only in rather sophisticated cameras, to advanced amateur photographers. The Limited, Inc. has several different types of stores, each for a distinct target market: Express for trendy younger women, Lerner New York for budget-conscious women, and Henri Bendel for upscale, high-fashion women. These target markets are all part of the overall market for women's clothes.

The National Fluid Milk Processor Promotion Board creates ads targeted at different market segments to promote the consumption of milk. It targets the youth market with ads featuring celebrities such as NASCAR driver Jeff Gordon.

Identifying a target market helps a company focus its marketing efforts on those who are most likely to buy its products or services. Concentrating on potential customers lets the firm use its resources efficiently. The target markets for Marriott International's lodging alternatives are shown in Exhibit 11-1. The latest in the Marriott family is SpringHill Suites. The SpringHill idea came from another Marriott chain, Fairfield Suites, an offshoot of Marriott's Fairfield Inns. The suites, opened in 1997, were roomy but devoid of most frills: the closets didn't have doors, and the lobby floors were covered with linoleum. Some franchisees com-

exhibit 11-1 | The Target Markets for Marriott International

	Price Range	Target Market
Fairfield Inn	$45–65	Economizing business and leisure travelers
TownePlace Suites	$55–70	Moderate-tier travelers who stay three to four weeks
SpringHill Suites	$75–95	Business and leisure travelers looking for more space and amenities
Courtyard	$75–105	Travelers seeking quality and affordable accommodations designed for the road warrior
Residence Inn	$85–110	Travelers seeking a residential-style hotel
Marriott Hotels, Resorts, and Suites	$90–235	Grounded achievers who desire consistent quality
Renaissance Hotels and Resorts	$90–235	Discerning business and leisure travelers who seek creative attention to detail
Ritz-Carlton	$175–300	Senior executives and entrepreneurs looking for a unique, luxury, personalized experience

SOURCE: Christina Binkley, "Marriott Outfits an Old Chain for New Market," *Wall Street Journal* (October 13, 1998), pp. B1, B3.

plained to Marriott that the suites were *under*priced: Fairfield Suites guests were saying they would pay a little more for a few more frills.

So Marriott began planning an upgrade. To create each of the first 20 or so SpringHill locations, Marriott spent $200,000 renovating an existing Fairfield Suites unit, adding ergonomic chairs, ironing boards, and other amenities. Lobbies at SpringHill hotels are fancier than the rooms themselves: the lobbies have fireplaces, breakfast rooms, crown moldings at the ceiling, and granite or ceramic tile floors.

HOT links

Look for other ways Marriott builds customer relationships at

http://www.marriott.com

Creating a Competitive Advantage

competitive advantage

A set of unique features of a company and its products that are perceived by the target market as significant and superior to those of the competition; also called *differential advantage.*

A **competitive advantage**, also called a differential advantage, is a set of unique features of a company and its products that are perceived by the target market as significant and superior to those of the competition. As Andrew Grove, former CEO of Intel, says, "You have to understand what it is you are better at than anybody else and mercilessly focus your efforts on it." Competitive advantage is the factor or factors that cause customers to patronize a firm and not the competition. There are three types of competitive advantage: cost, product/service differential, and niche.

cost competitive advantage

A firm's ability to produce a product or service at a lower cost than all other competitors in an industry while maintaining satisfactory profit margins.

Cost Competitive Advantage A firm that has a **cost competitive advantage** can produce a product or service at a lower cost than all its competitors while maintaining satisfactory profit margins. Firms become cost leaders by obtaining inexpensive raw materials, making plant operations more efficient, designing products for ease of manufacture, controlling overhead costs, and avoiding marginal customers. DuPont, for example, has an exceptional cost competitive advantage in the production of titanium dioxide. Technicians created a production process using low-cost feedstock that gives DuPont a 20 percent cost advantage over its competitors. The cheaper feedstock technology is complex and can be accomplished only by investing about $100 million and several years of testing time.

A cost competitive advantage enables a firm to deliver superior customer value. Chaparral Steel, for example, is the leading low-cost U.S. steel producer because it uses only scrap iron and steel and a very efficient continuous-casting process to make new steel. In fact, Chaparral is so efficient that it is the only U.S. steel producer that ships to Japan.

differential competitive advantage
A firm's ability to provide a unique product or service that offers something of value to buyers besides simply a lower price.

Differential Competitive Advantage A product/service **differential competitive advantage** exists when a firm provides something unique that is valuable to buyers beyond simply offering a low price. Differential competitive advantages tend to be longer lasting than cost competitive advantages because cost advantages are subject to continual erosion as competitors catch up. Cost advantages fail to last for two reasons. For one thing, technology is transferable. For example, Bell Labs invented fiber optic cable that reduced the cost of voice and data transmission by dramatically increasing the number of calls that could be transmitted simultaneously through a two-inch cable. Within five years, however, fiber optic technology had spread throughout the industry. Second, for most production processes or product categories (e.g., running shoes and laptop computers), there are alternative suppliers. Over time, high-cost producers tend to seek out lower-cost suppliers and they can compete more effectively with the industry's low-cost producers.

The durability of a differential competitive advantage tends to make this strategy more attractive to many top managers. Common differential advantages are brand names (Lexus), a strong dealer network (Caterpillar Tractor for construction work), product reliability (Maytag washers), image (Neiman Marcus in retailing), and service (Federal Express). Brand names such as Coca-Cola, BMW, and Cartier stand for quality the world over. Through continual product and marketing innovations and attention to quality and value, managers at these organizations have created enduring competitive advantages.

niche competitive advantage
A firm's ability to target and effectively serve a single segment of the market within a limited geographic area.

Niche Competitive Advantage A company with a **niche competitive advantage** targets and effectively serves a single segment of the market within a limited geographic area. For small companies with limited resources that potentially face giant competitors, "niche-ing" may be the only viable option. A market segment that has good growth potential but is not crucial to the success of major competitors is a good candidate for a niche strategy. Once a potential segment has been identified, the firm needs to make certain it can defend against challengers through its superior ability to serve buyers in the segment. For example, A Pea in the Pod is a small chain of retail stores that sells maternity clothes. Its quality materials, innovative designs, and reasonable prices serve as a barrier against competition.

concept check

- What is environmental scanning?
- What is a target market, and why should a company have one?
- What is a competitive advantage?
- Explain the three types of competitive advantages.

DEVELOPING A MARKETING MIX

>lg 3

Once a firm has defined its target market and identified its competitive advantage, it can create the **marketing mix,** that is, the blend of product offering, pricing, promotional methods, and distribution system that brings a specific group

marketing mix
The blend of product offering, pricing, promotional methods, and distribution system that brings a specific group of consumers superior value.

four Ps
Product, price, promotion, and place (distribution), which together make up the marketing mix.

of consumers superior value. Distribution is sometimes referred to as place, so the marketing mix is based on the **four Ps:** product, price, promotion, and place. Every target market requires a unique marketing mix to satisfy the needs of the target consumers and meet the firm's goals. A strategy must be constructed for each of the four Ps and blended with the strategies for the other elements. Thus, the marketing mix is only as good as its weakest part. An excellent product with a poor distribution system could be doomed to failure.

Compare McDonald's and Wendy's marketing efforts by visiting their home pages at http://www.mcdonalds.com and http://www.wendys.com

A successful marketing mix requires careful tailoring. For instance, at first glance you might think that McDonald's and Wendy's have roughly the same marketing mix. After all, they are both in the fast-food business. But McDonald's targets parents with young children through Ronald McDonald, heavily promoted children's Happy Meals, and playgrounds. Wendy's is targeted to a more adult crowd. Wendy's has no playgrounds but it does have carpeting (a more adult atmosphere), and it pioneered fast-food salad bars.

Product Strategy

product strategy
The part of the marketing mix that involves choosing a brand name, packaging, colors, a warranty, accessories, and a service program for the product.

Marketing strategy typically starts with the product. You can't plan a distribution system or set a price if you don't know what you're going to market. Marketers use the term *product* to refer to both *goods,* such as tires, stereos, and clothing, and *services,* such as hotels, hair salons, and restaurants. Thus, the heart of the marketing mix is the good or service. Creating a **product strategy** involves choosing a brand name, packaging, colors, a warranty, accessories, and a service program.

Marketers view products in a much larger context than you might imagine. They include not only the item itself but also the brand name and the company image. The names Yves St. Laurent and Gucci, for instance, create extra value for everything from cosmetics to bath towels. That is, products with those names sell at higher prices than identical products without the names. We buy things not only for what they do, but also for what they mean.

Pricing Strategy

pricing strategy
The part of the marketing mix that involves establishing a price for the product based on the demand for the product and the cost of producing it.

Pricing strategy is based on demand for the product and the cost of producing it. Some special considerations can also influence the price. Sometimes, for instance, a special introductory price is used to get people to try a new product. Some firms enter the market with low prices and keep them low, such as Carnival Cruise Lines and Suzuki cars. Others enter a market with very high prices and then lower them over time, such as producers of high-definition televisions and personal computers.

Distribution Strategy

distribution strategy
The part of the marketing mix that involves deciding how many stores and which specific wholesalers and retailers will handle the product in a geographic area.

Distribution is the means (the channel) by which a product flows from the producer to the consumer. One aspect of **distribution strategy** is deciding how many stores and which specific wholesalers and retailers will handle the product in a geographic area. Cosmetics, for instance, are distributed in many different ways. Avon has a sales force of several hundred thousand representatives who call directly on consumers. Clinique and Estée Lauder are distributed through selected department stores. Cover Girl and Del Laboratories use mostly chain drugstores and other mass merchandisers. Redken sells through beauticians. Revlon uses several of these distribution channels.

Promotion Strategy

promotion strategy
The part of the marketing mix that involves personal selling, advertising, public relations, and sales promotion of the product.

Many people feel that promotion is the most exciting part of the marketing mix. **Promotion strategy** covers personal selling, advertising, public relations, and sales promotion. Each element is coordinated with the others to create a promotional blend. An advertisement, for instance, helps a buyer get to know the company and paves the way for a sales call. A good promotion strategy can dramatically increase a firm's sales.

Public relations plays a special role in promotion. It is used to create a good image of the company and its products. Bad publicity costs nothing to send out, but it can cost a firm a great deal in lost business. Good publicity, such as a television or magazine story about a firm's new product, may be the result of much time, money, and effort spent by a public relations department.

Sales promotion directly stimulates sales. It includes trade shows, catalogs, contests, games, premiums, coupons, and special offers. McDonald's contests offering money and food prizes are an example. The company also issues discount coupons from time to time.

Considering a career in marketing? Visit http://www.marketingpower.com

MAKING ETHICAL CHOICES

OMNILIFE: THE STORY OF A CONTEMPORARY MEDICINE MAN?

Jorge Vergara got his start in the weight-loss and nutritional supplement business by working for Herbalife when it expanded into Mexico following investigations into its sales methods by the U.S. Food and Drug Administration and the California attorney general's office. To satisfy the investigating authorities, Herbalife agreed to stop making excessive product claims and engaging in questionable sales practices.

Thinking he could do better on his own, Vergara left Herbalife in 1991 and started his own business, Omnilife, geared to the Mexican market. Rather than selling diet pills and diet formulas, Vergara put vitamins and minerals in sweetened canned drinks, teas, coffees, and chewing gum. He focused on smaller communities where nutritional products are rare. Additionally, he used cash-and-carry distribution centers to supply the company's distributors, who operated in a multilevel marketing system similar to that used by Herbalife and Amway, among others.

Arturo Rodriguez, an Omnilife distributor, says the company is concerned about customers' health and consequently sells delicious products that make customers feel better. Another distributor, Pepe Vergara, who is also Jorge Vergara's cousin, provides a different perspective on Omnilife products. He says the company sells junk food—but that it is nutritional junk food!

Omnilife's sales pitches rely heavily on testimonials. They include claims that Omnilife products have helped customers "to avoid cancer operations or to walk again." Jorge Vergara admits "that he and his distributors sometimes make claims that wouldn't pass regulatory muster in the U.S." The spouse of an Omnilife distributor compares Vergara to the "medicine men who can still be found touting herbal potions in town squares throughout Latin America."

Critical Thinking Questions

1. How would you describe Omnilife's marketing mix?
2. Is Omnilife's marketing mix managed in an ethical fashion? Explain your answer.

Not-for-Profit Marketing

Profit-oriented companies are not the only ones that analyze the marketing environment, find a competitive advantage, and create a marketing mix. The application of marketing principles and techniques is also vital to not-for-profit organizations. Marketing helps not-for-profit groups identify target markets and develop effective marketing mixes. In some cases, marketing has kept symphonies, museums, and other cultural groups from having to close their doors. In other organizations, such as the American Heart Association and the U.S. Army, marketing ideas and techniques have helped managers do their jobs better. The army, for instance, has identified the most effective ways to get men and women between the ages of 18 and 24 to visit a recruiter.

In the private sector, the profit motive is both an objective for guiding decisions and a criterion for evaluating results. Not-for-profit organizations do not seek to make a profit for redistribution to owners or shareholders. Rather, their focus is often on generating enough funds to cover expenses. For example, the Methodist Church does not gauge its success by the amount of money left in offering plates. The Museum of Science and Industry does not base its performance evaluations on the dollar value of tokens put into the turnstile.

social marketing
The application of marketing techniques to social issues and causes.

Not-for-profit marketing is also concerned with **social marketing,** that is, the application of marketing to social issues and causes. The goals of social marketing are to effect social change (for instance, by creating racial harmony), further social causes (for instance, by helping the homeless), and evaluate the relationship between marketing and society (for instance, by asking whether society should allow advertising on television shows for young children). Individual organizations also engage in social marketing. The Southern Baptist Radio and Television Convention promotes brotherhood and goodwill by promoting religion and good deeds. M.A.D.D. counsels against drunk driving, and the National Wildlife Federation asks your help in protecting endangered animals and birds.

concept check

- What is meant by the marketing mix?
- What are the components of the marketing mix?
- How can marketing techniques help not-for-profit organizations?
- Define social marketing.

BUYER BEHAVIOR

>lg 4

buyer behavior
The actions people take in buying and using goods and services.

An organization cannot reach its goals without understanding buyer behavior. **Buyer behavior** is the actions people take in buying and using goods and services. Marketers who understand buyer behavior, such as how a price increase will affect a product's sales, can create a more effective marketing mix.

To understand buyer behavior, marketers must understand how consumers make buying decisions. The decision-making process has several steps, which are shown in Exhibit 11-2. The entire process is affected by a number of personal and social factors. A buying decision starts (step 1) with a stimulus. A *stimulus* is anything that affects one or more of our senses (sight, smell, taste, touch, or hearing). A stimulus might be the feel of a sweater, the sleek shape of a new-model car, the design on a package, or a brand name mentioned by a friend. The stimulus leads to problem recognition (step 2): "This sweater feels so soft and looks good on me. Should I buy it?" In other words, the consumer decides that there's a purchase need.

The consumer next gets information about the purchase (step 3). What other styles of sweaters are available? At what price? Can this sweater be bought at a lower price elsewhere? Next, the consumer weighs the options and decides whether to make the purchase (step 4). If the consumer buys the product (step

5), certain outcomes are expected. These outcomes may or may not become reality: the sweater may last for years, or the shoulder seams may pull out the first time it's worn. Finally, the consumer assesses the experience with the product (step 6) and uses this information to update expectations about future purchases (step 7).

Influences on Consumer Decision-Making

As Exhibit 11-2 shows, individual and social factors can influence the consumer decision-making process. *Individual factors* are within the consumer and are unique to each person. They include perception, beliefs and attitudes, values, learning, self-concept, and personality. Companies often conduct research to better understand individual factors that cause consumers to buy or not to buy. For instance, Hyatt Hotels found that people who stayed at Hyatt while on business chose other hotels when they traveled on vacation with their children.

exhibit 11-2 | Consumer Decision-Making Process

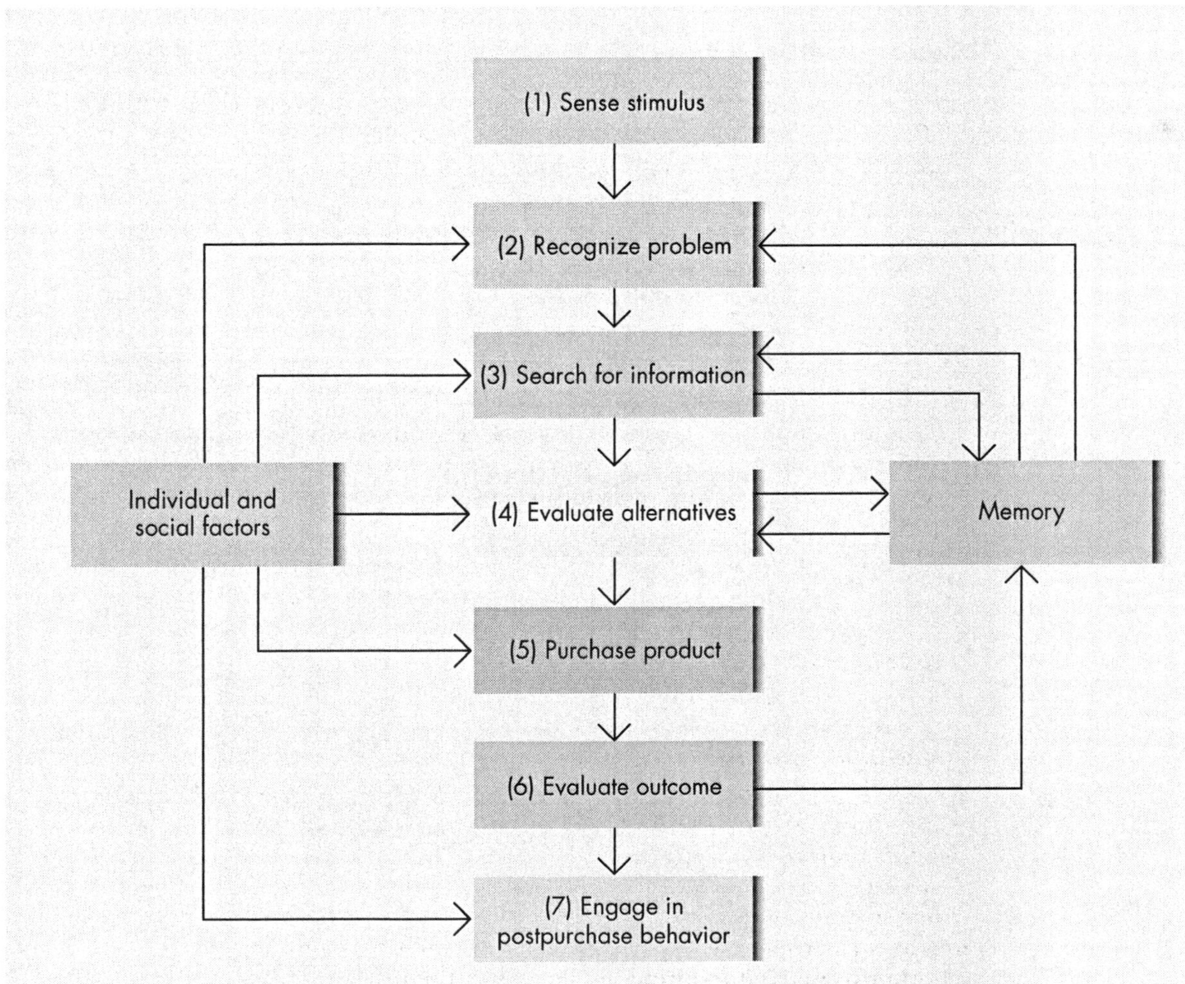

Hyatt was perceived as a businessperson's hotel. So Hyatt came up with a program called Camp Hyatt, which caters to children with a year-round program that varies by season. It combines attractive rates that appeal to parents with lots of activities for kids.

Social factors that affect the decision-making process include all interactions between a consumer and the external environment: family, opinion leaders, social class, and culture. Families may be the most important of these social factors. Yet families have limited resources, so many buying decisions are compromises. Since a number of decisions include input from several family members, marketing managers sometimes promote products using a family theme, such as Camp Hyatt.

Business-to-Business Purchase Decision-Making

Business buyer behavior and business markets are different from consumer markets. Business markets include institutions such as hospitals and schools, manufacturers, wholesalers and retailers, and various branches of government. The key difference between a consumer product and a business product is the intended use. If you purchase a certain model Dell computer for your home so you can surf the Internet, it is a consumer good. If a purchasing agent for MTV buys exactly the same computer for an MTV scriptwriter, it is a business good. Why? The reason is that MTV is a business, so the computer will be used in a business environment.

Characteristics of the Business-to-Business Market The main differences between consumer markets and business markets are as follows:

1. *Purchase volume.* Business customers buy in much larger quantities than consumers. Think how many truckloads of sugar Mars must purchase to make one day's output of M&Ms.
2. *Number of customers.* Business marketers usually have far fewer customers than consumer marketers. As a result, it is much easier to identify prospective buyers and monitor current needs. Think about how few customers for airplanes or industrial cranes there are compared to the more than 70 million consumer households in the United States.
3. *Location of buyers.* Business customers tend to be much more geographically concentrated than consumers. Aircraft manufacturing is found in Seattle, St. Louis, and Dallas/Fort Worth. Suppliers to these manufacturers often locate close to the manufacturers to lower distribution costs and facilitate communication.
4. *Direct distribution.* Business sales tend to be made directly to the buyer because such sales frequently involve large quantities or custom-made items like heavy machinery. Consumer goods are more likely to be sold through intermediaries like wholesalers and retailers.
5. *Rational purchase decisions.* Unlike consumers, business buyers usually approach purchasing rather formally. Businesses use professionally trained purchasing agents or buyers who spend their entire career purchasing a limited number of items.

concept check

- Explain the consumer decision-making process.
- How do business markets differ from consumer markets?

MARKET SEGMENTATION

>lg 5

The study of buyer behavior helps marketing managers better understand why people make purchases. To identify the target markets that may be most

market segmentation
The process of separating, identifying, and evaluating the layers of a market in order to design a marketing mix.

profitable for the firm, managers use **market segmentation,** which is the process of separating, identifying, and evaluating the layers of a market to design a marketing mix. For instance, a target market might be segmented into two groups: families with children and families without children. Families with young children are likely to buy hot cereals and presweetened cereals. Families with no children are more likely to buy health-oriented cereals. You can be sure that cereal companies plan their marketing mixes with this difference in mind. A business market may be segmented by large customers and small customers or by geographic area.

The five basic forms of consumer market segmentation are demographic, geographic, psychographic, benefit, and volume. Their characteristics are summarized in Exhibit 11-3 and discussed in the following sections.

Demographic Segmentation

demographic segmentation
The differentiation of markets through the use of categories such as age, education, gender, income, and household size.

Demographic segmentation uses categories such as age, education, gender, income, and household size to differentiate among markets. This form of market segmentation is the most common. The U.S. Census Bureau provides a great deal of demographic data. For example, marketing researchers can use census data to find areas within cities that contain high concentrations of high-income consumers, singles, blue-collar workers, and so forth.

Find a vast array of census data at
http://www.census.gov

You don't have to be an adult to have market clout. One study found that aggregate spending by or on behalf of children ages 4 to 12 roughly doubled every decade in the 1960s, 1970s, and 1980s. It tripled in the 1990s to more than $24 billion.[8] And whereas children in the 1960s spent almost all their money on candy, today only one-third of the money goes to food and drink, with the balance spent on toys, clothes, movies, and games.

Mature Americans (those born before 1945), baby boomers (consumers born between 1946 and 1964), and Generation Xers (younger consumers born between 1965 and 1978) all have different needs, tastes, and consumption pat-

exhibit 11-3 | Forms of Consumer Market Segmentation

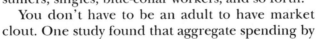

Form	General Characteristics
Demographic segmentation	Age, education, gender, income, race, social class, household size
Geographic segmentation	Regional location (e.g., New England, Mid-Atlantic, Southeast, Great Lakes, Plains States, Northwest, Southwest, Rocky Mountains, Far West); population density (urban, suburban, rural); city or county size; climate
Psychographic segmentation	Lifestyle, personality, interests, values, attitudes
Benefit segmentation	Benefits provided by the good or service
Volume segmentation	Amount of use (light versus heavy)

terns. Exhibit 11-4 shows some of these generational differences; note that baby boomers tend to be nostalgic and prefer the old to the new, whereas Generation Xers tend to be video oriented and would rather see the movie than read the book.

Certain markets are segmented by gender. These include clothing, cosmetics, personal care items, magazines, jewelry, and footwear. Gillette, for example, is one of the world's best-known marketers of personal care products and has historically targeted men for the most part. Yet women's products have generated most of Gillette's growth since 1992. Gillette's shaving line for women has expanded into a $400 million global business, growing nearly 20 percent annually.

Income is another popular way to segment markets. Income level influences consumers' wants and determines their buying power. Housing, clothing, automobiles, and alcoholic beverages are among the many markets segmented by income. Budget Gourmet frozen dinners are targeted to lower-income groups, whereas the Le Menu line is aimed at higher-income consumers.

Geographic Segmentation

geographic segmentation
The differentiation of markets by region of the country, city or county size, market density, or climate.

Geographic segmentation means segmenting markets by region of the country, city or county size, market density, or climate. *Market density* is the number of people or businesses within a certain area. Many companies segment their markets geographically to meet regional preferences and buying habits. Pizza Hut, for instance, gives easterners extra cheese, westerners more ingredients, and midwesterners both. Both Ford and Chevrolet sell more pickup trucks and

exhibit 11-4 | Preferences of Mature Adults, Baby Boomers, and Generation Xers

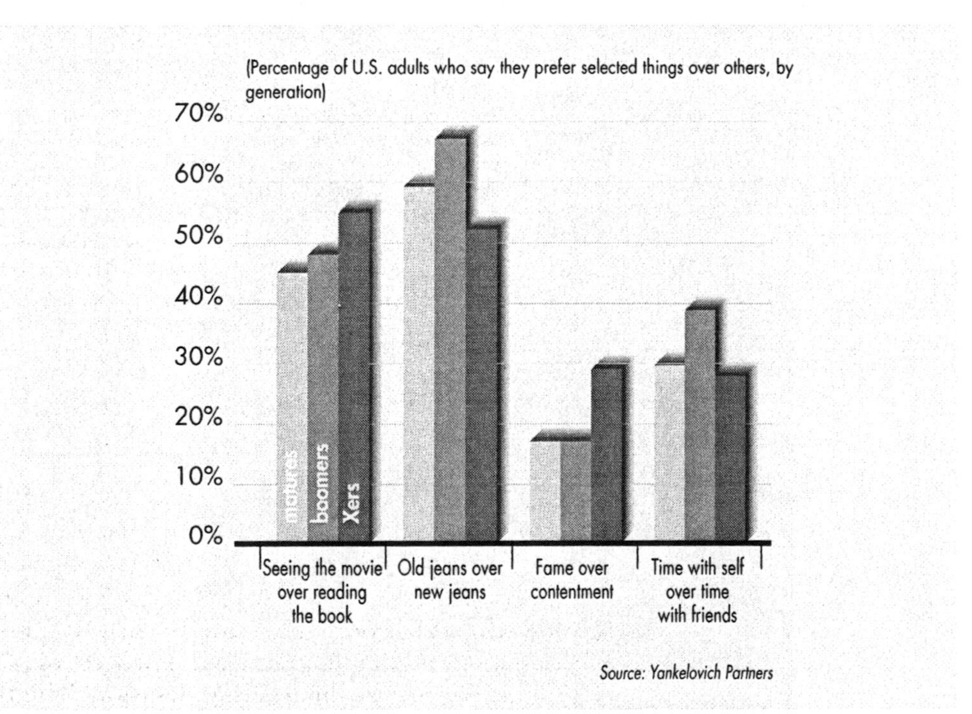

Source: Yankelovich Partners

truck parts in the middle of the country than on either coast. The well-defined "pickup truck belt" runs from the upper Midwest south through Texas and the Gulf states. Ford "owns" the northern half of this truck belt, and Chevrolet the southern half.

Psychographic Segmentation

Race, income, occupation, and other demographic variables help in developing strategies but often do not paint the entire picture of consumer needs. Demographics provide the skeleton, but psychographics add meat to the bones. **Psychographic segmentation** is market segmentation by personality or lifestyle. People with common activities, interests, and opinions are grouped together and given a "lifestyle name."

psychographic segmentation
The differentiation of markets by personality or lifestyle.

Benefit Segmentation

benefit segmentation
The differentiation of markets based on what a product will do rather than on customer characteristics.

Benefit segmentation is based on what a product will do rather than on consumer characteristics. For years Crest toothpaste was targeted toward consumers concerned with preventing cavities. Recently, Crest subdivided its market. It now offers regular Crest, Crest Tartar Control for people who want to prevent cavities and tartar buildup, Kid's Crest with sparkles that taste like bubble gum, and another Crest that prevents gum disease. Another toothpaste, Topol, targets people who want whiter teeth—teeth without coffee, tea, or tobacco stains. Sensodyne toothpaste is aimed at people with highly sensitive teeth.

Volume Segmentation

volume segmentation
The differentiation of markets based on the amount of the product purchased.

The fifth main type of segmentation is **volume segmentation**, which is based on the amount of the product purchased. Just about every product has heavy, moderate, and light users, as well as nonusers. Heavy users often account for a very large portion of a product's sales. Thus, a firm might want to target its marketing mix to the heavy-user segment. Kraft recently ran a $30 million advertising campaign directed at heavy users of Miracle Whip. A heavy user consumes 550 servings or 17 pounds of Miracle Whip a year.[9]

Links to major marketing research firms are available at http://www.quirks.com/source/links.htm

concept check

- Define market segmentation.
- List and discuss the five basic forms of market segmentation.

USING MARKETING RESEARCH TO SERVE EXISTING CUSTOMERS AND FIND NEW CUSTOMERS

>lg 6

How do successful companies learn what their customers value? Through marketing research, companies can be sure they are listening to the voice of the customer. **Marketing research** is the process of planning, collecting, and analyzing data relevant to a marketing decision. The results of this analysis are then communicated to management. The information collected through marketing

marketing research
The process of planning, collecting, and analyzing data relevant to a marketing decision.

research includes the preferences of customers, the perceived benefits of products, and consumer lifestyles. Research helps companies make better use of their marketing budgets. Marketing research has a range of uses from fine-tuning products to discovering whole new marketing concepts.

This section examines the marketing research process, which consists of the following steps:

1. Define the marketing problem.
2. Choose a method of research.
3. Collect the data.
4. Analyze the research data.
5. Make recommendations to management.

Define the Marketing Problem

The most critical step in the marketing research process is defining the marketing problem. This involves either writing a problem statement or a list of research objectives. If the problem is not defined properly, the remainder of the research will be a waste of time and money. Two key questions can help in defining the marketing problem correctly:

APPLYING TECHNOLOGY

USING THE WEB TO GATHER DECISION-MAKING INFORMATION

Web-based marketing research studies are changing the way marketing research will be conducted in the future. Web-based surveys have many advantages over traditional methods. For starters, no interviewers are involved, so interviewer errors are eliminated, as is interviewer bias. If the interviewer is in a bad mood or doesn't like certain types of people or subjects, then the data can be affected. In Web-based surveys, every respondent has exactly the same interviewer—one that is never tired, moody, prejudiced, impatient, or opinionated. Telephone interviews are limited to audio, but Web surveys can be truly multimedia. For example, a recent study of a new computer game showed respondents a variety of screen shots as well as a video clip of sample game play.

In contrast to traditional market research surveys, which can take six weeks to process, Web-based surveys are fast. Questionnaires are posted on a secure Web site, and respondents are directed to the site from banner ads or personal invitations issued by e-mail. Respondents drop by the survey site whenever they want to (even at 3 A.M.) and complete their surveys. Often, a sufficiently large sample, say, 300 or 400 respondents, can be completed over a weekend.

Any research project has two major cost components: data collection and analysis. Data collection costs for a Web-based survey are almost zero. With over 170 million Internet users worldwide in 2001, you can find just about any type of respondent on the Web. Analysis costs are also reduced because with advanced software programs data can be analyzed as quickly as consumers fill out a questionnaire online.

Overall, Web-based surveys offer tremendous potential to the marketing research industry because they are faster, generate more accurate information, and cost less than traditional surveys. Used properly, Web-based marketing research soon will vastly increase the amount of customer feedback on which managers base critical business decisions.

Critical Thinking Questions

1. Do you see any disadvantages of Internet surveys?
2. Would you participate in a Web survey? Why or why not?

Interviewing people in a shopping mall is a popular survey research method that allows firms to gather information about consumer opinions and attitudes.

1. Why is the information being sought? By discussing with managers what the information is going to be used for and what decisions might be made as a result, the researcher can get a clearer grasp of the problem.
2. Does the information already exist? If so, money and time can be saved and a quick decision can be made.

Choose a Method of Research

After the problem is correctly defined, a research method is chosen. There are three basic research methods: survey, observation, and experiment.

With **survey research,** an interviewer interacts with respondents, either in person or by mail, to obtain facts, opinions, and attitudes. A questionnaire is used to provide an orderly and structured approach to data gathering. Face-to-face interviews may take place at the respondent's home, in a shopping mall, the Internet, or at a place of business.

Observation research is research that monitors respondents' actions without direct interaction. In the fastest grow-ing form of observation research, researchers use cash registers with scanners that read tags with bar codes to identify the item being purchased. Technological advances are rapidly expanding the future of observation research. For example, ACNielsen has been using black boxes for years on television sets to silently obtain information on a family's viewing habits. But what if the set is on and no one is in the room? To overcome that problem, researchers will soon rely on infrared passive "people meters" that will identify the faces of family members watching the television program. Thus, the meter will duly record when the set is on and no one is watching.

In the third research method, **experiment,** the investigator changes one or more variables—price, package, design, shelf space, advertising theme, or advertising expenditures—while observing the effects of those changes on another variable (usually sales). The objective of experiments is to measure causality. For example, an experiment may reveal the impact that a change in package design has on sales.

survey research
A marketing research method in which an interviewer interacts with respondents, either in person, by mail, at a mall, or through the Internet to obtain facts, opinions, and attitudes.

observation research
A marketing research method in which the investigator monitors respondents' actions without interacting directly with the respondents; for example, by using cash registers with scanners.

experiment
A marketing research method in which the investigator changes one or more variables—price, packaging, design, shelf space, advertising theme, or advertising expenditures—while observing the effects of these changes on another variable (usually sales).

primary data
Information collected directly from the original source to solve a problem.

secondary data
Information that has already been collected for a project other than the current one, but which may be used to solve the current problem.

Collect the Data

Two types of data are used in marketing research: **primary data,** which are collected directly from the original source to solve a problem; and **secondary data,** which is information that has already been collected for a project other than the current one but may be used to help solve it. Secondary data can come from a number of sources, among them government agencies, trade associations, research bureaus, universities, the Internet, commercial publications, and internal company records. Company records include sales invoices, accounting records, data from previous research studies, and historical sales data.

See examples of the secondary research available from CACI at

http://demographics.caci.com

Primary data are usually gathered through some form of survey research. As described earlier, survey research often relies on interviews (see Exhibit 11-5 for the different types of interviews). Today, conducting surveys over the Internet is the fastest growing form of survey research, as the Applying Technology box on p. 329 describes.

Analyze the Data

After the data have been collected, the next step in the research process is data analysis. The purpose of this analysis is to interpret and draw conclusions from the mass of collected data. Many software statistical programs such as SAS and SPSS are available to make this task easier for the researcher.

Make Recommendations to Management

After completing the data analysis, the researcher must prepare the report and communicate the conclusions and recommendations to management. This is a key step in the process because marketing researchers who want their

exhibit 11-5 | Types of Interviews Used in Survey Research

Type	Description
Door-to-door	Interviewer interviews consumer in consumer's home (this practice is almost extinct).
Executive interview	Interviewer interviews industrial product user (e.g., engineer, architect, doctor, executive) or decision maker at place of business regarding an industrial product.
Mall intercept	Interviewer interviews consumer in shopping mall or other high-traffic location. Interviews may be done in public areas of the mall, or the respondent may be taken to a private test area.
Central location telephone interview	Interviewing is conducted from a telephone facility set up for that purpose. These facilities typically have equipment that permits the supervisor to unobtrusively monitor the interview while it is taking place. Some facilities have Wide Area Telephone Service (WATS) to permit national sampling from a single location. The questionnaire is programmed into a computer. The interviewer enters responses directly.
Self-administered questionnaires	These are most frequently employed at high-traffic locations such as shopping malls or in captive audience situations such as classrooms and airplanes. Respondents are given general information on how to fill out the questionnaire and are left to complete it on their own.
Ad hoc (one-shot) mail surveys	Questionnaires are mailed to a sample of consumers or industrial users. Instructions are included. Respondents are asked to fill out the questionnaire and return it via mail. Sometimes a gift or monetary incentive is provided.
Mail panels	Several companies, including Market Facts, The NPD Group, and National Family Opinion, operate large (more than 100,000 households) consumer panels and ad hoc mail surveys. The company has contacted the people on the panel earlier and explained the panel concept to them. They have agreed to participate for a certain period of time. In addition, participants are offered gratuities to participate in mail panels.
Point-of-service touch-screen monitors	Kiosks, equipped with touch-screen monitors, provide a new way to capture information from individuals in stores, health clinics, and other shopping or service environments.
Internet surveys	This is the fastest growing form of survey research. As the number of individuals connected to the Internet increases, this approach will become increasingly attractive. Internet surveys are discussed in the Applying Technology box.

conclusions acted upon must convince the manager that the results are credible and justified by the data collected. Today, presentation software like PowerPoint and Astound provides easy-to-use tools for creating reports and presentations that are more interesting, compelling, and effective than was possible just a few years ago.

concept check

- Define marketing research.
- Explain the marketing research process.
- What are the three basic marketing research methods?

CAPITALIZING ON TRENDS IN BUSINESS

To discover exactly what customers value most, organizations are using innovative techniques for collecting customer information. Some of the more sophisticated marketing research techniques that are growing in popularity are advanced observation research methods, decision support systems (DDSs), and database marketing.

Advanced Observation Research Methods

All forms of observation research are increasingly using more sophisticated technology. The major television networks, for example, are supporting an advanced technology that provides highly accurate market data about television viewers' behavior. The networks have been discouraged by the data flowing from ACNielsen media research, which indicate that the networks are losing market share. The networks say that ACNielsen's research is faulty and are backing a new measurement system created by Statistical Research Inc. (SRI), which in 2001 merged with Knowledge Networks. The stakes are about $13 billion in advertising revenue generated annually by the major networks.[10] During the 1990s SRI developed Systems for Measuring And Reporting Television, or SMART, at a cost of $160 million. The SMART setup consists of meters with sensors that can pick up signals from the air. The meter looks like a VCR and sits on top of the television. Users log in and out before and after watching television by pressing a device similar to a TV remote control, which was designed for ease of use. The device accurately tracks which program is being watched and by whom.

Perhaps most astounding of all is the new technology that is allowing us to learn how the brain receives and processes information. Brain science has come so far that researchers are now able to routinely eavesdrop on brains while they think. The new technology offers insights about how we perceive, think, and make decisions. This information will enable researchers to uncover consumers' root motivations—or hot buttons. These come from the subliminal regions of our brains, where values, needs, and motivations originate.[11]

decision support system (DSS)
An interactive, flexible, computerized information system that allows managers to make decisions quickly and accurately; used to conduct sales analyses, forecast sales, evaluate advertising, analyze product lines, and keep tabs on market trends and competitors' actions.

Decision Support Systems

More and more managers are turning to another form of technology called a **decision support system (DSS),** an interactive, flexible computerized information system that allows managers to make decisions quickly and accurately. Managers use DSS to conduct sales analyses, forecast sales, evaluate advertising, analyze product lines, and keep tabs on market trends and competitors' actions. A DSS not only allows managers to ask "what if" questions, but enables them to slice the data any way they want. A DSS has the following characteristics:

1. *Interactive.* The manager gives simple instructions and sees results generated on the spot. The process is under the manager's direct control; no computer programmer is needed.
2. *Flexible.* It can sort, regroup, total, average, and manipulate the data in a variety of ways. It will shift gears as the user changes topics, matching information to the problem at hand. For example, the chief executive can see highly aggregated figures, while the marketing analyst views detailed breakouts.
3. *Discovery oriented.* It helps managers probe for trends, isolate problems, and ask new questions.
4. *Easy to learn and use.* Managers need not be particularly computer knowledgeable. Novice users can elect a standard, or "default," method of using the system that enables them to bypass optional features and work with the basic system while they gradually learn its possibilities. This minimizes the frustration that frequently accompanies new computer software.

Using Databases for Micromarketing

database marketing
The creation of a large computerized file of the profiles and purchase patterns of customers and potential customers; usually required for successful micromarketing.

Perhaps the fastest growing use of DSS is for **database marketing,** which is the creation of a large computerized file of the profiles and purchase patterns of customers and potential customers. Using the very specific information in the database, a company can, if it wishes, direct a different individualized message to every customer or potential customer.

Beginning in the 1950s, network television enabled advertisers to "get the same message to everyone simultaneously." Database marketing can get a customized, individual message to everyone simultaneously through direct mail. This is why database marketing is sometimes called *micromarketing.* Specifically, database marketing can:

- Identify the most profitable and least profitable customers.
- Identify the most profitable market segments or individuals and target efforts with greater efficiency and effectiveness.
- Aim marketing efforts to those goods, services, and market segments that require the most support.
- Increase revenue through repackaging and repricing products for various market segments.
- Evaluate opportunities for offering new products and services.
- Identify products and services that are best-sellers and most profitable.

Database marketing can create a computerized form of the old-fashioned relationship that people used to have with the corner grocer, butcher, or baker. "A database is sort of a collective memory," says Richard G. Barlow, president of Frequency Marketing, Inc., a Cincinnati-based consulting firm. "It deals with you in the same personalized way as a mom-and-pop grocery store, where they knew customers by name and stocked what they wanted."[12] American Express, for example, can pull from its database all cardholders who made purchases at golf pro-shops in the past six months, attended symphony concerts, or traveled to Europe more than once in the last year.

concept check

- How is technology being used in marketing research?
- What is a decision support system (DSS) and what is its purpose?
- Explain what database marketing is and describe some of its uses.

APPLYING THIS CHAPTER'S TOPICS

As a consumer, you participate in shaping consumer products by the choices you make and the products and services you buy. You can become a better consumer by actively participating in marketing surveys and learning more about the products you buy.

Participate in Marketing Research Surveys

All of us get tired of telephone solicitations where people try to sell us everything from new carpet to chimney cleaning. Recognize that marketing research surveys are different. A true marketing research survey will *never* involve a sales pitch nor will the research firm sell your name to a database marketer. The purpose of marketing research is to build better goods and services for you and me. Help out the researchers and ultimately help yourself. The Council for Marketing and Opinion Research (CMOR) is an organization of hundreds of marketing research professionals that is dedicated to preserving the integrity of the research industry. If you receive a call from someone who tries to sell you something under the guise of marketing research, get the name and address of the organization. Call CMOR at 1-800-887-CMOR and report the abuse.

Understand Cognitive Dissonance

cognitive dissonance
The condition of having beliefs or knowledge that are internally inconsistent or that disagree with one's behavior.

When making a major purchase, particularly when the item is expensive and choices are similar, consumers typically experience **cognitive dissonance;** that is, they have beliefs or knowledge that are internally inconsistent or that disagree with their behavior. In other words, instead of feeling happy with their new purchase, they experience doubts, feel uneasy, and wonder if they have done the right thing. Understand that this feeling of uneasiness is perfectly normal and goes away over time. Perhaps the best way to avoid cognitive

TRY IT NOW!

1. **Stop junk mail** If you are upset about junk mail, contact the Direct Marketing Association and have your name removed from mailing lists. The email address is **http://www.the-dma.org/.** You can also join an umbrella organization dedicated to stopping the flood of junk email, intrusive telemarketing calls, and junk mail. One such organization is Junkbusters. It can be found at **http://www.junkbusters.com.**
2. **Know Your Profile** Do you wonder where marketers place you in their psychographic profiles? To find out, go to **http://www.future.sri.com/vals/presurvey.shtml** and take the Values and Life-Styles self-test. Where do you fit in?

dissonance is to insist on a strong warranty or money-back guarantee. A second approach is to read everything you can find about your purchase. Go to the Internet and use the search engines to find articles relevant to your purchase. Find Internet chat rooms about your product and join in the discussion. And, before you buy, check out the *Consumer Reports* ratings on your product at **http://www.consumerreports.org.**

SUMMARY OF LEARNING GOALS

>lg 1 **What are the marketing concept and relationship building?**

Marketing includes those business activities that are designed to satisfy consumer needs and wants through the exchange process. Marketing managers use the "right" principle—getting the right goods or services to the right people at the right place, time, and price, using the right promotional techniques. Today, many firms have adopted the marketing concept. The marketing concept involves identifying consumer needs and wants and then producing goods or services that will satisfy them while making a profit. Relationship marketing entails forging long-term relationships with customers, which can lead to repeat sales, reduced costs, and stable relationships.

>lg 2 **How do managers create a marketing strategy?**

A firm creates a marketing strategy by understanding the external environment, defining the target market, determining a competitive advantage, and developing a marketing mix. Environmental scanning enables companies to understand the external environment. The target market is the specific group of consumers toward which a firm directs its marketing efforts. A competitive advantage is a set of unique features of a company and its products that are perceived by the target market as significant and superior to those of the competition.

>lg 3 **What is the marketing mix?**

To carry out the marketing strategy, firms create a marketing mix—a blend of products, distribution systems, prices, and promotion. Marketing managers use this mix to satisfy target consumers. The mix can be applied to nonbusiness as well as business situations.

>lg 4 **How do consumers and organizations make buying decisions?**

Buyer behavior is what people and businesses do in buying and using goods and services. The consumer decision-making process consists of the following steps: responding to a stimulus, recognizing a problem or opportunity, seeking information, evaluating alternatives, purchasing the product, judging the purchase outcome, and engaging in postpurchase behavior. A number of factors influence the process including individual and social factors. The main differences between consumer and business markets are purchase volume, number of customers, location of buyers, direct distribution, and rational purchase decisions.

>lg 5 **What are the five basic forms of market segmentation?**

Success in marketing depends on understanding the target market. One technique used to identify a target market is market segmentation. The five basic forms of segmentation are demographic (population statistics), geographic (location), psychographic (personality or lifestyle), benefit (product features), and volume (amount purchased).

>lg 6 **How is marketing research used in marketing decision-making?**

Much can be learned about consumers through marketing research, which involves collecting, recording, and analyzing data important in marketing goods and services and communicating the results to management. Marketing researchers may use primary data, which are gathered through door-to-door, mall-intercept, telephone, the Internet, and mail interviews. Secondary data are available from a variety of sources including government, trade, and commercial associations. Both primary and secondary data give researchers a better idea of how the market will respond to the product. Thus, they reduce the risk of producing something the market doesn't want.

>lg 7 What are the trends in understanding the consumer?

New technology has increased the sophistication of observation research techniques and improved the accuracy of data, such as measurements of the size of television audiences. Researchers are also analyzing the brain to better understand how people think. A second trend is the growing use of decision support systems. These enable managers to make decisions quickly and accurately. A third trend is the growing use of databases for micromarketing.

>looking ahead at DaimlerChrysler

Before a company can create a marketing mix, it must identify the target market for the product. Thus, DaimlerChrysler first had to identify the target market for the 300M. To be successful, the company had to identify one or more competitive advantages unique to the 300M. DaimlerChrysler used marketing research to identify the target market for the 300M and then determined the needs and desires of these potential buyers. With this information, the company could build customer value into the 300M. The automaker must continue to use marketing research to identify the ever-changing desires of the target market. DaimlerChrysler can retain its leadership position with the 300M by continuing to deliver value to target buyers.

PREPARING FOR TOMORROW'S WORKPLACE

1. Can the marketing concept be applied effectively by a sole proprietorship, or is it more appropriate for larger businesses with more managers? Explain.
2. Write a memo to your manager explaining why it is important for his small business (a restaurant) to have a competitive advantage.
3. Divide the class into two groups. Debate the following propositions: (1) business buyer behavior can be just as emotional as consumer buyer behavior; (2) consumer buyer behavior can be just as rational as business buyer behavior.
4. "Market segmentation is the most important concept in marketing." Why do you think some marketing professionals make this statement? Give an example of each form of segmentation.
5. Write a paper explaining when a marketer would want to use primary data and when it would be better to use secondary data.
6. Divide the class into two teams. Debate the concept that marketing research is an invasion of privacy.
7. Can marketing research be carried out in the same manner all over the world? Why or why not?

WORKING THE NET

1. You've been hired by a snack food manufacturer that is interested in adding popcorn snacks to its product line. First, however, the company asks you to

KEY TERMS

benefit segmentation 328
buyer behavior 323
cognitive dissonance 334
competitive advantage 319
cost competitive advantage 319
customer satisfaction 315
customer value 315
database marketing 333
decision support system (DSS) 332
demographic segmentation 326
differential competitive advantage 320
distribution strategy 321
environmental scanning 318
exchange 314
experiment 330
four Ps 321
geographic segmentation 327
market segmentation 326
marketing 314
marketing concept 314
marketing mix 320
marketing research 328
niche competitive advantage 320
observation research 330
pricing strategy 321
primary data 330
product strategy 321
production orientation 315
promotion strategy 322
psychographic segmentation 328
relationship marketing 316

find some secondary data on the current market for popcorn. Go to the Dogpile Search Engine **(http://www.dogpile.com)** and do a search for "popcorn consumption." Can you find how much popcorn is sold annually? The geographic locations with the highest popcorn sales? The time of the year when the most popcorn is sold? What are the limitations of doing research like this on the Internet?

2. You and a friend want to start a new magazine for people who work at home. Do a search of the U.S. Census database at **http://www.census.gov** to get information about the work-at-home market.
3. Take the VALS lifestyle survey at **http://www.future.sri.com/vals/presurvey.shtml** and find out which psychographic segment you're in. Do you agree or disagree with the results? Why or why not?

CREATIVE THINKING CASE

The American Automobile Association—Building Long-Term Relationships?

This case is built upon the experience of Don Schultz, a marketing professor at Northwestern University. He tells his story in the first person.

Almost every car owner knows about the American Automobile Association. They're the people who slog through rain and snow to rescue stranded motorists. Whether it's a flat tire on the expressway or a broken axle or keys locked in a car parked in a lot, the AAA professionals come running. And they do a good job. I've been a member of the Chicago Motor Club, a "Triple A" affiliate, for 20 years. They have given good service to me, my wife, my children, and my mother.

In recent months, my car has had a problem. For reasons known only to the car, the battery discharges at random. Sometimes it happens overnight, sometimes weeks go by without a problem. When the battery discharges itself, I call AAA. No matter where I am, they come out and give me a jump. Seemingly my problem is no problem for them. They provide cheerful, friendly service, day and night.

Until recently, that is, when apparently I triggered their brand relationship destroying mechanism. While other service suppliers were sending end-of-the-year calendars and thank-you letters, I got threats from AAA. In a letter, Gerald F. Svarz, manager of member relations, wrote:

> Our records indicate that you have requested Emergency Road Service four times during the past 12 months. As outlined in the Member's Handbook, the Club reserves the right to notify a member when they have used four or more service calls in the previous 12 months. Excessive use of Emergency Road Service can result in the nonrenewal or the cancellation of a membership. The nonrenewal or cancellation of membership is based solely on the number of calls in a membership year.

Wow, talk about *building* brand *relationships!* Here's an organization that's going to kick me out of its club, whose primary claim to fame and only reason for being—at least for most of its members—is emergency road service. Only don't use our service too much, they say, or we'll cancel your membership. We reserve that right.

Just to make sure I wasn't overlooking something, I checked out AAA in the Yellow Pages. "Emergency Road Service," the ad says. Same for the newspaper ads I found. And "Emergency Road Service" is splashed all over the relation-*building* magazine they send me every few months. Their promotional literature says "Emergency Road Service" in big bold letters.

secondary data 330
social marketing 323
survey research 330
target market 318
volume segmentation 328

The problem is, they reserve the right to limit the Emergency Road Service you need. Am I a better AAA *customer* if I don't ever use their services? It sure sounds like it. What about all those years I paid the membership fee and never used the service? They didn't write to thank me for that, nor did they adjust my membership fee the way auto insurance companies do for safe drivers.

Critical Thinking Questions

1. Is AAA following the marketing concept?
2. Doesn't it make economic sense to "weed out" people who use the service too much?
3. Insurance companies cancel people's auto insurance if they get too many speeding tickets. Isn't AAA's policy the same thing?
4. Would you make any changes in AAA's operations? If so, what?

VIDEO CASE

Burke Marketing Research

Burke Marketing Research (**http://www.burke.com**), with offices and affiliates in 40 countries throughout the world, provides marketing research services to a wide range of clients. They include companies in the following industries: agricultural/chemical; computer hardware and software; communications/technology; consumer goods and services; entertainment, television, and cable; insurance and financial; pharmaceutical and health care; consulting; and industrial/business-to-business. Across this broad spectrum of industries, Burke deals with both quantitative and qualitative marketing issues. Each project is customized to fit the specific client's marketing needs and decision-making requirements.

As a partly employee-owned firm, Burke has a special commitment to its clientele. "Every employee is personally committed to providing the best possible service" to clients. Clients work directly with an account team which is charged with ensuring that the client's "objectives are met efficiently, economically, and on time."

To generate information for its studies, Burke uses a variety of data collection methods including focus groups, mail surveys, Internet online surveys, phone surveys, and mall intercept interviews. From its experience in "dealing with recurrent marketing problems across many industry and product categories," the company has developed a variety of marketing research protocols for examining and diagnosing common marketing problems. These protocols include onsite vendor/customer focus groups, image and positioning analysis, advertising campaign evaluation, new product demand and pricing analysis, product testing analysis, brand equity analysis, marketing performance analysis, and an integrated concept evaluation system. Each account team shapes the protocols to deal with the client's unique issues. In using each protocol, Burke follows a generally accepted approach to marketing research: defining the marketing problem; selecting and adapting the appropriate protocol for collecting the data; collecting and analyzing the data; and, finally, generating a report for the client that contains useful results and recommendations.

Burke's executives believe that effective "marketing research consists of much more than telephone surveys." They say that good marketing research requires knowledgeable, experienced people who are familiar with the client's industry and the challenges the client faces every day. Good marketing research also requires "attention to detail and a commitment to finding . . . results."

Critical Thinking Questions

1. How would you describe Burke's competitive advantage in the marketing research marketplace?
2. How does Burke Marketing Research use market segmentation in its own business?
3. Do you think Burke's approach to marketing research is effective? Why or why not?

---

ecommerce

Case: Boo.com's Big Boo-Boo

When Ernst Malmsten and Kajsa Leander announced the launch of Boo.com, they promised that their online shopping site would be a "gateway to world cool." They planned to sell international sportswear brands to fashion-savvy customers in Europe and North America. The pair quickly lined up over $130 million in capital and opened offices in New York and London.

Malmsten and Leander seemed to epitomize their target market. Both Swedish, they were in their late 20s and dressed in stylish clothes. Making sure the site focused on the coolest fashions was a critical factor, they decided, so they designated employees as "cool hunters" who observed what hip consumer groups were wearing. For example, one group of "cool hunters" spent time watching what young, chic architects in New York were wearing.

Several months before the Boo.com site was launched, the firm's public relations team started publicizing its debut. A multimillion-dollar advertising campaign also began to generate interest in the site.

Products on the site were shown in three-dimensional pictures that could be rotated for a closer look. Virtual mannequins let shoppers mix and match outfits and accessories. Miss Boo, an animated personal shopping assistant, stood ready to help customers with shopping advice and witty banter. However, the site had problems. It was built for high-speed access and the most advanced browsers but few Internet users had those tools. Technological and design problems meant the site couldn't start taking orders until months after its launch was announced.

Although Boo.com seemed off to a promising start, the firm closed its doors just a year after it opened. Some business analysts said the firm had spent too much too quickly on advertising while ignoring issues like merchandise selection. Others blamed the site's technological glitches for turning off customers. At least one analyst noted that younger women shoppers enjoy the social process of going shopping with friends, something that an online store couldn't duplicate.

Two months later, Fashionmall.com, a six-year-old fashion Internet portal, purchased the rights to use Boo.com's name, Web design elements, and editorial concepts. Fashionmall.com eventually relaunched Boo.com as one of its "floors."

Questions for Critical Thinking

1. Analyze Boo.com's marketing strategy and explain possible reasons for its failure.
2. What additional marketing research would you have recommended Boo.com conduct?
3. What advice would you have given to Fashionmall.com before it relaunched the Boo.com Web site?

SOURCES: William Echikson, "Designers Climb on the Virtual Catwalk," *BusinessWeek Online* (September 27, 1999), downloaded from **http://www.businessweek.com**; Ellen Neuborne, "Why Boo Really Went Bust," *BusinessWeek Online* (June 12, 2000), downloaded from **http://www.businessweek.com**; Bernhard Warner, "Boo.com Scares Up a Buyer," *The Standard* (June 1, 2000), downloaded from **http://www.thestandard.com**.

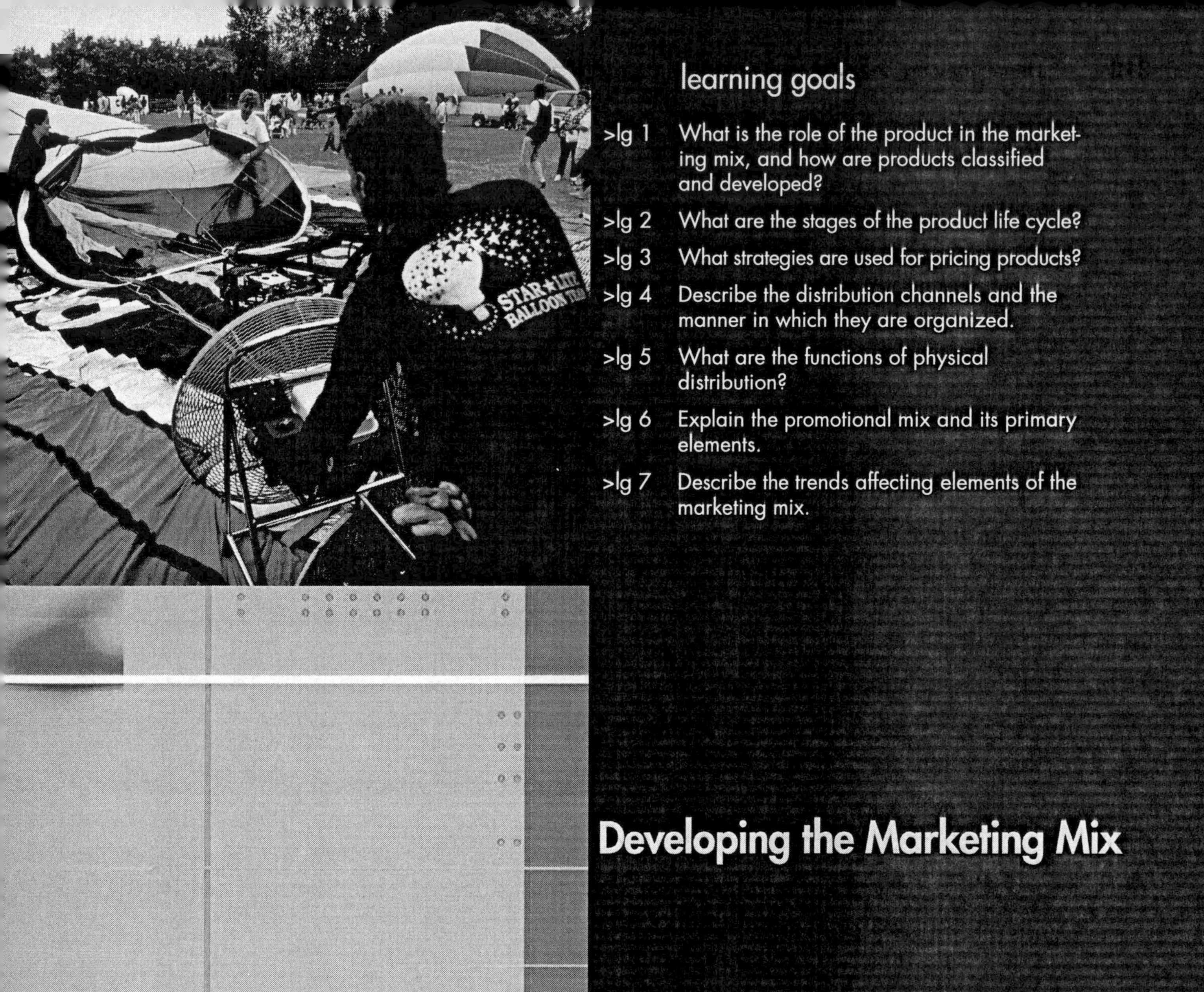

learning goals

- >lg 1 What is the role of the product in the marketing mix, and how are products classified and developed?
- >lg 2 What are the stages of the product life cycle?
- >lg 3 What strategies are used for pricing products?
- >lg 4 Describe the distribution channels and the manner in which they are organized.
- >lg 5 What are the functions of physical distribution?
- >lg 6 Explain the promotional mix and its primary elements.
- >lg 7 Describe the trends affecting elements of the marketing mix.

Developing the Marketing Mix

9

Hot Air to Ride

Each May, an eclectic group of inventor-aeronauts from all over the country converges on a grass airstrip in central Vermont. Officially, the event is the Experimental Balloon and Airship Meet. Unofficially it's "Brian's parts," in honor of Brian Boland, the shaggy-haired, bushy-bearded 51-year-old who owns the property. The beer drinking starts early, and before long a replica Viking ship built on the chassis of an '86 Chevy Astro swoops on the grass in big, crazy circles with a crew of shirtless, whooping men hanging over the gunwales.

A little context. Commercial blimps, the kind that fly corporate logos over sporting arenas, float on helium. The gas is expensive, so the blimps have to stay inflated all the time. Starting at $2 million a pop, with as much again in yearly upkeep, helium blimps are wildly impractical for private owners.

But there's an alternative: hot air. It's cheap, and you don't have to worry about storage. The era of personal blimping dawned in 1973 when an Englishman named Don Cameron showed up at a balloon meet with a rumpled-looking hot-air dirigible powered by a Volkswagen engine. Zipping out from over the tree line, he astonished the crowd by actually being able to steer his craft.

On paper, personal blimps are a can't-miss proposition, combining the grace of hot-air ballooning with the control of powered flight. A new top-of-the-line model starts at $150,000, about the same as a new single-engine Cessna. The reality, however, is that in this country personal blimping hardly exists. There are 530,000 private airplane pilots in the United States. The number flying their own blimps is two.

Boland wants blimping to take off, but he's less hepped on creating a business plan. He just wants to have as much fun as possible, and hopes someone else out there has the same definition of fun that he does. His most practical contribution to the field is a craft he dubs the Pocket Blimp. Designed to break down into pieces small enough to bring on a plane as check-in baggage, the model is just 70 feet long—one-third as long as a Goodyear blimp. Unlike top-end hot-air airships, the Pocket Blimp is unpressurized, lending it a fairly baggy appearance and reducing its practical speed to about six mph, barely enough to handle even the lightest breezes. But the Pocket Blimp is cheap—$30,000—and so simple that the FAA doesn't require certification for would-be pilots.

Sales, though, have been lackluster. "It would be great if someone would buy one," sighs Boland.[1]

Critical Thinking Questions

As you read this chapter, consider these questions as they relate to the Pocket Blimp:

- Is the Pocket Blimp a consumer product or a business product?
- Where is the Pocket Blimp in the product life cycle?
- What price strategy should be used for the Pocket Blimp?

BUSINESS IN THE 21ST CENTURY

As discussed in Chapter 11, the marketing mix is the blend of product, pricing, distribution and promotion strategies designed to produce mutually satisfying exchanges with a target market. Each element of the marketing mix can be manipulated to fine-tune the customer offering and achieve competitive success. This chapter examines each element of the marketing mix.

THE ROLE OF THE PRODUCT IN THE MARKETING MIX

LG 1

product
In marketing, any good or service, along with its perceived attributes and benefits, that creates value for the customer.

In marketing, a **product** is any good or service, along with its perceived attributes and benefits, that creates value for the customer. Attributes can be tangible or intangible. Among the tangible attributes are packaging and warranties as illustrated in Exhibit 12-1. Intangible attributes are symbolic, such as brand image. People make decisions about which products to buy after considering both tangible and intangible attributes of a product. For example, when you buy a pair of jeans, you consider price, brand, store image, and style before you buy. These factors are all part of the marketing mix.

Types of Consumer Products

Because most things sold are a blend of goods and services, the term *product* can be used to refer to both. After all, consumers are really buying packages of benefits that deliver value. The person who buys a plane ride on United

exhibit 12-1 | Tangible and Intangible Attributes of a Product Create Value for the Buyer

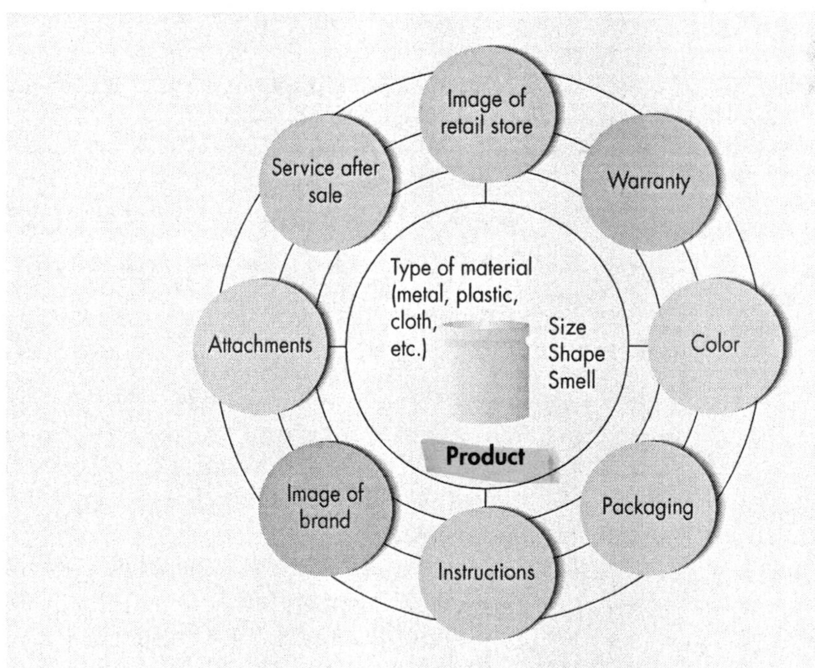

Airlines is looking for a quick way to get from one city to another (the benefit). Providing this benefit requires goods (a plane, food) and services (ticketing, maintenance, piloting).

Marketers must know how consumers view the types of products their companies sell so that they can design the marketing mix to appeal to the selected target market. To help them define target markets, marketers have devised product categories. Products that are bought by the end user are called *consumer products.* They include electric razors, sandwiches, cars, stereos, magazines, and houses. Consumer products that get used up, such as Breck hair mousse and Lays potato chips, are called *consumer nondurables.* Those that last for a long time, such as Whirlpool washing machines and Apple computers, are *consumer durables.*

unsought products
Products that either are unknown to the potential buyer or are known but the buyer does not actively seek them.

convenience products
Relatively inexpensive items that require little shopping effort and are purchased routinely without planning.

shopping products
Items that are bought after considerable planning, including brand-to-brand and store-to-store comparisons of price, suitability, and style.

specialty products
Items for which consumers search long and hard and for which they refuse to accept substitutes.

Another way to classify consumer products is by the amount of effort consumers are willing to make to acquire them. The four major categories of consumer products are defined below:

- **Unsought products** are products unknown to the potential buyer or known products that the buyer does not actively seek. New products fall into this category until advertising and distribution increase consumer awareness of them. Insurance, burial plots, encyclopedias, and similar items require agressive personal selling and highly persuasive advertising.
- **Convenience products** are relatively inexpensive items that require little shopping effort. Soft drinks, candy bars, milk, bread, and small hardware items are examples.
- **Shopping products** are bought only after a brand-to-brand and store-to-store comparison of price, suitability, and style. Examples are furniture, automobiles, a vacation in Europe, and some items of clothing.
- **Specialty products** are products for which consumers search long and hard for which they refuse to accept substitutes. Expensive jewelry, designer clothing, state-of-the-art stereo equipment, limited-production automobiles, and gourmet dinners fall into this category.

Types of Business Products

capital products
Large, expensive items with a long life span that are purchased by businesses for use in making other products or providing a service.

expense items
Items, purchased by businesses, that are smaller and less expensive than capital products and usually have a life span of less than one year.

Products bought by businesses or institutions for use in making other products or in providing services are called *business* or *industrial products.* They are classified as either capital products or expense items. **Capital products** are usually large, expensive items with a long life span. Examples are buildings, large machines, and airplanes. **Expense items** are typically smaller, less expensive items that usually have a life span of less than a year. Examples are printer ribbons and paper. Industrial products are sometimes further classified in the following categories:

1. *Installations.* These are large, expensive capital items that determine the nature, scope, and efficiency of a company. Capital products like General Motors' Saturn assembly plant in Tennessee represent a big commitment against future earnings and profitability.
2. *Accessories.* Accessories do not have the same long-run impact on the firm as installations, and they are less expensive and more standardized. But they are still capital products. Minolta copy machines, IBM personal computers (PCs), and smaller machines such as Black and Decker table drills and saws are typical accessories.
3. *Component parts and materials.* These are expense items that are built into the end product. Some component parts are custom-made, such as a drive shaft for an automobile, a case for a computer, or a special pigment for painting U.S. Navy harbor buoys; others are standardized for sale to many industrial

users. Intel's Pentium chip for PCs and cement for the construction trade are examples of standardized component parts and materials.

4. *Raw materials.* Raw materials are expense items that have undergone little or no processing and are used to create a final product. Examples include lumber, copper, and zinc.
5. *Supplies.* Supplies do not become part of the final product. They are bought routinely and in fairly large quantities. Supply items run the gamut from pencils and paper to paint and machine oil.
6. *Services.* These are expense items used to plan or support company operations; for example, janitorial cleaning and management consulting.

Branding

brand
A company's product identifier that distinguishes the company's products from those of its competitors.

trademark
The legally exclusive design, name, or other identifying mark associated with a company's brand.

brand equity
The value of company and brand names.

Find out how to trademark a design, name or other identifying mark by visiting the U.S. Patent and Trademark Office at http://www.uspto.gov

Most industrial and consumer products have a brand name. If everything came in a plain brown wrapper, life would be less colorful and competition would decrease. Companies would have less incentive to put out better products because consumers would be unable to tell one company's products from those of another.

The product identifier for a company is its **brand.** Brands appear in the form of words, names, symbols, or designs. They are used to distinguish a company's products from those of its competitors. Examples of well-known brands are Kleenex tissues, Jeep automobiles, and IBM computers. A **trademark** is the legally exclusive design, name, or other identifying mark associated with a company's brand. No other company can use that same trademark.

These brand names for laundry detergents are effective because they are short, distinctive, and easy to pronounce, recognize, and remember.

Benefits of Branding Branding has three main purposes: product identification, repeat sales, and new product sales. The most important purpose is *product identification.* Branding allows marketers to distinguish their products from all others. Many brand names are familiar to consumers and indicate quality. The term **brand equity** refers to the value of company and brand names. A brand that has high awareness, perceived quality, and brand loyalty among customers has high brand equity. Brand equity is more than awareness of a brand—it is the personality, soul, and emotion associated with the brand. Think of the feelings you have when you see the brand name Harley-Davidson, Nike, or even Microsoft. A brand with strong brand equity is a valuable asset. Some brands such as Coke, Kodak, Marlboro, and Chevrolet are worth millions of dollars.

FOCUSING ON SMALL BUSINESS

LITTLE GUYS CAN WIN THE BRANDING WAR

Small companies are embracing branding in part because they've seen the Fortune 500 corporations concentrating on building and leveraging their brands more than ever before. Coca-Cola Co. made the new Braves baseball stadium in Atlanta a shrine to Coke; giant Niketown stores extend the icon of the Nike Swoosh into the realm of "experiential" retailing.

Entrepreneurs thinking about creating their own brands should consider these suggestions:

1. *Establish your uniqueness.* That's what Cape Cod Potato Chips has done as it has battled with snack-industry giants for supermarket shelf space and a share of the dollars spent by potato chip lovers across the country. The company, which is based in Hyannis, Massachusetts, focuses on its self-developed "batch" processing of potatoes, which yields a distinctive taste and texture; extends its product line with chips made from different varieties of potatoes rather than just dusting on flavorings as some of its bigger competitors do; relies on product sampling instead of traditional advertising as its marketing workhorse; and supports its regional identity with everything from tours of its factory to its product packaging, which features a lighthouse.
2. *Stay within your core.* China Mist Tea Co. in Scottsdale, Arizona, has grown to a $5 million company in just a few years by providing only iced tea and selling only to restaurants and institutions. Along with that growth, however, has come the temptation to expand beyond its core business or to partner with a beverage giant such as Coca-Cola or PepsiCo. "We have such fanatically loyal customers that even Coke has noticed it and commented to us about it, and that's the key to our growth," says Dan Schweiker, co-owner of the company. "The reason is we know what our niche is and pay attention to it. We're not trying to become Lipton tea."
3. *Dominate a geographic or niche market.* Coke may have taught the world to sing, but a savvy small brander can dominate southwestern Mississippi or Schenectady, New York. Utz Quality Foods, Inc. of Hanover, Pennsylvania, for instance, has built a whole advertising campaign around the fact that people outside the mid-Atlantic region can't buy Utz products in stores. Small regional brewer Stevens Point Brewery stopped a five-year sales decline last year by paring back to the 12-county region around its headquarters in Stevens Point, Wisconsin.

Critical Thinking Questions

1. Should all small businesses try to build a brand? Why or why not?
2. What other suggestions do you have for an entrepreneur attempting to build a brand?

manufacturer brands
Brands that are owned by national or regional manufacturers and widely distributed; also call *national brands.*

dealer brands
Brands that are owned by the wholesaler or retailer rather than the name of the manufacturer.

generic products
Products that carry no brand name, come in plain containers, and sell for much less than brand-name products.

Types of Brands Brands owned by national or regional manufacturers and widely distributed are **manufacturer brands.** (These brands are sometimes called national brands, but since some of the brands are not owned by nationwide or international manufacturers, *manufacturer brands* is a more accurate term.) A few well-known manufacturer brands are Polaroid, Liz Claiborne, Nike, and Sony.

Brands that are owned by the wholesaler or retailer, rather than that of the manufacturer, are **dealer brands.** Sears has several well-known dealer (or private) brands, including Craftsman, DieHard, and Kenmore. The Independent Grocers Alliance (IGA), a large wholesale grocery organization, uses the brand name Shurfine on its goods. Dealer brands tie consumers to particular wholesalers or retailers. If you want a Kenmore washing machine, you must go to Sears.

Many consumers don't want to pay the costs of manufacturer or dealer brands. One popular way to save money is to buy **generic products.** These products carry no brand name, come in plain containers, and sell for much less than brand-name products. The most popular generic products are garbage bags, jelly, paper towels, coffee cream substitutes, cigarettes, and paper napkins.

Curious about how generic and private label products are manufactured? Visit the Private Label Manufacturers Association at

http://www.plma.com

Packaging

Just as a brand gives a product identity, its packaging also distinguishes it from competitors' products and increases its customer value. When you go to the store and reach for a bottle of dishwashing detergent, the package is the last chance a manufacturer has to convince you to buy its brand over a competitor's. A good package may cause you to reach for Joy rather than Palmolive.

The Functions of a Package A basic function of packaging is to protect the product from breaking or spoiling and thus extend its life. A package should be easy to ship, store, and stack on a shelf and convenient for the consumer to buy. Many new packaging methods have been developed recently. Aseptic packages keep foods fresh for months without refrigeration. Examples are Borden's "sipp' packs" for juices, the Brik Pak for milk, and Hunt's and Del Monte's aseptic boxes for tomato sauce.

A second basic function of packaging is to help promote the product by providing clear brand identification and information about the product's features. For example, Ralston Purina Co.'s Dog Chow brand, the leading dog food, was losing market share. The company decided that the pictures of dog breeds on the package were too old-fashioned and rural. With a new package featuring a photo of a dog and a child, sales have increased.

Developing New Products

New products pump life into company sales, enabling the firm not only to survive but also to grow. Companies like Allegheny Ludlum (steel), Corning (fiber optics), Dow (chemicals), Hewlett-Packard (computers), Campbell Soup (foods), and Stryker (medical products) get most of their profits from new products. Companies that lead their industries in profitability and sales growth get 49 percent of their revenues from products developed within the last five years.

How New Products Are Developed

Developing products is both costly and risky. About two-thirds of all new products fail. To increase their chances for success, most firms use the following product development process, which is also summarized in Exhibit 12-2.

1. *Set new product goals.* New product goals are usually stated as financial objectives. For example, a company may want to recover its investment in three years or less. Or it may want to earn at least a 15 percent return on the investment. Nonfinancial goals may include using existing equipment or facilities.

2. *Develop new product ideas.* Smaller firms usually depend on employees, customers, investors, and distributors for new ideas. Larger companies use these sources and more structured marketing research techniques, such as focus groups and brainstorming. A **focus group** consists of 8 to 12 participants led by a moderator in an in-depth discussion on one particular topic or concept. The intent is to find out how they feel about a product, concept, idea, or organization, how it fits into their lives, and their emotional involvement

focus group
A group of 8 to 12 participants led by a moderator in an in-depth discussion on one particular topic or concept.

exhibit 12-2 | Steps to Develop New Products That Satisfy Customers

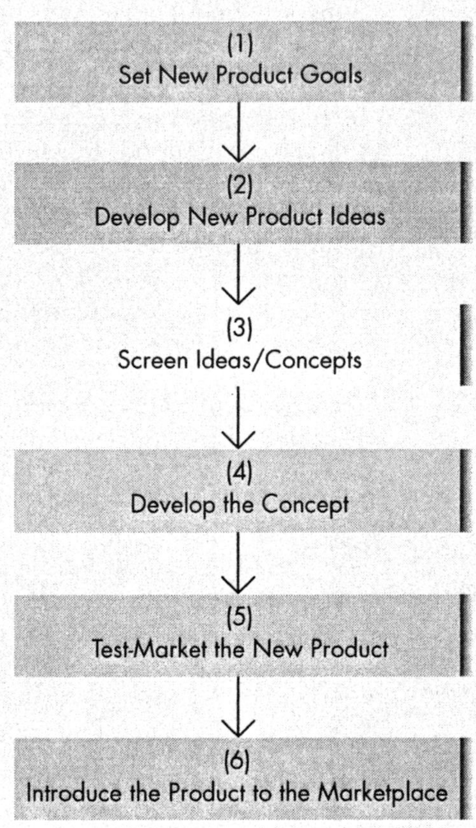

with it. Focus groups often generate excellent product ideas. A few examples are the interior design of the Ford Taurus, Stick-Up room deodorizers, Dustbusters, and Wendy's salad bar. In the industrial market, machine tools, keyboard designs, aircraft interiors, and backhoe accessories evolved from focus groups.

3. *Screen ideas and concepts.* As ideas emerge, they are checked against the firm's new product goals and its long-range strategies. Many product concepts are rejected because they don't fit well with existing products, needed technology is not available, the company doesn't have enough resources, or the sales potential is low.
4. *Develop the concept.* Developing the new product concept involves creating a prototype of the product, testing the prototype, and building the marketing strategy. The type and amount of product testing vary, depending on such factors as the company's experience with similar products, how easy it is to make the item, and how easy it will be for consumers to use it.

   As the marketing strategy and prototype tests mature, a communication strategy is developed. A logo and package wording are created. As part of the communication strategy, promotion themes are developed, and the product is introduced to the sales force.

test-marketing
The process of testing a new product among potential users.

5. *Test-market the new product.* **Test-marketing** is testing the product among potential users. It allows management to evaluate various strategies and to see how well the parts of the marketing mix fit together. Few new product concepts reach this stage. For those that pass this stage, the firm must decide whether to introduce the product on a regional or national basis.
6. *Introduce the product.* A product that passes test-marketing is ready for market introduction, called *rollout,* which requires a lot of logistical coordination. Various divisions of the company must be encouraged to give the new item the attention it deserves. Packaging and labeling in a different language may be required. Sales training sessions must be scheduled, spare parts inventoried, service personnel trained, advertising and promotion campaigns readied, and wholesalers and retailers informed about the new item.

Delve deeper into Procter & Gamble's marketing and brand management strategies at the firm's home page, http://www.pg.com

concept check

- Explain how business products are classified?
- What are the functions of a package?
- What are the steps in the new product development process?

PRODUCT LIFE CYCLE

>lg 2

product life cycle
The pattern of sales and profits over time for a product or product category; consists of an introductory stage, growth stage, maturity, and decline (and death).

Product managers create marketing mixes for their products as they move through the life cycle. The **product life cycle** is a pattern of sales and profits over time for a product (Ivory dishwashing liquid) or a product category (liquid detergents). As the product moves through the stages of the life cycle, the firm must keep revising the marketing mix to stay competitive and meet the needs of target customers.

As illustrated in Exhibit 12-3, the product life cycle consists of the following stages:

1. *Introduction.* When a product enters the life cycle, it faces many obstacles. Although competition may be light, the *introductory stage* usually features frequent product modifications, limited distribution, and heavy promotion. The failure rate is high. Production and marketing costs are also high, and sales volume is low. Hence profits are usually small or negative.
2. *Growth.* If a product survives the introductory stage, it advances to the *growth stage* of the life cycle. In this stage, sales grow at an increasing rate, profits are healthy, and many competitors enter the market. Large companies may start to acquire small pioneering firms that have reached this stage. Distribution becomes a major key to success during the growth stage, as well as in later stages. Manufacturers scramble to acquire dealers and distributors and to build long-term relationships. Without adequate distribution, it is impossible to establish a strong market position.

   Toward the end of the growth phase, prices normally begin falling and profits peak. Price reductions result from increased competition and from cost reductions from producing larger quantities of items (economies of scale). Also, most firms have recovered their development costs by now, and their priority is in increasing or retaining market share and enhancing profits.
3. *Maturity.* After the growth stage, sales continue to mount—but at a decreasing rate. This is the *maturity stage.* Most products that have been on the market for a long time are in this stage. Thus, most marketing strategies are de-

exhibit 12-3 | Sales and Profits during the Product Life Cycle

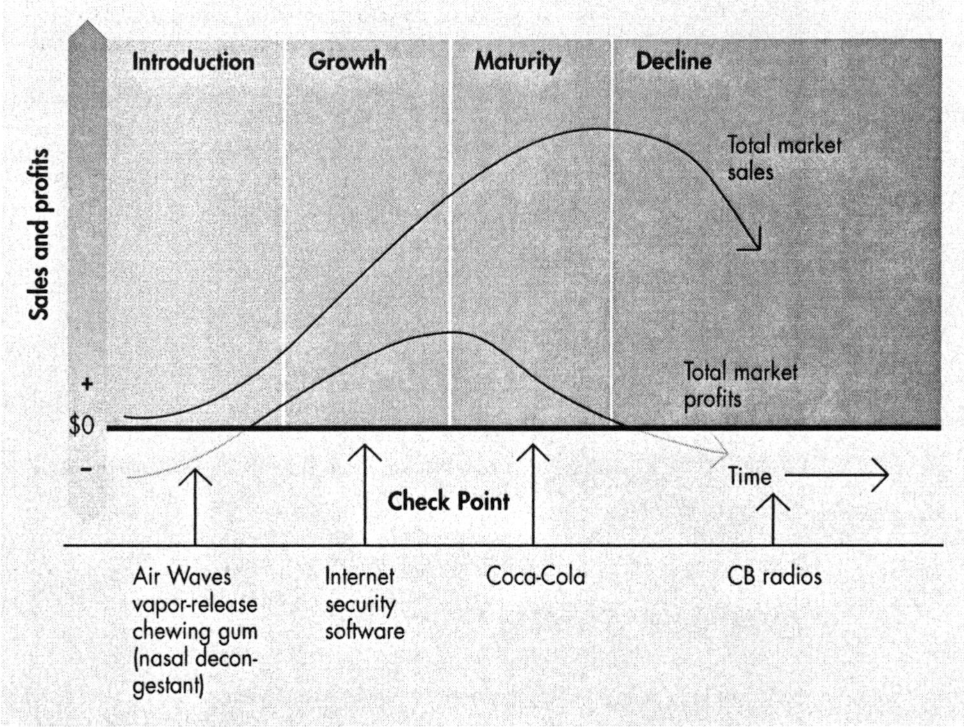

signed for mature products. One such strategy is to bring out several variations of a basic product (line extension). Kool-Aid, for instance, was originally offered in three flavors. Today there are twenty, as well as sweetened and unsweetened varieties.

4. *Decline (and death)*. When sales and profits fall, the product has reached the *decline stage*. The rate of decline is governed by two factors: the rate of change in consumer tastes and the rate at which new products enter the market. Sony turntables are an example of a product in the decline stage. The demand for turntables has now been surpassed by the demand for compact disc players and cassette players.

concept check

- What is the product life cycle?
- Describe each stage of the product life cycle.
- What are the marketing strategies for each stage of the product life cycle?

PRICING PRODUCTS RIGHT

>lg 3

Another component of the marketing mix is the price of the product. Price is the perceived value that is exchanged for something else. Value in our society is most commonly expressed in dollars and cents. Thus, price is typically the amount of money exchanged for a good or service. Note that *perceived value* refers to the time of the transaction. After you've used a product you've bought, you may decide that its actual value was less than its perceived value. Managers use various strategies when determining the price of a product, as this section explains.

Pricing Strategies

Price-skimming and penetration pricing are strategies used in pricing new products; other strategies such as odd-even pricing and prestige pricing and bundling may be used for established products as well.

price skimming
The strategy of introducing a product with a high initial price and lowering the price over time as the product moves through its life cycle.

Price Skimming The practice of introducing a new product on the market with a high price and then lowering the price over time is called **price skimming.** As the product moves through its life cycle, the price usually is lowered because competitors are entering the market. As the price falls, more and more consumers can buy the product.

Price skimming has four important advantages. First, a high initial price can be a way to find out what buyers are willing to pay. Second, if consumers find the introductory price too high, it can be lowered. Third, a high introductory price can create an image of quality and prestige. Fourth, when the price is lowered later, consumers may think they are getting a bargain. The disadvantage is that high prices attract competition. Price skimming can be used to price virtually any new products such as high-definition televisions, PCs, and color computer printers.

penetration pricing
The strategy of selling new products at low prices in the hope of achieving a large sales volume.

*hope to own the market

Penetration Pricing A company that doesn't use price skimming will probably use **penetration pricing.** With this strategy, the company offers new products at low prices in the hope of achieving a large sales volume. Penetration pricing requires more extensive planning than skimming does because the company must gear up for mass production and marketing. When Texas Instruments entered the digital-watch market, its facilities in Lubbock, Texas, could produce 6 million watches a year, enough to meet the entire world demand for low-priced watches. If the company had been wrong about demand, its losses would have been huge.

Penetration pricing has two advantages. First, the low initial price may induce consumers to switch brands or companies. Using penetration pricing on its jug wines, Gallo has lured customers away from Taylor California Cellars and Inglenook. Second, penetration pricing may discourage competitors from entering the market. Their costs would tend to be higher, so they would need to sell more at the same price to break even.

odd-even (psychological) pricing
The strategy of setting a price at an odd number to connote a bargain and at an even number to suggest quality.

prestige pricing
The strategy of increasing the price of a product so that consumers will perceive it as being of higher quality, status, or value.

Odd-Even Pricing Psychology often plays a big role in how consumers view prices and what prices they will pay. **Odd-even pricing** (or **psychological pricing**) is the strategy of setting a price at an odd number to connote a bargain and at an even number to imply quality. For years, many retailers have priced their products in odd numbers—for example, $99.95 or $49.95—to make consumers feel that they are paying a lower price for the product. Even-numbered pricing is sometimes used to denote quality. Examples include a fine perfume at $100 a bottle, a good watch at $500, or a mink coat at $3,000.

Prestige Pricing The strategy of raising the price of a product so consumers will perceive it as being of higher quality, status, or value is called **prestige pricing.** This type of pricing is common where high prices indicate high status. In the specialty shops on Rodeo Drive in Beverly Hills, which cater to the super-rich of Hollywood, shirts that would sell for $15 elsewhere sell for at least $50. If the price were lower, customers would perceive them as being of low quality.

concept check

- What is the difference between penetration pricing and price skimming?
- Describe odd-even pricing and prestige pricing.

THE ROLE OF DISTRIBUTION IN THE MARKETING MIX

distribution channel
The series of marketing entities through which goods and services pass on their way from producers to end users.

A successful marketing mix includes a distribution strategy that defines how the product moves through the **distribution channel,** a series of marketing entities through which goods and services pass on their way to end users and consumers. This section will look first at the entities that make up a distribution channel and then will examine the functions that channels serve.

Marketing Intermediaries in the Distribution Channel

marketing intermediaries
Organizations that assist in moving goods and services from producers to end users.

A distribution channel is made up of **marketing intermediaries,** or organizations that assist in moving goods and services from producers to end users and consumers. Marketing intermediaries are so called because they are in the middle of the distribution process between the producer and the end user. The following marketing intermediaries most often appear in the distribution channel:

agents
Sales representatives of manufacturers and wholesalers.

brokers
Go-betweens that bring buyers and sellers together.

industrial distributors
Independent wholesalers that buy related product lines from many manufacturers and sell them to industrial users.

wholesalers
Firms that sell finished goods to retailers, manufacturers, and institutions.

retailers
Firms that sell goods to consumers and to industrial users for their own consumption.

- *Agents and brokers.* **Agents** are sales representatives of manufacturers and wholesalers, and **brokers** are entities that bring buyers and sellers together. Both agents and brokers are usually hired on commission basis by either a buyer or a seller. Agents and brokers are go-betweens whose job is to make deals. They do not own or take possession of goods.
- *Industrial distributors.* **Industrial distributors** are independent wholesalers that buy related product lines from many manufacturers and sell them to industrial users. They often have a sales force to call on purchasing agents, make deliveries, extend credit, and provide information. Industrial distributors are used in such industries as aircraft manufacturing, mining, and petroleum.
- *Wholesalers.* **Wholesalers** are firms that sell finished goods to retailers, manufacturers, and institutions (such as schools and hospitals). Historically, their function has been to buy from manufacturers and sell to retailers.
- *Retailers.* **Retailers** are firms that sell goods to consumers and to industrial users for their own consumption.

At the end of the distribution channel are final consumers, like you and me, and industrial users. Industrial users are firms that buy products for internal use or for producing other products or services. They include manufacturers, utilities, airlines, railroads, and service institutions, such as hotels, hospitals, and schools.

Exhibit 12-4 shows various ways marketing intermediaries can be linked. For instance, a manufacturer may sell to a wholesaler that sells to a retailer that in turn sells to a customer. In any of these distribution systems, goods and services are physically transferred from one organization to the next. As each takes possession of the products, it may take legal ownership of them. As the exhibit indicates, distribution channels can handle either consumer products or industrial products.

Wholesalers

As described earlier, wholesalers are channel members that buy finished products from manufacturers and sell them to retailers. Retailers in turn sell the products to consumers. Wholesalers also sell products to institutions, such as manufacturers, schools, and hospitals, for use in performing their own missions. A manufacturer, for instance, might buy typing paper from Nationwide Papers, a wholesaler. A hospital might buy its cleaning supplies from Lagasse Brothers, one of the nation's largest wholesalers of janitorial supplies.

merchant wholesaler
An institution that buys goods from manufacturers (takes ownership) and resells them to businesses, government agencies, other wholesalers, or retailers.

Two main types of wholesalers are merchant wholesalers and agents and brokers. A **merchant wholesaler** is an institution that buys goods from manufactur-

exhibit 12-4 | Channels of Distribution for Industrial and Consumer Products

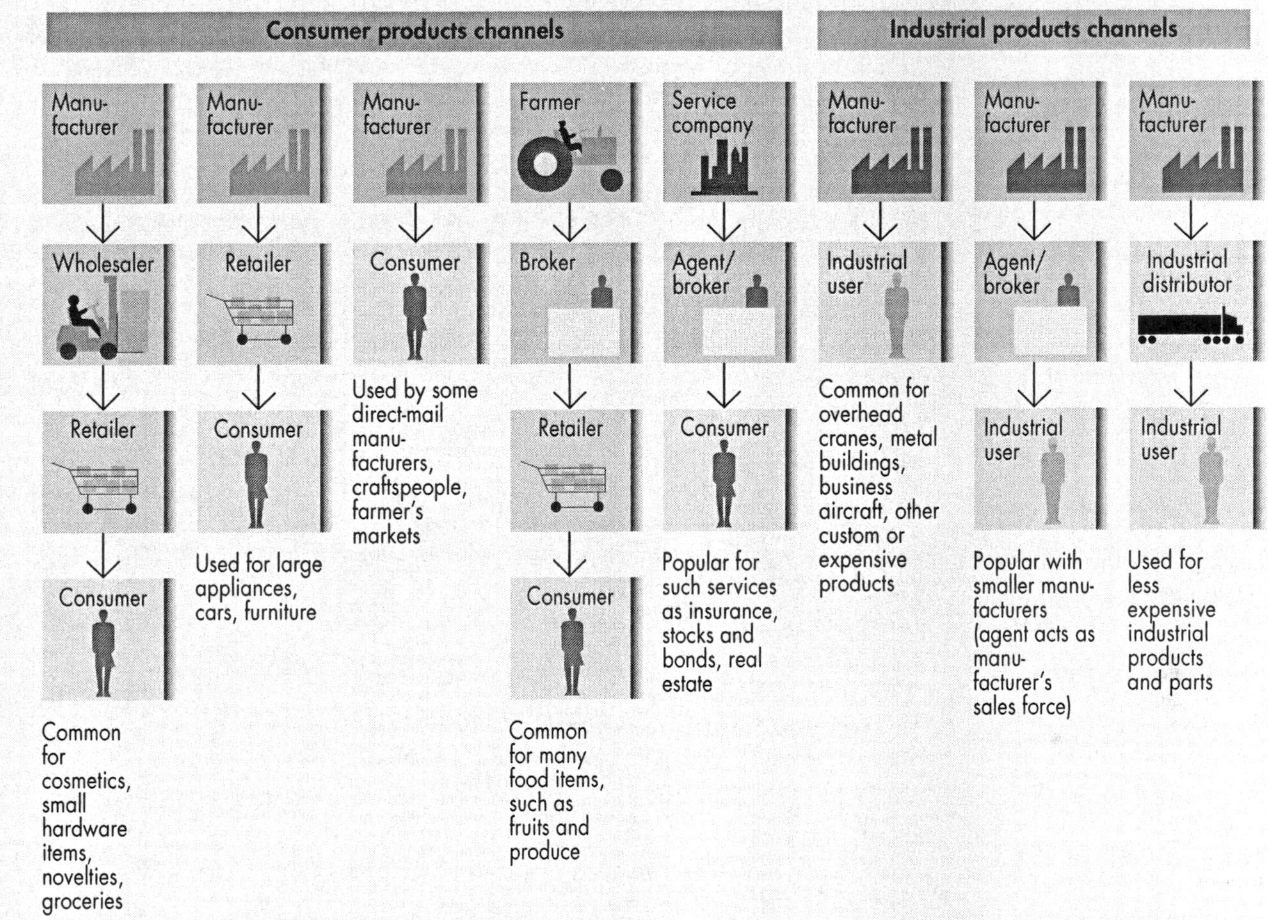

ers and resells them to businesses, government agencies, other wholesalers and retailers. Merchant wholesalers make up 80 percent of all wholesaling establishments and conduct slightly under 60 percent of all wholesale sales. All merchant wholesalers take title to the goods they sell.

manufacturers' representatives
Salespeople who represent noncompeting manufacturers; function as independent agents rather than as salaried employees of the manufacturers.

Agents and brokers, as described earlier, are another type of wholesaler. **Manufacturers' representatives** (also called manufacturers' agents) represent noncompeting manufacturers. These salespeople function as independent agents, not salaried employees of the manufacturer. They do not take title to or possession of merchandise. They get commissions if they make sales—and nothing if they don't. Brokers bring buyers and sellers together. Like agents, brokers do not take title to merchandise, they receive commisions on sales, and they have little say over company sale policies. They are frequently found in real estate, agriculture, insurance, and commodities.

Retailers

The major types of retailers are described in Exhibit 12-5, which divides them into two main categories: in-store retailing and nonstore retailing. Examples of *in-store retailing* include Sears, Wal-Mart, and Saks. These retailers get most of their revenue from people who come to the store to make purchases. *Nonstore retailing* involves selling products outside of the traditional bricks-and-mortar store. Nonstore retailing includes electronic retailing over the Internet (e-tailing), vending machines, direct selling (Mary Kay, Amway), home-shopping networks, and direct-response marketing (Land's End, Publisher's Weekly, J. Crew).

One of the challenges facing in-store and nonstore retailers is managing inventory. Managing inventory includes all aspects of moving goods from the seller to the retailer such as shipping, storing and stocking. The trick is to manage the inventory by cutting prices to move slow goods and by keeping adequate suppliers of hot-selling items in stock.

One of the more effificient new methods of managing inventory and streamlining the way products are moved from supplier to distributor to retailer is **efficient consumer response (ECR).** At the heart of ECR is **electronic data**

efficient consumer response (ECR)
A method of managing inventory and streamlining the movement of products from supplier to distributor to retailer; relies on electronic data interchange to communicate information such as automatic shipping notifications, invoices, inventory data, and forecasts.

exhibit 12-5 | In-Store and Nonstore Retailing

Types of In-Store Retailing	Description	Examples
Department store	Houses many departments under one roof with each treated as a separate buying center to achieve economies of buying, promotion, and control	JCPenney, Saks, May Co., Rich's, Bloomingdale's
Specialty store	Specializes in a category of merchandise and carries a complete assortment	Toys "R" Us, RadioShack, Zales Jewelers
Variety store	Offers a variety of inexpensive goods	Ben Franklin
Convenience store	Offers convenience goods with long store hours and quick checkout	7-Eleven, Circle K
Supermarket	Specializes in a wide assortment of food, with self-service	Safeway, Kroger, Winn-Dixie
Discount store	Competes on the basis of low prices and high turnover; offers few services	Wal-Mart, Target, Kmart
Off-price retailer	Sells at prices 25% or more below traditional department store prices in spartan environment	Robs, T.J. Maxx, Clothestime
Factory outlet	Owned by manufacturer; sells close-outs, factory seconds, and canceled orders	Levi Strauss, Ship 'n Shore, Dansk
Catalog store	Sends catalogs to customers and displays merchandise in showrooms where customers can order from attached warehouse	Best, Service Merchandise, Lurias
Hypermart	Offers huge selection of food and general merchandise with very low prices; sometimes called "mall without a wall"	Hypermart USA, American Fare
Types of Nonstore Retailing	**Description**	**Examples**
Vending machine	Sells merchandise by machine	Canteen
Direct selling	Sells face-to-face, usually in the person's home	Fuller Brush, Avon, Amway
Direct-response marketing	Attempts to get immediate consumer sale through media advertising, catalogs, or direct mail	K-Tel, L.L. Bean, Ronco
Home shopping networks	Selling via cable television	Home Shopping Network, QVC
Internet retailing (e-commerce)	Selling over the Internet	Bluefly.com, CDnow, eToys, Amazon.com

electronic data interchange (EDI)
Computer-to-computer exchange of information, including automatic shipping notifications, invoices, inventory data, and forecasts; used in efficient consumer response systems.

interchange (EDI), the computer-to computer exchange of information, including automatic shipping notifications, invoices, inventory data, and forecasts. Many retailers have successfully implemented ECR and EDI. The pioneer and market leader in ECR system is Wal-Mart, discussed in the Applying Technology box on page 356.

How Channels Organize and Cover Markets

In an efficient distribution channel, all the channel members work smoothly together and do what they're expected to do. A manufacturer expects wholesalers to promote its products to retailers and to perform several other functions as well. Not all channels have a leader or a single firm that sets channel policies. But all channels have members who rely on one another.

vertical marketing system
An organized, formal distribution channel in which firms are aligned in a hierarchy from manufacturer to wholesaler to retailer.

Vertical Marketing Systems To increase the efficiency of distribution channels, many firms have turned to vertical marketing systems. In a **vertical marketing system,** firms are aligned in a hierarchy (manufacturer to wholesaler to retailer). Such systems are planned, organized, formalized versions of distribution channels. The three basic types of vertical marketing systems are corporate, administrative, and contractual.

corporate distribution system
A vertical marketing system in which one firm owns the entire distribution channel.

In a **corporate distribution system,** one firm owns the entire channel of distribution. Corporate systems are tops in channel control. A single firm that owns the whole channel has no need to worry about channel members. The channel owner will always have supplies of raw materials and long-term contact with customers. It will have good distribution and product exposure in the marketplace. Examples of corporate distribution systems abound. Evans Products Co. (a manufacturer of plywood), for instance, bought wholesale lumber distributors to better market its products to retail dealers.

administrative distribution system
A vertical marketing system in which a strong organization takes over as leader and sets policies for the distribution channel.

In an **administrative distribution system,** a strong organization takes over as leader and sets channel policies. The leadership role is informal; it is not written into a contract. Companies such as Gillette, Hanes, Campbell's, and Westinghouse are administrative system leaders. They can often influence or control the policies of other channel members without the costs and expertise required to set up a corporate distribution system. They may be able to dictate how many wholesalers will be in the channel or require that the wholesalers offer 60-day credit to retail customers, among other things.

contractual distribution system
A vertical marketing system in which a network of independent firms at different levels (manufacturer, wholesaler, retailer) coordinate their distribution activities through a written contract.

The third form of vertical marketing is a **contractual distribution system.** It is a network of independent firms at different levels (manufacturer, wholesaler, retailer) that coordinate their distribution activities through a written contract. Franchises are a common form of the contractual system. The parent companies of McDonald's and ChemLawn, for instance, control distribution of their products through the franchise agreement each franchisee signs.

The Intensity of Market Coverage All types of distribution systems must be concerned with market coverage. How many dealers will be used to distribute the product in a particular area? The three degrees of coverage are exclusive, selective, and intensive. The type of product determines the intensity of the market coverage.

exclusive distribution
A distribution system in which a manufacturer selects only one or two dealers in an area to market its products.

When a manufacturer selects one or two dealers in an area to market its products, it is using **exclusive distribution.** Only items that are in strong demand can be distributed exclusively because consumers must be willing to travel some distance to buy them. If Wrigley's chewing gum were sold in only one drugstore per city, Wrigley's would soon be out of business. However, Bang and Olufsen stereo components, Jaguar automobiles, and Adrienne Vittadini designer clothing are distributed exclusively with great success.

selective distribution
A distribution system in which a manufacturer selects a limited number of dealers in an area (but more than one or two) to market its products.

A manufacturer that chooses a limited number of dealers in an area (but more than one or two) is using **selective distribution.** Since the number of retailers handling the product is limited, consumers must be willing to seek it out. Timberline boots, a high-quality line of footwear, are distributed selectively. So are Sony televisions, Maytag washers, Waterford crystal, and Tommy Hilfiger clothing.

A manufacturer that wants to sell its products everywhere there are potential customers is using **intensive distribution.** Such consumer goods as bread, tape, and lightbulbs are often distributed intensively. Usually, these products cost little and are bought frequently, which means that complex distribution channels are necessary. Coca-Cola is sold in just about every type of retail business, from gas stations to supermarkets.

concept check

- What is meant by an efficient channel of distribution?
- What are the three types of vertical marketing systems?
- Name the three degrees of market coverage.

intensive distribution
A distribution system in which a manufacturer tries to sell its products wherever there are potential customers.

Using Physical Distribution to Increase Efficiency and Customer Satisfaction

>lg 5

Physical distribution is an important part of the marketing mix. Retailers don't sell products they can't deliver, and salespeople don't (or shouldn't) promise deliveries they can't make. Late deliveries and broken promises may mean loss of a customer. Accurate order filling and billing, timely delivery, and arrival in good condition are important to the success of the product.

Distribution managers are responsible for making decisions that affect the successful delivery of a product to the end consumer. These decisions, presented in this section, include choosing a warehouse location and type, setting up a materials-handling system, and choosing among the available modes of transportation.

Choosing a Warehouse Location and Type Deciding where to put a warehouse is mostly a matter of deciding which markets will be served and where production facilities will be located. A *storage warehouse* is used to hold goods for a long time. For instance, Jantzen makes bathing suits at an even rate throughout the year to provide steady employment and hold down costs. It then stores them in a warehouse until the selling season.

distribution centers
Warehouses that specialize in changing shipment sizes, rather than in storing goods.

Distribution centers are a special form of warehouse. They specialize in changing shipment sizes rather than storing goods. Such centers make bulk (put shipments together) or break bulk. They strive for rapid inventory turnover. When shipments arrive, the merchandise is quickly sorted into orders for various retail stores. As soon as the order is complete, it is delivered. Distribution centers are the wave of the future, replacing traditional warehouses. Companies simply can't afford to have a lot of money tied up in idle inventory.

Setting Up a Materials-Handling System A materials-handling system moves and handles inventory. The goal of such a system is to move items as quickly as possible while handling them as little as possible. When Kodak built a new plant for making photographic coated paper, for example, it designed a way to minimize materials handling. It built a 10-level concrete rack to hold the one-ton rolls of raw paper. A computer handles inventory control and commands machines that can retrieve and carry the rolls without damage and then load the paper onto the assembly line.

concept check

- Discuss the functions of physical distribution.
- What is the goal of a materials-handling system?

Making Transportation Decisions Transportation typically accounts for between 5 and 10 percent of the price of goods. Physical distribution managers must decide which mode of transportation to use to

APPLYING TECHNOLOGY

WAL-MART KNOWS WHAT YOU LIKE

Many retailers talk a good game when it comes to mining data collected at cash registers as a way to build sales. Wal-Mart, the nation's largest retailer, has been doing it since about 1990. Now, it is sitting on a treasure trove of information so vast and detailed that it far exceeds what many manufacturers know about their own products.

Wal-Mart's database is second in size only to that of the U.S. government. Along with raw sales, profit margin, and inventory numbers, Wal-Mart also collects "market-basket data" from customer receipts at all its stores, so it knows what products are likely to be purchased together. The company receives about 100,000 queries a week from suppliers and its own buyers looking for purchase patterns or checking on a product.

At 192,000 square feet, Wal-Mart supercenters are about the size of four football fields. Wal-Mart quickly found customers were having trouble navigating them. To address customers' frustrations, Wal-Mart dug through heaps of purchase data from its supercenters and unearthed lots of ways to help people find things they didn't even know they needed. Kleenex tissues are in the paper-goods aisle and also mixed in with the cold medicine. Measuring spoons are in housewares and also hanging next to Crisco shortening. In October, flashlights are in the hardware aisle and also with the Halloween costumes.

To get real-time reports on sales, profitability, and inventory position, Wal-Mart managers can use a handheld computer that scans bar codes on store shelves. The information is crucial for pricing and shipping decisions, but it doesn't leave much room for creativity: "Everybody thinks they have a feel for what people like, but we keep data," says Randy Mott, Wal-Mart's chief information officer.

The data also help Wal-Mart time merchandise deliveries so that its shelves stay stocked—but not overstocked. The supercenters have cut back on how high they stack merchandise, making stores feel less crowded. The data have also helped keep inventory levels leaner and turning faster—a must for a retailer of perishable produce as well as of perishable fashion.

Critical Thinking Questions

1. Do you think that Wal-Mart's database could help in creating displays?
2. How can Wal-Mart's database be used in stocking a new Wal-Mart?
3. Is it a good idea to continually change a store's merchandise layout?

promotion
The attempt by marketers to inform, persuade, or remind consumers and industrial users to engage in the exchange process.

move products from producer to buyer. This decision is, of course, related to all other physical distribution decisions. The five major modes of transportation are railroads, motor carriers, pipelines, water transportation, and airways.

CREATING AN EFFECTIVE PROMOTION STRATEGY

Very few goods or services can survive in the marketplace without good promotion. Marketers, such as those touting Levi's Dockers, promote their products to build consumer demand. **Promotion** is an attempt by marketers to inform, persuade, or remind consumers and industrial users to engage in the exchange process. Once the product has been created, promotion is often used to convince target customers that it has a **differential advantage** over the competition. A differential advantage is a set of unique features that the target market perceives as important and better than the competition's features. Such features may include high quality, fast delivery, low price, good service, and the like. Lexus, for example, is seen as having a quality differential advan-

differential advantage
A set of unique features of a product that the target market perceives as important and better than the competition's features.

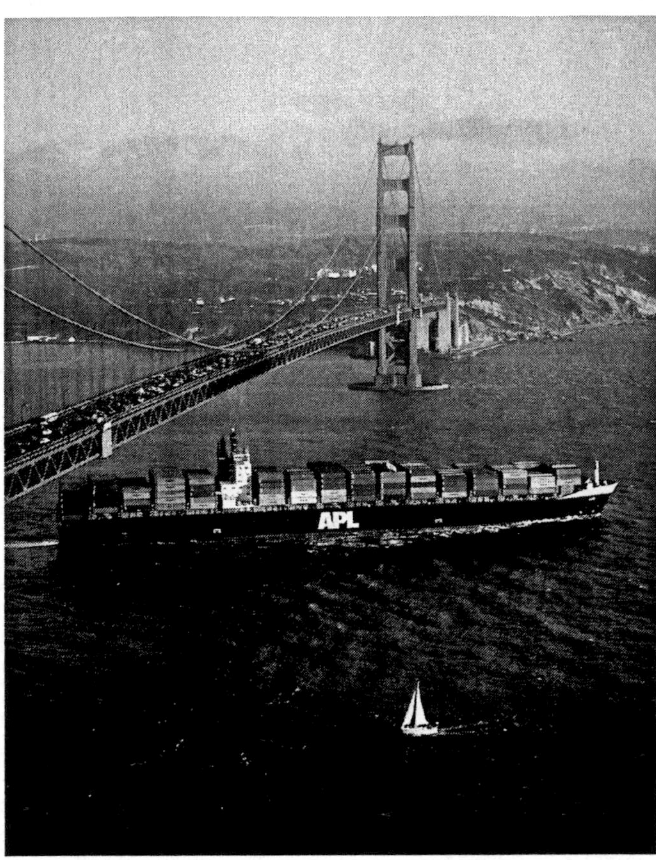

Water is one of the five major modes of transportation that distribution managers can choose from in moving products from the producer to the buyer.

tage over other luxury cars. Therefore, promotion for Lexus stresses the quality of the vehicle.

The Promotional Mix

The Freight World Web site offers detailed information on various transportation modes and links to transportation companies. Visit it at

http://www.freightworld.com

The combination of advertising, personal selling, sales promotion, and public relations used to promote a product is called the **promotional mix.** Each firm creates a unique mix for each product. But the goal is always to deliver the firm's message efficiently and effectively to the target audience. These are the elements of the promotional mix:

- *Advertising.* Any paid form of nonpersonal promotion by an identified sponsor.
- *Personal selling.* A face-to-face presentation to a prospective buyer.
- *Sales promotion.* Marketing activities (other than personal selling, advertising, and public relations) that stimulate consumer buying, including coupons and samples, displays, shows and exhibitions, demonstrations, and other types of selling efforts.
- *Public relations.* The linking of organizational goals with key aspects of the public interest and the development of programs designed to earn public understanding and acceptance.

The sections that follow examine the elements of the promotional mix in more detail.

promotional mix
The combination of advertising, personal selling, sales promotion, and public relations used to promote a product.

Advertising

Most Americans are bombarded daily with advertisements to buy things. **Advertising** is any paid form of nonpersonal presentation by an identified sponsor. It may appear on television or radio; in newspapers, magazines, books, or direct mail; or on billboards or transit cards.

The money that big corporations spend on advertising is mind-boggling. Total advertising expenses in this country are estimated at more than $190 billion a year. The largest percentage of the money goes to network television, followed closely by newspapers.[2] Nearly 12¢ of every dollar spent on perfume and cosmetics goes to advertising, and 15¢ out of every dollar spent on dolls and stuffed toys goes for advertising.[3] Even the missile and space industry spends nearly 2¢ of every sales dollar on ads. Spending by companies such as Procter & Gamble, Kraft-General Foods, Philip Morris, and General Motors averages more than $100,000 an hour, 24 hours a day; much of it is used in the prime evening hours on network television.

The channels through which advertising is carried to prospective customers are the **advertising media.** Both product and institutional ads appear in all the

advertising
Any paid form of nonpersonal presentation by an identified sponsor.

advertising media
The channels through which advertising is carried to prospective customers; includes newspapers, magazines, radio, television, outdoor advertising, direct mail, and the Internet.

major advertising media: newspapers, magazines, radio, television, outdoor advertising, direct mail, and the Internet.

cost per thousand (CPM)
Cost per thousand contacts is a term used in expressing advertising costs; refers to the cost of reaching 1,000 members of the target market.

reach
The number of different target consumers who are exposed to a commercial at least once during a specific period, usually four weeks.

frequency
The number of times an individual is exposed to an advertising message.

Media are evaluated on (1) **cost per thousand contacts (CPM)**; (2) **reach,** which is the number of different customers who are exposed to a commercial at least once per period of time (usually four weeks); and (3) **frequency,** which is the number of times an individual is exposed to a message.

Personal Selling

personal selling
A face-to-face sales presentation to a prospective customer.

sales prospects
The companies and people who are most likely to buy a seller's offerings.

Advertising acquaints potential customers with a product and thereby makes personal selling easier. **Personal selling** is a face-to-face sales presentation to a prospective customer. Sales jobs range from salesclerks at clothing stores to engineers with MBAs who design large, complex systems for manufacturers. About 6.5 million people are engaged in personal selling in the United States. Slightly over 45 percent of them are women. The number of people who earn a living from sales is huge compared, for instance, with the half a million workers employed in the advertising industry.

Selling is a process that can be learned. The steps in the selling process are as follows:

1. *Prospecting.* To start the process, the salesperson looks for **sales prospects,** those companies and people who are most likely to buy the seller's offerings.
2. *Approaching customers.* After identifying a prospect, the salesperson explains the reason for wanting an appointment and sets a specific date and hour. At the same time, the salesperson tries to build interest in the coming meeting.
3. *Presenting and demonstrating the product.* The presentation and demonstration can be fully automated, completely unstructured, or somewhere in between.
4. *Handling objections.* Almost every sales presentation, structured or unstructured, meets with some objection. Rarely does a customer say "I'll buy it" without asking questions or voicing concerns. The professional salesperson tries to anticipate objections so they can be countered quickly and with assurance.
5. *Closing the sale.* Asking the prospect to buy the product.
6. *Following up on the sale.* After the product is delivered to the customer, the salesperson must make a routine visit to see that the customer is satisified.

Sales Promotion

sales promotions
Marketing events or sales efforts—not including advertising, personal selling, and public relations—that stimulate buying.

Sales promotion helps make personal selling and advertising more effective. **Sales promotions** are marketing events or sales efforts—not including advertising, personal selling, and public relations—that stimulate buying. Today, sales promotion is an $80 billion industry and growing. Couponing alone is a $6 billion industry with over 275 billion coupons being distributed annually.[4] Sales promotion is usually targeted toward either of two distinctly different markets. Consumer sales promotion is targeted to the ultimate consumer market. Trade sales promotion is directed to members of the marketing channel, such as wholesalers and retailers.

The objectives of a promotion depend on the general behavior of target consumers. For ex-

concept check

- What are the elements of the promotional mix?
- How does sales promotion differ from advertising?
- Describe several types of sales promotion.

Entrepreneurs and small businesses don't always have big sales promotion budgets. For hundreds of low-cost promotion ideas, turn to the Guerrilla Marketing Web page at http://www.gmarketing.com.

ample, marketers who are targeting loyal users of their product don't want to change behavior. Instead, they want to reinforce existing behavior or increase product usage. Frequent-buyer programs that reward consumers for repeat purchases can be effective in strengthening brand loyalty. Other types of promotions are more effective with customers prone to brand switching or with those who are loyal to a competitor's product. Cents-off coupons, free samples, or an eye-catching display in a store will often entice shoppers to try a different brand.

Sales promotion offers many opportunities for entrepreneurs. Entrepreneurs design contests and sweepstakes, fabricate displays, manufacture premiums, and deliver free samples, among other things.

Public Relations

public relations

Any communication or activity designed to win goodwill or prestige for a company or person.

publicity

Information about a company or product that appears in the news media and is not directly paid for by the company.

Like sales promotion, public relations can be a vital part of the promotional mix. **Public relations** is any communication or activity designed to win goodwill or prestige for a company or person. Its main form is **publicity,** information about a company or product that appears in the news media and is not directly paid for by the company. Publicity can be good or bad. Children dying from eating tainted Jack in the Box hamburgers is an example of negative publicity.

Learn how to write a press release at http://www.publicrelationscentral.com/article1002.html

Naturally, firms' public relations departments try to create as much good publicity as possible. They furnish company speakers for business and civic clubs, write speeches for corporate officers, and encourage employees to take active roles in such civic groups as the United Way and the Chamber of Commerce. The main tool of the public relations department is the *press release,* a formal announcement of some newsworthy event connected with the company, such as the start of a new program, the introduction of a new product, or the opening of a new plant.

CAPITALIZING ON TRENDS IN BUSINESS

>lg 7

As customer expectations increase and competition becomes fiercer, perceptive managers will find innovative strategies to satisfy demanding consumers and establish unique products in the market. The key to success is to build a marketing mix that delivers value to the target customer.

Mass Customization

A silent revolution is changing the way many goods are made and services are delivered. Companies as diverse as BMW, Dell Computer, Levi Strauss, Mattel, McGraw-Hill, Wells Fargo, and many leading Web businesses are adopting mass customization to maintain or obtain a competitive edge. As we described in an earlier chapter, **mass customization** involves tailoring mass-market goods and services to the unique needs of the individuals who buy them.

mass customization

A flexible manufacturing technique in which mass-market goods and services are tailored to the unique needs of the individuals who buy them.

Mass producers dictate a one-to-many relationship, whereas mass customizers engage in a continual dialogue with customers. Although production is cost-efficient, the flexibility of mass customization can cut inventory. And mass customization offers two other advantages over mass production: it provides superior customer service, and it makes full use of cutting-edge technology.

concept check

- How can a new company build immediate brand recognition?
- What advantages does mass customization offer over mass production?
- What advantages do Internet auctions offer to companies and to consumers?

Services and Physical Distribution

The fastest-growing part of our economy is the service sector. Although distribution in the service sector is difficult to visualize, the same skills, techniques, and strategies used to manage goods inventory can also be used to manage service inventory, such as hospital beds, bank accounts, or airline seats. The quality of the planning and execution of distribution can have a major impact on costs and customer satisfaction. Because service industries are so customer oriented, customer service is a priority. Service distribution focuses on three main areas:

- *Minimizing wait times.* Minimizing the amount of time customers wait to deposit a check, obtain their food at a restaurant, or see a doctor for an appointment is a key factor in maintaining the quality of service. FedEx, for example, revolutionized the delivery market when it introduced guaranteed overnight delivery of packages and documents to commercial and residential customers.
- *Managing service capacity.* For a product manufacturer, inventory acts as a buffer, enabling it to provide the product during periods of peak demand without extraordinary efforts. Service firms don't have this luxury. If they don't have the capacity to meet demand, they must either turn down some prospective customers, let service levels slip, or expand capacity.
- *Improving delivery through new distribution channels.* Like manufacturers, service firms are now experimenting with different distribution channels for their services. These new channels can increase the time that services are available (like round-the-clock automated teller machines) or add to customer convenience (like pizza delivery or walk-in medical clinics).

Integrated Marketing Communications

Ideally, marketing communications from each promotional mix element (personal selling, advertising, sales promotion, and public relations) should be integrated. That is, the message reaching the consumer should be the same regardless of whether it comes from an advertisement, a salesperson in the field, a magazine article, or a coupon in a newspaper insert.

From the consumer's standpoint, a company's communications are already integrated. Typical consumers do not think in terms of advertising, sales promotion, public relations, or personal selling. To them, everything is an "ad." Unfortunately, many marketers neglect this fact when planning promotional messages and fail to integrate the various elements of their communication efforts. The most common rift typically arises between personal selling and the other elements of the promotional mix.

integrated marketing communications (IMC)
The careful coordination of all promotional activities—media advertising, sales promotion, personal selling, and public relations, as well as direct marketing, packaging, and other forms of promotion—to produce a consistent, unified message that is customer focused.

This unintegrated, disjointed approach to promotion has propelled many companies to adopt the concept of **integrated marketing communications (IMC)**. IMC involves carefully coordinating all promotional activities—media advertising, sales promotion, personal selling, and public relations, as well as direct marketing, packaging, and other forms of promotion—to produce a consistent, unified message that is customer focused. Following the concept of IMC, marketing managers carefully work out the roles the various promotional elements will play in the marketing mix. Timing of promotional activities is coordinated, and the results of each campaign are carefully monitored to improve future use of the promotional mix tools. Typically, a marketing communications director is appointed who has overall responsibility for integrating the company's marketing communications.

APPLYING THIS CHAPTER'S TOPICS

This chapter makes several important points that can affect your life right now. First, businesses are using mass customization to deliver low-cost, specialized products and services that meet the unique needs of individual customers. The Internet has helped usher in mass customization and has opened up vast sources of information on business and consumer products as explained in this section.

Custom Products and Services

Mass customization means that now, more than ever, you can get exactly the product that will fit your needs. A number of companies have adapted this strategy for competition, including AT&T, Coke and Pepsi, and fast-food companies such as McDonald's. The Internet is frequently the primary avenue for delivering customized products, giving you easy access to product and pricing information.

Looking for cheap airfares? Priceline.com lets consumers bid on air and hotel rates. Check out http://www.priceline.com

Always Sell Yourself

If you stop and think about it, all of us must be salespeople. If you are going to be successful in business, and in life in general, you must be a salesperson. You must be able to effectively explain and sell your plans, ideas, and hopes. A straight "A" student who can't do this will not be successful. Conversely, a "C" student who can will be successful. *Always* be prepared to sell yourself and your ideas. It's the best way to get ahead in business and in life.

TRY IT NOW!

1. **Comparison Shop** A beauty of the Internet is the ability to comparison shop like never before. To compare brands, features, and prices of products, go to one of these sites: **http://www.bottomdollar.com**, **http://www.mysimon.com**, or **http://www.compare.net.**
2. **Kick the Tires Before You Buy** At some point you are going to buy a car. The Web can simplify the process, help you make an intelligent decision, and save you money. Start at **http://www.edmunds.com.** The online version of the respected car-buying guide is crammed with information about new and used cars. The site offers thousands of car reviews and current loan rates. Once you decide what you want, go to one or all of these sites to get the best price: **http://www.autobytel.com**, **http://www.autotrader.com**, or **http://www.autoweb.com.** If you decide to buy a used car but are not sure about the strange sound or unexplained dent, go to **http://www.carfax.com** and plug in the car's vehicle identification number. In return you will get an immediate report of the car's public history that will tell you such things as whether the car has been auctioned and its emission test results. The report costs $20, but if there are no data, you don't pay. Once you have found the car of your dreams, go to **http://www.carfinance.com** for a loan or a lease plan at no charge.

>looking ahead at the Pocket Blimp

The Pocket Blimp could be a consumer or business product depending on use. If a person bought one for personal enjoyment, it would be a consumer good. If a company bought a Pocket Blimp to be used as an advertising vehicle, then it would be a business good. The Pocket Blimp is in the early part of the introductory stage of the product life cycle. Since the Pocket Blimp is a specialty product, a skimming price strategy would probably be best.

SUMMARY OF LEARNING GOALS

>lg 1 **What is the role of the product in the marketing mix, and how are products classified and developed?**

A product is any good or service, along with its perceived attributes and benefits, that creates customer value. Tangible attributes include the good itself, packaging, and warranties. Intangible attributes are symbolic like a brand's image.

Most items are a combination of goods and services. Services and goods are often marketed differently. Products are categorized as either consumer products or industrial products. Consumer products are goods and services that are bought and used by the end users. They can be classified as unsought products, convenience products, shopping products, or specialty products, depending on how much effort consumers are willing to exert to get them.

Industrial products are those bought by organizations for use in making other products or in rendering services. Capital products are usually large, expensive items with a long life span. Expense items are typically smaller, less expensive items that usually have a life span of less than a year.

Products usually have brand names. Brands identify products by words, names, symbols, designs, or a combination of these things. The two major types of brands are manufacturer (national) brands and dealer (private) brands. Generic products carry no brand name. Branding has three main purposes: product identification, repeat sales, and new product sales.

Often the promotional claims of well-known brands are reinforced in the printing on the package. Packaging is an important way to promote sales and protect the product. A package should be easy to ship, store, and stack on a store shelf.

The steps in new product development are setting new product goals, exploring ideas, screening ideas, developing the concept (creating a prototype and building the marketing strategy), test-marketing, and introducing the product. When the product enters the marketplace, it is often managed by a product manager.

>lg 2 **What are the stages of the product life cycle?**

After a product reaches the marketplace, it enters the product life cycle. This cycle typically has four stages: introduction, growth, maturity, and decline (and possibly death). Profits usually are small in the introductory phase, reach a peak at the end of the growth phase, and then decline.

>lg 3 **What strategies are used for pricing products?**

Price indicates value, helps position a product in the marketplace, and is the means for earning a fair return on investment. If a price is too high, the product won't sell well, and the firm will lose money. If the price is too low, the firm may lose money even if the product sells well.

The two main strategies for pricing a new product are price skimming and penetration pricing. Price skimming involves charging a high introductory price and then, usually, lowering the price as the product moves through its life cycle. Penetration pricing involves selling a new product at a low price in the hope of achieving a large sales volume.

Pricing tactics are used to fine-tune the base prices of products. Among these tactics are odd-even pricing and prestige pricing. Setting a price at an odd number tends to create a perception that the item is cheaper than the actual price. Prices in even numbers denote quality or status. Raising the price so an item will be perceived as having high quality and status is called prestige pricing. Consumers pay more because of the perceived quality or status.

>lg 4 **Describe the distribution channels and the manner in which they are organized.**
Distribution channels are the series of marketing entities through which goods and services pass on their way from producers to end users. Distribution systems focus on the physical transfer of goods and services and on their legal ownership at each stage of the distribution process.

A vertical marketing system is a planned, hierarchically organized distribution channel. There are three types of vertical marketing systems: corporate, administrative, and contractual. In a corporate system, one firm owns the entire channel. In an administrative system, a strong organization takes over as leader and sets channel policies. In a contractual distribution system, the independent firms coordinate their distribution activities by written contract.

>lg 5 **What are the functions of physical distribution?**
The functions of physical distribution include choosing a warehouse location and type, setting up a materials-handling system, and choosing modes of transportation (air, highway, rail, water, or pipeline). Criteria for selecting a mode of transportation include cost, transit time, reliability, capability, accessibility, and traceability.

>lg 6 **Explain the promotional mix and its primary elements.**
The unique combination of advertising, personal selling, sales promotion, and public relations used to promote a product is the promotional mix. Advertising is any paid form of nonpersonal promotion by an identified sponsor. Personal selling consists of a face-to-face presentation in a conversation with a prospective purchaser. Sales promotion consists of marketing activities—other than personal selling, advertising, and public relations—that stimulate consumers to buy. These activities include coupons and samples, displays, shows and exhibitions, demonstrations, and other selling efforts. Public relations is the marketing function that links the policies of the organization with the public interest and develops programs designed to earn public understanding and acceptance.

The main types of advertising media are newspapers, magazines, radio, television, outdoor advertising, direct mail, and the Internet. Newspaper advertising delivers a local audience but has a short life span. Magazines deliver special-interest markets and offer good detail and color. Radio is an inexpensive and highly portable medium but has no visual capabilities. Television reaches huge audiences and offers visual and audio opportunities, but it can be very expensive. Outdoor advertising requires short messages but is only moderately expensive. Direct mail can reach targeted audiences, but it is only as good as the mailing list. The Internet is global in scope and can offer a personalized message response by email, but as yet not everyone is on the Net. Media are evaluated on a CPM (cost per thousand contacts) basis and by reach and frequency.

About 6.5 million people in the United States are directly engaged in personal selling. Personal selling enables a salesperson to demonstrate a product and tailor the message to the prospect; it is effective in closing a sale.

Immediate purchase is the goal of sales promotion whether it is aimed at consumers or the trade (wholesalers and retailers). The most popular sales promotions are coupons, samples, premiums, contests, and sweepstakes. Public relations is mostly concerned with getting good publicity for companies. Public relations helps build a positive image for an organization, which is a good backdrop for selling its products.

>lg 7 **Describe the trends affecting the marketing mix.**

Mass customization, the growth of Internet auctions, improved techniques for managing service inventories, and integrated marketing communications are key trends in maximizing the effectiveness of the marketing mix.

KEY TERMS

administrative distribution system 354
advertising 357
advertising media 357
agents 351
brand 344
brand equity 344
brokers 351
capital products 343
contractual distribution system 354
convenience products 343
corporate distribution system 354
cost per thousand (CPM) 358
dealer brands 345
differential advantage 356
distribution centers 351
distribution channel 355
efficient consumer response (ECR) 353
electronic data interchange (EDI) 354
exclusive distribution 354
expense items 343
focus group 346
frequency 358
generic products 345
industrial distributors 351
integrated marketing communications (IMC) 360
intensive distribution 355
manufacturer brands 345
manufacturers' representatives 352
marketing intermediaries 351
mass customization 359
merchant wholesaler 351
odd-even (psychological) pricing 350
penetration pricing 350
personal selling 358

PREPARING FOR TOMORROW'S WORKPLACE

1. Under what circumstances would a jeans maker market the product as a convenience product? A shopping product? A specialty product?
2. Go to the library and look through magazines and newspapers to find examples of price skimming and penetration pricing. Make copies and show them to the class.
3. Explain how something as obvious as a retail price can have a psychological dimension.
4. Divide the class into teams of four. Trace the channel for some familiar product. Each group should tell why they think the channel has evolved as it has and how it is likely to change.
5. Go to a successful, independent specialty store in your area that has been in business for quite a while. Interview the manager and try to determine how the store successfully competes with the national chains.
6. Choose a current advertising campaign, determine whether it is effective, and then explain why or why not. Present your results to the class.
7. How can advertising, sales promotion, and publicity work together? Give an example.

WORKING THE NET

1. Visit an online retailer such as Amazon.com **(http://www.amazon.com)** or eToys **(http://www.eToys.com)**. At the site, try to identify examples of leader pricing, bundling, odd pricing, and other pricing strategies. Do online retailers have different pricing considerations than real-world retailers? Explain.
2. What are some of the logistics problems facing firms that operate internationally? Visit the *Logistics Management & Distribution Report* Web site at **http://www.manufacturing.net/lm** and see if you can find information about how firms manage global logistics.
3. The Zenith Media site at **http://www.zenithmedia.com** is a good place to find links to Internet resources on advertising. At the site, click on "category sites" and then click on one of the categories. Pick three of the company sites listed and review them, using the concepts in this chapter.

prestige pricing 350
price skimming 350
product 342
product life cycle 348
promotion 356
promotional mix 357
public relations 359
publicity 359
reach 358
retailers 351
sales promotions 358
sales prospects 358
selective distribution 354
shopping products 343
specialty products 343
test-marketing 348
trademark 344
unsought products 343
vertical marketing system 354
wholesalers 351

CREATIVE THINKING CASE

Personality Puffs and Cardio Chips

There was a time when potato chips were just potato chips, their greasy crunch leaving the snacker with an aftertaste of delicious guilt. No more. A new kind of chip aims at tackling the psyche rather than tickling the taste bud, promising to turn Americans into kinder, happier, and gentler souls.

The secret? Herbs and plant extracts, such as St. John's wort, ginkgo biloba, and kava kava, are added to the chips along with essences of edible flowers—violet, chamomile, peppermint, and passion flower—to help combat depression, promote long life, and improve memory. "It's just one of those next steps in the evolution of snacks and food," said the chips' manufacturer, Robert Ehrlich. "There are definitely benefits from the product."

But not everyone is swallowing that claim. Some nutritionists have expressed concern that all the feel-good messages about the snacks are just advertising gimmicks to sell chips. "They're just ridiculous," said Norman Rosenthal, clinical professor of psychiatry and author of *St. John's Wort: The Herbal Way to Feeling Good.* "It would be like having a penicillin pie or an antibiotic apple strudel."

Ehrlich founded Robert's American Gourmet, which began making his mood-enhancing snacks four years ago. A group of herbalists, zen masters, a psychiatrist, and young consumers help put the products together. At 99 cents for a 2-ounce bag, the chips are sold in supermarkets—in the health food section—in the United States and in some parts of Europe, Asia, and South America.

Low-fat Cardio Chips containing a blend of natural herbs to improve cardiovascular health, metabolic conditions, the immune system, and aging are one of Ehrlich's products. His other herbal products include St. John's Wort Tortilla Chips to improve moods, Ginkgo Biloba Rings to enhance memory, and Kava Corn Chips to promote relaxation. Personality Puffs, which come in the shape of little people, are made up of a blend of flowers, St. John's wort, and ginkgo biloba.

Unlike other herbal products, Personality Puffs come with a set of printed rules that will "open you to the magic that is ready to happen in your life." Snackers are asked to buy at least two bags and give one away to a stranger within one hour of purchase. That, Ehrlich said, will create goodwill and kindness.

Critical Thinking Questions

1. How would you classify these consumer goods?
2. Describe the pricing strategy for the herbal chips.
3. What distribution channel should be used for the chips?
4. What media would you recommend and what would you suggest as a promotional theme?

VIDEO CASE

The Internet and Burton Snowboards' Distribution System: Reaching Out to Newbies

Burton Snowboards **(http://www.burton.com)**, a manufacturer of snowboards and outerwear for snowboard riders, is located in Burlington, Vermont. Burton Snowboards uses its Web site to promote the sport of snowboarding as well as to market its products to professionals and amateurs alike.

Selected retailers sell Burton Snowboards' products to newbies as well as to those with more snowboarding experience. The products are intended to appeal to the discriminating buyer regardless of experience or ability level. Burton's snowboards are premium products—"equipment that starts where many companies reach their 'high-end.'"

Burton's also produces clothing to wear while snowboarding or in the lodge afterward. Emphasizing a layered approach for maximum comfort and warmth, Burton's produces a first layer, a thermal layer, a heater layer, and an outer layer of snowboarding outerwear. Burton's sells gloves, hats, and lodge clothing as well.

Although Burton Snowboards maintains distribution relationships with selected retailers, it has discovered that the Internet can be an important vehicle for developing customer traffic to those retailers.

Critical Thinking Questions

1. What function does Burton Snowboards' Web site serve in its distribution channel?
2. What does the Learn to Ride (LTR) Guide, available by clicking *LTR* at the Burton Snowboard home page, accomplish in terms of servicing Burton's distribution channel?
3. Do you think using the Internet to reach prospective customers is a wise business decision?

ecommerce

Case: Video on Demand

Feel like renting a movie tonight? Don't hop in your car for a run to your local video store. Instead, turn on your computer, log onto the Internet, and download the latest hit flick.

MGM and Blockbuster Video hope that consumers will soon welcome "video on demand" delivered via the Internet. MGM owns the world's largest movie library with 4,100 titles. Blockbuster Video is one of the world's largest video rental chains with over 7,700 retail stores in 27 countries. Under an Internet movie distribution agreement recently signed by both companies, Blockbuster will charge a fee for films ordered and delivered to customers through digital streaming or downloads. The two companies will split profits from movies sold this way. The deal is nonexclusive, meaning either firm can form partnerships with other firms in addition to this one.

"This is an exciting announcement for movie lovers," says John Antioco, Blockbuster's chief executive officer. "It underscores our goal to provide quality, in-home entertainment, in whatever form our consumers want it delivered, whether through our stores or other channels such as electronic delivery."

MGM already offers video clips at its corporate Web site, but hasn't yet made full-length feature films available for download. MGM isn't the only major movie studio looking at Internet distribution. Miramax Films plans to offer 12 full-length films for downloading in an agreement with multimedia distribution company SightSound.com. Miramax will set up an individual Web site for each film.

Online movie distribution has been discussed in the entertainment industry for over a decade, but no movie studio has yet utilized the Internet as a major distribution channel. One problem is the lack of widespread availability of the high-speed, high-capacity Internet access necessary to download movies quickly. However, as more consumers get faster Internet access, studios are hopeful that Internet distribution will debut to consumer applause.

Questions for Critical Thinking

1. Analyze the risks and benefits of their Internet distribution agreement for both Blockbuster and MGM.
2. Explain how Miramax's decision to offer films directly to consumers over the Internet could affect its relationships with customers and other channel members.
3. Do you think Internet movie distribution will succeed? Why or why not?

SOURCES: Mary Hullebrand, "Miramax Films Inks Online Distribution Deal," *E-Commerce Times* (April 19, 2000), downloaded from **http://www.ecommercetimes.com**; Robert La Franco, "Hype on Demand," *Redherring.com* (August 1, 2000), downloaded from **http://www.redherring.com**; Ken Yamada, "Digital Entertainment's Growing Pains," *Redherring.com* (August 2, 2000), downloaded from **http://www.redherring.com**; "MGM.com and Microcast Lead the Way in the Convergence of Film and Internet," *PR Newswire* (August 14, 2000), downloaded from **http://www.prnewswire.com**; "MGM and Blockbuster Announce Agreement to Develop Digital Streaming Model for Selected MGM Film Library Titles," Blockbuster Inc. company press release (January 18, 2000), downloaded from **http://www.blockbuster.com**.

learning goals

- >lg 1 Why is production and operations management important in both manufacturing and service firms?
- >lg 2 What types of production processes are used by manufacturers and service firms?
- >lg 3 How do organizations decide where to put their production facilities? What choices must be made in designing the facility?
- >lg 4 Why are resource planning tasks like inventory management and supplier relations critical to production?
- >lg 5 How do operations managers schedule and control production?
- >lg 6 How can quality management and lean manufacturing techniques help firms improve production and operations management?
- >lg 7 What roles do technology and automation play in manufacturing and service industry operations management?
- >lg 8 What key trends are affecting the way companies manage production and operations?

Achieving World-Class Operations Management

10

Harley-Davidson Revs up Production

Harley-Davidsons (**http://www.harley-davidson.com**) aren't just motorcycles. They're an American legend, known for their unique style, sound, and power ever since the first one was assembled in a backyard workshop in 1903. "People want more than two wheels and a motor," explains Harley-Davidson CEO Jeffrey Bleustein. "Harleys represent something very basic—a desire for freedom, adventure, and individualism."

Back in the 1980s, Harleys also represented everything that was wrong with American manufacturing. The company's main factory in York, Pennsylvania, was outdated and inefficient, keeping prices high. Quality was so poor that owners sometimes joked they needed two Harleys—one to ride and one for parts. Fed-up consumers started buying motorcycles made by Japanese and German manufacturers. Harley-Davidson's future looked grim.

To turn things around, the company designed new models and borrowed state-of-the-art quality and production techniques from Japanese manufacturers. It cut the number of parts stored in inventory at the company's factories, keeping costs—and prices—under control. As quality improved and prices stabilized, Harley-Davidson's sales began to climb.

By the mid-1990s, however, Harley's existing factories were having trouble keeping up with demand. Customers often had to wait a year or longer to get a new Harley. The choice was clear: either the firm must rev up its production capability, or it would risk losing customers to foreign competitors once again.

First order of business? A new $86 million factory in Kansas City. The 330,000-square-foot plant, opened in 1998, puts Harley-Davidson at the forefront of modern manufacturing and management practice.

In a special lightproof room, lasers automatically pierce holes in fenders for taillights and other attachments. Robots then polish the finished fenders, along with gas and oil tanks, while other robots paint the various components needed to build a Harley. The components are loaded onto three dozen specially designed carts that swivel 360 degrees and can be lowered or raised to suit different workers or tasks. The carts move among workstations where employees assemble motorcycle frames. By the end of the line, 70 employees have assembled 650 parts at 20 different workstations.

No motorcycle leaves the plant without a final stop at Station 20. A team of test drivers revs up and rides each motorcycle, checking operating quality and listening for the classic

Critical Thinking Questions

As you read this chapter, consider the following questions as they relate to Harley-Davidson:

- How has a focus on manufacturing supported Harley-Davidson's growth?
- What factors outside the company have led to this focus?
- What future production changes will Harley need to make in order to continue to grow?

Harley sound. Any bikes that don't meet rigid standards are sent back to the factory for adjustments and fine-tuning.

Employees are integral to the success of Harley's new factory. They are grouped in work teams, and every employee is cross-trained to perform a variety of production tasks. Each work team must constantly look for ways to build a better Harley. The result has been many employee-generated ideas for better equipment, factory layout, and production processes.

Looking back, CEO Bleustein believes production and operations have been vital to Harley-Davidson's continued growth. "In the last 10 years, we were very much internally focused," he says. "We had to fix our manufacturing and bring it to a new level. With that in place, our focus can be more external, bringing new and exciting products to the marketplace."[1]

BUSINESS IN THE 21ST CENTURY

Finding the most efficient and effective methods of producing the goods or services it sells to customers is an ongoing focus of nearly every type of business organization. Today more than ever, changing consumer expectations, technological advances, and increased competition are all forcing business organizations to rethink where, when, and how they will produce products or services.

Assembly-line employees at Harley-Davidson's new Kansas City plant suggested production process improvements that contributed to their firm's continued growth.

Like Harley-Davidson in the chapter's opening story, manufacturers are discovering that it is no longer enough to simply push products through the factory and onto the market. Consumers are demanding higher quality at reasonable prices. They also expect products to be delivered in a timely manner. Firms that can't meet these expectations often face strong competition from businesses that can. To compete, many manufacturers are reinventing how they make their products by automating their factories, developing new production processes, and tightening their relationships with suppliers.

Service organizations are also facing challenges. Their customers are demanding better service, shorter waits, and more individualized attention. Just like manufacturers, service organizations are using new methods to deliver what customers need and want. Banks, for example, are using technology such as ATMs and the Internet to make their services more accessible to customers. Many colleges now offer weekend courses for working students. Tax services are filing tax returns via computer.

In this chapter, we will examine how manufacturers and service firms manage and control the creation of products and services. Following a brief overview, we'll discuss production planning, including the choices firms must make concerning the type of production process they will use, the location where production will occur, and the management of resources needed in production. Next, we'll explain routing and scheduling, two critical tasks for controlling production and operations efficiency. Many businesses are improving productivity by employing new methods like quality control and automation. We'll discuss these methods before summarizing some of the trends affecting production and operations management.

PRODUCTION AND OPERATIONS MANAGEMENT—AN OVERVIEW

production >lg 1
The creation of products and services by turning inputs, such as natural resources, raw materials, human resources, and capital, into outputs, products and services.

operations management
Management of the production process.

Production, the creation of products and services, is an essential function in every firm. Production turns inputs, such as natural resources, raw materials, human resources, and capital, into outputs, products and services. This process is shown in Exhibit 8-1. Managing this conversion process is the role of **operations management.**

In the 1980s, many U.S. industries, such as automotive, steel, and electronics, lost customers to foreign competitors because their production systems could not provide the quality customers demanded. As a result, most American companies, both large and small, now consider a focus on quality to be a central component of effective operations management.

The goal of customer satisfaction, closely linked to quality, is also an important part of effective production and operations. In the past, the manufacturing

exhibit 8-1 | Production Process for Products and Services

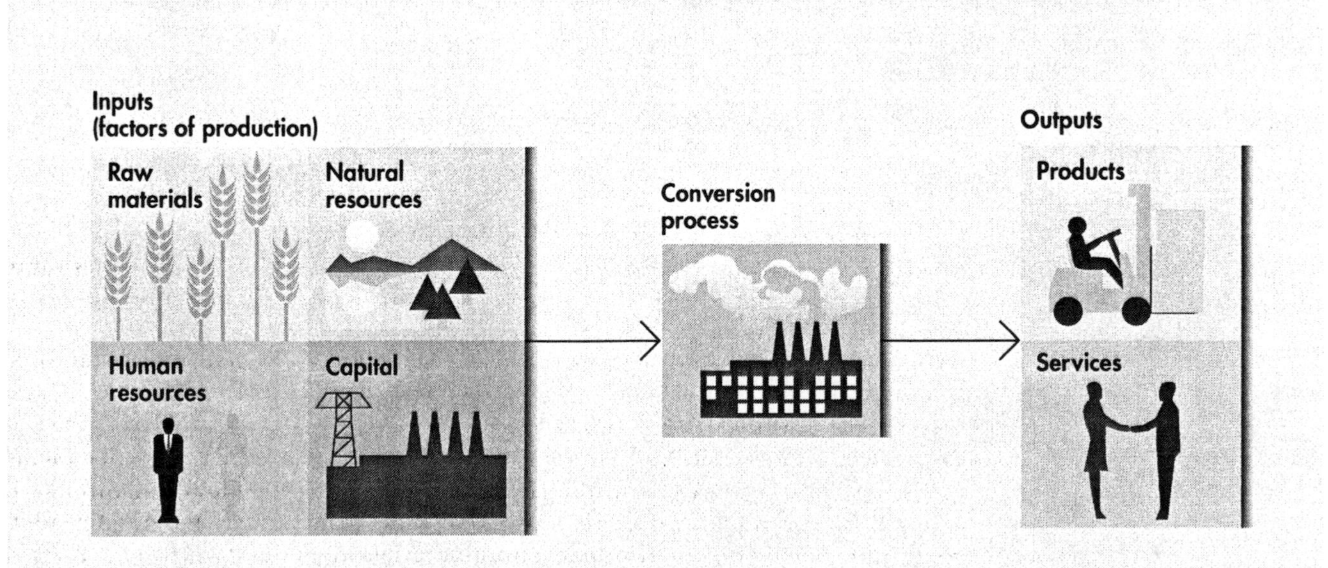

function in most companies was inwardly focused. Manufacturing had little contact with customers and didn't always understand their needs and desires. Today, however, stronger links between marketing and manufacturing have encouraged production managers to be more outwardly focused and to consider decisions in light of their effect on customer satisfaction. Service companies have also found that making operating decisions with customer satisfaction in mind can be a competitive advantage.

Operations managers, the personnel charged with managing and supervising the conversion process, play a vital role in today's firm. They control about three-fourths of a firm's assets, including inventories, wages, and benefits. They work closely with other major functions of the firm, such as marketing, finance, accounting, and human resources, to help ensure that the firm continually provides customer satisfaction. They face the challenge of combining people and other resources to produce high-quality goods, on time and at a reasonable cost. Working with marketing, they help to decide which products to make or which services to offer. They become involved with the development and design of goods and determine what production processes will be most effective.

Production and operations management involves three main types of decisions that are made at three different stages:

1. *Production planning.* The first decisions facing operations managers come at the *planning stage.* At this stage, decisions are made regarding where, when, and how production will occur. Resources are obtained and site locations determined.
2. *Production control.* At this stage, the decision-making process focuses on scheduling, controlling quality and costs, and the actual day-to-day operations of running a factory or service facility.
3. *Improving production and operations.* In the final stage, operations management focuses on developing more efficient methods of producing the firm's goods.

It is important to remember that these three types of decisions are ongoing and often occur simultaneously. In the following sections, we will take a closer look at the decisions and considerations firms face in each of these stages of production and operations management.

concept check

- Define production and explain how operations management is related to it.
- What are the three main types of decisions operations managers must make?

PRODUCTION PLANNING

production planning
The aspect of operations management in which the firm considers the competitive environment and its own strategic goals in an effort to find the best production methods.

An important part of operations management is **production planning.** During production planning, the firm considers the competitive environment and its own strategic goals in an effort to find the best production methods. Good production planning balances goals that may conflict such as providing high-quality service while keeping operating costs down, or keeping profits high while maintaining adequate inventories of finished products. Sometimes accomplishing all of these goals is quite difficult.

Production planning involves three phases. Long-term planning has a time frame of three to five years. It focuses on which goods to produce, how many to produce, and where they should be produced. Medium-term planning decisions cover about two years. They concern the layout of factory or service facilities, where and how to obtain the resources needed for production, and labor issues. Short-term planning, with a one-year time frame, converts these broader goals into specific production plans and materials management strategies.

Four important decisions must be made in production planning. They involve the type of production process that will be used, site selection, facility layout, and resource planning.

Production Process

In production planning, the first decision to be made is which type of **production process**—the way a good is made—best fits with the company's goals and customer demands. Another important consideration is the type of good or service being produced, as different goods may require different production processes. In general, there are three types of production: mass production, mass customization, and customization.

production process
The way a good is made.

mass production
The ability to manufacture many identical goods at once.

Mass Production **Mass production,** the ability to manufacture many identical goods at once, was a product of the Industrial Revolution. Henry Ford's Model-T automobile is a good example of mass production. Each car turned out by Ford's factory was identical, right down to its color. If you wanted a car in any color except black, you were out of luck. Canned goods, over-the-counter drugs, and household appliances are examples of goods that are still mass-produced. The emphasis in mass production is on keeping manufacturing costs low by producing highly uniform products.

A quality control employee inspects the uniformity of Trix yogurt, a product that is mass-produced to keep manufacturing costs low.

Increasingly, however, manufacturers are finding that mass production is becoming more complex. Many products are more complicated to produce. Automobile manufacturers, for example, are incorporating more sophisticated electronics into their car designs. As a result, the number of assembly stations in an auto assembly plant has increased. In many industries, customers are also demanding a wider array of choices and even customization. These trends have led to changes in the processes used to produce many goods.

Mass Customization and Customization In **mass customization,** a relatively new concept in manufacturing, goods are produced using mass production techniques, but only up to a point. At that point, the product or service is custom tailored to the needs or desires of individual customers. Golf club maker Taylor Made Golf devotes part of its production plant to mass customization. Customers needing longer club shafts, customized grips, or other options order through pro shops and golf instructors. Workers at Taylor Made's plant add the parts to the clubs based on the customer's requirements.[2]

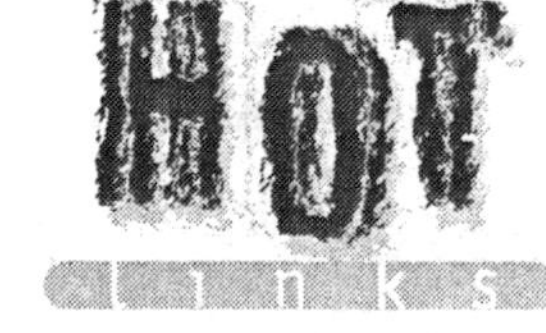

Can customized Taylor Made clubs improve your golf game? Find out more about how Taylor Made Golf uses mass customization at http://www.taylormadegolf.com

mass customization
A manufacturing process in which goods are mass-produced up to a point and then custom tailored to the needs or desires of individual customers.

customization
The production of goods or services one at a time according to the specific needs or wants of individual customers.

job shop
A manufacturing firm that produces goods in response to customer orders.

Customization is the opposite of mass production. In customization, the firm produces goods one at a time according to the specific needs or wants of individual customers. Unlike mass customization, each product or service produced is unique. For example, a print shop may handle a variety of projects, including newsletters, brochures, stationery, and reports. Each print job varies in quantity, type of printing process, binding, color of ink, and type of paper. A manufacturing firm that produces goods in response to customer orders is called a **job shop.**

Some types of service businesses also deliver customized services. Doctors, for instance, usually must consider the individual illnesses and circumstances of each patient before developing a customized treatment plan. Real estate agents also develop a customized service plan for each customer based on the type of house the person is selling or wants to buy. The differences between mass production, mass customization, and customization are summarized in Exhibit 8-2.

In addition to production type, operations managers also classify production processes in two ways: (1) by how inputs are converted into outputs and (2) by the timing of the process.

Converting Inputs to Outputs Production involves converting inputs (raw materials, parts, human resources) into outputs (products or services). In a manufacturing company, the inputs, the production process, and the final outputs are usually obvious. Harley-Davidson, for instance, converts steel, rubber, paint, and other inputs into motorcycles. The production process in a service company involves a less obvious conversion. For example, HCA–The Health Care Company converts the knowledge and skills of its medical personnel, along with equipment and supplies from a variety of sources, into health care services for patients. Examples of the inputs and outputs used by other types of businesses are shown in Exhibit 8-3.

There are two basic processes for converting inputs into outputs. In **process manufacturing,** the basic input (raw materials, parts) is *broken down* into one or more outputs (products). For instance, bauxite (the input) is processed to extract aluminum (the output). The **assembly process** is just the opposite. The basic inputs, like parts, raw materials, or human resources, are either *combined* to create the output or *transformed* into the output. An airplane, for example, is created by assembling thousands of parts. Iron and other materials are combined and transformed by heat into steel. In services, customers may play a role in the transformation process. For example, a tax preparation service combines the knowledge of the tax preparer with the customer's information about personal finances in order to complete tax returns.

process manufacturing
A production process in which the basic input is *broken down* into one or more outputs (products).

assembly process
A production process in which the basic inputs are either *combined* to create the output or *transformed* into the output.

continuous process
A production process that uses long production runs lasting days, weeks, or months without equipment shutdowns; generally used for high-volume, low-variety products with standardized parts.

Production Timing A second consideration in choosing a production process is timing. A **continuous process** uses long production runs that may last days, weeks, or months without equipment shutdowns. It is best for high-volume, low-variety products with standardized parts, such as nails, glass, and paper.

exhibit 8-2 | Classification of Production Types

Mass Production	Mass Customization	Customization
Highly uniform products or services. Many products made sequentially.	Uniform and standardized production to a point, then unique features added to each product.	Each product or service produced according to individual customer requirements.
Examples: Breakfast cereals, soft drinks, and computer keyboards.	Examples: Dell computers, tract homes, and Taylor Made Golf clubs.	Examples: Custom homes, legal services, and haircuts.

exhibit 8-3 | Converting Inputs to Outputs

Type of Organization	Input	Output
Airline	Pilots, crew, flight attendants, reservations system, ticketing agents, customers, airplanes, fuel, maintenance crews, ground facilities	Movement of customers and freight
Grocery store	Merchandise, building, clerks, supervisors, store fixtures, shopping carts, customers	Groceries for customer sales
High school	Faculty, curriculum, buildings, classrooms, library, auditorium, gymnasium, students, staff, supplies	Graduates, public service
Manufacturer	Machinery, raw materials, plant, workers, managers	Finished products for consumers and other firms
Restaurant	Food, cooking equipment, serving personnel, chefs, dishwashers, host, patrons, furniture, fixtures	Meals for customers

Some services also use a continuous process. Your local electric company is one example. Per-unit costs are low and production is easy to schedule.

intermittent process

A production process that uses short production runs to make batches of different products; generally used for low-volume, high-variety products.

In an **intermittent process,** short production runs are used to make batches of different products. Machines are shut down to change them to make different products at different times. This process is best for low-volume, high-variety products such as those produced by mass customization or customization. Job shops are examples of firms using an intermittent process.

Although some service companies use continuous processes, most service firms rely on intermittent processes. For instance, a restaurant preparing gourmet meals, a physician performing physical examinations or surgical operations, and an advertising agency developing ad campaigns for business clients all customize their services to suit each customer. They use the intermittent process. Note that their "production runs" may be very short—one grilled salmon or one eye exam at a time.

Site Selection

One big decision that must be made early in production and operations planning is where to put the facility, be it a factory or a service office. Site selection affects operating costs, the price of the product or service, and the company's ability to compete. For instance, the costs of shipping raw materials and finished goods can be as much as 25 percent of a manufacturer's total cost. Locating a factory where these and other costs are as low as possible can make a major contribution to a firm's success. Mistakes made at this stage can be expensive. It is hard and costly to move a factory or service facility once production begins. Firms must weigh a number of factors to ensure that the right decision is made.

Ohio? France? Sri Lanka? Get a clear picture of what these and other business locations offer at the Economic Development Directory

http://www.ecodevdirectory.com

Availability of Production Inputs As we discussed earlier, organizations need certain resources in order to produce products and services for sale. Access to these resources, or inputs, is a huge consideration in site selection. For example, the availability and cost of labor are very important to both manufacturing and service businesses. Payroll costs can vary widely from one location to another because of differences in the cost of living, the number of jobs available, and the skills and productivity of the local workforce. The unionization of the local labor force is another point to consider in many industries. Low labor costs were one reason Honeywell, a U.S. manufacturer, chose Ireland as the site for a new factory. Ireland has a skilled workforce, but high unemployment rates in the country have kept the cost of labor down. Honeywell and other companies pay employees significantly less in salary and fringe benefits in Ireland than they do in the United States.[3]

Learn more about Honeywell's worldwide operations at

http://www.honeywell.com

Executives must also assess the availability of raw materials, parts, and equipment for each production site under consideration. It can be costly to ship these resources long distances so companies that use heavy or bulky raw materials may choose to be located near suppliers. Mining companies want to be near ore deposits, oil refiners near oil fields, paper mills near forests, and food processors near farms.

Marketing Factors Businesses must also evaluate how the location of their facility will affect their ability to serve their customers. For some firms, it may not be necessary to be located near customers. Instead, the firm will need to assess the difficulty and costs involved with distributing its goods to customers from the location chosen.

Other firms may find that locating near customers can provide marketing advantages. When a factory or service center is close to customers, the firm can often offer better service at a lower cost. Other firms may gain a competitive advantage by locating their facilities so that customers can easily buy their products or services. The location of competitors may also be a factor. Businesses with more than one facility may also need to consider how far to spread their locations in order to maximize market coverage.

Detroit, Michigan, is a world-class manufacturing city where a high percentage of the local workforce is employed by General Motors and other firms in the automotive industry.

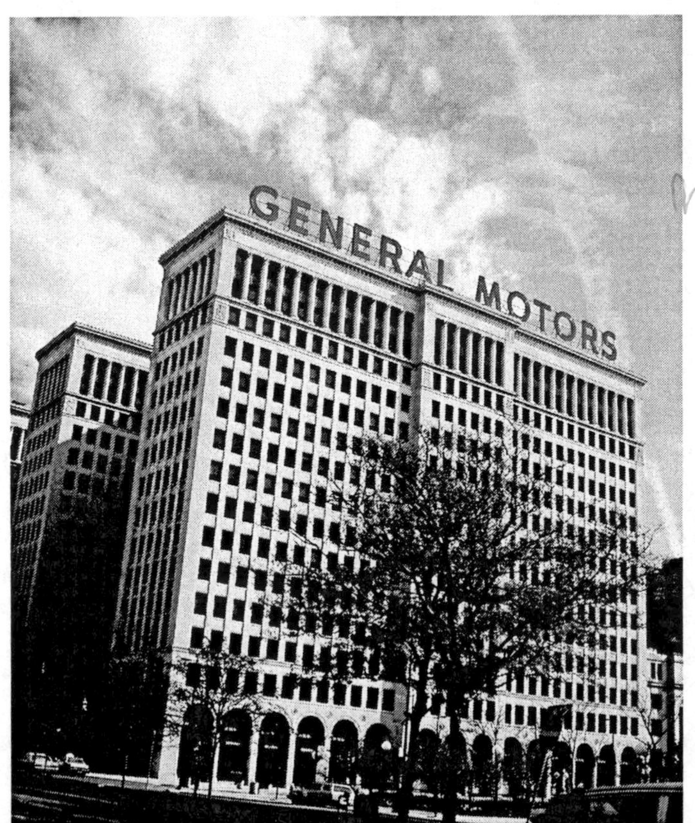

Local Incentives Incentives offered by countries, states, or cities may also influence site selection. Tax breaks are a common incentive. The locality may reduce the amount of taxes the firm will pay on income, real estate, utilities, or payroll. Tax incentives offered by state and city governments were a deciding factor in Mitsubishi's selection of Illinois as the site for its factory. For 13 years, Mitsubishi has enjoyed a 50 percent exemption from real estate taxes and receives a 50 percent rebate on its utility taxes.[4]

Other government incentives can also convince businesses to choose one location over another. Local governments sometimes offer exemption from certain regulations or financial assistance in order to attract or keep production facilities in their area. When financial services firm Fidelity Mutual was looking for a site for its administrative and customer service operations, the company chose Cincinnati, Ohio. Cincinnati officials gave the firm a tax break equal to about 5 percent of the firm's construction costs. The city also constructed a free highway to the new site and built a center at Northern Kentucky University. There, 200 students answer customer telephone inquiries for less pay than Fidelity's former telephone center employees.[5]

Manufacturing Environment Another factor to consider is the manufacturing environment in a potential location. Some localities have a strong existing manufacturing base. When a large number of manufacturers, perhaps in a certain industry, are already located in an area, that area is likely to offer greater availability of resources, such as manufacturing workers, better accessibility to suppliers and transportation, and other factors that can increase a plant's operating efficiency.

Every year, *Industry Week* evaluates the manufacturing climate of 315 U.S. cities. Each city is rated based on the productivity of its manufacturing sector, the percentage of the local workforce employed by manufacturing firms, the contribution of manufacturing to the area's overall economy, and several other factors. Though not necessarily the largest manufacturing cities in the United States, the top-ranked cities are considered "world-class" manufacturing cities by *Industry Week*. As Exhibit 8-4 shows, San Jose, California, and Houston, Texas, topped the most recent *Industry Week* survey.

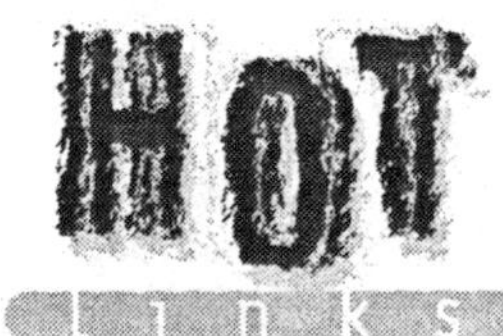

What characteristics make a city a world-class manufacturing site? Read the *Industry Week* articles at http://www.industryweek.com/iwinprint/communities

International Location Considerations In recent years, manufacturers in many industries have opened new production facilities outside the United States. There are often sound financial reasons for considering a foreign location. Labor costs are considerably lower in countries like Singapore, Ireland, and

exhibit 8-4 | Top 10 World-Class U.S. Manufacturing Cities

1. San Jose, California
2. Houston, Texas
3. Portland, Oregon
4. Dallas, Texas
5. Boston, Massachusetts
6. Chicago, Illinois
7. Austin, Texas
8. Los Angeles, California
9. Phoenix-Mesa, Arizona
10. Atlanta, Georgia

SOURCE: "The Atlas of U.S. Manufacturing," *Industry Week Special Report* (April 3, 2000), downloaded from *Industry Week* Web site, **http://www.industryweek.com**.

Mexico. Foreign countries may also have fewer regulations governing how factories operate. Or with a foreign location, production may be closer to new markets. That's exactly why Cabot Corp.'s Microelectronics Materials Division decided to open a plant in Japan. The company, which makes industrial slurries that are used to form computer chips, recognized a growing demand for its product in Asia. Opening a plant in Japan gave the company the ability to take advantage of this market growth.[6]

Facility Layout

After the site location decision has been made, the next focus in production planning is the facility's layout. Here, the goal is to determine the most efficient and effective design for the particular production process. A manufacturer might opt for a U-shaped production line, for example, rather than a long, straight one, to allow products and workers to move more quickly from one area to another.

Service organizations must also consider layout, but they are more concerned with how it affects customer behavior. It may be more convenient for a hospital to place its freight elevators in the center of the building, but doing so may block the flow of patients, visitors, and medical personnel between floors and departments.

There are three main types of facility layouts: process, product, and fixed-position layouts. All three layouts are illustrated in Exhibit 8-5.

process layout
A facility arrangement in which work flows according to the production process. All workers performing similar tasks are grouped together, and products pass from one workstation to another.

Process Layout The **process layout** arranges work flow around the production process. All workers performing similar tasks are grouped together. Products pass from one workstation to another (but not necessarily to every workstation). For example, all grinding would be done in one area, all assembling in another, and all inspection in yet another. The process layout is best for firms that produce small numbers of a wide variety of products, typically using general-purpose machines that can be changed rapidly to new operations for different product designs. For example, a manufacturer of custom machinery would use a process layout.

product (assembly-line) layout
A facility arrangement in which workstations or departments are arranged in a line with products moving along the line.

Product Layout The **product (or assembly-line) layout** is used for a continuous or repetitive production process. When large quantities of a product must be processed on an ongoing basis, the workstations or departments are arranged in a line with products moving along the line. Automobile and appliance manufacturers, as well as food-processing plants, usually use a product layout. Service companies may also use a product layout for routine processing operations. For example, overnight film processors use assembly-line techniques.

fixed-position layout
A facility arrangement in which the product stays in one place and workers and machinery move to it as needed.

Fixed-Position Layout Some products cannot be put on an assembly line or moved about in a plant. A **fixed-position layout** lets the product stay in one place while workers and machinery move to it as needed. Products that are impossible to move—ships, airplanes, and construction projects—are typically produced using a fixed-position layout. Limited space at the project site often means that parts of the product must be assembled at other sites, transported to the fixed site, and then assembled. The fixed-position layout is also common for on-site services like housecleaning services, pest control, and landscaping.

Resource Planning

As part of the production planning process, firms must ensure that the resources needed for production, such as raw materials, parts, and equipment, will be available at strategic moments in the production process. This can be a

exhibit 8-5 | Facility Layouts

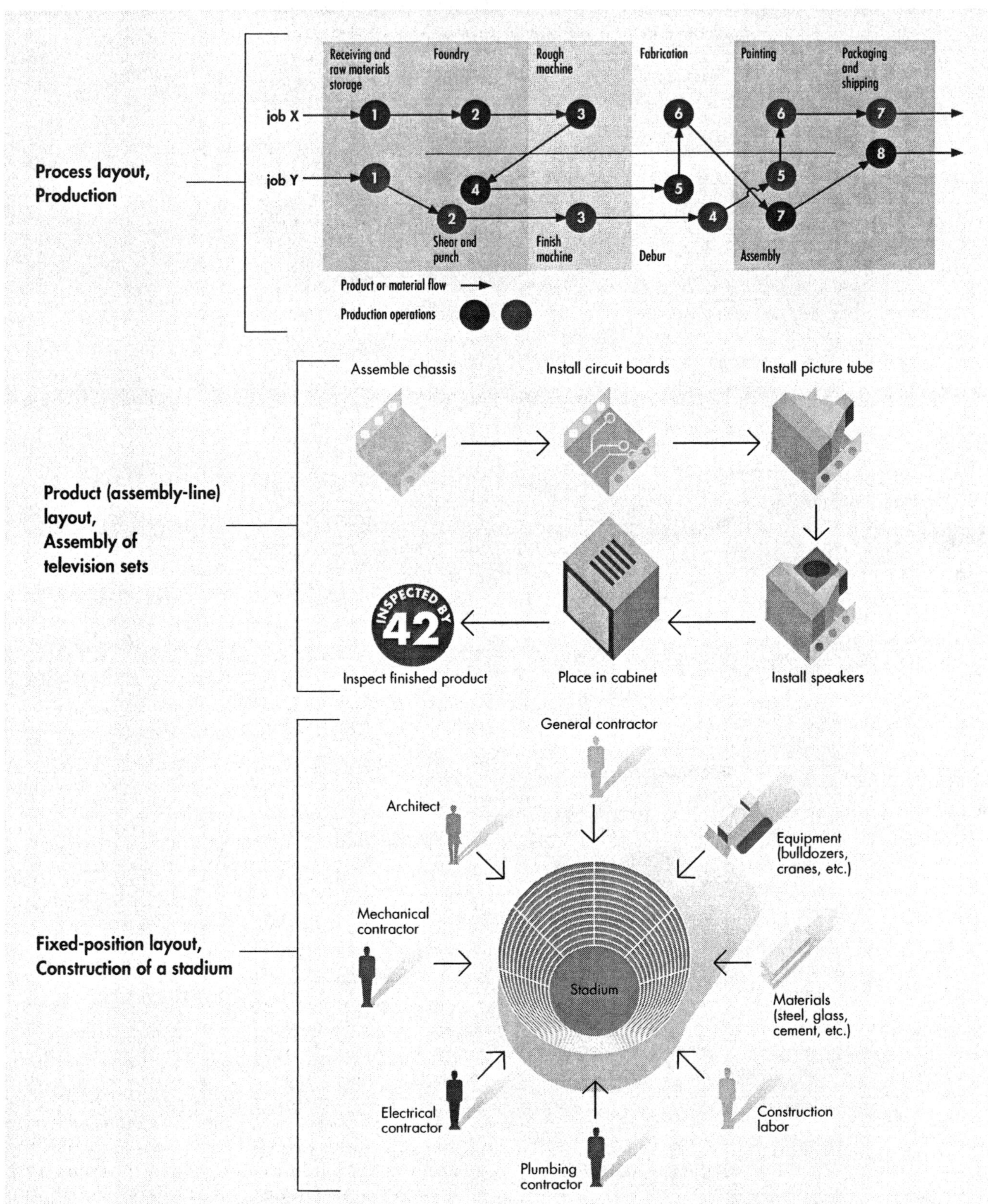

SOURCE: From *Production and Operations Management, 8th edition*, by Gaither/Frazier. © 1999. Reprinted with permission of South-Western College Publishing, a division of Thomson Learning. Fax 800-730-2215

MAKING ETHICAL CHOICES

TWISTING SUPPLIERS' ARMS

In recent years, General Motors (GM)—like some other companies—has been using aggressive tactics to wring concessions out of its suppliers in order to cut the costs of the parts going into the vehicles that it manufactures. Purchased materials represent 50 to 60 percent of a new automobile's cost. Consequently, cost concessions from suppliers can result in enormous savings for GM.

Since the early 1990s, GM has used tactics such as "tearing up contracts and running multiple rounds of bidding to grind down prices." Harold Kutner, vice-president and group executive in charge of GM's worldwide purchasing, defends these tactics. He does not apologize for GM's unrelenting efforts to cut costs. According to Kutner, if a supplier can provide units less expensively a year from now, then the supplier ought to be able to meet the lower cost now. "We're trying to drive tomorrow's savings into today's programs. Some suppliers can't do that, so they write a check to give us those savings." A few suppliers say that "this amounts to demanding a rebate in return for new contracts." Kutner says that GM does not require these payments. Yet he concedes that "we open the door to any scheming by suppliers to find cost savings."

Critical Thinking Questions

1. Is it ethical for a business to use "strong-arm" tactics to pressure its suppliers for concessions? Why or why not?
2. How might Kutner's attitude affect the propensity of GM's suppliers and employees to behave ethically or unethically?

huge challenge. The components used to build just one Boeing airplane, for instance, number in the millions. Cost is also an important factor. In many industries, the cost of materials and supplies used in the production process amounts to as much as half of sales revenues. Resource planning is therefore a big part of any firm's production strategy. The process of buying production inputs from various sources is called **purchasing,** or *procurement.*

purchasing
The process of buying production inputs from various sources; also called *procurement.*

bill of material
A list of the items and the number of each required to make a given product.

make-or-buy decision
The determination by a firm of whether to make its own production materials or buy them from outside sources.

Resource planning begins by specifying which raw materials, parts, and components will be required, and when, to produce finished goods. To determine the amount of each item needed, the expected quantity of finished goods to be produced must be forecast. A **bill of material** is then drawn up that lists the items and the number of each required to make the product.

Insourcing and Outsourcing Next, the firm must decide whether to make its own production materials or buy them from outside sources. This is the **make-or-buy decision.** The quantity of items needed is one consideration. If a part is used in only one of many products, buying the part may be more cost-effective than making it. Buying standard items, such as screws, bolts, rivets, and nails, is usually cheaper and easier than producing them internally. Sometimes purchasing larger components from another manufacturing firm is cost-effective as well. Purchasing items from an outside source instead of making them internally is called **outsourcing.** Harley-Davidson, for example, purchases its tires, brake systems, and other motorcycle components from other businesses that make them to Harley's specifications. If a product has special design features that need to be kept secret to protect a competitive advantage, however, a firm may decide to produce all parts internally.

outsourcing
The purchase of items from an outside source rather than making them internally.

In deciding whether to make or buy, a firm must also consider whether outside sources can provide high-quality supplies in a reliable manner. Having to shut down production because vital parts weren't delivered on time can be a costly disaster. For example, General Motors relies on hundreds of suppliers for parts. When workers in two of the plants that supplied parts went on strike, GM was forced to shut down virtually all of its North American production.[7] Just as bad are inferior parts or materials, which can damage a firm's reputation for producing high-quality goods. Therefore, firms that buy some or all of their production materials from outside sources need to pay close attention to building strong relationships with quality suppliers.

inventory
The supply of goods that a firm holds for use in production or for sale to customers.

Inventory Management A firm's **inventory** is the supply of goods it holds for use in production or for sale to customers. Deciding how much inventory to keep on hand is one of the biggest challenges facing operations managers. On the one hand, with large inventories, the firm can meet most production and customer demands. Buying in large quantities can also allow a company to take advantage of quantity discounts. On the other hand, large inventories can tie up the firm's money, are expensive to store, and can become obsolete.

inventory management
The determination of how much of each type of inventory a firm will keep on hand and the ordering, receiving, storing, and tracking of inventory.

Inventory management involves deciding how much of each type of inventory to keep on hand and the ordering, receiving, storing, and tracking of it. The goal of inventory management is to keep down the costs of ordering and holding inventories while maintaining enough on hand for production and sales. Good inventory management enhances product quality, makes operations more efficient, and increases profits. Poor inventory management can result in dissatisfied customers, financial difficulties, and even bankruptcy.

One way to determine the best inventory levels is to look at three costs: the cost of holding inventory, the cost of reordering frequently, and the cost of not keeping enough inventory on hand. Managers must measure all three costs and try to minimize them.

perpetual inventory
A continuously updated list of inventory levels, orders, sales, and receipts.

To control inventory levels, managers often track the use of certain inventory items. Most companies keep a **perpetual inventory,** a continuously updated list of inventory levels, orders, sales, and receipts, for all major items. Today, companies often use computers to track inventory levels, calculate order quantities, and issue purchase orders at the right times.

materials requirement planning (MRP)
A computerized system of controlling the flow of resources and inventory. A master schedule is used to ensure that the materials, labor, and equipment needed for production are at the right places in the right amounts at the right times.

Computerized Resource Planning Many manufacturing companies have adopted computerized systems to control the flow of resources and inventory. **Materials requirement planning (MRP)** is one such system. MRP uses a master schedule to ensure that the materials, labor, and equipment needed for production are at the right places in the right amounts at the right times. The schedule is based on forecasts of demand for the company's products. It says exactly what will be manufactured during the next few weeks or months and when the work will take place. Sophisticated computer programs coordinate all the elements of MRP. The computer comes up with materials requirements by comparing production needs to the materials the company already has on hand. Orders are placed so items will be on hand when they are needed for production. MRP helps ensure a smooth flow of finished products.

manufacturing resource planning II (MRPII)
A complex computerized system that integrates data from many departments to control the flow of resources and inventory.

Manufacturing resource planning II (MRPII) was developed in the late 1980s to expand on MRP. It uses a complex computerized system to integrate data from many departments, including finance, marketing, accounting, engineering, and manufacturing. MRPII can generate a production plan for the firm, as well as management reports, forecasts, and financial statements. The system lets managers make more accurate forecasts and assess the impact of production plans on profitability. If one department's plans change, the effects of these changes on other departments are transmitted throughout the company.

enterprise resource planning (ERP)
A computerized resource planning system that includes information about the firm's suppliers and customers as well as data generated internally.

Whereas MRP and MRPII systems are focused internally, **enterprise resource planning (ERP)** systems go a step further and incorporate information about the firm's suppliers and customers into the flow of data. ERP unites all of a firm's major departments into a single software program. For instance, production can call up sales information and know immediately how many units must be produced to meet customer orders. By providing information about the availability of resources, including both human resources and materials needed for production, the system allows for better cost control and eliminates production delays. The system automatically notes any changes, such as the closure of a plant for maintenance and repairs on a certain date or a supplier's inability to meet a delivery date, so that all functions can adjust accordingly. ERP is being used to improve operations not only in large corporations, such as Boeing, Lockheed Martin, and General Motors, but in small businesses as well, as the Focusing on Small Business box describes.

FOCUSING ON SMALL BUSINESS

PUTTING ANTHRO'S PRODUCTION TOGETHER WITH ERP

Anthro Corp. (**http://www.anthro.com**) executives are clear about their strategic goal. They want to be the McDonald's of the furniture industry. To get there, they know they must find a way to make producing custom office furniture as simple as turning out burgers.

In its plant in Tualatin, Oregon, Anthro's 65 employees make furniture to hold electronic gear like personal computers, medical instruments, and video equipment. Once customers place their orders over the phone, the manufacturing workers assemble prefabricated parts to each customer's specifications. Anthro promises to ship the finished furniture within 24 hours.

Anthro's problems began when sales took off. Suddenly, the company was struggling to keep up with the 30,000 different production orders that streamed in each year. Managing inventory also became more difficult. The plant sometimes ran out of critical items like castors just when workers needed them.

The solution? Anthro purchased an enterprise resource planning (ERP) system from software maker SAP. The $500,000 system runs on 30 PCs and links together everyone from senior executives to production workers. When a customer places an order, it is immediately entered into the ERP system, which automatically calculates the costs of producing the order.

At the same time, the system releases a production order to the factory floor that alerts workers to the details of the customer's order. The system also checks on-hand inventory. If a part needed for assembly isn't available, the system either sends a purchase order to Anthro's suppliers or tells assembly workers what needs to be done.

It took Anthro six months to implement the system, but company president Shoaib Tareen says he expects benefits like faster production times to continue for many years. "You have to have a long-term focus, because the advantage is, once you get it going, you can grow with it."

Critical Thinking Questions

1. How might the benefits from ERP affect Anthro's other functions such as marketing, human resources, or financial management?
2. Why do you think Anthro decided to install an ERP system instead of an MRP or MRPII system?
3. Do you agree with Anthro's president that the $500,000 investment in ERP was worthwhile? What other changes in production planning could the company have made to improve operating efficiency?

Supply Chain Management

In the past, the relationship between purchasers and suppliers was often competitive and antagonistic. Businesses used many suppliers and switched among them frequently. During contract negotiations, each side would try to get better terms at the expense of the other. Communication between purchasers and suppliers was often limited to purchase orders and billing statements.

supply chain
The entire sequence of securing inputs, producing goods, and delivering goods to customers.

Today, however, many firms are moving toward a new concept in supplier relationships. The emphasis is increasingly on developing a strong **supply chain.** The supply chain can be thought of as the entire sequence of securing inputs, producing goods, and delivering goods to customers. If any of the links in this process are weak, chances are customers—the end point of the supply chain—will end up dissatisfied.

supply chain management
The process of smoothing transitions along the supply chain so that the firm can satisfy its customers with quality products and services; focuses on developing tighter bonds with suppliers.

Strategies for Supply Chain Management Ensuring a strong supply chain requires that firms implement supply chain management strategies. **Supply chain management** focuses on smoothing transitions along the supply chain, with the ultimate goal of satisfying customers with quality products and services. A critical element of effective supply chain management is to develop tighter bonds with suppliers. In many cases, this means reducing the number of suppliers used and asking those suppliers to offer more services or better prices in return for an ongoing relationship. Instead of being viewed as "outsiders" in the production process, many suppliers are now playing an important role in supporting the operations of their customers. They are expected to meet higher quality standards, offer suggestions that can help reduce production costs, and even contribute to the design of new products.

One company that is seeking to forge stronger bonds with its suppliers is AMD. AMD manufactures integrated circuits that are used to build computers and communications equipment. The company has manufacturing facilities in the United States, Asia, and Europe and regards its suppliers as partners in the production process. Before a company can sell to AMD, it must pass a rigorous evaluation by AMD managers and executives. Each supplier must show that it is willing to match AMD's dedication to quality, reliability, service, and flexibility in meeting demand. Suppliers who meet AMD's requirements are rewarded with a long-term relationship with the company.[8]

Get a bird's eye view of AMD's manufacturing by viewing the quick-time video at
http://www.amd.com/video/manufac-qt.html

Improving Supplier Communications Underlying supply chain management is the development of strong communications with suppliers. Technology is providing new ways to do this. Some manufacturing firms are using the Internet to keep key suppliers informed about their requirements. Intel, for example, has set up a special Web site for its suppliers and potential suppliers. Would-be suppliers can visit the site to get information about doing business with Intel; once they are approved, they can access a secure area to make bids on Intel's current and future resource needs. The Internet also streamlines purchasing

Want to do business with Intel? Check out the company's supplier site at
http://supplier.intel.com

by providing firms with quick access to a huge database of information about the products and services of hundreds of potential suppliers. The number of businesses using the Internet to buy materials, supplies, and services is skyrocketing. According to industry analysts, business-to-business purchases over the Internet will grow from $20 billion in 2000 to over $13 trillion in 2004, an increase of 650 percent.[9]

Another communications tool is **electronic data interchange (EDI),** in which two trading partners exchange information electronically. EDI can be conducted via a linked computer system or over the Internet. The advantages of exchanging information with suppliers electronically include speed, accuracy, and lowered communication costs.

concept check

- What are the four main types of decisions that must be made in production planning, and what does each entail?
- Describe the various types of production processes and explain for what type of firm each is best suited.
- What factors does a firm consider when making a site selection decision?
- Describe the various types of facility layouts and explain for what type of production each is best suited.
- How is technology being used in resource planning?

PRODUCTION AND OPERATIONS CONTROL

>lg 5

Every company needs to have systems in place to see that production and operations are carried out as planned and to correct errors when they are not. The coordination of materials, equipment, and human resources to achieve production and operating efficiencies is called production control. Two of its key aspects are routing and scheduling.

electronic data interchange (EDI)
The electronic exchange of information between two trading partners.

Routing Production

Routing is the first step in controlling production. It sets out a work flow, that is, the sequence of machines and operations through which a product or service progresses from start to finish. Routing depends on the type of goods being produced and the facility layout. Good routing procedures increase productivity and cut unnecessary costs.

McDonald's is experimenting with new food preparation routes in many of its restaurants. The changes are part of McDonald's "Made For You" program, a strategic decision to offer customers more choices in how their orders are prepared. First, the restaurant chain redesigned its kitchens to improve the way orders are prepared and routed through the kitchen. New high-tech food preparation equipment that automates much of the order preparation process was added. Finally, a centralized computer system improved the flow of communications between the customer counter and the kitchen. When a customer orders a Big Mac, the order taker enters it into a specially designed cash register that simultaneously sends the information to a video screen in the kitchen. Before the customer has even finished paying, kitchen workers have almost a third of the order completed. Within a few moments, the order, including customizations such as extra ketchup or tomatoes, is on its way out to the customer.[10]

Redesigned food preparation routes and a computer system that links kitchen workers with order takers is helping McDonald's to serve customized food quickly.

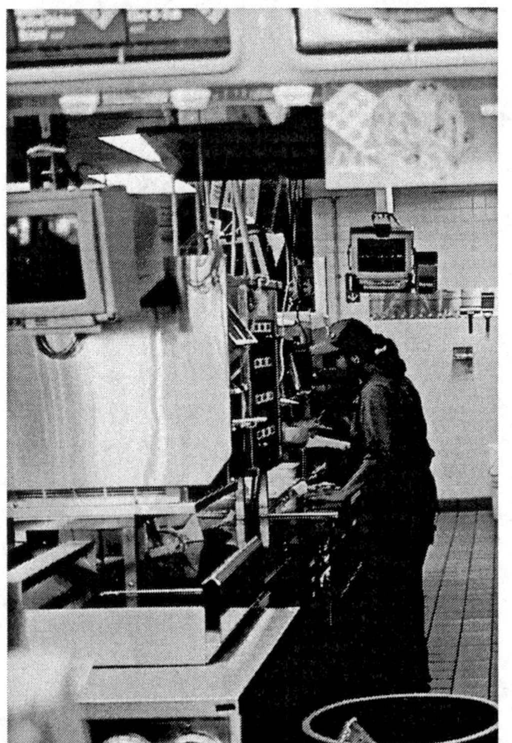

Scheduling

Closely related to routing is **scheduling.** Scheduling involves specifying and controlling the time required for each step in the production process. The operations manager prepares timetables showing the most efficient sequence of production and then tries to ensure that the necessary materials and labor are in the right place at the right time.

routing
The aspect of production control that involves setting out the work flow—the sequence of machines and operations through which the product or service progresses from start to finish.

scheduling
The aspect of production control that involves specifying and controlling the time required for each step in the production process.

Scheduling is important to both manufacturing and service firms. The production manager in a factory schedules material deliveries, work shifts, and production processes. Trucking companies schedule drivers, clerks, truck maintenance, and repair with customer transportation needs. Scheduling at a college entails deciding when to offer which courses in which classrooms with which instructors. A museum must schedule its special exhibits, ship the works to be displayed, market its services, and conduct educational programs and tours.

Scheduling can range from simple to complex. Giving numbers to customers waiting in a bakery and making interview appointments with job applicants are examples of simple scheduling. Organizations that must produce large quantities of products or services, or service a diverse customer base, face more complex scheduling problems.

Three common scheduling tools used for complex situations are Gantt charts, the critical path method, and PERT.

Gantt charts
Bar graphs plotted on a time line that show the relationship between scheduled and actual production.

Gantt Charts Named after their originator, Henry Gantt, **Gantt charts** are bar graphs plotted on a time line that show the relationship between scheduled and actual production. Exhibit 8-6 is an example. On the left, the chart lists the activities required to complete the job or project. Both the scheduled time and the actual time required for each activity are shown, so the manager can easily judge progress.

Gantt charts are most helpful when only a few tasks are involved, when task times are relatively long (days or weeks rather than hours), and when job routes are short and simple. One of the biggest shortcomings of Gantt charts is that they are static. They also fail to show how tasks are related. These problems can be solved, however, by using two other scheduling techniques, the critical path method and PERT.

exhibit 8-6 | A Typical Gantt Chart

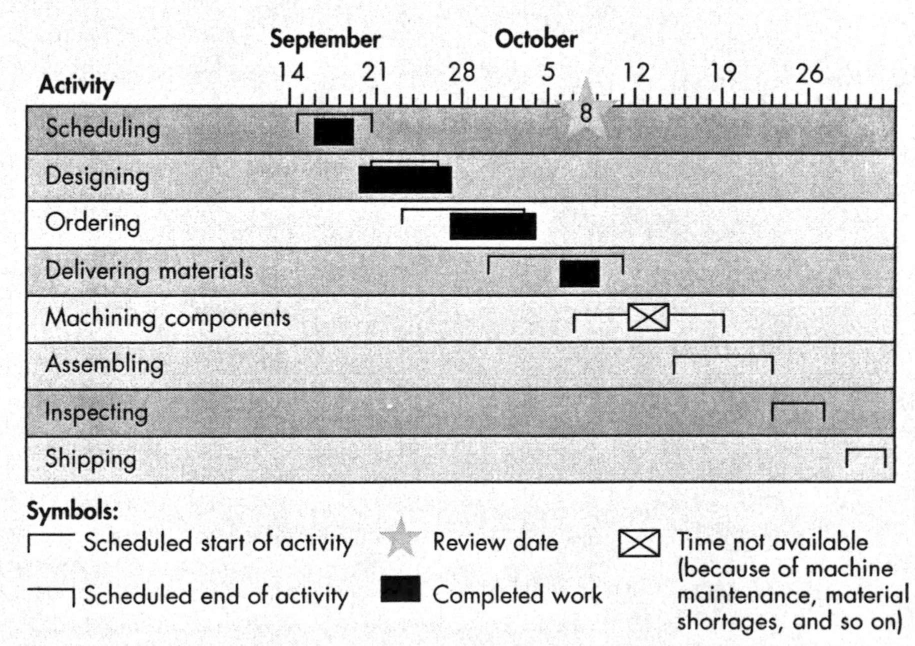

critical path method (CPM)
A scheduling tool that enables a manager to determine the critical path of activities for a project—the activities that will cause the entire project to fall behind schedule if they are not completed on time.

critical path
In a critical path method network, the longest path through the linked activities.

program evaluation and review technique (PERT)
A scheduling tool that is similar to the CPM method but assigns three time estimates for each activity (optimistic, most probable, and pessimistic); allows managers to anticipate delays and potential problems and schedule accordingly.

The Critical Path Method and PERT To control large projects, operations managers need to closely monitor resources, costs, quality, and budgets. They also must be able to see the "big picture"—the interrelationships of the many different tasks necessary to complete the project. Finally, they must be able to revise scheduling and divert resources quickly if any tasks fall behind schedule. The critical path method (CPM) and the program evaluation and review technique (PERT) are related project management tools that were developed in the 1950s to help managers accomplish this.

In the **critical path method (CPM)**, the manager identifies all of the activities required to complete the project, the relationships between these activities, and the order in which they need to be completed. Then, the manager develops a diagram that uses arrows to show how the tasks are dependent on each other. The longest path through these linked activities is called the **critical path.** If the tasks on the critical path are not completed on time, the entire project will fall behind schedule.

To better understand how CPM works, look at Exhibit 8-7, which shows a CPM diagram for constructing a house. All of the tasks required to finish the house and an estimated time for each have been identified. The arrows indicate the links between the various steps and their required sequence. As you can see, most of the jobs to be done can't be started until the house's foundation and frame are completed. It will take five days to finish the foundation and another seven days to erect the house frame. The activities linked by red arrows form the critical path for this project. It tells us that the fastest possible time the house can be built is 38 days, the total time needed for all of the critical path tasks. The noncritical path jobs, those connected with black arrows, can be delayed a bit or done early. Short delays in installing appliances or roofing won't delay construction of the house because these activities don't lie on the critical path.

Like CPM, **program evaluation and review technique (PERT)** helps managers identify critical tasks and assess how delays in certain activities will affect operations or production. In both methods, managers use diagrams to see how

exhibit 8-7 | A CPM Network for Building a House

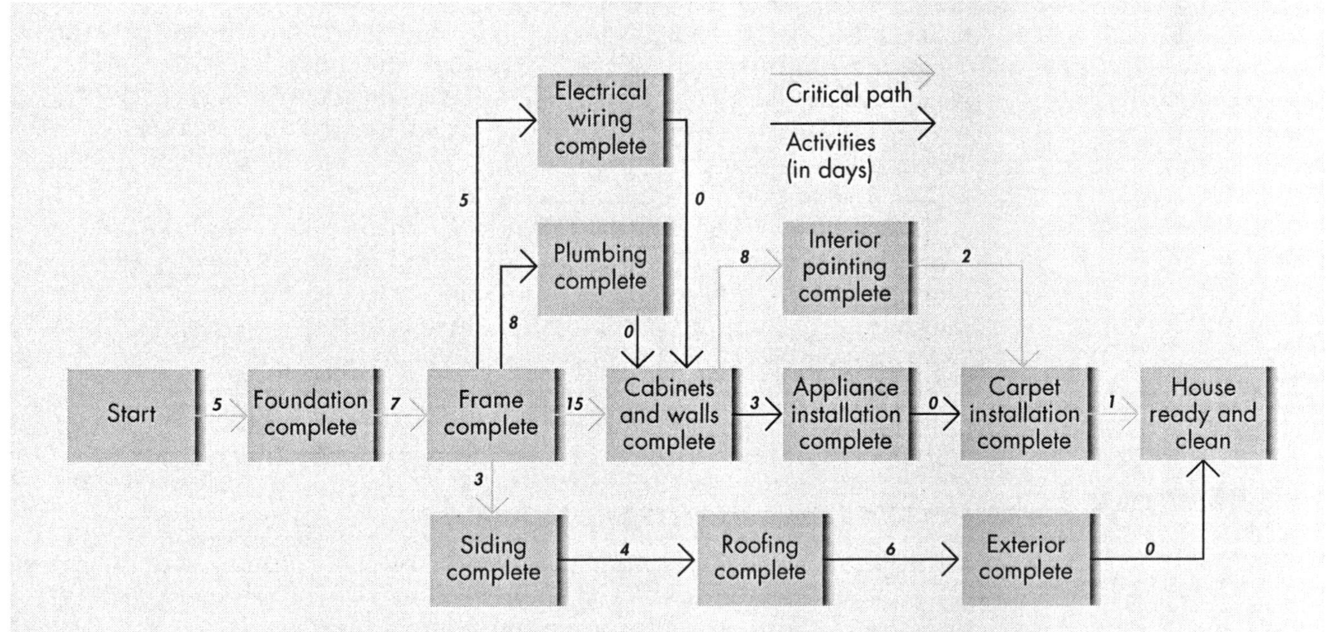

operations and production will flow. PERT differs from CPM in one important respect, however. CPM assumes that the amount of time needed to finish a task is known with certainty; therefore, the CPM diagram shows only one number for the time needed to complete each activity. In contrast, PERT assigns three time estimates for each activity: an optimistic time for completion, the most probable time, and a pessimistic time. These estimates allow managers to anticipate delays and potential problems and schedule accordingly.

concept check

- What is production control, and what are its key aspects?
- Identify and describe three commonly used scheduling tools.

IMPROVING PRODUCTION AND OPERATIONS

Competing in today's business world is difficult. The process of producing and delivering goods and services is becoming increasingly complex. Customers are demanding higher levels of quality and satisfaction. The lower production costs enjoyed by many foreign competitors can be difficult to compete against. In light of these challenges, businesses are continually looking for new ways to keep quality high, costs low, and production processes flowing smoothly. Among the methods that many companies have successfully implemented are total quality management, lean manufacturing, and automation.

Total Quality Management

Successful businesses recognize that quality and productivity must go hand in hand. Defective products waste materials and time, increasing costs. Worse, poor quality causes customer dissatisfaction, which usually means lost sales.

To a consumer, quality is how well a good serves its purpose. From the company's point of view, quality is the degree to which a good conforms to a set of predetermined standards. **Quality control** involves creating those quality standards and measuring finished products and services against them. Once quality control was simply a matter of inspecting products before they went out the door. Today, it's a company-wide commitment that involves every facet of operations.

quality control
The process of creating standards for quality and then measuring finished products and services against them.

One of the first to say that quality control should be a company-wide goal was an American, Dr. W. Edwards Deming. His ideas were adopted by the Japanese in the 1950s but largely ignored in the United States until the 1970s. Deming suggested that merely inspecting products after they are produced is not enough to ensure quality. He believed that quality control must start with top management, who must foster a culture dedicated to producing quality. Teamwork between managers and workers helps to identify ways to improve the production process, leading to better quality.

Total quality management (TQM) refers to the use of quality principles in all aspects of a company's production and operations. It emphasizes that all employees involved with bringing a product or service to customers—marketing, purchasing, accounting, shipping, manufacturing—contribute to its quality. TQM focuses on improving operations to achieve greater efficiency and, in turn, higher quality. Nearly every decision involved in production and operations management can affect a firm's ability to produce high-quality products and services.

total quality management (TQM)
The use of quality principles in all aspects of a company's production and operations.

The Move toward Lean Manufacturing

lean manufacturing
Streamlining production by eliminating steps in the production process that do not add benefits that customers are willing to pay for.

Manufacturers are discovering that they can better respond to rapidly changing customer demands, while keeping inventory and production costs down, by adopting lean manufacturing techniques. **Lean manufacturing** can be defined as streamlining production by eliminating steps in the production process that do not add benefits that customers are willing to pay for. In other words, non-value-added production processes are cut so that the company can concentrate its production and operations resources on items essential to satisfying customers. Toyota was a pioneer in developing these techniques, but today manufacturers in many industries have also adopted the lean manufacturing philosophy.

just-in-time (JIT)
A system in which materials arrive exactly when they are needed for production, rather than being stored on site.

Another Japanese concept, **just-in-time (JIT),** goes hand in hand with lean manufacturing. JIT is based on the belief that materials should arrive exactly when they are needed for production, rather than being stored on site. Relying closely on computerized systems such as MRP, MRPII, and ERP, manufacturers determine what parts will be needed and when, and then order them from suppliers so they arrive "just in time." Under the JIT system, inventory and products are "pulled" through the production process in response to customer demand. JIT requires close teamwork between vendors and production and purchasing personnel because any delay in deliveries of supplies could bring JIT production to a halt. If employed properly, however, a JIT system can greatly reduce inventory holding costs and can also smooth production highs and lows.

Automation in Productions and Operations Management

>lg 7

Technology is helping many firms improve their operating efficiency and ability to compete. Computer systems, in particular, are enabling manufacturers to automate factories in ways never before possible.

Consider how technology and automation have helped Winnebago. Plagued with production problems, the recreational-vehicle maker decided to use technology to streamline production and improve product quality. Since 1995, the company has spent approximately $5 million annually to automate its factory. Now a single worker is able to oversee the routing of panels needed to produce customized models with the touch of a button. A $400,000 computer tells the plant's production machines how to cut materials to fit the desired floor plan and accessories. Using computerized equipment, one worker can now do tasks that previously required several workers.[11]

Travel through Winnebago's production processes company info section at http://www.winnebagoind.com

Among the technologies helping to automate manufacturing are computer-aided design and manufacturing, robotics, flexible manufacturing systems, and computer-integrated manufacturing.

computer-aided design (CAD)
The use of computers to design and test new products and modify existing ones.

computer-aided manufacturing (CAM)
The use of computers to develop and control the production process.

CAD/CAM systems
Linked computer systems that combine the advantages of computer-aided design and computer-aided manufacturing. The system helps design the product, control the flow of resources, and operate the production process.

Computer-Aided Design and Manufacturing Systems Computers have transformed the design and manufacturing processes in many industries. In **computer-aided design (CAD),** computers are used to design and test new products and modify existing ones. Engineers use these systems to draw products and look at them from different angles. They can analyze the products, make changes, and test prototypes before making even one item. **Computer-aided manufacturing (CAM)** uses computers to develop and control the production process. The systems analyze the steps required to make the product. They then automatically send instructions to the machines that do the work. **CAD/CAM systems** combine the advantages of CAD and CAM by integrating design, testing, and manufacturing control into one linked computer system. The system helps design the product, control the flow of resources needed to produce the product, and operate the production process.

robotics
The technology involved in designing, constructing, and operating (computer-controlled machines that can perform tasks independently).

flexible manufacturing system (FMS)
A system that combines automated workstations with computer-controlled transportation devices—automatic guided vehicles (AGVs)—that move materials between workstations and into and out of the system.

computer-integrated manufacturing (CIM)
The combination of computerized manufacturing processes (like robots and flexible manufacturing systems) with other computerized systems that control design, inventory, production, and purchasing.

Automakers like General Motors have relied on CAD/CAM technology for some time. Using CAD/CAM systems, automotive designers are able to see a three-dimensional version of the car they are designing and make subtle adjustments to the design that can make a car model stand out in consumers' minds. The systems also detail and track all of the materials, parts, and processes necessary to move each car from the design stage to the showroom.[12]

Robotics *Robots* are computer-controlled machines that can perform tasks independently. **Robotics** is the technology involved in designing, constructing, and operating robots. The first robot, or "steel-collar worker," was used by General Motors in 1961.

Robots can be mobile or fixed in one place. Fixed robots have an arm that moves and does what the computer instructs. Some robots are quite simple, with limited movement for a few tasks such as cutting sheet metal and spot welding. Others are complex, with hands or grippers that can be programmed to perform a series of movements. Some robots are even equipped with sensing devices for sight and touch.

Robots usually operate with little or no human intervention. Replacing human effort with robots is most effective for tasks requiring accuracy, speed, or strength. Although manufacturers, such as Harley-Davidson as described at the beginning of this chapter, are most likely to use robots, some service firms are also finding them useful. Loyola University Medical Center in Maywood, Illinois, uses a $500,000 robot to sort and process hundreds of blood samples daily, freeing medical personnel from a tedious, and sometimes hazardous, repetitive task. The hospital estimates it saves about $200,000 a year in lab operating costs.[13]

Flexible Manufacturing Systems A relatively new way to automate a factory is to blend computers, robots, machine tools, and materials- and parts-handling machinery into a **flexible manufacturing system (FMS).** These systems combine automated workstations with computer-controlled transportation devices. Automatic guided vehicles (AGVs) move materials between workstations and into and out of the system.

Flexible manufacturing systems are expensive. Once in place, however, a system requires little labor to operate and provides consistent product quality. The system can be changed easily and inexpensively. FMS equipment can be programmed to perform one job and then quickly be reprogrammed to perform another. These systems work well when small batches of a variety of products are required or when each product is made to individual customer specifications.

With computer-aided design, engineers can design, analyze, modify, and test prototypes before products are manufactured.

Computer-Integrated Manufacturing **Computer-integrated manufacturing (CIM)** combines computerized manufacturing processes (like robots and FMS) with other computerized systems that control design, inventory, production, and purchasing. With CIM, when a part is redesigned in the CAD system, the changes are quickly transmitted both to the machines producing the part and to all other departments that need to know about and plan for the change.

Technology and Automation in Nonmanufacturing Operations

Manufacturers are not the only businesses benefiting from technology. Nonmanufacturing firms are also using automation to improve customer service and productivity. Banks now offer services to customers through automated teller machines (ATMs), via automated telephone systems, and even over the Internet. Retail stores of all kinds use point-of-sale (POS) terminals that track inventories, identify items that need to be reordered, and tell which products are selling well. Wal-Mart, the leader in retailing automation, has its own satellite system connecting POS terminals directly to its distribution centers and headquarters. As the Applying Technology box discusses, the restaurant industry is also streamlining operations with automation technology.

concept check

- Define total quality management, lean manufacturing, and just-in-time, and explain how each can help a firm improve its production and operations.
- How are both manufacturing and nonmanufacturing firms using technology and automation to improve operations?

APPLYING TECHNOLOGY

AUTOMATION SPEEDS UP FAST FOOD

Tired of long lines at fast-food restaurants? Chains like McDonald's, Arby's, and Burger King are hoping technology can put the "fast" back into fast food by automating many of the processes used in taking and preparing food orders.

You may have already noticed changes on drive-thru menu boards. McDonald's and Hardee's restaurants have rotating menu boards that automatically change according to the time of day. Pull up at breakfast and the board will show only breakfast items. Visit at lunchtime and you'll see lunch items. By limiting the choices displayed on the menu board, the restaurant makes it easier and quicker for customers to order. McDonald's and Burger King have also put special LCD screens at the drive-thru that show what you've ordered so you can instantly see if your order isn't right. Next innovation for the drive-thru? Face-to-face video technology that will let you see the face of the cashier (and let the cashier see you) as you're ordering.

Inside, fast-food restaurants are also changing. Most chains have high-tech point-of-sale (POS) computer systems. When you order at the counter, the clerk enters the information at the register, and it is automatically transmitted to the kitchen. These systems also let managers keep track of customer sales and operating efficiency. Soon, some fast-food chains will be adding self-service terminals so that you can punch in and pay for your order without waiting in line.

In the kitchen, technology is speeding up food preparation. FAST, Inc. (**http://www.fastinc.com**), a computer automation company, has developed the SMART Commercial Kitchen system, which links computer technology with the cooking controls of all the kitchen's appliances. The system automatically tells appliances such as ovens, fryers, and holding cabinets when to turn on, how long and at what temperature to cook, and when to turn off. Arby's has connected its SMART system to its POS system. When customer orders reach a certain level, the SMART system tells workers in the kitchen to put more beef in the ovens and then instantly sets the right cooking times.

Perhaps the most intriguing technologies on the horizon are automated handwashing systems. Spurred by recent incidents of food contamination, many chains are looking into equipping workers with electronic handwashing badges. The badges will beep at selected intervals to remind employees to wash their hands or change their gloves. They'll also keep track of whether the employee does as told—and report any handwashing deadbeats to the restaurant manager!

Critical Thinking Questions

1. How is automation likely to change customers' opinions of fast-food restaurants? Why?
2. Discuss the effect of automation and technology on the employees of fast-food restaurants.
3. Do you think some of the technology being used in fast-food restaurants would work for the cafeteria in your school? How about for an expensive steakhouse? Defend your answers.

CAPITALIZING ON TRENDS IN BUSINESS

>lg 8

The past decade has seen the U.S. economy grow at an unprecedented rate. Stock prices and corporate profits in many industries have soared, and unemployment and inflation have plummeted. Changes in production and operations management have made a huge contribution to this success and are likely to continue to propel productivity and economic growth in the new millennium.

Manufacturing continues to play a huge role in the U.S. economy. The 380,000 manufacturing firms in this country contributed $1.43 trillion to the national Gross Domestic Product (GDP) in 1998. While the economy grew as a whole by 29 percent between 1992 and 1999, manufacturing output grew 42 percent. Although the number of people employed by manufacturing firms declined in the 1980s, in the 1990s the number stabilized at about 18.5 million. The United States continues to have the most productive manufacturing workers in the world.[14] In order to maintain this level of productivity in the face of growing global competition, more complex products, and more demanding consumers, manufacturers are having to rethink how, when, and where they produce the goods they sell. New production techniques and manufacturing technologies are vital to keep production costs as low as possible and productivity high.

Nonmanufacturing firms also face operating challenges. Like manufacturers, they must keep up with the constant pace of change and carefully manage how they use and deploy resources. As the service sector grows, so do customer expectations about the speed and quality of service. This puts increased pressure on nonmanufacturing firms to be ever vigilant in their search for new ways of streamlining service production and operations. In this section, we will look at some of the trends likely to alter how companies manage and control the production of goods and services in the future.

Modular Production

The executives at Palm Computing knew they had a good idea: a small electronic personal organizer called the Pilot. They also knew that their competitive advantage would depend on getting the Pilot on the market as quickly as possible, a schedule that would be impossible to meet without help. The Pilot's designers wrote detailed specifications for how the product should be produced; then the company invited 3,500 other firms to create different parts of the product. Working together, Palm and its suppliers soon had the Pilot on the market. It became one of history's hottest products, selling more than 1 million units in its first 18 months.

Palm Computing's success highlights a growing trend in the business world, *modular production.* Modular production involves breaking a complex product, service, or process into smaller pieces that can be created independently and then combined quickly to make a whole. Modular production not only cuts the cost of developing and designing innovative products, but it also gives businesses a tool for meeting rapidly changing conditions. Modular production also makes it easier to implement mass customization or pure customization strategies. With access to a variety of components that can be assembled in different ways, endless combinations of product features are possible.

Agile Manufacturing

Another concept businesses are using to stay flexible and move fast is *agile manufacturing.* Investing millions of dollars in production processes, resources, and equipment that can be used only to produce one particular product doesn't always make economic sense. When customer demands shift or new technological innovations occur, the firm must be able to adapt. In agile manufacturing, firms strive to develop a production system comprised of flexible tools and processes that can be quickly changed to produce new or different products. Toyota uses agile manufacturing methods at its Kentucky plant. The factory builds both Camry and Avalon cars and the Siena minivans on the same assembly line. All three vehicles basically rely on the same underlying body platform. As the vehicles move through the plant, different components and parts are added depending on whether workers are producing a car or a minivan.[15]

Trends in Facility Layout

Work cell design, also sometimes called module design or cellular manufacturing, is an innovation that some manufacturers are finding can help improve quality and production efficiency. Work cells are small, self-contained production units that include several machines and workers arranged in a compact, sequential order. Each work cell performs all or most of the tasks necessary to complete either a product or a major production sequence. There are usually between 5 and 10 workers in a cell, and they are trained to be able to do any of the steps in the production process. The goal is to create a team environment where team members are involved in production from beginning to end.

Work cell design can have dramatic results. Berne Apparel, a maker of cotton coveralls and jackets, has been using the concept for more than a year. Workers in each group now work together to complete entire garments, rather than just parts of a garment. Because they can communicate with each other better and fill different production roles to get the job done, production time has been cut and quality improved. The company also has less employee turnover.[16]

concept check

- Explain modular production.
- How can agile manufacturing help a company obtain a competitive advantage?
- Explain how work cell design can help a company improve quality and efficiency.

APPLYING THIS CHAPTER'S TOPICS

As we've seen throughout this chapter, every organization produces something. Cereal manufacturers turn grains into breakfast foods. Law firms turn the skills and knowledge of attorneys into legal services. Retailers provide a convenient way for consumers to purchase a variety of goods. Colleges and universities convert students into educated individuals. Therefore, no matter what type of organization you end up working for in the future, you will be involved, to one degree or another, with your employer's production and operations processes.

In some jobs, such as plant manager and quality control manager, you will have a direct role in the production process. But employees of manufacturing firms are not the only ones involved with production. Software developers, bank tellers, medical personnel, magazine writers, and a host of other jobs are also actively involved in turning inputs into outputs. If you manage people in these types of jobs, you'll need insight into the tools used to plan, schedule, and control production processes. Understanding production processes, resource management, and techniques for increasing productivity is vital to be-

TRY IT NOW!

Track a Project with a Gantt Chart Your teacher has just announced a huge assignment, due in three weeks. Where do you start? How can you best organize your time? A Gantt chart can help you plan and schedule more effectively. First, break the assignment down into smaller tasks. Say, for instance, that you have a 10-page research paper due in three weeks. Your list of tasks would include picking a topic, researching information at the library and on the Internet, organizing your notes, developing an outline, and writing and proofreading the paper. Next, estimate how much time each task will take.

Try to be realistic. There's no sense saying it will only take you a day to write the paper when you know you have spent a week or more writing similar papers in the past. At the top of a piece of paper, list all of the days until the assignment is due. Along the side of the paper, list all of the tasks you've identified in the order they need to be done. Starting with the first task, block out the number of days you estimate each task will take. If you run out of days, you'll know you need to adjust how you've scheduled your time. If you know that you will not be able to work on some days, note them on the chart as well. Hang the chart where you can see it. Your Gantt chart will give you a visual tool for tracking your progress. Instead of worrying about the entire project all at once, you'll be able to see exactly what you should be doing on a particular day. The end result should be a terrific paper turned in on time!

coming a more valuable employee, who sees how his or her job fits into "the big picture" of the firm's operating goals.

Other professionals also need to understand production and operations management in order to help the firm reach its goals. Want to be a sales representative? An awareness of how, when, and where goods or services are made will help you better serve customer needs. Or, perhaps you plan to work in new product development. The best idea for a new product will fail if production cannot produce it in a timely, cost-effective manner. Human resource managers need to know the type of work operations personnel do in order to do a good job of recruiting and retaining employees. Financial personnel, such as accountants, also need to understand what goes on in production and operations. That knowledge helps them in budgeting, pricing products, and managing financial resources.

If you plan to start your own business, you'll also face many production and operations decisions. You can use the information from this chapter to help you find suppliers, design an operating facility (no matter how small), and put customer-satisfying processes in place. This information can also help you make decisions about whether to manufacture goods yourself or rely on outside contractors to handle production.

SUMMARY OF LEARNING GOALS

>lg 1 **Why is production and operations management important in both manufacturing and service firms?**

In the 1980s, many U.S. manufacturers lost customers to foreign competitors because their production and operations management systems did not support the high-quality, reasonably priced products consumers demanded. Service organizations also rely on effective operations management in order to satisfy consumers.

Operations managers, the personnel charged with managing and supervising the conversion of inputs into outputs, work closely with other functions in organizations to help ensure quality, customer satisfaction, and financial success.

>lg 2 What types of production processes are used by manufacturers and service firms?

Products are made using one of three types of production processes. In mass production, many identical goods are produced at once, keeping production costs low. Mass production, therefore, relies heavily on standardization, mechanization, and specialization. When mass customization is used, goods are produced using mass production techniques up to a point, after which the product or service is custom tailored to individual customers by adding special features. In general, mass customization is more expensive than mass production, but consumers are often willing to pay more for mass-customized products. When a firm's production process is built around customization, the firm makes many products one at a time according to the very specific needs or wants of individual customers.

>lg 3 How do organizations decide where to put their production facilities? What choices must be made in designing the facility?

Site selection affects operating costs, the price of the product or service, and the company's ability to compete. In choosing a production site, firms must weigh the availability of resources—raw materials, human resources, and even capital—needed for production, as well as the ability to serve customers and take advantage of marketing opportunities. Other factors include the availability of local incentives and the manufacturing environment. Once a site is selected, the firm must choose an appropriate design for the facility. The three main production facility designs are process, product, and fixed-position layouts.

>lg 4 Why are resource planning tasks like inventory management and supplier relations critical to production?

Production converts input resources, such as raw materials and labor, into outputs, finished products and services. Firms must ensure that the resources

>looking ahead

at Harley-Davidson

Harley-Davidson's Kansas City plant has helped rev up the company's sales and profits. The new plant is so efficient that when daily production was recently increased from 161 bikes a day to 180, the factory only needed to hire 11 new workers. The factory's quality is high, too. The number of parts or sections rejected because of poor quality is only 5 percent at the Kansas City plant, compared with 20 percent at Harley's other finishing plants. Thanks in part to the greater efficiency of the new plant, the company was able to manufacture 204,000 motorcycles in 2000, up from just 177,000 the previous year. "That means we will have accomplished our goal of producing 200,000 units per year by 2003 a full three years ahead of our original schedule," says CEO Bleustein. The company also exceeded its target for 2001 (233,000 units) by almost 10,000 units and has set a 2002 goal of 256,000 units.

Harley-Davidson continues to increase production while slashing costs by making an enormous investment in new technology. New computer systems in its factories automate how production and operations information is managed and used throughout the company.

The company has also launched a new computer system that has improved its relationships with suppliers. Since 1995, the company has cut the number of its suppliers from 1,000 to just over 400. The new system allows the company to order parts, components, and materials electronically and involves suppliers more closely in the design and development of new products.

Although some analysts criticize Harley-Davidson's slow and deliberate pace of incorporating technology and other changes into production, others are convinced that's the secret to the motorcycle manufacturer's growing profits and success. "This is a company that gets better every quarter," says one analyst. "There's nothing wrong with being an intelligent tortoise as opposed to a hare."[17]

KEY TERMS

assembly process 228
bill of material 234
CAD/CAM systems 242
computer-aided design (CAD) 242
computer-aided manufacturing (CAM) 242
computer-integrated manufacturing (CIM) 243
continuous process 228
critical path 240
critical path method (CPM) 240
customization 227
electronic data interchange (EDI) 238
enterprise resource planning (ERP) 236
fixed-position layout 232
flexible manufacturing system (FMS) 243
Gantt charts 239
intermittent process 229
inventory 235
inventory management 235
job shop 227
just-in-time (JIT) 242
lean manufacturing 241
make-or-buy decision 234
manufacturing resource planning II (MRPII) 235
mass customization 227
mass production 227
materials requirement planning (MRP) 235
operations management 225
outsourcing 234
perpetual inventory 235
process layout 232
process manufacturing 228

needed for production will be available at strategic moments in the production process. If they are not, productivity, customer satisfaction, and quality may suffer. Carefully managing inventory can help cut production costs while maintaining enough supply for production and sales. Through good relationships with suppliers, firms can get better prices, reliable resources, and support services that can improve production efficiency.

>lg 5 **How do operations managers schedule and control production?**
Routing is the first step in scheduling and controlling production. Routing analyzes the steps needed in production and sets out a work flow, the sequence of machines and operations through which a product or service progresses from start to finish. Good routing increases productivity and can eliminate unnecessary cost. Scheduling involves specifying and controlling the time and resources required for each step in the production process. It can range from simple to complex. Operations managers use three methods to schedule production: Gantt charts, the critical path method, and PERT.

>lg 6 **How can quality management and lean manufacturing techniques help firms improve production and operations management?**
Quality and productivity go hand in hand. Defective products waste materials and time, increasing costs. Poor quality also leads to dissatisfied customers. By implementing quality-control methods, firms often reduce these problems and streamline production. Lean manufacturing also helps streamline production by eliminating unnecessary steps in the production process. When activities that don't add value for customers are eliminated, manufacturers can respond to changing market conditions with greater flexibility and ease.

>lg 7 **What roles do technology and automation play in manufacturing and service industry operations management?**
Many firms are improving their operational efficiency by using technology to automate parts of production. Computer-aided design and manufacturing systems, for example, help design new products, control the flow of resources needed for production, and even operate much of the production process. By using robotics, human time and effort can be minimized. Robots are especially useful for tasks that require accuracy, speed, and strength. Factories are being automated by blending computers, robots, and machinery into flexible manufacturing systems that require less labor to operate. Service firms are automating operations too. Banks, law firms, and utility companies have used technology to cut labor costs and control quality.

>lg 8 **What key trends are affecting the way companies manage production and operations?**
Faced with growing global competition, increased product complexity, and more demanding consumers, manufacturers are rethinking how, when, and where they produce the goods they sell. Agile manufacturing is a concept that helps manufacturers stay fast and flexible. Firms strive to develop production systems composed of tools and processes that can be quickly changed to produce new or different products. Cellular manufacturing creates small, self-contained production units that include several machines and workers. Each work cell performs all or most of the tasks necessary to complete a product or production sequence. Because of these trends and the increased use of technology in production, firms are recognizing that smarter, better motivated workers are an asset. Both manufacturing and nonmanufacturing firms are therefore putting new emphasis on empowering employees—giving them greater say in deciding how their jobs should be done and a larger role in company decision making.

product (or assembly-line) layout 232
production 225
production planning 226
production process 227
program evaluation and review technique (PERT) 240
purchasing 234
quality control 241
robotics 243
routing 238
scheduling 238
supply chain 237
supply chain management 237
total quality management (TQM) 241

PREPARING FOR TOMORROW'S WORKPLACE

1. Reliance Systems, headquartered in Oklahoma City, is a manufacturer of computer keyboards. The company plans to build a new factory and hopes to find a location with access to low-cost but skilled workers, national and international transportation, and favorable government incentives. The company has zeroed in on three possible states for the site: Connecticut, Kentucky, and Louisiana. Divide the class into three groups. Assign one state to each of the three groups. The state groups should start at **http://www.ecodevdirectory.com** to find URLs for their statewide agency, and use that information to develop a case for that state. Each group will make a brief presentation on behalf of their state.
2. Tom Lawrence and Sally Zickle are co-owners of L-Z Marketing, an advertising agency. Last week, they landed a major aerospace manufacturer as a client. The company wants the agency to create its annual report. Tom, who develops the art for the agency, needs about a week to develop the preliminary report design, another two weeks to set the type, and three weeks to get the report printed. Sally writes the material for the report and doesn't need as much time: two days to meet with the client to review the company's financial information and about three weeks to write the report copy. Of course, Tom can't set type until Sally has finished writing the report. Sally will also need three days to proofread the report before it goes to the printer. Develop either a Gantt chart or a critical path diagram for Tom and Sally to use in scheduling the project. Explain why you chose the method you did. How long will it take Tom and Sally to finish the project if there are no unforeseen delays?
3. Look for ways that technology and automation are used at your school, in the local supermarket, and at your doctor's office. As a class, discuss how automation affects the service you receive from each of these organizations. Does one organization use any types of automation that might be effectively used by one of the others? Explain.
4. Pick a small business in your community. Make a list of the resources critical to the firm's production and operations. What would happen if the business suddenly couldn't acquire any of these resources? Divide the class into small groups and discuss strategies that small businesses can use to manage their supply chain.

WORKING THE NET

1. Go to **http://purchasing.miningco.com/msub-corp.htm.** Pick two or three of the companies listed and visit their supplier information Web sites. Compare the requirements the companies set for their suppliers. How do the requirements differ? How are they similar?
2. Manufacturers face many federal, state, and local regulations. Visit the National Association of Manufacturers at **http://www.nam.org.** Pick two or three of the legislative or regulatory issues discussed there and use a search engine like Yahoo! (**http://www.yahoo.com**) to find more information.
3. Using a search engine like Google (**http://www.google.com**) or Info Seek (**http://www.infoseek.com**), search for information about technologies like robotics, CAD/CAM systems, or ERP. Find at least three suppliers for one of these technologies. Visit their Web sites and discuss how their clients are using their products to automate production.

CREATIVE THINKING CASE

New Patterns for Jody B Fashions

Jody Branson is the owner of Jody B Fashions, a small manufacturer of women's dresses. Jody designs the dresses herself and personally orders fabrics, trims, and other materials needed for production from a number of different suppliers. Jody has a work crew of 40. Production begins when the fabric is cut using Jody's patterns. After cutting, the pieces for each dress style are placed into bundles, which are then moved through the factory from worker to worker. Each worker opens each bundle and does one assembly task, such as sewing on collars, hemming the dresses, or adding decorative items like appliqués and lace. Then the worker puts the bundle back together and passes it on to the next person in the production process. Finished dresses are pressed and packaged for shipment.

Things were running smoothly until recently when Jody sold her first big order to Kmart. Unlike the small boutique stores Jody usually sells to, Kmart wants to buy hundreds of dresses in different style and fabric combinations all at one time. If Kmart is pleased with this first order, chances are good it will give Jody a steady stream of future business. In the past, some of Jody's suppliers haven't sent their fabrics on time, so she has always ordered extra material to avoid shortages. She tried to do the same to prepare for the Kmart order, but her inventory room has become a disorganized nightmare. Jody had to shut down production twice this week because the workers who do the cutting couldn't find the fabric she had specified.

Jody knows she is beginning to fall behind on the Kmart order. She needs to cut the amount of time her workers take to finish each dress, but she doesn't want to sacrifice quality. Luckily, Jody has set aside some emergency capital that she can use to help solve this problem. She sees only three options:

- Hire additional workers for her production crew and hope to speed up production.
- Automate some of her production systems.
- Call Kmart's buyer and ask for an extension on the order delivery deadline.

Critical Thinking Questions

1. Evaluate Jody's production processes. Could she change them in any way to increase production?
2. Discuss the effectiveness of Jody's supply chain. Make recommendations for improvement.
3. Draw a diagram of how work flows through Jody's factory. Could Jody improve production by using a different layout? Draw a diagram of how this might look.
4. What do you think Jody should do? Are there any other options she could consider? Discuss whether each option is a short-term or long-term solution.

VIDEO CASE

The Vermont Teddy Bear Company

The Vermont Teddy Bear Co. (**http://www.vermontteddybear.com**) in Shelburne, Vermont, produces handcrafted teddy bears of such quality that each bear is guaranteed for life. Vermont Teddy Bears are targeted toward customers seeking quality, personalized gifts.

A Vermont Teddy Bear can easily be personalized for a specific occasion because the company produces a wide variety of teddy bears. There are numerous birthday teddy bears, get-well bears, new baby bears, "I love you" bears, summer bears, sports and hobby bears, holiday bears, graduation bears, bears for kids, occupation bears, and all-occasion bears. The occupation bears include a businessman and businesswoman, a doctor, a nurse, a teacher, and a police officer. The sports and hobby bears include a soccer bear, a golfer bear, a martial arts bear, a cheerleader bear, and a fitness bear.

A Vermont Teddy Bear can also be personalized with a creative card message of 35 words or less that accompanies the gift. To help customers who are at a loss for a personalized message, the company offers a variety of suggestions that can be used as is or adapted.

Another personalized service is the Bear-Gram delivery service, which is the company's core business. By calling 1-800-829-BEAR, a customer is assisted by a Bear Counselor sales agent to design a perfect gift for a special holiday, to commemorate a life event such as a birthday, an anniversary, or the birth of a new baby, or to wish someone well during a stay in the hospital. The added value to the Bear-Gram delivery service includes a Vermont Teddy Bear customized to fit the occasion, optional embroidery, a personalized greeting card, a colorful gift box equipped with an AirHole and B'Air Bag to ensure a safe journey, all delivered with a candy treat.

The Vermont Teddy Bear Co. strives to make the best teddy bears in the world by "combining unparalleled design innovation, unmatched product quality, and a passion for service."

Employees, who are viewed as internal customers, function in "a results-oriented environment that encourages fairness, collaboration, mutual respect, and pride" in the company. The company also engages vendors in a partnership focusing on innovative product development and unsurpassed customer service.

Critical Thinking Questions

1. What characteristics of the Vermont Teddy Bear Co.'s manufacturing operations point to the use of mass customization?
2. How does mass customization benefit the Vermont Teddy Bear Co.?
3. Why is quality control important for the Vermont Teddy Bear Co.?

Case: AviationX Prepares for Take-Off

The average commercial airplane is an engineering marvel, with more than 3 million parts. Unfortunately, keeping those 3 million parts in working order is a gigantic operational task. Airlines spend $32 billion each year just on the parts they need to keep their airplanes flying safely and on-time. Major U.S. carriers often issue 3,000 purchase orders a day and buy parts from more than 13,000 suppliers around the world. Because airlines often can't wait when a part is needed to repair a plane, they keep up to 300,000 spare parts in inventory at all times. One major carrier estimates its parts inventory is worth $1.5 billion.

Airlines have to be extremely careful about the parts they buy. One bad screw can lead to catastrophe if it causes a plane crash. Airlines also operate on a very thin profit margin. In order to attract customers, they have to keep ticket prices low and that means operating costs need to be cut or controlled whenever possible.

AviationX (**http://www.aviationx.com**), a small start-up in Arlington, Virginia, thinks the Internet can help. AviationX is planning to set up an e-commerce marketplace where airlines and suppliers can connect and do business. Instead of having to research the prices and availability of parts by phone, fax, or electronic data interchange, airlines will be able to sign on to AviationX's Web site and instantly find and order what is needed. AviationX says that the streamlined ordering process, combined with the ability to automatically compare the prices of different suppliers online, will save airlines at least 10 percent on every transaction, for an industry-wide savings of $300 million a year. To make money, AviationX will charge buyers a monthly fee and ask suppliers to pay a small commission on each sale.

AviationX isn't the only company planning to bring e-commerce to the airline industry. Several other small firms are launching their own online trading sites. Major parts manufacturers like Boeing and Airbus have also started their own e-commerce sites. Boeing's site handled $400 million in orders its first year.

In spite of these new sites, only about 3 percent of airline procurement is currently done through the Internet. Airlines aren't yet convinced of e-commerce's benefits. "We're entering an industry which, by nature, is rather prone to not making a change," admits Henrik Schroder, AviationX's CEO.

Questions for Critical Thinking

1. Evaluate the advantages and disadvantages for airlines if they buy parts through AviationX's e-commerce system. If you were in charge of purchasing for a major airline, would you sign up with AviationX? Why or why not?
2. Evaluate the advantages and disadvantages for suppliers and manufacturers if they sell parts through AviationX's e-commerce system. If you were a small manufacturer, would you sign up with AviationX? Why or why not?
3. What are the main challenges you see AviationX facing? Make suggestions for how the biggest challenges should be addressed.

SOURCES: Gregory Dalton, "Taxiing to the Net," *The Industry Standard* (February 28, 2000), downloaded from **http://www.thestandard.com**; Mickey Alam Khan, "iMarketing: AviationX Flies with Aerospace BTB Market," *dmnews.com* (March 7, 2000), downloaded from **http://www.dmnews.com**; Mark Roberti, "AviationX Charts Flight Plan," *InformationWeek Online* (March 27, 2000), downloaded from **http://www.informationweek.com**; "A New Kind of Hub: How B2B E-Marketplaces Will Revolutionize the Aviation Industry," AviationX company white paper, no date, downloaded from **http://www.aviationx.com**.

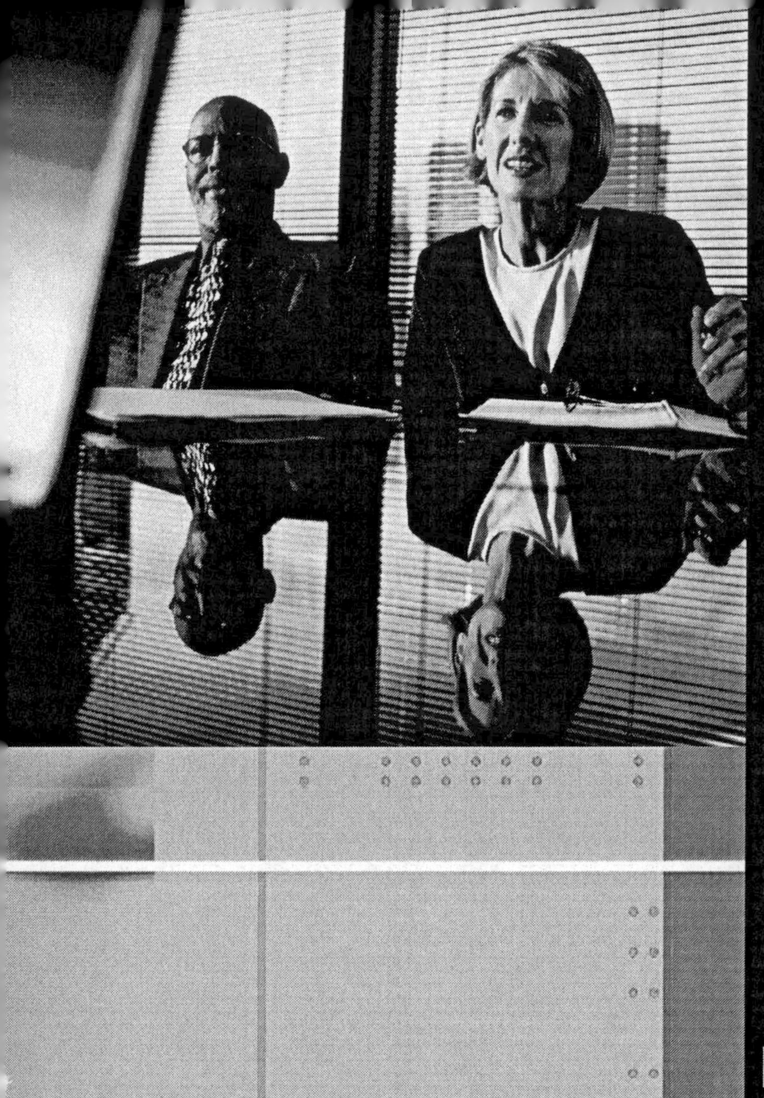

learning goals

>lg 1 How do finance and the financial manager affect the firm's overall strategy?

>lg 2 What types of short-term and long-term expenditures does a firm make?

>lg 3 What are the main sources and costs of unsecured and secured short-term financing?

>lg 4 What are the key differences between debt and equity, and the major types and features of long-term debt?

>lg 5 When and how do firms issue equity, and what are the costs?

>lg 6 How do securities markets help firms raise funding, and what securities trade in the capital markets?

>lg 7 What are the major U.S. securities exchanges and how are they regulated?

>lg 8 What are the current developments in financial management and the securities markets?

Financial Management and Securities Markets

11

Continental Airlines' New Routes to Profitability

What does it take to be a successful chief financial officer (CFO) today? CFOs are no longer behind-the-scenes players but key members of the executive team, setting the firm's overall strategy and participating in managerial activities that go well beyond traditional areas. Team building, strategic and operational planning, managing risks, selling and acquiring companies—it's all in a day's work for financial managers like Larry Kellner, executive vice president and CFO of Continental Airlines.

When Kellner took over the financial pilot's seat in 1995, the airline was about to crash into bankruptcy for the third time. At the end of 1994, Continental reported a net loss of $613 million, and its stock price was a mere $4.63 per share. The airline had very little credibility with investors and lenders: its debt amounted to more than $500 million, it owed $1 billion in overdue payments on leases from aircraft manufacturers, and it needed billions of dollars in additional financing to survive. "We had basically run out of cash," says Kellner.

Kellner and his financial staff set out to rebuild Continental's relationships with investors, analysts, banks, and trade creditors. They had to convince these key groups that the airline would not only take off but keep on flying this time.

The first step was to make sure Continental had the financial resources it needed to operate. Navigating through turbulent financial skies, Kellner negotiated with lenders and aircraft manufacturers to restructure high-interest debt on more favorable terms. From 1994 to 1998, annual interest expense dropped from $204 million to $64 million.

Kellner also tapped the securities markets to raise over $6 billion in new financing at advantageous rates and increase cash reserves to over $1 billion. As a result, Continental operated more efficiently and had the resources to weather a future economic downturn. By the end of 1999, the company's net income was $485 million, earnings per share were $6.66, and its stock was selling for about $44 in October 2000—quite a change from the situation when Kellner came on board.

Once the airline's financial house was in order, operational performance and customer service also improved. The airline had the resources to upgrade and expand its fleet, add services, and enter more international markets through partnerships with other airlines. Continental's reputation within the airline industry and the investment community soared. So did Kellner's; he was awarded a CFO Excellence Award from *CFO* magazine in 1998, 1999, and 2000.[1]

Critical Thinking Questions

As you read this chapter, consider the following questions as they relate to Continental Airlines:

- In addition to raising funds for Continental Airlines, what other types of financial activities would Larry Kellner oversee?
- Did Kellner's actions help to achieve the financial manager's primary goal of maximizing the value of the firm to its owners?
- Why is it important for financial managers to understand how securities markets operate?

BUSINESS IN THE 21ST CENTURY

In today's fast-paced global economy, managing a firm's finances is more complex than ever. For managers like Larry Kellner, a thorough command of traditional finance activities—financial planning, investing money, and raising funds—is only part of the job. Financial managers are more than number crunchers. As part of the top management team, chief financial officers (CFOs) need a broad understanding of their firm's business and industry, as well as leadership ability and creativity. They must never lose sight of the primary goal of the financial manager: to maximize the value of the firm to its owners.

Financial management—raising and spending a firm's money—is both a science and an art. The science part is analyzing numbers and flows of cash through the firm. The art is answering questions like these: Is the firm using its financial resources in the best way? Aside from costs, why choose a particular form of financing? How risky is each option?

This chapter focuses on the financial management of a firm and the securities markets in which firms raise funds. We'll start with an overview of the role of finance and of the financial manager in the firm's overall business strategy. Discussions of investment decisions and sources of short- and long-term financing follow. Next we'll examine the function, operation, and regulation of securities markets. Finally, we'll look at key trends affecting financial management and securities markets in the 21st century.

THE ROLE OF FINANCE AND THE FINANCIAL MANAGER

Finance is critical to the success of all companies. It may not be as visible as marketing or production, but management of a firm's finances is just as much a key to its success.

financial management
The art and science of managing a firm's money so that it can meet its goals.

Financial management—the art and science of managing a firm's money so it can meet its goals—is not just the responsibility of the finance department. All business decisions have financial consequences. Managers in all departments must work closely with financial personnel. If you are a sales representative, for example, the company's credit and collection policies will affect your ability to make sales.

Any company, whether it's a two-attorney law partnership or General Motors, needs money to operate. To make money, it must first spend money—on inventory and supplies, equipment and facilities, and employee wages and salaries.

When you come across a finance term you don't understand, visit the Hypertextual Finance Glossary at http://www.duke.edu/~charvey/Classes/wpg/glossary.htm.

Revenues from sales of the firm's products should be the chief source of funding. But money from sales doesn't always come in when it's needed to pay the bills. Financial managers must track how money is flowing into and out of the firm (see Exhibit 16-1). They work with the firm's other department managers to determine how available funds will be used and how much money is needed. Then they choose the best sources to obtain the required funding.

For example, a financial manager will track day-to-day operational data such as cash collec-

exhibit 16-1 | How Cash Flows through a Business

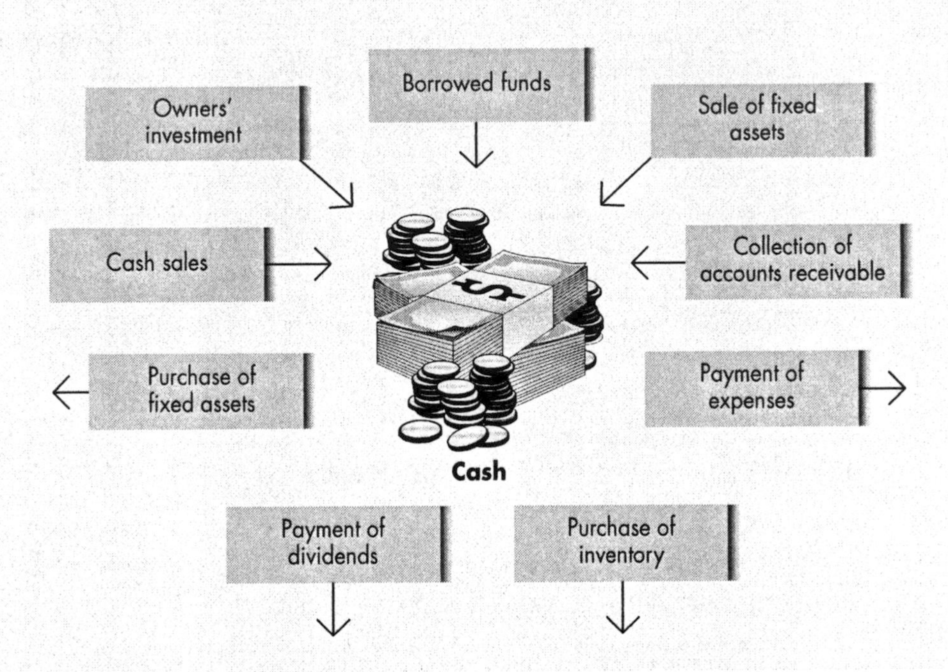

tions and disbursements to ensure that the company has enough cash to meet its obligations. Over a longer time horizon, the manager will thoroughly study whether and when the company should open a new manufacturing facility. The manager will also suggest the most appropriate way to finance the project, raise the funds, and then monitor the project's implementation and operation.

cash flows
The inflow and outflow of cash for a firm.

Financial management is closely related to accounting. In most firms both areas are the responsibility of the vice president of finance or the CFO. But accountants' main function is to collect and present financial data. Financial managers use financial statements and other information prepared by accountants to make financial decisions. Financial managers focus on **cash flows,** the inflow and outflow of cash. They plan and monitor the firm's cash flows to ensure that cash is available when needed.

Financial managers at Ford Motor Company plan and monitor cash flow to ensure that funds are available to finance the labor and material costs of producing vehicles.

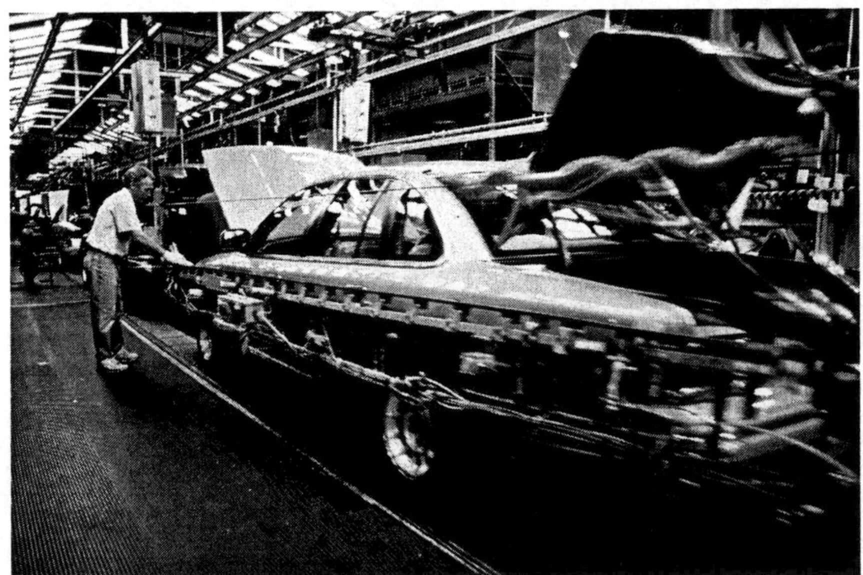

The Financial Manager's Responsibilities and Activities

Financial managers have a complex and challenging job. They analyze financial data prepared by accountants, monitor the firm's financial status, and prepare and implement financial plans. One day they may be developing a better way to automate cash collections,

What challenges do today's financial managers face? To find out, browse through recent issues of *CFO* magazine at http://www.cfo.com

the next they may be analyzing a proposed acquisition. The key activities of the financial manager are:

- *Financial planning.* Preparing the financial plan, which projects revenues, expenditures, and financing needs over a given period.
- *Investment (spending money).* Investing the firm's funds in projects and securities that provide high returns in relation to the risks.
- *Financing (raising money).* Obtaining funding for the firm's operations and investments and seeking the best balance between debt (borrowed funds) and equity (funds raised through the sale of ownership shares in the business).

The Goal of the Financial Manager

return
The opportunity for profit.

risk
The potential for loss or the chance that an investment will not achieve the expected level of return.

risk-return trade-off
A basic principle in finance that holds that the higher the risk, the greater the return that is required.

How can financial managers make wise planning, investment, and financing decisions? The main goal of the financial manager is *to maximize the value of the firm to its owners.* The value of a publicly owned corporation is measured by the share price of its stock. A private company's value is the price at which it could be sold.

To maximize the firm's value, the financial manager has to consider both short- and long-term consequences of the firm's actions. Maximizing profits is one approach, but it should not be the only one. Such an approach favors making short-term gains over achieving long-term goals. What if a firm in a highly technical and competitive industry did no research and development? In the short run, profits would be high because research and development is very expensive. But in the long run, the firm might lose its ability to compete because of its lack of new products.

Financial managers constantly strive for a balance between the opportunity for profit and the potential for loss. In finance, the opportunity for profit is termed **return;** the potential for loss, or the chance that an investment will not achieve the expected level of return, is **risk.** A basic principle in finance is that the higher the risk, the greater the return that is required. This widely accepted concept is called the **risk-return trade-off.** Financial managers consider many risk and return factors when making investment and financing decisions. Among them are changing patterns of market demand, interest rates, general economic conditions, market conditions, and social issues (such as environmental effects and equal employment opportunity policies).

concept check

- What is the role of financial management in a firm?
- How do the three key activities of the financial manager relate?
- What is the main goal of the financial manager? How does the risk-return trade-off relate to the financial manager's main goal?

HOW ORGANIZATIONS USE FUNDS

>lg 2

To grow and prosper, a firm must keep investing money in its operations. The financial manager decides how best to use the firm's money. Short-term expenses support the firm's day-to-day activities. For instance, athletic apparel maker Nike regularly spends money to buy such raw materials as leather and fabric and to pay employee salaries. Long-term expenses are typically for fixed assets. For Nike, these would include outlays to build a new factory, buy automated manufacturing equipment, or acquire a small manufacturer of sports apparel.

Short-Term Expenses

Short-term expenses, often called *operating expenses,* are outlays used to support current production and selling activities. They typically result in current assets, which include cash and any other assets (accounts receivable and inventory) that can be converted to cash within a year. The financial manager's goal is to manage current assets so the firm has enough cash to pay its bills and to support its accounts receivable and inventory.

Cash Management: Assuring Liquidity Cash is the lifeblood of business. Without it, a firm could not operate. An important duty of the financial manager is **cash management,** or making sure that enough cash is on hand to pay bills as they come due and to meet unexpected expenses.

cash management
The process of making sure that a firm has enough cash on hand to pay bills as they come due and to meet unexpected expenses.

Businesses estimate the cash requirements for a specific period. Many companies keep a minimum cash balance to cover unexpected expenses or changes in projected cash flows. The financial manager arranges loans to cover any shortfalls. If the size and timing of cash inflows closely match the size and timing of cash outflows, the company needs to keep only a small amount of cash on hand. A company whose sales and receipts are fairly predictable and regular throughout the year needs less cash than a company with a seasonal pattern of sales and receipts. A toy company, for instance, whose sales are concentrated in the fall, spends a great deal of cash during the spring and summer to build inventory. It has excess cash during the winter and early spring, when it collects on sales from its peak selling season.

Because cash held in checking accounts earns little, if any, interest, the financial manager tries to keep cash balances low and to invest the surplus cash. Surpluses are invested temporarily in **marketable securities,** short-term investments that are easily converted into cash. The financial manager looks for low-risk investments that offer high returns. Three of the most popular marketable securities are Treasury bills, certificates of deposit, and commercial paper. (**Commercial paper** is unsecured short-term debt—an IOU—issued by a financially strong corporation.)

marketable securities
Short-term investments that are easily converted into cash.

commercial paper
Unsecured short-term debt (an IOU) issued by a financially strong corporation.

In addition to seeking the right balance between cash and marketable securities, the financial manager tries to shorten the time between the purchase of inventory or services (cash outflows) and the collection of cash from sales (cash inflows). The three key strategies are to collect money owed to the firm (accounts receivable) as quickly as possible, to pay money owed to others (accounts payable) as late as possible without damaging the firm's credit reputation, and to minimize the funds tied up in inventory.

Find an introduction to the types of cash management services banks offer their customers at Centura Bank's site

http://www.centura.com/business/cash_management/indx.cfm

Managing Accounts Receivable **Accounts receivable** represent sales for which the firm has not yet been paid. Because the product has been sold but cash has not yet been received, an account receivable amounts to a use of funds. For the average manufacturing firm, accounts receivable represent about 15 to 20 percent of total assets.

accounts receivable
Sales for which a firm has not yet been paid.

The financial manager's goal is to collect money owed to the firm as quickly as possible—while offering customers credit terms attractive enough to increase sales. Accounts receivable management involves setting *credit policies,* guidelines on offering credit, and *credit terms,* specific repayment conditions, including how long customers have to pay their bills and whether a cash discount is given for quicker payment. Another aspect of accounts receivable management is deciding on *collection policies,* the procedures for collecting overdue accounts.

Setting up credit and collection policies is a balancing act for financial managers. On the one hand, easier credit policies or generous credit terms (a longer repayment period or larger cash discount) result in increased sales. On the other hand, the firm has to finance more accounts receivable. The risk of uncollectible accounts receivable also rises.

Technology can also help firms speed up collections. To cope with the meteoric rise in sales and, hence, accounts receivable, Dell Computer implemented an automated receivables collection system. Customized software improved order processing and collection methods. The new system also took over labor-intensive tasks such as sending letters to overdue accounts at specified times and creating activity reports with current account status. Dell's days receivables outstanding dropped from 50 to 37 days, freeing up a significant amount of cash.[2]

Inventory In a typical manufacturing firm, inventory is nearly 20 percent of total assets. The cost of inventory includes not only its purchase price, but also ordering, handling, storage, interest, and insurance costs. Financial managers must work closely with production and marketing managers to minimize the amount of inventory the firm carries without harming production efficiency or sales. Techniques for reducing the investment in inventory—efficient order quantities, the just-in-time system, and materials requirement planning—were described in Chapter 8.

Long-Term Expenditures

capital expenditures
Investments in long-lived assets, such as land, buildings, machinery, and equipment, that are expected to provide benefits over a period longer than one year.

capital budgeting
The process of analyzing long-term projects and selecting those that offer the best returns while maximizing the firm's value.

A firm also uses funds for its investments in long-lived assets, such items as land, buildings, machinery, and equipment. These are called **capital expenditures.** Unlike operating expenses, which produce benefits within a year, the benefits from capital expenditures extend beyond one year. For instance, a printer's purchase of a new printing press with a usable life of seven years is a capital expenditure. It appears as a fixed asset on the firm's balance sheet. Paper, ink, and other supplies, however, are expenses. Mergers and acquisitions, discussed in Chapter 4, are also considered capital expenditures.

Firms make capital expenditures for many reasons. The most common are to expand and to replace or renew fixed assets. Another reason is to develop new products. Most manufacturing firms have a big investment in long-term assets. Boeing Co., for instance, puts millions of dollars a year into airplane-manufacturing facilities.

Because capital expenditures tend to be costly and have a major effect on the firm's future, the financial manager must analyze long-term projects and select those that offer the best returns while maximizing the firm's value. This process is called **capital budgeting.** Decisions involving new products or the acquisition of another business are especially important. Another challenge managers face is assessing the value of proposed information technology expenditures, as the Applying Technology box demonstrates.

concept check

- Distinguish between short- and long-term expenses.
- What is the financial manager's goal in cash management? List the three key cash management strategies.
- Describe the firm's main motives in making capital expenditures.

OBTAINING SHORT-TERM FINANCING

>lg 3

How do firms raise the funding they need? They borrow money (debt), sell ownership shares (equity), and retain earnings (profits). The financial manager must assess all these sources and choose the one most likely to help maximize the firm's value.

Like expenses, borrowed funds can be divided into short- and long-term loans. A short-term loan comes due within one year; a long-term loan has a maturity greater than a year. Short-term financing is shown as a current liability on the balance sheet. It is used to finance current assets and support operations. Short-term loans can be unsecured or secured.

APPLYING TECHNOLOGY

NET PAYOFFS

Do investments in the latest technology pay off? So far, the results are mixed. According to International Data Corp., a major information technology research firm, through 1998 companies received only $1.00 back for every $1.50 they invested.

One exception to this rule is Loanshop.com, the first online mortgage company. Profitability in this high-volume business depends on a company's ability to generate high-quality loan transactions at the lowest possible cost.

The company gets over half of its customer communications via e-mail, and quick response was the key to converting leads to sales. The conversion rate was greatest for replies within an hour of receipt and then dropped quickly, to less than 1 percent after 24 hours. Unless Loanshop could quickly separate incoming e-mail according to priority, it would miss promising sales opportunities.

Loanshop.com had two options to speed up the process of separating serious leads from routine questions: hire more staff or invest in special software to filter e-mail and route high-priority inquiries to mortgage counselors. But what were the relevant financial, operating, or process measurements that showed whether the new technology added value? While many of its rivals focused on the number of visitors to the Web site, Loanshop.com president Jack Rodgers disagreed: "It's a meaningless number if no one buys our product."

Loanshop.com's managers knew that one person could process 100 e-mail messages in an eight-hour day. The e-mail automation system could perform this task in just 15 minutes—a 96 percent reduction. Armed with these data, managers performed a capital budgeting analysis and determined that the technology solution was the better choice.

The new software acts as the company's inbound e-mail telemarketing agent. It filters e-mail, answers routine inquiries, and sends loan requests directly to loan counselors. It also can forward completed loan applications to the Federal National Mortgage Association's automated underwriting system. The results speak for themselves: Loanshop.com doubled its mortgage counselors' sales, reduced the number of employees handling e-mail by over one-third, and earned a 40 percent return on investment in 14 months. Customers are happy, too: they learn whether they qualify for a loan in five minutes and save an average of $1,500 in administrative costs.

Critical Thinking Questions

1. Describe the steps a company should take to evaluate a proposed investment in new information technology equipment.
2. What measures and performance outcomes were relevant for Loanshop.com's capital budgeting decision?
3. What mistakes could a company make by investing in new technology? How did Loanshop.com avoid them?

Unsecured Short-Term Loans

unsecured loans
Short-term loans for which the borrower does not have to pledge specific assets as security.

Unsecured loans are made on the basis of the firm's creditworthiness and the lender's previous experience with the firm. An unsecured borrower does not have to pledge specific assets as security. The three main types of unsecured short-term loans are trade credit, bank loans, and commercial paper.

trade credit
The extension of credit by the seller to the buyer between the time the buyer receives the goods or services and when it pays for them.

accounts payable
Purchase for which a buyer has not yet paid the seller.

Trade Credit: Accounts Payable When Goodyear sells tires to General Motors, GM does not have to pay cash on delivery. Instead, Goodyear regularly bills GM for its tire purchases, and GM pays at a later date. This is an example of **trade credit**—the seller extends credit to the buyer between the time the buyer receives the goods or services and when it pays for them. Trade credit is a major source of short-term business financing. The buyer enters the credit on its books as an **account payable.** In effect, the credit is a short-term loan from the seller to the buyer of the goods and services. Until GM pays

Goodyear, Goodyear has an account receivable from GM—and GM has an account payable to Goodyear.

Bank Loans Unsecured bank loans are another source of short-term business financing. Companies often use these loans to finance seasonal (cyclical) businesses. Unsecured bank loans include lines of credit and revolving credit agreements. A **line of credit** specifies the maximum amount of unsecured short-term borrowing the bank will allow the firm over a given period, typically one year. The firm either pays a fee or keeps a certain percentage of the loan amount (10 to 20 percent) in a checking account at the bank. Another bank loan, the **revolving credit agreement,** is basically a guaranteed line of credit that carries an extra fee in addition to interest. Revolving credit agreements are often arranged for a two- to five-year period.

line of credit
An agreement between a bank and a business that specifies the maximum amount of unsecured short-term borrowing the bank will allow the firm over a given period, typically one year.

revolving credit agreement
A guaranteed line of credit whereby a bank agrees that a certain amount of funds will be available for a business to borrow over a given period.

Commercial Paper Financially strong major corporations issue commercial paper in multiples of $100,000 for periods ranging from 30 to 270 days. Many big companies use commercial paper instead of short-term bank loans because the interest rate on commercial paper is usually 1 to 3 percent below bank rates.

BetzDearborn, a Pennsylvania manufacturer of water treatment chemicals, saved $800,000 a year by replacing a portion of its short-term financing with a $500 million commercial paper program.[3]

Secured Short-Term Loans

Secured loans require the borrower to pledge specific assets as *collateral,* or security. The secured lender can legally take the collateral if the borrower doesn't repay the loan. Commercial banks and commercial finance companies are the main sources of secured short-term loans to business. Borrowers whose credit is not strong enough to qualify for unsecured loans use these loans.

secured loans
Loans for which the borrower is required to pledge specific assets as collateral, or security.

factoring
A form of short-term financing in which a firm sells its accounts receivable outright at a discount to a *factor.*

Typically, the collateral for secured short-term loans is accounts receivable or inventory. Because accounts receivable are normally quite liquid (easily converted to cash), they are an attractive form of collateral. The appeal of inventory—raw materials or finished goods—as collateral depends on how easily it can be sold at a fair price.

Another form of short-term financing using accounts receivable is **factoring.** A firm sells its accounts receivable outright to a *factor,* a financial institution (usually a commercial bank or commercial finance company) that buys accounts receivable at a discount. Factoring is widely used in the clothing, furniture, and appliance industries. Factoring is more expensive than a bank loan, however, because the factor buys the receivables at a discount from their actual value.

Learn about the services and current rates offered by 21st Capital Corp., a factoring firm, at http://www.21stcapital.com.

concept check

- Distinguish between unsecured and secured short-term loans.
- Briefly describe the three main types of unsecured short-term loans.
- Discuss the two ways that accounts receivable can be used to obtain short-term financing.

RAISING LONG-TERM FINANCING

>lg 4

A basic principle of finance is to match the term of the financing to the period over which benefits are expected to be received from the associated outlay. Short-term expenses should be financed with short-term funds, and long-term expenses should be financed with long-term funds. Long-term financing sources include both debt (borrowing) and equity (ownership). Equity financing comes either from selling new ownership interests or from retaining earnings.

MAKING ETHICAL CHOICES

SHAKY FINANCIAL MANAGEMENT

Paul Nussbaum assembled a $7 billion hotel empire in less than three years when he was CEO of Patriot American Hospitality, Inc. Patriot acquired a 450-hotel portfolio that included boutique hotels in England and the Wyndham Hotels chain in the United States, among others.

Patriot's buying spree was financed with large amounts of short-term debt and financial instruments called equity forward contracts, which were to be repaid in the future with Patriot stock. "The contracts were, in essence, a huge bet that Patriot's stock price would climb." If the stock price rose, Patriot would be able to pay off the equity forward contracts with fewer shares. If the stock price fell, more shares would be required to pay off the contracts.

Patriot's stock price declined during most of 1998, compromising the company's financial stability. Moreover, the company was forced to issue additional shares of common stock to cover its equity forward contracts, thereby "diluting its existing pool of stock and pushing its share price into a potentially fatal nose dive."

Patriot's financial position was further compromised by its load of short-term debt. Hundreds of millions of dollars of short-term debt were due in the first quarter of 1999. Nussbaum had planned to pay off that debt by selling long-term debt to investors, but because of the credit crunch set off by Russia's debt default, Patriot was unable to float its bond offering.

Patriot was hurt by other events as well. Nussbaum never established effective financial controls. Appropriate financial oversight was lacking for several months due to conflicts among the firm's key financial managers and the voluntary departure of the person who shared the chief financial officer's duties. Nussbaum also "lost credibility on Wall Street when the company repeatedly failed to meet earnings targets."

Critical Thinking Questions

1. Does Patriot's financial situation reflect questionable business ethics, or is it simply a case of poor management or unfortunate circumstances?
2. Is it unethical for a business firm to assume a high level of risk in its financial management?
3. Do publicly traded business firms have an ethical responsibility to their investors? Why or why not?

Debt versus Equity Financing

Say that the Boeing Co. plans to spend $2 billion over the next four years to build and equip new factories to make jet aircraft. Boeing's top management will assess the pros and cons of both debt and equity and then consider several possible sources of the desired form of long-term financing. The overall goal is to choose the mix of debt and equity to balance cost and risk.

The major advantage of debt financing is the deductibility of interest expense for income tax purposes, which lowers its overall cost. In addition, there is no loss of ownership. The major drawback is **financial risk**—the chance that the firm will be unable to make scheduled interest and principal payments. The lender can force a borrower that fails to make scheduled debt payments into bankruptcy. Most loan agreements have restrictions to ensure that the borrower operates efficiently.

financial risk
The chance that a firm will be unable to make scheduled interest and principal payments on its debt.

Equity, on the other hand, is a form of permanent financing that places few restrictions on the firm. The firm is not required to pay dividends or repay the investment. However, equity financing gives common stockholders voting rights that provide them with a voice in management. Equity is more costly than debt. Unlike the interest on debt, dividends to owners are not tax-deductible expenses.

Debt Financing

Long-term debt is used to finance long-term (capital) expenditures. The maturities of long-term debt typically range between 5 and 20 years. Three important forms of long-term debt are term loans, bonds, and mortgage loans.

term loan
A business loan with a maturity of more than one year; can be unsecured or secured.

bonds
Long-term debt obligations (liabilities) issued by corporations and governments.

interest
A fixed amount of money paid by the issuer of a bond to the bondholder on a regular schedule, typically every six months; stated as the *coupon rate.*

principal
The amount borrowed by the issuer of a bond; also called *par value.*

mortgage loan
A long-term loan made against real estate as collateral.

A **term loan** is a business loan with a maturity of more than one year. Term loans generally have 5- to 12-year maturities and can be unsecured or secured. They are available from commercial banks, insurance companies, pension funds, commercial finance companies, and manufacturers' financing subsidiaries. A contract between the borrower and the lender spells out the amount and maturity of the loan, the interest rate, payment dates, the purpose of the loan, and other provisions such as operating and financial restrictions on the borrower to control the risk of default. The payments include both interest and principal, so the loan balance declines over time. Borrowers try to arrange a repayment schedule that matches the forecast cash flow from the project being financed.

Bonds are long-term debt obligations (liabilities) of corporations and governments. A bond certificate is issued as proof of the obligation. The issuer of a bond must pay the buyer a fixed amount of money—called **interest,** stated as the *coupon rate*—on a regular schedule, typically every six months. The issuer must also pay the bondholder the amount borrowed—called the **principal,** or *par value*—at the bond's maturity date (due date). Bonds are usually issued in units of $1,000—for instance, $1,000, $5,000, or $10,000. They may be secured or unsecured, include special provisions for early retirement, or be convertible to common stock. Exhibit 16-2 summarizes the features of some popular types of corporate bonds.

A **mortgage loan** is a long-term loan made against real estate as collateral. The lender takes a mortgage on the property, which lets the lender seize the property, sell it, and use the proceeds to pay off the loan if the borrower fails to make the scheduled payments. Long-term mortgage loans are often used to finance office buildings, factories, and warehouses. Life insurance companies

exhibit 16-2 | Popular Types of Corporate Bonds

Bond Type	Characteristics
Collateral trust bonds	Secured by securities (stocks and bonds) owned by the issuer. Value of collateral is generally 25 to 35 percent higher than the bond's par value.
Convertible bonds	Unsecured bonds that can be exchanged for a specified number of shares of common stock.
Debenture	Unsecured bonds typically issued by creditworthy firms.
Equipment trust certificates	Used to finance "rolling stock"—airplanes, ships, trucks, railroad cars. Secured by the assets financed.
Floating-rate bonds	Bonds whose interest rate is adjusted periodically in response to changes in specified market interest rates. Popular when future inflation and interest rates are uncertain.
High-yield (junk) bonds	Bonds rated Ba or lower by Moody's or BB or lower by Standard & Poor's. High-risk bonds with high returns to investors. Frequently used to finance mergers and takeovers.
Mortgage bonds	Secured by property, such as land, equipment, or buildings.
Zero-coupon bonds	Issued with no coupon rate and sold at a large discount from par value. "Zeros" pay no interest prior to maturity. Investor's return comes from the gain in value (par value minus purchase price).

are an important source of these loans. They make billions of dollars' worth of mortgage loans to businesses each year.

Bond Ratings

Bonds vary in quality, depending on the financial strength of the issuer.

bond ratings
Letter grades assigned to bond issues to indicate their quality, or level of risk; assigned by rating agencies such as Moody's and Standard & Poor's.

Bond ratings are letter grades assigned to bond issues to evaluate their quality or level of risk. Higher ratings indicate lower risk of *default*—the failure of a company to make scheduled principal or interest payments. Ratings for corporate bonds are easy to find. The two largest and best-known rating agencies are Moody's and Standard & Poor's (S&P), whose publications are in most libraries and in stock brokerages. Exhibit 16-3 lists the letter grades assigned by Moody's and S&P. A bond's rating may change with events.

For the latest news about bond rating upgrades and downgrades, visit Moody's Investor Services at

http://www.moodys.com/

Equity Financing

lg 5

Equity is the owners' investment in the business. In corporations, the preferred and common stockholders are the owners. A firm obtains equity financing by selling new ownership shares (external financing) or by retaining earnings (internal financing).

common stock
A security that represents an ownership interest in a corporation.

Selling New Issues of Common Stock **Common stock** is a security that represents an ownership interest in a corporation.

When a high-growth company *goes public*, it has an *initial public offering (IPO)* to raise more funds to finance continuing growth. (Companies that are already public can issue and sell additional shares of common stock to raise equity funds.) An IPO often enables existing stockholders, usually employees, family, and friends who bought the stock privately, to earn big profits on their investment.

exhibit 16-3 | Moody's and Standard & Poor's Bond Ratings

Moody's Ratings	S & P Ratings	Description
Aaa	AAA	**Prime-quality investment bonds:** Highest rating assigned; indicates extremely strong capacity to pay.
Aa A	AA A	**High-grade investment bonds:** Also considered very safe bonds, although not quite as safe as Aaa/AAA issues; Aa/AA bonds are safer (have less risk of default) than single As.
Baa	BBB	**Medium-grade investment bonds:** Lowest of investment-grade issues; seen as lacking protection against adverse economic conditions.
Ba B	BB B	**Junk bonds:** Provide little protection against default; viewed as highly speculative.
Caa Ca C	CCC CC C D	**Poor-quality bonds:** Either in default or very close to it.

Yahoo co-founder Jerry Yang held a press conference to announce that his Internet search engine firm was going public to finance the expansion of Yahoo's online services.

But going public has some drawbacks. For one thing, there is no guarantee an IPO will sell. It is also expensive. Big fees must be paid to investment bankers, brokers, attorneys, accountants, and printers. Once the company is public, it is closely watched by regulators, stockholders, and securities analysts. The firm must reveal such information as operating and financial data, product details, financing plans, and operating strategies. Providing this information is often costly.

Going public can be successful when a company is well established and market conditions are right. Strong equity markets in the late 1990s prompted many companies to go public, especially very young Internet-related companies. Frequently companies that were only a year or two old rushed to go public to take advantage of market conditions. Online toy retailer eToys went public in May 1999 at \$20 a share. Its shares soared to \$76.56 the first day of trading—even though the company was less than two years old and had not shown any profits. However, by October 2000, the stock had plunged to about \$3.50 as e-commerce stocks fell from investor favor.[4] The company filed for bankruptcy in March 2001.

Dividends and Retained Earnings **Dividends** are payments to stockholders from a corporation's profits. A company does not have to pay dividends to stockholders. But if investors buy the stock expecting to get dividends and the firm does not pay them, the investors may sell their stock. If too many sell, the value of the stock decreases. Dividends can be paid in cash or in stock. **Stock dividends** are payments in the form of more stock. Stock dividends may replace or supplement cash dividends. After a stock dividend has been paid, more shares have a claim on the same company, so the value of each share often declines.

dividends
Payments to stockholders from a corporation's profits.

stock dividends
Payments to stockholders in the form of more stock; may replace or supplement cash dividends.

At their quarterly meetings, the company's board of directors (with the advice of its financial managers) decides how much of the profits to distribute as dividends and how much to reinvest. A firm's basic approach to paying dividends can greatly affect its share price. A stable history of dividend payments indicates good financial health. If a firm that has been making regular dividend payments cuts or skips a dividend, investors start thinking it has serious financial problems. The increased uncertainty often results in lower stock prices. Thus, most firms set dividends at a level they can keep paying.

Retained earnings, profits that have been reinvested in the firm, have a big advantage over other sources of equity capital: they do not incur underwriting costs. Financial managers strive to balance dividends and retained earnings to maximize the value of the firm. Often the balance reflects the nature of the firm and its industry. Well-established firms and those that expect only modest growth, like public utilities, typically pay out much of their earnings in dividends. High-growth companies, like those in the computer and biotechnology fields, finance most of their growth through retained earnings and pay little or no dividends to stockholders.

retained earnings
Profits that have been reinvested in a firm.

Preferred Stock Another form of equity is **preferred stock.** Unlike common stock, preferred stock usually has a dividend amount that is set at the time the stock is issued. These dividends must be paid before the company can pay any dividends to common stockholders. Also, if the firm goes bankrupt and sells its assets, preferred stockholders get their money back before common stockholders do.

preferred stock
An equity security for which the dividend amount is set at the time the stock is issued.

Like debt, preferred stock increases the firm's financial risk because it obligates the firm to make a fixed payment. But preferred stock is more flexible. The firm can miss a dividend payment without suffering the serious results of failing to pay back a debt. Most preferred stock is *cumulative preferred stock* that requires issuers to repay all unpaid dividends before any dividends can be paid to the holders of common stock.

Preferred stock is more expensive than debt financing, however, because preferred dividends are not tax-deductible. Also, because the claims of preferred stockholders on income and assets are second to those of debt holders, preferred stockholders require higher returns to compensate for the greater risk.

Venture Capital As we learned in Chapter 5, *venture capital* is another source of equity capital often used by small and growing firms that aren't big enough to sell securities to the public. This type of financing is especially popular among high-tech companies that need large sums of money.

Venture capitalists invest in new businesses in return for part of the ownership, sometimes as much as 60 percent. They look for new businesses with high growth potential, and they expect a high investment return within 5 to 10 years. By getting in on the ground floor, venture capitalists buy stock at a very low price. They earn profits by selling the stock at a much higher price when the company goes public. Venture capitalists generally get a voice in management through a seat on the board of directors. For example, in October 2000 two-year-old Thoughtworks, which develops customized business-to-business systems, raised $28 million from two venture capital firms. Representatives of the investing firms joined Thoughtworks' board and are using their expertise and industry contacts to help the company expand.[5]

Getting venture capital is difficult, even though there are hundreds of private venture capital firms in this country. Most venture capitalists finance only about 1 to 5 percent of the companies that apply.

concept check

- Compare the advantages and disadvantages of debt and equity to the issuer.
- Discuss the costs involved in issuing common stock.
- Briefly describe these sources of equity: retained earnings, preferred stock, venture capital.

SECURITIES MARKETS

Securities markets facilitate the transfer of funds from lenders and investors to corporate and governmental borrowers. Stocks, bonds, and other securities trade in securities markets. These markets streamline the purchase and sales activities of investors by allowing transactions to be made quickly and at a fair price from lenders to borrowers much easier. **Securities**—investment certificates issued by corporations or governments—represent either equity (ownership in the issuer) or debt (a loan to the issuer).

securities
Investment certificates issued by corporations or governments that represent either equity or debt.

Securities markets are busy places. On an average day, individual and institutional investors trade more than 1.8 billion shares of stock in over 10,000 companies. They also trade bonds, mutual funds, futures contracts, and options. *Individual investors* invest their own money to achieve their personal financial goals. About 70 million individual investors (representing about 50 percent of U.S. households) hold about 64 percent of the more than $5 trillion total U.S. equities outstanding, either directly or through mutual funds.

institutional investors
Investment professionals who are paid to manage other people's money.

Institutional investors are investment professionals who are paid to manage other people's money. Most of these professional money managers work for financial institutions, such as banks, mutual funds, insurance companies, and pension funds. Institutional investors control very large sums of money, often buying stock in 10,000-share blocks. They aim to meet the investment goals of their clients. Institutional investors are a major force in the securities markets, accounting for about half of the dollar volume of equities traded.

Businesses and governments also take part in the securities markets. Corporations issue bonds and stocks to raise funds to finance their operations. They are also among the institutional investors that purchase corporate and government securities. Federal, state, and local governments sell securities to finance specific projects and cover budget deficits.

primary market
The securities market where *new* securities are sold to the public.

secondary market
The securities market where (already issued) old securities are traded among investors; includes the organized stock exchanges, the over-the-counter market, and the commodities exchanges.

investment bankers
Firms that act as underwriters, buying securities from corporations and governments and reselling them to the public.

underwriting
The process of buying securities from corporations and governments and reselling them to the public; the main activity of investment bankers.

stockbroker
A person who is licensed to buy and sell securities on behalf of clients.

Types of Markets

Securities markets can be divided into primary and secondary markets. The **primary market** is where *new* securities are sold to the public, usually with the help of investment bankers. In the primary market, the issuer of the security gets the proceeds from the transaction. A security is sold in the primary market just once—when it is first issued by the corporation or government.

Later transactions take place in the **secondary market,** where *old* (already issued) securities are bought and sold, or traded, among investors. The issuers generally are not involved in these transactions. The vast majority of securities transactions take place in secondary markets, which include the organized stock exchanges, the over-the-counter securities market, and the commodities exchanges.

The Role of Investment Bankers and Stockbrokers

Two types of investment specialists play key roles in the functioning of the securities markets. **Investment bankers** help companies raise long-term financing. These firms act as intermediaries, buying securities from corporations and governments and reselling them to the public. This process, called **underwriting,** is the main activity of the investment banker, which acquires the security for an agreed-upon price and hopes to be able to resell it at a higher price to make a profit. Investment bankers advise clients on the pricing and structure of new securities offerings, as well as on mergers, acquisitions, and other types of financing. Well-known investment banking firms include Goldman Sachs Group, Merrill Lynch & Co., Morgan Stanley Dean Witter, First Boston, UBS PaineWebber, and Salomon Smith Barney (a division of Citigroup).

A **stockbroker** is a person who is licensed to buy and sell securities on behalf of clients. Also called *account executives,* these investment professionals work for brokerage firms and execute the orders customers place for stocks, bonds, mutual funds, and other securities. We'll discuss the different types of brokers later in this chapter.

concept check

- How do securities markets help businesses and investors?
- Distinguish between primary and secondary securities markets.
- How does an investment banker work with companies to issue securities?

Most securities transactions take place in secondary markets such as on the trading floor of the New York Stock Exchange, shown here.

Other Popular Securities

In addition to corporate issues of equity and debt, securities markets trade several other types of securities. These include Treasury securities, municipal bonds, mutual funds, futures contracts, and options. The first three appeal to a wide range of investors. Futures contracts and options are more complex investments for experienced investors.

U.S. Government Securities and Municipal Bonds The U.S. Treasury sells three major types of debt securities, commonly called "governments": Treasury bills, Treasury notes, and Treasury bonds. All three are viewed as risk-free because they are backed by the U.S. government. *Treasury bills* mature in less than a year and are issued with a minimum par value of $1,000. *Treasury notes* have maturities of 10 years or less, and *Treasury bonds* have maturities as long as 25 years or more. Both notes and bonds are sold in denominations of $1,000 and $5,000. The interest earned on government securities is subject to federal income tax but is free from state and local income taxes.

municipal bonds

Bonds issued by states, cities, counties, and other state and local government agencies.

Municipal bonds are issued by states, cities, counties, and other state and local government agencies. These bonds typically have a par value of $5,000 and are either general obligation or revenue bonds. *General obligation bonds* are backed by the full faith and credit (and taxing power) of the issuing government. *Revenue bonds,* on the other hand, are repaid only from income generated by the specific project being financed. Examples of revenue bond projects include toll highways and bridges, power plants, and parking structures. Because the issuer of revenue bonds has no legal obligation to back the bonds if the project's revenues are inadequate, they are considered more risky and therefore have higher interest rates than general obligation bonds.

You'll find a minicourse on municipal bonds when you click on municipal bonds at the top of the page at http://www.investingbonds.com

Municipal bonds are attractive to investors because interest earned on them is exempt from federal income tax. For the same reason, the coupon interest rate for a municipal bond is lower than for a similar-quality corporate bond. In addition, interest earned on municipal bonds issued by governments within the taxpayer's home state is exempt from state income tax as well. In contrast, all interest earned on corporate bonds is fully taxable.

Mutual Funds Suppose that you have $1,000 to invest but don't know which stocks or bonds to buy, when to buy them, or when to sell them. By investing in a mutual fund, you can buy shares in a large, professionally managed *portfolio,* or group, of stocks and bonds. A **mutual fund** is a financial service company that pools its investors' funds to buy a selection of securities—marketable securities, stocks, bonds, or a combination of securities—that meet its stated investment goals.

mutual fund

A financial service company that pools investors' funds to buy a selection of securities that meet its stated investment goals.

Each mutual fund focuses on one of a wide variety of possible investment goals, such as growth or income. Many large financial service companies, like Fidelity Investments and Vanguard, sell a wide variety of mutual funds, each with a different investment goal. Investors can pick and choose funds that match their particular interests. Some specialized funds invest in a particular type of company or asset—in one industry such as health care or technology, a geographical region such as Asia, or an asset such as precious metals. To help investors find the right fund for their needs, many mutual fund companies are using the Internet to good advantage.

futures contracts

Legally binding obligations to buy or sell specified quantities of commodities or financial instruments at an agreed-on price at a future date.

Futures and Options **Futures contracts** are legally binding obligations to buy or sell specified quantities of commodities (agricultural or mining products) or financial instruments (securities or currencies) at an agreed-on price at a future date. An investor can buy commodity futures contracts in cattle, pork bellies (large slabs of bacon), eggs, frozen orange juice concentrate, gasoline, heating oil, lumber, wheat, gold, and silver. Financial futures include Treasury securities and foreign currencies, such as the euro or Japanese yen.

Futures contracts do not pay interest or dividends. The return depends solely on favorable price changes. These are very risky investments because the prices can vary a great deal.

Options are contracts that entitle holders to buy or sell specified quantities of common stocks or other financial instruments at a set price during a specified time. As with futures contracts, investors must correctly guess future price movements in the underlying financial instrument to earn a positive return. Unlike futures contracts, options do not legally obligate the holder to buy or sell and the price paid for an option is the maximum amount that can be lost. But because options have very short maturities, it is easy to quickly lose a lot of money with them.

concept check

- Who issues municipal bonds and why?
- Why do mutual funds appeal to investors? Discuss some of the investment goals pursued by mutual funds.
- What are futures contracts? Why are they risky investments? How do options differ from futures contracts?

SECURITIES EXCHANGES

>lg 7

The two key types of securities exchanges are organized stock exchanges and the over-the-counter market. **Organized stock exchanges** are organizations on whose premises securities are resold. They operate using an auction-style trading system. All other securities are traded in the over-the-counter market.

To make transactions in an organized stock exchange, an individual or firm must be a member and own a "seat" on that exchange. Owners of the limited number of seats must meet certain financial requirements and agree to observe a broad set of rules when trading securities.

options
Contracts that entitle holders to buy or sell specified quantities of common stocks or other financial instruments at a set price during a specified time.

organized stock exchanges
Organizations on whose premises securities are resold using an auction-style trading system.

U.S. Stock Exchanges

The oldest and most prestigious U.S. stock exchange is the *New York Stock Exchange (NYSE),* which has existed since 1792. Often called the Big Board, it is located on Wall Street in downtown New York City. The NYSE, which lists the securities of about 2,800 corporations, handles most of the shares traded on organized stock exchanges in the United States. Major companies like IBM, Coca-Cola, AT&T, Procter & Gamble, Ford Motor Co., and Chevron list their shares on the NYSE. In 1999, 204 billion shares were traded on the NYSE, with a total dollar value of over $8.9 trillion. The NYSE is also popular with non-U.S. companies. About 400 foreign companies now list their securities on the NYSE.

HOT links

How many shares traded hands today? Find out at the New York Stock Exchange site

http://www.nyse.com/floor/floor.html

Another national stock exchange, the American Stock Exchange (AMEX), lists the securities of about 700 corporations. With 1999 trading volume of just over 7 billion shares, it is dwarfed by the NYSE. Because the AMEX's rules are less strict than those of the NYSE, most firms traded on the AMEX are smaller and less well known than NYSE-listed corporations.

In addition to the NYSE and AMEX, several regional exchanges list about 100 to 500 securities of firms located in their area. Regional exchange membership rules are much less strict than for the NYSE. The top regional exchanges are the Boston, Cincinnati, Chicago, and Pacific exchanges. An electronic network linking the NYSE and many of the regional exchanges allows

Many U.S. and other firms outside of Japan list their stock on the Tokyo Stock Exchange, one of the world's largest foreign exchanges.

brokers to make securities transactions at the best prices.

Global Trading and Foreign Exchanges

Improved communications and the elimination of many legal barriers are helping the securities markets go global. The number of securities listed on exchanges in more than one country is growing. Foreign securities are now traded in the United States. Likewise, foreign investors can easily buy U.S. securities.

Stock exchanges also exist in foreign countries. The London and Tokyo Stock Exchanges rank behind the NYSE and Nasdaq (described below). Other important foreign stock exchanges include those in Toronto, Montreal, Buenos Aires, Zurich, Sydney, Paris, Frankfurt, Hong Kong, and Taiwan. The number of big U.S. corporations with listings on foreign exchanges is growing steadily, especially in Europe. For example, over 10 percent of the daily activity in NYSE-listed stocks is due to trades on the London Stock Exchange.

The Over-the-Counter Market

over-the-counter (OTC) market
A sophisticated telecommunications network that links dealers throughout the United States and enables them to trade securities.

National Association of Securities Dealers Automated Quotation (Nasdaq) system
The first electronic-based stock market and the fastest-growing part of the stock market.

Unlike the organized stock exchanges, the **over-the-counter (OTC) market** is not a specific institution with a trading floor. It is a sophisticated telecommunications network that links dealers throughout the United States. The **National Association of Securities Dealers Automated Quotation (Nasdaq) system,** the first electronic-based stock market, is the fastest-growing part of the stock market. It provides up-to-date bid and ask prices on about 4,100 of the most active OTC securities, with a 1999 market value totaling $5.2 trillion. Its sophisticated electronic communication system is the main reason for the popularity and growth of the OTC market. In 1999, 270 billion shares with a value of $10.8 trillion exchanged hands, gains of 34 percent and 88 percent, respectively, over the preceding year.

The securities of many well-known companies, some of which could be listed on the organized exchanges, trade on the OTC market. Examples include Apple Computer, Coors, Dell Computer, Intel, MCI WorldCom, Microsoft, Nordstrom Department Stores, Qualcomm, and Starbucks. The stocks of most commercial banks and insurance companies also trade in this market, as do most government and corporate bonds. About 440 foreign companies also trade OTC.

What makes the Nasdaq different from an organized exchange? On the NYSE, one specialist handles all transactions in a particular stock, but on the Nasdaq system, a number of dealers handle ("make a market in") a security. For instance, about 40 dealers make a market in Apple Computer stock. Thus, dealers compete, improving investors' ability to get a good price.

Regulation of Securities Markets

The securities markets are regulated by both state and federal governments. The states were the first to pass laws aimed at preventing securities fraud. But most securities transactions occur across state lines, so federal securities laws are more effective. In addition to legislation, the industry has self-regulatory groups and measures.

Securities Legislation The *Securities Act of 1933* was passed by Congress in response to the 1929 stock market crash and subsequent problems during the Great Depression. It protects investors by requiring full disclosure of information about new securities issues. The issuer must file a *registration statement* with the Securities and Exchange Commission (SEC), which must be approved by the SEC before the security can be sold.

The *Securities Exchange Act of 1934* formally gave the SEC power to control the organized securities exchanges. The act was amended in 1964 to give the SEC authority over the OTC market as well. The amendment included rules for operating the stock exchanges and granted the SEC control over all participants (exchange members, brokers, dealers) and the securities traded in these markets.

insider trading
The use of information that is not available to the general public to make profits on securities transactions.

The 1934 act also banned **insider trading,** the use of information that is not available to the general public to make profits on securities transactions. Because of lax enforcement, however, several big insider trading scandals occurred during the late 1980s. The *Insider Trading and Fraud Act of 1988* greatly increased the penalties for illegal insider trading and gave the SEC more power to investigate and prosecute claims of illegal actions. The meaning of insider was expanded beyond a company's directors, employees, and their relatives to include anyone who gets private information about a company.

Other important legislation includes the *Investment Company Act of 1940,* which gives the SEC the right to regulate the practices of investment companies (such as mutual funds), and the *Investment Advisers Act of 1940,* which requires investment advisers to disclose information about their background. The *Securities Investor Protection Corporation (SIPC)* was established in 1970 to protect customers if a brokerage firm fails by insuring each customer's account for up to $500,000.

circuit breakers
Measures that, under certain conditions, stop trading in the securities markets for a short cooling-off period to limit the amount the market can drop in one day.

Self-Regulation The investment community also regulates itself, developing and enforcing ethical standards to reduce the potential for abuses in the financial marketplace. The National Association of Securities Dealers (NASD), the parent organization of the Nasdaq-Amex Market Group, oversees the nation's 5,600 brokerage firms and more than half a million registered brokers. It develops rules and regulations, provides a dispute resolution forum, and conducts regulatory reviews of member activities for the protection and benefit of investors.

In response to "Black Monday"—October 19, 1987, when the Dow Jones Industrial Average plunged 508 points and the trading activity severely overloaded the exchange's computers—the securities markets instituted corrective measures to prevent a repeat of the crisis. Now, under certain conditions, **circuit breakers** stop trading for a short cooling-off period to limit the amount the market can drop in one day. The NYSE circuit breaker levels are set quarterly based on the Dow Jones Industrial Average closing values of the previous month, rounded to the nearest 50 points.

concept check

- Describe the organized stock exchanges. How does the OTC market differ from them? What role does each type of market play?
- What is insider trading, and how can it be harmful?
- Briefly describe the key provisions of the main federal laws designed to protect securities investors. How does the securities industry regulate itself?

CAPITALIZING ON TRENDS IN BUSINESS

>lg 8

Many of the key trends shaping financial management as we enter the new millennium echo those in other disciplines. For example, technology is improving the efficiency with which financial managers run their operations and securities markets operate. As in other areas, the increasing interdependence of the world's economies requires an international approach to finance. One different note, however, is the expanding role of the financial manager in risk management.

Just as venturing overseas affects marketing, production, and general management practices, globalization brings additional complexity to financial management. Today's financial managers can make investments and raise financing both in the United States and overseas. They may have to compare the costs, risks, and benefits of relocating manufacturing facilities to another country versus expanding at home. And they must pay attention not only to the U.S. economy, but to economic developments in Japan, Russia, Germany, and other nations as well.

Risk Management

risk management
The process of identifying and evaluating risks and selecting and managing techniques to adapt to risk exposures.

The 1998 turmoil in Asian and Russian financial markets proved that going global increases a company's risk, whether or not the company has operations in those regions. As a result, financial managers are spending more time on **risk management,** the process of identifying and evaluating risks and selecting and managing techniques to adapt to risk exposures. Companies face a wide range of risks, including:

- *Credit risk.* Exposure to loss as a result of default on a financial transaction or a reduction in a security's market value due to decline in the credit quality of the debt issuer.
- *Market risk.* Risk resulting from adverse movements in the level or volatility of market prices of securities, commodities, and currencies.
- *Operational risk.* The risk of unexpected losses arising from deficiencies in a firm's management information, support, and control systems and procedures.

The job of Microsoft's financial managers is complex as they manage the company's global manufacturing, licensing, and wholesale and retail distribution of more than 200 products, such as the software sold by the retailer in Hong Kong shown here.

A failure in a company's risk control procedures can lead to substantial financial losses. Major financial institutions like Daiwa and Sumitomo Corp. lost huge amounts of money because their control systems collapsed. A breakdown in risk control eventually costs the shareholders money. They may have to invest more capital to bail out the troubled firm. Otherwise their equity investment will decline in value when the company's problems become known to the public.[6]

Recently, some insurance companies have entered the risk management arena. They offer new types of policies to protect companies against disappointing financial results. Reliance Group, a New York insurer, introduced Enterprise Earnings Protection Insurance. This policy reimburses a company for any operating earnings shortfall that is due to forces beyond management's control, such as drought, floods, or the Asian

GOING DIRECT WITH NIPHIX

Companies that are too small to trade in the OTC market no longer have to wait to qualify for Wall Street to tap the equity markets. Electronic trading networks like Niphix Investments provide an alternate route to the capital markets.

Niphix—itself a small company—is the first Internet-based direct stock market. "We cater to companies that are too small for Nasdaq, but we hope they can grow at Niphix," says Nimish Ghandi, Niphix's founder. At Niphix, microcap companies (with a market capitalization—the value of their equity—under $50 million) find services designed for their needs. Niphix helps small companies market and sell their stock without using an underwriter. Such issues are called direct public offerings (DPOs). Niphix's goal is to be a starting point for high-growth companies that will eventually move up to the more established exchanges.

To be listed on Niphix, a company must agree to full disclosure, including quarterly and annual audited reports using GAAP (generally accepted accounting principles) accounting. Standard & Poor's has agreed to cover all companies listed with Niphix.

Investors who want to buy and sell shares in Niphix-listed companies simply open a standard brokerage account with Niphix. Unlike similar trading systems, Niphix operates a matching system rather than acting as an intermediary. Buyers and sellers conduct their own online negotiations until they agree on a price. Then Niphix immediately executes the trade using its staff of registered brokers. Niphix also offers low transaction fees, ranging from $24 to $44.

Niphix is still young, and it is too soon to know if it will improve the liquidity of shares of companies going the DPO route. Thus far, the number of companies and investors using Niphix remains small. Tom Stewart-Gordon, editor of a DPO report, believes that investors who buy DPO shares focus on the company's products or philosophy rather than its liquidity. Supporters of exchanges like Niphix think that having a place to sell their securities will encourage more investors to consider DPOs.

Critical Thinking Questions

1. What advantages does Niphix offer a small company?
2. If you were a company owner planning to go public, would you consider Niphix? Justify your answer.
3. How does the availability of research reports for Niphix companies from a major firm like Standard & Poor's help both Niphix and the companies?

economic crisis. Reliance is hoping that CFOs will buy its policies to prevent earnings surprises. Guaranteeing results is likely to be an expensive proposition, however. And predicting the volatility of a client's earnings is a new area for insurers.[7]

Market Competition Heats Up

Whereas the NYSE was once the undisputed leader among stock exchanges, the Nasdaq has successfully challenged its position. The largest electronic exchange in the world, Nasdaq captures about 54 percent of total U.S. trading volume compared to the NYSE's 43 percent—reversing their positions of five years earlier. The Nasdaq lists 4,100 companies versus 2,800 on the NYSE.

As a result, the competition between the two institutions is intense. Each promotes itself as the best place for a major corporation to list its securities. The NYSE touts its prestige to convince Nasdaq and AMEX companies to switch their listings to the NYSE. Even though it spent millions on new information technology and uses order-matching technology for almost half its trades, the NYSE still lags behind the Nasdaq and major foreign exchanges technologically, however.[8]

The Nasdaq, calling itself "The market for the next 100 years" due to its emphasis on technology, merged with the AMEX in early 1999 to create what it termed a "market of markets." They operate as separate markets under the management of the Nasdaq-Amex Market Group, a subsidiary of the National Association of Securities Dealers, Inc. (NASD). This merger could pressure the remaining regional exchanges to find partners.

Threatening both the NYSE and the Nasdaq is the emergence of other electronic exchanges called *electronic communications networks (ECNs)*. ECNs allow institutional traders and some individuals to make direct transactions, without using brokers, securities exchanges, or the Nasdaq, in what is called the *fourth market*. Because they deal mostly in Nasdaq stocks, ECNs are taking trading volume away from the Nasdaq. ECNs are most effective for high-volume, actively traded stocks. Money managers and institutions such as pension funds and mutual funds with large amounts of money to invest like ECNs because they cost less than other trading venues.[9]

Starting in April 1999, the SEC allowed ECNs to register as exchanges. Orders could bypass members of the NYSE entirely. Discount brokerage firm Datek Online was the first to petition the SEC to turn its ECN, Island, into a self-regulated stock exchange. Niphix Investments, the ECN described in the Focusing on Small Business box, specializes in helping small companies go public.

APPLYING THIS CHAPTER'S TOPICS

Whether you are a marketing manager, purchasing agent, or systems analyst, knowledge of finance will help you to do your job better. You'll be able to understand your company's financial statements, its financial condition, and management's investment and financing decisions. Financial information also provides feedback on how well you are doing and identifies problems. On a more practical note, you may be asked to prepare a budget for your department or unit. Employees who understand the financial decision-making process will be able to prepare proposals that address financial concerns. As a result, they will be more likely to get the resources they require to accomplish the firm's goals.

If you own a business, you must pay close attention to financial management. Without financial plans you may find yourself running out of cash. It's easy to get so caught up in growing sales that you neglect your billing and collection methods. In fact, managing accounts receivable is often one of the more challenging aspects of running a young company. But you can't rely on revenue increases to solve your cash flow problems. Good receivables practices start with credit policies. Be choosy when it comes to offering trade credit and check customers' credit references and payment history thoroughly. Set the initial credit limit fairly low until the customer establishes a prompt payment history. Here are some other ways to improve collections:

- Bill frequently, not just at the end of the month, so that money flows in throughout the month.
- Clearly state payment terms.
- Establish regular and frequent follow-up procedures. Some companies call to notify the customer that the bill has been sent and to make sure the customer is satisfied. Weekly calls are in order for late payments.
- Monitor results of outstanding receivables collection.
- Don't fill new orders from customers who are continually delinquent.[10]

TRY IT NOW!

1. Small Business Loans, **http://www.smallbusinessloans.com,** offers a wide range of loans for small businesses. Choose five types of loans and describe the reasons businesses choose each type. Look at the application and summarize the type of information required to start the loan process. What other information do you think the lender will require before granting a loan?

2. The MaxFunds University, **http://www.maxfunds.com/content/university.html,** offers a course on investing in mutual funds: Maxuniversity–Part II. Use it to learn about the basics of mutual funds. Prepare a presentation for the class based on the materials.

SUMMARY OF LEARNING GOALS

>lg 1 **How do finance and the financial manager affect the firm's overall strategy?**

Finance involves managing the firm's money. The financial manager must decide how much money is needed and when, how best to use the available funds, and how to get the required financing. The financial manager's responsibilities include financial planning, investing (spending money), and financing (raising money). Maximizing the value of the firm is the main goal of the financial manager, whose decisions often have long-term effects.

>lg 2 **What types of short-term and long-term expenditures does a firm make?**

A firm invests in short-term expenses—supplies, inventory, and wages—to support current production, marketing, and sales activities. The financial manager manages the firm's investment in current assets so that the company has enough cash to pay its bills and support accounts receivable and inventory. Long-term expenditures (capital expenditures) are made for fixed assets such as land, buildings, and equipment. Because of the large outlays required for capital expenditures, financial managers carefully analyze proposed projects to determine which offer the best returns.

>lg 3 **What are the main sources and costs of unsecured and secured short-term financing?**

Short-term financing comes due within one year. The main sources of unsecured short-term financing are trade credit, bank loans, and commercial paper. Secured loans require a pledge of certain assets, such as accounts receivable or inventory, as security for the loan. Factoring, or selling accounts receivable outright at a discount, is another form of short-term financing.

>lg 4 **What are the key differences between debt and equity and the major types and features of long-term debt?**

Financial managers must choose the best mix of debt and equity for their firm. The main advantage of debt financing is the tax-deductibility of interest. But debt involves financial risk because it requires the payment of interest and principal on specified dates. Equity—common and preferred stock—is considered a permanent form of financing on which the firm may or may not pay dividends. Dividends are not tax-deductible.

The main types of long-term debt are term loans, bonds, and mortgage loans. Term loans can be secured or unsecured and generally have 5- to 12-year maturities. Bonds usually have maturities of 10 to 30 years. Mortgage loans are secured by real estate. Long-term debt usually costs more than

>looking ahead at Continental Airlines

After years of shaky financial skies, Continental Airlines is flying high. Its solid financial condition has paid off in many areas. With improved access to the financial markets, the airline has been able to finance the acquisition of new aircraft and retire old ones, giving Continental one of the youngest fleets in the industry. Newer planes appeal to business travelers and allow Continental to offer higher quality service and comfort. Airlines are now eager to form alliances with the revitalized Continental. Recently, Continental expanded its domestic and international route networks through a strategic partnership with Northwest and marketing alliances with Alaska, Air France, British Midland, Virgin, and other airlines.

Employees and passengers like the new Continental as well. In 2001, *Fortune* magazine named Continental one of its "100 Best Companies to Work for in America," and Continental was also on *Fortune*'s "World's Most Admired Companies" list. It has been praised for it its innovative use of information technology among airlines, thanks in large part to Larry Kellner's emphasis on upgrading Continental's communication and information systems. Gordon Bethune, Continental's chairman and chief executive officer, praised employees' efforts to focus on eliminating non-value-added costs.[11]

short-term financing because of the greater uncertainty that the borrower will be able to make the scheduled loan payments.

>lg 5 When and how do firms issue equity, and what are the costs?
The chief sources of equity financing are common stock, retained earnings, and preferred stock. The cost of selling stock includes issuing costs and potential dividend payments. Retained earnings are profits reinvested in the firm. For the issuing firm, preferred stock is more expensive than debt because its dividends are not tax-deductible and its claims are secondary to those of debtholders, but less expensive than common stock. Venture capital is often a source of equity financing for young companies.

>lg 6 How do securities markets help firms raise funding, and what securities trade in the capital markets?
Securities markets allow stocks, bonds, and other securities to be bought and sold quickly and at a fair price. New issues are sold in the primary market. After that, securities are traded in the secondary market. Investment bankers specialize in issuing and selling new security issues. Stockbrokers are licensed professionals who buy and sell securities on behalf of their clients.

In addition to corporate securities, investors can trade U.S. government Treasury securities and municipal bonds, mutual funds, futures, and options. Mutual funds are financial service companies that pool the funds of many investors to buy a diversified portfolio of securities. Investors choose mutual funds because they offer a convenient way to diversify and are professionally managed. Futures contracts are legally binding obligations to buy or sell specified quantities of commodities or financial instruments at an agreed-on price at a future date. They are very risky investments because the price of the commodity or financial instrument may change drastically. Options are contracts that entitle the holder the right to buy or sell specified quantities of common stock or other financial instruments at a set price during a specified time. They, too, are high-risk investments.

>lg 7 What are the major U.S. securities exchanges and how are they regulated?
Securities are resold on organized stock exchanges, like the New York Stock Exchange and regional stock exchanges, and in the over-the-counter market, a telecommunications network linking dealers throughout the United States. The most actively traded securities are listed on the Nasdaq system, so dealers and brokers can perform trades quickly and efficiently.

The Securities Act of 1933 requires disclosure of important information regarding new securities issues. The Securities Exchange Act of 1934 and its 1964 amendment formally empowered the Securities and Exchange Commission and granted it broad powers to regulate the organized securities exchanges and the over-the-counter market. The Investment Company Act of 1940 places investment companies such as mutual funds under SEC control. The securities markets also have self-regulatory groups like the NASD and measures such as "circuit breakers" to halt trading if the Dow Jones Industrial Average drops rapidly.

>lg 8 **What are the current developments in financial management and the securities markets?**

Globalization brings additional complexity to financial management. Financial managers must be prepared to invest and raise funds overseas and make transactions in multiple currencies. Financial managers are spending more time on risk management, identifying and evaluating risks, and selecting techniques to control and reduce risk. Companies face a wide range of risks, including credit risk, market risk, and operational risk.

The securities markets and investment industry are in the midst of considerable change. No longer does the New York Stock Exchange dominate equity market activity. The Nasdaq is challenging the Big Board, and the emergence of electronic exchanges could further alter the market positions of these two securities marketplaces.

KEY TERMS

accounts payable 445
accounts receivable 443
bond ratings 449
bonds 448
capital budgeting 444
capital expenditures 444
cash flows 441
cash management 443
circuit breakers 456
commercial paper 443
common stock 449
dividends 450
factoring 446
financial management 440
financial risk 447
futures contracts 453
insider trading 456
institutional investors 451
interest 448
investment banker 452
line of credit 446
marketable securities 443
mortgage loan 448
municipal bonds 453
mutual fund 453
National Association of Securities Dealers Automated Quotation (Nasdaq) system 455
options 454
organized stock exchanges 454
over-the-counter (OTC) market 455
preferred stock 450
primary market 451
principal 448
retained earnings 450
return 442
revolving credit agreement 446
risk 442
risk management 457
risk-return trade-off 442
secondary market 452
secured loans 446

PREPARING FOR TOMORROW'S WORKPLACE

1. The head of your school's finance department has asked you to address a group of incoming business students about the importance of finance to their overall business education. Develop an outline with the key points you would cover in your speech.
2. Edward M. Kerschner, a securities analyst at Wall Street's UBS PaineWebber, considers dividends a terribly tax-inefficient way of delivering returns to investors, because they are taxed twice, at the corporate and individual level. Many industries that traditionally pay large dividends—telecommunications and utilities, for example—are allocating funds to acquisitions, debt paydown, and other uses, and raising dividends more slowly as they face intensified competition. Divide the class into two teams to debate Kerschner's statement that dividends no longer add value.
3. You are the chief financial officer of Discovery Labs, a privately held, five-year-old biotechnology company that needs to raise $3 million to fund the development of a new drug. Prepare a report for the board of directors that discusses the types of long-term financing available to the firm, their pros and cons, and the key factors to consider in choosing a financing strategy.
4. Research the trends in the IPO marketplace from 1995 to 2000. Then select two IPO success stories and two failures. Prepare a report for the class on their performance. What lessons about the securities markets can you learn from their stories? Is it better to wait longer to go public or to use one of the alternative exchanges like Niphix to go public while the firm is still fairly small?
5. While having dinner at a Manhattan restaurant, you overhear two investment bankers at the next table. They are discussing the takeover of Bellamco Industries by Gildmart Corp., a deal that has not yet been announced. You have been thinking about buying Bellamco stock for a while, so the next day you buy 500 shares for $30 each. Two weeks later, Gildmart announces its acquisition of Bellamco at a price of $45 per share. Have you fairly earned a profit, or are you guilty of insider trading? What's wrong with insider trading?

securities 451
stockbroker 452
stock dividends 450
term loan 448
trade credit 445
underwriting 452
unsecured loans 445

WORKING THE NET

1. If factorig accounts receivable is still a mystery to you, visit the Global Financial Group site, **http://www.global-factoring.com.** Click on the top buttons to get information on "What is Factoring?", "Reasons to Factor," "How Does it Work?" "Factoring Terminology," "FAQs," and "How Do I Qualify?" Summarize your findings.
2. Go to vFinance.com, **http://www.vfinance.com,** and link to three different venture capital firms. Compare the firms' investment strategies (industry specialization, age of companies in which they invest, etc.).
3. The International Finance and Commodities Institute (IFCI) Financial Risk Site, **http://riskinstitute.ch**, offers an excellent introduction to risk management concepts. Explore the site, especially the Key Concepts page, develop a list of sources and types of financial risks, and give an example of each. Discuss briefly the consequences of not controlling these risks. How can companies implement sound risk management procedures?
4. Compare the listing requirements of the NYSE, Nasdaq, and AMEX using the information at their Web sites: **http://www.nyse.com** and **http://www.nasdaq.com-amex.com.** Search the sites for listing requirements. What types of companies qualify for listing on each exchange? Why do the Nasdaq and AMEX offer alternative listing standards?
5. Become a pro at researching companies on the Web. Take the tutorial on Researching Companies Online at **http://home.sprintmail.com/~debflanagan/index.html**. Put your newfound skills to use by researching the investment potential of a company of your choice.

CREATIVE THINKING CASE

Nonstop Trading

For many do-it-yourself investors, the normal trading day—9:30 A.M. to 4:00 P.M. Eastern time for the NYSE and Nasdaq—is not long enough. Now that they can research companies online at all hours, they want to manage their portfolios when they get home from work or react to late-breaking news outside normal trading hours. West Coast investors, for whom regular trading ends at 1:00 P.M. Pacific time, have long been unhappy about losing afternoon trading hours. Day traders, who buy and sell stocks the same day to capture tiny differences in stock prices, also want longer hours.

In 1999, brokers rushed to respond to the demand for longer trading hours by tapping into the resources of electronic stock trading systems. Datek was one of the first, extending its trading day with a 4:00 P.M. to 5:15 P.M. Eastern time session. Discover Brokerage and Dreyfus Brokerage Services added a session from 6:00 P.M. to 8:00 P.M. Eastern time. E*Trade allowed individual investors to join major traders such as mutual fund managers and institutional investors and trade from 4:00 P.M. to 6:30 P.M. through Instinet, a major ECN. "What our customers want is access to opportunity and a level playing field with larger institutional investors," says Christos Cotsakos, chairman of E*Trade. "It's all part of democratizing personal investing."

Following suit, the NYSE and Nasdaq announced plans for longer hours as well. Starting in fall 1999, investors could trade 100 of the largest Nasdaq stocks during a 5:30 P.M. to 10:00 P.M. after-hours session. The NYSE delayed the introduction of after-hours trading for about 500 of its stocks until 2000. By limiting trading to major companies, these exchanges hope to generate sufficient demand to avoid sharp price swings.

Not everyone is in favor of after-hours trading sessions, however. Conditions in after-hours trading could be different from regular daytime trading sessions. Prices could be more volatile, increasing the risk for small investors. As Alan Davidson, president of the Independent Broker-Dealer Association, says, "It extends the stock market into a casino . . . and emphasizes short-term over long-term investment."

Critical Thinking Questions

1. What are some of the advantages and disadvantages of extended trading hours?
2. Do you think it's important to have a "resting period" to allow investors to reflect on the day's market activity?
3. Why are smaller online brokerages and ECNs in the forefront of the push toward longer trading hours, while the NYSE and Nasdaq are following a more conservative approach?

VIDEO CASE

Growth through Acquisitions

Scotsman Industries (**http://www.scotsman-ice.com**) manufactures and markets refrigerated display cases, food preparation and storage equipment, beverage systems, ice machines, and walk-in coolers and freezers. Its primary customers are supermarkets, restaurants, lodging and health care facilities, and convenience stores. The company's goals include increasing sales and earnings by 15 to 20 percent annually. Internal growth should account for about 6 to 8 percent of the increase, with the rest from acquisitions.

The company's acquisition strategy targets companies that either strengthen existing product lines or add new but related areas. Since 1990 Scotsman has used acquisitions to transform itself from a company highly dependent on one product line to a more diversified company with product lines marketed to similar customer groups worldwide. In 1994 Scotsman acquired commercial foodservice equipment manufacturer Delfield Co. (**http://www.delfield.com**). With the 1997 acquisition of Kysor Industrial Corp., Scotsman entered the markets for walk-in coolers and freezers and supermarket and convenience store environmental control systems. Other acquisitions expanded Scotsman's global reach. Its Whitlenge and Homark subsidiaries in the United Kingdom and Hartek unit in Germany and Austria produce and sell beverage systems in Europe.

These acquisitions fueled Scotsman's growth as sales and earnings tripled during the 1990s. According to Richard Osborne, Scotsman's chairman, president, and CEO, the company will continue to acquire companies with strong fundamentals and complementary products, using these acquisitions to improve the strategic positions of current business lines.

Critical Thinking Questions

1. What are the financial management implications of growing the company through acquisitions?
2. Should a company finance acquisitions with debt or equity? Explain your answer.
3. What does Osborne mean when he says future acquisitions will focus on companies with strong fundamentals and complementary products?

e-commerce

Case: Pets.com Ends Up in the Doghouse

Pets.com was the cat's meow of online pet stores. Founded in February 1999, it caught the fancy of investors who were looking to grab some dot.com riches for themselves. Money flowed in from major venture capital firms and partners like Amazon.com. By December 1999, Pets.com raised $110 million in four financing rounds and seemed destined for Internet stardom. It scheduled its initial public offering (IPO) for its first birthday in February 2000.

With a lavish $27 million advertising campaign featuring their Sock Puppet mascot, Pets.com courted pet lovers who spared no expense on their pets, dressing them in diamond-studded collars, special coats, and other pricey accessories. However, the business model for pet e-tailers was not sustainable. "Pet products simply do not lend themselves very well to online purchases," says Andrew Bartels of Giga Information Group. "You can certainly order a 50-pound bag of dry dog food online, but think about the overnight shipping costs." To counter high shipping costs, Pets.com offered discounts to attract customers. As a result, it sold most products below cost, losing as much as $5 for every $1 of merchandise sold in the first quarter of 2000 alone.

"It was astounding to see how few pure dot.com e-tailers had a grasp of their gross margins," says Jim Breyer, managing partner at Accel Partners, a venture capital firm. They assumed that building sales to a high enough level would bring profits. Instead they discovered that expenses like marketing and personnel rose along with sales. At Pets.com, overall sales volume was slow to build; customers never returned to buy the higher-margin pet toys. The company quickly ran through their cash on hand.

By the time Pets.com went public, investors shunned Internet companies with small revenues, heavy losses, and no profits in sight. The stock never sold above the $11 offering price as the once-hot market for dot-coms fizzled. From there it was all downhill. Pets.com launched a private-label food line, started selling sock-puppet merchandise, and built a second distribution center to improve profitability and develop brand awareness. However, these strategies failed to interest new investors in providing the additional $20 million necessary for Pets.com to continue operations. On November 7, 2000, Pets.com stock closed its doors.

Questions for Critical Thinking

1. In an interview just after the company's demise, Pets.com chairman and chief executive Julie Wainwright said, "In the end, we thought [closing the company] was the best thing for our shareholders, who are our primary concern, since we're a public company." Do you agree with Wainwright, and why? How does being a public company change the picture for Pets.com? What additional responsibilities and risks does it involve?
2. How could better financial planning have helped Pets.com in the early stages of its life?
3. Assume you were Pets.com's chief financial officer in early 2000. What steps could you have taken to possibly avoid the company's downfall?

SOURCES: Timothy Hanrahan, Danielle Sessa, et. al, "Dot-Com Dominoes," *The Wall Street Journal Interactive Edition* (November 7, 2000), downloaded from **www.wsj.com**; Suzanne Koudsi, "Dot-Com Deathwatch: Why Is This Sock Puppet Still Smiling?" *Fortune* (June 26, 2000), p. 54; Pui-Wing Tam and Mylene Mangalindan, "Pets.com Will Shut Down, Citing Insufficient Funding," *The Wall Street Journal Interactive Edition,* November 8, 2000, downloaded from **www.wsj.com**; Fred Vogelstein, Janet Rae-Dupree, Paul Sloan, and William J. Holstein; "Easy Dot Com, Easy Dot Go," *U.S. News & World Report,* May 1, 2000, p. 42; Jerry Useem, "Dot-coms: What Have We Learned?" *Fortune* (October 30, 2000), pp. 82–104.

12

2

Explain how market prices are determined.

How Market Prices Are Determined

The performance of firms is affected by changes in the prices they charge for products (which influence their revenue) and the prices they pay for supplies and materials (which influence their operating expenses). The prices of products and supplies are influenced by demand and supply conditions.

The following framework uses demand and supply conditions to explain how prices of products change over time. The market price of a product is influenced by the total demand for that product by all customers. It is also affected by the supply of that product produced by firms. The interaction between demand and supply determines the price, as explained in detail next.

Demand Schedule for a Product

demand schedule a schedule that indicates the quantity of a product that would be demanded at each possible price

The demand for a product can be shown with a **demand schedule,** or a schedule that indicates the quantity of the product that would be demanded at each possible price. Consider personal computers as an example. Assume that the demand schedule for a particular type of personal computer is as shown in the first and second columns in Exhibit 4.6 for a given point in time. If the price is relatively high, the quantity demanded by consumers is relatively low. For example, if the price is $3,000, only 8,000 of these computers will be demanded (purchased) by consumers. At the other extreme, if the price is $1,000, a total of 25,000 of these computers will be demanded by customers. The quantity of personal computers demanded is higher when the price is lower.

Exhibit 4.6

How the Equilibrium Price Is Determined by Demand and Supply

If the Price of a Particular Computer Is:	The Amount of These Computers Demanded by Consumers Will Be:	The Amount of These Computers Supplied (Produced) by Firms Will Be:
$3,000	8,000	30,000
2,500	14,000	24,000
2,000	18,000	18,000
1,500	22,000	16,000
1,000	25,000	10,000

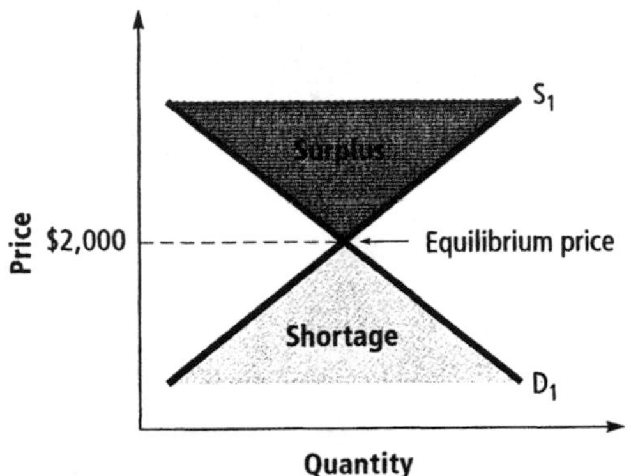

The graph in Exhibit 4.6, which is based on the table, shows the relationship between the price of a computer and the quantity of computers demanded by consumers. The demand curve (labeled D_1) shows that as the price decreases, the quantity demanded increases.

Supply Schedule for a Product

supply schedule a schedule that indicates the quantity of a product that would be supplied (produced) by firms at each possible price

The supply of a product can be shown with a **supply schedule,** or a schedule that indicates the quantity of the product that would be supplied (produced) by firms at each possible price. Assume that the supply schedule for the type of personal computer already discussed is as shown in the first and third columns of Exhibit 4.6 for a given point in time. When the price at which the personal computer can be sold is relatively high, firms will produce a large supply of this computer. For example, if the price is $3,000, 30,000 of these computers will be produced. Firms are willing to produce the computers at this price because they will earn a high profit if they can sell the computers at such a high price.

At the other extreme, if the price of computers is only $1,000, only 10,000 of these computers will be produced. The quantity supplied is much smaller at a low price because some firms will be unwilling to produce the computers if they can sell them for only $1,000. If some firms' actual cost of producing the computers is above this price of $1,000, these firms will be unwilling to produce the computers.

The graph accompanying Exhibit 4.6, which is based on the table, shows the relationship between the price of a computer and the quantity of computers supplied (produced) by firms. The supply curve (labeled S_1) shows that as price increases, the quantity of computers supplied increases.

AP Photo/ Keith Srakocic

A group of visitors to a Porsche and Audi dealership demonstrates North American desires for foreign-made cars, TVs and clothes.

Interaction of Demand and Supply

The interaction of the demand schedule and supply schedule determines the price. Notice from Exhibit 4.6 that at relatively high prices of computers (such as $3,000), the quantity supplied by firms exceeds the quantity demanded by customers, resulting in a so-called **surplus** of computers. For example, at the price of $3,000 the quantity supplied is 30,000 units and the quantity demanded is 8,000 units, resulting in a surplus of 22,000 units. This surplus occurs because consumers are unwilling to purchase computers when the price is excessive.

surplus the situation when the quantity supplied by firms exceeds the quantity demanded by customers

When the price of a computer is relatively low, the quantity supplied by firms will be less than the quantity demanded by customers, resulting in a so-called **shortage** of computers. For example, at a price of $1,000, the quantity demanded by customers is 25,000 units, while the quantity supplied by firms is only 10,000 units, causing a shortage of 15,000 units.

shortage the situation when the quantity supplied by firms is less than the quantity demanded by customers

Notice from Exhibit 4.6 that at a price of $2,000, the quantity of computers supplied by firms is 18,000 units, and the quantity demanded by customers is also 18,000 units. At this price, there is no surplus and no shortage. The price at which the quantity of a product supplied by firms equals the quantity of the product demanded by customers is called the **equilibrium price.** This is the price at which firms normally attempt to sell their products.

equilibrium price the price at which the quantity of a product supplied by firms equals the quantity of the product demanded by customers

At any price above the equilibrium price, the firms will be unable to sell all the computers they produce, resulting in a surplus. Therefore, they would need to reduce their prices to eliminate the surplus. At any price below the equilibrium price, the firms will not produce a sufficient quantity of computers to satisfy all the customers willing to pay that price (resulting in a shortage). The firms could raise their price to correct the shortage.

The demand and supply concepts just applied to a particular type of computer can also be applied to every product or service that firms produce. Each product or service has its own demand schedule and supply schedule, which will determine its own equilibrium price.

Exhibit 4.7

How the Equilibrium Price Is Affected by a Change in Demand

If the Price of a Particular Computer Is:	The Quantity of These Computers Demanded by Consumers Was:	But the Quantity of These Computers Demanded by Consumers Will Now Be:
$3,000	8,000	18,000
2,500	14,000	24,000
2,000	18,000	28,000
1,500	22,000	32,000
1,000	25,000	35,000

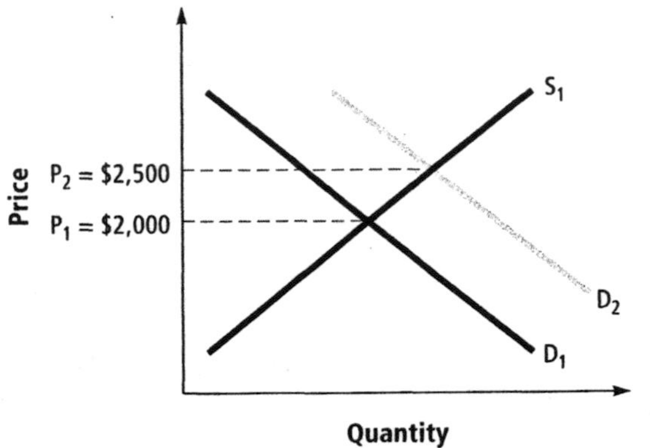

Effect of a Change in the Demand Schedule

As time passes, changing conditions can cause a demand schedule or a supply schedule for a specific product to change. Consequently, the equilibrium price of that product will also change. Reconsider the previous example and assume that computers become more desirable to potential consumers. Assume that the demand schedule for the computer changes as shown at the top of Exhibit 4.7. At any given price, the quantity demanded is now 10,000 units higher than it was before the computer became more popular. The graph accompanying Exhibit 4.7 shows how the demand curve shifts outward from D_1 to D_2.

Now consider the effect of this change in the demand schedule on the equilibrium price of computers. Assuming that the supply schedule remains unchanged, the effect of the change in the demand schedule on the equilibrium price is shown in Exhibit 4.7. At the original equilibrium price of $2,000, the quantity of computers demanded is now 28,000, while the quantity of computers supplied is still 18,000. A shortage of computers occurs at that price. At a price of $2,500, however, the quantity of computers supplied by firms equals the quantity of computers demanded by customers. Therefore, the new equilibrium price is $2,500. The graph at the bottom of Exhibit 4.7 confirms that the shift in the demand schedule from D_1 to D_2 causes the new equilibrium price of computers to be $2,500.

The graph illustrating the effect of a shift in the demand schedule on the equilibrium price of a product can be supplemented with simple logic. When a product becomes more popular, consumers' demand for that product increases, resulting in a shortage. Under these conditions, firms

Exhibit 4.8

How the Equilibrium Price Is Affected by a Change in Supply

If the Price of a Particular Computer Is:	The Quantity of These Computers Supplied by Firms Was:	But the Quantity of These Computers Supplied by Firms Will Now Be:
$3,000	30,000	36,000
2,500	24,000	30,000
2,000	18,000	24,000
1,500	16,000	22,000
1,000	10,000	16,000

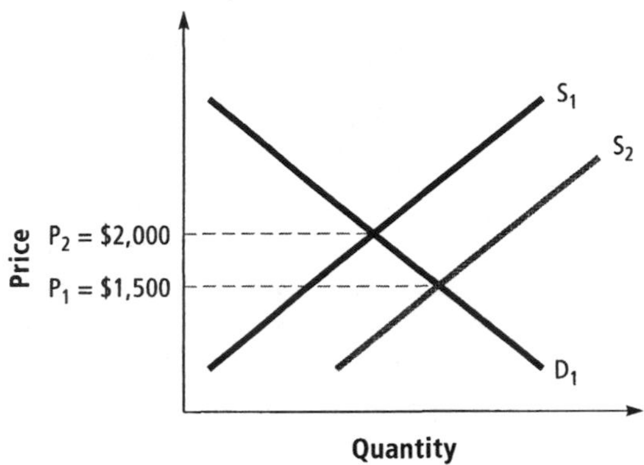

recognize that they can sell whatever amount they produce at a higher price. Once the price is raised to the level at which the quantity supplied is equal to the quantity demanded, the shortage is corrected.

Effect of a Change in the Supply Schedule

Just as the demand for a product may change, so may the supply. A change in the supply can also affect the equilibrium price of the product. To illustrate this effect, reconsider the original example in which the equilibrium price of computers was $2,000. Now assume that improved technology allows firms to produce the computer at a lower cost. In this case, firms will be willing to produce a larger supply of computers at any given price, which reflects a change in the supply schedule.

Assume that as a result of the improved technology (lower production costs), the supply schedule changes as shown in Exhibit 4.8. At any given price, the quantity supplied is now 6,000 units higher than it was before the improved technology. The graph accompanying Exhibit 4.8 shows how the supply schedule shifts outward from S_1 to S_2.

Now consider the effect of this change in the supply schedule on the equilibrium price of computers. Assuming that the demand schedule remains unchanged, the effect of the change in the supply schedule on the equilibrium price is shown in Exhibit 4.8. At the original equilibrium price of $2,000, the quantity of computers demanded is 18,000, while the quantity of computers supplied (produced) is now 24,000. A surplus of computers occurs at that price. At a price of $1,500, however, the quantity of computers supplied by firms equals the quantity of computers demanded by consumers. Therefore, the new equilibrium price is $1,500. The graph at the bottom of Exhibit 4.8 confirms that the shift in the supply schedule from S_1 to S_2 causes the new equilibrium price of computers to be $1,500.

The graph illustrating the effect of a shift in the supply schedule on the equilibrium price of a product can be supplemented with simple logic. When improved technology allows firms to produce a product at a lower cost, more firms will be willing to produce the product. This results in a larger supply produced, which causes a surplus. Firms recognize that the only way they will be able to sell all that is supplied (produced) is to lower the price of the product. Once the price is lowered to the level at which the quantity supplied is once again equal to the quantity demanded, the surplus is eliminated.

Effect of Demand and Supply on the General Price Level

The discussion so far of demand and supply has focused on one product to show how the equilibrium price of that product might change. Now consider how the general price level for all products might change. The general price level is an average of prices of all existing products and services. If the total (aggregate) demand by consumers for all or most products suddenly increases (perhaps because of an increase in the income level of most consumers), the general level of prices could rise. The general price level may also be affected by shifts in the supply schedules for all goods and services. If the supply schedule of all or most products suddenly decreases (perhaps because of increasing expenses when producing the products), the general level of prices should rise.

Factors That Influence Market Prices

Thus far, examples have illustrated how the demand by customers or the supply produced by firms can change, causing a new market price. Shifts in the demand schedule or the supply schedule can be caused by several factors, some of which are identified next.

Consumer Income

Consumer income determines the amount of products and services that individuals can purchase. A high level of economic growth results in more income for consumers. When consumers' income rises, they may demand a larger quantity of specific products and services. That is, the demand schedules for various products and services may shift out in response to higher income, which could result in higher prices.

Conversely, when consumers' income level declines, they may demand a smaller quantity of specific products. For example, in the early 1990s, the average income level in the United States declined substantially in specific areas where firms relied on government contracts (such as for building missiles and so on). The federal government's cutbacks on such expenditures resulted in less work for firms in specific regions of the country. As income declined, the demand for new homes in these areas declined, causing a surplus of new homes. The firms that were building new homes were forced to lower their prices because of the surplus.

Consumer Preferences

As consumer preferences (or tastes) for a particular product change, the quantity of that product demanded by consumers may change. There are numerous examples of products whose prices rose in response to increased demand. For example, the price of a scalped ticket at a sold-out event such as a concert, the World Series, or the Super Bowl may easily exceed $300.

When a product becomes less popular, the demand for the product declines. The resulting surplus may force firms to lower their prices to sell what they produce. For example, when specific clothes become unpopular, clothing manufacturers sell these clothes at discounted prices just to eliminate the surplus.

Production Expenses

Another factor that can affect equilibrium prices is a change in production expenses. When firms experience lower expenses, they are willing to supply (produce) more at any given price (as explained earlier). This results in a surplus of the product, forcing firms to lower their price to sell all that they have produced. For example, the prices of musical compact discs have declined every year since they were first introduced.

When expenses of firms increase, the opposite result occurs. For example, insurance companies that had insured South Florida homes in the early 1990s incurred high expenses in the aftermath of Hurricane Andrew. Some of these companies decided that they would no longer supply this insurance service in South Florida. Those companies that were still willing to provide insurance were able to raise their prices.

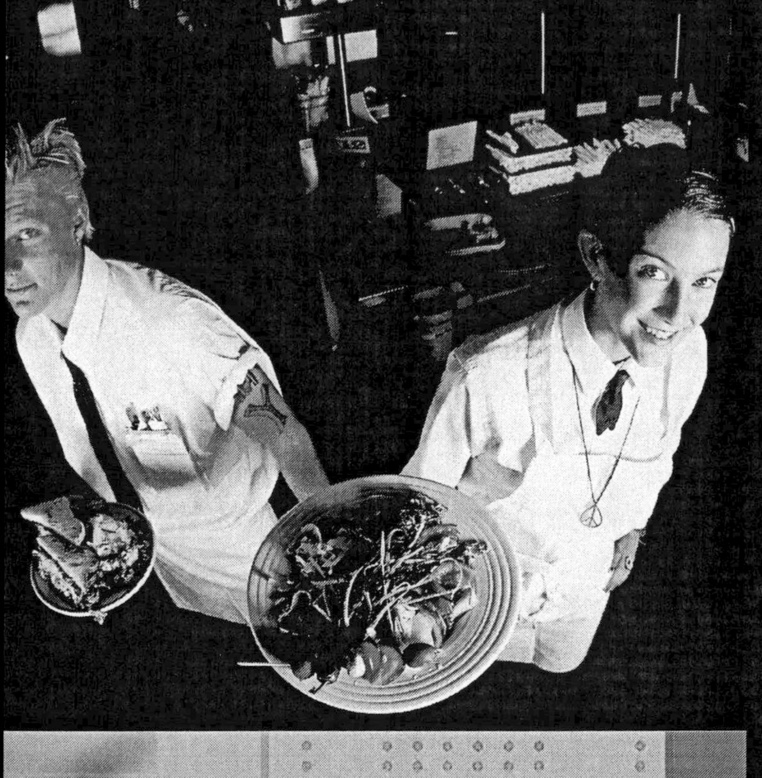

learning goals

- >lg 1 What is the human resource management process?
- >lg 2 How are human resource needs determined?
- >lg 3 How do human resource managers find good people to fill the jobs?
- >lg 4 What is the employee selection process?
- >lg 5 What types of training and development do organizations offer their employees?
- >lg 6 What is a performance appraisal?
- >lg 7 How are employees compensated?
- >lg 8 What is organizational career management?
- >lg 9 What are the key laws and federal agencies affecting human resource management?
- >lg 10 What trends are affecting human resource management?

Managing Human Resources

13

An Employee Problem at Don Pablo's

James Taylor is an assistant restaurant manager at Don Pablo's **(http://www.avado.com)**, a Mexican restaurant chain of more than 130 units, many of which are located in larger cities of the East. In addition to being a shift manager several days a week, he is responsible for hiring and training employees and scheduling their weekly shift assignments. Most of the wait staff work part-time and attend the local university. After the restaurant closes at 11:00 P.M., James stays to check liquor and food inventories, count cash and credit card receipts, and clean. One recent morning, he came early to the restaurant to prepare work schedules for the next two weeks, check employee time sheets, prepare payroll information for electronic transfer to corporate headquarters, and decide how to address a performance problem with Sharon Young, a waitress who has worked at the restaurant for nearly a year.

Sharon had been 30 minutes late for work the previous night, the fifth time in the last four weeks she had been late. Her attendance record for the last three months revealed six absences; each time she called only a few minutes before the start of her work shift to say she could not come to work. Punctuality and attendance had obviously become a problem. As a part-time employee, Sharon was not eligible for any paid sick leave or health insurance coverage. At the same time, James was aware that Sharon was an excellent waitress; her service and customer relations skills are the best among the current wait staff, and several repeat customers ask for her table.

As James contemplated his approach and options in dealing with Sharon, he quickly reviewed job and performance requirements for wait staff employees. They had to have good communication skills, a strong service (or helpfulness) orientation, reasonably detailed knowledge of menu items, be neat and clean in physical appearance, and possess sufficient strength to carry large trays of food. Most importantly, however, they had to be dependable, or work when scheduled and report to work a few minutes before the start of the work shift. Sharon was obviously becoming less dependable. Training, counseling, a disciplinary warning, or termination were feasible options for dealing with her situation. Discharging her, however, won't improve her performance or correct her behavior.

Critical Thinking Questions

As you read this chapter, consider the following questions as they relate to Don Pablo's Mexican restaurant:

- Is James faced with a typical human resource problem?
- What areas does human resource management cover?
- How should James proceed in solving this employee problem?

BUSINESS IN THE 21ST CENTURY

Human resource management in contemporary organizations is instrumental in driving an organization toward its objectives. Today, human resource professionals face numerous challenges in recruiting, selecting, and retaining employees:

Human resource managers at FedEx train employees to use computer technology that improves communication among employees and increases worker efficiency and productivity.

- Organizations are competing with each other for a shrinking pool of applicants.
- Workers seek to balance work and home/life activities.
- Technology is reshaping the way business is done.
- Laws govern many aspects of the employee-employer relationship.

Each day, human resource experts and front line supervisors deal with these challenges while sharing responsibility for attracting and retaining skilled, motivated employees. Whether faced with a large or small human resource problem, managers like James at Don Pablo's need to understand the process for finding and retaining excellent employees.

In this chapter, you will learn about the role of human resource management in building and maintaining an exceptional workforce. We will explore human resource planning, recruiting and selection, training, and motivating employees toward reaching organizational objectives. The chapter will also cover employee job changes within an organization and the laws guiding human resource decisions. Finally, we will look at important trends influencing human resource management.

DEVELOPING PEOPLE TO HELP REACH ORGANIZATIONAL GOALS

>lg 1

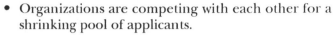

human resource management

The process of hiring, developing, motivating, and evaluating employees to achieve organizational goals.

Human resource management is the process of hiring, developing, motivating, and evaluating employees to achieve organizational goals. Organizational strategies and objectives form the basis for making all human resource management decisions. All companies strive to hire and develop well-trained, motivated employees. The human resources management process includes these steps, illustrated in Exhibit 9-1:

- Job analysis and design
- Human resource planning and forecasting
- Employee recruitment
- Employee selection
- Training and development
- Performance planning and evaluation

exhibit 9-1 Human Resource Management Process

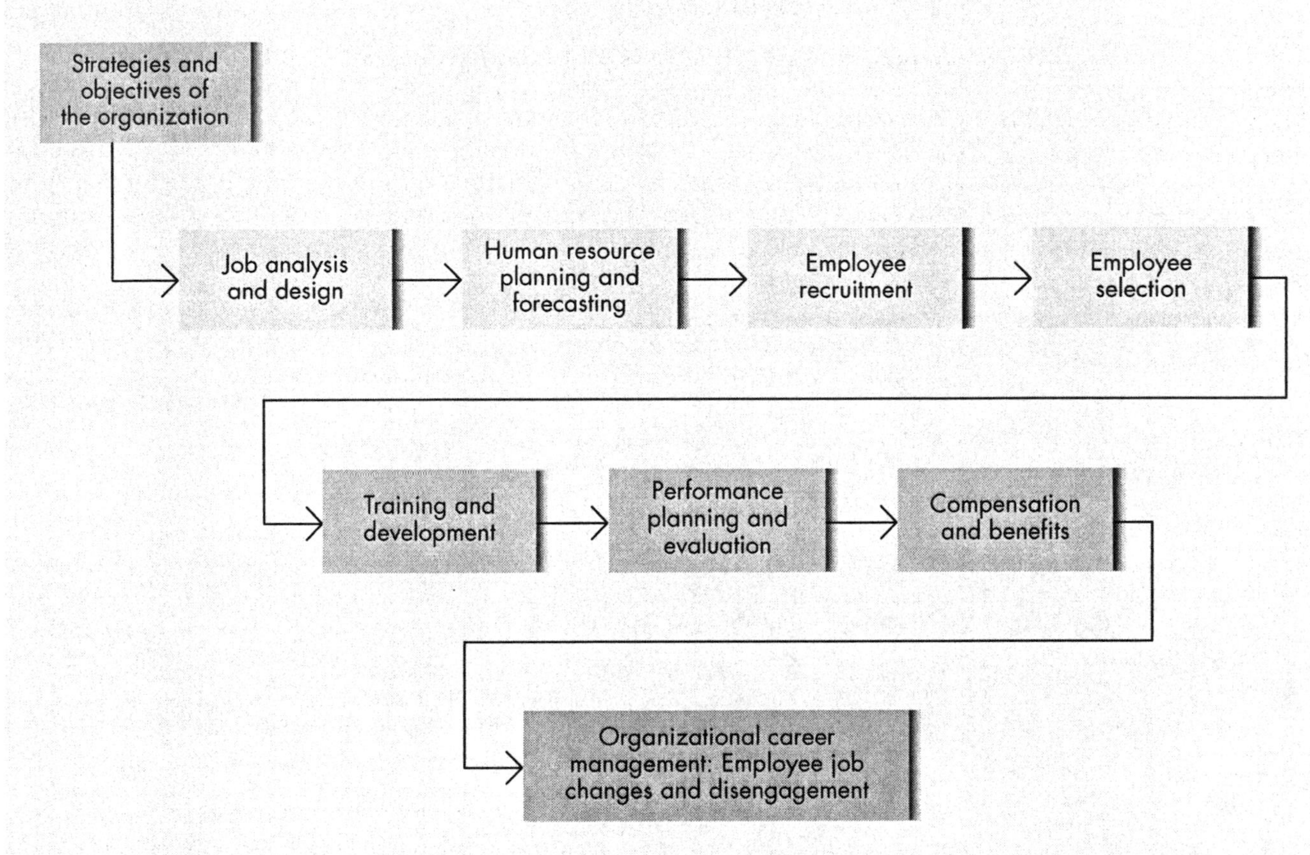

- Compensation and benefits
- Organizational career management: employee job changes and disengagement.

In the following sections, you will learn more about each of these important functions.

concept check

- Define human resource management.
- Describe the human resource management process.

HUMAN RESOURCE PLANNING

>lg 2

Firms need to have the right number of people, with the right training, in the right jobs, to do the organization's work when it needs to be done. Human resource specialists are the ones who must determine future human resource needs. Then they assess the skills of the firm's existing employees to see if new people must be hired or existing ones retrained.

human resource (HR) planning
Creating a strategy for meeting future human resource needs.

Creating a strategy for meeting future human resource needs is called **human resource (HR) planning.** Two important aspects of HR planning are job analysis and forecasting the firm's people needs. The HR planning process begins with a review of corporate strategy and policy. By understanding the mission of the organization, planners can understand its human resource needs. When Compaq Computer bought Digital Equipment Corp. (DEC), the acquisition resulted in several thousand DEC employees losing their jobs, while hundreds of

Compaq employees were transferred to DEC's former headquarters in Boston. Many transferred employees assumed managerial positions.

Job Analysis and Design

job analysis
A study of the tasks required to do a particular job well.

job description
The tasks and responsibilities of a job.

job specification
A list of the skills, knowledge, and abilities a person must have to fill a job.

Human resource planners must know what skills different jobs require. Information about a specific job is typically assembled through a **job analysis,** a study of the tasks required to do a job well. This information is used to specify the essential skills, knowledge, and abilities. For instance, when General Dynamics was awarded the contract for a new military plane, several new jobs were created for industrial engineers. Job analysts from the company's human resource department gathered information from other department heads and supervisors to help recruiters hire the right people for the new jobs.

The tasks and responsibilities of a job are listed in a **job description.** The skills, knowledge, and abilities a person must have to fill a job are spelled out in a **job specification.** These two documents help human resource planners find the right people for specific jobs. A sample job description is shown in Exhibit 9-2.

exhibit 9-2 | Job Description

Position: College Recruiter
Location: Corporate Offices
Reports to: Vice President of Human Resources
Classification: Salaried/Exempt

Job Summary: Member of HR corporate team. Interacts with managers and department heads to determine hiring needs for college graduates. Visits 20 to 30 college and university campuses each year to conduct preliminary interviews of graduating students in all academic disciplines. Following initial interviews, works with corporate staffing specialists to determine persons who will be interviewed a second time. Makes recommendations to hiring managers concerning best qualified applicants.

Job Duties and Responsibilities:

Estimated time spent and importance

- 15% Working with managers and department heads, determines college recruiting needs.
- 10% Determines colleges and universities with degree programs appropriate to hiring needs to be visited.
- 15% Performs college relations activities with numerous colleges and universities.
- 25% Visits campuses to conduct interviews of graduating seniors.
- 15% Develops applicant files and performs initial applicant evaluations.
- 10% Assists staffing specialists and line managers in determining who to schedule for second interviews.
- 5% Prepares annual college recruiting report containing information and data about campuses, number interviewed, number hired, and related information.
- 5% Participates in tracking college graduates who are hired to aid in determining campuses that provide the most outstanding employees.

Job Specification (Qualifications):

Bachelor's degree in human resource management or a related field. Minimum of two years of work experience with the firm in HR or department that annually hires college graduates. Ability to perform in a team environment, especially with line managers and department heads. Very effective oral and written communication skills. Reasonably proficient in Excel, Word, and Windows computer environment and familiar with People Soft.

Human Resource Planning and Forecasting

Does TeamStaff, a PEO, live up to its motto "Simply a better way to employ people"? Find out at

http://www.teamstaff.com

Forecasting an organization's human resource needs, known as an HR *demand forecast,* is an essential aspect of HR planning. This process involves two forecasts: (1) determining the number of people needed by some future time (in one year, for example), and (2) estimating the number of people currently employed by the organization who will be available to fill various jobs at some future time. This is an *internal* supply forecast.

By comparing human resource demand and supply forecasts, a future personnel surplus or shortage can be determined and appropriate action taken. For example, United Airlines hired approximately 2,000 additional flight attendants when it developed the Star Alliance, an air transport network consisting of United, Lufthansa, SAS, Thai, Varig, and Air Canada. On the other hand, One Plus Financial terminated hundreds of employees when it withdrew from the mortgage banking industry. Exhibit 9-3 summarizes the process of forecasting an organization's needs.

exhibit 9-3 | Human Resource Planning Process

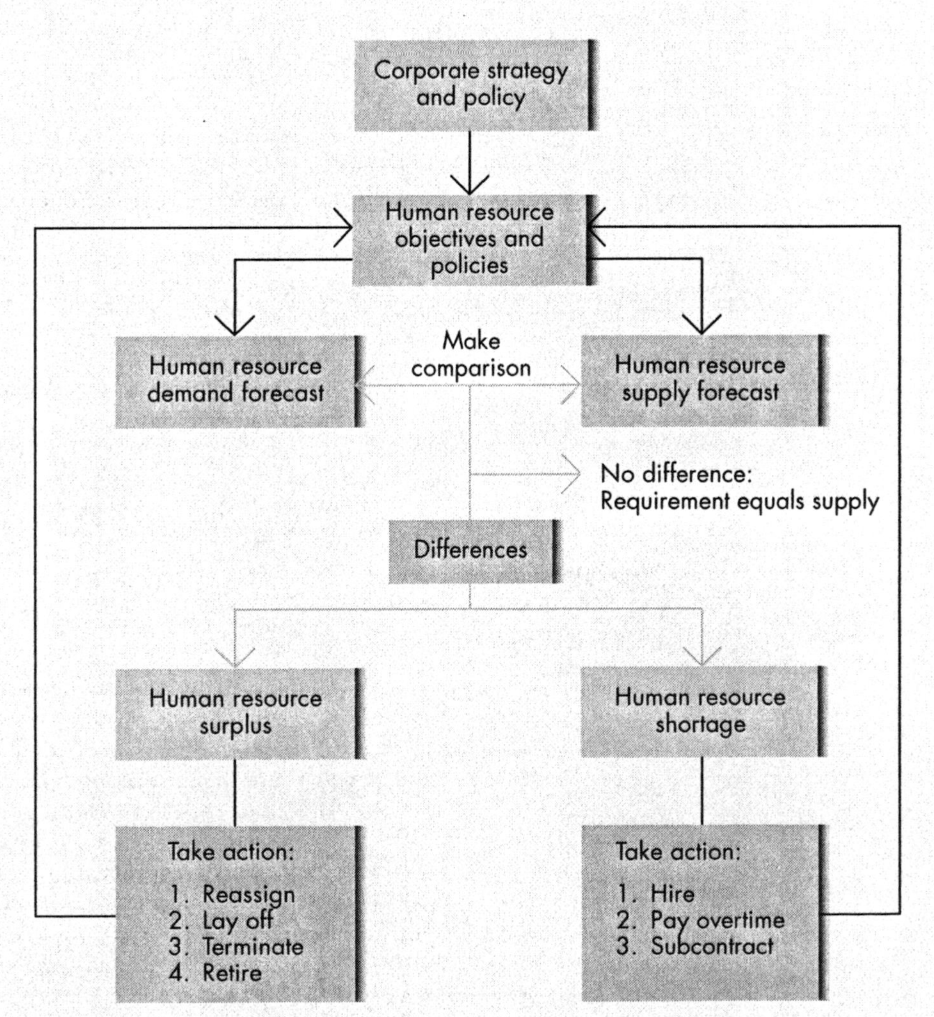

contingent workers
Persons who prefer temporary employment, either part-time or full-time.

In recent years many firms with employee shortages are hiring **contingent workers,** or persons who prefer temporary employment, either part-time or full-time. College students and retired persons comprise a big portion of America's contingent workforce. Other people who want to work but don't want to be permanent employees join a professional employer organization (PEO). A PEO performs staffing, training, and compensation functions by contracting with a business to provide employees for a specified period of time. A firm with a shortage of accountants can rent or lease an accountant from the PEO for the expected duration of the shortage.

concept check

- Describe the job analysis and design process.
- What is the process for human resource forecasting?

EMPLOYEE RECRUITMENT

>lg 3

When a firm creates a new position or an existing one becomes vacant, it starts looking for people with qualifications that meet the requirements of the job. Two sources of job applicants are the internal and external labor markets. The internal labor market consists of employees currently employed by the firm; the external labor market is the pool of potential applicants outside the firm.

Most companies including UPS, Southwest Airlines, and Wal-Mart follow a policy of promotion from within and try to fill positions with their existing employees. The internal search for job applicants usually means that a person must change his or her job. People are typically either promoted or transferred. A firm's *skills inventory* can help find the right person for a job opening. A skills inventory is a computerized employee database containing information on each employee's previous work experience, educational background, performance records, career objectives, and job location preferences. General Electric has used a skills inventory for many years as a means of determining promotions and transfers.

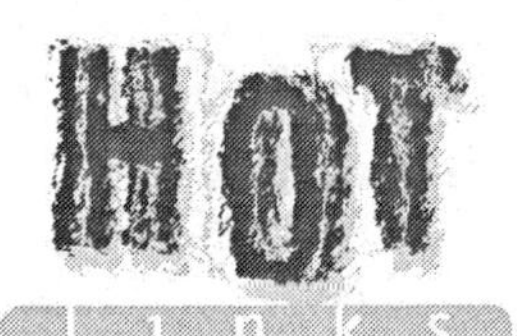

Search the database of CareerBuilder.com (**http://www.careerbuilder.com**) for a job in a new city. It combines the listings of *The New York Times, Washington Post, Boston Globe, Chicago Tribune, Los Angeles Times,* and *San Jose Mercury News.*

recruitment
The attempt to find and attract qualified applicants in the external labor market.

If qualified job candidates cannot be found inside the firm, the external labor market must be tapped. **Recruitment** is the attempt to find and attract qualified applicants in the external labor market. The type of position determines which recruitment method will be used and which segment of the labor market will be searched. Boeing will not recruit an experienced engineer the same way it would recruit a secretary or clerk typist.

Many organizations find qualified job applicants for professional positions through recruitment programs at college campuses.

Nontechnical, unskilled, and other nonsupervisory workers are recruited through newspaper, radio, and sometimes even television help wanted ads in local media. Starbucks placed ads in the *Beijing Youth Daily* to attract workers for its Beijing coffee shops.[1] Entry-level accountants, engineers, and systems analysts are commonly hired through college campus recruitment efforts. Each year Texas Instruments sends recruiters to dozens of colleges across the United States that have engineering degree programs. To recruit inexperienced technicians, National SemiConductor visits junior and community college campuses with electronic and related technical programs that are within 50 to 100 miles of its facilities.

A firm that needs executives and other experienced professional, technical, and managerial employees may employ the services of an executive search firm such as Korn/Ferry. The hiring firm pays the search firm a fee equivalent to one to four months of the employee's first-year salary. Many search firms specialize in a particular occupation, industry, or geographic location.

job fair
An event, typically one day, held at a convention center to bring together thousands of job seekers and hundreds of firms searching for employees.

Many firms participate in local job fairs. A **job fair** is typically a one-day event held at a convention center to bring together thousands of job seekers and hundreds of firms searching for employees.

Some firms now use the Internet exclusively to attract new employees. A firm can post job announcements at its Web site, and applicants send their résumés via the Internet. Beacon Application Services Corp., a systems integration company, recruits only over the Internet. According to Dan Maude, president of the firm, "A year's worth of Web recruiting for us costs less than one agency fee. . . . it's also faster."[2] The Applying Technology box describes how Career Central uses the Internet to match job applicants with job openings.

APPLYING TECHNOLOGY

INTERNET HIRING AND E-RECRUITING: THE "TIDAL WAVE" OF THE FUTURE

Internet hiring is a tidal wave that keeps on growing. There are several approaches being used in e-recruiting. These include:

- **Job Boards.** You can search for candidates by region, industry, or demographics. Problems: Candidate quality is questionable.
- **Professional Portals.** Companies can add content other than job listings in their information. Benefits include direct marketing of jobs and the ability of employers to promote their brands to candidates.
- **Database Models.** These allow for fast "matches" and potentially broader selection pools. Companies pay per candidate. Problems: Data might not be fresh.

The Fortune 500's best practices to optimize internet use in corporate recruiting include:

- 73% link their careers section directly to their home page.
- 56% adhere to the "one click to apply" practice.
- 55% publish information on employee benefits.
- 44% publish information on corporate culture.
- 42% have a separate college recruiting section.
- 42% allow job seekers to search a database of open job positions.

A second study found that the most effective online sites share many of these characteristics:

- They allow candidates to navigate the site easily and use links to career pages and job openings.
- They describe career opportunities and individual jobs in greater detail than do typical help-wanted ads.
- Their information about the company, including profiles of archetypal employees, gives candidates a sense of what it would be like to work there.
- They let candidates paste resumes to an application page, e-mail then to a recruiter, or create online applications that allow information to be entered with a few clicks.

Critical Thinking Questions

1. What are the benefits of an electronic job search for an applicant?
2. What are the benefits to the employer?
3. How can an electronic job search improve the match between the applicant's skills and the job's requirements?
4. Would you consider applying for a job online? Why or why not?

Source: "Is Online Recruiting Becoming a Tidal Wave?" *HR Focus*, April 2001.

concept check

- What is a skills inventory, and what are the two labor markets?
- Describe different ways that employees are recruited.
- How is technology helping firms find the right recruits?

Other firms including Coca-Cola, UBS PaineWebber, and NationsBank utilize artificial intelligence software to scan and track résumés.[3] Webhire, Inc. and HotJobs.com scan résumés for key words to identify qualified job candidates. Each system can scan and search thousands of résumés in minutes. With such systems, the words you use to describe your education, background, and work experience become very important.

EMPLOYEE SELECTION

selection
The process of determining which persons in the applicant pool possess the qualifications necessary to be successful on the job.

After a firm has attracted enough job applicants, employment specialists begin the selection process. **Selection** is the process of determining which persons in the applicant pool possesses the qualifications necessary to be successful on the job. The steps in the employee selection process are shown in Exhibit 9-4 and described below:

1. *Initial screening.* During the initial screening, an applicant usually completes an application form and has a brief interview of 30 minutes or less. The application form includes questions about education, work experience, and previous job duties. A personal résumé may be substituted for the application form. The interview is normally structured and consists of a short list of specific questions. For example: Are you familiar with any accounting software packages? Did you supervise anyone in your last job? Did you use a company car when making sales calls?
2. *Employment testing.* Following the initial screening, an applicant may be asked to take one or more employment tests, such as the Minnesota Clerical Test or the Wonderlic Personnel Test, a mental ability test. Some tests are designed to measure special job skills, others measure aptitudes, and some are intended to capture characteristics of one's personality. The Myers-Briggs

exhibit 9-4 | Steps of the Employee Selection Process

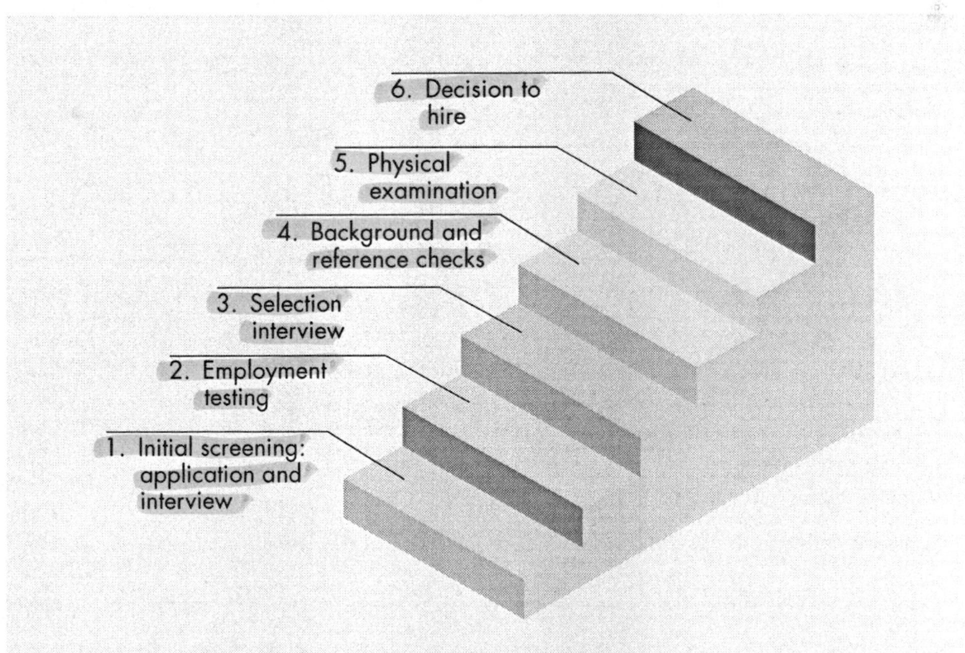

Type Indicator is a personality and motivational test widely used on college campuses as an aid in providing job and career counseling. Companies are increasingly using general attitude tests in job screening. John Pate, vice president of BT: Employee Screening Services, says, "You like to know what people are thinking. You don't want to hire their problems."[4]

selection interview
An in-depth discussion of an applicant's work experience, skills and abilities, education, and career interests.

3. *Selection interview.* The tool most widely used in making hiring decisions by Intel, Merck, and other firms is the **selection interview,** an in-depth discussion of an applicant's work experience, skills and abilities, education, and career interests. For managerial and professional positions, an applicant may be interviewed by several persons, including the line manager for the position to be filled. This interview is designed to determine an applicant's communication ability and motivation. It is also a means for gathering additional factual information from the applicant such as college major, years of part-time work experience, computer equipment used, and reason for leaving the last job. The applicant may be asked to explain how to solve a particular management problem or how she or he provided leadership to a group in a previous work situation when an important problem had to be solved quickly. United Airlines asks prospective flight attendants how they handled a conflict with a customer or coworker in a previous job.

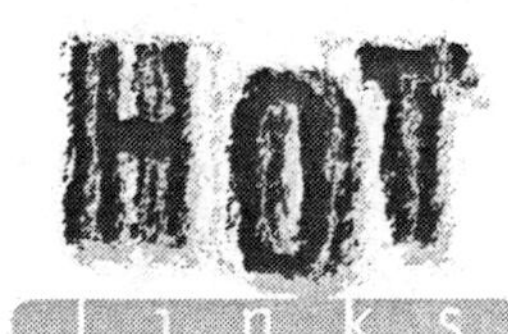

Get advice for brushing up your interview skills at the Job Hunting Advice page of *The Wall Street Journal*'s Career site, http://www.careerjournal.com

Carolyn Murray, a recruiter for W. L. Gore and Associates, makers of Gore-Tex, says she pays little attention to a candidate's carefully scripted responses to her admittedly easy questions. Instead, she listens for a casual remark that reveals the reality behind an otherwise thought-out reply. Using a baseball analogy, Carolyn gives examples of how three job candidates struck out in Exhibit 9-5.[5]

4. *Background and reference check.* If applicants pass the selection interview, most firms examine their background and check their references. In recent years an increasing number of employers such as American Airlines, Disney, and Microsoft are carefully researching applicants' backgrounds, particularly

exhibit 9-5 | Striking Out with Gore-Tex

The Pitch (Question to Applicant)	The Swing (Applicant's Response)	The Miss (Interviewer's Reaction to Response)
"Give me an example of a time when you had a conflict with a team member."	"Our leader asked me to handle all of the FedExing for our team. I did it, but I thought that FedExing was a waste of my time."	"At Gore, we work from a team concept. Her answer shows that she won't exactly jump when one of her teammates needs help."
"Tell me how you solved a problem that was impeding your project."	"One of the engineers on my team wasn't pulling his weight, and we were closing in on a deadline. So I took on some of his work."	"The candidate may have resolved the issue for this particular deadline, but he did nothing to prevent the problem from happening again."
"What's the one thing that you would change about your current position?"	"My job as a salesman has become mundane. Now I want the responsibility of managing people."	"He's not maximizing his current position. Selling is never mundane if you go about it in the right way."

their legal history, reasons for leaving previous jobs, and even creditworthiness. Retail firms such as Men's Warehouse, JCPenney, RadioShack, and TD Industries, where employees have extensive contact with customers, tend to be very careful about checking applicant backgrounds. Some checking can be easily done using the Internet. In fact, many retired law enforcement officers have started their own firms that specialize in these investigations.

5. *Physical exams.* Companies frequently require job candidates to have a medical checkup to ensure they are physically able to perform a job. Drug testing is becoming a routine part of physical exams. Companies such as American Airlines, Burlington Northern Santa Fe Railway, and the U.S. Postal Service use drug testing for reasons of workplace safety, productivity, and employee health. A comprehensive study by the Postal Service found that employees who tested positive for drugs were 50 percent more likely to be fired, injured, disciplined, or absent than those who tested negative. Drug users also had lower performance ratings.[6]
6. *Decision to hire.* If an applicant progresses satisfactorily through all the selection steps, a decision to hire the individual is made. The decision to hire is nearly always made by the manager of the new employee.

concept check

- What are the steps in the employee selection process?
- Describe some ways that applicants are tested.

EMPLOYEE TRAINING AND DEVELOPMENT

>lg 5

training and development
Activities that provide learning situations in which an employee acquires additional knowledge or skills to increase job performance.

To ensure that both new and experienced employees have the knowledge and skills to perform their jobs successfully, organizations invest in training and development activities. **Training and development** involves learning situations in which the employee acquires additional knowledge or skills to increase job performance. Training objectives specify performance improvements, reductions in errors, job knowledge to be gained, and/or other positive organizational results. The design of training programs at General Electric, for example, includes determining instructional methods, number of trainees per class, printed materials (cases, notebooks, manuals, and the like) to be used, location of training, use of audiovisual equipment and software, and many other matters. The process of creating and implementing training and development activities is shown in Exhibit 9-6.

exhibit 9-6 | Employee Training and Development Process

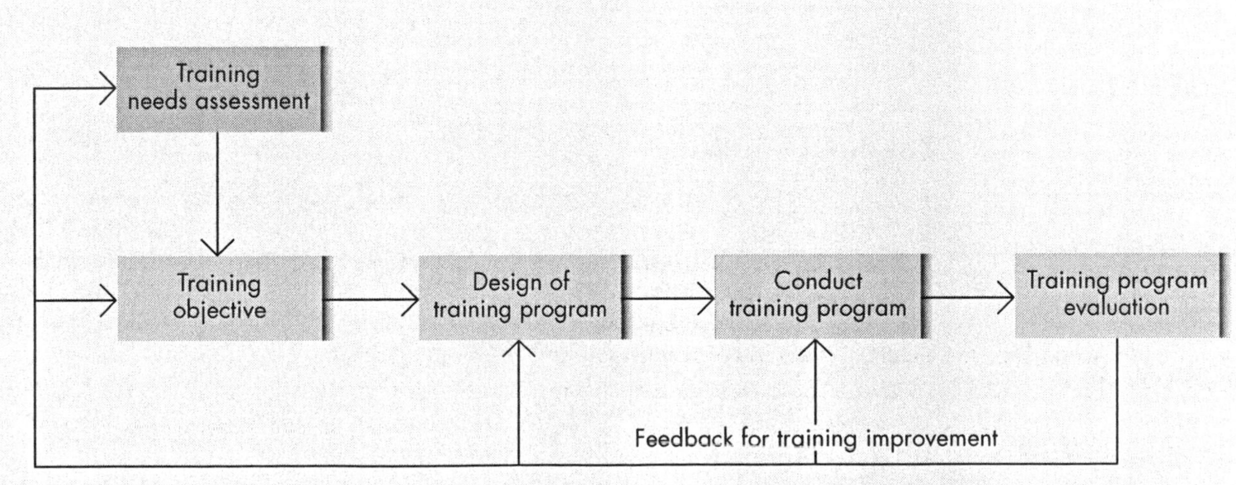

Training for new employees is instrumental in getting them up to speed and familiar with their job responsibilities. A study at MCI WorldCom found that in the first three months a new hire can accomplish only 60 percent as much as an experienced worker. And even a 5 percent drop in overall employee efficiency can cut MCI WorldCom's annual revenue by "several hundred million dollars."[7] The first type of training that new employees experience is **employee orientation,** which entails getting the new employee ready to perform on the job. Formal orientation (a half-day classroom program) provides information about company policies, salary and benefits, and parking. Although this information is very helpful, the more important orientation is about job assignments, work rules, equipment, and performance expectations provided by the new employee's supervisor and coworkers. This second briefing tends to be more informal and may last for several days or even weeks.

employee orientation
Training that prepares a new employee to perform on the job; includes information about job assignments, work rules, equipment, and performance expectations, as well as about company policies, salary and benefits, and parking.

On-the-Job Training

Continuous training for both new and experienced employees is important to keep job skills fresh. Job-specific training, designed to enhance a new employee's ability to perform a job, includes **on-the-job training,** during which the employee learns the job by doing it with guidance from a supervisor or experienced coworker.

on-the-job training
Training in which the employee learns the job by doing it with guidance from a supervisor or experienced coworker.

On-the-job training takes place at the job site or workstation and tends to be directly related to the job. This training involves specific job instructions, coaching (guidance given to new employees by experienced ones), special project assignments, or job rotation. **Job rotation** is the reassignment of workers to several different jobs over time. At Sears, management trainees work sequentially in two or three merchandise departments, customer service, credit, and human resources during their first year on the job.

job rotation
Reassignment of workers to several different jobs over time so that they can learn the basics of each job.

An **apprenticeship** usually combines specific on-the-job instruction with classroom training. It may last as long as four years and can be found in the skilled trades of carpentry, plumbing, and electrical work.

apprenticeship
A form of on-the-job training that combines specific job instruction with classroom instruction.

With **mentoring,** another form of on-the-job training, a senior manager or other experienced employee provides job- and career-related information to a protégé. Mentoring is becoming increasingly popular with many firms, including Federal Express, Texaco, Merrill Lynch, and Bank of America, which uses "quad squads" composed of a mentor and three new hires (a male, female, and a minority group member). At Coca-Cola Roberto Goizueta mentored Douglas Ivester to become CEO of the company. When Goizueta died suddenly in 1997, Ivester's transition to CEO went very smoothly. The company clearly benefited from this mentoring relationship.

mentoring
A form of on-the-job training in which a senior manager or other experienced employee provides job- and career-related information to a protégé.

The primary benefits of on-the-job training are that it provides instant feedback about performance and is inexpensive. Trainees produce while learning, and no expensive classroom or learning tools are needed.

Off-the-Job Training

Even with the advantages of on-the-job training, many firms recognize that it is often necessary to train employees away from the workplace. With off-the-job training, employees learn the job away from the job. There are numerous popular methods of off-the-job training. Frequently, it takes place in a classroom where cases, role-play exercises, films, videos, lectures, and computer demonstrations are utilized to develop workplace skills.

Another form of off-the-job training takes place in a facility called a vestibule or a training simulator. In **vestibule training,** used by Honda and Kroger, trainees learn about products, manufacturing processes, and selling in a scaled-down version of an assembly line or retail outlet. When mistakes

vestibule training
A form of off-the-job training in which trainees learn in a scaled-down version or simulated work environment.

By using vestibule training, airlines can teach pilots flight maneuvers and the controls of new aircraft in a safe and controlled off-the-job training environment.

are made, no customers are lost or products damaged. A training simulator, such as American Airlines' flight simulator for pilot training, is much like a vestibule facility. Pilots can practice hazardous flight maneuvers or learn the controls of a new aircraft in a safe, controlled environment with no passengers.

In a very rapidly developing trend that will undoubtedly accelerate in the 21st century, many companies including Compaq and Microsoft are using computer-assisted, electronically delivered training and development courses and programs. Many of these courses have their origins in **programmed instruction,** a self-paced, highly structured training method that presents trainees with concepts and problems using a modular format. Each module consists of a set of concepts, math rules, or task procedures with test questions at the end of the module. When the trainee or student masters all material presented in a module, he or she advances to the next module, which is somewhat more difficult. Some courses taught on your campus probably use programmed instructional materials.

Finally, trade associations, colleges and universities, and professional organizations offer professional and executive education courses at training centers or professional organization meetings.

Usually, off-the-job training is more expensive than on-the-job training, and its impact is less direct or the transfer of learning to the job is less immediate. Nevertheless, despite these shortcomings, some training can only be done away from the job.

concept check

- Describe several types of on-the-job training.
- Explain vestibule training and programmed instruction.

PERFORMANCE PLANNING AND EVALUATION

programmed instruction
A form of computer-assisted off-the-job training.

performance appraisal
A comparison of actual performance with expected performance to assess an employee's contributions to the organization.

Along with employee orientation and training, new employees learn about performance expectations through performance planning and evaluation. Managers provide employees with expectations about the job. These are communicated as job objectives, schedules, deadlines, and product and/or service quality requirements. As an employee performs job tasks, the supervisor periodically evaluates the employee's efforts. A **performance appraisal** is a comparison of actual performance with expected performance to assess an employee's contributions to the organization and to make decisions about training, compensation, promotion, and other job changes. The performance planning and appraisal process is shown in Exhibit 9-7 and described below.

1. The manager establishes performance standards.
2. The employee works to meet the standards and expectations.
3. The employee's supervisor evaluates the employee's work in terms of quality and quantity of output and various characteristics such as job knowledge, initiative, relationships with others, and attendance and punctuality.
4. Following the performance evaluation, reward (pay raise) and job change (promotion) decisions can be made.
5. Rewards are positive feedback and provide reinforcement, or encouragement, for the employee to work harder in the future.

exhibit 9-7 | Performance Planning and Evaluation

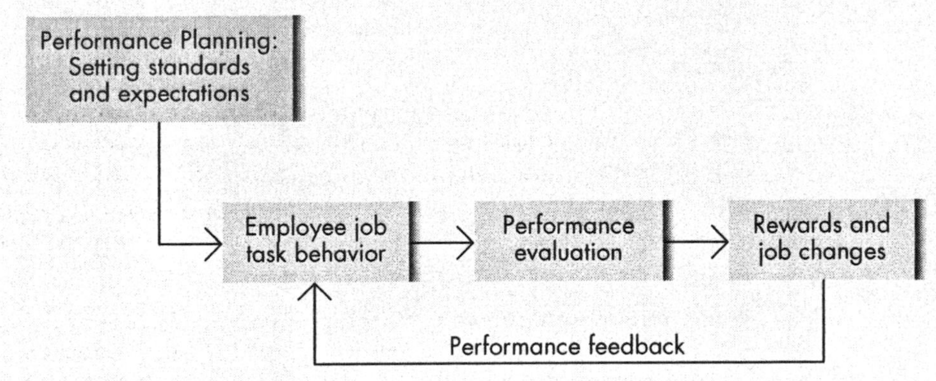

concept check

- What are the steps in the performance planning and appraisal process?
- What purposes do performance appraisals serve?

Performance appraisals serve a number of purposes, but they are most often used to make decisions about pay raises, training needs, and advancement opportunities.

EMPLOYEE COMPENSATION AND BENEFITS

>lg 7

External influences affect employee pay and benefits. With a high demand for skilled workers and high turnover rates, firms in the information technology industry offer high wages and many benefits to attract and retain workers like this Netscape employee.

Compensation, which includes both pay and benefits, is closely connected to performance appraisal. Employees who perform better tend to get bigger pay raises.[8] Several factors affect an employee's pay.

1. *Pay structure and internal influences.* Wages, salaries, and benefits usually reflect the importance of the job. The jobs that management considers more important are compensated at a higher rate; president, chief engineer, and chief financial officer are high-paying jobs. Likewise, different jobs of equal importance to the firm are compensated at the same rate. For instance, if a drill-press operator and a lathe operator are considered of equal importance, they may both be paid $21 per hour.
2. *Pay level and external influences.* In deciding how much to pay workers, the firm must also be concerned with the salaries paid by competitors. If competitors are paying much higher wages, a firm may lose its best employees. Larger firms conduct salary surveys to see what other firms are paying. Wage and salary surveys conducted by the Chamber of Commerce or the U.S. Department of Labor can also be useful.

   An employer can decide to pay at, above, or below the going rate. Most firms try to offer competitive wages and salaries within a geographic area or an industry. If a company pays below-market wages, it may not be able to hire skilled people. The level, or competitiveness, of a firm's compensation is determined by the firm's financial condition (or profitability), efficiency, and employee productivity, as well as the going rates paid by competitors. Miller Brewing Co. is considered a high-paying firm ($22–$25 per hour for production employees); McDonald's is a lower paying company ($6–$8 per hour for counter employees).

Types of Compensation or Pay

There are two basic types of compensation: direct and indirect. Direct pay is the wage or salary received by the employee; indirect pay consists of various employee benefits and services. Employees are usually paid directly on the basis of the amount of time they work, the amount they produce, or some combination of time and output. The following are the most common types of compensation:

- *Hourly wages.* Technicians, machinists, and assembly-line workers at Miller Brewing Co. are paid by the hour with wages ranging from $22.50 to $26.50 per hour.
- *Salaries.* Managerial and professional employees are paid an annual salary either on a biweekly or a monthly basis. The annual salary of our U.S. president is $400,000.
- *Piecework and commission.* Some employees are paid according to how much they produce or sell. A car salesperson might be paid $500 for each car sold or a 3 percent commission on the car's sale price. Thus, a salesperson who sold four cars in one week at $500 per car would earn $2,000 in pay for that week. Alternatively, a 3 percent commission on four cars sold with total sales revenue of $70,000 would yield $2,100 in pay.

  Increasingly, business firms are paying employees using a base wage or salary and an incentive. The incentive feature is designed to increase individual employee, work group, and/or organizational performance. Incentive pay plans are commonly referred to as variable or contingent pay arrangements.

- *Accelerated commission schedule.* A salesperson could be paid a commission rate of 3 percent on the first $50,000 of sales per month, 4 percent on the next $30,000, and 5 percent on any sales beyond $80,000. For a salesperson who made $90,000 of sales in one month, the monthly pay would be as follows:

$$
\begin{array}{rcr}
3\% \times \$50{,}000 & = & \$1{,}500 \\
4\% \times \$30{,}000 & = & \$1{,}200 \\
5\% \times \underline{\$10{,}000} & = & \underline{\$\ \ 500} \\
\$90{,}000 & & \$3{,}200
\end{array}
$$

- *Bonus.* A bonus is a payment for reaching a specific goal; it may be paid on a monthly, quarterly, or annual basis. A bank with several offices or branches might set monthly goals for opening new accounts, making loans, and customer service. Each employee of a branch that meets all goals would be paid a monthly bonus of $100. Although the bonuses are paid to the employees individually, the employees must function as an effective, high-performing group to reach the monthly goals.
- *Profit sharing.* A firm that offers profit sharing pays employees a portion of the profits over a preset level. For example, profits beyond 10 percent of gross sales might be shared at a 50 percent rate with employees. The company retains the remaining profits. All employees may receive the same profit shares, or the shares may vary according to base pay.
- *Fringe benefits.* **Fringe benefits** are indirect compensation and include pensions, health insurance, vacations, and many others. Some fringe benefits are

fringe benefits

Indirect compensation such as pensions, health insurance, and vacations.

required by law: unemployment compensation, worker's compensation, and Social Security, which are all paid in part by employers. *Unemployment compensation* provides former employees with money for a certain period while they are unemployed. To be eligible, the employee must have worked a minimum number of weeks, be without a job, and be willing to accept a suitable position offered by the state Unemployment Compensation Commission. Some state laws permit payments to strikers. *Workers' compensation* pays employees for lost work time caused by work-related injuries and may also cover rehabilitation after a serious injury. *Social Security* is mainly a government pension plan, but it also provides disability and survivor benefits and benefits for people undergoing kidney dialysis and transplants. Medicare (health care for the elderly) and Medicaid (health care for the poor) are also part of Social Security.

Many employers also offer fringe benefits not required by law. Among these are paid time off (vacations, holidays, sick days, even pay for jury duty), insurance (health and hospitalization, disability, life, dental, vision, and accidental death and dismemberment), pensions and retirement savings accounts, and stock purchase options.

Some firms with numerous fringe benefits allow employees to mix and match benefit items or select items based on individual needs. This is a flexible or cafeteria-style benefit plan. A younger employee with a family may desire to purchase medical, disability, and life insurance, whereas an older employee may want to put more benefit dollars into a retirement savings plan. All employees are allocated the same number of benefit dollars but can spend these dollars on different items and in different amounts.

concept check

- How does a firm establish a pay scale for its employees?
- What is the difference between direct and indirect pay?

ORGANIZATIONAL CAREER MANAGEMENT

>lg 8

An important aspect of the human resource management process is organizational career management, or facilitating employee job changes, including promotions, transfers, demotions, layoffs, terminations, and retirements.

Job Changes within the Organization

promotion
An upward move in an organization to a position with more authority, responsibility, and pay.

A **promotion** is an upward move in an organization to a position with more authority, responsibility, and pay. Promotion decisions are usually based on merit (ability and performance) and seniority (length of service). Union employees usually prefer a strict seniority system for employee advancement. Managers and technical employees strongly prefer promotions based on merit.

transfer
A horizontal move in an organization to a position with about the same salary and at about the same organizational level.

A **transfer** is a horizontal move in an organization to a position with about the same salary and at about the same organizational level. An employee may seek a transfer for personal growth, for a more interesting job, for convenience (better work hours, work location, or training opportunity), or for a job that offers more potential for advancement. Employers may transfer workers from positions where they are no longer needed to ones where they are needed. Or the goal may be to find a better fit for the employee within the firm. Sometimes transfers are made to give employees a different perspective or to reenergize them. Consider Randy Lagman, a staff support technician for Internet operations at Lands' End, a billion-dollar clothing catalog company based in Dodgeville, Wisconsin. Randy was transferred from a self-described "Web-geek" position to a job with the title "technical adventurer outfitter."

Randy's transfer had a big impact on his work style. For most people, bringing work home means reading reports in front of the TV or analyzing spreadsheets in an office carved out of a spare bedroom. For Lagman, it means wearing a raincoat, sitting under a lawn sprinkler, and testing a weatherproof laptop. "I'm getting a reputation as the neighborhood crackpot," he jokes. His work has also had an impact on his understanding of risk and stress. Lots of information technology people believe that they work in high-stakes, high-pressure environments. But Lagman's role as technical adventurer outfitter brings him into contact with people who know the *real* meaning of risk.[9]

demotion
The downgrading or reassignment of an employee to a position with less responsibility.

When a person is downgraded or reassigned to a position with less responsibility, it is called a **demotion.** This usually occurs when an employee isn't performing satisfactorily. In most companies, a person is given several warnings before a demotion takes place.

Separations

separation
The departure of an employee from the organization; can be a layoff, termination, resignation, or retirement.

A **separation** occurs when an employee leaves the company. Layoffs, terminations, resignations, and retirements are all types of separations. Sometimes separations occur because companies are trying to remain competitive in the global marketplace. When oil prices dropped significantly early in 1997, many energy firms laid off or terminated workers. UPR, Inc., an oil exploration and drilling company, initially terminated 400 employees and later offered early retirement packages to other employees to encourage them to retire.

layoff
A temporary separation of an employee from the organization; arranged by the employer, usually because business is slow.

A **layoff** is a temporary separation arranged by the employer, usually because business is slow. Layoffs can be planned, such as seasonal reductions of employees, or unplanned, as when sales unexpectedly decline. Generally, employees with the least seniority are laid off first.

There are several alternatives to a layoff. With a *voluntary reduction in pay,* all employees agree to take less pay so that everyone can keep working. Other firms arrange to have all or most of their employees take vacation time during slow periods. Major league baseball teams, the Houston Astros, for example, encourage their full-time year-round employees to take vacations during the off-season from November through April. Other employees agree to take *voluntary time off,* or work fewer hours, which again has the effect of reducing the employer's payroll and avoiding the need for a layoff. Control Data Corp. avoids layoffs with what it calls a *rings of defense* approach. Temporary employees are hired with the specific understanding that they may be laid off at any time. When layoffs are needed, the temporary workers are the first "ring of defense." Permanent Control Data employees know they probably will never be laid off.

termination
A permanent separation of an employee from the organization, arranged by the employer.

A **termination** is a permanent separation arranged by the employer. Reasons for terminations include failure to perform as expected, violation of work rules, dishonesty, theft, sexual harassment, excessive absenteeism, or insubordination (disobedience).

Most companies follow a series of steps before terminating an employee. First, the employee is given an oral warning. The second step is a written statement that the employee's actions are not acceptable. If the employee fails to improve, he or she is suspended from work for a time. If the employee persists in wrongdoing after suspension, his or her employment is terminated.

resignation
A permanent separation of an employee from the organization, done voluntarily by the employee.

Resignation is a permanent form of separation that is undertaken voluntarily by the employee, whereas layoff and termination are involuntary. An employee may resign for almost any reason: to seek a new career, move to a different part of the country, accept an employment offer with a significant pay raise, or join a fast-growing firm with numerous advancement opportunities.

For companies in high-growth industries, keeping employees from resigning and moving to "greener pastures" is a number-one priority. This is particularly true in smaller entrepreneurial firms where losing a key employee can be disastrous. A good example of a company that emphasizes employee retention is Trilogy Software, discussed in the Focusing on Small Business box.

FOCUSING ON SMALL BUSINESS

AT TRILOGY SOFTWARE, RESIGNATION IS A DIRTY WORD

At age 28, Danielle Rios has it all—a BS degree in computer science from Stanford, a great track record as a software developer for IBM, and the energy and savvy to market herself. With all that going for her, Rios could be a free-agent winner in the new economy, adding value by juggling different projects with different firms. Or she could have her pick of well-established corporate launch pads for her career.

But for the last three years, Rios has worked with Trilogy Software, Inc., a small, rapidly growing software firm based in Austin, Texas. Trilogy is on the cutting edge of sales-and-marketing software, and Rios is part of a team that shows potential customers how the software can work for them.

Joe Liemandt founded Trilogy in 1989, after dropping out of Stanford only a few months before graduation. To finance the start-up, Liemandt charged up 22 credit cards. Four years ago, Trilogy had 100 employees. Today it has almost 1,000 and plans to add another 1,000 soon. But to call Trilogy workers "employees" misses the point. They're all shareholders. They're all managers. They're all partners. That's how Liemandt, Trilogy's CEO, has chosen to run his company—and that's what makes it successful.

Liemandt knows that Trilogy depends on talented people. He also knows that people can go anywhere. Which means that his biggest competitive headache isn't companies like SAP AG, Baan Co., and PeopleSoft, Inc.—businesses he has to face down in the marketplace. His biggest worry is holding on to people like Rios. "There's nothing more important than recruiting and growing people," he says. "That's my number-one job."

It's a seller's market for talent. People with the right combination of savvy and ambition can afford to shop for the right boss, the right colleagues, the right environment. In the old economy, it was a buyer's market: Companies had their pick of the crop, and the question they asked was "Why hire?" Now the question is "Why join up?"

Critical Thinking Questions

1. Do you think that Trilogy overemphasizes the importance of employees?
2. What are some things that Trilogy can do to keep those workers in high demand?
3. Would you want to work for Trilogy?

retirement
The separation of an employee from the organization at the end of his or her career.

Retirement usually ends one's career. Common retirement ages are 55, 62, 65, and 70, but no one can be required to retire, according to the Age Discrimination in Employment Act. The law does, however, allow mandatory retirement in a few occupations, such as firefighter, police officer, and commercial airline pilot.

Workers in companies with too many employees may be offered early-retirement incentives. This option offers retirement benefits to younger employees or adds extra retirement benefits or both. Employees can thus retire more comfortably without working longer. Xerox, General Motors, IBM, Hewlett-Packard, and Phillips Petroleum, among others, have used early-retirement plans to reduce their workforces.

concept check

- What is organizational career management?
- Define promotion, transfer, termination, and retirement.

LAWS AFFECTING HUMAN RESOURCE MANAGEMENT

>lg 9

Federal laws help ensure that job applicants and employees are treated fairly and not discriminated against. Hiring, training, and job placement must be unbiased. Promotion and compensation decisions must be based on

MAKING ETHICAL CHOICES

AN UNFAIR DISMISSAL?

Alex Lambros, Jr., a stockbroker, has had just one customer complaint in 25 years in the business. Recruited in 1989 to work for Merrill Lynch & Co., Lambros soon became a top producer. He developed an "$88 million book of brokerage business" and was recognized by the company as one of the elite performers in the brokerage industry.

Several years later, when he was the acting branch manager of a Merrill Lynch office in Cape Coral, Florida, Lambros was fired for destroying company property. His apparent offense was that he tore open a payroll envelope addressed to the office's branch manager.

Lambros filed a complaint of wrongful termination and defamation with the New York Stock Exchange—one of several oversight authorities for the brokerage industry. Lambros contended that he was terminated because he "had repeatedly questioned the propriety of actions by superiors." He further contended that Merrill Lynch's managers were tempted by his "lush client base." High-performing brokers get a larger share of the commissions paid by clients. By redistributing Lambros's client base to brokers with lower commissions or by having managers take over the accounts, the company could retain a greater percentage of the commissions, and the managers would benefit. In addition, a brokerage firm benefits if client accounts are actively traded—"something that top producers with trusted relationships with their clients don't always do." Were Lambros's claims true? Merrill Lynch contends that his claims "were baloney from the start."

Critical Thinking Questions

1. In your opinion, was Lambros's dismissal fair and just?
2. How would you evaluate the action of a brokerage firm's managers who obtain new clients by firing a broker and taking his accounts?

performance. These laws help all Americans who have talent, training, and the desire to get ahead.

New legislation and the continual interpretation and reinterpretation of existing laws will continue to make the jobs of human resource managers challenging and complicated. In 1999, for example, the National Academy of Sciences reported a link between muscle and skeletal injuries and certain workplace activities, such as lifting. In response, OSHA, a federal agency discussed below, issued new standards for the handling and lifting of objects by employees. Of course, human resource managers must now integrate these standards into their organizations. The key laws that currently affect human resource management are shown in Exhibit 9-8.

Several laws govern wages, pensions, and unemployment compensation. For instance, the Fair Labor Standards Act sets the minimum wage, which is periodically raised by Congress. Many minimum-wage jobs are found in service businesses, such as restaurants and car washes. The Pension Reform Act protects the retirement income of employees and retirees. Federal tax laws also affect compensation, including employee profit-sharing and stock purchase plans.

Employers must also be aware of changes to laws concerning employee safety, health, and privacy. The Occupational Safety and Health Act requires employers to provide a workplace free of health and safety hazards. For instance, manufacturers must require employees working on loading docks to wear steel-toed shoes so their feet won't be injured if materials are dropped. Drug and AIDS testing are also governed by federal laws.

exhibit 9-8 | Laws Impacting Human Resource Management

Law	Purpose	Agency of Enforcement
Social Security Act (1935)	Provides for retirement income and old age health care	Social Security Administration
Fair Labor Standards Act (1938)	Sets minimum wage, restricts child labor, sets overtime pay	Wage and Hour Division, Department of Labor
Equal Pay Act (1963)	Eliminates pay differentials based on gender	Equal Employment Opportunity Commission
Civil Rights Act (1964), Title VII	Prohibits employment discrimination based on race, color, religion, gender, or national origin	Equal Employment Opportunity Commission
Age Discrimination in Employment Act (1967)	Prohibits age discrimination against those over 40 years of age	Equal Employment Opportunity Commission
Occupational Safety and Health Act (1970)	Protects worker health and safety, provides for hazard-free workplace	Occupational Safety and Health Administration
Vietnam Veterans Readjustment Act (1974)	Requires affirmative employment of Vietnam War veterans	Veterans Employment Service, Department of Labor
Employee Retirement Income Security Act (1974)—also called Pension Reform Act	Establishes minimum requirements for private pension plans	Internal Revenue Service, Department of Labor, and Pension Benefit Guaranty Corporation
Pregnancy Discrimination Act (1978)	Treats pregnancy as a disability, prevents employment discrimination based on pregnancy	Equal Employment Opportunity Commission
Immigration Reform and Control Act (1986)	Verifies employment eligibility, prevents employment of illegal aliens	Employment Verification Systems, Immigration and Naturalization Service
Americans with Disabilities Act (1990)	Prohibits employment discrimination based on mental or physical disabilities	Department of Justice, Equal Employment Opportunity Commission, others
Family and Medical Leave Act (1993)	Requires employers to provide unpaid leave for childbirth, adoption, or illness	Department of Labor

Human resource managers must ensure that their firms accommodate the needs of disabled employees like wheelchair-bound workers who need ramps to facilitate their mobility.

Another employee law that continues to strongly affect the work of human resource managers is the Americans with Disabilities Act. To be considered disabled, a person must have a physical or mental impairment that greatly limits one or more major life activities. More than 54 million Americans fall into this category.[10] Employers may not discriminate against disabled persons. They must make "reasonable accommodations" so that qualified disabled employees can perform the job, unless doing so would cause "undue hardship" for the business. Altering work schedules, modifying equipment so a wheelchair-bound person can use it, and making buildings accessible by ramps and elevators are considered reasonable. Two companies often praised for their efforts to hire the disabled are McDonald's and DuPont.

The Family and Medical Leave Act went into effect in 1993. The law applies to employers with 50 or more employees. It requires these employers to provide unpaid leave of up to 12 weeks during any 12-month period to workers who have been employed for at least a year and work a minimum of 25 hours a week. The reasons for the leave include the birth or adoption of a child; the serious illness of a child, spouse, or parent; or a serious illness that prevents the worker from doing the job. Upon return, the employee must be given her or his old job back. The worker cannot collect unemployment compensation while on leave. A company can deny leave to a salaried employee in the highest-paid 10 percent of its workforce, if letting the worker take leave would create a "serious injury" for the firm.

The Role of Government Agencies in Human Resource Management

Several federal agencies oversee employment, safety, compensation, and related areas. The Occupational Safety and Health Administration (OSHA) sets workplace safety and health standards, provides safety training, and inspects places of work (assembly plants, construction sites, and warehouse facilities, for example) to determine employer compliance with safety regulations.

The Wage and Hour Division of the Department of Labor enforces the federal minimum-wage law and overtime provisions of the Fair Labor Standards Act. Employers covered by this law must pay certain employees a premium rate of pay (or time and one-half) for all hours worked beyond 40 in one week.

How does the Equal Employment Opportunity Commission promote equal opportunity in employment? Visit **http://www.eeoc.gov** to learn what the agency does.

The Equal Employment Opportunity Commission, created by the 1964 Civil Rights Act, investigates and resolves charges of discrimination. It also files lawsuits on its own against employers. Violators can be forced to promote, pay back wages to, or provide additional training for employees against whom they discriminated. Sears, Motorola, and AT&T have had to make large back-pay awards and to offer special training to minority employees after the courts found they had been discriminated against.

The Office of Federal Contract Compliance Programs (OFCCP) oversees firms with U.S. government contracts to make sure that applicants and employees get fair treatment. A big part of its job is to review federal contractors' affirmative action programs. Employers set up **affirmative action programs** to expand job opportunities for women and minorities. In the case of a major violation, the OFCCP can recommend cancellation of the firm's government contract.

affirmative action programs
Programs established by organizations to expand job opportunities for women and minorities.

Making Affirmative Action Work

Many firms have appointed an affirmative action officer to help ensure that they comply with antidiscrimination laws. At firms such as Coca-Cola, Snap-on Tools, Hilton Hotels, and Burlington Northern Santa Fe Railway, the affirmative action officer makes sure that job applicants and employees get fair treatment. He or she often reports directly to the company president rather than to the vice president of human resources.

Affirmative action officers watch for signs of *adverse impact,* or unfair treatment of certain classes of employees. **Protected classes** are the specific groups (women, African Americans, Native Americans, and others) who have legal protection against employment discrimination.

protected classes
The specific groups who have legal protection against employment discrimination; include women, African Americans, Native Americans, and others.

One example of adverse impact is a job qualification that tends to weed out more female applicants than male applicants. Suppose that an airline automatically rules out anyone under five feet seven inches tall who wants to be a pilot. Many more female applicants than male applicants would be rejected because women tend to be shorter than men. But height has nothing to do with a pilot's ability, so this height requirement would be discriminatory.

The overall affirmative action record of the past decade has been mixed. The employment of women in professional occupations continues to grow, but minority representation among professionals has not significantly increased, even though professional jobs have been among the fastest growing areas. Technical jobs have the most equitable utilization rates of minorities.

concept check

- What are the key federal laws affecting employment?
- List and describe the functions of the two federal agencies that enforce employment discrimination laws.
- What is affirmative action?

CAPITALIZING ON TRENDS IN BUSINESS

>lg 10

Social change, evolving demographics, advancing technology, and global competition are driving the trends in human resource management in the 21st century.

Social Change

The most dramatic social change that is occurring is the increasing number of women joining the labor force—a trend that began in the 20th century and continues today. Today, women comprise about 45 percent of the American labor force. The entry of women into the workforce has created some new human resource management issues including dual-career couples, child and elder care, and workplace sexual harassment. American Airlines, for example, recently offered a new employee benefit called Life Balance Work/Life Services to assist employees in coping with some nonwork lifestyle issues. According to Allison Payne, the airline's vice president of human resources, Life Balance functions like a personal assistant who can help with child care arrangements, car repair services, mortgage rate information, parenting, and many other personal and family issues.[11]

For the latest news in the human resources field, visit the Web site of the Society for Human Resource Management at

http://www.shrm.org

Another social change is the new attitude toward changing jobs. Only a few years ago, recent college graduates could expect to change jobs and employers three to five times during their 25 to 40 years of professional experience. Now, a 22- to 25-year-old college graduate can expect six to ten of these changes and one or two significant occupational changes, such as from engineer to accountant. This increased frequency of job changes may mean that employees and employers are less loyal to one another.

Demographics

Changes in demographics have resulted in a more diverse workforce, as shown in Exhibit 9-9. **Diversity** refers to employee differences in age, race and ethnicity, gender, educational background, and work experiences. Managing a diverse work group is more difficult than managing a homogeneous group, such as all white males, for example, because each group brings its own ideas, habits, culture, and communication skills to the work environment. Progressive human

diversity
Employee differences in age, race and ethnicity, gender, educational background, and work experience.

exhibit 9-9 | The Diversity of the American Labor Force

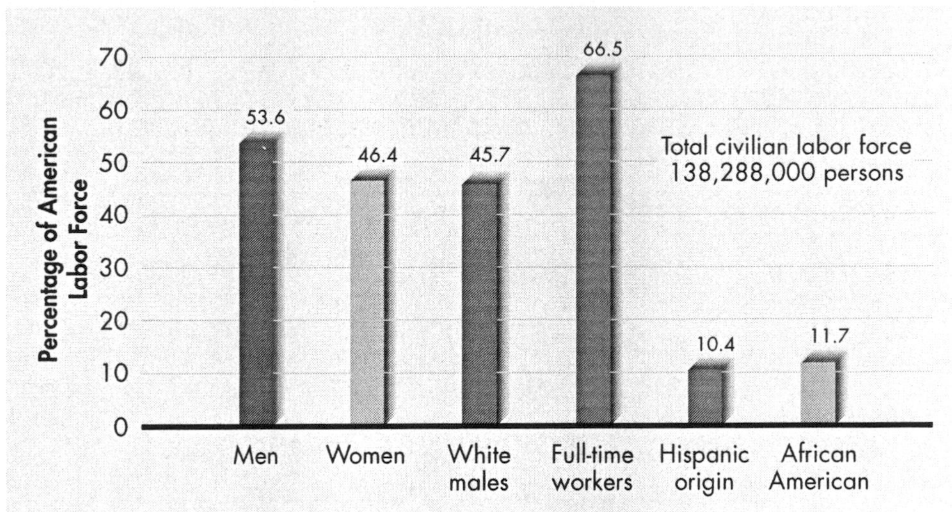

resource practices of diversity management focus on mentoring women and minority persons and removing the *glass ceiling,* or the invisible barrier in many firms that prevents women, minorities, and others from advancing to high-level management and executive positions. Nothing has prevented Darla Moore from advancing in her professional fields of banking and investments. She is CEO of Rainwater, Inc., and in 1998 she became the first woman ever to have a college of business named for her—the Moore School of Business at the University of South Carolina.[12]

Advancing Technology

Advances in information technology have greatly improved the efficiency of handling many transaction-based aspects (payroll and expense reimbursement) of employee services. Technology enables instant communication of human resource data from far-flung branches to the home office. Ease of communication has also led many companies to outsource some or all of their human resource functions. **Outsourcing** is the assignment of various functions, like human resources, accounting, or legal work, to outside organizations. The National Geographic Society outsourced all of its employee benefits programs to Workforce Solutions. Administaff is a large company that handles compensation and benefits processing, training, and even performance appraisal for many large corporate clients. Without computer databases and networks, such outsourcing would be impossible.

outsourcing
The assignment of various functions, such as human resources, accounting, or legal work, to outside organizations.

Technology has also made telecommuting a reality for almost 29 million workers. **Telecommuting** is now commonplace. In this arrangement, employees work at home and are linked to the office by phone, fax, and computer.[13] At Cisco Systems, a computer-networking giant based in San Jose, California, telecommuters have improved their productivity by up to 25 percent, while the company has saved about $1 million on overhead and retained key employees who might otherwise have left. What's more, those who have traded suits for sweats say they love setting their own schedules, skipping rush hour, spending more time with their kids, and working at least part-time in comfortable surroundings. "It's surprising the number of engineers who will respond to a question at 11:00 on a Saturday night," says John Hotchkiss, Cisco's human resource manager. "We can solve a problem that would not have been solved until Monday morning."[14]

telecommuting
An arrangement in which employees work at home and are linked to the office by phone, fax, and computer.

Telecommuting has also grown because of a strong economy in which employers must do what they can to attract the best and brightest workers. Telecommuting also offers environmental and political benefits as companies respond to Clean Air Act provisions aimed at reducing traffic. It also enables businesses to cut real estate costs by creating "hoteling" arrangements in which, say, 10 people share a single cubicle on an as-needed basis. Exhibit 9-10 lists some of the companies most friendly to telecommuting.

Global Competition

As more firms "go global," they are sending an increasing number of employees overseas. Procter & Gamble, IBM, Caterpillar, Microsoft, Federal Express, and many others have tens of thousands of employees abroad. Such companies face somewhat different human resource management issues than do firms that operate only within the United States. For example, criteria for selecting employees include not only technical skills and knowledge of the business, but also the ability to adapt to a local culture and to learn a foreign language.

Once an individual is selected for an overseas assignment, language training and cultural orientation become important. Salary and benefits, relocation expenses, and special allowances (housing, transportation, and education) can increase human resource costs by as much as three times normal annual costs. After an overseas assignment of one year or more, the firm must repatriate the employee, or bring the individual back home. Job placement and career progression frequently become issues during repatriation because the firm has changed and the employee's old job may no longer exist. After spending a year in Brussels, Belgium, Mike Rocca, a financial executive with Honeywell, experienced "reentry shock" when he returned to his corporate office in Minneapolis and saw how new software had changed accounting.

concept check

- How is the entry of more women into the workforce affecting human resource management?
- What is diversity, and how does it affect human resource management?
- What benefits does telecommuting offer?
- What issues does "going global" present for human resource management?

exhibit 9-10 | Telecommuting-Friendly Employers

Company	Percentage of Workforce that Telecommutes	Special Features
Aetna	2%	Telecommuter is assigned an office "buddy."
Arthur Andersen	20	Conducts safety inspections of home offices.
AT&T	55	Manager and employee work out details.
Boeing	1	Rules differ for each business unit.
Cisco Systems	66	24-hour technical support, ergonomic furniture required.
Georgia Power	5	May soon allow some to work at company sites near home.
Hewlett-Packard	8	Recommends ergonomically correct office.
IBM	20	Teleworkers use shared space in the office.
Merrill Lynch	5	Employees can test telecommuting in two-week simulation.
The Leisure Co./America West	16	Arranges monthly potluck team dinners to keep everyone in touch.

SOURCE: Reprinted *Business Week* from October 12, 1998, by special permission, copyright © 1998 by The McGraw-Hill Companies, Inc.

APPLYING THIS CHAPTER'S TOPICS

It's never too early to start thinking about your career in business. No, you don't have to decide today, but it's important to decide fairly soon how you will spend your life's work. A very practical reason for doing so is that it will save you a lot of time and money. We have seen too many juniors, seniors, or even graduate students who aren't really sure what they want to do upon graduation. The longer you wait to choose a profession, the more credit hours you may have to take in your new field and the longer it will be before you start earning real money.

Interested in a career in human resources? At **http://www.ipma-hr.org/public/research_index.cfm** you'll find valuable tips to point you in the right direction.

A second reason to choose a career field early is that you can get a part-time or summer job and "test-drive" the profession. If it's not for you, you will find out very quickly.

Your school placement office can give you plenty of information about various careers in business. We also describe many career opportunities at the end of each part of this text. Another source of career information is the Internet. Go to any search engine,

TRY IT NOW!

Make Telecommuting Work for You Maybe a part-time job might require too much driving time. Perhaps there are simply no jobs in the immediate area that suit you. Try telecommuting right now. Is telecommuting for you? Nearly 75 percent of teleworkers responding to an AT&T survey said they were more satisfied with their personal and family lives than before they started working at home.[15] But telecommuting is not for every person or every job, and you'll need plenty of self-discipline to make it work for you. Ask yourself if you can perform your duties without close supervision. Also, think about whether you would miss your coworkers.

If you decide to give telecommuting a try, consider these suggestions to maintain your productivity:

- *Set ground rules with your family.* Spouses and small children have to understand that even though you're in the house, you are busy earning a living. It's fine to throw in a few loads of laundry or answer the door when the plumber comes. It's another thing to take the kids to the mall or let them play games on your office PC.
- *Clearly demarcate your work space by using a separate room with a door you can shut.* Let your family know that, emergencies excepted, the space is off-limits during working hours.
- *If you have small children, you may want to arrange for child care during your working hours.*
- *Stay in touch with your coworkers and professional colleagues.* Go into the office from time to time for meetings to stay connected.

Above all, you can make telecommuting work for you by being productive. Doing your job well whether on-site or telecommuting will help assure you of a bright future.

such as Excite or Lycos, and enter "careers in business," or narrow your search to a specific area such as management or marketing.

Career planning will not end when you find your first professional job. It is a life-long process that ends only with retirement. Your career planning will include conducting a periodic self-assessment of your strengths and weaknesses, gathering information about other jobs both within the firm and externally, learning about other industries, and setting career goals for yourself.[16] You must always think about your future in business.

You Will Be Involved in Human Resources Decision Making

During your professional career in business, you will likely have the opportunity to become a manager. As a manager, you will have to make many human resource decisions, including hiring, firing, promoting, giving a pay raise, sending an employee to a training program, disciplining a worker, approving a college tuition reimbursement request, and reassigning an employee to a different job. In short, you will be involved in virtually every human resource decision or activity affecting the employees you manage.

Always treat people as you wish to be treated when making human resource decisions. Be fair, be honest, offer your experience and advice, and communicate frequently with your employees. If you follow this simple advice, you will be richly rewarded in your own career.

>looking ahead at Don Pablo's

James was faced with a typical human resource problem with Sharon, the tardy waitperson. As presented in this chapter, James should utilize his human resource management skills and redirect Sharon toward improved performance. One approach is to offer additional training on company policies and the importance of good customer service. He might remind her that if she is late or doesn't come to work on a particular day, then her work must be shared by other waitpersons, which may lead to poor customer service. Finally, James may have to make the difficult decision to demote or fire Sharon if her performance does not meet desired levels.

Don Pablo's is expanding the number of its units and is part of a larger organization called Avado Brands. In addition to Don Pablo's, the company owns Canyon Cafe restaurants (southwestern theme) and Hops (a microbrewery with an American-style menu). The firm plans to open dozens of new restaurants over the next five years, which will create many new human resource challenges and opportunities.

SUMMARY OF LEARNING GOALS

>lg 1 What is the human resource management process?

The human resource management process consists of a sequence of activities that begins with job analysis and HR planning; progresses to employee recruitment and selection; then focuses on employee training, performance appraisal, and compensation; and ends when the employee leaves the organization. Human resource decisions and activities along this series of events increase the value and contributions the employee makes to the firm. Over several years for a given employee, training, performance appraisal, and changes in compensation form a repeated set of activities that facilitate career development and increase a person's contributions to the firm.

>lg 2 How are human resource needs determined?

Creating a strategy for meeting human resource needs is called human resource planning, which begins with job analysis. Job analysis is a process for studying a job to determine its tasks and duties for setting pay, determining

KEY TERMS

affirmative action programs 274
apprenticeship 265
contingent workers 260
demotion 270
diversity 275
employee orientation 265
fringe benefits 268
human resource (HR) planning 257
human resource management 256
job analysis 258
job description 258
job fair 261
job rotation 265
job specification 258
layoff 270
mentoring 265
on-the-job training 265
outsourcing 276
performance appraisal 266
programmed instruction 266
promotion 269
protected classes 274
recruitment 260
resignation 270
retirement 271
selection 262
selection interview 263
separation 270
telecommuting 276
termination 270
training and development 264
transfer 269
vestibule training 265

employee job performance, specifying hiring requirements, and designing training programs. Information from the job analysis is used to prepare a job description, which lists the tasks and responsibilities of the job. A job specification describes the skills, knowledge, and abilities a person needs to fill the job described in the job description. By examining the human resource demand forecast and the *internal* supply forecast, human resource professionals can determine if the company faces a personnel surplus or shortage.

>lg 3 **How do human resource managers find good people to fill the jobs?**
When a job vacancy occurs, most firms begin by trying to fill the job from within. If a suitable *internal* candidate is not available, the firm begins an external search. Firms use local media to recruit nontechnical, unskilled, and nonsupervisory workers. To locate highly trained recruits, employers use college recruiters, executive search firms, job fairs, and company Web sites to promote job openings.

>lg 4 **What is the employee selection process?**
Typically, an applicant submits an application, or résumé, and then receives a short, structured interview. If an applicant makes it past the initial screening, he or she may be asked to take an aptitude, personality, or skills test. The next step is the selection interview which is an in-depth discussion of the applicant's work experience, skills and abilities, education, and career interests. An applicant seeking a professional or managerial position will typically be interviewed by several people. After the selection interview, successful applicants may be asked to undergo a physical exam before being offered a job.

>lg 5 **What types of training and development do organizations offer their employees?**
Training and development programs are designed to increase employees' knowledge, skills, and abilities in order to foster job performance improvements. Formal training (usually classroom in nature and off-the-job) takes place shortly after being hired. Development programs prepare employees to assume positions of increasing authority and responsibility. Job rotation, executive education programs, mentoring, and special project assignments are examples of employee development programs.

>lg 6 **What is a performance appraisal?**
A performance appraisal compares an employee's actual performance with the expected performance. Performance appraisals serve several purposes but are typically used to determine an employee's compensation, training needs, and advancement opportunities.

>lg 7 **How are employees compensated?**
Direct pay is the hourly wage or monthly salary paid to an employee. In addition to the base wage or salary, direct pay may include bonuses and profit shares. Indirect pay consists of various benefits and services. Some benefits are required by law: unemployment compensation, workers' compensation, and Social Security. Others are voluntarily made available by employers to employees. These include paid vacations and holidays, pensions, health and other insurance products, employee wellness programs, and college tuition reimbursement.

>lg 8 **What is organizational career management?**
Organizational career management is the facilitation of employee job changes, including promotions, transfers, layoffs, and retirements. A promotion is an upward move with more authority, responsibility, and pay. A transfer is a horizontal move in the organization. When a person is downgraded to a position with less responsibility, it is a demotion. A layoff is a temporary separation arranged by the employer, usually when business is slow. A termination is a permanent separation arranged by the employer. A resignation is a voluntary separation by the employee. Retirement is a permanent separation that ends one's career.

>lg 9 **What are the key laws and federal agencies affecting human resource management?**

A number of federal laws (listed in Exhibit 9-8) affect human resource management. Federal law prohibits discrimination based on age, race, gender, color, national origin, religion, or disability. The Americans with Disabilities Act bans discrimination against disabled workers and requires employers to change the work environment to accommodate the disabled. The Family and Medical Leave Act requires employers, with certain exceptions, to provide employees up to 12 weeks of unpaid leave a year. The leave can be for the birth or adoption of a child or due to serious illness of a family member.

Federal agencies that deal with human resource administration are the Equal Employment Opportunity Commission (EEOC), the Occupational Safety and Health Administration (OSHA), the Office of Federal Contract Compliance Programs (OFCCP), and the Wage and Hour Division of the Department of Labor. The EEOC and OFCCP are primary agencies for enforcement of employment discrimination laws; OSHA enforces safety regulation; and the Wage and Hour Division enforces the minimum wage and related laws. Many companies employ affirmative action and safety officers to ensure compliance with antidiscrimination and workplace safety laws.

>lg 10 **What trends are affecting human resource management?**

Women now comprise 45 percent of the workforce in America. As a result, we are seeing growing numbers of dual-career couples. In turn, companies are now facing issues like sexual harassment and nonwork lifestyle issues such as child care and elder care. Workers also now change jobs three to five times during their career. This lessens the loyalty between employer and employee. As the American workforce becomes increasingly more diverse, companies are offering diversity training and mentoring of minorities.

Technology continues to improve the efficiency of human resource management. It also enables firms to outsource many functions done internally in the past. Telecommuting is becoming increasingly popular among employers and employees.

As more firms enter the international market, they are sending an increasing number of employees overseas. In addition to normal job requirements, selected workers must have the ability to adapt to a local culture and perhaps to learn a foreign language.

PREPARING FOR TOMORROW'S WORKPLACE

1. Divide the class into teams of five. Each group should select a form of applicant testing and defend why their form of testing should be used to screen applicants.
2. What kind of training and development program would be best for assembly-line workers? For first-line supervisors? For industrial sales representatives? For maintenance workers? For computer programmers?
3. Would an overseas job assignment be good for your career development? If you think so, what country would you prefer to live and work in for two or three years, and what type of job would you like to have in that country?
4. The fringe benefit package of many employers includes numerous voluntarily provided items such as health insurance, life insurance, pension plan, paid vacations, tuition reimbursement, employee price discounts on products of the firm, and paid sick leave. At your age, what are the three or four most important benefits? Why? Twenty years from now, what do you think will be your three or four most important benefits? Why?

5. Select two teams of five. One team will take the position that employees are simply a business expense to be managed. The second team will argue that employees are an asset to be developed to enable the firm to gain a competitive advantage. The remainder of the class will judge which team provided the stronger argument.
6. How important is training likely to be in the future? What changes that are facing organizations will increase the importance of training?
7. Is reducing the number of employee resignations always a good thing? Why or why not?
8. You are applying for a job as a manager. Write down five critical questions that you would ask your prospective employer. Share these with the class.

WORKING THE NET

1. Go to Monster.com at **http://content.monster.com/resume/** to learn how to prepare an electronic résumé that will get results. Develop a list of rules for creating effective electronic résumés, and revise your own résumé into electronic format.
2. Working as a contingent employee can help you explore your career options. Visit the Manpower Web site at **http://www.manpower.com,** and search for several types of jobs that interest you. What are the advantages of being a temporary worker? What other services does Manpower offer job seekers?
3. As a corporate recruiter, you must know how to screen prospective employees. The Integrity Center Web site at **http://www.integctr.com** offers a brief tutorial on pre-employment screening, a glossary of key words and phrases, and related information. Prepare a short report that tells your assistant how to go about this process.
4. You've been asked to give a speech about the current status of affirmative action and equal employment to your company's managers. Starting with the Web site of the American Association for Affirmative Action (**http://www.affirmativeaction.org**) and its links to related sites, research the topic and prepare an outline for your talk. Include current legislation and recent court cases.
5. Web-based training is becoming popular at many companies as a way to bring a wider variety of courses to more people at lower costs. The Web-Based Training Information Center site at **http://www.filename.com/wbt** provides a good introduction. Learn about the basics of online training at its Primer page. Then link to the Resources section, complete a survey, and explore other areas that interest you.

CREATIVE THINKING CASE

"Do-It-Yourself" Human Resource Management at Spectrum Signal Processing

Some companies are now managing all or part of their human resource functions with employee teams. Martin McConnell decided that this was the way to go at Spectrum Signal Processing, Inc. McConnell is vice president of finance for Spectrum, a hardware and software designer with 155 employees in Burnaby, British Columbia. He says his company has no human resource department at all. Instead, it uses rotating human resource committees.

In a 1996 employee-satisfaction survey, Spectrum's managers discovered that its employees were not all that satisfied with the way the company was dealing with human resource issues. So Spectrum created a cross-functional employee team to focus on those issues. McConnell initially thought the committee would be only short term; it would deal with the immediate problems and then disband. "But it gained so much interest and momentum, it became part of our culture," he says.

Now the committee regularly discusses and addresses most of the company's typical human resource functions: performance appraisals and the employee handbook, as well as company training, recognition, mentoring, and orientation programs. (Payroll and benefits administration are handled by the accounting department.)

The committee consists of 12 elected members from various job functions. Member-involvement dates are staggered, so the committee is constantly getting new members and perspectives. McConnell and CEO Barry Jinks also serve on the team, albeit in an advisory role. According to group chair Carol Schulz, the bosses' presence doesn't present a hindrance. "They have the same say as anybody else," says Schulz. "Plus it gives employees the feeling that they really do care."

McConnell admits that at first he worried that the committee might establish some overly expensive policies. "But it's not us versus them," he says. "Whatever decision they made would be modified for what works for the environment. Or maybe we'd implement it in stages."

Critical Thinking Questions

1. What are the advantages and possible disadvantages of a do-it-yourself human resource department?
2. Would this concept work at a large company like Ford Motor Co., or is it best suited for smaller organizations?
3. One problem that has surfaced at Spectrum is that serving on the committee takes a lot of time and distracts committee members from their jobs. McConnell is thinking about using a co-op student from a local university to do detail and legwork. Do you think that this is a good idea? Why or why not?

VIDEO CASE

Valassis Communications: Matching People to the Company's Culture

Valassis Communications, Inc.(**http://www.valassis.com:**), headquartered in Livonia, Michigan, has been a leader in marketing services for over a quarter of a century. Valassis maintains that it has set the standard in its industry "for quality, reliability, service and expertise." A publicly held company with annual sales exceeding $740 million, Valassis has more than 1,300 employees across the United States and Canada.

The company's flagship product is the Free-Standing Insert (FSI), which is "distributed through newspapers to over 57 million households nearly every Sunday." The FSI is a booklet containing coupons, refunds, and other values from America's largest packaged goods companies. Other Valassis products include solo inserts that promote a single company's products or services; delivery of manufacturers' product samples and promotional messages through Sunday newspapers; direct placement of newspaper ads for clients; and oversight of clients' games and sweepstakes promotions.

Valassis Communications has a unique corporate culture that it calls "Change to Grow." The Change to Grow philosophy and culture are based on eight fundamental principles:

- Change is good.
- Don't point fingers—solve problems.
- Go—with speed.
- Create positive energy.
- Set the high bar high—don't fear failure.
- Be empowered, and be accountable.
- Communicate clearly and openly.
- Stick to fundamentals.

Executives at Valassis Communications believe the company's competitive advantage in the marketplace is based on its very capable and highly motivated employees. Accordingly, Valassis strives to match the abilities and motivation of the people it hires with the company's Change to Grow culture. With over 14,000 applicants for approximately 100 job openings annually, Valassis puts prospective employees through a rigorous screening and interview process to determine which individuals are most likely to embody and adhere to the eight fundamental principles of the "Change to Grow" culture.

Those who are fortunate enough to be hired by Valassis embark on unique career paths. The company does not "believe in rigid, standardized training methods or career paths, because . . . each employee has their own strengths, talents, and ultimate career goals."

Valassis also prefers to promote from within the company. Consequently, it invests heavily in employee training. Valassis University, a company-run educational program, "offers professional and personal development courses, as well as courses that cover specific areas and functions of the company. . . . Employees can work toward a variety of Valassis 'degrees' including a Bachelor and Master of Leadership." Valassis also supports continuing education for employees through an educational assistance reimbursement program.

When it comes to people, the bottom line for Valassis is to hire the right people through its recruitment and selection process and then to develop those people with appropriate training.

Critical Thinking Questions

1. What are the advantages of Valassis Communications' approach of hiring people with abilities and motivation that match the company's Change to Grow culture?
2. How does the Valassis approach to training and development help reinforce the company's culture?
3. Would you like to work for a company like Valassis Communications, given its Change to Grow culture? Why or why not?

Case: Value America Says Goodbye

Jennifer and Shawn Messmer were thrilled when Value America, a fast-growing Internet retailer, offered Jennifer a job as director of communications. Not only would Jennifer have a new job, but Value America also offered Shawn, a schoolteacher, a position in the company's merchandising department. It seemed like the perfect opportunity, so in September the couple packed up and moved to Value America's headquarters in Charlottesville, Virginia.

The three-year-old company sold everything from cheesecake to computers on its Web site. When a customer ordered a product, the order was sent directly to the product manufacturer who then shipped it to the customer. Founder Craig Winn had lined up top-notch investors in the firm, including Federal Express Chairman Fred Smith. Jennifer and Shawn weren't the only new employees. Sales were growing at 348 percent a year; to meet demand, the company had expanded its payroll by 78 percent in the past year alone.

On December 29, just four months after the Messmers had joined the company, all employees were summoned to a meeting at a local hotel. No one was quite sure why they were there. Maybe, some thought, the firm's executives were going to thank them for the long hours they'd just put in trying to process the rush of orders right before Christmas. Others, however, noticed an ominous sign. Instead of the soda, pizza, and snacks that were usually served at company meetings, only pitchers of water stood on the tables in the meeting room.

The company's new CEO, Glenda Dorchak, stood up in front of the room. Although sales were up, she said, the company was losing money at an alarming rate. The board of directors had decided that drastic measures were called for so, in addition to dropping 25 product categories from the Web site, 47 percent of Value America's staff—some 300 people—would be fired immediately. They were to return to their offices where their supervisors would let them know who would be laid off. Jennifer and Shawn Messmer both lost their jobs.

Questions for Critical Thinking

1. Suggest human resource strategies Value America could have used to avoid overstaffing.
2. In addition to financial considerations, what are some other human resource issues fast-growing Internet firms need to address when expanding their workforce?
3. Evaluate the effectiveness of Value America's method of terminating nearly half of its workforce. What effect do you think this had on remaining employees?

SOURCES: Keith Perine, "When Heads Roll," *The Standard* (May 8, 2000), downloaded from **http://www.thestandard.com**; Keith Perine, "Value America Files for Bankruptcy," *The Standard* (August 11, 2000), downloaded from **http://www.thestandard.com**.

An Introduction to Information Systems in Organizations

14

PRINCIPLES

The value of information is directly linked to how it helps decision makers achieve the organization's goals.

Knowing the potential impact of information systems and having the ability to put this knowledge to work can result in a successful personal career, organizations that reach their goals, and a society with a higher quality of life.

System users, business managers, and information systems professionals must work together to build a successful information system.

The use of information systems to add value to the organization can also give an organization a competitive advantage.

Information systems personnel are the key to unlocking the potential of any new or modified system.

LEARNING OBJECTIVES

- Distinguish data from information and describe the characteristics used to evaluate the quality of data.
- Identify the basic types of business information systems and discuss who uses them, how they are used, and what kinds of benefits they deliver.
- Identify the major steps of the systems development process and state the goal of each.
- Identify the value-added processes in the supply chain and describe the role of information systems within them.
- Identify some of the strategies employed to lower costs or improve service.
- Define the term *competitive advantage* and discuss how organizations are using information systems to gain such an advantage.
- Define the types of roles, functions, and careers available in information systems.

[Merck-Medco]

A Pharmacy for the Future

In the not-too-distant future, the corner pharmacy and the pleasant pharmacist who fills your prescriptions each month may become a fond memory from bygone days; they will, that is, if Merck-Medco has anything to say about it. Merck-Medco, which will be called Medco Health in the future, is one of the country's largest pharmacy-benefits managers (PBMs) and a pioneer in a brand-new method for distributing prescription drugs.

The pharmaceutical industry is big business today and will continue growing over the next several years. "Some of the growth stems from new drugs being introduced in the market, but the larger factor is that the population keeps growing older," says Eric Veiel, an analyst with Deutsche Bank. "The older we get, the more drugs we tend to take." Merck-Medco believes that by restructuring the traditional prescription medicine distribution system and automating the process of filling prescriptions, it can satisfy the increasing demand more efficiently.

Merck-Medco contracts with large employers and unions and collects a fee for processing patients' prescriptions and billing the patients' health-plan providers. Merck-Medco customers include United Airlines and its 80,000 U.S. employees, General Motors' 300,000 employees, and Oxford Health Plans' 1.5 million members, to name a few. Prescriptions are placed by physicians via e-mail, phone, or fax to any of Merck-Medco's 13 pharmacies and may be conveniently refilled by the patient at Merck-Medco's Web site or by phone. Once a prescription request is submitted, it starts a chain of events that involves several employees and processes at multiple locations.

A prescription request begins its journey at one of Merck-Medco's processing pharmacies, such as the Liberty Lake Plant in Washington state. Here prescriptions are entered into a proprietary electronic system, which first checks the patient's records to see if it is time to refill the medication and then evaluates the prescription from a clinical standpoint. Are there harmful side effects if the drug is combined with other medications the patient is taking? Is there a generic equivalent or a more effective medication? In about one third of the cases, a Merck-Medco pharmacist will phone the physician to discuss other options for the patient or ask for clarification. Bob Blyskal, senior vice president of operations, says this initial screening is all-important. "We use technology to dramatically improve quality of care through accuracy, and it allows us to remove pharmacists from counting pills and devote them to real value-added types of activities—drug utilization, generic substitution." Once the prescription is approved and in the system, it is transmitted to a dispensary such as the one at Willingboro, New Jersey.

"Willingboro is the world's largest pharmacy and the most advanced," company president Richard T. Clark said. In its 280,000 square foot facility, as big as six football fields, it dispenses about 200,000 mail-order prescriptions a week. This number is expected to quadruple by 2003. The dispensing process starts in the command center, a central monitoring system that manages the entire dispensing process and allows employees to track a bottle through various machines. The first step is to print the medication documentation, up to eight pages of patient-specific directions, drug warnings, and billing information. Then the command center gives instructions to the automated pill-counting mechanism and instructs a printer to generate a label and apply it to an empty bottle. The bottle, held in a rack with 23 others, moves to the dispensing lane on a two-mile conveyor belt. Once the bottle gets to the proper dispensing channel, the command center releases the pills. A bar code reader ensures that the right bottle is under the right dispensing channel. Once filled, the bottle, along with the documentation, is put in a bag, heat-sealed, and bar-code labeled. Scanners do a final accuracy check, and the package goes to the mail-sorting area. The whole trip down the conveyor belt takes about 15 minutes.

Merck-Medco provides its customers with a Web site that provides useful information concerning their prescriptions and other health-care issues. The site, located at http://www.merck-medco.com, provides easy and secure methods for members to fill

prescriptions, review prescription prices and copayments based on their health plans, check prescription records and benefits, receive e-mail reminders for refills, order nonprescription general health items through its relationship with on-line drugstore CVS.com, and research a wide variety of healthcare information.

Through seamless interaction among its Web site, pharmacist screening, and automated dispensing systems, Merck-Medco is often able to mail prescription refills on the same day they are requested. Are we wise to trust machines to fill our prescriptions? Merck-Medco claims that its system has never put a wrong pill in a wrong bottle.

As you read this chapter, consider the following:

- In what ways has Merck-Medco's new process for filling prescriptions improved the business of the organizations (such as United Airlines) that make use of its services, the lives of employees/members of those organizations, the practice of physicians, and the work of pharmacists and other employees of Merck-Medco? Are there any drawbacks to this new system?
- Besides pharmacies, what other traditional businesses might profit from this type of automation?

information system
a set of interrelated components that collect, manipulate, and disseminate data and information and provide a feedback mechanism to meet an objective

An **information system (IS)** is a set of interrelated components that collect, manipulate, store, and disseminate data and information and provide a feedback mechanism to meet an objective. The feedback mechanism helps organizations achieve their goals, such as increasing profits or improving customer service. We all interact daily with information systems, both personally and professionally. We use automatic teller machines at banks, checkout clerks scan our purchases using bar codes and scanners, we access information over the Internet, and we get information from kiosks with touchscreens. Major *Fortune* 500 companies are spending in excess of $1 billion per year on information technology. In the future, we will depend on information systems even more. General Motors, for example, has teamed up with Fidelity Investments to allow people to get information on investments and trade stocks using voice commands from a car or truck.[1] Knowing the potential of information systems and having the ability to put this knowledge to work can result in a successful personal career, organizations that reach their goals, and a society with a higher quality of life.

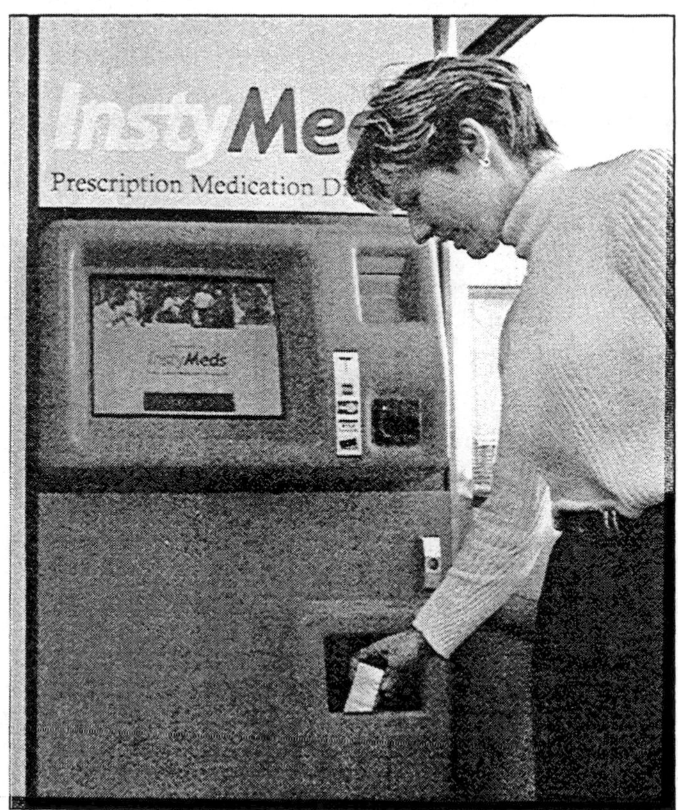

Information systems are everywhere. An advanced information system can be used to obtain prescriptions from automated kiosks: Customers respond to questions on a touchscreen and pay with a credit card, and the dispenser delivers the medication.

(Source: AP/Wide World Photos.)

Regardless of your career choice, information systems will play an important role in your future. If you work in the IS field, you will find good salaries and advancement opportunities. Most students, however, will not work in the IS field. Most will work for a business or organization in an area such as sales, marketing, accounting, finance, production, or research and development. As you will see throughout this text, information systems play a critical role in all these areas. We show you how information systems can be used to advance your career and help your organization achieve its goals in an ever-changing environment.

Computers and information systems are constantly changing the way organizations conduct business. We saw in the opening vignette, for example, how Merck-Medco was able to speed the delivery of prescriptions while maintaining a high degree of accuracy. Today we live in an information economy. Information itself has value, and commerce often involves the exchange of information, rather than tangible goods. Systems based on computers are increasingly being used to create, store, and transfer information. Investors are using information systems to make multimillion-dollar decisions, financial institutions are employing them to transfer billions of dollars around the world electronically, and manufacturers are using them to order supplies and distribute goods faster than ever before. Computers and information systems will continue to change our society, our businesses, and our lives. In this chapter, we present a framework for understanding computers and information systems and discuss why it is important to study information systems. This understanding will help you unlock the potential of properly applied information systems concepts.

INFORMATION CONCEPTS

Information is a central concept throughout this book. The term is used in the title of the book, in this section, and in almost every chapter. To be an effective manager in any area of business, you need to understand that information is one of an organization's most valuable and important resources. This term, however, is often confused with the term *data*.

DATA VERSUS INFORMATION

data
raw facts, such as an employee's name and number of hours worked in a week, inventory part numbers, or sales orders

information
a collection of facts organized in such a way that they have additional value beyond the value of the facts themselves

Data consists of raw facts, such as an employee's name and number of hours worked in a week, inventory part numbers, or sales orders. When these facts are organized or arranged in a meaningful manner, they become information. **Information** is a collection of facts organized in such a way that they have additional value beyond the value of the facts themselves. For example, a particular manager might find the knowledge of total monthly sales to be more suited to his or her purpose (i.e., more valuable) than the number of sales for individual sales representatives. Providing information to customers can also help companies increase revenues and profits. Uniglobe.com, Inc., provides fast and accurate information to people considering a cruise.[2] According to Mike Dauberman, senior vice president of business operations, "If you can grab a customer while they're on their peak of interest in a cruise, they're considerably more likely to buy it."

Turning data into information is a *process*, or a set of logically related tasks performed to achieve a defined outcome. The process of defining relationships among data to create useful information requires knowledge. *Knowledge* is an awareness and understanding of a set of information and ways that information can be made useful to support a specific task or reach a decision. Part of the knowledge needed for building a railroad layout, for instance, is understanding how large an area is available for the layout, how many trains will run on the track, and how fast they will travel. The act of selecting or rejecting facts based on their relevance to particular tasks is also based on a type of knowledge used in the process of converting data into information. Therefore, information can be considered data made more useful through the application of knowledge. Trimac, a Canadian bulk hauling company, for example, computerized its data to produce useful information to help it analyze profit potential.[3] According to a Trimac manager, "This technology facilitates the implementation of data ... used for trip analysis, haul analysis, and profitability, either by customer or equipment."

In some cases, data is organized or processed mentally or manually. In other cases, a computer is used. What is important is not so much where the data comes from or how it is processed but whether the results are useful and valuable. This transformation process is shown in Figure 1.1.

FIGURE 1.1

The Process of Transforming Data into Information

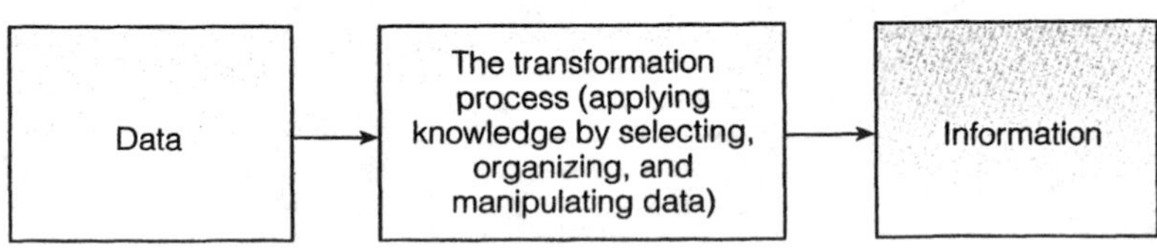

THE CHARACTERISTICS OF VALUABLE INFORMATION

To be valuable to managers and decision makers, information should have the characteristics described in Table 1.1. These characteristics also make the information more valuable to an organization. United Parcel Service (UPS) is able to determine the exact location of every package in its system.[4] This increased accuracy saves the company both time and money. According to one UPS executive, "That saves us from having to unload 20 trucks to find one little package, the way we had to do it five years ago." In addition, if an organization's information is not accurate or complete, people can make poor decisions, costing organizations and individuals thousands, or even millions, of dollars. Many believe, for example, that the collapse of energy-trading firm Enron in 2001 was a result of inaccurate accounting and reporting information, which led investors and employees alike to misjudge the actual state of the company's finances and suffer huge personal losses. Some believe that Enron's inaccurate accounting was intentional and designed to deceive employees and investors and not a simple accounting mistake. In any event, if information is not pertinent to the situation, not delivered to decision makers in a timely fashion, or too complex to understand, it may be of little value to the organization.

TABLE 1.1

Characteristics of Valuable Data

Characteristics	Definitions
Accurate	Accurate information is error free. In some cases, inaccurate information is generated because inaccurate data is fed into the transformation process (this is commonly called garbage in, garbage out [GIGO]).
Complete	Complete information contains all the important facts. For example, an investment report that does not include all important costs is not complete.
Economical	Information should also be relatively economical to produce. Decision makers must always balance the value of information with the cost of producing it.
Flexible	Flexible information can be used for a variety of purposes. For example, information on how much inventory is on hand for a particular part can be used by a sales representative in closing a sale, by a production manager to determine whether more inventory is needed, and by a financial executive to determine the total value the company has invested in inventory.
Reliable	Reliable information can be depended on. In many cases, the reliability of the information depends on the reliability of the data collection method. In other instances, reliability depends on the source of the information. A rumor from an unknown source that oil prices might go up may not be reliable.
Relevant	Relevant information is important to the decision maker. Information that lumber prices might drop may not be relevant to a computer chip manufacturer.
Simple	Information should also be simple, not overly complex. Sophisticated and detailed information may not be needed. In fact, too much information can cause information overload, where a decision maker has too much information and is unable to determine what is really important.
Timely	Timely information is delivered when it is needed. Knowing last week's weather conditions will not help when trying to decide what coat to wear today.
Verifiable	Information should be verifiable. This means that you can check it to make sure it is correct, perhaps by checking many sources for the same information.
Accessible	Information should be easily accessible by authorized users to be obtained in the right format and at the right time to meet their needs.
Secure	Information should be secure from access by unauthorized users.

THE VALUE OF INFORMATION

The value of information is directly linked to how it helps decision makers achieve their organization's goals. For example, the value of information might be measured in the time required to make a decision or in increased profits to the company. Consider a market forecast that predicts a high demand for a new product. If market forecast information is used to develop the new product and the company is able to make an additional profit of $10,000, the value of this information to the company is $10,000 minus the cost of the information. Valuable information can also help managers decide whether to invest in additional information systems and technology. A new computerized ordering system may cost $30,000, but it may generate an additional $50,000 in sales. The *value added* by the new system is the additional revenue of $20,000 from the increased sales. Most corporations have cost reduction as a primary goal. BASF, a large chemical company headquartered in Germany, spends nearly $100 million in distributing its inventory to North American customers.[5] Using a computerized inventory information system, BASF was able to reduce annual inventory distribution costs by 6 percent, or $6 million.

WHAT IS AN INFORMATION SYSTEM?

As mentioned previously, an information system is a specialized type of system and can be defined in a number of different ways. But an information system (IS) is typically considered to be a set of interrelated elements or components that collect (input), manipulate (process), and disseminate (output) data and information and provide a feedback mechanism to meet an objective (see Figure 1.2).

INPUT, PROCESSING, OUTPUT, AND FEEDBACK

Input

input
the activity of gathering and capturing raw data

In information systems, **input** is the activity of gathering and capturing raw data. In producing paychecks, for example, the number of hours every employee works must be collected before paychecks can be calculated or printed. In a university grading system, individual instructors must submit student grades before a summary of grades for the semester or quarter can be compiled and sent to the students.

Input can take many forms. In an information system designed to produce paychecks, for example, employee time cards might be the initial input. Car manufacturers are experimenting with a fingerprint identification input device in their car security systems.[6] You may soon be able to gain entry to a car and start it with the touch of a finger. This unique input device will also adjust mirrors, the steering-wheel position, the temperature, and the radio for an individual's size and preferences. Regardless of the system involved, the type of input is determined by the desired output of the system.

Input can be a manual or automated process. A scanner at a grocery store that reads bar codes and enters the grocery item and price into a computerized cash register is a type of automated input process. Regardless of the input method, accurate input is critical to achieve the desired output.

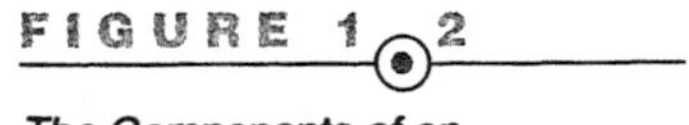
FIGURE 1.2

The Components of an Information System

Feedback is critical to the successful operation of a system.

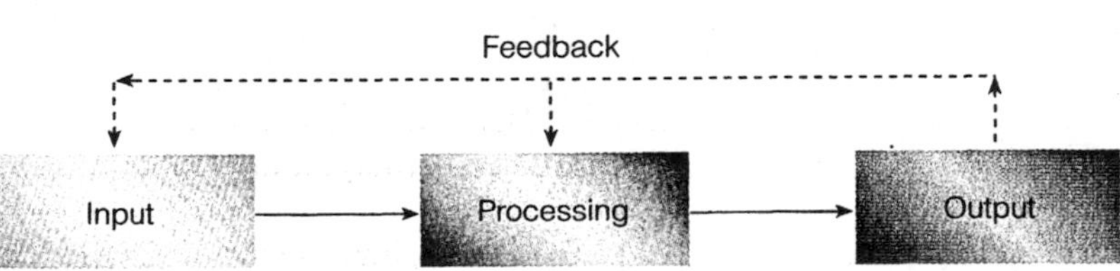

processing
converting or transforming data into useful outputs

Processing

In information systems, **processing** involves converting or transforming data into useful outputs. Processing can involve making calculations, making comparisons and taking alternative actions, and storing data for future use. Processing data into useful information is critical in business settings. Airline manufacturer Boeing, for example, streamlined its processing operations for needed parts.[7] According to Candace Ismael, director of supplier management and procurement, "The vision was to create a single process and supporting system for purchasing indirect parts."

Processing can also be done manually or with computer assistance. In the payroll application, each employee's number of hours worked must be converted into net, or take-home, pay. The required processing can first involve multiplying the number of hours worked by the employee's hourly pay rate to get gross pay. If weekly hours worked exceed 40 hours, overtime pay may also be included. Then deductions—for example, federal and state taxes, contributions to health and life insurance or savings plans—are subtracted from gross pay to get net pay.

output
production of useful information, usually in the form of documents and reports

Output

In information systems, **output** involves producing useful information, usually in the form of documents and reports. Outputs can include paychecks for employees, reports for managers, and information supplied to stockholders, banks, government agencies, and other groups. In some cases, output from one system can become input for another. For example, output from a system that processes sales orders can be used as input to a customer billing system.

Output can be produced in a variety of ways. For a computer, printers and display screens are common output devices. Output can also be a manual process involving handwritten reports and documents.

feedback
output that is used to make changes to input or processing activities

Feedback

In information systems, **feedback** is output that is used to make changes to input or processing activities. For example, errors or problems might make it necessary to correct input data or change a process. Consider a payroll example. Perhaps the number of hours an employee worked was entered into a computer as 400 instead of 40 hours. Fortunately, most information systems check to make sure that data falls within certain ranges. For number of hours worked, the range might be from 0 to 100 hours because it is unlikely that an employee would work more than 100 hours for any given week. So, the information system would determine that 400 hours is out of range and provide feedback, such as an error report. The feedback is used to check and correct the input on the number of hours worked to 40. If undetected, this error would result in a very high net pay on the printed paycheck!

Feedback is also important for managers and decision makers. For example, bedding maker Sealy Corp. used a computerized feedback system to link its suppliers and plants.[8] According to Jim Packer, director of procurement, "We're building 90% of our products to order, and this communications link between us, our suppliers, and the transportation network and plants closes the loop." For Sealy, output from an information system might indicate that inventory levels for a few items are getting low—a potential problem. A manager could use this feedback to decide to order more inventory from a supplier. The new inventory orders then become input to the system. In addition to this reactive approach, a computer system can also be proactive—predicting future events to avoid problems. This concept, often called **forecasting**, can be used to estimate future sales and order more inventory before a shortage occurs.

forecasting
predicting future events to avoid problems

MANUAL AND COMPUTERIZED INFORMATION SYSTEMS

As discussed earlier, an information system can be manual or computerized. For example, some investment analysts manually draw charts and trend lines to assist them in making investment decisions. Tracking data on stock prices (input) over the last few months or years, these analysts develop patterns on graph paper (processing) that help them determine what stock prices are likely to do in the next few days or weeks (output). Some investors have made millions of dollars using manual stock analysis information systems. Of course, today many excellent computerized information systems have been developed to follow stock indexes and markets and to suggest when large blocks of stocks should be purchased or sold (called *program trading*) to take advantage of market discrepancies. It is important to stress, however, that simply computerizing a manual information system does not guarantee improved system performance. If the underlying information system is flawed, the act of computerizing it might only magnify the impact of these flaws.

COMPUTER-BASED INFORMATION SYSTEMS

computer-based information system (CBIS)
hardware, software, databases, telecommunications, people, and procedures that are configured to collect, manipulate, store, and process data into information

A **computer-based information system (CBIS)** consists of hardware, software, databases, telecommunications, people, and procedures that are configured to collect, manipulate, store, and process data into information. For example, a company's payroll systems, order entry system, or inventory control systems are examples of a CBIS. (*Information technology*, abbreviated *IT*, is a related term. For our purposes, IT refers to the technology components of hardware, software, databases, and telecommunications.) The components of a CBIS are illustrated in Figure 1.3.

Hardware

hardware
computer equipment used to perform input, processing, and output activities

Hardware consists of computer equipment used to perform input, processing, and output activities. Input devices include keyboards, automatic scanning devices, equipment that can read magnetic ink characters, and many other devices. Investment firm T. Rowe Price, for example, uses voice response to allow customers to get their balances and other information using ordinary spoken sentences.[9] Processing devices include the central processing unit and main memory. There are many storage and output devices, including secondary storage devices, printers, and computer screens. One company, for example, uses computer hardware in its stores to allow customers to order items that are not on store shelves.[10] The hardware helps the company "save the sale" and increase revenues.

FIGURE 1.3

The Components of a Computer-Based Information System

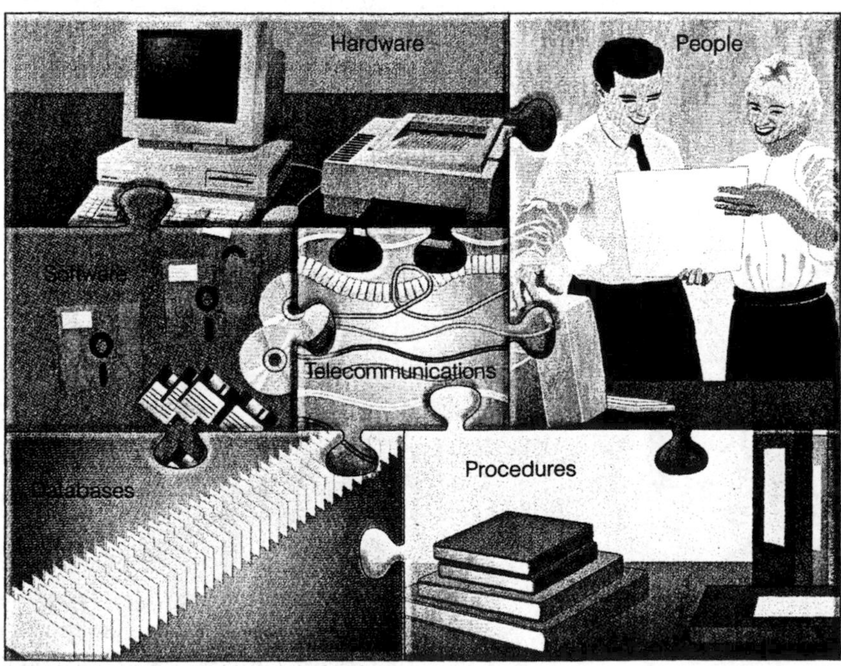

Software

software
the computer programs that govern the operation of the computer

Software consists of computer programs that govern the operation of the computer. These programs allow a computer to process payroll, send bills to customers, and provide managers with information to increase profits, reduce costs, and provide better customer service. There are two basic types of software: system software, such as Windows XP and the older Windows 2000, which controls basic computer operations such as start-up and printing, and applications software, such as Office XP and the older Office 2000, which allows specific tasks to be accomplished, such as word processing or tabulating numbers.[11]

Databases

database
an organized collection of facts and information

A **database** is an organized collection of facts and information, typically consisting of two or more related data files. An organization's database can contain facts and information on customers, employees, inventory, competitors' sales information, on-line purchases, and much more. Most managers and executives believe a database is one of the most valuable and important parts of a computer-based information system.[12] A database management system (DBMS) consists of software used to create, maintain, and manipulate a database to produce useful reports and outputs.

Telecommunications, Networks, and the Internet

telecommunications
the electronic transmission of signals for communications; enables organizations to carry out their processes and tasks through effective computer networks

networks
connected computers and computer equipment in a building, around the country, or around the world to enable electronic communications

Internet
the world's largest computer network, actually consisting of thousands of interconnected networks, all freely exchanging information

Telecommunications is the electronic transmission of signals for communications, which enables organizations to carry out their processes and tasks through effective computer networks. Bob Evans Farms, for example, uses a telecommunications system and satellites to link its 459 restaurants to its plants and headquarters in Columbus, Ohio, to speed credit card authorization and report sales and payroll data.[13] **Networks** are used to connect computers and computer equipment in a building, around the country, or around the world to enable electronic communications. Merrill Lynch, for example, uses a wireless network that sends data through the air to connect 2,000 people between Manhattan and New Jersey.[14]

Telecommunications and networks help people communicate using electronic mail (e-mail) and voice mail. These systems also help people work in groups. The **Internet** is the world's largest computer network, actually consisting of thousands of interconnected networks, all freely exchanging information. Research firms, colleges, universities, high schools, and businesses are just a few examples of organizations using the Internet. But anyone who can gain access to the Internet can communicate with anyone else on the Internet, including those who are in flight. American and Delta Air Lines in 2001 announced plans to launch Internet service on 1,500 aircraft.[15]

The World Wide Web is a network of links on the Internet to documents containing text, graphics, video, and sound. Information about the documents and access to them are controlled and provided by tens of thousands of special computers called Web servers. The Web is one of many services available over the Internet and provides access to literally millions of documents.

intranet
an internal network based on Web technologies that allows people within an organization to exchange information and work on projects

extranet
a network based on Web technologies that allows selected outsiders, such as business partners and customers, to access authorized resources of the intranet of a company

The technology used to create the Internet is now also being applied within companies and organizations to create an **intranet**, which allows people within an organization to exchange information and work on projects.[16] Read the "Ethical and Societal Issues" box to see how some companies are helping people balance their work and personal life with use of corporate Web and intranet technology. An **extranet** is a network based on Web technologies that allows selected outsiders, such as business partners and customers, to access authorized resources of the intranet of a company. Lisa Boothe, the global e-business leader at Du Pont, reported that her company plans to move all of its fabric, chemical, and biotechnology businesses to its extranet site for corporate customers.[17] Many people use extranets every day without realizing it—to track shipped goods, order products from their suppliers, or access customer assistance from other companies. Log on to the FedEx site to check the status of a package, for example, and you are using an extranet.

Xylo, Inc., Creates Work/Life Solutions

"The remarkable, and partly fortuitous, coming together of the technologies that make up what we label IT—information technologies—has begun to alter, fundamentally, the manner in which we do business and create economic value, often in ways that were not readily foreseeable even a decade ago," remarked Alan Greenspan, chairman of the Federal Reserve System, to university students in Grand Rapids, Michigan. "As a consequence, growth in output per work hour has accelerated, elevating the standards of living of the average American worker."

Being more productive has been a morale booster for U.S. workers. A recent survey of U.S. adults over the age of 18 showed that 92 percent found meaning and purpose in their work. But as people become more involved with their careers, they often find it difficult to participate fully in their career and have enough time for their other life obligations. Work commitments may compete with life commitments, known as the work/life dilemma. A college student experiences this dilemma when he or she has to pass up an outing with friends to finish a class project due the next day. Working students have an even more complex dilemma by having to balance school commitments, work commitments, and a personal life—the work/student/life dilemma. As we take on full-time careers and full-time family responsibilities, the stakes in this balancing act become high. With the increase in dual-income homes and single working parents, employees are feeling the pull between work and home responsibilities more than ever. Businesses have recognized this problem and are investing in tools to help their employees successfully meet this challenge.

Xylo, Inc., which is being acquired by Workstream, Inc., is a leading provider of Web-based work/life solutions used by *Fortune* 500 and other leading companies to attract and retain employees. Xylo clients include Charles Schwab, EDS, Eddie Bauer, Hewlett-Packard, Microsoft, Nordstrom, Northwest Airlines, Sodexho, and many more. "These companies are gaining a competitive edge in the labor market and sending a powerful message to employees about their strong commitment to work/life," said Xylo Senior Vice President of Marketing Judy Meleliat.

Work/life solutions such as Xylo's provide the tools for employees to strike a balance between their work demands and personal lives, while allowing their companies to increase loyalty and reward their employees' commitment. Xylo provides its clients with a custom-designed, password-protected Web site tailored to fit the client's corporate objectives, culture, and values. The Web site offers employees direct access to a wide variety of services and information. It also includes a link to the company intranet for access from any computer with an Internet connection. The Web site is organized into three areas:

1. *Co-worker Connection:* join a company team or interest group, post a classified ad, join a carpool
2. *My Company:* company news, company links, employee birthdays, suggestion box, on-line surveys
3. *Discounts & Services:* the mall, travel, entertainment, financial matters, healthy living, family matters

The Co-worker Connection area nurtures a community atmosphere among the members of the organization. The My Company area provides two-way communication between members and management and also can act as a gateway to the corporate intranet. Discounts & Services offers employees a convenient place to shop, make travel arrangements, and access helpful information. This area offers discounts from well-known Xylo marketing partners in travel, entertainment, and retail industries, and it can be edited to include local advertisements and discounts from the client company's own corporate partners.

Some might argue that allowing employees to shop on-line during work hours is distracting and counterproductive. But in the new work environment, with employees juggling so many responsibilities, many employers are finding that when they take an active role in helping employees handle work/life issues, employees become more content and focused, and the whole company benefits. Work/life solutions such as Xylo's exploit the benefits of modern-day telecommunications to build community, commitment, and contentment in the workforce.

Discussion Questions

1. How have work/life issues changed over the past 20 years? What impact, if any, have information systems had on the way society views work?
2. What types of industry would benefit most from a work/life solution such as Xylo's? Is there any type of business in which this solution might be inappropriate?

Critical Thinking Questions

3. Many companies establish policies regarding appropriate use of the corporate intranet and the Internet. What policies would you create to accompany a product such as Xylo's?
4. Are we moving to a point where we no longer differentiate between a professional life and personal life? Are there any hazards in doing so?

Sources: "EDS Selects Xylo's Web-based Work/Life Solution," *Business Wire,* November 6, 2001; "Majority of Americans Find Work Meaningful and Purposeful," *Business Wire,* October 30, 2001; Xylo Web site, http://www.xylo.com.

People

People are the most important element in most computer-based information systems. Information systems personnel include all the people who manage, run, program, and maintain the system.[18] Bank One Corp., for example, recently hired 600 information systems personnel to speed up its computer-related projects.[19]

Users are any people who use information systems to get results. Users include financial executives, marketing representatives, manufacturing operators, and many others. Certain computer users are also IS personnel.

Procedures

procedures
the strategies, policies, methods, and rules for using a CBIS

Procedures include the strategies, policies, methods, and rules for using the CBIS. For example, some procedures describe when each program is to be run or executed. Others describe who can have access to facts in the database. Still other procedures describe what is to be done in case a disaster, such as a fire, an earthquake, or a hurricane, that renders the CBIS unusable.

Now that we have looked at computer-based information systems in general, we briefly examine the most common types used in business today. These IS types are covered in more detail later in the book.

BUSINESS INFORMATION SYSTEMS

The most common types of information systems used in business organizations are electronic commerce systems, transaction processing systems, management information systems, and decision support systems. In addition, some organizations employ special-purpose systems such as artificial intelligence systems, expert systems, and virtual reality systems. Together, these systems help employees in organizations accomplish both routine and special tasks—from recording sales, to processing payrolls, to supporting decisions in various departments, to providing alternatives for large-scale projects and opportunities.

e-commerce
involves any business transaction executed electronically between parties such as companies (business-to-business), companies and consumers (business-to-consumer), consumers and other consumers, (consumer to consumer), business and the public sector, and consumers and the public sector

ELECTRONIC COMMERCE

E-commerce involves any business transaction executed electronically between parties such as companies (business-to-business), companies and consumers (business-to-consumer), consumers and other consumers (consumer-to-consumer), business and the public sector, and consumers and the public sector. People may assume that e-commerce is reserved mainly for consumers visiting Web sites for on-line shopping. Web shopping, however, is only a small part of the e-commerce picture; the major volume of e-commerce—and its fastest-growing segment—is business-to-business transactions that make purchasing easier for corporations. This growth is being stimulated by increased Internet access, user confidence, better payment systems, and rapidly improving Internet and Web security. E-commerce offers opportunities for small businesses, too, by enabling them to market and sell at a low cost worldwide, thus offering them an opportunity to enter the global market right from start-up. Figure 1.4 provides a brief example of how e-commerce can simplify the process for purchasing new office furniture from an office supply company. Under the manual system, a corporate office worker must get approval for a purchase that costs more than a certain amount. That request goes to the purchasing department, which generates a formal purchase order to procure the goods from the approved vendor. Business-to-business e-commerce automates the entire process. Employees go directly to the supplier's Web site, find the item in its catalog, and order what they need at a price prenegotiated by the employee's company.

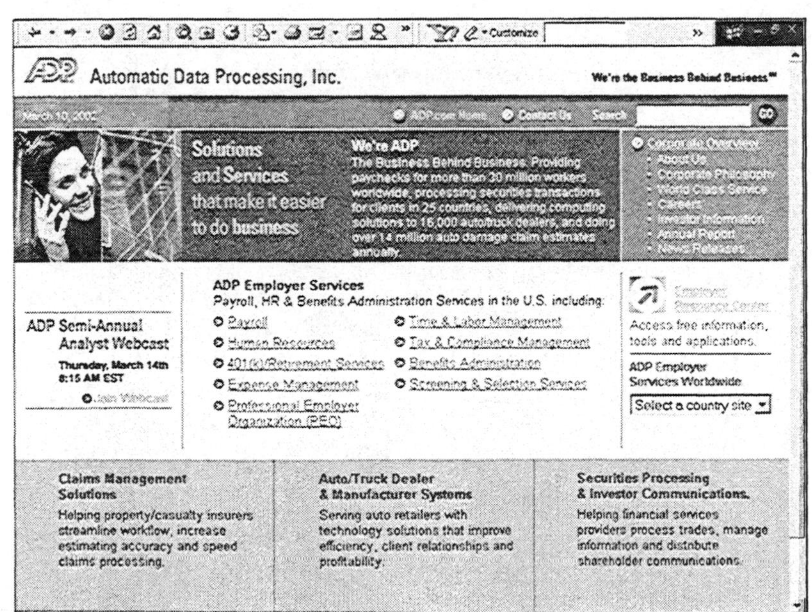

Already a huge portion of the e-commerce market, business-to-business transactions—such as this paycheck service by Automated Data Processing—are projected to pass the $1 trillion mark at the beginning of 2003.

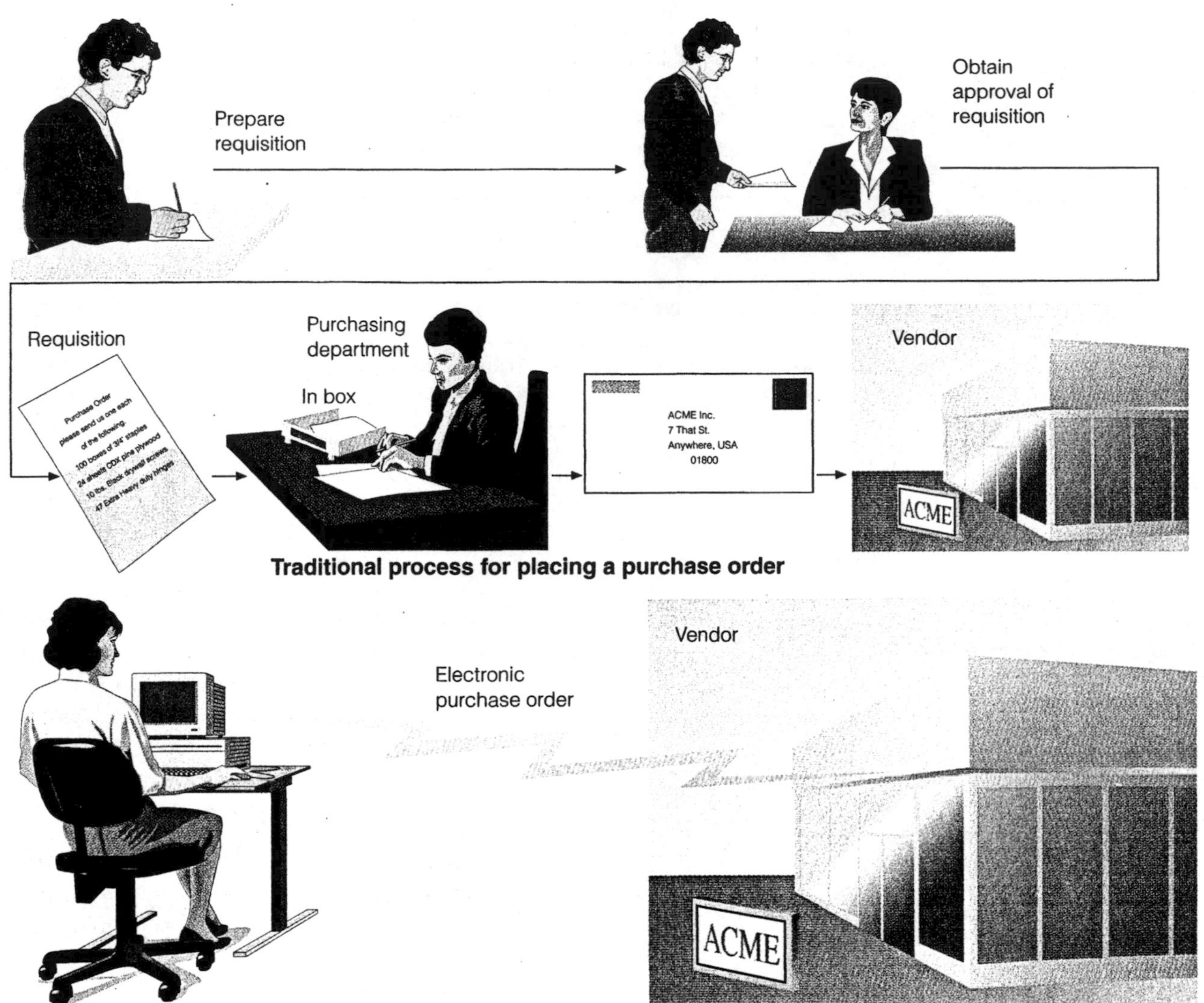

FIGURE 1.4

E-commerce greatly simplifies the purchasing process.

Today, several e-commerce firms have teamed up with more traditional brick-and-mortar firms to draw from each's strengths. Amazon.com, for example, is joining forces with Circuit City Stores, Inc.[20] With the new venture, customers will be able to order products through Amazon on the Internet and pick up products at one of the 600 local Circuit City stores or get them shipped to their address through Amazon.com's home or office delivery system.

TRANSACTION PROCESSING SYSTEMS AND ERP

Transaction Processing Systems

Since the 1950s computers have been used to perform common business applications. The objective of many of these early systems was to reduce costs by automating many routine, labor-intensive business systems. A **transaction** is any business-related exchange such as payments to employees, sales to customers, or payments to suppliers. Thus, processing business transactions was the first application of computers for most organizations. A **transaction processing system (TPS)** is an organized collection of people, procedures, software, databases, and devices used to process completed business transactions. To understand a transaction processing system is to understand basic business operations and functions.

transaction
any business-related exchange such as payments to employees, sales to customers, and payments to suppliers

transaction processing system (TPS)
an organized collection of people, procedures, software, databases, and devices used to process completed business transactions

One of the first business systems to be computerized was the payroll system (see Figure 1.5). The primary inputs for a payroll TPS are the numbers of employee

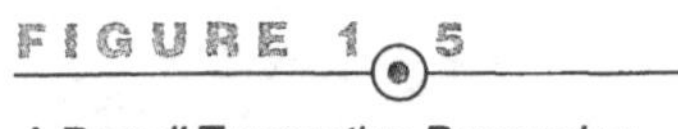

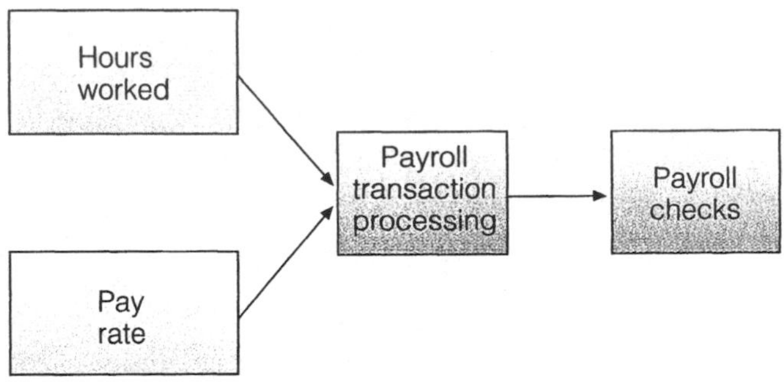

A Payroll Transaction Processing System

The inputs (numbers of employee hours worked and pay rates) go through a transformation process to produce outputs (paychecks).

hours worked during the week and the pay rate. Other inputs often include employee ID number and department. The primary output consists of paychecks. Early payroll systems were able to produce employee paychecks, along with important employee-related reports required by state and federal agencies, such as the Internal Revenue Service. Simultaneously, other routine processes, including sales ordering, customer billing, and inventory control, were computerized as well.

Enterprise Resource Planning

enterprise resource planning (ERP system)
a set of integrated programs that is capable of managing a company's vital business operations for an entire multisite, global organization

An **enterprise resource planning (ERP) system** is a set of integrated programs that is capable of managing a company's vital business operations for an entire multisite, global organization. An ERP system can take a large number of separate systems developed over a number of years by the organization and replace them with one unified set of programs. This can make the system easier to use and more effective.

Although the scope of an ERP system may vary from company to company, most ERP systems provide integrated software to support the manufacturing and finance business functions of an organization. In such an environment, a demand forecast is prepared that estimates customer demand for several weeks. The ERP system checks what is already available in finished product inventory to meet the projected demand. Any shortcomings then need to be produced. In developing the production schedule, the ERP system checks the raw material and packing material inventory and determines what needs to be ordered to meet the planned production schedule. Most ERP systems also have a purchasing subsystem that orders the items required. In addition to these core business processes, some ERP systems may be capable of supporting additional business functions such as human resources, sales, and distribution. PeopleSoft, for example, recently launched an Internet-based ERP to manage customer relationships.[21] The primary benefits of implementing an ERP system include easing adoption of improved work processes and improving access to timely data for operational decision making.

INFORMATION AND DECISION SUPPORT SYSTEMS

The benefits provided by an effective transaction processing system are tangible and can be used to justify their cost in computing equipment, computer programs, and specialized personnel and supplies. They speed business activities and reduce clerical costs. Although early accounting and financial transaction processing systems were already valuable, companies soon realized that the data stored in these systems can be used to help managers make better decisions in their respective business areas, whether human resources, marketing, or administration. Satisfying the needs of managers and decision makers continues to be a major factor in developing management information and decision support systems.

Management Information Systems

management information system (MIS)
an organized collection of people, procedures, software, databases, and devices used to provide routine information to managers and decision makers

A **management information system (MIS)** is an organized collection of people, procedures, software, databases, and devices used to provide routine information to managers and decision makers. The focus of an MIS is primarily on

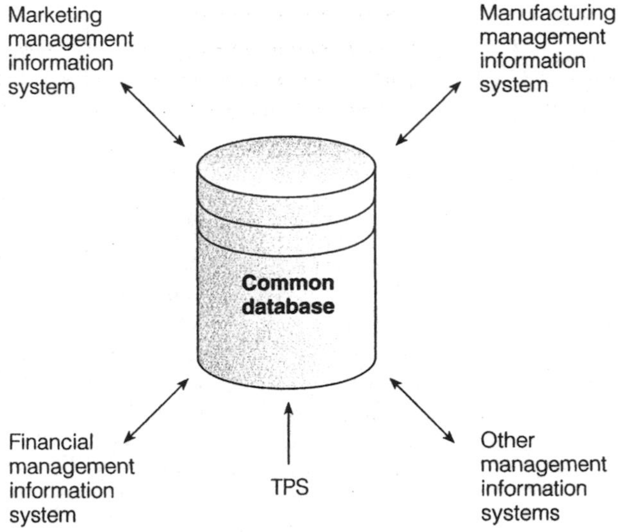

FIGURE 1.6

Functional management information systems draw data from the organization's transaction processing system.

operational efficiency. Marketing, production, finance, and other functional areas are supported by management information systems and linked through a common database. Management information systems typically provide standard reports generated with data and information from the transaction processing system (see Figure 1.6).

Decision Support Systems

By the 1980s, dramatic improvements in technology resulted in information systems that were less expensive but more powerful than earlier systems. People at all levels of organizations began using personal computers to do a variety of tasks; they were no longer solely dependent on the information systems department for all their information needs. So, people quickly recognized that computer systems could support additional decision-making activities. A **decision support system (DSS)** is an organized collection of people, procedures, software, databases, and devices used to support problem-specific decision making. The focus of a DSS is on decision-making effectiveness. Whereas an MIS helps an organization "do things right," a DSS helps a manager "do the right thing."

decision support system (DSS)
an organized collection of people, procedures, software, databases, and devices used to support problem-specific decision making

A DSS supports and assists all aspects of problem-specific decision making. As seen in the "IS Principles in Action" box, a DSS can also support customers by rapidly responding to their phone and e-mail inquiries.

The essential elements of a DSS include a collection of models used to support a decision maker or user (model base), a collection of facts and information to assist in decision making (database), and systems and procedures (user interface) that help decision makers and other users interact with the DSS (see Figure 1.7).

SPECIAL-PURPOSE BUSINESS INFORMATION SYSTEMS: ARTIFICIAL INTELLIGENCE, EXPERT SYSTEMS, AND VIRTUAL REALITY

In addition to TPSs, MISs, and DSSs, organizations often use special systems. One of these systems is based on the notion of **artificial intelligence (AI)**, where the computer system takes on the characteristics of human intelligence. The field of artificial intelligence includes several subfields (see Figure 1.8).

artificial intelligence (AI)
a field in which the computer system takes on the characteristics of human intelligence

Robotics is an area of artificial intelligence in which machines take over complex, routine, boring, or dangerous tasks, such as welding car frames or assembling computer systems and components. Vision systems allow robots and other devices to have "sight" and to store and process visual images. Natural language processing involves the ability of computers to understand and act on verbal or written commands in English, Spanish, or other human languages. Learning systems give computers the ability to learn from past mistakes or experiences,

IS Principles in Action

PRINCIPLE

Knowing the potential impact of information systems and having the ability to put this knowledge to work can result in a successful personal career, organizations that reach their goals, and a society with a higher quality of life.

Home Depot Invests Big in Information Systems

Although 2002 was a year of caution for most businesses when it came to information system spending, research shows that hard-goods retailers may increase their investment in information systems. Greg Buzek, president of IHL Consulting Group, which produced a report on the subject, stated that "leading-edge home improvement and electronics retailers like Home Depot, Lowes, Best Buy, and Circuit City will continue to invest heavily in new information technology. These retailers achieved their dominant market positions by deploying advanced technology during the slower economic times of the early 1990s. We are looking at another period where there will be favorable vendor and lender terms on capital IT spending. As a result, we expect to see these types of retailers maintain or even increase their level of capital spending to take advantage of these favorable terms."

Home Depot's recent commitments to major information system overhauls certainly bear this out. The Atlanta-based retailer of home improvement goods has embarked on a sweeping plan to tie together thousands of its software applications, stores, and systems in real time. The new unified system will provide relevant and up-to-date data and information for use in the company's MISs and DSSs to assist top management in making critical corporate decisions. Charlie Weston, director of information services at Home Depot, said the EAI implementation will probably run into millions of dollars but should pay for itself in the next several years.

Home Depot isn't stopping there—it is also changing the way it handles customer phone and e-mail inquiries. In the past, when customers phoned their local Home Depot with questions, the operator would connect them with a salesperson on the floor. Overburdened salespeople sometimes had to choose between either leaving the person waiting on the phone or making customers on the floor wait. Now Home Depot routes its calls to regional call centers. The Tampa call center employs 1,000 customer agents who handle customer calls in the company's southern division. These agents are able to access specific, detailed information for each store location using customer relationship management (CRM) solutions from Avaya Inc. Avaya's Interaction Management software links multiple databases in local stores and then delivers information to the regional agents, who seamlessly respond to customers by phone, e-mail, or other electronic media. By handling all contacts regionally, Home Depot frees store associates to spend more time with in-store customers. Customers contacting the company by phone or e-mail also receive more efficient and accurate service, with little or no time spent on hold or waiting for a response.

"For us, contact center technology is more than getting a call to an agent," said Ed Buter, senior manager—information services, Home Depot. "We have approximately a million products in more than 1,200 stores, with numerous databases kept at the stores for things like product orders, delivery and installation schedules, tool rentals, or promotional events. Our challenge is to get this information to the agents while quickly and effectively integrating all channels of communication into a system that supports the business."

It's clear that Home Depot understands that the quality of information flow within an organization is critical to the organization's ability to gain a competitive advantage. By connecting all its stores in a real-time network, Home Depot can more effectively view its stores (expected to number more than 2,300 by 2005) as a single entity. Such collective information allows the chain's management to examine up-to-the-minute nationwide statistics and trends, which ultimately supports more effective and timely decisions. With the addition of regional call centers, Home Depot makes more effective use of its employees' time to serve their customers. Add to this the services offered at the Web site, homedepot.com, and it's hard to imagine what more this company could do to improve itself.

Discussion Questions

1. What types of information, statistics, and trends might Home Depot managers be interested in tracking with their new system in order to meet the organization's goals?
2. Before you visit homedepot.com, list some valuable services you think Home Depot could offer its customers on the Web.

Critical Thinking Questions

3. If you were a Home Depot competitor, what type of services might you offer customers above and beyond those mentioned here so that your organization could compete with Home Depot?
4. Consider the expense involved in opening regional call centers. How does this investment assist Home Depot in being a more efficient and effective company?

Sources: "Home Improvement and Electronics Retailers Lead IT Spending Growth in Retail," *Business Wire*, January 8, 2002; Marc Songini, "Home Depot Launches Major Integration," CRM projects, *Computerworld*, June 29, 2001, http://www.computerworld.com; Avaya Inc.'s Web site, http://www.avaya.com.

such as playing games or making business decisions, and neural networks is a branch of artificial intelligence that allows computers to recognize and act on patterns or trends. Some successful stock, options, and futures traders use neural networks to spot trends and make them more profitable with their investments. **Expert systems** give the computer the ability to make suggestions and act like an expert in a particular field.[22] The unique value of expert systems is that they

expert system
a system that gives a computer the ability to make suggestions and act like an expert in a particular field

FIGURE 17

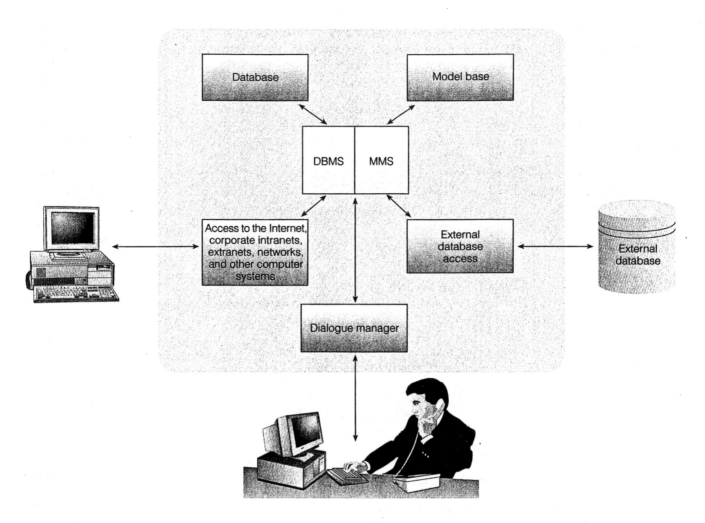

Essential DSS Elements

allow organizations to capture and use the wisdom of experts and specialists. Therefore, years of experience and specific skills are not completely lost when a human expert dies, retires, or leaves for another job. Expert systems can be

FIGURE 18

The Major Elements of Artificial Intelligence

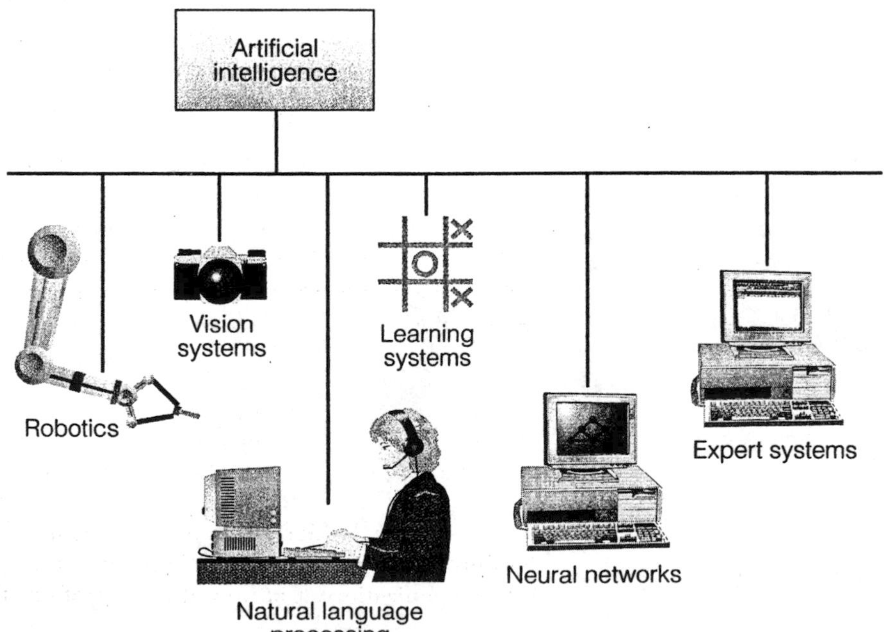

applied to almost any field or discipline. Expert systems have been used to monitor complex systems such as nuclear reactors, perform medical diagnoses, locate possible repair problems, design and configure information system components, perform credit evaluations, and develop marketing plans for a new product or new investment strategies.

Originally, the term **virtual reality** referred to immersive virtual reality, which means the user becomes fully immersed in an artificial, three-dimensional world that is completely generated by a computer. A variety of input devices such as head-mounted displays (see Figure 1.9), data gloves (see Figure 1.10), joysticks, and handheld wands allow the user to navigate through a virtual environment and to interact with virtual objects. Today, virtual reality systems that are not fully immersed can be utilized on personal computers to allow people to take a virtual tour of real estate, sporting events, space exploration, and more.

Now that we have reviewed the basic types of business information systems, we turn to a brief discussion of how systems are developed in organizations. Systems development is a critical function in today's organizations—and one that can often take many resources to accomplish well.

FIGURE 1.9

A Head-Mounted Display

The head-mounted display (HMD) was the first device of its kind providing the wearer with an immersive experience.

(Source: Courtesy of Virtual Research Systems, Inc.)

virtual reality
originally the term referred to immersive virtual reality, which means the user becomes fully immersed in an artificial, three-dimensional world that is completely generated by a computer

systems development
the activity of creating or modifying existing business systems

SYSTEMS DEVELOPMENT

Systems development is the activity of creating or modifying existing business systems. Developing information systems to meet business needs is highly complex and difficult—so much so that it is common for information systems projects to overrun budgets and exceed scheduled completion dates. Business managers would like the development process to be more manageable, with predictable costs and timing. Systems development includes investigation, analysis, design, implementation, and maintenance and review.

The goal of the *systems investigation* is to gain a clear understanding of the problem to be solved or opportunity to be addressed. Once this is understood, the next question to be answered is, "Is the problem worth solving?" Given that organizations have limited resources—people and money—this question deserves careful consideration. If the decision is to continue with the solution, the next step, *systems analysis*, defines the problems and opportunities of the existing system. *Systems design* determines how the new system will work to meet the business needs defined during systems analysis. *Systems implementation* involves creating or acquiring the various system components (hardware, software, databases, etc.) defined in the design step, assembling them, and putting the new system into operation. The purpose of *systems maintenance and review* is to check and modify the system so that it continues to meet changing business needs.

Systems development allows an organization to effectively utilize computer technology to increase revenues and reduce costs. Well-designed and -implemented information systems can help organizations achieve their goals. We discuss the use of information systems in organizations next.

ORGANIZATIONS AND INFORMATION SYSTEMS

organization
a formal collection of people and other resources established to accomplish a set of goals

An **organization** is a formal collection of people and other resources established to accomplish a set of goals. The primary goal of a for-profit organization is to maximize shareholder value, often measured by the price of the company stock. Nonprofit organizations include social groups, religious groups, universities, and other organizations that do not have profit as the primary goal.

FIGURE 1.10

A Data Glove

Realistic interactions with virtual objects via such devices as a data glove that senses hand position allow for manipulation, operation, and control of virtual worlds.

(Source: Courtesy of Virtual Technologies, Inc.)

An organization is a system. Money, people, materials, machines and equipment, data, information, and decisions are constantly in use in any organization. As shown in Figure 1.11, resources such as materials, people, and money are input to the organizational system from the environment, go through a transformation mechanism, and are output to the environment. The outputs from the transformation mechanism are usually goods or services. The goods or services produced by the organization are of higher relative value than the inputs alone. Through adding value or worth, organizations attempt to achieve their goals.

All business organizations contain a number of value-added processes. Providing value to a stakeholder—customer, supplier, manager, or employee—is the primary goal of any organization. The value chain, first described by Michael Porter in a 1985 *Harvard Business Review* article, is a concept that reveals how organizations can add value to their products and services. The **value chain** is a series (chain) of activities that includes inbound logistics, warehouse and storage, production, finished product storage, outbound logistics, marketing and sales, and customer service (Figure 1.12). Each of these activities is investigated to determine what can be done to increase the value perceived by a customer. Managing these activities is often called *supply chain management.*[23] Depending on the customer, value may mean lower price, better service, higher quality, or uniqueness of product.[24] The value comes from the skill, knowledge, time, and energy invested by the company. By adding a significant amount of value to their products and services, companies will ensure further organizational success.

value chain
a series (chain) of activities that includes inbound logistics, warehouse and storage, production, finished product storage, outbound logistics, marketing and sales, and customer service

What role does an information system play in these value-added processes? A traditional view of information systems holds that they are used by organizations to control and monitor value-added processes to ensure effectiveness and efficiency. An information system can turn feedback from the value-added process subsystems into more meaningful information for employees' use within an organization. This information might summarize the performance of the systems and be used as the basis for changing the way the system operates. Such changes could involve using different raw materials (inputs), designing new assembly-line procedures (product transformation), or developing new products and services (outputs). In this view, the information system is external to the process and serves to monitor or control it.

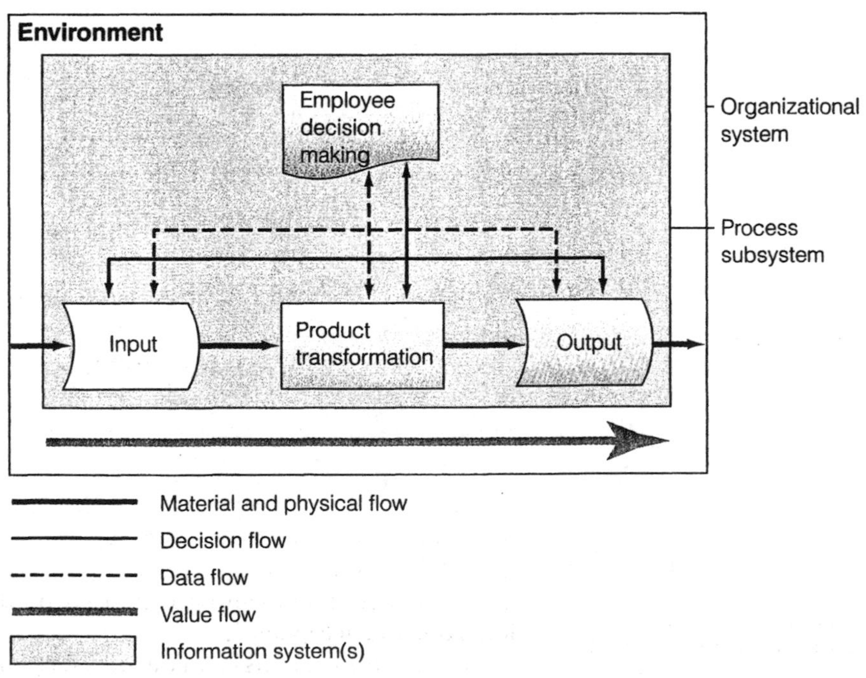

FIGURE 1.11

A General Model of an Organization

Information systems support and work within all parts of an organizational process. Although not shown in this simple model, input to the process subsystem can come from internal and external sources. Just prior to entering the subsystem, data is external. Once it enters the subsystem, it becomes internal. Likewise, goods and services can be output to either internal or external systems.

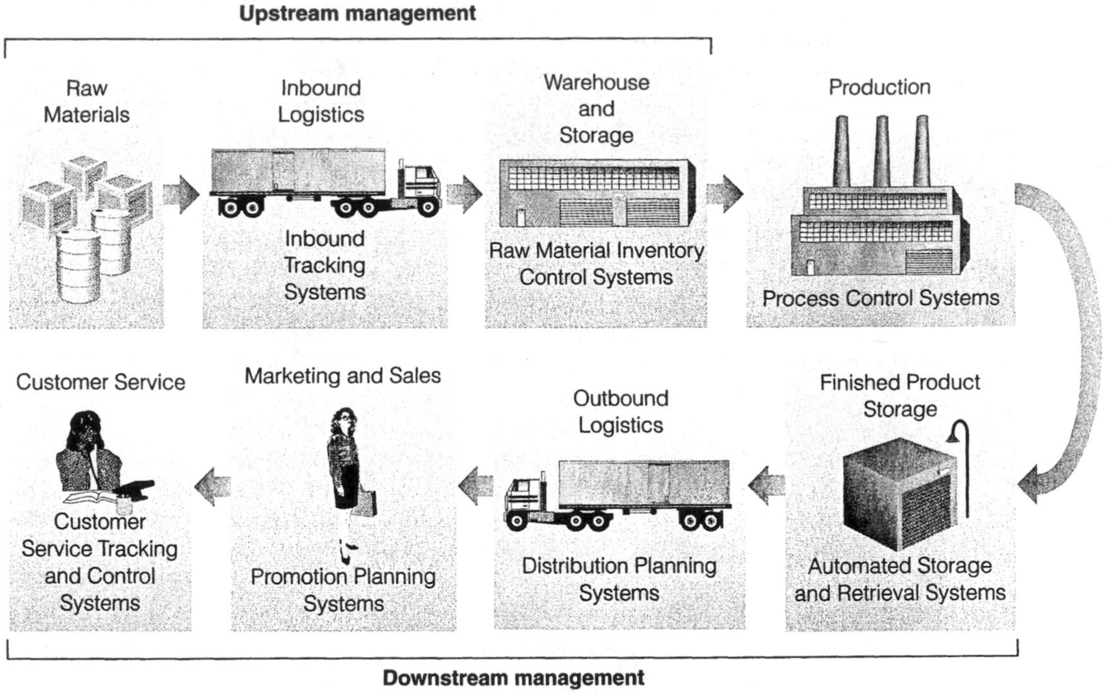

FIGURE 1.12

The Value Chain of a Manufacturing Company

The management of raw materials, inbound logistics, and warehouse and storage facilities is called upstream management, *and the management of finished product storage, outbound logistics, marketing and sales, and customer service is called* downstream management.

A more contemporary view, however, holds that information systems are often so intimately intertwined with the underlying value-added process that they are best considered *part of* the process itself. From this perspective, the information system is internal to and plays an integral role in the process, whether providing input, aiding product transformation, or producing output. Consider a phone directory business that creates phone books for international corporations. A corporate customer requests a phone directory listing all steel suppliers in Western Europe. Using its information system, the directory business can sort files to find the suppliers' names and phone numbers and organize them into an alphabetical list. The information system itself is an integral part of this process. It does not just monitor the process externally but works as part of the process to transform raw data into a product. In this example, the information system turns raw data input (names and phone numbers) into a salable output (a phone directory). The same system might also provide the input (data files) and output (printed pages for the directory).

The latter view brings with it a new perspective on how and why information systems can be used in business. Rather than searching to understand the value-added process independently of information systems, we consider the potential role of information systems within the process itself, often leading to the discovery of new and better ways to accomplish the process. Thus, the way an organization views the role of information systems will influence the ways it accomplishes its value-added processes.

TECHNOLOGY DIFFUSION, INFUSION, AND ACCEPTANCE

Even if a company buys or develops new computerized systems, managers and employees may never use the new systems. In other cases, new computerized systems are not used to their potential. Millions of dollars can be wasted as a result. The extent to which new computerized systems are used throughout an organization is critical and can be measured by the amount of technology diffusion, infusion, and acceptance.

technology diffusion
a measure of how widely technology is spread throughout the organization

Technology diffusion is a measure of how widely technology is spread throughout an organization. An organization in which computers and information systems are located in most departments and areas has a high level of technology diffusion.[25] Some on-line merchants, such as Amazon.com, have a high level of diffusion and use computer systems to perform most of their business functions, including marketing, purchasing, and billing. **Technology infusion**, on the other hand, is the extent to which technology permeates an area or department. In other words, it is a measure of how deeply imbedded technology is in an area of the organization. Some architectural firms, for example, use computers in all aspects of designing a building or structure. This design area thus has a high level of infusion. Of course, it is possible for a firm to have a high level of infusion in one aspect of its operations and a low level of diffusion overall. The architectural firm may use computers in all aspects of design (high infusion in the design area) but may not use computers to perform other business functions, including billing, purchasing, and marketing (low diffusion).

technology infusion
the extent to which technology is deeply integrated into an area or department

Although an organization may have a high level of diffusion and infusion, with computers throughout the organization, it does not necessarily mean that information systems are being used to their full potential. In fact, the assimilation and use of expensive computer technology throughout organizations vary greatly.[26] One reason is a low degree of acceptance and use of the technology among some managers and employees. Research has attempted to explain the important factors that enhance or hinder the acceptance and use of information systems.[27] A number of possible explanations of technology acceptance and usage have been studied.[28] The **technology acceptance model (TAM)** specifies the factors that can lead to higher acceptance and usage of technology in an organization, including the perceived usefulness of the technology, the ease of its use, the quality of the information system, and the degree to which the organization supports the use of the information system.[29] Companies hope that a high level of diffusion, infusion, and acceptance will lead to greater performance and profitability.[30]

technology acceptance model (TAM)
description of the factors that can lead to higher acceptance and usage of technology in an organization, including the perceived usefulness of the technology, the ease of its use, the quality of the information system, and the degree to which the organization supports the use of the information system

COMPETITIVE ADVANTAGE

A **competitive advantage** is a significant and (ideally) long-term benefit to a company over its competition. Establishing and maintaining a competitive advantage is complex, but a company's survival and prosperity depend on its success in doing so.

competitive advantage
a significant and (ideally) long-term benefit to a company over its competition

FACTORS THAT LEAD FIRMS TO SEEK COMPETITIVE ADVANTAGE

A number of factors can lead to the attainment of competitive advantage. Michael Porter, a prominent management theorist, suggested a now widely accepted **five-forces model**. The five forces include (1) rivalry among existing competitors, (2) the threat of new entrants, (3) the threat of substitute products and services, (4) the bargaining power of buyers, and (5) the bargaining power of suppliers. The more these forces combine in any instance, the more likely firms will seek competitive advantage and the more dramatic the results of such an advantage will be.

five-force model
a widely accepted model that identifies five key factors that can lead to attainment of competitive advantage, including (1) rivalry among existing competitors, (2) the threat of new entrants, (3) the threat of substitute products and services, (4) the bargaining power of buyers, and (5) the bargaining power of suppliers

Rivalry among Existing Competitors

The rivalry among existing competitors is an important factor leading firms to seek competitive advantage. Typically, highly competitive industries are characterized by high fixed costs of entering or leaving the industry, low degrees of product differentiation, and many competitors. Although all firms are rivals with their competitors, industries with stronger rivalries tend to have more firms seeking competitive advantage.

Threat of New Entrants

The threat of new entrants is another important force leading an organization to seek competitive advantage. A threat exists when entry and exit costs to the industry are low and the technology needed to start and maintain the business is

In the restaurant industry, competition is fierce because entry costs are low. So a small restaurant that enters the market can be a threat to existing restaurants.

(Source: © Owen Franken/CORBIS.)

commonly available. For example, consider a small restaurant. The owner does not require millions of dollars to start the business, food costs do not go down substantially for large volumes, and food processing and preparation equipment is commonly available. When the threat of new market entrants is high, the desire to seek and maintain competitive advantage to dissuade new market entrants is usually high.

Threat of Substitute Products and Services

The more consumers are able to obtain similar products and services that satisfy their needs, the more likely firms are to try to establish competitive advantage. Such an advantage often creates a "new playing field" in which "substitute" products are no longer considered as such by the consumer. Consider the personal computer industry and the introduction of low-cost computers. A number of consultants and computer manufacturers made much of the high cost of ownership associated with personal computers in the mid-1990s. They introduced low-cost network computers with minimal hard disk space, slower CPUs, and less main memory than some consumers desired, but at half the cost of a standard workstation. There was considerable interest in these new machines for a while, but traditional personal computer manufacturers fought back. They developed a class of powerful workstations and implemented new pricing strategies to make them available at under $1,000. This eliminated the primary advantage of the stripped-down network computers and regained lost customers.

Bargaining Power of Customers and Suppliers

Large buyers tend to exert significant influence on a firm. This influence can be diminished if the buyers are unable to use the threat of going elsewhere. Suppliers can help an organization obtain a competitive advantage. In some cases, suppliers have entered into strategic alliances with firms. When they do so, suppliers act like a part of the company. Suppliers and companies can use telecommunications to link their computers and personnel to obtain fast reaction times and the ability to get the parts or supplies when they are needed to satisfy customers.

STRATEGIC PLANNING FOR COMPETITIVE ADVANTAGE

To be competitive, a company must be fast, nimble, flexible, innovative, productive, economical, and customer oriented. It must also align the information system strategy with general business strategies and objectives. Given the five market forces just mentioned, Porter proposed three general strategies to attain competitive advantage: altering the industry structure, creating new products and services, and improving existing product lines and services. Subsequent research into the use of information systems to help an organization achieve a competitive advantage has confirmed and extended Porter's original work to include additional strategies—such as forming alliances with other companies, developing a niche market, maintaining competitive cost, and creating product differentiation.[31]

Altering the Industry Structure

Altering the industry structure is the process of changing the industry to become more favorable to the company or organization. This strategy can be accomplished by gaining more power over suppliers and customers. Some automobile manufacturers, for example, insist that their suppliers be located close to major plants and manufacturing facilities and that all business transactions be accomplished using

With soft sales in the PC market, Hewlett-Packard and Compaq agreed to a merger to make them more competitive. The strategic alliance was expected to help H-P compete in the larger computer server hardware market and in IS consulting services.

(Source: © AFP/CORBIS.)

electronic data interchange (EDI, direct computer-to-computer communications with minimal human effort). This system helps the automobile company control the cost, quality, and supply of parts and materials.

A company can also attempt to create barriers to new companies entering the industry. An established organization that acquires expensive new technology to provide better products and services can discourage new companies from getting into the marketplace. Creating strategic alliances may also have this effect. A *strategic alliance*, also called a *strategic partnership*, is an agreement between two or more companies that involves the joint production and distribution of goods and services.

Creating New Products and Services

Creating new products and services is always an approach that can help a firm gain a competitive advantage, and this is especially true of the computer industry and other high-tech businesses. If an organization does not introduce new products and services every few months, the company can quickly stagnate, lose market share, and decline. Companies that stay on top are constantly developing new products and services. Equifax, the largest credit-reporting agency in the United States, uses its information system to help it explore new products and services in new markets.[32] According to Equifax's Chief Financial Officer (CFO) Phil Mazzilli, "I'm involved in all strategic decisions, including how we use technology to get ourselves into new markets and improve efficiency, profitability, and shareholder value."

Improving Existing Product Lines and Services

Improving existing product lines and services is another approach to staying competitive. The improvements can be either real or perceived. Manufacturers of household products are always advertising new and improved products. In some cases, the improvements are more perceived than real refinements; usually, only minor changes are made to the existing product. Many food and beverage companies are introducing "healthy" and "light" product lines. A popular beverage company introduced "born on" dating for beer.

Using Information Systems for Strategic Purposes

In its simplest terms, competitive advantage is usually embodied in either a product or a service that has the most added value to consumers and that is unavailable from the competition or in an internal system that delivers benefits to a firm not enjoyed by its competition. Although it can be difficult to develop information systems to provide a competitive advantage, some organizations have done so with success. A classic example is SABRE, a sophisticated computerized reservation system installed by American Airlines and one of the first CBISs recognized for providing competitive advantage. Travel agents used this system for rapid access to flight information, offering travelers reservations, seat assignments, and ticketing. The travel agents also achieved an efficiency benefit from the SABRE system. Because SABRE displayed American Airlines flights whenever possible, it also gave the airline a long-term, significant competitive advantage.

Quite often, the competitive advantage a firm gains with a new information system is only temporary—competitors are quick to copy a good idea. So, although the SABRE system was the first on-line reservation system, other carriers soon developed similar systems. However, SABRE has maintained a leadership position in the past because it was the first system available, has been aggressively marketed, and has had continual upgrades and improvements over time. Maintaining a competitive advantage takes effort and is not guaranteed. SABRE's competitive advantage, for example, is being challenged with the many Internet-based travel sites becoming popular with today's travelers.

The extent to which companies are using computers and information technology for competitive advantage continues to grow. Many companies have even instituted a new position—chief knowledge officer—to help them maintain a competitive advantage. Forward-thinking companies must constantly update or acquire new systems to remain competitive in today's dynamic marketplace. In addition to using information systems to help a company achieve a competitive advantage internally, companies are increasingly investing in information systems to support their suppliers and customers. Investments in information systems that result in happy customers and efficient suppliers can do as much to achieve a competitive advantage as internal systems, such as payroll and billing. Table 1.2 lists several examples of how companies have attempted to gain a competitive advantage.

TABLE 1.2

Competitive Advantage Factors and Strategies

	Strategies		
Factors That Lead to Attainment of a Competitive Advantage	**Alter Industry Structure**	**Create New Products and Services**	**Improve Existing Product Lines and Services**
Rivalry among existing competitors	Blockbuster changes the industry structure with its chain of video and music stores.	Dell, Gateway, and other PC makers develop computers that excel at downloading Internet music and playing the music on high-quality speakers.	Food and beverage companies offer "healthy" and "light" product lines.
Threat of new entrants	AOL and Time Warner merge to form a large Internet and media company.	Apple Computer introduces an easy-to-use iMac computer that can be used to create and edit home movies.	Starbucks offers new coffee flavors at premium prices.
Threat of substitute products and services	Ameritrade and other discount stockbrokers offer low fees and research on the Internet.	Wal-Mart uses technology to monitor inventory and product sales to determine the best mix of products and services to offer at various stores.	Cosmetic companies add sunscreen to their product lines.
Bargaining power of buyers	Ford, GM, and others require that suppliers locate near their manufacturing facilities.	Investors and traders on the Chicago Board of Trade (CBOT) put pressure on the institution to implement electronic trading.	Retail clothing stores require manufacturing companies to reduce order lead times and improve materials used in the clothing.
Bargaining power of suppliers	American Airlines develops SABRE, a comprehensive travel program used to book airline, car rental, and other reservations.	Intel develops SpeedStep, a chip for laptop computers that operates at faster speeds when connected to an electrical outlet.	Hayworth, a supplier of office furniture, has a computerized-design tool that helps it design new office systems and products.

PERFORMANCE-BASED INFORMATION SYSTEMS

There have been at least three major stages in the business use of IS. The first stage started in the 1960s and was oriented toward cost reduction and productivity. This stage generally ignored the revenue side, not looking for opportunities to increase sales via the use of IS. The second stage started in the 1980s and was defined by Porter and others. It was oriented toward gaining a competitive advantage. In many cases, companies spent large amounts on ISs and ignored the costs. Today, we are seeing a shift from strategic management to performance-based management in many IS organizations. This third stage carefully considers both strategic advantage and costs. This stage uses productivity, return on investment (ROI), net present value, and other measures of performance. Figure 1.13 illustrates these stages.

PRODUCTIVITY

productivity
a measure of the output achieved divided by the input required

Developing information systems that measure and control productivity is a key element for most organizations.[33] **Productivity** is a measure of the output achieved divided by the input required. A higher level of output for a given level of input means greater productivity; a lower level of output for a given level of input means lower productivity. Consider a tax preparation firm, where productivity can be measured by the hours spent on preparing tax returns divided by the

FIGURE 1.13

Three Stages in the Business Use of IS

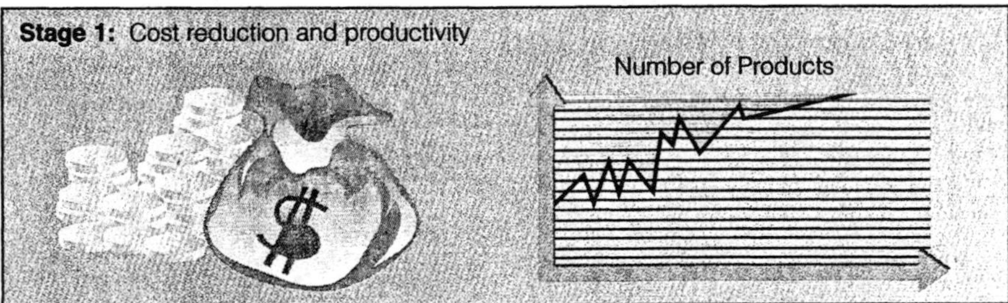

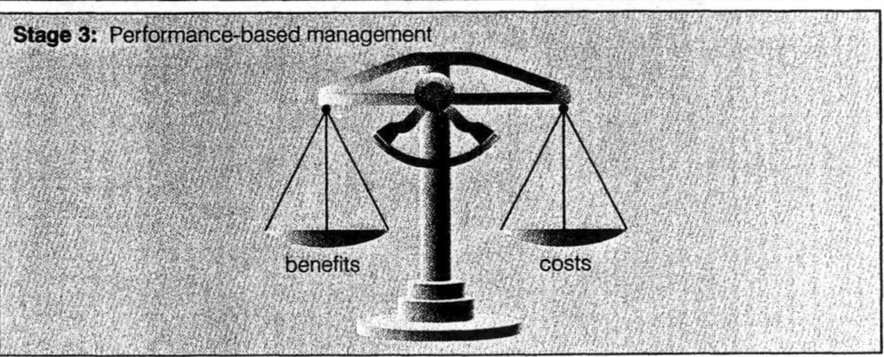

total hours the employee worked. For example, in a 40-hour week, an employee may have spent 30 hours preparing tax returns. The productivity is thus equal to 30/40, or 75 percent. With administrative and other duties, a productivity level of 75 may be excellent. The numbers assigned to productivity levels are not always based on labor hours—productivity may be based on factors like the amount of raw materials used, resulting quality, or time to produce the goods or service. In any case, what is important is not the value of the productivity number but how it compares with other time periods, settings, and organizations.

Productivity = (Output/Input) × 100%

Measuring productivity is important because improving productivity boosts a nation's standard of living. In an era of intense international competition, the need to improve productivity is critical to the well-being of any enterprise or country. If a company does not take advantage of technological and management innovation to improve productivity, its competitors will. The ability to apply information technology to improve productivity will separate successful enterprises from failures.

QUALITY

quality
the ability of a product (including services) to meet or exceed customer expectations

The definition of the term *quality* has evolved over the years. In the early years of quality control, firms were concerned with meeting design specifications—that is, conformance to standards. If a product performed as designed, it was considered a high-quality product. A product can perform its intended function, however, and still not satisfy customer needs. Today, **quality** means the ability of a product (including services) to meet or exceed customer expectations. This view of quality is completely customer oriented. A high-quality product will satisfy customers by functioning correctly and reliably, meeting needs and expectations, and being delivered on time with courtesy and respect. Companies such as Boeing combine computer technology and continuous improvement programs to both enhance quality and cut costs.[34] Boeing uses portable computing devices to monitor the quality of its airplane manufacturing process. After the quality data is entered into the portable computer, it is transferred to larger computers for analysis and report writing.

RETURN ON INVESTMENT AND THE VALUE OF INFORMATION SYSTEMS

return on investment (ROI)
one measure of IS value that investigates the additional profits or benefits that are generated as a percentage of the investment in information systems technology

One measure of IS value is **return on investment (ROI)**. This measure investigates the additional profits or benefits that are generated as a percentage of the investment in information systems technology. A small business that generates an additional profit of $20,000 for the year as a result of an investment of $100,000 for additional computer equipment and software would have a return on investment of 20 percent ($20,000/$100,000).

Because of the importance of ROI, many computer companies provide ROI calculators to potential customers. ROI calculators are typically found on a vendor's Web site and can be used to estimate returns in ten minutes or less. Plumtree Software, for example, provided Suncor Energy with an ROI calculator to help Suncor determine whether Plumtree's Internet software was worth the investment.[35] John Wharton, the e-business manager for Suncor, used the ROI calculator from Plumtree and decided to invest in the software.

Earnings Growth

Another measure of IS value is the increase in profit, or earnings growth, it brings. For instance, suppose a mail-order company, after installing an order processing system, had a total earnings growth of 15 percent compared with the previous year. Sales growth before the new ordering system was only about 8 percent annually. Assuming that nothing else affected sales, the earnings growth brought by the system, then, was 7 percent.

Market Share

Market share is the percentage of sales that one company's products or services have in relation to the total market. If installing a new on-line Internet catalog increases sales, it might help a company increase its market share by 20 percent. First Data Corp. embarked on a massive information systems upgrade to help it maintain its leading position in market share in automatic payment systems.[36] Denver-based First Data is the world's largest third-party transaction processor, with over 300 million accounts.

Customer Awareness and Satisfaction

Although customer satisfaction can be difficult to quantify, about half of today's best global companies measure the performance of their information systems based on feedback from internal and external users. Some companies use surveys and questionnaires to determine whether the investment in information systems has increased customer awareness and satisfaction.

Total Cost of Ownership

total cost of ownership (TCO) measurement of the total cost of owning computer equipment, including desktop computers, networks, and large computers

In addition to such measures as return on investment, earnings growth, market share, and customer satisfaction, some companies are also tracking total costs. One measure, developed by the Gartner Group, is the **total cost of ownership (TCO)**. This approach breaks total costs into such areas as the cost to acquire the technology, the cost of technical support, administrative costs, and the cost of end-user operations. Other costs in TCO include retooling and training costs. TCO can be used to get a more accurate estimate of the total costs for systems that range from small PCs to large mainframe systems. Market research groups often use TCO to compare different products and services.[37] In reviewing messaging products, Sara Radicati, president of a marketing research firm, said, "The market for messaging solutions is on the rise, but total cost of ownership continues to be a major issue for service providers."

Most organizations today realize that they must look at both sides of the equation—benefits as well as costs—in evaluating potential information system investments. Also, determining return on investment can help the IS organization prove its contribution to the organization and ensure that its efforts are aligned with the company's overall business objectives.

INFORMATION SYSTEMS PERSONNEL AND CAREERS IN INFORMATION SYSTEMS

Realizing the benefits of any information system requires competent and motivated information systems personnel, and many companies offer excellent job opportunities.[38] *Computerworld* reported the best ten places to work in IS based on training the company provides; recruiting, hiring, and retention practices; and day-to-day work environment (see Table 1.3).[39] Note the broad range of industries in which those companies operate—further proof of the widespread use of information systems and the value of an IS background whatever your career choice.

Numerous schools have degree programs with such titles as information systems, computer information systems, and management information systems. These programs are typically in business schools and within computer science departments. Degrees in information systems have provided high starting salaries for many students after graduation from college. Demand for IS professionals has also grown in nonprofit organizations and in government.[40] In 2001, the federal government had about 60,000 people employed as IS professionals.

Many global opportunities in information systems also exist. In addition, some companies seek skilled IS employees from foreign countries, including Russia and India.[41] "I'm finding the technical expertise in Russia is very high," says Ken Pocek, a manager for an Intel lab in Russia. The U.S. H-1B visa

TABLE 1.13

The 10 Best Places to Work for IS

Rank	Company	Average Training Days	Average Cost of Training
1	The Home Depot	17	$9,200
2	Nationwide Insurance	15	$7,652
3	The Vanguard Group	15	$8,000
4	Forsythe Technology	15	$10,000
5	Avon Products	10	$11,000
6	FleetBoston Financial	7	$9,200
7	Towers Perrin	10	$10,000
8	PricewaterhouseCoopers	15	$7,907
9	Harrah's Entertainment	14	$7,000
10	USAA	8	$7,200

Source: Data from Leslie Goff, "The Best Places to Work," *Computerworld*, June 25, 2001, p. 38.

program is another approach to getting skilled employees from foreign lands to the United States under a special visa program.[42] Congress recently raised the cap on H-1B visas from 115,000 to 195,000 through 2003. But not everyone is happy with the H-1B program. Some companies may be firing U.S. workers and hiring less expensive workers under the H-1B program. Both men and women are finding global opportunities in information systems.[43]

ROLES, FUNCTIONS, AND CAREERS IN THE INFORMATION SYSTEMS DEPARTMENT

Information systems personnel typically work in an information systems department that employs Web developers, computer programmers, systems analysts, computer operators, and a number of other information systems personnel. They may also work in other functional departments or areas in a support capacity. In addition to technical skills, information systems personnel also need skills in written and verbal communication, an understanding of organizations and the way they operate, and the ability to work with people (the system users).[44] In general, information systems personnel are charged with maintaining the broadest perspective on organizational goals. For most medium- to large-sized organizations, information resources are typically managed through an IS department. In smaller businesses, one or more people may manage information resources, with support from outside services—outsourcing. As shown in Figure 1.14, the information systems organization has three primary responsibilities: operations, systems development, and support.

Operations

The operations component of a typical IS department focuses on the use of information systems in corporate or business unit computer facilities. It tends to focus more on the *efficiency* of information system functions rather than their effectiveness.

The primary function of a system operator is to run and maintain IS equipment. System operators are responsible for starting, stopping, and correctly operating mainframe systems, networks, tape drives, disk devices, printers, and so on. System operators are typically trained at technical schools or through on-the-job experience. Other operations include scheduling, hardware maintenance, and preparation of input and output. Data-entry operators convert data into a form the computer system can use. They may use terminals or other devices to enter business transactions, such as sales orders and payroll data. Increasingly, data entry is being automated—captured at the source of the transaction rather than being entered later. In addition, companies may have local area network and Web or Internet operators who are responsible for running the local network and any Internet sites the company may have.

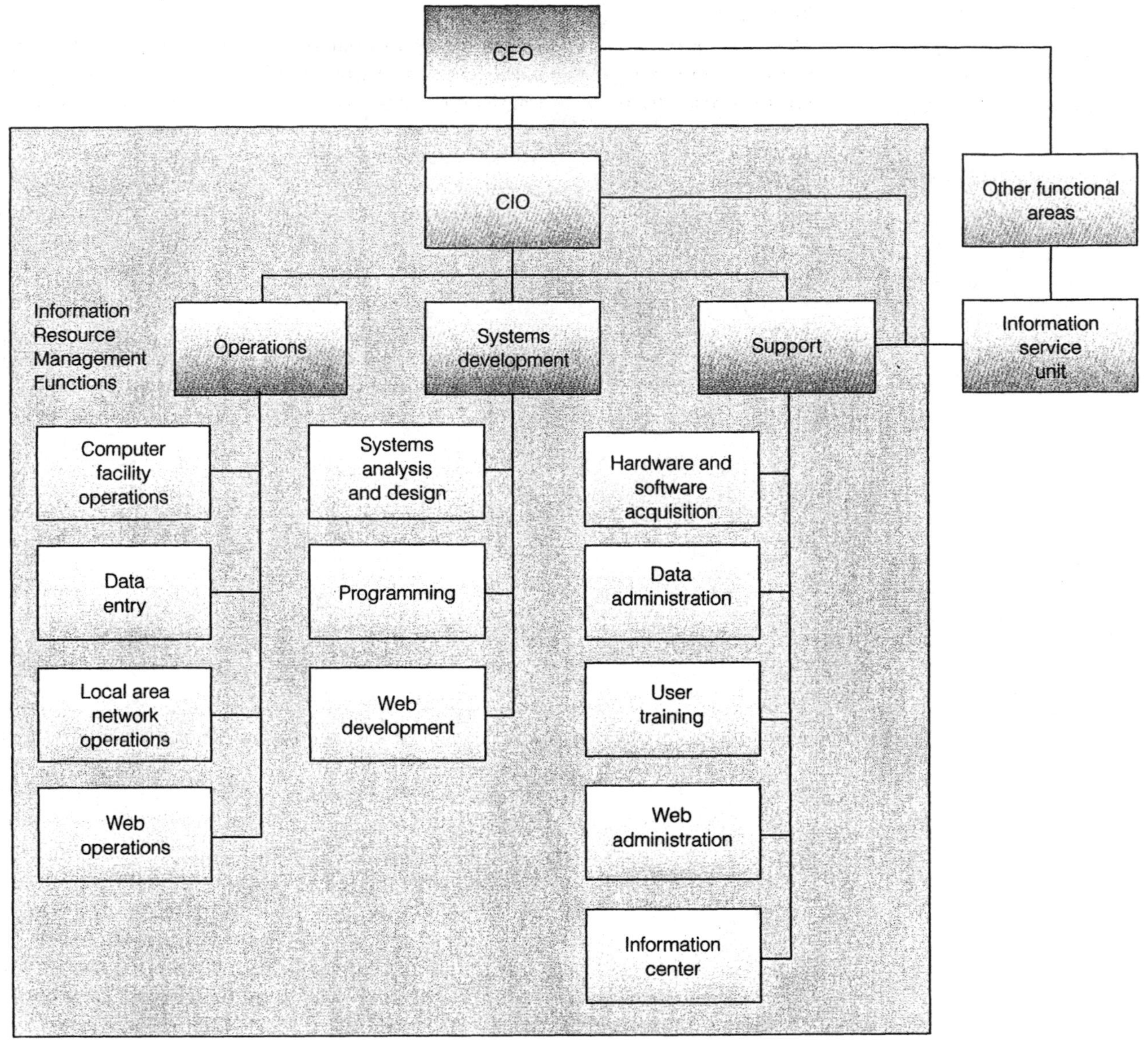

FIGURE 14.14

The Three Primary Responsibilities of Information Systems

Each of these elements—operations, systems development, and support—contains subelements critical to the efficient and effective operation of the organization.

Systems Development

The systems development component of a typical IS department focuses on specific development projects and ongoing maintenance and review. Systems analysts and programmers, for example, focus on these concerns.

The role of a systems analyst is multifaceted. Systems analysts help users determine what outputs they need from the system and construct the plans needed to develop the necessary programs that produce these outputs. Systems analysts then work with one or more programmers to make sure that the appropriate programs are purchased, modified from existing programs, or developed. The major responsibility of a computer programmer is to use the plans developed by the systems analyst to develop or adapt one or more computer programs that produce the desired outputs. The main focus of systems analysts and programmers is to achieve and maintain information system effectiveness.

With the dramatic increase in the use of the Internet, intranets, and extranets, many companies have Web or Internet developers who are responsible for developing effective and attractive Internet sites for customers, internal personnel, suppliers, stockholders, and others with a business relationship with the company.

Support

The support component of a typical IS department focuses on providing user assistance in the areas of hardware and software acquisition and use, data administration, user training and assistance, and Web administration. In many cases, the support function is delivered through an information center.

Because information systems hardware and software are costly, especially if mistakes are made, the acquisition of computer hardware and software is often managed by a specialized support group. This group sets guidelines and standards for the rest of the organization to follow in making purchases. Gaining and maintaining an understanding of available technology is an important part of the acquisition of information systems. Also, developing good relationships with vendors is important.

Firms may look to one outside source to supply part or all of their information systems needs—a single-vendor solution. There are advantages to this approach, such as potential cost savings and built-in compatibility. But using single vendors also involves risks, including lack of flexibility, vendor complacency due to lack of competitive bidding, and the possibility of missing out on new products from other vendors. Having an in-house specialist who focuses on the acquisition of information systems may also be wise when using the outsourcing approach.

A database administrator focuses on planning, policies, and procedures regarding the use of corporate data and information. For example, database administrators develop and disseminate information about the corporate databases for developers of information system applications. In addition, the database administrator is charged with monitoring and controlling database use.

User training is a key to getting the most from any information system. The support area ensures that appropriate training is available to users. Training can be provided by internal staff or from external sources. For example, internal support staff may train managers and employees in the best way to enter sales orders, to receive computerized inventory reports, and to submit expense reports electronically. Companies also hire outside firms to help train users in other areas, including the use of word processing, spreadsheet, and database programs.

Web administration is another key area of the support function. With the increased use of the Internet and corporate Web sites, Web administrators are sometimes asked to regulate and monitor Internet use by employees and managers to make sure that it is authorized and appropriate. Web administrators also are responsible for maintaining the corporate Web site. Keeping corporate Web sites accurate and current can require substantial resources.

information center
a support function that provides users with assistance, training, application development, documentation, equipment selection and setup, standards, technical assistance, and troubleshooting

The support component typically operates the information center. An **information center** provides users with assistance, training, application development, documentation, equipment selection and setup, standards, technical assistance, and troubleshooting. Although many firms have attempted to phase out information centers, others have changed the focus of this function from technical training to helping users find ways to maximize the benefits of the information resource.

TYPICAL IS TITLES AND FUNCTIONS

The organizational chart shown in Figure 1.14 is a simplified model of an IS department in a typical medium- or large-sized organization. Many organizations have even larger departments, with increasingly specialized positions such as librarian, quality assurance manager, and the like. Smaller firms often combine the roles depicted in Figure 1.14 into fewer formal positions.

The Chief Information Officer

The overall role of the chief information officer (CIO) is to employ an IS department's equipment and personnel in a manner that will help the organization attain its goals. The CIO is usually a manager at the vice president level concerned with the overall needs of the organization. He or she is responsible for corporatewide policy, planning, management, and acquisition of information systems. Some of the CIO's top concerns include integrating information systems operations with corporate strategies, keeping up with the rapid pace of technology, and defining and assessing the value of systems development projects in terms of performance, cost, control, and complexity. The high level of the CIO position is consistent with the idea that information is one of the organization's most important resources. This individual works with other high-level officers of an organization, including the chief financial officer (CFO) and the chief executive officer (CEO), in managing and controlling total corporate resources.

Increasingly, CIOs have to deal with international information systems. Chris Scalet, CIO for International Paper Co., has to manage information systems in the United States, Europe, South America, and Asia from his offices in New York.[45] According to Scalet, "It's a situation where you just have to communicate and recommunicate—you have to overcommunicate."

Depending on the size of the information systems department, there may be several people at senior IS managerial levels. Some of the job titles associated with information systems management are the CIO, vice president of information systems, and manager of information systems. A central role of all these individuals is to communicate with other areas of the organization to determine changing needs. Often these individuals are part of an advisory or steering committee that helps the CIO and other IS managers with their decisions about the use of information systems. Together they can best decide what information systems will support corporate goals. CIOs must work closely with advisory committees, stressing effectiveness and teamwork and viewing information systems as an integral part of the organization's business processes—not as an adjunct to the organization. Thus, CIOs need both technical and business skills. Some companies, like discount broker Ameritrade, have co-CIOs.[46] One Ameritrade co-CIO has technical skills in developing computer programs, and the other has financial skills in developing planning tools for clients.

LAN Administrators

Local Area Network (LAN) administrators set up and manage the network hardware, software, and security processes. They manage the addition of new users, software, and devices to the network. They isolate and fix operations problems. LAN administrators are in high demand and often solve both technical and nontechnical problems. According to Chris Holmes of J. P. Morgan, "I transitioned into technology, where I am currently a LAN administrator and troubleshooter. I now have the opportunity to work directly with technology and solve problems, and that brings me much more satisfaction."[47]

Internet Careers

The recent bankruptcy of some Internet start-up companies, called the dot-gone era by some, has resulted in layoffs for some firms.[48] Some executives of these bankrupt start-up Internet companies lost hundreds of millions of dollars in a few months. Yet, the growth in the use of the Internet to conduct business continues and has caused a steady need for skilled personnel to develop and coordinate Internet usage. As seen in Figure 1.14, these careers are in the areas of Web operations, Web development, and Web administration. As with other areas in IS, there are a number of top-level administrative jobs related to the Internet. These career opportunities are with traditional companies and companies that specialize in the Internet.

Internet jobs within a traditional company include Internet strategists and administrators, Internet systems developers, Internet programmers, and Internet or Web site operators. The Internet has become so important to some companies that some have suggested a new position, chief Internet officer, with responsibilities and salary similar to the CIO's.

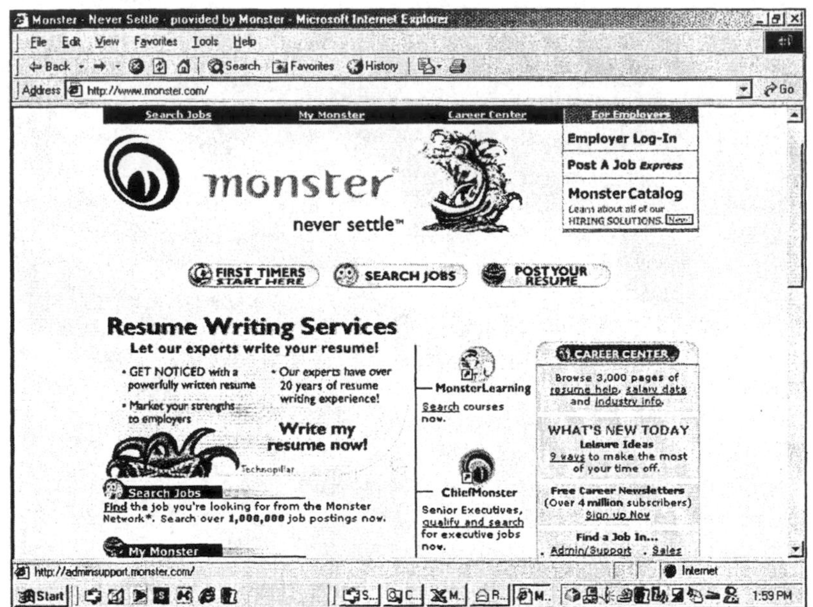

Internet job sites such as Monster.com allow job hunters to browse job opportunities and post their résumés.

In addition to traditional companies, there are many exciting career opportunities in companies that offer products and services over the Internet. These companies include Amazon.com, Yahoo!, eBay, and many others. Systest, for example, specializes in finding and eliminating digital bugs that could halt the operation of a computer system.

A number of Internet sites post job opportunities for Internet careers and more traditional careers, such as Monster.com. These sites allow prospective job hunters to browse job opportunities, job locations, salaries, benefits, and other factors. In addition, some of these sites allow job hunters to post their résumés.

Quite often the people filling IS roles have completed some form of certification. **Certification** is a process for testing skills and knowledge resulting in an endorsement by the certifying authority that an individual is capable of performing a particular job. Certification frequently involves specific, vendor-provided or vendor-endorsed coursework. There are a number of popular certification programs, including Novell Certified Network Engineer, Microsoft Certified Professional Systems Engineer, Certified Project Manager, and others.[49] The Certified Information Systems Security Professional (CISSP) is also becoming increasingly important to companies.[50] The federal government is helping military personnel get IS certification. GI Bill beneficiaries, for example, can now get reimbursed for technology certification through the Computing Technology Industry Association.[51]

certification
process for testing skills and knowledge that results in a statement by the certifying authority that says an individual is capable of performing a particular kind of job

One of the greatest fears of every IS manager is spending several thousand dollars to help an employee get certified and then losing that person to a higher-paying position with a new firm. As a consequence, some organizations request a written commitment from individuals to stay a certain time after obtaining their certification. Needless to say, this requirement can create some ill will with the employee. To provide newly certified employees with incentives to remain, other organizations provide salary increases based on additional credentials acquired.

OTHER IS CAREERS

In addition to working for an information systems department in an organization, information systems personnel can work for one of the large consulting firms, such as Accenture, EDS, and others. These jobs often entail a large amount of travel, because consultants are assigned to work on various projects wherever the client is. Such roles require excellent people and project management skills in addition to IS technical skills.

Another IS career opportunity is to be employed by a hardware or software vendor developing or selling products. Such a role enables the individual to work on the cutting edge of technology and can be extremely challenging and exciting!

WHY LEARN ABOUT INFORMATION SYSTEMS?

Studies have shown that the involvement of managers and decision makers in all aspects of information systems is a major factor for organizational success, including higher profits and lower costs. A knowledge of information systems will help you make a significant contribution on the job. It will also help you advance in your chosen career or field. Managers are expected to identify opportunities to implement information systems to improve the business. They are also expected to be able to lead information system projects in their area of the business.

Information systems play a fundamental and ever-expanding role in all business organizations. If you are to have a solid understanding of how organizations operate, it is imperative that you understand the role of information systems within these organizations. Moreover, in this new century, business survival and prosperity continue to become more difficult. For example, increased mergers among former competitors to create global conglomerates, continued downsizing of corporations to focus on their core businesses and to improve efficiencies, efforts to reduce trade barriers, and the globalization of capital all point to the increased internationalization of business organizations and markets. In addition, business issues and decisions are becoming more complex and must be made faster. An understanding of information systems will help you cope, adapt, and prosper in this challenging environment.

Regardless of your chosen field or the organization for which you may work, it is likely that you will use information systems. Why study information systems? A knowledge of information systems will help you advance in your career, solve problems, realize opportunities, and meet your own personal goals.

SUMMARY

PRINCIPLE ***The value of information is directly linked to how it helps decision makers achieve the organization's goals.***

Data consists of raw facts; information is data transformed into a meaningful form. The process of defining relationships between data requires knowledge. Knowledge is an awareness and understanding of a set of information and how that information can be made useful to support a specific task. To be valuable, information must have several characteristics: it should be accurate, complete, economical to produce, flexible, reliable, relevant, simple to understand, timely, verifiable, accessible, and secure. The value of information is directly linked to how it helps people achieve their organization's goals.

Information systems are sets of interrelated elements that collect (input), manipulate and store (process), and disseminate (output) data and information. Input is the activity of capturing and gathering new data; processing involves converting or transforming data into useful outputs; and output involves producing useful information. Feedback is the output that is used to make adjustments or changes to input or processing activities. The components of a computer-based information system include hardware, software, databases, telecommunications and networks, people, and procedures.

PRINCIPLE ***Knowing the potential impact of information systems and having the ability to put this knowledge to work can result in a successful personal career, organizations that reach their goals, and a society with a higher quality of life.***

Information systems play an important role in today's businesses and society. The key to understanding the existing variety of systems begins with learning their fundamentals. The types of systems used within organizations can be classified into four basic groups: (1) e-commerce, (2) TPS, (3) MIS and DSS, and (4) special-purpose business information systems.

E-commerce involves any business transaction executed electronically between parties such as companies (business-to-business), companies and consumers (business-to-consumer), consumers and other consumers, (consumer-to-consumer), business and the public sector, and consumers and the public sector. The major volume of e-commerce and its fastest-growing segment is business-to-business transactions that make purchasing easier for big corporations. E-commerce offers opportunities for small businesses by enabling them to market and sell at a low cost worldwide, thus enabling them to enter the global market.

The most fundamental system is the transaction processing system (TPS). A transaction is any business-related exchange. The TPS handles the large volume of business transactions that occur daily within an organization. TPSs include order processing, purchasing, accounting, and related systems.

An enterprise resource planning (ERP) system is a set of integrated programs that is capable of managing a company's vital business operations for an entire multisite, global organization. Although the scope of an ERP system may vary from company to company, most ERP systems provide integrated software to support the manufacturing and finance business functions of an organization.

A management information system (MIS) uses the information from a TPS to generate information useful for management decision making. The focus of an MIS is primarily on operational efficiency.

A decision support system (DSS) is an organized collection of people, procedures, databases, and devices used to support problem-specific decision making. The DSS differs from an MIS in the support given to users, the decision emphasis, the development and approach, and system components, speed, and output.

The special-purpose business information systems include artificial intelligence systems, expert systems, virtual reality systems, and other specialized information systems. Artificial intelligence (AI) includes a wide range of systems, in which the computer system takes on the characteristics of human intelligence. An expert system (ES) is designed to act as an expert consultant to a user who is seeking advice about a specific situation. Originally, the term *virtual reality* referred to immersive virtual reality, in which the user becomes fully immersed in an artificial, three-dimensional world that is completely generated by a computer. Virtual reality can also refer to applications that are not fully immersive, such as mouse-controlled navigation through a three-dimensional environment on a graphics monitor, stereo viewing from the monitor via stereo glasses, stereo projection systems, and others.

PRINCIPLE ***System users, business managers, and information systems professionals must work together to build a successful information system.***

Systems development involves creating or modifying existing business systems. The major steps of this process and their goals include systems investigation (gain a clear understanding of what the problem is); systems analysis (define what the system must do to solve the problem); systems design (determine exactly how the system will work to meet the business needs); implementation (create or acquire the various systems components defined in the design step); and maintenance and review (maintain and then modify the system so that it continues to meet changing business needs).

PRINCIPLE ***The use of information systems to add value to the organization can also give an organization a competitive advantage.***

An organization is a formal collection of people and various other resources established to accomplish a set of goals. The primary goal of a for-profit organization is to maximize shareholder value. Nonprofit organizations include social groups, religious groups, universities, and other organizations that do not have profit as the primary goal. Organizations are systems with inputs, transformation mechanisms, and outputs.

Value-added processes increase the relative worth of the combined inputs on their way to becoming final outputs of the organization. The value chain is a series (chain) of activities that includes (1) inbound logistics, (2) warehouse and storage, (3) production, (4) finished product storage, (5) outbound logistics, (6) marketing and sales, and (7) customer service.

Organizations use information systems to support organizational goals. Because information systems typically are designed to improve productivity, methods for measuring the system's impact on productivity should be devised.

The extent to which technology is used throughout an organization can be a function of technology diffusion, infusion, and acceptance. Technology diffusion is a measure of how widely technology is in place throughout an organization. Technology infusion is the extent to which technology permeates an area or department. The technology acceptance model (TAM) investigates factors, such as perceived usefulness of the technology, ease of use of the technology, the quality of the information system, and the degree to which the organization supports the use of the information system, to predict information system usage and performance.

Competitive advantage is usually embodied in either a product or a service that has the most added value to consumers and that is unavailable from the competition or in an internal system that delivers benefits to a firm not enjoyed by its competition. A five-force model covers factors that lead firms to seek competitive advantage: rivalry among existing competitors, the threat of new market entrants, the threat of substitute products and services, the bargaining power of buyers, and the bargaining power of suppliers. Three strategies to address these factors and to attain competitive advantage include altering the industry structure, creating new products and services, and improving existing product lines and services.

The ability of an information system to provide or maintain competitive advantage should also be determined. Several strategies for achieving competitive advantage include enhancing existing products or services or developing new ones, as well as changing the existing industry or creating a new one.

Developing information systems that measure and control productivity is a key element for most organizations. A useful measure of the value of an information system project is return on investment (ROI). This measure investigates the additional profits or benefits that are generated as a percentage of the investment in information systems technology. Total cost of ownership (TCO) can also be a useful measure.

PRINCIPLE ***Information systems personnel are the key to unlocking the potential of any new or modified system.***

Information systems personnel typically work in an information systems department that employs a chief information officer, systems analysts, computer programmers, computer operators, and a number of other people. The overall role of the chief information officer (CIO) is to employ an IS department's equipment and personnel in a manner that will help the organization attain its goals. Systems analysts help users determine what outputs they need from the system and construct the plans for developing the necessary programs that produce these outputs. Systems analysts then work with one or more programmers to make sure that the appropriate programs are purchased, modified from existing programs, or developed. The major responsibility of a computer programmer is to use the plans developed by the systems analyst to develop or adapt one or more computer programs that produce the desired outputs.

Computer operators are responsible for starting, stopping, and correctly operating mainframe systems, networks, tape drives, disk devices, printers, and so on. LAN administrators set up and manage the network hardware, software, and security processes. Trained personnel are also increasingly needed to set up and manage a company's Internet site, including Internet strategists, Internet systems developers, Internet programmers, and Web site operators. Information systems personnel may also work in other functional departments or areas in a support capacity. In addition to technical skills, information systems personnel also need skills in written and verbal communication, an understanding of organizations and the way they operate, and the ability to work with people (users). In general, information systems personnel are charged with maintaining the broadest enterprisewide perspective.

In addition to working for an information systems department in an organization, information systems personnel can work for one of the large information systems consulting firms, such as Accenture, EDS, and others. Another IS career opportunity is to be employed by a hardware or software vendor developing or selling products.

CHAPTER 1 SELF-ASSESSMENT TEST

The value of information is directly linked to how it helps decision makers achieve the organization's goals.

1. A (An) ________________ is a set of interrelated components that collect, manipulate, and disseminate data and information and provide a feedback mechanism to meet an objective.
2. The value of data is measured by the increase in revenues. True False

Knowing the potential impact of information systems and having the ability to put this knowledge to work can result in a successful personal career, organizations that reach their goals, and a society with a higher quality of life.

3. A (An) ________________ consists of hardware, software, databases, telecommunications, people, and procedures.
4. Computer programs that govern the operation of a computer system are called
   A. feedback
   B. feedforward
   C. software
   D. transaction processing systems

5. Payroll and order processing are examples of a computerized management information system.
True False

System users, business managers, and information systems professionals must work together to build a successful information system.

6. What involves creating or acquiring the various system components (hardware, software, databases, etc.) defined in the design step, assembling them, and putting the new system into operation?
   A. systems implementation
   B. systems review
   C. systems development
   D. systems design

7. ______________ involves creating or acquiring the various system components, such as hardware, software, databases, and other components.

The use of information systems to add value to the organization can also give an organization a competitive advantage.

8. A (An) ______________ is a formal collection of people and other resources established to accomplish a set of goals.

9. Today, quality means
   A. achieving production standards
   B. meeting or exceeding customer expectations
   C. maximizing total profits
   D. meeting or achieving design specifications

10. Technology diffusion is a measure of how widely technology is spread throughout an organization.
True False

Information systems personnel are the key to unlocking the potential of any new or modified system.

11. Who is involved in helping users determine what outputs they need and constructing the plans needed to produce these outputs?
   A. the CIO
   B. the applications programmer
   C. the systems programmer
   D. the systems analyst

12. The systems development component of a typical IS department focuses on specific development projects and ongoing maintenance and review.
True False

13. The ______________ is typically in charge of the information systems department or area in a company.

Chapter 1 Self-Assessment Test Answers

1. information system, 2. False, 3. computer-based information system (CBIS), 4. C, 5. False, 6. A., 7. Systems implementation, 8. organization, 9. B, 10. True, 11. D, 12. True, 13. chief information officer (CIO)

REVIEW QUESTIONS

1. What are the components of any information system?
2. How would you distinguish data and information? Information and knowledge?
3. Identify at least six characteristics of valuable information.
4. What is a computer-based information system? What are its components?
5. What are the most common types of computer-based information systems used in business organizations today? Give an example of each.
6. Identify three functions of a transaction processing system.
7. What are some of the benefits organizations seek to achieve through using information systems?
8. What is a value-added process? Give several examples.
9. What is the technology acceptance model (TAM)?
10. What are some general strategies employed by organizations to achieve competitive advantage?
11. What are the five common justifications for implementation of an information system?
12. Define the term *productivity*. Why is it difficult to measure the impact that investments in information systems have on productivity?
13. What is the total cost of ownership?
14. What is the operations component of a typical IS department?
15. What is the role of the systems analyst?

DISCUSSION QUESTIONS

1. Describe the "ideal" automated auto license plate renewal system for the drivers in your state. Describe the input, processing, output, and feedback associated with this system.
2. How is it that useful information can vary widely from the quality attributes of valuable information?
3. What is the difference between MIS and DSS?
4. Discuss the potential use of virtual reality to enhance the learning experience for new automobile drivers. How might such a system operate? What are the benefits and potential drawbacks of such a system?
5. Discuss how information systems are linked to the business objectives of an organization.
6. You have been hired to work in the IS area of a manufacturing company that is starting to use the Internet to order parts from its suppliers and offer sales and support to its customers. What types of Internet positions would you expect to see at the company?
7. You have been asked to participate in the preparation of your company's strategic plan. Specifically, your task is to analyze the competitive marketplace using Porter's five-force model. Prepare your analysis, using your knowledge of a business you have worked for or have an interest in working for.
8. Based on the analysis you performed in the preceding discussion question, what possible strategies could your organization adopt to address these challenges? What role could information systems play in these strategies? Use Porter's strategies as a guide.
9. Imagine that you are the CIO for a large, multinational company. Outline a few of your key responsibilities.
10. What sort of information systems position would be most appealing to you—working as a member of an IS organization, being a consultant, or working for an information systems hardware or software vendor? Why?
11. What are your career goals, and how can a computer-based information system be used to achieve them?

PROBLEM-SOLVING EXERCISES

1. Prepare a data disk and a backup disk for the problem-solving exercises and other computer-based assignments you will complete in this class. Create one directory for each chapter in the textbook (you should have nine directories). As you work through the problem-solving exercises and complete other work using the computer, save your assignments for each chapter in the appropriate directory. On the label of each disk be sure to include your name, course, and section. On one disk write "working copy"; on the other write "backup."
2. Search through several business magazines (*Business Week, Computerworld, PC Week,* etc.) for a recent article that discusses the use of information technology to deliver significant business benefits to an organization. Now use other resources to find additional information about the same organization (*Reader's Guide to Periodical Literature,* on-line search capabilities available at your school's library, the company's public relations department, Web pages on the Internet, etc.). Use word processing software to prepare a one-page summary of the different resources you tried and their ease of use and effectiveness.
3. Create a table that lists all the courses you are taking in the first column. The other columns of the table should be the weeks of the semester or quarter, such as Week 1, Week 2, etc. The body of the table should contain the actual assignments, quizzes, exams, the final exam, etc., for each course. Place the table into a database and print the results. Create a table in the database for the first three weeks of class and print the results. Create another table in the database for your two hardest classes for all weeks and print the results.

TEAM ACTIVITIES

1. Before you can do a team activity, you need a team! The class members may self-select their teams, or the instructor may assign members to groups. Once your group has been formed, meet and introduce yourselves to each other. You will need to find out the first name, hometown, major, and e-mail address and phone number of each member. Find out one interesting fact about each member of your team, as well. Come up with a name for your team. Put the information on each team member into a database and print enough copies for each team member and your instructor.
2. Have your team interview a company that recently introduced new technology. Write a brief report that describes the extent of technology infusion and diffusion.
3. Have your team interview a company, university, or governmental agency that is quality conscious. Write a brief report that describes the quality efforts taken and the impact of these quality initiatives on the success the organization has had in achieving its goals.

WEB EXERCISES

1. Throughout this book, you will see how the Internet provides a vast amount of information to individuals and organizations. We will stress the World Wide Web, or simply the Web, which is an important part of the Internet. Most large universities and organizations have an address on the Internet, called a Web site or home page. The address of the Web site for the publisher of this text is http://www.course.com. You can gain access to the Internet through a browser, such as Internet Explorer or Netscape. Using an Internet browser, go to the Web site for this publisher. What did you find? Try to obtain information on this book. You may be asked to develop a report or send an e-mail message to your instructor about what you found.
2. Go to an Internet search engine, such as http://www.yahoo.com, and search for information about a company, including its Web site. Write a report that summarizes the size of the company, the number of its employees, its products, the location of its headquarters, and its profits (or losses) for last year. Would you want to work for this company?

CASES

CASE 1

Expert Systems Simplify Life for Automotive Manufacturers

Infomedia is a successful Australian software developer that specializes in designing information systems for the automotive industry. The company's primary product, Microcat, has developed the reputation of being the best electronic parts catalog (EPC) for the global automotive industry. It is shipped to more than 32,000 subscribers in over 100 countries and 22 languages. Infomedia produces versions of its electronic parts catalog products for the majority of leading car manufacturers in Australia, including Daewoo, Daihatsu, Ford, General Motors Holden, Honda, Hyundai, Isuzu, Mitsubishi, Suzuki, and Toyota. International versions have been produced for Daihatsu, Ford, Hyundai, and Land Rover.

Microcat is popular in part because it adds "intelligence" and communications capabilities to the cataloging methods, transforming them from simple table/code reference tools to interactive technical selling systems. By programming expert knowledge into the system, users can quickly and accurately identify repair jobs and identify and request related parts and fluids for the required repairs. Infomedia works with the manufacturer to custom design a Microcat system for cataloging automotive parts. For example, in the case of a European automaker, details on more than 500,000 parts and 19.5 million vehicles are stored and processed within Microcat. An examination of Infomedia's development process provides examples of many of the concepts discussed in this chapter.

Step 1—Preparation: Manufacturers who choose to implement the Microcat electronic parts sales and cataloging system for their replacement parts operations begin with a thorough analysis of their situation and requirements with a Microcat data engineer. This engineer is assigned to work with the manufacturer's implementation team. This team generally includes a representative from cataloging, replacement parts marketing, and information services. During this early stage business rules, logic algorithms, interpretation rules, and data parsing gathered from the human experts are programmed into the system and tested on a reasonably sized data sample. After much tweaking, when the system provides intelligent and accurate responses to parts inquiries, it is time to load in the parts data.

Step 2—Source Material: To create the initial electronic catalog, the team gathers data from a number of original sources, including electronic data and images, microfiche images, paper drawings, and photographs. The Microcat production team devises a "harmonizing" approach to represent all of the manufacturer's data in a consistent and intuitive fashion.

Step 3—Preprocessing: With the expert system and parts-related data in hand, Infomedia's production processing team goes to work preparing the first Microcat master catalog implementation of the manufacturer's product lines. At this stage, Infomedia's preprocessing systems integrate the two—expert system and parts data—into one uniform digital continuum. Secondary preprocessing then optimizes all the data for speed and encrypts it for security. This step can take anywhere from a few weeks to several months.

Step 4—Preproduction: Before a broad release to parts centers, a "beta," or trial, version of the new Microcat system is prepared. Infomedia trainers work with the manufacturer and selected parts center staff to test and fine-tune the beta system. User recommendations and observations are given to the Microcat data engineers to consider and incorporate, where appropriate.

Step 5—Communications: Microcat engineers work to integrate the Microcat system with existing systems in the corporation. From Microcat, employees can access customer information, pricing and stock availability, and other business-related data. This approach eliminates much time-consuming duplication of effort.

Step 6—Periodic Update Process: Once the product is completed, it is delivered to each of the manufacturer's facilities on CD/DVD-ROM. The software is updated to reflect changes in prices, inventory, parts specifications, and other fluctuating variables at agreed-upon time intervals. For example, a manufacturer may receive an updated CD every month. The on-line and network versions of Microcat can update information in real time.

Microcat's development process is typical of the systems development process used in most information systems. The goals of the Microcat system are also typical of most information systems:

1. Improve access to the data to improve customer service
2. Use Microcat's interpretation capabilities to rely less on an individual's component knowledge
3. Reduce chances of inaccurate or out-of-date data
4. Increase sales of genuine parts by freeing up more time for sales staff to sell
5. Reduce credit returns caused by inaccuracy of spare parts selection
6. Interface with other computer systems
7. Provide the opportunity to add specific or local knowledge to the data
8. Simplify distribution of all the manufacturer's parts information
9. Take advantage of technological advancements as they can be introduced

Even if automotive parts are not your cup of tea, there is a lot to be learned about information systems from this very successful Australian company.

Discussion Questions

1. What advantages does an automotive manufacturer who uses Microcat have over a manufacturer who has developed and maintains its own electronic parts catalog?
2. What types of products might Microcat be enhanced to handle? If you owned Microcat, what industry would you pursue next?

Critical Thinking Questions

3. Microcat is an expert system because it includes the knowledge, logic, algorithms, and interpretation rules of human experts. How will the implementation of this tool affect the jobs of those human experts who helped design it?
4. How does Microcat allow automotive manufacturers to be more effective and efficient?

Sources: "Smart Cars Put Infomedia in Fast Lane," *australianIT.com*, January 4, 2002; "Infomedia and Toyota Motor Europe Sign Five-Year Data License Agreement," *Business Wire*, January 3, 2002; "Infomedia Releases the Next Generation in Automotive Dealership Management Systems," *Business Wire*, October 18, 2001; http://www.infomedia.com.au.

CASE 2

Delta and Tellabs Seek Higher Return on Investment

In these days of performance-based information systems, managers have to work hard to get their information system requests approved. Requests to develop a new information system or improve on existing systems are closely scrutinized by senior managers to assure that the investment is effectively supporting corporate goals and will bring in a quick return.

Delta Technology, the IT arm of $16 billion Atlanta-based Delta Air Lines, presents a good example of this trend. "We have been carefully reviewing every project and every spend [expense] with approvals at the senior vice president level. Before, we delegated decisions to a lower level," says Curtis Robb, senior vice president and chief technology officer. "Finance is also much more actively involved in business cases that are developed [for IT projects]." In other words, Delta and many other companies have found it necessary to implement return on investment (ROI) standards and procedures for measuring return on information system investment.

Curtis Robb says there are critical issues that businesses must address to ensure ROI. The first is total cost of ownership. Each of Delta's business teams must develop plans that look ahead four years, he says. They look at not only the purchase price but also the "tail behind that purchase price"—hardware, software, maintenance, and support, Robb says. The second issue is finding the right level of support for the system once it is in place. Rightsizing maintenance contracts has helped Delta shed $10 million in expenses. Standardizing technology has also helped the company save on training and development costs. Rather than building new systems from scratch, Delta designs generic systems to allow portions of systems to be reused on new projects as they arise. The final issue is time to market. At Delta, "solution architects" are assigned to projects from the start to help create a blueprint and determine a timeline.

Once an information system project is under way, it is important to provide oversight to ensure that the project brings in a return. Some companies create technology review boards to provide monthly reviews of IS proposals. Projects are reviewed each month to make sure scope, costs, and time frames are on target.

Implementing a system such as Delta's often meets with a considerable amount of cultural resistance. Tellabs, a Naperville, Illinois–based communications equipment maker, has faced obstacles in implementing its new procedures for measuring return on IT investment. When information system proposals were reviewed for approval, CIO Cathy Kozik found a number of inaccuracies and a general lack of honesty. Managers and staffers were finding it hard to be objective due to concerns over budget cuts and worries about automating themselves out of their jobs. To overcome the honesty and accuracy problems, Kozik asked financial controllers from each unit to oversee the calculations of each proposal.

Implementing ROI standards must be a gradual process, Kozik warns. If Tellabs had forced its ROI process on workers, "it would have collapsed under its own weight," she says. "Instead of going from 0 to 120, we're going from 0 to 30, 30 to 60."

The role of the CIO becomes all the more valuable to an organization when it is striving toward a high ROI. The CIO bridges the gap between top-level executives who may be technically naïve and lower-level staff who may be more interested in preserving their jobs than saving the company money. Only the CIO can assure that the organization is getting the highest possible return on its information system investments to gain an advantage over the competition.

Discussion Questions

1. How might a CIO motivate the information system staff to assist in assessing return on investment and to overcome fears of job loss?
2. How does the trend of involving upper management in information system management decisions affect the balance of power within the organization? Does this undermine previous efforts to empower lower-level employees? Is it possible to have both a high ROI and empowered employees?

Critical Thinking Questions

3. How will the quest for leaner, meaner information systems affect innovation in the industry? Which IS employees are in danger of losing their jobs?
4. As Delta and its competitors strive for higher return on investment, what types of initiatives will give these companies a competitive advantage?

Sources: Melissa Solomon, "ROI: It's about People, Not Numbers," *Computerworld*, January 14, 2002, http://www.computerworld.com; Julia King, "ROI: Make It Bigger, Better, Faster," *Computerworld*, January 1, 2002, http://www.computerworld.com.

CASE 3

Pressplay: Defining the Internet Music Industry

The digitized world in which we now exist has brought with it wonderful conveniences, along with legal and ethical challenges. The digitization of data, information, and other media makes it possible to electronically store, access, and transfer a wide variety of material. This innovation has posed serious legal concern over copyright infringement and ethical dilemmas for users who find it possible to share copyrighted materials such as books, music, and video conveniently over the Internet. Sharing the intellectual and creative property of others deprives the copyright owners of the financial rewards they are due. Should this trend continue unchecked, some of the greatest creative minds in our society would no longer be able to make a living. In the year 2000, this problem exploded when the MP3 music file format was introduced, making it very easy to share music files over the Internet.

With every problem comes an opportunity. Here the challenge was to design a system that provides Internet users with a method for accessing music, while respecting copyrights, at an acceptable cost to compensate the record companies and musicians. The first company that could bring such a product to market would establish a solid competitive advantage in what could be a highly profitable industry.

The first companies to step up to the plate were Pressplay and Musicnet. Releasing their products within a week of each other, these two companies partnered with popular music Web sites to offer a platform for music subscription services. Pressplay offered a more robust set of services through popular sites such as Microsoft Network, Yahoo!, and MP3.com. Pressplay gained even greater popularity when it partnered with MediaUnbound to offer its subscribers a personalized service.

Pressplay is a global joint venture created by French media and communications group Vivendi Universal and Sony of Japan. Pressplay offers consumers on-demand access to a wide variety of music that can be streamed, downloaded, or burned onto a CD while respecting and protecting artists' rights. Pressplay offers music from the world's three largest record companies—Sony, Universal, and EMI—as well as many independent labels. It offers memberships at different levels ranging in price from $9.95 per month to $24.95. The more expensive memberships allow greater access to music and more freedom for burning CDs.

Why might Internet users choose Pressplay over free file swapping? By its partnership with MediaUnbound, Pressplay tracks its subscribers' musical interests and makes intelligent suggestions for future listening. This service assists subscribers in discovering new music. Also, Pressplay hopes that users' consciences will drive them to subscribe so that they can access music legally. As the music industry creates a new electronic distribution system, through the efforts of pioneers like Pressplay, we can be assured that copyrighted material is safeguarded. Since Pressplay was responsible for creating this technology, they are sure to be a major player in the industry as it develops.

Discussion Questions

1. In what ways can Pressplay entice users to its services over free file swapping?
2. Now that Pressplay has gained a competitive advantage with its music distribution solution, how can it maintain its competitive advantage as new companies enter the market?

Critical Thinking Questions

3. Besides the music industry, what other industries are affected by digitization, the Internet, and copyright law issues? Would a solution similar to Pressplay's be effective in those industries also?
4. Being first to market with technological solutions gives a company a huge competitive advantage. What are some current problems that technology could help solve?

Sources: "BMI Announces Licensing Agreement with Pressplay," *Business Wire*, January 28, 2002; Pete Barlas, "Pressplay to Personalize Song Listings for Its Users," *Investor's Daily*, January 28, 2002; Dave Gussow, "Net Music Takes a Big Step Forward," *St. Petersburg Times*, January 28, 2002, http://www.sptimes.com; Pressplay Web site, http://www.pressplay.com; Musicnet Web site, http://www.musicnet.com.

NOTES

Sources for the Opening Vignette on p. 3: "Taking the Drugstore to the Customers: A New Automated Pharmacy: Merck-Medco's Opened N.J. Facility to Dispense Mail-Order Prescriptions," *Investor's Business Daily*, January 14, 2002; "'Pharmacy for the Future' Officially Opens in Willingboro, N.J.," *The Philadelphia Inquirer*, November 13, 2001; "Merck-Medco Discovers Prescription for Success while Others Struggle," *The Associated Press State & Local Wire*, November 28, 2001; Merck-Medco Web site, http://www.merck-medco.com.

1. Jennifer Disabantino, "GM's OnStar Puts Stock in Service," *Computerworld*, February 26, 2001, p. 48.
2. Mathew Schwartz, "The Care and Keeping of Customers," *Computerworld*, January 8, 2001, p. 58.
3. Linda Rosencrance, "Data Warehouse Gives Trimac Information for the Long Haul," *Computerworld*, July 2, 2001, p. 47.
4. Charles Haddad, "How UPS Delivered through the Disaster," *Business Week*, October 1, 2001, p. 66.
5. Slava Sery, et al., "Optimization Models for Restructuring BASF," *Interfaces*, May–June, 2001 p. 55.
6. Allison Wright, "Custom Cars for Every Driver," *Computerworld*, March 12, 2001, p. 60.
7. J. Vijayan, "Procurement Network Harnesses Buying Power," *Computerworld*, June 4, 2001, p. 33.
8. Lee Gladwin, "Users Extend Use of Web Portals to Supply Chain for Materials Procurement," *Computerworld*, June 11, 2001, p. 7.
9. Theo Francis, "T. Rowe Price Rolls Out Voice Response," *The Wall Street Journal*, May 30, 2001, p. C21.
10. Stacy Collett, "Retailers, Travel Companies Deploy Thousands of Kiosks," *Computerworld*, August 6, 2001, p. 18.
11. Jay Greene, "Microsoft: How It Became Stronger Than Ever," *Business Week*, June 4, 2001, p. 75.
12. Dan Verton, "Oracle Launches Technology Offensive," *Computerworld*, June 25, 2001, p. 8.
13. Sami Lais, "Satelittes Link Bob Evans Farms," *Computerworld*, July 2, 2001, p. 51.
14. Dennis Berman, "Disaster Gives New Life to Wireless Telecom Firms," *The Wall Street Journal*, October 3, 2001, p. B1.
15. Bob Brewin, "Airlines Take Internet to the Skies," *Computerworld*, June 18, 2001, p. 10.
16. Neil Randall, "Instant Intranet," *PC Magazine*, August 2001, p. 76.
17. Michael Meehan, "Exects: Building Consensus is Biggest B2B Challenge," *Computerworld*, June 18, 2001, p. 14.
18. Laura Stevens, "Job Hunting," *Forbes*, June 25, 2001, p. 76.
19. Lucas Mearian, "Bucking the Trend, Bank to Hire 600 IT Workers," *Computerworld*, December 3, 2001, p. 61.
20. "Amazon.com Looks for Sales Boost in Circuit City," *Information Week Online*, August 21, 2001.
21. Marc Songini, "PeopleSoft Kicks Off Web-Based CRM Suite," *Computerworld*, June 4, 2001, p. 14.
22. Laura Landro, "New Medical Software Gives Physians Clues When They're Stumped," *The Wall Street Journal*, June 29, 2001, p. B1.
23. Russell Kay, "Supply Chain Management," *Computerworld*, December 17, 2001, p. 32.

24. Clayton Christensen, "Understanding Your Value Chain," *The Australian Financial Review*, January 11, 2002.
25. Christoph Loch and Berndao Huberman, "A Punctuated-Equilibrium Model of Technology Diffusion," *Management Science*, February 1999, p. 160.
26. Curtis Armstrong and V. Sambamurthy, "Information Technology Assimilation in Firms," *Information Systems Research*, December 1999, p. 304.
27. Ritu Agarwal and Jayesh Prasad, "Are Individual Differences Germane to the Acceptance of New Information Technology," *Decision Sciences*, spring 1999, p. 361.
28. V. Venkatesh, "Determinants of Perceived Ease of Use: Integrating Control, Intrinsic Motivation, and Emotion into the Technology Acceptance Model," *Information Systems Research*, December 2000, p. 342.
29. Kwon, et al., "A Test of the Technology Acceptance Model," Proceedings of the Hawaii International Conference on System Sciences, January 4–7, 2000.
30. Je-Won Moon, et al., "Extending the TAM for a World Wide Web Context," *Information and Management*, February 2001, p. 217.
31. M. Porter and V. Millar, "How Information Systems Give You Competitive Advantage," *Journal of Business Strategy*, winter 1985. See also M. Porter, *Competitive Advantage* (New York: Free Press, 1985).
32. Eric Chabrow, et al., "Facing an IT Future," *Information Week Online*, June 18, 2001.
33. Edie Schmidt, et al., "Using Cyclic Planning to Manage Capacity at Aloca," *Interfaces*, June 2001, p. 14.
34. Matt Hamblen, "Handhelds Help Boeing Boost Quality Inspections," *Computerworld*, November 8, 1999, p. 38.
35. Steve Hamm, "Sizing Up Your Payoff," *Business Week*, October 29, 2001, p. EB24.
36. Michael Meehan, "First Data Overhauling Backbone for E-Payments," *Computerworld*, July 9, 2001, p. 18.
37. "Mirapoint's Total Cost of Ownership Significantly Lower," *PR Newswire*, December 18, 2001.
38. Laura Stevens, "Job Hunting," *Forbes*, June 25, 2001, p. 76.
39. Leslie Goff, "The Best Places to Work," *Computerworld*, June 25, 2001, p. 38.
40. Patrick Thibodeau, "Feds Cast Bait to Lure IT Workers from Private Sector," *Computerworld*, August 2001, p. 7.
41. Guy Chazan, "Now Available from Russia," *The Wall Street Journal*, August 6, 2001, p. B1.
42. Andrew Wilson, "H-1Bs Are Still Needed, Despite Slower Economy," *Computerworld*, June 4, 2001, p. 25.
43. Kathleen Melymuka, "Global Woman," *Computerworld*, August 6, 2001, p. 34.
44. Terry Byrd and Douglas Turner, "An Exploratory Analysis of the Value of Skills of IT Personnel," *Decision Sciences*, winter 2001, p. 21.
45. Patrick Thibodeau, "CIOs at Global Firms Face Cultural and Logistical Challenges," *Computerworld*, January 15, 2001, p. 40.
46. Linda Rosencrance, "Broker Revamps IT to Support New Strategy," *Computerworld*, July 2, 2001, p. 6.
47. "The Career Column," *The Dallas Morning News*, October 7, 2001.
48. Andy Serwer, "15 Minutes of Obscene Wealth," *Fortune*, June 11, 2001, p. 110.
49. Carol Sliwa, "Microsoft Tweaks Windows Certification," *Computerworld*, January 1, 2001, p. 10.
50. Mathias Thurman, "Security Certification: It's Worth the Effort," *Computerworld*, November 5, 2001, p. 56.
51. Julekha Dash, "GI Bill to Cover Cost of IT Certification Examinations," *Computerworld*, June 25, 2001, p. 12.

Hardware and Software

15

PRINCIPLES

Information system users must work closely with information system professionals to define business needs, evaluate options, and select the hardware and software that provide a cost-effective solution to those needs.

LEARNING OBJECTIVES

- Identify and discuss the role of the essential hardware components of a computer system.
- List and describe popular classes of computer systems and discuss the role of each.
- Outline the role of the operating system and discuss how operating systems have evolved over time.
- Identify and briefly describe the functions of the two basic kinds of software.

Organizations do not develop proprietary application software unless doing so will meet a compelling business need that can provide a competitive advantage.

- Discuss how application software can support personal, workgroup, and enterprise business objectives.
- Identify three basic approaches to developing application software.

End users and IS professionals use a programming language whose functional characteristics are appropriate to the task at hand.

- Outline the overall evolution of programming languages and highlight the differences between programming languages used by end users and IS professionals.

The information system industry continues to undergo constant change; users need to be aware of recent trends and issues in software licensing to be effective in their business and personal life.

- Identify several key issues and trends in licensing that have an impact on organizations and individuals.

[Flextronics]

Global Deployment of Software Improves Key Business Process

Flextronics is a multinational manufacturer that designs products, manufactures them, and delivers them to its client companies in 28 countries on four continents. Flextronics has headquarters in both San Jose, California, and Singapore and has established a network of facilities in key markets to provide top service to its customers while efficiently controlling its operations. As a contract manufacturer, Flextronics specializes in building other companies' high-tech hardware—everything from Microsoft's new Xbox video-game system to Ericsson's cell phones. Flextronics does 29 percent of its business in large computer servers and peripheral equipment but also gets more than half its revenue from communications equipment. Key customers include such well-known information system hardware providers as Cisco Systems, Ericsson, Hewlett-Packard, Microsoft, Nokia, and Philips. Its major competitors are Solectron, SCI Systems, and Celestica. Recent annual revenue exceeded $12 billion, and its employees number more than 70,000.

Operating as a contract manufacturer requires lots of quoting and bidding on the various components for each job. The number and complexity of quotes require Flextronics to use personal computers and software to manage them. To streamline the complex bidding process, Flextronics began using an on-line software package called QuoteWin to generate its quotes electronically. As the company became more familiar with the software program, Flextronics management was so impressed with the results that they decided to implement the system globally. In addition to simplifying and streamlining the quoting and bidding process, they hoped to develop a consistent work process and establish standard hardware and software across all divisions of the company.

The use of personal computers and the QuoteWin software system helps simplify and reduce the time required to create quotes by passing information back and forth over networks to Flextronics's suppliers and to clients once a bid has been compiled. In fact, it takes only minutes to gather contract pricing data. As a result, Flextronics was able to cut the average time to prepare a quote from three weeks to two. The QuoteWin system also maintains an accurate database of all quotes associated with each job on a mainframe computer. The availability of historical data, coupled with good reporting tools in the software, enables business managers to do a thorough "what-if" analysis of each quote. (E.g., managers can ask, "If this part is eliminated, how much money can we save the customer?")

Flextronics hopes to convert all its suppliers to the new system; however, many smaller suppliers are concerned with the cost. Also, some suppliers have been less than enthusiastic about adopting the QuoteWin software because they work with other manufacturers who use a variety of quote preparation systems. The suppliers would naturally prefer to see some standardization in the software to help streamline the process for everyone.

Flextronics currently has six global "quote hubs," which manage its bidding and quoting activities. It evaluated the use of QuoteWin in each region and now has over 60 users on the system. The global rollout of the software package was scheduled hub by hub based on the number of quotes generated. Europe was the first region to get up and running because that hub generated the most quotes.

In the future, Flextronics plans to enhance the bid and quote process even further with the implementation of a custom-built software package called FlexDesign. This system will compile company rules and guidelines about product design and components. Engineers involved in the bid and quote process can use this information to choose components based on proven business practices and technical expertise, including such factors as whether the component is from an approved supplier or whether it's been tested elsewhere in the company.

As you read this chapter, consider the following:

- What are the various kinds of hardware and software and how are they used?
- Where can software be obtained, and what are the pros and cons of each approach?

Appropriate use of information systems can reap huge benefits in business, as when Flextronics accelerated and improved its bidding and quoting process. Employing information systems and providing additional processing capabilities can increase employee productivity, expand business opportunities, and allow for more flexibility. Information system users must work closely with information system professionals to define business needs, evaluate options, and select the hardware and software that provide a cost-effective solution to those needs. To meet this responsibility in your career, you must understand the basic concepts of hardware and software presented in this chapter.

OVERVIEW OF HARDWARE

In building a car, manufacturers try to match the intended use of the vehicle to its components. Racing cars require special types of engines, transmissions, and tires. The selection of a transmission for a racing car, then, requires consideration not only of how much of the engine's power can be delivered to the wheels (efficiency and effectiveness) but also of how expensive the transmission is (cost), how reliable it is (control), and how many gears it has (complexity). Similarly, organizations assemble the hardware components of a computer system so that they are effective, efficient, and well suited to the tasks that need to be performed. Users and IS professionals often need to make these decisions together, combining their knowledge of systems and business functions as well as forecasting their future needs.

Because business needs and their importance vary at different companies, the information system solutions chosen can be quite different.

- Mike Meinz, director of IT at General Mills, was facing a merger with Pillsbury and wanted to simplify the combined companies' computing infrastructure. He believed that the best way to do this was to minimize the number of hardware and software vendors, so he chose Hewlett-Packard as a key vendor and purchased three of its newest, most powerful computers.
- Homestore.com is a home improvement and real estate company that has seen a rapid increase in the number of visitors to its Web site. Scott Sullivan, vice president for technology and operations, needed flexible technology that could be expanded quickly, easily, and inexpensively when business demanded. As a result, he elected to go with Dell computers because of Dell's ability to tailor computer systems to client needs.
- United Airlines needed powerful computers to plan flights based on passenger loads and to access large databases of passenger information. It chose IBM to provide the hardware to meet this need because of its experience in large-capacity computer systems.
- Bell South's Vice President of Enterprise Data and Infrastructure Rich Liddell needed outstanding service and support. He elected to go with Sun Microsystems because it had helped work out problems with software vendors in the past and also installed additional computing capacity over a weekend.[1]

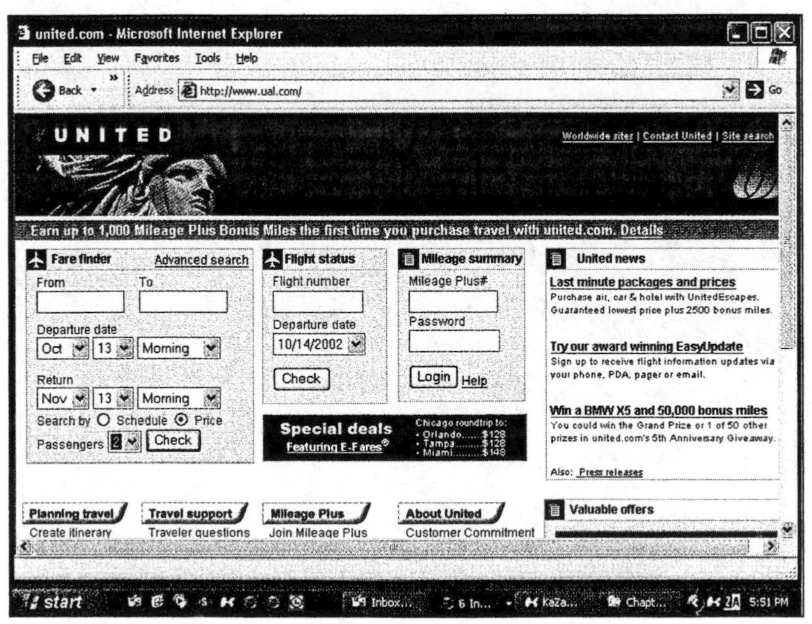

United Airlines needed a powerful computer system to manage the large volume of flight and passenger data.

As each of these examples demonstrates, assembling a computer subsystem requires an understanding of its relationship to the information system and the needs of the organization. Although we generally refer to the computer subsystem as simply a computer system, we must remember that the computer system objectives are subordinate to, but supportive of, the information system and the needs of the organization.

central processing unit (CPU)
the part of the computer that consists of two primary elements: the arithmetic/logic unit and the control unit

arithmetic/logic unit (ALU)
portion of the CPU that performs mathematical calculations and makes logical comparisons

control unit
part of the CPU that sequentially accesses program instructions, decodes them, and coordinates the flow of data in and out of the ALU, primary storage, and even secondary storage and various output devices

HARDWARE COMPONENTS

Computer system hardware components include devices that perform the functions of input, processing, data storage, and output (Figure 2.1). To understand how these hardware devices work together, consider an analogy from a paper-based office environment. Imagine a one-room office occupied by a single individual. The human (the central processing unit) organizes and manipulates data. The person's mind (primary storage) and the desk occupied by the human (secondary storage) are places to temporarily store data. Filing cabinets provide additional data storage (secondary storage). In this analogy, the incoming and outgoing mail trays can be understood as sources of new data (input) or as a place to put the processed paperwork (output).

The ability to process (organize and manipulate) data is a critical aspect of a computer system, in which processing is accomplished by an interplay between one or more of the central processing units and primary storage. Each **central processing unit (CPU)** consists of two primary elements: the arithmetic/logic unit and the control unit. The **arithmetic/logic unit (ALU)** performs mathematical calculations and makes logical comparisons. The **control unit** sequentially accesses program instructions, decodes them, and coordinates the flow of data in and out of the ALU, primary storage, and even secondary storage and various output devices.

Primary memory, which holds program instructions and data, is closely associated with the CPU. To understand the function of processing and the interplay between the CPU and memory, let's examine the way a typical computer executes a program instruction.

FIGURE 2.1

Computer System Components

These components include input devices, output devices, communications devices, primary and secondary storage devices, and the central processing unit (CPU). The control unit, the arithmetic/logic unit (ALU), and register storage area constitute the CPU.

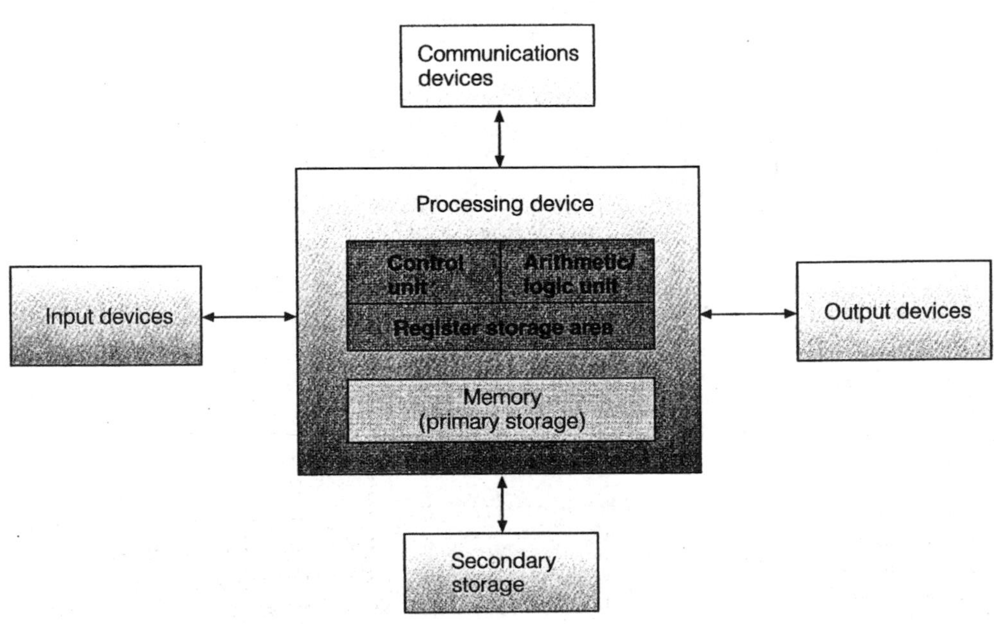

HARDWARE COMPONENTS IN ACTION

The execution of any machine-level instruction involves two phases: the instruction phase and the execution phase. During the instruction phase, the following takes place:

- *Step 1: Fetch instruction.* The instruction to be executed is accessed from memory by the control unit.
- *Step 2: Decode instruction.* The instruction is decoded so the central processor can understand what is to be done, relevant data is moved from memory, and the location of the next instruction is identified

instruction time (I-time)
the time it takes to perform the fetch-instruction and decode-instruction steps of the instruction phase

Steps 1 and 2 are called the instruction phase, and the time it takes to perform this phase is called the **instruction time (I-time)**.

The second phase is the execution phase. During the execution phase, the following steps are performed:

- *Step 3: Execute the instruction.* The ALU does what it is instructed to do. This could involve making either an arithmetic computation or a logical comparison.
- *Step 4: Store results.* The results are stored in memory.

execution time (E-time)
the time it takes to execute an instruction and store the results

machine cycle
the instruction phase followed by the execution phase

Steps 3 and 4 are called the execution phase. The time it takes to complete the execution phase is called the **execution time (E-time)**.

After both phases have been completed for one instruction, they are again performed for the second instruction, and so on. The instruction phase followed by the execution phase is called a **machine cycle** (Figure 2.2). Some central processing units can speed up processing by using *pipelining*, where the CPU gets one instruction, decodes another, and executes a third at the same time. The Pentium processor, for example, uses two execution unit pipelines, which gives the processing unit the ability to execute two instructions in a single machine cycle.

Now that you have learned about the basic hardware components and the way they function, we turn to an examination of processing power, speed, and capacity. These three attributes determine the capabilities of a hardware device.

PROCESSING AND MEMORY DEVICES: POWER, SPEED, AND CAPACITY

The components responsible for processing—the CPU and memory—are housed together in the same box or cabinet, called the *system unit.* All other computer system devices, such as the monitor and keyboard, are linked either directly or indirectly into the system unit housing. As discussed previously, achieving information system objectives and organizational goals should be the primary consideration in selecting processing and memory devices. In this section, we investigate the characteristics of these important devices.

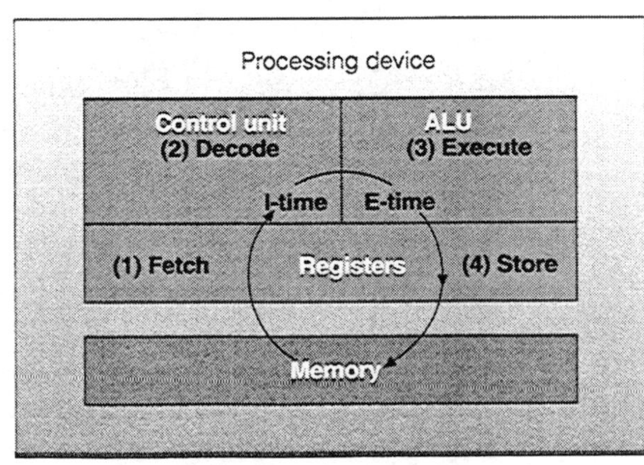

FIGURE 2.2

Execution of an Instruction

In the instruction phase, the computer's control unit fetches the instruction to be executed from memory (1). Then the instruction is decoded so the central processor can understand what is to be done (2). In the execution phase, the ALU does what it is instructed to do, making either an arithmetic computation or a logical comparison (3). Then the results are stored in memory (4). The instruction and execution phases together make up one machine cycle.

PROCESSING CHARACTERISTICS AND FUNCTIONS

Because efficient processing and timely output are important, organizations use a variety of measures to gauge processing speed. These measures include the time it takes to complete a machine cycle, clock speed, and others.

Machine Cycle Time

The time it takes to execute the instruction phase and the execution phase is the machine cycle time. Machine cycle time is one measure of processing speed.

Clock Speed

clock speed
a series of electronic pulses, produced at a predetermined rate, that affect machine cycle time

Each CPU produces a series of electronic pulses at a predetermined rate, called the **clock speed,** which affects machine cycle time. The control unit executes an instruction in accordance with the electronic cycle, or pulses of the CPU "clock." Each instruction takes at least the same amount of time as the interval between pulses. The shorter the interval between pulses, the faster each instruction can be executed. Clock speed is often measured in megahertz (MHz), or millions of cycles per second. The clock speed for personal computers is in the multiple GHz range.[2]

Wordlength

wordlength
the number of bits the CPU can process at one time

Data is moved within a computer system in units called *bits.* A bit is a binary digit—0 or 1. Another factor affecting overall system performance is the number of bits the CPU can process at one time, or the **wordlength** of the CPU. Early computers were built with CPUs that had a wordlength of 4 bits, meaning that the CPU was capable of processing 4 bits at one time. The 4 bits could be used to represent actual data, an instruction to be processed, or the address of data to be accessed. The 4-bit limitation was quite confining and greatly constrained the power of the computer. Over time, CPUs have evolved to 8-, 16-, 32-, and 64-bit machines with dramatic increases in power and capability. Computers with larger wordlengths can transfer more data between devices in the same machine cycle. They can also use the larger number of bits to address more memory locations and hence are needed for systems with large memory requirements.

The Itanium processor is Intel's first microprocessor that is based on the 64-bit architecture called IA-64. It was codeveloped with Hewlett-Packard at a cost of over $1 billion. The 64-bit chip allows the CPU to directly address 16 quintrillion (billion billion) unique address locations compared with 4.3 billion for a 32-bit processor. The ability to directly access a larger address space is critical for multimedia, imaging, and database applications.

Physical Characteristics of the CPU

CPU speed is also limited by physical constraints. Most CPUs are collections of digital circuits imprinted on silicon wafers, or chips, each no bigger than the tip of a pencil eraser. To turn a digital circuit within the CPU on or off, electrical current must flow through a medium (usually silicon) from point A to point B.

The speed at which it travels between points can be increased by either reducing the distance between the points or reducing the resistance of the medium to the electrical current.

Moore's Law
a hypothesis that states that transistor densities on a single chip will double every 18 months

Reducing the distance between points has resulted in ever-smaller chips, with the circuits packed closer together. In the 1960s, shortly after patenting the integrated circuit, Gordon Moore, former chairman of the board of Intel (the largest microprocessor chip maker), formulated what is now known as **Moore's Law**. This hypothesis states that transistor (the microscopic on/off switches, or the microprocessor's brain cells) densities on a single chip will double every 18 months. Moore's Law has held up amazingly well over the years. In June 2001, Intel reported that the company had successfully made a handful of silicon transistors 80 atoms wide and three atoms thick, capable of switching on and off 1.5 trillion times a second. This breakthrough will make it possible to build a CPU with

1 billion transistors operating at 20 GHz by around 2007. Such a computer will have 12 times the number of transistors and be more than five times faster than the computers of 2003. Many researchers now forecast that it will be possible to continue doubling the number of transistors on a chip every 18 months until at least 2014.[3]

In addition to increased speeds, Moore's Law has had an impact on costs and overall system performance. As seen in Figure 2.3, the number of transistors on a chip continues to climb.

superconductivity
a property of certain metals that allows current to flow with minimal electrical resistance

Another substitute material for silicon chips is superconductive metal. **Superconductivity** is a property of certain metals that allows current to flow with minimal electrical resistance. Traditional silicon chips create some electrical resistance that slows processing. Chips built from less resistant, superconductive metals offer increases in processing speed.

Researchers are also experimenting with chips called *optical processors* that use light waves instead of electrical current to represent bits. The primary advantage of optical processors is their speed. Optical processors have the potential to be 500 times faster than traditional electronic circuits.

MEMORY CHARACTERISTICS AND FUNCTIONS

byte
eight bits together that represent a single character of data

Located physically close to the CPU (to decrease access time), memory provides the CPU with a working storage area for program instructions and data. The chief feature of memory is that it rapidly provides the data and instructions to the CPU.

Storage Capacity

Like the CPU, memory devices contain thousands of circuits imprinted on a silicon chip. Each circuit is either conducting electrical current (on) or not (off). By representing data as a combination of on or off circuit states, the data is stored in memory. Usually eight bits are used to represent a character, such as the letter *A*. Eight bits together form a **byte**. Table 2.1 summarizes commonly

FIGURE 2.3

Moore's Law

(Source: Data from "Moore's Law: Overview," Intel Web site, http:// www. Intel.com/research/silicon/mooreslaw. htm, accessed July 22, 2002.)

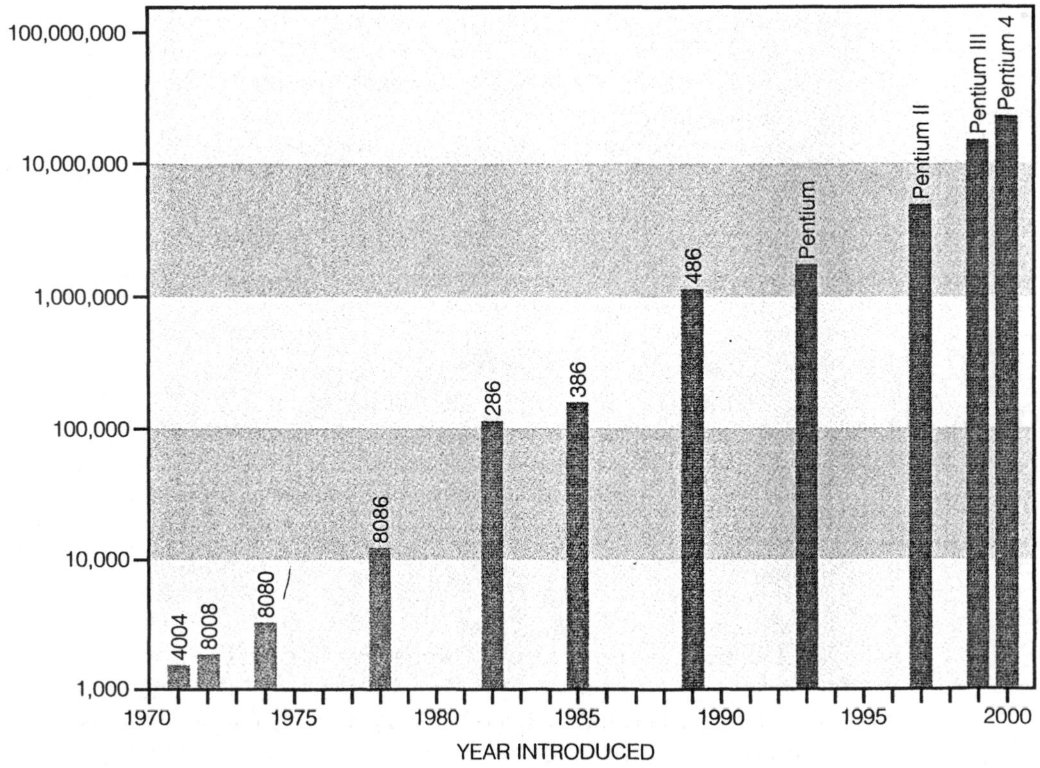

Name	Abbreviation	Exact Number of Bytes	Approximate Number of Bytes
Byte	B	1	1
Kilobyte	KB	1,024 bytes	1 thousand
Megabyte	MB	1,024 kilobytes	1 million
Gigabyte	GB	1,024 megabytes	1 billion
Terabyte	TB	1,024 gigabytes	1 trillion
Petabyte	PB	1,024 terabytes	1 quadrillion

TABLE 2.1

Number of Bytes

used measurements. Storage capacity is measured in bytes, abbreviated with the letter *B*, with one byte usually equal to one character.

Types of Memory

There are several forms of memory, as shown in Figure 2.4. Instructions or data can be temporarily stored in **random access memory (RAM)**. RAM is temporary and volatile—RAM chips lose their contents if the current is turned off or disrupted (as in a power surge, brownout, or electrical noise generated by lightning or nearby machines). RAM chips are mounted directly on the computer's main circuit board or in chips mounted on peripheral cards that plug into the computer's main circuit board. These RAM chips consist of millions of switches that are sensitive to changes in electric current.

random access memory (RAM)
a form of memory in which instructions or data can be temporarily stored

RAM comes in many different varieties. The mainstream type of RAM is *extended data out,* or *EDO RAM.* Another kind of RAM memory is called *SDRAM,* or *synchronous DRAM,* which has the advantage of a faster transfer speed between the microprocessor and the memory. *Dynamic RAM (DRAM)* chips need high or low voltages applied at regular intervals—every few milliseconds (two one-thousandths of a second)—or they will lose their information.

Another type of memory, **ROM**, an acronym for **read-only memory**, is usually nonvolatile. In ROM, the combination of circuit states is fixed, and therefore its contents are not lost if the power is removed. ROM provides permanent storage for data and instructions that do not change, such as programs and data from the computer manufacturer.

read-only memory (ROM)
a nonvolatile form of memory

There are other types of nonvolatile memory as well. Programmable read-only memory (PROM) is a type in which the desired data and instructions—and hence the desired circuit state combination—must first be programmed into the memory chip. After that, PROM behaves like ROM. PROM chips are used where the CPU's data and instructions do not change but the application is so

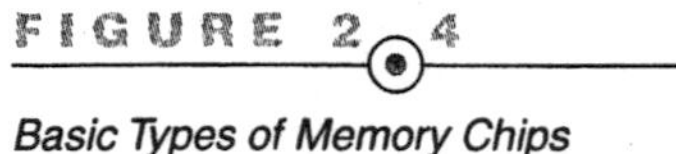

Basic Types of Memory Chips

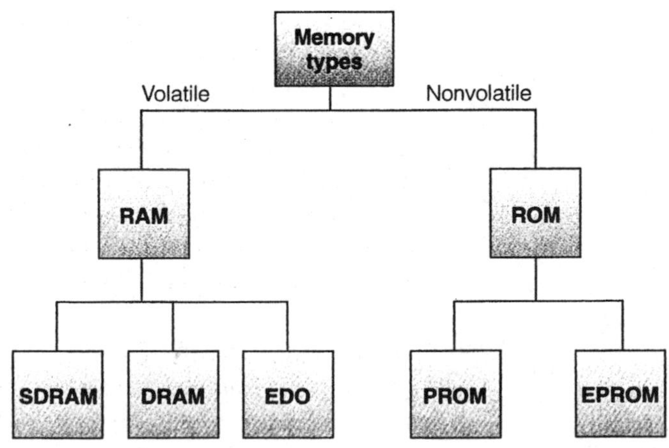

specialized or unique that custom manufacturing of a true ROM chip would be too costly. A common use of PROM chips is for storing the instructions for popular video games, such as those from Nintendo and Sega. Game instructions are programmed into the PROM chips by the game manufacturer. Instructions and data can be programmed into a PROM chip only once. Erasable programmable read-only memory (EPROM) is similar to PROM except, as the name implies, the memory chip can be erased and reprogrammed. An automobile manufacturer, for example, might use an industrial robot to perform repetitive operations on a certain car model. When the robot is performing its operations, the nonvolatility and rapid accessibility to program instructions offered by EPROM are an advantage. Once the model year is over, however, the EPROM controlling the robot's operation will need to be erased and reprogrammed to accommodate a different car model.

MULTIPROCESSING

multiprocessing
simultaneous execution of two or more instructions

coprocessor
part of the computer that speeds processing by executing specific types of instructions while the CPU works on another processing activity

There are a number of forms of **multiprocessing**, which involves the simultaneous execution of two or more instructions. One form of multiprocessing involves **coprocessors**. A coprocessor speeds processing by executing specific types of instructions while the CPU works on another processing activity. Coprocessors can be internal or external to the CPU and may have different clock speeds than the CPU. Each type of coprocessor best performs a specific function. For example, a math coprocessor chip can be used to speed mathematical calculations, and a graphics coprocessor chip decreases the time it takes to manipulate graphics.

Parallel Processing

parallel processing
a form of multiprocessing that speeds processing by linking several processors to operate at the same time, or in parallel

Another form of multiprocessing, called **parallel processing**, speeds processing by linking several processors to operate at the same time, or in parallel. The most frequent business uses for parallel processing are modeling, simulation, and analysis of large amounts of data. In today's marketplace, consumers demand quick response and customized service, so companies are gathering and reporting more information about their customers. Collecting and organizing the enormous amount of customer data is no easy task, but parallel processing can help companies organize data on existing consumer buying patterns and process them more quickly to build an effective marketing program. As a result, a company can gain a competitive advantage.

SECONDARY STORAGE AND INPUT AND OUTPUT DEVICES

secondary storage
devices that store larger amounts of data, instructions, and information more permanently than allowed with main memory; also called *permanent storage*

As we have seen, memory is an important factor in determining overall computer system power. However, memory provides only a small amount of storage area for the data and instructions the CPU requires for processing. Computer systems also need to store larger amounts of data, instructions, and information more permanently than main memory allows. **Secondary storage**, also called *permanent storage*, serves this purpose.

Compared with memory, secondary storage offers the advantages of nonvolatility, greater capacity, and greater economy. Most forms of secondary storage are considerably less expensive than memory (see Figure 2.5). Because of the electromechanical processes involved in using secondary storage, however, it is considerably slower than memory. The selection of secondary storage media and devices requires an understanding of their primary characteristics—access method, capacity, and portability.

SECONDARY STORAGE ACCESS METHODS

sequential access
retrieval method in which data must be accessed in the order in which it is stored

Data and information access can be either sequential or direct. **Sequential access** means that data must be accessed in the order in which it is stored. For

Data Storage Media	Data tape cartridge	Data tape cartridge	Rewritable optical disk	Jaz disk	Zip disk	Zip disk	Floppy diskette	SDRAM
Capacity	30 GB	2 GB	2.6 GB	2 GB	200 MB	100 MB	1.44 MB	128 MB
Cost	$366.77	$40.45	$58.91	$98.34	$15.02	$9.45	$0.50	$111.93
Cost/MB	0.012	0.020	0.023	0.049	0.075	0.095	0.347	0.874

FIGURE 2.5

Cost Comparison for Various Forms of Data Storage

All forms of secondary storage cost considerably less per megabyte of capacity than RAM, although they have slower access times. A diskette costs about 35 cents per megabyte, while RAM can cost around $.90 per megabyte, three times more.

(Source: Data from CompUSA Direct Catalog, January 2002.)

example, inventory data stored sequentially may be stored by part number, such as 100, 101, 102, and so on. If you want to retrieve information on part number 125, you need to read and discard all the data relating to parts 001 through 124.

Direct access means that data can be retrieved directly, without having to pass by other data in sequence. With direct access, it is possible to go directly to and access the needed data—say, part number 125—without reading through parts 001 through 124. For this reason, direct access is usually faster than sequential access. The devices used to sequentially access secondary storage data are simply called **sequential access storage devices (SASDs)**; those used for direct access are called **direct access storage devices (DASDs)**.

SECONDARY STORAGE DEVICES

The most common forms of secondary storage include magnetic tapes, magnetic disks, and optical disks. Some of these media (magnetic tape) allow only sequential access, while others (magnetic and optical disks) provide direct and sequential access. Figure 2.6 shows some different secondary storage media.

Magnetic Tapes

One common secondary storage medium is **magnetic tape**. Similar to the kind of tape found in audio- and videocassettes, magnetic tape is a Mylar film coated with iron oxide. Portions of the tape are magnetized to represent bits. Magnetic tape is a sequential access storage medium. Although access is slower, magnetic tape is usually less expensive than disk storage. In addition, magnetic tape is often used to back up disk drives and to store data off-site for recovery in case of disaster. Tape technology is improving to provide tape drives

direct access
retrieval method in which data can be retrieved without the need to read and discard other data

sequential access storage device (SASD)
device used to sequentially access secondary storage data

direct access storage device (DASD)
device used for direct access of secondary storage data

magnetic tape
common secondary storage medium; Mylar film coated with iron oxide, with portions of the tape magnetized to represent bits

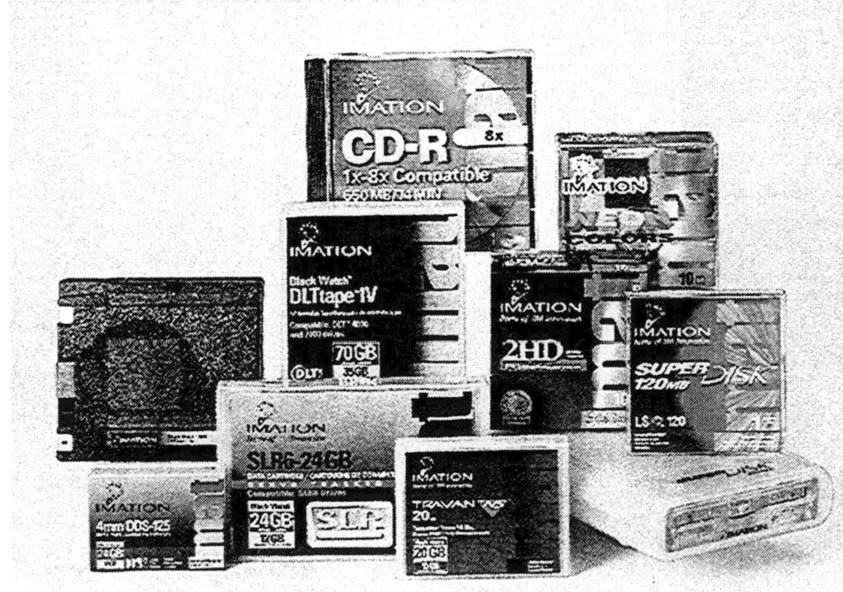

FIGURE 2.6

Types of Secondary Storage

Secondary storage devices such as magnetic tapes and disks, optical disks, CD-ROMs, and DVDs are used to store data for easy retrieval at a later date.

(Source: Courtesy of Imation.)

FIGURE 2.7

Hard Disk

Hard disks give direct access to stored data. The read/write head can move directly to the location of a desired piece of data, dramatically reducing access times, as compared with magnetic tape.

(Source: Courtesy of Seagate Technology.)

magnetic disk
common secondary storage medium; bits are represented by magnetized areas

redundant array of independent/inexpensive disks (RAID)
method of storing data that allows the system to create a "reconstruction map" so that if a hard drive fails, it can rebuild lost data

storage area network (SAN)
technology that uses computer servers, distributed storage devices, and networks to tie the storage system together

with greater capacities and faster transfer speeds. For example, Sony Electronics Inc.'s AIT-3 cartridges offer a 100 GB capacity per cartridge, with a transfer rate of 11 MB/second.

Magnetic Disks

Magnetic disks are also coated with iron oxide; they can be thin steel platters (see Figure 2.7) or Mylar film (diskettes). As with magnetic tape, magnetic disks represent bits by small magnetized areas. When reading from or writing onto a disk, the disk's read/write head can go directly to the desired piece of data. Thus, the disk is a direct access storage medium and allows for fast data retrieval. For example, if a manager needs information on the credit history of a customer, the information can be obtained in a matter of seconds if the data is stored on a direct access storage device. Magnetic disk storage varies widely in capacity and portability.

RAID

Companies' data storage needs are expanding rapidly. Today's storage configurations routinely entail many hundreds of gigabytes. However, putting the company's data on-line involves a serious business risk—the loss of critical business data can put a corporation out of operation. The concern is that the most critical mechanical components inside a disk storage device—the disk drives, the fans, and other input/output devices—can break.

Organizations now require that their data storage devices be fault tolerant—have the ability to continue with little or no loss of performance in the event of a failure of one or more key components. **Redundant array of independent/inexpensive disks (RAID)** is a method of storing data that, if a hard drive fails, allows the lost data on that drive to be rebuilt. With this approach, data is stored redundantly on different physical disk drives using a technique called *stripping* to evenly distribute the data.

Las Vegas casinos employ highly reliable computers that guarantee constant uptime. RAID storage devices are commonly used to prevent downtime or data loss. In addition, backup tapes are created each day and go out in armored trucks to a facility unknown to the casino and managed by a company that doesn't give its name out.

SAN

Storage area network (SAN) uses computer servers, distributed storage devices, and networks to tie everything together, as shown in Figure 2.8. To increase the speed of storing and retrieving data, fiber-optic channels are often used. Although

FIGURE 2.8

Storage Area Network

SAN provides high-speed connections between data storage devices and computers over a network.

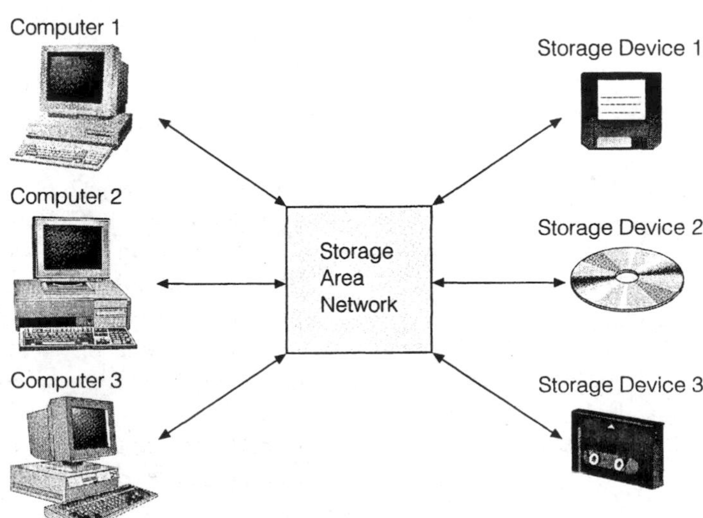

SAN technology is relatively new, a number of companies are using SAN to successfully and efficiently store critical data. Cox Communications Inc., a $3 billion cable TV and telecom services vendor in Atlanta, added a Dell storage area network so it can connect five storage systems of over 3.5 TB of data to all of its 300 Dell servers. Data moves at speeds of 100 MB per second over the SAN, compared with the speeds of 20 MB per second Cox got with standard connections.[4]

Optical Disks

optical disk
a rigid disk of plastic onto which data is recorded by special lasers that physically burn pits in the disk

Another type of secondary storage medium is the **optical disk,** a rigid plastic disk onto which data is recorded by special lasers that physically burn pits in the disk. Data is directly accessed from the disk by an optical disk device that uses a low-power laser to measure the difference in reflected light caused by a pit (or lack thereof) on the disk. Each pit represents the binary digit 1; each unpitted area represents the binary digit 0. Once a master optical disk has been created, duplicates can be manufactured using techniques similar to those used to produce music CDs.

compact disk read-only memory (CD-ROM)
a common form of optical disk on which data, once it has been recorded, cannot be modified

A common form of optical disk is called **compact disk read-only memory (CD-ROM)**. Once data has been recorded on a CD-ROM, it cannot be modified—the disk is "read only." CD-writable (CD-W) disks allow data to be written once to a CD disk. CD-rewritable (CD-RW) technology allows personal computer users to replace their diskettes with high-capacity CDs that can be written upon and edited over. The CD-RW disk can hold roughly 500 times the capacity of a 1.4-MB diskette. A popular use of writable and rewritable CD technology is to enable users to burn a CD of their favorite music for their later listening pleasure.

Magneto-Optical Disk

magneto-optical disk
a hybrid between a magnetic disk and an optical disk

A **magneto-optical disk** combines magnetic disk technologies with CD-ROM technologies. Like magnetic disks, MO disks can be read from and written to. And like diskettes, they are removable. However, their storage capacity can exceed 5 GB, much greater than magnetic diskettes, and their data access speed is faster than diskettes but not as fast as hard disk drives.

A 2.3-GB MO disk format, nicknamed GigaMO, was jointly developed by Fujitsu and Sony in 2001. It can transfer data at the rate of 8.3 MB/second. Meanwhile, Hewlett-Packard and Sony have developed a 5.2 GB magneto-optical drive.[5]

The primary advantage of optical disks is their huge storage capacities, compared with other secondary storage media. Optical disks can store large applications and programs that contain graphics and audio data. They also allow for storage of data that is not needed at a given moment but could possibly be useful later.

Digital Versatile Disk

digital versatile disk (DVD)
storage format used to store digital video or computer data

Digital Versatile Disk Player

DVD disks look like CDs but have a much greater storage capacity and can transfer data at a much faster rate.

(Source: Courtesy of Sony Electronics.)

The **digital versatile disk (DVD)** brings together the formerly separate worlds of home computing and home video (Figure 2.9). A DVD is a five-inch CD-ROM look-alike with the ability to store about 135 minutes of digital video. When it is used to store video, the picture quality far surpasses anything seen on tape, cable, or standard broadcast TV—sharp detail, true color, no flicker, no snow. The sound is recorded in digital Dolby, creating clear "surround" effects by completely separating all the audio channels in a home theater. The DVD costs less to duplicate and ship than the videocassette, takes less shelf space, and delivers higher quality.

The DVD can double as a computer storage disk and provide up to a 17-GB capacity. The physical disks resemble CD-ROMs, but they are thinner, so DVD players can also read current CD-ROMs, but current CD-ROM players cannot read DVDs. The access speed of a DVD drive is faster than the typical CD-ROM drive. DVD manufacturers include Sony, Philips, and Toshiba. These companies are also actively involved in making and improving standard CD-ROM drives. Newer DVD technology

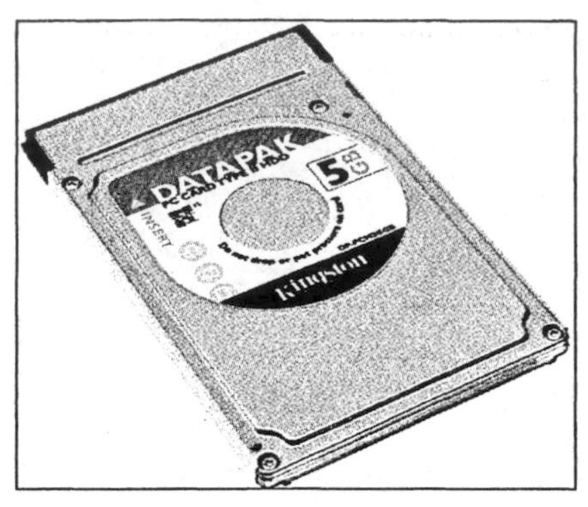

The PC memory card is like a portable hard disk that fits into any Type II PC card slot and can store up to 5 gigabytes.

(Source: Courtesy of Kingston Technology.)

provides write-once disks and rewrite disks, often called DVD RAM. There are also combo DVD/CD-ROM drives that can read both DVDs and CD-ROMs.

Memory Cards

A group of computer manufacturers formed the Personal Computer Memory Card International Association (PCMCIA) to create standards for a peripheral device known as a PC memory card. These PC memory cards are credit-card-size devices that can be installed in an adapter or slot in many personal computers. To the rest of the system, the PC memory card functions as though it were a fixed hard disk drive. Although the cost per megabyte of storage is greater than for traditional hard disk storage, these cards are less failure prone than hard disks, are portable, and are relatively easy to use. Software manufacturers often store the instructions for their program on a memory card for use with laptop computers.

Expandable Storage

expandable storage devices storage that uses removable disk cartridges to provide additional storage capacity

Expandable storage devices use removable disk cartridges (Figure 2.10). Expandable storage devices can be internal or external, and a few personal computers now include internal expandable storage devices as standard equipment. CD-RW drives by Hewlett-Packard, Iomega, and others can also be used for expandable storage. These expandable storage devices are ideal for backups of the critical data on your hard drive. They can hold at least 80 times as much data and operate five times faster than the existing 1.44-MB diskette drives. Although more expensive than fixed hard disks, removable disk cartridges combine hard disk storage capacity and diskette portability.

The overall trend in secondary storage is toward more direct-access methods, higher capacity, and increased portability. The business needs and needs of individual users should be considered when selecting a specific type of storage. In general, the ability to store large amounts of data and information and access it quickly can increase organizational effectiveness and efficiency. Table 2.2 lists the most common secondary storage devices and their capacities for easy reference.

INPUT DEVICES

A user's first experience with computers is usually through input and output devices. Through these devices—the gateways to the computer system—people provide data and instructions to the computer and receive results from it. Input and output devices are part of the overall user interface, which includes other hardware devices and software that allow humans to interact with a computer system.

As with other computer system components, the selection of input and output devices depends on the needs of the users and business objectives. For example, many restaurant chains use handheld input devices or computerized terminals that let waiters enter orders quickly and accurately. These systems have also cut costs by making inventory tracking more efficient and marketing to customers more effective.

Literally hundreds of devices can be used for data input, ranging from special-purpose devices used to capture specific types of data to more general-purpose input devices. We will now discuss several.

FIGURE 2.10

Expandable Storage

Expandable storage drives allow users to add storage capacity by simply inserting a removable disk or cartridge. The disks can be used to back up hard disk data or to transfer large files to colleagues.

(Source: Courtesy of Iomega.)

Personal Computer Input Devices

A keyboard and a computer mouse are the most common devices used for entry and input of data such as characters, text, and basic commands. Some companies are developing newer keyboards that are more comfortable, adjustable, and faster to use. These keyboards, such as the split keyboard by Microsoft and others, are designed to avoid wrist and hand injuries caused by hours of keyboarding. Using the same keyboard, you can enter sketches on the touchpad and text using the keys.

Storage Device	Year First Introduced	Maximum Capacity
3.5-inch diskette	1987	1.44 MB
CD-ROM	1990	650 MB
Zip	1995	100–250 MB
DVD	1996	17 GB

TABLE 2.2

Comparison of Secondary Storage Devices

A computer mouse is used to point to and click on symbols, icons, menus, and commands on the screen. The computer responds by taking a number of actions, such as copying data into the computer system or opening files.

Voice-Recognition Devices

voice-recognition device
an input device that recognizes human speech

Another type of input device can recognize human speech. Called **voice-recognition devices,** these tools use microphones and special software to record and convert the sound of the human voice into digital signals. Speech recognition can be used on a factory floor to allow equipment operators to give basic commands to machines while their hands perform other operations. Voice recognition can also be used by security systems to allow only authorized personnel into restricted areas. Voice-recognition systems now available on many makes of autos and trucks allow a driver to activate radio programs and CDs. They can even tell you the time. Asking "What time is it?" will get a response such as, "Eleven thirty-four AM."

Digital Computer Cameras

digital computer camera
input device used with a PC to record and store images and video in digital form

Some personal computers work with **digital computer cameras,** which record and store images and video in digital form. When you take pictures, the images are electronically stored in the camera. A cable is then connected from the camera to a port on the computer, and the images can be downloaded. During the download, the visual images are converted into digital codes by a computer board. Once in digital format, the images can be modified and included in other applications. For example, a photo of the company office recorded by a digital computer camera can be captured and then pasted into a word processing document for a company brochure. Some digital cameras, like the Sony Mavica, can store images on diskettes. The diskettes can then be inserted into a computer to transfer the photos to a hard disk where they can be edited, sent to another location, pasted into another application, or printed. Some personal computers, as shown in Figure 2.11, have a video camera that records full-motion video.[6]

pixel
a dot of color on a photo image or a point of light on a display screen

Uninformed buyers assume that the number of **pixels** (or points of data) that a camera can capture is the definitive measure of image quality. However, resolution is simply the measure of the amount of data saved in the picture file. This relates to how large an image may be printed or displayed, but not to how well the picture will appear. The key is to choose a camera with a resolution suited to your output purpose. A 1-megapixel resolution is good for 5 × 7 inch print, but a 2-megapixel resolution is needed for a good 8 × 10 inch picture.

An ergonomic keyboard is designed to be more comfortable to use.

(Source: Courtesy of Kinesis Corporation, http://www.kinesis-ergo.com.)

Terminals

Inexpensive and easy to use, terminals are input devices that perform data input. A terminal is connected to a complete computer system, including a processor, memory, and secondary storage. General commands, text, and other data are entered via a keyboard or mouse, converted into machine-readable form, and transferred to the processing portion of the computer system. Terminals are normally connected directly to the computer system by telephone lines or cables and can be placed in offices, in warehouses, and on factory floors.

FIGURE 2.11

A PC Equipped with a Computer Camera

Digital video cameras make it possible for people at distant locations to conduct videoconferences, eliminating the need for expensive travel to attend physical meetings.

(Source:© Andreas Pollok/Stone.)

Scanning Devices

Image and character data can be input using a scanning device. A page scanner is like a copy machine. The page to be scanned is typically inserted into the scanner or placed face down on the glass plate of the scanner, covered, and scanned. With a handheld scanner, the scanning device is moved or rolled manually over the image to be scanned. Both page and handheld scanners can convert monochrome or color pictures, forms, text, and other images into machine-readable digits. Many companies use scanning devices to help them manage their documents and cut down on the high cost of using and processing paper.

Magnetic Ink Character Recognition (MICR) Devices

In the 1950s, the banking industry became swamped with paper checks, loan applications, bank statements, and so on. To remedy this overload and process documents more quickly, the industry developed **magnetic ink character recognition (MICR)**, a system for reading this data quickly. With MICR, data is placed on the bottom of a check or other form using a special magnetic ink. Data printed with this ink using a special character set can be read by both people and computers.

magnetic ink character recognition (MICR)
system for reading data on the bottom of a check or other form using magnetic ink

Optical Data Readers

A special scanning device called an *optical data reader* can also be used to scan documents. The two categories of optical data readers are for optical mark recognition (OMR) and optical character recognition (OCR). People completing OMR forms use pencils to fill in boxes on OMR paper, which is also called a "mark sense form." OMR is used in standardized tests (including SAT and GMAT tests), surveys, and census taking. In comparison, most OCR readers use reflected light to recognize various characters. With special software, OCR readers can convert handwritten or typed documents into digital data.

Point-of-Sale (POS) Devices

Point-of-sale (POS) devices are terminals used in retail operations to enter sales information into the computer system. The POS device then computes the total charges, including tax. Many POS devices also use other types of input and output devices, such as keyboards, bar code readers, printers, and screens. A large portion of the money that businesses spend on computer technology involves POS devices.

point-of-sale (POS) devices
terminals used in retail operations to enter sales information into the computer system

Automatic Teller Machine (ATM) Devices

Another type of special-purpose input/output device, the automatic teller machine (ATM), is a terminal most bank customers use to perform withdrawals and other transactions for their bank accounts. The ATM, however, is no longer used only for cash and bank receipts. Companies use various ATM devices to support their business processes. Some ATMs dispense tickets for airlines, concerts, and soccer games. Some colleges use them to output transcripts. For this reason, the input and output capabilities of ATMs are quite varied. Like POS devices, ATMs may combine other types of input and output devices. Unisys, for example, has developed an ATM kiosk that allows bank customers to make cash withdrawals and pay bills and also receive advice on investments and retirement planning.[7]

Touch-Sensitive Screens

Advances in screen technology allow display screens to function as input as well as output devices. By touching certain parts of a sensitive screen, you can execute a program or cause the computer to take an action. Touch-sensitive screens are frequently used at gas stations for customers to select grades of gas and request a receipt, at fast-food restaurants for order clerks to enter customer choices, at information centers in hotels to allow guests to request facts about local eating and drinking establishments, and at amusement parks to provide directions to patrons. They also are used in kiosks at airports and department stores.

Bar Code Scanners

A bar code scanner employs a laser scanner to read a bar-coded label. This form of input is used widely in grocery store checkouts and in inventory control. Owens & Minor is a medical and surgical supply company that has equipped hospital operating rooms with supplies and labeled each item with a bar code. When an item is used during surgery, a wireless handheld computer scans its bar code to update a computerized inventory system. The system tracks how much inventory is left and automatically places an order for refills when an item falls below the reorder point.[8]

OUTPUT DEVICES

Computer systems provide output to decision makers at all levels of an organization to solve a business problem or capitalize on a competitive opportunity. In addition, output from one computer system can be used as input into another computer system within the same information system. The desired form of this output might be visual, audio, and even digital. Whatever the output's content or form, output devices function to provide the right information to the right person in the right format at the right time.

Display Monitors

The display monitor is a TV-screen-like device on which output from the computer is displayed. Because traditional monitors use a cathode ray tube to display images, they are sometimes called *CRTs*. The monitor works in much the same way as a TV screen—one or more electron beams are generated from cathode ray tubes. As the beams strike a phosphorescent compound (phosphor) coated on the inside of the screen, a dot on the screen called a *pixel* lights up. The electron beam sweeps back and forth across the screen so that as the phosphor starts to fade, it is struck and lights up again.

With today's wide selection of monitors, price and overall quality can vary tremendously. The quality of a screen is often measured by the number of horizontal and vertical pixels used to create it. A larger number of pixels per square inch means a higher resolution, or clarity and sharpness of the image. For example, a screen with a 1,024 x 768 resolution (786,432 pixels) has a higher sharpness than one with a resolution of 640 x 350 (224,000 pixels). The distance between one pixel on the screen and the next nearest pixel is known as dot pitch. The common range of dot pitch is from .25 mm to .31 mm. The smaller the number, the better the picture. A dot pitch of .28 mm or smaller is considered good. Greater pixel densities and smaller dot pitches yield sharper images of higher resolution.

A monitor's ability to display color is a function of the quality of the monitor, the amount of RAM in the computer system, and the monitor's graphics adapter card. The color graphics adapter (CGA) was one of the first technologies to display color images on the screen. Today, super video graphics array (SVGA) displays are standard, providing vivid colors and superior resolution.

Liquid Crystal Displays (LCDs)

Because CRT monitors use an electron gun, there must be a distance of one foot between the gun and screen, causing them to be large and bulky. Thus, a different technology, flat-panel display, is used for portable personal computers and laptops. One common technology used for flat-screen displays is the same liquid crystal display technology used for pocket calculators and digital watches. LCD monitors are flat displays that use liquid crystals—organic, oil-like material placed between two polarizers—to form characters and graphic images on a backlit screen.

CRT monitors are large and bulky in comparison with LCD monitors (flat displays).

(Source: Courtesy of ViewSonic Corporation.)

The primary choices in LCD screens are passive-matrix and active-matrix LCD displays. In a passive-matrix display, the CPU sends its signals to transistors around the borders of the screen, which control all the pixels in a given row or column. In an active-matrix display, each pixel is controlled by its own transistor attached in a thin film to the glass behind the pixel. Passive-matrix displays are typically dimmer and slower, but less expensive than active-matrix ones. Active-matrix displays are bright and clear and have wider viewing angles than passive-matrix displays. Active-matrix displays, however, are more expensive and can increase the weight of the screen.

LCD technology is also being used to create thin and extremely high-resolution monitors for desktop computers. Although the screen may measure just 13 inches from corner to corner, the display's extremely high resolution—1,280 × 1,280 pixels—lets it show as much information as a conventional 20-inch monitor. And while cramming more into a smaller area causes text and images to shrink, you can comfortably sit much closer to an LCD screen than a conventional CRT monitor.

Printers and Plotters

Hard copy is paper output from a device called a printer. Printers with different speeds, features, and capabilities are available. Some can be set up to accommodate different paper forms such as blank check forms, invoice forms, and so forth. Newer printers allow businesses to create customized printed output for each customer from standard paper and data input using full color.

MP3
music format for the Internet; abbreviation for Motion Picture Experts Group Audio Layer 3

The speed of the printer is typically measured by the number of pages printed per minute (ppm). Like a display screen, the quality, or resolution, of a printer's output depends on the number of dots printed per inch. A 600-dpi (dots-per-inch) printer prints more clearly than a 300-dpi printer. A recurring cost of using a printer is the ink-jet or laser cartridge that must be replaced every few thousand pages of output. Figure 2.12 shows a laser printer.

Plotters are a type of hard-copy output device used for general design work. Businesses typically use these devices to generate paper or acetate blueprints, schematics, and drawings of buildings or new products onto paper or transparencies. Standard plot widths are 24 inches and 36 inches, and the length can be whatever meets the need—from a few inches to several feet.

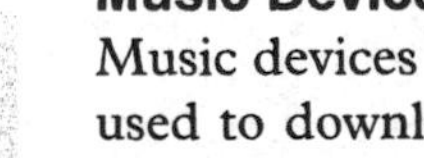

Music Devices

Music devices are about the size of a cigarette pack and can be used to download music from the Internet and other sources. These devices have no moving parts and can store hours of music. When you get tired of the music, you can always download new pieces. **MP3** is an abbreviation for Motion Picture Experts Group Audio Layer 3, a popular music format for the Internet that requires about 1 MB of storage for every minute of music—about a tenth of the storage required for music on a standard CD. The MP3 standard allows the music to be compressed, so it takes less time to download from the Internet and takes up less space on the computer's hard drive. While MP3 is currently the leading digital audio format, it is facing competition

FIGURE 2.12

Laser Printer

Laser printers, available in a wide variety of speeds and price ranges, have many features, including color capabilities. They are the most common solution for outputting hard copies of information.

(Source: Courtesy of Epson America, Inc.)

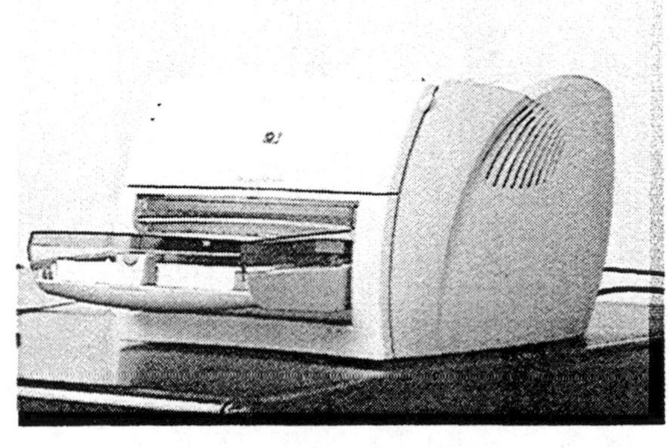

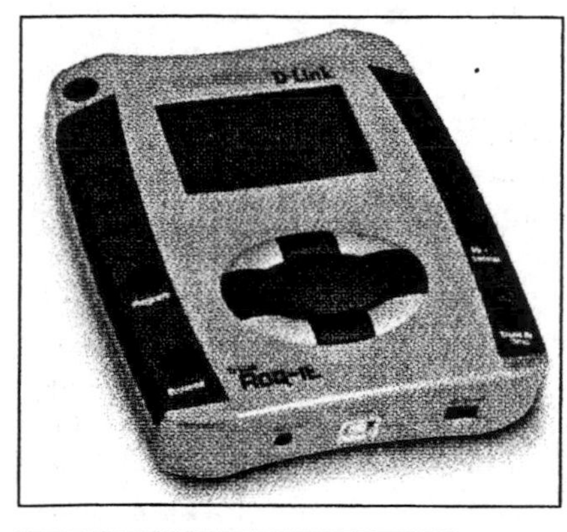

D-Link offers an MP3 player with a 10-GB storage capacity that can hold 150 hours of music.

(Source: Courtesy of D-Link Systems, Inc.)

from Microsoft's Windows Media, RealNetwork's Real Audio, and an upgraded version of MP3 called mp3PRO, which will cut the storage space required in half. A number of Internet sites allow people to share music using the MP3 format.

COMPUTER SYSTEM TYPES

Computer systems can range from desktop (or smaller) portable computers to massive supercomputers that require housing in large rooms. Let's examine the types of computer systems in more detail. Table 2.3 shows general ranges of capabilities for various types of computer systems.

PERSONAL COMPUTERS

personal computer (PC) relatively small, inexpensive computer system, sometimes called a microcomputer

As previously noted, **personal computers (PCs)** are relatively small, inexpensive computer systems. Although personal computers are designed primarily for single users, they are often tied into larger computer systems as well. Personal computers can be purchased from retail stores or on-line. Over half the households in the United States have at least one personal computer, and nearly 90 percent of children use a personal computer in school.[9]

There are several types of personal computers. Desktop computers are the most common personal computer system configuration. Increasingly powerful desktop computers can provide sufficient memory and storage for most business

TABLE 2.3

Types of Computer Systems

Type of computer	Typical Processor Speed	Weight	Cost	How Used	Example
Handheld	> 200 MHz	< .5 lb	< $500	Personal organizer	Palm
Notebook	> 1 GHz	< 4 lbs	< $1,000	Improvement of individual worker's productivity	IBM
Laptop	> 1 GHz	< 7 lbs	< $2,000	Improvement of individual worker's productivity	Apple iBook Hewlett-Packard
Network	> 400 MHz	< 15 lbs	< $750	Support for data entry and Internet connection	Oracle
Desktop	> 2 GHz	< 25 lbs	< $2,000	Improvement of individual worker's productivity	Apple iMac Dell
Workstation	> 2 GHz	< 30 lbs	$4,000 – $40,000	Engineering, CAD, software development	Sun Microsystems
Midrange	> 2 GHz	> 50 lbs	$20,000 – $250,000	Computing for a department or small company	IBM AS/400
Mainframe	> 600 MIPS	> 200 lbs	> $250,000	Computing for a large company	IBM Z/900
Supercomputer	> 4 Teraflops	> 200 lbs	> $1,000,000	Scientific applications, marketing, customer support, product development	Compaq Terascale

computing tasks. Desktop PCs have become standard business tools; more than 30 million are in use in large corporations.

In addition to traditional PCs that use Intel processors and Microsoft software, there are other options. In January 2002, Apple announced three models of its new iMac personal computer with a design that represents a radical departure from the previous version. Its base is a small half sphere with a flat-panel monitor attached to the base by a jointed chrome neck that can be adjusted to position the monitor. Some say that the new machine looks more like a desk lamp than a desktop computer. The SuperDrive is a popular option and enables the user to read and write both CDs and DVDs. The machines come loaded with the new Mac OS X version 10.1 operating system and a number of multimedia software applications including iDVD, which allows users to make DVD movies; iMovie, a video-editing application; iPhoto, a new digital photo-editing tool; and iTunes, which lets users convert CD music into MP3 files for use on Apple's iPod portable MP3 music player.[10]

Various smaller personal computers can be used for a variety of purposes. A *laptop computer* is a small, lightweight PC about the size of a briefcase. Apple, for example, has the iBook computer, which is a laptop system compatible with the iMac. Newer PCs include the even smaller and lighter *notebook* and *subnotebook* computers, which provide similar computing power. Some notebook and subnotebook computers fit into docking stations of desktop computers to provide additional storage and processing capabilities. Ultraportable notebooks are the fastest-growing segment of the notebook-class computer. Dell, Fujitsu, Hewlett-Packard, IBM, and Sharp all sell highly portable notebook computers that measure 1.0 × 11.0 × 9.0 inches or less and weigh under four pounds.

network computer
a cheaper-to-buy and cheaper-to-run version of the personal computer that is used primarily for accessing networks and the Internet

Handheld (palmtop) computers often include a wide variety of software and communications capabilities. Palm was the company that invented the Palm Pilot organizer and its successors. Palm signed licensing agreements with Handspring, IBM, Sony, and many other manufacturers, permitting them to make what amounts to Palm clones. These computers are compatible and able to communicate with desktop computers over wireless networks.

Typical handhelds cost less than $600, come with a 200+-MHz processor, have 64+ MB of RAM, contain a speaker and a microphone for voice notes, offer a headphone jack for listening to digital music files and audio books, and have a connection cradle that keeps the address book, calendar, and e-mail synchronized with data on the user's desktop computer. They can run up to 14 hours between battery charges.[11] Such portability and power can streamline business processes. The *Atlanta Journal-Constitution* expects to save more than $250,000 a year on newspaper delivery services using palmtop computers to assist with the return of unsold papers at more than 15,000 locations around Atlanta. Each newspaper rack is given a unique bar code, and delivery people scan in the location and enter the number of newspapers that weren't purchased at that rack. This information is then relayed to corporate information systems to calculate the retailer's bill, saving hours of manual calculations. Delivery people can also get up-to-date delivery information in sequential order throughout their route via the palmtop computers, simplifying their task.[12]

Handheld (palmtop) computers such as this Handspring Treo 90 pack powerful features into small spaces. This device weighs only four ounces but has 16 MB of memory—enough to keep anyone organized on the go.

(Source: Courtesy of Handspring.)

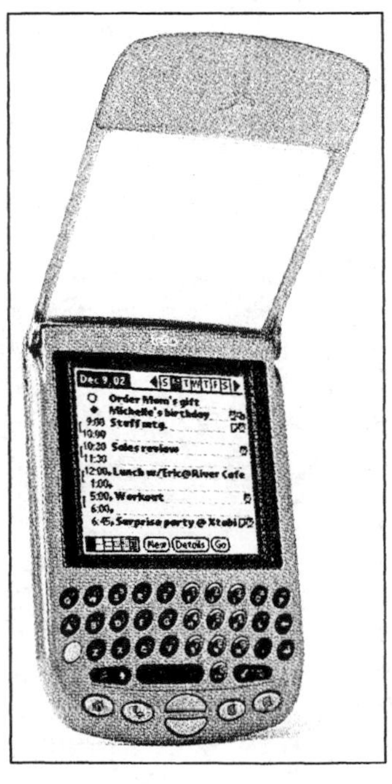

Embedded computers are computers placed inside other products to add features and capabilities. In automobiles, embedded computers can help with navigation, engine performance, braking, and other functions. Household appliances, stereos, and some phone systems also use embedded computers. In a unique application, Raven Shoes from VectraSense Technologies feature embedded computers that monitor a jogger's level of activity and increase or decrease the support offered by the shoes accordingly.[13]

A **network computer** is a cheaper-to-buy and cheaper-to-run version of the personal computer that is used primarily for network access and e-mail. These stripped-down computers do not have the storage capacity or power of typical desktop computers, nor do they need it for the role they play. Unlike personal computers, network computers download software from a network when needed. This feature can make it much easier and less expensive to manage the support, distribution, and updating of software applications. The initial target user is someone who performs what is called heads-down data entry—customer inquiry, phone order taking, and classic data entry. The network computer is designed to have no moving parts to avoid expensive equipment repairs. IBM, Oracle, and Sun Microsystems were the first companies to develop prototypes of such systems, with a purchase price in the $500 to $1,500 range. Advocates of network computers argue that they not only cost less to purchase compared with a standard desktop PC but also cost less to operate. However, the network computer's flexibility is extremely limited when compared with the PC. In addition, PC companies have responded strongly to network computers with lower prices and more competitive products. Only about 150,000 such devices shipped in the United States in 2000, and it is debatable how successful this type of computer will ultimately be.[14]

workstation
computer that fits between high-end microcomputers and low-end midrange computers in terms of cost and processing power

Web appliance
A device that can connect to the Internet, typically through a phone line

midrange computer
formerly called minicomputer, a system about the size of a small three-drawer file cabinet that can accommodate several users at one time

mainframe computer
large, powerful computer often shared by hundreds of concurrent users connected to the machine via terminals

Workstations are computers that fit between high-end personal computers and low-end midrange computers in terms of cost and processing power. They cost from $3,000 to $40,000. Workstations are small enough to fit on an individual's desktop. Workstations are used to support engineering and technical users who perform heavy mathematical computing, computer-aided design (CAD), and other applications requiring a high-end processor. Such users need very powerful CPUs, large amounts of main memory, and extremely high-resolution graphic displays to meet their needs. Engineers use CAD programs to create two- and three-dimensional engineering drawings and product designs.

Many companies, including Microsoft and Intel, are developing inexpensive **Web appliances**, devices that can connect to the Internet. They can be used to check stock prices, check e-mail messages, search the Internet for information, and more. Web appliances come in a variety of configurations. Some have a keyboard, a passive-matrix display, a 200-MHz processor, and Web and e-mail software. These devices can cost under $200 to purchase and about $20 per month for an Internet connection. Some Web appliances have the appearance of a cellular phone, with the capabilities of a standard phone and basic Internet connections. Other Web appliances are being attached to everyday products, such as TVs, stoves, and refrigerators. Once attached, the Web appliance can get movie schedules, alert people when their stove may require maintenance, or advertise grocery specials. In the future, Web appliances may be built into many of the products we use every day.

Mainframe computers have been the workhorses of corporate computing for more than 50 years. They can support hundreds of users simultaneously and handle all of the core functions of a corporation.

(Source: Courtesy of IBM Corporation.)

MIDRANGE COMPUTERS

Midrange computers are systems about the size of a three-drawer file cabinet and can accommodate several users at one time. These systems often have secondary storage devices with more capacity than workstation computers and can support a variety of transaction processing activities, including payroll, inventory control, and invoicing. Midrange computers often have excellent processing and decision support capabilities. Many small- to medium-size organizations—such as manufacturers, real estate companies, and retail operations—use midrange computers.

MAINFRAME COMPUTERS

Mainframe computers are large, powerful computers often shared by hundreds of concurrent users connected to the machine via terminals. The mainframe computer must reside in an environment-controlled computer room or data center with special heating, venting, and air-conditioning (HVAC) equipment to control the temperature, humidity, and dust levels around the computer.

In addition, most mainframes are kept in a secured data center with limited access to the room through some kind of security system. The construction and maintenance of such a controlled-access room with HVAC can add hundreds of thousands of dollars to the cost of owning and operating a mainframe computer. Mainframe computers also require specially trained individuals (called *system engineers* and *system programmers*) to care for them. Mainframe computers start at $250,000 for a fully configured system.

The role of the mainframe is to act as a large information processing and data storage utility for a corporation—running jobs too large for other computers, storing files and databases too large to be stored elsewhere, and storing backups of files and databases created elsewhere (these large stores of data are sometimes called *data warehouses*). The mainframe is capable of handling the millions of daily transactions associated with airline, automobile, and hotel/motel reservation systems. It can process the tens of thousands of daily queries necessary to provide data to decision support systems. Its massive storage and input/output capabilities enable it to play the role of a video computer, providing full-motion video to users. Over time, mainframes have been evolving into smaller, faster, less expensive systems as a result of *complementary metal oxide semiconductor (CMOS)*, a computer chip fabrication technology that uses special semiconductor material. Mainframe computers provide support for large packaged software products, Web technologies, and communications protocols, much like their smaller cousins, the midrange computers.

supercomputers
the most powerful computer systems, with the fastest processing speeds

Wal-Mart upgraded its mainframes and associated disk storage at a cost of $50 million. The project replaced a number of IBM S/390 mainframes with IBM's newer z900 computers. The new 64-bit mainframes include a very fast coprocessor designed to support the complex operations used in communicating secure e-business applications over the Internet. The mainframes are being used to run core business applications such as invoicing, replenishing product inventories, and processing credit card transactions for over 4,000 stores.[15]

SUPERCOMPUTERS

Supercomputers are the most powerful computer systems, with the fastest processing speeds. Supercomputers are used by government agencies to perform the high-speed number crunching needed in weather forecasting and military applications. They are also used by universities and large corporations involved with research or high-technology businesses. Some large oil companies, for example, use supercomputers to perform sophisticated analysis of detailed data to help them explore for oil.

ASCI White is a powerful supercomputer at Lawrence Livermore Laboratory in Livermore, California. It is capable of 12.3 trillion operations per second, more than a person with a calculator could do in 10 million years, and is used by the lab to simulate nuclear weapons tests.

(Source: AP/Wide World Photos.)

Compaq's Terascale Computing System at the Pittsburgh Supercomputing Center was rated the world's most powerful supercomputer committed to unclassified research in November 2001. This system is used for a wide variety of research projects, including simulation of the blood flow in the human body, space weather modeling, virtual tests for therapeutic cancer drugs, global modeling of the earth's magnetic field, and simulation of shock waves and eddies in turbulent fluids. The system has over 3 TB of total RAM, with a hard-disk array of 50 TB of primary storage and an additional 300 TB of disk or tape storage available as needed. The system has a peak processing capability exceeding 6 trillion calculations per second (teraflops).[16] Read the "Ethical and Societal Issues" special-interest feature to gain an appreciation of how even the most powerful computers and simulation models are sometimes still inadequate.

Although all of the preceding computer system types can be used for general processing tasks, they can also serve a specific and unique purpose, such as supporting Internet and network applications. A **computer server** is a computer designed for a specific task, such as network or Internet applications. Servers typically have large memory and storage capacities, along with fast and efficient communications abilities. They can range in size from a PC to a mainframe system, depending on the needs of the organization. A Web server is used to handle Internet traffic and communications. An Internet caching server stores Web sites that are frequently used by a company. A file server stores and coordinates program and data files. An application server provides services to support Web-based applications that connect users to corporate databases. As with general computers, there are benchmarks to help a company determine the performance of a server, such as ZD ServerBench, WebBench, and NetBench.

computer server
a computer designed for a specific task, such as network or Internet applications

We now turn to the other critical component of effective computer systems—software. Like hardware, software has made technological leaps in a relatively short time span.

OVERVIEW OF SOFTWARE

In the 1950s, when computer hardware was relatively rare and expensive, software costs were a comparatively small percentage of total information systems costs. Today, that situation has dramatically changed. Software can represent 75 percent or more of the total cost of an information system for three major reasons: advances in hardware technology have dramatically reduced hardware costs, increasingly complex software requires more time to develop and so is more costly, and salaries for software developers have increased because the demand for these workers far exceeds the supply. In the future, software is expected to make up an even greater portion of the cost of the overall information system. The critical functions software serves, however, make it a worthwhile investment.

One of software's most critical functions is to direct the workings of the computer hardware. **Computer programs** are sequences of instructions for the computer. **Documentation** describes the program functions and helps the user operate the computer system. A program displays some of its documentation on screen, and other forms appear in external resources, such as printed manuals. There are two basic types of software: systems software and application software. **Systems software** is the set of programs designed to coordinate the activities and functions of the hardware and various programs throughout the computer system. A particular systems software package is designed for a specific CPU design and class of hardware. The combination of a particular hardware configuration and systems software package is known as a **computer system platform**. **Application software** consists of programs that help users solve particular computing problems.

computer programs
sequences of instructions for the computer

documentation
text that describes the program functions and helps the user operate the computer system

systems software
the set of programs designed to coordinate the activities and functions of the hardware and various programs throughout the computer system

computer system platform
the combination of a particular hardware configuration and system software package

application software
programs that help users solve particular computing problems

Both systems and application software can be used to meet the needs of an individual, a group, or an enterprise. Application software can support individuals, groups, and organizations to help them realize business objectives. Application software has the greatest potential to affect the processes that add value to a business because it is designed for specific organizational activities and functions, as we saw in the case of Flextronics. The effective implementation and use of application software can provide significant internal efficiencies and support corporate goals. Before an individual, a group, or an enterprise decides on the best approach for acquiring application software, goals and needs should be analyzed carefully.

Ethical and Societal Issues

European Weather Forecasters Rely on Blue Storm

Few things affect us so profoundly as the weather. It affects our food supply and the way we live. It even inflicts untold damage when it turns savage. Although we can never control the weather, we can try to predict its changes and avoid loss of life and property. But predicting weather on a large scale takes some massive computing power. The European Center for Medium-range Weather Forecasts (ECMWF) is an international organization headquartered in the United Kingdom. Its purpose is to prepare medium-range (up to ten-day) weather forecasts for distribution to the weather services of 23 European countries. These countries use the forecasts to issue warnings of severe storms and floods, present daily television weather forecasts throughout Europe, and provide specialized services to their many commercial and governmental users (e.g., optimal routing of ships at sea). The ECMWF also conducts research to improve these forecasts.

The behavior of the Earth's atmosphere follows a set of physical laws that can be expressed in extremely complex mathematical equations. Using these equations, scientists can forecast how temperature, wind speed and direction, and humidity will change over time. They use actual weather conditions for initial starting values for computer modeling and then calculate the weather at each point throughout the model atmosphere. The ECMWF model has 21 million grid points distributed throughout the atmosphere between the surface and a height of 63 kilometers (39 miles, if you don't like metrics). The complete weather forecast is made in a series of short steps, each about 20 minutes ahead, with each intermediate forecast serving as the starting conditions for the next forecast step.

The ECMWF recently ordered a supercomputer nicknamed Blue Storm and a data storage network from IBM to help scientists improve their forecasting abilities. The system is an IBM supercomputer capable of performing 7 trillion calculations per second (7 teraflops). The supercomputer will be expanded in stages so that by 2004 the machine should run at more than 20 teraflops. At that point, the Blue Storm system will be roughly five times more powerful than ECMWF's current systems.

ECMWF employees will access Blue Storm using powerful IBM IntelliStation workstations, and researchers throughout Europe will be able to access the system via a network. Blue Storm is expected to contain a storage capacity of 1.5 PB (petabytes). Memory capacity is 4.1 TB.

Unfortunately, the goal of achieving precise, long-term forecasting (many weeks in advance) has proven difficult for several reasons. Small errors in the initial weather conditions and the approximations of atmospheric processes (e.g., variable cloud conditions) in the models are the two main sources of inaccurate forecasts. In addition, minor natural events that may seem trivial can result in larger-magnitude atmospheric changes, so accounting for those seemingly insignificant changes can be mind- and computer-boggling. In addition, gaps in our understanding of weather phenomena can confound even the best models. Much remains to be known about basic processes in our atmosphere. For example, scientists only recently discovered the existence of massive electrical discharges into the atmosphere above thunderstorms (called *sprites* and *blue jets*)—some of them many miles across. Still, Blue Storm is helping the ECMWF to advance weather forecasting by providing awesome computing power.

Discussion Questions

1. There is great room for improvement in weather forecasting by gathering more detailed and accurate weather data and conducting basic research into atmospheric processes. How can the ECMWF justify the expenditure of tens of millions of dollars for a faster computer with all these shortcomings?
2. Do weather forecasting organizations have a responsibility to do a better job of communicating the uncertainty associated with their forecasts? If so, how might this be done effectively?

Critical Thinking Questions

3. Conduct a little research of your own to find out what other forecasting models scientists use. How likely is it that problems exist in these models?
4. If Moore's Law continues in effect until at least 2012, what sort of computers will be available? Will these machines be capable of more accurate forecasts?

Sources: Adapted from Clint Boulton, "BM Supercomputers Tabbed by Agencies," *Internet News*, November 9, 2001, http://www.internetnews.com; Clint Boulton, "IBM Commences Operation 'Blue Storm,'" *Internet News*, December 21, 2001, http://www.internetnews.com; Martin J. Garvey, "IBM to Build Supercomputer to Help Forecast Weather," *InformationWeek*, December 21, 2001, http://www.informationweek.com; John Marchese, "Forecast Hazy," *Discover*, June 21, 2001, pp. 44–51; "Forecasting by Computer," the European Center for Medium-range Weather Forecasts Web site, http://www.ecmwf.int, accessed January 2, 2001.

SUPPORTING INDIVIDUAL, GROUP, AND ORGANIZATIONAL GOALS

Every organization relies on the contributions of individuals, groups, and the entire enterprise to achieve business objectives. To help them achieve these objectives, the organization provides them with specific application software and information systems. One useful way of classifying the many potential uses of information systems is to identify the scope of the problems and opportunities addressed by a particular organization, called the **sphere of influence**. These spheres of influence are personal, workgroup, and enterprise, as shown in Table 2.4.

sphere of influence
the scope of problems and opportunities addressed by a particular organization

Software	Personal	Workgroup	Enterprise
Systems software	Personal computer and workstation operating systems	Network operating systems	Midrange computer and mainframe operating systems
Application software	Word processing, spreadsheet, database, graphics	Electronic mail, group scheduling, shared work	General ledger, order entry, payroll, human resources

TABLE 2.4

Classifying Software by Type and Sphere of Influence

personal productivity software
software that enables users to improve their personal effectiveness, increasing the amount of work they can do and its quality

Information systems that operate within the *personal sphere of influence* serve the needs of an individual user. These information systems enable users to improve their personal effectiveness, increasing the amount of work that can be done and its quality. Such software is often referred to as **personal productivity software**. There are many examples of such applications operating within the personal sphere of influence—a word processing application to enter, check spelling of, edit, copy, print, distribute, and file text material; a spreadsheet application to manipulate numeric data in rows and columns for analysis and decision making; a graphics application to perform data analysis; and a database application to organize data for personal use.

A *workgroup* is two or more people who work together to achieve a common goal. A workgroup may be a large, formal, permanent organizational entity such as a section or department or a temporary group formed to complete a specific project. The human resource department of a large firm is an example of a formal workgroup. It consists of several people, is a formal and permanent organizational entity, and appears on a firm's organization chart. An information system that operates in the *workgroup sphere of influence* supports a workgroup in the attainment of a common goal. Users of such applications are operating in an environment where communication, interaction, and collaboration are critical to the success of the group. Applications include systems that support information sharing, group scheduling, group decision making, and conferencing. These applications enable members of the group to communicate, interact, and collaborate.

Information systems that operate within the *enterprise sphere of influence* support the firm in its interaction with its environment. The surrounding environment includes customers, suppliers, shareholders, competitors, special-interest groups, the financial community, and government agencies. Every enterprise has many applications that operate within the enterprise sphere of influence. The input to these systems is data about or generated by basic business transactions with someone outside the business enterprise. These transactions include customer orders, inventory receipts and withdrawals, purchase orders, freight bills, invoices, and checks. One of the results of processing transaction data is that the records of the company are updated. The order entry, finished product inventory, and billing information systems are examples of applications that operate in the enterprise sphere of influence. These applications support interactions with customers and suppliers.

Regardless of the sphere of influence that software supports, all information systems need software programs to control basic computer functions such as memory management and providing an interface for users. Such software is called *systems software* and is the foundation on which applications are built.

SYSTEMS SOFTWARE

Controlling the operations of computer hardware is one of the most critical functions of systems software. Systems software also supports the application programs' problem-solving capabilities. Different types of systems software include operating systems and utility programs.

OPERATING SYSTEMS

operating system (OS)
a set of computer programs that control the computer hardware and act as an interface to application programs

An **operating system (OS)** is a set of computer programs that control the computer hardware and act as an interface with application programs (Figure 2.13). The operating system, which plays a central role in the functioning of the complete computer system, is usually stored on disk. After a computer system is started, or "booted up," portions of the operating system are transferred to memory as they are needed. The group of programs, collectively called the operating system, executes a variety of activities, including the following:

- Performing common computer hardware functions
- Providing a user interface
- Providing a degree of hardware independence
- Managing system memory
- Managing processing tasks
- Providing networking capability
- Controlling access to system resources
- Managing files

Common Hardware Functions

All application programs must perform certain tasks—for example, getting input from the keyboard or some other input device, retrieving data from disks, storing data on disks, and displaying information on a monitor or printer. Each of these basic functions requires a more detailed set of instructions to complete. The operating system converts a simple, basic instruction into the set of detailed instructions the hardware requires. In effect, the operating system acts as intermediary between the application program and the hardware. The typical OS performs hundreds of such functions, each of which is translated into one or more instructions for the hardware. The OS notifies the user if input/output devices need attention, if an error has occurred, or if anything abnormal occurs in the system.

user interface
element of the operating system that allows individuals to access and command the computer system

command-based user interface
a user interface that requires that text commands be given to the computer to perform basic activities

graphical user interface (GUI)
an interface that uses icons and menus displayed on screen to send commands to the computer system

User Interface

One of the most important functions of any operating system is providing a **user interface**. A user interface allows individuals to access and command the computer system. The first user interfaces for mainframe and personal computer systems were command based.

A **command-based user interface** requires text commands to be given to the computer to perform basic activities. For example, the command ERASE 00TAXRTN would cause the computer to erase or delete a file called 00TAXRTN. RENAME and COPY are other examples of commands used to rename files and copy files from one location to another.

A **graphical user interface (GUI)** uses pictures called *icons* and menus displayed on screen to send commands to the computer system. Many people find that GUIs are easier to use because users intuitively grasp the functions. Today, the most widely used graphical user interface is Windows by Microsoft. As the name suggests, Windows is based on the use of a window, or a portion of the display

FIGURE 2.13

The role of the operating system and other systems software is as an interface or buffer between application software and hardware.

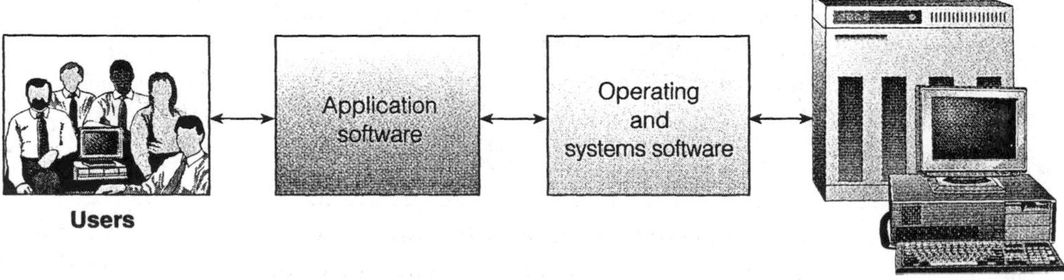

screen dedicated to a specific application. The screen can display several windows at once. The use of GUIs has contributed greatly to the increased use of computers because users no longer need to know command-line syntax to accomplish a task.

Hardware Independence

application program interface (API)
interface that allows applications to make use of the operating system

The applications use the operating system by making requests for services through a defined **application program interface (API),** as shown in Figure 2.14. Programmers can use APIs to create application software without understanding the inner workings of the operating system.

Memory Management

The memory management feature of operating systems converts a user's request for data or instructions (called a *logical view* of the data) to the physical location where the data or instructions are stored. A computer understands only the *physical view* of data—that is, the specific location of the data in storage or memory and the techniques needed to access it. This concept is described as logical versus physical access. For example, the current price of an item, say, a Texas Instruments BA-35 calculator with an item code of TIBA35, might always be found in the logical location "TIBA35$." If the CPU needed to fetch the price of TIBA35 as part of a program instruction, the memory management feature of the operating system would translate the logical location "TIBA35$" into an actual physical location in memory or secondary storage (Figure 2.15).

Processing Tasks

multitasking
capability that allows a user to run more than one application at the same time

time-sharing
capability that allows more than one person to use a computer system at the same time

Task management features of today's operating systems manage all processing activities. Task management allocates computer resources to make the best use of each system's assets. Task management software can permit one user to run several programs or tasks at the same time (multitasking) and allow several users to use the same computer at the same time (time-sharing). With **multitasking,** a user can run more than one application at the same time. Without having to exit a program, you can work in one application, easily pop into another, and then jump back to the first program, picking up where you left off. Better still, while you're working in the *foreground* in one program, one or more other applications can be churning away, unseen, in the *background*—sorting a database, printing a document, or performing other lengthy operations that otherwise would monopolize your computer and leave you staring at the screen unable to get other work done. Multitasking can save users a considerable amount of time and effort.

Time-sharing allows more than one person to use a computer system at the same time. For example, 15 customer service representatives may be entering

FIGURE 2.14

Application Program Interface Links Application Software to the Operating System

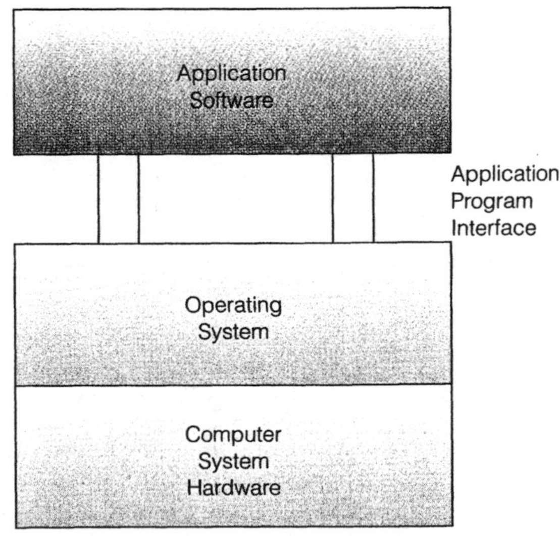

FIGURE 2.15

An Example of the Operating System Controlling Physical Access to Data

The user prompts the application software for specific data. The operating system translates this prompt into instructions for the hardware, which finds the data the user requested. Having completed this task, the operating system then relays the data back to the user via the application software.

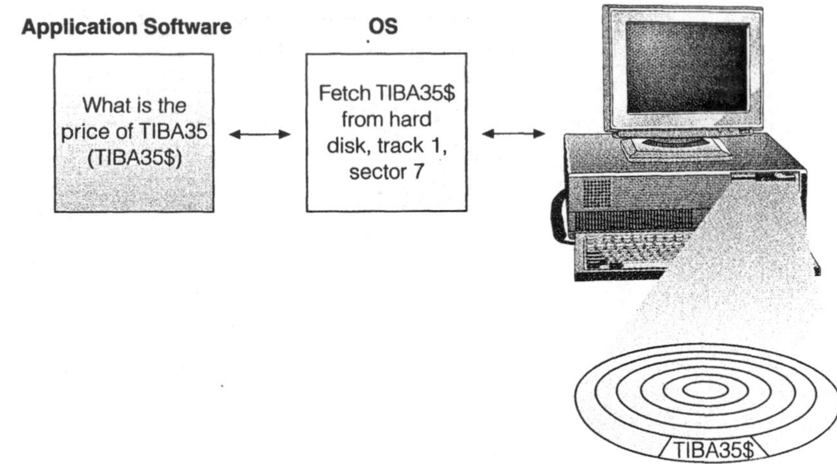

sales data into a computer system for a mail-order company simultaneously. In another case, thousands of people may be simultaneously using an on-line computer service to get stock quotes and valuable business news. Time-sharing works by dividing time into small CPU processing time slices, which can be a few milliseconds or less in duration. During a time slice, some tasks for the first user are done. The computer then goes from that user to the next and completes some tasks for that user during that time slice. This process continues for each user and cycles back to the first user. Because the CPU processing time slices are small, it appears that tasks for all users are being completed at the same time. In reality, each user is sharing the time of the computer with other users.

scalability
the ability of the computer to handle an increasing number of concurrent users smoothly

The ability of the computer to handle an increasing number of concurrent users smoothly is called **scalability**. Scalability is a critical feature for systems that must handle a large number of users, such as a mainframe computer or a Web server. Because personal computer operating systems usually are oriented toward single users, management of multiple-user tasks often is not needed.

Networking Capability

The operating system can provide features and capabilities that aid users in connecting to a computer network. For example, Apple computer users have built-in network access through the AppleTalk feature, and the Microsoft Windows operating systems come with the capability to link users to the Internet.

Access to System Resources

Computers often handle sensitive data that can be accessed over networks, so the operating system needs to provide a high level of security against unauthorized access to users' data and programs. Typically, the operating system establishes a log-on procedure that requires users to enter an identification code and a matching password. If the identification code is invalid or if the password does not match the identification code, the user cannot gain access to the computer. The operating system also requires that user passwords be changed frequently—say, every 30 days. If the user is successful in logging on to the system, the operating system records who is using the system and for how long. In some organizations, such records are also used to bill users for time spent using the system. The operating system also reports any attempted breaches of security.

File Management

The operating system performs a file management function to ensure that files in secondary storage are available when needed and that they are protected from unauthorized access. Many computers support multiple users who store files on centrally located disks or tape drives. The operating system keeps track of where each file is stored and who may access it. The operating system must also be able to resolve what to do if more than one user requests access to the same file at the same time.

PERSONAL COMPUTER OPERATING SYSTEMS

Early operating systems for personal computers were very basic. In the last several years, however, more advanced operating systems have been developed, incorporating some features previously available only with mainframe operating systems. Table 2.5 classifies a number of current operating systems by sphere of influence. This section reviews selected popular personal computer operating systems.

Microsoft PC Operating Systems

There has been a continuous and steady evolution of personal computer operating systems since a formerly small company called Microsoft developed PC-DOS and MS-DOS to support the IBM personal computer, introduced in the 1970s.

TABLE 2.5

Popular Operating Systems

Personal	Workgroup	Enterprise	Consumer
Windows 98			
Windows NT	Windows NT Server	Windows NT Server	
Windows 2000	Windows 2000 Server		
		Windows Advanced Server, Limited Edition	
Windows ME			
Windows XP	Windows XP	Windows XP	Windows XP Embedded
MAC OS			
MAC OS X	MAC OS Server		
Unix	Unix	Unix	
Solaris	Solaris	Solaris	
Linux	Linux	Linux	Linux
Red Hat Linux	Red Hat Linux	Red Hat Linux	
	Netware		
	IBM OS/390	IBM OS/390	
	IBM z/OS	IBM z/OS	
	HP MPE/iX	HP MPE/iX	
			Windows CE.Net
			Pocket PC
			Handheld PC
			Palm OS

Each new version of the operating system has improved in terms of ease of use, processing capability, reliability, and ability to support new computer hardware devices.

Windows 98 let an organization's IS department install and configure the operating system and all applications on one machine and then copy the configuration to each end user's machine. System start-up and shutdown were also speeded up.

The *Windows New Technology (NT) Workstation* operating system was designed to take advantage of the newer 32-bit processors, and it featured multitasking and advanced networking capabilities. NT can also run programs written for other operating systems. NT supports symmetric multiprocessing, the ability to simultaneously use multiple processors. The many features and capabilities of NT made it very attractive for use on many computers. Microsoft renamed the next release of the Windows NT line of operating systems *Windows 2000.* This operating system, with 30 million lines of code, took four years to complete and cost Microsoft more than $1 billion to develop. Microsoft designed Windows 2000 to be easy to use, and it contained many high-level security features and significant enhancements for laptop users. The operating system was also designed to provide high reliability.

Windows Millennium Edition (ME) was designed for home use and enables even novice computer users to organize photos, make home movies and records, and play music, as well as the usual computer tasks such as accessing the Internet, playing games, and performing word processing.

Windows XP (XP reportedly stands for the wonderful experience that you will have with your personal computer) was released in fall 2001. Previous consumer versions of Windows were notably unstable and crashed frequently, requiring frustrating and time-consuming reboots. With XP, Microsoft hopes to bring the reliability of Windows 2000 to the consumer. The operating system is enormous—requiring more than 2 GB of hard drive space and more than an hour to install. It only works well on personal computers with at least 128 megabytes of RAM and a 400 MHz or faster processor. Its redesigned icons, task bar, and window borders make for more pleasant viewing. The Start menu is two columns wide, with recently used programs in the left column and everything else (e.g., My Documents, My Computer, and Control Panel) in the right column. It comes with Internet Explorer 6 browser software, which boasts improved security and reliability features, including a one-way firewall that blocks hacker invasions coming in from the Internet. It also offers fast user switching, a feature that essentially allows multiple users to share the computer. With fast user switching, one user can stop what he or she is doing and allow another user to log on to the same PC—without making the first user close applications, save files, and log off. Users can specify that certain files and folders not be accessible to other users sharing the computer.

Apple Computer PC Operating Systems

While IBM system platforms traditionally use Intel microprocessors and one of the Windows operating systems, Apple computers typically use Motorola microprocessors and a proprietary Apple operating system—the Mac OS. Although IBM and IBM-compatible computers hold the largest share of the business PC market, Apple computers are also quite popular, especially in the fields of publishing, education, and graphic arts. The Apple operating systems have also evolved over a number of years and often provide features not available from Microsoft.

The *MAC OS X* ("Ten") operating system is a completely new implementation of the Mac operating system that includes an entirely new user interface called "Aqua," which provides a new visual appearance for users—including luminous and semitransparent elements such as buttons, scroll bars, windows, and fluid animation to enhance the user's experience. One goal of the new software is to provide an extremely stable computing environment. It also comes with new features like automatic networking and an instant wake-from-sleep capability for portable computers.[17] Cline, Davis & Mann Inc., a New York advertising agency, specializes in healthcare industry campaigns with major pharmaceutical clients such as Pfizer (Viagra), GlaxoSmithKline (Serevent, an asthma inhaler), and Janssen Pharmaceutica (Risperdal for schizophrenia and Reminyl for Alzheimer's disease). About 90 percent of the computers for the ad agency's 360 employees are Macs, which are used mainly for graphics and creative work. The firm moved to Mac OS X to take advantage of the improved reliability and new features.[18]

Linux

Linux is an operating system whose source code is freely available to everyone. This doesn't mean, however, that Linux and its assorted distributions are free—companies and developers may charge money for it as long as the source code remains available. Linux is actually only the *kernel* of an operating system, the part that controls hardware, manages files, separates processes, and so forth. Several combinations of Linux are available with sets of utilities and applications to form a complete operating system. Each of these combinations is called a *distribution* of Linux.

WORKGROUP OPERATING SYSTEMS

To keep pace with today's high-tech society, the technology of the future must support a world in which network usage, data storage requirements, and data processing speeds increase at a dramatic rate. This rapid increase in communications and data processing capabilities pushes the boundaries of computer science and physics. Powerful and sophisticated operating systems are needed to run the servers that meet these business needs for workgroups.

Windows 2000 Server

Microsoft designed *Windows 2000 Server* to do a host of new tasks that are vital for Web sites and corporate Web applications on the Internet. Besides being more reliable than Windows NT, this operating system is capable of handling extremely demanding computer tasks such as order processing. It can be tuned to run on machines with up to 32 microprocessors—satisfying the needs of all but the most demanding of Web operators. Four machines can be clustered together to prevent service interruptions, which are disastrous for Web sites. With Windows 2000, Microsoft introduced Active Directory, which lets corporations keep track of every employee, computer, software package, and even scrap of data in one place.

Unix

Unix is a powerful operating system originally developed by AT&T for minicomputers. Unix can be used on many computer system types and platforms, from personal computers to mainframe systems. Unix also makes it much easier to move programs and data among computers or to connect mainframes and personal computers to share resources. Unix is considered to have a complex user interface with strange and arcane commands, so software developers have provided shells such as Motif from Open Systems Foundation and Open Look from Sun Microsystems. These shells provide a graphical user interface and shield the users from the complexity of the underlying operating system. There are many variants of Unix, including HP/UX from Hewlett-Packard, AIX from IBM, UNIX SystemV from UNIX Systems Lab, and SCO from Santa Cruz Operations.

Solaris is the Sun Microsystems variation of the Unix operating system, and Solaris is the current server operating system of choice for large Web sites. Solaris is highly reliable and handles the most demanding tasks. It can supervise servers with as many as 64 microprocessors, and eight such computers can be clustered together to work as one. The Solaris operating system can run on Sun's Sparc family of microprocessors, as well as computers with Intel microprocessors. An example of the unique features of Solaris is fault detection and analysis that lets IS administrators establish policies for problematic conditions. For example, if a processor gets too hot, the capability may instruct a system to shut down the processor and reboot.

Cleveland-based paint manufacturer and retailer Sherwin-Williams is deploying IBM PCs running the Turbolinux operating system to replace existing Unix-based systems. Under the multimillion-dollar deal, IBM is installing nearly 10,000 desktop personal computers—along with monitors, printers, cash drawers, and related products—in 2,500 Sherwin-Williams stores across North America. The new Turbolinux-equipped systems run all store functions, including customer transactions, inventory management, and software applications used for paint mixing and tinting.[19]

NetWare

NetWare is a network operating system sold by Novell that can support end users on Windows, Macintosh, and Unix platforms. NetWare provides directory software to track computers, programs, and people on a network, making it easier for large companies to manage complex networks. NetWare users can log in from any computer on the network and still get their own familiar desktop with all their applications, data, and preferences.

Red Hat Linux

Red Hat Software offers the *Red Hat Linux* network operating system, which taps into the talents of tens of thousands of volunteer programmers who generate a steady stream of improvements for the Linux operating system. The Red Hat Linux network operating system is very efficient at serving up Web pages and can manage a cluster of up to eight servers. Burlington Coat Factory needed a new operating system on more than 1,250 of its personal computers to support functions such as shipping, receiving, and order processing at 250 stores. Red Hat Linux was chosen because the operating system is inexpensive and runs on standard industry hardware, so that any risks were minimal. In addition, Linux environments typically have fewer virus and security problems than other operating systems. Red Hat Linux has proven to be a very stable and efficient operating system—it doesn't crash.[20]

Mac OS X Server

The *Mac OS X Server* is the first modern server operating system from Apple Computer. It provides Unix-style process management. Protected memory puts each service in its own well-guarded chunk of dynamically allocated memory, preventing a single process from going awry and bringing down the system or other services. Preemptive multitasking ensures that each process gets the right amount of CPU time and the system resources it needs for optimal efficiency and responsiveness.

Red Hat Linux 7.2 is a network operating system from Red Hat Software.

(Source: Box shot copyright © 2002 Red Hat, Inc. All rights reserved. Reprinted with permission from Red Hat, Inc.)

ENTERPRISE OPERATING SYSTEMS

The new generation of mainframe computers provides the computing and storage capacity to meet massive data processing requirements and provide a large number of users with high performance and excellent system availability, strong security, and scalability. In addition, a wide range of application software has been developed to run in the mainframe environment, making it possible to purchase software to address almost any business problem. As a result, mainframe computers remain the computing platform of choice for mission-critical business applications for many companies. *OS/390* and *z/OS* from IBM, *MPE/iX* from Hewlett-Packard, and *Red Hat Linux* are examples of mainframe operating systems.

In recognition of the widespread popularity of a competing operating system, z/OS allows partitions to run a version of the Linux operating system. Russell Corporation, an apparel maker in Atlanta, recently upgraded from an

IBM S/390 mainframe to a z800 mainframe computer. The company was attracted by the z800's faster processor speed and support for up to 32 GB of memory. In addition, Russell can use the z800 to run the Linux operating system if it decides to adopt the open-source operating system because of the virtual partitioning technology that IBM ships with its zSeries mainframes.[21] Z/OS also makes it safer to run Internet and intranet applications by providing new intrusion-detection services and support for services that are frequently used in e-commerce applications.[22]

The Red Hat Software Linux mainframe operating system is optimized for IBM's S/390 Parallel Enterprise and Multiprise 3000 servers, but it can also run on the IBM's zSeries 800 and 900 servers. This version of Red Hat Linux means that the company now has Linux versions for everything from handheld devices to the largest enterprise mainframes.[23]

CONSUMER APPLIANCE OPERATING SYSTEMS

New operating systems and other software are changing the way we interact with personal digital assistants (PDAs), mobile phones, digital cameras, TVs, and other appliances. Here are some of the more popular operating systems for such devices.

Windows CE.Net

Windows CE.Net is an embedded operating system for use in mobile devices, such as smart phones and PDAs, and can also be used in a variety of other devices, such as digital cameras, thin clients, TV set-top boxes, and automotive computers. PDAs with Windows CE try to bring as much of the functionality of a desktop PC as possible to a handheld device.[24] Microsoft hopes to entice hardware developers away from using rival operating systems such as Linux by providing both tools to customize Windows CE.Net to a specific device and specific software applications. Such features could enable hardware developers to get their products to market faster.[25]

Windows XP Embedded

The *Windows XP Embedded* operating system is used in devices such as handheld computers, TV set-top boxes, and automated industrial machines. It is based on Microsoft's Windows XP Professional desktop operating system and includes more than 10,000 software components, including such features as a built-in chat feature, which is Microsoft's answer to America Online Inc.'s popular Instant Messaging, and support for several network variations. As with Windows CE.Net, hardware developers can choose the pieces of the operating system they need for certain devices.[26]

Handheld PC

Handheld PC is a Microsoft operating system designed to manage a wide range of Windows-powered mobile devices including the Pocket PC and Handheld PCs. The operating system supports forms-based applications used for data collection, connects the user to a server to run desktop applications, and enables connections to the Internet.

Pocket PC

Pocket PC 2002 provides several features including handwriting recognition, the ability to beam information to devices running either Pocket PC or Palm Inc.'s competing operating system, Microsoft's instant messaging technology, and support for more secure Internet connections.[27] In June 2002, China Merchants Bank and Legend Group Ltd. began offering on-line banking services for Chinese users of Legend's Tianji XP personal digital assistant (PDA) as part of an effort to improve the bank's service. The PDA uses Microsoft's Pocket PC 2002 software and provides the ability to check account balances, transfer funds, and trade securities on-line. The service can be accessed over any Internet connection.[28]

Palm OS

The strategy Palm has taken with its *Palm OS* operating system and Palm PDA is to extend these devices from single-purpose schedule managers to more general-purpose devices. The company has added features to allow better integration with desktop PCs and enabled users to add applications to the device. Such flexibility has enabled the Palm to remain relatively easy to use while adding some expandability and capability as a general-purpose computing platform. Palm has licensed its operating system to major chip makers including Intel, Motorola, and Texas Instruments for use in all kinds of mobile devices, from handheld computers to cell phones (Figure 2.16) and even wristwatches. Office Depot completed a yearlong nationwide rollout of wireless devices containing the Palm OS to its 2,000 truck drivers. Drivers use the system to scan shipments, create an electronic manifest as deliveries are loaded on a truck, and capture customer signatures electronically. Future enhancements include enabling customers to track the status of their orders via its Web site.[29]

APPLICATION SOFTWARE

proprietary software
a one-of-a-kind program for a specific application

off-the-shelf software
existing software program

contract software
software developed for a particular company

As discussed earlier, the primary function of application software is to apply the power of a computer to give individuals, workgroups, and the entire enterprise the ability to solve problems and perform specific tasks. Application programs perform those specific computer tasks by interacting with systems software to direct the computer hardware. Programs that complete sales orders, control inventory, pay bills, write paychecks to employees, and provide financial and marketing information to managers and executives are examples of application software. Most of the computerized business jobs and activities discussed in this book involve the use of application software.

TYPES AND FUNCTIONS OF APPLICATION SOFTWARE

The key to unlocking the potential of any computer system is application software. A company can either develop a one-of-a-kind program for a specific application (called **proprietary software**) or purchase and use an existing software program (sometimes called **off-the-shelf software**). It is also possible to modify some off-the-shelf programs, giving a blend of off-the-shelf and customized approaches. These different sources of software are shown in Figure 2.17. The relative advantages and disadvantages of proprietary software and off-the-shelf software are summarized in Table 2.6.

FIGURE 2.16

Not only is the new Nokia 7650 a phone, it's also an integrated imaging device. Point, use the color display as a viewfinder, and snap a picture. Images can be stored on the device and sent to a friend.

(Source: Courtesy of Nokia.)

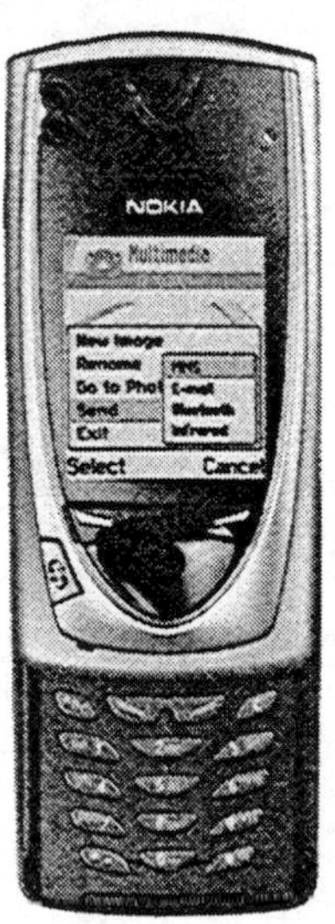

Proprietary Application Software

Software to solve a unique or specific problem is called *proprietary application software*. This type of software is usually built, but it can also be purchased from an outside company. If an organization has the time and IS talent, it may opt for *in-house development* for all aspects of the application programs. Alternatively, an organization may obtain customized software from external vendors. For example, a third-party software firm, often called a *value-added software vendor*, may develop or modify a software program to meet the needs of a particular industry or company. A specific software program developed for a particular company is called **contract software**.

Off-the-Shelf Application Software

Software can also be purchased, leased, or rented from a software company that develops programs and sells them to many computer users and organizations. Software programs developed for a general market are called off-the-shelf software packages because they can literally be purchased "off the shelf" in a store. Many companies use off-the-shelf software to support business processes.

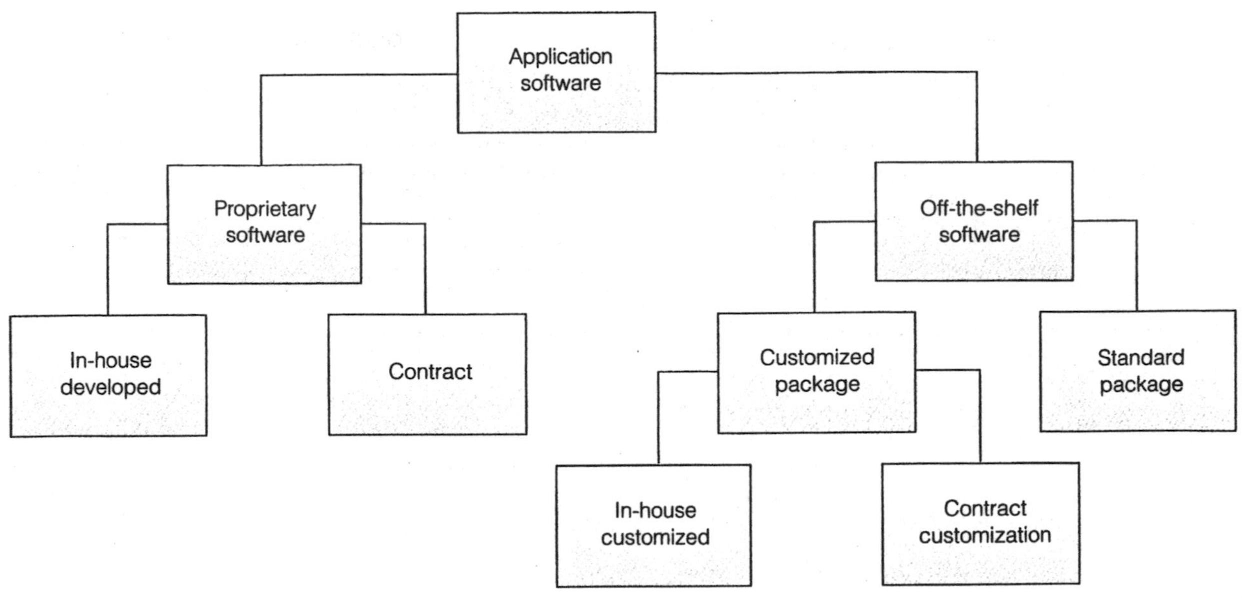

FIGURE 2.17

Sources of Software: Proprietary and Off-the-Shelf

Some off-the-shelf software may be modified to allow some customization.

Customized Package

In some cases, companies use a blend of external and internal software development. That is, off-the-shelf software packages are modified or customized by in-house or external personnel. For example, a software developer may write a collection of programs to be used in an auto body shop that includes features to generate estimates, order parts, and process insurance. Designed properly—and allowing for minor tailoring for each body shop—the same software package can be sold to many businesses. However, since each body shop has slightly different requirements, software vendors would probably provide a wide range of services, including installation of their standard software, modifications for unique customer needs, training of end users, and other consulting services.

Some software companies encourage their customers to make changes to their software and will sometimes make the necessary changes themselves for a fee. Other software companies will not allow their software to be modified by those purchasing or renting it.

application service provider (ASP)
a company that provides both end-user support and the computers on which to run the software from the user's facilities

Another approach to obtaining a customized software package is to use an **application service provider (ASP)**—a company that provides both end-user support and the computers on which to run the software from the user's facilities. Such companies can also simplify a complex corporate software package for users so that it is easier to set up and manage. ASPs also provide contract customization of off-the-shelf software, assist in speeding deployment of new applications, and help IS managers avoid implementation headaches, reducing the need for skilled IS staff members and reducing project start-up expenses. Perhaps the biggest advantage of employing an application service provider is that it frees in-house corporate resources from staffing and managing complex computing projects so that they can focus on more important things.

Using an application service provider is not without risks—sensitive information could be compromised in a number of ways, including unauthorized access by employees or computer hackers, the application service provider being unable to keep its computers and network up and running as consistently as is needed, or a disaster disabling the application service provider's data center, temporarily putting an organization out of business. These are legitimate concerns that the application service provider must address.

Proprietary Software		Off-the-Shelf Software	
Advantages	**Disadvantages**	**Advantages**	**Disadvantages**
You can get exactly what you need in terms of features, reports, and so on.	It can take a long time and significant resources to develop required features.	The initial cost is lower since the software firm is able to spread the development costs over a large number of customers.	An organization might have to pay for features that are not required and never used.
Being involved in the development offers a further level of control over the results.	In-house system development staff may become hard pressed to provide the required level of ongoing support and maintenance because of pressure to get on to other new projects.	There is a lower risk that the software will fail to meet the basic business needs—you can analyze existing features and the performance of the package.	The software may lack important features, thus requiring future modification or customization. This can be very expensive because users must adopt future releases of the software as well.
There is more flexibility in making modifications that may be required to counteract a new initiative by one of your competitors or to meet new supplier and/or customer requirements. A merger with another firm or an acquisition also will necessitate software changes to meet new business needs.	There is more risk concerning the features and performance of the software that has yet to be developed.	Package is likely to be of high quality since many customer firms have tested the software and helped identify many of its bugs.	Software may not match current work processes and data standards.

TABLE 2.6

A Comparison of Proprietary and Off-the-Shelf Software

Ingersoll-Rand Co. is an industrial and commercial equipment manufacturer with recent annual sales in excess of $9 billion. In May 2002, it rolled out a hosted version of Oracle software to 1,000 of its shared services employees, with the help of application service provider Corio, Inc. Ingersoll's shared services employees manage finances, human resources, and procurement for several departments within the company. Under the terms of the five-year contract, Corio runs the application from one of its data centers in San Jose, California, and provides access to Ingersoll-Rand's shared services employees worldwide.[30]

PERSONAL APPLICATION SOFTWARE

Literally hundreds of computer applications exist to help individuals at school, home, and work. For example, a graphics program can help a sales manager develop an attractive sales presentation to give at the annual sales meeting. A spreadsheet program allows a financial executive to test possible investment outcomes. The primary personal application programs are word processing, spreadsheet analysis, database, graphics, and on-line services. Advanced software tools—such as project management, financial management, desktop publishing, and creativity software—are finding more and more use in business. The features of personal application software are summarized in Table 2.7.

In addition, there are literally thousands of other personal computer applications to perform specialized tasks: to help you do your taxes, get in shape, lose weight, get medical advice, write wills and other legal documents, repair your

Type of Software	Explanation	Example	Vendor
Word processing	Creates, edits, and prints text documents	Word WordPerfect	Microsoft Corel
Spreadsheet	Provides a wide range of built-in functions for statistical, financial, logical, database, graphics, and data and time calculations	Excel Lotus 1-2-3 Quattro Pro	Microsoft Lotus/IBM Originally developed by Borland
Database	Stores, manipulates, and retrieves data	Access Approach FoxPro dBASE	Microsoft Lotus/IBM Microsoft Borland
On-line information services	Obtains a broad range of information from commercial services	America Online CompuServe Prodigy	America Online CompuServe Prodigy
Graphics	Develops graphs, illustrations, and drawings	Illustrator FreeHand	Adobe Macromedia
Project management	Plans, schedules, allocates, and controls people and resources (money, time, and technology) needed to complete a project according to schedule	Project for Windows On Target Project Schedule Time Line	Microsoft Symantec Scitor Symantec
Financial management	Provides income and expense tracking and reporting to monitor and plan budgets (some programs have investment portfolio management features)	Managing Your Money Quicken	Meca Software Intuit
Desktop publishing (DTP)	Works with personal computers and high-resolution printers to create high-quality printed output, including text and graphics; various styles of pages can be laid out; art and text files from other programs can also be integrated into "published" pages	QuarkXPress Publisher PageMaker Ventura Publisher	Quark Microsoft Adobe Corel
Creativity	Helps generate innovative and creative ideas and problem solutions. The software does not propose solutions, but provides a framework conducive to creative thought. The software takes users through a routine, first naming a problem, then organizing ideas and "wishes," and offering new information to suggest different ideas or solutions	Organizer Notes	Macromedia Lotus

TABLE 2.7

Examples of Personal Productivity Software

computer, fix your car, write music, and edit your pictures and videos (see Figures 2.18 and 2.19). This type of software, often called *user software* or *personal productivity software,* includes general-purpose tools and programs that support individual needs.

Word Processing

If you write reports, letters, or term papers, word processing applications can be indispensable. Word processing applications can be used to create, edit, and print documents (Figure 2.20). Most come with a vast array of features, including those for checking spelling, creating tables, inserting formulas, creating graphics,

FIGURE 2.18

TurboTax

Tax preparation programs can save hours of work and are typically more accurate than doing a tax return by hand. Programs can check for potential problems and give you help and advice about what you may have forgotten to deduct.

(Source: Courtesy of Intuit.)

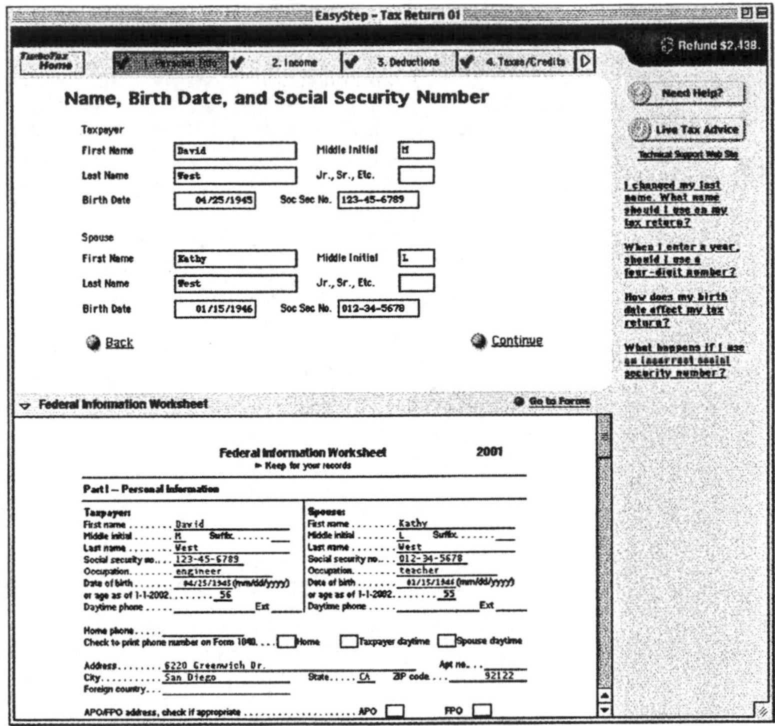

and much more. This book (and most like it) was entered into a word processing application using a personal computer.

Spreadsheet Analysis

People use spreadsheets to prepare budgets, forecast profits, analyze insurance programs, summarize income tax data, and analyze investments. Whenever numbers and calculations are involved, spreadsheets should be considered. Features of spreadsheets include graphics, limited database capabilities, statistical analysis, built-in business functions, and much more (Figure 2.21).

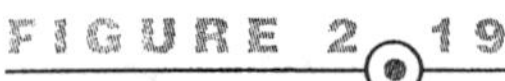

FIGURE 2.19

Quicken

Off-the-shelf financial management programs are useful for paying bills and tracking expenses.

(Source: Courtesy of Intuit.)

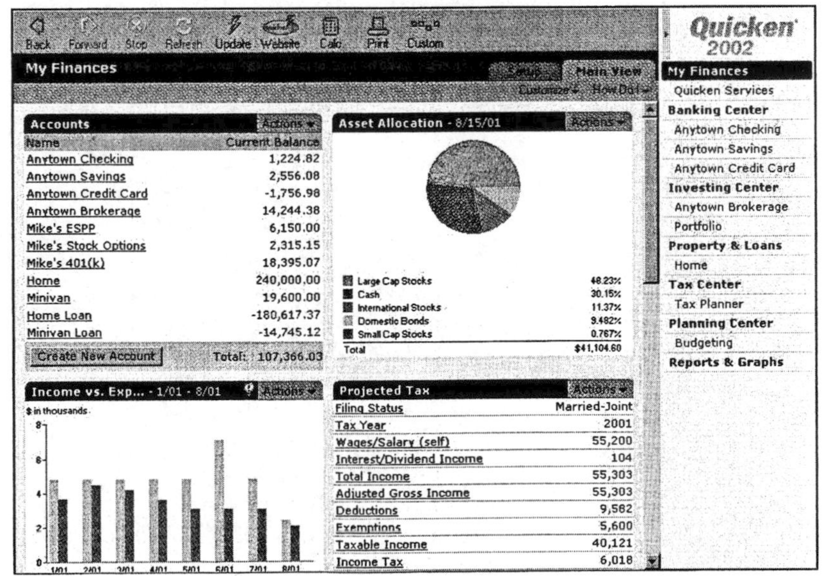

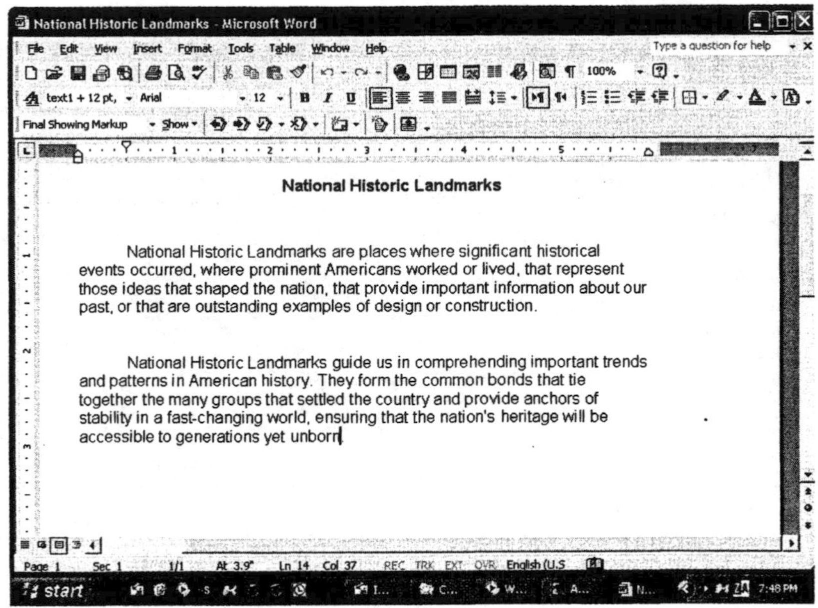

FIGURE 2.20

Word Processing Program

Word processing applications can be used to write letters, holiday greeting cards, work reports, and term papers.

Database Applications

Database applications are ideal for storing, manipulating, and retrieving data. These applications are particularly useful when you need to access a large amount of data and produce reports and documents. The uses of a database application are varied. You can keep track of a CD collection, the items in your apartment, and tax records using a database application. In business, a database application can help process sales orders, control inventory, order new supplies, send letters to customers, and pay employees. A database can also be a front end to another application. For example, a database application can be used to enter and store income tax information. The stored results can then be exported to other applications, such as a spreadsheet or tax preparation application (Figure 2.22).

FIGURE 2.21

Spreadsheet Program

Spreadsheet programs should be considered when calculations are required.

Microsoft Excel - Book Warehouse Inventory

	A	B	C	D	E	F	G
1	Catalog No.	Description	Price	Current Inventory	Current Inventory Value	Inventory Reorder Point	
2	0-590-84735-X	A Guide to National Parks	$29.95	4320	$129,384.00	4000	
3	1-55858-024-7	Tracing Your Geneology	$99.95	652	$65,167.40	600	
4	1-55858-092-1	History of Our Flag	$17.95	232	$4,164.40	200	
5	1-55858-024-7	Women in History	$59.95	192	$11,510.40	200	
6	0-316-18820-4	Computer Security	$27.95	542	$15,148.90	400	
7	0-670-82238-8	Modern Décor	$22.95	365	$8,376.75	300	
8	1-57064-043-2	Nutrition	$43.95	241	$10,591.95	200	
9	0-590-45855-8	Engineering Marvels	$35.95	854	$30,701.30	800	
10	1-85714-046-X	Managing Your Finances	$43.95	795	$34,940.25	700	
11	0-15-207124-5	Music of the 21st Century	$62.95	864	$54,388.80	800	
12	0-399-22421-1	Creating a Winning Webpage	$21.95	1654	$36,305.30	1000	
13	0-399-21395-3	Time Management Skills	$21.95	4613	$101,255.35	4000	
14	0-399-23208-7	Networking Know-How	$19.95	631	$12,588.45	600	
15	0-8167-1091-0	Natural Fractals	$28.95	1185	$34,305.75	1000	
16	0-14-050534-2	El Nino!	$32.95	584	$19,242.80	500	
17	0-590-43172-2	The History of Dance	$39.95	6921	$276,493.95	6000	
18	0-590-40264-1	Gothic Architecture	$29.95	1486	$44,505.70	1000	
19	0-590-41800-9	Touring Finland	$17.95	1583	$28,414.85	1000	

Sheet1 / Sheet2 / Sheet3

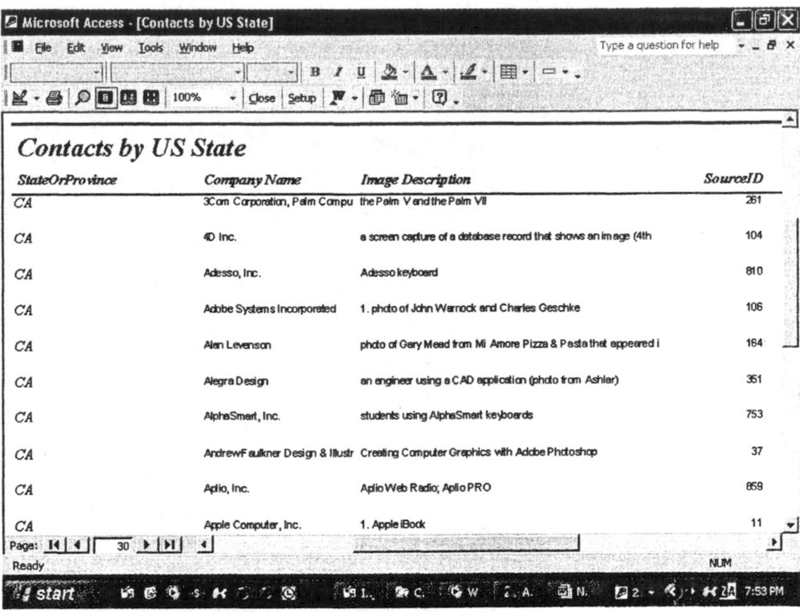

FIGURE 2.22

Database Program

Once entered into a database application, information can be manipulated and used to produce reports and documents.

Graphics Programs

With today's graphics programs, it is easy to develop attractive graphs, illustrations, and drawings. Graphics programs can be used to develop advertising brochures, announcements, and full-color presentations. If you are asked to make a presentation at school or work, you can use a graphics program to develop and display slides while you are giving your talk. A graphics program can be used to help you make a presentation, a drawing, or an illustration (Figure 2.23).

Software Suites

software suite
a collection of single-application software packages in a bundle

A **software suite** is a collection of single-application software packages in a bundle. Software suites can include word processors, spreadsheets, database management systems, graphics programs, communications tools, organizers, and more. There are a number of advantages to using a software suite. The software programs have been designed to work similarly, so once you learn the basics for one application, the other applications are easier to learn and use. Buying software in a bundled suite is cost-effective: the programs usually sell for a fraction of what they would cost individually.

FIGURE 2.23

Graphics Program

Graphics programs can help you make a presentation at school or work. They can also be used to develop attractive brochures, illustrations, drawings, and maps.

(Source: Courtesy of Adobe Systems, Incorporated.)

Microsoft Office, Corel's WordPerfect Office, Lotus SmartSuite, and Sun Microsystems's StarOffice are examples of popular general-purpose software suites for personal computer users (Table 2.8). Each of these software suites includes a spreadsheet program, word processor, database program, and graphics package with the ability to move documents, data, and diagrams among them. Thus, a user can create a spreadsheet and then cut and paste that spreadsheet into a document created using the word processing application.

Since one or more applications in a suite may not be as desirable as the others, some people still prefer to buy separate packages. Another issue with the use of software suites is the large amount of main memory required to run them effectively. For example, many users find that they must spend hundreds of dollars for additional internal memory to upgrade their personal computer to be able to run a software suite.

WORKGROUP APPLICATION SOFTWARE

Workgroup application software, often called *groupware,* helps groups of people work together more efficiently and effectively toward a common goal. Such software can support a team of managers working on the same production problem, letting them share their ideas and work via connected computer systems. Examples of such software include group scheduling software, electronic mail, and other software that enables people to share ideas. Read the "IS Principles in Action" special feature to learn more about collaborative computing software.

Lotus Notes and Domino

Lotus, now a division of IBM, has defined *knowledge management* as the ability to provide individuals and groups of users with a method to find, access, and deliver valuable information in a coherent fashion. Its Lotus Notes product is an attempt to provide this ability. Lotus Notes gives companies the capability of using one software package, and one user interface, to integrate many business processes. For example, it can allow a global team to work together from a shared set of documents, have electronic discussions using common threads of discussion, and schedule team meetings. As Lotus Notes matured, Lotus added services to it and renamed it Domino, and now an entire market has emerged to build collaborative software based on Domino. For example, Domino.Doc is a Domino-based document management application with built-in workflow and archiving capabilities. Its "life cycle" feature tracks a document through the review, approval, publishing, and archiving processes. Similarly, the workflow integration adds support for multiple roles, log tracking, and distributed approval.

Group Scheduling

Group scheduling is another form of workgroup software, but not all software schedulers approach their tasks the same way. Some schedulers, known as personal information managers (PIMs), tend to focus on personal schedules and

TABLE 2.8

Major Components of Leading Software Suites

Personal Productivity Function	Microsoft Office XP	Lotus SmartSuite Millennium Edition	Corel WordPerfect Office 2002	Sun Microsystems
Word Processing	Word	WordPro	WordPerfect	Writer
Spreadsheet	Excel	Lotus 1-2-3	Quattro Pro	Calc
Presentations	PowerPoint	Freelance Graphics	Presentations	Impress
Database	Access	Lotus Approach	Paradox	

IS Principles in Action

PRINCIPLE

Organizations do not develop proprietary application software unless doing so will meet a compelling business need that can provide a competitive advantage.

Honda Uses Collaboration Software to Speed Product Development

Honda is the world's largest motorcycle maker and Japan's third largest automaker behind Toyota and Nissan. It also has a power products division that manufactures lawn mowers, snow blowers, portable generators, and outboard motors. The company's car models include the Accord, Acura, Civic, Legend, Prelude, and Insight—a gasoline-electric hybrid.

The automobile industry is intensely competitive, with manufacturers facing cut-throat global competition. They are under pressure to reduce costs to the minimum and pass the savings along to customers. They must also reduce the time to produce new models that appeal to customers in many parts of the world while tailoring automobiles to customer specifications. To overcome these challenges, manufacturers are turning over an increasing portion of their design, development, production, and customer-support activities to multiple suppliers and other business partners. Such collaborative product development is changing the way Honda brings products to market.

The research and development activities for Honda use software called eMatrix from MatrixOne to support collaborative product development. This Internet-based system helps document and manage the product's bill of materials (BOM)—a list that describes all components of the finished product, such as part numbers, quantity, measurements, and labor and material costs. An accurate and complete BOM is critical to the manufacturing process—any mistake can cost the manufacturer in loss of labor and materials and valuable time-to-market.

eMatrix enables Honda research and design engineers to share design information from the early stages of product development so that the accuracy of the engineering BOM is greatly improved. The system supports engineers as they manage and configure all the details that go into a product: basic car design, options, features, local variations, components and larger assembled parts, specifications, supporting documentation, costs, and engineering changes. The single, accurate view of the engineering BOM across all organizations involved in the product ensures that most design and development issues are identified and resolved earlier in the design and manufacturing cycle. Such coordination leads to the early detection and resolution of many problems—saving time and resources. The bottom line is higher quality, decreased costs, and the ability to bring automobiles to market faster.

The eMatrix system is being deployed in multiple stages with the ultimate goal of linking Honda's global research and design activities wherever they are located. The first phase of the rollout was completed in October 2001 and connected several thousand design engineers throughout Japan, the United States, the United Kingdom, and Thailand. The software vendor, MatrixOne, partnered with Fujitsu to deploy the eMatrix platform and integrate it with Honda's other key information systems.

Discussion Questions

1. Product design has always been a collaborative process. How has Honda brought collaboration to a new level?
2. Why is the BOM such a critical element of collaborative product development?

Critical Thinking Questions

3. Why did Honda resort to a software package to support this critical business process rather than develop a custom application to meet its needs?
4. What issues do you anticipate Honda must overcome in trying to implement this standard software to support its worldwide research and design activities?

Sources: Adapted from Antone Gonsalves, "It's the Tiger in Their Tanks," *InformationWeek*, September 17, 2001, http://www.informationweek.com; Demir Sarias, "Honda's E-Business Strategy," *Line 56*, December 11, 2001, http://www.line56.com; Honda Motor Co., Ltd., Company Report, http://www.moneycentral.msn.com, accessed December 28, 2001; "Automotive Solutions," MatrixOne Web site, http://www.matrixone.com, accessed December 28, 2001; "MatrixOne Solutions Drive New Paradigm for Automobile Design at Honda," About Us, Press Box, MatrixOne Web site, http://www.matrixone.com, accessed December 28, 2001.

lists, as opposed to coordinating the schedules and meetings of a team or group. Schedulers do not suit everyone's needs, and if they are not truly required, they could impede efficiency.

ENTERPRISE APPLICATION SOFTWARE

Software that benefits the entire organization can also be developed or purchased. A fast-food chain, for example, might develop a materials ordering and distribution program to make sure that each fast-food franchise gets the necessary raw materials and supplies during the week. This materials ordering and distribution program can be developed internally using staff and resources in the IS department or purchased from an external software company. Table 2.9 lists a number of applications that can be addressed with enterprise software.

TABLE 2.9

Examples of Enterprise Application Software

Accounts receivable	Sales ordering
Accounts payable	Order entry
Airline industry operations	Payroll
Automatic teller systems	Human resource management
Cash-flow analysis	Check processing
Credit and charge card administration	Tax planning and preparation
Manufacturing control	Receiving
Distribution control	Restaurant management
General ledger	Retail operations
Stock and bond management	Invoicing
Savings and time deposits	Shipping
Inventory control	Fixed asset accounting

Many organizations are moving to integrated enterprise software that supports supply chain management (movement of raw materials from suppliers through shipment of finished goods to customers), as shown in Figure 2.24.

Organizations can no longer respond to market changes using nonintegrated information systems based on overnight processing of yesterday's business transactions, conflicting data models, and obsolete technology. As a result, many corporations are turning to *enterprise resource planning (ERP)* software, a set of integrated programs that manage a company's vital business operations for an entire multisite, global organization. An ERP system must be able to support multiple legal entities, multiple languages, and multiple currencies. Although the scope of an ERP system varies from vendor to vendor, most ERP systems provide integrated software to support manufacturing and finance. In addition to these

FIGURE 2.24

Use of Integrated Supply Chain Management Software

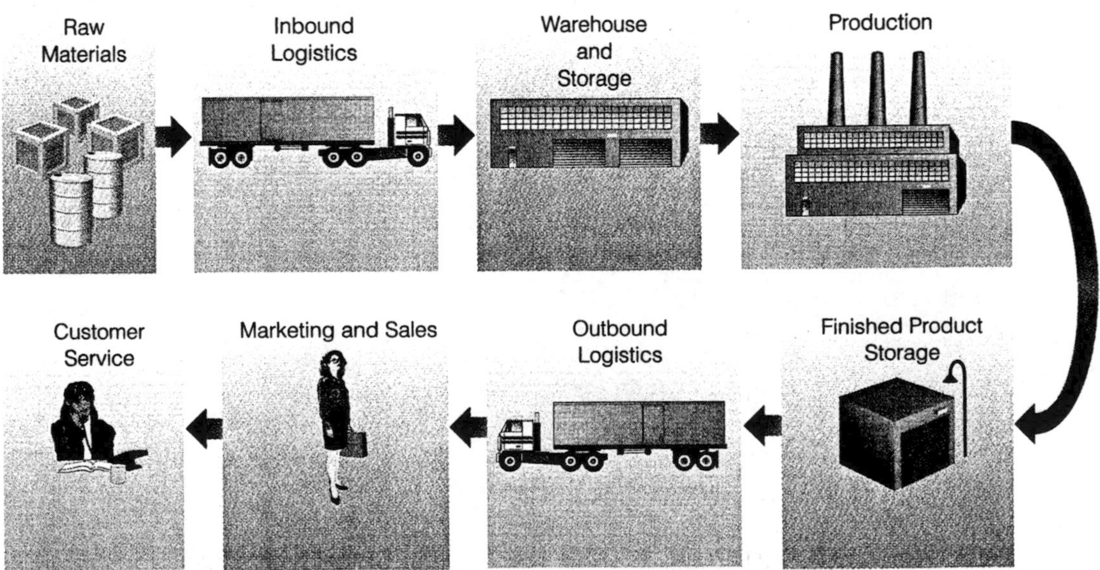

Integrated Enterprise Software to Support Supply Chain Management

core business processes, some ERP systems support additional business functions such as human resources, sales, and distribution. Software vendors that provide integrated enterprise software are listed in Table 2.10.

Most ERP vendors specialize in software that addresses the needs of well-defined markets, such as automotive, semiconductor, petrochemical, and food/beverage manufacturers, with solutions targeted to meet their specific needs. Increased global competition, new executive management needs for control over the total cost and product flow through their enterprises, and more customer interactions are driving the demand for enterprisewide access to current business information. ERP offers integrated software from a single vendor that helps meet those needs. The primary benefits of implementing ERP include eliminating inefficient systems, easing adoption of improved work processes, improving access to data for operational decision making, standardizing technology vendors and equipment, and enabling the implementation of supply chain management.

Now that we have discussed the software that businesses use to accomplish their daily tasks, we turn to a brief discussion of programming languages—the programs that IS professionals—and even everyday users today—can use to write new applications.

PROGRAMMING LANGUAGES

programming languages
coding schemes used to write both systems and application software

syntax
a set of rules associated with a programming language

Both systems and application software are written in coding schemes called **programming languages.** The primary function of a programming language is to provide instructions to the computer system so that it can perform a processing activity. IS professionals work with programming languages, which are sets of symbols and rules used to write program code. Programming involves translating what a user wants to accomplish into instructions that the computer can understand and execute. Like writing a report or a paper in English, writing a computer program in a programming language requires that the programmer follow a set of rules. Each programming language uses a set of symbols that have special meaning. Each language also has its own set of rules, called the **syntax** of the language. The language syntax dictates how the symbols should be combined into statements capable of conveying meaningful instructions to the CPU. The desire to use the power of information processing efficiently in problem solving has pushed development of literally thousands of programming languages, but only a few dozen are in common use today. A brief summary of the various programming language generations is provided in Table 2.11.

The various languages have certain characteristics that make them appropriate for particular types of problems or applications. Among the third-generation languages, COBOL has excellent file-handling and database-handling capabilities for manipulating large volumes of business data, while FORTRAN is better suited for scientific applications. Java is an obvious choice for Web developers. End users will choose one of the fourth- or fifth-generation languages to develop programs. Although many programming languages are used to write new

TABLE 2.10

Selected Enterprise Resource Planning Vendors

SAP	Baan
Oracle	SSA
PeopleSoft	Marcam
Dun & Bradstreet	QAD
J.D. Edwards	Ross Systems

Generation	Key Characteristics	Examples
First	Computer instructions written in machine code (0s and 1s) directly executable by the computer. Very tedious and time-consuming to create.	Machine language
Second	Abbreviations used for common operations (such as ADD, MOV, JMP). Each operation was followed by the address of one or more parameters. Recognizable names replaced numerical addresses. Assemblers were required to convert code into the machine language of a specific manufacturer's computer.	Assembly language
Third	Computer instructions became even more English-like and easier to read. Software programs called compilers or interpreters were required to convert instructions into machine language.	FORTRAN COBOL
Fourth	Language was easy enough for nonprogrammers to use. Computer instructions became very powerful, telling the computer what was to be done, without requiring step-by-step instructions on how to do it.	Focus Powerhouse SAS Essbase
Visual programming languages	Enabled developers to create applications using point-and-click and drag-and-drop techniques instead of text-oriented methods.	Visual Basic Visual C++
Object-oriented languages	Objects contain the data, instructions, and procedures. The same objects can be easily reused in different programs for a variety of applications, greatly increasing program quality and programmer productivity.	Eiffel C++ C# Java SmallTalk

TABLE 2.11

Summary of Programming Languages

business applications, more lines of code are written in COBOL in existing business applications than in any other programming language.

SOFTWARE BUGS

To detect computer program logic errors, programmers run through test data and check the results of the program against the results of running the same data by hand or calculator. Most computer programs involve thousands of lines of code, so it can take years to debug programs such as those used to control emergency shutdown systems on nuclear reactors. According to the Pentagon and the Software Engineering Institute at Carnegie Mellon University, typically five to 15 bugs exist in every 1,000 lines of code. Most software bugs arise because manufacturers release new software as early as possible instead of waiting until all bugs are identified and removed. They are under intense pressure from customers to deliver the software they have announced and from shareholders to begin selling the new product to increase sales. Software companies must then issue bug fixes, product updates, and new releases—all of which further complicates the life of software users and IS organizations. We briefly discuss the types of licensing agreements for software next.

SOFTWARE LICENSING

In general, software manufacturers want to license their software to lock in a steady, predictable stream of revenue from customers. Software manufacturers also want to encourage customers to move to the latest releases of their software products to minimize the effort required to support out-of-date products. They offer numerous types of software licenses to help accomplish these objectives.

In a *usage-based license* arrangement, software fees are based on the amount of actual usage of the manufacturer's products. Licensees are charged in much the same way that utility firms charge their customers-increasing fees for increased use of power or water. With *capacity-based licenses,* the fees paid to the software manufacturer are based on the processing power of the computer on which the software is installed. Users who run their software on a more powerful processor pay more for the software. When software is accessed as a *network service,* the software manufacturer makes its products available through the Internet. The advantage of this form of usage is that the software manufacturer automatically offers users bug fixes, enhancements, and other updates over the Web and charges a subscription fee for the software and associated services. With *subscription licensing,* user companies sign a multiyear deal with a manufacturer for individual products or a collection of products and then pay annual subscription fees based on how many PCs they have.

In July 2002, Microsoft put into effect its Version 6 *volume licensing* program. Under this program, companies that enroll in Microsoft's new Software Assurance program are entitled to receive the latest versions of Microsoft products during their contract term. The annual cost is 25 percent of the volume license fee for server software products and 29 percent for desktop products. To be eligible for this program, the company must already be running the most current version of the product. Many users and companies viewed this program as a way to ensure that they stay on current software releases, but at a substantial increase in their software budget.[31]

With all of the options available for obtaining software, day-to-day users—as well as IS personnel—need to be aware of the pros and cons of each alternative. Informed users are wiser consumers, both in their personal and work lives.

SUMMARY

PRINCIPLE ***Information system users must work closely with information system professionals to define business needs, evaluate options, and select the hardware and software that provide a cost-effective solution to those needs.***

Hardware devices work together to perform input, processing, data storage, and output. Processing is performed by an interplay between the central processing unit (CPU) and memory. Primary storage, or memory, provides working storage for program instructions and data to be processed and provides them to the CPU. Together, a CPU and memory process data and execute instructions.

Processing that uses several processing units is called *multiprocessing.* One form of multiprocessing uses coprocessors; coprocessors execute one type of instruction while the CPU works on others. Parallel processing involves linking several processors to work together to solve complex problems.

Computer systems can store larger amounts of data and instructions in secondary storage, which is less volatile and has greater capacity than memory. Storage media can be either sequential access or direct access. Common forms of secondary storage include magnetic tape, magnetic disk, optical disk storage, and PC memory cards. Redundant array of independent/inexpensive disks (RAID) is a method of storing data that allows the system to more easily recover data in the event of a hardware failure. Storage area network (SAN) uses computer servers, distributed storage devices, and networks to provide fast and efficient storage.

Input and output devices allow users to provide data and instructions to the computer for processing and allow subsequent storage and output. These devices are part of a user interface through which humans interact with computer systems. Input and output devices vary widely, but they share common characteristics of speed and functionality.

Scanners are input devices that convert images and text into binary digits. Point-of-sale (POS) devices are terminals with scanners that read and enter codes into computer systems. Automatic teller machines (ATMs) are terminals with keyboards used for transactions.

Output devices provide information in different forms, from hard copy to sound to digital format. Display monitors are standard output devices; monitor quality is determined by size, number of colors that can be displayed, and resolution. Other output devices include printers and plotters.

The main computer system types are personal computers, midrange computers, mainframe computers, and supercomputers. Personal computers (PCs) are small, inexpensive computer systems. Two major types of PCs are desktop and laptop computers. Handheld (palmtop) computers are increasingly popular for portable computing and communications needs. Embedded computers add features and capabilites to other products such as automobiles and household appliances. The network computer is a diskless, inexpensive computer used for accessing server-based applications and the Internet. Web appliances connect users to the Internet. Workstations are advanced PCs with greater memory, processing, and graphics abilities. Midrange computers are filing cabinet–size computers that have greater secondary storage and support transaction processing. Even larger mainframes have higher processing capabilities, while supercomputers are extremely fast computers used to solve the most intensive computing problems.

There are two main categories of software: systems software and application software. Systems software is a collection of programs that act as a buffer between hardware and application software. Application software enables people to solve problems and perform specific tasks.

An operating system (OS) is a set of computer programs that controls the computer hardware to support users' computing needs. OS hardware functions convert an instruction from an application into a set of instructions needed by the hardware. The OS also serves as an intermediary between application programs and hardware, allowing hardware independence. Memory management involves controlling storage access and use by converting logical requests into physical locations and by placing data in the best storage space. Task management allocates computer resources through multitasking and time-sharing. With multitasking, users can run more than one application at a time. Time-sharing allows more than one person to use a computer system at the same time. An OS also provides a user interface, which allows users to access and command the computer.

Over the years, several popular operating systems have been developed. These include several proprietary operating systems used primarily on mainframes. MS-DOS is an early OS for IBM-compatibles. Newer versions, such as Windows 98, Windows 2000, Windows NT, Windows ME, and Windows XP are fully functional operating systems with graphical user interfaces. Apple computers typically use a proprietary operating system, the Mac OS. Unix is the leading portable operating system, usable on many computer system types and platforms. Linux is an operating system whose source code is available to everyone.

Application software may be proprietary or off-the-shelf. Although there are literally hundreds of computer applications that can help individuals at school, home, and work, the primary ones are word processing, spreadsheet analysis, database, graphics, and on-line services.

PRINCIPLE ***Organizations do not develop proprietary application software unless doing so will meet a compelling business need that can provide a competitive advantage.***

Application software applies the power of the computer to solve problems and perform specific tasks. Application software can support individuals, groups, and organizations. User software, or personal productivity software, includes general-purpose programs that enable users to improve their personal effectiveness, increasing the amount of work and its quality. Software that helps groups work together is often referred to as *groupware.* Enterprise software that benefits the entire organization can also be developed or purchased.

Three approaches organizations use to obtain applications are as follows: (1) build proprietary application software, (2) buy existing programs off the shelf, or (3) use a combination of customized and off-the-shelf application software.

PRINCIPLE ***End users and IS professionals use a programming language whose functional characteristics are appropriate to the task at hand.***

There are five generations of programming languages, plus object-oriented programming languages. End users learn and typically use fourth-generation programming languages such as Visual C++, Visual Basic, Focus, Powerhouse, and SAS. These fourth-generation languages are less procedural and more Englishlike than the first three generations of programming languages, which are typically used by IS professionals.

Object-oriented programming languages, such as Smalltalk, C++, C#, and Java, use groups of related data, instructions, and procedures called objects, which serve as reusable modules in various programs. These languages can reduce program development and testing time. Java can be used to develop applications on the Internet.

According to the Pentagon and the Software Engineering Institute at Carnegie Mellon University, there are typically five to 15 bugs in every 1,000 lines of code.

PRINCIPLE ***The information system industry continues to undergo constant change; users need to be aware of recent trends and issues in software licensing to be effective in their business and personal life.***

Software manufacturers want to license their software to lock in a steady, predictable stream of revenue from customers and to encourage customers to move to the latest releases of their software products to minimize the effort required to support out-of-date products. There are numerous types of software licenses to help accomplish these objectives including capacity based, network service, subscription, and volume based.

CHAPTER 2 SELF-ASSESSMENT TEST

Information system users must work closely with information systems professionals to define business needs, evaluate options, and select the hardware and software that provide a cost-effective solution to those needs.

1. The overriding consideration in making hardware decisions in a business should be how hardware can be used to support the objectives of the information system and the goals of the organization. True False
2. ________________ is a property of certain metals that lets current flow with minimal resistance.
3. A petabyte represents about 1,024 gigabytes. True False
4. A form of memory that loses its contents if power is lost is called
   A. ROM
   B. PROM
   C. CD-ROM
   D. RAM
5. Which of the following is a sequential access storage media?
   A. magnetic tape
   B. RAID
   C. magnetic disk
   D. optical disk
6. On a megabyte-to-megabyte basis, memory is still more expensive than most forms of secondary storage. True False
7. The relative clock speed of two CPUs from different manufacturers is a good indicator of their relative processing speed. True False
8. ________________ is the ability to increase the capability of a computer system to process more transactions in a given period by adding more, or more powerful, processors.

Organizations do not develop proprietary application software unless doing so will meet a compelling business need that can provide a competitive advantage.

9. The primary function of application software is to apply the power of the computer to give individuals, workgroups, and the entire enterprise the ability to solve problems and perform specific tasks. True False
10. Software that enables users to improve their personal effectiveness, increasing the amount of work they can do and its quality, is called ________________.
    A. personal productivity software
    B. operating system software
    C. utility software
    D. graphics software
11. Which of the following is NOT a characteristic of ERP software?
    A. ability to support a multisite, global organization
    B. ability to support multiple legal entities, multiple languages, and multiple languages
    C. ability to integrate software to support manufacturing and finance functions
    D. ability to let individual users set up their own systems and work practices the way they like it
12. Software used to solve a unique or specific problem that is usually built, but that can also be purchased from an outside company, is called ________________.
13. Software that has the greatest potential to affect the processes that add value to a business because it is designed for specific organizational activities and functions is called ________________.
    A. personal productivity software
    B. operating system software
    C. utility softwarc
    D. applications software

14. A class of applications software that helps groups work together and collaborate is called ________________.

End users and IS professionals use a programming language whose functional characteristics are appropriate to the task at hand.

15. Each language also has its own set of rules, called the ________________ of the language.
16. A special software program called a *compiler* converts a third-generation programming language into the machine language instructions consisting of binary digits. True False

The information system industry continues to undergo constant change; users need to be aware of recent trends and issues in software licensing to be effective in their business and personal life.

17. A licensing option where the software manufacturer makes its products available through the Internet and automatically offers updates, bug fixes, and other enhancements is called ________________.

Chapter 2 Self-Assessment Test Answers:

1. True, 2. Superconductivity, 3. False, 4. D., 5. A, 6. True, 7. False, 8. Scalability, 9. True, 10. A, 11. D, 12. proprietary software, 13. D, 14. groupware or collaborative computing software, 15. syntax, 16. True, 17. network service

REVIEW QUESTIONS

1. Describe a storage area network (SAN) system.
2. Why is it said that the components of all information systems are interdependent?
3. Explain the two-phase process for executing instructions.
4. Identify the three components of the CPU and explain the role of each.
5. What is Moore's Law?
6. Describe the various types of memory.
7. What is the difference between sequential and direct access of data?
8. Identify and briefly describe the various classes of personal computers.
9. What are the computer system types? How do these types differ?
10. State three reasons the relative cost of hardware and software has shifted so dramatically.
11. Give four examples of personal productivity software.
12. What are the two basic types of software? Briefly describe the role of each.
13. Identify the two primary sources for acquiring application software.
14. Describe the term *enterprise resource planning (ERP) system*. What functions does such a system perform?
15. Identify and briefly discuss four different types of software licenses.

DISCUSSION QUESTIONS

1. What are the implications of Moore's Law—that is, continuing the trend of increased computing power at lower costs? Use Moore's Law to forecast the PC computing power that could be available in three years. What sort of applications could benefit from that level of computer power?
2. Imagine that you are the business manager for your university. What type of computer would you recommend for broad deployment in the university's computer labs—a standard desktop personal computer or a network computer? Why?
3. If cost were not an issue, describe the characteristics of your ideal laptop computer—hard disk capacity, processor speed, screen resolution, amount of main memory, types of secondary storage, etc.
4. What if you discovered that your favorite recording group composes, edits, and records all its music using multimedia computer technology? How would you feel? Does the use of computer technology to create original works of art or music diminish or enhance the accomplishment? Should such artists be considered as great as others who do not use computer technology?

5. Assume that you must take a computer programming course next semester. What language do you think would be best for you to study? Why? Do you think that a professional programmer needs to know more than one programming language? Why or why not?
6. Identify the three spheres of influence and briefly discuss the software needs of each.
7. What are some of the benefits associated with implementation of an enterprise resource planning system? What are some of the issues that could keep the use of enterprise resource planning software from being successful?
8. Define the term *application service provider.* What are some of the advantages and disadvantages of employing an ASP? What precautions might you take to minimize the risk of using one?
9. Briefly outline the evolution of programming languages. Use your imagination and creativity to develop a brief description of the sixth generation of programming languages. How would they work? What sort of features might be included?
10. Identify four types of software licenses frequently used. Which approach does the best job of ensuring a steady, predictable stream of revenue from customers? Which approach is most fair for the small company that makes infrequent use of the software?

PROBLEM-SOLVING EXERCISES

1. Do research (read various trade journals and search the Internet) on companies that make rewritable DVD devices. Use your word processing program to write a short report summarizing your findings. Make sure to include the speed, features, and price of the various devices. Be sure to discuss the compatability of each device with movie DVD devices. Develop a simple spreadsheet to compare the features and costs of the rewritable DVD devices you found.

2. Choose a programming language of interest to you and develop a six-slide presentation on its history, current level of usage, typical applications, ease of use, etc.

3. Use a spreadsheet package to prepare a simple monthly budget and forecast your cash flow—both income and expenses—for the next six months (make up numbers rather than using actual ones). Now use a graphics package to plot your total monthly income and monthly expenses for six months. Cut and paste both the spreadsheet and the graph into a word processing document that summarizes your financial condition.

TEAM ACTIVITIES

1. With two of your classmates, visit a major computer retail store (e.g., Gateway, CompUSA, MicroCenter). Spend a couple of hours there, during which each of you concentrates on identifying the latest developments in storage, input, and output devices. Write a brief report summarizing your findings.
2. With two or three of your classmates, visit the main computer facility of your college or university. Find out the manufacturer and model number as well as the specifications (speed of CPU, amount of main memory, disk drive capacity, etc.) of a mainframe or midrange computer. How long has it been in use? How much longer does the university plan to use it before replacing it with something different? What business processes have changed that spurred this alteration? Will your college or university upgrade the computer or buy a new one?
3. Form a group of three or four classmates. Identify and contact an information systems professional with a local firm. Interview the individual to discover the relative level of use of custom software versus standard application packages. If you uncover examples of the use of custom software, find out why the software was developed this way. Write a brief report summarizing your findings.

WEB EXERCISES

1. Microsoft, IBM/Lotus, Sun Microsystems, and Corel are the four main providers of personal productivity software suites. Do research to assess the relative success of these companies' products in terms of sales of their software suites. Do you think it is possible that Microsoft will become the only provider of such software? Would this be good or bad? Why? Write a brief report summarizing your findings and conclusions.
2. Search the Web for companies that make secondary storage devices and systems, including disk, tape, RAID, SAN, and others. Summarize your findings using your word processing device.
3. Visit the Web sites of three manufacturers of handheld computers. Make a list of features and software applications available from each. Develop a spreadsheet that compares features and prices. Which system and manufacturer do you prefer? Why?

CASES

CASE 1

Australia Experiments with Electronic Voting

Government exists at three levels in Australia—Commonwealth (federal), state, and local. Australia is divided into six self-governing states (New South Wales, Queensland, South Australia, Tasmania, Victoria, and Western Australia) and two mainland territories (Australian Capital Territory and Northern Territory). Canberra, the capital of Australia, is situated in the Australian Capital Territory (ACT) and has a population of around 313,000. Federal Parliament passed the Australian Capital Territory (Self-Government) Act in 1988, which established self-government in the ACT. The ACT Legislative Assembly has 17 elected members.

In October 2001, roughly 215,000 Canberrans went to the polls to elect their local 17-member Legislative Assembly. At eight booths across the city, 16,500 voters elected to participate in a pilot test of a new electronic voting system (at an estimated cost of $400,000) rather than use the traditional paper-and-pencil method. These electronic voters were issued a bar code that gave them secure, once-only access to the electronic voting system. They then viewed lists of candidates on a screen-based ballot-recording system and selected their preferred candidates using a keypad. Votes were confirmed by another bar code swipe, and then the bar code was dropped into the ballot box.

The Australian Capital Territory uses a complex balloting system called Hare-Clark. Under this method of balloting, voters express their first, second, and third preferences, and so on, for each candidate for each office. A candidate is elected if he or she gains 50 percent of the votes plus one (an absolute majority). But if no candidate achieves such a majority, the lowest vote-getter is excluded, and that candidate's second preferences are distributed on a proportional basis to the remaining candidates as full votes. This process repeats until one of the candidates gains the required absolute majority.

All 16,500 electronic votes were recorded and stored on a secure, stand-alone computer and then transferred to a Zip disk for transport to the central database on election night. It took a full week to read the hand-marked paper ballots, perform the necessary data entry to capture the votes in an electronic format, and then transfer the results to the central computer system. Twelve days were required to complete the count, including a built-in delay of six days to allow for postal votes to come in. The accuracy of the count eliminated the need for time-intensive hand recounts. A recount in 1998 resulted in a delay of 22 days before a result was known.

Members of Australia's other electoral commissions across the country watched the pilot of the new system closely. While they were impressed, they were not eager to expand use of the electronic system. They thought that Canberra, with its high number of computer technology users, was atypical of the rest of the country and that unequal access to technology would inhibit broad-scale acceptance of electronic voting. Also, Canberra's relatively small geographic area means fewer ballot locations and thus means that less computer hardware is required to implement an electronic system. The electoral commissioners also raised concerns about security.

Discussion Questions

1. What percentage of Canberrans voted in this election? What percentage of the voters tried the new electronic system? Do you find these percentages surprising? Why?
2. The electoral commissioners observing the pilot raised several issues. Which of these issues do you think are most significant? Which issues were raised that were not so significant or that can be easily overcome?

Critical Thinking Questions

3. What suggestions for improvement would you make for conducting a second pilot—either in the voting and counting process itself or in the technology used?
4. Do you think such a voting system would be successful in the United States? Why or why not?

Sources: Adapted from Selina Mitchell, "Canberra Leads Way in E-Voting," *Australian IT*, October 9, 2001, http://www.AustralianIT.news.com.AU; Selina Mitchell, "States Say E-Vote Cost Is Too High," *Australian IT*, November 13, 2001, http://www.AustralianIT.news.com.AU; "Legislative Council and Periodic Elections," Tasmanian Parliamentary Library Web site, http://www.parliament.tas.gov.au, accessed January 3, 2002.

CASE 2

Infosys Uses Offshore Outsourcing Model to Provide Contract Software

Infosys is one of India's best-known technology companies. It has been in operation for over 20 years and has 10,000 employees in 30 offices worldwide, providing software and services to large companies. Much of the work that information systems professionals do can be done anywhere—on a company's premises or thousands of miles away in a foreign country. But to make this process work well, someone must provide strong project management, ensure good communications, provide high-quality products, meet deadlines, and stay within budget constraints. Infosys has gained such a reputation with its clients.

Infosys's strategy is to set up world-class software development campuses to ensure itself a good supply of well-trained employees. For example, Infosys signed an agreement with the local Indian government to establish a software development campus in Hyderabad, India. Eventually, this campus will provide training facilities for 2,500 software professionals.

Infosys has also been highly successful in forming partnerships with major U.S. companies to provide programming expertise. Three of its customers are Aetna, Kansas City Southern, and SunAmerica. Aetna, one of the leading U.S. providers of health care and related financial services, is using more than 500 Infosys employees to create on-line financial and retirement benefit services to complement Aetna's growing line of "E-health" initiatives. Aetna retains control of the overall system design process, but it uses Infosys to program, test, and deliver the various system components. Aetna turned to Infosys for part of its software needs because the cost of hiring in-house programming staff in the United States is seven times higher than in India. As an additional benefit, time-zone differences mean that work can be done around the clock—one shift of workers in the United States and two shifts of workers from Infosys at locations around the world keep the projects moving. With the shortage of United States programmers, the use of offshore outsourcing was an alternative to hiring inexperienced college graduates or enticing seasoned IT veterans out of retirement.

Infosys worked with Kansas City Southern to build a $50 million management control system to help the railway guarantee on-time shipments and cut freight cycle times. Kansas City Southern (KCS) carries automotive and computer parts from Canada and Chicago to Mexico City and brings finished Volkswagen Beetles and PCs back north. The new system helps customers order and track freight shipments on-line, replaces paper records used by train engineers and customer service agents, and provides business managers with a more effective way to track costs such as those of leased freight cars. When Infosys came on board, software development occurred around the clock, in tandem with developers from Infosys in Madras, India, with some 1.5 million worker hours expended in the effort.

Infosys has contracted with SunAmerica, a financial services company, to transform its old policy administration system into a new Web-based, thin client system. The new system will improve the policy administration process for SunAmerica and redesign its output systems to print policies for some 130,000 users.

Discussion Questions

1. Briefly describe the offshore outsourcing model for delivering contract software. Why have many major U.S. companies turned to this approach to develop their key applications?
2. What are some of the potential negatives associated with offshore outsourcing?

Critical Thinking Questions

3. What unique risks are associated with the execution of an offshore outsourcing project?
4. What specific actions can be taken to reduce these risks?

Sources: Adapted from Business Editors/High-Tech Writers, "Infosys Signs MoU with the Government of Andhra Pradesh to Establish a Software Development Campus in Hyderabad," *BusinessWire,* January 11, 2001, http://www.businesswire.com; Matt Hamblen, "The Little Engine That Might," *Computerworld,* August 6, 2001, http://www.computerworld.com; Saritha Rai, "World Business Briefing/Asia: India: High-Technology Optimism," *The New York Times,* June 5, 2001, late edition; "SunAmerica Selects Infosys to Transform Core Policy Systems," *The New York Times on the Web,* December 4, 2001, http://www.nytimes.com; Business Editors/High-Tech Writers, "Infosys Expands Strategic Relationship with Aetna," *BusinessWire,* March 14, 2001, http://www.businesswire.com.

CASE 3

Crystal Flash Opts for Application Service Provider

Crystal Flash is a supplier of energy-related products and services serving the state of Michigan. It employs 600 workers and is owned by Heritage, one of the largest oil producers in the United States. Crystal Flash's retail food and fuel stores, with their bright yellow canopies, are highly visible and instantly recognizable in western Michigan. Its fleet of 100 trucks delivers propane and heating oil to thousands of homes in rural areas, plus gasoline and diesel fuel to trucking companies, construction firms, and farms.

In 2000, Crystal Flash decided to revamp its outdated sales practices, which led to customers being called on by more than one salesperson and created heavy administrative workloads. A committee consisting of representatives from sales, marketing, and information systems was formed to determine how to establish a more uniform and efficient set of sales processes. The group focused on implementing a sales management software application. After six months of work, they decided that a custom sales management application would be too expensive due to the required consulting, hardware, ongoing maintenance, and licensing fees. They spent the next six months reviewing and evaluating existing sales management software packages. The solution they chose was Salesnet Sales Force Automation, a software application that runs on server hardware owned and operated by Salesnet Inc., a sales software application service provider.

The Salesnet Process Builder software module enables sales organizations to define and build their own sales processes. Crystal Flash was able to define a set of standard sales processes that will reinforce effective selling/closing behaviors among all its sales reps. No longer are Crystal Flash's sales reps spending time completing unnecessary paperwork, and they are able to use the software's calendar, scheduling, and contact management features to support greater teamwork. In addition, use of the software enables Crystal Flash managers to access real-time information about sales team activities and to obtain sales reports, forecasts, and customer information.

Sales reps can access the Internet-based application through desktop PCs, by dialing up through notebook computers, or wirelessly on smaller devices.

Because Salesnet is a hosted application, there is no up-front capital investment in software, hardware, IT resources, or ongoing maintenance fees. As a result, Crystal Flash saved up to $100,000 over other solutions. The standard version of Salesnet costs $59 per user per month.

Discussion Questions

1. In addition to economic factors, why would a small company such as Crystal Flash find the use of an application service provider especially attractive?
2. What are the biggest benefits of this system for Crystal Flash?

Critical Thinking Questions

3. Check out the Salesnet Web site at http://www.salesnet.com. Can you identify any limitations of its software that might make its use inappropriate for a large sales organization?
4. Can you identify any potential problems or risks with Crystal Flash's choice to use an application service provider?

Sources: Adapted from Linda Formichelli, "Sovereign Tracks Processes, Prospects, with Salesnet," *CRM White Paper*, June 18, 2002, http://www.searchcrm.com; Stacy Crowley, "Salesnet Preps 'Extended' Version, Offline App," *Computerworld*, June 24, 2002, http://www.computerworld.com; Eric M. Zeman, "A Flash of Brilliance," *Field Force Automation*, May 2002, http://www.ffa.com; Crystal Flash Web site, "About Us," http://www.crystalflash.com, accessed July 28, 2002.

NOTES

Sources for the opening vignette on p. 47: Adapted from Corporate Information—Flextronics Web site, http://www.flextronics.com, accessed December 27, 2001; PolyDyne Software Inc. Web site, http://www.polydyne.com, accessed December 27, 2001; David Hannon, "Contract Manufacturer Moves to Online Quoting," *Purchasing*, August 23, 2001, p. 23; Jeff Sweat, "Customer Collaboration Counts—Flextronics Depends on Collaborative Tools to Work with Clients and Connect Co-Workers," *InformationWeek*, December 10, 2001, http://www.informationweek.com.

1. Paul McDougall, "Lowdown on the High-End," *InformationWeek*, June 11, 2001, http://www.informationweek.com.
2. "Intel and AMD Set to Unveil New Chips on Monday," *The New York Times on the Web*, January 4, 2002, http://www.nytimes.com.
3. John Markoff, "Intel Makes an Ultra-Tiny Chip," *The New York Times on the Web*, June 10, 2001, http://www.nytimes.com.
4. Martin J. Garvey, "Cox Adds Dell to Its Storage Lineup," *InformationWeek*, September 3, 2001, http://www.informationweek.com.
5. Martyn Williams, "Fujitsu Begins Sampling 2.3 GB Magneto-Optical Disk Drive," *Computerworld*, July 5, 2001, http://www.computerworld.com.
6. David Pogue, "Digital Cameras for Less: How Much Will $300 Buy?" *The New York Times on the Web*, December 20, 2001, http://www.nytimes.com.
7. Unisys Web site, http://www.unisys.com, accessed January 16, 2002.
8. David M. Ewalt, "Staying Healthy with Wireless," *InformationWeek*, September 17, 2001, http://www.informationweek.com.
9. "Report Counts Computers in Majority of U.S. Homes," *The New York Times on the Web*, September 7, 2001, http://www.nytimes.com.
10. Sumner Lemon and Matt Berger, "Jobs Unveils New iMac, Calls Apple's 'i' Products a Success," *IDG News Service*, January 7, 2002, http://www.computerworld.com.
11. David Pogue, "An Elegant New Sony Handlheld," *The New York Times on the Web*, November 29, 2001, http://www.nytimes.com.
12. Aishia M. Williams, "Doing Business without Wires," *InformationWeek*, January 15, 2001, http://www.informationweek.com.
13. Matt Hamblen, "The Wireless Geek Can Be Tres Chic," *Computerworld*, March 20, 2002, http://www.computerworld.com.
14. Ian Fried, "Ellison's NIC Co. to Team with Sun," *Cnet News.com*, http://news.com.com., accessed June 25, 2001.
15. Lucas Mearian, "Wal-Mart Deal Boosts IBM in Storage Wars," *Computerworld*, October 22, 2001, http://www.computerworld.com.
16. Mark K. Anderson, "Public Computing on a Super Scale," *Wired News*, October 4, 2001, http://www.wirednews.com.
17. David Pogue, "A New Face (and Heart) for the Mac," *The New York Times on the Web*, March 29, 2001, http://www.nytimes.com.
18. Leslie Jaye Goff, "Supporting Creativity," *Computerworld*, December 10, 2001, http://www.computerworld.com.
19. Todd R. Weiss, "Sherwin-Williams Brushes SCO Unix Aside, Adopts Linux," *Computerworld*, May 27, 2002, http://www.computerworld.com.
20. Todd R. Weiss, "Burlington Coat Factory Warehouse Corp," *Computerworld*, March 11, 2002, http://www.computerworld.com.
21. Jaikumar Vijayan, "Mainframe Users Turn to IBM's z800 for Cost Savings," *Computerworld*, June 24, 2002, http://www.computerworld.com.
22. Jaikumar Vijayan, "What's New in z/OS?" *Computerworld*, November 19, 2001, http://www.computerworld.com.
23. Todd R. Weiss, "Red Hat Linux Now Available for IBM S/390 Mainframes," *Computerworld*, December 18, 2001, http://www.computerworld.com.
24. Larry Mittag, "Palm OS or Windows CE?" *Computerworld*, May 10, 2001, http://www.computerworld.com.
25. Sumner Lemon, "Windows CE.Net Ready for January Launch," *Computerworld*, December 27, 2001, http://www.computerworld.com.
26. Matt Berger, "Microsoft Offers Test Version of Windows XP Embedded," *Computerworld*, September 24, 2001.
27. Douglas F. Gray, "Vendors Unleash New Handhelds for Pocket PC 2002," *Computerworld*, October 4, 2001.
28. Summer Lemon, "China Merchant's Bank, Legend Offer PDA Banking Service," *Computerworld*, June 25, 2002, http:www.computerworld.com.
29. "Palm on Your Wristwatch," *Wired*, July 24, 2001, http://www.wired.com.
30. Larry Greenemeier, "Ingersoll-Rand and Cosio Get Cozier on ASP Front," *InformationWeek*, May 1, 2002, http://www.informationweek.com.
31. Carol Sliwa, "License Tracker Launched as Microsoft Deadline Looms," *Computerworld*, July 15, 2002, http://www.computerworld.com.

Organizing Data and Information

16

PRINCIPLES

LEARNING OBJECTIVES

The database approach to data management provides significant advantages over the traditional file-based approach.

- Define general data management concepts and terms, highlighting the advantages and disadvantages of the database approach to data management.
- Name three database models and outline their basic features, advantages, and disadvantages.

A well-designed and well-managed database is an extremely valuable tool in supporting decision making.

- Identify the common functions performed by all database management systems and identify three popular end-user database management systems.

Further improvements in the use of database technology will continue to evolve and yield real business benefits.

- Identify and briefly discuss recent database applications.

[Valio]

Building Brand Loyalty with Better Decision-Making Data

Valio is the largest dairy company in Finland, generating annual sales in excess of $1.5 billion. Founded in 1905, Valio is a farmer's cooperative that supplies nearly 80 percent of Finland's fresh milk. The 33 owner dairies collect milk from some 17,200 dairy farms, and Valio processes the milk into 800 dairy products. Valio then markets the products at home and in 60 other countries under various brand names.

Valio's probiotic dairy products and food supplements are especially profitable. (Probiotics are food supplements or dairy products containing live bacteria that are beneficial to the health of the consumer.) Valio owns the worldwide patent for Lactobacillus GG, one of the leading probiotic bacterial strains, and it allows other companies to use the bacteria in their products through licensing agreements. Fermented dairy products, "sweet milk," fresh cheeses, ripened cheeses, infant foods, dairy and nondairy drinks, and food supplements all can contain the bacteria.

Long known for its high-quality products, Valio must now compete in the global marketplace for shelf space with aggressively priced rival products. As part of its strategy to remain successful, Valio built a huge database with information from multiple sources that feeds a number of smaller databases with subsets of its data. For example, one smaller database contains information on domestic markets, and another has data on export markets. Company decision makers can access the data from anywhere in the world via the Internet. They then use software to analyze the data to track brand and product performance by location and customer and to track sales, profits, and inventory. These tools and the data enable employees to focus on customer needs, cut costs, and increase revenue.

Data consistency is a key benefit derived from use of the large database. All employees—including sales managers, sales reps, and marketing teams—work with the same data, so they start with a common set of facts about the current state of the company.

The system was designed for ease of use, so even workers who are new to PCs can use the system with minimal training. Standard formatted reports enable managers to quickly view the latest business developments. If necessary, workers can drill down into the data to obtain more in-depth analyses.

Valio made a strategic decision to offer its customers Internet access to a special database that contains market data—its own and suppliers'—as well as raw materials forecasts. Customers can then modify their orders, and Valio can alter its production schedules to match consumer buying habits. This collaboration enables Valio and its customers to minimize their inventories and develop a more competitive supply chain. Valio's efforts to build a larger and more sophisticated database than its rivals have provided it with a competitive edge and strengthened consumer loyalty to its brands.

As you read this chapter, consider the following:

- How can databases be used to support critical business objectives?
- What are some of the issues associated with compiling and managing massive amounts of data?

As we saw in Chapter 1, a database is a collection of data organized to meet users' needs. Throughout your career, you will be directly or indirectly accessing a variety of databases, ranging from a simple roster of departmental employees to a fully integrated corporate database. You will probably access these databases using software called a **database management system (DBMS)**. A DBMS consists of a group of programs that manipulate the database and provide an interface between the database and the user of the database and other application programs. A database, a DBMS, and the application programs that use the data in the database make up a database environment. Understanding basic database system concepts can enhance your ability to use the power of a computerized database system to support organizational goals and advance your career.

database management system (DBMS)
a group of programs that manipulate the database and provide an interface between the database and the user of the database and other application programs

The bane of modern business is too much data and not enough information. Computers are everywhere, accumulating gigabytes galore. Yet it only seems to get harder to find the forest for the trees—that is, to extract significance from the blizzard of numbers, facts, and statistics. After careful consideration of what data was needed, Valio developed a database to enable decision makers to track brand and product performance by location and customer and to track sales, profits, and inventory. This is an example of delivering the right information to the right people in the right fashion and at the right time to improve and ensure organizational effectiveness and efficiency. Such careful consideration of decision makers' needs helps avoid data overload.

Like other components of a computer-based information system, the overall objective of a database is to help an organization achieve its goals. A database can contribute to organizational success in a number of ways, including the ability to provide managers and decision makers with timely, accurate, and relevant information based on data. As we saw in the case of Valio, a database can help companies organize data to learn from this valuable resource. Databases also help companies generate information to reduce costs, increase profits, track past business activities, and open new market opportunities. In fact, the ability of an organization to gather data, interpret it, and act on it quickly can distinguish winners from losers in a highly competitive marketplace. It is critical to the success of the organization that database capabilities be aligned with the company's goals. Because data is so critical to an organization's success, many firms develop databases to help them access data more efficiently and use it more effectively. In this chapter, we will investigate the development and use of different types of databases.

DATA MANAGEMENT

Without data and the ability to process it, an organization would not be able to complete most business activities successfully. It could not pay employees, send out bills, order new inventory, or produce information to assist managers in decision making. As you recall, data consists of raw facts, such as employee numbers and sales figures. For data to be transformed into useful information, it must first be organized meaningfully.

THE HIERARCHY OF DATA

Data is generally organized in a hierarchy that begins with the smallest piece of data used by computers (a bit) and progresses through the hierarchy to a database. As discussed in Chapter 2, a bit (a binary digit) represents a circuit that is either on or off. Bits can be organized into units called bytes. A byte is typically eight bits. Each byte represents a **character**, which is the basic building block of information. A character may consist of uppercase letters (A, B, C, ..., Z), lowercase letters (a, b, c, ..., z), numeric digits (0, 1, 2, ..., 9), or special symbols (.![+][-]/...).

character
basic building block of information, consisting of uppercase letters, lowercase letters, numeric digits, or special symbols

field
typically a name, number, or combination of characters that describes an aspect of a business object or activity

record
a collection of related data fields

file
a collection of related records

hierarchy of data
bits, characters, fields, records, files, and databases

Characters are put together to form a **field**. A field is typically a name, number, or combination of characters that describes an aspect of a business object (e.g., an employee, a location, a truck) or activity (e.g., a sale). A collection of related data fields is a **record**. By combining descriptions of various aspects of an object or activity, a more complete description of the object or activity is obtained. For instance, an employee record is a collection of fields about one employee. One field would be the employee's name, another her address, and still others her phone number, pay rate, earnings made to date, and so forth. A collection of related records is a **file**—for example, an employee file is a collection of all company employee records. Likewise, an inventory file is a collection of all inventory records for a particular company or organization. PC database software often refers to files as tables.

At the highest level of this hierarchy is a *database*, a collection of integrated and related files. Together, bits, characters, fields, records, files, and databases form the **hierarchy of data** (Figure 3.1). Characters are combined to make a field, fields are combined to make a record, records are combined to make a file, and files are combined to make a database. A database houses not only all these levels of data but the relationships among them.

DATA ENTITIES, ATTRIBUTES, AND KEYS

entity
generalized class of people, places, or things for which data is collected, stored, and maintained

attribute
a characteristic of an entity

data item
the specific value of an attribute

Entities, attributes, and keys are important database concepts. An **entity** is a generalized class of people, places, or things (objects) for which data is collected, stored, and maintained. Examples of entities include employees, inventory, and customers. An **attribute** is a characteristic of an entity. For example, employee number, last name, first name, hire date, and department number are attributes for an employee (Figure 3.2). Inventory number, description, number of units on hand, and the location of the inventory item in the warehouse are examples of attributes for items in inventory. Customer number, name, address, phone number, credit rating, and contact person are examples of attributes for customers. Attributes are usually selected to capture the relevant characteristics of entities such as employees or customers. The specific value of an attribute, called a **data item**, can be found in the fields of the record describing an entity.

FIGURE 3.1

The Hierarchy of Data

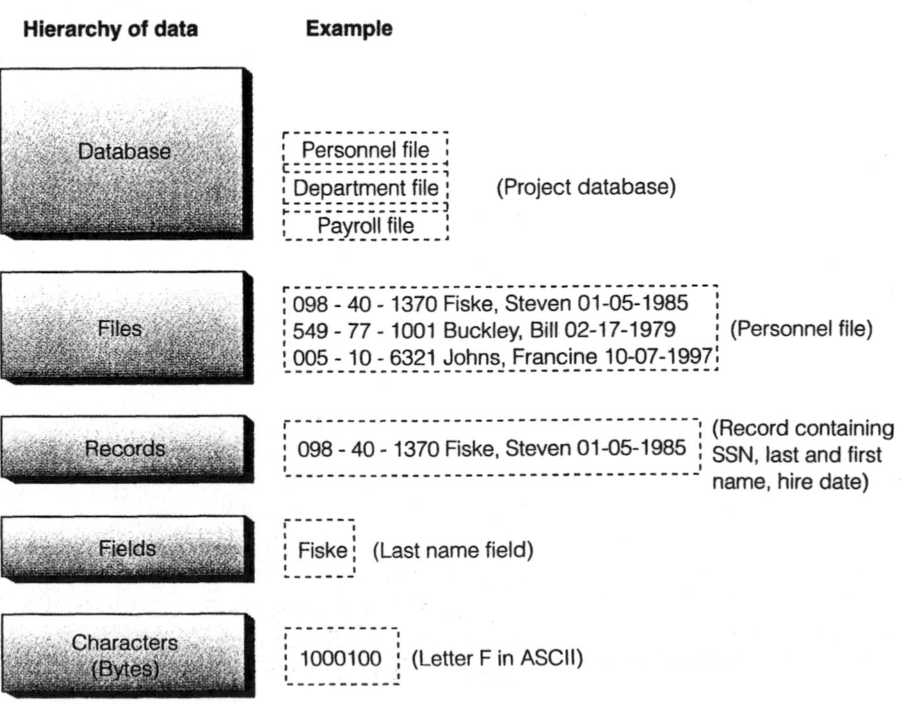

FIGURE 3.2

Keys and Attributes

The key field is the employee number. The attributes include last name, first name, hire date, and department number.

Employee #	Last name	First name	Hire date	Dept. number
005-10-6321	Johns	Francine	10-07-1997	257
549-77-1001	Buckley	Bill	02-17-1979	632
098-40-1370	Fiske	Steven	01-05-1985	598

Entities (records)

Key field

Attributes (fields)

key
a field or set of fields in a record that is used to identify the record

primary key
a field or set of fields that uniquely identifies the record

As we mentioned, a collection of fields about a specific object is a record. A **key** is a field or set of fields in a record that is used to identify the record. A **primary key** is a field or set of fields that uniquely identifies the record. No other record can have the same value for its primary key. The primary key is used to distinguish records so that they can be accessed, organized, and manipulated. For an employee record such as the one shown in Figure 3.2, the employee number is an example of a primary key.

Locating a particular record that meets a specific set of criteria may require the use of a combination of secondary keys. For example, a customer might call a mail-order company to place an order for clothes. If the customer does not know his primary key (such as a customer number), a secondary key (such as last name) can be used. In this case, the order clerk enters the last name, such as Adams. If there are several customers with the last name of Adams, the clerk can check other fields, such as address, first name, and so on, to find the correct customer record. Once the correct customer record is obtained, the order can be completed and the clothing items shipped to the customer.

THE TRADITIONAL APPROACH VERSUS THE DATABASE APPROACH

Traditionally, organizations collected data within each department of a business. Customer order data was maintained within the sales and order fulfillment department, invoicing data was kept in the billing department, and tax information was logged in the accounting department. Today, organizations have begun to tie functions together to streamline their information systems and avoid unnecessary duplication. Let's look at both the traditional and database approaches to information systems.

The Traditional Approach

One of the most basic ways to manage data is via files. Because a file is a collection of related records, all records associated with a particular application (and therefore related by the application) could be collected and managed together in an application-specific file. At one time, most organizations had numerous application-specific data files; for example, customer records often were maintained in separate files, with each file relating to a specific process completed by the company, such as shipping or billing. This approach to data management, in which separate data files are created and stored for each application program, is called the **traditional approach**. For each particular application, one or more data file is created (Figure 3.3).

traditional approach to data management
an approach whereby separate data files are created and stored for each application program

data redundancy
duplication of data in separate files

One of the flaws in this traditional file-oriented approach to data management is that much of the data—for example, customer name and address—is duplicated in two or more files. Such duplication is called **data redundancy** and creates the possibility that changes to the data (e.g., a new customer address) might be made in one file and not the other. The order-processing department

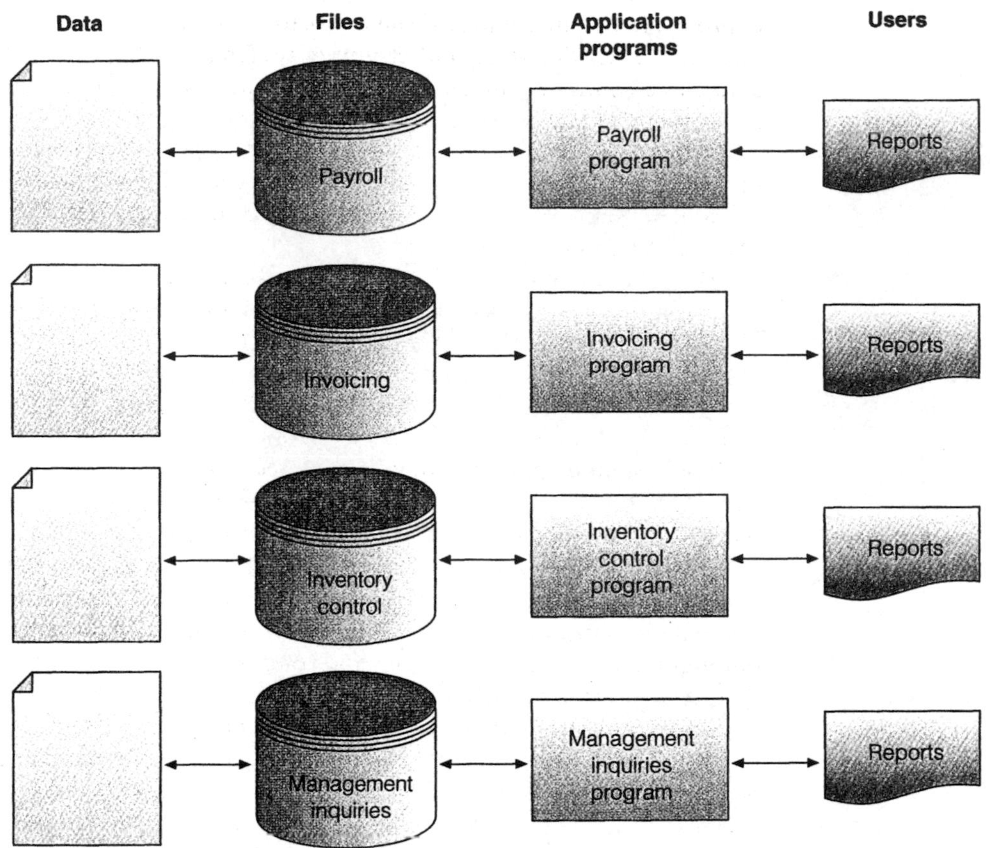

FIGURE 3.3

The Traditional Approach to Data Management

With the traditional approach, one or more data files is created and used for every application. For example, the inventory control program would have one or more files containing inventory data, such as the inventory item, number on hand, and item description. Likewise, the invoicing program can have files on customers, inventory items being shipped, and so on. With the traditional approach to data management, it is possible to have the same data, such as inventory items, in several different files used by different applications.

data integrity
the degree to which the data in any one file is accurate

database approach to data management
an approach whereby a pool of related data is shared by multiple application programs

might have updated its file to the new address, but the billing department is still sending bills to the old address. Data redundancy, therefore, conflicts with **data integrity**—the degree to which the data in any one file is accurate and consistent. Keeping a customer's address in only one file decreases the possibility that the customer will have two different addresses stored in different locations. The efficient operation of a business requires a high degree of data integrity.

Despite the drawbacks of using the traditional file approach in computerized database systems, some organizations continue to use it. For these firms, the cost of converting to another other approach is too high.

The Database Approach

The **database approach** to data management is a more efficient and effective means of organizing data, with a pool of related data shared by multiple application programs. Rather than having separate data files, each application uses a collection of data that is either joined or related in the database.

The database approach offers significant advantages over the traditional file-based approach. For one, by controlling data redundancy, the database approach can use storage space more efficiently and increase data integrity. The database approach can also increase an organization's flexibility in the use of data. Because data once kept in two files is now located in the same database, it is easier to locate and request data for many types of processing, and departments can share data and information resources. This flexibility can be critical when coordinating organizationwide responses across diverse functional areas of a corporation. However, some consistency needs to be established among software programs.

As an example of the advantages gained using the database approach, consider SWISS, a Swiss intercontinental airline formed from the Crossair, Swissair, and SairGroup merger. Its planes began flying in March 2002. The airline, which served almost 2 million passengers in its first quarter, is using the database approach to organize and store all its customer data, historical flight information, sales and marketing data, and customer preference information. The database is a valuable source of information for the entire organization. SWISS sales and marketing employees use the data to segment its customers and develop targeted marketing campaigns to appeal to each resulting group. Operational personnel use the database to monitor postflight activities, such as claims handling and resolution, and analyze customer feedback data received at its call centers to identify necessary improvements.[1]

To use the database approach to data management, additional software—a database management system (DBMS)—is required. As previously discussed, a DBMS consists of a group of programs that can be used as an interface between a database and the user or the database and application programs. Typically, this software acts as a buffer between the application programs and the database itself. Figure 3.4 illustrates the database approach.

The database approach to data management involves a combination of hardware and software. Tables 3.1 and 3.2 list some of the primary advantages and disadvantages of the database approach and explore some of these issues.

Because of the many advantages of the database approach, most businesses use databases to store data on customers, orders, inventory, employees, and suppliers. This data is used as the input to the various information systems throughout an organization. For example, the transaction processing system can use the data to support daily business processes such as billing, inventory tracking, and ordering. This same data can be processed by a management information system to create reports or a decision support system to provide information to aid managerial decision making.

Much planning and organization go into the development of corporate databases. For example, Best Buy is a specialty retailer of consumer electronics, personal

The Database Approach to Data Management

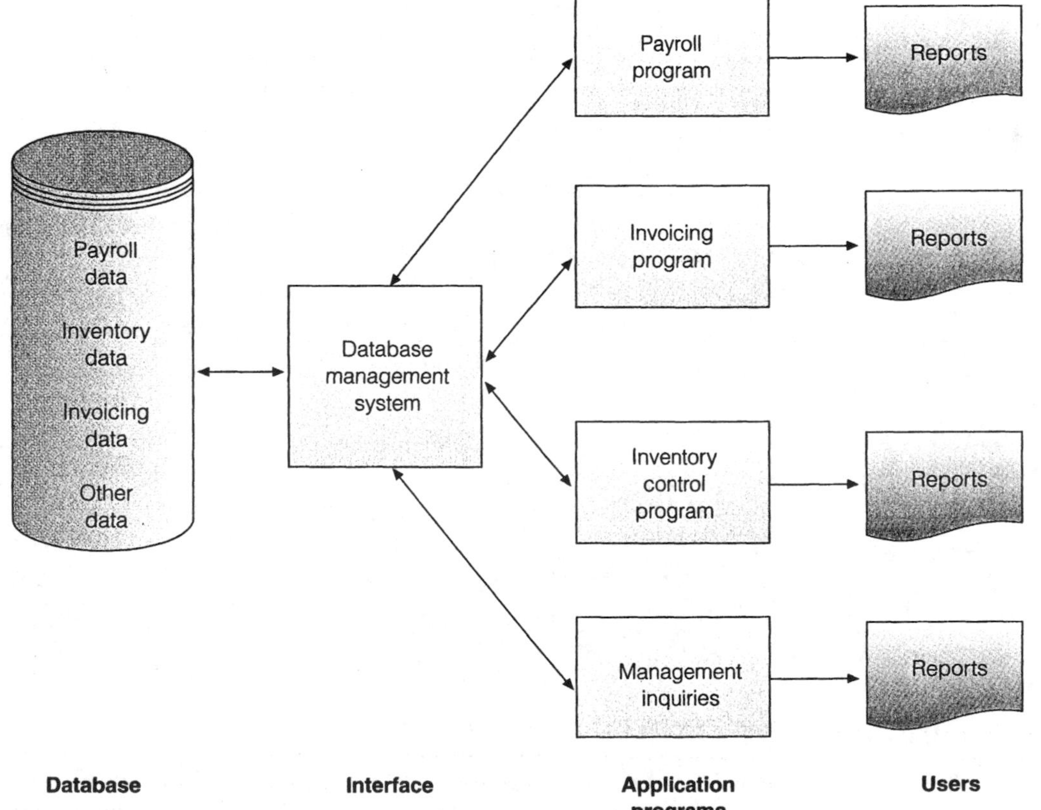

Advantages	Explanation
Improved strategic use of corporate data	Accurate, complete, up-to-date data can be made available to decision makers where, when, and in the form they need it.
Reduced data redundancy	The database approach can reduce or eliminate data redundancy. Data is organized by the DBMS and stored in only one location. This results in more efficient utilization of system storage space.
Improved data integrity	With the traditional approach, some changes to data were not reflected in all copies of the data kept in separate files. This is prevented with the database approach because there are no separate files that contain copies of the same piece of data.
Easier modification and updating	With the database approach, the DBMS coordinates updates and data modifications. Programmers and users do not have to know where the data is physically stored. Data is stored and modified once. Modification and updating is also easier because the data is stored at only one location in most cases.
Data and program independence	The DBMS organizes the data independently of the application program. With the database approach, the application program is not affected by the location or type of data. Introduction of new data types not relevant to a particular application does not require the rewriting of that application to maintain compatibility with the data file.
Better access to data and information	Most DBMSs have software that makes it easy to access and retrieve data from a database. In most cases, simple commands can be given to get important information. Relationships between records can be more easily investigated and exploited, and applications can be more easily combined.
Standardization of data access	A primary feature of the database approach is a standardized, uniform approach to database access. This means that the same overall procedures are used by all application programs to retrieve data and information.
A framework for program development	Standardized database access procedures can mean more standardization of program development. Because programs go through the DBMS to gain access to data in the database, standardized database access can provide a consistent framework for program development. In addition, each application program need address only the DBMS, not the actual data files, reducing application development time.
Better overall protection of the data	The use of and access to centrally located data are easier to monitor and control. Security codes and passwords can ensure that only authorized people have access to particular data and information in the database, thus ensuring privacy.
Shared data and information resources	The cost of hardware, software, and personnel can be spread over a large number of applications and users. This is a primary feature of a DBMS.

TABLE 3.1

Advantages of the Database Approach

computers, entertainment software, and appliances. It operates nearly 2,000 retail stores and commercial Web sites under the names Best Buy, Magnolia Hi-Fi, Media Play, On Cue, Sam Goody, and Suncoast. Best Buy uses information about the business and its customers to tailor the product mix to its customer base, minimize the time items are held in inventory to reduce costs, and respond quickly to customer needs. At the center of this strategic information is a database, which consolidates information from about 350 different sources across the enterprise.[2]

DATA MODELING AND DATABASE MODELS

It is critical to keep business data organized so that it can be used effectively. A database should be designed to store all data relevant to the business and provide

A corporate database enables Best Buy to reduce inventory costs and provide customers with the products they demand. The database pulls information from 350 sources across the enterprise.

(Source: AP/Wide World Photos.)

quick access and easy modification. In addition, it must reflect the business processes of the organization. When building a database, careful consideration must be given to these questions:

- *Content:* What data should be collected and at what cost?
- *Access:* What data should be provided to which users and when?
- *Logical structure:* How should data be arranged so that it makes sense to a given user?
- *Physical organization:* Where should data be physically located?

DATA MODELING

Key considerations in organizing data in a database include determining what data is to be collected, who will have access to it, and how they might use it. Based on these determinations, a database can then be created. Building a database requires two different types of designs: a logical design and a physical design. The logical design of a database shows an abstract model of how the data should be structured and arranged to meet an organization's information needs. The logical design of a database involves identifying relationships among the different data items and grouping them in an orderly fashion. Because databases provide both input and output for information systems throughout a business, users from all functional areas should assist in creating the logical design to ensure that their needs are identified and addressed. Physical database design starts from the logical database design and fine-tunes it for performance and cost considerations (e.g., improved response time, reduced storage space, lower operating cost). The person identified to fine-tune the physical design must have an in-depth knowledge of the DBMS to implement the database. For example, the logical database design may need to be altered so that certain data entities are combined, summary totals are carried in the data records rather than recalculated, and some data attributes are repeated in more than one data entity. These are examples of **planned data redundancy**. It is done to improve the system performance so that user reports or queries can be created more quickly.

planned data redundancy
a way of organizing data in which the logical database design is altered so that certain data entities are combined, summary totals are carried in the data records rather than calculated from elemental data, and some data attributes are repeated in more than one data entity to improve database performance

data model
a diagram of data entities and their relationships

One of the tools database designers use to show the logical relationships among data is a data model. A **data model** is a diagram of entities and their relationships. Data modeling usually involves understanding a specific business problem and analyzing the data and information needed to deliver a solution. When

TABLE 3.2

Disadvantages of the Database Approach

Disadvantages	Explanation
Relatively high cost of purchasing and operating a DBMS in a mainframe operating environment	Some mainframe DBMSs can cost hundreds of thousands of dollars.
Increased cost of specialized staff	Additional specialized staff and operating personnel may be needed to implement and coordinate the use of the database. However, some organizations have been able to implement the database approach with no additional personnel.
Increased vulnerability	Even though databases offer better security because security measures can be concentrated on one system, they also make more data accessible to the trespasser if security is breached. In addition, if for some reason there is a failure in the DBMS, multiple application programs are affected.

enterprise data modeling
data modeling done at the level of the entire enterprise

done at the level of the entire organization, this is called **enterprise data modeling**. Enterprise data modeling is an approach that starts by investigating general data and information needs of the organization at the strategic level and then examining more specific data and information needs for the various functional areas and departments within the organization. Various models have been developed to analyze data and information needs. An entity-relationship diagram is an example of such a data model.

entity-relationship (ER) diagrams
a data model that uses basic graphical symbols to show the organization of and relationships between data

Entity-relationship (ER) diagrams use basic graphical symbols to show the organization of and relationships between data. In most cases, boxes are used in ER diagrams to indicate data items or entities, and connecting lines show relationships between data items and entities. ER diagrams function as a blueprint for the individuals building the database. ER diagrams ensure that the relationships among the data entities in a database are correctly structured so that any application programs developed are consistent with business operations and user needs. In addition, ER diagrams can serve as reference documents once a database is in use. If changes need to be made to the database, ER diagrams can help design them.

Figure 3.5 shows an ER diagram for an order database. In this database design, one salesperson serves many customers. This is an example of a one-to-many relationship, as shown by the one-to-many symbol ("crow's foot") shown in Figure 3.5. The ER diagram also shows that each customer can place one-to-many orders, each order includes one-to-many line items, and many line items can specify the same product (a many-to-one relationship). There can also be one-to-one relationships. For example, one order generates one invoice. ER diagrams help ensure that the relationships among the data entities in a database are logically structured so that application programs can be developed to serve user needs. In addition, ER diagrams can be used as reference documents once a database is in use. If changes are to be made in the database, ER diagrams can help design them.

DATABASE MODELS

The structure of the relationships in most databases follows one of three logical database models: hierarchical, network, and relational. Hierarchical and network models were used to build older databases; most new databases are built based on the relational database model. It is important to remember that the records represented in the models are actually linked or related logically to one another.

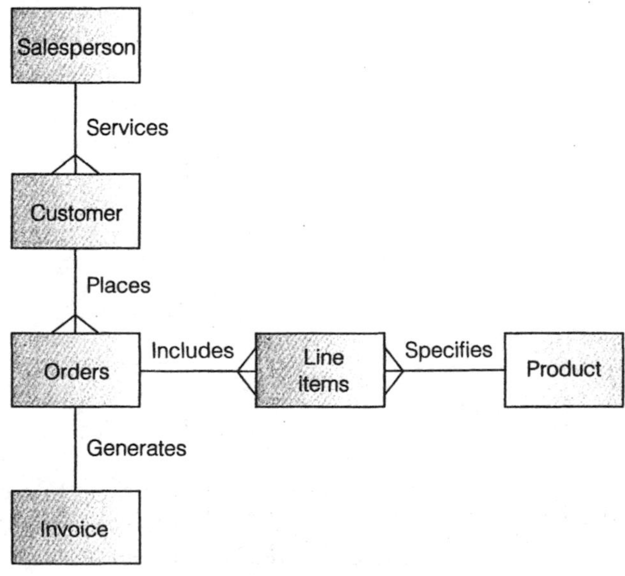

FIGURE 3.5

An Entity-Relationship (ER) Diagram for a Customer Ordering Database

Development of this type of diagram helps ensure the logical structuring of application programs that are able to serve users' needs and are consistent with the data relationships in the database.

These links dictate the way users can access data with application programs. Because the different models involve different links between data, each model has unique advantages and disadvantages.

hierarchical database model
a data model in which data is organized in a top-down, or inverted tree, structure

network model
an expansion of the hierarchical database model with an owner-member relationship in which a member may have many owners

relational database model
a database model that describes data in which all data elements are placed in two-dimensional tables, called *relations*, that are the logical equivalent of files

domain
the allowable values for data attributes

selecting
data manipulation that chooses rows according to certain criteria

Hierarchical (Tree) Models

In many situations, data follows a hierarchical structure. In a **hierarchical database model,** the data is organized in a top-down, or inverted tree, structure. For example, data about a project for a company can follow this type of model, as shown in Figure 3.6. The hierarchical model is best suited to situations in which the logical relationships between data can be properly represented with the one-to-many approach.

Network Models

In the **network model** there is an owner-member relationship in which a member may have many owners (Figure 3.7). Thus, the network model is capable of supporting many-to-many relationships.

Databases structured according to either the hierarchical model or the network model suffer from the same deficiency: once the relationships are established between data elements, it is difficult to modify them or to create new relationships.

Relational Models

The **relational database model** describes data using a standard tabular format with all data elements placed in two-dimensional tables, called *relations*, that are the logical equivalent of files. The tables in relational databases organize data in rows and columns, simplifying data access and manipulation. It is easier to understand the relational model (Figure 3.8) than hierarchical and network models.

In the relational model, each row of a table represents a data entity, with the columns of the table representing attributes. Each attribute can take on only certain values. The allowable values for these attributes are called the **domain.** The domain for a particular attribute indicates what values can be placed in each of the columns of the relational table. For instance, the domain for an attribute such as gender would be limited to male or female. A domain for pay rate would not include negative numbers. Defining a domain can increase data accuracy. For example, a pay rate of -$5.00 could not be entered into the database because it is a negative number and not in the domain for pay rate.

Once data has been placed into a relational database, users can make inquiries and analyze data. Basic data manipulations include selecting, projecting, and joining. **Selecting** involves choosing rows according to certain criteria. Suppose a

FIGURE 3.6

A Hierarchical Database Model

Project 1 is the top, or root, element. Departments A, B, and C are under this element, with Employees 1 through 6 beneath them as follows: Employees 1 and 2 under Department A, Employees 3 and 4 under Department B, and Employees 5 and 6 under Department C. Thus, there is a one-to-many relationship among the elements of this model.

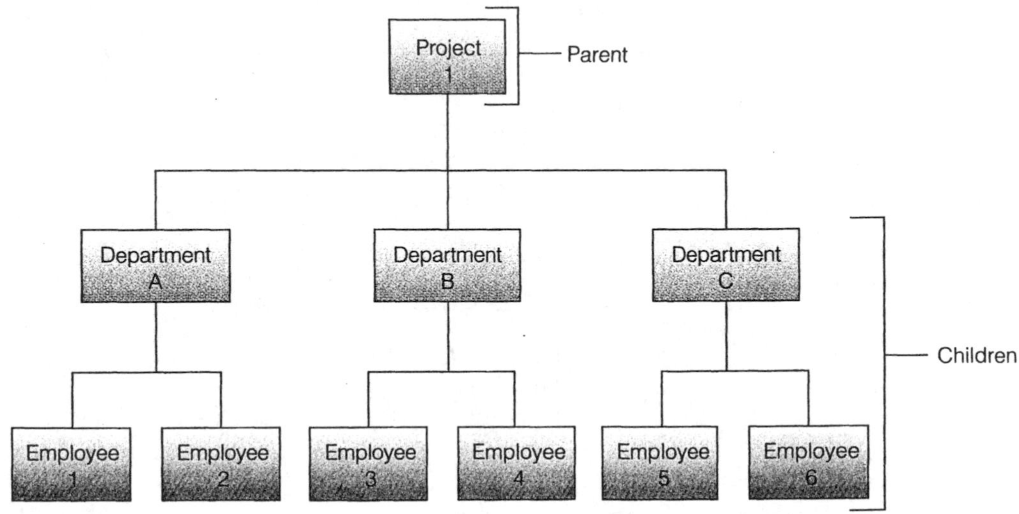

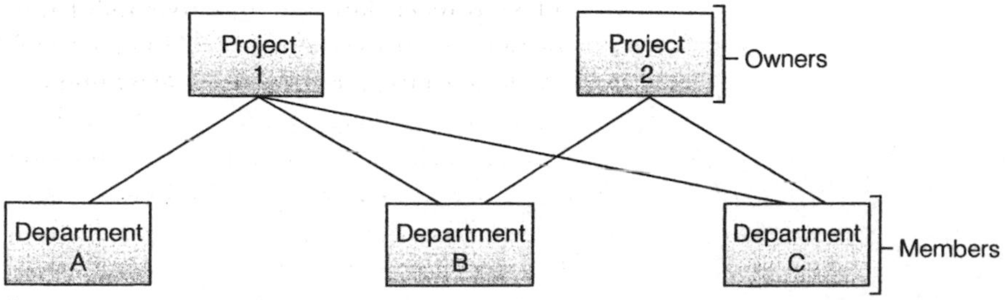

FIGURE 3.7

A Network Database Model

In this network model, two projects are at the top. Departments A, B, and C are under Project 1; Departments B and C are under Project 2. Thus, the elements of this model represent a many-to-many relationship.

project table contains the project number, description, and department number for all projects being performed by a company. The president of the company might want to find the department number for Project 226, a sales manual project. Using selection, the president can choose the row for Project 226 and see that the department number for the department completing the sales manual project is 598.

projecting
data manipulation that chooses columns in a table

Projecting involves choosing columns in a table. For example, we might have a department table that contains the department number, department name, and social security number (SSN) of the manager in charge of the project. The sales manager might want to create a new table with only the department number and the social security number of the manager in charge of the sales manual project. Projection can be used to create a new table containing only department number and SSN.

joining
data manipulation that combines two or more tables

Joining involves combining two or more tables. For example, we can combine the project table and the department table to get a new table with the project

FIGURE 3.8

A Relational Database Model

In the relational model, all data elements are placed in two-dimensional tables, or relations. As long as they share at least one common element, these relations can be linked to output useful information.

Data table 1: Project table

Project number	Description	Dept. number
155	Payroll	257
498	Widgets	632
226	Sales Manual	598

Data table 2: Department table

Dept. number	Dept. name	Manager SSN
257	Accounting	005-10-6321
632	Manufacturing	549-77-1001
598	Marketing	098-40-1370

Data table 3: Manager table

SSN	Last name	First name	Hire date	Dept. number
005-10-6321	Johns	Francine	10-07-1997	257
549-77-1001	Buckley	Bill	02-17-1979	632
098-40-1370	Fiske	Steven	01-05-1985	598

number, project description, department number, department name, and social security number for the manager in charge of the project.

As long as the tables share at least one common data attribute, the tables in a relational database can be **linked** to provide useful information and reports (see Figure 3.9). Being able to link tables to each other through common data attributes is one of the keys to the flexibility and power of relational databases. Suppose the president of a company wants to find out the name of the manager of the sales manual project and how long the manager has been with the company. The president would make the inquiry to the database. The DBMS would start with the project description and search the project table to find out the project's department number. It would then use the department number to search the department table for the department manager's social security number. The department number is also in the department table and is the common element that allows the project table and the department table to be linked. The DBMS then uses the manager's social security number to search the manager table for the manager's hire date. The manager's social security number is the common element between the department table and the manager table. The final result: the manager's name and hire date are presented to the president as a response to the inquiry.

linked
data manipulation that combines two or more tables using common data attributes to form a new table with only the unique data attributes

The relational database model is easier to control, more flexible, and more intuitive than the others because it organizes data in tables. As seen in Figure 3.10, a relational database management system, such as Access, provides a number of tips and tools for building and using database tables. This figure shows the database displaying information about data types and indicating that additional help is available.

Galileo International is one of four major worldwide reservation systems that handle travel industry bookings. In 2002, it implemented a new fare-pricing

FIGURE 3.9

Linking Data Tables to Answer an Inquiry

In finding the name and hire date of the manager working on the sales manual project, the president needs three tables: project, department, and manager. The project description (Sales Manual) leads to the department number (598) in the project table, which leads to the manager's SSN (098-40-1370) in the department table, which leads to the manager's name (Fiske) and hire date (01-05-1985) in the manager table.

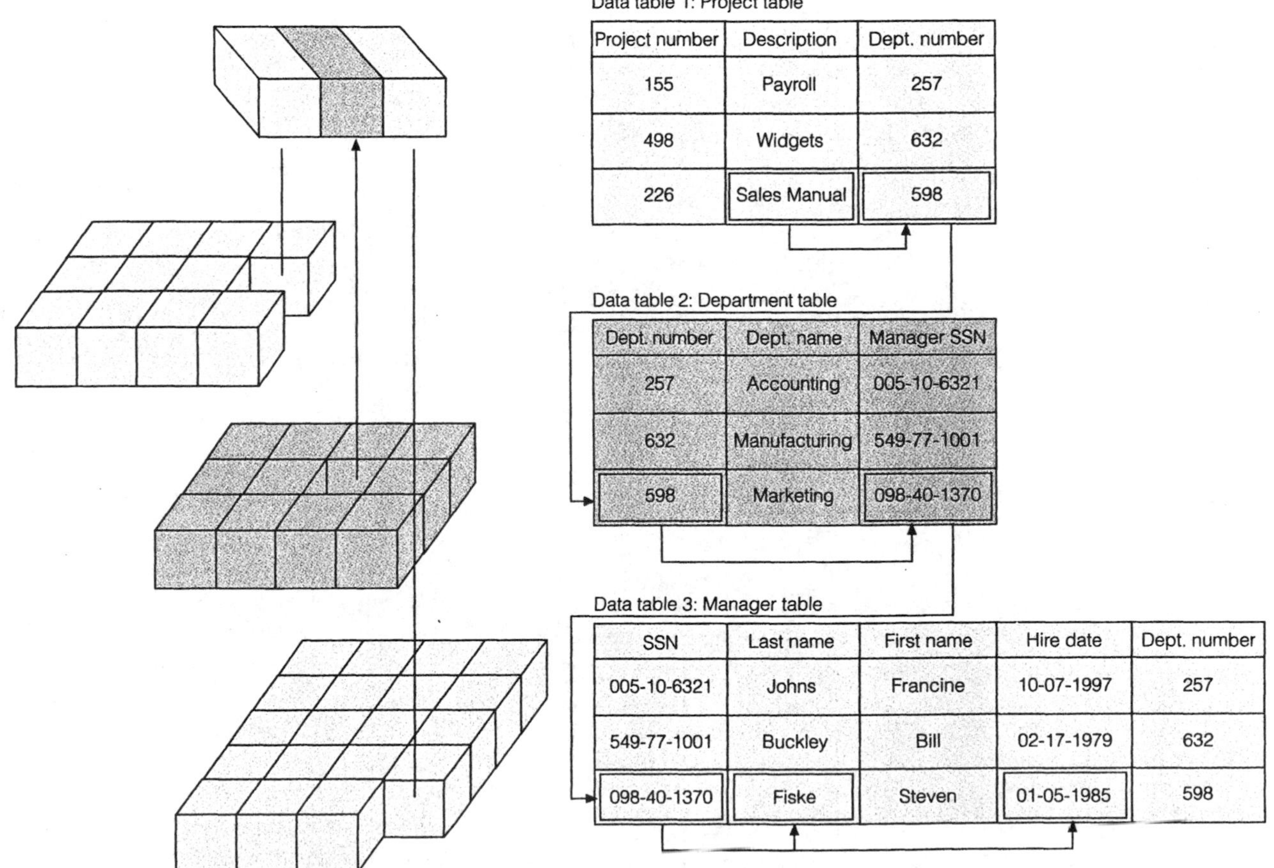

Data table 1: Project table

Project number	Description	Dept. number
155	Payroll	257
498	Widgets	632
226	Sales Manual	598

Data table 2: Department table

Dept. number	Dept. name	Manager SSN
257	Accounting	005-10-6321
632	Manufacturing	549-77-1001
598	Marketing	098-40-1370

Data table 3: Manager table

SSN	Last name	First name	Hire date	Dept. number
005-10-6321	Johns	Francine	10-07-1997	257
549-77-1001	Buckley	Bill	02-17-1979	632
098-40-1370	Fiske	Steven	01-05-1985	598

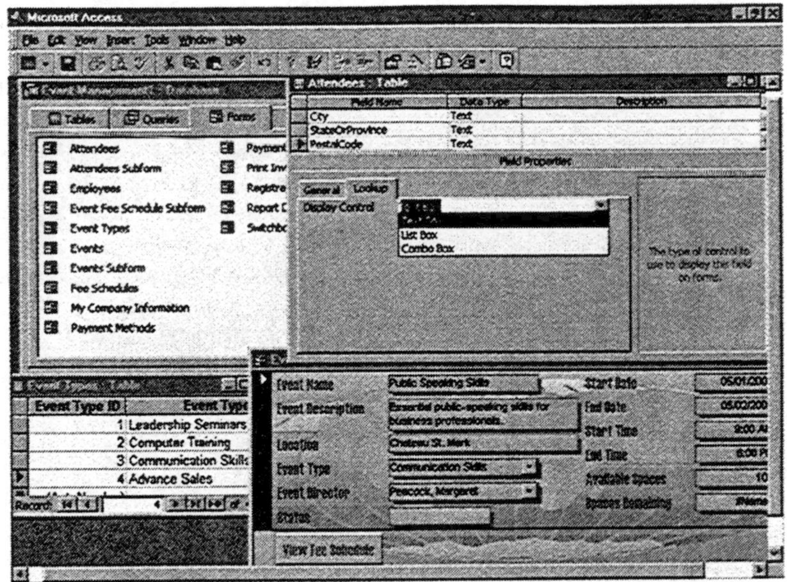

FIGURE 3.10

Building and Modifying a Relational Database

Relational databases provide many tools, tips, and tricks to simplify the process of creating and modifying a database.

system based on the use of relational database technology. The millions of daily queries from on-line travel companies, such as Expedia, Travelocity, and Orbitz, plus the need to adjust pricing rapidly for those sites, require the most efficient database management technology possible. With the new system and the use of relational database technology, Galileo can also accept lists of airline airfares automatically from ATPco, the industry-funded company that publishes airfares.[3]

DATABASE MANAGEMENT SYSTEMS (DBMSs)

Creating and implementing the right database system ensures that the database will support an organization's business activities and goals. But how do we actually create, implement, use, and update a database? The answer is found in the database management system. DBMSs are classified by the type of database model they support. For example, a relational database management system supports the relational model. Access by Microsoft is a popular relational DBMS for personal computers. Other popular relational DBMSs include Microsoft SQL; DB2 and Informix from IBM; Oracle; and Sybase. A number of open source database management systems are also available, including MySQL, PostgreSQL, and Berkeley DB. These DBMSs come with open source licenses so they are free. Yahoo and Slashdot are two Web sites that rely on open source databases to store articles and comments.[4]

PROVIDING A USER VIEW

schema
a description of the entire database

Because the DBMS is responsible for access to a database, one of the first steps in installing and using a database involves defining the logical and physical structure of the data and relationships among the data in the database. This description is called a **schema** (as in schematic diagram). A schema can be part of the database or a separate schema file. The DBMS can reference a schema to find where to access the requested data in relation to another piece of data.

subschema
a file that contains a description of a subset of the database and identifies which users can view and modify the data items in the subset

A DBMS also acts as a user interface by providing a view of the database. A user view is the portion of the database a user can access. To create different user views, subschemas are developed. A **subschema** is a file that contains a description of a subset of the database and identifies which users can modify the data items in that subset. While a schema is a description of the entire database, a subschema shows only some of the records and their relationships in the database.

For example, a sales representative might need only data describing customers in her region, not the sales data for the entire nation. A subschema could be used to limit her view to data from her region. With subschemas, the underlying structure of the database can change, but the view the user sees might not change. For example, even if all the data on the southern region changed, the northeast region sales representative's view would not change if she accessed data on her region.

A number of subschemas can be developed for different users and the various application programs. Typically, the database user or application will access the subschema, which then accesses the schema (Figure 3.11). Subschemas can also provide additional security because various users are typically allowed to view only certain parts of the database.

CREATING AND MODIFYING THE DATABASE

Schemas and subschemas are entered into the DBMS via a data definition language. A **data definition language (DDL)** is a collection of instructions and commands used to define and describe data and data relationships in a specific database. A DDL allows the database's creator to describe the data and the data relationships that are to be contained in the schema and the many subschemas. In general, a DDL describes logical access paths and logical records in the database.

data definition language (DDL)
a collection of instructions and commands used to define and describe data and data relationships in a specific database

data dictionary
a detailed description of all the data used in the database

Another important step in creating a database is to establish a **data dictionary**, a detailed description of all data used in the database. The data dictionary contains the name of the data item, aliases or other names that may be used to describe the item, the range of values that can be used, the type of data (such as alphanumeric or numeric), the length of the data item in bytes, a notation of the person responsible for updating it and the various users who can access it, and a list of reports that use the data item. Following are some of the typical uses of a data dictionary.

- *Provide a standard definition of terms and data elements.* Standardization can help in programming by providing consistent terms and variables to be used for all programs. Programmers know what data elements are already "captured" in the database and how they relate to other data elements.
- *Assist programmers in designing and writing programs.* Programmers do not need to know which storage devices are used to store needed data. Using the

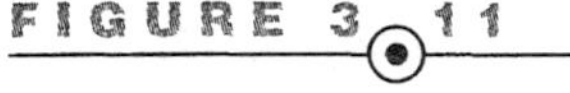

The Use of Schemas and Subschemas

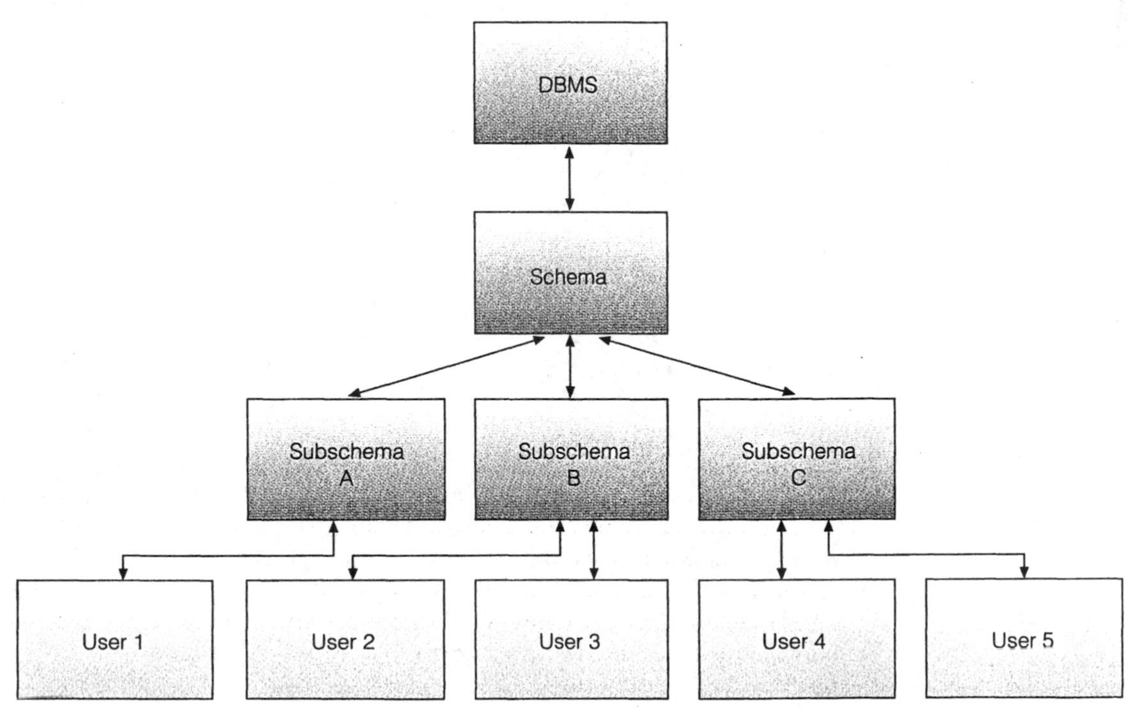

data dictionary, programmers specify the required data elements. The DBMS locates the necessary data. More important, programmers can use the data dictionary to see which programs already use a piece of data and, if appropriate, copy the relevant section of the program code into their new program, thus eliminating duplicate programming efforts.

- *Simplify database modification.* If for any reason a data element needs to be changed or deleted, the data dictionary would point to specific programs that use the data element that may need modification. Use of a data dictionary helps achieve the advantages of the database approach in these ways:
- *Reduced data redundancy.* With standard definitions of all data, it is less likely that the same data item will be stored in different places under different names. For example, a data dictionary would reduce the likelihood that the same part number would be stored as two different items, such as PTNO and PARTNO.
- *Increased data reliability.* A data dictionary and the database approach reduce the chance that data will be destroyed or lost. In addition, it is more difficult for unauthorized people to gain access to sensitive data and information.
- *Faster program development.* With a data dictionary, programmers can develop programs faster. They don't have to develop names for data items because the data dictionary does that for them.
- *Easier modification of data and information.* The data dictionary and the database approach make modifications to data easier because users do not need to know where the data is stored. The person making the change indicates the new value of the variable or item, such as part number, that is to be changed. The database system locates the data and makes the necessary change.

STORING AND RETRIEVING DATA

When an application program needs data, it requests that data through the DBMS. Suppose that to calculate the total price of a new car, an auto dealer pricing program needs price data on the engine option-six cylinders instead of the standard four cylinders. The application program requests this data from the DBMS. In doing so, the application program follows a logical access path. Next, the DBMS, working in conjunction with various system software programs, accesses a storage device, such as a disk or tape, where the data is stored. When the DBMS goes to this storage device to retrieve the data, it follows a path to the physical location (physical access path) where the price of this option is stored. In the pricing example, the DBMS might go to a disk drive to retrieve the price data for six-cylinder engines. This relationship is shown in Figure 3.12.

This same process is used if a user wants to get information from the database. First, the user requests the data from the DBMS. For example, a user might give a command, such as LIST ALL OPTIONS WHERE PRICE IS 200. This is the logical access path (LAP). Then the DBMS might go to the options price sector of a disk to get the information for the user. This is the physical access path (PAP).

When two or more people or programs attempt to access the same record in the same database at the same time, there can be a problem. For example, an inventory control program might attempt to reduce the inventory level for a product by ten units because ten units were just shipped to a customer. At the same time, a purchasing program might attempt to increase the inventory level for the same product by 200 units because more inventory was just received. Without proper database control, one of the inventory updates may not be correctly made, resulting in an inaccurate inventory level for the product. **Concurrency control** can be used to avoid this potential problem. One approach is to lock out all other application programs from access to a record if the record is being updated or used by another program.

concurrency control
a method of dealing with a situation in which two or more people need to access the same record in a database at the same time

FIGURE 3.12

Logical and Physical Access Paths

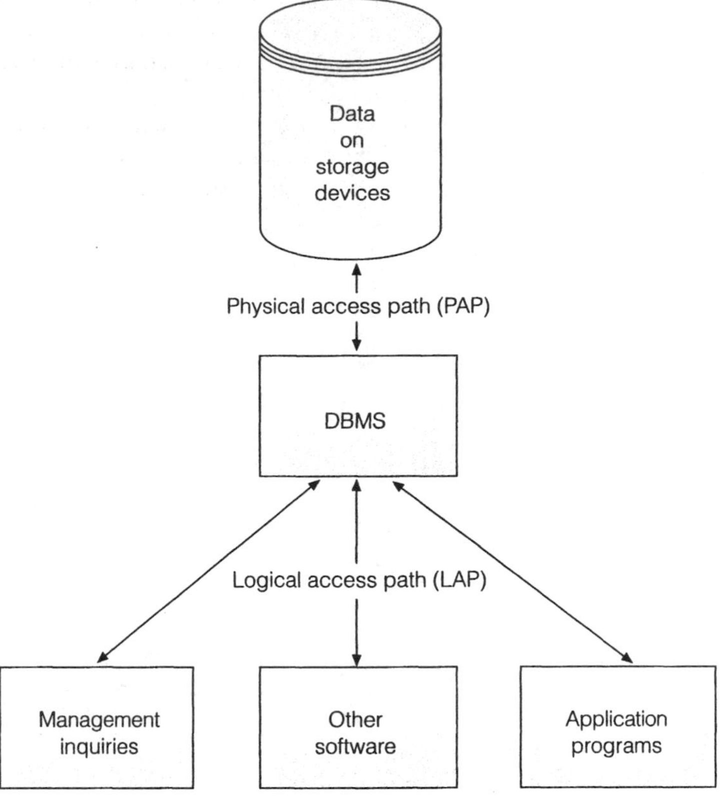

MANIPULATING DATA AND GENERATING REPORTS

Once a DBMS has been installed, the system can be used by all levels of employees via specific commands in various programming languages. For example, COBOL commands can be used in simple programs that will access or manipulate certain pieces of data in the database. Here's another example of a DBMS query: SELECT * FROM EMPLOYEE WHERE JOB_CLASSIFICATION = "C2." The * tells the program to include all columns from the EMPLOYEE table for just those employees with a C2 job classification. In general, the commands that are used to manipulate the database are part of the **data manipulation language (DML)**. This specific language, provided with the DBMS, allows managers and other database users to access, modify, and make queries about data contained in the database to generate reports. Again, the application programs go through subschemas, schemas, and the DBMS before actually getting to the physically stored data on a device such as a disk.

data manipulation language (DML)
the commands that are used to manipulate the data in a database

Structured query language (SQL) was developed in the 1970s and adopted by the American National Standards Institute as the standard query language for relational databases in 1986. SQL lets programmers and end users learn one powerful query language for accessing databases and use it on systems ranging from PCs to the largest mainframe computers (Figure 3.13). Because SQL uses standardized and simplified procedures for retrieving, storing, and manipulating data in a database system, the popular database query language can be easy to understand and use. The various database management software manufacturers have developed their own variations of SQL that work with their DBMSs. All variations of SQL allow for users to SELECT data FROM various tables WHERE certain conditions are met. SELECT, FROM, and WHERE are three key SQL operators.

Once a database has been set up and loaded with data, it can produce output—usually in the form of screen displays or hard-copy printouts (Figure 3.14). The output-control features of a database program allow you to select the records and fields to appear in reports. You can also complete calculations specifically

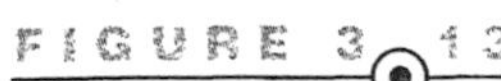

Structured Query Language

SQL has become an integral part of most relational database packages, as shown by this screen from Microsoft Access.

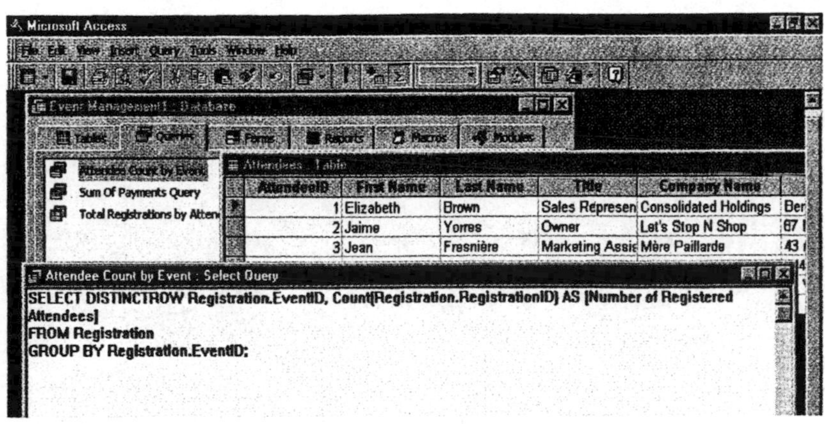

for the report by manipulating database fields. Formatting controls and organization options (such as report headings) help you customize reports and create flexible, convenient, and powerful information-handling tools.

A database program can produce a wide variety of documents, reports, and other outputs that can help organizations achieve their goals. The most common reports select and organize data to present summary information about some aspect of company operations. For example, accounting reports often summarize financial data such as current and past-due accounts. Many companies base their routine operating decisions on regular status reports that show the progress of specific orders toward completion and delivery. Increasingly, companies are using databases to provide improved customer services.

Exception, scheduled, and demand reports highlight events that require urgent management attention. Exception reports are produced only when some predefined exception condition occurs—for example, a sales change by +/–10 percent. Scheduled reports are produced according to a predetermined time schedule—for example, the fourth work night of the month. Demand reports are produced only when a user explicitly requests them. Database programs can produce various documents and reports. A few examples include these:

- Form letters with address labels
- Payroll checks and reports

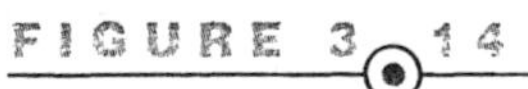

Database Output

A database application offers sophisticated formatting and organization options to produce the right information in the right format.

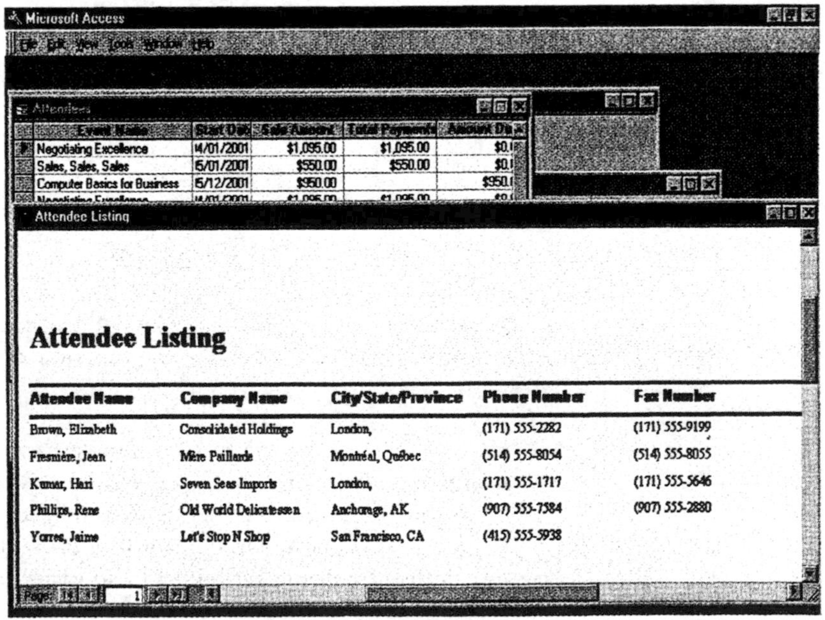

- Invoices
- Orders for materials and supplies
- A variety of financial performance reports

ADMINISTERING DATABASES

database administrator (DBA)
a highly skilled and trained systems professional who directs or performs all activities related to maintaining a successful database environment

With the proliferation of databases today, organizations need personnel who can oversee their selection and use for critical processes. A **database administrator (DBA)** is a highly skilled and trained information systems professional who directs or performs all activities related to maintaining a successful database environment. The DBA's responsibilities include designing, implementing, and maintaining the database system; establishing policies and procedures pertaining to the management, security, maintenance, and use of the database management system; and training employees in database management and use. A DBA is expected to understand the fundamental business of the organization, be proficient in the use of selected database management systems, and stay abreast of emerging technologies and new design approaches. Typically, a DBA has either a degree in computer science or management information systems and some on-the-job training with a particular database product or more extensive experience with a range of database products.

data administrator
a nontechnical but important person who ensures that data is managed as an important organizational resource

Some organizations have created a position called **data administrator**, a nontechnical but important role that ensures that data is managed as an important organizational resource. The data administrator is responsible for defining and implementing a consistent set of principles for a variety of data issues, including setting data standards and data definitions that apply across the many databases that an organization may have. For example, this would ensure that a term such as *customer* is defined and treated consistently in all corporate databases. The data administrator also works with business managers to identify who should have read and/or update access to certain databases and to selected attributes within those databases. This information is then communicated to the database administrator to execute the technical details of implementation. The database administrator and data administrator must work together as a team to meet the database needs of the organization.

POPULAR DATABASE MANAGEMENT SYSTEMS

The latest generation of database management systems makes it possible for end users to build their own database applications. End users are using these tools to address everyday problems such as how to manage a mounting pile of information on employees, customers, inventory, and sales or how to organize wine lists, CD collections, and video libraries. These database management systems are an important personal productivity tool, along with word processing, spreadsheet, and graphics software.

A key to making DBMSs easier to use is the incorporation of "wizards" that walk you through how to build customized databases, modify ready-to-run applications, use existing record templates, and quickly locate the data you want. These applications also include powerful features such as help systems and Web-publishing capabilities. For example, users can create a complete inventory system and then instantly post it to the Web, where it does double duty as an electronic catalog. Some of the more popular DBMSs for end users include Corel's Paradox, FileMaker's FileMaker Pro, Microsoft's Access, and Lotus's Approach.

The complete database management software market encompasses software that is used by professional programmers and that runs on midrange, mainframe, and supercomputers. The entire market generates $10 billion per year in revenue, with IBM, Oracle, and Microsoft the leaders (Figure 3.15). Although Microsoft rules in desktop PC software, its share of database software on mainframe computers is small.

FIGURE 3.15

Worldwide Database Market Share, 2001—Based on Percentage of Worldwide New License Revenue from DBMSs

(Source: Data from James Niccolai, "Gartner: IBM Steals Database Crown from Oracle," *Computerworld,* May 7, 2002, http://www.computerworld.com.)

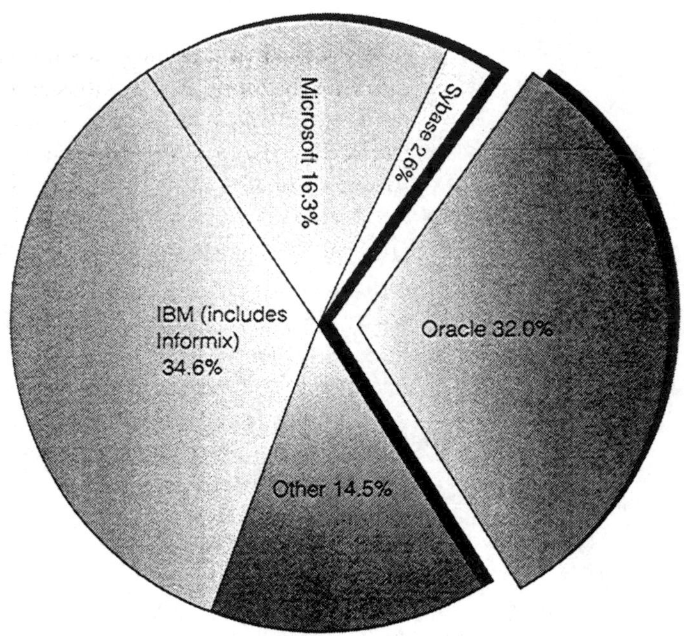

SELECTING A DATABASE MANAGEMENT SYSTEM

Selecting the best database management system begins by analyzing database needs and characteristics. The information needs of the organization affect what type of data is collected and what type of database management system is used. Important characteristics of databases include the size of the database, number of concurrent users, performance, the ability of the DBMS to integrate with other systems, the features of the DBMS, vendor considerations, and the cost of the database management system.

Database Size

The database size depends on the number of records or files in the database. The size determines the overall storage requirement for the database. Most database management systems can handle relatively small databases of less than 100 million bytes; fewer can manage terabyte-size databases.

Number of Concurrent Users

The number of simultaneous users that can access the contents of the database is also an important factor. Clearly, a database intended for use by a large workgroup must be able to support a number of concurrent users; if it cannot, then the efficiency of the members of the workgroup will be lowered. The term *scalability* is sometimes used to describe how well a database performs as the size of the database or the number of concurrent users is increased. A highly scalable database management system is desirable to provide flexibility. Unfortunately, many companies make a poor DBMS choice in this regard and then later are forced to convert to a new DBMS when the original does not meet expectations.

Performance

How fast the database can update records can be the most important performance criterion for some organizations. Credit card and airline companies, for example, must have database systems that can update customer records and check credit or make a plane reservation in seconds, not minutes. Other applications, such as payroll, can be done once a week or less frequently and do not require immediate processing. If an application demands immediacy, it also demands rapid recovery facilities in the event the computer system shuts down temporarily. Other performance considerations include the number of concurrent users that can be supported and how much main memory is required to execute the database management program.

Integration

A key aspect of any database management system is its ability to integrate with other applications and databases. A key determinant here is what operating systems it can run under—such as Unix, Windows XP, and Linux. Some companies use several databases for different applications at different locations. A manufacturing company with four plants in three different states might have a separate database at each location. The ability of a database program to import data from and export data to other databases and applications can be a critical consideration.

Features

The features of the database management system can also make a big difference. Most database programs come with security procedures, privacy protection, and a variety of tools. Other features can include how easy the database package is to use and the availability of manuals and documentation that can help the organization get the most from the database package. Additional features such as wizards and ready-to-use templates help improve the product's ease of use and are very important.

Vendor

The size, reputation, and financial stability of the vendor should also be considered in making any database purchase. Some vendors are well respected in the information systems industry and have a large staff of support personnel to give assistance, if needed. A well-established and financially secure database company is more likely to remain in business than others.

The ability of the vendor to provide global support for large, multinational companies or companies outside the United States is becoming increasingly important. CERN is the European Organization for Nuclear Research located near Geneva, Switzerland. It is building a particle accelerator that will give scientists new insights into the structure of matter. When the Large Hadron Collider begins operation in 2006, it will generate a prodigious amount of information—between 5 and 20 PB (petabytes) of raw data each year. CERN information systems people are considering using Oracle9i rather than the Objectivity database software that has so far been an unofficial standard among nuclear research labs. The primary reason is that Oracle has extensive European operations while Objectivity does not.[5]

Cost

Database packages for personal computers can cost a few hundred dollars, while large database systems for mainframe computers can cost hundreds of thousands of dollars. In addition to the initial cost of the database package, monthly operating costs should be considered. Some database companies rent or lease their database software. Monthly rental or lease costs, maintenance costs, additional hardware and software costs, and personnel costs can be substantial.

Databases continually evolve to include new capabilities and make work processes more efficient. In addition, they allow organizations to perform functions that were unheard of only a few years ago. We explore some interesting database applications next.

DATABASE APPLICATIONS

A number of developments in the use of databases and database management systems can help managers meet changing business needs, including providing access to the company's databases by the Internet, setting up data warehouses and marts, gathering and disseminating business intelligence, distributing data to where it can be used most effectively, analyzing large amounts of data, sharing data across different DBMSs, using the object-oriented approach in database development, and storing and retrieving spatial data.

LINKING THE COMPANY DATABASE TO THE INTERNET

Customers, suppliers, and company employees must be able to access corporate databases through the Internet, intranets, and extranets to meet various business needs. For example, when they are shopping, Internet customers need to access the corporate product database to obtain product information, including size, color, type, and price details. Suppliers use the Internet and corporate extranets to view inventory databases to check levels of raw materials and the current production schedule to determine when and how much of their products must be delivered to support just-in-time inventory management. Company employees need to be able to access corporate databases to support decision making even when they are off-site. In such cases, they may use laptop computers and access the data via the Internet or company intranet.

In enabling such access of corporate databases, it is important that any software installation required at the user end be extremely simple. In addition, only authorized users should be able to access the databases. As a result, organizations are using application servers—software packages that connect end users to the databases holding the information they need to access by setting up an application session for each user, checking each user's identification and password, fetching requested information from the appropriate database, and building the data into a Web page for display to the users. Application server software packages, offered by more than three-dozen vendors, also provide application management services such as monitoring system performance to identify any system bottlenecks.

DATA WAREHOUSES, DATA MARTS, AND DATA MINING

The raw data necessary to make sound business decisions is stored in a variety of locations and formats—hierarchical databases, network databases, flat files, and spreadsheets, to name a few. This data is initially captured, stored, and managed by transaction processing systems that are designed to support the day-to-day operations of the organization. For decades, organizations have collected operational, sales, and financial data with their on-line transaction processing (OLTP) systems.

Traditional OLTP systems are designed to put data into databases very quickly, reliably, and efficiently, but they are not good at supporting meaningful analysis of the data. In fact, tuning a system to provide speedy performance for OLTP often sacrifices data analysis capabilities. Also, data stored in OLTP databases is inconsistent and constantly changing. The database contains the current transactions required to operate the business, including errors, duplicate entries, and reverse transactions, which get in the way of a business analyst, who needs stable data. Historical data is missing from the OLTP database, which makes trend analysis impossible. Because of the application orientation of the data, the variety of nonintegrated data sources, and the lack of historical data, companies were limited in their ability to access and use the data for other purposes. So, although the amount of data collected by OLTP systems can double every two years, it does not meet the needs of the business decision maker—those systems are data rich but information poor.

data warehouse
a database that collects business information from many sources in the enterprise, covering all aspects of the company's processes, products, and customers

A **data warehouse** is a database that collects business information from many sources in the enterprise, covering all aspects of the company's processes, products, and customers. The data warehouse provides business users with a multidimensional view of the data they need to analyze business conditions. Data warehousing is designed specifically to support management decision making, not to meet the needs of transaction processing systems. The data warehouse provides a specialized decision support database that manages the flow of information from existing corporate databases and external sources to end-user decision support applications. A data warehouse stores historical data that has been extracted from operational systems and external data sources (Figure 3.16). This

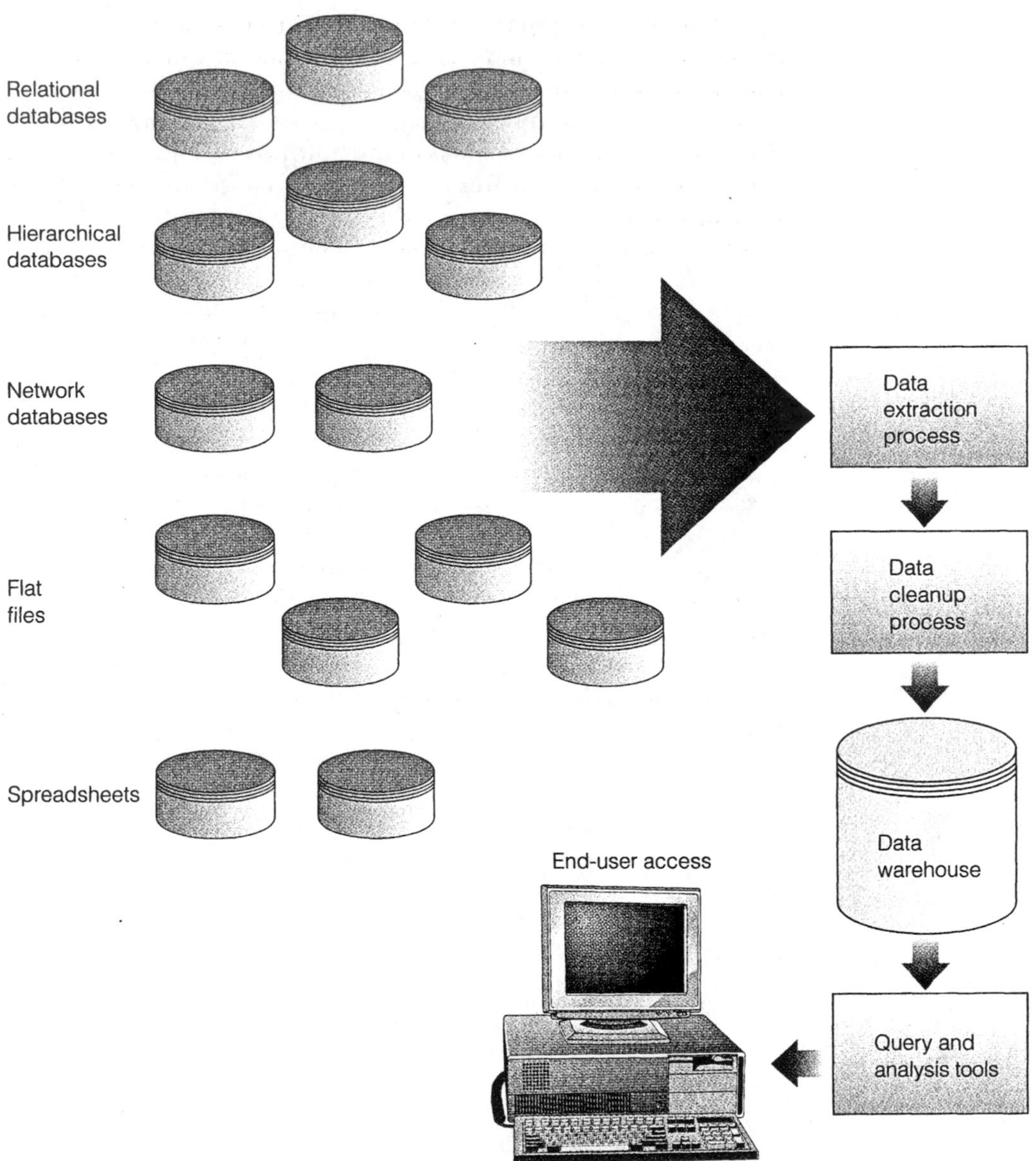

FIGURE 3.16

Elements of a Data Warehouse

operational and external data is "cleaned up" to remove inconsistencies and integrated to create a new information database that is more suitable for business analysis.

Data warehouses typically start out as very large databases containing millions and even hundreds of millions of data records. As this data is collected from the various production systems, a historical database is built that business analysts can use. To remain fresh and accurate, the data warehouse receives regular updates, and old data that is no longer needed is purged. Updating the data warehouse must be fast, efficient, and automated, or its ultimate value is sacrificed. It is common for a data warehouse to contain from three to ten years of current and historical data. Data cleaning tools can merge data from many sources into one database, automate data collection and verification, delete unwanted data, and maintain data in a database management system. The amount of data the average business collects and stores is doubling each year. If that holds true at a company such as Sears Roebuck and Co., which is combining its customer and inventory data warehouses to create a 70-TB system, the retailer will hit the 1-PB threshold (approximately 1,000 TB) within four years. A petabyte of data is the equivalent of 250 billion pages of text, enough to fill 20 million four-drawer filing cabinets.[6]

The primary advantage of data warehousing is the ability to relate data in new, innovative ways. However, a data warehouse can be extremely difficult to establish, with the average cost of building one estimated at over $2 million.

data mart
a subset of a data warehouse

A **data mart** is a subset of a data warehouse. Data marts bring the data warehouse concept—on-line analysis of sales, inventory, and other vital business data that has been gathered from transaction processing systems—to small and medium-size businesses and to departments within larger companies. Rather than store all enterprise data in one monolithic database, data marts contain a subset of the data for a single aspect of a company's business—for example, finance, inventory, or personnel. In fact, there may even be more detailed data for a specific area in a data mart than a data warehouse would provide.

Data marts are most useful for smaller groups who want to access detailed data, typically for use in some sort of decision support system. A warehouse is used for summary data for the rest of the company. Because data marts typically contain tens of gigabytes of data, as opposed to the hundreds of gigabytes in data warehouses, they can be deployed on less powerful hardware with smaller disks, delivering significant savings to an organization. Although any database software can be used to set up a data mart, some vendors deliver specialized software designed and priced specifically for data marts. Already, companies such as Sybase, Software AG, and Microsoft have products and services that make it easier and cheaper to deploy these scaled-down data warehouses. The selling point is that data marts put targeted business information into the hands of more decision makers.

data mining
an information analysis tool that involves the automated discovery of patterns and relationships in a data warehouse

Data mining is an information analysis tool that involves the automated discovery of patterns and relationships in a data warehouse. Data mining represents the next step in the evolution of decision support systems. It makes use of advanced statistical techniques and machine learning to discover facts in a large database, including databases on the Internet. Unlike query tools, which require users to formulate and test a specific hypothesis, data mining uses built-in analysis tools to automatically generate a hypothesis about the patterns and anomalies found in the data and then from the hypothesis to predict future behavior.

Data mining's objective is to extract patterns, trends, and rules from data warehouses to evaluate (i.e., predict or score) proposed business strategies, which in turn will improve competitiveness, improve profits, and transform business processes. It is used extensively in marketing to improve customer retention; cross-selling opportunities; campaign management; market, channel, and pricing analysis; and customer segmentation analysis (especially one-to-one marketing). In short, data mining tools help end users find answers to questions they never even thought to ask.

Jiffy Lube uses data mining to attract new customers. The company keeps records on millions of vehicles, tracking how often the owners come in and for what services. Using this data, it has profiled its best customers so its service centers can custom design direct mailings to locals who match its best customers' profiles but haven't yet visited Jiffy Lube.[7] United Airlines built a data warehouse that eventually will hold 6 TB of customer, reservation, and flight data. United will use data mining to better manage customer data, improve its frequent-flier programs, study flight data, and analyze reservation patterns. The airline will also use the data to identify high-value customers who were inconvenienced by delays and offer them some sort of compensation.[8]

E-commerce presents another major opportunity for effective use of data mining. Attracting customers to on-line Web sites is tough; keeping them can be next to impossible. For example, when on-line retail Web sites launch deep-discount sales, they cannot easily figure out how many first-time customers are likely to come back and buy again. Nor do they have a way of understanding which customers acquired during the sale are price sensitive and more likely to jump on future sales. As a result, companies are gathering data on user traffic through their

Todd & Holland Tea Merchants used predictive analysis data mining software to redefine its target market—to include professional women from 25 to 35 years of age. Previously, the company had overlooked that customer segment.

Web sites. This data is then analyzed using data mining techniques to personalize the Web site and develop sales promotions targeted at specific customers.

Predictive analysis is a form of data mining that combines historical data with assumptions about future conditions to predict outcomes of events such as future product sales or the probability that a customer will default on a loan. Retailers use predictive analysis to upgrade occasional customers into frequent purchasers by predicting what products they will buy if offered an appropriate incentive. Genalytics, Magnify, NCR Teradata, SAS Institute, Sightward, SPSS, and Quadstone have developed predictive analysis tools. Todd & Holland Tea Merchants sells specialty tea over the Internet and in a retail shop. The company used predictive analysis software from SPSS to analyze the company's customer list and a year's worth of sales data. The resulting recommendation was that Todd & Holland should market the tea to professional women between 25 and 35—a market segment that had gone unrecognized by the owners.[9]

Table 3.3 summarizes a few of the most frequent applications for data mining. Also, read the "Ethical and Societal Issues" special-interest box to see how predictive analysis and data mining can be used along with database management technology to help make the skies safer for all of us.

BUSINESS INTELLIGENCE

Closely linked to the concept of data mining is use of databases for business intelligence purposes. **Business intelligence** is the process of gathering enough of the right information in a timely manner and usable form and analyzing it so that it can have a positive impact on business strategy, tactics, or operations. Business intelligence involves turning data into useful information that is then distributed throughout an enterprise. Companies use this information to make improved

TABLE 3.3

Common Data Mining Applications

Application	Description
Branding and positioning of products and services	Enable the strategist to visualize the different positions of competitors in a given market using performance (or importance) data on dozens of key features of the product in question and then to condense all that data into a perceptual map of just two or three dimensions
Customer churn	Predict current customers who are likely to go to a competitor
Direct marketing	Identify prospects most likely to respond to a direct marketing campaign such as telephone solicitation or direct mailing
Fraud detection	Highlight transactions most likely to be deceptive or illegal
Market-basket analysis	Identify products and services that are most commonly purchased at the same time (e.g., nail polish and lipstick)
Market segmentation	Group customers based on who they are or on what they prefer
Trend analysis	Analyze how key variables (e.g., sales, spending, promotions) vary over time

Ethical and Societal Issues

Database Technology Improves Airport Security

The Transportation Security Administration is evaluating various approaches to harness database technology in its efforts to improve airport security. Unfortunately, any such system may require airlines to invest in additional information systems technology—at a time when they are suffering from a lack of revenue. One major airline has already declared bankruptcy.

One idea is to develop a database system that links every airline reservation system in the country with a number of private and government databases. Data mining and predictive analysis would be used to sort through personal travel histories, the backgrounds of passengers aboard particular flights, and a wealth of other data to assign numerical "threat ratings" to individuals. Warnings would be sent electronically to workers at airport screening locations to inspect individuals with high threat ratings more closely.

Another approach would allow prescreened "trusted travelers" to pass through airport security checkpoints quickly, avoiding long lines and congestion. This system would devote more time and resources to screening other travelers whose level of risk is higher or unknown. Those who apply for the "trusted traveler" program would have to pass a background check using data from a number of state and federal databases. Once at the airport, "trusted traveler" passengers would be identified, perhaps by scanning their fingerprints or retinas or requiring some form of identification card. (The federal government is considering developing a security ID card for airline passengers that would rely on biometric identification and be linked to government databases.) The system would also cross-check the passenger's identification with the FBI's watch list database and a federal passenger profiling system known as Computer-Assisted Passenger Screening. Provided everything was clear, the passenger could then proceed to his or her airplane using expedited security check-in procedures.

Discussion Questions

1. Which approach is best in terms of improving airport security: assigning a threat rating to individuals or prescreening individuals to identify "trusted travelers"? Why do you think this approach is best?
2. Identify specific data that could be used to assign numeric threat ratings to individuals. Describe how the system would work.

Critical Thinking Questions

3. Briefly discuss the data integrity or data privacy issues associated with the two approaches outlined in the box.
4. Identify other technical and economic issues that may make it difficult to implement either approach. Should the federal government help pay the cost of implementing these safeguards?

Sources: Adapted from Dan Verton, "Feds Mulling New Airline Surveillance," *Computerworld*, February 1, 2002, http://www.computerworld.com; Matt Berger, "'Trusted Traveler' Aims to Streamline Flight Security," *Computerworld*, March 18, 2002, http://www.computerworld.com; Brian Sullivan, "EPIC Files Suit against the Bush Administration," *Computerworld*, April 2, 2002, http://www.computerworld.com; Larry Greenemeier, "Security Technology Modeled on Israeli Example," *Information Week*, March 11, 2002, http://www.informationweek.com.

strategic decisions about which markets to enter, how to select and manage key customer relationships, and how to select and effectively promote products to increase profitability and market share.

predictive analysis
a form of data mining that combines historical data with assumptions about future conditions to predict outcomes of events such as future product sales or the probability that a customer will default on a loan

business intelligence
the process of getting enough of the right information in a timely manner and usable form and analyzing it so that it can have a positive impact on business strategy, tactics, or operations

competitive intelligence
a continuous process involving the legal and ethical collection of information, analysis, and controlled dissemination of information to decision makers

AXA Financial, a member of Paris-based AXA Group, is one of the world's largest providers of insurance and financial services, with over 4.5 million customers. It subdivided its large DB2-based data warehouse into data marts, with each focused on a different business area. This approach enables workers to use business intelligence tools to gain an in-depth understanding of AXA's customers—the profits they generate, their rate of retention, and the opportunities they offer to cross-sell the company's products.[10] Employees can obtain the data needed to zero in on problem areas, obtain a detailed picture of the profitability of any customer, and see which products are selling and which are not. If sales decline, they can track those declines to specific offices or even to individual sales reps to pinpoint problems and take immediate steps to remedy them.

Competitive intelligence is one aspect of business intelligence and is limited to information about competitors and the ways that knowledge affects strategy, tactics, and operations. Effective **competitive intelligence** is a continuous process, involving the legal and ethical collection of information, analysis that doesn't avoid unwelcome conclusions, and controlled dissemination of that information to decision makers. To stay ahead in the marketplace, you must be able to integrate competitive intelligence into your company's strategic plans and decisions. Competitive intelligence is a critical part of a company's ability to see and respond quickly and appropriately to the changing marketplace.

Competitive intelligence is not espionage—the use of illegal means to gather information. In fact, almost all the information a competitive intelligence professional needs can be collected by examining published information sources, conducting interviews, and using other legal, ethical methods. Using a variety of analytical tools, a skilled competitive intelligence professional can by deduction fill the gaps in information already gathered.

counterintelligence
the steps an organization takes to protect information sought by "hostile" intelligence gatherers

knowledge management
the process of capturing a company's collective expertise wherever it resides—in computers, on paper, in people's heads—and distributing it wherever it can help produce the biggest payoff

The term **counterintelligence** describes the steps an organization takes to protect information sought by "hostile" intelligence gatherers. One of the most effective counterintelligence measures is to define "trade secret" information relevant to the company and control its dissemination.

Knowledge management is the process of capturing a company's collective expertise wherever it resides—in computers, on paper, or in people's heads—and distributing it wherever it can help produce the biggest payoff. The goal of knowledge management is to get people to record knowledge (as opposed to data) and then share it. Although a variety of technologies can support it, knowledge management is really about changing people's behavior to make their experience and expertise available to others. Knowledge management had its start in large consulting firms and has expanded to nearly every industry. Pharmaceutical companies must have access to various databases from different biotechnology companies to ensure they make informed decisions. Kyowa Pharmaceutical depends on access to multiple databases to facilitate the flow of information throughout the clinical trials of its new products. It uses IBM Life Sciences' DiscoveryLink software to connect information from distributed databases and makes the data available to biotechnology researchers via the Internet.[11]

DISTRIBUTED DATABASES

A distributed database is a database in which the data may be spread across several smaller databases connected via telecommunications devices. Distributed databases give corporations more flexibility in how databases are organized and used. Local offices can create, manage, and use their own databases, and people at other offices can access and share the data in the local databases. Giving local sites more direct access to frequently used data can improve organizational effectiveness and efficiency significantly.

Swiss Federal Railways (SBB) carries more than 85 percent of Switzerland's passenger traffic. It uses distributed databases to maintain its reputation for punctuality, safety, and reliability. An Oracle database is stored in Bern, Switzerland, and holds data on SBB's passenger service operation, including data on fares, routes, and other essential information. The database is continually replicated and downloaded from the master database to 176 satellite servers across the country. The satellite locations can only read the data. Then they send back the latest figures on ticket sales and reservations for high-speed and InterCity services.[12]

Integrating the various distributed databases can be a challenge because some organizations use more than one database management system. A hierarchical database management system may be used at the headquarters of a large manufacturing company, and different relational DBMSs may be used by the various regional offices. Businesses must develop a solution that enables them to access data in these different DBMSs. IBM, Oracle, and Microsoft all are pursuing approaches that would enable a user to access all of a company's computerized data, no matter where it is stored (file servers, e-mail servers, corporate databases, and employees) with a single query. IBM calls its approach the *federated data concept*, and it relies on special software to seek out the data wherever it might be (including on non-IBM databases) and return the results to the user. Oracle calls for users to combine all data into a few central databases.[13] Microsoft is taking an approach similar to IBM's and creating tools and mechanisms that would allow a user to go get the data wherever it might be.[14]

ON-LINE ANALYTICAL PROCESSING (OLAP)

Most industry surveys today show that the majority of data warehouse users rely on spreadsheets, reporting and analysis tools, or their own custom applications to retrieve data from warehouses and format it into business reports and charts. In general, these approaches work fine for questions that can be answered when the amount of data involved is relatively modest and can be accessed with a simple table lookup.

For nearly two decades, multidimensional databases and their analytical information display systems have provided flashy sales presentations and trade show demonstrations. All you have to do is ask where a certain product is selling well, for example, and a colorful table showing sales performance by region, product type, and time frame automatically pops up on the screen. Called **on-line analytical processing (OLAP)**, these programs are now being used to store and deliver data warehouse information. OLAP allows users to explore corporate data from a number of different perspectives.

on-line analytical processing (OLAP)
software that allows users to explore data from a number of different perspectives

OLAP servers and desktop tools support high-speed analysis of data involving complex relationships, such as combinations of a company's products, regions, channels of distribution, reporting units, and time periods. Speed is essential as businesses grow and accumulate more and more data in their operational systems and data warehouses. Long popular with financial planners, OLAP is now being put in the hands of other professionals. The leading OLAP software vendors include Cognos, Comshare, Hyperion Solutions, Oracle, MineShare, WhiteLight, and Microsoft. Blockbuster Inc. is working a half-dozen OLAP projects with a total potential savings of $30 million in operational costs. Blockbuster currently uses Hyperion's Essbase to extract budgeting and planning data from its enterprise systems and analyze how the weather or given movie titles affect sales in its stores. It also uses the software to help in planning how to exploit peak rental times.[15]

Access to data in multidimensional databases can be very quick because they store the data in structures optimized for speed, and they avoid SQL and index processing. But multidimensional databases can take a great deal of time to update; in very large databases, update times can be so great that they force updates to be made only on weekends. Some software providers are attempting to counteract this flaw through the use of partitioning and calculation-on-the-fly capabilities. Despite this flaw, multidimensional databases have continued to prosper because of their great retrieval speed.

Consumer goods companies use OLAP to analyze the millions of consumer purchase records captured by scanners at the checkout stand. This data is used to spot trends in purchases and to relate sales volume to promotions and store conditions, such as displays, and even the weather. OLAP tools let managers analyze business data using multiple dimensions, such as product, geography, time, and salesperson. The data in these dimensions, called *measures*, is generally aggregated—for example, total or average sales in dollars or units, or budget dollars or sales forecast numbers. Rarely is the data studied in its raw, unaggregated form. Each dimension also can contain some hierarchy. For example, in the time dimension, users may examine data by year, by quarter, by month, by week, and even by day. A geographic dimension may compile data from city, state, region, country, and even hemisphere. Read the "IS Principles in Action" special feature to learn more about the use of data warehouses and OLAP tools.

The value of data ultimately lies in the decisions it enables. Powerful information-analysis tools in areas such as OLAP and data mining, when incorporated into a data warehousing architecture, bring market conditions into sharper focus and help organizations deliver greater competitive value. OLAP provides top-down, query-driven data analysis; data mining provides bottom-up, discovery-driven analysis. OLAP requires repetitive testing of user-originated

IS Principles in Action

PRINCIPLE

Further improvements in the use of database technology will continue to evolve and yield real business benefits.

Sears Competes Using Data Warehouse and OLAP Tools

Sears, Roebuck and Co. is completing a project that will allow it to combine information about customer buying trends with inventory and sales data. As part of the project, Sears is buying more EMC Symmetrix disk arrays, a new WorldMark Unix server, and a Teradata database from NCR. The additional hardware and data storage devices will allow Sears to combine its inventory and sales data warehouse with a customer data warehouse onto a single server and provide access to 140 TB of data. Sears is also working with EMC to build a 25-TB storage area network (SAN) to link additional data from Unix and Windows NT servers for use in product assortment planning, human resources, and enterprise resource planning. The new hardware costs in the neighborhood of $15 million.

The recent downturn in retailing as well as competitive pricing and merchandising have made Sears recognize that it must use the huge amounts of data it gathers more wisely. Consolidating its inventory and sales data with its customer information data will enable Sears's employees to analyze customer buying habits, inventory levels, and sales data. The goal is to gain a better understanding of customer shopping habits through market-basket analysis—identification of products and services that are most commonly purchased at the same time. Such knowledge enables Sears to better merchandise and promote its products, thus improving its ability to market goods and control inventory. To remain competitive, Sears must ensure that its customers find the merchandise and service they want in its stores, while eliminating what they don't want—faster than the competition.

Prior to the data consolidation, Sears could track sales down to basic store levels, such as how many size-36 walking shorts it sold in any of its stores on a particular day. But the $41 billion retailer couldn't link the data to customer purchases—to see whether any of the buyers of those shorts also bought a swimsuit that day, indicating that they might be taking a vacation. The consolidated data will support such analysis, and with that kind of knowledge, Sears can target its promotional mailings on other products, such as offering discounts on golf shirts to those it thinks are planning vacations.

Sears sees many other opportunities arising from the merger of its inventory and sales data with customer data. Executives recently used the data to determine that Sears wasn't making money on cosmetics and bicycles, two product lines it has decided to drop.

Sears uses on-line analytical processing (OLAP) software to run complex queries, create different scenarios, and detect patterns in sales and financial data. Hyperion's Essbase OLAP software is used by workers at headquarters to manipulate financial data about store profitability and costs. The data can be analyzed many different ways using the OLAP software—by geography, lines of business, store size, and other factors. Sears eventually will provide store managers the ability to access the data using the Essbase software. The holdup is a lack of training and cultural resistance. Many store managers prefer to remain on the store floor rather than crunch numbers on a computer.

Discussion Questions

1. How can analyzing sales by customer purchases help Sears improve its ability to market goods and control inventory?
2. Identify three additional examples of how the new sales data could be used in decision making.

Critical Thinking Questions

3. What can be done to overcome store managers' resistance to the use of data and analytical tools? Is their resistance to analysis necessarily a bad thing?
4. How might Sears try to quantify the benefits derived from the use of the consolidated data and analysis tools?

Sources: Adapted from Lucas Mearian, "Sears Triples Its Storage Capacity," *Computerworld*, January 28, 2002, http://www.computerworld.com; Lucas Mearian, "Sears to Build Huge Storage Network for CRM," *Computerworld*, January 24, 2002, http://www.computerworld.com; Marc L. Songini, "Firms Face Barriers in Push for Data Analysis," *Computerworld*, April 30, 2001, http://www.computerworld.com; Rick Whiting, "Tower of Power," *Information Week*, February 11, 2002, http://www.InformationWeek.com.

theories; data mining requires no assumptions and instead identifies facts and conclusions based on patterns discovered. OLAP, or multidimensional analysis, requires a great deal of human ingenuity and interaction with the database to find information in the database. A user of a data mining tool does not need to figure out what questions to ask; instead, the approach is, "Here's the data, tell me what interesting patterns emerge." For example, a data mining tool in a credit card company's customer database can construct a profile of fraudulent activity from historical information. Then, this profile can be applied to all incoming transaction data to identify and stop fraudulent behavior, which may otherwise go undetected. Table 3.4 compares the OLAP and data mining approaches to data analysis.

Characteristic	OLAP	Data Mining
Purpose	Supports data analysis and decision making	Supports data analysis and decision making
Type of analysis supported	Top-down, query-driven data analysis	Bottom-up, discovery-driven data analysis
Skills required of user	Must be very knowledgeable of the data and its business context	Must trust in data mining tools to uncover valid and worthwhile hypothesis

TABLE 3.4

Comparison of OLAP and Data Mining

open database connectivity (ODBC) standards
standards that ensure that software written to comply with them can be used with any ODBC-compliant database

OPEN DATABASE CONNECTIVITY (ODBC)

To help with database integration, many companies rely on **open database connectivity (ODBC) standards**. Software written to comply with these standards can be used with any ODBC-compliant database, making it easier to transfer and access data among different databases. For example, a manager might want to take several tables from one database and incorporate them into another database that uses a different database management system. Or, a manager might want to transfer one or more database tables into a spreadsheet program. If all this software meets ODBC standards, the data can be imported, exported, or linked to other applications (see Figure 3.17). For example, a table in an Access database can be exported to a Paradox database or a spreadsheet. Tables and data can also be imported using ODBC. For example, a table in a FileMaker Pro database or an Excel spreadsheet can be imported into an Access database. Linking allows an application to use data or an object stored in another application without actually importing the data or object into the application. The Access database, for example, can link to a table in the Lotus 1-2-3 spreadsheet or the Sybase database. Applications that follow the ODBC standard can use these powerful ODBC features to share data between different applications stored in different formats.

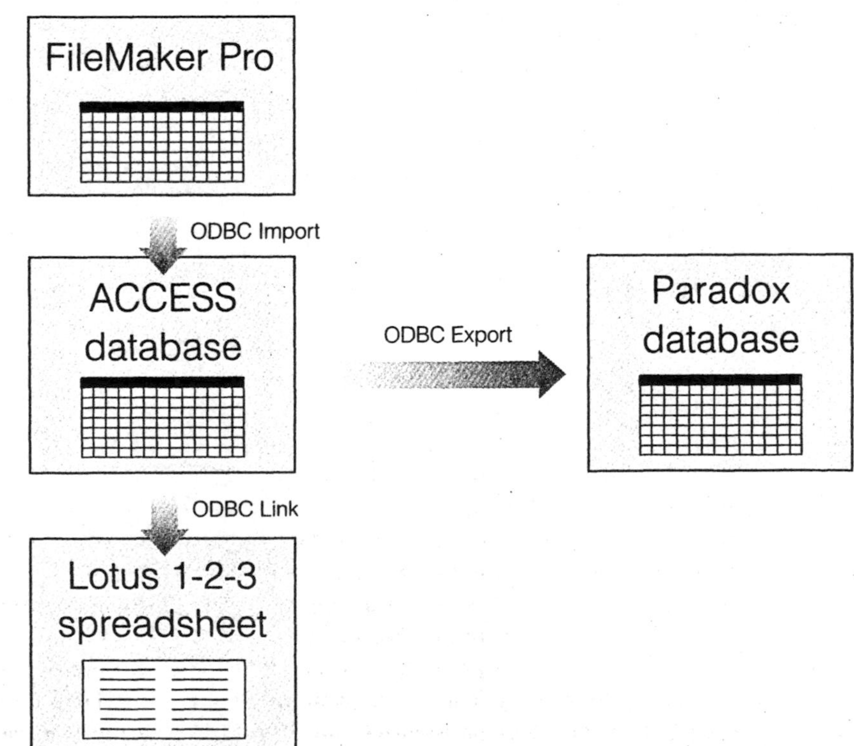

FIGURE 3.17

Advantages of ODBC

ODBC can be used to export, import, or link tables between different applications.

OBJECT-RELATIONAL DATABASE MANAGEMENT SYSTEMS

Many of today's newer application programs require the ability to manipulate audio, video, and graphical data. Conventional database management systems are not well suited for this, because these types of data cannot easily be stored in rows or tables. Manipulation of such data requires extensive programming so that the DBMS can translate data relationships. An **object-relational database management system (ORDBMS)** provides a complete set of relational database capabilities plus the ability for third parties to add new data types and operations to the database. These new data types can be audio, images, unstructured text, spatial data, or time-series data that require new indexing, optimization, and retrieval features.

object-relational database management system (ORDBMS)
a DBMS capable of manipulating audio, video, and graphical data

In such a database, these types of data are stored as objects, which contain both the data and the processing instructions needed to complete the database transaction. The objects can be retrieved and related by an ORDBMS. Businesses can then mix and match these elements in their daily search for clues and information. For example, by clicking on a picture of a red Corvette, a market analyst at General Motors might be able to call up a profile of red Corvette buyers. If he wants to break that up by geographic region, he might circle and click on a map. All in the same motion, he might view a GM sales-training film to see whether the sales pitch is appropriate, given the most recent market trends. Chances are the analyst will do all this using an Internet site tied into a database. As another example, MasterCard is interested in object-oriented technology to combine transactional data with cardholder fingerprints to prevent fraud.

Each of the vendors offering ORDBMS facilities provides a set of application programming interfaces to allow users to attach external data definitions and methods associated with those definitions into the database system. They are essentially offering a standard socket into which users can plug special instructions. DataBlades, Cartridges, and Extenders are the names applied by Informix, Oracle, and IBM to describe the plug-ins to their respective products. Other plug-ins serve as interfaces to Web servers.

Web-based applications increasingly require complex object support to link graphical and other media components back to the database. These systems make sense for developers of systems that are highly dependent on complex data types, particularly Web and multimedia applications. Because it supports so many applications, an ORDBMS is also called a *universal database server.*

An increasing amount of data that organizations use is in the form of images, which can be stored in object-relational databases. Credit card companies, for example, input pictures of charge slips into an image database using a scanner. The images can be stored in the database and later sorted by customer, printed, and sent to customers along with their monthly statements. Image databases are also used by physicians to store X rays and transmit them to clinics away from the main hospital. Financial services, insurance companies, and government branches are also using image databases to store vital records and replace paper documents.

Spatial data technology is used by NASA to store data from satellites and earth stations. Location-specific information can be accessed and compared.

(Source: Courtesy of NASA.)

SPATIAL DATA TECHNOLOGY

Spatial data technology involves the use of an object-relational database to store and access data according to the locations it describes and to permit spatial queries and analysis. MapExtreme is spatial technology software from MapInfo that extends a user's database so it can store, manage, and manipulate location-based data. New York City police use the software to bring together crime data and map the data visually so that patterns are easier to analyze. Commanders can select and work with spatial data at a specified location, within a rectangle, a given radius, or a polygon such as a precinct. For example, a commander can request a list of all liquor stores within a two-mile radius of the precinct.[16]

From spatial data technology, to multimedia capabilities, to data mining and warehousing, to relational capabilities, today's databases are essential business tools. They store, retrieve, and help users sort through and make sense of the mountains of data that organizations collect, turning data into useful information.

SUMMARY

PRINCIPLE ***The database approach to data management provides significant advantages over the traditional file-based approach.***

Data is one of the most valuable resources a firm possesses. It is organized into a hierarchy that builds from the smallest element to the largest: bit, byte, field, record, file, and database.

An entity is a generalized class of objects for which data is collected, stored, and maintained. An attribute is a characteristic of an entity. Specific values of attributes—called *data items*—can be found in the fields of the record describing an entity. A data key is a field within a record that is used to identify the record. A primary key uniquely identifies a record, while a secondary key is a field in a record.

The traditional approach to data management has been from a file perspective. Separate files are created for each application. This approach can create problems over time: as more files are created for new applications, data that is common to the individual files becomes redundant. Also, if data is changed in one file, those changes might not be made to other files, reducing data integrity.

To address problems of traditional file-based data management, the database approach was developed. Benefits of this approach include reduced data redundancy, improved data consistency and integrity, easier modification and updating, standardization of data access, and more efficient program development.

Potential disadvantages of the database approach include the relatively high cost of purchasing and operating a DBMS in a mainframe operating environment; specialized staff required to implement and coordinate the use of the database; and increased vulnerability if security is breached and there is a failure in the DBMS.

When building a database, careful consideration must be given to content and access, logical structure, and physical organization. One of the tools database designers use to show the relationships among data is a data model that shows data entities and their relationships. Enterprise data modeling involves analyzing the data and information needs of the entire organization. Entity-relationship (ER) diagrams can be employed to show the relationships between entities in the organization.

Databases typically use one of three common models: hierarchical (tree), network, and relational. The relational model, the most widely used database model, is easier to control, more flexible, and more intuitive than the other models because it organizes data in tables.

PRINCIPLE ***A well-designed and well-managed database is an extremely valuable tool in supporting decision making.***

A DBMS is a group of programs used as an interface between a database and application programs. When an application program requests data from the database, it follows a logical access path. The actual retrieval of the data follows a physical access path. Records can be considered in the same way: a logical record is what the record contains; a physical record is where the record is stored on storage devices. Schemas are used to describe the entire database, its record types, and their relationships to the DBMS.

A database management system provides four basic functions: providing user views, creating and modifying the database, storing and retrieving data, and manipulating data and generating reports.

Subschemas are used to define a user view, the portion of the database a user can access and/or manipulate. Schemas and subschemas are entered into the computer via a data definition language, which describes the data and relationships in a specific database. Another tool used in database management is the data dictionary, which contains detailed descriptions of all data in the database.

Once a DBMS has been installed, the database may be accessed, modified, and queried via a data manipulation language. SQL is used in several popular database packages today and can be installed on PCs and mainframes.

Popular end-user DBMSs include Microsoft Access, Lotus Approach, Corel Paradox, and FileMaker's FileMaker Pro. IBM, Oracle, Microsoft, and Sybase are the leading DBMS vendors.

A database administrator (DBA) is a highly skilled and trained systems professional who directs or performs all activities related to maintaining a successful database environment. The role of the data administrator is a nontechnical but important one that ensures that data is managed as an important organizational resource.

PRINCIPLE *Further improvements in the use of database technology will continue to evolve and yield real business benefits.*

Organizations are building data warehouses, which are relational database management systems specifically designed to support management decision making. Data mining, which is the automated discovery of patterns and relationships in a data warehouse, is emerging as a practical approach to generate a hypothesis about the patterns and anomalies in the data that can be used to predict future behavior.

Business intelligence is the process of getting enough of the right information in a timely manner and usable form and analyzing it so that it can have a positive impact on business strategy, tactics, or operations. Competitive intelligence is one aspect of business intelligence limited to information about competitors and how that information affects strategy, tactics, and operations. Counterintelligence describes the steps an organization takes to protect information sought by "hostile" intelligence gatherers. Knowledge management is the process of capturing a company's collective expertise wherever it resides—in computers, on paper, or in people's heads—and distributing it wherever it can help produce the biggest payoff.

A distributed database is a database in which the data may be spread across several smaller databases connected via telecommunications devices.

Multidimensional databases and on-line analytical processing (OLAP) programs are being used to store data and allow users to explore the data from a number of different perspectives.

An object-relational database management system (ORDBMS) provides a complete set of relational database capabilities, plus the ability for third parties to add new data types and operations to the database. These new data types can be audio, images, unstructured text, spatial data, or time series data that require new indexing, optimization, and retrieval features.

Spatial data technology involves the use of an object-relational database to store and access data according to the locations it describes and to permit spatial queries and analysis.

CHAPTER 3 SELF-ASSESSMENT TEST

The database approach to data management provides significant advantages over the traditional file-based approach.

1. A group of programs that manipulate the database and provide an interface between the database and the user of the database and other application programs is called a(n)
   A. GUI
   B. operating system
   C. DBMS
   D. productivity software
2. A characteristic of an entity is called a(n) ________________.
3. A primary key is a field or set of fields that uniquely identifies the record. True False
4. The duplication of data in separate files is known as
   A. data redundancy
   B. data integrity
   C. data relationships
   D. data entities
5. ________________ is a data modeling approach that starts by investigating the general data and information needs of the organization at the strategic level and then examining more specific data and information needs for the various functional areas and departments within the organization.
6. The structure of the relationships in most databases follows one of three logical database models:
   A. hierarchical, network, and relational
   B. enterprise, departmental, and distributed
   C. normalized, unnormalized, and standard
   D. tactical, strategic, and global

A well-designed and well-managed database is an extremely valuable tool in supporting decision making.

7. Once data has been placed into a relational database, users can make inquiries and analyze data. Basic data manipulations include selecting, projecting, and verifying. True False

8. Because the DBMS is responsible for access to a database, one of the first steps in installing and using a database involves telling the DBMS the logical and physical structure of the data and relationships among the data in the database. This description is called a(n) ________________.
9. The commands that are used to access and report information from the database are part of the
   A. data definition language
   B. data manipulation language
   C. data redundancy process
   D. subschema
10. Three popular DBMSs for end users are ________________, ________________, and ________________.
11. The ability of a vendor to provide global support for large, multinational companies or companies outside the United States is becoming increasingly important. True False

Further improvements in the use of database technology will continue to evolve and yield real business benefits.

12. A(n) ________________ holds business information from many sources in the enterprise, covering all aspects of the company's processes, products, and customers.
13. An information analysis tool that involves the automated discovery of patterns and relationships in a data warehouse is called
    A. data mart
    B. data mining
    C. predictive analysis
    D. business intelligence
14. ________________ is a continuous process involving the legal and ethical collection of information, analysis that doesn't avoid unwelcome conclusions, and controlled dissemination of that information to decision makers.

Chapter 3 Self-Assessment Test Answers

1. C, 2. Attribute, 3. True, 4. A, 5. Enterprise data modeling, 6. A, 7. False, 8. Schema, 9. B, 10. any of three of the following: Corel's Paradox, FileMaker's FileMaker Pro, Microsoft's Access, and Lotus's Approach, 11. True, 12. data warehouse, 13. B, 14. Competitive intelligence

REVIEW QUESTIONS

1. What is an attribute? How is it related to an entity?
2. Define the term *database*. How is it different from a database management system?
3. What is data redundancy? Why is it a problem?
4. How would you describe the traditional approach to data management? How does it differ from the database approach?
5. What is data modeling? What is its purpose? Briefly describe three commonly used data models.
6. What is a database schema, and what is its purpose?
7. Identify important characteristics in selecting a database management system.
8. What is the difference between a data definition language (DDL) and a data manipulation language (DML)?
9. What is a distributed database system?
10. What advantages does the open database connectivity (ODBC) standard offer?
11. What is data mining? What is OLAP? How are they different?
12. What is an ORDBMS? What kind of data can it handle?
13. What is business intelligence? How is such information gathered?
14. What is spatial data technology? How might it be used?
15. What is predictive analysis?

DISCUSSION QUESTIONS

1. You have been selected to represent the student body on a project to develop a new student database for your school. What actions might you take to fulfill this responsibility to ensure that the project meets the needs of students and is successful?
2. Your company is releasing a major new product. To announce the product, you, the advertising manager in charge of the new product launch, need to develop advertising and other promotions. What counterintelligence initiatives might you undertake?
3. What is a data model, and what is data modeling? Why is data modeling an important part of strategic planning?

4. You are going to design a database for your cooking club to track its recipes. Identify the database characteristics most important to you in choosing a DBMS. Which of the database management systems described in this chapter would you choose? Why? Is it important for you to know what sort of computer the database will run on? Why or why not?
5. Distinguish OLAP from predictive analysis. Under what conditions would you use one technique over the other?
6. Make a list of the databases in which data about you exists. How is the data in each database captured? Who updates each database, and how often? Is it possible for you to request a printout of the contents of your data record from each database? What data privacy concerns do you have?
7. You are the vice president of information technology for a large, multinational, consumer packaged goods company (e.g., Procter & Gamble, Unilever, or Gillette). You must make a presentation to persuade the board of directors to invest $5 million to establish a competitive intelligence organization—including people, data gathering services, and software tools. What key points do you need to make in favor of this investment? What arguments can you anticipate others might make?

PROBLEM-SOLVING EXERCISES

1. Develop a simple data model for an end-user database management system to record your personal items and home/apartment furnishings so that you have a log of all valuable items for insurance purposes in case of theft, fire, or a natural disaster. For each item, what attributes should you capture? What will be the unique key for the records in your database?
2. A video rental store is using a relational database to store information on movie rentals to answer customer questions. Each entry in the database contains the following items: Movie ID No. (primary key), Movie Title, Year Made, Movie Type, MPAA Rating, Number of Copies on Hand, and Quantity Owned. Movie types are comedy, family, drama, horror, science fiction, and western. MPAA ratings are G, PG, PG-13, R, X, and NR (not rated). Use an end-user database management system to build a data entry screen to enter this data. Build a small database with at least ten entries.
3. To improve service to their customers, the salespeople at the video rental store have proposed a list of changes being considered for the database in the previous exercise. From this list, choose two database modifications and modify the data entry screen to capture and store this new information. Proposed changes:
   A. Add the date that the movie was first available to help locate the newest releases
   B. Add the director's name
   C. Add the names of three primary actors in the movie
   D. Add a rating of one, two, three, or four stars
   E. Add the number of Academy Award nominations

TEAM ACTIVITIES

1. In a group of three or four classmates, do research to identify the largest existing data warehouse. Write a brief paragraph about the data warehouse and how it is used. Try to identify any unique problems due to the size of the data warehouse.
2. As a team of three or four classmates, interview business managers from three different businesses that use databases to help them in their work. What data entities and data attributes are contained in each database? How do they access the database to perform analysis? Have they received training in any query or reporting tools? What do they like about their database, and what could be improved? Do any of them use data mining or OLAP techniques? Weighing the information obtained, select one of these databases as being most strategic for the firm and briefly present your selection and the rationale for the selection to the class.
3. Imagine that you and your classmates are a research team developing an improved process for evaluating auto loan applicants. The goal of the research is to predict which applicants will become delinquent or forfeit their loan. Those who score

well on the application will be accepted; those who score exceptionally well will be considered for lower-rate loans. Prepare a brief report for your instructor addressing these questions:

A. What data do you need for each loan applicant?
B. What data might you need that is not typically requested on a loan application form?
C. From where might you get this data?

Take a first cut at designing a database for this application. Using the chapter material on designing a database, show the logical structure of the relational tables for this proposed database. In your design, include the data attributes you believe are necessary for this database and show the primary keys in your tables. Keep the size of the fields and tables as small as possible to minimize required disk drive storage space. Fill in the database tables with the sample data for demonstration purposes (ten records). Once your design is complete, implement it using a relational DBMS.

WEB EXERCISES

1. Use a Web search engine to find information on one of the following topics: business intelligence, knowledge management, predictive analysis. Find a definition of the term, an example of a company using the technology, and three companies that provide such software. Cut graphics and text material from the Web pages and paste them into a word processing document to create a two-page report on your selected topic. At the home page of each software company, request further information from the company about its products.
2. Use a Web search engine to find three companies that provide competitive intelligence services. How are the services that they provide similar? How are they different? Which companies seem to be the most ethical? Why?

CASES

CASE 1

VNU, International Media and Information Company

In 1994, VNU NV was a Netherlands-based owner of Dutch newspapers and television stations and European magazines. Over the next seven years, it spent a total of $8 billion acquiring other companies to transform itself into a leading provider of information about media and consumers for use by media companies and advertisers. Today VNU owns 145 trade newspapers and magazines; Soundscan, which tracks retail sales of recorded music; Nielsen Media Research, which rates television shows; and ACNielsen, which compiles market data on the sales of packaged goods. With operations in over 100 countries and employing 35,000 people, VNU provides millions of people around the world with business intelligence.

Its marketing information activities are built on the data collected, edited, and stored by its ACNielsen subsidiary. The basic data collection process begins with in-store scanning of product codes at the checkout and observations of professional auditors during store visits. This data is gathered from retail outlets wherever food, household, health and beauty, durables, confectionery, and beverage products are sold. The data can be used to track sales volume, selling price, and effectiveness of promotions and merchandising—not just of your own company's products but of competitors as well. The data can also be used to measure overall product performance, assess the extent of product distribution in area stores, quantify the effectiveness of special promotions such as sales or advertisements, and measure consumers' reactions to changes in price.

Recognizing the need to support global decision making, ACNielsen introduced an Internet service to deliver its information products in 1996. This expansion on-line allows people within client organizations to obtain ACNielsen information, regardless of their location.

In addition to its information products, ACNielsen markets a broad range of advanced decision support software that helps more than 9,000 clients spread across 100 countries to obtain large volumes of information, evaluate it, make judgments about their growth opportunities, and plan future marketing and sales campaigns. The software includes tools that perform sophisticated multidimensional reporting, data mining, analytical modeling, graphical presentations, and expert systems. The goal is to enable decision makers to make sound recommendations to optimize their business: price levels, promotion methods, media spending, product portfolio mix, retail category optimization, and other choices. If made correctly, these key decisions can generate increased sales and profits.

Discussion Questions

1. What issues might be involved in collecting, editing, and storing the ACNielsen data? Identify some specific issues related to data privacy.
2. What concerns might be associated with providing customers around the world with access to the ACNielsen data via the Internet?

Critical Thinking Questions

3. What ethical issues might arise for VNU in providing marketing data, tools, and services to two major multinational companies that are competitors (e.g., Procter & Gamble and Unilever)? How might these issues be minimized?
4. Which do you think is more important to VNU customers—good data or good tools for the analysis of data? Why?

Sources: Adapted from Geraldine Fabrikant, "MEDIA: Big Makeover for Dutch Media Data Company," *The New York Times*, August 13, 2001, late edition-final, section C, p. 9; "About VNU," VNU Web site, at http://www.vnu.com, accessed February 25, 2002; "Sybase Solution Analyzes Television Viewing Trends for Nielsen Research," Sybase press release, October 22, 2001.

CASE 2

Wells Fargo Bank Uses Predictive Analysis to Improve Profits

Banks are major investors in information systems. In fact, the largest banks spend 20 to 25 percent of their overall budgets in this area. Much of this spending is driven by the ongoing consolidation of banks and the intense pressures to remain profitable. One area of spending is for predictive analysis to improve profitability and increase revenue.

Wells Fargo Home Mortgage is a subsidiary of Wells Fargo & Co. in San Francisco. The company is one of the top providers of home loans in the United States, handling one of every 12 U.S. mortgages. Wells Fargo built a data warehouse that contains more than 200 million payment records on 12 million borrowers and 5 million home loans. It uses this data and predictive analysis software to forecast the performance of its mortgage loan portfolio and individual mortgage loans. The goal is to manage the risk of loan defaults. Too tight a credit policy means the bank loses revenue by refusing loans that would be paid back. Too loose a credit policy means the bank loses money on defaulted loans.

A credit-scoring model helps loan officers evaluate new applications and predict the likelihood of default. Completing such an analysis gives loan officers a better sense of the potential risk up front so that they can price the loan accordingly. Other models predict the performance of the entire loan portfolio to help managers assess the potential loss from bad loans. Loan portfolio analysis looks at the payment history of millions of customers over two or three years—often examining between 40 million and 50 million payment records, plus quarterly credit reports for each loan. With this knowledge, the company can then price loans appropriately and market various loans to different segments of consumers. Such thorough analysis of its home mortgage portfolio has helped Wells Fargo extend credit to customers who might not otherwise be eligible for a home loan.

Consolidating data from multiple sources to build a single, companywide data warehouse has helped Wells Fargo ensure accurate and consistent results. This increased reliability has led to savings in human and computer resources by cutting the turnaround time on data requests from many days to just a few hours or minutes.

Wells Fargo used the data warehouse and predictive analysis tools to carefully analyze loan performance over time. What it learned was that its loan default rates were half as much as rating services such as Moody's and Standard & Poor's had predicted. Based on the new, lower default rate, Wells Fargo was able to renegotiate the loans and assume more risk, thus saving $250,000 per month in interest expenses.

The system also helped Wells Fargo enter into new partnerships with mortgage insurance companies and generate more than $30 million a year in additional revenues. Without the system, Wells Fargo would not be able to meet stringent legal reporting requirements for these partnerships.

Discussion Questions

1. What benefits has Wells Fargo achieved through the use of a data warehouse and predictive analysis tools?
2. Why is it important to have multiple years of consolidated data for all types of customers when performing predictive analyses? Why wouldn't the analysis be as worthwhile if it were done with a representative subset of the data?

Critical Thinking Questions

3. How important is data completeness and quality to the predictive analysis process? What actions might Wells Fargo take to ensure the accuracy and completeness of its data?
4. What other predictive analyses or models would be useful to Wells Fargo besides those already mentioned?

Sources: Adapted from "Success Stories—Wells Fargo Manages Credit Risk of 12 Million Borrowers with SAS," SAS Institute Web site, http://www.SAS.com, accessed February 27, 2002; Lucas Mearian, "Study: IT Spending at Banks to Increase in 2002," *Computerworld*, January 14, 2002, http://www.computerworld.com; Rick Whiting, "Companies Boost Sales Efforts with Predictive Analysis," *Information Week*, February 25, 2002, http://www.informationweek.com.

CASE 3

J. Crew Turns to Data Warehousing to Increase On-line Sales

J. Crew is a global retailer and catalog merchant of prestige fashions with headquarters in New York City. It offers a wide range of men's, women's, and children's apparel, shoes, accessories, and personal-care products through its fast-expanding retail network of 133 U.S. stores and 76 licensed stores in Japan.

When J. Crew set up its jcrew.com site in June 1997, it was one of the first apparel sites on the Web. Today the Web site is J. Crew's fastest-growing distribution channel. Part of the reason for its huge success is that J. Crew uses a data warehouse and software tools to identify for on-line shoppers what J. Crew clothes, shoes, and accessories customers frequently purchase together. That information is fed to applications running the Web site so that when on-line shoppers click on an item, the Web site recommends complementary products that the customer might be interested in buying. Delivering dynamic, relevant product recommendations to shoppers has increased the average order size and raised customer satisfaction and loyalty.

J. Crew uses DigiMine's Enterprise Analytics data mining software to analyze sales data from its Web site, retail stores, and catalog sales operation. All of this data is collected and stored in a 500-GB data warehouse running on a Microsoft SQL Server database, which took J. Crew and DigiMine six months to develop. J. Crew combines the data generated by visitors clicking on its Web pages with product sales data from corporate systems that process order data from catalog and retail operations. The consolidation of all this data gives J. Crew a complete view of its customers' preferences and enables it to analyze sales trends, build customer profiles, and generate product recommendations for e-mail marketing campaigns. It also uses this pooled data to pair products and advise shoppers which shoes customers most often buy with which slacks. As a result, every shopper at jcrew.com can view compelling apparel, shoe, or accessory suggestions, based on their browsing and purchasing behavior.

Discussion Questions

1. Visit the J. Crew Web site at http://www.jcrew.com and shop for some apparel. Be alert for the site's attempts to increase your order size through recommendations of complementary apparel, shoe, or accessories. Write a paragraph summarizing your experience.
2. In serving their on-line shoppers, most retailers do not combine data from the brick-and-mortar stores and catalog purchases with browsing and shopping data from their Web sites. J. Crew does. How does this provide J. Crew a competitive advantage?

Critical Thinking Questions

3. Identify some potential data privacy issues that might arise with the capture, storage, and analysis of customers' on-line shopping data from the J. Crew Web site.
4. Imagine that J. Crew is considering offering a new service for on-line customers—help in shopping for gifts for friends and family members. Interested customers would register friends and family members, along with their birth dates, anniversaries, and other pertinent information such as sizes and color preferences. J. Crew would send an e-mail reminding the customer that a friend's birth date or other special occasion was near and suggest that they visit the Web site for help in choosing a gift. What are the pros and cons of such a service? What additional information would need to be captured in the data warehouse to support this service? Would you be in favor of this service? Why or why not?

Sources: Adapted from Ann Bednarz, "Cents and Retail Sensibility," *Computerworld*, January 7, 2002, http://www.computerworld.com; Mark Hall, "Finding Answers in Data Haystacks," *Computerworld*, April 23, 2001, http://www.computerworld.com; Rick Whiting, "Retailer Seeks Success in How Customers Dress," *Information Week*, November 26, 2001, http://www.informationweek.com; "J. Crew Deploys DigiMine's Data Mining Solutions," DigiMine company press release, November 13, 2001, http://www.digimine.com/; J. Crew Web site, http://www.JCrew.com.

NOTES

Sources for the opening vignette on p. 99: Adapted from "Finland's Largest Dairy Company Farms Profitable Pastures," Success Stories, Compaq Web site, http://www.compaq.com, accessed February 20, 2002; "Company and Functional Products," Valio Web site, http://valio.com, accessed February 20, 2002; "Carton Finds Its Thrills ... with a Blueberry-Flavored Milk Drink," *Packaging Digest*, April 2001, http://www.findarticles.com; "Valio's Profit Surges in First Eight Months," *Eurofood*, November 8, 2001, http://www.findarticles.com.

1. Jennifer Maselli, "Swiss Hopes to Reach New Heights," *Information Week*, June 24, 2002, http://www.informationweek.com.
2. Lucas Mearian and Linda Rosencrance, "Police Pleased with Data Mining Engines," *Computerworld*, April 2, 2001, http://www.computerworld.com.
3. Jennifer DiSabatino, "Galileo Moves Fare Pricing onto Unix-based System," *Computerworld*, March 1, 2002, http://www.computerworld.com.
4. Peter Wayner, "Open Source Databases Bloom," *Computerworld*, September 10, 2001, http://www.computerworld.com.
5. Rick Whiting, "CERN Project Will Collect Hundreds of Petabytes of Data," *Information Week*, February 11, 2002, http:/informationweek.com.
6. Rick Whiting, "Tower of Power," *Information Week*, February 11, 2002, http://www.informationweek.com.
7. Bill Miles, "Slick," *Darwin*, June 21, 2001, http://www.darwinmag.com.
8. Rick Whiting, "United Building 6-Terabyte Warehouse," *Information Week*, April 1, 2002, http://www.informationweek.com.
9. Rick Whiting, "Companies Boost Sales Efforts with Predictive Analysis," *Information Week*, February 25, 2002, http://www.informationweek.com.
10. Rick Whiting, "United Building 6-Terabyte Warehouse," *Information Week*, April 1, 2002, http://www.informationweek.com.
11. Larry Greenemeier, "The IT Prescription for Faster Drug Delivery," *Computerworld*, February 25, 2002, http://www.computerworld.com.
12. "Oracle Enterprise Manager Helps SBB Reduce Costs by Enabling a Seamless Operation of a Replicated Environment," Oracle Web Site, http://www.oracle.com, accessed August 1, 2002.
13. Gary H. Anthes, "Agreeing to Disagree," *Computerworld*, August 5, 2002, http://www.computerworld.com.
14. Gary Anthes, "Database Horizons," *Computerworld*, August 5, 2002, http://www.computerworld.com.
15. Marc L. Songini, "Firms Face Barriers in Push for Data Analysis," *Computerworld*, April 30, 2001, http://www.computerworld.com.
16. Linda Rosencrance, "NYPD Selects MapInfo for Citywide Crime Analysis," *Computerworld*, January 4, 2002, http://www.computerworld.com.

Electronic Commerce and Transaction Processing Systems

17

PRINCIPLES	LEARNING OBJECTIVES
E-commerce is a new way of conducting business, and as with any other new application of technology, it presents both opportunities for improvement and potential problems.	• Identify several advantages of e-commerce. • Identify several e-commerce applications.
E-commerce requires the careful planning and integration of a number of technology infrastructure components.	• Outline the key components of technology infrastructure that must be in place for e-commerce to succeed. • Discuss the key features of the electronic payments systems needed to support e-commerce.
An organization's transaction processing system (TPS) must support the routine, day-to-day activities that occur in the normal course of business and help a company add value to its products and services.	• Identify the basic activities and business objectives common to all transaction processing systems. • Discuss the importance of business resumption planning and disaster recovery for key transaction processing systems.
Implementation of an enterprise resource planning (ERP) system enables a company to achieve numerous business benefits through the creation of a highly integrated set of systems.	• Define the term *enterprise resource planning system* and discuss the advantages and disadvantages associated with the implementation of such a system.

[Tesco]

Grocer Implements Successful E-Commerce Business Model

As the death of many dot.coms has shown, conducting business on-line involves much more than simply setting up a Web site and raking in profits. On-line grocers offer a good example of why pure e-commerce operations can encounter serious new business problems compared with Web sites that add an on-line component to existing brick-and-mortar sales (sales out of physical stores). Solid sales and operations experience must be combined with good technical knowledge to create a successful e-commerce Web site.

A number of existing grocery chains and dot.com start-ups have tried to enter the on-line grocery business—unsuccessfully. One on-line grocer that is profitable is U.K.-based Tesco. Through its Web site, Tesco.com, the company serves 1 million registered customers in the United Kingdom, handles more than 85,000 orders per week with an average order of $133, and generates nearly $500 million in annual sales. Tesco.com operates in four countries—the U.K., the Republic of Ireland, South Korea, and the United States.

Tesco has been the most successful of the on-line grocers largely because net margins for grocers in England are close to 8 percent versus 2 percent for U.S.-based grocers. Another reason for its success is that it has kept things simple. When shoppers log on to Tesco.com, they key in their postal code, and their order is routed to their local Tesco store. Once it is received, workers pick items from the store shelves to fill the order. Tesco has not invested in multimillion-dollar automated distribution facilities or fancy conveyor belts that zip products through warehouses. However, it has required considerable effort to integrate its on-line customer ordering system with its inventory control transaction processing system.

Albertson's (U.S.) and Royal Ahold (Netherlands) have followed this "keep things simple" model for e-business and fill orders from their own brick-and-mortar stores. Filling on-line orders directly out of a local store instead of from a warehouse results in lower costs for the company and faster service for customers.

On the other side of the coin, numerous on-line grocers have failed with different business models. After fewer than eight months of its on-line shopping trial, Safeway plc in the United Kingdom shut down its on-line service in November 2000. The chain did not even deliver to customers; they ordered via the Web and picked up their groceries at a store at a prearranged time. Webvan is another notable failure. It filed for bankruptcy in July 2001 after spending more than $800 million in two years. HomeRuns.com, in business since 1996, also shut down in July 2001. Both the Webvan and HomeRuns.com business models were based on establishing expensive warehouses in many locations and required costly fleets of delivery personnel and equipment. The companies simply couldn't recover the heavy start-up costs until their customer bases grew much larger. Furthermore, since neither operated brick-and-mortar stores, they relied on a major behavior change in the way that people buy groceries to become profitable.

As you read this chapter, consider the following:

- How are organizations using e-commerce, transaction processing systems, and enterprisewide systems to provide improved customer service, become more productive, and remain competitive?
- How does a company's business strategy affect the types of systems it uses?

AN INTRODUCTION TO ELECTRONIC COMMERCE

business-to-consumer (B2C) e-commerce
a form of e-commerce in which customers deal directly with the organization, avoiding any intermediaries

business-to-business (B2B) e-commerce
a form of e-commerce in which the participants are organizations

consumer-to-consumer (C2C) e-commerce
a form of e-commerce in which the participants are individuals, with one serving as the buyer and the other as the seller

Dot.com companies take many forms. Early e-commerce news profiled start-ups that used Internet technology to compete with the traditional players in an industry. For example, Amazon.com challenged well-established booksellers Walden Books and Barnes and Noble. Like Amazon, Tesco (the grocer discussed in the opening vignette) provides an example of **business-to-consumer (B2C) e-commerce,** in which customers deal directly with an organization and avoid any intermediaries. Other types of e-commerce are **business-to-business (B2B) e-commerce,** in which the participants are organizations, and **consumer-to-consumer (C2C) e-commerce,** in which consumers sell directly to other consumers. Neoforma.com is a B2B e-commerce company that received more than $80 million in financing to create an Internet marketplace to take on the $140 billion hospital supply industry. eBay is an example of a C2C e-commerce site; customers buy and sell items directly to each other through the site.

Aside from the major categories of e-commerce, companies are also using Internet technologies to enhance their current operations, such as inventory control and distribution. But whatever model is used, successful implementation of e-business requires significant changes to existing business processes and substantial investment in information systems technology.

Over the past few years, we have learned a lot about the practical limitations of e-commerce. It has become painfully clear that before companies can achieve profits, they must understand their business, their consumers, and the constraints of e-commerce. Although it once seemed so, selling cheap consumer goods on-line in a virtual storefront may not always be a great way to compete. And inventing a new use for cutting-edge technology isn't necessarily enough to guarantee a successful business. Starting up a dot.com company, taking it public, and selling shares at inflated stock prices before the company has earned a profit doesn't work anymore either—investors have become wary of flimsy schemes.

Still, e-commerce is not dead; it is maturing and evolving, with the focus currently shifted from B2C to B2B. E-commerce is a useful tool for connecting business partners in a virtual supply chain to cut resupply times and reduce costs. Noted research firm International Data Corporation (IDC) predicts B2B e-commerce will have a $5.3 trillion impact on the worldwide economy by 2005.[1] As far as B2C e-commerce is concerned, consumers spent about $10.5 billion per quarter on-line in 2002, excluding travel. With travel, annual on-line spending was about $85 billion in 2002.[2] Yet traditional retail sales figures still dwarf on-line sales—total on-line sales are approximately 2 to 3 percent of total retail sales.[3]

Businesses and individuals use e-commerce to reduce transaction costs, speed the flow of goods and information, improve the level of customer service, and enable close coordination among manufacturers, suppliers, and customers. E-commerce also enables consumers and companies to gain access to worldwide markets. E-commerce is not limited to use by manufacturing firms; many service firms have also implemented successful e-commerce projects. Blue Cross/Blue Shield's Federal Employee Program moved onto the Web, enabling the health insurer to provide real-time claims processing and interactive customer service. The company processes medical, dental, and pharmacy claims for half the government employees across the country. The new system gives the plan's customers, healthcare providers, and claims processors access to pertinent information quickly over the Internet.[4]

Business processes that are strong candidates for conversion to e-commerce are those that are paper based and time-consuming and those that can make business more convenient for customers. Thus, it comes as no surprise that the first business processes that companies converted to an e-commerce model were those related to buying and selling. For example, after Cisco Systems, the maker of Internet routers and other telecommunications equipment, put its procurement operation on-line in 1998, the company reported that it halved cycle times and saved an additional $170 million in material and labor costs. Similarly, Charles Schwab & Co. slashed transaction costs by as much as 80 percent by shifting brokerage transactions from traditional channels like retail and phone centers to the Internet.[5]

Some companies, such as those in the automotive and aerospace industries, have been conducting e-commerce for decades through the use of electronic data interchange (EDI), which involves application-to-application communications of business data (invoices, purchase orders, etc.) between companies in a standard data format. Many companies have now gone beyond simple EDI-based applications to launch e-commerce initiatives with suppliers, customers, and employees to address business needs in new areas.

Because of the costs involved in buying new technology, the EDI capabilities of most small businesses are nonexistent or extremely limited. A few major retailers and manufacturers have enlisted the help of third parties to bring smaller firms into their EDI supply chain. For example, SPS Commerce specializes in hooking up small businesses like American Outdoor Products (25 employees) to big supply chains like Recreational Equipment Incorporated (REI). SPS built an Internet-based application that translates EDI ordering and shipping requirements so that workers can access them through a Web browser on their PC.[6]

VALUE CHAINS IN E-COMMERCE

supply chain management
a key value chain composed of demand planning, supply planning, and demand fulfillment

All business organizations contain a number of value-added processes. The supply chain management process is a key value chain that, for most companies, offers tremendous business opportunities if converted to e-commerce. **Supply chain management** is composed of three subprocesses: demand planning to anticipate market demand, supply planning to allocate the right amount of enterprise resources to meet demand, and demand fulfillment to fill customer orders quickly and efficiently (Figure 5.1). The objective of demand planning is to understand customers' buying patterns and develop overall long-term, intermediate-term, and short-term forecasts of customer demand. Supply planning includes strategic planning, inventory planning, distribution planning, procurement planning, transportation planning, and supply allocation. The goal of demand fulfillment is to provide fast, accurate, and reliable delivery of customer orders. Demand fulfillment includes order capturing, customer verification, order promising, backlog management, and order fulfillment.

FIGURE 5.1

Supply Chain Management

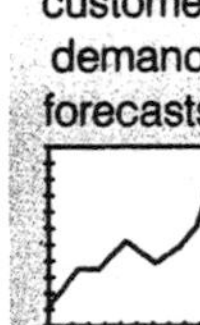

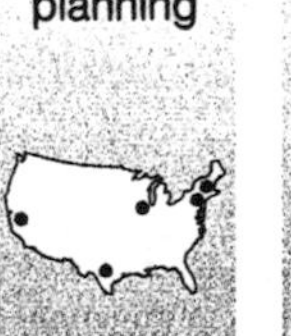

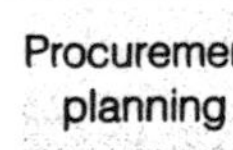

Conversion to e-commerce supply chain management provides businesses an opportunity to (1) increase revenues or decrease costs by eliminating time-consuming and labor-intensive steps throughout the order and delivery process, (2) improve customer satisfaction by enabling customers to view detailed information about delivery dates and order status, and (3) reduce inventory including raw materials, safety stocks, and finished goods. Achieving these goals requires integrating all subprocesses that exchange information and move goods between suppliers and customers, including manufacturers, distributors, retailers, and any other enterprise within the extended supply chain.

BUSINESS TO BUSINESS (B2B)

Business-to-business e-commerce offers enormous opportunities. It is considerably larger and expected to grow much more rapidly than business-to-consumer (B2C) e-commerce is. Not only does B2B e-commerce allow manufacturers to buy at a low cost worldwide, but it also offers enterprises the chance to sell to a global market right from the start. In addition, e-commerce offers great promise for developing countries, helping them enter the prosperous global marketplace and so helping reduce the gap between rich and poor countries.

The rapid development of e-commerce presents great challenges to society, however. Even though e-commerce is creating new job opportunities, it could also cause a loss of employment in some traditional jobs such as order processing or customer service areas. And as we are already seeing, many companies may fail in the intense competitive environment of e-commerce. Because of these threats, it is vital that the opportunities and implications of e-commerce be understood.

BUSINESS TO CONSUMER (B2C)

Even though it has attracted a lot of media attention, e-commerce for consumers is still in its early stages. Some shoppers are not yet convinced that it is worthwhile to connect to the Internet, search for shopping sites, wait for the images to download, try to figure out the ordering process, and then worry about whether their credit card numbers will be stolen by a hacker. But attitudes are changing, and an increasing number of shoppers are beginning to appreciate the convenience of e-commerce. For time-strapped households, consumers wonder, why waste time fighting crowds in shopping malls when from the comfort of home, you can shop on-line anytime and have the goods delivered directly? These shoppers have found that many goods and services are cheaper when purchased via the Web—for example, stocks, books, newspapers, airline tickets, and hotel rooms. They can also get information about automobiles, cruises, and homes to cut better deals. Internet shoppers can unleash shopping bots to browse the Internet and obtain lists of items, prices, and merchants. More than a new way to place orders, the Internet is emerging as a paradise for comparison shoppers.

Many manufacturers and retailers have outsourced the physical logistics of delivering merchandise to cybershoppers—the storing, packing, shipping, and tracking of products. To provide this service, DHL, Federal Express, United Parcel Service, and other delivery firms have developed software tools and interfaces that directly link customers' ordering, manufacturing, and inventory systems with their own system of highly automated warehouses, call centers, and worldwide shipping network. The goal is to make the transfer of all information and inventory—from the manufacturer to the delivery firm to the consumer—fast and simple.

For example, when a customer orders a printer at the Hewlett-Packard Web site, that order actually goes to FedEx, which stocks all the products that HP sells on-line at a dedicated e-distribution facility in Memphis, a major FedEx shipping hub. FedEx ships the order, which triggers an e-mail notification to the customer that the printer is on its way and an inventory notice to HP that the FedEx warehouse now has one fewer printer in stock (Figure 5.2). For product returns, HP

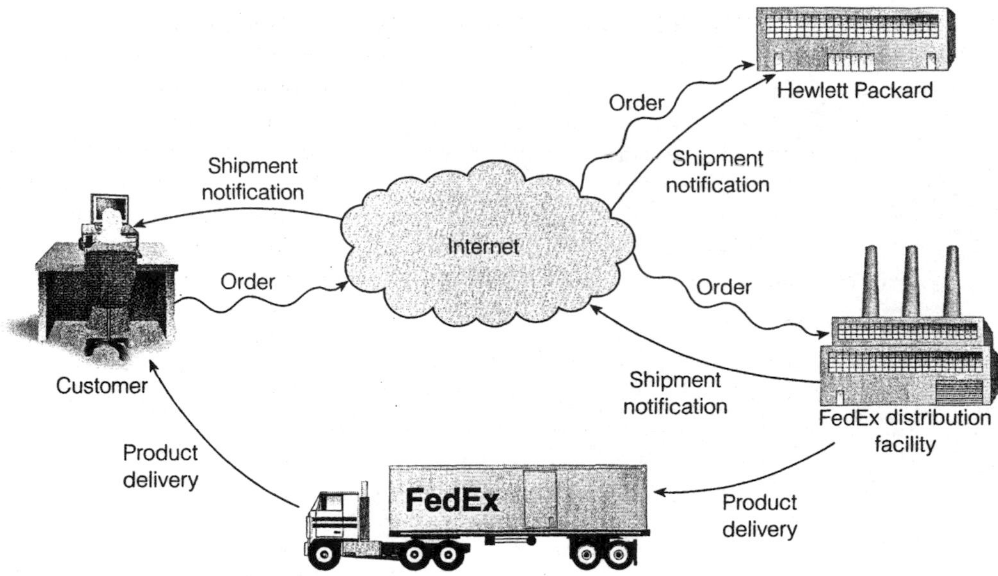

FIGURE 5.2

Product and Information Flow for HP Printers Ordered over the Web

enters return information into its own system, which is linked to FedEx. This signals a FedEx courier to pick up the unwanted item at the customer's house or business. Customers don't need to fill out shipping labels or package the item. Instead, the FedEx couriers use information transmitted over the Internet to a computer in their trucks to print a label from a portable printer attached to their belts. FedEx has control of the return, and HP can monitor its progress from start to finish.

CONSUMER TO CONSUMER (C2C)

Consumer-to-consumer (C2C) e-commerce involves consumers selling directly to other consumers. Often this exchange is done through Web auction sites such as eBay, which enabled people to sell over $9 billion in merchandise in 2001 to other consumers by auctioning items off to the highest bidder. The growth of C2C is responsible for reducing the use of the classified pages of the newspaper to advertise and sell personal items.

E-COMMERCE APPLICATIONS

E-commerce is being applied to retail and wholesale, manufacturing, marketing, investment and finance, on-line stock trading, and auctions. Here are some current uses in those areas.

RETAIL AND WHOLESALE

electronic retailing (e-tailing)
the direct sale from business to consumer through electronic storefronts, typically designed around an electronic catalog and shopping cart model

cybermall
a single Web site that offers many products and services at one Internet location

Many examples of e-commerce in retail and wholesale exist. **Electronic retailing,** sometimes called *e-tailing*, is the direct sale from business to consumer through electronic storefronts, which are typically designed around the familiar electronic catalog and shopping cart model. Companies such as Office Depot, Wal-Mart, and many others have used the same model to sell wholesale to employees of corporations. There are tens of thousands of electronic retail Web sites—selling literally everything from soup to nuts. In addition, cybermalls are another means to support retail shopping. A **cybermall** is a single Web site that offers many products and services at one Internet location—the basic idea of a regular shopping mall. An Internet cybermall pulls together multiple buyers and sellers into one virtual place, easily reachable through a Web browser.

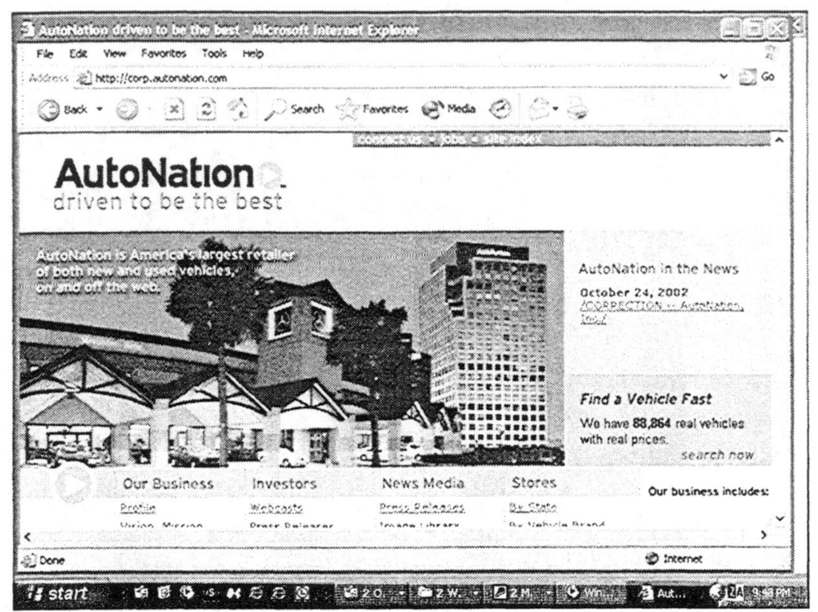

AutoNation.com is the largest auto dealership network and employs 30,000 people at 286 dealerships with $20 billion in annual revenue, $1.8 billion of it from Internet sales.

Giant retailer Sears, Roebuck and Co. provides an example of how e-commerce is transforming retail selling. Sears gives its shoppers the chance to order on-line and pick up items in its stores. To offer that capability, Sears had to implement technology to enable near-real-time inventory checks so customers can determine whether an item is in stock at a given store. The item is then plucked from the shelf and sent to merchandise pickup, triggering an e-mail confirmation to the customer. Sears joins trailblazer Circuit City Stores as one of the few retailers that can perform the inventory checks necessary to enable in-store pickup.[7]

Office Depot and Amazon.com provide yet another example of how e-commerce is transforming retail selling. In September 2002, Amazon.com signed an e-commerce alliance deal with Office Depot to host an office products store on its site. More than 50,000 office products are available for sale on-line. While Office Depot has long had its own on-line sales operation, this deal greatly expands its sales market. Customers can pick up their on-line purchases in one of Office Depot's U.S. stores. Amazon.com processes the transaction for the customer while Office Depot manages inventory and product fulfillment. This deal is one of several Amazon marketing alliances with other companies, including Circuit City, Marshall Field's, Target, and Toys 'R' Us.[8]

MANUFACTURING

electronic exchange
an electronic forum where manufacturers, suppliers, and competitors buy and sell goods, trade market information, and run back-office operations

One approach many manufacturers take to raise profitability and improve customer service is to move their supply chain operations onto the Internet. Here they can form an **electronic exchange** to join with competitors and suppliers alike using computers and Web sites to buy and sell goods, trade market information, and run back-office operations, such as inventory control, as shown in Figure 5.3. With such an exchange, the business center is not a physical building but a network-based location where business interactions occur. This approach has greatly speeded the movement of raw materials and finished products among all members of the business community, thus reducing the amount of inventory that must be maintained. It has also led to a much more competitive marketplace and lower prices.

Private exchanges are owned and operated by a single company. The owner uses the exchange to trade exclusively with established business partners. Public exchanges are owned and operated by industry groups. They provide services and a common technology platform to their members and are open, usually for a fee, to any company that wants to use them.

At the turn of the 21st century, nearly 1,000 on-line marketplaces in 70 industries had been announced by Internet and brick-and-mortar companies, including the following: the Worldwide Retail Exchange (http://www.worldwideretail exchange.org), currently led by 62 retailers around the world; Covisint (http://www.covisint.com), a global exchange for the auto industry originally formed by automakers Ford, General Motors, and DaimlerChrysler; and TradeRanger in the energy and petrochemical industry (http://www.trade ranger.com). More than 10,000 on-line exchanges are expected to be operational by late 2003; however, it's anyone's guess how many will survive. To date, only a

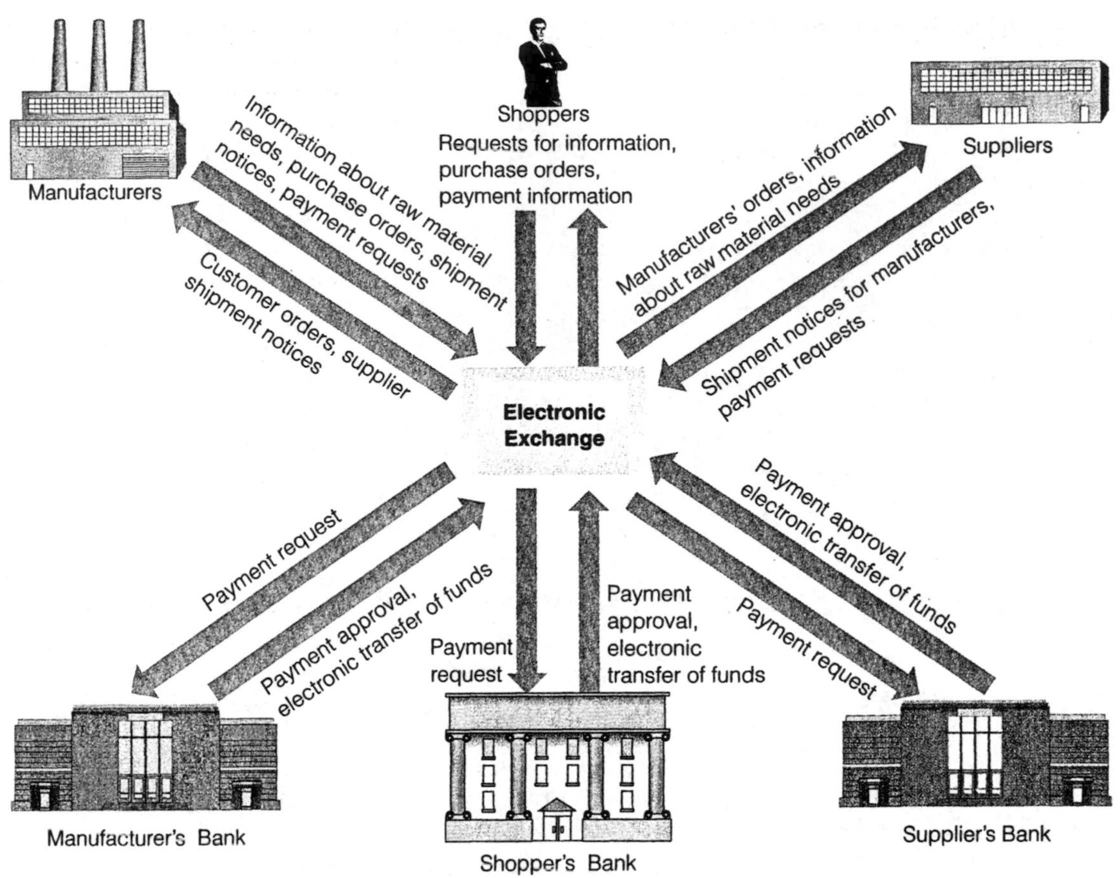

Model of an Electronic Exchange

few exchanges are seeing trickles of revenue from transaction fees, software licensing, and other charges; none is believed to be profitable yet.

Several strategic and competitive issues are associated with the use of exchanges. Many companies distrust their corporate rivals and fear they may lose trade secrets through participation in such exchanges. Suppliers worry that the on-line marketplaces and their auctions will drive down the prices of goods and favor buyers. Suppliers also can spend a great deal of money in the setup to participate in multiple exchanges. For example, more than a dozen new exchanges appeared in the oil industry, and the printing industry was up to more than 20 on-line marketplaces. Until a clear winner emerges in particular industries, suppliers are more or less forced to sign on to several or all of them. Yet another issue is potential government scrutiny of exchange participants—any time competitors get together to share information, it raises questions of collusion or antitrust behavior.

Airbus, headquartered in Toulouse, France, is a leading aircraft manufacturer. Its market share includes about half of all orders for airliners with more than 100 seats, including the double-deck A380, the world's largest commercial airliner. It spends in excess of $13 billion per year, with thousands of suppliers involved with the design and development of new aircraft. While the company considered participating in public e-marketplaces, it rejected that idea because of security and competitive considerations. Instead, Airbus formed its own private B2B marketplace using software from Ariba to support its procurement strategy, establish contracts with suppliers, maintain information on suppliers, and hold auctions for commodities or general procurement. Using this system, Airbus is able to publish its procurement needs and invite suppliers from around the world to bid on them. This enables Airbus to select the best suppliers and enter into negotiations on major purchases.[9]

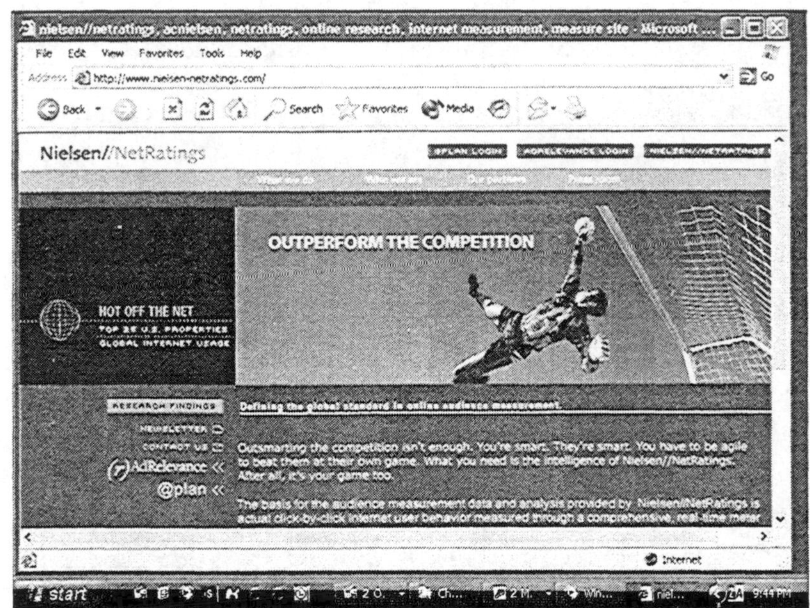

On-line marketing firm Nielsen/Net Ratings provides its clients with customized media and market research services, helping them to gain a competitive edge.

Many companies that already use the Internet for their private exchanges have no desire to share their on-line expertise with competitors. At Wal-Mart, the world's number-one retail chain, executives turned down several invitations to join exchanges in the retail and consumer goods industries. Wal-Mart is pleased with its in-house exchange, Retail Link, which connects the company to 7,000 worldwide suppliers that sell everything from toothpaste to furniture.

MARKETING

The nature of the Web allows firms to gather much more information about customer behavior and preferences than they could with other marketing approaches. Marketing organizations can measure a large number of activities as customers and potential customers gather information and make their purchase decisions. Analysis of this data is complicated because of the Web's interactivity and because each visitor voluntarily provides or refuses to provide personal data such as name, address, e-mail address, telephone number, and demographic data. Internet advertisers use the data they gather to identify specific portions of their markets and target them with tailored advertising messages. This practice, called **market segmentation**, divides the pool of potential customers into smaller groups, which are usually defined in terms of demographic characteristics such as age, gender, marital status, income level, and geographic location.

market segmentation
the identification of specific markets to target them with advertising messages

Technology-enabled relationship management has become possible when promoting and selling on the Web. **Technology-enabled relationship management** occurs when a firm obtains detailed information about a customer's behavior, preferences, needs, and buying patterns and uses that information to set prices, negotiate terms, tailor promotions, add product features, and otherwise customize its entire relationship with that customer.

technology-enabled relationship management
the use of detailed information about a customer's behavior, preferences, needs, and buying patterns to set prices, negotiate terms, tailor promotions, add product features, and otherwise customize the entire relationship with that customer

DoubleClick is a leading global Internet advertising company that leverages technology and media expertise to help advertisers use the power of the Web to build relationships with customers. The DoubleClick Network is its flagship product, a collection of high-traffic and well-recognized sites on the Web (AltaVista, Dilbert, US News, Macromedia, and more than 1,500 others). This network of sites is coupled with DoubleClick's proprietary DART targeting technology, which allows advertisers to target their best prospects based on the most precise profiling criteria available. DoubleClick then places a company's ad in front of those best prospects. Comprehensive on-line reporting lets advertisers know how their campaign is performing and what type of users are seeing and clicking on their ads. This high-level targeting and real-time reporting provide speed and efficiency not available in any other medium. The system is also designed to track advertising transactions, such as impressions and clicks, to summarize these transactions in the form of reports, and to compute DoubleClick Network member compensation.

INVESTMENT AND FINANCE

The Internet has revolutionized the world of investment and finance. Perhaps the changes have been so great because this industry had so many built-in inefficiencies and so much opportunity for improvement.

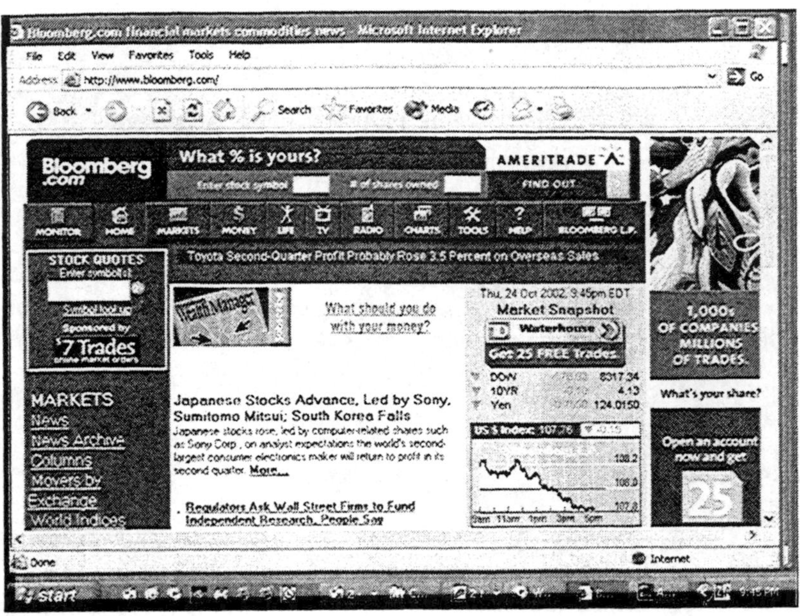

Investment and finance sites provide a multitude of services with the click of a mouse. Bloomberg.com is one of the top sites on the Web for news and financial information. Browsers can find stock market, mortgage, and other financial tracking information, as well as tips and advice on many finance subjects.

On-Line Stock Trading

Before the World Wide Web, if you wanted to invest in stocks, you called your broker and asked what looked promising. He'd tell you about two or three companies and then would try to sell you shares of a stock or perhaps a mutual fund. The sales commission was well over $100 for the stock (depending on the price of the stock and the number of shares purchased) or as much as an 8 percent sales charge on the mutual fund. If you wanted information about the company before you invested, you would have to wait two or three days for a one-page Standard and Poor's stock report providing summary information and a chart of the stock price for the past two years to arrive in the mail. Once you purchased or sold the stock, it would take two days to get an order confirmation in the mail, detailing what you had paid or received for the stock.

The brokerage business adapted to the Internet faster than any other arm of finance, with Net brokers grabbing 45 percent of the New York Stock Exchange and NASDAQ trades by early 2000. But with the stock market decline of 2000 through 2002 and with day traders counting their losses, that share is down to 22 percent.[10] Still, to make a trade, all you need to do is log on to the Web site of your on-line broker; with a few keystrokes and a few clicks of your mouse to identify the stock and number of shares, you can buy and sell securities in seconds. In addition, an overwhelming amount of free information is available to on-line investors—from the latest Securities & Exchange filings to the rumors spread in chat rooms. See Table 5.1 for a short list of the more valuable sites.

One indispensable tool of the on-line investor is a portfolio tracker. This tool allows you to enter information about the securities you own—ticker symbol, number of shares, price paid, and date purchased—at a tracker Web site. You can then access the tracker site to see how your stocks are doing. (There is typically a 15- to 20-minute delay between the price displayed at the site and the price at which the stock is actually being sold.) In addition to reporting the current value of your portfolio, most sites provide access to news, charts, company profiles, and analyst ratings on each of your stocks. You can also program many of the trackers to watch for certain events (e.g., stock price change of more than +/– 3 percent in a single day). When one of the events you specified occurs, an "alert" symbol is posted next to the affected stock. Table 5.2 lists a number of the more popular tracker Web sites.

On-Line Banking

On-line banking customers can check balances of their savings, checking, and loan accounts; transfer money among accounts; and pay their bills. With on-line banking, these customers think they can gain a better current knowledge of how much they have in the bank, eliminate the need to write checks in longhand, and reduce how much they spend on envelopes and stamps. All of the nation's major banks and many of the smaller banks enable their customers to pay bills on-line. In 2001, 15 million Americans paid bills on-line, and Americans took out at least $160 billion in mortgages on-line in 2001, 8 percent of the total market. The number of Americans who pay bills on-line is expected to reach 46 million by 2005.[11]

Name of Site	URL	Description
411 Stocks	www.411.stocks.com	One-stop location to get lots of information about a stock—price data, news, discussion groups, charts, basic data, financial statements, and delayed quotes
MarketReporter	www.marketreporter.com	Provides financial news, recommendations, upgrades, downgrades, message boards, stock market simulation game
Thomson Investors Network	www.thomsoninvest.com	Financial commentary from a number of stock market publications, including *First Watch* and *Stocks to Watch*
Elite Trader	www.elitetrader.com	Virtual gathering place for day traders with bulletin boards and chat rooms
Dayinvestor.com	www.dayinvestor.com	News and stock alerts with frequent briefs on market activity and rumors
DRIP Advisor	www.dripadvisor.com	Covers the basics of dividend reinvestment programs (DRIPs), what companies offer DRIPs, and how to start a DRIP
The Raging Bull	ragingbull.lycos.com	Contains lots of message boards; guest experts produce news, commentary, and analysis
EDGAR Online	www.edgar-online.com	Provides access to company filings with the Securities and Exchange Commission (SEC)
Federal Filings Online	www.fedfil.com	Dow Jones directory of documents filed with the federal government, including bankruptcy proceedings, initial public offering (IPO) filings, SEC reports, and court cases

TABLE 5.1

Web Sites Useful to Investors

Here's how electronic bill payment works. You first set up a list of frequent payees, along with their addresses and a code describing the type of payment, such as "home mortgage." Then when you go on-line to pay your bills, you simply enter the code or name assigned to the check recipient, the amount of the check, and the date you want it paid. In many cases, the bank still prints and mails a check, so you have to time your on-line transactions to allow for bank processing and mail delays. But most bill-paying programs allow you to schedule recurring payments for every week, month, or quarter, which you might want to do for your auto loan or health insurance bill.

electronic bill presentment
a method of billing whereby the biller posts an image of your statement on the Internet and alerts you by e-mail that your bill has arrived

The next advance in on-line bill paying is **electronic bill presentment,** which eliminates all paper, right down to the bill itself. Under this process, the biller posts an image of your statement on the Internet and alerts you by e-mail that your bill has arrived. You then direct your bank to pay it. CheckFree (http://www.checkfree.com) offers such a service, enabling more than 5.9 million consumers to

TABLE 5.2

Popular Stock Tracker Web Sites

Name of the Web Stock Tracker Site	URL
MSN MoneyCentral	moneycentral.msn.com/investor
Quicken.com	www.quicken.com
The Motley Fool	www.fool.com
Yahoo!	quote.yahoo.com
Morningstar	www.morningstar.com

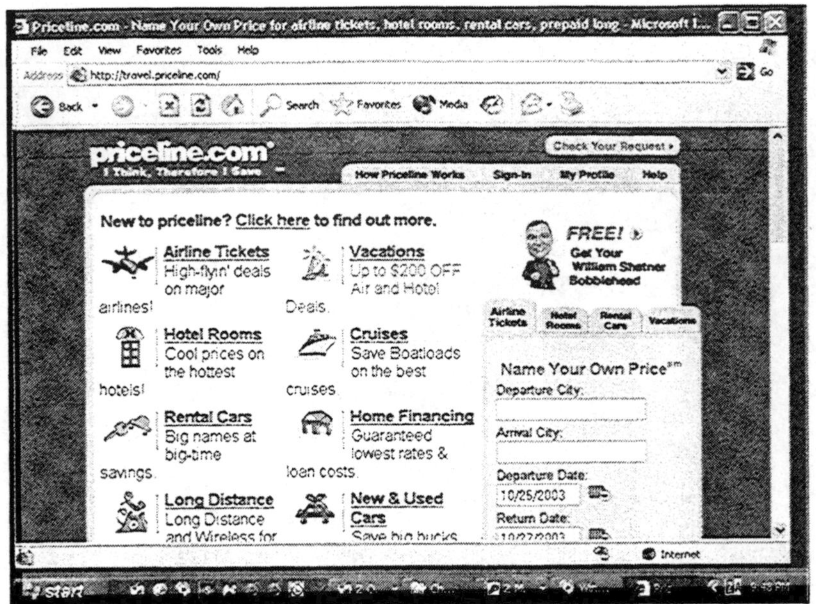

Priceline.com is a patented Internet bidding system that enables consumers to save money by naming their own price for goods and services.

receive and pay bills over the Internet or electronically with over 430 companies. Several major banks, including Union Bank of California, J. P. Morgan Chase & Co., Wachovia, and Wells Fargo, have contracted with on-line bill payment company Metavante to offer consumers the ability to view and pay bills.[12]

AUCTIONS

The Internet has created many new options for C2C, including electronic auctions, where geographically dispersed buyers and sellers can come together. A special type of auction called *bidding* allows a prospective buyer to place only one bid for an item or a service. We already discussed the on-line auction success of eBay in Chapter 4, but other auction sites and models exist. Priceline.com is the patented Internet bidding system that enables consumers to achieve significant savings by naming their own price for goods and services. Priceline.com takes these consumer offers and then presents them to sellers, who can fill as much of that guaranteed demand as they wish at price points determined by buyers.

reverse auction
an auction in which the role of the bidder is switched from the buyer to the seller; multiple sellers post prices for a single buyer

In a **reverse auction,** the role of the bidder is switched from the buyer to the seller. In other words, multiple sellers post prices for a single buyer. Many companies consider on-line reverse auctioning to be a vast improvement over the traditional sealed-bid process for procuring goods and services because it increases competition and creates market transparency by allowing vendors to submit multiple bids in real time. Vendors' identities are concealed during the auction event, but their bids are not. Once the reverse auction event is completed, the seller may evaluate the bids, weigh the other variables to be considered, and then make the procurement. In August 2002, Orbis Online was selected as a contractor by the General Services Administration (GSA) to conduct on-line reverse auctions. The goal is to achieve the best competitive pricing and help automate the way government agencies purchase products and services.[13]

Now that we've examined some of the applications of e-commerce, let's look at some technical issues related to information systems and technology that make it possible.

TECHNOLOGY, INFRASTRUCTURE, AND DEVELOPMENT

For e-commerce to succeed, a complete set of hardware, software, and network components must be chosen carefully and integrated to support a large volume of transactions with customers, suppliers, and other business partners worldwide. On-line consumers frequently complain that poor Web site performance (e.g., slow response time and "lost" orders) drives them to abandon some e-commerce sites in favor of those with better, more reliable performance. This section provides a brief overview of the key technology infrastructure components (Figure 5.4).

HARDWARE

A Web server complete with the appropriate software is key to successful e-commerce. The amount of storage capacity and computing power required of the Web server depends primarily on two things—the software that must run on the server and the volume of e-commerce transactions that must be processed.

FIGURE 5.4

Key E-Commerce Technical Components

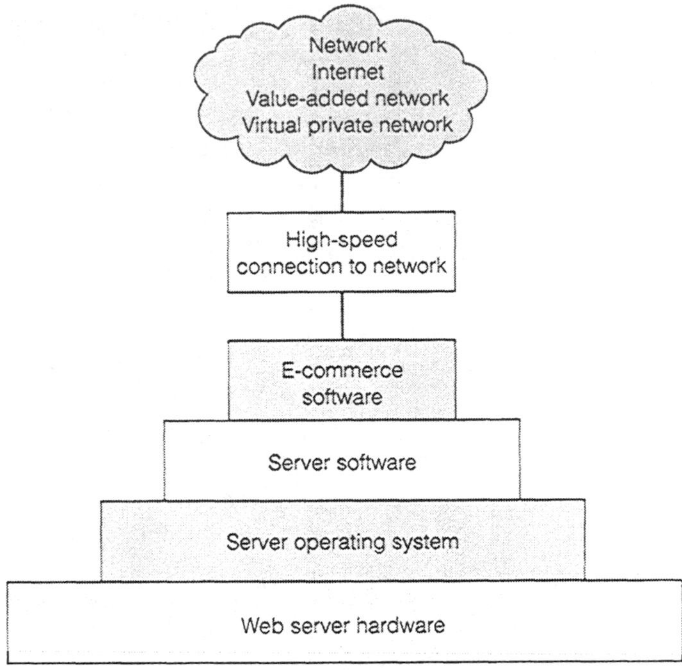

Although business managers and information systems staff can define the software to be used, it is difficult for them to estimate how much traffic the site will generate. As a result, the most successful e-commerce solutions are designed to be highly scalable so that they can be upgraded to meet unexpected user traffic.

Many companies decide that a third-party Web service provider is the best way to meet their initial e-commerce needs. A Web service rents out space on its computer system and provides a high-speed connection to the Internet, which minimizes the initial setup costs for e-commerce. The service provider can also provide personnel trained to operate, troubleshoot, and manage the Web server. Other companies decide to take full responsibility for acquiring, operating, and supporting their own Web server hardware and software, but this approach requires considerable up-front capital and a set of skilled and trained individuals. Whichever approach is taken, there must be adequate hardware backup to avoid a major business disruption in case of a failure of the primary Web server.

SOFTWARE

Each e-commerce Web server must have software to perform a number of fundamental services, including security and identity authentication, retrieval and sending of Web pages, and Web page construction. The two most popular Web server software packages are Apache HTTP Server and Microsoft Internet Information Server.

Web site development tools
tools used to develop a Web site, including HTML or visual Web page editor, software development kits, and Web page upload support

Web site development tools include features such as an HTML/visual Web page editor (e.g., Microsoft's FrontPage, NetStudio's NetStudio, SoftQuad's HoTMetaL Pro), software development kits that include sample code and code development instructions for languages such as Java or Visual Basic, and Web page upload support to move Web pages from a development PC to the Web site. Which tools are bundled with the Web server software depends on which Web server software you select.

Web page construction software
software that uses Web editors and extensions to produce both static and dynamic Web pages

Web page construction software uses Web editors to produce Web pages—either static or dynamic. *Static Web pages* always contain the same information—for example, a page that provides text about the history of the company or a photo of corporate headquarters. *Dynamic Web pages* contain variable information and are built in response to a specific Web visitor's request. For example, if a Web site visitor inquires about the availability of a certain product by entering a product identification number, the Web server will search the product inventory database and generate a dynamic Web page based on the current product information it found, thus fulfilling the visitor's request. This same request by another visitor later in the day may yield different results due to ongoing changes in product inventory. A server that handles dynamic content must be able to access information from a variety of databases. The use of open database connectivity enables the Web server to assemble information from different database management systems, such as SQL Server, Oracle, and Informix.

Once you have located or built a host server, including the hardware, operating system, and Web server software, you can begin to investigate and install e-commerce software. There are three core tasks that **e-commerce software** must support: catalog management, product configuration, and shopping cart facilities.

e-commerce software
software that supports catalog management, product configuration, and shopping cart facilities

catalog management software
software that automates the process of creating a real-time interactive catalog and delivering customized content to a user's screen

Any company that offers a wide range of product offerings requires a real-time interactive catalog to deliver customized content to a user's screen. **Catalog management software** combines different product data formats into a standard format for uniform viewing, aggregating, and integrating catalog data into a central repository for easy access, retrieval, and updating of pricing and availability changes. The data required to support large catalogs is almost always stored in a database on a computer that is separate from, but accessible to, the e-commerce server machine. The effort to build and maintain on-line catalogs can be substantial. For example, Fastenal is a leading distributor of nuts, bolts, screws, and other products used by manufacturing and construction companies. The company has a group of more than two-dozen product marketers and information systems staff who help the company assemble and update its e-commerce catalogs. Its goal is to expand its on-line catalog to the full line of over 1 million products that it distributes.[14]

product configuration software
software used by buyers to build the product they need on-line

Customers need help when an item they are purchasing has many components and options. **Product configuration software** tools were originally developed in the 1980s to assist B2B salespeople in matching their company's products to customer needs. Buyers use the new Web-based product configuration software to build the product they need on-line with little or no help from salespeople. For example, Dell customers use product configuration software to build the computer of their dreams. Use of such software can expand into the service arena as well, with consumer loans and financial services to help people decide what sort of loan or insurance is best for them.

electronic shopping cart
a model commonly used by many e-commerce sites to track the items selected for purchase, allowing shoppers to view what is in their cart, add new items to it, and remove items from it

Today many e-commerce sites use an **electronic shopping cart** to track the items selected for purchase, allowing shoppers to view what is in their cart, add new items to it, or remove items from it, as shown in Figure 5.5. To order an item, the shopper simply clicks that item. All the details about it—including its price, product number, and other identifying information—are stored automatically. If the shopper later decides to remove one or more items from the cart, he or she can do so by viewing the cart's contents and removing any unwanted items. When the shopper is ready to pay for the items, he or she clicks a button (usually labeled "proceed to checkout") and begins a purchase transaction. Clicking the "Checkout" button displays another screen that usually asks the shopper to fill out billing, shipping, and payment method information and to confirm the order.

ELECTRONIC PAYMENT SYSTEMS

Electronic payment systems are a key component of the e-commerce infrastructure. The U.S. Federal Reserve System released results of a November 2001 survey that suggested that check writing is giving way to electronic payments. The Fed found that the use of checks has declined from approximately 85 percent of

Electronic Shopping Cart
An electronic shopping cart (or bag) allows on-line shoppers to view their selections and add or remove items.

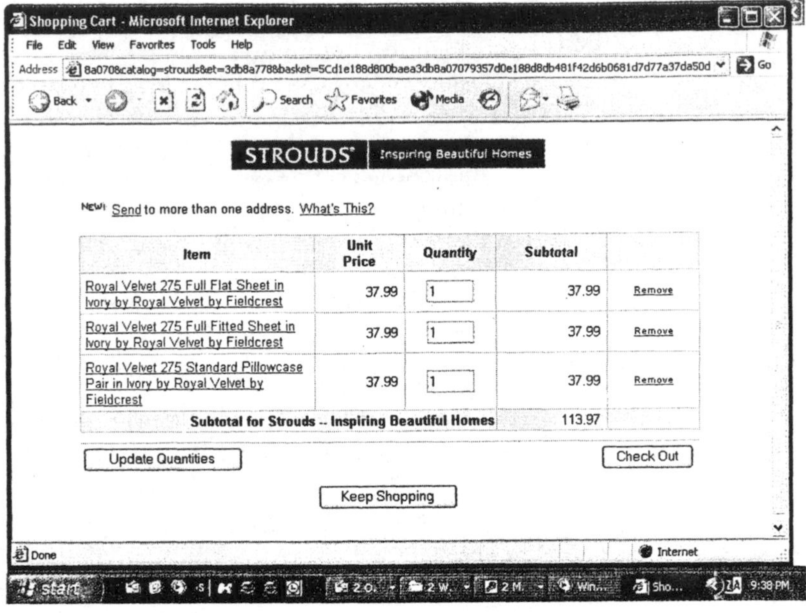

noncash payments since the last study in 1979 to about 60 percent, with an estimated 50 billion checks written annually in the United States, for a total of $48 trillion in payments.[15] Current e-commerce technology relies on user identification and encryption to safeguard business transactions. Actual payments are made in a variety of ways, including electronic cash; electronic wallets; and credit, charge, debit, and smart cards.

electronic cash
an amount of money that is computerized, stored, and used as cash for e-commerce transactions

Authentication technologies are used by organizations to confirm the identity of a user requesting access to information or assets. A digital certificate is an attachment to an e-mail message or data embedded in a Web site that verifies the identity of a sender or Web site.

A security system assures customers that information they provide to retailers, such as credit card numbers, cannot be viewed by anyone else on the Web.

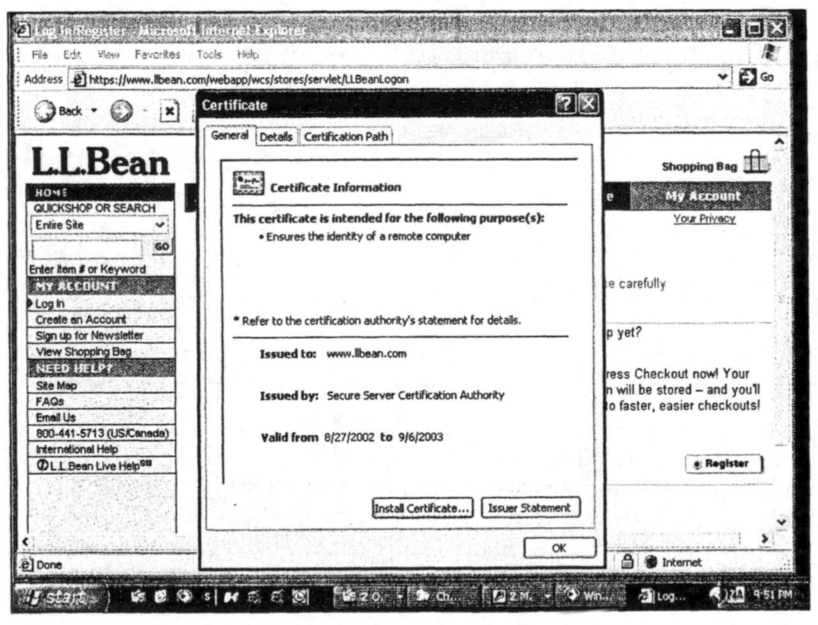

One indicator of the security associated with a Web site is visible on screen. Look at the bottom left corner of your browser before sending your credit card number to an e-commerce vendor. If you use Netscape Navigator, make sure you see a solid key in a small blue rectangle. If you use Microsoft Internet Explorer, the words "Secure Web site" appear near a little gold lock. If you're worried about how secure a secure connection is, visit the Netcraft.com site. At this site you can type in any Web site address and determine the equipment being used for secure transactions. One more tip: To ensure security, you should always use the newest browser available. The newer the browser, the better the security.

Electronic Cash

Electronic cash is an amount of money that is computerized, stored, and used as cash for e-commerce transactions. A consumer must open an account with a bank to obtain electronic cash. Whenever the consumer wants to withdraw electronic cash to make a purchase, he or she accesses the bank via the Internet and presents proof of identity—typically a digital certificate. After the bank verifies the consumer's identity, it issues the consumer the requested amount of electronic cash and deducts the same amount from the consumer's account. The electronic cash is stored in the consumer's electronic wallet on his or her computer's hard drive or on a smart card (both are discussed later).

Consumers can spend their electronic cash when they locate e-commerce sites that accept electronic cash for payment. The consumer sends electronic cash to the merchant for the specified cost of the goods or services. The merchant validates the electronic cash to be certain it is not forged and belongs to the customer. Once the goods or services are shipped to the consumer, the merchant presents the electronic cash to the issuing bank for deposit. The bank then credits the merchant's account for the transaction amount, minus a small service charge.

Electronic Wallets

electronic wallet
a computerized stored value that holds credit card information, electronic cash, owner identification, and address information

On-line shoppers quickly tire of repeatedly entering their shipment and payment information each time they make a purchase. An **electronic wallet** holds credit card information, electronic cash, owner identification, and address information. It provides this information at an e-commerce site's checkout counter. When consumers click on items to purchase, they can then click on their electronic wallet to order the item, thus making on-line shopping much faster and easier.

Household International, a leading provider of consumer finance, credit card, auto finance, and credit insurance products, in partnership with General Motors Corporation and CyberCash (acquired by VeriSign), a provider of e-commerce technologies and services for merchants, introduced the GM Card easyPay electronic wallet marketed to a large portion of GM card members. The GM Card easyPay Wallet stores a shopper's name, credit card information, shipping details, and other pertinent facts that can be called up to make an on-line purchase with a single click of a computer mouse. The wallet is available to GM card members and interested consumers at http://www.gmcard.com.[16]

Credit, Charge, Debit, and Smart Cards

On-line shoppers use credit and charge cards for the majority of their Internet purchases. A credit card, such as Visa or MasterCard, has a preset spending limit based on the user's credit limit, and each month the user can pay off a portion of the amount owed or the entire credit card balance. Interest is charged on the unpaid amount. All credit card customers are protected by law from paying any more than $50 for fraudulent transactions. At Visa, on-line purchases account for the highest amount of purchase fraud—24 cents for every $100 spent, compared with 6 cents for every $100 overall.[17] In fact, the risk of bogus credit card transactions has slowed the growth of e-commerce by exposing merchants to substantial losses and making on-line shoppers nervous. Credit card fraud accounted for $1.2 billion of total on-line sales of $65 billion in 2001, with merchants forced to cover most of those losses. Banks charge merchants an average fee of 2.5 percent for on-line transactions compared with 1.5 percent for in-store purchases to offset the costs of credit card fraud.[18]

On-line payment processor VeriSign processes about one in every four on-line transactions in the United States. It recently adopted a credit card identification system developed by MasterCard to reduce credit card fraud. The system relies on a "Universal Cardholder Authentication Field" that enables merchants to verify that on-line shoppers are using credit cards that actually belong to them by entering a special password associated with the card. MasterCard is providing merchants with a powerful incentive to sign up for the new program—merchants who verify transactions through the new system won't have to pay for losses should the transaction turn out to be illegitimate. Instead, the card issuer will be liable.[19]

A charge card, such as American Express, carries no preset spending limit, and the entire amount charged to the card is due at the end of the billing period. Charge cards do not involve lines of credit and do not accumulate interest charges.

Debit cards look like credit cards or automated teller machine (ATM) cards, but they operate like cash or a personal check. While a credit card is a way to "buy now, pay later," a debit card is a way to "buy now, pay now." Debit cards allow you to spend only what is in your bank account. It is a quick transaction between the merchant and your personal bank account. When you use a debit card, your money is quickly deducted from your checking or savings account. Credit, charge, and debit cards currently store limited information about you on a magnetic stripe. This information is read each time the card is swiped to make a purchase.

smart card
a credit card–sized device with an embedded microchip to provide electronic memory and processing capability

The **smart card** is a credit card–sized device with an embedded microchip to provide electronic memory and processing capability. Smart cards can be used for a variety of purposes, including storing a user's financial facts, health insurance data, credit card numbers, and network identification codes and passwords. They can also store monetary values for spending.

Smart cards are better protected from misuse than conventional credit, charge, and debit cards because the smart card information is encrypted. Conventional credit, charge, and debit cards clearly show your account number on the face of the card. The card number, along with a forged signature, is all that a thief needs to purchase items and charge them against your card. A smart card makes credit theft practically impossible because a key to unlock the encrypted information is required, and there is no external number that a thief can identify and no physical signature a thief can forge.

Smart cards have been around for over a decade and are widely used in Europe, Australia, and Japan, but they have not caught on in the United States. Use has been limited because there are so few smart card readers to record payments, and U.S. banking regulations have slowed smart card marketing and acceptance as well. American Express launched its Blue card smart card in 1999. You can use a smart card reader that attaches to your PC monitor to make on-line purchases with your American Express card. You must visit the American Express Web site to get an electronic wallet to store your credit card information and shipping address. When you want to buy something on-line, you go to the checkout screen of a Web merchant, swipe your Blue card through the reader, type in a password, and you're done. The digital wallet automatically tells the vendor your credit card number, its expiration date, and your shipping information.[20] Read the "IS Principles in Action" special interest box to find out more about smart cards.

As we pointed out earlier, e-commerce applications often provide customers the ability to order and pay for products and request service and information. As such, these applications form the basis for a class of information systems called *transaction processing systems*, which we discuss next.

AN OVERVIEW OF TRANSACTION PROCESSING SYSTEMS

Every organization has manual and automated transaction processing systems (TPSs), which process the detailed data necessary to update records about the fundamental business operations of the organization. These systems include order entry, inventory control, payroll, accounts payable, accounts receivable, and general ledger, to name just a few. The input to these systems includes basic business transactions such as customer orders, purchase orders, receipts, time cards, invoices, and payroll checks. The result of processing business transactions is that the organization's records are updated to reflect the status of the operation at the time of the last-processed transaction. Automated TPSs consist of databases, telecommunications, people, procedures, software, and hardware devices used to process transactions. The processing activities include data collection, data edit, data correction, data manipulation, data storage, and document production.

IS Principles in Action

PRINCIPLE

E-commerce requires the careful planning and integration of a number of technology infrastructure components.

Visa Implements Smart Card Technology

Visa cards today can be used to pay for purchases at more than 42 million merchant locations in 300 countries and territories. They can also be used to obtain cash at over 700,000 ATMs in 136 countries. More than 14,000 U.S. financial institutions rely on the VisaNet processing system to facilitate over $765 billion in annual transaction volume—including more than half of all Internet payments.

Visa continues to work on behalf of its member financial institutions, merchants, and consumers to continually deliver better ways to pay. The company announced the smart Visa card in May 2001 as a means of providing a highly personalized card capable of changing as your needs change and as new services become available. The Visa smart card uses an embedded chip that is programmed to accept, store, and send data. It is also designed to minimize card duplication and forgery. An especially useful feature of the smart Visa is that it enables you to consolidate many of the store and discount cards filling your wallet onto its memory chip. Visa's vision is that smart cards will continue to add new services and levels of convenience to consumers' everyday lives by, for example, functioning as electronic keys for a home, office, or car or offering payment services through a personal computer, mobile phone, or personal digital assistant (PDA).

Smart Visa card readers are credit card–sized devices that connect to your personal computer to provide additional features. You can pay for on-line purchases by simply inserting your smart Visa card into the reader. The password-protected smart Visa card works with Verified by Visa to authenticate your identity and your card. Verified by Visa allows you to add a personal password to your existing Visa card. When you make purchases at participating on-line stores, you validate your identity by entering your password in a special Verified by Visa window. This gives you added safety and reassurance that only you can use your Visa card on-line.

As smart card technology evolves and new services become available, you will be able to use the reader to download these new features onto your smart Visa card. The smart Visa card and reader also provide secure access to your account through your financial institution's Web site. You can obtain smart Visa card readers from the financial institutions that issue the smart Visa cards or from a variety of consumer electronics retailers.

Visa is confident that smart card acceptance and usage will increase significantly in the United States. However, for this to happen, merchants must pay up to $1,000 for new point-of-sale (POS) devices that are smart card–enabled. As a critical first step in providing smart card payments, Visa brought together key industry players, including Hypercom, Ingenico Fortronic, and VeriFone, to build smart card POS devices, networking equipment, and software. Importantly, all hardware and software had to conform to EMV (Europay Co., Master Card International, and Visa International) standards. These standards cover specifications for financial transaction systems and smart card–based credit cards, and they must be adhered to for smart cards to be universally compatible in world markets.

Discussion Questions

1. What are the advantages of a smart card over an ordinary credit card or debit card? Are there any disadvantages?
2. What can be done to spread the use of smart cards? Does it need to start with businesses or with customers?

Critical Thinking Questions

3. Why would competitors Europay, Master Card, and Visa work together to develop smart card standards?
4. Imagine that you are the owner of a small, local retail store with annual sales in the $2 to $5 million range. What would cause you to install three or four new POS terminals at a cost of $1,000 to accept the new smart cards?

Sources: Adapted from the Visa-USA Web site, http://www.usa.visa.com; Business Editors, "Visa U.S.A. Drives Industry Collaboration to Build Smart Card Acceptance in U.S," *Business Wire*, May 7, 2001, http://www.businesswire.com; Lucas Mearian, "Visa Smart Card Technology Almost Ready for Prime Time," *Computerworld*, May 8, 2001, http://www.computerworld.com; Maria Trombly, "Visa Offers to Help E-merchants Meet New Security Guidelines," *Computerworld*, March 2, 2001, http://www.computerworld.com.

Because TPSs often perform activities related to customer contacts—such as order processing and invoicing—these information systems play a critical role in providing value to the customer. For example, by capturing and tracking the movement of each package, United Parcel Service (UPS) can provide timely and accurate data on the exact location of a package. Shippers and receivers can access an on-line database and, by providing the airbill number of a package, find the package's current location. Such a system provides the basis for added value through improved customer service.

Without transaction processing information systems, recording and processing business transactions would consume huge amounts of an organization's resources. The transaction processing system (TPS) also provides employees

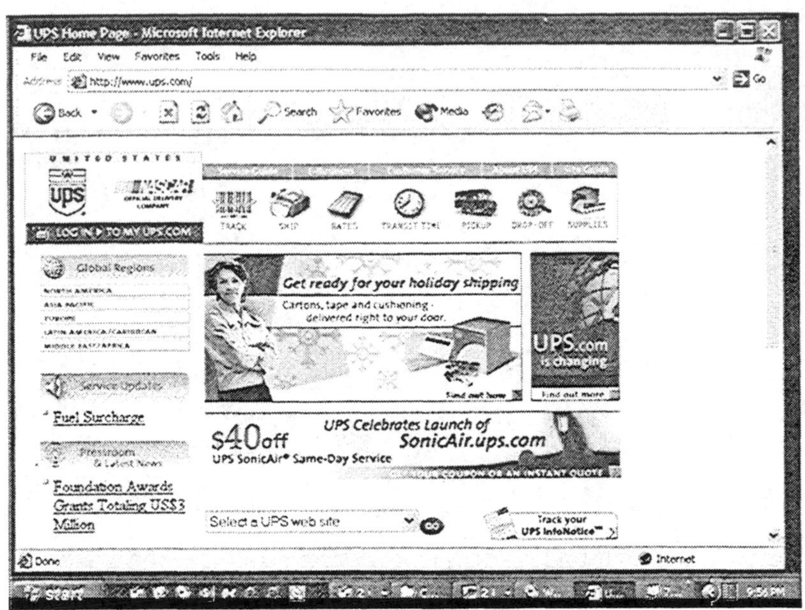

UPS adds value to its service by providing timely and accurate data on-line on the exact location of a package.

involved in other business processes—the management information system/decision support system (MIS/DSS) and the special purpose information systems—with data to help them achieve their goals. So a transaction processing system serves as the foundation for the other systems (Figure 5.6). Transaction processing systems perform routine operations such as sales ordering and billing, often performing the same operations daily or weekly. The amount of support for decision making that a TPS directly provides managers and workers is low.

These systems require a large amount of input data and produce a large amount of output without requiring sophisticated or complex processing. As we move from transaction processing to management information/decision support and to special-purpose information systems, we see less routine, more decision support, less input and output, and more sophisticated and complex processing and analysis. But the increase in sophistication and complexity in moving from transaction processing does not mean that it is less important to a business. In most cases, all these systems start as a result of one or more business transactions.

TRADITIONAL TRANSACTION PROCESSING METHODS AND OBJECTIVES

batch processing system
method of computerized processing in which business transactions are accumulated over a period of time and prepared for processing as a single unit or batch

With **batch processing systems**, business transactions are accumulated over a period of time and prepared for processing as a single unit or *batch* (Figure 5.7a). The time period during which transactions are accumulated is whatever length of time is needed to meet the needs of the users of that system. For example, it may be important to process invoices and customer payments for the accounts receivable system daily. On the other hand, the payroll system may receive time cards and process them biweekly to create checks and update employee earnings records as well as to distribute labor costs. The essential characteristic of a batch processing system is that there is some delay between the occurrence of the event and the eventual processing of the related transaction to update the organization's records.

on-line transaction processing (OLTP)
computerized processing in which each transaction is processed immediately, without the delay of accumulating transactions into a batch

With **on-line transaction processing (OLTP)**, each transaction is processed immediately and the affected records are updated, without the delay of accumulating transactions into a batch (Figure 5.7b). Consequently, at any time, the data in an on-line system always reflects the current status. When you make an airline reservation, for instance, the transaction is processed and all databases, such as seat occupancy and accounts receivable, are updated immediately. This type of processing is absolutely essential for businesses that require data quickly and

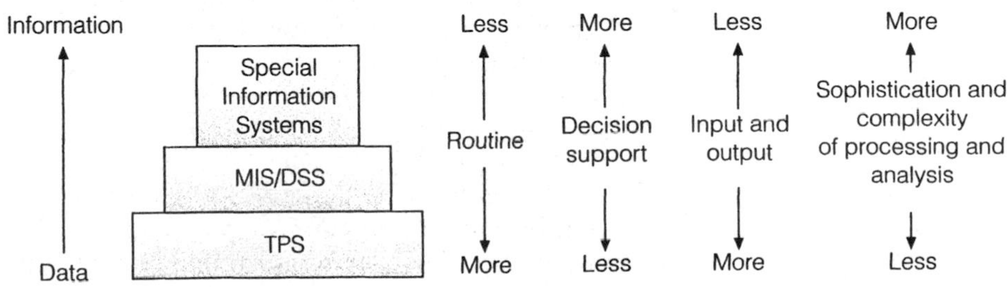

FIGURE 5.6

TPS, MIS/DSS, and Special-Purpose Information Systems in Perspective

FIGURE 5.7

Batch versus On-Line Transaction Processing

Batch processing (a) inputs and processes data in groups. In on-line processing (b), transactions are completed as they occur.

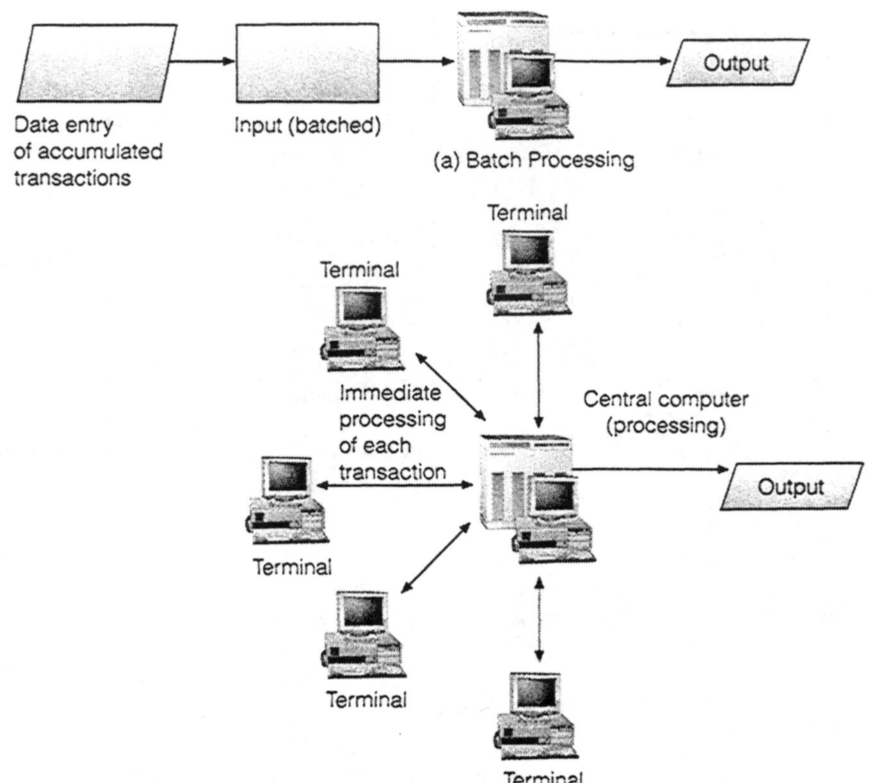

update it often, such as airlines, ticket agencies, and stock investment firms. Many companies have found that OLTP helps them provide faster, more efficient service—one way to add value to their activities in the eyes of the customer. Increasingly, companies are using the Internet to perform many OLTP functions.

Even though the technology exists to run TPS applications using on-line processing, it is not done for all applications. For many applications, batch processing is more appropriate and cost-effective. Payroll transactions and billing are typically done via batch processing. Specific goals of the organization define the method of transaction processing best suited for the various applications of the company. Figure 5.8 shows the total integration of a firm's transaction processing systems.

One objective of any TPS is error-free data input and processing. An editing program, for example, should have the ability to determine that an entry that should read "40 hours" is not entered as "400 hours" or "4000 hours" because of a data-entry error.

When a TPS is developed or modified, the personnel involved should carefully consider how the new or modified system might provide a significant and long-term benefit or competitive advantage. Such an advantage is typically gained through providing superior customer service (e.g., use of tracking systems that are accessible by customers to determine shipping status) or dramatically cutting costs (e.g. use of warehouse management systems employing scanners and bar-coded products to reduce labor hours and improve inventory accuracy).

TRANSACTION PROCESSING ACTIVITIES

All transaction processing systems perform common data processing activities. TPSs capture and process data that describes fundamental business transactions. This data is used to update databases and to produce a variety of reports for use by

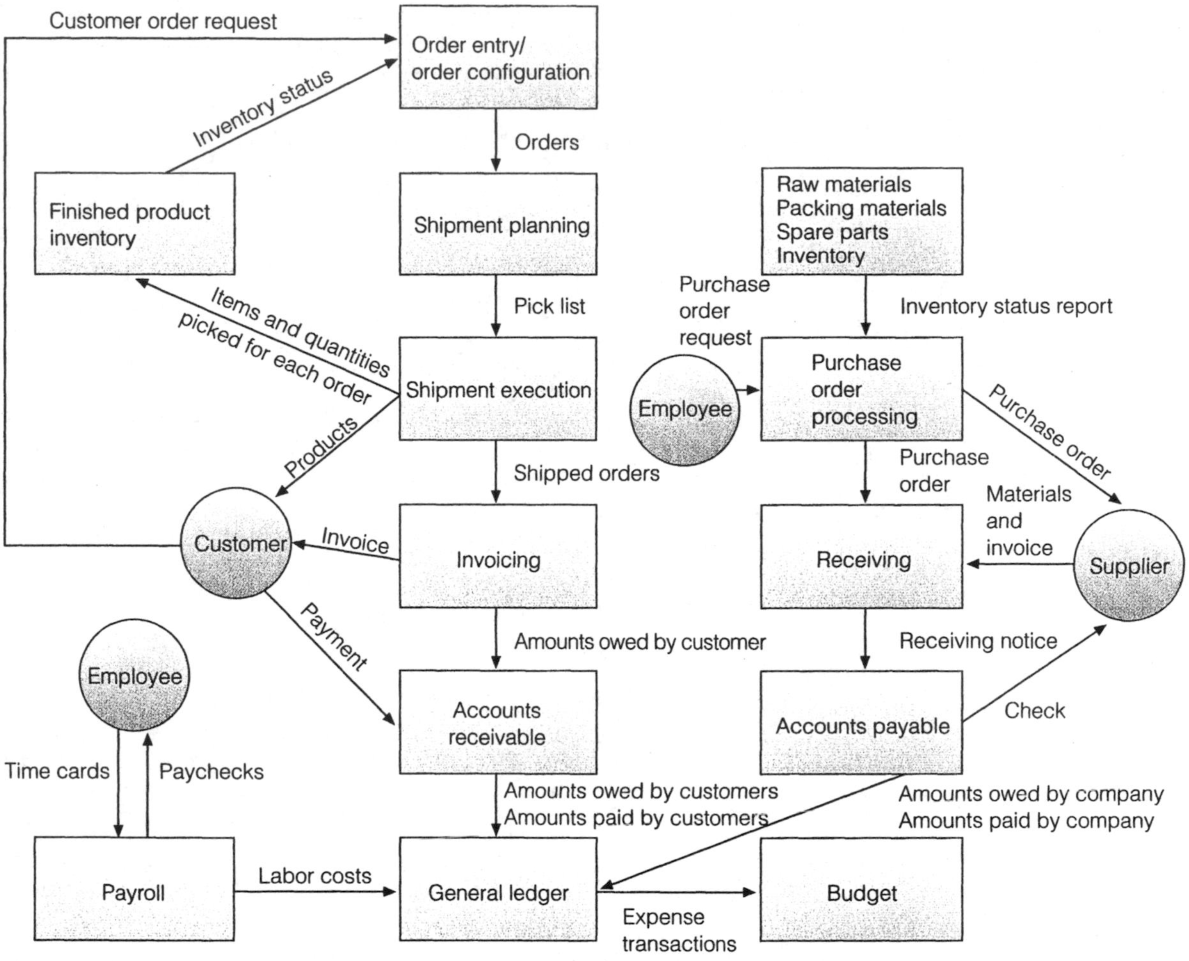

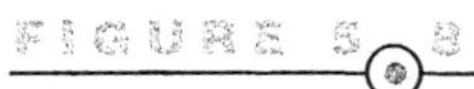

FIGURE 5.8

Integration of a Firm's TPSs

transaction processing cycle
the process of data collection, data editing, data correction, data manipulation, data storage, and document production

data collection
the process of capturing and gathering all data necessary to complete transactions

people both within and outside the enterprise. The business data goes through a **transaction processing cycle** that includes data collection, data editing, data correction, data manipulation, data storage, and document production (Figure 5.9).

Data Collection

The process of capturing and gathering all data necessary to complete transactions is called **data collection.** In some cases, this can be done manually, such as by collecting handwritten sales orders or changes to inventory. In other cases, data collection is automated via special input devices such as scanners, point-of-sale devices, and terminals.

Data should be captured at its source, and it should be recorded accurately, in a timely fashion, with minimal manual effort, and in a form that can be directly entered to the computer rather than keying the data from some type of document. This approach is called *source data automation.* An example of source data automation is the use of scanning devices at the grocery checkout to read the Universal Product Code (UPC) automatically. Reading the UPC bar codes is quicker and more accurate than having a cash register clerk enter codes manually. The scanner reads the bar code for each item and looks up its price in the item database. The point-of-sale transaction processing system uses the price data to determine the customer's bill. The number of units of this item purchased, the date, the time, and the price are also used to update the store's inventory database, as well as its database of detailed purchases. The inventory database is used to generate a management report notifying the store manager to reorder items whose sales have reduced the stock below the reorder quantity. The detailed purchases database

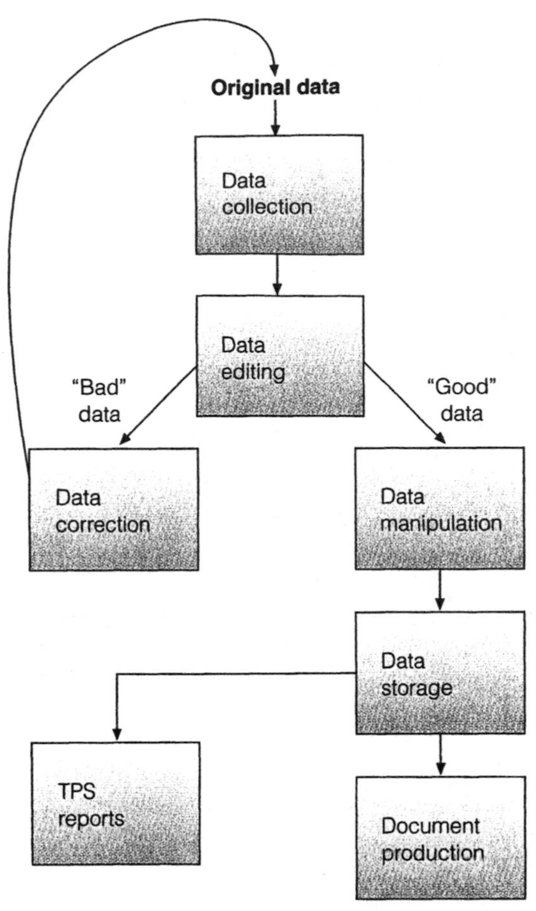

FIGURE 5.9

Data Processing Activities Common to Transaction Processing Systems

data editing
the process of checking data for validity and completeness

data correction
the process of reentering miskeyed or misscanned data that was found during data editing

data manipulation
the process of performing calculations and other data transformations related to business transactions

data storage
the process of updating one or more databases with new transactions

can be used by the store (or sold to market research firms or manufacturers) for detailed analysis of sales (Figure 5.10).

Many grocery stores combine point-of-sale scanners and coupon printers. The systems are programmed so that each time a specific product—say, a box of cereal—crosses a check-out scanner, an appropriate coupon—perhaps a milk coupon—is printed. Companies can pay to be promoted through the system, which is then reprogrammed to print those companies' coupons if the customer buys a competitive brand. These TPSs help grocery stores to increase profits by improving their repeat sales and bringing in revenue from other businesses.

Data Editing

An important step in processing transaction data is to perform **data editing** for validity and completeness to detect any problems with the data. For example, quantity and cost data must be numeric and names must be alphabetic; otherwise, the data is not valid. Often the codes associated with an individual transaction are edited against a database containing valid codes. If any code entered (or scanned) is not present in the database, the transaction is rejected.

Data Correction

It is not enough to reject invalid data. The system should provide error messages that alert those responsible for the data edit function. These error messages must specify what problem is occurring so that corrections can be made. **Data correction** involves reentering miskeyed or misscanned data that was found during data editing. For example, a UPC that is scanned must be in a master table of valid UPCs. If the code is misread or does not exist in the table, the checkout clerk is given an instruction to rescan the item or key in the information manually.

Data Manipulation

Another major activity of a TPS is **data manipulation**, the process of performing calculations and other data transformations related to business transactions. Data manipulation can include classifying data, sorting data into categories, performing calculations, summarizing results, and storing data in the organization's database for further processing. In a payroll TPS, for example, data manipulation includes multiplying an employee's hours worked by the hourly pay rate. Overtime calculations, federal and state tax withholdings, and deductions are also performed.

Data Storage

Data storage involves updating one or more databases with new transactions. Once the update process is complete, this data can be further processed and manipulated by other systems so that it is available for management decision making. Thus, although transaction databases can be considered a by-product of transaction processing, they affect nearly all other information systems and decision-making processes in an organization.

Document Production and Reports

TPSs produce important business documents that may be paper reports or displays on computer screens. Paychecks, for example, are hard-copy documents produced by a payroll TPS, while an outstanding balance report for invoices might be displayed by an accounts receivable TPS. Often, results from one TPS are passed downstream as input to other systems. For example, the results of updating

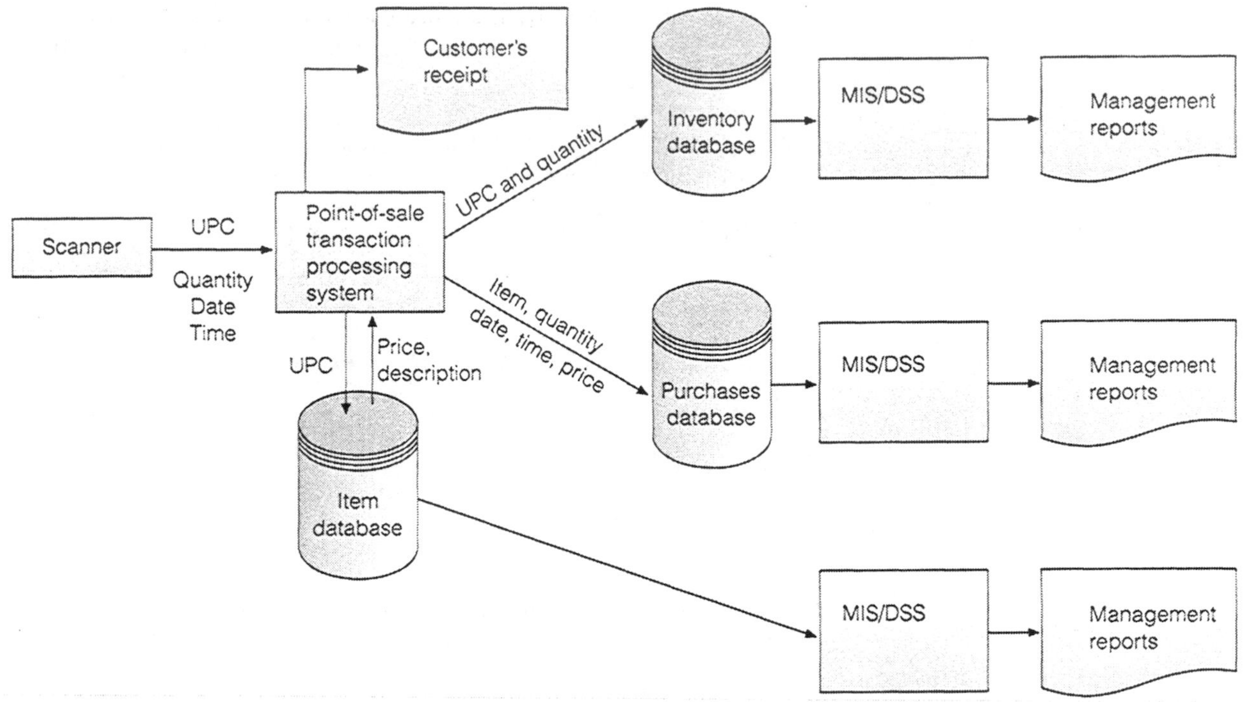

Point-of-Sale Transaction Processing System

Scanning items at the checkout stand results in updating a store's inventory database and its database of purchases.

the inventory database are used to create the stock exception report (a type of management report) of items whose inventory level is less than the reorder point.

In addition to major documents such as checks and invoices, most transaction processing systems provide useful reports that help managers and employees perform various activities. These reports can be printed or displayed on a computer screen. A report showing current inventory is one example; another might be a document listing items ordered from a supplier to help a receiving clerk check the order for completeness when it arrives. A TPS can also produce reports required by local, state, and federal agencies, such as statements of tax withholding and quarterly income statements.

ORDER PROCESSING SYSTEMS

Since transaction processing systems were first built to handle the give and take between customers and product suppliers, we can gain a better understanding of how they work by examining several common transaction processing systems that support order processing (Table 5.3).

order processing systems
systems that process order entry, sales configuration, shipment planning, shipment execution, inventory control, invoicing, customer relationship management, and routing and scheduling

Order processing systems include order entry, sales configuration, shipment planning, shipment execution, inventory control, invoicing, customer resource management, and routing and scheduling. The business processes supported by these systems are so critical to a firm's operation that collectively they are sometimes referred to as the "lifeblood of the organization." Figure 5.11 is a system-level flowchart that shows the various systems and the information that flows between them. A rectangle represents a system, a line represents the flow of information from one system to another, and a circle represents any entity outside the system—in this case, the customer. What is key to note here is how these transaction processing systems work together as an integrated whole to support major business processes.

PURCHASING AND ACCOUNTING SYSTEMS

Transaction processing systems support many areas of the business. For example, the purchasing transaction processing systems include inventory control, purchase order processing, receiving, and accounts payable. This integrated set of systems

Order Processing System	Purpose
Order entry	Captures the basic data needed to process a customer order
Sales configuration	Ensures that the products and services ordered are sufficient to accomplish the customer's objectives and will work well together
Shipment planning	Determines which open orders will be filled and from which location they will be shipped
Shipment execution	Coordinates the outflow of all products from the organization, with the objective of delivering quality products on time to customers
Inventory control (finished product)	Updates computerized inventory records to reflect the exact quantity on hand of each stock-keeping unit
Invoicing and billing	Generates customer invoices based on records received from the shipment execution transaction processing system
Customer resource management	Monitors and tracks each customer contact with the company
Routing and scheduling	Determines the best way to get products from one location to another

TABLE 5.3

Systems That Support Order Processing

enables an organization to plan, manage, track, and pay for its purchases of raw materials, parts, and services. There are accounting transaction processing systems including budget, accounts receivable, payroll, asset management, and general ledger systems. This integrated set of systems enables an organization to plan, manage, track, and control its cash flow and revenue.

FIGURE 5.11

Order Processing Systems

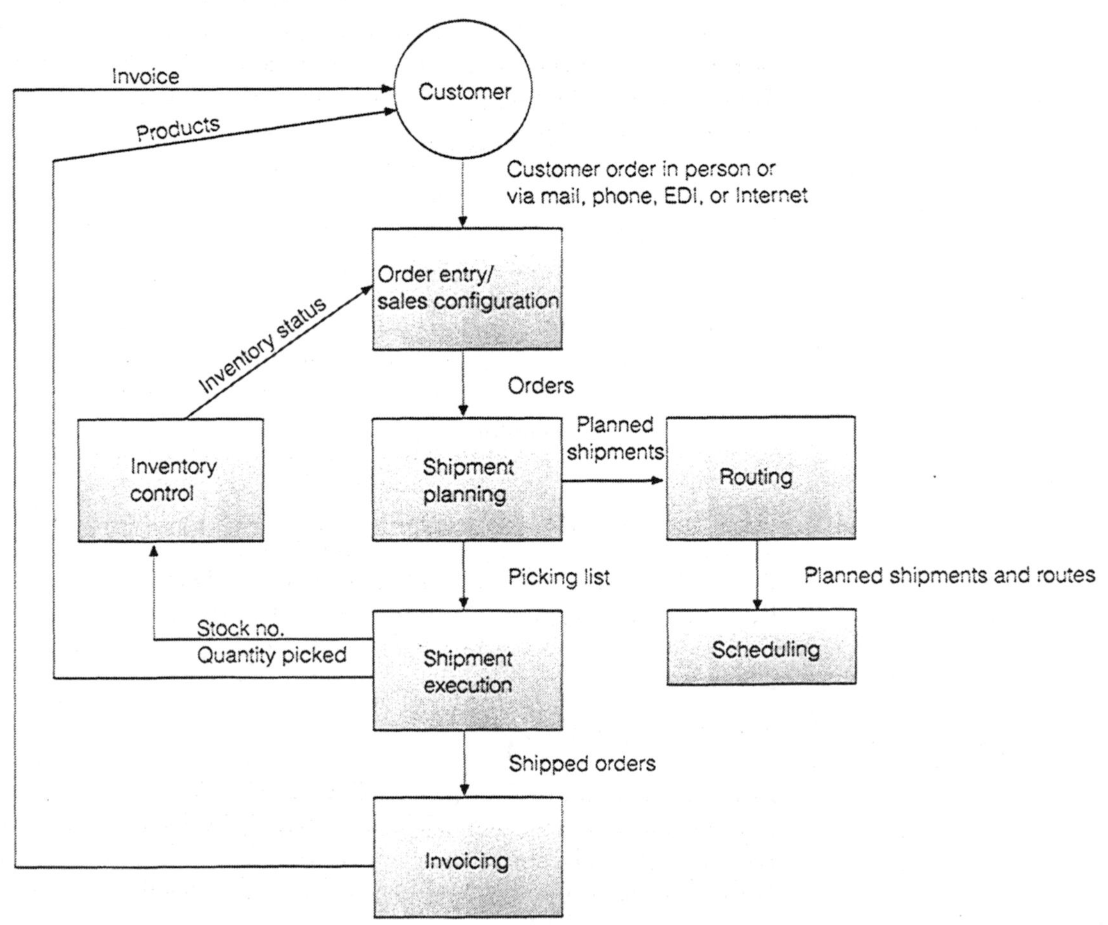

Companies like Iron Mountain provide a secure, off-site environment for records storage. In the event of a disaster, vital data can be recovered.

(Source: © 2002 PhotoDisc.)

BUSINESS RESUMPTION PLANNING

Most organizations would grind to a screeching halt if their transaction processing systems failed. **Business resumption planning** is the process of anticipating and minimizing the effects of disasters. Disasters can be natural emergencies such as a flood, a fire, or an earthquake or interruptions in business processes due to such causes as labor unrest or erasure of an important file. Business resumption planning focuses primarily on two issues: maintaining the integrity of corporate information and keeping key information systems running until normal operations can be resumed.

business resumption planning
the process of anticipating and providing for disasters

One of the first steps of business resumption planning is to identify potential threats or problems, such as natural disasters, employee misuse of personal computers, and poor internal control procedures. Business resumption planning also involves disaster preparedness. The primary tools used in disaster planning and recovery are backups for hardware, software and databases, telecommunications, and personnel. A common backup for hardware is a similar or compatible computer system owned by another company or a specialized backup system provided by an organization from which a written hardware backup agreement is obtained. Software and databases can be backed up by making duplicate copies of all programs and data. Some business recovery plans call for the backup of vital telecommunications, with the most critical nodes on the network backed up by duplicate components. Business and IS managers should occasionally hold an unannounced "disaster test"—similar to a fire drill—to ensure that the disaster plan is effective.

disaster recovery
the implementation of the business resumption plan

The value of backup and recovery for critical systems was brought home on September 11, 2001. Nearly 3,000 people perished in those terrorist attacks. But even as they mourned the human losses, companies with offices in the World Trade Center towers had to execute **disaster recovery** plans to resume business. Companies varied widely in the thoroughness and effectiveness of their contingency planning, and some had a harder time resuming business than others. One of the hardest hit yet best prepared was Morgan Stanley, a $54 billion investment banking firm. The firm had 3,700 employees located on 25 floors in the two World Trade Center buildings; only six were killed. In addition to the loss of life, the firm suffered property damages and a loss of revenue due to business downtime valued at $150 million. Morgan Stanley had revamped its disaster recovery plan when the Persian Gulf War began in 1990, specifying everything from where employees meet after a crisis to how data is protected. As a result, backup data centers in Manhattan and New Jersey were able to keep all critical information systems running without interruption. There was no loss of any computer-based data, and its e-mail service was restored within 72 hours. On the other extreme of preparedness was May Davis Group, a privately held financial services firm with 13 employees on the 87th floor of 1 World Trade Center. The firm had no disaster recovery plan at the time of the attack. One employee perished in the attack, property damage exceeded $100,000, and the loss of revenue due to business downtime and data loss exceeded $1 million.[21]

ENTERPRISE RESOURCE PLANNING

Flexibility and quick response are hallmarks of business competitiveness. Access to information at the earliest possible time can help businesses serve customers better, raise quality standards, and assess market conditions. Enterprise resource planning (ERP) is a key factor in instant access. Although some think that ERP systems are

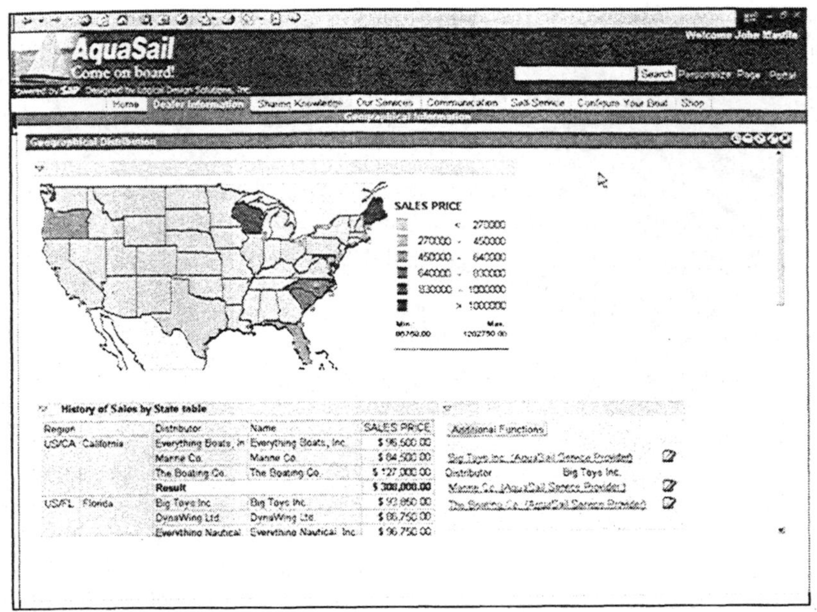

SAP R/3 software provides comprehensive solutions for companies of all sizes in all industry sectors.

(Source: Copyright by SAP AG. All rights reserved.)

only for extremely large companies, this is not the case. Medium-sized companies can also benefit from the ERP approach. A few leading vendors of ERP systems are listed in Table 5.4.

AN OVERVIEW OF ENTERPRISE RESOURCE PLANNING

The key to ERP is real-time monitoring of business functions, which permits timely analysis of key issues such as quality, availability, customer satisfaction, performance, and profitability. Financial and planning systems receive "triggered" information from manufacturing and distribution. When something happens on the manufacturing line that affects a business situation—for example, packing material inventory drops to a certain level, delaying delivery of a customer's order—a message is triggered for the appropriate person in purchasing. In addition to manufacturing and finance, ERP systems can also support human resources, sales, and distribution. This sort of integration is breaking through traditional corporate boundaries.

ERP systems accommodate the different ways each company runs its business by either providing vastly more functions than one business could ever need or including customization tools that allow firms to fine-tune what should already be a close match. SAP R/3 is the undisputed king of the first approach. R/3 is easily the broadest and most feature-rich ERP system on the market. Thus, rather than compete on size, most rivals focus on customizability. ERP systems have the ability to configure and reconfigure all aspects of the IS environment to support whatever way your company runs its business.

ERP vendors have also developed specialized systems for specific applications and market segments. Developing custom packages for every market need and segment would be a huge undertaking for ERP vendors. As a result, major ERP vendors are increasingly seeking help from other software vendors to develop specialized programs to tie directly into their ERP systems. Most companies have found it surprisingly difficult to justify implementation of an ERP system based strictly on cost savings.

TABLE 5.4

Some ERP Software Vendors

Software Vendor	Name of Software
Oracle	Oracle Manufacturing
SAP America	SAP R/3
Baan	Triton
PeopleSoft	PeopleSoft
J. D. Edwards	WorldSoftware and One World
Ross Systems	iRenaissance
QAD	MFG/Pro

COMMONALITIES AMONG ERP SYSTEMS

Almost all ERP systems are based on a similar set of basic design elements. This section summarizes the design elements common to Baan, J. D. Edwards, Oracle, PeopleSoft, SAP, Ross Systems, QAD, and other major ERP vendors.

Integrated Data

ERP systems are designed so that data is entered only once in the system and that data is easily accessible by all ERP programs. Each data item is clearly documented in a data dictionary. The software is flexible enough to be configured to meet the customer's business requirements.

Operate in Client/Server Environment

The applications run in a multilevel client/server architecture consisting of clients, application servers, and database servers. The clients are usually desktop computers with fast processors and more than 32 MB of RAM. Users of the client computers request services from the application servers. The application servers are powerful midrange or even mainframe computers. The job of the server is to reply to all requests made of it, including requests for data, communication of messages, and update of master files. The request from the client travels via a network to the application server. A database server in the ERP system holds the data and is accessed and updated constantly.

Based on Objects

Many ERP systems are built using the object-oriented programming approach discussed in Chapter 2. An object is a collection of data and programs. "Purchase order" and "customer" are examples of ERP business objects used in business processes. Attributes contain the details of an object, such as name, date of employment, and address of an employee.

Employ Tables

ERP systems employ three major types of tables: system configuration tables, control tables, and application data tables. System configuration tables define the structure of the system; only the software manufacturer changes these tables. The ERP system customer's project team uses both control tables to configure the software to meet the customer's specific business requirements. Control tables define functions that guide the user in his or her activities. For example, a control table might be set up to require a customer service representative to enter a line item to reference data about the product from the material master table before a purchase order is accepted.

ADVANTAGES AND DISADVANTAGES OF ERP

Increased global competition, new needs of executives for control over the total cost and product flow through their enterprises, and ever-more-numerous customer interactions are driving the demand for enterprisewide access to real-time information. ERP offers integrated software from a single vendor to help meet those needs. The primary benefits of implementing ERP include elimination of inefficient systems, easing adoption of improved work processes, improving access to data for operational decision making, and technology standardization. Disadvantages include the considerable time and expense in getting an ERP system up and running, compatibility problems with other systems, and the risk inherent in having only one vendor. Let's look at these pros and cons more closely.

Elimination of Costly, Inflexible Legacy Systems

Adoption of an ERP system enables an organization to eliminate dozens or even hundreds of separate systems and replace them with a single integrated set of applications for the entire enterprise. In many cases, these systems are decades old, the original developers are long gone, and the systems are poorly documented. As a result, they are extremely difficult to fix when they break, and adapting them to meet new business needs takes too long. They become an anchor on the organization that keeps it from moving ahead and remaining competitive. An ERP system helps match the capabilities of an organization's information systems to its business needs—even as these needs evolve.

Improvement of Work Processes

Competition requires companies to structure their business processes to be as effective and customer-oriented as possible. ERP vendors do research to define the best business processes. They gather requirements of leading companies within the same industry and combine them with findings from research institutions and consultants. The individual application modules included in the ERP system are then designed to support these **best practices**, the most efficient and effective ways to complete a business process. As a result, implementation of an ERP system ensures good work processes based on best practices. For example, for managing customer payments, the ERP system's finance module can be configured to reflect the most efficient practices of leading companies in an industry. This increased efficiency ensures that everyday business operations follow the optimal chain of activities, with all users supplied the information and tools they need to complete each step.

best practices
the most efficient and effective ways to complete a business process

Increase in Access to Data for Operational Decision Making

ERP systems operate via an integrated database and use essentially one set of data to support all business functions. So decisions on optimal sourcing or cost accounting, for instance, can be run across the enterprise from the start, rather than looking at separate operating units and then trying to integrate that information manually or reconciling data with another application. The result is an organization that looks seamless, not only to the outside world but also to the decision makers who are deploying resources within the organization.

The data is integrated to provide excellent support for operational decision making and allows companies to provide greater customer service and support, strengthen customer and supplier relationships, and generate new business opportunities. For example, once a salesperson makes a new sale, the business data captured during the sale is available to the financial, sales, distribution, and manufacturing business functions in other departments.

Upgrade of Technology Infrastructure

An ERP system provides an organization with the opportunity to upgrade and simplify the information technology it employs. In implementing ERP, a company must determine which hardware, operating systems, and databases it wants to use. Centralizing and formalizing these decisions enables the organization to eliminate the hodgepodge of multiple hardware platforms, operating systems, and databases it is currently using—most likely from a variety of vendors. Standardization on fewer technologies and vendors reduces ongoing maintenance and support costs as well as the training load for those who must support the infrastructure. Remy Corporation, a $22 million Denver-based professional services firm, needed its front-office applications (those that interact directly with customers) to more easily integrate with its back-office systems. It decided to eliminate its collection of systems from a variety of software manufacturers and move to a PeopleSoft ERP system to avoid potential system integration issues.[22]

Despite its benefits, moving to ERP can also have drawbacks. Chief among the problems that organizations have encountered are the sizable cost and time needed to implement a system, difficulties in linking with a company's other systems, and the risks of consolidating products and services into only one ERP vendor.

Expense and Time in Implementation

Getting the full benefits of ERP is not simple or automatic. Although ERP offers many strategic advantages by streamlining a company's transaction processing system, ERP is time-consuming, difficult, and expensive to implement. Some companies have spent years and tens of millions of dollars implementing ERP systems. And when there are problems with an ERP implementation, it can be expensive to fix. GM Locomotive Group, a $2 billion subsidiary of the auto manufacturer that makes locomotives, diesel engines, and armored vehicles such as tanks, installed an ERP system to improve its financial reporting and its ability to forecast spare parts needs. It encountered such severe problems during system rollout that its spare parts business virtually ground to a halt and caused GM to launch an emergency turnaround effort. The software wasn't configured well enough to match internal business processes, and mainframe data wasn't properly formatted for the new system.[23]

Difficulty Integrating with Other Systems

Most companies have other systems that must be integrated with the ERP. These systems can include financial analysis programs, Internet operations, and other applications. Many companies have experienced difficulties making these other systems operate with their ERP system. Other companies employ additional software to create these links. General Mills uses Tidal Software's Enterprise Scheduler to link the systems used to manage customer orders and its SAP R/3 ERP system. The Enterprise Scheduler converts 2.5 million orders sent annually via EDI transactions to SAP's format and imports them to R/3. It then routes orders within the company and alerts General Mills's personnel to any problems associated with the orders, such as difficulties in scheduling production or meeting customer desired delivery dates.[24]

Risks in Using One Vendor

The high cost to switch to another vendor's ERP system makes it extremely unlikely that a firm will do so. So once a company has adopted an ERP system, the vendor knows it has a "captive audience" and has less incentive to listen and respond to customer issues. The high cost to switch also creates a high level of risk—in the event the ERP vendor allows its product to become outdated or goes out of business. Picking an ERP system involves not just choosing the best software product but also choosing the right long-term business partner.

Implementing an ERP system is extremely challenging and requires tremendous amounts of resources, the best IS people, and plenty of management support. Many companies have failed with their initial attempts, causing major business disruptions. Companies, facing quarterly financial pressures from stockholders and analysts, have become more willing to hold software suppliers publicly responsible for problems tied to the use of their products. The negative impact on the software supplier can be severe. Read the "Ethical and Societal Issues" special-interest box for an example of what can go wrong.

Obviously, firms that decide to implement ERP systems should do so with careful planning and a clear idea of gains they can make competitively. The positives can then significantly outweigh the negatives.

Ethical and Societal Issues

Nike Stumbles Implementing ERP

Nike is the world's leading shoe company and sells its products throughout the United States and 140 other countries. Nike also sells Cole Haan dress and casual shoes and a line of athletic apparel and equipment. In addition, Nike operates Niketown shoe and sportswear stores and is opening Nike Goddess stores catering to women.

The firm issued an earnings warning in February 2001, blaming its $400 million project to roll out a new demand- and inventory-management system—as well as lower shoe sales—for an expected earnings shortfall of $100 million. Nike said that after implementing a new ERP system in the summer of 2000, orders for some shoes were placed twice—once by the new system and once by its existing order-management system. Also, orders for many new shoe styles were lost and never processed. The heavily customized ERP system included modules from Dallas-based i2 Technologies Inc. i2 provides software that helps manufacturers plan and schedule production and related operations such as raw materials procurement and product delivery.

In its defense, i2 said the company's software modules represented only about 10 percent of the $400 million ERP project. The installation was also large and complex, requiring a high degree of customization of the i2 applications that were then linked with other ERP and back-end systems. In addition, the wide range of apparel products sold in a multitude of sizes and styles led to further difficulties in tailoring the i2 software to match Nike's internal business processes. i2 said that Nike failed to follow i2's recommendation to minimize customization, to adopt i2's best practices for the footwear and apparel business, and to deploy the system gradually and in stages. Instead, Nike heavily customized the software and brought the system to thousands of suppliers and distributors at once.

The Nike announcement created a serious public relations problem for i2, and potential customers began to question the viability of the company's software. Shares of i2 stock dropped from just over $25 in March 2001 to under $4 in May 2002. (The stock had been as high as $104 in March 2000.) The Nike incident was not the sole or even primary cause, but it was certainly a contributing factor.

Interestingly, brokerage firm Wells Fargo Van Kasper lowered its rating of Nike in December 2001, in part based on the perceived problem with Nike's implementation of SAP software. In addition to the difficulties Nike has already encountered, investors were concerned that the installation of a new SAP software system in the company's core U.S. business segment would impede the flow of Nike's spring 2002 merchandise line.

Discussion Questions

1. What business benefits would Nike likely gain from the successful implementation of an ERP system?
2. Do research on the Web on i2 Technologies and write a paragraph summarizing its current business state.

Critical Thinking Questions

3. Supply chain software vendor i2 says Nike pushed the $400 million system into production too quickly, insisted on too much customization, and went live with too many suppliers and distributors at once. That could be, but for $400 million, did Nike have a right to set some high expectations of the software vendors?
4. This isn't the first time a company has attributed lowered earnings to new software mishaps. How might a financial auditor or IS consultant pinpoint the amount of the earnings shortfall due to weak sales and the amount due to IS problems? Would knowing this information make any difference?

Sources: Adapted from Bob Evans, "Listening Post," *Information Week*, June 4, 2001, http://www.informationweek.com; Marc Songini, "Nike Says Profit Woes IT Based," *Computerworld*, March 5, 2001, http://wwwcomputer world.com; John Soat, "IT Confidential," *Information Week*, March 5, 2001, http://www.informationweek.com; Steve Konicki, "Nike Just Didn't Do It Right," *Information Week*, March 5, 2001, http://www.informationweek.com; Aaron Ricadela, "The State of Software Quality," *Information Week*, May 21, 2001, http://www.informationweek.com; John Soat, "IT Confidential," *Information Week*, December 17, 2001, http://www.informationweek.com.

SUMMARY

PRINCIPLE ***E-commerce is a new way of conducting business, and as with any other new application of technology, it presents both opportunities for improvement and potential problems.***

Businesses and individuals use e-commerce to reduce transaction costs, speed the flow of goods and information, improve the level of customer service, and enable the close coordination of actions among manufacturers, suppliers, and customers. E-commerce also enables consumers and companies to gain access to worldwide markets.

Business-to-business e-commerce allows manufacturers to buy at a low cost worldwide, and it offers enterprises the chance to sell to a global market right from the start.

Although it is gaining acceptance, business-to-consumer, or e-commerce for consumers, is still in its early stages. Yet, e-commerce offers great promise for developing countries, helping them to enter the prosperous global marketplace and hence helping reduce the gap between rich and poor countries. By using business-to-consumer e-commerce to sell directly to consumers, a producer or provider of consumer services can eliminate the middlemen, or intermediaries, between them and the end consumer. In many cases, this squeezes costs and inefficiencies out of the supply chain and can lead to higher profits and/or lower prices for consumers.

Consumer-to-consumer (C2C) e-commerce involves consumers selling directly to other consumers.

Supply chain management is composed of three subprocesses: demand planning to anticipate market demand, supply planning to allocate the right amount of enterprise resources to meet demand, and demand fulfillment to fulfill demand quickly and efficiently. Conversion to e-commerce supply chain management provides businesses an opportunity to achieve excellence by increasing revenues, decreasing costs, improving customer satisfaction, and reducing inventory. But to achieve this goal requires integrating all subprocesses that exchange information and move goods between suppliers and customers, including manufacturers, distributors, retailers, and any other enterprise within the extended supply chain.

Many manufacturers and retailers have outsourced the physical logistics of delivering merchandise to cybershoppers. To provide this service, delivery firms have developed software tools and interfaces that directly link customers' ordering, manufacturing, and inventory systems with their own system of highly automated warehouses, call centers, and worldwide shipping network. The goal is to make the transfer of all information and inventory—from the manufacturer to the delivery firm to the consumer—fast and simple.

Electronic retailing (e-tailing) is the direct sale from business-to-consumer through electronic storefronts designed around an electronic catalog and shopping cart model. A cybermall is a single Web site that offers many products and services at one Internet location. Manufacturers are joining electronic exchanges, where they can join with competitors and suppliers to use computers and Web sites to buy and sell goods, trade market information, and run back-office operations such as inventory control. They are also using e-commerce to improve the efficiency of the selling process by moving customer queries about product availability and prices on-line. The nature of the Web allows firms to gather much more information about customer behavior and preferences than they could using other marketing approaches. This new technology has greatly enhanced the practice of market segmentation and enabled companies to establish closer relationships with their customers. Detailed information about a customer's behavior, preferences, needs, and buying patterns allows companies to set prices, negotiate terms, tailor promotions, add product features, and otherwise customize a relationship with a customer. The Internet has also revolutionized the world of investment and finance, especially on-line stock trading and on-line banking. The Internet has also created many options for electronic auctions, where geographically dispersed buyers and sellers can come together.

PRINCIPLE ***E-commerce requires the careful planning and integration of a number of technology infrastructure components.***

A number of infrastructure components must be chosen and integrated to support a large volume of transactions with customers, suppliers, and other business partners worldwide. These components include hardware, Web server software, e-commerce software, and network and packet switching.

Current e-commerce technology relies on the use of identification and encryption to safeguard business transactions. Web site operators must protect against a denial-of-service attack, where the attacker takes command of many computers on the Internet and causes them to flood the target Web site with requests for data and other small tasks that keep the target machine too busy to serve legitimate users. A digital certificate is an attachment to an e-mail message or data embedded in a Web page that verifies the identity of a sender or a Web site. Actual payments are made in a variety of ways including electronic cash; electronic wallets; and credit, charge, debit, and smart cards.

PRINCIPLE ***An organization's transaction processing system (TPS) must support the routine, day-to-day activities that occur in the normal course of business and help a company add value to its products and services.***

Transaction processing systems (TPSs) are at the heart of most information systems in businesses today. TPSs consist of all the components of a CBIS, including databases, telecommunications, people, procedures, software, and hardware devices to process transactions. All TPSs perform the following basic activities: data collection involves the capture of source data to complete a set of transactions; data edit checks for data validity and completeness; data correction involves providing feedback of a potential problem and enabling users to change the data; data manipulation is the performance of calculations, sorting, categorizing, summarizing, and storing for further processing; data storage involves placing transaction data into one or more databases; and document production involves outputting records and reports.

The methods of transaction processing systems include batch and on-line processing. Batch processing involves the collection of transactions into batches, which are entered into the system at regular intervals as a group. On-line transaction processing (OLTP) allows transactions to be entered as they occur. Organizations expect TPSs to accomplish a number of specific objectives, including processing data generated by and about transactions, maintaining a high degree of accuracy, ensuring data and information integrity, compiling accurate and timely reports and documents, increasing labor efficiency, helping provide increased and enhanced service, and building and maintaining customer loyalty.

TPS applications are seen throughout an organization. The order processing systems include order entry, sales configuration, shipment planning, shipment execution, inventory control, invoicing, customer relationship management, and routing and scheduling.

The purchasing transaction processing systems include inventory control, purchase order processing, accounts payable, and receiving. The accounting systems include the budget, accounts receivable, payroll, asset management, and general ledger.

Because of the importance of a transaction processing system to the ongoing operation of an organization, a business resumption plan that anticipates and minimizes the effects of disasters is mandatory. Business resumption planning focuses primarily on two issues: maintaining the integrity of corporate information and keeping the information system running until normal operations can be resumed. Disaster recovery is the implementation of the business resumption plan. Although companies have known about the importance of disaster planning and recovery for decades, many still do not adequately prepare.

PRINCIPLE ***Implementation of an enterprise resource planning (ERP) system enables a company to achieve numerous business benefits through the creation of a highly integrated set of systems.***

Enterprise resource planning (ERP) software is a set of integrated programs that manage a company's vital business operations for an entire multisite, global organization. It must be able to support multiple legal entities, multiple languages, and multiple currencies. Although the scope of an ERP system may vary from vendor to vendor, most ERP systems provide integrated software to support manufacturing and finance. In addition to these core business processes, some ERP systems are capable of supporting additional business functions such as human resources, sales, and distribution.

Almost all ERP systems are based on a set of common basic design elements. They are designed so that data is entered only once in the system and that data is easily accessible by all ERP programs. Each data item is clearly documented in a data dictionary. The software is flexible enough to be configured to meet the customer's business requirements. The applications run in a multilevel client/server architecture consisting of clients, application servers, and database servers. Many ERP systems are built using the object-oriented programming approach. ERP systems employ three major types of tables: system configuration tables, control tables, and application data tables.

Implementation of an ERP system can provide many advantages, including elimination of costly, inflexible legacy systems; providing improved work processes; providing access to data for operational decision making; and creating the opportunity to upgrade technology infrastructure. Some of the disadvantages associated with an ERP system are that they are time-consuming, difficult, and expensive to implement.

CHAPTER 5 SELF-ASSESSMENT TEST

E-commerce is a new way of conducting business, and as with any other new application of technology, it presents both opportunities for improvement and potential problems.

1. Which of the following statements is NOT a reason for the success of U.K.–based on-line grocer Tesco?
   A. It has a profit margin of 8 percent compared with 2 percent for most U.S.-based grocers.
   B. It made a multimillion-dollar investment in automated distribution facilities.
   C. Workers, not automated conveyors, are used to pick items to fill customer orders.
   D. Orders are routed directly from the Web site to the customer's local Tesco store.
2. eBay is an example of what form of e-commerce?
   A. A2B
   B. B2B
   C. C2B
   D. C2C
3. On-line sales of products to consumers now exceed traditional retail sales. True False
4. Business processes that are strong candidates for conversion to e-commerce are those that are paper based and time-consuming and those that can make business more convenient for customers. Thus, it comes as no surprise that the first business processes that companies converted to an e-commerce model were those related to ________________ and ________________.
5. B2C e-commerce generates greater total revenue than B2B e-commerce. True False

E-commerce requires the careful planning and integration of a number of technology infrastructure components.

6. The physical logistics of delivering merchandise to cybershoppers—the storing, packing, shipping, and tracking of products—is so critical to the success of an organization that few manufacturers and retailers have outsourced these activities. True False
7. Which of the following contain variable information and are built in response to a specific Web visitor's request?
   A. static pages
   B. artificial pages
   C. dynamic pages
   D. virtual pages

An organization's transaction processing system (TPS) must support the routine, day-to-day activities that occur in the normal course of business and help a company add value to its products and services.

8. All transaction processing systems perform a set of basic data processing activities. Which of the following is NOT one of the basic data processing activities?
   A. data collection and data editing
   B. data correction and data manipulation
   C. data storage and document production
   D. data duplication and data elimination
9. Data should be captured at its source, and it should be recorded accurately, in a timely fashion, with minimal manual effort, and in a form that can be directly entered into the computer rather than keying the data from some type of document. True False
10. Which of the following statements is TRUE?
    A. Disaster recovery is the implementation of the business resumption plan.
    B. Business resumption planning is the process of anticipating and minimizing the effects of disasters.
    C. September 11 led a number of companies to rethink their business resumption plan.
    D. All of the above.

Implementation of an enterprise resource planning (ERP) system enables a company to achieve numerous business benefits through the creation of a highly integrated set of systems.

11. Which of the following is a primary benefit of implementing an ERP system?
    A. elimination of inefficient systems
    B. easing adoption of improved work processes
    C. improving access to data for operational decision making
    D. all of the above
12. The individual application modules included in an ERP system are designed to support the ________________ ________________, the most efficient and effective ways to complete a business process.
13. Because it is so critical to the operation of an organization, most companies are able to implement an ERP system without major difficulty. True False

Chapter 5 Self-Assessment Test Answers

1. B, 2. D, 3. False, 4. buying, selling, 5. False, 6. False, 7. C, 8. D, 9. True, 10. D, 11. D, 12. best practices, 13. False.

REVIEW QUESTIONS

1. Define the term *e-commerce.* Identify and briefly describe three different forms of e-commerce. Which form is the largest in terms of dollar volume?
2. What sort of business processes are good candidates for conversion to e-commerce?
3. A major challenge for companies moving to business-to-consumer e-commerce is the need to change distribution systems and work processes to be able to manage shipments of individual units directly to consumers. What sort of changes are required and why?
4. Briefly describe the three subprocesses that make up supply chain management.
5. Briefly describe how on-line banking works.
6. What is an electronic exchange? How does it work?
7. What are some of the issues associated with the use of electronic exchanges?
8. Briefly explain the differences among credit, charge, debit, and smart cards.
9. What specific objectives do organizations hope to accomplish through the use of transaction processing systems?
10. What is the common set of basic transaction processing activities performed by all transaction processing systems?
11. What is an enterprise resource planning system?
12. A business resumption plan focuses on what two issues?
13. What is the difference between business resumption planning and disaster recovery?
14. What systems are included in the purchasing family of systems?
15. What systems are included in the accounting family of systems?

DISCUSSION QUESTIONS

1. Why is it important in effective e-commerce for front-end Web-enabled applications like order taking to be tightly integrated with back-end applications like inventory control and production planning?
2. Why are many manufacturers and retailers outsourcing the physical logistics of delivering merchandise to shoppers? What advantages does such a strategy offer? Are there any potential issues or disadvantages?
3. Distinguish between a B2B and a B2C e-commerce company.
4. Would you agree with the statement that e-commerce is dead or dying? Why or why not?
5. Wal-Mart, the world's number-one retail chain, has turned down several invitations to join exchanges in the retail and consumer goods industries. Is this good or bad for the overall U.S. economy? Why?
6. Assume that you are the owner of a small dry cleaning business. Describe the day-to-day transaction processing activities that you would encounter.
7. Your company is a medium-sized service company with revenue of $500 million per year. You've decided that the organization will implement a new order processing system. What are some of the key questions that must be answered to further define the scope of this effort?
8. Imagine that you are the new IS manager for a *Fortune* 1000 company. Your internal information systems audit has revealed that your firm's systems are lacking disaster recovery plans and backup procedures. How would you decide whether your firm should invest in the development of a disaster recovery plan and backup procedures?
9. What is the advantage of implementing ERP as an integrated solution to link multiple business processes? What are some of the issues and potential problems?
10. How would you develop a business resumption plan and prepare for a potential disaster recovery? What steps would you use to plan for a potential disaster?

PROBLEM-SOLVING EXERCISES

1. As a team, develop a set of criteria you would use to evaluate various business-to-consumer Web sites on the basis of ease of use, protection of consumer data, security of payment process, etc. Develop a simple spreadsheet containing these criteria and use it to evaluate five different Web sites.
2. Do research to get current data about the growth of B2B, B2C, or C2C e-commerce—either in the United States or worldwide. Use a graphics software package to create a line graph representing this growth. Extend the growth line five years beyond the available data using two different modeling tools available with the software package. Write a paragraph discussing the issues and assumptions that affect the accuracy of your five-year projection and the likelihood that e-commerce will achieve this forecast.

TEAM ACTIVITIES

1. As a team, conduct an interview with a member of a company's IS organization on the subject of its transaction processing systems. Identify each of the company's major TPS systems. For each TPS, define its primary purpose, identify when the system was implemented, and classify the system as a proprietary system or a software package.
2. As a team, choose an idea for a Web site—products or services you would provide. Develop an implementation plan that outlines the steps you need to take and the decisions you must make to set up the Web site and make it operational.
3. Assume that your team has formed a consulting firm to evaluate the business resumption plans of companies. Develop a list of at least ten questions you would ask as you audit a firm's plan. Visit a company and perform the audit based on these questions.

WEB EXERCISES

1. Access the Web sites of two package-delivery services and document the services they provide for cybershoppers in terms of product delivery and return. Which company offers superior services? Why do you think so?
2. Identify and visit the Web sites of three public exchanges that are owned and operated by an industry group. Write a brief summary of each exchange outlining its purpose, members, and information about its operation.
3. A number of companies sell ERP software. Search the Internet to get more information about one of the companies that makes and sells this powerful software. Develop a one-page report or send an e-mail message to your instructor about what you found.

CASES

CASE 1

DaimlerChrysler Joins Covisint Exchange

Procurement decisions affect long-term supplier relations and directly determine product costs and quality. DaimlerChrysler, the German-based company, is using e-commerce to optimize the core tasks of supply and parts procurement, including the analysis of information on suppliers and markets; preparation of procurement criteria with product development and logistics; price research procedures; and contract management. Improving the procurement process has the potential to significantly reduce processing times and expenditures, which can translate into lower costs and reduced time to market.

Recognizing the potential benefits of a streamlined procurement system, Ford and General Motors sought to establish competing automotive procurement marketplaces (Ford's Auto-Xchange and GM's TradeXchange). The two companies eventually dropped those plans and decided to work with Covisint to develop a worldwide portal for the automobile industry that would ensure a standard method of connecting suppliers and manufacturers on the Internet—from development through logistics.

DaimlerChrysler (Germany), Renault (France), Nissan (Japan), and Peugeot Citroen (France) agreed to join Ford and GM in the development of Covisint and to use this electronic trade exchange. Automobile industry suppliers benefit from the industry standard electronic marketplace, as well as from the elimination of time-consuming and costly separate interfaces and applications to the various manufacturers and their own suppliers.

The Covisint exchange uses Commerce One's MarketSite software to process transactions, conduct on-line auctions, and manage the content of a parts catalog. Covisint uses Oracle's enterprise resource planning applications to run its internal operations and Oracle's Exchange Marketplace to provide security, single sign-on, and registration capabilities. (Single sign-on is a session/user authentication process that permits a user to access all the applications he or she has been given the rights to on the server and eliminates future authentication prompts when the user switches applications during that particular session.) The portal integrates all original equipment manufacturers and supplier applications worldwide via one common framework. Covisint's backers hope to channel more than $300 billion in annual transactions through the exchange.

Over a 12-month period, DaimlerChrysler managed 512 on-line bidding events valued at $9 billion using Covisint. In May 2001, DaimlerChrysler staged an on-line bidding event with an order volume of $3 billion in just four days. In total, 43 percent of the total value of the parts for a future Chrysler model series was negotiated on-line, with over 50 on-line bidding events in the third quarter of 2001 alone.

The business benefits from finding new suppliers and reducing the price of products are substantial; however, the biggest benefits come from reducing the time it takes to close deals. DaimlerChrysler (and the other automakers) are trying to reduce the time required to get new products to market. The use of e-commerce has reduced the time required for order placement by up to 80 percent, cutting both time and business process costs. As a result, DaimlerChrysler's management stated that the economic effects achieved with e-commerce in the first year of implementation had already covered the costs of its investment and that it holds great potential for the future, too.

Discussion Questions

1. Why would Ford and GM scrap plans to build their own exchanges in favor of an industrywide standard electronic marketplace?
2. Are there any disadvantages or potential problems in the use of the Covisint electronic exchange?

Critical Thinking Questions

3. If the major automobile manufacturers and parts suppliers all use the same industrywide electronic marketplace, is it possible for DaimlerChrysler to gain an advantage over the others in the important area of procurement? Why or why not?
4. What issues might there be for a small parts supplier in getting connected to Covisint?

Sources: Adapted from "e-Business at DaimlerChrysler Is Paying Off: Savings Exceed Present Investment," February 4, 2002, DaimlerChrysler Web site, http://www.daimlerchrysler.de; "DaimlerChrysler Meets Combined Global Procurement Requirements for PCs via Online Bidding Event," November 5, 2001, DaimlerChrysler Web site, http://www.daimlerchrysler.de; "DaimlerChrysler Selects Covisint to Develop New Global Supplier Portal," January 23, 2002, DaimlerChrysler Web site, http://www.daimlerchrysler.de; Lee Copeland, "Covisint's Stalled Start," *Computerworld*, December 17, 2001, http://www.computerworld.com; Lee Copeland, "Covisint Technology Partners Sign Equity Agreements," *Computerworld*, January 1, 2001, http://www.computerworld.com; Heather Harreld, "Covisint Taps MatrixOne for Collaboration Tools," *Computerworld*, September 5, 2001, http://www.computerworld.com.

CASE 2

Lowe's Fights Tooth and Nail to Be No. 1

Lowe's employs over 100,000 people and is the 14th-largest U.S. retailer, with more than 750 stores in 42 states. Lowe's caters to the do-it-yourselfer, as well as to the commercial business customer. Its stores carry more than 40,000 home improvement items including plumbing and electrical products, tools, building materials, hardware, outdoor equipment, appliances, lumber, nursery and gardening products, millwork, paint, sundries, cabinets, and furniture.

Annual sales exceed $22 billion, making the company no. 2 behind industry leader Home Depot. However, competition is heating up. Home Depot is looking over its shoulder at a rival that is coming on strong. Lowe's is in the midst of an aggressive $2 billion expansion plan, opening more than two stores every week. Its new superstores are the largest in the industry—at approximately 150,000 square feet of retail space. And Lowe's is a leader among home improvement stores in having a presence on the Web—beating Home Depot by five months in offering its products on-line.

While neither company provides on-line sales figures, both acknowledge that the volume is small so far. It is clear, however, that both have identified e-commerce as a growth area and are investing in it even as they scale back in some other areas. Competition for in-store sales is getting so intense that the incremental business gained from a well-designed Web site can make a difference in the battle for no. 1.

For its part, Lowe's is continuing to build its business on the Internet by opening a new portal, Accent & Style, which offers home decorating tips. The goal is for this site to drive on-line sales and draw people into stores. Lowe's executives believe that the biggest opportunity on the Internet is to educate customers and prepare them to make buying decisions.

Most shoppers still want to see and touch what they're buying, but there is evidence that appliances—a major growth category for Lowe's and Home Depot—can sell well on the Internet. Maytag, the nation's third-largest appliance maker, launched its Maytag.com Web site in January 2001 and has derived 70 percent of its sales from major appliances costing $600 or more. Lowe's understands that the Web has its limits, and so it carries only about 35 percent of its total store inventory on-line.

Lowe's has its eye on controlling the fulfillment costs of on-line orders to ensure that its e-commerce initiative becomes profitable. Lowe's customers can choose to have items delivered or pick them up at the store. Lowe's contracts with NFI Interactive, a logistics company, to make its home deliveries. Often, orders above a certain amount are delivered for no additional charge. For customer pickups, Lowe's store personnel package orders that come in from the Web.

Discussion Questions

1. Do some quick research to compare total sales for Lowe's versus Home Depot for the past two years. Which one is no. 1 in sales? Is the gap closing or increasing?
2. Visit the Web site of each company. Write a brief paragraph describing your on-line experience as you try to find the closest store and purchase some items of interest to you. Which Web site would you rate as being better? Why?

Critical Thinking Questions

3. Do you agree with the Lowe's company executives who think that the biggest opportunity on the Internet is to educate customers and prepare them to make buying decisions? Or should increasing on-line sales be the goal of the company Web site?
4. What is your opinion in terms of how important an on-line presence is for Lowe's?

Sources: Adapted from "About Lowe's," Lowe's Web site, http://www.lowes.com, Accessed April 7, 2002; Eric Young, "Home Improvement Chains Battle Online," *Computerworld*, May 14, 2001, http://www.computerworld.com; Amy Tsao, "How Home Depot and Lowe's Measure Up," *Business Week Online*, December 5, 2001, http://www.businessweek.com; Steve Ulfelder, "The Web's Last Gap," *Computerworld*, June 18, 2001, http://www.computerworld.com.

CASE 3

MetLife Implements Customer-Centric Service Strategy

MetLife is a leading provider of insurance and other financial services to individual and institutional customers. It serves 10 million individual U.S. households and 64,000 companies and institutions with 33 million employees and members. MetLife is one of the largest U.S. insurers, offering life and property/ casualty insurance (including home and auto coverage), as well as savings, retirement, and other financial services for groups and individuals. It also has international insurance operations in 13 countries. MetLife demutualized and sold about a third of the company to the public in 2000.

The business environment for insurance companies has changed dramatically in recent years. Consumers have many more purchasing options thanks to the 1999 Gramm-Leach-Bliley Act, which allowed banks to merge with securities and insurance companies. The act enabled insurance companies and financial institutions to sell a broader array of products and, in turn, created a highly competitive environment. Insurance consumers' buying habits have changed—instead of agents pushing products, consumers are now seeking out information, often from both insurance companies and banks that are developing hybrid insurance and securities products.

Insurance companies are aggressively pursuing new business strategies that will help them keep their existing customers and win new customers from new and old competitors. MetLife, in particular, is concentrating its efforts on implementing a customer-centric service strategy to help it retain consumers and, in turn, boost sales.

MetLife has been working with software vendor DWL Inc. since 2000 to develop and deploy DWL Customer, a real-time transactional application that consolidates customer data. This application creates a single master record for each customer by pulling information from over 30 transaction processing systems. The goal is to ensure that every business unit and every MetLife employee has a consistent and current view of a customer's data. Doing so enables the sales department to better target customers for cross-selling opportunities. For example, a service rep could sell a life-insurance policy to someone who holds a health-insurance policy with the company.

Creating a master record for each customer will also help MetLife keep records up to date and identify any data accuracy problems. For example, if a customer has a life-insurance policy that states his age is 32, but he later opens a mutual fund and gives his age to the agent as 52, the system will alert the agent of the problem.

Successful implementation of this system inevitably will change the way MetLife employees do their jobs. Sales and service representatives, for example, will be expected to deal with all aspects of their customers' financial needs, not just the one or two product lines they've traditionally handled. MetLife's management believes that customer service is imperative not only to MetLife's ability to grow but also to its ability to survive. Changes in work processes and roles, coupled with successful implementation of the system, will enable the company to connect with customers in a way that provides intrinsic value and growth for the future.

Discussion Questions

1. What challenges is MetLife facing that are driving it to implement a customer-centric service strategy?
2. What benefits does MetLife expect to achieve through successful implementation of this new strategy?

Critical Thinking Questions

3. Gaining the desired business benefits from customer-centric service requires people to change the way they operate. What sort of changes must be made? What can MetLife management do to help ensure that employees are willing to make these changes?
4. Imagine that you are a MetLife service agent with 15 years of experience. Make a list of all the pros and cons you can imagine that such an individual would associate with moving to the new way of doing business.

Sources: Adapted from Jennifer Maselli, "Data Central," *Information Week*, January 21, 2002, 45–46; Jennifer Maselli, "Insurers Look to CRM For Profits," *Information Week*, May 6, 2002, http://www.informationweek.com; "MetLife Launches New Company Web Site," *BusinessWire*, April 30, 2002, accessed at http://www.news.moneycentral.msn.com; "About Us," MetLife Web site, http://www.metlife.com, accessed May 12, 2002.

NOTES

Sources for the opening vignette on p.181: Adapted from "Preliminary Statement of Results, 52 Weeks, Ending 23 February 2002," http://www.tesco.com; Christopher T. Heun, "Grocers Count on IT to Keep Cash Registers Ringing," *InformationWeek*, December 24, 2001, http://informationweek.com; Todd R. Weiss, "Online Grocer Webvan Crashes with a Thud," *Computerworld*, July 16, 2001, http://www.computerworld.com; Todd R. Weiss, "HomeRuns.com Latest Online Grocer to Bow Out," *Computerworld*, July 13, 2001, http://www.computerworld.com.

1. Don Blancharski, "Is E-Commerce Dead?" ITT World.com, October 23, 2001, http://www.itworld.com.
2. Marianne Kolbasuk McGee, "Online Shoppers Keep Buying. But Does the Dow Really Care?" *Information Week*, September 16, 2002, http://www.informationweek.com.
3. Linda Rosecrance, "Online Sales Hit $10 Billion in Q4 2001," *Computerworld*, February 20, 2002, http://www.computerworld.com.
4. Jane Black, "Online Extra: Where the Web Is Really Revolutionizing Business," *BusinessWeek Online*, August 27, 2001, http://businessweek.com.
5. Linda Rossetti, "The Big Bounce," *Computerworld*, March 12, 2001, http://www.computerworld.com.
6. Mark Hall, "The Weakest Link," *Computerworld*, December 17, 2001, http://www.computerworld.com.
7. Carol Sliva, "Online Sales Strong, but E-tailers Cautious on Spending," *Computerworld*, December 10, 2001, http://www.computerworld.com.
8. Beth Cox, "Office Depot Scores Amazon Deal," *InternetNews*, September 6, 2002, http://www.internetnews.com.
9. Tom Smith, "Airbus Automates Sup@ir-Sized Supply Chain," *InternetWeek*, August 22, 2002, http://www.internetweek.com.
10. Timothy J. Mullaney and Darnell Little, "Online Finance Hits Its Stride," *Business Week Online*, April 22, 2002, http://www.businessweek.com.
11. Timothy J. Mullaney and Darnell Little, "Online Finance Hits Its Stride," *Business Week Online*, April 22, 2002, http://www.businessweek.com.
12. Linda Rosencrance, "Metavante to Acquire Assets of Rival," *Computerworld*, July 30, 2002, http://www.computerworld.com.
13. Orbis Online Web site, press releases http://www.orbison-line.com, accessed November 22, 2002.
14. Alorie Gilbert, "E-Catalogs: Long Journey to Rewards," *Information Week*, August 6, 2001, 51–52.
15. Lucas Mearian, "Research Points to Sharp Rise in Number of E-billing Users," *Computerworld*, December 3, 2001, http://www.computerworld.com.
16. About the Card, http://www.Gmcard.com, accessed April 19, 2002.
17. Lucas Mearian, "Visa Pushes On-line Security Software on Merchants and Banks," *Computerworld*, May 11, 2001, http://www.computerworld.com.
18. Michael Liedtke, "VeriSign Embraces MasterCard's On-line Anti-Fraud System," *Information Week*, September 4, 2002, http://www.informationweek.com.
19. Michael Liedtke, "VeriSign Embraces MasterCard's Online Anti-Fraud System," *Information Week*, September 4, 2002, http://www.informationweek.com.
20. "Blue from American Express," American Express Web site, http://home4americanexpress4.com, accessed April 20, 2002.
21. Deirdre Lanning, "The I.T. Toll," *Business 2.0*, December 2001, http://www.business2.com.
22. Steve Konicki, "With Applications, Less Is More," *Information Week*, February 5, 2002, 45.
23. Marc L. Songini, "GM Locomotive Unit Puts ERP Rollout Back on Track," *Computerworld*, February 11, 2002, http://www.computerworld.com.
24. Steve Konicki, "Job Scheduling Puts General Mills on Top of Orders," *Information Week*, February 4, 2002, p. 45.

INDEX

D

E

Q

R